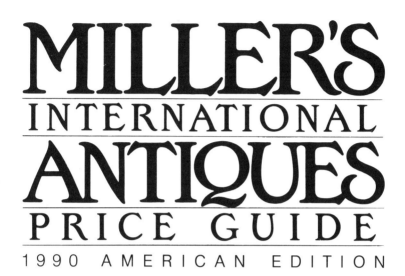

MILLER'S
INTERNATIONAL
ANTIQUES
PRICE GUIDE

1990 AMERICAN EDITION

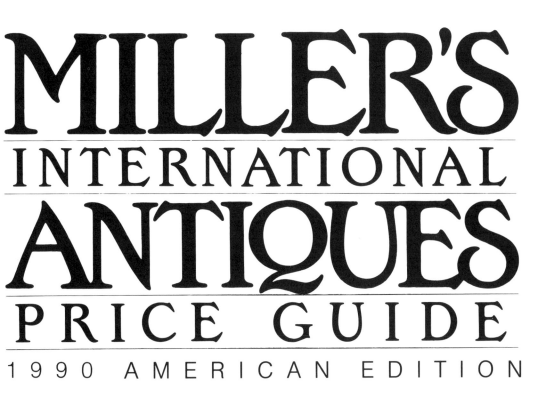

MILLER'S INTERNATIONAL ANTIQUES PRICE GUIDE

1990 AMERICAN EDITION

COMPILED AND EDITED BY
JUDITH AND MARTIN MILLER

VIKING

HOW TO USE THE BOOK

Miller's uniquely practical *International Antiques Price Guide* has been compiled to make detailed information immediately available to the consumer.

The book is organized by category of antique: e.g. Pottery, Porcelain, Furniture, etc. (see Contents List on page 6); within each major category there are sub-categories of items in alphabetical order: e.g. basket, bowl, candlestick, etc., and these in turn are ordered by date. There are around 9,000 photographs of antiques and collectibles, each with a detailed description and price range. There is also a fully cross-referenced index at the back of the book.

This 1990 Edition contains 144 pages in full color – 24 more than last year – illustrating over 1,000 exceptional or attractive pieces including a range of fine rugs and carpets.

In addition to individual entries there are special features throughout the book, giving pointers for the collector – likely condition, definitions of specialist terms, history, etc – together with general articles, chapter introductions, glossaries, bibliographies where further reading is important, tables of marks etc. As all the pictures and captions are new every year the selection of items included quickly builds into an enormously impressive and uniquely useful reference set.

PRICES

All the price ranges are based on actual prices of items bought and sold during the year prior to going to press. Thus the guide is fully up-to-date.

Prices are *not* estimates: because the value of an antique is what a willing buyer will pay to a willing seller, we have given not just one price per item but a range of prices to take into account regional differences and freak results.

This is the best way to give an idea of what an antique will *cost*, but should you wish to *sell* remember that the price you receive could be 25-30% less – antique dealers have to live too!!

Condition

All items were in good merchantable condition when last sold unless damage is noted.

ACKNOWLEDGEMENTS

Judith and Martin Miller wish to thank a large number of International auctioneers, dealers and museums who have helped in the production of this edition. The auctioneers can be found in our specialist directory towards the back of this edition.

Viking Penguin, a division of Penguin Books U.S.A. Inc., 40 West 23rd Street, New York, New York 10010, U.S.A.

Penguin Books Canada Ltd., 2801 John Street, Markham, Ontario, Canada L3R 1B4

Designed and created by
Millers Publications
Sissinghurst Court
Sissinghurst
Cranbrook
Kent, England

First published in 1989 by Viking Penguin, a division of Penguin Books U.S.A. Inc.
Published simultaneously in Canada
ISBN: 0-670-82938-2
ISSN: 0893-8857

Typeset in England by Ardek Photosetters, St. Leonards-on-Sea, England.
Color originated by Scantrans, Singapore
Printed and bound in England by William Clowes Ltd, Beccles

Editor's Introduction
by
Judith Miller

Martin and I started *Miller's Antiques Price Guide* in 1979. We produced a book which we believed was greatly needed by virtually everyone who had some interest in antiques, whether professional or as a collector.

We firmly believed that what was needed was a guide to the antiques market which was photographically illustrated, with detailed, concise descriptions and price ranges. The last ten years have convinced me that this is what the buying public want. Initially, of course, we produced the kind of book that Martin and I wanted – and since we now sell well in excess of 100,000 copies of the British edition, it would seem we were not alone. The book in its various editions is now used all over the world as a major reference work to antiques and since we use in the region of 10,000 new photographs every year, the issues of the British Guide provide an unrivalled source to 100,000 different antiques.

Five years ago we decided, in conjunction with Viking Penguin, to produce a U.S. edition of the Guide. We were convinced that the U.S. market needed the clear, high quality photographs, detailed descriptions, and the price ranges which give a "ball-park" figure for the thousands of items featured in *Miller's International Antiques Price Guide.* These price ranges are researched from sold items and give readers an essential tool for buying and selling antiques and collectibles. We are constantly trying to improve our product and give the U.S. consumer information relevant to the antiques market in the States.

One interesting development I have noticed over the years is that the antiques market is becoming more international. Of course, each country has a special interest in items made by native craftsmen and it is the general trend that such pieces will sell better at a major saleroom in their country of origin. However, to balance this, when general prices achieved at auction in New York, London, Geneva and Hong Kong are compared, they show a striking similarity.

We try to include as many color photographs as is possible, and this year we have well over 1,000 items illustrated in color, all of which have been on the market in the year prior to compilation. All the pieces included, either in color or black and white, are antiques which have been available through dealers or auction houses; they are not museum pieces. The result is a strongly visual and encyclopedic reference guide to recognizing and buying antiques, to detecting trends and to planning one's future collecting. On my monthly trips to the U.S. I am in constant touch with dealers, antiques centers and auction houses to check and verify prices.

Finally our thanks are due to all those experts whose invaluable help and guidance has contributed so much toward this new edition.

CONTENTS

A French bronze figure of an acrobat, attributed to Barthelemy Prieur, cracked, repaired, early 17thC, 12in (30.5cm) high, with late 18thC base.
$60,000-70,000

POTTERY

Following the trend of recent years there has been a continued strong interest in unusual or rare pieces. Neales of Nottingham sold a mid-18thC redware teapot, with some damage to the spout and decorated in a style similar to white saltglaze wares of the period, for $3,500. For a damaged piece of redware of a relatively late type this was an excellent price and illustrates the fact that even damaged rarities find a ready market in today's saleroom climate. A similar, slightly larger pot had sold, at a less publicised sale, for $1,900 some months previously.

The policy adopted by some auction rooms of holding back pieces for special sales seems to pay dividends with higher than anticipated prices at Bonhams' 'Commemoratives' sale and Phillips' decorative tile sale. Both sales averaged some 30% above estimate with noted enthusiasm for inscribed delft, William de Morgan tiles and large tile murals. Damaged delft, if well restored (usually by careful glueing rather than overpainting), seems to be popular, perhaps because of its decorative appeal. Good, well-decorated chargers are especially desirable.

Overall the pottery market remains buoyant with stoneware, maiolica, delft and lead glazed earthenwares continuing to increase in value. Rarity and condition remain important considerations. However a rare damaged piece will sell more easily than an ordinary perfect one. The market for large decorative pieces of no particular academic importance is still strong. The improvement in the Irish economy in 1989 should stimulate the Irish delftware market with new collectors entering the fray.

Baskets

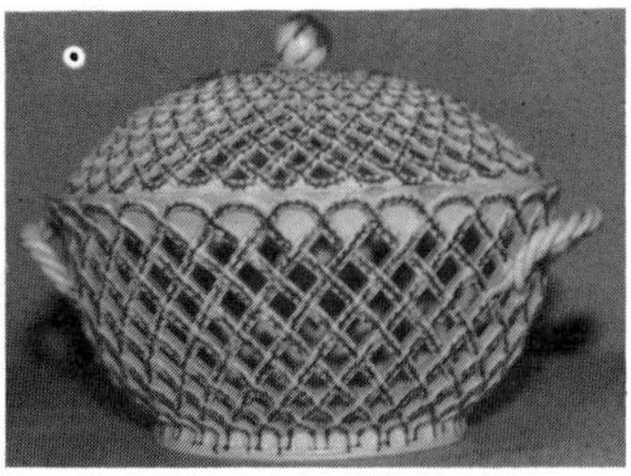

An early pearlware basket, decorated in blue, slight damage, c1785, 10in (25.5cm) wide.
$630-720

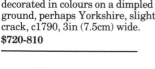

A creamware miniature basket, decorated in colours on a dimpled ground, perhaps Yorkshire, slight crack, c1790, 3in (7.5cm) wide.
$720-810

Bellarmines

A German bellarmine, c1620.
$1,000-1,400

A Rhenish bellarmine jug, moulded with a mask and rosette, 16th/17thC, 9in (22.5cm).
$270-360

Bottles

A Continental saltglazed bottle, early 19thC, 17½in (44.5cm).
$90-140

A Fulham impressed saltglazed bottle, c1835, 15in (38cm).
$70-100

A black glazed bottle, possibly Yorkshire, 19thC, 8in (20.5cm).
$70-100

A London delft blue and white bottle, inscribed and dated, chip to foot, 1651, 5½in (16.5cm).
$6,000-8,000

Bowls

An English delft polychrome fluted bowl, painted in underglaze blue, green and overglaze iron red, the interior with a blue flower spray, London or Bristol, cracked and glaze flaking to rim, c1725, 11in (26.5cm) diam.
$1,800-2,700

A Bristol delft blue and white bleeding bowl, the interior painted with bird in flight above flowering shrubs, the initials B.S. and the date 1730, cracks to rim and glaze missing, 7½in (19.5cm) wide.
$2,700-3,500

A Staffordshire pearlware punch bowl, transfer printed with various wild fowl, butterflies and trellis border, damaged, c1800, 19¼in (49cm) diam.
$1,800-2,700

A Bristol delft polychrome punch bowl, painted in iron red, blue and green, the interior with a flowering plant, cracks, chipped and flaking, c1730, 12½in (32cm) diam.
$2,700-3,600

A Bristol delft polychrome teabowl, painted in iron red with a landscape of blue rockwork and green sponged trees, slight glaze flaking, manganese 10 mark, c1730, 3in (7.5cm) diam.
$1,700-2,000

A gravel finish sugar bowl, decorated with blue bands, 19thC, 5½in (14cm).
$90-140

A Bristol delft powdered manganese ground bowl, painted in underglaze blue with fish, the interior with a flower spray, cracks and slight glaze flaking, c1740, 9in (23cm) diam.
$5,500-6,500

A thrown slipware dish with combed decoration, Fremington, North Devon, c1890, 12in (30.5cm) diam.
$225-270

A blue and white transfer printed teabowl and saucer, unrecorded pattern, marked Semi China in diamond frame, c1820.
$180-220

A Staffordshire saltglazed scratch blue teabowl, incised with 3 flowers beneath a herringbone rim, c1750, 3½in (8.5cm) diam.
$800-900

Devon Pottery posy bowls.
$18-25

Miller's is a price Guide not a price List

The price ranges given reflect the average price a purchaser should pay for similar items. Condition, rarity of design or pattern, size, colour, provenance, restoration and many other factors must be taken into account when assessing values.
When buying or selling, it must always be remembered that prices can be greatly affected by the condition of any piece. Unless otherwise stated, all goods shown in Miller's are of good merchantable quality, and the valuations given reflect this fact.
Pieces offered for sale in exceptionally fine condition or in poor condition may reasonably be expected to be priced considerably higher or lower respectively than the estimates given herein

A Wedgwood pedestal bowl designed by Keith Murray, covered in a white glaze, slight chip, printed marks, 9in (22cm) diam.
$550-650

An English delft bowl, the exterior decorated in iron red, blue and yellow, the interior painted blue, probably Liverpool, 10in (25.5cm) diam.
$800-900

A Liverpool delft blue and white bowl, the interior with a man holding an axe with the initials B A*E and the date 1769, the exterior with trailing flowering branches beneath a diaper border, rim chips, 7in (18.5cm) diam.
$3,500-4,500

Busts

A pair of Copeland parianware busts of Queen Victoria and Prince Albert, after W. Theed, 30½in (77.5cm) high.
$1,000-1,200

A mug commemorating Nelson's victories, 2 small chips to base, c1805, 5in (12.5cm).
$550-650

Commemorative

A European subject 'famille rose' tankard, painted with the Duke of Cumberland, within a gilt frame, with the words 'In Remembrance of the Glorious Victory at Culloden Apl 16th 1746', beneath a gilt spearhead border to the lip, restored handle, Qianlong, 4½in (12cm).
$2,000-2,500

A Rogers Reform commemorative blue and white plate, c1810, 10in (25cm).
$130-180

A bone china loving cup, with gilt inscription 'In Commemoration of the Exhibition of the Works of Art of all Nations, held in London in the year 1851', with print of Crystal Palace to reverse, 4in (10cm).
$180-230

A Staffordshire jug, commemorating the Coronation of William IV and Adelaide, c1831, 7½in (19cm).
$650-700

A Doulton Lambeth jug, 1897 Jubilee, moulded in green, blue and brown, with portraits and inscriptions.
$270-320

A Methodist centenary jug, c1838, 6in (15cm).
$200-270

A Wedgwood plate, 1902 Coronation, printed in blue with portrait and the Dominions.
$180-225

A mug printed in black with a portrait of Victoria, inscribed 'Liverpool Shipperies Exhibition, Opened . . . May 11th, 1886'.
$270-360

A commemorative mug, George VI and Queen Elizabeth.
$35-90

A 1937 Coronation basket, with wicker handle, in the form of a caravan, printed in colours with portraits and flags.
$270-320

A commemorative mug, the Battle of Inkerman, 5in (12.5cm).
$270-320

A Claypits pottery tyg, 5½in (14cm).
$200-250

A Copeland tazza, made for the Art Union of London in memory of Prince Albert, decorated in brown and ochre, on a revolving foot, printed marks, 16½in (41.5cm).
$650-720

A treacle glazed jug, commemorating the death of Wellington, c1853, 7in (18cm)
$180-270

A Royal Doulton loving cup, commemorating the Coronation of King Edward VIII, designed by Charles Noke and Harry Fenton, No. 653 of a limited edition of 2,000, complete with certificate.
$400-500

A Victorian railway commemorative jug, c1840, 5½in (14cm).
$570-630

A mug commemorating the Coronation of Edward VIII.
$40-50

A Victorian Coronation commemorative mug, printed in puce, cracked and chipped, base marked R and C, 4in (10cm).
$720-800

A Prince Albert memorial jug, South Wales Pottery, 8½in (22cm).
$540-630

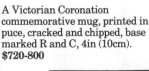

Make the Most of Miller's

In the commemorative section we have included both pottery and porcelain, as most dealers and collectors are more interested in the subject matter rather than the material.

A William Brownfield Cobridge moulded parian Royal Commemorative jug, for Edward and Alexander, registration mark for 1863, 6½in (17cm).
$180-220

Cottages

A Staffordshire model of Windsor Lodge, modelled as a pastille burner, outlined with coloured flowersprays and gilt, named in script, slight staining, c1840, 5in (12.5cm).
$450-540

A Staffordshire pottery lighthouse, Prattware type, c1820, 3in (7.5cm) high.
$350-450

A Staffordshire cottage, c1850.
$300-400

A Staffordshire pastille burner, c1845.
$500-600

A Staffordshire pastille burner, c1850.
$250-350

Cow Creamers

A Staffordshire creamware cow creamer milking group of Whieldon type, the cow spotted in brown and the milkmaid in a brown coat, with green glazed base, slight restoration, c1765, 7in (18cm) long.
$1,600-2,000

A St. Anthony's Pottery, Newcastle-upon-Tyne cow creamer, impressed Sewell, 19thC.
$2,000-2,700

Cups

A Staffordshire saltglazed coffee cup, moulded and splashed in underglaze blue with panels of birds, beasts and figures, c1750, 2½in (6cm).
$1,200-2,000

A London delft white fuddling cup, the 3 vases joined with entwined handles, bearing the date 1661 and the initials I E, chips to feet and glaze flaking, 5in (12.5cm).
$4,500-6,000

A Swansea pottery teabowl and saucer, with black transfer ware pattern showing the Chateau, by Thomas Rothwell, late 18thC, cup 2in (5cm).

A London delft blue and white two-handled beaker, with scroll blue dash handles, restoration, cracked and rim chips, c1720, 2¼in (7cm).
$600-800

A copper lustreware goblet, c1855, 4in (10cm).
$125-150

A faience chocolate cup, Northern France, c1870, 4in (10cm).
$35-75

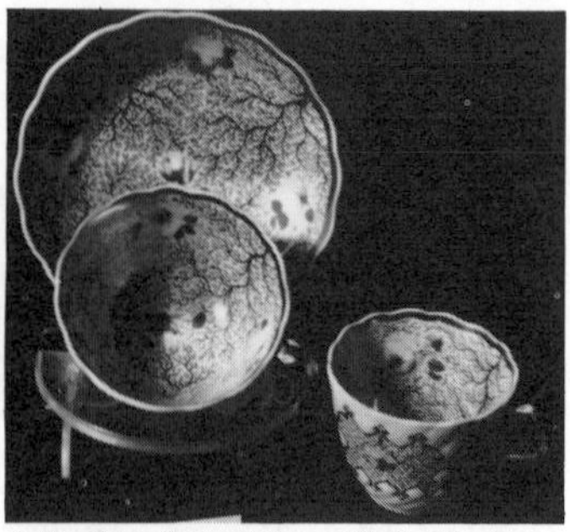

A Rockingham trio, with basket weave moulding, painted with roses and gilded, puce griffin mark, c1835.
$450-500

A Staffordshire saltglazed polychrome teabowl and saucer, painted in a bright 'famille rose' palette, with puce loop and dot pattern yellow borders, damaged and restored, c1760.
$900-1,200

A Liverpool delft polychrome coffee cup, with blue dash loop handle, painted in blue and green, rim chips, c1760, 2½in (6cm).
$1,400-1,800

Ewers

A Wedgwood black basalt ewer, surmounted by Bacchus, decorated with vines and grapes in relief, 17½in (44.5cm).
$1,000-1,200

A Ralph Wood figure of a ram, 6½in (16.5cm) wide.
$2,200-2,700

Figures – Animals

A pair of Brameld creamware figures of does, with dappled brown markings and black ears and hooves, on green mound bases, one ear chipped, c1820, 7½in (18.5cm) wide.
$2,700-3,500

CREAMWARE

- ★ a low fired earthenware first produced c1740
- ★ Josiah Wedgwood perfected the body in the mid-1760s. This perfected body he named Queen's Ware in honour of Queen Charlotte
- ★ Wedgwood sold Queen's Ware in the white and with overglaze enamel decoration
- ★ the body was well suited to overglaze transfer printing
- ★ other potteries also produced creamware in large quantities, notably Leeds, Melbourne, Cockpit Hill (Derby) and Liverpool

A Staffordshire miniature sheep, c1860, 4in (10cm).
$140-180

A pair of Staffordshire giraffes, 19thC, 6in (15.5cm).
$800-1,000

A pair of early Staffordshire figures of a lion and lioness with cupids, c1815, 5½in (14cm).
$4,000-5,500

A pair of pearlware figures of sheep, enriched in black, on green mound bases, edged with black and ochre sponging, perhaps Yorkshire, ram repaired, ewe with restoration to base, c1800, 6in (15cm) wide.
$1,600-2,200

A Staffordshire dog, c1850, 8½in (22cm).
$450-50

A Staffordshire group of a ewe and her lamb, splashed in yellow glazes, on green and blue lined base, c1790, 4in (10cm).
$1,300-2,000

A Staffordshire group of poodles, c1860, 6in (15cm).
$180-220

A Victorian Staffordshire poodle inkwell, c1870, 5½in (14cm).
$210-270

A pair of Staffordshire spill vases, horses with foals, restored, c1860, 12in (30.5cm).
$600-700

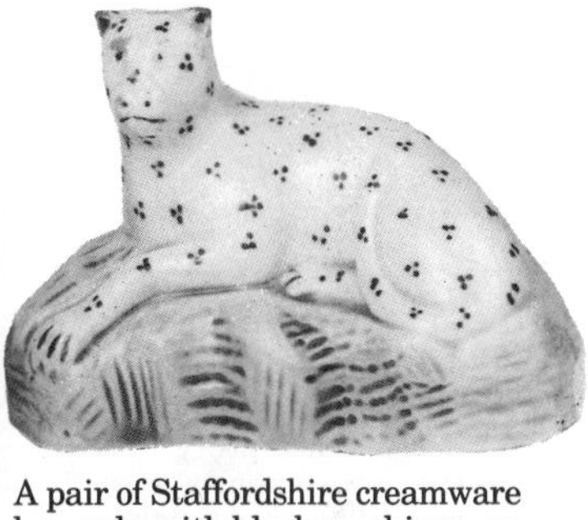
A pair of Staffordshire creamware leopards, with black markings, on green mound bases, one restored, minute chipping to ears, c1780, 3½in (9cm) wide.
$1,200-1,500

A pair of Staffordshire figures, decorated in Pratt colours, c1800.
$3,600-4,500

An English cow and calf group, splashed in brown, probably Yorkshire, c1810, 6in (15cm) wide.
$1,000-1,200

A Staffordshire miniature group of poodles, c1860, 2in (5cm).
$240-300

A Staffordshire bull baiting group, on oval base, enamels flaking, c1820, 6in (15cm).
$1,000-1,200

A pair of Yorkshire type sheep, c1800, 5in (12.5cm).
$2,000-3,000

A pair of Staffordshire spaniels, with gilt markings, slight wear to enamels, c1860, 16in (40.5cm).
$630-720

A pottery figure of a ram, marked Fell, c1830, 5½in (14cm) wide.
$1,300-1,400

A pearlware figure of a stallion, with brown harness and blue patterned saddle cloth, perhaps Yorkshire, ears chipped, c1800, 6in (15.5cm).
$4,500-5,500

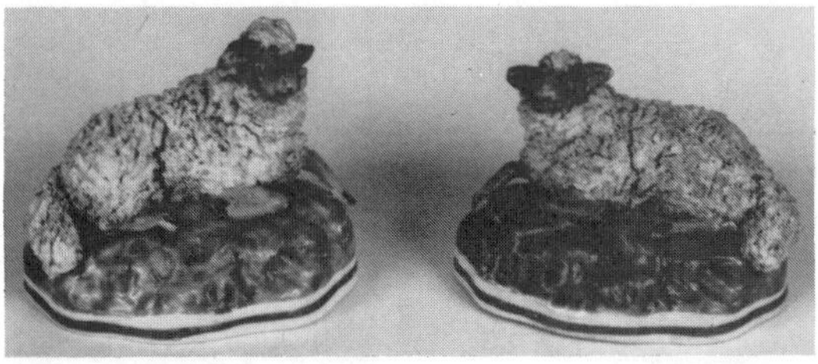

A pair of Samuel Alcock sheep, c1835, 3in (7.5cm).
$450-540

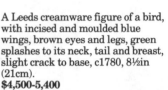

A Staffordshire pottery figure of a lion, his foreleg resting on a globe, raised on a marble plinth with red and black border, restored, late 18thC, 10½in (27cm).
$2,800-3,600

A pair of Staffordshire greyhounds, each presenting their prey, decorated in fawn enamels on a white base with gilt line, slight damage, late 19thC, 8in (20.5cm).
$400-600

A Leeds creamware figure of a bird, with incised and moulded blue wings, brown eyes and legs, green splashes to its neck, tail and breast, slight crack to base, c1780, 8½in (21cm).
$4,500-5,400

A pair of greyhounds, c1860, 11in (29cm).
$720-800

A Yorkshire pottery model of a horse, with black mane, docked tail and pink and purple splashed decoration to the body, on a green splashed waisted plinth, ears restored, 6in (15cm).
$3,600-4,500

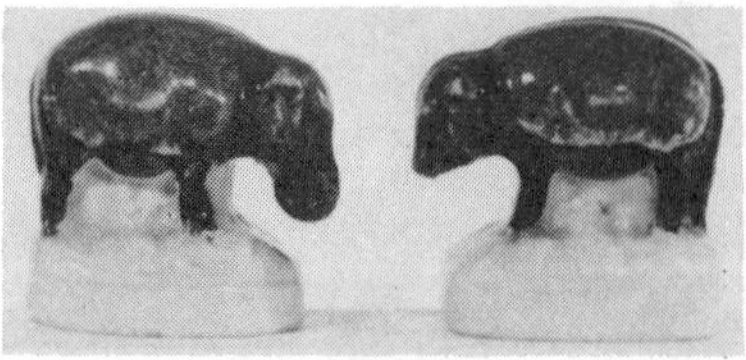

A pair of Staffordshire miniature elephant models, painted in green and dark brown, one with trunk missing, c1890, 2½in (6.5cm) wide.
$400-450

A pair of Staffordshire dog models, with black markings, one with turquoise collar, the other with a re collar, enamels flaking, glaze crazed, one forepaw cracked, c1870 10in (25.5cm).
$990-1,100

A pair of Staffordshire sheep, Whieldon type, 5½in (14cm) wide.
$2,200-2,500

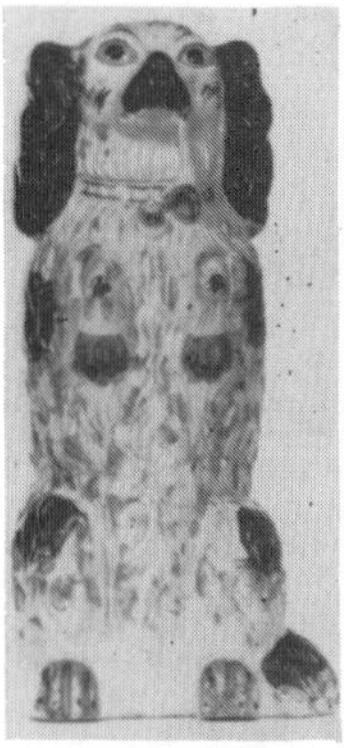

A Staffordshire model of a spaniel, with iron red markings, base with small glaze flake, c1850, 14in (35.5cm).
$1,600-2,100

A pair of Staffordshire pigeons on nests, c1835, 3½in (9cm) wide.
$900-1,000

A miniature whippet, c1840, 3in (7.5cm).
$170-200

A Bretby pottery six-piece animal orchestra, each painted in muted colours, impressed pottery marks, largest 12in (30cm) high.
$1,600-2,000

A pair of Cerreto Sannita pottery aquamanile, modelled as crouching lions, enriched with yellow and green glazes, minor chips and glaze flakes, 18thC, 7in (18cm).
$1,000-1,400

A majolica camel and rider group, impressed Brown – Westhead, Moore & Co., 19thC, 16in (40.5cm) wide.
$1,800-2,200

A Staffordshire creamware figure of a greyhound of Whieldon type, lightly splashed in grey, on a rockwork base, some chipping, c1770, 3½in (9.5cm).
$1,600-2,200

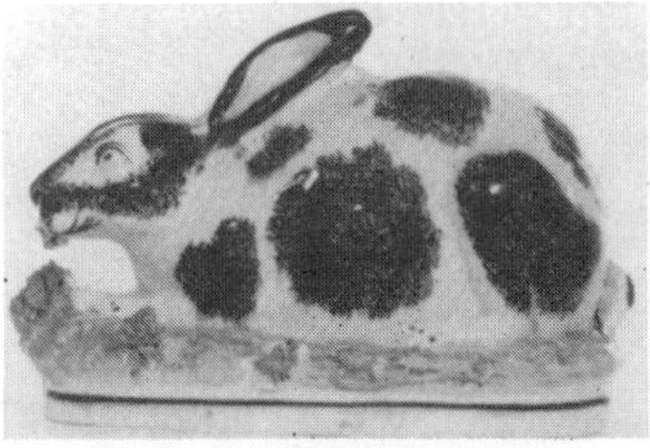

A Staffordshire model of a rabbit, with sponged black markings, the green base with applied clay grass, one ear restored, c1840, 9in (23cm) wide.
$1,800-2,100

A pair of Staffordshire tigers, by William Kent, c1870, 5½in (14cm) wide.
$2,100-2,700

A Staffordshire spill vase, lion with cubs, c1850.
$600-700

A pair of Staffordshire dalmatians, c1850.
$600-800

A pair of Staffordshire rabbits.
$800-1,000

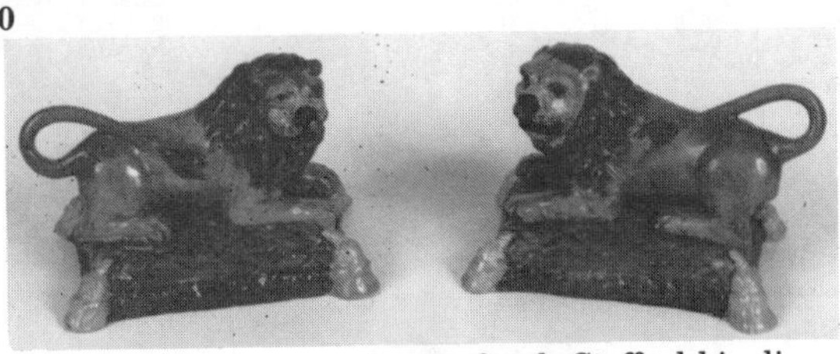

A pair of early Staffordshire lions, c1820, 5in (13cm) wide.
$2,700-3,600

A pair of Staffordshire figures of zebras, c1850.
$500-700

A pair of Staffordshire creamware figures of cattle of Whieldon type, splashed in mottled brown glazes, applied with green foliage and flowerheads, restoration, c1755, 7½ and 8½in (19 and 21cm) wide.
$20,000-28,000

A Ralph Wood spaniel, c1780, 7in (18cm).
$2,200-3,000

Figures – People

A pair of Staffordshire jockeys, c1875, 9in (22.5cm).
$500-550

A pair of Staffordshire figures of Turkish musicians, c1860, 4½in (11cm).
$350-400

A Whieldon type creamware figure, c1770, 3in (7.5cm).
$450-540

A Swansea figure with basket of flowers, c1805, 4½in (11cm).
$1,000-1,200

A Charles Vyse pottery figure of a pedlar, in the form of a brilliantly attired Indian, inscribed Vyse Chelsea, c1935, on wood plinth, 13in (33cm) high overall.
$900-1,000

A Staffordshire creamware figure of a shepherdess, of Ralph Wood type, in dark brown hat, green bodice, brown jacket and skirt, and white under-skirt, restored, c1780, 9in (22.5cm).
$1,200-1,800

A Staffordshire group of the Dandies, c1820, 7½in (19cm).
$1,000-1,200

A Staffordshire hollow cast figure of a girl in long robes, splashed in green and dark brown glazes, holding a doll, head re-stuck, c1780, 3in (8cm).
$400-500

A Prattware figure of Bacchus, painted in typical palette of orange, yellow, blue, brown and green, c1800, 10in (26cm).
$720-800

An Obadiah Sherratt group of a street entertainer in eastern costume with red hat, pink jacket, floral shirt and yellow breeches, standing beside a dancing bear, damaged and restored, c1830, 9in (22.5cm).
$2,500-3,000

A pair of Ralph Wood figures of gardeners, c1780, 8in (20cm).
$3,500-4,000

A Staffordshire pearlware group of a town lady with a boy, she in brown stole, yellow dress and iron red coat, the boy in black hat, green jacket and brown breeches, on marbled base, c1800, 8½in (21.5cm).
$1,300-2,000

In the Ceramics section if there is only one measurement it usually refers to the height of the piece

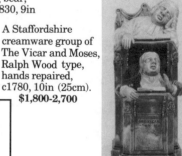

A Staffordshire creamware group of The Vicar and Moses, Ralph Wood type, hands repaired, c1780, 10in (25cm).
$1,800-2,700

A Staffordshire pearlware group of St. George slaying the Dragon, of Ralph Wood type, restoration, replacement spear, c1800, 11½in (29cm).
$1,400-1,800

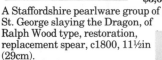

An Obadiah Sherratt group of Romulus and Remus, bocage restored, enamel worn, c1830, 7in (17.5cm).
$3,600-4,500

A Staffordshire group of Minerva in purple, yellow and green robes, perhaps Wood and Caldwell, head restored, base with firing damage, c1830, 10½in (26cm).
$1,400-1,800

An early Staffordshire figure, c1800, 4in (10cm).
$360-440

A Staffordshire pearlware group of a country woman with a boy, she in black plumed bonnet, iron red cape and black spotted dress, the boy in black jacket and yellow trousers, her neck restored, c1820, 9in (23.5cm).
$1,000-1,400

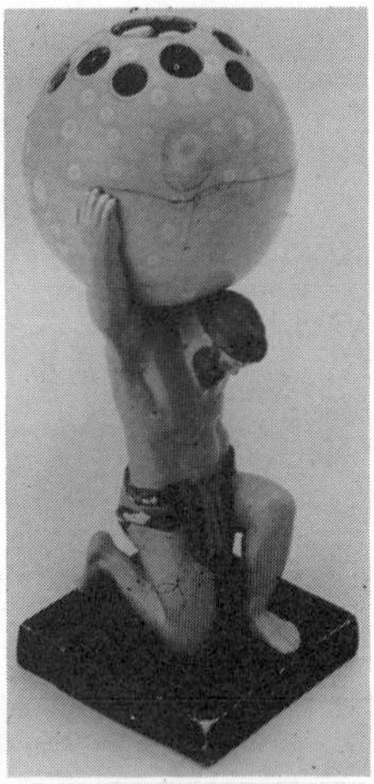

A Staffordshire pottery figural pot pourri of Atlas, supporting a yellow globe, probably Wood and Caldwell, on a black base, damaged, c1810, 11in (28cm).
$550-650

A Staffordshire cock-fighting group, c1815.
$2,000-2,700

A Staffordshire pearlware group of a gallant and companion, wearing their best clothes, in brown, green and yellow, on marbled base edged in black, her neck repaired, c1820, 9in (22cm).
$1,300-1,400

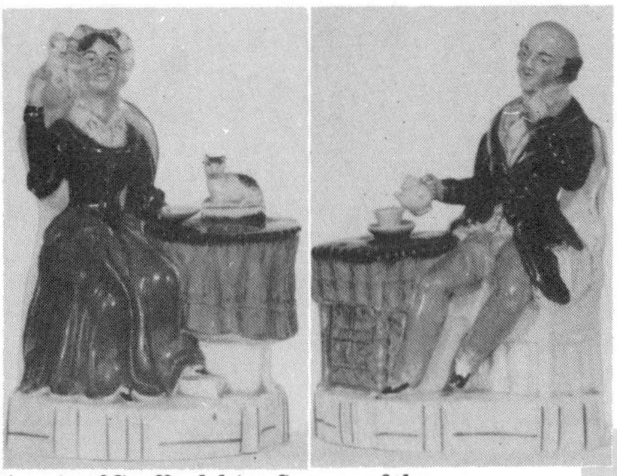

A pair of Staffordshire figures of the Dickens characters, Mr. Dick and Betsy Trottwood, some wear, c1850, 7in (18cm).
$1,300-2,000

A pair of Staffordshire figures of children on zebras, c1855, 6½in (16cm).
$600-700

A Staffordshire figure, probably Lord Byron, c1830, 5½in (14cm).
$250-300

An Obadiah Sherratt set of 3 figures, depicting Faith, Hope and Charity, decorated in colours, the bases with feather and shell moulding, Faith with restored arm, c1810, 9in (23cm).
$540-720

A pair of royal children with dogs, c1850, 5½in (14cm).
$650-700

A Staffordshire figure of a brigand in Spanish costume, with purple cape and holding a pistol, on mound and square base, repaired, glaze crazed, c1850, 13in (32cm).
$200-300

A pair of Staffordshire figures, the Welsh Tailor and his wife, c1840, 5in (12.5cm).
$900-1,100

A Staffordshire figure of the Leopard Slayer, c1855, 11½in (29cm).
$550-650

A Staffordshire figure of a boy with a rabbit, c1860, 9½in (24cm).
$360-400

A pair of Staffordshire figures, each modelled as a girl standing beside a hutch with 2 rabbits, on rockwork bases, one cracked, one head re-stuck, c1855, 6in (15cm).
$180-200

A group, Flight from Egypt, c1820, 7½in (19cm).
$1,400-1,600

A pair of Staffordshire figures of the Prince of Wales and the Princess Royal, standing with deer, c1855, 9in (22.5cm).
$750-850

A Staffordshire group of children with rabbit, c1860, 6½in (16cm).
$200-270

A garniture of 3 Staffordshire figures of a young boy and girl, kneeling before pianos, and a central piano fitted as a watch holder, with a recumbent dog underneath, c1875, 7½ to 9in (19 to 22.5cm).
$750-800

A Staffordshire lady with dog and kennel, c1860, 3in (7.5cm).
$250-300

A pair of Staffordshire cows, with cowman and milkmaid, c1860, 10in (25cm).
$900-1,000

A rare enamelled figure of a hawker, Leeds, c1790.
$900-1,000

A Staffordshire group of figures, 21st Lancers and a Sailor, c1890, 12in (30cm).
$400-450

A Staffordshire figure of Red Riding Hood, c1850, 14in (35cm).
$700-800

A tithe pig group, c1815, 7in (17.5cm).
$1,500-2,000

A French maiolica figure of a putto seated on the back of a dolphin, coloured in blue and yellow, outlined in black, base chipped and cracked, early 18thC, 7in (17.5cm).
$300-400

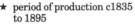

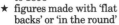

A Staffordshire figure of the Prince Regent and his pet dog, c1850, 8½in (21cm).
$1,200-1,600

A Ralph Wood figure of Neptune, c1780, 9in (22.5cm).
$1,200-1,500

STAFFORDSHIRE FIGURES

- ★ period of production c1835 to 1895
- ★ figures made with 'flat backs' or 'in the round'
- ★ material used varies from pottery to porcelain type body
- ★ many figures do not appear in the standard reference book 'Staffordshire Portrait Figures' by P D Gordon Pugh. However, some collectors only buy figures which appear in Pugh
- ★ many fakes and restored pieces appear on the market
- ★ value is affected by damage, poorly defined features, flaked overglaze enamel or rubbed gilding
- ★ unusual animals and theatrical figures particularly collectable

Punch and Judy riding on goats, c1850.
$700-800

A pottery group, New Marriage Act, c1825, 7in (17.5cm).
$2,000-2,500

In mint condition.

A Staffordshire figure of a man riding an elephant, probably by Thomas Parr.
$700-800

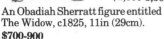

An Obadiah Sherratt figure entitled The Widow, c1825, 11in (29cm).
$700-900

A Prattware type figure of St. George and the Dragon, 11in (28cm).
$2,500-3,500

A Charles Vyse figure of 'The Piccadilly Rose Woman', naturalistically coloured, base inscribed C. Vyse Chelsea, c1900, 9in (23cm).
$800-1,000

A Staffordshire figure of a girl at a well, c1855.
$200-270

A pottery group, Dr. Syntax playing cards, c1830, 8in (20cm).
$1,800-2,100

A Staffordshire pearlware figure of a nymph, with a dolphin at her side, wearing a green robe lined in purple, the base marbled in ochre, some damage, 8in (20cm).
$400-450

A Staffordshire musical group, c1810, 10½in (26cm).
$1,300-1,400

A Staffordshire group, Rural Pastimes, enamel chipped, bocage restored, 9in (22.5cm).
$800-1,000

A pair of Staffordshire spill holders, c1860, 9in (22.5cm).
$600-900

Victorian Staffordshire Portrait Figures

A figure of Abraham Lincoln, titled on the base, 15½in (38cm), (B).
$450-550

Staffordshire figures of the Prince of Wales and Princess Royal, c1843, 7in (18cm), (A,137 and A,138).
$300-350

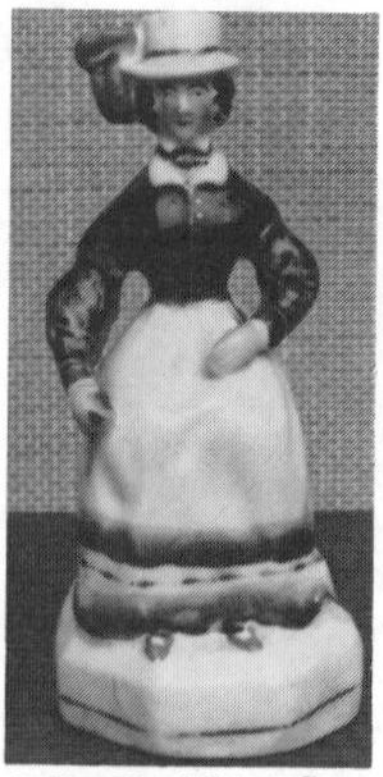

A Staffordshire figure of Queen Victoria, c1848.
$350-400

STAFFORDSHIRE FIGURES

Where the description of a piece includes an identifying number (e.g. E,80/158), this number refers to its listing in P. D. Gordon Pugh's standard reference book 'Staffordshire Portrait Figures'. As such it is an additional indication of authenticity

A Staffordshire group of the Dandies, the lady in plumed yellow hat and floral dress, standing arm in arm with a gentleman in black hat, long dark brown jacket and yellow trousers, on base with black line, c1820, 8in (20cm).
$1,200-1,800

A Staffordshire bust of Wesley, c1850.
$400-600

A figure of Jenny Lind in the part of Alice from Meyerbeer's opera of Robert the Devil, in blue bodice and yellow dress, named in gilt script, c1847, 13in (32.5cm), (E,80/158).
$1,400-1,500

A Staffordshire figure of Robert Evans, c1850.
$1,000-1,200

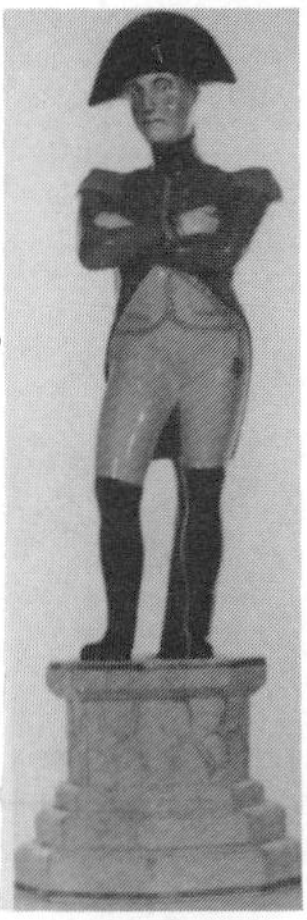

A large Staffordshire figure of Napoleon in black hat, green and red uniform with yellow breeches and black boots, restoration, c1835, 20½in (51cm), (C,263/23A).
$1,000-1,500

A Staffordshire figure of Man Friday, c1840, 7in (17cm), (E,478/144).
$450-550

A Staffordshire group of Esmeralda and Gringoire, she in dark blue and pink costume holding a tambourine with a leaping goat at her side, he with iron red cap, blue jacket and brown breeches, c1850, 9in (22.5cm), (E,31/65).
$160-200

A Staffordshire group of the British Lion seated on a recumbent figure of Napoleon III, c1860, 9in (23cm), (93/277).
$360-450

A Staffordshire group, Musicians, c1850, 10in (25.5cm), (E,298).
$250-300

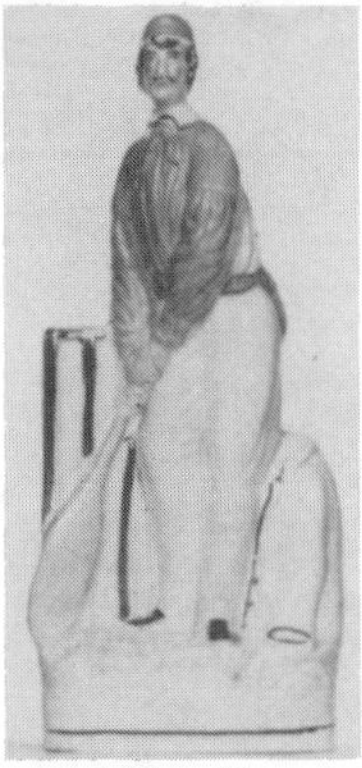

A Staffordshire figure possibly depicting the batsman Julius Caesar, in red cap and blue shirt, standing before the wicket with a yellow bat, cracked, 14in (35cm), (F,51/14).
$900-1,000

A Victorian Staffordshire figure of a shepherdess and sheep.
$100-200

A Staffordshire model of Potash Farm, home of James Rush, c1860, 6in (15cm), (G,556/20).
$400-450

A Staffordshire house with a figure of a troubadour, c1855, 8½in (21cm).
$450-540

A Staffordshire watch-holder, c1850, 11in (28cm).
$500-700

Prince Llewellyn returned from hunting to find his son lying dead and his pet hound Gelert covered in blood. In anguish he killed the dog, realising too late that Gelert had been trying to protect his son from the wolf.

A Staffordshire painted pottery group of a family of 3, beneath a floral bower, 9in (22.5cm).
$180-200

A Staffordshire figure of Eliza Cook, with tartan bodice and pink dress, some chipping, enamel flaking, c1850, 10in (25cm), (H,10/367).
$180-360

A rare Staffordshire figure, with inscription, c1865, 7½in (19cm).
$200-250

A group depicting 2 young women known as the Alphington Ponies, identically dressed with yellow hats, orange coats and pale blue dresses, 4½in (12cm), (I,18/41).
$700-800

A figure group of 3 naval officers, painted and gilt, 8½in (21cm).
$450-550

A Staffordshire figure of a forester, c1860, 11in (28cm).
$240-300

A Staffordshire lighthouse, Grace Darling, c1838.
$250-300

Flatware

A Brameld plate transfer printed in green with Don Quixote pattern, impressed Brameld, c1820.
$70-100

A Castleford platter, blue and white transfer printed with Buffalo and Ruins pattern, impressed D. Dunderdale & Co, c1800.
$700-800

A Bristol delft polychrome plate, boldly painted in blue, yellow, manganese and ochre, 18thC, 9in (22cm).
$1,300-1,500

An English delft blue dash tulip charger, boldly painted in colours, crack repaired, glaze flaking at back, London or Bristol, c1690, 14in (34.5cm).
$750-1,000

A pair of Bristol delft powdered manganese ground lobed plates, the centres painted in underglaze blue with boats at sail, slight rim chips, c1740, 9in (22cm).
$3,600-4,500

A Bristol delft Adam and Eve charger, boldly painted, within a blue triangle, dot and grass pattern rim, c1740, 13½in (34cm).
$5,500-6,500

An English delft powdered blue ground plate, the centre painted with an Oriental in a fenced garden, perhaps Liverpool, minute rim chips, c1750, 9in (22cm).
$3,000-4,000

An English delft powdered manganese ground plate, the centre painted in underglaze blue with 2 Orientals, slight rim chips, Bristol or Wincanton, c1745.
$1,800-2,800

A Lambeth delft ballooning saucer dish, painted in underglaze blue, grey/green and manganese, within a manganese 'feuille-de-choux' rim suspending X-pattern swags and manganese roses, minute rim flaking, c1785, 9in (22.5cm).
$2,000-3,000

An English delft plate, possibly Liverpool, c1750, 9in (22.5cm).
$110-130

A children's plate, marked Wallace & Co, Newcastle-upon-Tyne, c1850, 7in (17cm).
$90-100

A London delft dated blue and white armorial plate, painted in a dark blue with the arms of The Clothworkers Company, slight rim chips and flaking, 1701, 9in (22.5cm).
$21,000-27,000

A Liverpool delft dish, the polychrome decoration in blue, manganese, yellow and green, mid-18thC, 13½in (34cm).
$1,200-1,600

A pair of dessert plates by H. & R. Daniel, 8½in (21cm).
$900-1,000

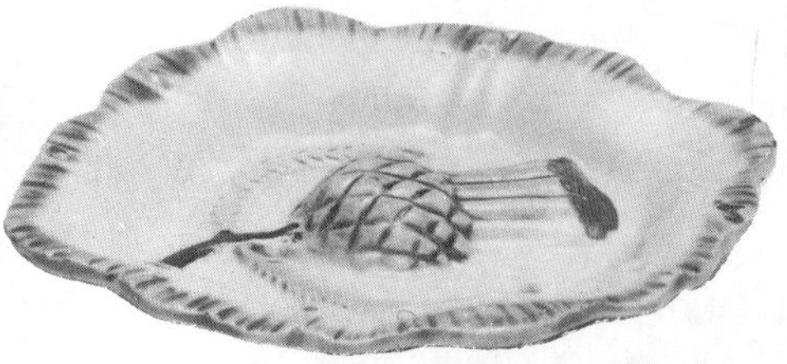

A pearlware miniature dish, the centre moulded and coloured with a thistle, within a green rim, slight rim chip, c1780, 5in (12cm).
$750-1,000

A creamware transfer printed plate, possibly Leeds, c1770, 10in (25cm).
$360-420

A Staffordshire saltglazed leaf dish, with green stalk handle and moulded with a green fern, on a ground of raised veins, restored, c1755, 6in (15cm).
$500-900

A Ferrybridge pearlware stand, with polychrome decoration, impressed Wedgwood & Co, c1800.
$150-180

A Staffordshire creamware plate of Whieldon type, enriched in conventional splashed glazes, c1760, 8½in (21.5cm).
$1,800-2,700

A Staffordshire slipware dish of deep form, with slip decoration on a terracotta ground, early 18thC, 12in (30cm) wide.
$550-650

A Staffordshire saltglazed white heart-shaped dish, moulded with anthemion and scrolls, c1760, 4in (10cm).
$550-650

A Brameld caneware plate with raised flower border, impressed Brameld, c1820.
$250-300

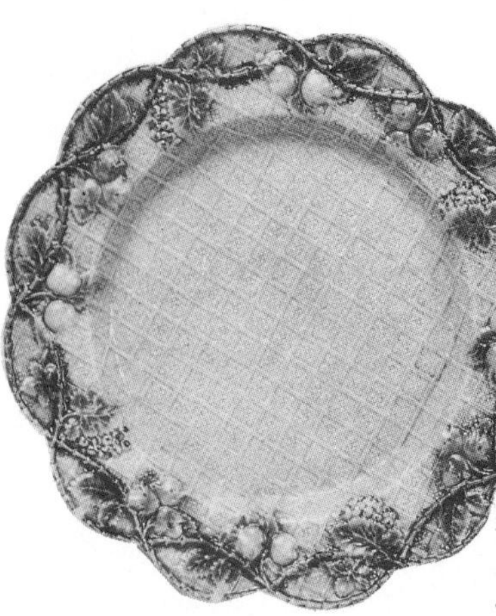

A Staffordshire creamware plate of Whieldon type, rim restored in 2 places, c1760, 9½in (23.5cm).
$1,000-1,500

A Staffordshire slipware dish, the dark brown ground with a light brown slip star edged in cream, with brown and cream flowerheads, mid-18thC, 17in (42cm).
$10,500-14,000

A Staffordshire pearlware tray, painted flowers on an ochre ground within a deep blue border, richly gilt with a garland of flowers and with a moulded yellow and gilt rim, gilding worn, 6in (15cm).
$550-650

A Staffordshire earthenware plate, printed in blue with Buffalo pattern, c1820, 10in (25cm).
$70-90

A Swansea, Dillwyn, children's plate, c1840, 6in (15.5cm).
$100-150

A Swansea child's plate, c1850, 5½in (14cm).
$100-120

A Whieldon plate, c1780, 9in (22.5cm).
$250-300

A Swansea, Dillwyn, plate, c1820, 9in (22.5cm).
$300-350

A Llanelli blue transfer plate, with damask pattern border, impressed and printed mark, South Wales pottery, 10½in (26cm).
$70-100

A Swansea child's plate, c1840, 7½in (19cm).
$180-220

A large Watcombe charger, hand painted and dated 1870.
$110-150

A Swansea transfer ware plate showing rural scene, c1805, 10in (25cm).
$120-150

A Welsh blue transfer plate, Whampoa pattern, c1835, 5in (12.5cm) diam.
$90-120

A Swansea pottery dish, Lady of Llangollen pattern, c1820, 17in (42cm).
$750-1,000

A Swansea blue and white transfer ware platter, 19in (46cm) wide.
$900-1,300

Jugs

A Minton majolica jug, with vine twist handle, moulded and painted with figures dancing around a castle wall, impressed mark and date code for 1873, 10in (24.5cm).
$400-450

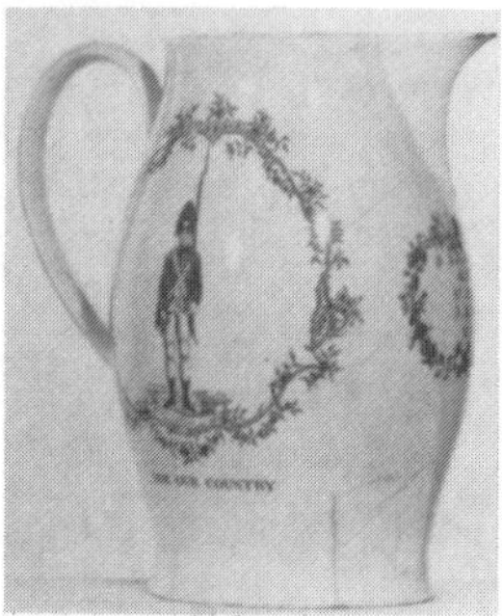

A creamware baluster jug printed in black, inscribed For Our Country on one side, the reverse with Masonic emblems, with inscription beneath the lip, rim chipped, some cracks, c1785, 11in (27.5cm).
$750-800

A Prattware jug, decorated on each side with scenes of young children, coloured under the glaze in typical palette, the base moulded with stiff leaves, c1800, 6in (15cm).
$450-700

A Staffordshire saltglazed polychrome creamboat, with iron red, yellow, black, green and puce decoration, slight cracks, c1760, 4½in (11.5cm) wide.
$2,000-3,000

A spongeware jug and basin set, damaged, 12½in (32cm).
$250-350

An English delft puzzle jug, dated 1732, 7in (18cm).
$5,000-7,500

A Staffordshire creamware baluster cream jug, streaked in brown, green and grey glazes, handle repaired, c1760, 4in (9.5cm).
$600-900

A Llanelli pottery copper lustre jug, 7½in (19cm).
$350-450

A Prattware jug with maroon ground, printed with a scene of a windmill, marked, c1850.
$160-200

A pearlware jug, transfer printed in sepia, c1795, 5½in (14cm).
$300-400

A Staffordshire saltglazed white pecten shell moulded cream jug, of baluster shape, handle and lip restored, c1745, 3in (7.5cm).
$1,000-1,400

A Sunderland pottery purple lustre transfer printed jug, with floral patterns, Masonic and Crimean emblems, probably Southwick, c1855, 9in (22.5cm).
$600-800

A white stoneware jug, decorated in blue slip, probably Turner, slight damage, c1800, 6in (15cm).
$200-260

A Verwood pottery jug, c1880, 7½in (19cm).
$100-200

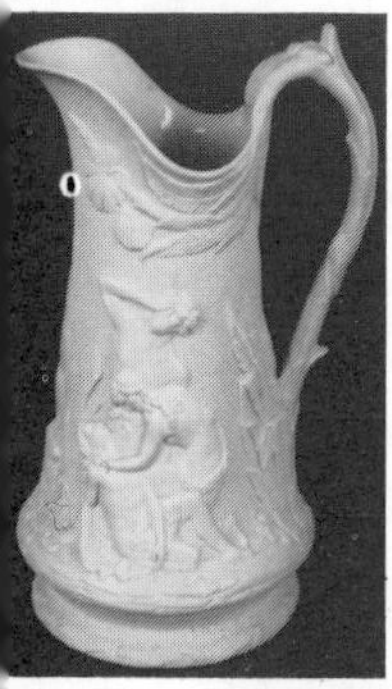

A relief moulded jug in white stoneware, with Biblical scenes, attributed to Thomas Till & Son, c1855, 9½in (24cm).
$200-350

A pearlware oviform jug, moulded and coloured with The Miser, perhaps Yorkshire, c1800, 5in (13cm).
$600-900

A pearlware jug, with loop handle, perhaps Yorkshire, c1800, 5in (13cm).
$1,000-1,400

A lustre jug decorated with children's figures, small chip, c1890, 4½in (11cm).
$75-150

A Van Ambrugh jug, c1845, 8½in (21cm).
$250-350

A Max Läuger pottery jug, decorated in slip with green flowers against a deep blue ground with slight iridescence, Kandern Tonwerk mark, including ML monogram numbered 50, 10in (24cm).
$750-1,000

A Brussels Delft baluster shaped jug, mid-18thC, set with a 19thC Dutch silver rim and a coin, 10in (25cm).
$1,500-2,500

A Pesaro documentary tri-lobed jug, with scroll handle, the body with an inscription in Greek within a starburst cartouche, flowering branches and scattered flowers to the spreading foot, inscribed Callegari, Pesaro, chips to foot, c1790, 9in (22cm).
$4,000-5,000

A creamware jug, c1780, 11in (29cm).
$1,000-1,400

A Savona blue and white puzzle jug, the neck pierced with florets, inscribed Chi Beve Nopca, c1700, 8in (21cm).
$1,500-1,600

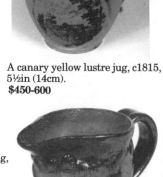

A canary yellow lustre jug, c1815, 5½in (14cm).
$450-600

A yellow printed brown jug, c1820, 4½in (11cm).
$100-200

A London saltglazed satyr jug, c1840, 4in (10cm).
$150-200

A pair of Sweney Mountain type jugs, c1800, 6½in (16cm).
$75-150

A saltglazed game jug, c1840, 11in (29cm).
$350-450

A blue banded jug, c1880, 4½in (11cm).
$60-100

A transfer printed jug, c1850, 7½in (19cm).
$200-350

A lustre jug, with the Volunteer Rifle, c1860, 7in (17cm).
$200-350

Toby Jugs

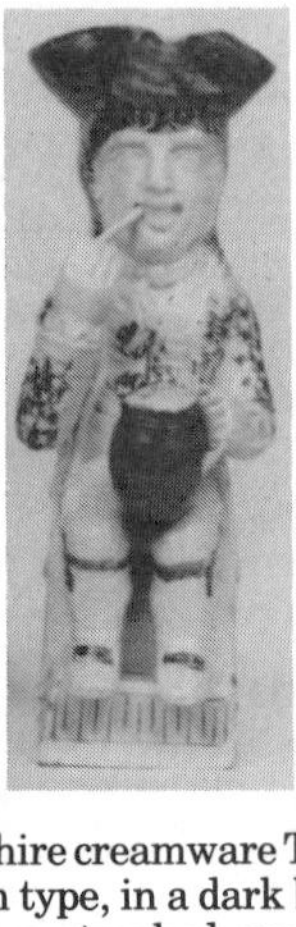

A Staffordshire creamware thin-man Toby jug of Whieldon type, in streaked brown hat and sponged brown coat and waistcoat, seated on a brown chair with green stretchers, c1765, 10in (25cm).
$6,000-8,000

A Staffordshire creamware Toby jug of Whieldon type, enriched in manganese, hat and handle chipped, c1760, 7in (18cm).
$6,000-8,000

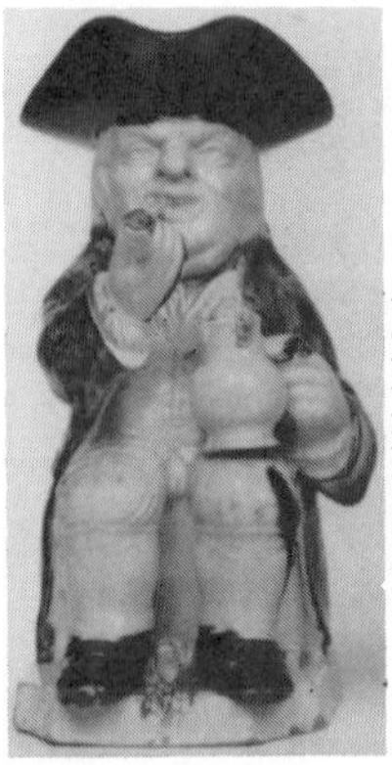

A Staffordshire creamware Toby jug of Whieldon type, in a dark brown hat and shoes, streaked grey and manganese jacket, a dog between his feet, restorations, c1765, 10in (25cm).
$1,400-1,600

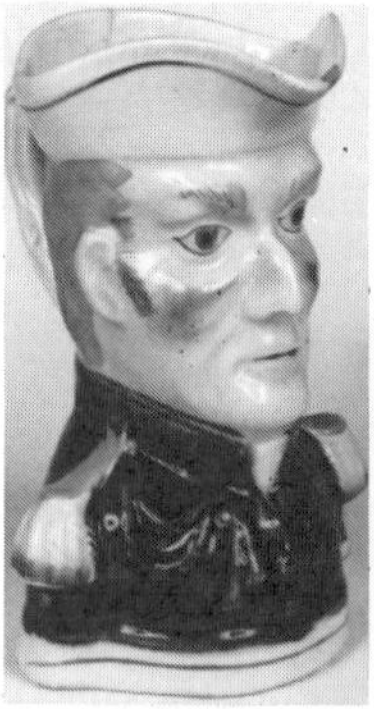

A Staffordshire Toby jug of Wellington, c1840, 7in (17cm).
$300-400

A Staffordshire Toby jug, late 18thC.
$800-1,000

Iugs

child's mug, c1860,
½in (9cm).
100-130

A Swansea cottage mug, c1860, 2½in (6cm).
$100-140

A Swansea cottage 2-pint mug, c1860, 5in (13cm).
$180-220

An English pottery mug, with black transfer print, c1820, 5in (13cm).
$200-300

A Sunder-land lustre mug, c1850, 2½in (6cm).
$75-150

Staffordshire Swansea cottage
nug, c1870, 3in (7.5cm).
100-150

A blue and white Willow pattern mug, c1840, 5in (12cm).
$150-200

A copper lustre mug, c1800, 4in (10cm).
$100-150

A pair of mugs, Tam O'Shanter,
1845, 3in (7.5cm).
$200-400

A child's mug, Steady Bow-Wow, c1880, 3in (7cm).
$80-90

A Staffordshire creamware mug, printed and painted with the Arms of the Friendly Society of Cordwainers of England, enamel damaged, c1790, 6in (15cm).
$400-600

A copper lustre mug with embossed
sprigs, c1860, 4in (10cm).
$140-200

A child's mug entitled Football, c1880, 2½in (6cm).
$100-110

A slip banded mug, c1850, 4in
(10cm).
$50-100

A miniature transfer printed Continental tankard, c1810, 1½in (4cm).
$20-40

A mochaware mug with pad mark, c1850, 6in (15cm).
$200-250

A pair of novelty chamber pots, painted with floral sprigs in brown, blue and green, and inscribed with names, one damaged, early 19thC, 4½in (11cm) wide.
$600-800

A Wedgwood terracotta two-handled pot and cover, for pot pourri, colourfully enamelled, impressed Wedgwood, c1810, 9½in (24cm).
$500-600

Redware

An American slip decorated redware platter, 17½in (45cm) diam.
$1,200-1,600

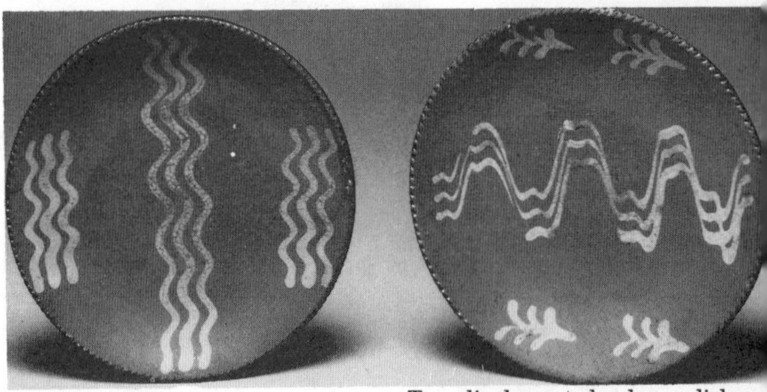

Two slip decorated redware dishes, Pennsylvania, damaged, 19thC, 9½in (25cm) diam.
$800-1,000

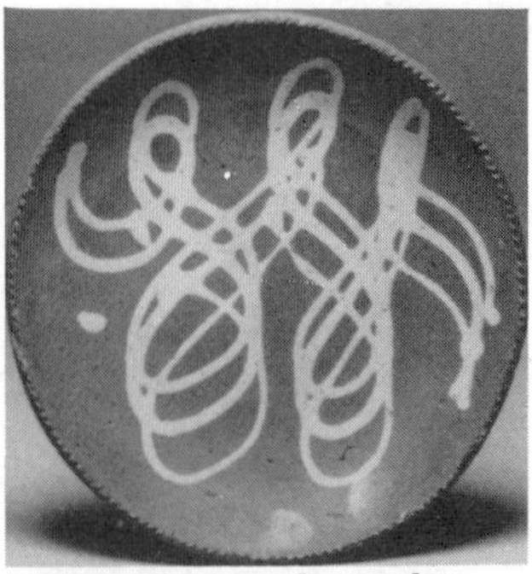

A slip decorated redware plate, Pennsylvania, mid-19thC, 10in (26cm) diam.
$1,500-2,000

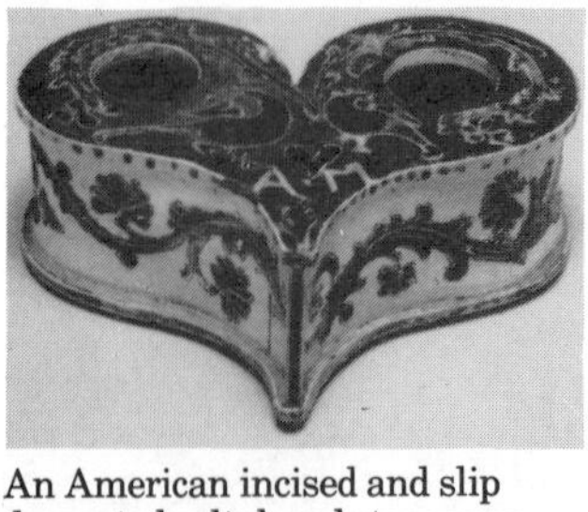

An American incised and slip decorated saltglazed stoneware inkwell, repair and chip to rim, c1800.
$8,500-9,500

Although stoneware inkwells were made in most potteries, this heart-shaped example is very rare and was most probably made as a presentation piece, perhaps as a wedding gift.

Stoneware

A saltglazed stoneware jug, by Noah White, Utica, New York, c1835, 13½in (34cm).
$900-1,200

A saltglazed slip decorated and incised stoneware pitcher, Pennsylvania, 19thC, damaged 12½in (32cm) high.
$2,000-3,000

A slip decorated stoneware butter churn, by W. A. Macquoid & Co., New York, cracks, c1865, 15in (38cm) high.
$600-700

A saltglazed slip decorated stoneware pot, by Samuel Hart & Sons, Fulton, New York, cracks an abrasions, c1850, 10½in (26cm) high.
$1,200-1,700

'ea Caddies

Bristol delftware tea caddy, c1760.
,000-1,500

Staffordshire creamware tea ddy of Whieldon type, with green aze, c1760, 3½in (9cm).
,400-1,600

A documentary Bovey Tracey saltglazed scratch-blue tea caddy, inscribed and dated 1768, neck and cover with later silver replacement, 4½in (11.5cm).
$3,000-4,000

A Staffordshire tea caddy with puce transfer ware decoration, c1815, 5in (13cm).
$400-500

A Staffordshire creamware tea caddy of Whieldon type, streaked brown glaze, slight rim chips, c1760, 4in (9.5cm).
$1,000-1,200

Tea & Coffee Pots

A Bristol glazed stoneware teapot in the form of a Toby jug, 19thC, 8in (20cm).
$100-150

creamware teapot and cover, with abstock moulded spout and twined reeded handle, painted in e manner of Robinson and nodes, in iron red and black, storation to spout and cover, rhaps Leeds, c1770, 5½in 3.5cm).
1,200-1,600

A Leeds creamware bullet shaped teapot, decorated with iron red portrait, hairline cracks and chips, mid-18thC, 5in (12.5cm).
$5,000-6,000

A Leeds creamware coffee pot and domed cover, the green striped body with foliage moulded spout and flower finial, minute cracks to handle, finial restored, c1775, 9in (22.5cm).
$7,000-8,000

Staffordshire saltglazed eart-shaped teapot and cover, with roll handle, the body and cover oulded with trailing vine, the ver with button finial, slight crack shoulder, c1755, 5in (12.5cm).
5,000-6,000

A Creil majolica teapot and cover, potted in the Minton manner, in the form of a monkey wearing a decorated blue jacket clasping a large nut, impressed mark, mid-19thC.
$400-600

A Staffordshire teapot with original gilding, c1755.
$1,800-2,200

A Staffordshire saltglazed coffee pot and cover, painted in a bright 'famille rose' palette, some cracks and chips, spout restored, c1755, 9in (22cm).
$6,000-7,000

A Staffordshire saltglazed white teapot and cover, with moulded bird's head and foliage spout and faceted scroll handle, finial chipped, spout repaired, c1755, 6in (15cm).
$14,000-19,000

A Staffordshire creamware teapot and cover of Whieldon type, crispl moulded with trailing vine beneat rich brown and grey glazes, tip of spout mounted in white metal, slight damage, c1755, 4in (9.5cm).
$2,500-3,000

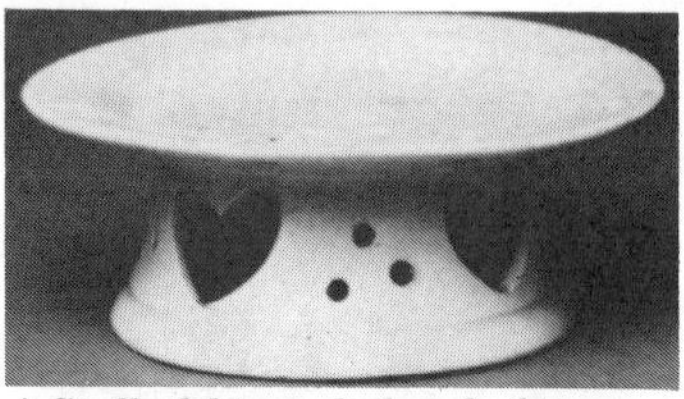

A Staffordshire saltglazed white teapot stand, c1760, 5½in (13.5cm) diam.
$1,500-1,800

A Staffordshire creamware teapot and cover of Wedgwood-Whieldon type, with alternating green and ochre stripes, some restoration, c1760, 5in (12.5cm).
$9,000-10,000

A Staffordshire creamware baluste coffee pot and cover of Whieldon type, streaked in brown, damage and restoration, c1760, 8in (19cm).
$2,000-3,000

A Staffordshire saltglazed miniature coffee pot and cover, slight restoration, c1760, 4½in (11.5cm).
$1,200-1,500

A Staffordshire saltglazed teapot and cover, boldly painted in pink with roses on a dense ground of black circles and dots, some chips c1760, 7in (17cm) wide.
$2,000-2,500

A Staffordshire saltglazed teapot with applied vine decoration, c176
$12,000-14,000

A Staffordshire saltglazed polychrome punch pot, finely painted with Bacchus astride a barrel, replacement cover painted with a tree, restored, c1760, 8in (19cm).
$8,000-10,000

A Staffordshire coffee pot, with mottled underglaze greens and browns, c1765.
$8,000-9,000

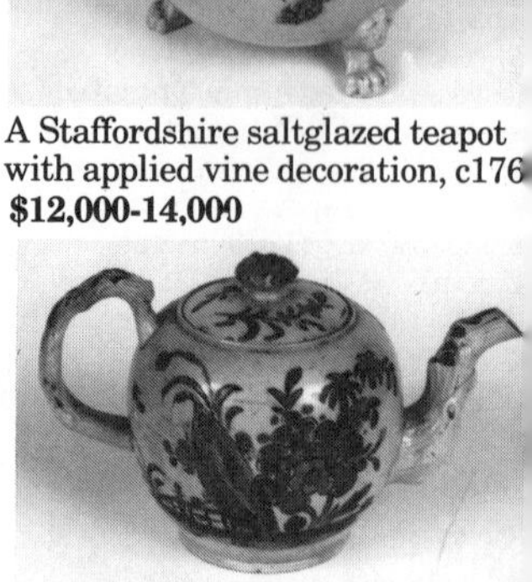

A saltglazed teapot, c1750, 4i (10cm).
$800-1,000

A miniature redware teapot, c1745, 3in (7.5cm).
$450-500

A Staffordshire teapot, c1770.
$1,200-1,400

, Staffordshire creamware globular punch
ot and cover of Whieldon type, with
pplied trailing vine beneath a streaked
rown glaze, chipped, c1760, 8½in (21cm).
5,000-7,000

A Staffordshire saltglaze bear jug and
over, damage, c1750, 10½in (26.5cm).
$8,000-12,000

\ Staffordshire creamware
igure of Whieldon type,
1760, 3½in (8.5cm) long.
12,000-14,000

A Staffordshire pottery jug,
inscribed R. Woodman, 9½in
23cm). **$80-100**

A Staffordshire creamware
figure, restoration and
damage, 10in (25.5cm).
$25,000-30,000

A Chelsea coffee pot and
cover, damage, incised
mark, c1745, 8½in (22cm).
$40,000-50,000

A Staffordshire creamware baluster coffee
pot and cover, chipped, c1760, 9in (23cm).
$10,000-12,000

A Staffordshire saltglaze baluster coffee
pot and cover, slight damage, c1755.
$11,000-13,000

An Obadiah Sherratt group of Polito's
Menagerie, damage and repairs, c1830,
13½in (35cm) wide.
$30,000-32,000

A Staffordshire saltglaze footed bowl,
depicting 'The 7 Champions of
Christendom', damaged and repaired,
c1745, 11in (28cm). **$12,000-14,000**

A Staffordshire slipware drinking vessel,
lecorated in cream slip beneath a rich
reacle glaze, cracked and chipped, dated
700, 5½in (13.5cm) wide.
9,000-11,000

A Staffordshire saltglaze two-handled cup
incised RSB and dated 1761, the reverse
with a bird, handles cracked, 13in (33cm)
wide.
$24,000-30,000

A Staffordshire and solid
agate chocolate pot and
domed cover, cover
restored, c1750, 9in
(22.5cm). **$12,000-14,000**

A Chelsea silver shaped dish, with shell-moulded thumbpieces, painted in the Kakiemon palette with a sinuous dragon looking towards an iron red tiger, raised anchor mark, c1750, 9½in (24.5cm) wide.
$14,000-16,000

A Dutch Delft Doré plate, painted with Chinese ladies, insects and leaves, with a foliate border, gilt rim, slight chips, red monogram APK, c1700, 9in (23cm) diam.
$7,000-9,000

An Urbino Istoriato dish, painted in the Fontana workshop with Proserpine and her companions, chips repaired, the reverse inscribed Le Compagnie L Prozerpina, c1570, 10½in (27.5cm) diam.
$35,000-40,000

A Venice Istoriato saucer dish, painted with Apollo slaying the children of Niobe, minor rim chips, c1560, 11½in (29.5cm) diam.
$36,000-40,000

A Pallisy oval dish, moulded in relief with fishes, molluscs and frogs, the border with leaves, shells and other aquatic fauna, the reverse mottled in blue and manganese, firing cracks and old damage to rim, 16thC, 19½in (49.5cm) wide.
$5,000-10,000

A Pesaro fluted crespina, painted with the sacrifice of Isaac, chips to rim, reduced, footrim missing, c1570, 9½in (24.5cm) diam.
$12,000-16,000

An Urbino Istoriato dish, painted in the Patanazzi workshop, with the Menapiars surrendering to Caesar, damage, c1580, 10½in (27cm) diam.
$40,000-45,000

An Urbino Istoriato charger, painted in the Fontana workshop, with Deucalion and Pyrrha after the flood, hair crack and repaired chips, c1560, 16in (40.5cm).
$40,000-45,000

A Pesaro fluted crespina, painted with Christ on the road to Calvary, chips and some repainting, c1570, 9in (23.5cm).
$8,000-12,000

An Urbino dish, painted with the Flagellation, re-stuck, c1570, 12½in (31.5cm).
$14,000-18,000

An Urbino dish, painted in the Patanazzi workshop, with the Carnutes and the Senones surrendering to Caesar, repaired, c1580, 10½in (27cm).
$12,000-14,000

A Faenza documentary compendiaro crespina, painted in the workshop of Maestro Virgiliotto Calamelli, damage, c1565, 12in (30cm). **$10,000-12,000**

A Capodimonte beaker, minor rim chips, blue stylised fleur-de-lys mark, c1745, 3in (8cm).
$1,600-2,000

A Reval rococo baluster vase, chips, blue monogram TRF, c1780, 10in (25.5cm).
$10,000-12,000

Two Castelli baluster vases, painted in the manner of Antonio Saverio Grue, damage and repairs, c1730, 13in (32.5cm). **$20,000-24,000**

A pair of Meissen teacups and saucers, one cup damaged, blue crossed swords mark, c1730.
$12,000-16,000

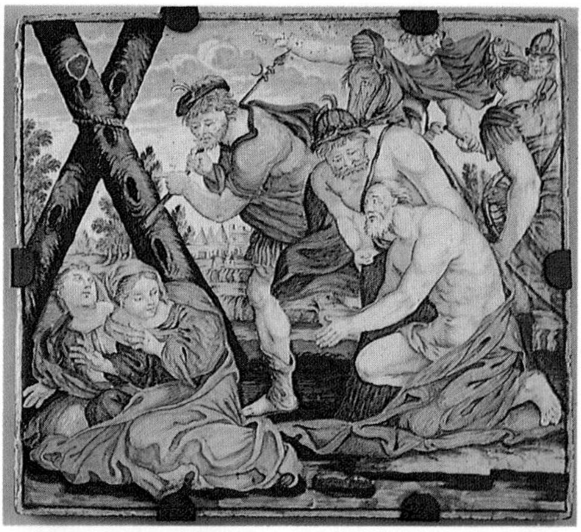

A Castelli plaque, painted in the manner of Carlo Antonio Grue, with St. Andrew's adoration of the Cross, c1725, 12in (30cm) high.
$4,000-5,000

A Staffordshire saltglaze polychrome pepper pot, painted in a 'famille rose' palette, c1755, 4½in (12cm).
$11,000-13,000

A Meissen Kakiemon bowl, painted with chrysanthemum issuing from a rocky terrace, the reverse with a similar spray and an insect in flight, blue crossed swords mark, c1730, 11½in (29.5cm) diam.
$4,000-5,000

A Staffordshire saltglaze sauceboat, crisply moulded and painted with trailing vine, the interior painted in a 'famille rose' palette within a diaper pattern border, c1755, 7in (18cm) long. **$8,000-10,000**

A London delft Royal Portrait plaque of Queen Anne, minute chipping, dated 1704, pierced for hanging, 9in (23.5cm).
$30,000-35,000

A pair of Meissen celadon fond bottles, AR monogram and incised former's marks, c1732, 12in (30cm). **$90,000-100,000**

A Chamberlain's Worcester porcelain cup and saucer inscribed 'Sherbourn', marked in red, c1815, saucer 5½in (14cm).
$3,000-4,000

A Meissen Kakiemon beaker and saucer, blue crossed swords mark and incised mark, c1735. **$3,000-4,000**

A Meissen Hausmalerei tea-bowl and saucer, painted at Bayreuth, c1725.
$28,000-32,000

A Meissen chocolate cup and saucer, from the Swan service, blue crossed swords mark, c1737.
$40,000-50,000

A Meissen Kakiemon beaker, the handle enriched with gilding, crossed swords mark and incised mark, c1725, 3½in (8.5cm). **$8,000-10,000**

A Meissen chinoiserie beaker, painted by J. G. Hörold, c1728, with almost contemporary trembleuse stand, 3in (8cm)
$9,000-10,000

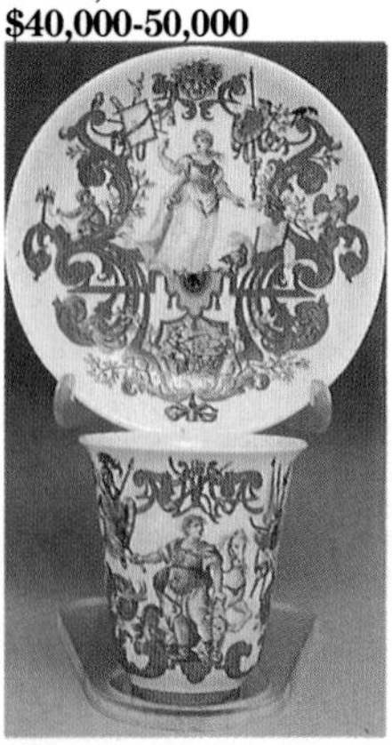

A Böttger Hausmalerei beaker and saucer, painted by Ignaz Bottengrüber, c1725.
$50,000-60,000

A Meissen bowl, probably painted by J. E. Mehlhorn, c1730, 7in (18cm) diam.
$8,000-10,000

A Meissen teacup from the Swan service, rim chip, c1740.
$12,000-14,000

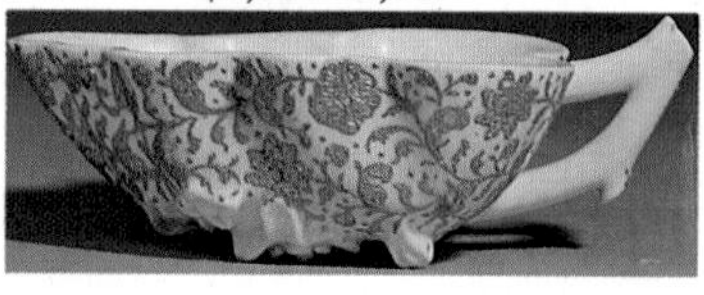

A Böttger porcelain Hausmalerei cup, gilded, minute chips, c1715, decorated later, 5in (12.5cm). **$5,000-6,000**

A Meissen cup and saucer, various marks, c1736.
$5,000-7,000

A Sèvres cup and trembleuse saucer, various marks, c1816.
$36,000-40,000

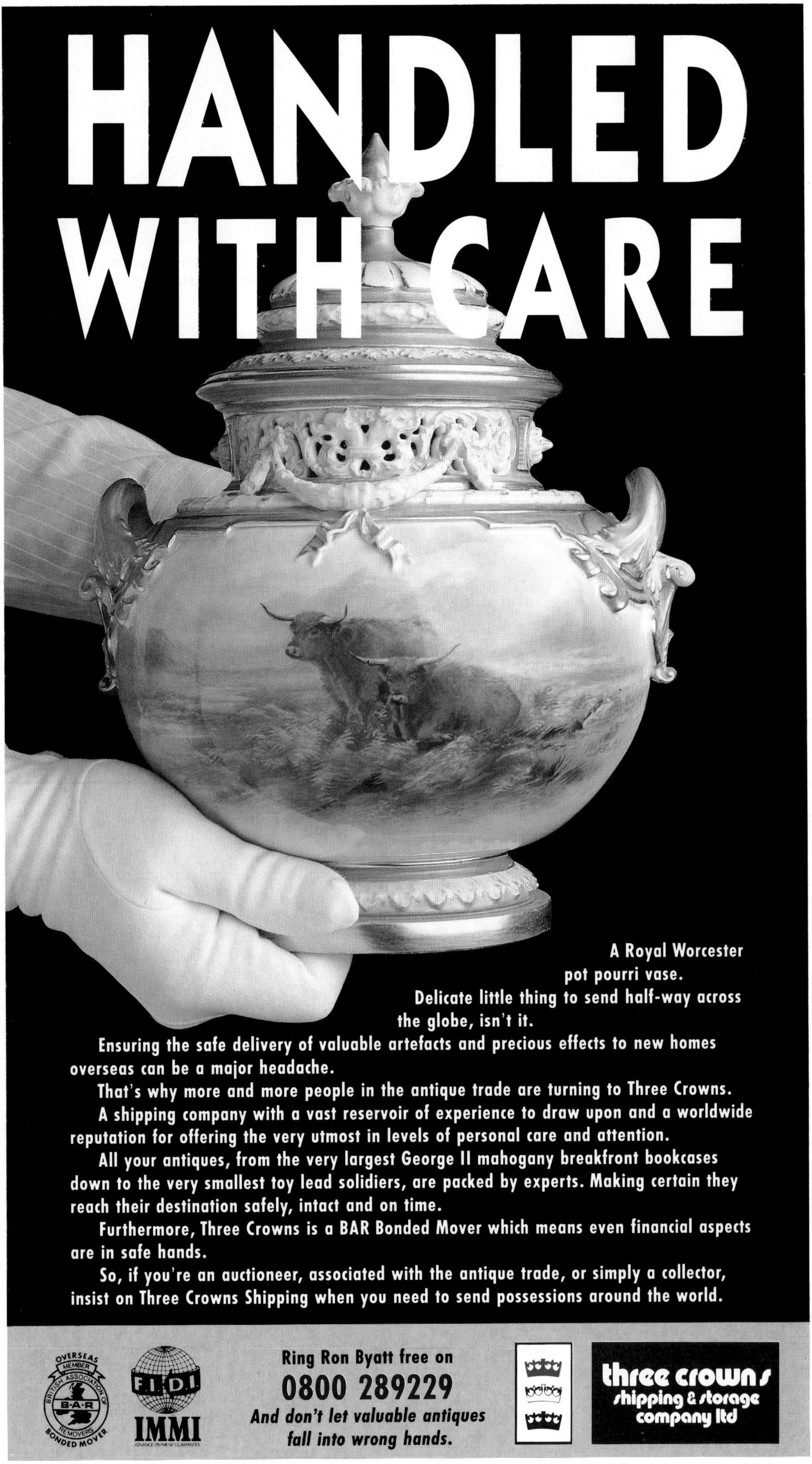
HANDLED
WITH CARE
A Royal Worcester
pot pourri vase.
Delicate little thing to send half-way across
the globe, isn't it.
Ensuring the safe delivery of valuable artefacts and precious effects to new homes overseas can be a major headache.
That's why more and more people in the antique trade are turning to Three Crowns.
A shipping company with a vast reservoir of experience to draw upon and a worldwide reputation for offering the very utmost in levels of personal care and attention.
All your antiques, from the very largest George II mahogany breakfront bookcases down to the very smallest toy lead soldiers, are packed by experts. Making certain they reach their destination safely, intact and on time.
Furthermore, Three Crowns is a BAR Bonded Mover which means even financial aspects are in safe hands.
So, if you're an auctioneer, associated with the antique trade, or simply a collector, insist on Three Crowns Shipping when you need to send possessions around the world.
OVERSEAS MEMBER
BRITISH ASSOCIATION OF REMOVERS
B·A·R
BONDED MOVER
F.I.D.I.
IMMI
Ring Ron Byatt free on
0800 289229
And don't let valuable antiques fall into wrong hands.
three crowns
shipping & storage
company ltd

A Meissen Hausmalerei coffee pot, chipped, crossed swords mark, c1725 and later, 8in (21cm). **$28,000-30,000**

A Meissen teapot and cover, painted in the manner of J. G. Höroldt, blue AR mark and gilder's mark 72, c1728, 4½in (11.5cm). **$48,000-52,000**

A Böttger porcelain coffee pot and cover, chips repaired, c1722, 8in (20cm). **$50,000-60,000**

A Meissen Imari teapot and cover, chipped, blue crossed swords and incised marks, c1725, 6in (14.5cm). **$12,000-16,000**

An early Meissen teapot and cover, KPM and crossed swords marks, c1725, 6½in (16.5cm). **$36,000-40,000**

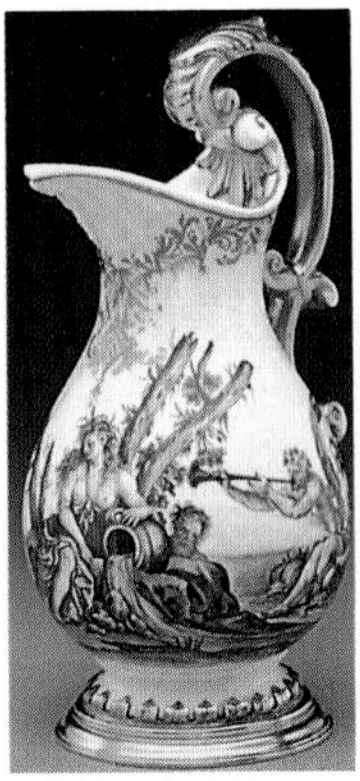

A Meissen Hausmalerei jug, damaged, marked, c1740 and later. **$12,000-14,000**

A Meissen wine pot, painted with 'indianische Blumen', chipped spout, blue crossed swords mark, c1728, 6in (15cm). **$28,000-32,000**

A Worcester figure of a gardener, damage, c1770, 7in (17cm). **$16,000-20,000**

l. A Frankenthal chinoiserie figure, c1760, 11in (28cm). **$18,000-20,000**

r. A Ludwigsburg figure of the Abbé, c1765, 6in (15cm). **$14,000-18,000**

A pair of Royal Dux figures, in the form of young women holding lamps, applied pink triangle mark, 32in (81.5cm). **$5,000-6,000**

A 'Girl in a Swing' group of Leda and the Swan, damage, c1750, 6in (15cm). **$36,000-40,000**

. Ridgway leaf-shaped dish, with broad
ilt rim and heavily raised and gilt
ıttice and leaf decorated border, red
ainted mark 893, c1825, 9½in (24cm).
400-600

Meissen figures, modelled by
J. J. Kändler, damage and repairs,
blue crossed swords marks:
l. Hofnarr Frölich, c1739,
9½in (24.5cm). **$14,000-16,000**
r. The Cherry Pickers, c1770, 11in
(28.5cm). **$6,000-8,000**

A Wurzburg figure of a girl,
allegorical of Autumn,
damage, c1770, 7½in (18.5cm).
$15,000-16,000

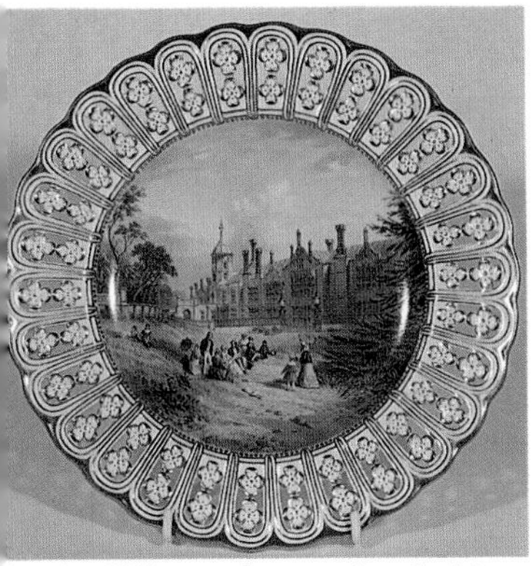

\ pair of Minton plates, painted with
ountry scenes, inscribed 'Cobham Hall,
Kent' and 'Penshurst from the Park',
mpressed Minton and mark for 1862,
in (23cm). **$3,000-4,000**

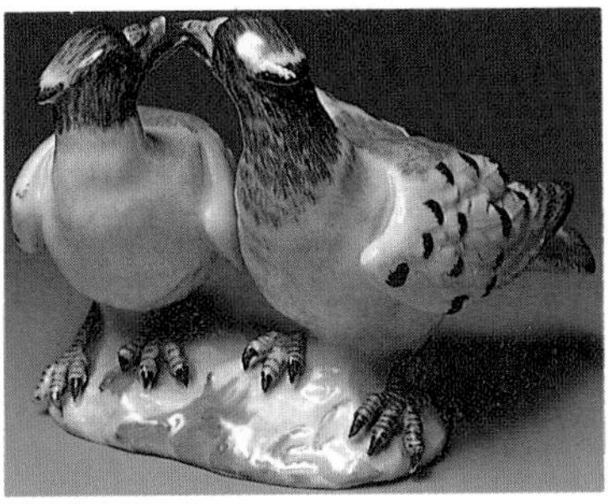

A Meissen group of doves, modelled by
J. J. Kändler, their plumage incised and
painted, chip to one talon and beaks,
c1750, 4½in (12cm) wide.
$5,000-6,000

A Louis XV ormolu mounted
Frankenthal group, restored,
7½in (19cm).
$4,000-5,000

\ Meissen Jagd group,
nodelled by J. J. Kändler,
ne leg broken and repaired,
1745, 7in (18cm).
10,000-12,000

Two Meissen figures, Pantalone and Scapin,
from the Commedia dell'Arte, modelled by
J. J. Kändler and P. Reinicke, chips,
one marked, c1743, 5½in (14.5cm).
$5,000-7,000 each

A Meissen group, La Toilette
Der Prinzessin, blue crossed
swords marks, c1761, 9in
(23cm) wide.
$7,000-9,000

\ Höchst Turkish orchestra, by J. P.
Melchior, damage and restored, blue
vheel marks, c1770, 7½in (19cm).
35,000-40,000

A Ridgway trio, with gold beaded rims, bold acanthus
leaf gilt painted and moulded decoration on blue ground,
c1840, orange painted mark 5/1745, the saucer 5½in
(14cm). **$400-500**

A Worcester dish, painted in the manner of Jefferyes Hamett O'Neale, blue square seal mark, c1770, 10½in (26.5cm) wide.
$12,000-16,000

A pair of blue and white plates, after a design by Cornelius Pronk, one with firing crack, c1735, 8½in (22cm).
$14,000-16,000

A pair of Vienna dishes, painted with fruit and vegetables, blue beehive marks, various impressed marks, and 34 in red enamel c1770, 14½in (36.5cm).
$14,000-16,000

A Chamberlain's Worcester centrepiece with gilt handles, gilt rim, raised leaf decorated border, painted with flowers, the underside and foot similarly painted, 13½in (34cm) wide.
$900-1,200

A Meissen deep plate from the Swan service, rim chips, blue crossed swords mark and Dreyer's mark of Rehschuh, c1741, 9in (23cm).
$18,000-24,000

A Worcester dish, from the Duke of Gloucester Service, gold crescent mark, c1775, 13½in (34cm).
$20,000-24,000

A Meissen plate, from the Hollandisches service, painted with a view of St. Jans Kerkhof in Utrecht, blue crossed swords mark and dot mark, Pressnummer 46 and painter's mark, c1763, 8in (20.5cm).
$5,000-6,000

A Barr, Flight & Barr plate, attributed to Samuel Astles, impressed BFB and printed puce marks, c1805, 9in (23cm).
$3,000-4,000

A Meissen armorial dish, from the service made for Graf Johann Christian von Hennicke, blue crossed swords mark, Pressnummer 20 and Dreher's mark 4, c1740, 15in (38.5cm).
$7,000-8,000

Three Nicholas I Imperial porcelain military plates, signed S. Doladugine, some wear to painting and one plate repaired, c1840, 10½in (27cm).
$6,000-8,000

A Sèvres déjeuner, blue interlaced L's enclosing date letter E for 1757, and painter's mark for Rocher, incised marks.
$24,000-28,000

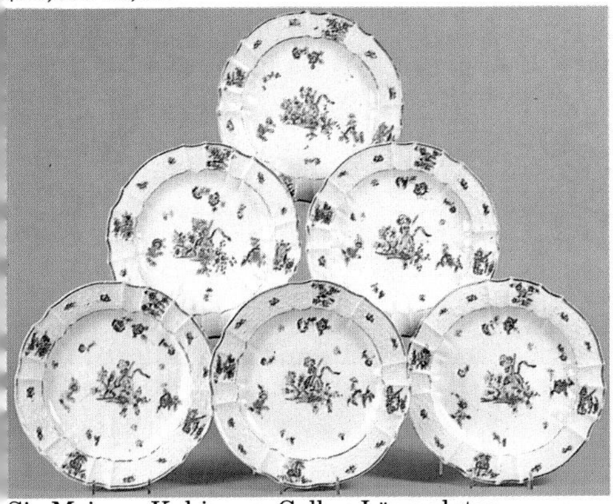

Six Meissen Kakiemon Gelber Löwe plates, crossed swords marks, Pressnummer 22, c1738, 10in (25.5cm). **$11,000-12,000**

A Derby part dessert service, marked, c1795. **$140,000-150,000**

A pair of Vincennes seaux à demi bouteille, painter Taillandier's marks, c1753, 4½in (11cm) high.
$20,000-24,000

A Newhall part tea and coffee service, painted by Fidelle Duvivier, some rubbing to gilt rims, pattern No. 11 to major pieces, c1785.
$50,000-60,000

A Meissen (Punkt) déjeuner, crossed swords and dot marks, c1775, the tray 17½in (44cm) wide.
$16,000-20,000

A Furstenberg part tea and coffee service, blue script F and Pressnummern to most pieces, c1775.
$5,000-6,000

A Coalport part dessert service, probably painted by S. Lawrence, impressed pattern No. 4/412, c1840.
$8,000-10,000

A Ludwigsburg tête á tête, painted 'en grisaille' with oval cartouches, blue crowned interlaced C marks, c1775.
$12,000-16,000

A Meissen garniture of 5 vases, with applied May blossom, cartouches of raised flowering branches enclosing scenes of birds and fowl, c1760, tallest 10½in (26.5cm). **$14,000-16,000**

A Höchst tureen, cover and stand, painted in the manner of Andreas Öttner, minor damage, the tureen incised IH±, the stand with crowned blue wheel mark and IN, c1760, 13in (33.5cm) wide. **$10,000-12,000**

Two Volkstedt relief moulded portrait plaques, the borders modelled as gilded frames, chips, c1785, 9½in (24cm) high. **$32,000-36,000**

A pair of Sèvres pattern plaques, late 19thC, in later gilded frames, the plaques 17½in (45cm) diam. **$24,000-30,000**

l. A Meissen double-ended snuff box, c1765, 3in (7.5cm) wide. **$16,000-20,000**

r. A pair of Sèvres pattern vases, 20thC. **$10,000-12,000**

A pair of Louis XVI style ormolu mounted Samson vases and covers, restoration, 19thC, 13in (33cm). **$16,000-20,000**

A pair of Sèvres plaques, signed Micaud Pinx, dated 1804, minor damage, 13in (33cm). **$30,000-32,000**

A Flight & Barr Worcester sauce tureen, cover and stand, script marks, c1800, the stand 8½in (21cm) wide. **$12,000-14,000**

A pair of Worcester Imari pattern vases and covers, c1770, 12in (30.5cm). **$60,000-65,000**

A pair of ormolu mounted Meissen candlesticks, the porcelain c1755. **$7,000-8,000**

A Meissen armorial sugar bowl and cover from the Swan service, modelled by J. J. Kändler and J. F. Eberlein, blue crossed swords mark, c1741, 7in (18cm) high. **$60,000-70,000**

A Kakiemon deep bowl, with enamels on underglaze blue, damage and repairs, Fuku mark, late 17thC, 10½in (26cm). **$4,000-6,000**

A Ming box and cover, body crack, Longqing six-character mark within double square and of the period, 4½in (11cm) square. **$24,000-28,000**

A Yuan dish, restored, c1350, 19in (48cm) diam. **$16,000-20,000**

A Yaozhou celadon bowl, with deeply carved interior under a lightly crackled glaze, glaze crack, Song Dynasty, 8½in (21cm) diam. **$14,000-16,000**

A Canton 'famille rose' initialled punchbowl, enamelled with audience scenes on a butterfly and foliage ground beneath a band of figures at the rim, centred to one side with the initials GF, restored, 19thC, 21½in (54.5cm). **$7,000-9,000**

A 'famille rose' Masonic armorial punch bowl, with the motto 'Holiness to the Lord', Qianlong, c1775. **$14,000-16,000**

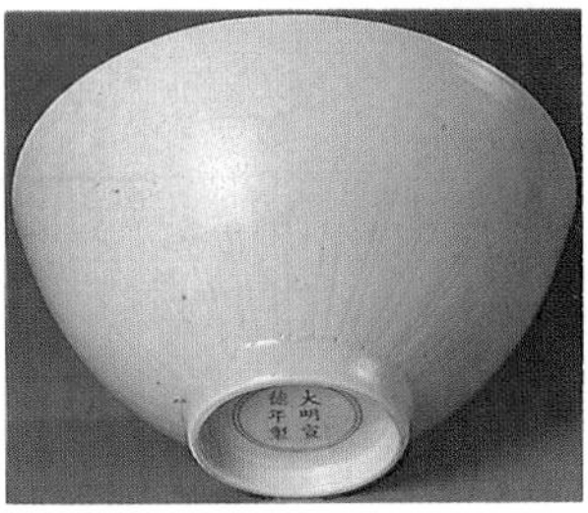

A white glazed anhua-decorated bowl, encircled Xuande six-character mark and of the period, 8in (20.5cm) diam, fitted box. **$40,000-50,000**

A Meissen tea caddy and cover, pressnummer 49 to base and gilder's 11, c1745, 5in (13cm). **$6,000-7,000**

A late Ming box and pierced cover, fritted, chipped, Wanli six-character mark within a double rectangle and of the period, 10½in (27cm) wide. **$14,000-16,000**

An early Ming deep bowl, the mouth bound with copper, possibly reduced, chips, Yongle/Xuande, 14½in (36.8cm) wide. **$400,000+**

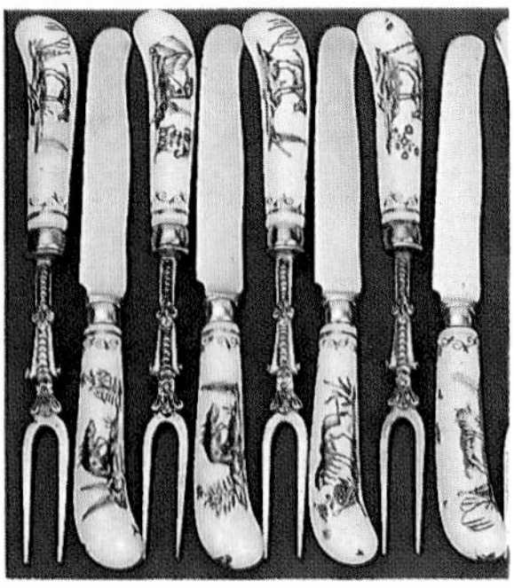

A set of 12 Meissen knife and fork handles, enriched with gilding, c1735, with old silver blades and forks, 7½in (19.5cm). **$7,000-8,000**

A Shufu bowl, moulded with lotus scrolls and 'shu' and 'fu', under an opaque glaze tinged with blue, Yuan Dynasty, 4½in (12cm) diam. **$10,000-12,000**

Two bowls, Tongzhi six-character marks and of the period. **$4,000-6,000**

A pair of 'famille rose' bowls, restored, Jiaqing seal mark and of the period, 6in (15cm) diam. **$15,000-16,000**

A pair of 'famille rose' medallion bowls, Jiaqing six character marks and of the period, 5½in (15cm). **$35,000-40,000**

A pair of 'famille rose' bowls, Daoguang seal marks in underglaze blue and of the period, 6in (15cm) diam. **$10,000-12,000**

Two 'kraak porselein' dishes, discovered by Capt. M. Hatcher, c1643. **$12,000-16,000**

A pair of yellow glazed bowls, Guangxu six-character marks in underglaze blue and of the period, 4in (10cm), fitted box. **$1,500-2,000**

A Kenjo-Imari bowl, six-character mark, c1700. **$20,000-24,000**

A pair of ruby enamelled blue and white bowls, Guangxu six-character mark in underglaze blue and of the period, 9in (23cm) diam. **$6,000-8,000**

A pair of Wucai dragon and phoenix bowls, marked, 5½in (13cm) diam. **$32,000-36,000**

A pair of 'famille rose' bowls, Guangxu mark in underglaze blue and of the period, 4½in (12cm) diam. **$5,000-6,000**

A pair of 'famille verte' bowls, Yongzheng marks, 4in (10cm), boxed. **$50,000-60,000**

An Arita plate, painted with birds, flowers and fruit around a medallion with the letters VOC, late 17thC, 8in (20cm) diam. **$9,000-11,000**

A Longquan celadon dish, chipped, Southern Song Dynasty, 9in (23cm) diam.
$6,000-8,000

An Imari plate, painted after a design by Cornelius Pronk, cracked, early 18thC, 9in (23.5cm) diam.
$3,000-4,000

A Ko-Kutani dish, hairline crack to foot, Fuku mark in blue and black enamels, late 17thC, 8½in (21cm) diam.
$70,000-80,000

An Arita charger, with VOC centrally, chip restored, late 17thC.
$18,000-24,000

A circular dish, damage and repairs, late Yuan Dynasty, 18in (45.5cm) diam.
$40,000-50,000

A Ming Wucai saucer dish, restored, encircled Wanli six-character mark and of the period, 7½in (19cm).
$8,000-10,000

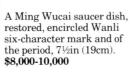

A Kakiemon foliate rimmed dish, rubbed enamels, late 17thC, 7½in (19cm).
$16,000-20,000

An Arita dish, with monogram, late 17thC, 9½in (24.5cm) diam.
$11,000-12,000

An Arita underglaze blue dish, in the Kakiemon manner, late 17thC, 12½in (31.5cm) diam.
$10,000-12,000

An Arita charger, with the letters VOC centrally, minor crack, late 17thC, 15½in (38.5cm) diam.
$20,000-24,000

An iron red dragon charger, Guangxu six-character mark in iron red and of the period, 20in (51cm). **$6,000-8,000**

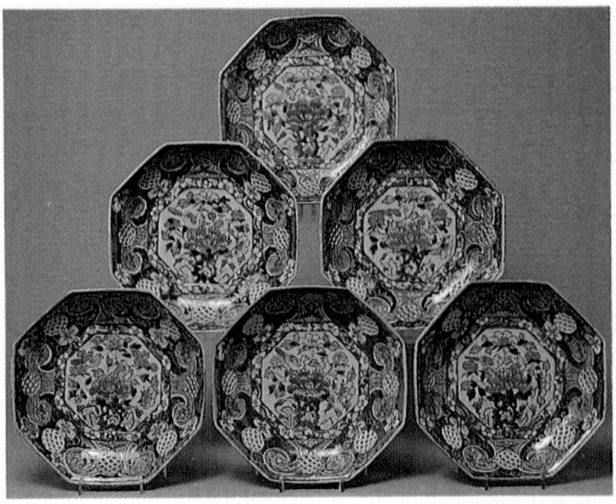

Six Imari dishes, decorated in enamel and gilt on underglaze blue, late 17th/early 18thC, 9½in (24.5cm). **$12,000-14,000**

A pair of Arita plates, c1700, 12½in (32cm). **$10,000-12,000**

A Chinese 'Imari' armorial barber's bowl, c1712, 13½in (35cm). **$8,000-10,000**

A pair of 'famille rose' saucer dishes, Qianlong, 15in (38cm). **$6,000-7,000**

A large Imari bowl Genroku period. **$12,000-14,000**

A Kakiemon bowl, moulded with interlocking rings around the sides, early 18thC, 8½in (22cm) wide. **$4,000-5,000**

A pair of Imari chargers. **$24,000-28,000**

A verte-Imari armorial plate, Yongzheng, c1730, 14in (35cm). **$18,000-20,000**

A Kakiemon dish, kiln mark, late 17thC. **$11,000-13,000**

A pair of saucer dishes, Qianlong seal marks and of the period, 5½in (13cm) diam. **$12,000-14,000**

A pair of Imari plates, damaged and restored, c1740, 9½in (23.5cm). **$7,000-8,000**

A Sancai glazed pottery head of a horse, ear restored, Tang Dynasty, 9½in (24cm) long. **$5,000-6,000**

A painted pottery figure of a horse, Six Dynasties/early Tang Dynasty, 18in (46cm) high.
$12,000-14,000

A pair of spaniels, each modelled in mirror image, one repaired, Qianlong, 9in (23cm) high.
$40,000-50,000

A group of painted pottery musicians and dancers, restored, Tang Dynasty. **$26,000-28,000**

A painted pottery figure of a horse, damaged and repairs, Tang Dynasty, 18in (46cm) high.
$16,000-20,000

A painted red pottery figure of a horse, Tang Dynasty.
$8,000-10,000

A 'famille rose' figure of a pheasant, chipped, late 18th/early 19thC, 14in (36cm) high.
$10,000-12,000

A painted grey pottery figure of a tricorn, late Eastern Han/Six Dynasties, 17in (44cm). **$15,000-17,000**

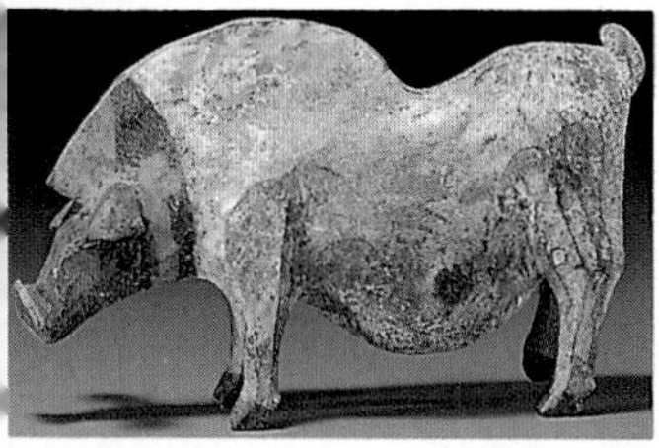

A painted pottery figure of a boar, restored, Northern Wei Dynasty, 6in (15cm) long.
$20,000-24,000

A pair of Imari models of cockerels, slight damage, late 17thC, 6½in (17cm) long. **$30,000-35,000**

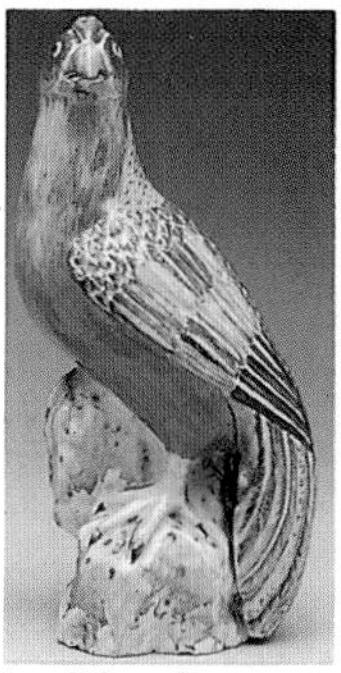

l. A pair of 'famille rose' figures of pheasants, repaired, Qianlong, 13in (33cm) high.
$50,000-60,000

r. A pottery figure of an equestrian flutist, Sui Dynasty, 11½in (29cm).
$12,000-14,000

A model of a Kakiemon seated tiger, restorations, late 17thC, 7½in (18.5cm). **$40,000-50,000**

A pair of Sancai Buddhistic lions, some chips, 42½in (107cm) high.
$8,000-10,000

A pair of Imari bijin, old damage and restoration, Genroku period, 12½in (31.5cm) high.
$30,000-40,000

An Arita model of a seated puppy, late 17thC, 7in (17.5cm). **$40,000-50,000**

A pair of Arita puppies, restored, late 17thC, 9½in (24cm). **$50,000-60,000**

An Arita model of a seated dog, some restoration, late 17thC, 16in (40cm).
$70,000-80,000

A painted figure of a kneeling woman, Han Dynasty. **$10,000-12,000**

Two painted pottery figures.
$28,000-32,000

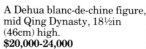

A pair of ormolu mounted Chinese export figures, the porcelain Qing, 16in (41cm).
$8,000-10,000

A Dehua blanc-de-chine figure, mid Qing Dynasty, 18½in (46cm) high.
$20,000-24,000

A painted and Sancai-glazed pottery equestrian, restored, Tang Dynasty, 15in (38cm).
$400,000+

An Imari jardinière, in enamels and gilt on underglaze blue, late 19thC, 18in (46cm) high.
$10,000-12,000

An Arita teapot and cover, damaged and repaired, early 18thC, 10½in (26cm) wide. **$5,000-7,000**

A Ming style bottle vase, Qianlong, 12in (30.5cm).
$140,000-150,000

A Kakiemon teapot and cover, c1680, 6in (15cm) wide.
$20-000-24,000

An Imari tureen and domed cover, chips and repairs, Genroku period, 12in (30cm) diam. **$20,000-24,000**

Three Imari jars and covers, damage and restorations, Genroku period, 24in (61cm) high.
$18,000-20,000

A 'famille rose' fish bowl, minor cracks, one mask repaired, Qianlong, 26½in (67cm) diam. **$24,000-30,000**

A baluster jar, painted with the '3 Friends', Yongzheng six-character mark and of the period, 3in (8cm).
$14,000-16,000

A pair of Chinese Imari tureens, covers and stands, chips and restored, early 18thC, stands 14½in (37.5cm).
$20,000-24,000

A pair of 'famille rose' tureens, covers and stands, Qianlong, stands 11in (28cm).
$14,000-18,000

A pair of jardinières, Yongzheng marks, 3in (7.5cm). **$10,000-12,000**

An Imari tureen and cover, slight damage, Genroku period, 9½in (23.5cm) high.
$6,000-8,000

A pair of Régence ormolu mounted Chinese porcelain jardinières, the porcelain c1650, 8in (21cm) high.
$35,000-40,000

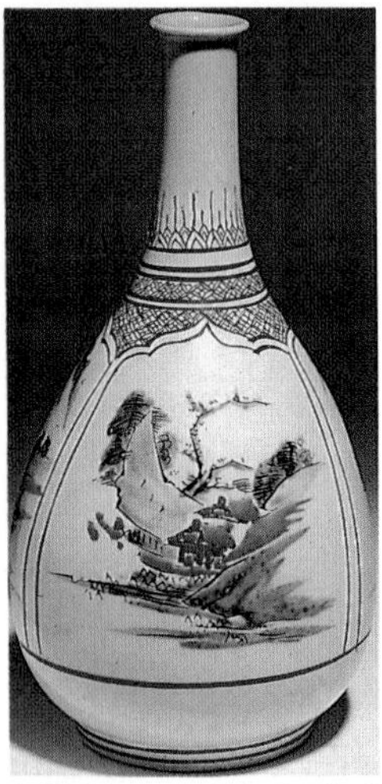

A Kakiemon globular bottle vase, c1680, 11in (28cm).
$30,000-35,000

A Kakiemon ovoid jar, chip to neck of rim, c1660, 8½in (21.5cm).
$90,000-100,000

A Ko-Imari oviform jar, decorated in enamels with peonies, foliage, stylised clouds above a leaf design band, the neck with geometric band, chip to rim, c1670, 11½in (29.5cm).
$44,000-50,000

A Kakiemon jar and cover, some damage, Empo/Jokyo period, 15in (38cm) high.
$100,000-120,000

A Transitional gu-shaped beaker vase, small rim chips, c1640, 16½in (41.5cm) high.
$14,000-16,000

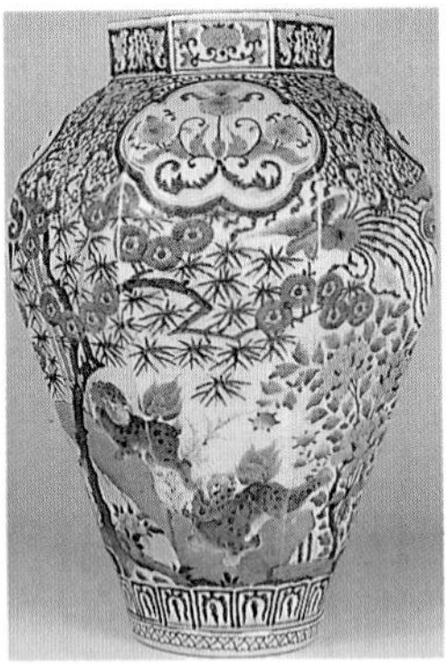

An Arita octagonal vase, minor rim chip and crack, late 17thC, 23½in (60cm).
$8,000-10,000

A Kakiemon underglaze blue vase and cover, cracked and restored, late 17thC, 14in (36cm) high.
$7,000-9,000

A Komai dish, slight old wear, signed Dai Nihon Kyoto ju Kakiya sei, late 19thC, 14½in (37cm).
$10,000-12,000

A Satsuma vase, signed, late 19thC, 22½in (57.5cm).
$12,000-16,000

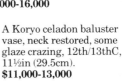

An Imari charger, decorated in enamels on underglaze blue, Genroku period, 19½in (49.5cm). **$12,000-16,000**

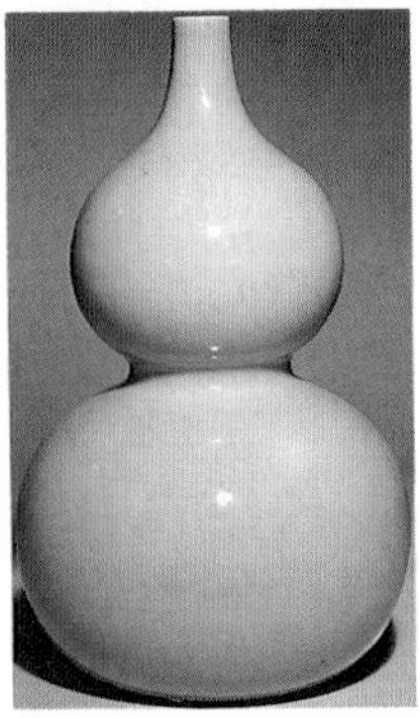

A celadon-glazed gourd vase, Jiaqing six-character mark and of the period, 12½in (33cm).
$8,000-10,000

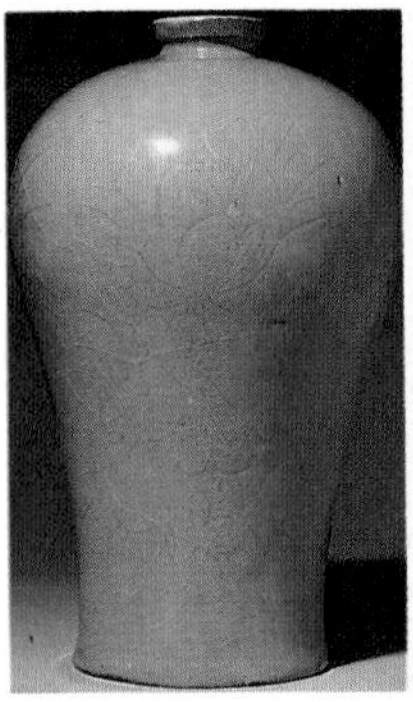

A Koryo celadon baluster vase, neck restored, some glaze crazing, 12th/13thC, 11½in (29.5cm).
$11,000-13,000

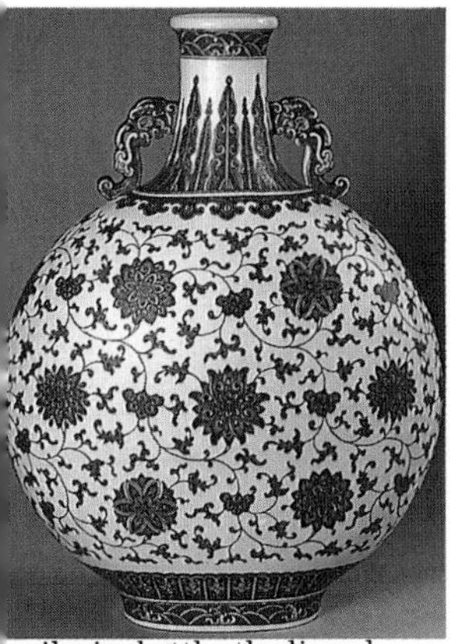

ı pilgrim bottle, the lipped
verted rim cracked, Qianlong
eal mark and of the period,
8½in (47cm), fitted box.
ı40,000-50,000

A pair of 'famille rose' vases, one repaired, late Qing Dynasty, 32½in (82.5cm).
$50,000-60,000

A five-piece garniture, comprising 3 vases and covers and 2 beaker vases, damage and restorations, Kangxi, baluster vases 17½in (44cm).
$24,000-26,000

A five-piece garniture of 'famille verte' vases, cracked and restored, Kangxi, beakers 10½in (26cm).
$12,000-14,000

ı 'famille rose'
ase, Jiaqing mark,
.1in (28cm).
ı20,000-24,000

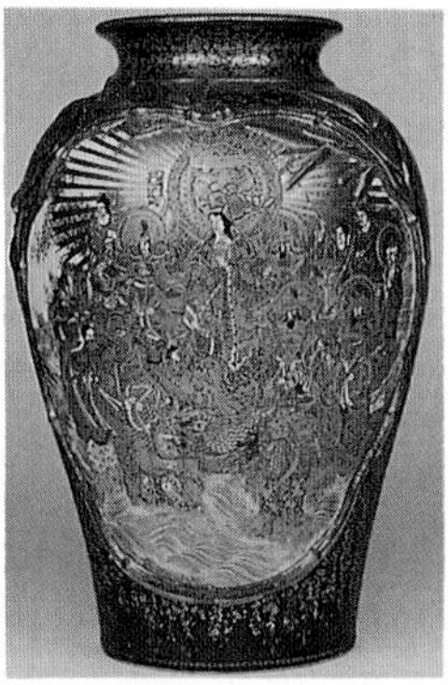

A Kinkozan vase, decorated in enamels, signed, late 19thC, 12½in (31cm).
$7,000-9,000

Eight Transitional vases, all with six-character marks within double squares, c1643, 4½in (11.5cm).
$24,000-30,000

\ 'famille rose'
vase, Qianlong mark,
25in (63.5cm).
$14,000-16,000

A 'famille rose' baluster vase, iron red Qianlong seal mark and of the period, 7½in (19cm).
$24,000-30,000

A Ge-type glazed Cong form vase, Qianlong seal mark in underglaze blue and of the period, 11½in (29cm).
$7,000-9,000

\ pair of Imari vases and
overs, cracks and restored,
Genroku period, 24½in
62.5cm). **$32,000-35,000**

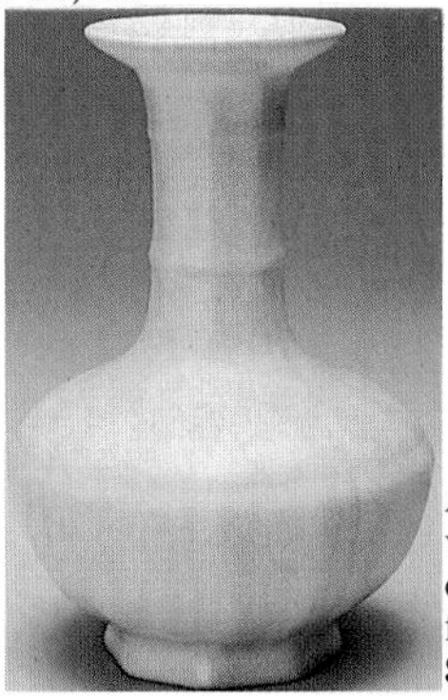

A moulded Guanyao-type bottle vase, Qianlong seal mark and of the period, 8½in (21cm), fitted box.
$12,000-14,000

A celadon glazed baluster vase, Qianlong seal mark and of the period, 16in (40cm).
$14,000-16,000

A Chinese Canton enamel tea table in 2 parts, early 19thC, 22½in (57cm) diam, wood stand. **$8,000-10,000**

A five-piece altar garniture, comprising a censer on lion's feet, 2 vases and 2 candlesticks, all painted with Immortals, beakers restored, 19thC, censer 19½in (50cm) high. **$7,000-9,000**

A five-piece garniture, comprising 3 jars and covers and 2 vases, decorated in enamel and gilt on underglaze blue, Genroku period, the jars and covers 13½in (21.5cm) high. **$6,000-8,000**

l. An Imperial bell, Nao, Qianlong Yuzhi mark, 7in (18cm). **$12,000-14,000**
r. An Imari moulded vase, repaired, Genroku period. **$7,000-9,000**

A green-glazed red pottery phoenix lamp, restored, Han Dynasty, 13in (33cm). **$8,000-10,000**

l. A 'famille rose' Tibetan style ewer and cover, Jiajing. **$8,000-10,000**
r. A Directoire ormolu and Chinese porcelain birdcage. **$16,000-20,000**

A Kakiemon kendi, restored, late 17thC, 8in (20cm). **$10,000-12,000**

An Imari tankard, decorated in iron red enamel and gilt on underglaze blue, Genroku period, 9in (22.5cm). **$10,000-12,000**

A Ko-Imari candlestick, minor chips to rim, inscribed ken, c1700, 7½in (19.5cm). **$7,000-8,000**

A Dayazhai 'famille rose' bottle vase, Yong Xing Chun mark, Tongzhi, 16in (40cm). **$15,000-17,000**

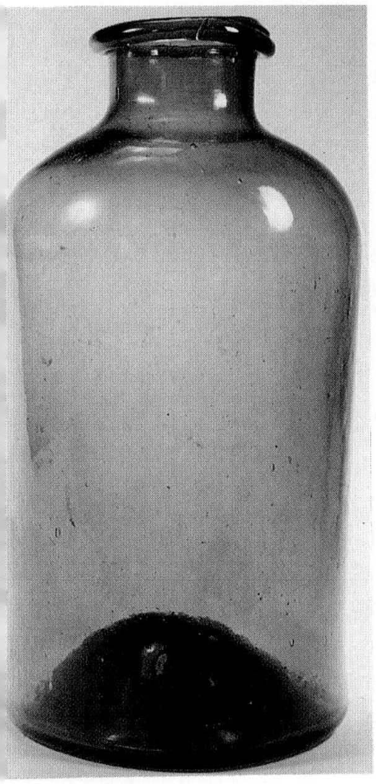

A pair of Beijing bottle vases, the globular bodies with tall necks flaring slightly towards the mouth, c1850, 9in (23cm), fitted box.
$10,000-12,000

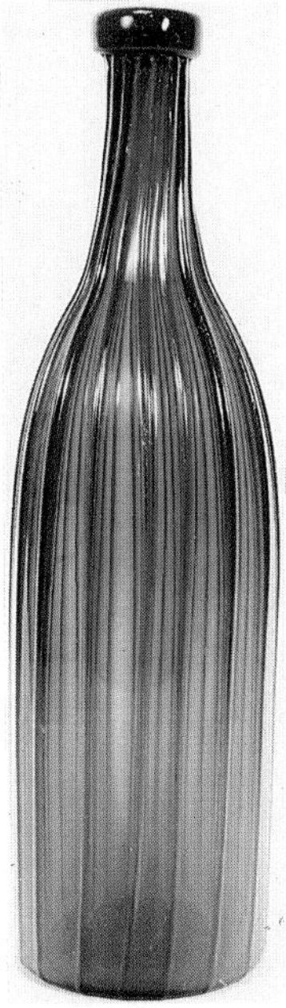

A Nailsea ovoid bottle glass flask, c1810, 8½in (21.5cm).
$600-700

ι 'Nailsea' crown glass
ıuff jar, with folded-over
im, c1800, 11½in (29.5cm).
250-300

A green ribbed spirit bottle, with folded rim, c1830, 11½in (29.5cm).
$600-700

A pair of octagonal beakers, with enamelled panels picked out in gilt, c1880, 3½in (9.7cm).
$200-300

An amber carafe, with flute and prism cut body, star cut base, c1830, 5in (13cm).
$400-500

A green wrythen moulded beaker, the wrythen cup-shaped body with folded rim and moulded scalloped foot, c1850, 4in (10cm).
$220-250

ι blue glass measure, the
ody with trailed neck ring,
ngraved in diamond point
William Parry, Silence,
Never 1852', glass c1820,
ngraving later, 4in (10.5cm).
400-500

An amethyst glass finger bowl and stand, c1850, stand 7½in (18.5cm) diam.
$160-200

A wrythen moulded sugar basin, with brown amethyst tint, c1820, 3in (7.5cm).
$240-300

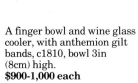

An amethyst wrythen moulded
ugar basin, with folded rim
ınd plain foot, c1820, 2½in
6.5cm).
$240-300

A finger bowl and wine glass cooler, with anthemion gilt bands, c1810, bowl 3in (8cm) high.
$900-1,000 each

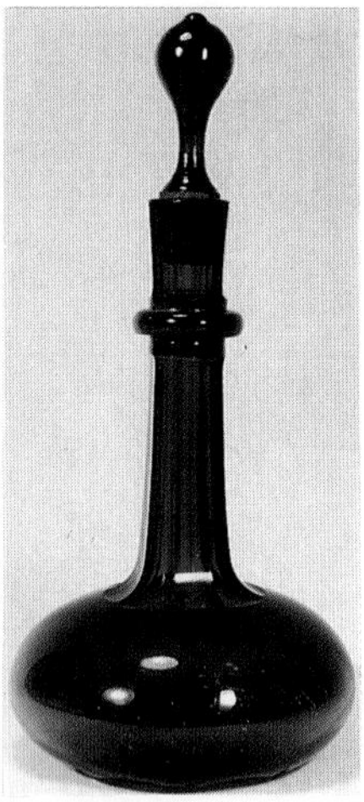

A decanter with flute cut neck, c1860, 8½in (22cm).
$140-200

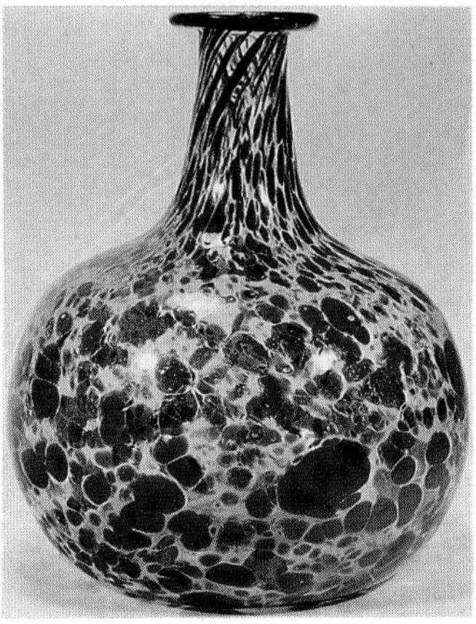

A Crown clear glass carafe, with red and blue marvered decoration, possibly Stourbridge, c1840, 8½in (21cm).
$450-500

l. & r. A pair of blue spirit decanters, with plain lozenge stoppers, c1800, 9½in (23.5cm). **$1,000-1,200**

c. A smaller decanter, 8in (20.5cm).
$250-300

A set of 3 barrel shaped spirit bottles, c1840, 6½in (16cm).
$2,000-2,500

A set of 3 spirit decanters, c1800, 7½in (19cm). **$2,200-2,600**

A spirit bottle, c1830, 6½in (17cm).
$450-500

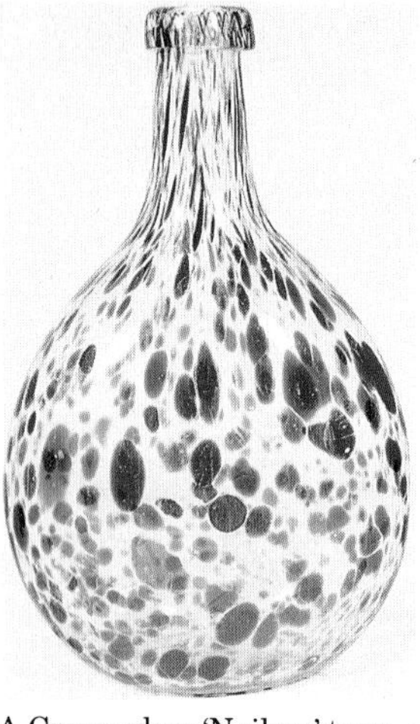

A Crown glass 'Nailsea' type carafe, c1860, 9in (23cm).
$500-600

A set of 3 spirit decanters, c1790, 7½in (19cm).
$2,500-3,000

Three decanters, with gilt decoration and lozenge stoppers, c1790, 7in (18cm).
$400-1,000 each

l. & r. A pair of Bristol blue decanters, with simulated gilt wine labels, 'Hollands' and 'Rum', gilt lozenge stoppers, c1790, 7½in (18.5cm). **$800-1,000**

c. A plain decanter with lozenge stopper, c1790, 7in (18cm). **$350-400**

A German enamelled Wagoner's Guild humpen, dated 1660, 6½in (17cm). **$28,000-32,000**

Three spirit flagons with loop handles and plated mounts, cork/metal stoppers, c1830, 8in (20cm).
$220-300 each

l. & r. A pair of blue flagons with loop handles and odd cork/metal stoppers, c1825, 7½in (19.5cm).
$500-600
c. A carafe, c1840. **$300-400**

l. A blue flagon for gin, c1820, 7½in (19cm).
$240-280
r. A spirit bottle, c1830, 12in (31cm).
$350-400

A Beilby enamelled decanter and stopper for beer, damage, c1775, 11in (28.5cm).
$14,000-16,000

An Irish decanter, c1810, 8in (20.5cm).
$750-800

An amethyst spirit flagon, with loop handle and brass mount, brass/cork stopper, c1830, 7½in (19.5cm).
$350-400

Two green flagons with loop handles, plated mounts and cork/metal stoppers, c1825, 4in (10.5cm).
$260-300 each

A green goblet, c1760, 5in (12.5cm).
$900-1,000

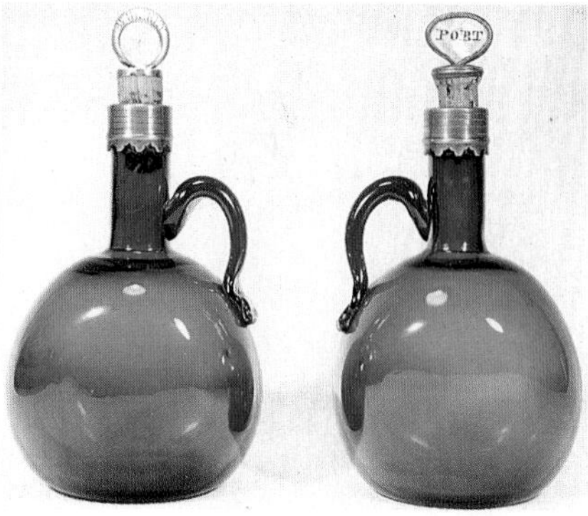

Two blue flagons with loop handles, metal mounts and cork/metal stoppers, c1825, 7½in (19cm).
$260-300 each

l. & r. A set of 6 wine glasses, c1830, 5in (12.5cm). **$600-700**
c. An amber wine glass, c1850. **$120-160**

l. & r. A pair of ribbed ovoid wines, c1830, 4in (10cm). **$220-250**
c. A green wine glass, c1830. **$100-120**

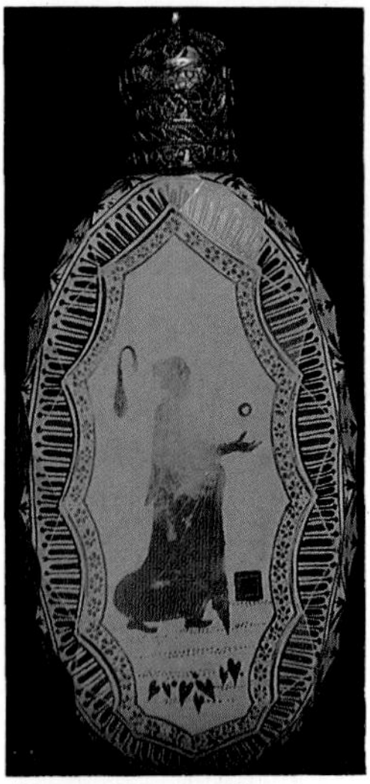

An opaque scent bottle, c1770, 4½in (11cm).
$1,600-1,800

A Potsdam-Zechlin engraved and gilt goblet and cover, c1740, 12½in (31cm).
$7,000-8,000

Two wine glasses, c1850, 5in (13cm).
l. **$140-160**
r. **$70-90**

Two scent bottles, c1780, 5in (12cm).
$500-600 each

Three Nailsea rolling pins, c1860, 14 to 15in (35 to 38cm)
$100-400 each

Two cream jugs. l. c1800, 2½in (7cm).
r. c1780, 3½in (9cm).
$300-400 each

Rolling pins, c1860.
Top. With verse.
Bottom 'Nailsea'.
$130-150 each

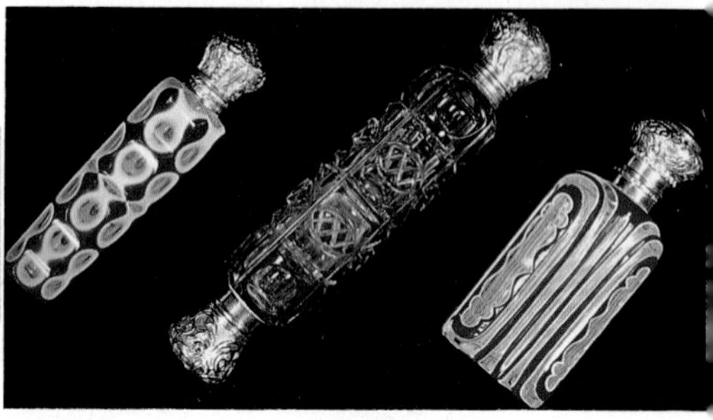

Blue and opaque white scent bottles, c1860. l. **$60-80**
c. & r. **$500-600 each**

A Williamite commemorative goblet, probably Irish, c1720, 10in (25cm).
$80,000-90,000

A cream jug with applied strap handle, 3½in (9cm).
$180-200

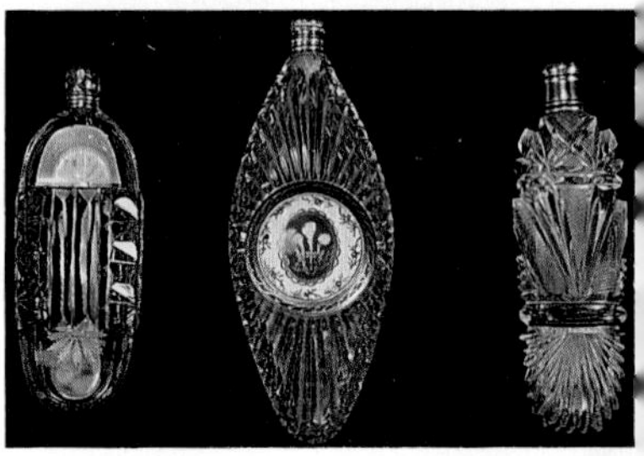

Scent bottles with white metal mounts, c1820. l. & r. **$180-200 each**
c. **$800-900**

Three rolling pins, with gilt and cold enamelled decoration, in good unrubbed condition, with verses, 13½ to 16½in (34 to 41cm). **$130-170 each**

Scent bottles, with white metal or brass mounts, c1860. l. **$550-600**
the others **$160-200 each**

iles

n ornamental grape tiles, painted colours, decorated with bunches grapes, Burgundian lily corners, thC.
00-700

Two ornamental tiles, painted in blue, depicting 4 circular cartouches containing Burgundian lilies separated by a canted cartouche with similar decoration, late 16thC.
$200-300

A children's games tile field, painted in blue, the border with ornamental foliate tiles, some chips, 17thC, framed.
$400-500

manganese tile picture by Aelmis, tterdam, one tile cracked, id-18thC, 20½in by 15in (51 by .5cm), framed.
,000-3,000

Fifteen tulip tiles, painted in colours, early 17thC.
$1,200-1,400

A Rotterdam tile picture comprising 6 tiles, painted in colours, decorated with a Louis XV clock, the centre inscribed Bakhuizen tot Rotterdam, 1768, one tile restored, framed.
$800-1,000

our ornamental tiles, painted in lours with a central foliated star otif, on a blue ground, quarter sette corners, c1580.
600-800

A large medallion soldier tile, painted in colours, c1600, 7in (17.5cm) square.
$1,500-2,500

A sgraffito tile field, painted in colours, some tiles restored, early 17thC.
$400-500

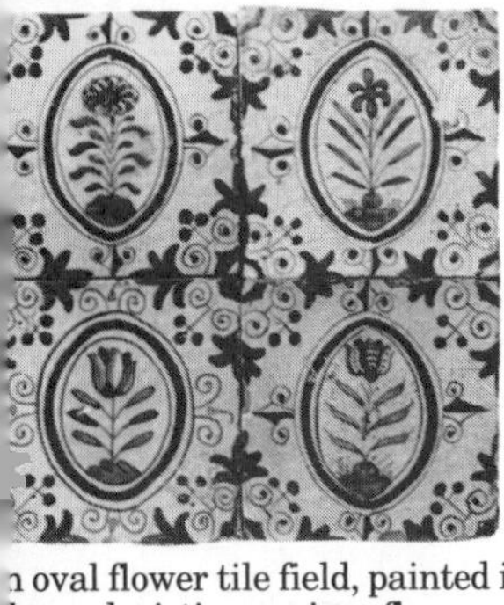

n oval flower tile field, painted in lours depicting various flowers, rgundian lily corners, early thC.
00-300

An animal medallion tile field, painted in colours depicting various animals and a bird, restored, early 17thC.
$3,000-4,000

A bird and flower tile field, probably Rotterdam, early 17thC.
$1,200-1,400

Seven unicorn tiles, some damage.
$1,300-1,500

A framed manganese tile picture, painted with Abraham dismissing Hagar and child, c1770, 20 by 24in (50 by 61cm).
$1,800-2,500

A Dutch Delft four tile picture, painted with a yellow bird in a manganese cage, with blue feeder, 18thC, 9½ by 9in (24 by 22.5cm), with wood frame, damaged.
$500-600

Eight ornamental bird tiles, painted in manganese purple, depicting 2 doves within an oval ring, suspended by ribbons, in the neo-classical style, 18thC.
$700-900

Twenty-one children's games tiles, painted in blue, some restored and chipped.
$600-800

A Rozenburg tile panel, after a painting by J. C. K. Klinkenberg, depicting a typical view of Amsterdam, year mark for 1902, 24 by 18in (60 by 44.5cm).
$2,500-3,000

A Foglie cherub tile, painted in colours with quarter rosette corners, early 17thC.
$700-800

A Frisian white ground tile picture, painted in colours depicting a young juggler with a striped costume, 18thC, some tiles later, 21 by 15½in (53 by 39.5cm).
$1,000-1,200

A Biblical tile picture comprising 2 tiles, painted in manganese purple restored, late 18thC, 20½ by 26in (51.5 by 65cm).
$1,400-1,600

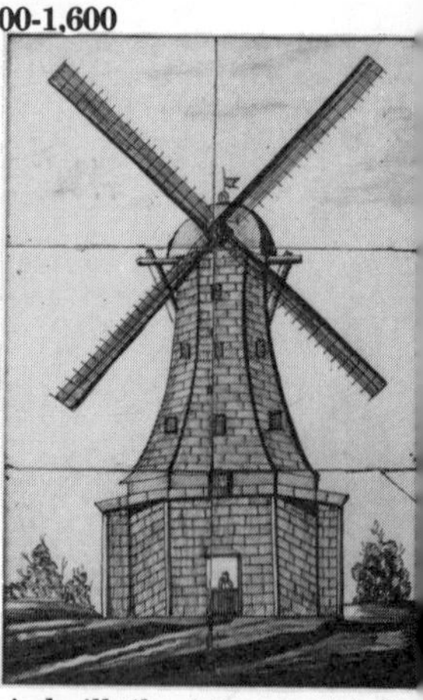

A windmill tile picture, painted i manganese purple, late 18thC, framed.
$1,200-1,400

Four animal tiles painted in colours depicting a bull, a goat and 2 dogs, early 17thC.
$900-1,000

Eight Amor tiles, painted in blue, depicting winged cherubs, late 17thC.
$400-600

Wemyss Ware

A Wemyss pig sponged with black, 6in (16cm) wide. **$1,000-1,200**

A Wemyss goose flower-holder, 8in (20cm).
$800-1,400

An oval dish and matching ring tree, decorated with roses, impressed marks, 5in (13cm).
$300-400

A Wemyss plate with raspberries, 7in (17.5cm) diam. **$100-150**

A Wemyss tablet painted with roses, 6in (15cm) wide.
$100-150

A duchess candlestick, painted with roses, 7in (17cm) diam.

$300-500

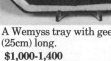

A Wemyss tray with geese, 10in (25cm) long.
$1,000-1,400

A Wemyss plate with cockerel decoration, 7in (17.5cm).
$300-400

A Wemyss foot bath.
$2,000-5,000

Wemyss is showing an increase in value and is proving a good investment.

A Wemyss tankard with plum decoration, 5½in (14cm).
$450-550

A heart shaped inkwell, decorated with forget-me-nots, 7½in (19cm).
$500-600

A heart shaped tray with cherries, 12in (30cm) long.
$400-600

A Wemyss jug and basin, painted with roses, 11in (28cm) diam.
$300-500

A Wemyss quaich with irises, 10in (25cm) wide including handles.
$500-600

A large Wemyss pig, 18in (45cm) long.
$1,500-3,000

MASON'S IRONSTONE

Mason's Ironstone is popular with collectors. Factory marks make it readily identifiable and the relatively long period of production coupled with the durability of the ware allow collectors opportunities to purchase fairly easily.

It is an enjoyable product to collect as a vast range of shapes, some now extremely rare, were made in a variety of colourful patterns.

Ironstone is full of character and so slight damage does little to detract from its visual appeal. Consequently if damage is reflected in the price, a rare damaged piece will find a ready market.

Background history

1752 Miles Mason born in Yorkshire.
1782 Married Elizabeth Farrer, daughter of Richard Farrer, a noted dealer in imported Chinese porcelain.
1783 Took over Farrer's business.
1791 The East India Company ceased importing Chinese porcelain due to losses incurred through the formation of 'rings' by dealers.
1795 Following completion of orders placed prior to the 1791 decision, the effects of the cessation of importation coupled with the difficulties caused by the war with France began to take effect.
1796 Mason sought to take advantage of the situation by producing his own Chinese-style porcelain to replace true Chinese wares in the market.
1796 Mason joined Thomas Wolfe and John Lucock in establishing a porcelain manufactory in Liverpool. Fashionable shapes with printed patterns in Nankin style were produced.
1800 The Liverpool factory closed.
1800-1804 Mason set up a factory at Lane Delph, Newcastle-under-Lyme, which was in operation by 1804. The name chosen for advertising the product, 'British Nankin', confirms the market Mason was trying to fill.
1805 Mason transferred his works to, Fenton, Staffordshire. Larger wares impressed M.MASON.
1806 Mason joined by his son, William. Larger wares impressed M.MASON and SON.
1813 Miles Mason ceased to be actively involved in the business which was taken over by his sons, William, Charles and George who quickly ran porcelain production down.

Type of Porcelain Produced

1796-1806 Mason produced a hard white porcelain fired at about 1,380°C. It was a hybrid hard paste without the addition of bone ash and was made to the standard formula of the period. From 1806 bone ash was added to an adjusted formula and a type of bone china produced. From 1796 to 1813 a very full range of shapes was produced including all the accoutrements of tea, dinner and dessert services as well as ornaments and other household goods. Shapes followed a range of fashions but patterns imitated Nankin wares. Types of decoration include Nankin-type wares printed in underglaze blue sometimes enhanced by overglaze gilding, bat-printed wares and wares decorated with overglaze colours in Chinese style.
Rarer are wares painted with European landscapes, European flowers or foliate and geometric patterns. These last named forms of decoration are particularly desirable.

A Mason's Patent Ironstone china sauce tureen and cover, painted in the Imari manner in typical enamel colours and gold, early 19thC, 8in (20cm).
$600-700

Mason's Patent Ironstone China

1800-1813 Mason's were producing some blue printed earthenware and pearlware as well as porcelain. One of Mason's sons, Charles, saw that there was a vast and growing middle class market and sought to find a product to exploit it. Porcelain was too refined and expensive a product so Charles experimented with earthenware formulae along the lines of patents taken out between 1800 and 1813 by William and John Turner, amongst others, for various durable earthenwares.
1813 Charles Mason's patent for 'Patent Ironstone China' was taken out. Production had already begun at Mason's Fenton manufactory. The formula used was for a very durable body combining ironstone slag with Cornish stone, Cornish clay and flint.
1813-1826 Charles and George Mason produced a full range of shapes decorated in bright colours with bold 'Chinese' patterns. Wares produced during the period include tea, supper, dinner and dessert services as well as a host of useful and decorative household items — candlesticks, flowerpots, inkstands, jugs, pen trays, toilet sets, watering cans, wine coolers and the like. Unlike the porcelain wares of Miles Mason most pieces are marked. Some earthenwares, including a number marked Cambrian Argil were produced, c1820.
1826 George Mason retired. Charles was joined by a partner, Samuel Faraday, and the style C. J. Mason and Co. was adopted.
1848 C. J. Mason was declared bankrupt and his stock in trade was sold. He salvaged some finished wares and continued in production for a short time, displaying garden seats, fish ponds, jugs, ewers and a variety of jars at the Great Exhibition of 1851.
1848-1858 Mason's moulds having been bought by Francis Morley, wares continued to be made under the name Morley and Co. Morley's marks being added below Mason's.
1858-1862 The firm continued as Morley and Ashworth.
1862 Ashworths.
1968 Ashworths were renamed 'Mason's Ironstone China Ltd.

l. A Mason's blue printed plate, impressed 'Mason's Cambrian Argil' mark, c1820, 9in (22cm).
$120-160

c. A Mason's hexagonal vase, printed mark, c1860, 3in (7.5cm).
$60-80

r. A Mason's blue printed plate, impressed 'Mason's Cambrian Argil' mark, c1820, 8½in (21cm).
$120-160

A Mason's Ironstone Japan pattern dessert dish and centrepiece dish, 13in (32cm), both with printed crown marks, c1820.
r. $450-550
l. $280-320

A Mason's Ironstone plate, with gilt enamels against an orange ground, separated by gilt and underglaze blue fish scale pattern, c1920, 10in (25cm).
$80-120

l. & r. A pair of Mason's Ironstone vases with the Landscape Scroll pattern, printed crown mark, c1840, 6in (15cm).
$300-350

c. A Mason's Ironstone plate, impressed mark, c1820, 8½in (21cm).
$120-150

A Mason's Ironstone Japan pattern inkstand with loose container, impressed mark, c1820, 3in (7.5cm).
$600-700

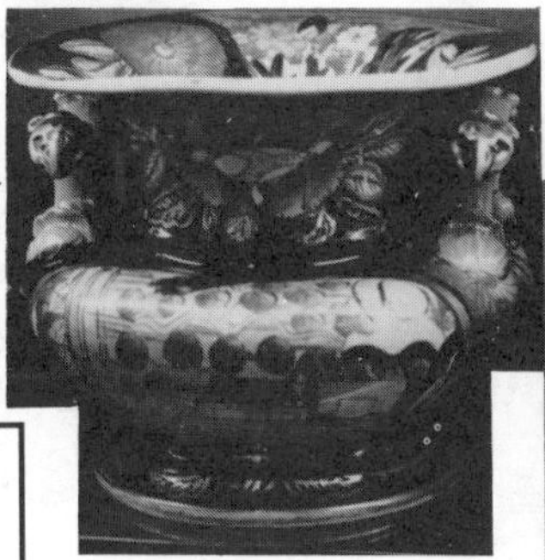

A Mason's Ironstone cooler, richly painted and gilded, impressed mark, c1820, 11in (28cm).
$900-1,000

A large Mason's pot pourri, in the Japan pattern, impressed mark, c1820, 9½in (24cm).
$3,000-4,000

DATING MASON'S IRONSTONE

- ★ as Mason's Ironstone was produced over a long period using the same moulds and patterns a great deal of reliance has to be put on marks. Marks should be scrutinised carefully as the marks of over 200 firms are known
- ★ the word 'patent' used in the mark should indicate a piece by Mason or a continuation partnership
- ★ pattern numbers alongside the mark usually indicate production after 1880
- ★ the words 'Made in England' or high pattern numbers by letters indicate a late 19thC or 20thC date

A Mason's Ironstone bowl, c1830, 12in (30cm) diam.
$800-900

A Mason's Ironstone toilet ewer and basin, with double panel pattern, printed crown mark, c1840.
$800-900

Miscellaneous

A dated slipware money box with unusual skull motifs, possibly Yorkshire, 5½in (14cm).
$250-350

A slipware money box, early 18thC, 5in (12.5cm).
$800-1,000

A Prattware money box, c1800, 5in (12.5cm).
$800-900

A saltglazed money box, early 19thC. 6½in (16cm).
$60-80

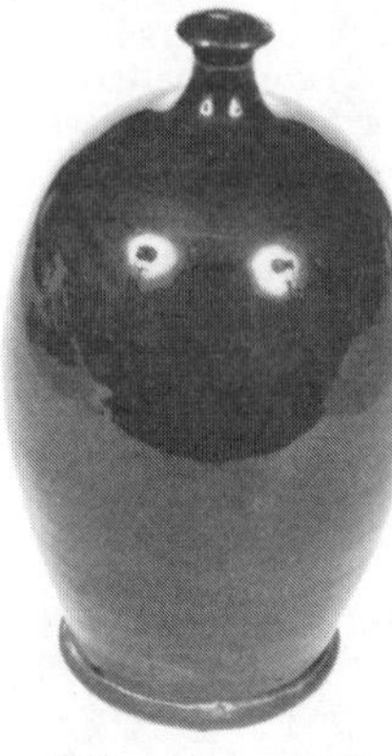

A pottery money box, c1880, 7½in (19cm).
$50-75

A Scottish agate bodied hen money box, mid-19thC, 4in (10cm).
$120-150

A hen and chicks money box, probably Yorkshire, c1860, 8½in (21cm).
$150-200

A saltglazed money box, c1835, 5½in (14cm).
$150-200

A Buckley money box c1860, 9½in (24cm).
$250-300

A majolica garden seat, with mottled green ground and prunus decoration, 19in (48cm).
$400-500

A Victorian blue and white lavatory pan, decorated with an Italian landscape, 14½in (36cm) wide.
$150-200

A blue and white lavatory pan, mid-19thC.
$300-350

A slipware strainer of Boney Pie pattern, c1780, 11½in (29cm) diam
$2,000-2,500

. manganese glazed red bodied
ɩcking chair, 19thC, 7½in (18.5cm).
240-260

A rocking chair in agate, with slip trailing, dated 1886, Halifax, 9in (22.5cm).
$360-400

Two Deruta holy water stoops, painted in colours and moulded in relief, some damage, early 17thC, 14½ and 16½in (36.5 and 42cm).
$3,000-3,500

A Staffordshire model of a greengage of Ralph Wood type, naturally modelled and resting on an oval basket, slight damage, c1780, 3in (8cm) wide.
$800-1,000

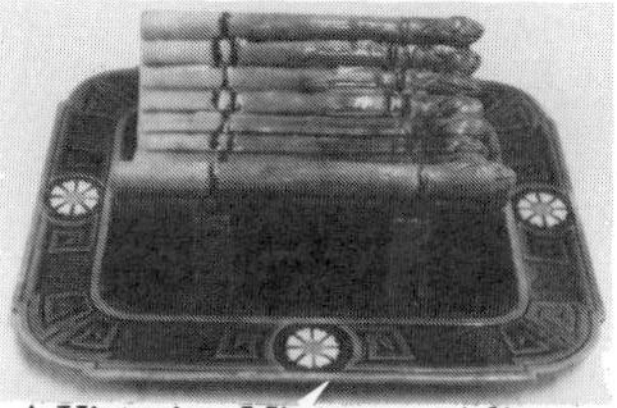

A Victorian Mintons majolica asparagus dish, with green and brown ground, 9in (23cm) wide.
$300-400

. miniature rustic chair, c1880, 6in
.5cm).
150-200

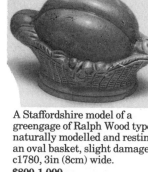

A Buckley slipware chest of drawers, c1860, 10½in (26cm).
$900-1,000

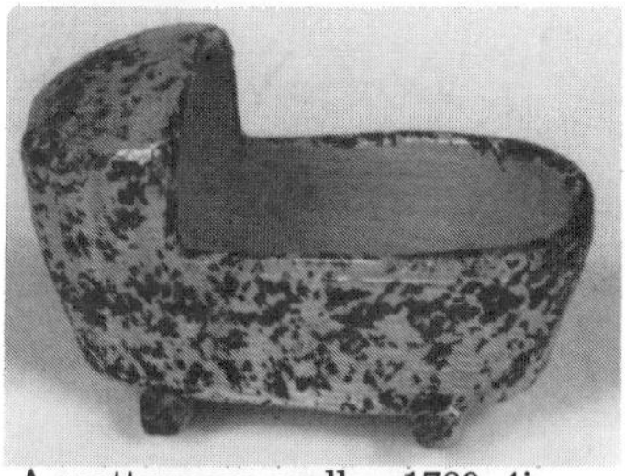

A spatterware cradle, c1780, 4in (10cm) wide.
$200-250

. Staffordshire pearlware clock
roup and cover of Walton type,
ıodelled as a vase with a clock dial,
n a green base with blue foliage,
ɔme restoration, c1820, 8in (20cm).
,800-2,000

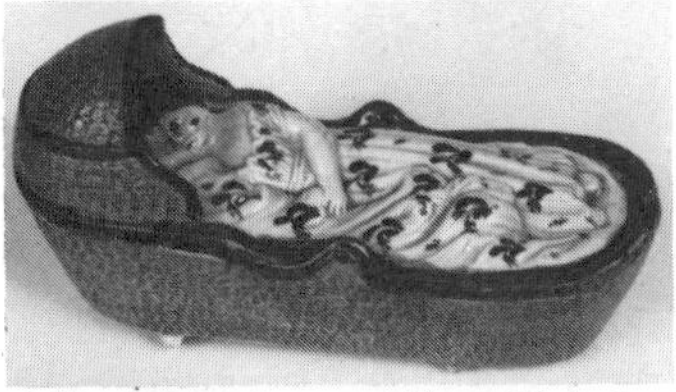

A Prattware type cradle, with baby, c1800, 8½in (21.5cm) wide.
$1,800-2,000

An early Staffordshire cradle, with baby, c1790, 4in (10cm).
$1,400-1,600

An early Staffordshire yellow cradle, 5in (12.5cm) wide.
$1,000-1,200

A Prattware longcase clock, the numerals and hands in brown, the case in ochre with yellow door, blue lower section, the back and sides streaked in ochre, yellow and blue, chipped, c1790, 7in (18cm).
$400-500

An early Staffordshire watch holder, possibly Sunderland, 11½in (29cm).
$1,400-1,600

A Winchcombe casserole, probably by Elijah Comfort, c1930.
$200-250

PORCELAIN

Although porcelain prices have remained steady during the year there have been some noticeable market trends with ordinary wares of the 1770-1800 period remaining in the doldrums whilst early rarities and decorative 19thC wares attract higher prices. Porcelain is still undervalued by comparison with pottery. A rare Bristol marked cream boat fetched a little over $6,000 in 1989 due to some damage, in line with estimate but seemingly good value for such a rarity.

Wares formerly attributed to William Ball have now been found on the site of Nicholas Crisp's factory at Vauxhall and this has given them a slight boost in the market.

As usual, prices fetched by porcelain in House Sales exceed expectation but these prices have to be viewed against the perspective of pieces fresh to the market and with good provenance. At Southwick House a pair of rare Derby figures in the white depicting the actor Henry Woodward and actress Kitty Clive fetched $64,000. At Hawling Manor a Derby service decorated with named botanical specimens also fetched $64,000, further recording the popularity of such wares.

An unexpectedly high price of $6,500 for a rare Capodimonte teapot lacking its cover (against an estimate of $800-$1,200) further illustrates the importance of rarity value.

Although a rarity and of a typ not seen on the market for a number of years the estimate seemed reasonable when seen in context of the incompletene of the pot. Most observers expected a top bid of $2,500-$3,000 but such was the enthusiasm for the piece that bidding easily exceeded both estimates.

It seems increasingly difficult find saleroom bargains these days, not necessarily because c improved cataloguing and marketing, though these are relevant factors, but because the numbers of dealers and the level of expertise has increase dramatically since the introduction of the antique 'fa and the knowledge available through specialist books.

Baskets

A Berlin Zwiebelmuster pierced blue and white basket, applied leaf and flower terminals to the entwined handles, blue sceptre mark and painter's B1, impressed IZ, H, and ii to base, c1785, 8½in (21cm).
$700-800

A Continental fruit basket with floral encrusted bowl, the column moulded with 2 lovers, a goat and a dog, 20½in (52cm).
$1,200-1,500

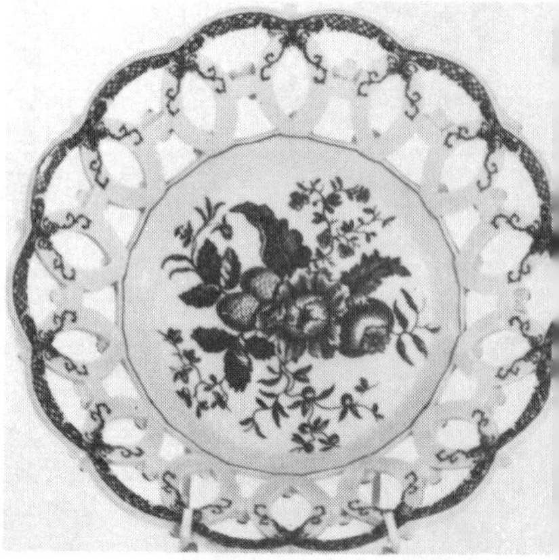

A Worcester blue and white baske with everted pierced sides and the exterior with five-petalled flowers at the intersections, the well printe with flowers, fruit and pine-cones, hatched crescent mark, slight damage, 8½in (22cm).
$500-600

A Rockingham basket, with entwined branch carrying-handle, the centre painted with Salisbury Cathedral named below, some chipping to flowers, puce griffin mark, c1835, 12½in (31cm) wide.
$1,800-2,000

Bottles

An Arita blue and white apothecary bottle, neck restored, late 17thC, 9in (23cm).
$1,300-1,500

An English Pilgrim bottle, with dolphin-like handles, on a gold and white decorated light green groun late 19thC, 11½in (28.5cm).
$500-600

Bowls

A Worcester posy bowl, c1894, 2in (5cm).
$120-150

A Worcester transfer printed bowl, in underglaze blue, with uncommon European landscapes, c1780, 4½in (11cm) diam.
$300-350

A Pennington's Liverpool teabowl and saucer, painted with floral sprays, c1780, saucer 5in (12.5cm) diam.
$200-250

A Royal Worcester crownware bowl, in orange, green and gilt, c1926, 2½in (6.5cm).
$120-150

A Davenport Imari powder bowl and cover, painted with the Witches pattern, c1880, 3in (7.5cm) diam.
$250-300

A deep bowl, transfer printed in blue with chinoiserie scenes and flying birds, possibly Swansea, late 18thC, 4½in (11cm).
$500-600

A Liverpool creamware bowl, the interior printed in black, the exterior with the Sailor's Farewell and the Sailor's Return divided by scenes of the Triumph of Neptune and the Triumph of Venus, cracked, c1800, 8½in (21.5cm) diam.
$250-300

A Sitzendorf bowl and cover, with moulded basket borders, painted with equestrian figures in landscapes, flowersprays and sprigs, the cover knop in the form of a young child and dog, 11in (28cm).
$700-800

Boxes

A Coalport jewelled box and cover, modelled as a pair of bellows, the cover enamelled in colours in imitation of opalescent stone and gilt, reserved on a gold ground enriched with turquoise beading, with pink ground base, green printed mark and pattern No. v 2258 and Ovington Brothers in iron red, c1894, 9½in (24cm) long.
$1,200-1,300

A Davenport Imari trinket box and cover, painted with the Witches pattern, c1880. 5in (12.5cm) wide.
$250-300

A Meissen snuff box and cover, with moulded ozier pattern and scattered 'deutsche Blumen', c1765, with contemporary chased silver gilt mounts, 3½in (8cm) wide.
$2,000-2,500

A pair of Meissen boxes and covers, modelled as a recumbent ewe and ram, the ram with beige patches, the ewe with charcoal patches, repaired, blue crossed swords marks to both pieces, c1755, contemporary gilt rim mount and horns to ram, 6½in (16cm) wide.
$2,000-3,000

Candelabra

A pair of Meissen three-light candelabra, slight damage, incised No. 128, crossed swords mark, 8in (20.5cm).
$2,500-3,000

A pair of German candelabra, in Meissen style, one damaged, underglaze blue double crossed baton marks, 19thC, 20in (51cm).
$900-1,000

A pair of Derby bocage candlestick groups, slight damage, late 18thC, 8½in (20.5cm).
$1,200-1,500

A Swansea chamber candlestick, with gilt scroll and bird's head handle and campana-shaped nozzle, the base painted by William Pollard, minute rubbing to gilding, c1815, 5in (12.5cm) diam.
$3,000-4,000

Centrepieces

A Derby centrepiece, probably by William 'Quaker' Pegg, the body painted in colours with flowers within gilt line borders, marked and inscribed in blue, late 18thC, 15in (38cm) wide.
$5,000-6,000

A Minton elephant centrepiece.
$1,500-1,800

A Worcester majolica comport, supported by 3 dolphins, mid-19thC, 7in (18cm).
$200-300

A pair of German comports, painted and applied with flowers, in bright enamel colours, one bowl damaged, 19½in (49cm).
$1,500-2,000

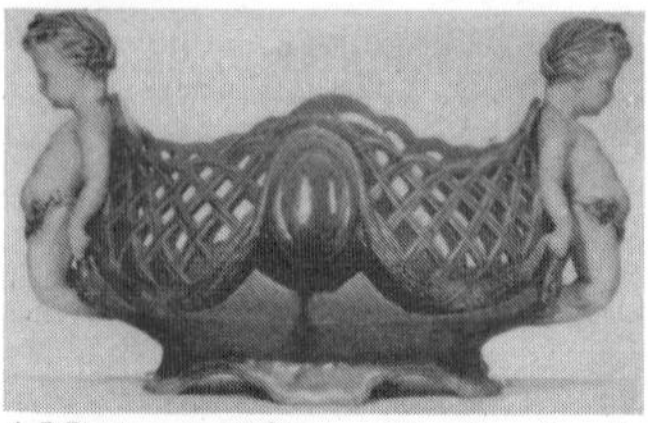

A Minton majolica centrepiece bowl, impressed factory marks, 11in (28cm) wide.
$500-700

A German porcelain centrepiece, damaged and gilding rubbed, 14in (35.5cm).
$600-800

Cottages & Pastille Burners

A Coalport pastille burner, c1830, 5in (12.5cm).
$2,500-3,000

A Spode pastille burner, in the form of a large house with 2 windows in the gable end and 3 doors with steps, the roof applied with colourful mosses and flowers, drawer missing, 9½in (23cm) wide.
$2,600-3,000

A pastille burner, the gold tiled roof edged with moss, the garden applied with flowers, 6½in (16.5cm).
$800-1,000

An English pastille burner, with detachable base, c1830, 6in (15cm).
$1,200-1,500

A pastille burner in the form of a house, containing a drawer for the pastille, set on a mound base, drawer interior broken, 6½in (16.5cm).
$2,500-3,000

A pastille burner in the form of a two-tier house, with a central chimney, detailed in gold, some damage, 9in (23cm) wide.
$500-600

A pastille burner and stand, in the form of a thatched cottage, painted in enamel colours and gold, slight damage, 6in (15cm).
$1,300-1,500

A pastille burner in the form of a two-tier house, detailed in gold, 6½in (16.5cm).
$600-700

Cups

A Coalport miniature cup and saucer, hand painted with gilt background, saucer 2in (5cm) diam.
$120-150

A miniature Minton hand painted two-handled loving cup, c1895.
$150-200

A Rockingham cup and saucer with scroll moulding, decorated with apple green borders, painted with a scene, puce griffin mark, c1835.
$400-450

A Coalport Batwing pattern coffee cup and saucer, c1900, 3in (7cm).
$100-120

A Staffordshire loving cup, painted in colours, with a gilt presentation inscription, to Messrs Cartlidge Brothers, China and Earthenware Retailers, 'During the Depression of Trade since the commencement of the Eastern Question from the manufacturers of the Staffordshire potteries', repaired, cracked and interior stained, 6in (15cm).
$200-250

A Swansea London-decorated cabinet cup, painted on a shaded brown ground between gilt band borders with white husks, slight crack, c1815, 3½in (9cm).
$1,000-1,200

A Swansea cabinet cup, painted by Henry Morris, c1820, 4½in (12cm).
$4,000-5,000

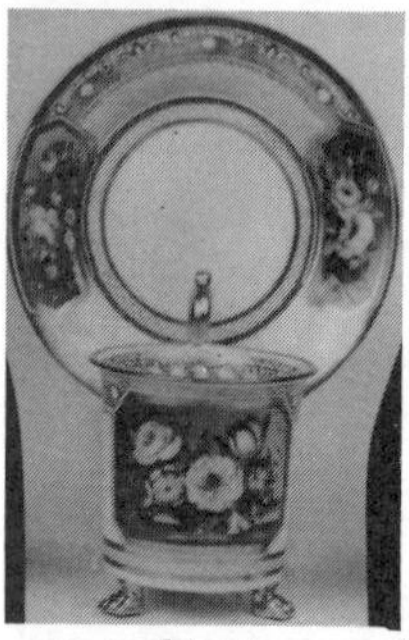

A Swansea cabinet cup and saucer, painted by Thomas Baxter, with gilt cartouches, the cup with pierced lotus scroll handle and 3 gilt paw feet, restoration, script mark in puce, c1815.
$2,250-3,000

A Nantgarw breakfast cup with floral decoration and landscape panel, script mark in puce, Caerphilly Castle, Glamorganshire, 3½in (9cm).
$1.800-2,000

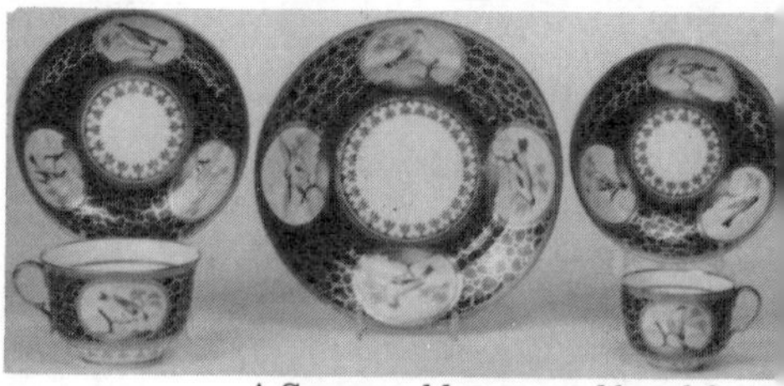

A Swansea blue ground breakfast cup and saucer, teacup and saucer and a plate, painted by William Pollard, with gilt cartouches on a gilt 'caillouté' ground, red stencil marks, c1815.
$4,000-4,500

A Worcester coffee cup, enamelled in red, blue and green, chips to rim, c1770, 2in (5cm).
$100-150

A Swansea cabinet cup, with beaded border, painted with basket and sprays of flowers, gilt scroll and seeded border.
$150-200

A Worcester coffee cup and saucer, painted by The Spotted Fruit Painter, underglaze blue crossed swords mark and figure 9, c1770, saucer 5in (12.5cm).
$900-1,000

A pair of Spode cabinet cups, covers and stands, painted on a gold ground, marked in puce Spode 711, c1805, 5in (12.5cm).
$5,000-6,000

A pair of Flight and Barr cups and covers, painted 'en grisaille', with shaped gilt border on a grey marbled ground, gilt enrichments, one restored and hairline crack, script mark in red, Flight and Barr Coventry St. London, Barr Flight and Barr Worcester, c1800, 5in (12.5cm).
$1,000-1,200

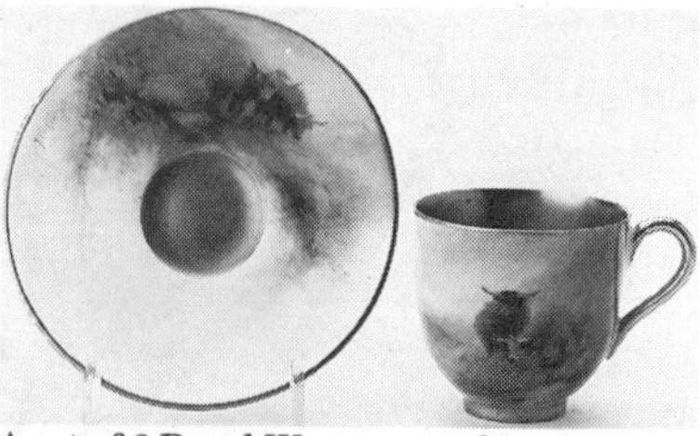

A set of 6 Royal Worcester cabinet coffee cups and saucers, signed H. Stinton, printed mark and date code for 1926.
$3,000-4,000

Flight, Barr and Barr cabinet cup
ıd saucer, painted within gilt
›rders, cup with minor rim chip,
:inted mark in full, c1820.
300-1,000

A Flight, Barr and Barr coffee can and saucer, decorated in Japan style with gilt, rust, blue, pink and green, impressed FBB mark, saucer 6in (15cm).
$700-800

A Royal Worcester blue and white coffee cup and saucer, c1877.
$40-50

transfer printed coffee can, with
ıstre decoration, c1800, 3in (7.5cm).
70-80

A bat printed coffee can, c1800, 2in (5cm).
$70-80

A coffee cup and saucer, damaged and unmarked, saucer 6in (15cm) diam.
$60-80

Meissen coffee cup, painted in
ıce enamel, crossed swords and dot
ark, late 18thC.
200-300

A late Berlin cabinet cup and saucer, painted 'en grisaille' with a view of Dunrobin Castle, named on the saucer, on a matt blue ground richly gilt, blue sceptre mark.
$600-700

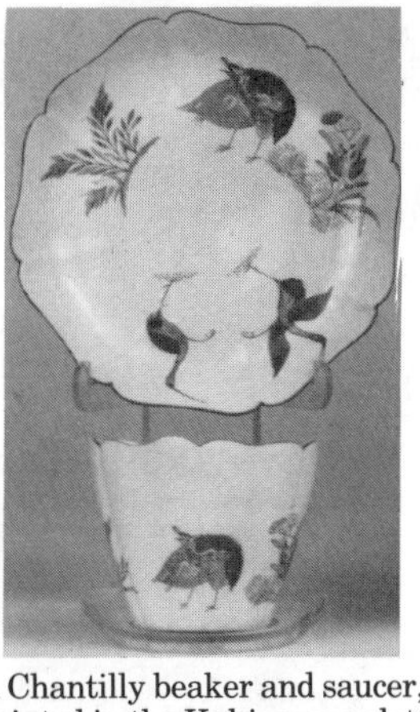

A Chantilly beaker and saucer, painted in the Kakiemon palette, with brown rims, repaired, red hunting horn marks, c1735.
$800-900

A Dresden cup and saucer, marked, saucer 5in (12.5cm) diam.
$50-60

Meissen Purpurmalerai
vo-handled cup and saucer,
ımaged.
1,200-1,600

A set of 6 Berlin footed ice cups, with C-scroll handles, enriched with green and puce feathering painted in colours, blue sceptre marks, c1780, 2½in (6.5cm).
$3,500-4,000

Figures – Animal

A pair of Bow figures of deer, naturally modelled with dappled brown hides, ears restored, stag's neck repaired and with restoration to right knee and antler sockets, antlers lacking, c1760, 4in (9.5cm) long.
$2,800-3,000

A Derby figure of a bird perched on a stump, heightened in yellow and brown, some chips, 2in (5cm).
$400-500

A Royal Dux model of a camel, with Arab mounted in the saddle, painted in typical muted enamel colours and gold, applied triangle mark, 19½in (50cm).
$2,000-3,000

A Plymouth white figural group of a ewe and suckling lamb, c1770, 3½in (9cm).
$1,400-1,600

A Meissen hunting group of 3 hounds bearing down on a bison, modelled by J. J. Kändler, painted in colours, one tail missing, blue crossed swords mark, c1700, 9in (22.5cm) wide.
$2,000-2,500

A Staffordshire model of a young giraffe, painted in green and edged in gilt, repaired and base chipped, 4in (10cm).
$400-500

A pair of Meissen rabbits, c1850, 2in (5cm) wide.
$400-500

A Meissen figure of a starling, modelled by J. J. Kändler, with black and green plumage, perched on rockwork base with fruiting foliage, some restoration to beak and feet, blue crossed swords mark at back, c1740, 6in (15cm).
$2,500-3,000

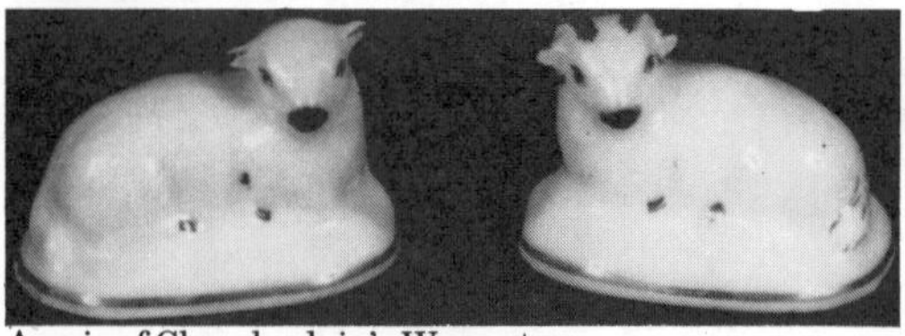

A pair of Chamberlain's Worcester sheep, marked, 3in (7.5cm) wide.
$900-1,000

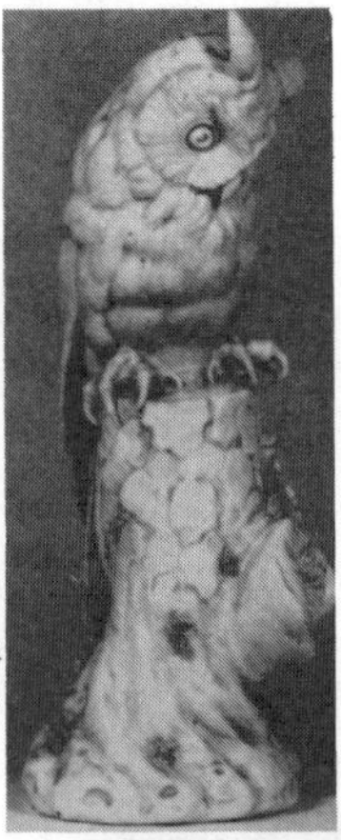

A German white glazed model of an owl perched on a tree stump, 13½in (34cm).
$300-400

A pair of English figures of peacocks, painted in gilt with blue and black eyes, damaged, puce crown crossed batons and D marks, 6½in (16.5cm).
$1,600-2,000

A Meissen figure of a nanny goat, modelled by J. J. Kändler, painted in colours, repairs, blue crossed swords mark to rear of base, c1745, 6½in (16.5cm) wide.
$3,500-4,000

A pair of Meissen groups of a fox attacking a cockerel and a hound attacking a hare, painted in colours the bases enriched with gilding, hare damaged, blue crossed swords and dot mark, c1765, 2½in (5.5cm) wide.
$4,000-5,000

Three Meissen miniature birds, c1850, 1½ to 2½in (4 to 6cm).
$800-1,000

A pair of late Meissen figures of jays, naturalistically painted, beaks restored and damaged, blue crossed swords and incised and impressed numerals, 15in (38cm).
$1,600-2,000

A late Meissen model of a cat, with brown markings and painted facial details, blue crossed swords and incised and impressed numerals, 6in (15cm) wide.
$1,200-1,750

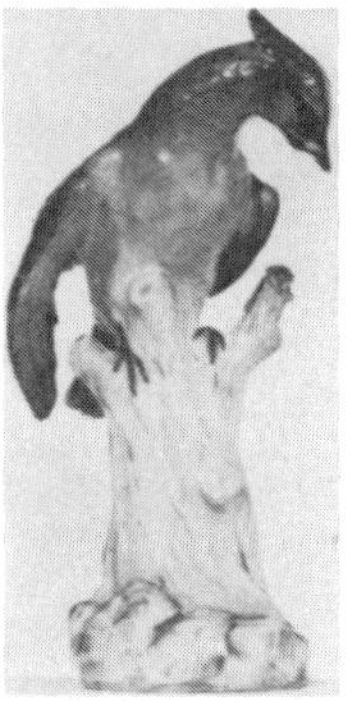

A late Meissen figure of a jay perched on a stump, naturalistically coloured, some restoration, blue crossed swords and incised numerals, 9in (23cm).
$300-400

Figures – People

A Bow figure of a putto emblematic of Autumn, on the back of a leopard in yellow with manganese spots, the base painted in puce with flowersprays, c1756, 6in (15.5cm).
$1,200-1,600

A similar figure with the T mark for the repairer Tebo is in the Museum of London.

A Bow white figure of Matrimony, loosely based on a Meissen original, a birdcage in her right hand and a sheep lying at her feet, on a scrolling base, some restoration, c1753, 9½in (24cm).
$800-1,000

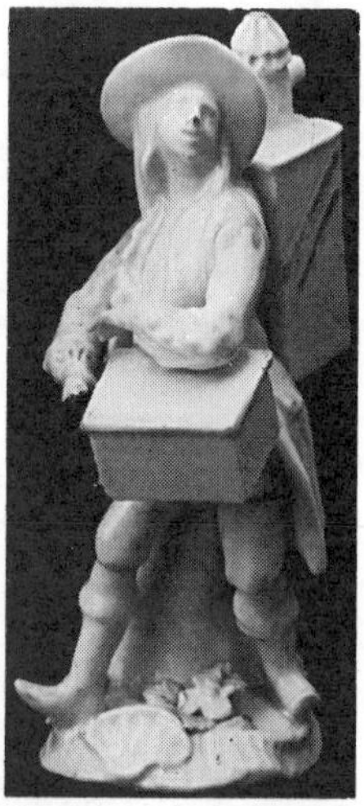

A Bow white figure of a peepshow man looking over his left shoulder, the shell and wave scroll base encrusted with flowers, c1755, 5½in (14cm).
$800-900

A pair of Bow figures of a sportsman and companion, in predominantly pale pink and yellow clothes lined in pale blue and iron red, some restoration, minor chips, c1758, 7½in (18.5cm).
$4,000-5,000

A pair of Bow figures of a shepherd and a shepherdess, he in pink jacket, white shirt and blue breeches, she in a flowered bodice and beige skirt, holding a white apron, restoration to recorder and her right arm, some minute chipping, c1758, 5½in (14.5cm).
$3,000-4,000

A Bow group of the Triumph of Bacchus, on a base moulded with scrolls picked out in puce, restoration, rim chips, c1760, 8in (20cm).
$1,400-2,000

A pair of Derby figures of a shepherd and a shepherdess, in pale pink, yellow, iron red and green flowered clothes, on scroll moulded bases enriched in puce and green, restoration, some chipping, Wm. Duesbury and Co, c1760, 10½ and 11in (26 and 27.5cm).
$3,000-4,000

Two Derby figures of seated musicians, some damage and restoration, c1768, 8in (20cm).
$1,500-2,000

A Derby shepherdess, c1770, 5½in (14cm).
$450-500

A Derby gardener, c1820, 5in (12.5cm).
$450-500

A Derby figure of a shepherd, c1770, 6½in (16cm).
$550-600

A Derby figure of a young man, slight damage, incised N51, late 18thC, 5in (12.5cm).
$900-1,000

A Derby figure, Goodnight, restored, c1820, 4in (10cm).
$200-250

A Derby figure of a boy in colourful costume, slight damage, incised N49, late 18thC, 6in (15cm).
$800-900

A Derby figure of a Turk, marked, c1825, 6in (15cm).
$450-500

A 'Girl in a Swing' white figure of a nymph, on rockwork base, some restoration, c1751, 5½in (14cm).
$8,000-9,000

This figure almost certainly emblematic of Winter, but possibly that of a vestal virgin tending the sacred flame, appears not to have been recorded elsewhere.

A pair of Derby figures of a gardener and his lady companion, each with a basket of fruit on their laps, restored, 5in (12.5cm).
$1,500-1,800

A Royal Dux figure, c1910, 14in (35cm).
$1,000-1,200

A Minton figure of a guitar player, c1835, 9in (23cm).
$700-900

An early Royal Worcester majolica figure, impressed mark, c1865, 5in (12.5cm).
$300-350

A pair of Royal Worcester tinted 'ivory' figures of a French fisherboy and companion, after the models by James Hadley, decorated in pale colours and enriched in gilding, impressed Hadley at back, puce printed marks, No. 1202, c1886, 18in (45cm).
$2,000-3,000

A Royal Worcester figure, Months of the Year series, by Freda Doughty, 5in (12.5cm).
$80-120

Three Royal Worcester 'ivory' figures from The Countries of the World series after James Hadley, modelled as a Yankee, John Bull and an Irishman, one incised Hadley, impressed and puce printed marks and various shape numbers, date codes for 1881, 1889 and 1897, 7in (17.5cm).
$1,500-1,800

A Royal Worcester figure of a boy wearing Queen Anne style rustic costume, glazed in shades of yellow, apricot and green, with gilt highlights, puce factory marks and impressed factory marks, 9in (23cm).
$900-1,000

A Royal Worcester figure of a girl in a Kate Greenaway style dress, with cream costume edged in gilt, gilt worn, impressed and printed marks and date code for c1888, 9in (23cm).
$900-1,000

A Royal Worcester figure of a maiden standing barefoot, wearing green and orange costume dusted in gilt, puce printed marks and impressed marks, c1890, 8in (20cm).
$700-800

A pair of parian figures, missing book from one figure, c1865, 11in (29cm).
$600-700

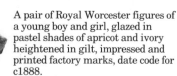

A pair of Royal Worcester figures of lady musicians, with gilded decoration.
$300-400

A pair of Royal Worcester figures of a young boy and girl, glazed in pastel shades of apricot and ivory heightened in gilt, impressed and printed factory marks, date code for c1888.
$1,500-1,800

A Frankenthal figure of a Chinaman modelled by K. G. Lück, wearing a white jacket with blue striped cummerbund, red and puce striped trousers, yellow shoes, enriched with gilding, repairs, crowned CT mark, c1765, 5in (13cm).
$1,400-1,800

A Frankenthal figure of a seated shepherd shearing a sheep, modelled by J. W. Lanz, on a rococo scroll moulded base enriched with gilding, repairs to hat and hand, blue crowned CT monogram and incised script b to base, c1760, 5½in (13.5cm).
$2,500-3,000

A Frankenthal figure of a lady modelled by K. G. Lück, wearing a yellow bonnet, black ruff collar, white bodice and skirt with orange florets, repairs, chips to hat, crowned CT monogram, c1765, 5½in (14cm).
$1,600-2,000

A Fürstenberg figure of a sailor wearing a soft hat, black waistcoat, orange sleeved shirt and striped pantaloons with black sandals, repaired, c1775, 7½in (18cm).
$1,000-1,500

A Höchst figure of a boy gardener, modelled by J. P. Melchior, hat repaired, blue wheel mark and incised HM, c1765, 6in (15cm).
$2,000-2,400

A Geva figure of a lady searching for fleas in her nightshirt, wearing a puce bonnet with a black headband, enriched with gilding, repaired, c1790, 4in (10cm).
$6,000-7,000

A Höchst figure of a seated drunkard modelled by Simon Feilner after Kändler, wearing orange jacket with yellow lining, a white shirt and braces holding up his black trousers, on treestump base, repaired, c1754, 7in (17cm).
$1,800-2,500

A Fürstenberg figure allegorical of Winter, script f mark on base, c1800, 5in (13cm).
$1,200-1,600

A Frankenthal pastoral group of a shepherd and his companion, emblematic of Spring, modelled by A. Bauer, painted in colours, minor damage and chips, crowned Carl Theodore mark, c1765, 6in (15cm) wide.
$3,000-4,000

A pair of Höchst figures of the Sultan and Sultana modelled by J. P. Melchior, some repairs, blue crowned wheel marks, c1765, 7½in (18.5cm).
$10,000-12,000

A Meissen figure of a trinket seller, wearing purple, blue, yellow, white and black, restorations, c1745, 6½in (16.5cm).
$3,000-4,000

A Meissen figure of a bagpiper modelled by J. J. Kändler, wearing a black hat with yellow band, brown cloak with yellow lining, red waistcoat with gilt buttons, white leggings, black shoes with red ribbons, repaired, chips to base, blue crossed swords mark, c1745, 9in (23cm).
$4,000-5,000

A Meissen figure of a grape seller from the Cris de Paris series, modelled by P. Reinicke, wearing a black hat, pale puce coat, yellow waistcoat, puce trousers and white leggings, on rococo scroll base encrusted with flowers, repaired, crossed swords mark to rear of base, c1745, 6in (14.5cm).
$4,000-5,000

A Meissen figure of a hurdy-gurdy player, in brown hat, yellow jacket, white shirt and breeches, with a satchel over his shoulder, minor restoration, traces of blue crossed swords mark, Pressnummer 33, c1740, 5½in (14cm).
$1,600-2,000

A Meissen figure of a shepherdess, wearing a green jacket with black bodice, her dress with scattered coloured 'indianische Blumen', on rococo base enriched with gilding, repaired, blue crossed swords mark to rear of base, c1750, 10½in (27cm).
$2,000-2,500

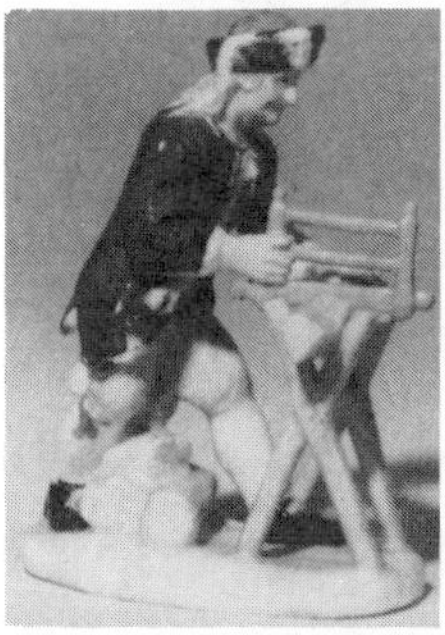

A pair of Meissen figures of woodcutters, modelled by J. J. Kändler and P. Reinicke, in black, iron red, buff, turquoise and blue, damaged, one with blue crossed swords mark at back, the other with blue crossed swords mark on base, c1745-50, 5in (13cm).
$4,000-5,000

A Meissen figure of a Hungarian mandolin player, modelled by Johann Georg Eberlein, wearing black, green, pale yellow and white, repaired, c1745, 7in (18cm).
$1,400-1,800

A pair of Meissen figures of Taste and Smell from the Five Senses, modelled by Friedrich Elias Meyer, in yellow lined cloaks with 'indianische Blumen', each with restoration to arms, blue crossed swords marked on the bases, c1745, 11in (28cm).
$3,000-3,500

A Meissen figure of a Dutch peasant, modelled by P. Reinicke, wearing an iron red waistcoat, yellow trousers and a soft green hat, repaired, crossed swords mark at back, c1745, 5½in (14cm).
$1,400-1,800

A Meissen figure of a pilgrim, modelled by J. F. Eberlein, wearing a broad-rimmed yellow hat and a grey cape, a pale green jacket and puce knee breeches, repaired, some damage, blue crossed swords mark to rear of base, c1745, 6in (15.5cm).
$1,000-1,200

A Meissen figure of a fisherboy, a fish in one hand and a basket of fish at his side, wearing a yellow headscarf, a lilac jacket with purple flowers, white shirt, pink breeches and black shoes with blue ribbons, on a base enriched with gilding, repaired, Pressnummer 11, c1770, 5in (12cm).
$1,200-1,400

A pair of Meissen figures, of a dairyman and female companion, blue crossed swords mark, 18thC, 3in (8cm).
$900-1,000

A Meissen porcelain figure of an 18thC lady, 8in (20cm), with a pair of Meissen figures of young girls in 18thC costume, all 19thC.
$1,300-1,500

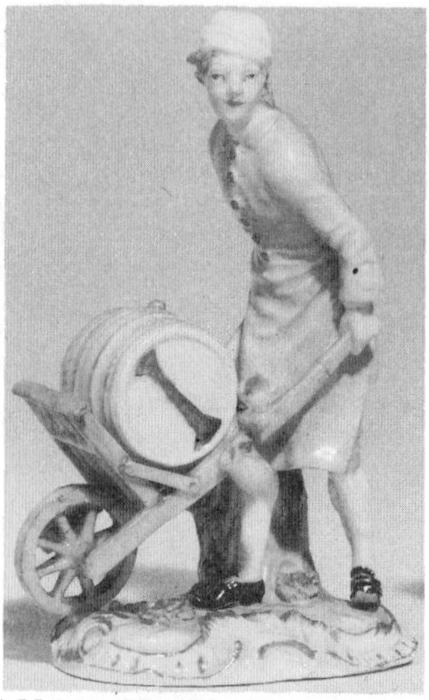

A Meissen Marcolini figure of a vinegar-seller from the Cris de Paris series, modelled by J. J. Kändler and P. Reinicke, wearing lilac and green, enriched with gilding, one shaft of wheelbarrow broken and repaired, blue crossed swords and star mark and painter's mark H, c1770, 5½in (14cm).
$2,000-2,400

A late Meissen figure of Venus clad in a blue drape studded with jewels, holding an apple and a flower garland, damaged, blue crossed swords mark, c1880, 7in (18cm).
$800-1,000

A pair of Meissen figures of young ladies, one in lace trimmed dress, the other in striped red and lilac dress, holding a toy sheep, damaged, blue crossed swords, impressed numerals, 6in (15cm).
$1,800-2,000

A Meissen group of 4 scantily clad children, warming themselves by an open fire, painted and incised marks, 7in (17.5cm).
$1,000-1,200

A Meissen figure of a drummer boy, with blue hat, purple jacket and yellow breeches and shoes, on a treestump base enriched with gilding, blue crossed swords mark and incised z2 to rear of base, c1765, 5in (13cm).
$900-1,000

A late Meissen figure of a putto emblematic of Air, from a set of the Elements, scantily clad in a turquoise drape, chipped, blue crossed swords and incised and impressed numerals, c1880, 5in (13cm).
$700-800

A Meissen group of children, on circular base, some restoration, crossed swords mark in blue, late 19thC, 13in (33cm).
$1,300-1,500

Flatware

A Chelsea plate painted with flowersprays and scattered flowers, the border crisply moulded with scrolls and trellis, red anchor mark, c1755, 11in (28cm).
$800-1,000

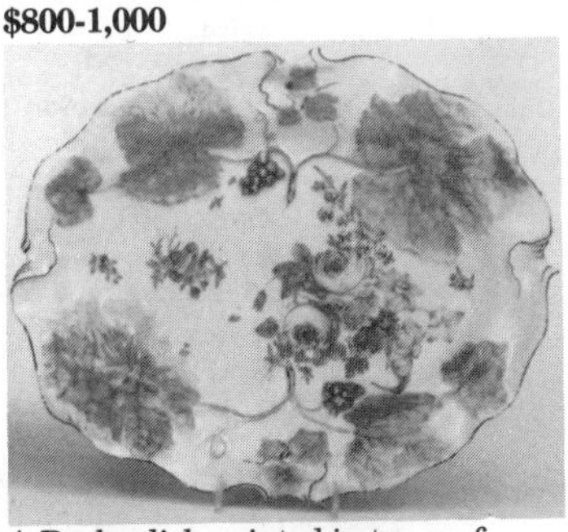

A Derby dish painted in tones of green and purple, within a shaped chocolate line rim, minute rim chips, Wm. Duesbury & Co., c1760, 12in (31cm) wide.
$1,800-2,000

A Derby plate, painted by George Complin, pattern No. 126, decorated within gilt borders, crown, crossed batons and D marks in puce, c1790, 9in (22cm).
$1,000-1,200

A pair of Copeland plates, hand painted in the Sèvres style, c1865, 9½in (24cm).
$300-350

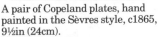

A Crown Derby Imari plate, impressed and printed mark with date code for 1885, 9in (22cm).
$250-300

A Bloor Derby oval meat dish, repaired, 18in (45cm) wide.
$100-150

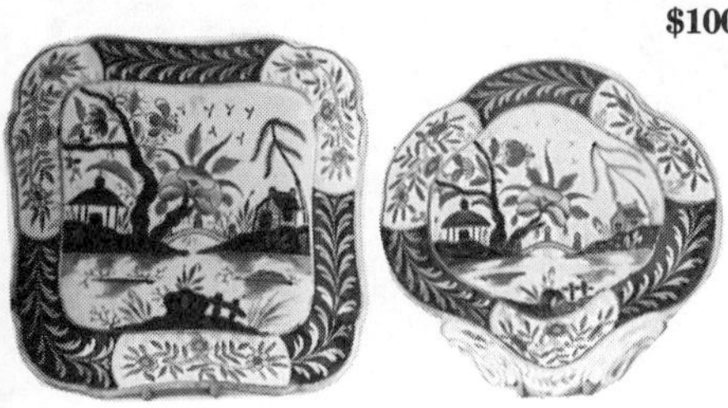

Two Coalport shaped dishes, both 8in (20cm) wide.
$300-350

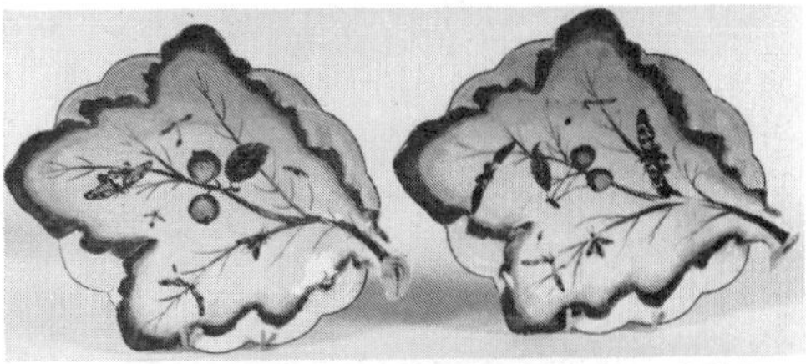

A pair of Derby leaf-shaped dishes, printed in colours within moulded basket borders, firing cracks, mid-18thC, 11½in (29cm) long.
$1,400-1,800

A Nantgarw lobed dish, with scattered floral decoration, London impressed mark, c1818, 11½in (29cm).
$1,000-1,500

SWANSEA PORCELAIN

★ factory produced high quality soft-paste porcelain from 1814-22
★ factory started by Dillwyn, Billingsley and Walker
★ superb translucent body, excellent glaze
★ in many ways one of the best porcelain bodies produced in the British Isles
★ also noted for delicacy of flower painting, usually attributed to Billingsley although much was obviously done by other decorators including Pollard and Morris
★ a close study of marked pieces will give one an idea of Billingsley's work but unless actually signed by him pieces should be marked 'possibly by Billingsley'
★ on pieces moulded with the floral cartouches the moulding can be detected on the other side of the rim, unlike the heavier Coalport wares which later utilised same moulds
★ especially notable are figure and bird paintings by T Baxter
★ the Swansea mark often faked, particularly on French porcelain at the end of the 19th, beginning of the 20thC
★ in 1816 Billingsley left to start up again at Nantgarw
★ many pieces were decorated in London studios

A J & W Ridgway plate, hand painted with pastoral scenes, c1825, 8½in (22cm).
$150-180

A Rockingham pin tray, applied with coloured roses within a gadroon and foliage rim, lightly enriched in gilding, Cl.2 in red, c1835, 4in (10cm).
$500-600

A Swansea London decorated plate, painted by J. Bradley & Co. with The Red-Breasted Goosander named in red script on the reverse, and with J. Bradley & Co. 47 Pall Mall, London, c1820, 8in (21cm).
$5,000-6,000

A Rockingham blue ground tray, the centre painted within a periwinkle blue border, edged with yellow flowers and gilt scrolls, puce griffin mark, c1835, 14½in (36.5cm) wide.
$1,800-2,000

A Swansea dish painted by George Beddow, with nr. Southampton within a double gilt line rim, impressed mark and crossed tridents, c1817, 11½in (29cm) wide.
$900-1,300

A First Period Worcester porcelain plate, with gilt wavy edge, painted with polychrome sprays of flowers in gilt scroll borders on blue scale ground, blue painted square mark, c1760, 8½in (22cm).
$200-300

A Worcester leaf dish, pencilled in black with a butterfly and gilt flowers, minute chips, slight rubbing, c1758, 7½in (18.5cm).
$1,200-1,600

A Swansea London decorated plate, painted with a lakeland scene within a gilt panelled diaper and seed pattern border, edged with C-scrolls, c1820, 8in (21cm).
$1,800-2,000

A Derby side plate with gilt rim, painted flowers within gilt leaf borders surrounded by gilt fern decoration on blue ground, orange painted Derby mark, 7in (17cm).
$400-500

A Worcester porcelain dish, from the Marchioness of Huntley service, c1770, 8in (20cm).
$1,000-1,200

A Worcester plate of the Lord Henry Thynne type, restoration to rim, open crescent mark, c1770, 14in (35cm).
$750-850

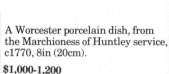

A Meissen blue and white dish, with indented corners, painted in the Transitional style, blue crossed swords mark and painter's circle, incised Dreher's mark 3R, c1732, 12in (30cm).
$9,000-10,000

A Frankenthal lobed dish, painted in colours, tiny chip to rim, crowned CT mark and painter's mark 80, incised H.110, c1765, 11in (27.5cm).
$3,000-4,000

A Meissen plate from the Möllendorf service, the centre painted in red with a spray of 'indianische Blumen', enriched with gilding, gilt dentil rim, blue crossed swords mark, Pressnummer 22 and impressed letter H, c1750, 10in (25cm).
$1,500-1,800

A Meissen Kakiemon moulded dish, painted with a tied spray of 'indianische Blumen', a blue bird on a scroll branch, two chips, blue enamel crossed swords mark, inventory No. N.5, incised Johanneum No. N=45W, c1730, 12½in (31.5cm).
$6,000-8,000

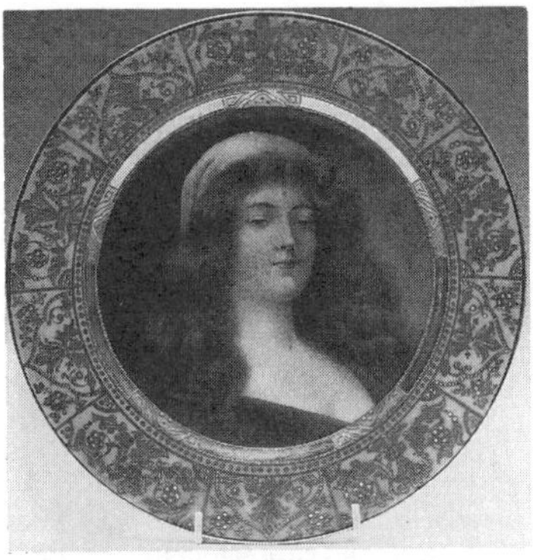

An Austrian porcelain plate, the centre painted with a portrait of a young woman with light brown hair, wearing a red dress, the violet border decorated with symmetrical designs in gold, 10in (24.5cm).
$500-600

A pair of Fürstenberg Berliner dessert plates, the borders painted in colours with sprays of flowers and puce ground shaped cartouches, the wells painted with figures, blue script F marks, c1775, 10in (25cm).
$1,500-2,000

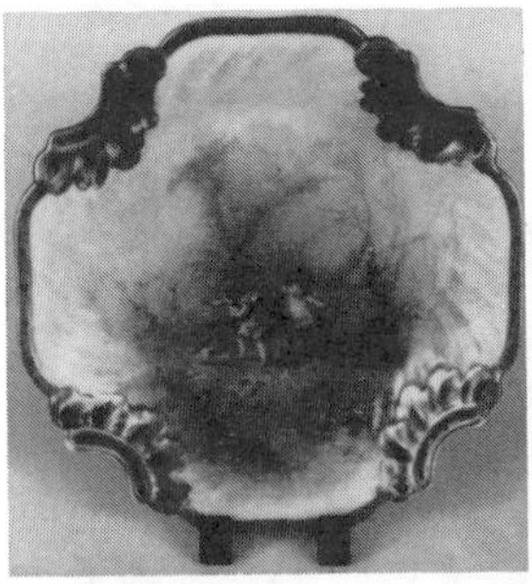

A Limoges hand painted plate, signed by A. Nicol, c1900, 9in (23cm).
$300-350

A Frankfurt blue and white dish painted with chinoiserie figures in the Transitional style, hairline crack and restored chips to rim, c1680, 15½in (39cm).
$1,000-1,200

A Du Paquier dish, painted with 4 iron red diaper panels above a continuous band of 'Laub-und-Bandelwerk', enriched with gilding, brown rim, the reverse with 3 iron red flowersprays, repaired, cracked, c1730, 18in (46cm).
$3,000-4,000

A blue and white transfer printed dish with The Beemaster pattern, c1815, 8½in (22cm) wide.
$300-400

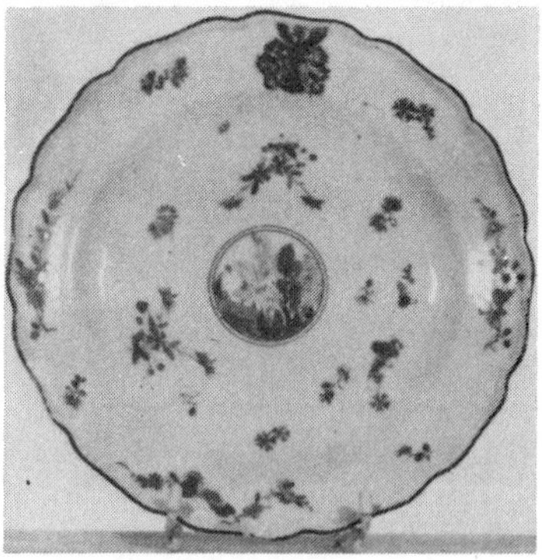

A pair of Meissen armorial plates from a service made for Graf Johann Christian von Hennicke, painted in the Kakiemon style, with central medallion outlined in black and red, both damaged, blue crossed swords mark, c1735.
$600-800

Jugs

A Worcester blue and white faceted cream jug, painted with The Root pattern, extending over the rim to the interior, painter's mark, c1758, 3½in (9cm).
$1,600-1,800

A Worcester mask jug, apple green ground and cabbage leaf moulded, painted within shaped gilt C-scroll cartouches, beneath a border of moulded gilt foliage, minor restoration, c1770, 8in (20.5cm).
$2,400-3,000

A Worcester cream jug, painted in pink 'camaieu' in the atelier of James Giles, the interior rim with trellis pattern, c1770, 4in (9cm).
$1,000-1,300

A Scottish jug printed with Oddfellows Arms, enamel decoration and inscription, dated 1823, 8in (20.5cm).
$280-320

A Royal Worcester jug, painted with a robin, signed by William Powell, c1928, 4in (10cm).
$400-450

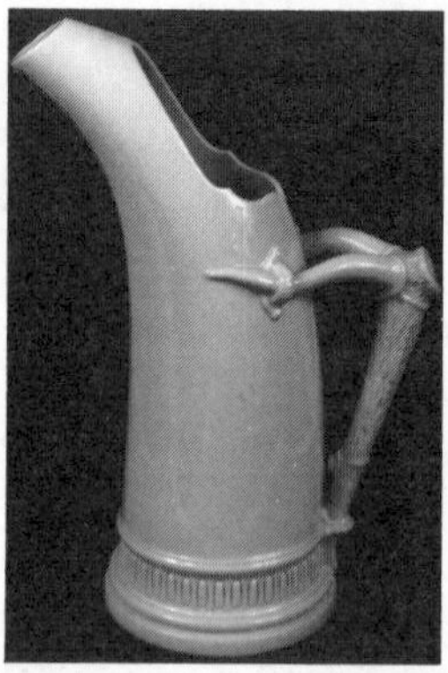

A Royal Worcester jug, Reg. No. 37112, marked, c1910, 10in (25.5cm).
$300-350

A Sèvres cream jug, with branch handle, heightened in gilt, the body painted in colours, blue interlaced L mark enclosing the letter H for 1760 and with painter's mark of Evans, 3½in (9cm).
$800-1,000

Mugs

A Worcester apple green ground mug, painted within gilt C-scroll mirror-shaped cartouches flanking the gilt monogram AB within a similar cartouche, crack to handle, c1780, the decoration perhaps later, 4½in (11.5cm).
$5,000-6,000

A Worcester transfer printed mug, after Robert Hancock, with The Milkmaids and May Day, slight hairline crack, c1765, 5in (12.5cm).
$650-700

A Chamberlain's Worcester beaker, inscribed 'Peace', possibly commemorating the battle of the Nile, painted in the manner of John Wood, chipped.
$1,500-1,600

Plaques

A German plaque, indistinctly signed and dated 1842, 13in (33cm).
$6,000-7,000

A German plaque, painted with the Madonna looking down on the Christ child, 7in (18cm), gilt metal frame.
$500-600

A Continental hand-painted plaque, 19thC, 5in (12.5cm) diam.
$30-40

Pots

A pair of Chelsea pots and covers, painted with bouquets and flowersprays, edged in gilding, the covers with turquoise branch finials, one cracked, red anchor, 9 and 14 marks, c1756, 3½in (9cm).
$2,000-2,500

A pair of Derby coral red ground D-shaped bough pots, with gilt ram's mask handles, decorated in gilt and white, minute chips, crown, crossed batons and D marks in carmine, Duesbury & Kean, c1800, 9½in (24cm) wide.
$2,000-3,000

A pair of Coalport flower pots and stands, with fixed gilt ring handles, c1810, 6½in (15.5cm).
$8,000-9,000

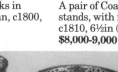

A Copeland Spode marmalade pot and bowl.
$40-60

A Bloor Derby bough pot and pierced cover, painted with flowers enclosed by gilt borders against cobalt blue reserves, gilding retouched and one foot restored, printed mark, c1820, 4½in (11.5cm).
$1,200-1,500

A St. Cloud white seau à demi-bouteille, with mask handles, c1730, 4½in (11cm).
$3,000-4,000

A Royal Worcester 'broken egg' jam pot, with original silver plated stand and spoon, shape No. 2218, c1902, 4in (10cm).
$400-500

A garniture of 3 Davenport D-shaped bough pots, with fixed gilt ring handles, some restoration, chips and retouching, impressed lower case marks above an anchor, c1805, 4½ and 6in (12 and 15.5cm).
$2,000-3,000

Services

A Samuel Alcock dessert service, with apple green borders, enriched with gilt and reserved with a salmon pink band, comprising: a sauce tureen, cover and stand, 7 dishes and 12 plates, pattern No. 3/1860, c1848. **$3,000-4000**

A John Rose Coalport part tea service, decorated with an Imari design within gold rims, comprising: a milk jug, sugar basin and cover, waste bowl, 3 plates, 18 cups and 12 saucers, some damage, pattern No. 159, early 19thC.
$1,500-1,600

A Coalport tea service, comprising: a teapot, restored, a stand, a matching cream jug, and cup and saucer, orange painted mark 875 and pink printed mark 'Patronised by the Society of Arts, The Gold Medal Awarded May 30th 1820, Coalport Improved Feldspar Porcelain, I. Rose & Co'. **$800-900**

A Coalport part tea service, comprising: a teapot, sucrier and cover, milk jug, slop bowl, bread and butter plate, and 2 cups and saucers, gold marks 2/587 and large plate with orange printed mark 'Patronised by the Society of Arts, the Gold Medal awarded May 30th 1820, Coalport Feldspar Porcelain', some restoration.
$400-500

A Coalport part dessert service, painted in polychrome, comprising a bowl, a dish and 9 plates.
$300-400

A Coalport botanical part dessert service, painted within pale yellow borders, comprising: 2 shaped dishes, one damaged, 2 square dishes, one riveted, and 8 plates, 2 cracked, one chipped, 1 stained, some rubbing to gilding, c1820.
$2,000-2,500

A Coalport dessert service, comprising: a comport, 2 oval dishes and 6 plates, painted within gold decorated blue ground, some pieces signed F. Howard, Waring & Gillow stamp, early 20thC.
$1,600-2,000

A Coalport dessert service, comprising: a large comport, 4 dishes and 12 plates, c1845, plate 9in (23cm).
$3,500-4,000

A Pinxton tea and coffee service, with burnt orange bellflowers within gilt line borders, comprising: 10 tea cups, 9 coffee cans, 10 saucers, slop basin, milk jug, bread and butter plate, a sugar basin on stand and teapot with domed cover, pattern No. 312.
$4,000-5,000

A Chamberlain's Worcester dinner service, decorated with underglaze blue and yellow, comprising: a soup tureen, 3 vegetable dishes and covers, 2 sauce tureens and covers, 4 meat dishes, 20 soup plates, 44 dinner plates and 35 dessert plates, some damage.
$2,000-2,500

A Chamberlain's Worcester part tea service of Admiral Lord Nelson pattern, with Imari style iron red, blue and gilt decoration, comprising: teapot, cover and stand, milk jug, sucrier and cover, 2 cups and saucers and a deep dish, painted mark No. 240.
$5,000-6,000

A Dr. Wall Worcester 8-piece tea service, decorated with the Bengal Tiger pattern, teapot with square seal mark, c1770.
$4,000-5,000

A Royal Worcester part dinner service, comprising 14 pieces, printed and painted in colours, printed marks in brown and numbered W over 3425 in red.
$4,000-5,000

A Worcester part tea service, all with blue seal mark.
$2,500-3,000

Fifteen pieces of Meissen 'blanc-de-chine' white prunus blossom moulded teawares, comprising: a teapot and cover, cracked, 2 tea caddies and covers, 2 hot water jugs and covers, one cover damaged, 5 saucers and 5 beakers, blue crossed swords marks to some pieces, c1750.
$2,000-3,000

A miniature part tea service, painted in colours, comprising: a teapot and cover, sugar bowl and cover and a milk jug, jug and bowl handles broken.
$300-400

A Grainger's Worcester tea service, comprising 38 pieces, various marks, pattern No. 102, c1825.
$1,200-1,300

Tea & Coffee Pots

A Coalport tea kettle, cover and stand, with green and gilt foliage moulded carrying handle, the cover with pink rose finial, minor chipping to flowers, the stand with script Coalport mark in gold, c1830, 8in (20cm).
$4,000-5,000

A Spode coffee pot and cover, with faceted spout and loop handle gilt with foliage, with gilt line rims, pattern No. 1914, c1815, 10½in (27cm).
$500-700

A Derby teapot, cover and stand, c1810, 6in (15cm).
$400-450

A Spode coffee pot and cover, with richly gilt faceted spout and loop handle, gilt with trailing foliage between diamond pattern rims, foot repaired, pattern No. 609, c1805, 10in (25cm).
$300-400

A Machin coffee pot and cover, bat-printed and coloured, the spout with gilt foliage, pattern No. 687, c1815, 9in (23.5cm).
$700-800

A Derby coffee pot and cover, painted with scattered cornflowers between gilt line rims, the cover with gilt ring finial, crown, crossed batons and D mark and pattern No. 129 in puce, Wm. Duesbury & Co, c1785, 10in (24.5cm).
$1,200-1,400

A Nymphenburg yellow ground teapot and cover, painted in colours, finial lacking, impressed Bavarian shield mark and 2, c1760, 4in (11cm).
$2,400-3,000

A Barr, Flight & Barr coffee pot and cover, painted with bands of sepia and gilt foliage between gilt line rims, minute rubbing to gilding near base of spout, c1800, 9in (23cm).
$800-1,000

A Meissen teapot and cover, painted with branches of blossom below a gold scrolling rim, 18thC, 3in (8cm).
$1,200-1,500

A Worcester, Grainger & Co, Imari pattern teapot and cover, boldly painted with iron red flowers with blue and gilt foliage, within gilt line rims, script mark inside cover, c1810, 11in (28cm) wide.
$800-900

'ureens & Butter 'ubs

A pair of Sèvres 'Seaux à Liqueur' with pierced dividers, painted in colours with blue and gilt dash lines to rims, one divider broken, interlaced L's enclosing date letter L for 1764, painter's mark PT for Petit to both pieces, 12½in (32cm) wide.
$4,000-5,000

'ases

pair of J. W. Hammann allendorf cornucopia vases, c1775, in (25.5cm) high.
00-900

A garniture of 3 Chelsea vases, with gilt scroll handles, the feet with pink scale pattern, handle cracked, c1765, smaller vases 11in (27cm) high.
$6,000-8,000

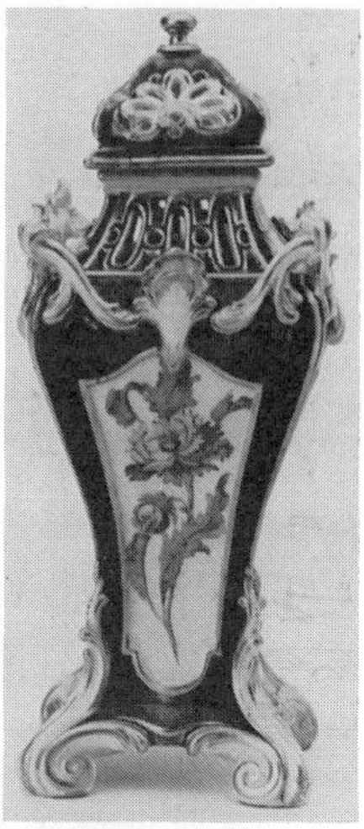

A Chelsea vase and cover, with gilt panel on each side enclosing floral spray against dark blue reserve, with pierced domed cover, some damage, c1770, 10in (25cm).
$800-1,000

pair of Chelsea blue ground vases, th pierced rococo scroll handles riched in gilding, painted with otic birds, richly gilt grounds and t line rims, with pendant scrolls d foliage, minute rubbing to ding, c1765, 7in (17cm).
,000-7,000

A pair of Coalport green ground vases with panels outlined in yellow and gilt, reserved with panels of flowers, cracked and chipped, 8½in (21cm).
$500-700

A Coalport vase and domed cover, enriched with gilt, gilt ampersand mark, c1865, 24½in (62cm).
$5,000-6,000

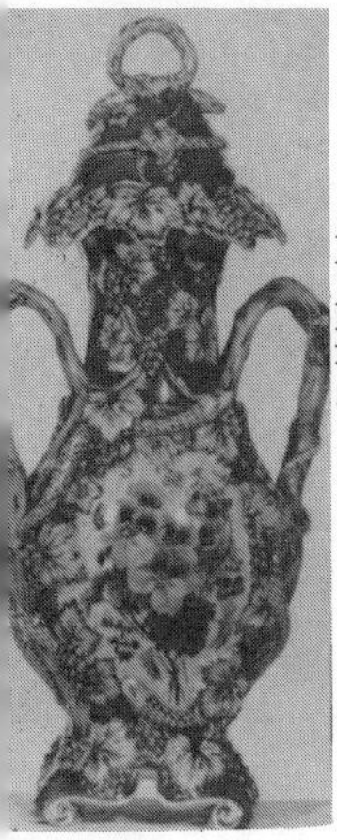

A pair of Coalport vases and covers, the blue grounds reserved with panels of flowers, both damaged and repaired, 13½in (34cm).
$1,000-1,400

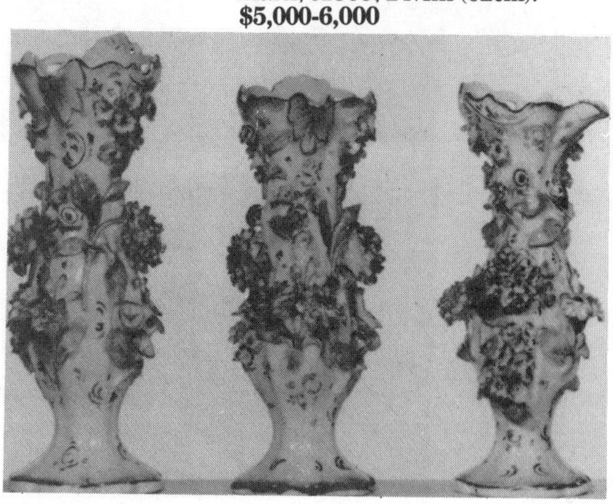

A Coalbrookdale type garniture of 3 vases, painted in colours, damaged, 9in (23cm).
$200-250

A pair of Vienna enamel bottle vases, with Bacchus figural stoppers, the bodies painted with classical scenes in yellow medallions on grey grounds enriched with scroll motifs, c1880, 12½in (31.5cm).
$4,000-5,000

A Chelsea midnight blue vase and cover, supported by 3 white caryatid figures, the body decorated in gold and applied with pink and white flowerheads, c1770, 11in (28cm).
$1.400-1.800

A Derby vase, boldly painted in the manner of George Rouse, the neck and pedestal painted in moss green within gold bands, one handle repaired, painted mark in red, c1800, 11in (29cm).
$400-600

A pair of Continental vases and covers, each painted on either side by E. Sieffert, with gilt enrichments and bronze elephant handles, bronze mounted covers and base, 19thC, 18½in (47cm).
$3,000-4,000

A pair of Sèvres pattern vases, painted within oval gilt line cartouches reserved on turquoise grounds, with gilt rims and footrims, hair crack to one, gilding rubbed, late 19thC, 38½in (98.5cm).
$7,000-8,000

A pair of Derby pedestal vases with swan handles, painted on a deep blue ground decorated in gold with scrolls and foliage, painted mark, early 19thC, 10in (24.5cm).
$2,500-3,000

A pair of English porcelain vases, of Vincennes Duplessis form, each painted blue in the manner of Viellard, with gilt enrichments, probably Coalport, some damage, early 19thC, 8in (20cm).
$1,200-1,500

A pair of Vienna vases with covers, decorated with classical figures on a navy blue ground and heavily gilt, one finial damaged, 11in (28cm).
$400-500

A Copeland & Garrett fluted vase, early 19thC, 6in (15cm).
$300-400

A Copeland & Garrett spill vase, c1840, 4in (10cm).
$150-200

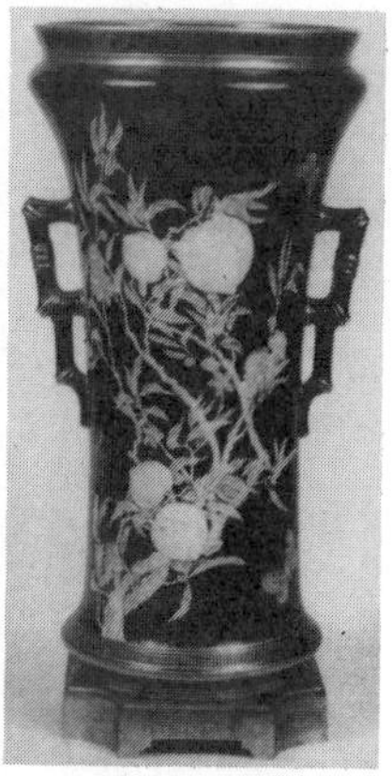

A Mintons 'pâte-sur-pâte' ormolu-mounted vase, decorated by C. Toft in white slip on a dark brown ground, with everted gilt dentil rim and the lower part with gilt radial bands, signed in white slip, c1875, 21in (54cm).
$1,500-2,000

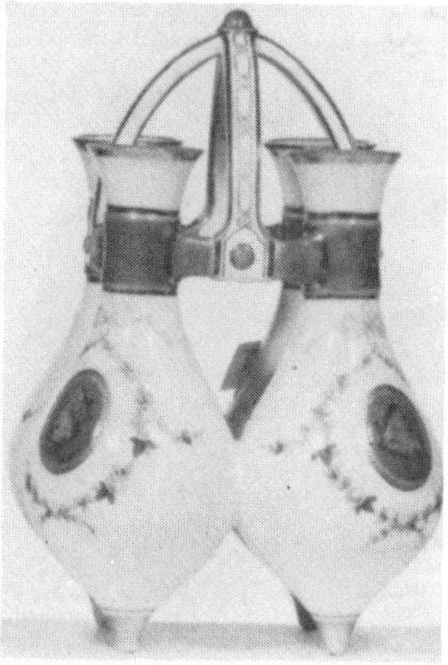

A Minton quadruple vase moulded as 4 joined bottle-shaped vases, their necks joined by strapwork, 9in (22cm).
$400-500

A Spode campana vase painted in gilt and pink with flowers, 4½in (11cm).
$100-140

A Rockingham pot pourri vase and pierced cover, with gilt scroll handles, the cover and foot with applied trailing flowers, c1835, 14in (35cm).
$4,000-5,000

A Rockingham green ground vase and cover, painted with flowers and insects, between gilt dentil and stiff leaf rims, the cover with gilt rose finial, restoration, red griffin mark, Cl.15 in puce, raised concentric ring mark, c1830, 18in (46cm).
$2,000-2,500

A Staffordshire hunting spill vase, c1850, 7½in (19cm).
$400-500

A Swansea vase, with gilt moulded fan and anthemion handles, the neck, lower part and stem enriched in gilding, impressed mark and trident, c1815, 10in (26cm).
$8,000-9,000

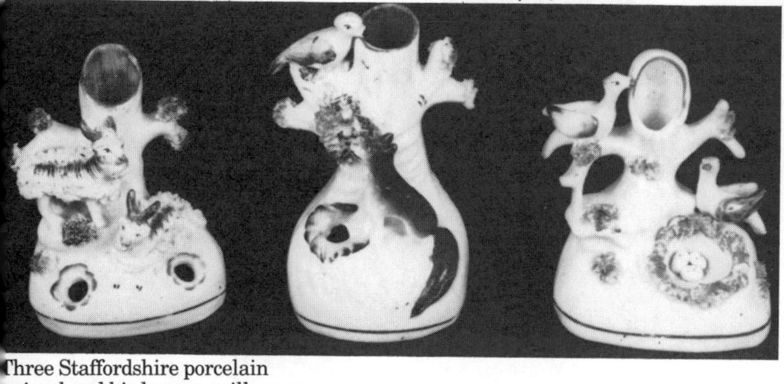

Three Staffordshire porcelain animal and bird group spill vases, c1850, 3in (7.5cm).
$180-200 each

A Staffordshire swan spill vase, c1850, 7in (17.5cm).
$400-450

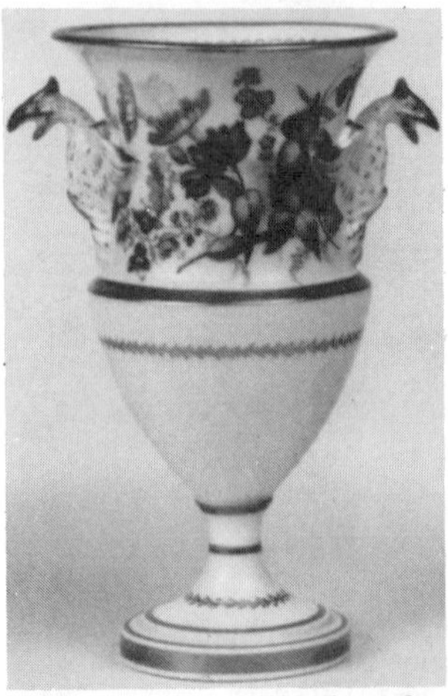

A Swansea vase with gilt eagle handles, painted by David Evans, the interior rim with gilt scrolls, handles restored, red stencil mark, c1815, 6in (15cm).
$4,000-5,000

A Swansea pot pourri vase and pierced cover, painted by David Evans, handles restored, script mark in red, c1820, 5½in (13.5cm).
$4,000-5,000

A pair of Wedgwood Fairyland Lustre vases with flared necks, designed by Daisy Makeig-Jones, signed in monogram D M-J, printed Portland vase mark and pattern No. Z.5360i, c1920, 11½in (29.5cm).
$8,000-10,000

A pair of early Worcester vases, painted in Kakiemon enamels with flowers, boughs of blossom and a banded hedge, damaged, mid-18thC, 5in (12cm).
$4,000-5,000

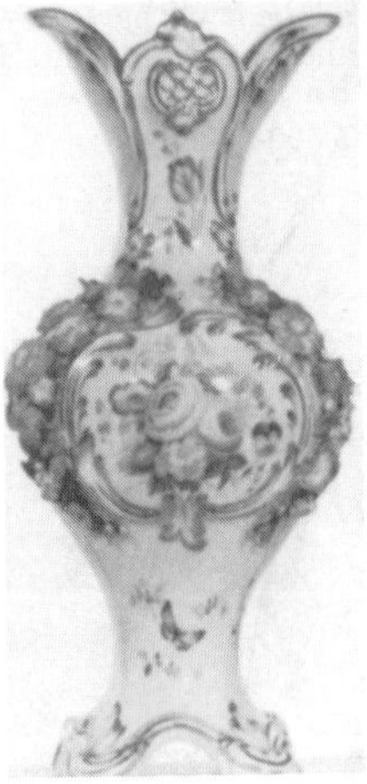

A George Sparks Worcester vase, painted with a NW view of Worcester, neck and foot outlined in gilt, minor chipping, painted mark in red script, c1840.
$200-300

A Wedgwood Fairyland Lustre Candlemas vase, 9½in (24cm).
$1,000-1,200

A Kerr & Binns Worcester 'Limoges enamel' two-handled vase, decorated by Thomas Bott, enamelled in blue/white slip with a portrait of Dante, named on the gilt oval cartouche, iron red painted shield mark including the date 1857 and TB monogram, 1857, 12½in (32.5cm).
$1,400-2,000

A pair of Grainger's Worcester 'pâte-sur-pâte' vases, in white on a blue ground, the handles, rim and foot painted in gold, impressed mark, c1880.
$1,200-1,500

A Kerr & Binns Worcester vase, painted by James Bradley Snr, c1853, 7in (18cm).
$500-600

A Locke Worcester vase, shape No. 291, c1900, 7in (18cm).
$200-300

Locke Worcester vase, painted
ıd signed by H. Wall, c1900, 5½in
4cm).
250-300

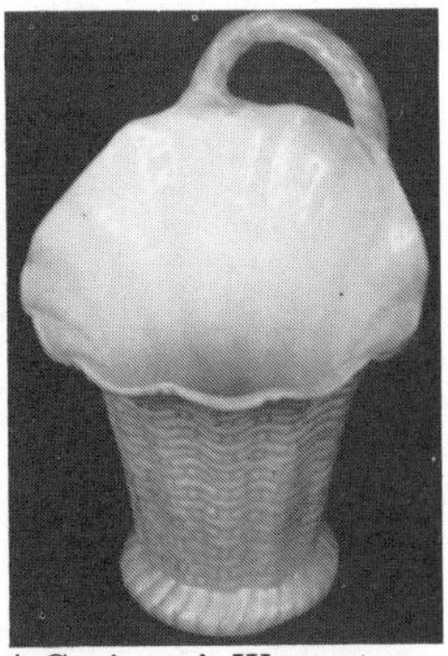

A Grainger's Worcester posy vase, c1900, 4in (10cm).
$100-120

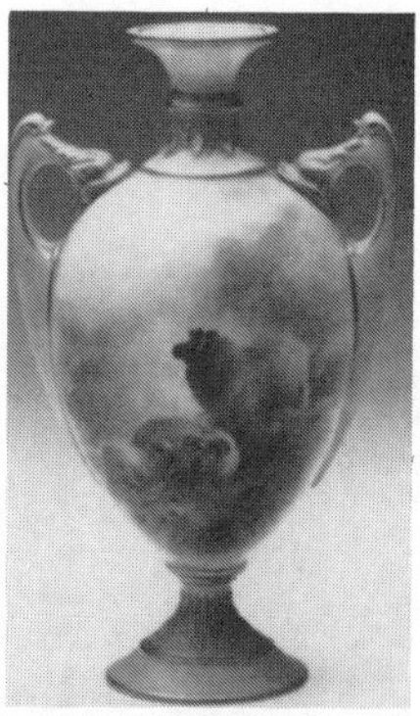

A Royal Worcester pedestal vase, painted by Harry Davis, shape No. 2158, printed mark and date code for 1907, 9½in (24cm).
$4,000-5,000

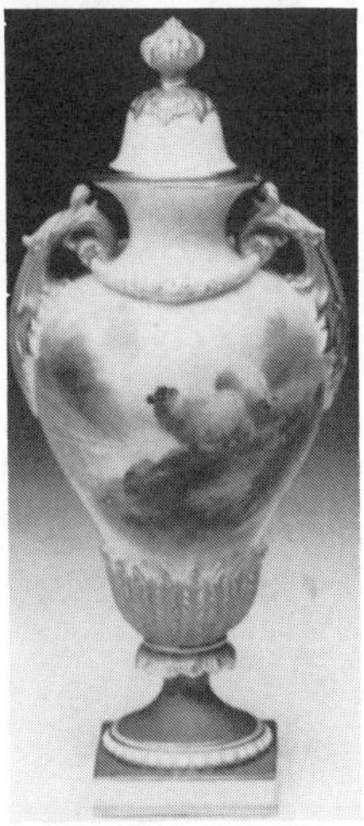

Royal Worcester pedestal jar and
ıver, painted by Harry Davis,
ıape No. 1937, printed mark and
ate code for 1907, 9½in (24cm).
6,000-7,000

A Royal Worcester vase/pot pourri, with inner and outer domed cover, hand painted on a pale blue ground with rich gilding, signed C. Baldwyn, shape No. 1995, green mark, 1902, 8in (20cm).
$4,000-5,000

A Royal Worcester vase, decorated with pink and yellow on a green and peach ground and gilt, signed R. Austin, green printed mark for 1907, 8in (20cm).
$500-600

Royal Worcester pierced
ıwo-handled vase, painted by
[. Chair, enriched with gilt dots
ıd gilding, signed, pattern
[o. 1399, puce printed marks, date
ıde for 1909, 6½in (16cm).
1,800-2,000

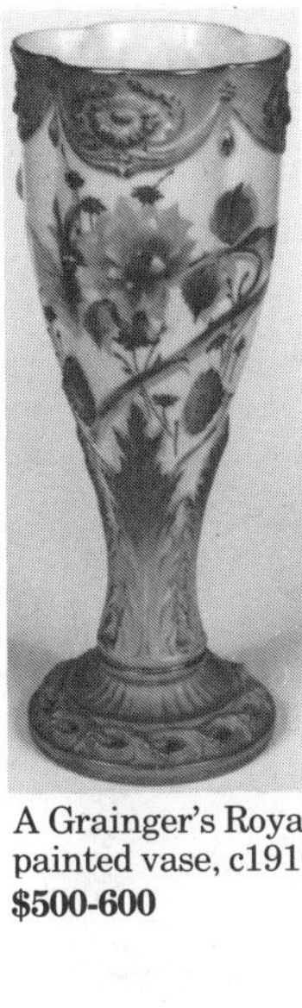

A Grainger's Royal Worcester hand painted vase, c1910, 9in (23cm).
$500-600

A Royal Worcester two-handled vase, by John Stinton, 1917.
$5,000-6,000

A Royal Worcester vase, painted and signed by Harry Stinton, Grainger's shape No. 702, c1912, 6in (15cm).
$1,600-1,800

A Royal Worcester posy vase, shape No. G.69, c1926, 2in (5cm).
$100-120

ORIENTAL POTTERY & PORCELAIN

Bottles

Two blue and white square bottles, painted with scenes after a Chinese novel, chips, mid-17thC, with silver stoppers.
$10,000-14,000

A moulded 'famille rose' bottle shaped as Liuhai, holding a string of cash in both hands, late 18th/early 19thC.
$800-1,000

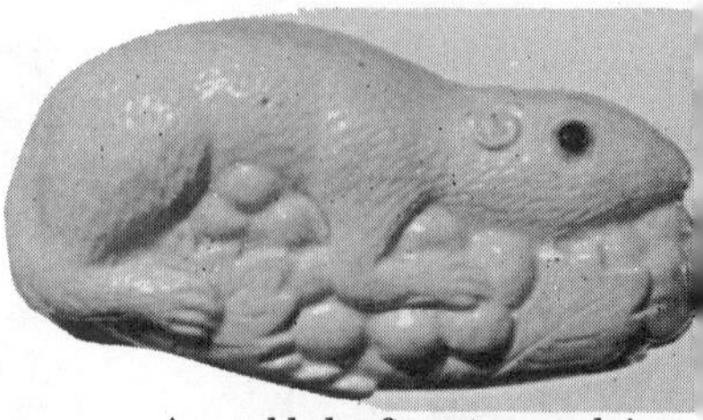

A moulded soft paste porcelain bottle shaped as a recumbent squirrel, the body markings finel incised, the ivory glaze of rich tor stopper missing, 19thC.
$800-1,000

Bowls

A Longquan celadon lotus bowl, the exterior lightly moulded, the glaze pooling slightly under the rim, damage, Song Dynasty, 6½in (16cm) diam.
$3,000-5,000

A Shufu stem bowl, with a line of lotus heads and floral sprays, under a bluish-white glaze pooling at the rim, slight chips and scratching, Yuan Dynasty, 5in (12.5cm) diam, with fitted box.
$2,000-3,000

Two Junyao bowls, covered in a crackled blue glaze, one with purpl splashes to the interior, Song Dynasty, 4in (10cm) diam.
$6,000-7,000

A Junyao stem bowl, heavily potted with shallow rounded sides, all under a widely crackled pale lavender glaze, with a purple splash inside and outside, Song/Yuan Dynasty, 5in (12.5cm) diam.
$1,500-2,000

A pair of blue and white saucer dishes with countersunk base, painted in strong blue tones, one with hair crack, encircled Jiajing six-character marks and of the period, 6in (15cm) diam.
$6,000-8,000

A Longquan celadon tripod vessel, moulded with a frieze, under a glaze of rich olive green hue, all supported on a dropped base within the tripod feet, Song/Yuan Dynasty, 5in (12.5cm) diam, with box.
$1,600-2,000

A Junyao saucer dish, with a thick bluish grey opalescent glaze thinning at the rim, revealing the dark stoneware body, Song Dynasty, 8in (19cm) diam, with box.
$4,000-5,000

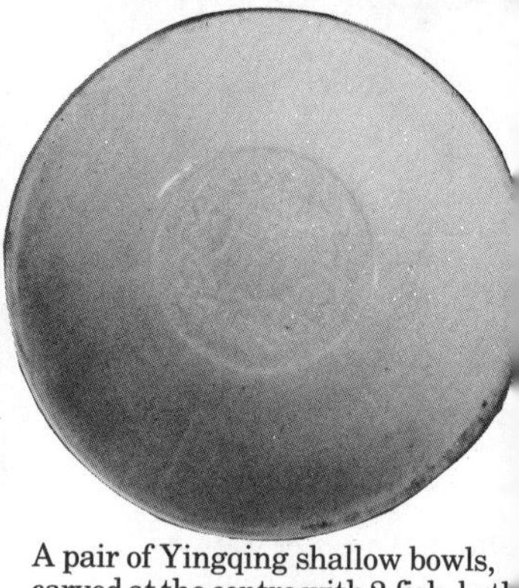

A pair of Yingqing shallow bowls, carved at the centre with 2 fish, botl bowls fired upside down on the unglazed rims, under a pale grey glaze, Southern Song/Yuan Dynasty, 6½in (16.5cm) diam.
$1,000-1,500

n early blue and white dish, the ıse unglazed with a continuous oove., Yuan Dynasty, 11in 7.5cm) diam.
12,000-14,000

A Ming blue and white saucer dish, painted in inky blue tones to the interior with a striding five-clawed dragon amidst fire and cloud scrolls, the exterior with a pair of similar dragons, encircled Jiajing six-character mark and of the period, 10in (24.5cm) diam.
$7,000-9,000

A Ming blue and white dish, painted at the centre with a leaping carp, the exterior painted with 4 similar fish, chipped and cracked, six-character Jiajing mark and of the period, 8in (20cm).
$2,000-3,000

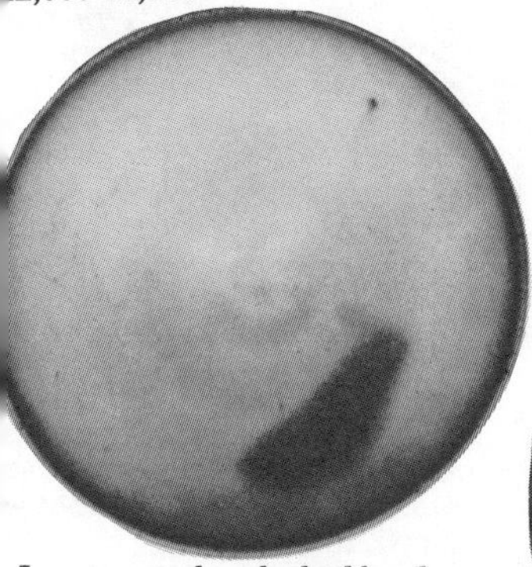

Junyao purple splashed bowl, nder a pale lavender glaze ıinning to celadon at the rim, on a ıff stoneware foot, Song/Yuan ynasty, 7in (18cm) diam.
,000-4,000

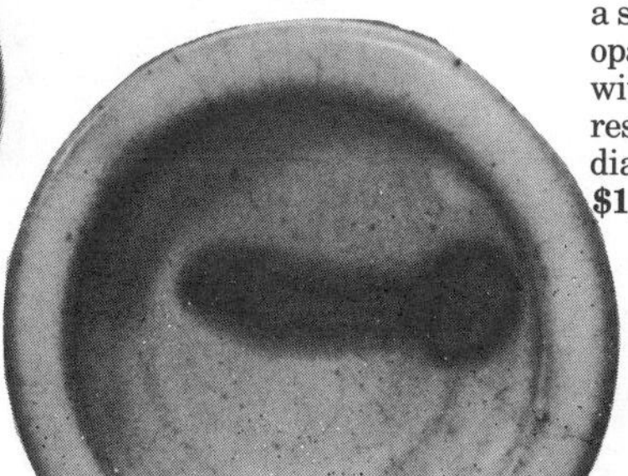

A Junyao dish, heavily potted with a straight rim, under a thick opalescent glaze of pale lavender with a splash of copper red, rim chip restored, Yuan Dynasty, 5in (12cm) diam, with box.
$1,000-1,500

A late Ming blue and white enamelled dish, with foliate rim, touches of green, yellow and iron red overall, cracks and chips, Wanli, 11in (27.5cm) diam.
$3,000-4,000

A late Ming blue and white shaped deep dish, Wanli, 14½in (36cm).
$800-1,000

A Longquan celadon foliate rim dish, with thickly potted sides, enclosing an inscription in the medallion, the rim with sketchy bracket pattern corresponding to the lobes, the underside moulded with petals, 14thC, 13½in (34cm) diam.
$1,500-2,000

A Longquan celadon dish, heavily potted and carved at the centre with diaper pattern, the exterior undecorated, all under a glaze of even olive green tones, 14thC, 14in (35.5cm).
$3,000-4,000

A rare enamelled bowl decorated in iron red, green, blue and black enamels, with a continuous band of flowerheads and scrolling foliage between narrow red lines, c1660, 6in (16cm).
$4,000-6,000

An iron red dragon bowl, painted in bright enamels, crack sealed, Kangxi six-character mark and of the period, 6in (15.5cm).
$1,500-2,000

A blue and white moulded foliate stem bowl, Kangxi, 8in (20cm).
$1,500-2,000

A 'famille verte' shallow bowl and domed cover, with animal head handles, painted in blue and green, Kangxi, 7½in (19cm) wide.
$800-1,000

A blue and white bowl with rounded sides and slightly everted rim, painted to the exterior with a flock of birds, under a sky with a star constellation, small chip, Kangxi six-character mark and of the period, 8in (20cm).
$3,000-4,000

A blue and white moulded foliate bowl, reserved on a diaper pattern ground at the rim, chips, crack and restoration, seal mark to the base, Kangxi, 13½in (34cm).
$2,400-3,000

A Kakiemon bowl, the exterior painted in blue, turquoise, iron red, green and gilt with bamboo, pine and prunus, the base with the black wheel engraved Dresden Palace collection mark: N=113 over a square, 18thC, 4in (10cm) diam.
$4,000-5,000

CHINESE PORCELAIN – VALUE POINTS

★ about 80% of the marks that appear on Chinese porcelain are retrospective
★ if a piece bears a correct, as opposed to a retrospective, reign mark then its value compared to an unmarked but comparable specimen would probably be of the magnitude of 3 to 4 times more
★ a piece of a known date but bearing the mark of an earlier reign would be adversely affected and could possible fetch less than an unmarked piece of the same vintage
★ as a rule condition will adversely affect a readily available type of ware more than a very rare or early type
★ original covers or lids can raise the price considerably – especially if the vessel appears more complete with it. Hence a baluster vase, for example, would be less affected than a wine ewer

An Arita moulded foliate rimmed bowl, decorated in various coloured enamels and gilt, the exterior with a band of hanabishi roundels, minor chip, 18thC, 7in (17.5cm).
$2,500-3,000

A Kakiemon two-handled bowl and domed cover, with lion finial, painted in blue and green enamels and iron red above underglaze blue rockwork, repaired, late 17thC, 6in (15cm) wide.
$4,000-5,000

Three Kakiemon foliate rimmed bowls, decorated in iron red, green and black enamels with gilt on underglaze blue, restoration, minor chips, c1700, 6in (15cm).
$2,500-3,000

Chinese blue and white bowl, ainted with a figure on a bridge vithin a river landscape of uildings, pine and rockwork, 1750, 7½in (19cm).
400-600

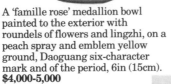

A 'famille rose' medallion bowl painted to the exterior with roundels of flowers and lingzhi, on a peach spray and emblem yellow ground, Daoguang six-character mark and of the period, 6in (15cm).
$4,000-5,000

A pair of teadust glazed stembowls, under an opaque olive green minutely dimpled glaze firing pale at the rim, incised three-character mark zhiden tang, mid-Qing Dynasty, 7in (17.5cm).
$2,000-2,500

An Imari bowl, decorated in iron ed, green, aubergine and black namels and gilt on underglaze lue, the base with a 'ju' character, Aeiji period, 10in (25cm).
4,000-5,000

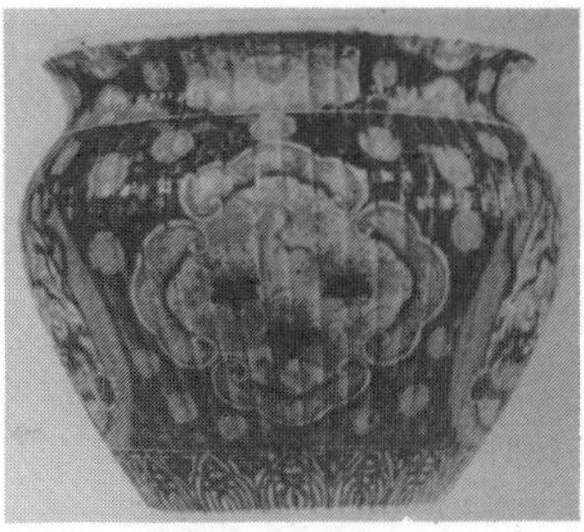

An Imari fluted oviform bowl with flared rim, painted on an underglaze blue ground reserved with iron red and gilt scrolling flowers and leaves, 18in (46cm) diam.
$3,000-4,000

A Wucai dragon and phoenix bowl, with lipped rim, decorated in 'famille verte' enamels and underglaze blue with 2 dragons in pursuit of flaming pearls, divided by a phoenix with outstretched wings, the interior with an iron red dragon and a pearl amidst green flames, Daoguang seal mark and of the period, 6in (15cm) diam, fitted box.
$5,000-7,500

Satsuma bowl painted in colours nd richly gilt in the interior, the xterior with a dark blue ground nriched with gilt flowers and 'ho-o', ½in (14cm).
800-1,000

A Satsuma thickly potted foliate rimmed bowl, painted in colours and richly gilt, 12in (30cm) diam.
$4,000-5,000

A Satsuma egg-shaped tripod bowl and cover, painted and heavily gilt, 7½in (19cm) wide.
$600-700

A Satsuma shallow bowl, painted in colours and gilt around the exterior, the interior with sprays of flowers on a fine gilt dot ground, 5in (13cm).
$4,000-5,500

An Oriental plique à jour bowl, 4in (10cm).
$1,800-2,000

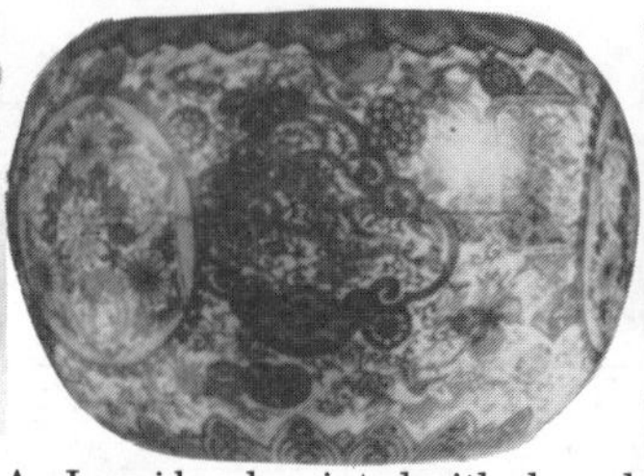

An Imari bowl, painted with shaped panels of 'ho-o' and roundels of stylised flowerheads on a ground of floral medallions, 18in (46cm) diam.
$2,000-2,500

Censers

A green-glazed red pottery tripod incense burner, lian, the glaze of deep green colour almost wholly iridescent to one side, Han Dynast 8in (20.5cm) diam.
$1,600-2,000

A Transitional blue and white tripod censer, lian, painted vividly with Daoist Immortals and monks, Jiajing six-character mark, c1640, 7½in (19cm) diam.
$5,000-6,000

Cups

A blue and white cup, painted to the exterior with the 8 Immortals and their attributes, Shoulao riding a deer and Xiwangmu on a phoenix, rim chip restored, Yongzheng six-character mark and of the period, 4in (10cm) diam.
$2,000-3,000

An Imari beaker, decorated in iron red, green and black enamels and gilt on underglaze blue, the interior with a single flowerspray, chip to rim, Genroku period, 3½in (9.5cm).
$1,400-1,600

A Chinese Imari mug, with C-scroll handle, painted with peony and chrysanthemum issuing from pierced blue rockwork, early 18thC, 6½in (16cm).
$1,200-1,400

A Longquan celadon stemcup, the interior incised with a spray of lotus, all under a celadon glaze of deep green tones, Yuan Dynasty, 5in (13cm) diam, box.
$900-1,000

A blue and white double-walled cup the exterior of the inner wall decorated with 3 couples visible through windows and lattice screens, small frittings, Kangxi.
$1,600-2,000

A Chinese mug, bearing a retrospective Qianlong seal mark, late 19thC, 4in (10cm).
$80-100

A Chinese export tankard, painted in 'famille rose' enamels with peonies and a tree hung with berries, Qianlong, 6½in (16cm).
$1,000-1,200

A Ming blue and white stemcup, painted in bright tones, cracked and restored, Zhengde six-character mark in a line to the foot interior and of the period, 6½in (16cm) diam.
$7,000-8,000

igures – Animal

pair of pale green glazed hawks, brown rockwork bases, the bodies inted with black feather arkings to the wings and bodies, e Qing Dynasty, 11in (27.5cm).
,200-1,500

A pair of Cantonese figures of Buddhistic lions, supporting candle holders on their backs, their bodies painted in iron red with gilt fur markings, gilt ears and tails, damage, 6in (15cm) wide.
$5,000-6,000

A white glazed dog with deep blue eyes, Qianlong, 9½in (24cm) long.
$6,000-7,000

igures – People

A painted grey pottery figure of a standing attendant, wearing a flowing robe, the hands clasped, concealed within the sleeves and pierced at the cuff, the head with almond shaped eyes, the hair parted in the centre and drawn up on top, traces of white slip overall and painted details, Han Dynasty, 26½in (67cm).
$25,000-30,000

A painted pottery figure of an attendant, the robe with brick red border, Han Dynasty, 16in (40.5cm).
$4,000-5,500

air of painted grey pottery ures of male officials, the robes inted in yellow, white and red ments flaring out sharply below knees, Han Dynasty, 14in .5cm).
,000-5,000

A brown glazed buff pottery figure of a standing groom, covered in brown glaze of dark amber hues, Tang Dynasty, 10½in (27cm), box.
$1,600-2,000

aubergine and turquoise glazed icial, holding an official plaque d wearing flowing robes, seated a low seat, Kangxi, 4in (10cm).
000-3,000

A white painted red pottery figure of a court lady, dressed in long loose robes, some damage, Tang Dynasty, 9in (23.5cm).
$250-300

A straw glazed pottery equestrian figure, wearing a long robe, the greenish glaze with traces of colouring, Sui/Tang Dynasty, 13in (33cm).
$6,000-7,000

A Chinese unglazed buff pottery figure of a standing attendant with clasped arms, his robe with orange pigment, Tang Dynasty, 8in (20cm).
$400-500

Flasks

A large pilgrim flask, heavily potted with 'chilong' handles, all under a crackled pale blue glaze, neck restored, base crack, Yongzheng six-character mark, 19thC, 20in (50.5cm).
$2,000-3,000

A Dingyao hexafoil dish, the centre delicately carved, under a glaze of fine ivory tone pooling into 'tear drops' near the foot, repaired, Northern Song Dynasty, 7in (17.5cm).
$5,000-6,000

A Ming celadon shaped fluted dish, moulded with a central flowerspray, 16thC, 14in (35cm).
$800-1,000

An Arita blue and white charger, the wide everted rim with flowerheads and scrolling foliage, star cracks to base, c1700, 25in (63cm).
$4,000-5,000

Flatware

A Yaozhou celadon lobed dish, freely carved with a duck swimming in stylised waves, under a glaze of pale olive green, the flared footrim unglazed, Song Dynasty, 7in (17cm).
$6,000-8,000

A Ming Green Dragon saucer dish, the interior incised and painted in bright green enamel on the biscuit, the exterior similarly decorated, old damage, encircled Hongzhi six-character mark and of the period, 8in (20cm).
$1,500-2,000

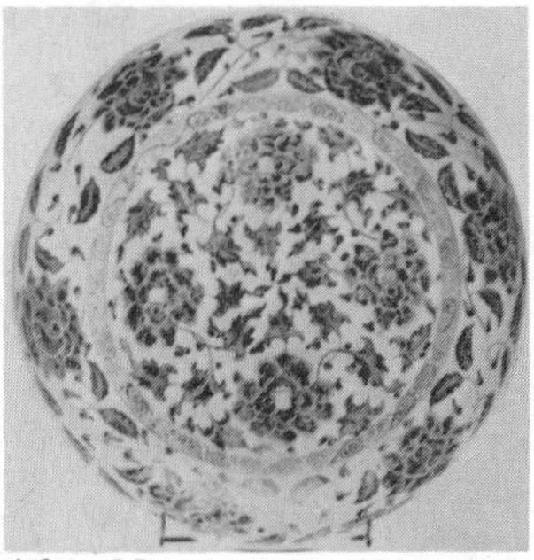

A late Ming provincial blue and white saucer dish, c1600, 16½in (42cm).
$3,500-4,000

An Arita blue and white kraak-style deep dish, painted wit flowers, butterflies, birds and emblems, cracked, chipped, late 17thC, 24in (60cm), and a wood frame.
$2,000-3,000

A late Ming blue and white Shonsui-type dish, with wavy brown dressed rim, painted with alternate panels of cell pattern, bamboo and cloud scrolls, the reverse with flowerheads and scrolling foliage, Chenghua mark, Chongzheng, 8in (20cm).
$1,200-1,500

A Swatow blue and white dish painted to the centre with a rounde of 2 recumbent deer in a landscape, below a bird perched on a tree, the everted rim with trellis pattern, wave pattern and panels of stylised flowers, rim chip, c1600, 16in (40cm).
$600-800

A Kakiemon type underglaze blue dish, decorated with 2 herons, c1680, 7in (18cm).
$2,500-3,000

Four Arita moulded dishes, lecorated in iron red enamel and gilt on underglaze blue, Ming six-character mark, Chenghua, early 18thC, 8½in (22cm).
$3,000-4,000

Two blue and white armorial plates, rim chips, Kangxi, 10in (25cm).
$5,000-6,000

A pair of 'famille verte' plates, painted with an equestrian figure and boy attendant before a fenced pagoda, Kangxi, 9in (22cm).
$1,800-2,000

A pair of Imari lobed saucer dishes, painted within bands of trailing pine, the borders with red and green ground panels, rim chip, early 18thC, 10in (25cm).
$3,000-4,000

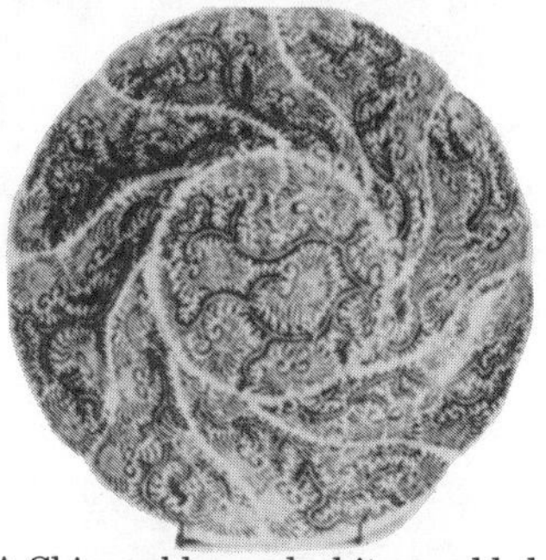

A Chinese blue and white moulded deep dish, painted with dense stylised formal scrolling flowers and leaves, small restoration, Kangxi, 19½in (49cm).
$2,000-2,500

\ polychrome basin, painted on an ron red Y-pattern ground below ron red lotus on a blue washed ground at the border, cracked and hipped, Kangxi, 15in (37cm).
$1,500-2,000

The base bears a four-character nscription which reads 'Yu Tang Jiaqi' – Jade hall precious vessel.

A pair of blue and white moulded deep plates, each painted at the centre with a crab amongst shells and water fronds, below a deep moulded border with wavy rim painted with fish, the reverse with further sprays, Kangxi, 8in (20cm).
$3,000-4,000

A blue and white saucer dish, Kangxi, 13½in (33.5cm).
$5,000-6,000

A Transitional blue and white dish, painted with a warrior and 2 dignitaries on a terrace, damage, mid-17thC, 19in (47cm).
$5,000-6,000

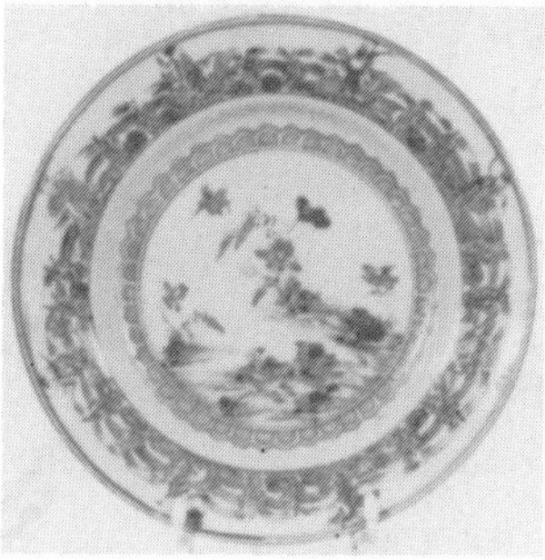

A pair of Doucai 'famille verte' plates, the borders with the Eight Daoist Immortals, each riding a fish and holding his attribute among green breaking waves, hairline crack, Kangxi, 9in (22cm).
$1,000-1,200

\ blue and white dish, small rim hips, crack to base, Chenghua nark, Kangxi, 15in (38cm).
$3,500-4,000

A blue and white saucer dish, the exterior with 5 lotus sprays, encircled six-character mark Jishibao .... zhezhen ...., mid-17thC, 6in (15cm), fitted box.
$2,000-3,000

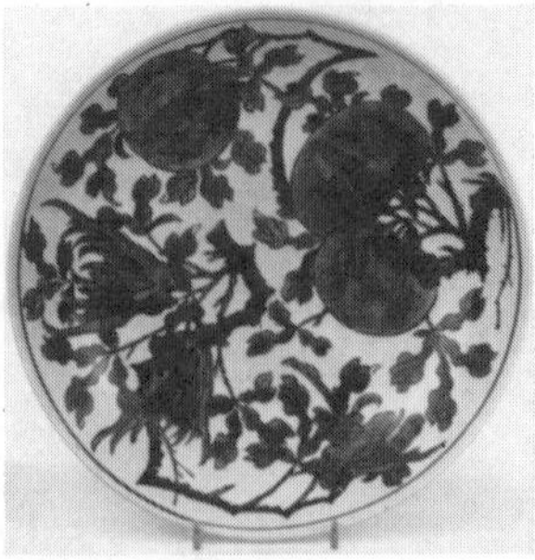

A blue and white dish, the heavily potted body painted with sprays of peach and finger citrus, on double foot rim, restored crack, Kangxi, 14½in (36cm).
$1,400-2,000

A blue and white and underglaze copper red bowl, haircrack sealed, underglaze blue mark to base, Kangxi, 8in (19cm).
$4,000-5,000

A pair of moulded Arita dishes, decorated in iron red, blue, green and black enamels and gilt, with panels each depicting the character 'ju', c1700, 8½in (21cm).
$3,200-3,500

A Doucai iron red enamel dish, painted with a five-clawed dragon rising out of the sea, the exterior similarly painted, small chips, encircled Kangxi six-character mark and of the period, 8½in (21cm).
$3,200-4,000

A 'famille verte' plate, Kangxi, 8½in (21cm).
$700-900

A pair of Kakiemon dishes, decorated in iron red, green, yellow and black enamels, on underglaze blue, with sprays of wild pinks and other flowers and foliage, 18thC, 6in (14.5cm).
$4,000-5,000

A foliate rimmed Kakiemon saucer dish, decorated in typical coloured enamels and gilt, c1700, 5in (13cm).
$1,800-2,000

A 'famille verte' dish with a rich blue translucent enamel, painted at the centre with a blue Buddhistic lion playing with a ribboned brocaded ball, damaged, Kangxi, 20½in (51.5cm).
$6,000-7,000

A blue and white and underglaze copper red dish, painted to the interior with a sage and attendant, below a three-line inscription, rim crack, minute glaze chip, early Kangxi, 10in (25cm).
$4,000-5,000

Two enamelled and underglaze blue and white armorial plates, painted at the centre with the gilt cypher S.W. on a central underglaze blue medallion beneath a simple coat-of-arms at the plain border, rim crack, star crack, gilding worn, Kangxi, c1720, 12 and 14in (30 and 35cm) diam.
$2,500-3,000

The arms are those of Winder, seated originally in Cumberland.

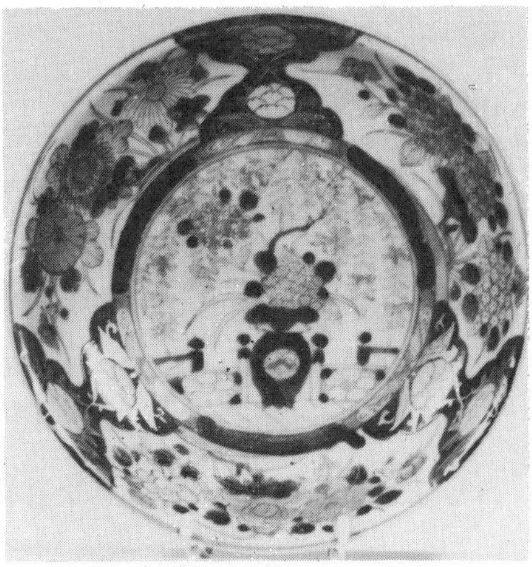

A pair of Imari dishes, centrally painted with baskets of flowers on fenced terraces, within borders of flowerheads, mid-18thC, 10in (25cm).
$800-1,200

A pair of Arita dishes with 3 projecting cusps, the centre of each painted in underglaze blue in the manner of Van Frytom, Ming/ Chenghua mark, c1700, 5in (12.5cm) diam.
$5,000-6,000

An Arita blue and white shallow dish, with the design of the Hall of One Hundred Boys, the centre with the characters Hyakushido, 18thC, 8in (20cm).
$3,000-3,500

A late Ming Swatow polychrome dish, painted to the centre in green and turquoise with 2 Daoist figures, one taking a flaming pearl from the dragon's mouth, the other waving 2 rings at a tiger, crack, 17thC, 15½in (39cm).
$1,400-1,800

The tiger and the dragon are representative of the good and evil forces in Nature.

A 'famille rose' deep dish, painted at he centre with a phoenix in flight above figures on a terrace, the well with cartouches containing ribboned vases reserved on a trellis pattern and flowerhead ground, Yongzheng, 12½in (31.5cm).
$7,000-8,000

An Imari foliate rimmed dish, decorated in iron red, yellow, green, aubergine and black enamels and gilt on underglaze blue, the reverse with scrolling karakusa, c1700, 11in (27cm).
$3,500-5,000

A pair of blue and white saucer dishes, painted with the Arbour pattern after a design by Cornelius Pronk, the wide borders reserved on a trellis pattern ground, one with chips, c1735, 9in (22.5cm).
$9,000-10,000

A pair of 'famille rose' armorial plates, painted with a central coat-of-arms below a crest with a lamb bearing the banner of St. George, chips, restoration, Qianlong, c1738, 9in (22.5cm).
$1,500-2,500

The arms are those of Roberts quartering Price.

A 'famille rose' Quail plate, painted with a pair of quail and flowers below a yellow spearhead at the well, 'bianco-sopra-bianco' floral and foliage sprays at the border, early Qianlong, 9in (22.5cm).
$1,200-1,500

A pair of pink 'camaieu' Judgment of Paris plates, painted at the centre with Juno, Minerva and Venus, below thin 'grisaille' and gilt rings at the well, some chips, Qianlong, c1750, 9in (23cm).
$2,800-3,500

TRANSITIONAL WARES

- ★ these wares are readily identifiable both by their form and by their style of decoration
- ★ Forms: sleeve vases, oviform jars with domed lids, cylindrical brushpots and bottle vases are particularly common
- ★ the cobalt used is a brilliant purplish blue, rarely misfired
- ★ the ground colour is of a definite bluish tone, probably because the glaze is slightly thicker than that of the wares produced in the subsequent reigns of Kangxi and Yongzheng
- ★ the decoration is executed in a rather formal academic style, often with scholars and sages with attendants in idyllic cloud-lapped mountain landscapes
- ★ other characteristics include the horizontal 'contoured' clouds, banana plantain used to interrupt scenes, and the method of drawing grass by means of short 'V' shaped brush strokes
- ★ in addition, borders are decorated with narrow bands of scrolling foliage, so lightly incised as to be almost invisible or secret (anhua)
- ★ these pieces were rarely marked although they sometimes copied earlier Ming marks

Three 'famille rose' armorial plates, painted with elaborate coat-of-arms, some cracks, Qianlong, c1740, 9in (23cm).
$5,000-6,000

Three 'famille rose' armorial soup plates, painted at the centre with a coat-of-arms within feathery mantling and below a crest, minute chips, Qianlong, c1750, 9in (22.5cm).
$3,000-3,500

A pair of 'famille rose' armorial sou plates, painted at the centre with a coat-of-arms within elaborate mantling below a wheatsheaf crest and above the motto 'desira nararo se', with iron red and gilt spearhea at the rim, minute chips, Qianlong c1765, 8½in (21cm).
$3,000-3,500

The arms are those of Moltby impaling Lyne.

A pair of 'famille rose' and underglaze blue and white armorial soup plates, painted in underglaze blue, some enamel rubbing, Qianlong, c1760, 10in (25cm).
$1,500-2,000

A 'famille rose' armorial soup plate, painted with a coat-of-arms within a band of iron red and gilt, minor chips, star crack, Qianlong, c1755, 9in (22cm).
$1,200-1,500

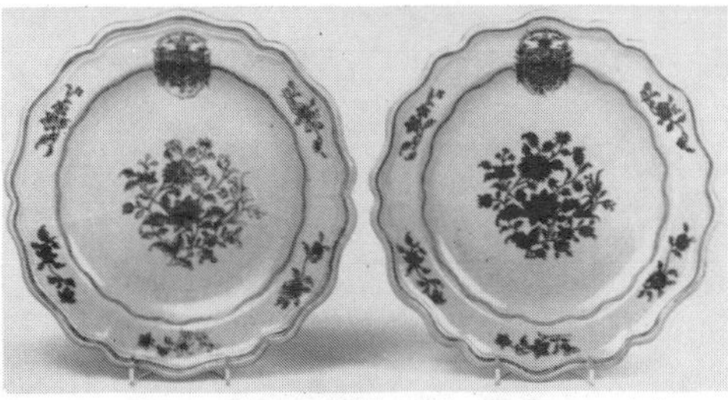

A pair of 'famille rose' armorial foliate plates, modelled on a European silver shape, painted in iron red and gilt at the centre, beneath a coat-of-arms surmounted by a ducal crest and the motto 'tu in ea et ego pro ea' (sic), chipped and cracked, Qianlong, c1770, 10in (25cm).
$6,000-7,000

A 'famille rose' basket, Qianlong, 10in (25cm).
$3,000-4,000

A pair of crested plates, painted in 'famille rose' enamels with mottos 'Bonaespei' and 'Brevis estusus', Qianlong, 6½in (16cm).
$900-1,000

A pair of blue and white plates, painted at the centre with peony and bamboo, the rim with a band of scrolling foliage, Qianlong, 13½in (34cm).
$1,400-2,000

A 'famille rose' dish, painted in bright enamelling with blue enamel borders, 2 chips to inner rim, Qianlong, 18in (45cm) wide.
$3,000-4,000

Eight 'famille rose' plates, reserved at the border on an iron red ground scattered with peony sprays, minor chipping, Qianlong, 9in (22.5cm).
$3,500-4,000

Six 'famille rose' plates, each painted with birds above prunus and bamboo, with floral borders, one restored, one cracked, chipped, Qianlong, 9in (22.5cm).
$1,400-1,800

Did you know

MILLER'S Antiques Price Guide builds up year by year to form the most comprehensive photo-reference system available

A 'famille rose' plate, painted with an elderly fisherman and 2 assistants, minor chips, Qianlong, 9in (22.5cm).
$800-1,200

A 'famille rose' European subject dish, painted at the centre with a naked European lady, with grisaille and gilt strapwork and cartouches containing pairs of doves at the rim, re-painted and restored, Qianlong, 16in (40cm).
$4,000-5,000

The scene is after an engraving of 1781 by Bonnet entitled 'Le Bain'.

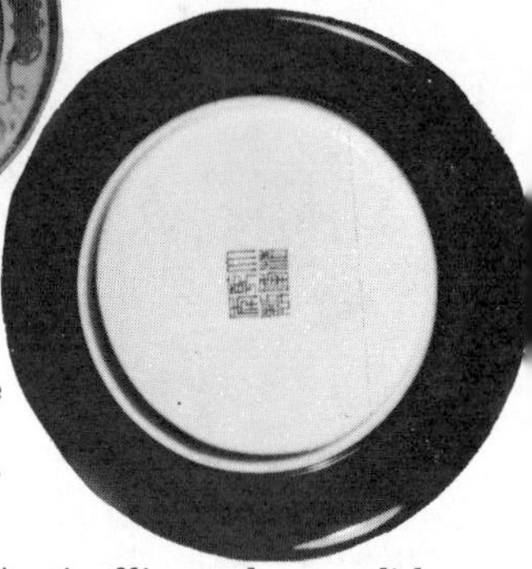

A pair of liver red saucer dishes, covered in an even glaze firing slightly darker below the white rim, glaze slightly rubbed, Qianlong seal marks and of the period, 6in (16cm).
$1,800-2,500

A pair of Chinese blue and white foliate dishes with raised central bosses, Qianlong, 12in (30cm).
$1,200-1,500

Two large 'famille rose' dishes, one painted with crabs, the other with flowers, Qianlong, 15in (37.5cm).
$1,200-1,600

A 'famille rose' meat dish, boldly painted with flowers, trailing fruit and leaves, Qianlong, 16in (40cm) wide.
$1,800-2,500

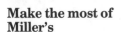

A blue and white Export serving dish, the centre painted with a Dutch coastal view, Qianlong, 18in (45cm) wide.
$1,000-1,400

A Chinese European subject plate, painted 'en grisaille' to the centre with a scene depicting Europa and the Bull, Qianlong, 9in (22.5cm).
$1,600-2,000

A blue and white dish, painted with a sampan moored at a promontory, Qianlong, 22in (55cm).
$3,200-3,600

Make the most of Miller's

Unless otherwise stated, any description which refers to 'a set' or 'a pair' includes a valuation for the entire set or the pair, even though the illustration may show only a single item

A pair of 'famille rose' dishes featuring 2 peacocks, small rim chips, Qianlong, 13in (33cm) wide.
$3,000-4,000

\ pair of Chinese blue and white
ıeat dishes, painted with figures on
ɔridges before buildings and
hrines, Qianlong, 18in (46cm) wide.
$1,000-1,200

A Chinese Imari meat dish, painted within a blue trellis pattern well, the border with sprays of flowers, Qianlong, 16in (41cm) wide.
$1,500-2,000

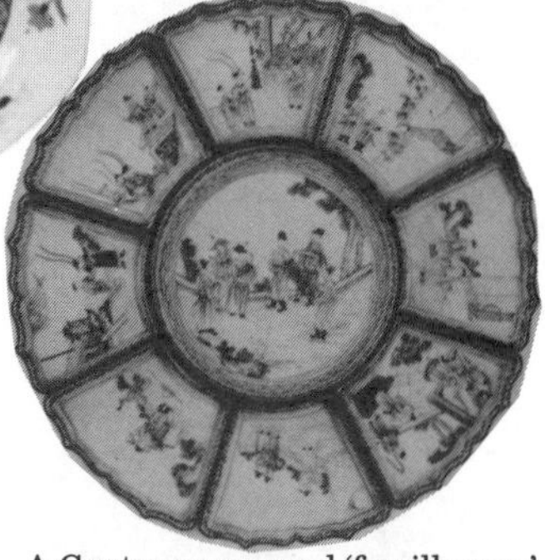

A Cantonese enamel 'famille rose' hors d'oeuvres set, comprising: 8 wedge shaped dishes around a central dish, within pale blue borders reserved with dark brown scrolling foliage, Qianlong, 17in (43cm).
$600-1,000

A 'famille rose' saucer dish, painted
vith chrysanthemum, peony and
ɔrunus issuing from pierced blue
ockwork within a gilt spearhead
ɔorder, Qianlong, 10in (25cm).
$400-600

Two 'famille rose' pseudo Tobacco Leaf plates and 2 large saucer dishes, restored, late Qianlong, 9½ and 11in (24 and 28cm).
$2,500-3,000

A pair of Chinese Export 'famille rose' plates, 18thC, 8½in (21cm).
$600-800

An orange Fitzhugh pattern dish, painted with 4 flowersprays and Daoist emblems within a band of trellis pattern at the border, c1800, 19in (48cm).
$6,000-7,000

An Imari charger, decorated in iron red, green and yellow enamels and gilt on underglaze blue, signed 'Hizen Kanyo Kajitoshi sei', late 19thC, 25½in (64cm).
$5,000-6,000

\n Imari charger, the reverse with
ɔeony sprays and scrolling
karakusa', on ring foot, 19thC,
2½in (56cm).
$4,000-5,000

An Imari dish, decorated in iron red enamel and gilt on underglaze blue, with gilt rims, late 19thC, 22½in (56cm).
$6,000-7,000

A Canton 'famille rose' plate, painted to the centre with the initials V.O.C. (Vereenigde Oostindische Compagnie), surrounded by panels of mandarins, ladies, butterflies and birds on flowersprays, 19thC, 15in (37.5cm).
$4,000-5,000

An Imari dish, having scalloped border, richly decorated, with gilding, c1900, 18in (45cm).
$400-500

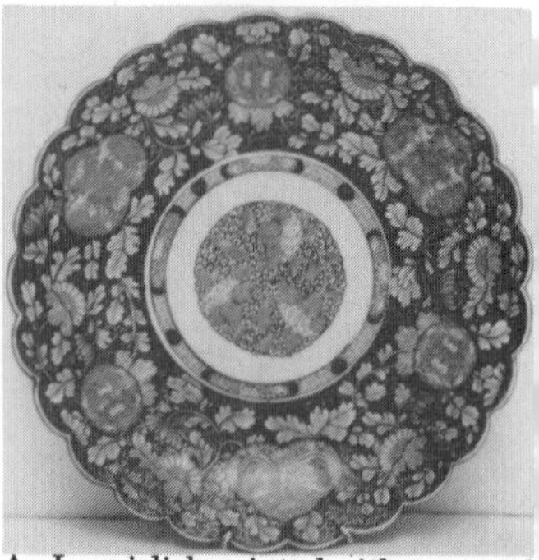

An Imari dish painted with a central blue floral medallion, the broad underglaze blue ground border reserved with iron red and gilt scrolling flowers and leaves, 25in (62.5cm).
$2,500-3,000

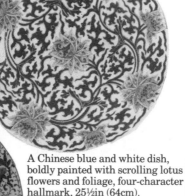

An Imari charger, in underglaze blue, iron red and coloured enamels, 22in (55cm).
$4,000-5,000

An Annamese blue and white charger, freely painted with a dragon amidst cloud forms, scalloped rim, cracked, 18½in (46cm).
$4,500-5,000

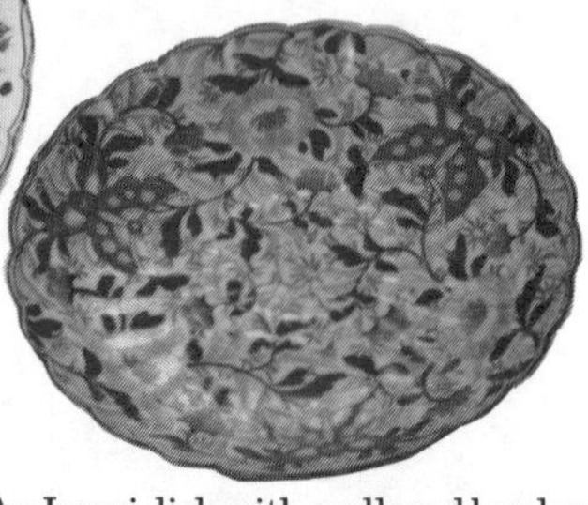

An Imari dish with scalloped border, richly decorated, with gilding, c1900, 12in (30cm).
$200-250

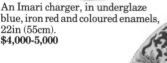

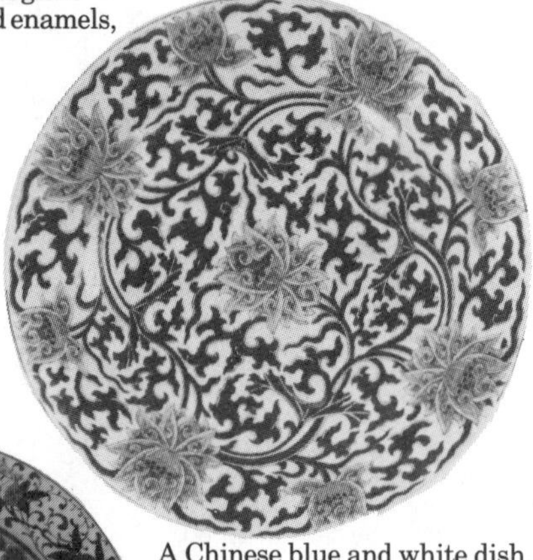

A Chinese blue and white dish, boldly painted with scrolling lotus flowers and foliage, four-character hallmark, 25½in (64cm).
$2,500-3,000

An Imari dish, decorated in iron red enamel and gilt on underglaze blue, the reverse with a band of scrolling peony flowerheads and foliage, beneath branches of plum blossom, Genroku period, 13in (32cm).
$3,000-3,500

An Imari dish, decorated in iron red and gilt on underglaze blue, Genroku period, 12½in (31cm).
$8,000-9,000

Did you know

MILLER'S Antiques Price Guide builds up year by year to form the most comprehensive photo-reference system available

A 'famille rose' saucer dish, painted with an iron red five-clawed dragon, below 4 paired groups of the 8 Buddhist emblems, 'Bajixiang' and key pattern at the rim, the exterior with 4 bats, Hongxian Yuzhi iron red mark to the base and probably of the period, 10in (24cm).
$2,500-3,000

Garden Seats

A pair of 'famille rose' garden seats, painted with 2 panels reserved on a yellow ground, late Qing Dynasty, 18in (46cm).
$6,000-7,000

An Oriental pottery garden seat, decorated with floral panels and insects.
$600-700

Jardinières

A late Ming blue and white jardinière, vividly painted in bright blue tones, Wanli, 13in (33cm) wide.
$8,000-9,000

A Chinese jardinière, painted with flowers in coloured enamels within blue and iron red borders, 19thC, 13in (33cm) diam.
$8,000-9,000

A blue and white jardinière, painted with 5 four-clawed dragons amongst clouds above breaking waves at the foot and below a bat and cloud band at the rim, 19thC, 18½in (46.5cm) diam, wood stand.
$3,000-4,000

A 'famille verte' jardinière with Buddhistic lion mask and ring handles, painted with flowers and birds below iron red scrolling foliage and above a band of stylised yellow ground panels, Kangxi six-character mark below the rim, 21½in (54cm) diam.
$4,000-5,000

A pair of blue and white jardinières, painted within key pattern and archaistic dragon bands, small chips, 19thC, 11in (28cm) wide.
$3,000-4,000

A pair of blue and white jardinières, painted with panels below a band of upright leaves and key pattern at the border, the bases pierced, rim chip, glaze bubbles, late 19thC, 17½in (44.5cm).
$7,000-9,000

Jars

A Ming blue and white jar, painted to each face with a five-clawed dragon, neck reduced, small hole to base where the body is thinly potted, Jiajing six-character mark in a double square and of the period, 4½in (11cm).
$1,200-1,500

A white glazed jar, covered with a slightly degraded whitish straw glaze, stopping just below mid-body revealing the fine grained body, kiln adhesion to body, Tang Dynasty, 9½in (24.5cm).
$1,600-1,800

A miniature phosphatic-splashed jarlet, with inverted mouth, the thick black glaze extending to mid-body with suffusions of pale lavender blue, Tang Dynasty, 2½in (5.5cm) wide.
$1,800-2,000

A Henan black glazed ribbed jar, with white slip-trailed ribs to the body, the black glaze pooling at the buff stoneware foot, the rim biscuit, chipped, Song Dynasty, 5in (12.5cm) wide.
$3,000-4,000

A late Ming blue and white jar, painted on a cell ground, with 4 lion mask handles, base restored, cracks, Wanli, 13½in (34cm).
$2,600-3,000

Two Transitional blue and white oviform jars and covers, each reserved on cracked ice grounds, c1643, 6½in (16.5cm).
$1,000-1,400

A Transitional blue and white jar and cover, painted with 2 panels, divided by leafy flowersprays, all reserved on a cracked-ice ground, a band of chevrons at the shoulder, the cover with Buddhist symbols, c1643, 7½in (19.5cm).
$600-800

A Chinese blue and white jar and cover, glaze scratches, rim crack, Transitional, c1640, 10in (26cm).
$1,200-1,600

A blue and white brush pot, painted in bright inky blue tones with a scene of a scholarly gathering, rim firing crack, early Kangxi, 7in (18cm) diam, wood stand.
$4,000-5,000

A Wucai baluster jar and cover, painted with ladies beside iron re swirling clouds, the cover with 3 jumping boys among rockwork, neck damaged, Transitional, 14in (35.5cm), with wood stand.
$2,000-2,500

A blue and white jar, painted on the sides in inky blue tones, the neck with a band of upright leaves, the flat base unglazed, minor rim fritting, Kangxi, 16½in (41.5cm).
$5,000-6,000

A blue and white baluster jar and cover, painted with a cloud collar reserved with scrolling peony on a blue washed ground above flowersprays and lappets at the foot Kangxi, 15½in (39.5cm).
$4,000-5,000

An Arita blue and white jar and cover, painted all over, body crack, rim chip, cover repaired and with chips, late 17thC, 25in (63cm).
$4,000-5,000

An Imari jar and domed cover with knop finial, painted and lightly moulded with flowering peony, chrysanthemum and plum, repaired, c1700, 17in (43cm).
$1,200-1,400

An underglaze copper red water pot, painted with flowers within an underglaze blue band at the inverted rim, the underglaze red of brownish tone, rim frits, six-character Kangxi mark and of the period, 3½in (9cm) wide.
$4,000-5,000

A ginger jar and cover, painted on a cracked ice ground, cover riveted, Kangxi, 9in (23cm).
$350-400

A pair of Chinese blue and white jars, painted with quatrefoil panels of archaistic vessels and emblems, on cracked-ice pattern grounds reserved with prunus heads, Kangxi, 7½in (19cm), wood covers and stands.
$1,200-1,400

A Swatow blue and white jar, painted in greyish blue tones, 17thC, 10½in (26cm).
$4,000-5,500

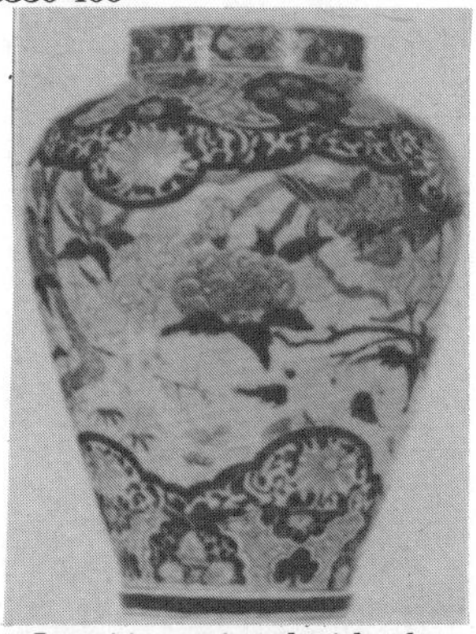

An Imari jar, painted with a broad band of 'ho-o' among flowering shrubs and trees, with underglaze blue scrolling foliage, gilt flowerheads and dragons above and below, late 17thC, 12½in (31.5cm).
$2,000-3,000

A blue and white jar, painted in a pencilled style with 2 five-clawed dragons, each chasing a flaming pearl amongst cloud and fire scrolls, Qianlong seal mark and of the period, 7½in (19.5cm).
$7,000-8,000

IMARI PATTERNS

- ★ Imari named after port of shipment
- ★ decoration of Japanese porcelain often based on brocade patterns
- ★ made at Arita, Hizen Province, from early 18thC to early 19thC
- ★ Imari patterns copied and adapted by Derby, Worcester, Spode, Minton, Mason and others
- ★ patterns also made in China

A Chinese blue and white jar and domed cover with Buddhistic lion finial, glaze cracks, cover chips, late Qianlong, 18in (45.5cm).
$1,200-1,400

An Imari jar, decorated in various coloured enamels and gilt on underglaze blue, gold lacquer repair, late 19thC, wood cover, 25in (63.5cm).
$1,800-2,000

A Satsuma pot pourri jar, finely painted, the shoulder with an overall foliate decoration, complete with embossed and pierced gilt metal cover, 7in (17.5cm).
$4,000-5,000

A blue and white jar and cover, the knop finial restored, the collar neck with scallop repairs.
$3,500-4,000

An Arita jar, decorated in underglaze blue with a continuous landscape of temples and trees, diapering and keywork, slight chipping to neck, 10½in (26cm).
$6,000-8,000

A pair of 'famille verte' jars and domed covers, the covers with knob finials, decorated with a defeated soldier kneeling before his conqueror, two chilong forming a roundel at the base in underglaze blue, 20in (51cm).
$5,000-6,000

Jugs

Two blue and white milk jugs, with scrolling S-shaped handles, the spouts moulded with bearded masks, the covers surmounted by bud finials, one handle cracked, chips and fritting, Qianlong, 5½in (15cm).
$1,200-1,400

Tea & Coffee Pots

An Imari moulded teapot, decorated in iron red and green enamels and gilt, with knop finial and a bamboo-shaped handle, c1700, 5½in (14cm).
$3,000-4,000

A blue and white teapot and cover with torii-shaped handle, painted with 2 panels, cover fritted, hairline crack to spout, Kangxi, 10½in (26cm).
$2,000-3,000

A Zhejiang celadon teapot and cover, with a glaze of deep olive green tones, Song/Yuan Dynasty, 4in (10cm) wide, box.
$1,400-1,600

A 'famille rose' teapot and cover, the sides, handle and spout moulded as bamboo, the flat cover applied with a twig finial, fritting, handle cracked, Qianlong, 5in (12.5cm).
$1,200-1,400

A 'famille rose' coffee pot and cover, painted with various figures below bird and cell cartouches at the neck, Qianlong, 9in (23cm).
$1,400-2,000

A Cantonese enamel 'famille rose' tea kettle and stand, with a swing handle, cover in plaited cane, fitted with a lamp, some damage, Qianlong, 11½in (29cm).
$1,800-2,000

A blue and white Makuzu Kozan teapot and cover, with 2 roundels containing 'ho-o' birds, the handle and spout formed as a serpent, signed on a square reserve Makuzu Kozan sei, late 19thC, 8in (20cm) wide.
$2,000-2,500

A Kyoto earthenware kettle, painted in enamels and gilding, on a seeded gilt ground, spout repaired, painted mark, Meiji period, 5in (12.5cm).
$1,000-1,200

A Cantonese teapot, decorated with landscapes and figures.
$300-400

Services

A Satsuma tea service, comprising: a teapot and cover, milk jug and cover, sucrier and cover, 6 tea cups and saucers, one cracked.
$700-800

A Qianlong 'famille rose' part service, enamelled with exotic birds and flowers, comprising: 4 dishes, 11 plates and 5 bowls, and 8 Spode pottery matching plates.
$8,000-9,000

Tureens

A pair of blue and white Fitzhugh pattern sauce tureens and covers, with bud finials and shell scroll handles, one shallow rim frit, c1800, 8in (20cm) wide.
$3,000-4,000

A 'famille rose' soup tureen and cover, and a similar meat dish, 18thC, 18in (45.5cm) wide.
$5,000-6,000

A 'famille rose' armorial tureen and cover, the tureen with iron red handles, body cracks, enamel slightly worn, Qianlong, c1760, 16in (40cm) diam.
$4,000-6,000

An export two-handled tureen, cover and stand, painted 'en grisaille' and gilt with the initials GEH within a shield on an ermine ground, some glaze crackling to cover, Qianlong, c1780, stand 8½in (21.5cm) wide.
$3,000-4,000

A 'famille rose' hen tureen and cover, with brightly enamelled wing and tail feathers, puce wattle and comb and iron red feathers, some restoration, Qianlong, 8in (20cm).
$6,000-8,000

A Chinese blue and white soup tureen and a cover, with pomegranate knop, painted with a river landscape, Qianlong, 12½in (32cm) wide.
$600-800

A Chinese blue and white tureen, cover and stand, with boar's head handles, pomegranate finial, minor damage, late 18thC, 12in (30.5cm) wide.
$2,000-3,000

Use the Index!

Because certain items might fit easily into any of a number of categories, the quickest and surest method of locating any entry is by reference to the index at the back of the book.
This has been fully cross-referenced for absolute simplicity

An Imari tureen and cover, decorated in coloured enamels and gilt on underglaze blue, the cover similarly decorated with knop finial, base restored, Genroku period, 13½in (34cm) diam.
$4,000-5,000

A moulded Imari tureen and cover, with loop handle, decorated in iron red enamel and gilt on underglaze blue, minor chip to rim, Genroku period, 6½in (17cm).
$3,000-4,000

An Imari tureen and cover, decorated in iron red enamel and gilt on underglaze blue, the cover with a finial of plum blossom on a looped strip imitating paper, Genroku period, 9½in (24.5cm) diam.
$3,000-4,000

An Imari tureen and cover, decorated in typical coloured enamels and gilt on underglaze blue, the cover similarly decorated with a finial modelled as cherry blossoms scattered on a piece of poem paper, Genroku period, 13½in (34.5cm) diam.
$4,000-5,000

An Imari tureen and cover, decorated in various enamels and gilt on underglaze blue, with a moulded foliate rimmed dish decorated in similar colours and gilt on underglaze blue with similar decoration, all pieces with restoration, Genroku period, the tureen and cover 11in (27.5cm).
$3,000-4,000

Vases

A green-glazed red pottery baluster vase, hu, under a rich golden-greenish glaze, Han Dynasty, 16in (40cm).
$2,000-2,500

A Cizhou vase, covered with a thick brownish-black glaze with a sgraffiato design, the shoulder with 2 lugs, Song Dynasty, 13½in (34cm) high, box.
$4,000-5,000

A Zhejiang celadon vase, freely combed and incised with a stylised leaf design, under an olive green glaze, left in the biscuit at the rim, Song Dynasty, 8in (20.5cm).
$1,400-1,800

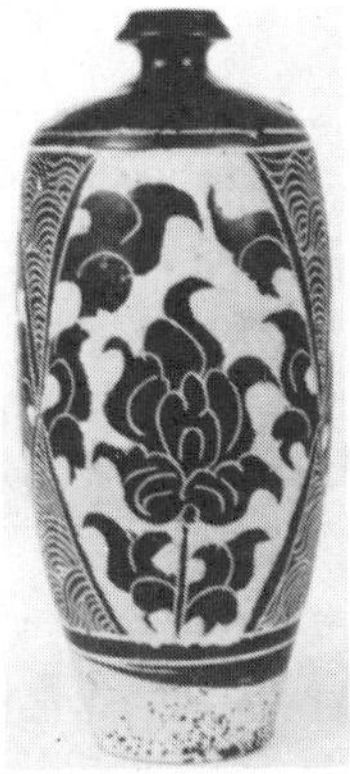

A Cizhou meiping, carved through a rich dark brown glaze to the buff pottery body with 3 large panels of peony divided by swirling waves, neck restored, Song Dynasty, 13½in (34cm).
$4,000-5,000

A blue and white vase, painted in strong blue tones, the neck with foliate scrolls, rim chip, c1500, 5in (13cm).
$2,500-3,000

A yellow glazed vase, incised with 2 pairs of contending scaly dragons, Longqing six-character mark, Qing Dynasty, 11½in (29cm).
$1,400-1,600

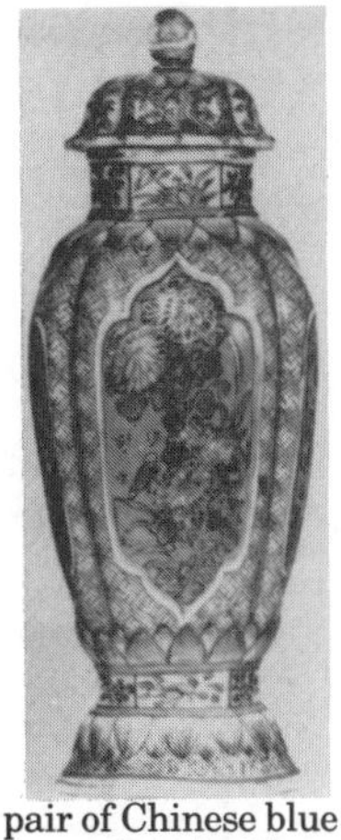

A blue and white vase and domed cover, minor interior glaze cracks, early Kangxi, 14in (35.5cm).
$2,000-2,500

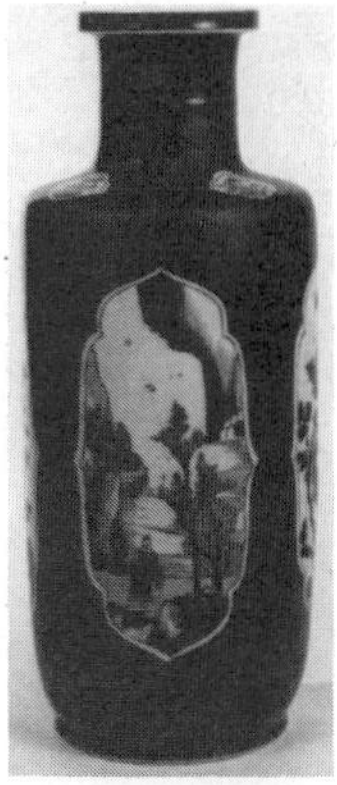

A powder blue and white rouleau vase, painted with upright ogival panels, all reserved on a powder-blue ground below smaller floral panels at the shoulder, glaze bubble to one side, Kangxi, 18in (45cm).
$2,500-3,000

pair of Chinese blue and white ɪses, painted with panels of ɪwering shrubs on grounds of ɪastika pattern, between moulded tus petals, later decorated in iron d, green, yellow and gilt, covers ɪmaged, the porcelain Kangxi, ʒin (33cm).
,400-1,600

A blue and white bottle vase, Kangxi, 12in (30cm).
$3,000-4,000

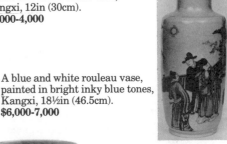

A blue and white rouleau vase, painted in bright inky blue tones, Kangxi, 18½in (46.5cm).
$6,000-7,000

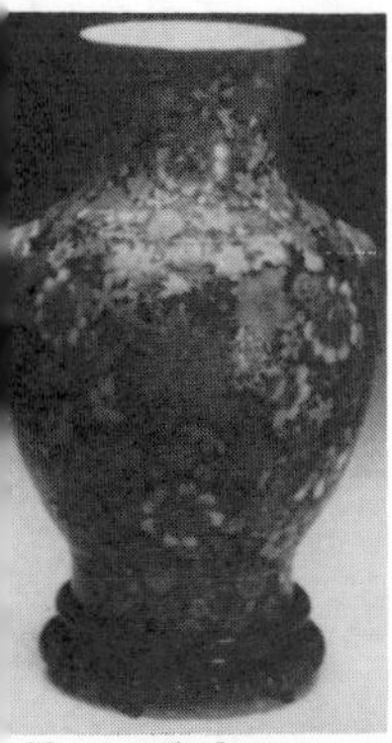

Chinese baluster vase, moulded ith elephant head and ring andles, covered overall with ightly coloured flowers and liage on a black ground, Kangxi ark but later period, 22½in 7cm), and carved wood stand.
,000-3,000

A 'famille verte' yanyan vase, painted with a dense scrolling ground of peony and foliage and long tailed flying phoenix, rim chips and polish, some glaze flakes, Kangxi, 18in (46cm).
$2,000-2,500

A blue and white bottle vase, painted with scrolling lotus and pomegranate and a band of reserve painted floral scrolls at the shoulder, the base with an underglaze blue G-mark, some staining, Kangxi, 8½in (21.5cm).
$5,000-6,000

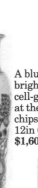

A blue and white vase, painted in bright blue, on a long life symbol cell-ground below stiff leaf lappets at the flaring neck, rim frits, foot chips, Chenghua mark, Kangxi, 12in (30.5cm).
$1,600-2,000

A blue and white sleeve vase, the rim brown dressed, Kangxi, 15½in (39cm).
$2,000-3,000

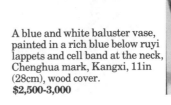

n Arita blue and white vase, ecorated with 3 panels, the neck ith a band of lappets, body and eck restored, late 17thC, 19in 8cm).
3,000-4,000

A blue and white baluster vase, painted in a rich blue below ruyi lappets and cell band at the neck, Chenghua mark, Kangxi, 11in (28cm), wood cover.
$2,500-3,000

A multi-faceted Kakiemon type vase, decorated in iron red enamel on underglaze blue, the shoulder with a band of cherry blossoms among scrolling 'karakusa', enamels and glaze rubbed, neck reduced, chip to rim, late 17thC, 7½in (19.5cm).
$14,000-16,000

A 'famille verte' vase, painted with baskets of flowers divided by butterflies in flight, below a band of lappets on the shoulder and stiff leaves and flowerheads at the slightly flaring neck, Kangxi, 9½in (23.5cm).
$1,600-1,800

A 'famille rose' vase, painted in bright enamels with a lady and a young boy holding a bird, Yongzheng, 8in (20cm).
$1,400-1,600

A 'famille rose' vase, painted with 2 oval panels, on a ground of butterflies among scrolling peony, on iron red and gilt cell pattern, restored, Qianlong, 16in (41cm).
$1,400-1,500

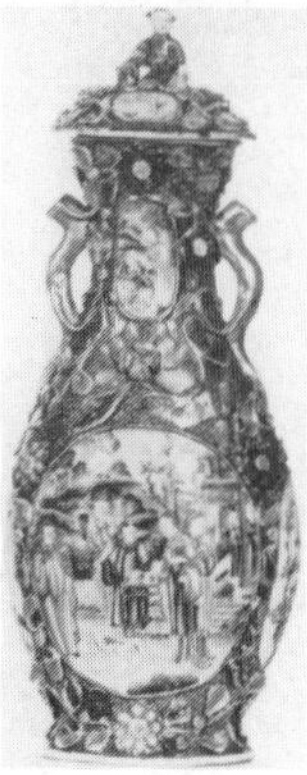

A 'famille rose' vase and domed cover, with seated figure finial a gilt branch handles, painted on a iron red, black and gilt Y-pattern ground heavily encrusted with scrolling flowers and leaves, restored, Qianlong, 14in (35.5cm
$1,200-1,400

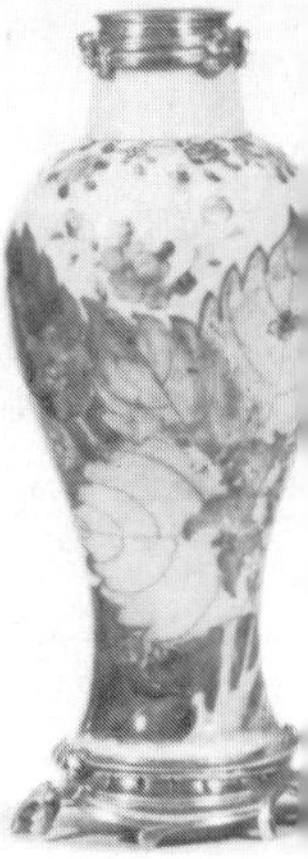

A 'famille rose' Tobacco leaf vase, neck crack, Qianlong, 6½in (16.5cm), gilt metal scroll rim mount and fixed stand.
$3,000-4,000

A 'famille rose' slender baluster vase, painted and lightly moulded with river landscapes on a turquoise raised dot ground, reserved with flowersprays, Qianlong, 11½in (29cm).
$700-800

A garniture of 5 Mandarin vases, some damage, Qianlong, 12½in (31.5cm).
$1,500-1,600

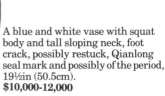

A pair of 'famille rose' vases and covers and one beaker vase, each painted with a duck swimming amongst lotus and iris, covers restored, Qianlong, baluster vas 11in (27cm).
$4,000-5,000

A 'famille rose' Mandarin pattern trumpet vase, reserved on a gilt floral scroll ground, the interior of the trumpet mouth with iron red and gilt vine scroll, chip to rim, Qianlong, 17in (43cm).
$2,500-3,000

A Chinese vase and cover, enamelled in 'famille rose' palette, the reserves with dense gilt tendril decoration, damaged, Qianlong, 14½in (37cm).
$600-800

A blue and white vase with squat body and tall sloping neck, foot crack, possibly restuck, Qianlong seal mark and possibly of the period, 19½in (50.5cm).
$10,000-12,000

A 'famille rose' vase, painted with peaches on a large spray, small rim chips, 19thC, 20½in (51.5cm).
$3,000-4,000

A Canton 'famille rose' vase, with embossed butterfly handles, the white ground painted with flowers, butterflies and utensils, 19thC, 23in (58cm).
$800-1,000

A pair of Imari vases and covers, each decorated in iron red, green, aubergine, yellow and black enamels and gilt on underglaze blue, the covers with large knop finials and similarly decorated to the vases, both covers damaged, Genroku period, 18in (46cm) high.
$9,000-10,000

A pair of Kutani style vases, the white ground richly decorated with Oriental figures, in burnt orange and charcoal-grey colour, with rich gilding, 19thC, 14in (35.5cm).
$2,500-3,000

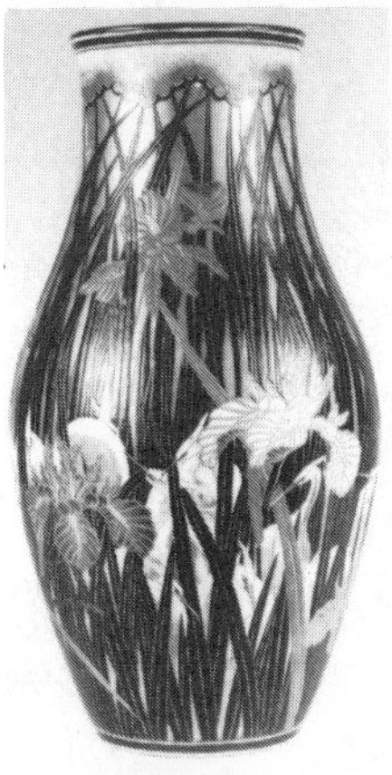

A Satsuma vase, decorated in various coloured thickly applied enamels and gilt with egrets among a profusion of iris beneath stylised clouds, signed Satsuma Hosai, with large Satsuma 'mon', late 19thC, 21in (53.5cm).
$7,000-8,000

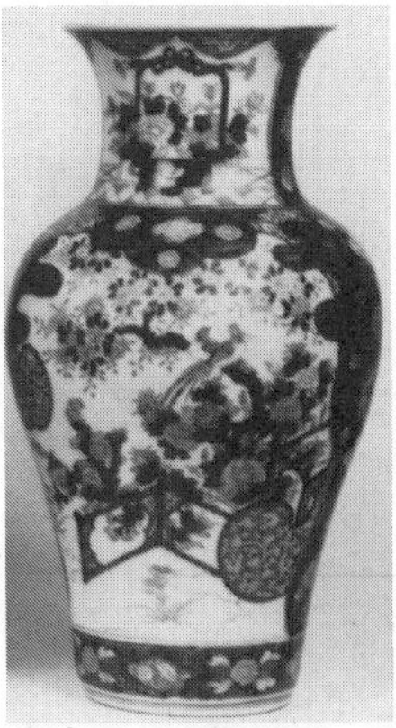

A pair of Imari vases, decorated in iron red, green and black enamels and gilt on underglaze blue, the everted rims with further flowers and foliage, late 19thC, 18½in (47cm).
$2,500-3,000

A pair of Cantonese vases, decorated with peacocks and other exotic birds in 'famille rose' flowering branches, 19thC, 24in (61cm).
$1,500-2,000

A pair of Japanese vases, painted on an orange ground, mid-19thC, 17½in (44.5cm).
$2,000-3,000

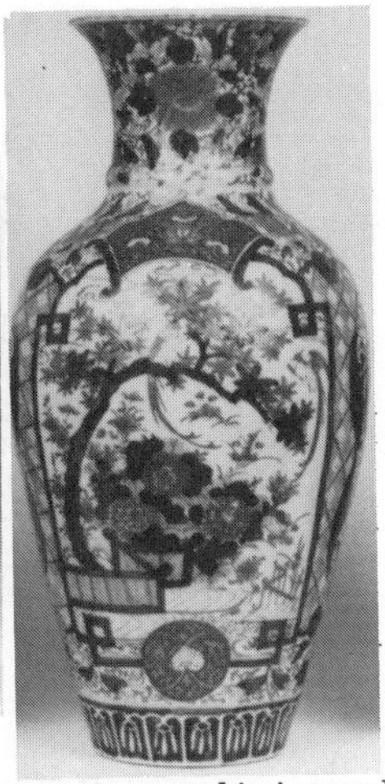

An Imari vase, decorated in iron red enamel and gilt on underglaze blue, late 19thC, 22½in (57cm).
$1,000-1,200

Price

Prices vary from auction to auction – from dealer to dealer. The price paid in a dealer's shop will depend on:
1) what he paid for the item
2) what he thinks he can get for it
3) the extent of his knowledge
4) awareness of market trends
It is a mistake to think that you will automatically pay more in a specialist dealer's shop. He is more likely to know the 'right' price for a piece. A general dealer may undercharge but he could also overcharge

An Imari vase, decorated in iron red and black enamels and gilt on underglaze blue, the everted neck with 'ho-o' birds divided by sacred pearls, the neck with some restoration, Genroku period, 24½in (62cm).
$6,000-8,000

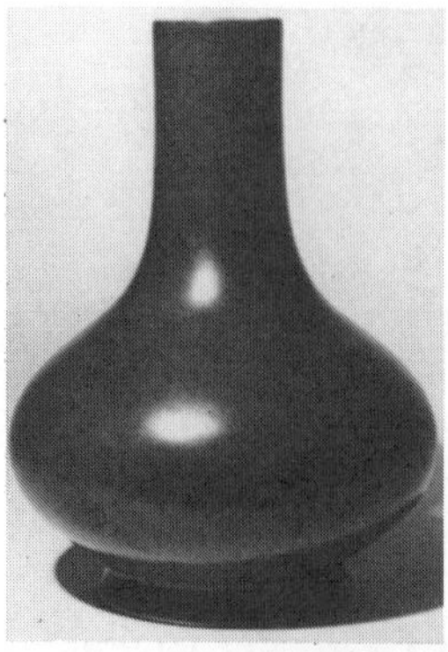

A teadust-glazed vase, under a speckled olive brown glaze thinning at the rim, the foot rim brown dressed, shallow foot rim chip, Xianfeng six-character mark and of the period, 13in (33cm).
$3,000-4,000

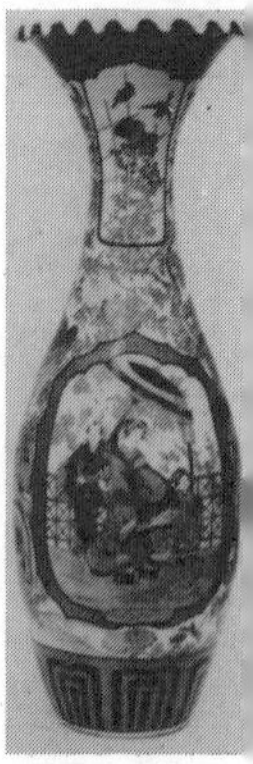

A pair of Japanese vases, with foliate rims, decorated in coloured enamels and gilt, on a ground of 'ho-o' on rockwork and flowers, 49in (124.5cm), wood stand.
$5,000-6,000

A pair of 'famille rose' broad gu-shaped beaker vases, painted on pink grounds, reserved with formal scrolling lotus below key pattern yellow ruyi heads at the rims, 15in (38cm).
$1,600-2,500

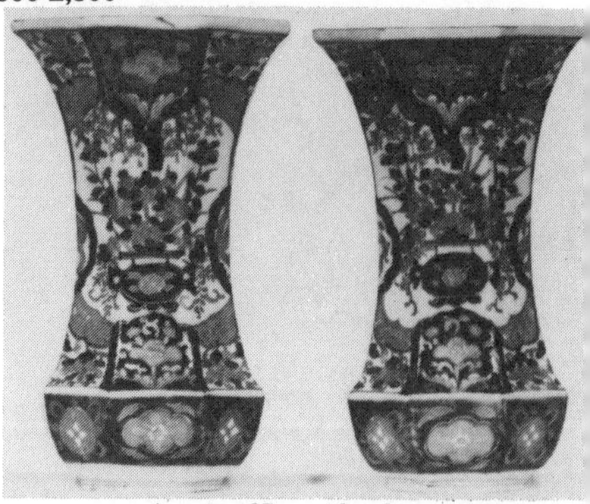

A pair of Imari beaker vases, painted with jardinières of flowers, divided by 'ho-o' roundels, with flowering shrubs above and below, 8½in (22cm).
$600-800

A pair of Kutani vases, moulded on either side with a fan and tassels, brightly painted with butterflies and exotic birds, on a gold decorated orange ground, 13½in (34cm).
$900-1,200

A pair of Kaga vases, painted with ladies in conversation in a garden, the reverses with flowers and fruit, 14½in (37cm).
$1,200-1,400

A pair of Imari lobed vases and domed covers, painted with shaped panels of 'ho-o', bats and objects before fenced landscapes, 18½in (46cm).
$1,800-2,000

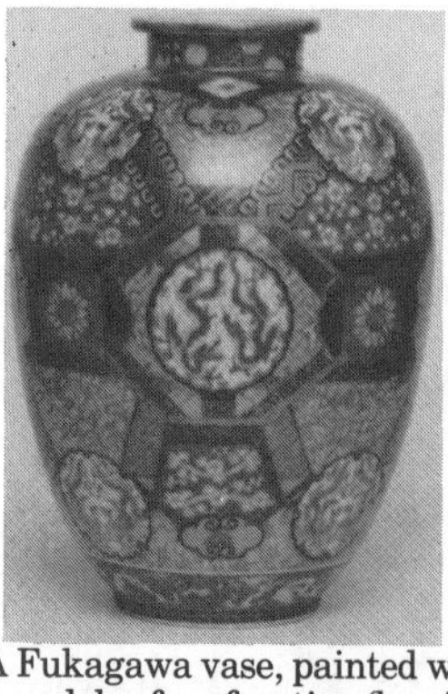

A Fukagawa vase, painted with roundels of confronting 'ho-o' or dragons divided by shaped panels of prunus, with underglaze blue and gilt geometric bands, 14½in (37cm).
$1,700-2,000

A Canton vase, applied at the shoulder and neck with Buddhist lions and dragons, reserved on a gold ground, painted with insects and flowers, 24½in (61.5cm).
$1,000-1,200

A Cantonese vase, decorated with scenes of Chinese elders, 17in (43cm).
$600-700

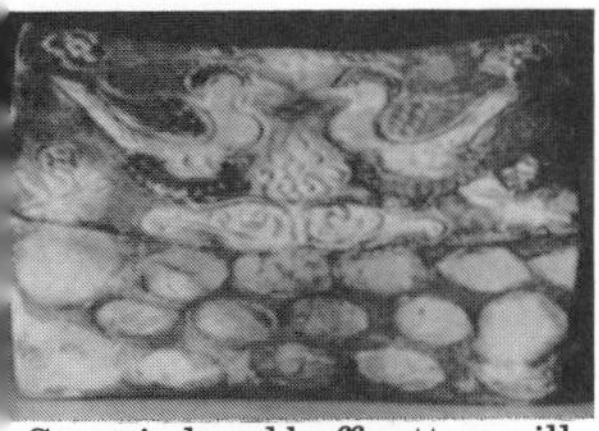

A Sancai glazed buff pottery pillow, the top impressed with a pair of confronted ducks, the sides reserved on an amber ground, the main face with an amber design on a green ground, Tang/Liao Dynasty, 6in (15cm) wide, box.
$2,000-2,500

A Transitional blue and white box and cover, the cover painted with a pheasant on pierced rockwork, the box with a band of running foliage and flowers, c1650, 9½in (23cm) diam.
$3,000-4,000

A Cizhou stoneware pillow with ogival shaped top painted with a striding tiger, the border in chocolate brown on a crackled white slip, the sides with freely drawn stylised foliage, chipped, Song Dynasty, 10in (25cm) wide.
$3,000-4,000

A Ming blue and white box and domed cover, painted in vibrant tones with a five-clawed dragon amidst clouds, cover restored, encircled six-character Jiajing mark and of the period, 6½in (16cm) diam.
$2,000-3,000

A 'famille rose' cafe-au-lait ground garniture comprising: 3 baluster vases and covers and 2 beaker vases, covers and one beaker vase fritted, Qianlong, baluster vases 11in (27cm).
$5,000-6,000

An Arita blue and white square tokkuri, the sides painted with panels of wooded rocky river landscapes surrounded by trellis pattern, with related domed stopper, c1800, 7½in (19cm).
$1,000-1,500

An Imari tapering cylindrical urn and shallow domed cover on 3 tall lappet-shaped feet, painted with linked panels of formal foliage divided by iron red and gilt flowers and leaves, damaged, c1700, 12in (30cm), metal tap.
$1,400-2,000

A Cizhou polychrome pillow, the centre carved and combed with a flowerspray, painted in green, yellow and amber on a colourless ground, the sides under a green glaze stopping above the base, the reverse with circular firing aperture, Jin Dynasty, 12in (30cm) wide.
$9,000-10,000

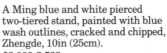

A Ming blue and white pierced two-tiered stand, painted with blue wash outlines, cracked and chipped, Zhengde, 10in (25cm).
$3,000-3,500

A Satsuma tripod koro with 2 high handles and pierced domed cover, with seated shishi finial, painted in colours and gilt, on a dense stylised floral ground, 12in (30cm).
$2,500-3,000

A pair of Canton stick stands, painted in bright enamel colours on a yellow ground within decorated turquoise rims, slight damage, 14in (35cm).
$1,500-2,000

Chinese dynasties and marks

Earlier Dynasties

Shang Yin, c.1532-1027 B.C.
Western Zhou (Chou) 1027-770 B.C.
Spring and Autumn Annals 770-480 B.C.
Warring States 484-221 B.C.
Qin (Ch'in) 221-206 B.C.
Western Han 206 BC-24 AD
Eastern Han 25-220
Three Kingdoms 221-265
Six Dynasties 265-589
Wei 386-557
Sui 589-617
Tang (T'ang) 618-906
Five Dynasties 907-960
Liao 907-1125
Sung 960-1280
Chin 1115-1260
Yüan 1280-1368

Ming Dynasty

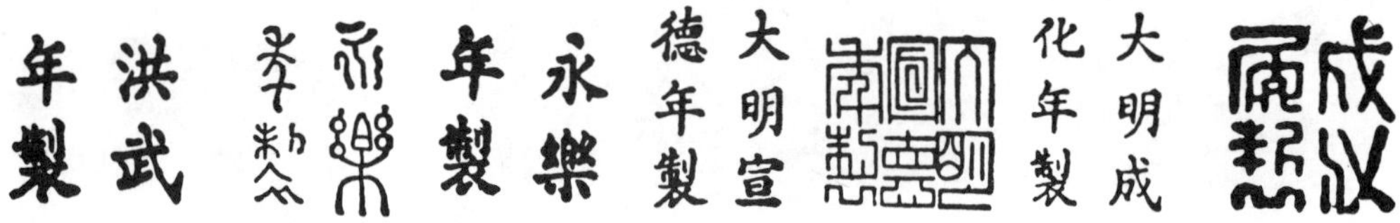

Hongwu (Hung Wu) 1368-1398 | Yongle (Yung Lo) 1403-1424 | Xuande (Hsüan Té) 1426-1435 | Chenghua (Ch'éng Hua) 1465-1487

Hongzhi (Hung Chih) 1488-1505 | Zhengde (Chéng Té) 1506-1521 | Jiajing (Chia Ching) 1522-1566 | Longqing (Lung Ching) 1567-1572 | Wanli (Wan Li) 1573-1620 | Tianqi (Tien Chi) 1621-1627 | Chongzhen (Ch'ung Chêng) 1628-1644

Qing (Ch'ing) Dynasty

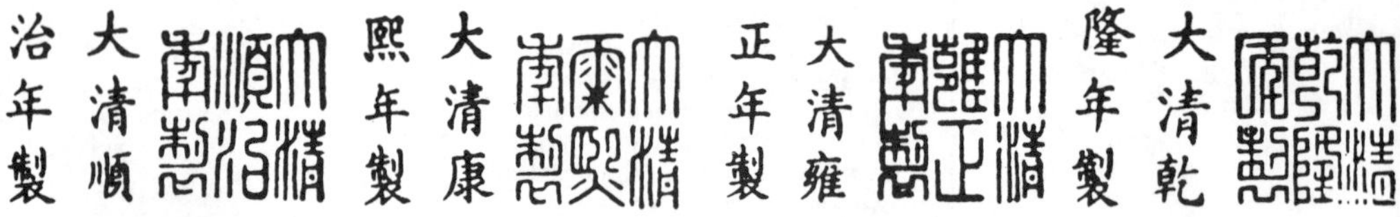

Shunzhi (Shun Chih) 1644-1661 | Kangxi (K'ang Hsi) 1662-1722 | Yongzheng (Yung Chêng) 1723-1735 | Qianlong (Ch'ien Lung) 1736-1795'

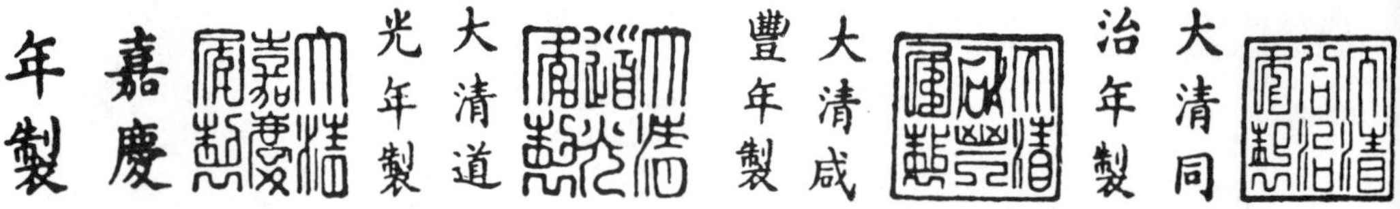

Jiaqing (Chia Ch'ing) 1796-1820 | Daoguang (Tao Kuang) 1821-1850 | Xianfeng (Hsien Féng) 1851-1861 | Tongzhi (T'ung Chih) 1862-1874

Guangxu (Kuang Hsu) 1875-1908 | Xuantong (Hsuan T'ung) 1909-1911 | Hongxian (Hung Hsien) 1916

LASS
ottles

set of 4 Bristol blue spirit bottles,
1800, 7½in (19cm).
1,600-1,800

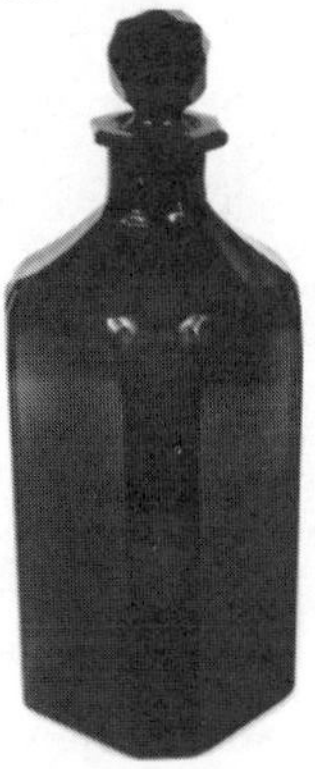

dark green brandy spirit bottle,
1800, 7½in (19cm).
350-370

An amber and white overlay wine bottle, with fruiting vine decoration, c1840, 12½in (32cm).
$350-400

A pair of blue spirit bottles, c1800, 9½in (24cm).
$800-900

A sealed and dated wine bottle, with olive green tint, the seal and shoulder inscribed, c1717, 6½in (16.5cm).
$3,000-4,000

Bowls

A set of 4 green glass finger bowls, c1870, 4½in (11cm) diam.
$550-650

A set of 12 blue tinted finger bowls, some damage, 5in (12cm) diam.
$800-1,000

n Irish cut fruit bowl, the body
vith a band of facets beneath a
urnover rim, with alternate prism
utting, supported on a triple knop
tem above a moulded fluted
preading foot, chip to footrim,
erhaps Cork, c1800, 12½in (32cm)
vide.
2,000-3,000

A green posy bowl, with vertical ribbing, c1860.
$90-100

Two blue glass posy bowls, c1860, 2 and 3in (5 and 7.5cm).
l. **$120-130**
r. **$80-100**

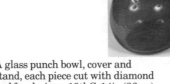

Three glass posy bowls/night lights:
l. Cranberry glass
c. Vaseline glass
r. Amber glass.
$80-100 each

A glass punch bowl, cover and stand, each piece cut with diamond and fan designs, 19thC, 14in (36cm).
$600-800

handmade Venetian glass
weetmeat dish, in the shape of an
xotic bird, 10in (25.5cm).
140-200

A sweetmeat bowl, with everted dentil rim, knopped stem and radially moulded foot, c1730, 3½in (9.5cm).
$600-800

A Venetian enamelled bowl, decorated with green dots on a gilt scale band edged with white and red and white dots beneath a slightly everted rim, small crack to base, c1500, 6in (15.5cm) diam.
$1,000-1,200

A cut bowl with bands of relief diamonds and Vandyke cut rim, with star cut base, c1790, 12½in (32cm) wide.
$400-600

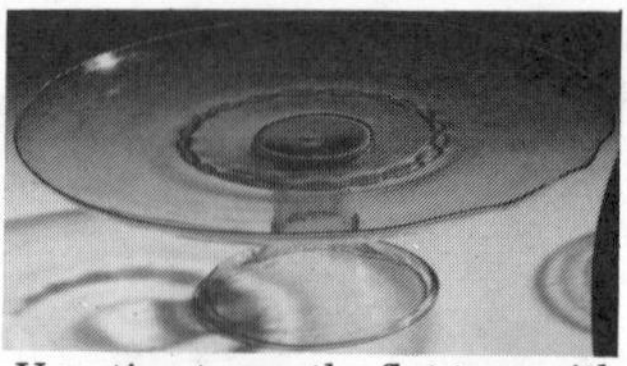

A Venetian tazza, the flat tray with everted rim, the underside applied with a band of turquoise chain ornament, supported on a high waisted spreading stem with upturned folded rim, early 17thC, 11½in (29.5cm) diam.
$1,600-2,000

Candelabra

A pedestal stemmed candlestick and a detachable wax pan, 18thC, 10in (25.5cm).
$1,000-1,200

A pedestal stemmed candlestick, c1750, 10in (25cm).
$900-1,000

A pedestal stemmed candlestick, mid-18thC, 7½in (19.5cm).
$400-600

A pair of twin-light candlesticks, with hobnail cut scalloped sconces and waterfall prism drops, some drops missing, c1812.
$2,000-3,000

A pair of vaseline moulded candlesticks, 19thC, 11in (28cm).
$300-350

Chandeliers

A cut glass eight-light chandelier, with associated moulded glass drip pans, 35in (89cm).
$12,000-14,000

A moulded cut glass eleven-light chandelier, with circular star cut corona, the ring turned gilt metal shaft with shepherds' crooks hung with beads and fillets, formerly twelve-light, 48in (122cm), fitted for electricity.
$1,100-1,300

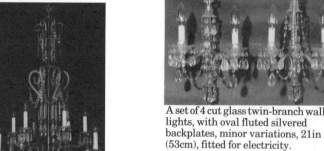

A set of 4 cut glass twin-branch wall lights, with oval fluted silvered backplates, minor variations, 21in (53cm), fitted for electricity.
$7,000-8,000

Decanters

A pair of decanters, engraved 'Claret' and 'Madeira' within hops and barley and fruiting vine cartouches, plain bevelled lozenge stoppers, c1780, 8in (20cm).
$3,000-3,500

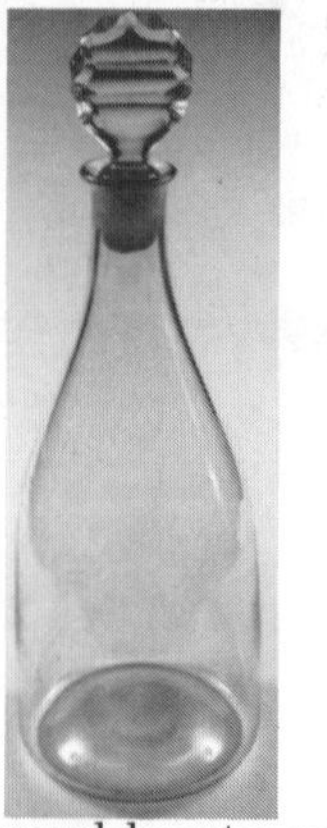

A plain tapered decanter, with cut lozenge stopper, c1780, 12in (30.5cm).
$450-500

A tapered 'Port' decanter, with fruiting vine cartouche, lunar cut lozenge stopper, c1780, 7½in (19cm).
$700-800

A set of 3 Bristol blue decanters, with simulated gilt wine labels, gilt lozenge stoppers, in a Sheffield plated trefoil frame, c1790, 7½in (19cm).
$2,800-3,000

Three plain decanters, c1800, 8½ to 9½in (21.5 to 24cm).
$400-500 each

A square cut spirit decanter, engraved 'Brandy' within a leaf and ribbon bow cartouche, with cut mushroom stopper, c1800, 8in (20.5cm).
$250-300

A Georgian decanter, with bull's eye stopper, c1810, 10½in (26cm).
$250-300

A cut and engraved decanter and stopper, inscribed 'Norwich A Port, Ships & Commerce', early 19thC, 11in (28cm).
$1,600-1,800

Three cut decanters, c1810, 9in (23cm).
$400-500 each

l. & r. Two flute moulded spirit decanters, with pouring necks and moulded mushroom stoppers, c1810, 7in (17.5cm).
$250-300
c. A flute moulded decanter, with wrythen ball stopper, c1810, 7in (17.5cm).
$130-170

A pair of ovoid decanters, with target stoppers, c1810, 9in (23cm).
$1,200-1,400

An Irish decanter, with 3 feather edge neck rings, c1810, 9in (22.5cm).
$600-700

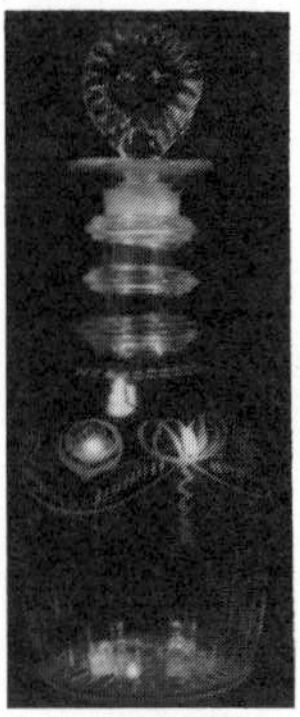

A spirit decanter, engraved with a ribbon bow and open rose decoration, marked Waterloo Co., Cork, c1815, 7½in (19.5cm).
$1,000-1,200

A pair of Prussian shaped decanters, with monogram 'ERR', target stoppers, c1830, 8½in (22cm).
$1,000-1,200

l. & r. A pair of spirit decanters, with cut blaze, prism and diamond cutting, cut hollow mushroom stoppers, c1830, 7in (18.5cm).
$650-700

c. A cut spirit decanter, c1820.
$180-250

A magnum decanter with wide vertical fluting, 3 neck rings and cut mushroom stopper, 11½in (29cm), and a pair of matching decanters, 8½in (22cm), c1840.
$4,500-5,000

A Victorian decanter, with hollow mushroom stopper, c1850, 11in (28cm).
$120-150

A heavy cut glass spirit decanter and stopper, 11in (28cm).
$160-200

l. & r. A pair of cylindrical decanters, with slice cut and vertically fluted bodies, with hollow cut mushroom stoppers, c1840, 8½in (21.5cm).
$700-800

c. An ovoid decanter with base and shoulder fluting, annulated neck rings and cut mushroom stopper, c1800.
$350-450

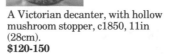

A pair of green wine flagons, with clear glass rope twist handles, c1850, 9in (23cm).
$250-300 each

A mallet-shaped blue tinted decanter, with related lozenge stopper, gilded bladed rings to the neck, decorated in gilt with a cartouche, 9½in (24cm).
$100-140

A green glass wine flagon, with brass mount, 7½in (19cm).
$250-300

An amber glass wine flagon, with brass mount, 8in (20.5cm).
$500-600

Drinking Glasses

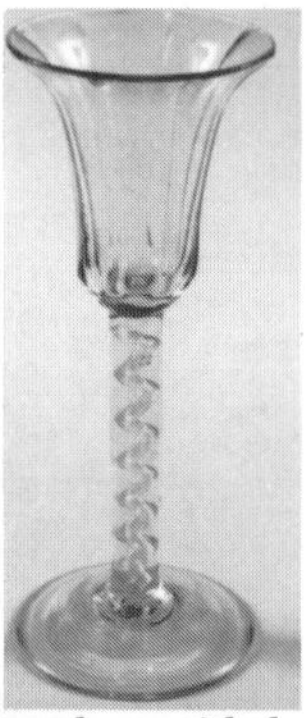

An air-twist wine glass, the bowl with vertical ribs, c1745, 6in (15cm).
$650-700

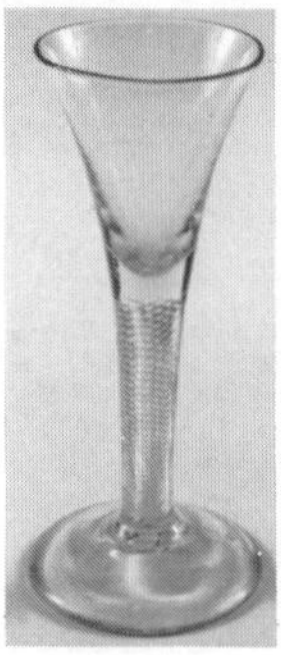

An air-twist wine glass, with drawn trumpet stem, c1740, 6in (15cm).
$350-400

An Excise glass with hollow stem, c1745, 5½in (14cm).
$400-440

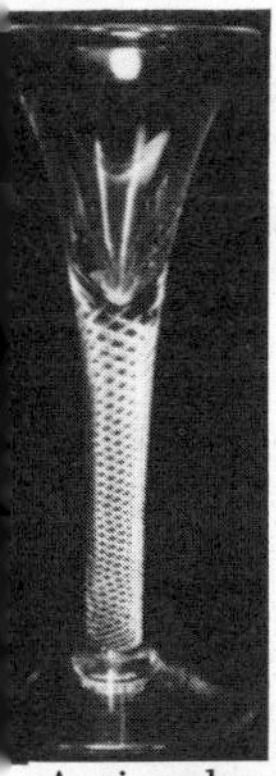

A wine glass with trumpet bowl, on a drawn stem with multiple spiral air-twist, plain conical foot, c1750, 7in (18cm).
$400-500

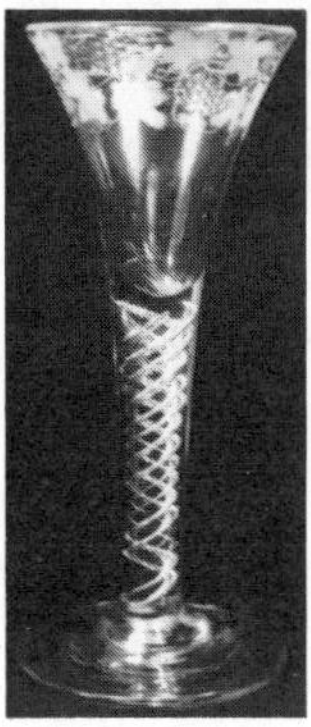

A wine glass, with air-twist multiple spiral, the bowl engraved with fruiting vine motif, plain conical foot, c1750, 6½in (17cm).
$550-650

DRINKING GLASSES

Ordered in line with the E Barrington Haynes system (see Pelican Books *Glass* by E Barrington Haynes)

Group	**I**	**Baluster Stems**	**1685-1725**
	II	**Moulded Pedestal Stems**	**1715-1765**
	III	**Balustroid Stems**	**1725-1755**
	IV	**Light (Newcastle) Balusters**	**1735-1765**
	V	**Composite Stems**	**1740-1770**
	VI	**Plain Straight Stems**	**1740-1770**
	VII	**Air Twist Stems**	**1740-1770**
	VIII	**Hollow Stems**	**1750-1760**
	IX	**Incised Twist Stems**	**1750-1765**
	X	**Opaque Twist Stems**	**1750-1780**
	XI	**Mixed and Colour Twist Stems**	**1755-1775**
	XII	**Faceted Stems**	**1760-1800**
	XIII	**Other glasses with short or rudimentary stems: Dwarf Ales; Jelly Glasses; Rummers; Georgian Ales, wines and drams; 18th-19thC**	

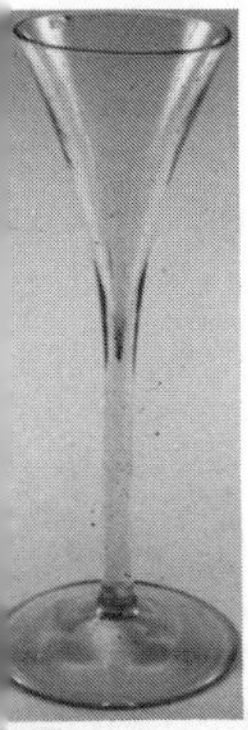

Toastmaster's glass, c1750, 7in
18cm).
600-700

A wine glass with ovoid bowl, plain conical foot, c1750, 6½in (16cm).
$500-600

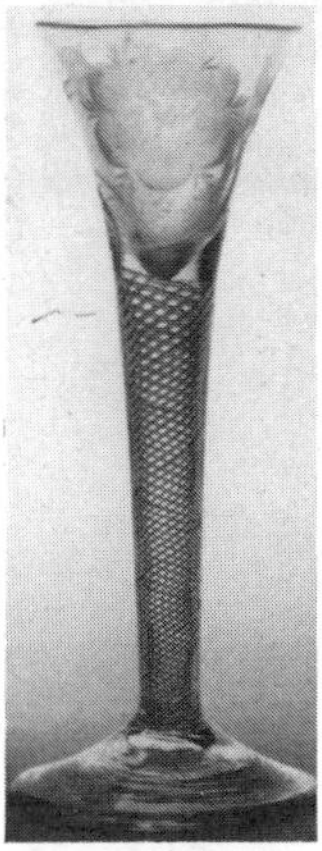

A Jacobite air-twist wine glass, the bowl engraved with a rose, the reverse with an oak leaf and a sun, the stem filled with spiral threads above a conical foot, c1750, 6½in (16cm).
$1,800-2,000

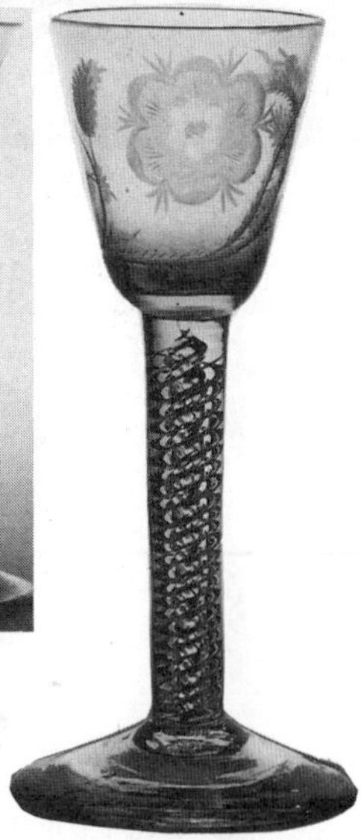

A Jacobite mercury twist wine glass, with engraved bowl, with conical foot, c1750, 5½in (14cm).
$1,600-2,000

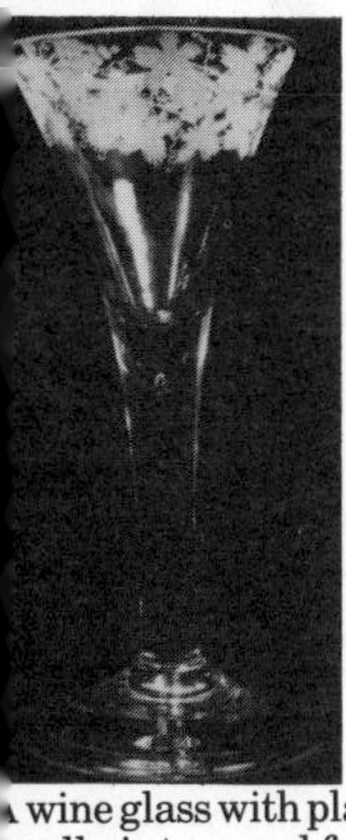

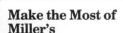

wine glass with plain drawn stem, mall air tear and folded conical ot, c1750, 7½in (19cm).
500-600

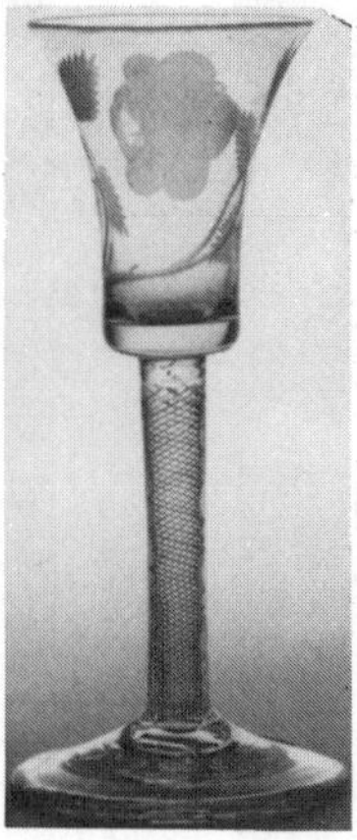

A Jacobite air-twist wine glass, with engraved bucket bowl, the stem filled with spirals and terminating with a conical foot, c1750, 6½in (16cm).
$1,000-1,200

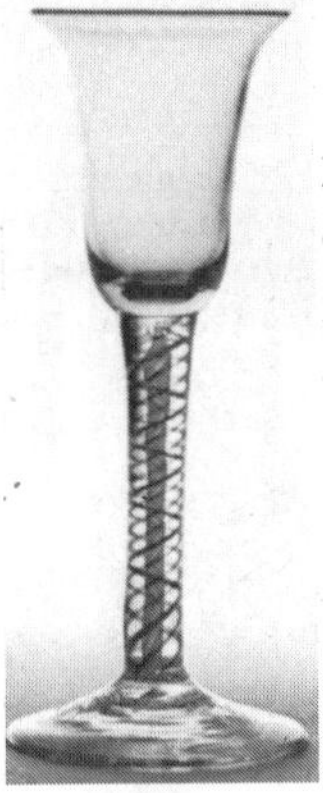

A colour twist wine glass, the stem with a gauze core entwined by opaque white and translucent red, green and blue threads, on a conical foot, c1760, 6in (15cm).
$1,500-1,700

Make the Most of Miller's

In Miller's we do NOT just reprint saleroom estimates. We work from realised prices either from an auction room or a dealer. Our consultants then work out a realistic price range for a similar piece. This is to try to avoid repeating freak results – either low or high

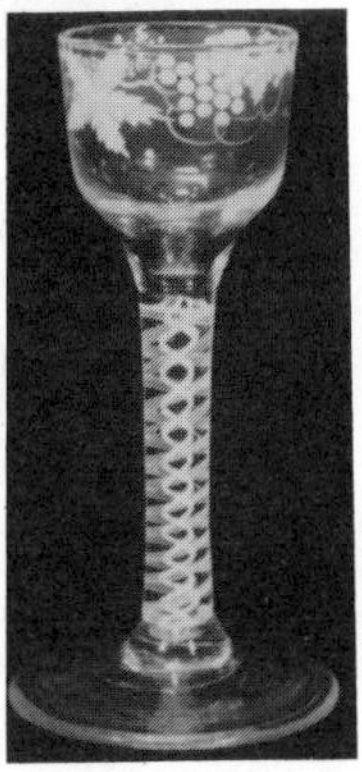

A Beilby wine glass, the ogee bowl with fruiting vine in white enamel, c1760, 5½in (14cm).
$3,500-4,000

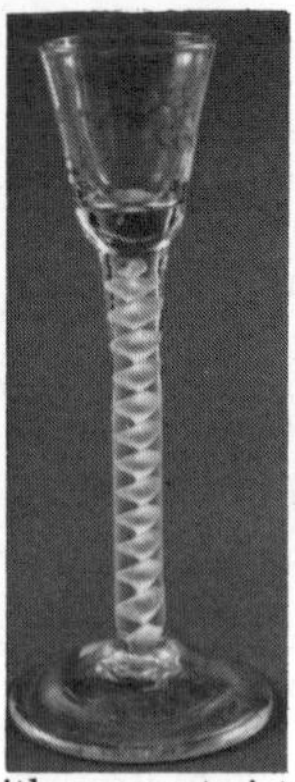

A cordial glass, with opaque twist, on conical foot, c1760, 7in (18cm).
$900-1,000

Two Lynn wine glasses, with radially moulded ribbed bowls, on stems with double series opaque twists, c1760, 5½ and 6in (14 and 15cm).
$1,400-1,600 each

Three wine glasses, with double series opaque twist stems and plain conical feet, c1760, tallest 7in (18cm).
$320-440 each

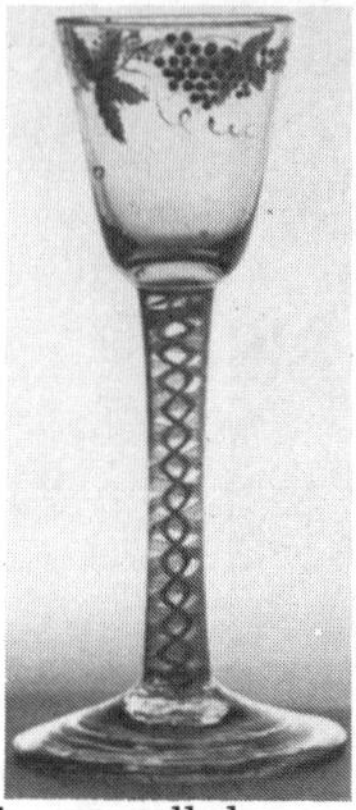

A Beilby enamelled opaque twist wine glass, stress cracks to footrim, c1770, 5in (15.5cm).
$1,300-1,500

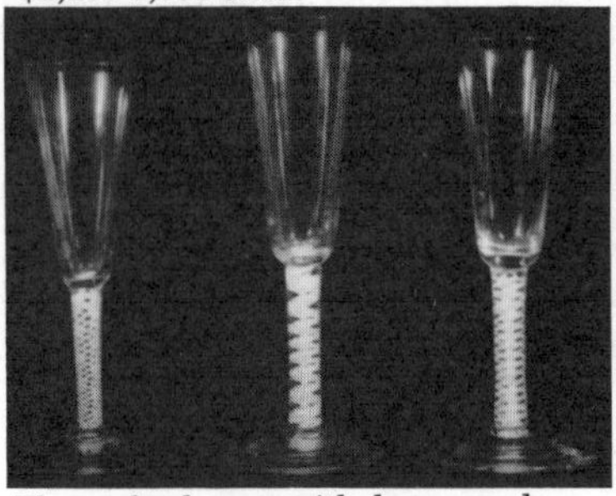

Three ale glasses, with deep round funnel bowls, on plain stems with double series opaque white twists, c1760, tallest 8in (20cm).
$350-500 each

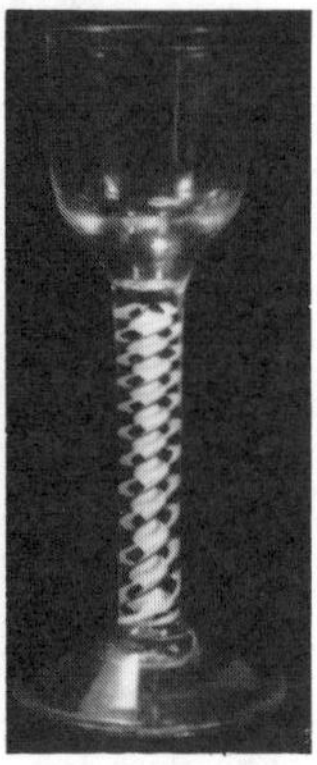

A colour twist wine glass, with central opaque cable and pair of outer spiralling tapes edged in translucent red, c1770, 7in (18cm).
$4,000-4,500

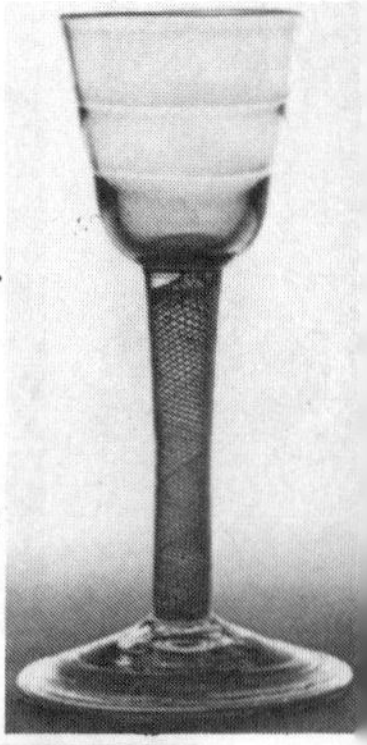

A 'Lynn' opaque twist wine glass, the stem filled with opaque spirals above a folded conical foot, c1770, 5½in (14.5cm).
$1,100-1,300

A set of 4 Beilby enamelled opaque twist wine glasses, one slightly chipped, one with replacement foot, c1775, 6in (15cm).
$3,500-4,000

Three amber wine glasses, with hollow stems, c1830, 4½in (11cm).
$160-190 each

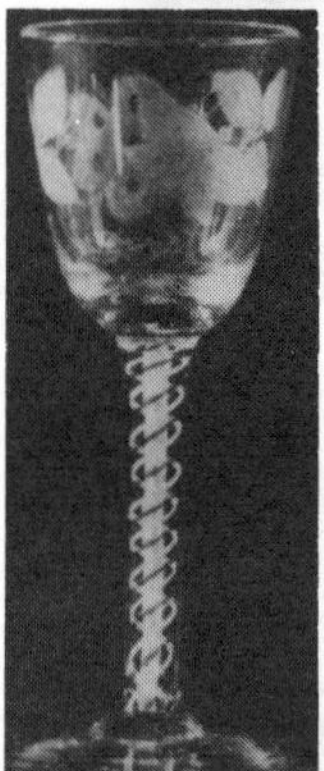

A pair of Continental colour twist Jacobite drinking glasses, on spreading feet engraved with flowers and moths, 6in (15cm).
$300-400

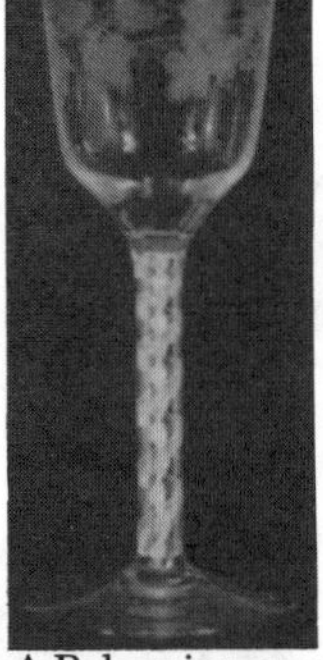

An ogee bowl drinking glass, on double series twist stem, the bowl engraved with fruiting vine, slight chip to base, 6½in (15cm).
$200-300

A small heavy baluster dram glass, the bowl set on a stem with cushion knop with air tear, on folded conical foot, c1710, 4in (10.5cm).
$1,000-1,200

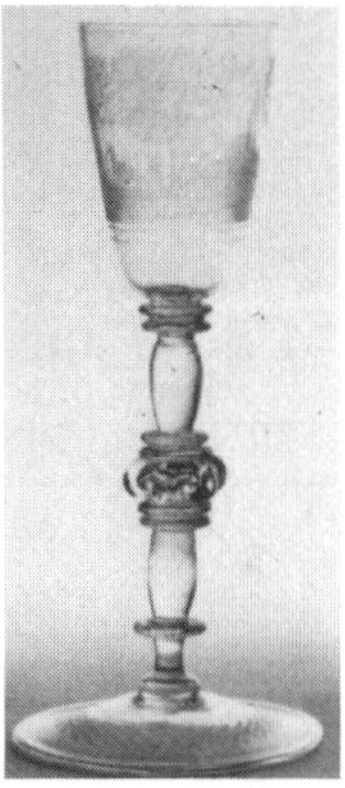

A Bohemian engraved goblet, the stem with a central moulded knop between 2 oviform sections divided by mereses, the conical foot with a foliate band and folded rim, the engraving perhaps Nuremburg, c1700, 9½in (24cm).
$3,000-4,000

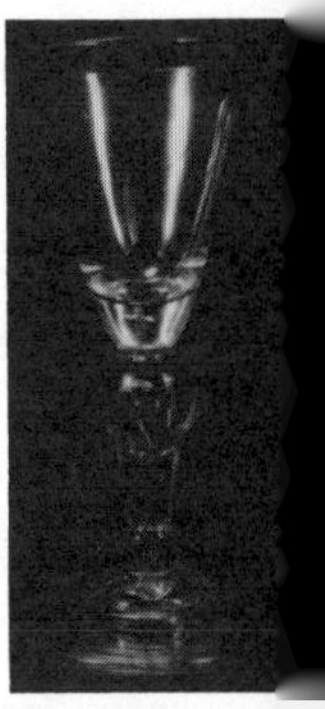

A heavy baluster wine glass, the bowl with solid section and air tear, inverted baluster knopped stem, with base knop and air tear, with domed folded foot, c1710, 6½in (17cm).
$1,800-2,000

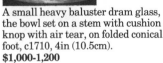

aluster goblet, on folded conical
, c1715, 6in (15.5cm).
100-1,200

A baluster wine glass, c1715, 6in (15.5cm).
$600-800

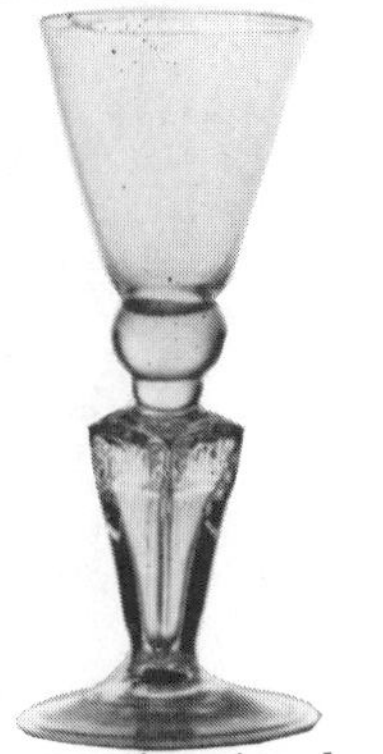

A commemorative wine glass, the upper part inscribed in relief 'God Save King George', and the shoulder with a crown at each angle, on folded conical foot, 1720, 6½in (16cm).
$10,000-12,000

A heavy baluster wine glass, on a stem with ball knop and air tear, folded conical foot, c1720, 6in (15cm).
$1,100-1,200

A balustroid wine glass, with trumpet bowl on a drawn stem with short inverted baluster and base knops, plain domed foot, c1740, 7in (18cm).
$1,100-1,200

A balustroid wine glass, engraved with fruiting vine with multi-knopped stem and folded conical foot, c1730, 6½in (17cm).
$1,600-1,800

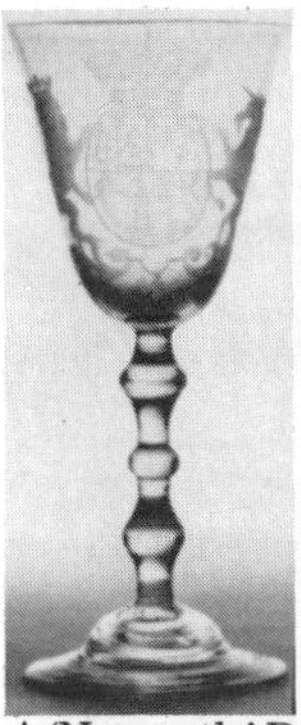

A 'Newcastle' Dutch engraved royal armorial light baluster goblet, the funnel bowl with the Royal Arms of England as borne by George II, on multi-knopped stem, with dome foot, mid-18thC, 8in (20cm).
$1,800-2,400

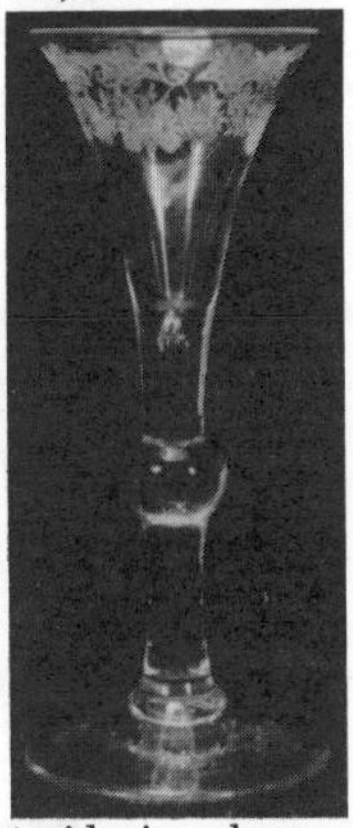

A balustroid wine glass, engraved with a band of floral decoration, on a stem with ball knop, with plain conical foot, c1740, 7in (14cm).
$1,600-1,700

alustroid wine glass, with a solid
se and collar, on domed folded
t, c1740, 5in (15cm).
00-1,000

A Silesian engraved wine glass, the fluted ogee bowl decorated with figures, flowers and birds, on a faceted inverted baluster stem, the foot cut with radiating petal ornament, c1745, 5in (12.5cm).
$900-1,000

A Silesian engraved wine glass, the fluted ogee bowl with a sailing scene, on a facet cut inverted baluster stem, the conical foot with a band of ovals, c1745, 5½in (14cm).
$1,200-1,400

Did you know
MILLER'S Antiques Price Guide builds up year by year to form the most comprehensive photo-reference system available

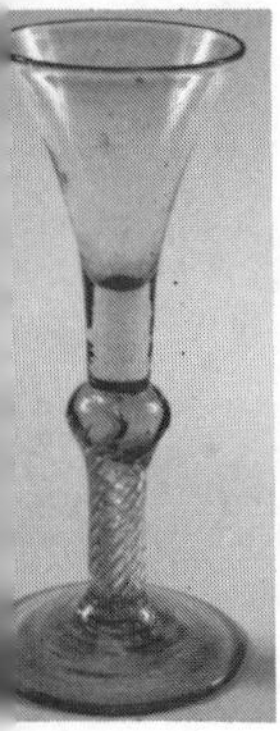

A composite stemmed wine glass, on conical foot, c1745, 6½in (17cm).
$800-850

A balustroid wine glass, the bell bowl engraved with a floral band, annulated knop to plain stem, plain conical foot, c1745, 6½in (16.5cm).
$900-1,000

A balustroid wine glass on a stem with centre and base ball knops, plain domed foot, c1750, 7in (17cm).
$900-1,000

A Jacobite light baluster wine glass, c1745, 7in (18cm).
$3,300-3,500

A Newcastle wine glass, engraved with a floral meander, with Newcastle air bead and knopped stem, on plain conical foot, c1750, 7in (18cm).
$1,800-2,000

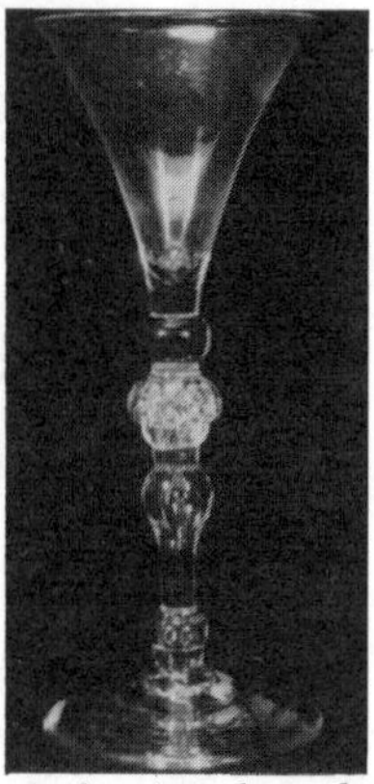

A Newcastle wine glass, the trumpet bowl on a stem with ball, air-beaded, inverted baluster with tear and base knops, c1750, 7½in (18.5cm).
$1,800-2,000

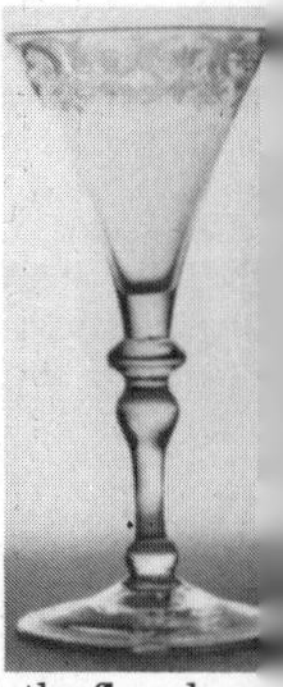

An engraved goblet, the flared funnel bowl with solid lower part, c a conical foot, c1750, 7½in (18.5cm
$1,500-1,600

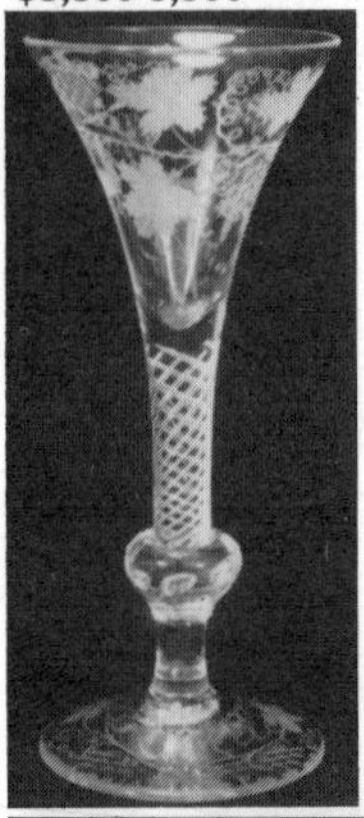

A composite stem wine glass, the engraved trumpet bowl with multiple spiral air-twist, c1750, 7½in (18cm).
$1,600-1,800

Three engraved wine glasses, c1750, 5 to 6in (12 to 15cm).
$240-360 each

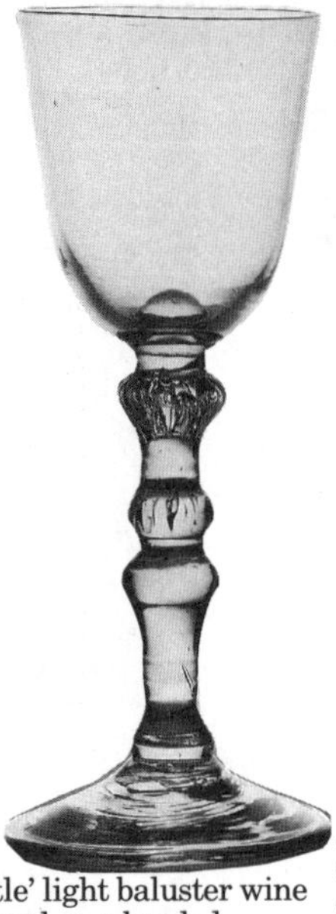

A 'Newcastle' light baluster wine glass, the bowl on a beaded dumb-bell knop above an inverted baluster section and basal knop, c1750, 7in (17cm).
$900-1,000

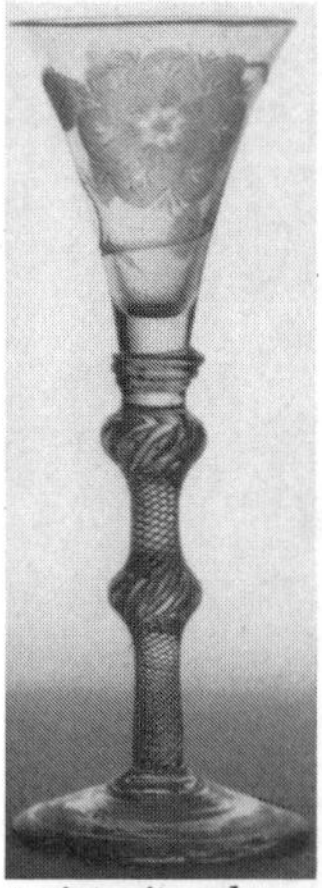

A Jacobite air-twist wine glass, wi engraved trumpet shaped bowl, th double knopped stem filled with spiral threads, c1750, 7in (17cm).
$3,500-4,000

A wine glass with multiple spiral air-twist stem, c1750, 7½in (18cm).
$350-400

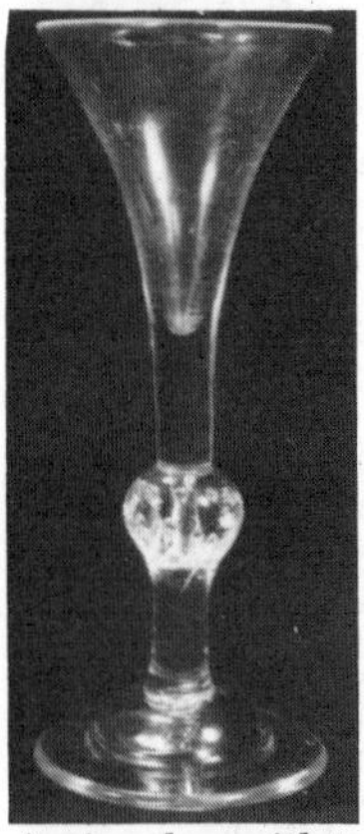

A wine glass with trumpet bowl on a drawn stem with air-beaded knop and plain section, c1750, 7in (17cm).
$1,200-1,300

A wine glass with a single series opaque twist stem, c1760, 6in (15cm).
$400-500

A wine glass with air-twist stem, shoulder and central ball knops, on plain conical foot, c1750, 7in (17cm).
$850-900

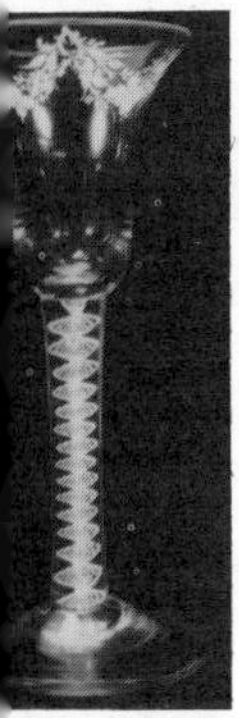

eilby wine glass, the bowl melled in white, the stem with a gle series lace spiral opaque te twist, c1775, 7in (17cm).
00-4,500

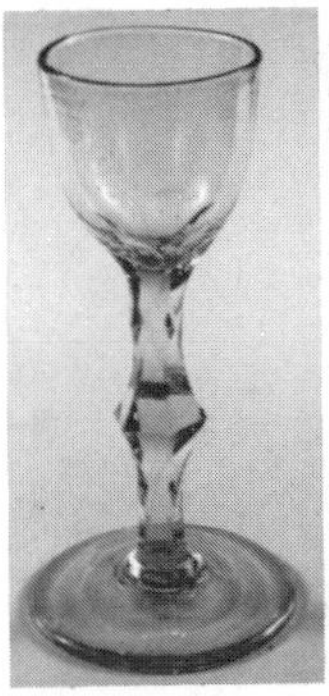

A facet cut knop stemmed wine glass, c1780, 6in (15cm).
$250-300

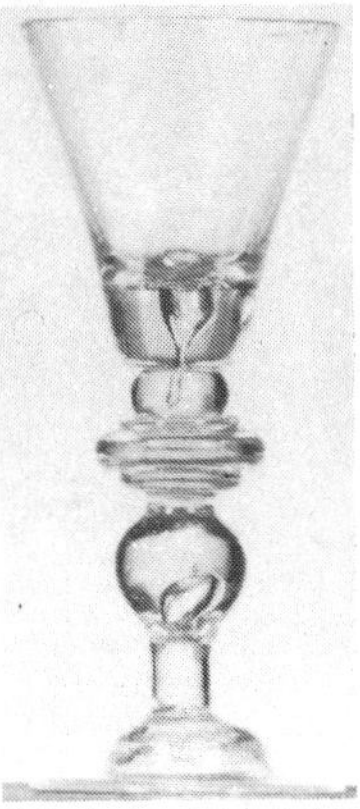

A balustroid drinking glass, with annulated knop and a domed folded foot, chip to rim, 6½in (16.5cm).
$400-500

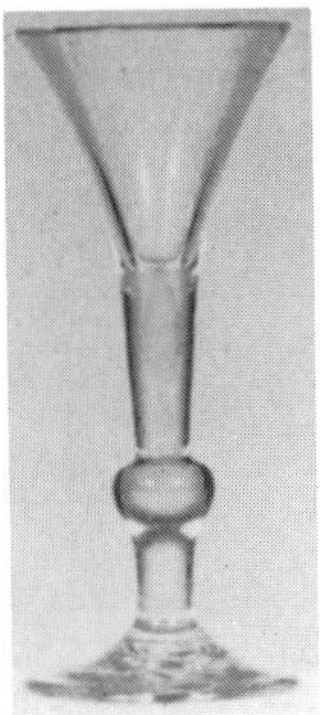

A balustroid trumpet drawn kit-kat glass on knopped stem, 6½in (16.5cm).
$200-300

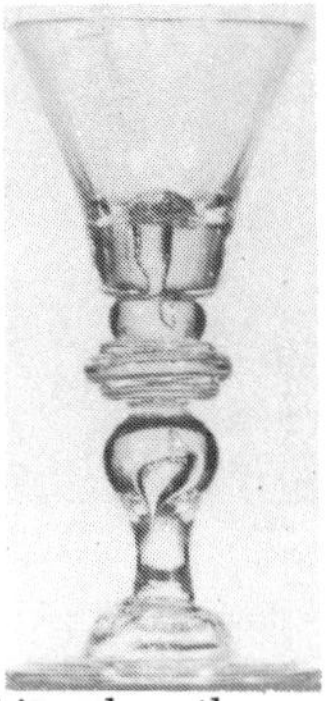

A balustroid drinking glass, the stem with annulated knop and swirling knop with tear inclusion, domed folded foot, 5½in (14cm).
$300-500

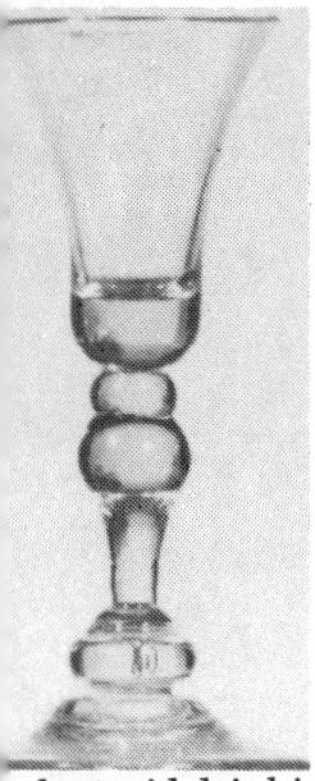

alustroid drinking glass, with ring bowl on swirling knopped l basal knopped stem, chips, 6½in .5cm).
0-600

A Bohemian goblet, engraved in the manner of Rugendas, supported on a multi-knopped section, on conical foot with upturned folded rim, c1700, 9in (22.5cm).
$2,500-3,000

A pair of Venetian Aventurine wine glasses with silver gilt mounts, of brown tint flecked with copper crystals, the fluted bell bowls on facet cut knopped stems, each section joined by rope twist silver gilt bands, the footrims similarly mounted, one glass slightly damaged, early 18thC, 3½in (8.5cm).
$3,000-4,000

A German diamond-engraved goblet, Bohemian, c1700, 9in (23cm).
$8,000-9,000

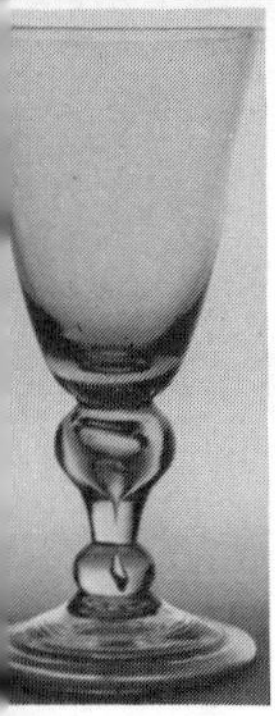

A large baluster goblet, c1700, 11½in (29cm).
$7,000-8,000

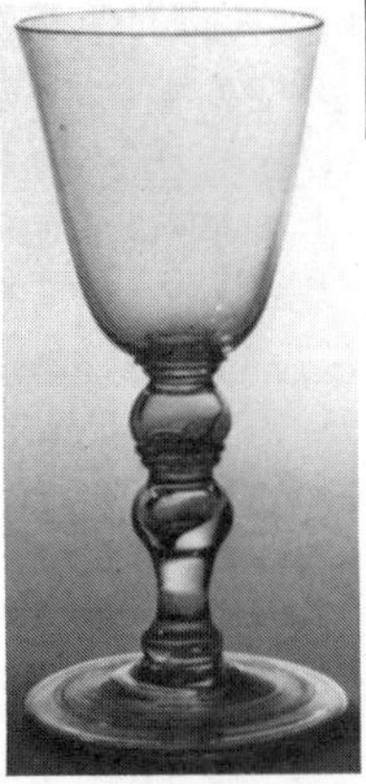

A baluster coin goblet, the bowl on a hollow ball knop containing a Charles II three-pence piece dated 1673, on an inverted baluster stem with a tear and base knop, early 18thC, 7½in (18.5cm).
$3,500-4,000

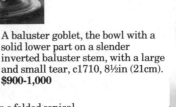

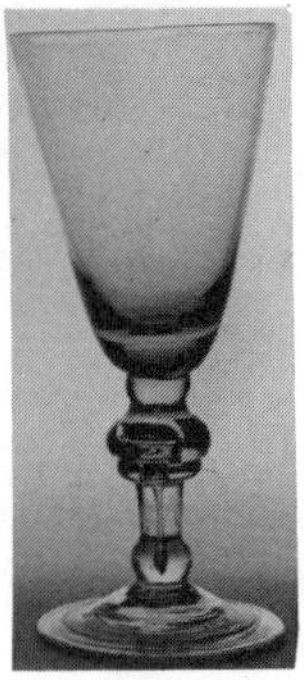

A baluster goblet, on a folded conical foot, c1710, 11in (28cm).
$4,000-5,000

A baluster goblet, the bowl with a solid lower part on a slender inverted baluster stem, with a large and small tear, c1710, 8½in (21cm).
$900-1,000

A baluster goblet, with tulip-shaped bowl, the solid lower part on a drop knop enclosing a tear, c1710, 8in (20cm).
$1,400-1,800

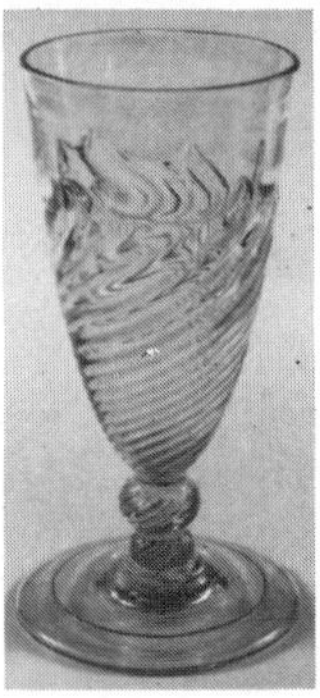

A flammiform ale glass on folded foot, c1720, 5½in (14cm).
$700-800

A Dutch engraved light baluster goblet, the funnel bowl inscribed 'MAAS/LUST', the multi-knopped stem including beaded sections an conical foot, mid-18thC, 7½in (18.5cm).
$1,200-1,400

A dark green goblet of Absolon type, the ogee bowl inscribed in gilt, the rim gilt, on knopped and inverted baluster stem and plain foot, early 19thC, 6½in (16cm).
$800-1,000

A Sunderland Bridge rummer, engraved with a sailing ship and inscribed in diamond point below, the reverse with the initials 'MCF', 19thC, 7in (17.5cm).
$800-1,000

A glass goblet engraved with ships, c1810, 5in (12.5cm).
$600-650

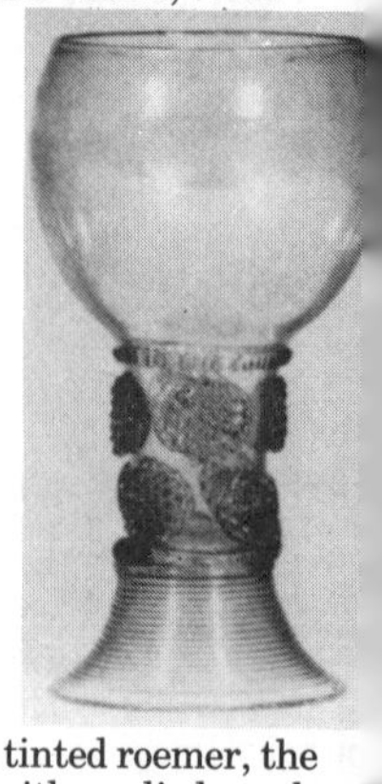

A pale green tinted roemer, the hollow stem with applied raspber prunts and threaded domed foot, 18thC, 5in (12.5cm).
$250-300

An engraved goblet, 'Speed the Plough', c1810, 5in (12.5cm).
$700-800

A pair of flute cut glasses with facet cut knop stems, c1810, 5in (12cm).
$130-150

l. & r. A pair of bucket rummers, c1820, 5in (13cm).
$200-250

c. A bucket shaped rummer with fluted base, c1820, 5½in (14.5cm).
$70-90

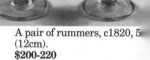

A pair of rummers, c1820, 5 (12cm).
$200-220

Three engraved rummers, c1820, largest 8in (20cm).
$800-1,000 each

A Masonic rummer, engraved with the initials 'CJK' and 'PSP', 'Joine Nov.15th 1840', with star cut foot, c1840, 6½in (17cm).
$950-1,000

A Sunderland Bridge rummer.
$400-500

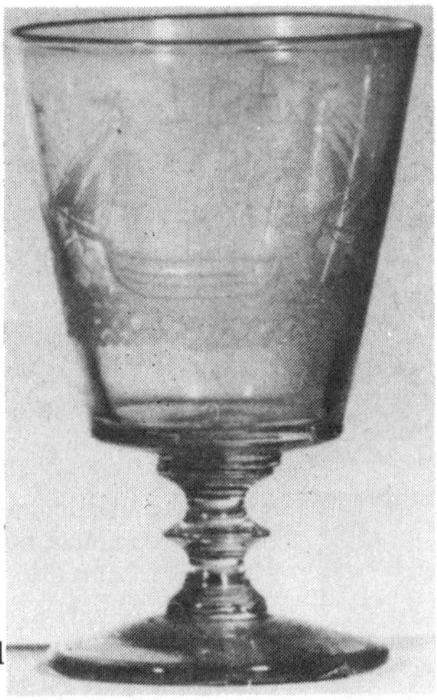

A bucket shaped rummer, on bladed knopped stem, the bowl engraved with ships, 5in (12.5cm).
$400-600

Flasks

A German dark blue 'Nabelflasche', each side with a central deep indentation, with pewter mount and screw cover, c1700, 10½in (26cm).
$1,100-1,200

A German dark blue 'Nabelflasche', of lightly ribbed flattened oviform, with pewter mount and screw cover, c1700, 8½in (21.5cm).
$3,600-4,000

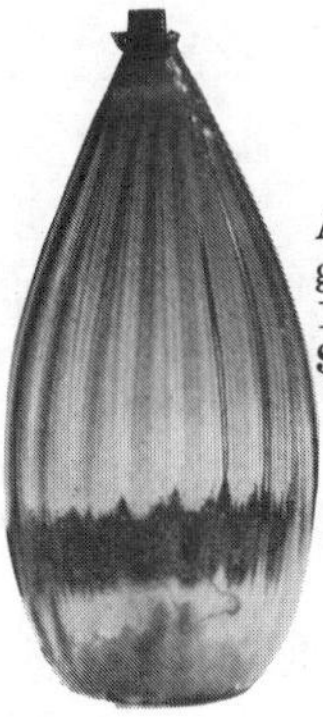

A German spirit flask, with pale green tint, with kick-in base, early 18thC, 9½in (24cm).
$1,200-1,400

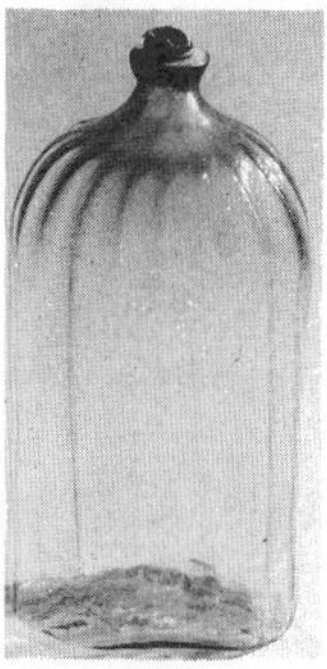

A Central European pewter mounted spirit flask, with lightly ribbed sides, slight damage to pewter mount, early 18thC, 6in (15cm).
$800-900

A German brown tinted spirit flask, with pewter mount, early 18thC, 6in (15.5cm).
$900-1,000

Two glass boots, c1830, 3in (7.5cm).
$90-130 each

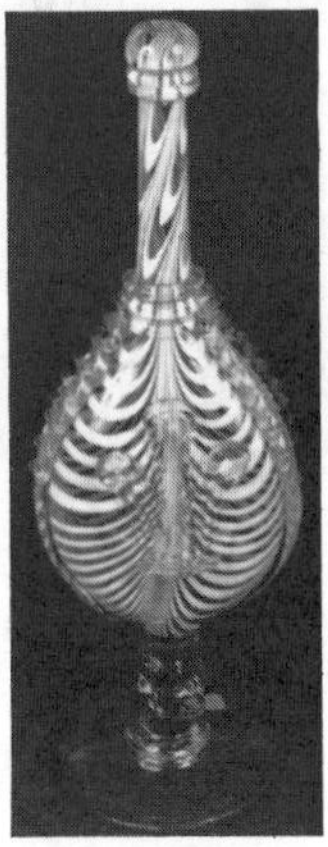

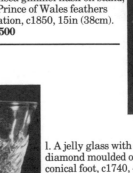

A Nailsea gimmel flask on stand, with Prince of Wales feathers decoration, c1850, 15in (38cm).
$450-500

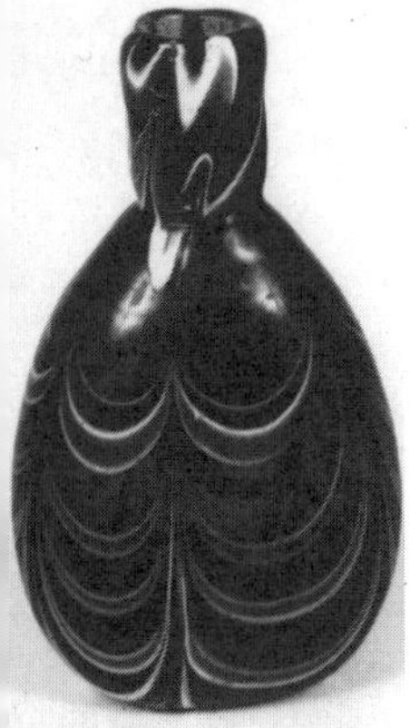

A Nailsea green and pink gimmel flask, c1850, 4in (10cm).
$2,900-4,000

Jelly Glasses

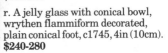

l. A jelly glass with conical bowl, diamond moulded overall, with conical foot, c1740, 4in (10cm).
$160-200

r. A jelly glass with conical bowl, wrythen flammiform decorated, plain conical foot, c1745, 4in (10cm).
$240-280

Three jelly glasses, c1750, tallest 4½in (11cm).
$180-250 each

Three hexagonal jelly glasses, c1770, largest 4in (10cm).
$180-220 each

l. & r. Two matching jelly glasses, with ribbed trumpet bowls, on air-beaded rudimentary stems, c1780, 3½in (9.5cm).
$80-120 each

c. A bell bowl jelly glass, with ribbed body, with air-beaded rudimentary stem, c1780, 3½in (9.5cm).
$80-120

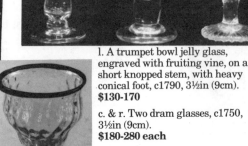

A set of 6 jelly glasses, the trumpet bowls with notched rims and plain feet, c1800, 4in (10cm).
$450-500

l. A trumpet bowl jelly glass, engraved with fruiting vine, on a short knopped stem, with heavy conical foot, c1790, 3½in (9cm).
$130-170

c. & r. Two dram glasses, c1750, 3½in (9cm).
$180-280 each

A blue rimmed bonnet glass, c1790, 3in (8cm).
$120-160

Jugs

A water jug engraved with an ironworker at his forge, the reverse with hops and barley, and the initials $^{W}{}_{H}{}^{N}$, the high hollow kick in the base containing a silver George II coin, with strap handle, stress crack to base, c1760, 6½in (17cm).
$600-700

An amethyst glass baluster cream jug and sugar bowl, early 19thC.
$200-300

An amethyst glass jug, c1800, 3in (7.5cm).
$240-260

A cranberry glass jug, c1880, 4in (10cm).
$150-180

A Victorian claret jug, decorated with polished ovals, c1860, 12in (30.5cm).
$240-280

A Georgian claret jug, with pillar cut body and single ringed neck, c1830, 12in (30.5cm).
$600-700

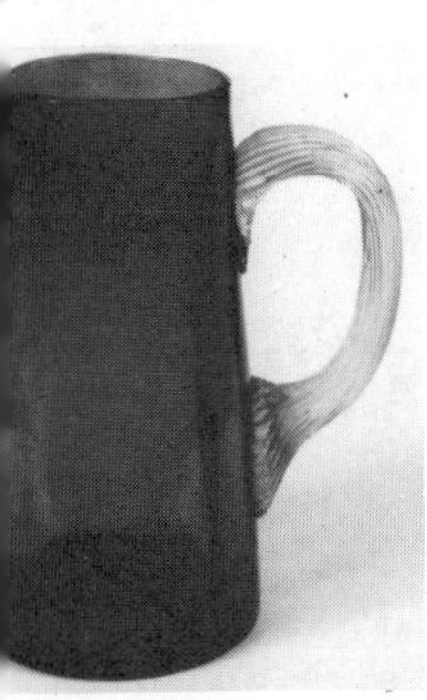

ranberry glass jug, c1880, 7in
cm).
50-180

A cranberry glass jug, c1880, 8in (20.5cm).
$300-350

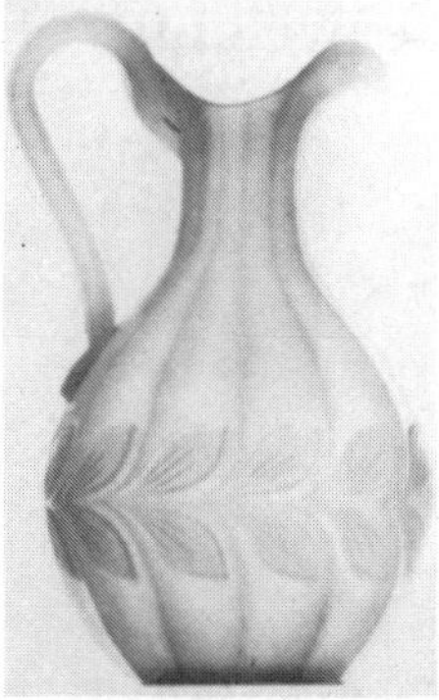

A Bohemian jug and matching goblet, the pink overlay cut away in flutes and stylised leaves, the jug with applied loop handle, 10½in (27cm).
$600-700

aperweights

lichy red ground concentric
lefiori weight, the central white
try-mould surrounded by
rcles of coloured canes, including
hite and green rose, mid-19thC,
n diam.
000-1,200

A Baccarat garlanded red and white flower weight, mid-19thC, 6.8cm diam.
$3,000-4,000

A Baccarat garlanded double-clematis weight, with star cut base, mid-19thC, 7.2cm diam.
$2,500-3,000

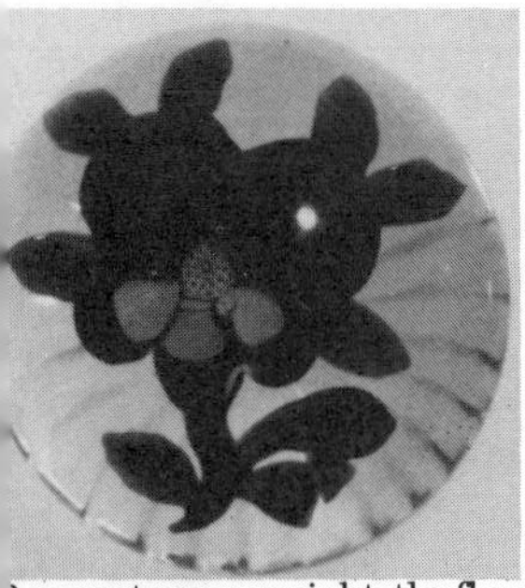

accarat pansy weight, the flower
h 2 plum coloured petals and
ellow and purple petals, on a star
base, mid-19thC, 7.3cm diam.
00-900

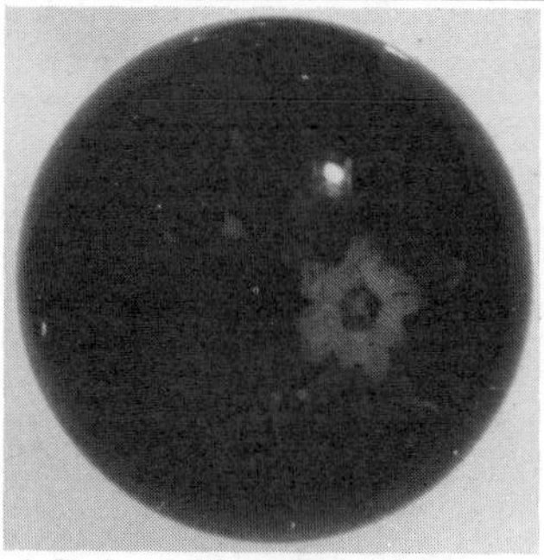

A St. Louis blue ground bouquet weight, in white, yellow, pink and red with green leaves, mid-19thC, 7.5cm diam.
$1,600-2,000

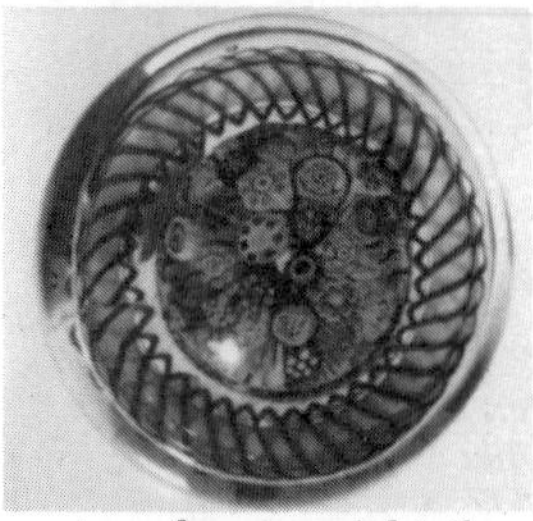

A Baccarat mushroom weight, the tuft of closely packed coloured canes, set within a torsade of white gauze entwined with spiral blue thread between mercury bands, on a star cut base, slight fritting to footrim, mid-19thC, 8.2cm diam.
$1,200-1,300

St. Louis faceted upright bouquet
ight, the bouquet with a large
ite and 2 smaller pink
ntian-type flowers and 2 florets
rrounded by green leaves, set
thin a white torsade of corkscrew
bon entwined by thread between
ercury bands, mid-19thC, 8cm
m.
,600-2,000

A Baccarat pansy weight, with plum coloured petals, blue and white cogwheel petals, green leaves and a dark purple bud, on a star cut base, mid-19thC, 6.8cm diam.
$2,800-3,200

A St. Louis fuchsia weight, with red buds and green leaves, mid-19thC, 6.5cm diam.
$2,000-2,500

Paperweights

A Russian facet-cut floral seal, the base engraved with monogram 'ID', 2 chips to rim of base, late 19thC, 6.5cm.
$2,200-2,500

A green glass dump, late 19thC, 6in (15cm).
$130-180

A Paul Stankard apple blossom and bee weight, signed with a black 'S' on a white dot and etched Experimental A317 1980, 7.8cm diam.
$600-700

A Paul Stankard faceted bouquet weight, signed with a black 'S' on a yellow dot, and etched B577 1982, 8cm diam.
$2,800-3,200

A Paul Stankard, strawberries, blossom and buds weight, with yellow and white flowers, red and green fruit and green leaves, signed with a black 'S' on a white dot and etched B318 1981, 7.5cm diam.
$1,600-1,800

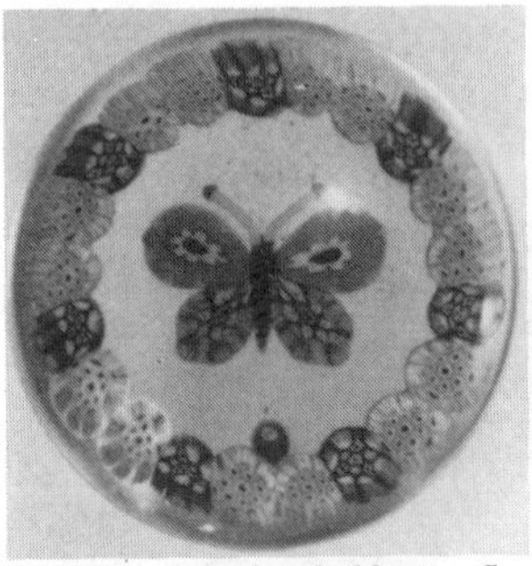

A Paul Ysart garlanded butterfly weight, the insect with an aventurine body, lime green and pink wings and white antennae with red tips, set within green, pink and white canes, inscribed 'PY', 20thC, 7cm diam.
$2,000-2,400

A Paul Stankard bouquet weight, signed with a blue 'S' on a white and orange dot, and etched 137 76, 7cm diam.
$1,700-2,000

Scent Bottles

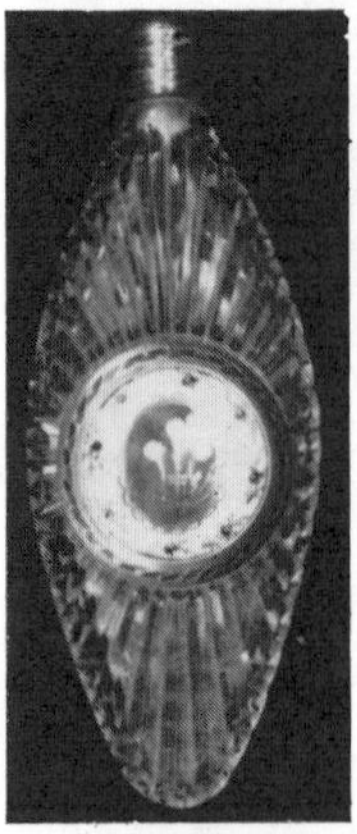

An oval cut scent bottle, with central metal plaque enamelled with floral motifs and fleur-de-lys, with silver screw cap, c1790, 4½in (11.3cm).
$600-700

A mercury glass perfume flask, with silver hinged top, c1840, 3½in (9cm).
$900-1,000

A cameo glass perfume flask, glass stopper, silver hinged top, c1840, 4in (10cm).
$1,100-1,200

A cameo scent bottle and stopper, the matt ground overlaid in white, c1880, 5½in (14.5cm).
$1,000-1,200

l. A yellow glass perfume bottle, with silver hinged top, c1900, 5½in (14cm).
$400-450

r. A cut crystal perfume bottle, 4½in (11.5cm).
$200-250

'ankards

Lynn ribbed crystal tankard, with
omed foot, slight crack to handle,
1775, 5in (12.5cm).
600-800

A mug with waisted body and ribbed rim, gadrooned lower half and foot ring, ribbed handle, c1780, 4in (11cm).
$500-600

Vases

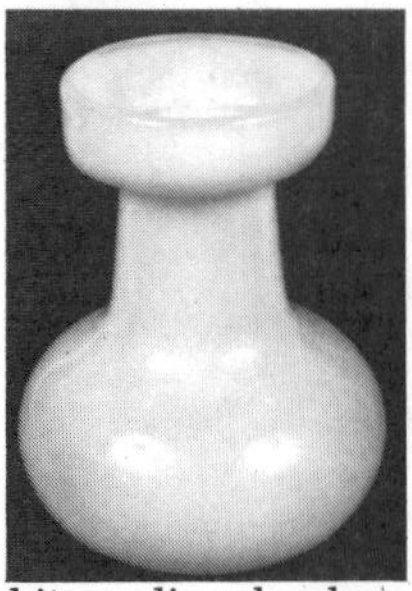

A white opaline glass hyacinth vase, c1820, 5in (12.5cm).
$300-350

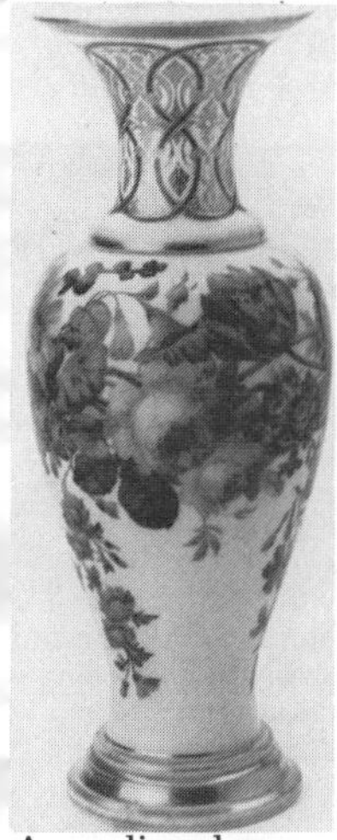

An opaline glass vase, the body colourfully painted, elaborate gilt enrichments, early 19thC, 18in (45.5cm).
$1,200-1,300

A celery vase, c1830, 10in (25.5cm).
$800-900

A celery glass, engraved with swan and trailing leaves, c1850, 8in (20.5cm).
$150-160

A celery vase, c1840, 7in (18cm).
$70-90

A Baccarat opaline two-handled vase, painted with flowers, gilt bands, gilding to rim and footrim rubbed, c1850, 15½in (39.5cm).
$3,600-4,000

n engraved celery vase,
1850, 8in (20.5cm).
130-150

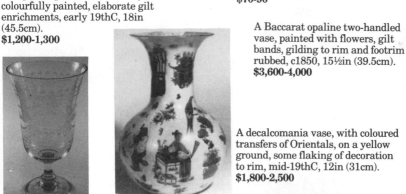

A decalcomania vase, with coloured transfers of Orientals, on a yellow ground, some flaking of decoration to rim, mid-19thC, 12in (31cm).
$1,800-2,500

A Mary Gregory amethyst glass hyacinth vase, c1860, 5½in (14cm).
$150-200

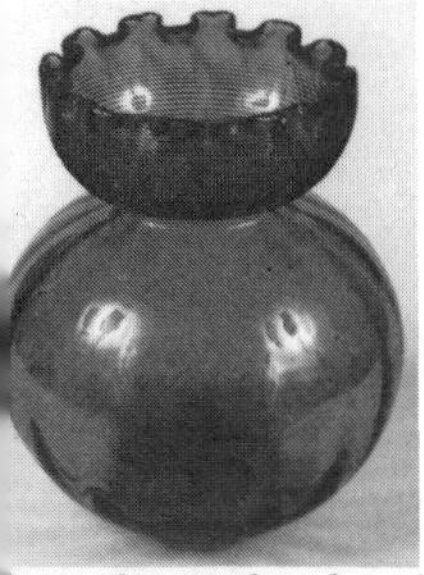

\ cranberry glass hyacinth vase,
vith gold trailing around rim,
1850.
300-400

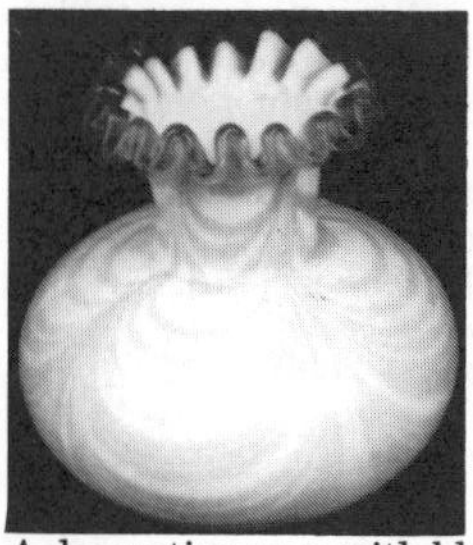

A decorative vase with blue and white overlay, amber rim, 19thC, 4½in (11cm).
$250-300

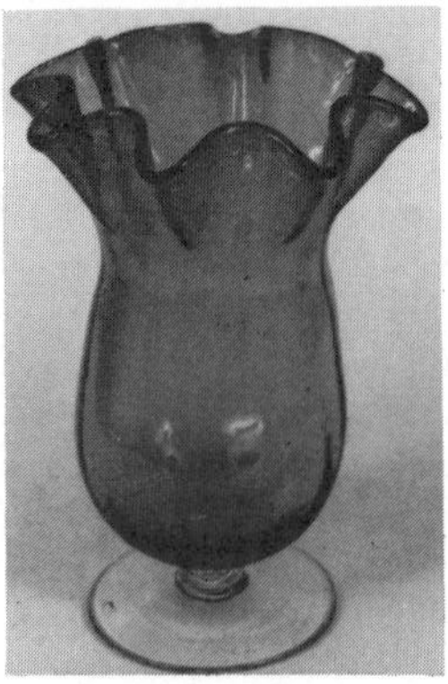

A cranberry vase, c1860, 7in (18cm).
$170-200

A pair of amethyst glass hyacinth vases, c1870, 8in (20.5cm).
$170-200

A pair of cranberry glass vases, c1880, 11in (28cm).
$550-600

A ruby and clear glass celery vase, c1840, 10in (25.5cm).
$220-250

An opaline glass vase, painted with swags of flowers, gilt enrichments, c1880, 14in (35.5cm).
$800-1,000

A Thomas Webb cameo two-handled vase, the brown ground overlaid in white with floral swags, impressed Thomas Webb & Sons, c1885, 8in (20.5cm) wide.
$2,500-3,000

A cameo glass vase, probably Webb, in red overlaid in white with flowers and insects, 9in (23cm).
$400-500

A pair of white overlay ruby glass lustre vases, painted with panels of flowers on a gold decorated ground, hung with prisms, 10½in (26cm).
$1,600-2,000

An amber glass hyacinth vase, c1880, 7½in (19cm).
$50-60

Miscellaneous

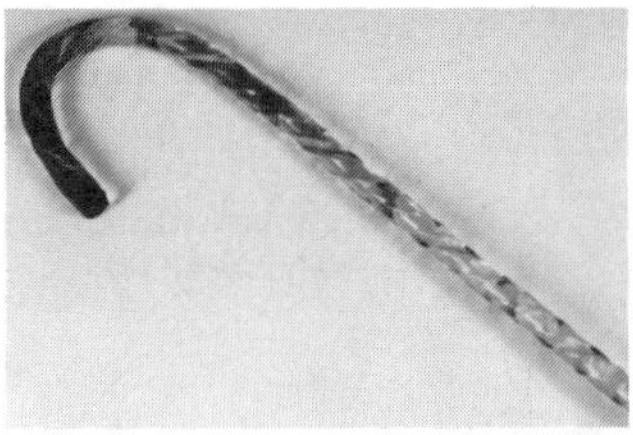

A Nailsea green glass walking stick, c1860, 45in (114cm) long.
$60-80

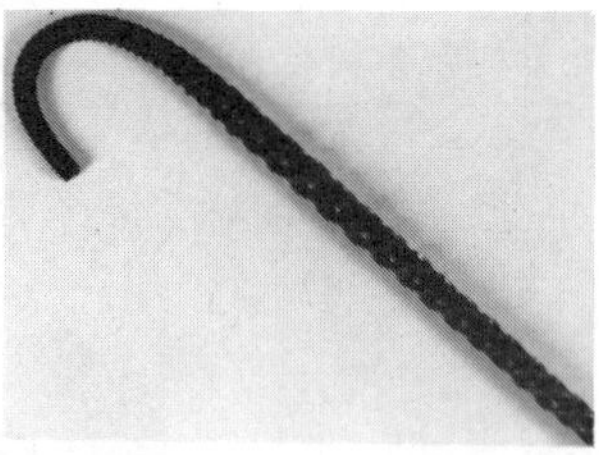

A Nailsea green glass walking stick, c1870, 50in (126cm).
$100-150

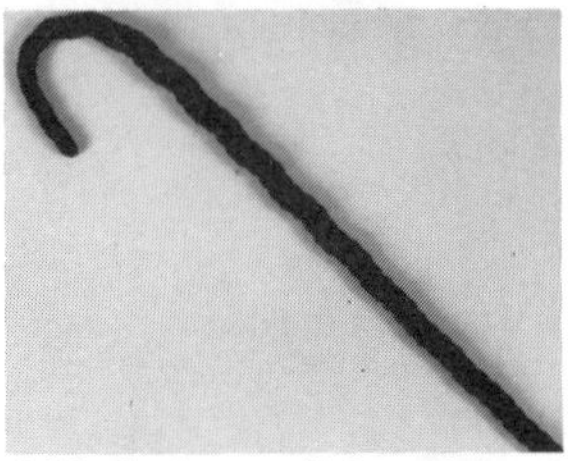

A black glass walking stick, c1870, 43in (109cm).
$100-150

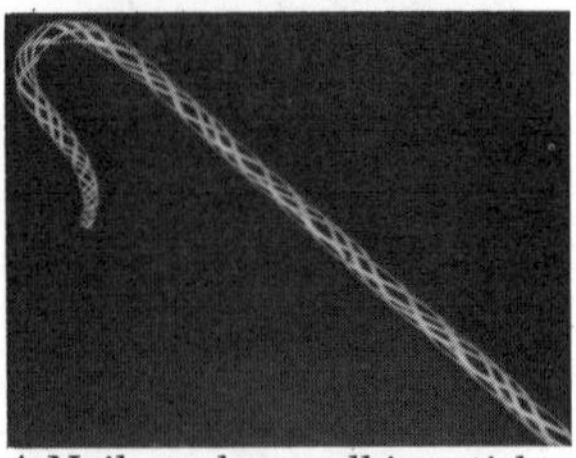

A Nailsea glass walking stick, c1860, 30in (76cm).
$80-120

A green tinted glass table service, engraved with seahorses and dolphins, comprising: a ribbed fruit dish, a jug with loop handle, a decanter with stopper, 2 candlesticks, 40 wine glasses, 8 finger bowls, 16 plates and a basket cover.
$5,000-6,000

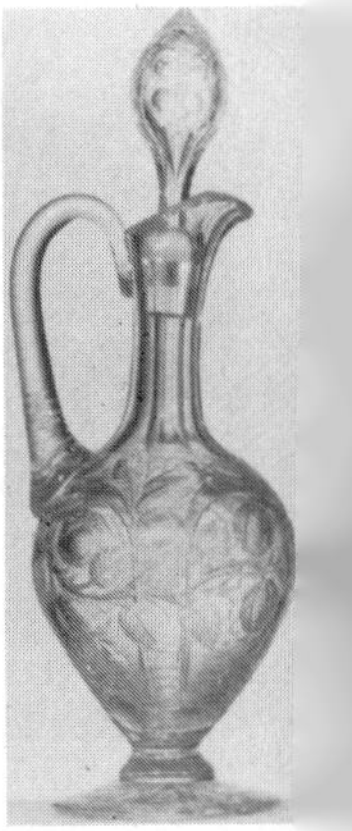

A Webb table service, comprising: a decanter jug and stopper, 47 glasses, 12 tumblers, 28 dishes, and 10 hock glasses, possibly Stevens and Brierly, some damaged.
$5,000-6,000

 set of 8 cups and saucers of blue nted glass, with white dot border nd painted in gilt with cherubs and uiting vine, gilding rubbed, slight hips.
450-600

A Continental crystal plaque, richly decorated and enamelled, 13in (33cm).
$150-250

A stained glass and leaded roundel by Jessie Jacobs, painted in colours, 10in (25cm) diam, with chain for suspension.
$450-600

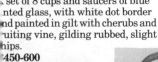

 moulded lacemaker's lamp, 1730, 6in (14.5cm).
1,800-2,000

A Venetian 'ice glass' bucket, late 16th/early 17thC, 5in (13cm) diam.
$600-900

An Irish piggin, with bands of flute, diamond, prism and blaze cutting, c1820, 5in (12.5cm).
$1,200-1,400

Two Nailsea crown glass snuff jars, in light green, c1800, 11in (28cm).
$250-350

Two Irish pickle jars and covers, 1815, 6 to 7in (15.5 to 17.5cm).
$250-350

A rectangular clear glass block decorated with fish, possibly by Gino Cenedese, Murano, 12in (32cm) wide.
$450-700

Two glass bird feeders, c1800, smallest with blue top, 5½in (14cm).
$75-150

An amethyst carafe, tumbler and plate, with gilt fruiting vine decoration, c1870, 7½in (19cm).
$400-600

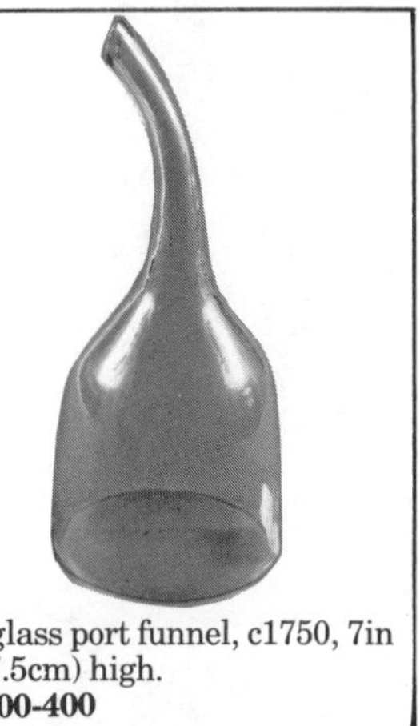

A glass port funnel, c1750, 7in (17.5cm) high.
$300-400

Two blue glass egg cups, c1830, 3in 7cm) high.
$150-200

A cranberry glass carafe with matching glass, c1820, 7in (17.5cm).
$250-350

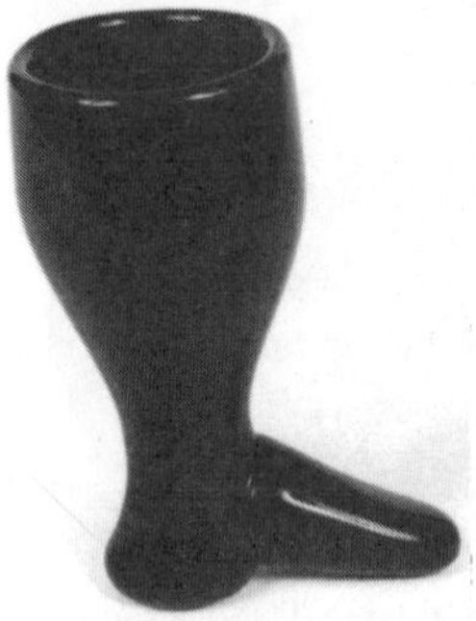

A dark blue stirrup cup, c1800, 3½in (9cm).
$500-600

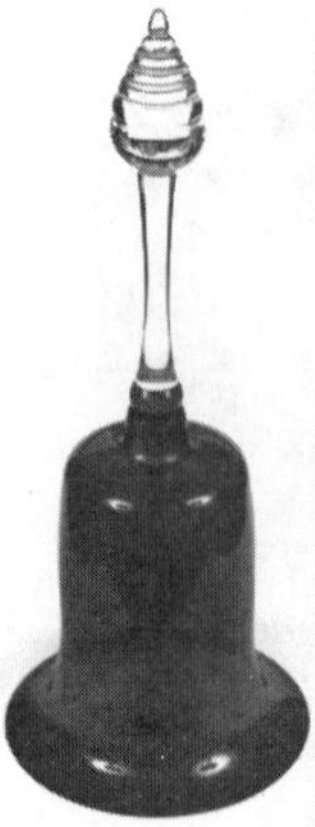

A cranberry glass bell, c1880, 15½in (39cm).
$250-300

An engraved bell decorated with a view of the High Level Bridge at Newcastle on Tyne, the reverse inscribed George Pedley, clapper lacking, hook chipped, c1849, 8in (20cm).
$1,000-1,200

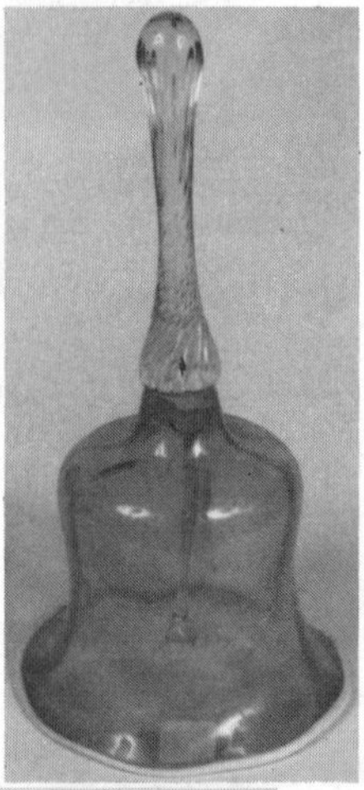

A vaseline glass bell with white rim, c1860, 11in (28cm).
$300-400

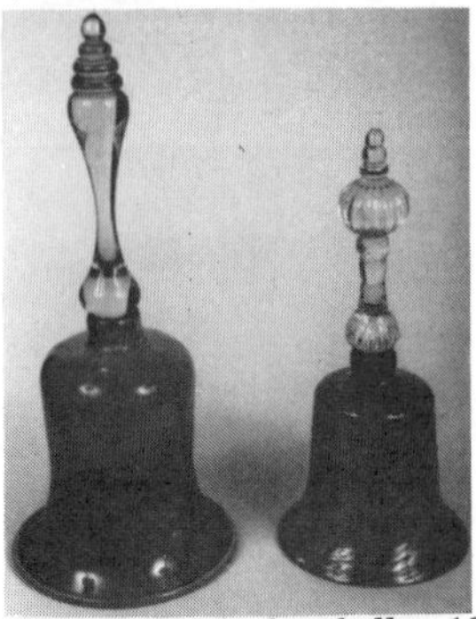

Two cranberry glass bells, c1860, 10 and 12½in (25 and 32cm).
$250-300 each

A French blue opaline glass casket, with gold metal mounts, late 19thC, 4in (10cm).
$900-1,000

A ruby casket, c1870, 5½in (14cm).
$1,200-1,500

A Bohemian casket with gilt metal mounts, the lid and sides engraved with deer in a forest, chip to lid, 4½in (11cm) wide.
$300-400

A confiture and cover, cut with bands of diamonds, set on a hexagonal foot, early 19thC, 18in (45cm).
$1,400-1,600

A pair of lustres, with scalloped rim and base, c1880, 10½in (26cm).
$1,100-1,300

A pair of lustres with scalloped top, c1830, 9½in (24cm).
$850-900

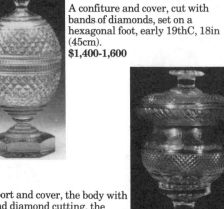

A comport and cover, the body with flute and diamond cutting, the domed cover with mushroom finial, c1820, 4½in (11cm).
$300-350

A Silesian tazza, c1740, 13in (33cm) diam.
$600-700

A George III clear comport, 12in (30.5cm) diam.
$500-600

pedestal stemmed tazza on high
med folded foot, 13½in (34cm)
de.
00-600

ı Irish oval dish with looped prism
coration and fan cut rim, c1790,
in (28cm) diam.
.,300-1,500

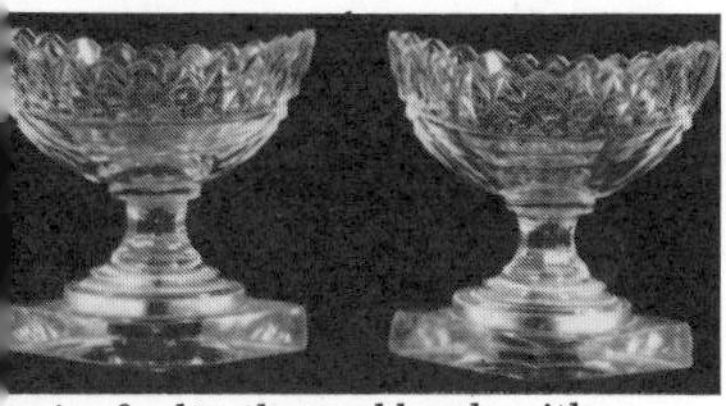

pair of salts, the oval bowls with
ism and diamond cutting,
alloped rims, c1820, 4in (9cm).
00-600

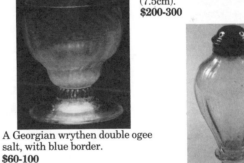

wo glass salts, c1790, 3 and 3½in
.5 and 9cm).
120-150

glass mustard pot, with lid, c1800,
½in (14cm).
50-350

An oval cut butter dish and cover, with star cut base, domed cover, c1825, 5½in (14.5cm) diam.
$600-700

A Georgian wrythen double ogee salt, with blue border.
$60-100

A cruet set, with silver tops, c1800.
$250-350

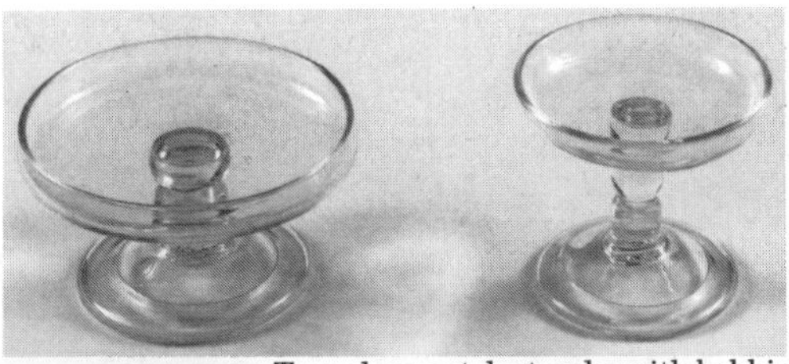

Two glass patch stands, with bobbin knopped stems on folded feet, c1750, 2½ and 3in (6 and 7.5cm) diam.
$400-500

A butter dish and cover, with broad flute and slice cutting, serrated rim, the domed lid with cut ball finial, c1820, 4in (11cm).
$300-400

A pair of salts on square lemon squeezer bases, c1790, 3½in (9cm).
$200-250

A pair of oval cut and moulded salts, on lemon squeezer feet, c1810, 3in (7.5cm).
$200-300

A glass pepper pot, on lemon squeezer base, with silver plated top, c1790, 5in (13cm).
$60-100

Three cut glass sugar sifters, c1810, 6in (15cm).
$100-120 each

An open topped fly trap, 19thC, 7in (18cm).
$75-150

A glass domed fly trap with 3 feet, the closed top pink tinged, c1850, 8½in (21.5cm).
$100-150

An open topped domed fly trap, 19thC, 7in (18cm).
$75-150

GLASS APPENDIX

Drinking glasses

STEM FORMATIONS

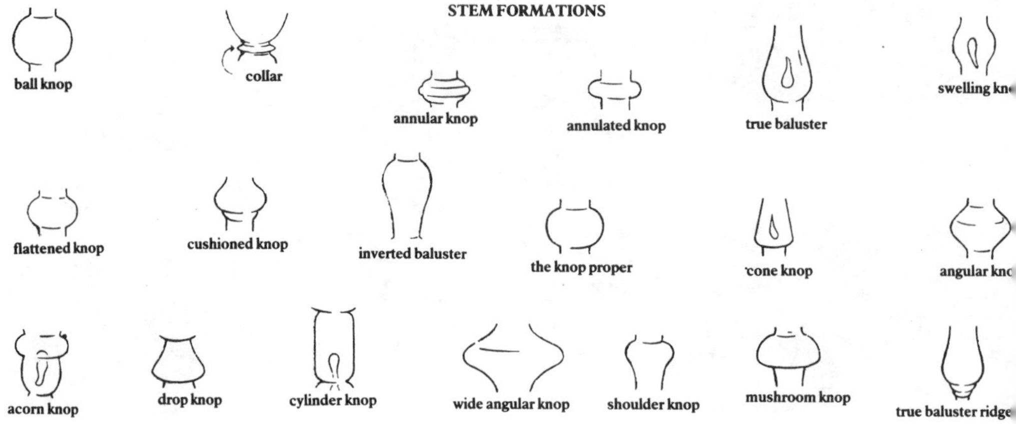

BOWL FORMS

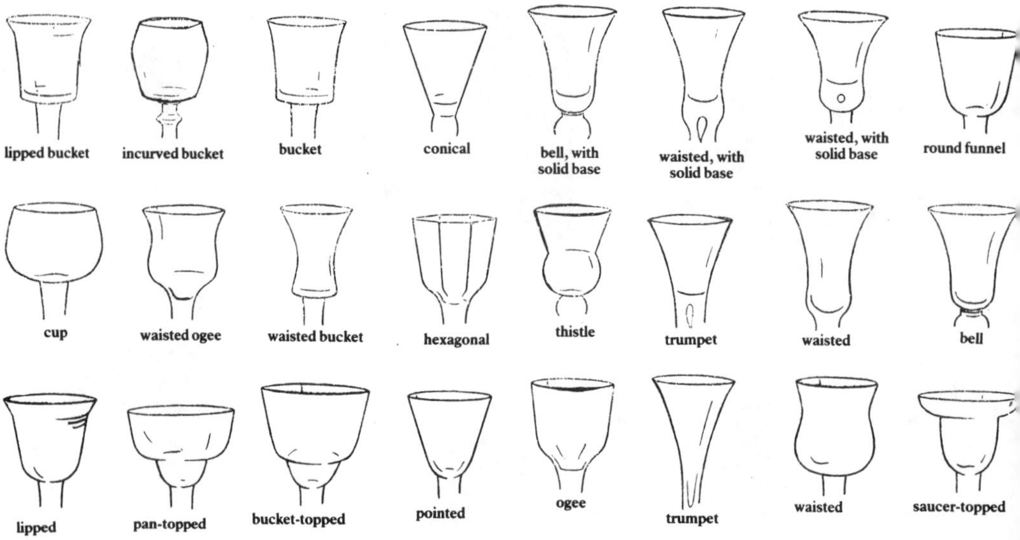

FOOT FORMS

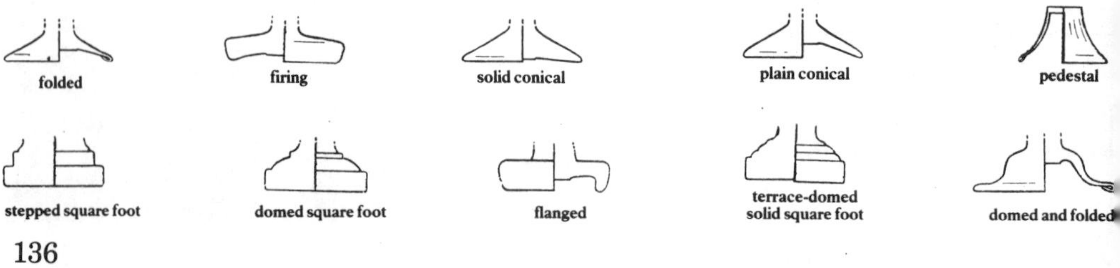

OAK & COUNTRY FURNITURE

Bureaux

A Queen Anne oak bureau, with well fitted interior, c1710.
$5,000-6,000

An oak bureau with fully fitted interior, 18thC, 30in (76cm).
$4,500-5,000

A George II oak bureau, the crossbanded sloping flap enclosing a fitted interior, 28½in (72cm).
$3,000-4,000

An oak bureau cabinet, the top section with a cavetto moulded cornice, the hinged sloping flap enclosing a fitted interior, adapted, 18thC, 38½in (98cm).
$2,000-3,000

A George II oak bureau cabinet, with swan neck pediment, the base with writing slope enclosing well fitted interior, 39½in (100cm).
$7,000-9,000

A William and Mary walnut bureau, with fitted interior, on turned gatelegs, lacks interior, has addition to rear, 38in (96.5cm).
$9,000-10,000

A mid-Georgian oak bureau, the hinged slope enclosing a fitted interior with stationery compartments, pen drawers and a well, 37in (94cm).
$2,000-3,000

A Queen Anne walnut bureau, with fitted interior including a document drawer. 36in (91.5cm).
$22,000-30,000

Did you know
MILLER'S Antiques Price Guide builds up year by year to form the most comprehensive photo-reference system available

Cabinets

A Provincial oak two-part corner cabinet, the moulded cornice above a pair of astragal glazed doors and a pair of panelled doors, late 18thC.
$1,400-1,600

An oak cabinet, with an inset glazed enamel clock face, the cupboard beneath with a diamond pendulum aperture flanked by a pair of glazed cupboards with glazed sides, one pane of glass missing, 18thC, 73in (185cm).
$6,000-10,000

A George II pollard oak bowfront hanging corner cabinet, with 4 enclosed shelves, 26½in (67cm).
$5,000-6,000

An oak hanging wall cabinet, with dentilled cornice and geometrically inlaid fruitwood frieze, above a glazed door enclosing 2 velvet-lined shelves, 33in (84cm).
$3,000-4,000

A Dutch oak cabinet, with green painted interior, the bowfronted base with a pair of fielded panelled doors, mid-18thC, 56½in (143cm).
$13,000-15,000

Chairs

An English oak carved and inlaid wainscot chair, c1680.
$7,000-10,000

An oak chair, with barley twist turning, 17thC.
$500-700

An oak dining chair, boldly carved with flowerhead and foliage, on turned supports with twin box stretchers, 17thC with later panel seat.
$400-500

An oak armchair, the panelled back carved with guilloches and foliage and inscribed several times HA, the arms on turned supports with solid seat, the turned legs joined by stretchers, 17thC with some later carving.
$1,500-2,000

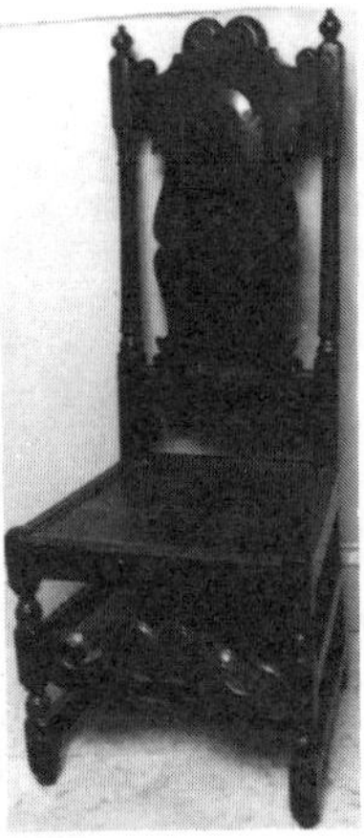

An oak chair with carved back and front stretcher, 17thC.
$600-700

An oak panelled back chair, 17thC.
$900-1,100

An oak wainscot lambing armchair, with serpentine cresting and panelled back, above a box seat enclosed by a panel door, basically 17thC.
$3,000-4,000

An oak armchair, with carved panelled back and inlaid cresting rail, the sloping arms on turned and finialled posts above a solid seat, on turned legs joined by stretchers, seat rail re-supported, mid-17thC.
$11,000-13,000

A William and Mary walnut caned chair.
$500-600

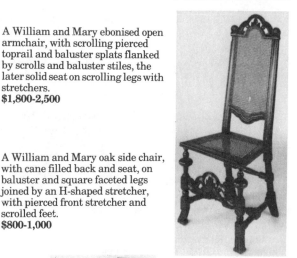

A William and Mary ebonised open armchair, with scrolling pierced toprail and baluster splats flanked by scrolls and baluster stiles, the later solid seat on scrolling legs with stretchers.
$1,800-2,500

A William and Mary oak side chair, with cane filled back and seat, on baluster and square faceted legs joined by an H-shaped stretcher, with pierced front stretcher and scrolled feet.
$800-1,000

An oak panelled back chair, late 17thC.
$1,400-2,000

A George I oak armchair, converted to a commode, with needlework seat, front cabriole legs shortened.
$400-600

A pair of oak side chairs, with solid panelled backs, solid seats and turned legs, late 17thC.
$1,400-2,000

A pair of Dutch walnut side chairs, in the style of Daniel Marot, with yellow padded seats and scrolling foliate aprons, on foliate cabriole legs with pierced scrolling front stretchers and baluster stretchers, late 17thC, later blocks.
$3,000-4,000

A set of 6 George III oak hall chairs, the backs fluted, applied with roundels and painted with crests, the dished seats on turned supports with X-stretcher rails.
$7,000-8,000

A George III applewood desk chair, c1785.
$1,200-1,500

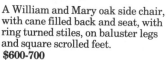

A set of 6 oak chairs,
$3,000-3,500

A William and Mary oak side chair, with cane filled back and seat, with ring turned stiles, on baluster legs and square scrolled feet.
$600-700

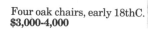

Four oak chairs, early 18thC.
$3,000-4,000

A sack back Windsor armchair, Philadelphia, c1790.
$3,500-4,000

A sack back Windsor armchair, branded L H., on bottom of seat, Philadelphia, c1800.
$2,500-3,000

A pair of bow back Windsor side chairs, 1 branded Sanborn, Boston, Massachusetts, c1799.
$4,500-5,000

A turned and joined cherrywood side chair, side stretchers restored, New Jersey, c1700.
$2,000-3,000

17thC turned chairs from New York are exceedingly rare.

A William and Mary painted bannister back armchair, New York or Connecticut, c1740.
$2,000-3,000

A sack back Windsor armchair, branded W. Cox, Philadelphia, c1800.
$4,000-5,000

A sack back Windsor armchair, Philadelphia, arm rail restored, c1800.
$1,500-2,000

A bow back Windsor armchair, Philadelphia, old repairs, c1810.
$1,500-2,000

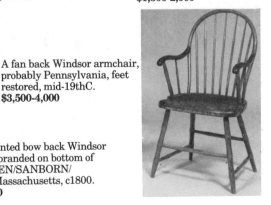

A pair of painted bow back Windsor side chairs, branded on bottom of seat, REUBEN/SANBORN/ BOSTON, Massachusetts, c1800.
$3,500-4,500

A fan back Windsor armchair, probably Pennsylvania, feet restored, mid-19thC.
$3,500-4,000

ʌ yew Windsor chair, early 19thC.
1,200-1,300

A comb-back Windsor chair, c1800.
$1,500-1,600

A Welsh primitive chair, with oak seat and sycamore spindles, c1800.
$800-1,000

A child's Windsor chair, with original green paint, c1800.
$500-600

ʌn elm chair, new rush seat, c1820.
ʻ300-400

A matched set of 6 wheel back Windsor elbow chairs, c1820.
$2,500-3,500

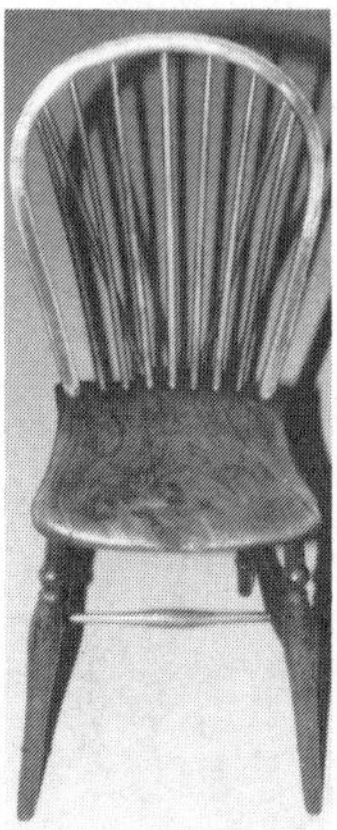

A set of 6 stick back Windsor chairs, c1820.
$1,300-1,400

ʌ set of 10 ash and elm wheel back Vindsor chairs, c1830.
ʻ3,000-3,500

An ash and elm Windsor rocking chair, c1830.
$600-700

An ash and elm comb back corner chair with rush seat, 18thC.
$1,400-1,600

ʌn ash and beech elbow chair, 9thC, 22in (56cm).
ʻ120-130

ʌ green painted bow back Windsor ɪrmchair, on bamboo turned ɪplayed legs, Philadelphia, feet ɪieced, c1800.
ʻ1,500-2,000

Two painted fan back Windsor side chairs, probably Rhode Island, late 18thC.
$2,000-3,000

A child's high chair in elm with rush seat, 19thC.
$450-500

A set of 6 ash and elm Windsor elbow chairs, with pierced splat backs, on turned legs and stretchers, 19thC.
$4,000-5,000

An elm Windsor elbow chair, 19thC 18in (46cm).
$500-600

A bow back Windsor armchair, probably Pennsylvania, early 19thC.
$2,000-3,000

A set of 7 oak framed ladderback dining chairs, late 19thC.
$400-600

A fruitwood ladderback elbow rocking chair, with rush seat, on turned supports, 19thC.
$300-400

A child's Windsor stick and wheel back elbow chair.
$300-400

A set of 8 ladderback period style chairs, by Tudor Oak of Cranbrook, with padded seats.
$800-1,000

A harlequin set of 8 elm and beech Windsor armchairs, with arched toprails and comb backs, mostly late 19thC.
$3,000-4,000

A carved walnut hall chair, the back scroll and guilloche carved with central satyr mask, panel seat, on carved panel supports.
$240-320

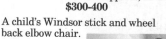

Two yew and elm Windsor armchairs, stamped Nicholson, Rockley.
$5,000-6,000

A set of 6 matched elm Windsor open arm elbow chairs, the saddle shaped seats on turned legs with stretchers.
$6,000-7,000

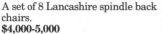

A Windsor chair.
$600-700

A set of 8 Lancashire spindle back chairs.
$4,000-5,000

A yew Windsor armchair, with crinoline stretcher.
$700-800

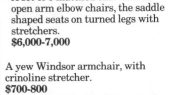

An oak desk chair, by Mouseman Thompson, the horseshoe top rail carved with masks above latticework splats and a leather upholstered seat, on faceted legs joined by a cross stretcher.
$600-1,000

A harlequin set of 3 Victorian elm, ash and beech Windsor armchairs, one stamped B and one stamped M.
$1,500-1,700

A child's oak rocking chair, the back panel carved depicting Richard the Lionheart above an inscription, 'Coeur de Lion receives his fatal wound'.
$800-1,000

A pair of Spanish walnut open armchairs, with padded backs surmounted by scroll carved finials, upholstered in red velvet embroidered with crests, the seat hung with tassels, on square legs joined by pierced scroll carved stretchers.
$1,400-2,000

A Windsor yew and elm armchair, the arched back with pierced splat and baluster supports, with moulded seat, on baluster legs, later rockers.
$2,500-3,000

A carved oak chair.
$1,300-1,500

A carved oak chair.
$1,000-1,100

A harlequin set of 6 Cromwellian oak chairs.
$3,000-4,000

A Charles II carved oak panelled box settle, North Yorkshire, c1680.
$8,000-10,000

An oak settle, with 2 drawers beneath the seat, c1700, 45in (114cm).
$6,000-7,000

A George II oak panelled back settle, c1740.
$2,000-3,000

An Austrian oak settle, painted and carved, above a hinged box seat with fielded panels and worded 'MARIATRINSISABET', late 17thC, 75in (190.5cm).
$4,000-5,000

An oak sofa, with concave cresting and vase-shaped splats, down curving arms and velvet upholstered seat, on cabriole legs with pad feet, parts 18thC, 73in (185cm).
$2,400-3,000

Chests

A panelled oak coffer, with original locks and hinges, early 17thC.
$1,800-2,000

An English oak coffer, c1630, 48in (122cm).
$1,600-1,800

An oak coffer, early 17thC, 62in (157cm).
$4,500-5,000

An oak chest, c1630, 52in (132cm).
$1,400-1,600

A carved oak coffer, c1650.
$700-900

A Jacobean oak and yew-wood chest, with 4 long graduated drawers, each with double raised panels of yew and burr oak within a moulded centre, with panelled sides, raised on stile feet, 38in (97cm).
$7,000-10,000

Did you know
MILLER'S Antiques Price Guide builds up year by year to form the most comprehensive photo-reference system available

ɪn oak chest, with moulded top and
entilled frieze above panelled
rawers, on block feet, mid-17thC,
he frieze later, 43½in (110cm).
2,000-3,000

A Welsh oak and pine panelled coffer, with original blue painted decoration, c1660.
$4,000-5,000

A Charles II oak coffer, with hinged triple panelled top, the frieze dated 1676 with the initials IW, 50½in (128cm).
$2,400-3,000

ɪ Charles II carved oak coffer, dated
669.
4,000-7,000

A Charles II West Country carved oak coffer, with drawer, c1670.
$3,000-5,000

A Charles II child's oak coffer, c1675.
$4,000-5,000

A Charles II carved oak panelled
coffer, c1675.
$2,000-4,000

An oak panelled coffer with inlays, North Yorkshire, c1680.
$4,000-6,000

An oak chest, 17thC, 38in (97cm).
$1,000-1,500

ɪ Charles II oak chest of drawers,
lecorated with plum wood split
ɔaluster, c1680.
$6,000-8,000

An oak chest of drawers, with cherrywood geometric cushion facings and split turned decoration, 17thC, 39in (99cm).
$5,000-7,000

An oak chest, c1680, 32in (81cm).
$7,000-8,000

A James II walnut and oak veneered cushion-moulded chest of drawers, 46in (116.5cm).
$8,000-9,000

An oak mule chest, the frieze carve with flowerheads and strapwork, the geometric panels incised with John Janis, 1688, the long drawer below also carved, 50in (127cm).
$1,600-2,000

An oak panelled carved coffer, Lake District, c1690.
$2,000-4,000

A panelled carved coffer, c169 36in (91.5cm).
$700-800

An English arcaded carved panelled coffer, c1690.
$1,600-2,500

An oak chest of drawers, 18thC, 37in (94cm).
$1,000-1,500

An oak carved panelled coffe c1695.
$2,000-4,000

A William and Mary oak chest of drawers, with ebony geometric line inlay, on deep moulded base and later turned feet, 34½in (88cm).
$5,000-6,000

An Italian walnut cassone, with hinged lid, above fielded front panels and 2 base drawers divided by fluted pilasters, on block feet, late 17thC, 60in (152cm).
$2,400-3,000

A large oak coffer, with pierced metal strapwork hinges, restorations, late 17thC, later carrying handles and supports, 56i (142cm).
$1,400-2,000

An oak coffer, with 4 inlaid panels initialled 'I.P.', 17thC, 59in (149.5cm).
$3,000-4,000

An oak chest, fitted with 4 long drawers of varying depths with geometrically panelled fronts, late 17thC, 39in (99cm).
$1,400-1,800

A reconstructed oak framed linen chest, heavily carved with scrolls and stylised flowerheads, 17thC, 50in (127cm).
$800-1,000

A Jacobean oak chest, with brass knobs and escutcheons, 17thC, 37in (94cm).
$1,100-1,200

An oak coffer, the triple panelled lid above a scrolled frieze above 3 diamond carved panels, on block feet, 17thC, 50in (127cm).
$2,000-3,000

A Spanish walnut coffer, with hinged top, the front carved with geometric roundels, minor restorations, 17thC, 66½in (168cm).
$1,400-1,500

An oak chest, carved with the Welsh King and Queen, the front panel with dragons, c1600.
$3,000-4,000

A carved oak coffer, with hinged top, 17thC, 47in (119cm).
$2,000-3,000

A carved oak coffer, 17thC.
$1,000-1,200

An oak plank coffer, with guilloche carving, late 17th/early 18thC, 44in (112cm).
$500-600

Make the most of Miller's

Every care has been taken to ensure the accuracy of descriptions and estimated valuations. Where an attribution is made within inverted commas (e.g. 'Chippendale') or is followed by the word 'style' (e.g. early Georgian style) it is intended to convey that, in the opinion of the publishers, the piece concerned is a later – though probably still antique – reproduction of the style so designated. Unless otherwise stated, any description which refers to 'a set', or 'a pair' includes a valuation for the entire set or the pair, even though the illustration may show only a single item

An oak coffer, 17thC, 24½in (62cm).
$900-1,300

An oak coffer, 17thC, 39in (99cm).
$3,000-4,000

A carved oak coffer, 17thC, 64in (164cm).
$900-1,300

An oak chest on stand, restored, 18thC.
$2,400-3,000

An oak and elm mule chest, 18thC, 56in (143cm).
$1,200-1,500

An elm coffer, 18thC, 55in (139cm).
$900-1,000

An oak and elm chest on stand, the top section with cavetto cornice, the stand with thumb-mould edge and shaped frieze, on bulbous turned supports, early 18thC, 39in (99cm).
$1,200-1,500

An oak coffer with hinged lid and guilloche frieze, 18thC, 38in (97cm).
$500-600

An oak chest with 2 short and 3 long drawers, all with raised shaped moulding, brass swan neck handles, on bracket feet, early 18thC, 39in (99cm).
$800-1,000

A Queen Anne walnut chest, crossbanded and outlined with feather stringing, the hinged top with engraved brass escutcheons, brass loop handles to the sides, 50in (128cm).
$7,000-9,000

A Queen Anne oak chest on stand, with 2 short and 3 graduated long drawers with brass drop handles and escutcheons, 39½in (100cm).
$2,000-3,000

An oak tallboy, with shaped apron and cabriole legs, 41in (104cm).
$6,000-8,000

A Westmorland oak panelled and carved coffer with drawer, dated 1703.
$2,000-3,000

A carved elm coffer, 18thC, 38in (96cm).
$800-900

A George I walnut veneered chest of drawers, c1705, 36in (91.5cm).
$5,000-6,000

An oak mule chest, dated 1707.
$1,200-1,400

A George I oak chest, on original stand, c1725.
$6,000-12,000

A George I walnut chest of drawers, 37in (94cm).
$7,000-8,000

An oak lowboy, c1740, 32in (81cm).
$1,800-2,500

A George II solid walnut chest of drawers, crossbanded in padouk, c1740.
$4,000-6,000

A George II oak chest on stand, inlaid with fruitwood and chequered inlay of boxwood and ebony, original brasses, c1745.
$8,000-12,000

A mid-Georgian burr elm and oak chest, the top and front re-veneered, 37in (94cm).
$2,000-3,000

A Welsh oak coffer bach, c1785.
$3,000-4,000

An oak dowry/mule chest, the hinged top above a fielded panelled front inlaid in boxwood with the initials 'M.M. A.G. 23 1775', above 3 short drawers and a shaped apron, on bracket feet, 64in (163cm).
$1,400-2,000

A small oak chest on chest, c1780.
$2,000-2,500

A mid-Georgian oak blanket chest, with hinged top, the frieze with 2 false drawers above 5 drawers crossbanded with walnut flanked by recessed fluted pilaster angles, on ogee bracket feet, 64½in (163cm).
$3,000-4,000

A George III oak chest of drawers, inlaid with bog oak and holly, c1785.
$3,000-5,000

A George III oak and mahogany banded mule chest, with hinged top, above a fielded panel front, with 3 short drawers and 2 long drawers below, on bracket feet, 64in (162.5cm).
$2,000-2,500

An oak mule chest, with hinged lid, above a foliate carved frieze with the initials 'W' and 'H', 57in (144.5cm).
$900-1,200

A carved oak chest, 37½in (95cm).
$4,000-6,000

An oak chest, the hinged plank top with moulded edge, the front with Gothic carved panels, 35in (89cm).
$10,000-11,000

A French coffer, with hinged moulded top, the front with 2 panels carved with a lady and a gentleman, on moulded plinth, 36in (91.5cm).
$600-1,000

An oak coffer, with fielded panels to front.
$400-500

A Spanish walnut coffer with hinged lid, 3 locks, pierced iron clasps and carrying handles, on plinth base, 40½in (102cm).
$1,000-1,200

A Dutch Colonial coffer, with plank top, 62½in (158cm).
$800-1,000

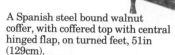

A Spanish steel bound walnut coffer, with coffered top with central hinged flap, on turned feet, 51in (129cm).
$1,400-2,000

An oak coffer, with panelled hinged top, inlaid with lozenge and star motifs, 45in (114cm).
$1,100-1,200

Cupboards

A Jacobean style oak press, with chip and carved strapwork borders, on block feet, 58½in (147cm).
$1,300-1,500

An oak press cupboard, with original carving, c1680.
$3,500-4,000

James I oak court cupboard, good our and patination, 54in (137cm).
0,000-12,000

ı oak court cupboard, carved with ;ures, masks and foliate scrolls, thC style, 61in (154cm).
,000-4,000

An oak court cupboard, 17thC, 55½in (139cm).
$3,000-4,000

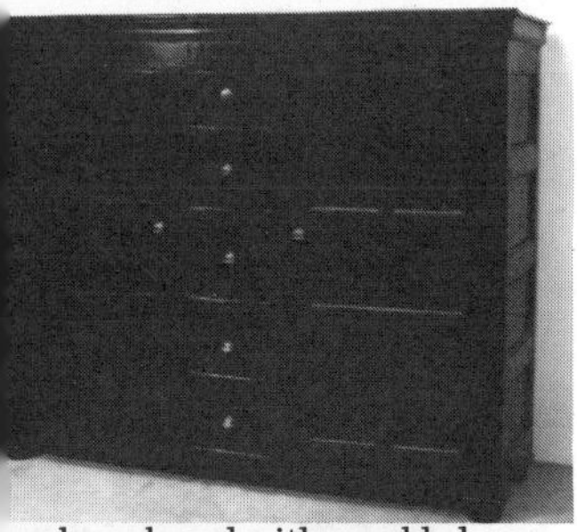

. oak cupboard with moulded nice, carved initials HR and date 33, panelled doors with H hinges ıking 5 central drawers with ıss knobs, early 18thC, 72in 3cm).
,000-4,000

A William and Mary oak court cupboard, the later top above a lunette carved frieze and recessed cupboards, 65½in (165cm).
$1,800-2,000

A Dutch rosewood and ebony veneered oak cupboard, with lion mask and drop ring handles, on large bun feet, 17thC, 66½in (167cm).
$4,000-5,000

An oak wardrobe with moulded cornice, 3 dummy drawers above central cupboard and 4 drawers below, brass drop handles, early 18thC, 60in (152cm).
$2,500-3,000

An oak wardrobe with 2 fielded panelled doors and central fielded panels, the base with 3 drawers with brass drop handles, replacement cornice, 18thC, 53½in (136cm).
$4,000-6,000

A North Wales oak panelled tridarn, good colour and patination, c1720, 52in (132cm).
$12,000-15,000

An oak spice cupboard, with geometric moulding, 17thC, 16½in (42cm).
$900-1,000

A carved oak court cupboard, mid-17thC, 55in (140cm).
$5,000-6,000

An oak and fruitwood chest in 2 parts, with arcaded sides, mid-17thC, 47in (119cm).
$3,000-4,000

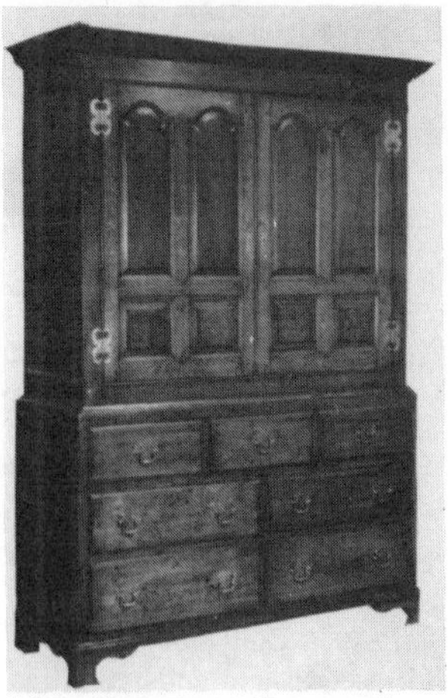

A late Georgian oak press, the top with moulded cornice above 2 arched fielded panel doors, above 3 dummy drawers and 4 short drawers, on bracket feet, 60in (152cm).
$3,000-4,000

An oak clothes cupboard with moulded cornice, 2 doors enclosing sliding trays, 2 similar doors below, 19thC, 48in (122cm).
$1,200-1,500

An oak court cupboard of panelled construction, on moulded plinth a block feet, 66in (168cm).
$1,400-2,000

An oak bow fronted corner cupboa with mahogany crossbanding to doors and reeding to the sides.
$700-900

An oak spice cupboard fitted with numerous small drawers.
$500-600

An oak bread and cheese cupboar with fielded and fretted door pane 2 drawers, on bracket feet.
$2,000-3,000

A carved buffet, with 2 cupboard doors centred by relief carved masks, 48in (122cm).
$600-1,000

An oak court cupboard, the upper section inlaid with light and dark wood strapwork and flanked by turned columns, the lower section with 2 fluted drawers above similarly inlaid cupboards, 61in (155cm).
$1,500-2,000

A Renaissance style oak press, carved with masks in gadrooned and strapwork borders applied wit points, the coffered top with 2 friez drawers above 2 fielded panel door applied with split mouldings between fluted column pilasters, o block feet, 73in (185cm).
$1,500-2,000

A Flemish oak and ebony press cupboard, with overhanging cornice, the base with a pair of conforming cupboard doors flanked by fluted pilasters above one drawer, with panelled sides, 57in (145cm).
$5,000-6,000

ressers

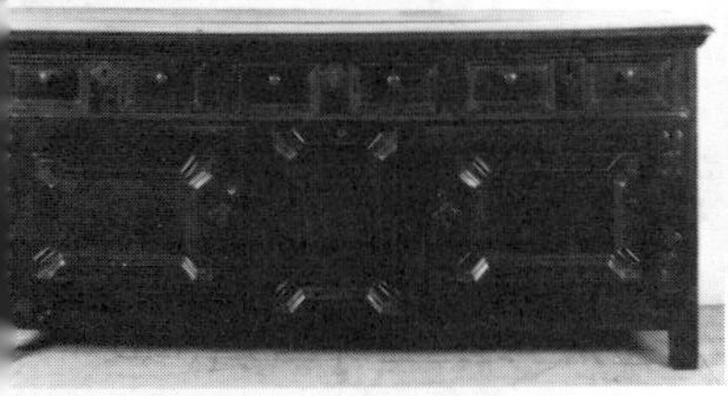

oak dresser base, with thumb
ılded top above 3 drawers and
ıpboard doors, mid-17thC, 72in
3cm).
,000-28,000

An oak Welsh dresser, on ring turned baluster legs, early 18thC, 75½in (193cm).
$5,000-6,000

An oak and mahogany banded dresser base, the top with a bevelled edge above 3 drawers and a shaped apron, on cabriole legs and pointed pad feet, early 18thC, 77in (196cm).
$6,000-8,000

oak dresser base with 5 moulded
ed long drawers, 2 fielded
elled cupboard doors with brass
handles, early 18thC, 72in
3cm).
00-6,000

An oak dresser, the drawers with brass handles and lock escutcheons, with cabriole front legs and plain square back legs, 18thC, 86in (220cm).
$8,000-9,000

hropshire oak dresser, with
awers with brass swan neck
dles and oval escutcheons, 72in
3cm).
00-3,500

An oak dresser with later plate rack, the base crossbanded with mahogany and fitted with 3 drawers above a shaped apron, restorations, 18thC, 76½in (194cm).
$3,000-5,000

A North Wales oak dresser, the rack with arched fielded panel cupboards and spice drawers, good colour and patination, c1720. **$18,000-25,000**

oak dresser, the superstructure
1 3 spice drawers, the 3 central
wers flanked by a pair of drawers
panelled cupboards, on plinth
e, 18thC, 72in (183cm).
00-10,000

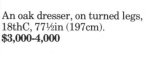

An oak dresser, on turned legs, 18thC, 77½in (197cm).
$3,000-4,000

An oak Welsh dresser with a three-tier back with iron hooks, 18thC, 54in (137cm).
$3,500-4,000

An oak dresser, on cabriole legs with claw and ball feet, 18thC and later, 74in (188cm).
$6,000-8,000

A Shropshire oak dresser, crossbanded with mahogany, c1770, 76in (193cm).
$10,000-12,000

A North Wales canopy dresser with small cupboards in the rack, good colour and patina, c1740.
$10,000-15,000

An oak dresser, the superstructur with 2 shelves and plain cornice, t base with 3 cockbeaded drawers, turned columns, mid-18thC, 73in (185cm).
$6,000-7,000

An oak Welsh dresser, the open top with 5 shallow drawers, 5 larger drawers to the base, above a central arched open dog kennel, flanked by shaped friezes, with pot board base, 18thC, 64in (163cm).
$12,000-14,000

A North Wales cupboard dresser with rack, mid-18thC.
$12,000-15,000

A mid-Georgian oak dresser with later plate rack, surmounted by a moulded cornice and centred by a pendulum clock with brass and ste dial, the base with 11 drawers, on later bracket feet, 94in (239cm).
$10,000-12,000

A George II oak dresser with mahogany crossbanding, pierced frieze, on 3 cabriole front supports, 68in (173cm).
$5,000-6,000

An oak dresser, the base mid-18thC, 69in (175cm).
$2,500-3,000

A George II oak dresser base, on cabriole legs, good colour and patin
$10,000-14,000

An oak dresser base, c1780.
$5,000-6,000

An oak dresser, with 3 short frieze drawers above 3 central drawers, flanked by a pair of panelled doors, late 18thC, 60in (152cm).
$2,500-3,000

A George III oak dresser base with cabriole legs, c1790.
$7,000-9,000

ieorge III oak dresser inlaid with
quered stringing and with
erae, 67in (170cm).
)00-6,000

oak dresser, with 3 short
wers with brass bail handles and
rced escutcheons, arcaded apron,
board and canted supports, 54in
7cm).
)00-8,000

ieorge III oak dresser, the later
ociated top with open shelves and
olection moulded cornice, on
ck feet, 55½in (141cm).
,000-5,000

oak joint stool with shaped
ze, 17thC, 17½in (45cm).
800-3,500

A George III oak low Welsh dresser, the planked top with 3 frieze drawers on baluster front legs and cross stretchers, adaptations, 83in (211cm).
$5,000-7,000

An oak Welsh dresser, with filled-in rack, breakfront base with 3 drawers, 2 cupboards and standing on bracket feet.
$4,000-5,000

An oak Welsh dresser having inlay to doors and drawers, with 2 cupboards, 6 drawers.
$3,500-4,000

An oak joint stool, with moulded rails, 17thC, 18in (46cm).
$2,000-2,500

An oak and mahogany dresser, the ogee moulded cornice above a lozenge inlaid frieze and 3 open shelves, on bracket feet, mid-19thC, 68in (173cm).
$3,000-4,000

An oak and mahogany breakfront dresser, 69in (175cm).
$3,000-4,000

Stools

An oak joint stool in original condition, c1630.
$1,600-2,000

A Welsh turned stool, in sycamore, 11in (29cm) high.
$120-200

An English oak joint stool, 17thC.
$2,000-3,000

An oak joint stool, early 18thC.
$600-700

An oak closed stool on cabriole le
c1740.
$800-1,000

A George II oak closed stool, with crossbanded hinged top, brass side handles, shaped aprons, on cabriole legs with pointed pad feet, 20½in (52cm).
$1,400-1,800

A walnut bench, c1800, 106
(269cm) long.
$300-400

An oak joint stool, the frieze carved with geometric half roundels, 20in (51cm).
$1,000-1,400

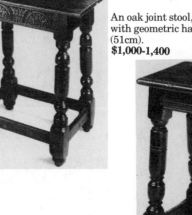

An oak joint stool with moulded frieze on turned legs.
$2,500-3,000

An oak joint stool with moulded rectangular top, carved frieze and baluster legs, 18½in (47cm).
$900-1,200

Tables

An oak refectory table, on baluster supports joined by stretchers, with renovations, 17thC, 95in (240cm).
$12,000-14,000

A William and Mary walnut veneered candle stand, 14in (35cm) diam.
$6,000-7,000

An oak refectory table with plank top, the frieze with floral lunette carving to 3 sides, on 4 baluster and ring turned legs, united by low stretchers, 17thC and later, 73in (183cm).
$2,000-3,000

An oak table with moulded top and one frieze drawer, on baluster legs joined by moulded stretchers, 17thC, 32in (81cm).
$5,000-7,500

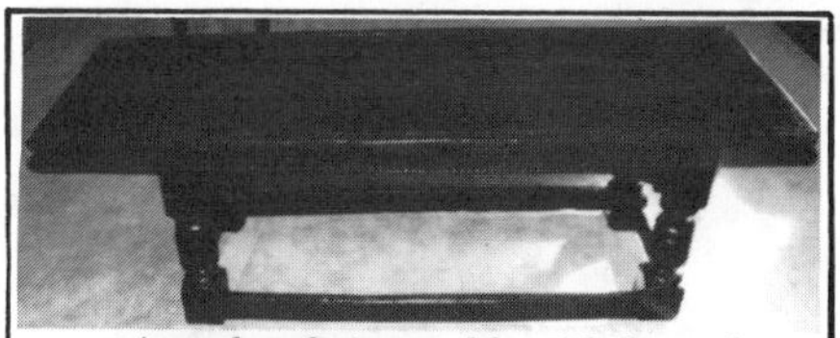

An oak refectory table with framed top and heavy turned legs, base shortened, one new stretcher, 17thC, 92in (230cm).
$14,000-19,000
If completely original **$35,000**

oak side table, in original
ndition with good patination,
thC, 26in (65cm).
,000-4,000

An oak side table, the top with moulded edge and frieze drawer over shaped front, c1690, 26in (65cm).
$3,000-4,000

An oak side table with bobbin turning, 17thC, 35½in (90cm).
$2,000-4,000

PATINATION

- ★ means layers of polish, dirt, dust, grease, etc, which have accumulated over the years — really the whole depth of surface of a piece of antique timber
- ★ the patination on different woods varies considerably but the same piece of wood will basically colour to the same extent (always allowing for bleaching by sunlight, etc)
- ★ walnut furniture often had an oil varnish applied to give it a good base to take the wax polish — this has led to the lovely mellow patina which is virtually impossible to fake
- ★ dirt and grease from handling are important guides (especially under drawer handles, on chair arms, etc) — these areas should have a darker colour — if they don't beware!
- ★ pieces which have carving or crevices will have accumulated dirt giving dark patches
- ★ colour and patination are probably the most important factors when valuing a piece of furniture
- ★ by repolishing a piece of furniture and removing evidence of patination, a dealer can conceal replacement or conversion

An oak gateleg table, 17thC, 33½in (85cm).
$2,500-3,000

An oak gateleg dining table, on bobbin turned legs, with square stretchers, top with later addition, mid-17thC.
$7,000-10,000

An oak and walnut side table, the plank top above a single drawer and wavy frieze, on part turned legs and stretchers, late 17thC, 34½in (88cm).
$2,500-3,000

An oak gateleg table with oval twin-flap top on spirally turned legs joined by conforming stretchers, basically 17thC, 60in (152cm) wide, open.
$6,000-7,000

An oak refectory table with plank top, moulded apron, shaped brackets and urn-shaped turned legs, late 17thC, 143in (359cm).
$9,000-10,000

An oak gateleg dining table, with plain edge on bobbin turned supports and moulded square stretchers, late 17thC, 60in (150cm) open.
$800-1,000

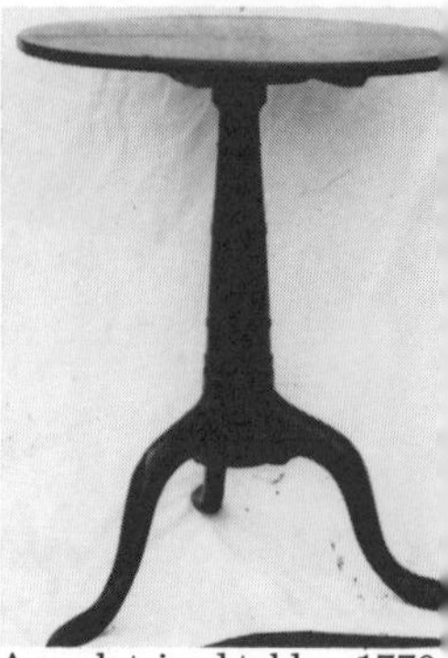
An oak tripod table, c1770.
$500-600

A Charles II oak gateleg dining table, with twin-flap top and spirally turned supports, joined by moulded stretchers, 59in (150cm).
$3,000-4,000

A Charles II oak side table, with planked top, the frieze with a moulded edge on bobbin turned legs and stretchers, 36in (91cm).
$8,000-9,000

A Charles II oak X-stretcher side table, c1685.
$3,000-5,000

An oak and walnut side table with Spanish feet, 17thC, 34½in (86cm).
$4,500-5,000

A William and Mary walnut side table, with single frieze drawer, on spiral turned supports with shaped X-stretcher, on bun feet, some restoration, 36in (91cm).
$5,000-6,000

A William and Mary oak side tab
c1690.
$4,000-6,000

An oak gateleg table, 17thC, 62in (154cm).
$2,500-3,000

An oak lowboy, 18thC, 38in (96cm).
$800-900

A small Queen Anne oak lowb
$3,000-5,000

An oak table with 2 drawers, early 18thC, 39in (99cm).
$6,000-7,000

Queen Anne oak gateleg table.
,000-4,000

A George I oak side table with one flap.
$3,000-4,000

A George II oak lowboy, crossbanded with mahogany.
$4,000-6,000

George II oak lowboy with star
lay and mahogany crossbanding.
,000-6,000

An oak tripod table, 18thC, 21in (53cm).
$400-500

A George II oak lowboy, crossbanded with mahogany.
$4,000-6,000

n oak side table with short
awers and shaped apron, the
rned supports joined with a
-stretcher, 18thC style, 30½in
7cm).
,000-5,000

A walnut and oak lowboy, the coffered top above 3 small drawers, on chamfered square moulded legs, basically 18thC, 31in (78cm).
$1,400-1,600

An early Georgian oak gateleg table, with oval twin-flap top, club legs and pad feet, 5 hinges stamped IP, 55in (140cm) open.
$2,500-3,000

small elm side table, with pad
et, 18thC, in mint condition, 22in
5cm).
1,800-2,000

An early Georgian crossbanded oak side table, with 3 short drawers, 33½in (84cm).
$3,000-4,000

An oak side table with a drawer, 19thC, 21½in (54cm).
$300-400

A Danish oak and pine centre table, with planked top and plain frieze previously fitted with a drawer, 3 feet replaced, basically 17thC, 55in (140cm).
$2,000-3,000

A Dutch oak draw-leaf table with moulded frieze fitted with a single drawer inlaid with ebony, 90in (228cm).
$2,000-2,500

A Dutch oak draw-leaf table, on bulbous turned supports joined by flat stretchers, on flattened bun fee basically 17thC, 77in (193cm).
$2,500-3,000

A Dutch oak refectory table with planked top with an undulating apron, on bulbous baluster legs joined by flat stretchers, 17thC style, 70½in (177cm).
$6,000-7,000

An oak table, probably French, c1680, 65in (164cm).
$2,500-3,000

A French provincial cherrywood wine table, 18thC, 57in (144cm).
$2,000-3,000

An elm and oak refectory table with solid figured elm top, the top 17th/18thC, the base early 19thC, 152½in (388cm).
$12,000-15,000

An oak lowboy, the top with thumb-moulded edge, fitted with one long and 2 short drawers, scrol shaped apron, on turned tapering supports, 33in (84cm).
$800-1,000

An oak candle stand, 18in (46cm) diam.
$400-600

An oak side table, with full width drawer, on turned legs, 31in (78cm).
$900-1,000

A drawing room sewing table, 16in (40cm) wide, closed.
$1,000-1,200

An oak side table, with single frieze drawer, on bobbin turned supports, pad feet, 27in (68cm).
$400-500

RNITURE

·ds

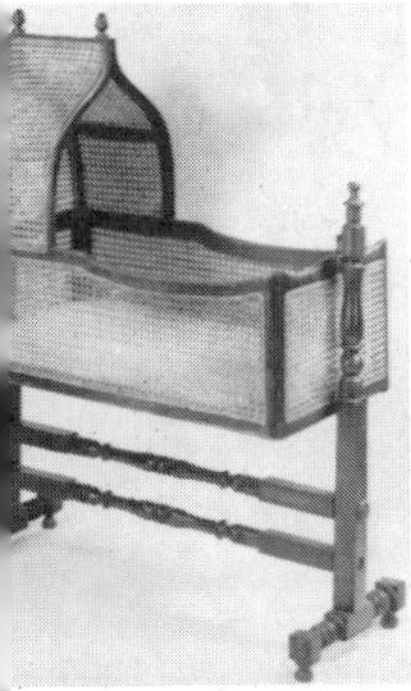

Regency mahogany cradle, with
ie filled rocking body, on turned
t with later oak finials, 38in
'cm).
000-1,400

Regency mahogany single
lstead, the ends with scrolled
esting, lacking sides, 42in (107cm)
le, and a pair of mahogany bed
es, 76½in (194cm) long.
800-2,000

nahogany four-poster bed, hung
h aquamarine watered silk
nbrequin hangings with bronze
oured tassels, with box spring,
ttress and valance, 54½in
9cm).
000-9,000

Charles X mahogany 'lit en
eau', with box spring and
ttress, 54in (137cm).
000-5,000

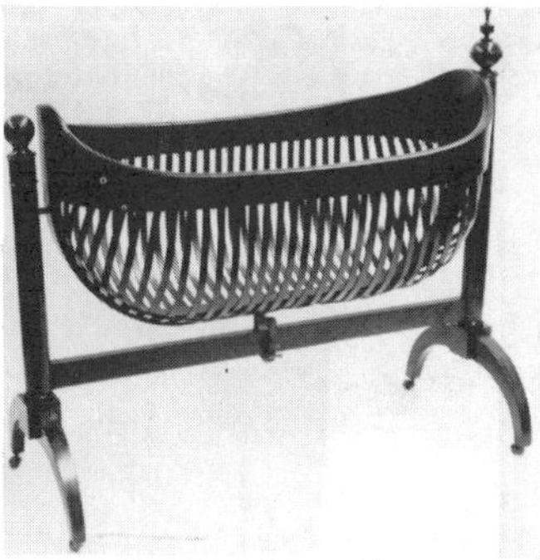

An early Victorian mahogany cradle, on caliper supports, 52in (132cm).
$900-1,000

A Charles X period carved walnut cradle, on scroll dolphin supports, on a cartouche shaped platform base.
$8,000-9,000

A Federal maple pencil post bedstead, New England, c1800, 72in (182.5cm).
$2,500-3,500

A mahogany four-poster bed in the manner of Chippendale, on fluted columns, each with a stiff leaf capital, on hipped cabochon headed cabriole legs and hairy paw feet, 84in (213cm).
$7,000-8,000

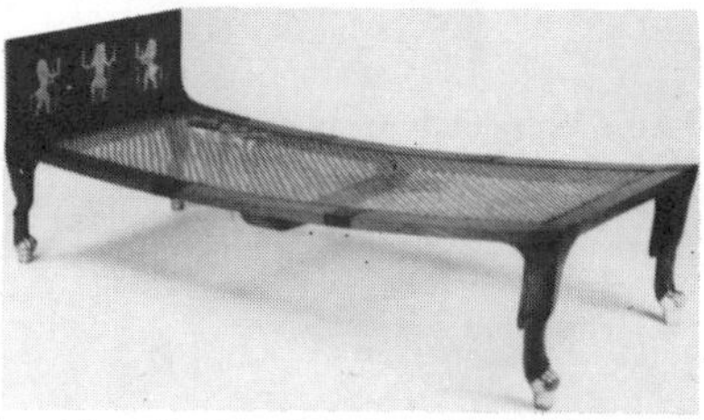

A walnut and ebonised Egyptian style day bed, in the style of J. Moyr Smith, the headboard with ebonised stringing and 3 carved and gilt panels, strung with webbed twine, on 4 stylised feline legs with gilt sabots, 28in (70cm).
$10,000-12,000

A mahogany four-poster bed, with pleated ivory silk canopy on spirally and ring-turned columns, with mattress and box spring, 78in (198cm).
$8,000-9,000

Bonheur du jour

In the Furniture section if there is only one measurement it usually refers to the width of the piece

A Regency style mahogany bonheur du jour, inlaid with brass, with cylinder roll top and hinged writing table with green baize lining, the base with full width drawer, which when opened rotates the cylinder top, 36in (92cm).
$2,000-3,000

A late Victorian painted rosewood bonheur du jour.
$3,000-3,500

A walnut bonheur du jour in the French manner, inlaid with satinwood panels, stringing and scrollwork, with 3 'Sèvres' porcelain plaques, 19thC, 43in (109cm).
$3,000-4,000

An Edwardian rosewood and boxwood strung bonheur du jour, with raised writing slope and 2 frieze drawers, on square tapering supports, 37in (94cm).
$1,500-2,000

A maple, inlaid and part ebonise[illegible] bonheur du jour, with applied ormolu decoration and inset paint[illegible] porcelain panels, 19thC, 49in (125cm).
$6,000-7,000

An Edwardian inlaid mahogany bonheur du jour, with brass galleried shelf, satinwood herringbone inlay and shell paterae, on square tapering supports and castors, 36in (92cm[illegible]
$800-1,000

An Edwardian mahogany bonheur du jour, inlaid with satinwood crossbanding and boxwood scroll motifs, with brass gallery and inset leather writing surface, the square tapering supports ending in brass castors, 36in (92cm).
$2,500-3,000

An Empire mahogany bonheur du jour, the top inset with mottled white marble with pierced three-quarter ormolu gallery, 34in (86cm).
$2,500-3,000

Breakfront Bookcases

An ormolu mounted kingwood, parquetry and Vernis Martin bonheur du jour, the sloping flap with a panel of frolicking cherubs below a tambour shutter enclosing a bird's-eye maple fitted interior, 25in (64cm).
$12,000-14,000

A George III mahogany breakfront bookcase, 96in (244cm).
$18,000-20,000

A late Georgian mahogany breakfront bookcase, the upper part with a moulded dentil cornice, enclosed by astragal glazed doors, on bracket feet, 96in (244cm).
$10,000-12,000

A George III mahogany breakfront bookcase, with pierced scrolled swan-neck pediment flanked by a later spindle gallery, 94½in (240cm).
$12,000-14,000

George III style mahogany reakfront bookcase, with dentil oulded cornice and fluted frieze, ie lower section with a gadrooned p fitted with 3 moulded panel oors between fluted uprights, on racket feet, 82in (208cm).
8,000-9,000

A Chippendale style mahogany breakfront bookcase, with gadrooned carved borders, the blind fret and moulded cornice above 4 astragal glazed doors, on cabriole legs with ball and claw feet, 67in (170cm).
$7,000-8,000

A William IV 'plum pudding' mahogany inverted breakfront library bookcase, by Thomas Mash, 102 Wardour St, on reduced plinth base, lacking cornice, 155in (394cm).
$5,000-6,000

A mahogany breakfront library bookcase, with swan neck pediment and urn finials, each section with adjustable shelves, mid-19thC, 105in (267cm).
$12,000-15,000

mahogany breakfront bookcase, ith secrétaire drawer, 19thC.
6,000-7,000

A mahogany breakfront bookcase, decorated with blind fret bands, on plinth base, 19thC, 75in (191cm).
$10,000-12,000

A figured mahogany breakfront library bookcase, in George III style, late 19thC, 78in (198cm).
$8,000-9,000

breakfront bookcase, the pilaster upports surmounted by carved canthus leaf brackets, the lower ection with 18 drawers with ooden knob handles and Bramah ocks, late 19thC, 144in (365cm).
10,000-12,000

A mahogany breakfront bookcase with the label of Edwards & Roberts, the glazed doors enclosing adjustable shelves, 78in (198cm).
$16,000-18,000

George III mahogany breakfront ookcase, the upper part with scroll ediment and fluted cornice, lower art with 4 panelled doors applied ith oval paterae medallions, on linth base, 98in (249cm).
24,000-28,000

Make the Most of Miller's

CONDITION is absolutely vital when assessing the value of an antique. Damaged pieces on the whole appreciate much less than perfect examples. However a rare, desirable piece may command a high price even when damaged

An early Victorian mahogany breakfront bookcase, applied with acanthus carved scroll mouldings, the top section with a banded cornice, the 3 panelled cupboard doors divided by pilasters, on plinth base, 55in (140cm).
$2,500-3,000

A Victorian burr walnut breakfront library bookcase, inlaid with marquetry arabesques and applied with cabochoned mouldings, on plinth base, 107in (272cm).
$8,000-10,000

A late Victorian mahogany breakfront library bookcase, the top section with a bolection moulded cornice, 102in (260cm).
$7,000-9,000

A Victorian walnut breakfront low bookcase, the frieze inlaid with boxwood scrolls, 66in (168cm).
$2,500-3,000

A Victorian burr walnut dwarf breakfront bookcase with scroll fretwork panels to the 2 doors, flanked by scroll brackets and open shelving, 72in (183cm).
$3,000-4,000

A mahogany dwarf breakfront bookcase, the moulded top above 4 glazed panelled doors, between fluted column pilasters, on turned bun feet, basically early 19thC, 63in (160cm).
$8,000-9,000

Bureau Bookcases

A mahogany bureau bookcase, the hinged slope enclosing a fitted interior above 4 long drawers, on bracket feet, 18thC associated, 39½in (100cm).
$6,000-7,000

A George III style mahogan[y] bookcase, 48in (122cm).
$800-1,000

An early George II walnut bureau bookcase, the upper section enclosing shelves and 3 drawers, the lower section with a herringbone banded fall front enclosing a fitted interior, 40in (102cm).
$11,000-13,000

A George III mahogany bureau and associated bookcase, 40in (102cm).
$2,000-3,000

A George III mahogany bureau bookcase, the top with 2 adjustable shelves enclosed by a pair of doors with outline moulded crossbanded panels, 42in (107cm).
$3,000-4,000

A George III mahogany bureau bookcase, with broken pediment and dentil moulded cornice above blind fret carved frieze and 2 astragal moulded glazed panel doors, the slope with fitted interio[r] on ogee bracket feet, 47in (119cm)
$7,000-8,000

A mahogany bureau bookcase, the sloping flap enclosing a fitted interior, adaptations, late 18th and 19thC, 42½in (108cm).
$3,000-4,000

ι George III mahogany bureau
ookcase with moulded cornice,
rossbanded glazed doors, quarter
eneered and inlaid fall front, with
ılly fitted marquetry inlaid
nterior, the drawers with brass
lrop handles, double pilaster
orners, 48in (122cm).
;6,000-8,000

A George IV mahogany bureau bookcase, the hinged sloping flap enclosing a fitted interior, above 4 long graduating drawers, on bracket feet, 46in (117cm).
$5,000-6,000

A Georgian mahogany bureau bookcase, the upper part enclosed by a pair of barred glass doors, the fall front enclosing a fitted interior, 47in (119cm).
$5,000-6,000

An inlaid mahogany bureau bookcase, the fall front enclosing fully fitted and inlaid interior, ogee bracket feet, early 19thC, 48in (122cm).
$4,000-5,000

ι late Regency mahogany cylinder
ureau bookcase, the top section
vith a bobbin moulded cornice
nclosed by a bevelled Gothic lancet
stragal glazed door, 44½in (113cm).
;3,000-4,000

A mahogany bookcase, the serpentine base fitted with 2 short and 3 long drawers, between fluted canted angles, on bracket feet, 19thC.
$5,000-6,000

A walnut double domed bureau bookcase, the top section with partly fitted interior and a pair of candle slides, the crossbanded sloping flap enclosing a fitted interior, above 3 graduated drawers, on bun feet, 41in (104cm).
$9,000-10,000

A mahogany and parcel gilt bureau bookcase, with dentilled cornice and blind fret frieze above 2 glazed doors, the bureau with hinged slope enclosing well fitted interior, on ogee bracket feet, 40in (101cm).
$6,000-7,000

\ Victorian 'plum pudding'
nahogany bookcase, the panelled
loors below enclosing a cellaret
lrawer, 52in (132cm).
$5,000-6,000

An Edwardian mahogany bureau bookcase, with architectural pediment above astragal glazed doors, the fall enclosing a satinwood interior, above a drawer and panelled cupboards, 37½in (96cm).
$3,000-4,000

A Victorian bowfronted bookcase, inlaid with foliate marquetry with satinwood banded and boxwood line borders, on square tapering legs, 35in (90cm).
$4,000-6,000

A mahogany bureau bookcase, the cylinder fall enclosing a well fitted interior, the whole with boxwood stringing, on bracket feet, 46in (117cm).
$4,000-6,000

Dwarf bookcases

A George III mahogany double-sided dwarf open bookcase, with stepped solid ends, 30in (76cm).
$6,000-7,000

A late Georgian mahogany dwarf bookcase, 45in (114cm).
$1,500-2,000

A pair of Regency gilt and cream painted dwarf bookcases, with mottled grey marble tops and adjustable shelves, on shaped feet carved with anthemions, re-decorated, 16½in (42cm).
$7,000-8,000

A pair of early Victorian satinwood dwarf bookcases, with moulded leaf cornices and adjustable shelves, the sides headed by leafy scrolls, 27in (69cm).
$7,000-8,000

A Regency mahogany dwarf open bookcase, with shaped gallery top, 3 shelves over a crossbanded and inlaid base fitted with 2 drawers, 22in (56cm).
$3,000-4,000

A parcel gilt and green painted revolving bookstand, the 4 tiers with leather book spine dividers, the faceted marbled central shaft on plinth base, 41in (104cm) high.
$5,000-6,000

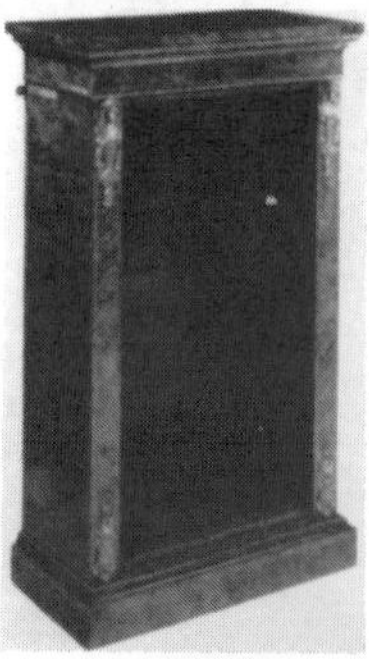

A burr walnut and gilt metal mounted dwarf bookcase, banded in tulipwood and inlaid with boxwood lines, 29in (74cm).
$2,500-3,000

A satinwood and yew-wood bookcase, early 19thC style, 28in (71cm).
$4,000-5,000

A mahogany dwarf bookcase, with one long drawer with metal knobs, 19thC, 23½in (60cm).
$700-900

A Regency rosewood open bookcase, with raised mirrored back, 44in (112cm).
$5,000-6,000

ibrary Bookcases

A William IV rosewood bookcase, with moulded cornice above a pair of panelled doors filled with leather book spines, stamped MANUFACTURED BY W & G POWELL, 6 Argyle Street, Bath, 34½in (88cm).
$5,000-6,000

A William IV mahogany bookcase, with 2 glazed upper doors and panelled doors below, 58in (147cm).
$3,000-4,000

William IV mahogany bookcase, e astragal glazed doors flanked by ain pilasters with palmette pitals and bases, on octagonal et, 45in (114cm), width reduced.
,000-4,000

A mahogany and rosewood glazed bookcase, 19thC.
$50,000-60,000

A William IV carved rosewood open bookcase, with graduated shelves surmounted by mirrored superstructure, with pierced fret cresting flanked by foliate S-scrolls, 36in (91cm).
$2,000-3,000

Victorian walnut bookcase, the wer section with 4 slim drawers bove 4 panelled doors between olute headed pilasters, 93in 236cm).
6,000-8,000

A late Victorian carved oak library bookcase, with moulded dentil carved top, 5 turned pilasters with Ionic capitals and reeded lower sections, the 4 apron drawers with brass drop handles, 130in (332cm).
$3,000-4,000

An Edwardian inlaid mahogany bookcase, with 2 bowfront drawers and serpentine undertier, on square tapering legs, 37in (94cm).
$1,000-1,300

A mahogany bookcase, the base fitted with a leather-lined slide above 2 short and 2 long drawers simulated as short drawers, on plinth base, 47in (119cm).
$4,000-5,000

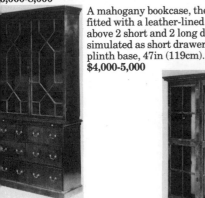

walnut bookcase, with moulded ornice above glazed cupboard oors, the stand with spirally turned egs and conforming stretchers, 49in 125cm).
3,000-10,000

A Victorian mahogany breakfront library bookcase, inlaid with satinwood urns, paterae and radial geometric lines, in blind fret banded borders, 116in (295cm).
$5,000-6,000

Secrétaire Bookcases

A Continental mahogany bookcase, with 2 glazed doors enclosing adjustable shelves, mid-19thC, 88in (224cm).
$2,000-3,000

A George III flamed mahogany secrétaire bookcase, with a drawer with fitted interior and pigeonholes, above a pair of figured cupboard doors, 50in (127cm).
$8,000-9,000

A George III mahogany secrétair bookcase, the top section with an inlaid cavetto moulded cornice, above a pair of mirrored and astragal glazed doors, on splayed bracket feet, adaptations, 34in (87cm).
$10,000-12,000

A George III mahogany secrétaire bookcase, with a drawer enclosing an interior of drawers and pigeonholes, the bracket feet flanking a waved apron, c1800, 38in (97cm).
$7,000-8,000

A Georgian mahogany secrétaire bookcase, with fitted interior and pigeonholes, 3 long drawers belo on bracket feet, alterations, 43in (109cm).
$4,000-5,000

A Regency mahogany and satinwood crossbanded secrétaire bookcase, the upper part with a shaped pediment enclosed by a pair of concentric lozenge panel doors with ebony stringing, 41in (104cm).
$8,000-12,000

A Regency mahogany secrétaire bookcase, the secrétaire drawer with camphorwood veneered drawers and pigeonholes, above 3 further drawers and a bowed apron, upper part restored, 36½in (92cm).
$2,000-3,000

A Regency mahogany secrétaire bookcase, the base with a fitted secrétaire drawer above 2 later inlaid panelled cupboards enclosin slides, on bracket feet, 46in (177cm)
$10,000-12,000

A Regency mahogany secrétaire bookcase, with arched cornice above a pair of rectilinear astragal glazed doors, the lower section with secrétaire drawer with fitted interior, above 3 further long drawers, 35in (90cm).
$3,000-4,000

A George III mahogany secrétaire bookcase, with arched cornice above 2 Gothic glazed doors, restorations, top and lower part possibly associated, 47½in (121cm).
$4,000-6,000

A late George III mahogany and satinwood secrétaire bookcase.
$6,000-7,000

A George III mahogany and tulipwood banded secrétaire bookcase, with arched dentil cornice surmounted by urn finials, the bowfront lower section with 2 small drawers above a secrétaire fitted with satinwood drawers and pigeonholes, 44in (112cm).
$20,000-22,000

A George III mahogany secrétaire bookcase, the drawer with boxwood and ebony stringing and enclosing pigeonholes and small drawers, 2 panelled doors below enclosing trays, 47½in (121cm).
$5,000-6,000

A William IV mahogany secrétaire library bookcase, applied with paterae and acanthus carved scroll mouldings, the top section with a bolection moulded cornice, 82in (208cm).
$7,000-8,000

A mahogany secrétaire bookcase, inlaid with boxwood lines, the deep writing drawer above 2 panelled cupboard doors, on splayed bracket feet, early 19thC, 42in (107cm).
$4,000-5,000

A Victorian oak secrétaire bookcase, with adjustable shelves, the secrétaire drawer flanked by 4 small drawers, 3 panelled doors below, centred with carved busts in relief, raised on a plinth base, 66in (168cm).
$2,500-3,000

A mahogany bookcase, the lower section with 2 cupboard doors as 8 dummy drawers, flanking 4 short drawers, on plinth base, 62in (157cm).
$4,000-6,000

Buckets

A George III brass bound mahogany plate bucket, with spiral turned swing handle, 16in (40cm) high.
$3,000-4,000

A George III brass bound mahogany plate bucket, with brass swing handle and pierced slatted sides, with later tin liner, 12in (30.5cm) diam.
$2,000-3,000

A George III brass bound mahogany coal bucket, with brass swing handle, slatted sides and brass liner, the base later, 14in (33.5cm) wide.
$2,000-3,000

A George III brass bound plate bucket, 14¼in (37cm) diam.
$2,000-3,000

A Dutch fruitwood and ebonised bucket, constructed with alternating strips, on a turned shaft and circular base, with ball feet, 17½in (45cm) high.
$2,000-2,500

A Dutch fruitwood and ebonised bucket of rippled tapering form, constructed of alternating strips, with brass swing handle, 12in (30.5cm) high.
$2,500-3,000

Bureaux

A Queen Anne walnut bureau, the crossbanded sloping flap enclosing a fitted interior, on later bracket feet, formerly with bun feet, restored, 36in (92cm).
$7,000-9,000

A walnut bureau, the fall front with feather stringing, the interior with well and stepped drawers, early 18thC, 34in (86cm).
$8,000-9,000

A walnut bureau with feather lined inlay, the flap enclosing a fitted interior and well above 2 simulated frieze drawers, on a double gate spiralled baluster frame, with Spanish scroll feet, joined by undulating flat cross-stretchers, part early 18thC, 36in (92cm).
$4,000-6,000

A George I style walnut bureau with feather lined inlay, the flap enclosing a fitted interior, on bracket feet, 25in (64cm).
$2,000-3,000

In the Furniture section if there is only one measurement it usually refers to the width of the piece

A walnut bureau, the crossbanded lid enclosing a fitted interior, above 2 short and 2 long graduated drawers, on bracket feet, parts 18thC, 36in (92cm).
$10,000-12,000

A George II walnut bureau with crossbanded fall enclosing a fitted stepped interior with well, column drawers, pigeonholes and crossbanded drawers, on ogee bracket feet, 37in (94cm).
$4,000-4,500

An elm, burr-veneered and crossbanded bureau, the walnut banded and feather strung fall enclosing a shaped fitted interior and well with slide, 18thC, with later top, 36in (92cm).
$6,000-7,000

A George II walnut bureau, inlaid overall with chevron bands, the sloping flap enclosing a fitted interior, on a later undulating bracket base, 37½in (95cm).
$5,000-7,000

George III mahogany and
ycamore bureau, the leather-lined
haped spreading fall flap enclosing
fitted interior above a pair of
upboard doors, on square tapering
et, 30in (76cm).
,000-5,000

An early George III mahogany bureau, the sloping fall front concealing a fully fitted interior, on ogee bracket feet, 41in (104cm).
$6,000-7,000

A George III mahogany bureau, the hinged slope enclosing a fitted interior, above 2 short and 3 long graduated drawers, on bracket feet, 36in (92cm).
$3,000-4,000

. George III mahogany bureau, the
ap enclosing fitted interior above
graduated long drawers, on
racket feet, 35½in (91cm).
3,000-4,000

A George III mahogany bureau, with boxwood and ebony string inlay, the sloping fall front enclosing a satinwood and ebony strung interior, above 2 short and 3 long drawers, on ogee bracket feet, 48in (122cm).
$2,500-3,000

A George III mahogany bureau, with later brass handles, 36in (92cm).
$2,500-3,000

George III mahogany bureau,
ith fitted interior, 39in (99cm).
,000-4,000

A George III inlaid mahogany bowfront secrétaire chest, with crossbanded top, the secrétaire drawer with maple faced fitted interior and 3 graduated long drawers below, shaped frieze on splayed supports, 45in (114cm).
$2,500-3,000

A Georgian mahogany bureau, with fitted interior, standing on bracket feet.
$2,000-3,000

A George III mahogany bureau, with sloping fall front enclosing a cupboard, drawers and pigeonholes, 4 graduated long drawers below, on shaped bracket feet, 43in (109cm).
$2,000-3,000

A George III mahogany bureau, with sloping flap enclosing a fitted interior, restorations, 37in (95cm).
$3,000-4,000

A George III mahogany bureau on stand, the sloping flap enclosing a fitted interior above a slide, 32in (81cm).
$8,000-9,000

A Georgian mahogany secrétaire, with fitted interior, inlay to drawer, with shaped apron and standing on bracket feet.
$2,000-2,500

A walnut bureau, with crossbanded sloping flap and fitted interior above 4 graduated long drawers, on bracket feet, 37½in (96cm).
$4,000-5,000

A mahogany and tulipwood banded bureau, the top centred by an inlaid classical urn, the fall front with an oval crossbanded panel inlaid with a flowering urn, enclosing a fitted interior, above 4 graduated drawers, on bracket feet, c1880, 33in (84cm).
$4,000-5,000

A mahogany bureau with 4 graduated drawers, on double ogee feet, early 19thC, 45in (114cm).
$1,200-1,500

A small mahogany bureau with well fitted interior, c1880.
$3,000-4,000

A golden burr walnut bureau with slide, c1900.
$3,000-4,000

A mahogany bureau, with 4 drawers and brass drop handles, 19thC, 26in (66cm).
$2,000-3,000

A William IV cylinder bureau.
$3,000-4,000

A Victorian mahogany cylinder bureau.
$4,500-5,000

An Edwardian satinwood, harewood and foliate marquetry cylinder bureau, the top with a mirror backed brass galleried superstructure, the cylinder enclosing a lined sliding writing surface, pen drawers, and stationery compartments, 2 short drawers below, 35in (90cm).
$5,000-6,000

A ladies writing bureau with floral marquetry, gilt metal mounts and brass gallery, on cabriole legs.
$5,000-6,000

ׂ Continental bombé shaped
vriting bureau, decorated with
•arquetry panels, gilt metal mounts
nd gallery to back.
1,200-1,500

A Dutch marquetry and walnut bureau, 18thC.
$12,000-13,000

A Dutch walnut and marquetry breakfront bureau, the hinged slope enclosing a fitted interior, on bun feet, adaptations, 18thC, 41in (104cm).
$7,000-8,000

ׂ Dutch mahogany and marquetry
•ombé bureau, the cylinder
·nclosing a fitted interior with
eather writing surface, the whole
nlaid with floral sprays, the sides
vith flowering urns, mid-18thC
·vith later inlay, 44in (112cm).
ι6,000-7,000

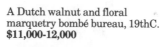

A Dutch walnut and marquetry bureau, the fall inlaid with an urn of flowers, birds and acanthus scrolls, enclosing a stepped interior, the waved front with 3 long drawers, the outset corners continuing to lion's paw feet, c1770, 46in (117cm).
$10,000-12,000

A Dutch marquetry writing bureau, decorated with floral and basket panels, with well interior, on bracket feet, 18thC.
$8,000-9,000

A Dutch marquetry writing bureau, with bombé base, fitted interior, floral inlays and ball and claw feet.
$11,000-12,000

A Dutch walnut and floral marquetry bombé bureau, 19thC.
$11,000-12,000

A Dutch marquetry miniature bureau, the hinged slope enclosing drawers and pigeonholes, on shaped bracket feet, 16in (41cm).
$6,000-8,000

A Louis Philippe ormolu mounted rosewood parquetry bureau de dame, with dished top and frieze drawer, the bombé fall front inlaid with floral marquetry, with 4 serpentine interior drawers and recess, on cabriole legs, 28in (70cm).
$4,000-5,000

A Dutch marquetry inlaid bureau, the shaped sloping flap enclosing a fitted interior, the waved frieze with one drawer, on cabriole legs, 36½in (92cm).
$4,000-5,000

A French mahogany and Vernis Martin bureau à cylindre, with red and white mottled marble top, with pierced three-quarter gallery, the cylinder and slide painted with romantic figures in a landscape, on brass filled fluted turned tapering legs, 36in (91cm).
$3,000-4,000

A South German walnut bureau, decorated with burr walnut panels, 18thC, 52in (132cm).
$18,000-20,000

A German mahogany and brass mounted cylinder bureau, in the Empire style, with 2 long drawers between brass stiles, on square tapered fluted legs terminating in block feet, 19thC, 49in (125cm).
$8,000-10,000

A burr walnut veneered bureau on stand, the sloping flap enclosing a mirrored interior, the stand with a gadrooned edge, 2 frieze drawers, on scroll carved end supports joined by spirally turned stretchers, probably German, 19thC, 38in (97cm).
$4,000-6,000

A South German burr elm and fruitwood bureau, the fall front inlaid with 2 panels of strapwork designs, enclosing a replaced interior, the serpentine lower section fitted with 2 long drawers, on cabriole legs, 33½in (84cm).
$1,500-2,000

Bureau Cabinets

A William and Mary walnut and chevron banded escritoire, with brass handles, later bun feet, 44in (112cm).
$8,000-10,000

A walnut bureau cabinet, with a pair of panelled cupboard doors and 2 candle slides, the crossbanded sloping flap enclosing a fitted interior, early 18thC, 41½in (105cm).
$6,000-8,000

A Georgian bureau bookcase, c1760, 42in (107cm).
$9,000-11,000

A walnut secrétaire cabinet with moulded dentilled cornice, the fall flap enclosing a fitted interior, the base with a pair of cupboard doors enclosing 2 short and 2 long drawers, possibly Dutch, late 17thC, 44in (112cm).
$6,000-8,000

A Queen Anne walnut crossbanded and featherstrung bureau cabinet, the upper part fitted with shelves and 2 drawers, enclosed by arched veneered panel doors, the lower part with sloping fall enclosing a fitted interior, 60in (163cm) high.
$8,000-10,000

A George I walnut bureau cabinet, the upper part with adjustable shelves, enclosed by a pair of fielded panel doors with re-entrant corners, 42in (106cm).
$15,000-18,000

A George III mahogany bureau cabinet with dentilled cornice, the frieze carved with blind fretwork above a pair of panelled cupboard doors and 2 candle slides, the flap enclosing a fitted interior, 47½in (120cm).
$9,000-10,000

A George III mahogany bureau cabinet, the bureau with a hinged slope enclosing a fitted interior, above 2 short and 3 graduated long drawers between canted angles inlaid with flowers, on shaped bracket feet, 48in (122cm).
$4,000-6,000

A George III mahogany bureau cabinet, the broken swan neck pediment centred by an urn finial, the lower section with 4 long drawers, on bracket feet, restorations, 2 parts associated, 41in (104cm).
$6,000-9,000

A mid-Georgian ash bureau cabinet, crossbanded and featherbanded, the bureau with hinged slope enclosing fitted interior, 40in (101cm).
$12,000-14,000

A walnut bureau cabinet, the top section with 2 panelled doors, the base with a featherbanded slope enclosing a fitted interior, 38½in (98cm).
$6,000-9,000

A mahogany secrétaire cabinet, inlaid with satinwood bands, radial boxwood lines and applied with leafy paterae, with a deep writing drawer and 3 long graduated drawers, on plinth base, 46in (117cm).
$2,000-3,000

A mahogany secrétaire of narrow proportions, the ogee moulded cornice above 4 graduated drawers and a secrétaire faced as 2 further drawers, a panelled cupboard below, 21in (53cm).
$3,000-4,500

A Louis XVI style mahogany secrétaire à abattant, the Carrara marble slab above a drawer and a figured fall, cupboards below, flanked by brass fitted pilasters continuing to toupie feet, c1860, 23½in (60cm).
$5,500-7,000

An Anglo-Dutch walnut and gilt embellished double dome bureau cabinet, the upper part with a fitted interior, enclosed by a pair of glazed panel doors between pilaster stiles, 2 candle slides below, the lower part with a sloping fall enclosing a fitted interior and parquetry slide, above 4 short and 2 long drawers, on later bun feet, early 18thC, 45in (115cm).
$40,000-52,000

Collectors' Cabinets

A mahogany numismatist's cabinet, fitted with 6 long graduated drawers, some with coin apertures, on brass castors, 19thC, 17½in (44cm).
$400-600

A mahogany artist's cabinet, the 22 drawers fitted with oil colour specimen palettes, enclosed by a glazed door, recessed carrying handle to the top, 19thC, 15in (38cm) high.
$200-400

Display Cabinets

A walnut display cabinet of Queen Anne style, on bracket feet, stamped Gill & Reigate, London, 27in (68cm).
$2,500-3,000

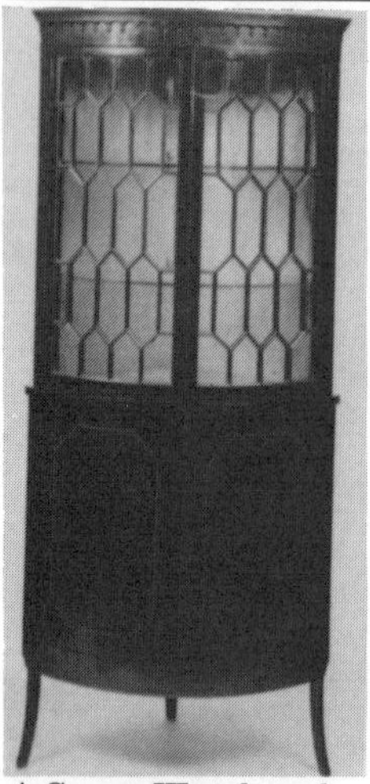

A George III style mahogany bowfront corner display cabinet, inlaid with chequered boxwood lines, with bolection moulded cornice and arcaded frieze, above a pair of astragal glazed doors and a pair of panel cupboard doors, 31in (78cm).
$1,400-1,600

A Boulle china display cabinet, mid-19thC, 44in (112cm).
$3,000-3,500

A pair of white lacquered and gilt metal mounted display cabinets, the lower section fitted with a single frieze drawer, on cabriole legs headed by foliate clasps, on sabots, late 19thC, 39½in (100cm).
$5,000-6,000

An ebonised wood and Boulle cabinet, with ormolu mountings, single glazed panel door, on shaped plinth base, 19thC, 29in (73cm).
$800-1,000

A satinwood, mahogany banded and ebony inlaid display cabinet, with broken architectural pediment, the whole inlaid with swags and ribbons, on tapering supports with spade feet, stamped Edwards & Roberts, late 19thC, 28in (70cm).
$6,000-7,000

A walnut display cabinet, with inlay and ormolu mounts, 19thC.
$800-1,000

A mahogany display cabinet, 19thC.
$1,400-1,600

ı Edwardian mahogany and
laid cabinet.
,000-4,000

An Edwardian Sheraton style mahogany corner cabinet, inlaid with vase, foliate scrolls and paterae, with ebony and boxwood stringing, 27in (69cm).
$3,000-4,000

An Edwardian mahogany bowfront display cabinet, inlaid with radial and chequered boxwood lines, the simulated dentilled cavetto moulded cornice above a glazed door, with serpentine undertier, 49in (125cm).
$3,000-4,000

n Edwardian mahogany display
ıbinet, outlined with satinwood
ınding, boxwood and ebony
ringing, on tapering square legs,
6in (91cm).
1,600-1,800

An Edwardian mahogany and satinwood inlaid two-tier display cabinet, with Gothic latticed glazed doors, raised on square tapering legs with spade feet, 30in (76cm).
$1,000-1,400

An Edwardian mahogany display cabinet, inlaid with satinwood bands and geometric boxwood line borders, on cabriole legs with pad feet, 72in (183cm).
$1,400-1,600

n Edwardian mahogany display
ıbinet on shaped legs, the door
ith carved beading, with piano top
splay section above, and shaped
irror surmount, 22in (56cm).
1,000-1,200

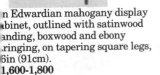

An Edwardian mahogany and marquetry display cabinet, inlaid throughout, the base with 2 doors inlaid with ribbon-tied baskets of flowers and sprays, 34in (86cm).
$7,000-8,000

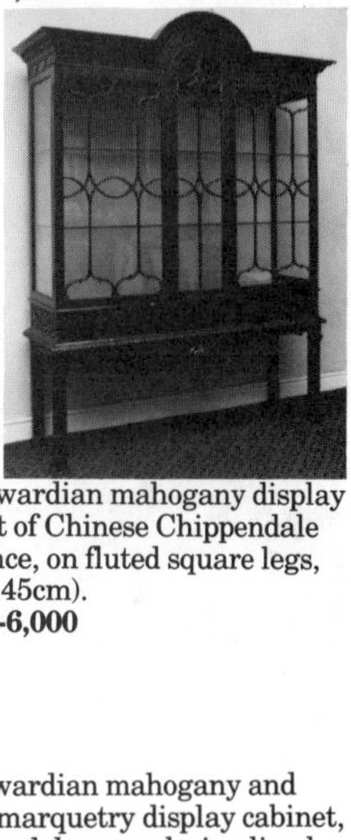

An Edwardian mahogany display cabinet of Chinese Chippendale influence, on fluted square legs, 57in (145cm).
$5,000-6,000

A walnut display cabinet with
ırched glazed door, standing on
arved cabriole legs with ball and
law feet.
$2,000-3,000

A mahogany and satinwood display cabinet, the top section with a domed cornice applied with finials and inlaid with a sunburst lunette, above a single glazed panel door, on square tapered legs, 30in (76cm).
$2,000-3,000

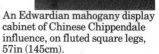

An Edwardian mahogany and foliate marquetry display cabinet, the glazed doors enclosing lined shelves, on square tapered legs joined by an undertier, 47½in (121cm).
$4,000-5,000

A mahogany display cabinet, with moulded cornice above 2 pointed arched astragal glazed doors enclosing lined shelves, the lower section fitted with 2 columns of 4 drawers, on bracket feet, 61½in (156cm).
$4,000-6,000

An Austrian Biedermeier cabinet, lined with original William Morris lining paper, 41½in (105cm).
$5,000-6,000

A Dutch walnut miniature display cabinet of 18thC design, with arched and moulded cornice, fitted with 2 velvet-lined shelves, enclosed by a pair of glazed doors, with 3 shaped drawers below.
$1,800-2,000

A Dutch walnut and marquetry display cabinet, the 2 panelled doors and angled sides inlaid with urns and trailing foliage motifs, late 18th/early 19thC, 51in (130cm).
$10,000-12,000

A Dutch walnut china cabinet of canted outline, the lower section of bombé form fitted with 3 long drawers between waved angles flanked by 2 cupboard doors, on ball and claw feet, 66in (168cm).
$3,000-4,000

A Louis XVI Transitional style mahogany vitrine, with fabric lined interior, profuse gilt metal mounts and borders, on cabriole supports, 46in (117cm).
$3,000-4,000

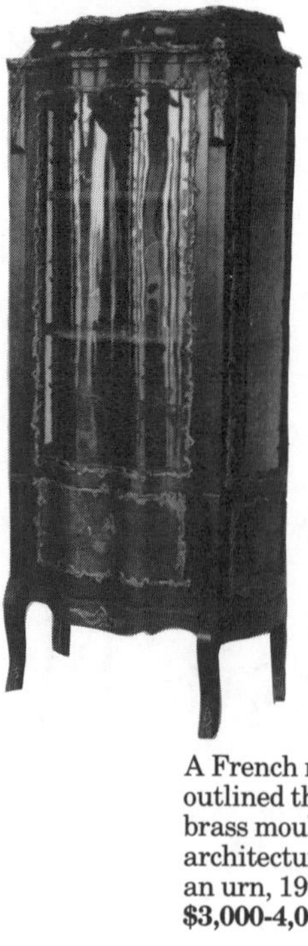

A French vitrine display cabinet, with shaped front, gilt metal mounts and Vernis Martin panels.
$3,000-4,000

A Louis XV Transitional style kingwood standing vitrine, applied with gilt metal mounts, on cabriole legs mounted with sabots and caryatid headings, 35in (89cm).
$2,000-3,000

A French kingwood breakfront display cabinet, applied with gilt metal mounts, with beige marble top above a parquetry frieze and 3 glazed doors enclosing glass shelves, late 19thC, 47in (119cm).
$4,000-5,000

A French mahogany vitrine, outlined throughout with plain gilt brass mouldings, the galleried architectural pediment centred by an urn, 19thC, 42in (107cm).
$3,000-4,000

FRENCH FURNITURE PERIODS

1610-1643	Louis XIII
1643-1715	Louis XIV
1715-1723	Regence
1723-1774	Louis XV
1774-1793	Louis XVI
DIRECTOIRE	
1793-1795	Revolution
1795-1799	Directoire
1799-1804	Consulate
1804-1815	Empire
RESTORATION	
1815-1824	Restoration
1824-1830	Charles X
LOUIS-PHILIPPE	
1830-1848	Louis-Philippe
1848-1852	2nd Republic
1852-1870	Napoleon III
1871-1940	3rd Republic

A French mahogany and ormolu mounted vitrine, surmounted by a marble top, on tapered legs headed with foliate ornament and terminating in sabots.
$2,000-3,000

Cabinets on Stands

A William and Mary style walnut and marquetry cabinet on stand, the floral inlaid frieze above a pair of panelled doors, similarly inlaid, on slender inverted baluster turned columns joined by scrolled stretchers, 38in (97cm).
$1,500-1,800

A walnut, tortoiseshell and Boulle cabinet on stand, the arched moulded cornice inlaid with pewter scrolls, the central cupboard door with conforming decoration, flanked by small drawers, the stand with false drawers, the cabinet partly 17thC, 45in (114cm).
$6,000-9,000

A Portuguese colonial rosewood cabinet on stand, the cabinet fitted with an arrangement of cushion moulded drawers, possibly Brazilian, with restorations, c1700, 41½in (105cm).
$3,000-4,500

A Flemish ebony and ebonised cabinet on stand, the moulded cornice above 8 drawers, each with a marble panel framed by a rippled moulding, the later stand with plain frieze, on baluster legs and bun feet, the cabinet late 17thC, 46in (117cm).
$8,000-10,000

A walnut cabinet on chest inlaid with marquetry bands, the top section with a moulded cornice and convex frieze drawer above 2 doors inlaid with arched panels and enclosing 9 drawers, the chest fitted with 2 short and 2 long drawers, on shaped bracket feet, early 18thC, 44in (112cm).
$10,000-13,500

A lacquer decorated cabinet on stand, the doors decorated with birds and foliage, with chased gilt brass hinges and elaborate escutcheons, the ebonised pine stand with pierced fret corner brackets, on square chamfered legs, 18thC, 38in (97cm).
$5,000-6,000

A walnut chest-on-stand, with crossbanded drawers, the stand with an ogee moulded frieze, on baluster turned legs tied by shaped stretchers, restorations, early 18thC, 41in (104cm) wide.
$3,000-4,500

A mahogany cabinet-on-stand, decorated with blind fret bands, the bolection moulded cornice above a pair of inset panel doors enclosing 10 small drawers, on chamfered square moulded legs, partly 18thC, 38½in (98cm).
$2,000-3,000

A figured walnut and feather banded cabinet-on-stand, the lower section with 2 short and 2 long drawers, on bracket feet, basically 18thC, 41½in (105cm).
$5,000-6,000

A George I black japanned cabinet-on-stand, decorated in gilt with chinoiseries and fitted with engraved brass hinges and lock-plate, on a later stand with cabriole legs and pad feet, restored, 41in (104cm).
$7,000-8,000

A Dutch walnut and marquetry cabinet, with single glazed door, inlaid with flowers and foliage, 32in (81cm).
$7,000-8,000

A Regency mahogany cabinet, decorated with boxwood stringing, each cupboard fitted with sliding shelves and enclosed by brass grille panelled doors, on turned supports, 33in (84cm).
$7,000-8,000

A cream painted cabinet-on-stand, the cupboard doors with tapestry panels depicting mediaeval pastoral scenes, enclosing a well fitted painted interior, the giltwood stand with a scroll moulded frieze on moulded scroll supports, tied by shaped stretchers, 38in (98cm).
$4,000-6,000

A yew-wood and marquetry cabinet-on-stand, the drawers of South German 17thC marquetry about a central cupboard door, the stand with a mahogany slide, on chamfered partly ribbed legs, the cabinet 35in (89cm).
$10,000-12,000

A mahogany side cabinet-on-stand, applied with C-scrolls and foliate carved mouldings, with mirror lined interior, above 2 frieze drawers and a pierced serpentine frieze, on square tapering legs with carved paw feet joined by finialled cross-stretchers, 27in (69cm).
$2,000-2,500

Side Cabinets

A George III mahogany serpentine side cabinet, the top above a figured panelled door, on spreading feet, 39½in (100cm).
$5,000-6,000

A Regency rosewood and cut brass side cabinet, with green mottled marble top, on scroll feet with acanthus, bird and floral brass inlays, 45in (114cm).
$4,000-5,000

A Regency mahogany side cabinet with later rounded top, 54½in (139cm).
$3,000-4,000

A Regency rosewood and parcel gilt side cabinet, with mottled green marble top above a frieze applied with gilt metal sunbursts, the cupboard doors with brass grilles and pleated silk backing, on beaded plinth base, restorations and later marble, 49½in (126cm).
$3,500-4,000

A Regency rosewood and brass inlaid side cabinet, the top with rounded corners above a frieze inlaid with brass foliate designs, the brass grille doors flanked by plain column pilasters headed by carved paterae, originally with superstructure, 44in (112cm).
$6,000-8,000

A Regency rosewood and parcel-gilt breakfront side cabinet, with mottled dark grey marble top and 2 pairs of cupboard doors filled with brass trellis, on a yellow pleated silk ground, the marble damaged, 69in (175cm).
$7,000-8,000

A Regency parcel gilt and simulated rosewood breakfront side cabinet, on bun feet, 49in (125cm).
$7,000-8,000

A Regency brass inlaid rosewood side cabinet, with eared top and frieze drawer, above a pair of panelled doors filled with pleated brown silk, flanked by canted scrolling angles, on later bun feet, 33in (84cm).
$2,000-3,000

A Regency mahogany side cabinet, the panelled doors filled with gilt trellis and backed with light brown silk, on later brass paw feet, the top possibly associated, 25in (63cm).
$5,000-6,000

A Regency mahogany breakfront side cabinet, inlaid with ebonised lines and foliate motifs, the 4 panelled doors enclosing shelves, on plinth base, 55½in (140cm).
$8,000-10,000

A Regency rosewood side cabinet of breakfront form, with marble top above 4 brass grille and pleated silk doors, flanked by moulded pilasters with scroll corbels, on lobed melon feet, 74in (188cm).
$16,000-18,000

A George IV rosewood breakfront side cabinet, with 4 brass grille doors backed with pleated yellow silk, on plinth base, 84in (213cm).
$9,000-11,000

An early Victorian rosewood secrétaire side cabinet of inverted form, the centre section with a deep secrétaire drawer above open shelves flanked by 2 tapestry panelled doors, on plinth base, 86in (219cm).
$8,000-11,000

A Victorian burr walnut veneered breakfront side cabinet, the end canted corners with leaf sprays, on a plinth base, 67in (170cm).
$3,000-4,000

A Victorian burr walnut breakfront side cabinet, inlaid with marquetry and geometric boxwood lines in gilt metal mounted borders, the panelled door inset with a painted porcelain plaque, on toupee feet, 61in (155cm).
$8,000-11,000

A Victorian burr walnut veneered breakfront side cabinet, the end canted corners with leaf sprays, on a plinth base, 67in (170cm).
$3,500-4,000

A Victorian figured walnut foliate marquetry and ormolu mounted side cabinet, 79in (200cm).
$10,000-12,000

A Victorian walnut side cabinet, the frieze and central panelled door inlaid with foliate arabesques, 60in (152cm).
$3,500-4,000

A late Victorian burr walnut side cabinet, crossbanded with kingwood, 74in (188cm).
$6,000-8,000

A Victorian thuya and ebonised breakfront side cabinet, with gilt metal mounts and mouldings, 71in (180cm).
$3,500-4,000

A Victorian burr walnut breakfront side cabinet, inlaid with marquetry, geometric boxwood lines, decorated with inset painted porcelain oval plaques, in gilt metal mounted borders, adaptations, 66in (168cm).
$6,000-8,000

A rosewood side cabinet, the 'verde antico' marble top with inverted front, 72in (182cm).
$7,000-8,000

A Sheraton style satinwood side cabinet, the crossbanded doors flanked by pilasters inlaid with husk chains, 43½in (110cm).
$3,000-4,000

A zebrawood and partridgewood crossbanded side cabinet, of serpentine form, in the Italian style, on square section cabriole legs, stamped Edwards and Roberts, c1890, 33in (84cm).
$4,000-5,000

ormolu mounted birch side
inet, the door applied with
ndels and anthemions, with
ee-quarter column angles, on
ned feet, 32in (81cm).
000-8,000

A French ebonised and Boulle breakfront side cabinet, with brass mouldings, the decorated plinth with gadrooned mouldings, on turned feet, mid-19thC, 71in (180cm).
$6,000-7,000

A pair of Louis XVI style ebonised side cabinets, applied with gilt metal mounts and inlaid with marquetry in geometric boxwood line borders, late 19thC, 29½in (75cm).
$1,500-2,000

ouis XVI style side cabinet, with
ned marble inset top, the
gswood cabinet having ebony
l floral marquetry panels, gilt
tal borders and caryatid mounts
he forecorners, 31in (79cm).
000-5,000

A Louis XVI style ebonised side cabinet, with brass geometric lines, inlaid with heartstone and applied with gilt metal mounts, the top enclosed by a hinged panelled lid, stamped C.T. Hayward.
$3,000-4,000

A French ebonised side cabinet, with Boulle decoration to the shaped back and panel door, late 19thC, 33in (84cm).
$1,500-2,000

An Italian green painted and gilded side cabinet, the lower section with 2 glazed doors flanked by reeded half-columns, on a foliate plinth, 52in (132cm).
$5,000-6,000

Canterburies

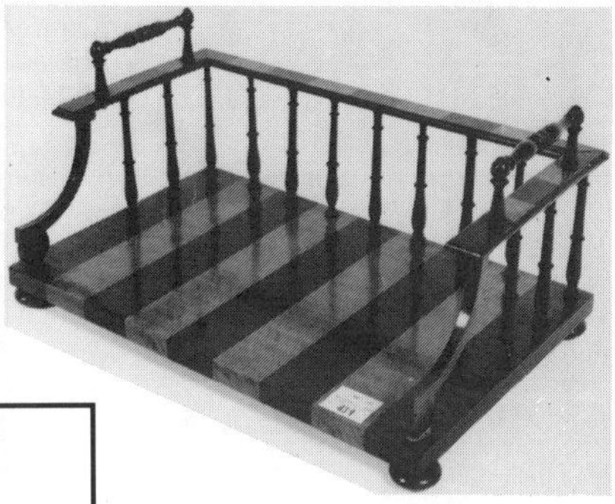

A Regency period rosewood and satinwood desk top canterbury, 14in (36cm).
$2,000-3,000

A Regency mahogany canterbury, the dished top with 4 compartments and ring turned baluster columns to the corners, a drawer below, on ring turned legs, 18in (46cm).
$3,000-3,500

Make the Most of Miller's

We do not repeat photographs in Miller's. However, the same item may appear in a subsequent year's edition if our consultants feel it is of interest to collectors and dealers

A Regency mahogany canterbury, on turned tapering legs, 18in (45cm).
$4,000-5,000

A Regency mahogany canterbury, with one frieze drawer, 19in (48cm).
$6,000-7,000

A Regency mahogany canterbury with slatted divisions, the frieze with a drawer, on square tapering legs, 18in (46cm).
$4,000-5,000

A William IV rosewood canterbury, with 4 curved compartments and ring turned supports above a shallow drawer, on turned tapered legs, 20in (51cm).
$2,000-3,000

A Regency mahogany canterbury, the base with a single drawer on turned tapered legs, brass caps and castors, 18in (46cm).
$2,500-3,000

A Regency rosewood canterbury, 18in (46cm).
$5,000-6,000

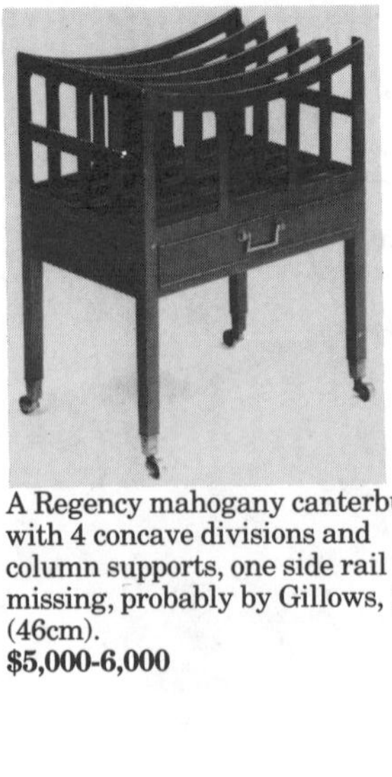
A Regency mahogany canterbury, with 4 concave divisions and column supports, one side rail missing, probably by Gillows, 18in (46cm).
$5,000-6,000

A Regency mahogany canterbury, with 4 slatted divisions and a drawer, on turned tapered legs with brass cappings and castors, 18in (46cm).
$4,000-5,000

A Regency rosewood canterbury, with single frieze drawer, on turned tapering supports with brass castors, 19½in (50cm).
$2,000-3,000

A George III period mahogany canterbury, with fitted drawer, on baluster supports, 21in (75cm).
$2,500-3,000

A George III mahogany and inlai canterbury, with 4 divisions and slatted sides, the drawer with boxwood and ebony stringing, on square tapered legs ending in bra cappings and castors, 20in (51cm
$3,000-4,000

nid-Victorian carved rosewood
ıterbury, with pierced leaf carved
isions, single drawer, on turned
;s and castors, 20½in (52cm).
600-1,800

A Victorian walnut canterbury, with arabesque fretwork panels, a drawer below, on turned legs, 23in (58cm).
$1,200-1,500

A Victorian canterbury-whatnot, with burr walnut veneer and fretwork panels, on barley twist supports.
$2,500-3,000

CANTERBURIES

- ★ name denotes a piece of movable equipment usually used for sheet music
- ★ first music canterburies appeared c1800
- ★ round tapered legs appeared in c1810
- ★ the canterbury shows quite well the stylistic development of the 19thC – from the quite straight, slender severe to the bulbous and heavily carved later examples
- ★ many Victorian examples with good carving fetch more than the earlier examples
- ★ elegance is one of the major criteria in this small expensive piece of furniture
- ★ note that some are made from the base of a whatnot or étagère but even more are modern reproductions

A Victorian walnut oval canterbury-table, the base with deep fretted gallery, the divisions on spindle turned supports, the inlaid oval top on turned and carved supports, 30in (76cm).
$1,800-2,500

In the Furniture section if there is only one measurement it usually refers to the width of the piece.

Open Armchairs

A Queen Anne walnut open armchair, with padded back and seat covered in buff damask, the back legs with restorations.
$3,000-4,000

A Charles II walnut open armchair, ‿he cane-filled back carved with ıcanthus S-scrolls, flanked by ıcanthus carved baluster uprights, ‿vith later upholstered seat, on ‿onforming legs with stretchers.
$3,000-4,000

A pair of Charles II beechwood open armchairs, with out-scrolled arms above split cane seat, the scrolling legs joined by an H-shaped stretcher and pierced foliate carved front stretcher, restorations, one front stretcher replaced.
$4,000-5,000

A Queen Anne style walnut armchair, with a scrolled crest rail and upholstered back continuing to moulded scroll arms, on shell carved cabriole legs and pad feet.
$800-1,000

A Queen Anne style stained maple armchair.
$2,500-3,500

A walnut open armchair of George I style, with arched upholstered back and foliate carved shepherd's crook arms, on palmette carved cabriole legs, with ball and claw feet.
$2,000-3,000

A mid-Georgian beechwood ope armchair, with vase shaped spla the drop-in seat covered in floral needlework.
$1,000-1,500

A pair of George II style mahogany library armchairs, upholstered in red floral damask, on cabriole legs and scrolled toes carved with foliag
$12,000-15,000

A George II style walnut framed library armchair, with conforming cabriole legs and scroll feet.
$3,000-4,000

A Regency rosewood grained armchair, the splats decorated with Greek key motifs and centred by lion masks, the caned seat on turned tapered legs.
$2,000-2,500

A Regency carved oak elbow chair in the Gothic taste in the manner of George Smith, with stuffover scroll back and padded scroll arm supports, a panel seat with quatrefoil panel seat rail, on sabre legs and casters.
$1,500-2,000

A pair of Regency mahogany open armchairs, the down scrolled arms headed by stiff leaves, on sabre legs.
$3,000-4,000

A mahogany framed elbow chair, with upholstered seat and bow stretcher frame base.
$200-300

A Regency mahogany armchair, with horsehair upholstered seat and brass mounted apron, on sabre legs, and a matching chair, renovations.
$1,800-2,500

A Regency parcel gilt and simulated rosewood open armchair, with shaped top rail and pierced tablet-centred splat, the cane filled seat on ring turned tapering legs, and a matching chair.
$2,000-2,500

A pair of Regency open armchairs, in the manner of George Smith, c1826.
$30,000-35,000

A pair of Regency mahogany armchairs, the gadrooned bowed bar and anthemion carved rail backs above upholstered seats, on ring turned tapering legs.
$1,500-2,000

A Regency ebonised and parcel gilt open armchair, redecorated.
$3,000-4,000

A Regency mahogany armchair, the top rail boldly carved as 2 anthemion scrolls, the foliate carved arms continuing to sabre legs.
$900-1,000

A George III mahogany library armchair, the arms with stop fluted supports, on square chamfered legs.
$8,000-9,000

A pair of Regency mahogany open armchairs.
$2,500-3,000

A George III mahogany open armchair, with tapestry drop-in seat, the square moulded legs joined by a stretcher.
$2,000-2,500

A George III mahogany open armchair, with padded back and seat, the frame inlaid with paterae, on channelled square tapering legs with spade feet.
$8,000-9,000

A pair of George III mahogany armchairs, the splats inlaid with satinwood panels, the reeded arms on slender baluster turned supports, on turned tapered legs with lobed collars.
$2,000-3,000

A pair of Regency style green painted armchairs, the backs with floral decorated panels above trellis splats, the arms on lion's paw supports continuing to baluster turned legs.
$1,800-2,500

A pair of late George III mahogany armchairs, with downswept arms on square tapering legs and spade feet, restorations, one chair re-railed.
$5,000-6,000

A George III mahogany open armchair in the Louis XV style, the padded back and seat upholstered in yellow velvet, on cabriole legs and pad feet, one front foot slightly reduced.
$3,000-4,000

A pair of George III carved mahogany elbow chairs, with trell splats and reeded arm supports on urn turned uprights, with stuffove seats on square tapered legs.
$2,000-2,500

A George III open armchair, the shaped top rail carved with scrolls and foliage with pierced interlaced splat, the drop-in seat covered in needlework, on square chamfered legs joined by stretchers.
$4,000-5,000

A George III giltwood open armchair, with cartouche shaped padded serpentine back and seat, the seat rail on turned fluted tapering legs, later gilded.
$1,200-1,500

A pair of George III mahogany open armchairs, the drop-in seats upholstered in brown cotton, on moulded tapering legs joined by stretchers.
$6,000-7,000

A George III mahogany open armchair, the shaped carved toprail above a scroll carved and pierced splat centred by a fretwork lozenge, with a needlework upholstered drop-in seat, restorations.
$3,000-4,000

A George III mahogany library armchair, upholstered in green damask, restorations.
$5,000-6,000

A George III cream and pink painted open armchair, the fluted seat rail on ribbed tapering legs with foliate bands.
$3,000-4,000

An early George III mahogany open armchair, with scroll carved top rail, pierced waisted splat, outswept arms with curved supports, the drop-in seat on tapering square legs with stretchers.
$1,500-2,000

A George III mahogany open armchair, the padded back, arms and seat upholstered in tan hide, restorations.
$3,000-4,000

Federal mahogany armchair,
assachusetts or Rhode Island,
800.
,000-7,000

A Chippendale carved mahogany lolling chair, small patches to each arm support, Philadelphia, c1780.
$25,000-30,000

A Federal carved mahogany armchair, minor repairs, Philadelphia, c1805.
$6,000-7,000

A Federal carved cherrywood lolling chair, small patches to each arm joint, Massachusetts, c1800.
$9,000-12,000

A pair of Federal mahogany armchairs, minor repairs to crest, Connecticut, c1805.
$6,000-7,000

Federal inlaid mahogany lolling
air, Eastern Connecticut, feet
paired, c1800.
,500-3,500

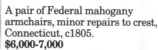

A pair of George III style mahogany open armchairs, the curved arm supports and square legs carved with blind fretwork joined by pierced stretchers, restorations, 19thC.
$10,000-12,000

A George III mahogany ladderback open armchair, with serpentine shaped crossbars, the drop-in seat on square legs joined by stretchers.
$1,200-1,500

A set of 12 George III style mahogany armchairs, the moulded wheel backs with a central roundel and pierced undulating splats, above brass studded bowed seats and armpads upholstered in red leather, with a fluted banded apron and turned tapering legs.
$8,000-10,000

A mid-Victorian walnut open tub armchair, with scrolled armrests on barley twist supports above a serpentine seat, on barley twist legs and casters.
$800-1,200

A set of Victorian mahogany chairs, possibly by Gillows, including a pair of armchairs, the arms with lion's mask finials, on lion monopodia legs with paw feet.
$7,000-8,000

A mahogany framed open armchair, with hide upholstery, c1880.
$900-1,000

A Victorian walnut gentleman's open armchair, and a lady's matching chair.
$5,000-6,000

A carved walnut chair with cane seat, c1870.
$800-1,000

A pair of Empire mahogany armchairs.
$4,000-5,000

An Edwardian mahogany open armchair, the pierced arched top rail above a marquetry inlaid splat, with needlework seat.
$800-1,000

An open arm elbow chair, with oriental style lacquered decoration, early 20thC.
$400-600

An Edwardian inlaid mahogany elbow chair.
$400-500

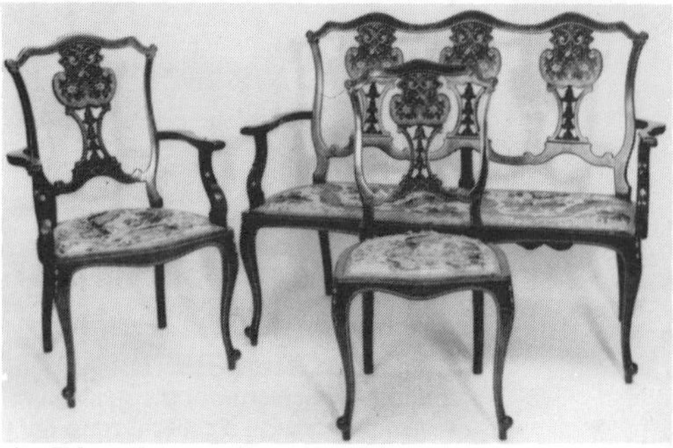

An Edwardian mahogany salon suite, comprising sofa, 2 carvers and 4 standard chairs, with inlaid panels of musical trophies and grotesques in bone and satinwood.
$5,000-6,000

A Louis XV walnut fauteuil, upholstered in tapestry.
$3,500-4,000

A pair of Louis XV provincial walnut fauteuils, the arm supports carved with acanthus, on cabriole legs with scrolling feet.
$4,000-5,000

A Louis XV style stained beech fauteuil, upholstered in gros point needlework.
$1,400-1,600

A Louis XVI grey painted salon suite, comprising a two-seater canape and 2 armchairs.
$6,000-8,000

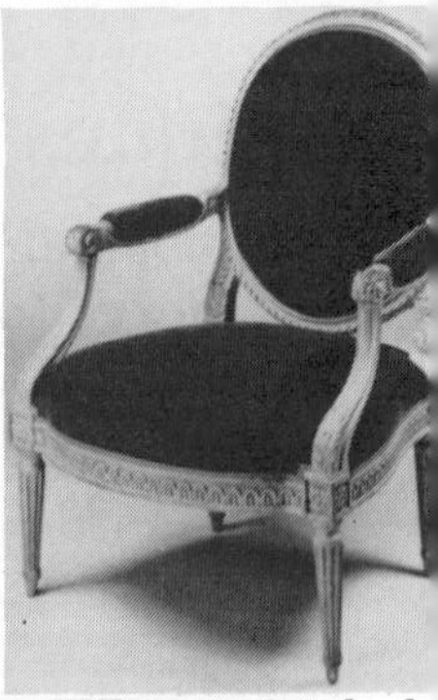

A Louis XVI grey painted salc suite, comprising a two-seater canape and 2 armchairs.
$6,000-7,000

A pair of Louis XVI style grey painted fauteuils, and a canape, the channelled frames carved with ribbon twist and foliage on turned tapering legs.
$5,000-6,000

A Louis XVI style giltwood suite, comprising 2 fauteuils and a canape.
$5,000-6,000

A pair of French Renaissance sty regal armchairs, the pinnacle lanc back carved with cusps and acanthus scrolls in high relief, wi close nailed upholstered panel, se and armpads in brown leather, stamped P. Mazarozer.
$5,000-6,000

A pair of Continental style gilt armchairs, 19thC.
$1,500-1,800

An Empire mahogany fauteuil, with curved and slightly scrolling solid back, scrolled arm supports and bow padded seat on gently scrolling legs.
$3,000-4,000

A pair of walnut fauteuils, the crestings carved with scallops an husks on turned tapering stop flu legs, formerly caned, possibly Austrian, late 18thC and later.
$3,500-4,000

A Continental blue painted walnut armchair, restorations, late 18thC.
$600-800

An Empire mahogany fauteuil, the yoke-shaped curved top rail with scrolling arm terminals and padded seat, covered in brown leather, restorations.
$3,000-4,000

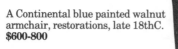

A Hepplewhite armchair, with tapestry seat.
$2,000-3,000

pair of Flemish 17thC style beech rmchairs, the high arched backs nd seats with gros point floral pestry, the acanthus carved rolled arms continuing to scroll apports tied by wavy H-stretchers.
2,500-3,000

A Dutch mahogany and marquetry open armchair, the padded back with a bowed top rail inlaid with cherubs supporting a basket of flowers, early 19thC.
$1,500-2,000

A mahogany bergère, with caned back and seat, in channelled frame, with spirally fluted baluster arm supports, late 19thC.
$1,000-1,200

pair of Italian grey painted and arcel gilt open armchairs, the pholstered back with rocaille arved crests and moulded frames, ie foliate carved arms continuing) cabriole legs.
1,800-2,500

A walnut Farthingale chair, the padded back and seat upholstered in red velvet, with spirally turned arms, legs and stretchers, 17thC and later.
$4,000-5,000

A giltwood fauteuil, with padded back, arms and bowed seat, the channelled frame with geometric flowerheads with winged lion monopodia, possibly Scandinavian, early 19thC.
$5,000-6,000

A beechwood fauteuil, with caned back and serpentine seat in a moulded frame, the seat frame replaced.
$5,000-7,500

A Lancashire mahogany spindle ack armchair, with slightly bowed rms, on square legs, c1790.
700-800

A Chippendale design mahogany armchair, converted to a commode, mid-19thC.
$800-1,000

A mahogany armchair, basically late 18thC.
$1,000-1,200

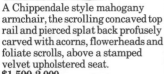

A Chippendale style mahogany armchair, the scrolling concaved top rail and pierced splat back profusely carved with acorns, flowerheads and foliate scrolls, above a stamped velvet upholstered seat.
$1,500-2,000

A pair of 17thC style walnut open armchairs, the arched backs with pierced acanthus top rail between finialled turned supports flanking a pierced splat, the arms terminating in scrolls above an upholstered seat on turned legs joined by a finialled cross stretcher.
$1,500-2,000

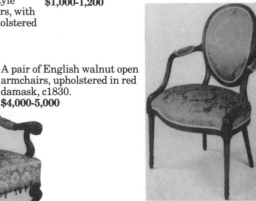

A pair of mahogany armchairs in Chinese Chippendale taste, the shaped top rails centred by a fan motif above trelliswork backs and acanthus moulded scrolled arms, on carved cabriole legs.
$1,000-1,200

A set of 6 Hepplewhite style mahogany open armchairs, with serpentine front and upholstered stuffover seats.
$2,500-3,000

A mahogany open armchair of Hepplewhite style, labelled Warings, Manchester, the seat upholstered over a cane panel, serpentine fronted on fluted square front supports with shaped feet.
$1,200-1,500

A pair of English walnut open armchairs, upholstered in red damask, c1830.
$4,000-5,000

A Hepplewhite style mahogany armchair in the French taste.
$1,000-1,200

A pair of rosewood framed armchairs, the upholstered serpentine fronted seats on moulded cabriole legs, mid-19thC.
$3,500-4,000

A set of 8 carved satinwood elbow chairs in the Sheraton style, some defective, early 19thC and later.
$8,000-10,000

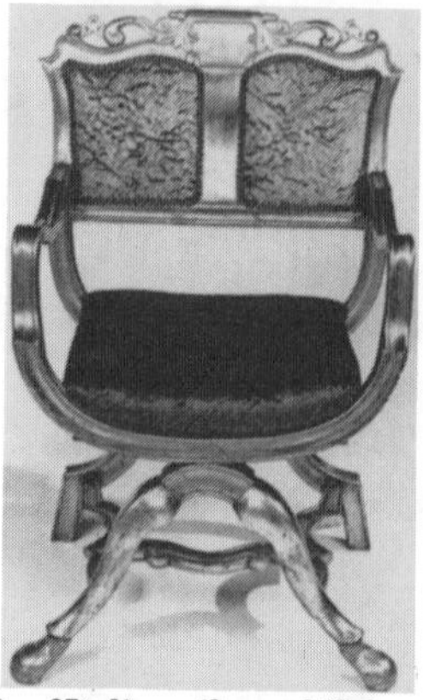

A pair of Italian giltwood X-framed armchairs, with pierced and scrolled crests and shaped arms, on angled cabriole legs.
$400-550

pholstered rmchairs

Federal carved mahogany wing
air, distressed.
,500-5,500

A mid-Georgian walnut wing armchair, the seat upholstered in yellow damask, re-railed and later blocks.
$6,000-7,000

A Regency mahogany tub bergère, with curved arched back and bowed seat in a moulded frame, on reeded tapering legs.
$3,000-4,000

Regency cream and green painted
rgère, on turned tapering front
d sabre back legs, re-supported.
4,000-15,000

A Regency mahogany folding campaign armchair, with leather-padded back, arms and seat, the hinged front with leather-lined flap.
$2,500-3,000

A late Regency mahogany bergère, with turned and reeded arm ends, continuing to similar supports, red leather upholstery.
$1,800-2,000

A Regency mahogany bergère, covered in blue leather, the plain channelled frame, on square legs with brass caps and casters, previously caned, distressed.
$8,000-9,000

Regency mahogany bergère,
vered in buttoned red repp, the
eded arm supports and seat rail,
turned tapering legs.
,500-2,500

A Regency mahogany bergère, with padded rectangular back, sides and cushion, on turned tapering baluster legs.
$2,000-3,000

A Regency painted bergère, attributed to Gillows, the seat with a later solid panel, on sabre legs with brass socket casters, stamped BB & Co patent, the caning in poor condition.
$1,500-2,000

George III mahogany frame wing
mchair, with serpentine stuffover
ck and outswept scroll arm
pports, on moulded chamfered
gs with casters.
,500-3,000

A Federal upholstered mahogany barrel back armchair, several old breaks and repairs, one rear foot repaired, Baltimore or Philadelphia, c1810.
$8,000-10,000

A Victorian carved mahogany hoopback drawing room chair, upholstered in red, on scroll supports, scroll feet and casters.
$800-1,000

A Victorian carved walnut balloon back armchair, with buttoned back and carved scroll arms, on cabriole legs.
$1,500-2,000

Two Victorian walnut framed armchairs, the oval buttoned back with moulded frames and carved crests, the open arms continuing to cabriole legs.
$3,500-4,000

A Victorian walnut framed button back armchair, with carved decoration, on cabriole legs.
$1,200-1,600

A Victorian button back armchair, with serpentine front, on reeded legs.
$1,200-1,600

A late Victorian armchair, attributed to Howard & Sons numbered 3718.
$2,000-3,000

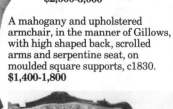

A late Victorian salon suite, comprising a settee, a pair of armchairs and 2 occasional chairs, with curved gadrooned and carved top rails, upholstered or carved and spindle backs, fluted arm supports.
$2,000-3,000

A mahogany and upholstered armchair, in the manner of Gillows, with high shaped back, scrolled arms and serpentine seat, on moulded square supports, c1830.
$1,400-1,800

A walnut button back chair, with shaped and carved back, on turned front supports and casters, 19thC.
$600-800

An upholstered armchair, on cabriole supports.
$1,200-1,300

pair of burr walnut Biedermeier
airs, upholstered in blue cotton,
thC.
00-1,000

A Chippendale style mahogany framed window seat, 42in (106.5cm).
$2,000-3,000

A pair of armchairs, with loose cotton covers concealing the original upholstery, on square tapered legs, brass caps and casters, stamped and labelled Howard.
$4,000-5,000

A mahogany wing armchair, upholstered in hide, on square legs joined by stretchers.
$2,500-3,000

A cream painted and parcel gilt bergère, with cartouche shaped padded back, arm rests, sides and squab covered in floral brocade.
$6,000-7,000

A five-piece walnut bergère suite, comprising a sofa, two armchairs and 2 tub armchairs.
$2,500-3,000

Louis XV walnut fauteuil, with
oulded frame, on cabriole legs and
rolled feet, restored.
3,000-4,000

A mahogany framed bergère suite, comprising settee and 2 armchairs, the cresting rails carved with ribbon and garlands of bellflowers, the loose cushions in gold damask.
$7,000-8,000

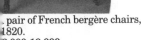

. pair of French bergère chairs,
1820.
8,000-10,000

A French suite, comprising a sofa and 2 chairs, early 19thC.
$3,600-4,000

Corner Chairs

A George II walnut corner library chair.
$1,300-1,500

A George II red walnut corner chair.
$4,000-5,000

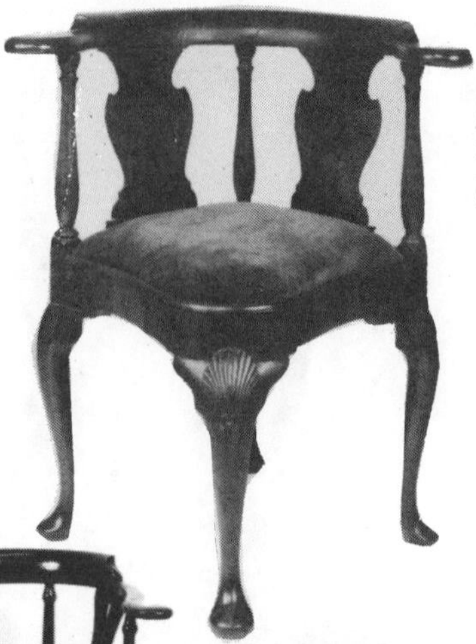

A George II walnut corner armchair, with upholstered drop-in seat, on cabriole legs with pad feet and shell headings, labelled E. Brian & Sons, 61 High Street, Princes End, Tipton.
$1,600-2,000

A late George II red walnut corne armchair, with pierced splats, on square chamfered legs joined by stretchers.
$1,800-2,500

Two mahogany framed corner chairs, with pierced vase splats and triple turned pillar supports, slip-in seats and square legs, mid-18thC.
$1,300-1,500

A carved mahogany corner chair, the carved backrest with Greek key top rail and ram's horn terminals above a curving seat rail with spiral carved supports, the upholstered seat above turned fluted legs with shaped stretchers.
$1,000-1,200

A mahogany corner chair, with shaped top rail and pierced splat, the drop-in seat on turned legs joined by stretchers with a cabriole front leg.
$1,400-1,800

Dining Chairs

A set of 6 walnut chairs, in the style of Daniel Marot, with upholstered seats on cabriole legs joined by conforming stretchers.
$4,000-5,000

A Queen Anne style walnut din chair, on shell carved cabriole le with pad feet.
$300-400

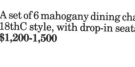

A set of 5 Queen Anne style dining chairs, with shell carvings and carved cabriole legs.
$700-800

A set of 6 mahogany dining chairs in 18thC style, with drop-in seats.
$1,200-1,500

set of 8 George III carved ahogany dining chairs, including carvers, chamfered legs united by retchers, bearing printed label 'roperty of the late J.R. Knott, sq., of Ixworth House, Ixworth'.
),000-10,000

A set of 8 George III mahogany dining chairs, including 2 carvers, with upholstered drop-in tapestry seats, on square moulded legs joined with stretchers, adapted.
$12,000-13,000

A set of 4 George III mahogany dining chairs, with brass inlaid reeded bar and rope carved rail backs, one leg repaired.
$1,500-1,800

. set of 8 George III style mahogany ining chairs, including 2 carvers.
5,000-6,000

A set of 4 George III mahogany chairs, on square tapered legs.
$3,000-4,000

A pair of mid-Georgian walnut dining chairs, each with a serpentine top rail and pierced splat carved with eagles' heads, the drop-in seats covered in brown repp, possibly Irish.
$5,000-6,000

A set of 6 George III mahogany dining chairs, with upholstered drop-in seats, on moulded square legs joined by stretchers.
$9,000-10,000

A pair of mid-Georgian mahogany dining chairs, with floral needlework drop-in seats, on square moulded legs joined by stretchers, one replaced.
$1,600-1,800

A set of 5 rosewood dining chairs, with turned vertical splats and supports, early 19thC.
$1,400-1,500

A set of 4 George III mahogany chairs, including a pair of armchairs, the shield backs carved with wheatears and inlaid with oval fan paterae, on moulded square section legs.
$5,000-6,000

Four George III mahogany framed dining chairs, with slip-in seats, the cabriole front legs with acanthus carved knees and ball-and-claw feet, some restoration.
$8,000-9,000

A harlequin set of 7 George III mahogany dining chairs, comprising a set of 4 and 3 odd, including an open armchair with later arms, some re-railed and later blocks.
$3,000-4,000

A set of 4 George III mahogany dining chairs, with woolwork tapestry drop-in seats, on square chamfered supports and H-stretchers.
$500-600

A set of 12 Georgian style mahogany ladderback dining chairs, with wavy, pierced backs, on chamfered square supports.
$6,000-7,000

A set of 6 Regency ebonised and decorated dining chairs in the Etruscan style, with cane seats.
$3,000-4,000

A set of 8 Georgian carved mahogany dining chairs, including 2 carvers, on tapered legs headed with paterae ornament, one with later top rail.
$20,000-24,000

A set of 4 Regency mahogany dining chairs, the banded bowed bar and reeded latticed rail backs applied with paterae, above upholstered seats, on sabre legs.
$2,500-3,000

A set of 6 Regency brass mounted stained beechwood dining chairs, 4 stamped IW, 2 possibly later.
$5,000-6,000

A set of 8 Regency mahogany dining chairs, with padded seats, on turned tapering legs, stamped IM.
$9,000-10,000

A set of 6 Regency carved mahogany and ebony strung dining chairs, including 2 carvers, with stuffover seats, on ring turned tapered legs.
$8,000-10,000

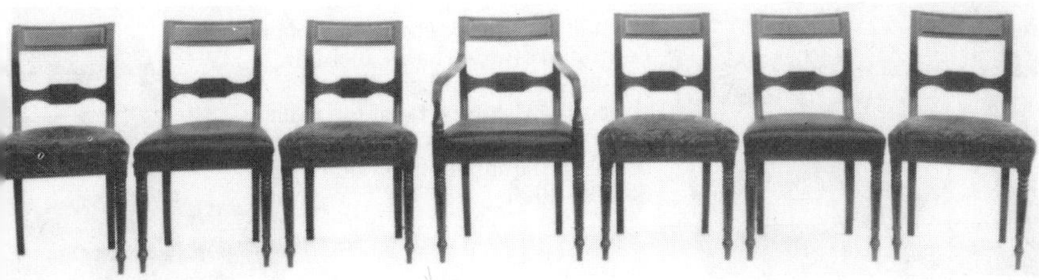

set of 7 Regency mahogany dining
airs, with brass line inlay.
,000-7,000

A set of 6 Regency mahogany dining chairs, including 2 open armchairs, one single chair with one leg spliced, one armchair with 2 legs spliced and front feet replaced.
£4,000-4,500 *C*

A set of 8 Regency dining chairs, including 2 open armchairs, the drop-in seats upholstered in silk, on sabre legs.
$6,000-8,000

set of 12 Regency carved
ahogany dining chairs, including
armchairs, with stuffover seats, on
ng turned tapered legs, restoration
ıd parts later.
4,000-16,000

A set of 4 Regency mahogany dining chairs, including 2 open armchairs, the seats upholstered in striped silk, on ring turned legs.
$1,500-2,000

A set of 6 Regency brass inlaid mahogany dining chairs, including a pair of armchairs, with upholstered seats, 2 partly re-railed.
$6,000-7,000

A set of 5 late Regency mahogany dining chairs, including an armchair with scroll arms.
$1,600-2,000

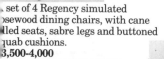

set of 4 Regency simulated
›sewood dining chairs, with cane
lled seats, sabre legs and buttoned
quab cushions.
3,500-4,000

A set of 4 Regency simulated rosewood dining chairs, the split cane seats with squab cushions, one side rail replaced.
$1,800-2,500

A set of 8 Regency style mahogany dining chairs, including 2 carvers.
$700-800

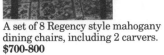

set of 3 Regency mahogany dining
hairs, each with curved back with
-shaped splat, the drop-in seats
pholstered in black horsehair, on
quare tapering legs joined by
retchers.
400-600

A set of 4 late Regency mahogany dining chairs, including an armchair, on sabre legs, adaptations.
$1,000-1,600

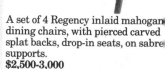

A set of 4 Regency mahogany dining chairs, the scrolling frames with fluted bowed bar and rail backs above graduated upholstered seats and side panels, on sabre legs.
$3,000-4,000

A set of 6 Regency ebonised and gilt decorated dining chairs, including an elbow chair with scroll arm supports, with rope twist top rails and cane panel backs, having cane panel and squab seats, on sabre legs.
$3,000-4,000

A set of 4 Regency inlaid mahogany dining chairs, with pierced carved splat backs, drop-in seats, on sabre supports.
$2,500-3,000

A set of 6 late Regency rosewood dining chairs, c1825.
$4,000-5,000

A set of 8 Regency mahogany dining chairs, including a pair of open armchairs, on ring turned tapering legs, one with later blocks.
$10,000-12,000

A set of 4 Regency brass inlaid rosewood dining chairs, 2 stamped WB.
$4,000-5,000

A set of 6 Regency brass inlaid simulated rosewood dining chairs, some re-railed, restorations.
$6,000-7,000

A set of 7 late Regency mahogany dining chairs, including 1 armchair, on ring turned tapered legs, tied by X-stretchers.
$2,000-3,000

Make the most of Miller's

Unless otherwise stated, any description which refers to 'a set' or 'a pair' includes a valuation for the entire set or the pair, even though the illustration may show only a single item

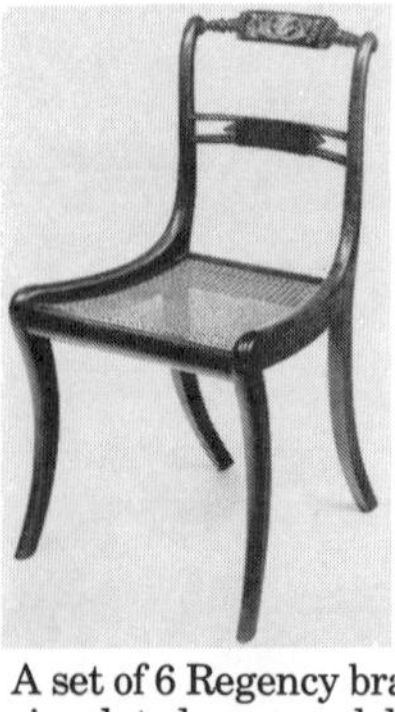

A set of 6 Regency brass inlaid and simulated rosewood dining chairs, with tablet centred ring turned top rails, horizontal splats and cane filled seats with squab cushions, on sabre legs.
$5,000-6,000

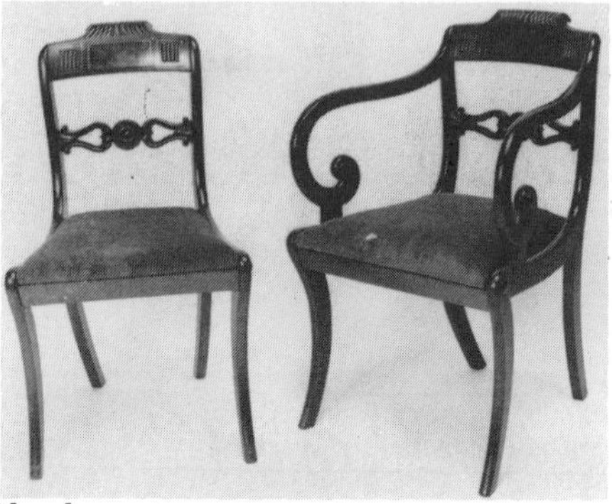

A set of 5 Regency mahogany dining chairs, including 1 carver, the top rail fluted and with brass inlaid panel, on sabre legs.
$2,000-2,500

REGENCY FURNITURE

★ really an expression of the neo-classical taste which was evident all over Europe
★ based on the French styles developed in the Consulate (1799-1804) and Empire (1804-15) periods
★ one of the greatest English exponents was Thomas Hope
★ mainly used mahogany and rosewood
★ the decoration was based on many classical forms, Roman, Egyptian, Greek and Etruscan – often all used on one piece
★ rosewood was often French polished and, when in short supply, was often simulated by painting on beech
★ often noted for good brass inlay

set of 7 late Regency mahogany
ining chairs, the brass inlaid bar
nd foliate carved rail backs above
pholstered drop-in seats, adapted,
tamped T.G.
5,000-6,000

A set of 6 Regency mahogany dining chairs, with figured top rails above scroll and sunburst horizontal splats, on sabre legs.
$2,000-2,500

A set of 7 Hepplewhite style mahogany dining chairs, including 1 carver, with shield-shaped backs, the bowed upholstered seats on square tapered moulded legs.
$2,000-3,000

Make the Most of Miller's

Every care has been taken to ensure the accuracy of descriptions and estimated valuations. Price ranges in this book reflect what one should expect to pay for a similar example. When selling one can obviously expect a figure below. This will fluctuate according to a dealer's stock, saleability at a particular time, etc. It is always advisable to approach a reputable specialist dealer or an auction house which has specialist sales

A set of 6 George III Hepplewhite style mahogany dining chairs, with drop-in seats, the carver armchair with shepherd's crook arms.
$2,000-2,500

A set of 6 Hepplewhite carved mahogany dining chairs, the backs with foliate splats surmounted by panels with paterae and husks, with stuffover bowed saddle seats, on moulded concave tapered legs.
$4,000-5,000

In the Furniture section if there is only one measurement it usually refers to the width of the piece.

A set of 18 Sheraton design mahogany framed dining chairs, the back inlaid with an oval trumpet shell medallion, inlaid overall with boxwood stringing.
$8,000-10,000

A set of 7 Hepplewhite style
nahogany chairs, including a pair
f armchairs, the shield-backs with
vheatear carved splats.
1,500-2,000

A set of 6 Hepplewhite style mahogany dining chairs, including 4 armchairs, with floral upholstered seats.
$4,000-5,000

A set of 6 Sheraton period mahogany dining chairs, with channelled vertical back splats, on square tapering legs, joined by stretchers.
$3,000-4,000

A set of 4 Sheraton style mahogany dining chairs, with arched top rails, above 3 pierced splats.
$1,000-1,200

A set of 8 Chippendale style carved mahogany dining chairs, including 2 carvers, on cabriole supports with ball-and-claw feet.
$3,500-4,000

A set of 8 Chippendale style mahogany dining chairs, including 2 armchairs, late 19thC.
$9,000-10,000

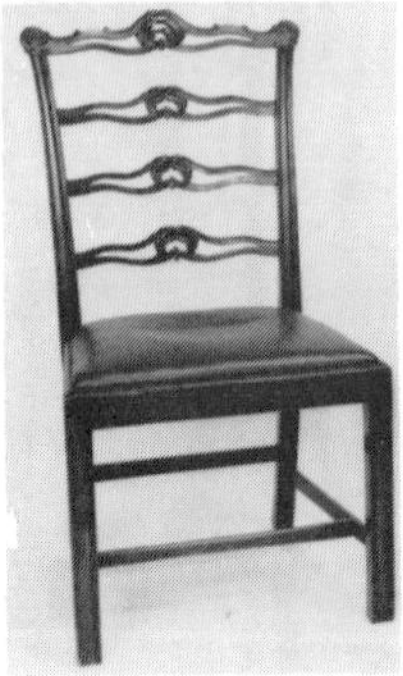

A set of 5 Chippendale style mahogany dining chairs, including 2 carvers, with pierced and carved ladderback, reeded legs, joined by stretchers.
$1,500-2,000

A set of 6 Chippendale style mahogany dining chairs, including 2 carvers.
$3,000-4,000

A set of 8 Chippendale style mahogany dining chairs, including 2 carvers, with pierced and carved back splats, the cabriole legs with foliate carved knees and ball-and-claw feet.
$4,000-5,000

A set of 8 Chippendale style dining chairs, including 2 carvers.
$4,000-5,000

A set of 8 Chippendale style mahogany dining chairs, including 2 armchairs, with interlaced vase splat, with drop-in seats, on cabriole supports with pad feet.
$1,500-2,000

A set of 8 William IV rosew
dining chairs, with tapestry
serpentine seats.
$6,000-8,000

A set of 8 Chippendale style mahogany dining chairs, including 2 armchairs.
$6,000-7,000

A pair of Chippendale style dining
chairs, with loose seats, on carved
cabriole legs with ball-and-claw fee
$200-400

set of 12 mahogany ladderback
ning chairs, including 2 carvers,
ith pierced wavy bars, mid-19thC.
,000-10,000

A set of 6 Victorian dining chairs.
$1,800-2,500

A set of 6 Victorian walnut dining chairs, with fluted column and acanthus carved arched crestings.
$2,500-3,000

A set of 6 Victorian walnut framed balloon backed dining chairs, the seats recovered in floral needlework.
$3,000-4,000

set of 6 late Victorian walnut
ning chairs, with inlaid
ecoration.
,800-2,500

A set of 6 Victorian rosewood chairs, with pierced and carved hooped backs, on cabriole legs.
$4,000-5,000

A set of 6 Victorian mahogany balloon back dining chairs, with turned tapered fluted legs.
$2,500-3,000

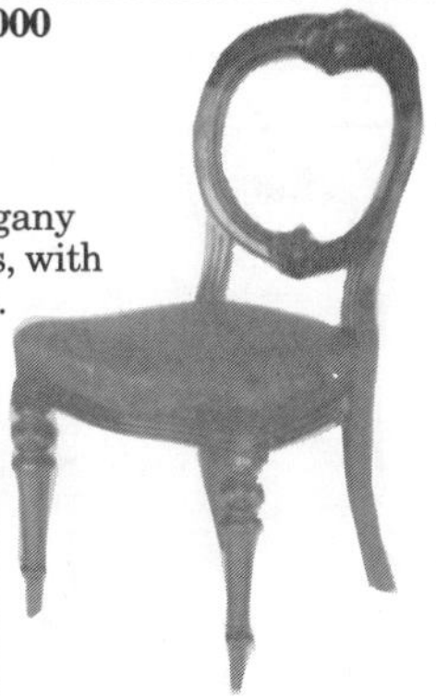

A set of 8 early Victorian mahogany dining chairs.
$5,000-6,000

set of 6 early Victorian walnut
ning chairs, with serpentine
holstered seats.
,000-4,000

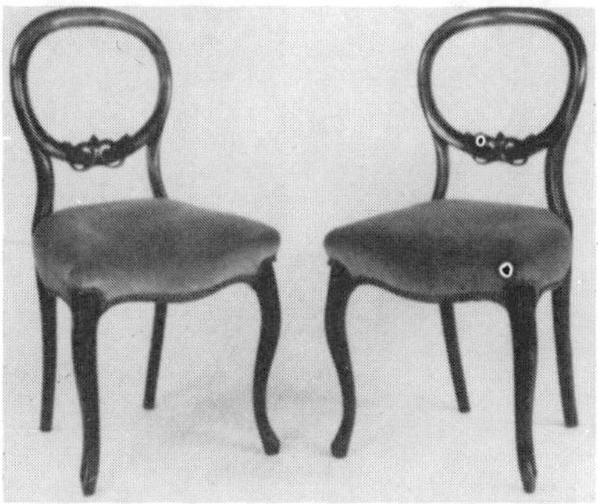

A set of 6 Victorian walnut dining chairs, the balloon moulded and foliate carved rail backs above upholstered serpentine seats.
$3,000-4,000

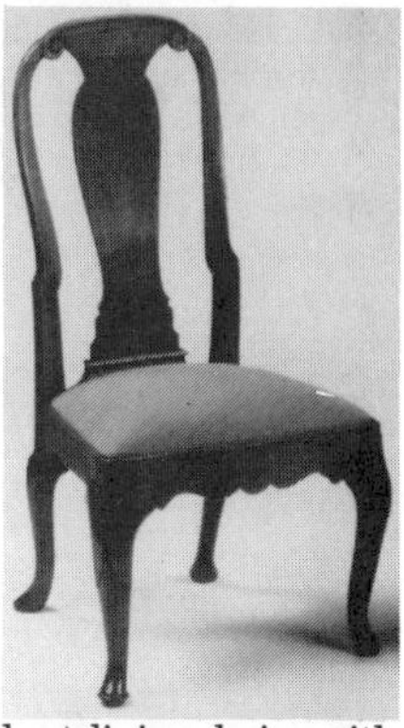

A set of 6 walnut dining chairs, with a scrolled carved top rail and vase shaped splat above a serpentine drop-in seat upholstered in blue, possibly Colonial, 19thC.
$7,000-8,000

A set of 6 William IV rosewood dining chairs, with bowed carved top rails and foliate carved splats, on tapered legs.
$3,500-4,000

A set of 6 early Victorian mahogany dining chairs.
$5,000-6,000

A set of 6 Victorian rosewood dining chairs, with cartouche shaped backs, scroll carved crossbars, upholstered seats and moulded cabriole legs.
$3,000-4,000

A set of 6 Victorian walnut dining chairs.
$3,000-4,000

A set of 7 early Victorian mahoga dining chairs, labelled T.H. Film & Son.
$4,000-5,000

A set of 6 Victorian mahogany dining chairs, the acanthus carved C-scrolling railed semi-balloon backs above upholstered serpentine seats.
$1,800-2,500

A set of 12 Victorian rosewood dining chairs, with serpentine upholstered seats, on slender French cabriole front supports.
$9,000-10,000

A set of 8 Victorian mahogany dining chairs, the buttoned and close nailed serpentine crested panelled backs and seats on reeded turned tapering legs.
$5,000-6,000

A set of 6 Victorian mahogany dining chairs, on turned front supports.
$1,200-1,600

A set of 8 Victorian walnut dining chairs.
$1,800-2,500

A set of 3 Chippendale style mahogany dining chairs, early 19thC.
$400-600

A set of 6 Victorian mahogany dining chairs.
$2,000-3,000

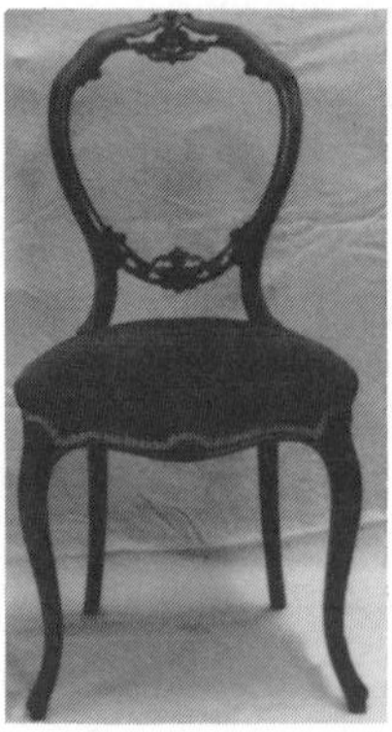

A set of 4 balloon back dining chairs, with upholstered seats on cabriole legs, 19thC.
$1,500-2,000

A set of 6 Victorian balloon back dining chairs, bearing maker's label William Johnson, Sheffield.
$3,000-4,000

A set of 6 early Victorian rosewood dining chairs.
$4,000-5,000

ʌ set of 6 Hepplewhite style dining hairs, including 2 carvers, with vheatear shield backs.
1,500-2,000

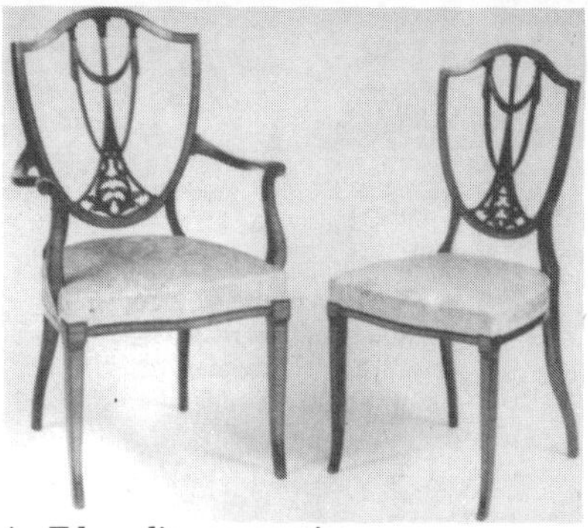

An Edwardian seven-piece mahogany suite, in Hepplewhite style, including 2 armchairs and a two-seater sofa, inlaid with satinwood bands and boxwood lines.
$5,000-6,000

A set of 6 dining chairs, including 2 carvers.
$600-800

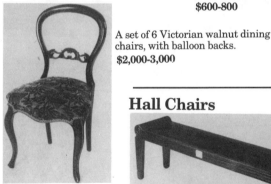

A set of 6 Victorian walnut dining chairs, with balloon backs.
$2,000-3,000

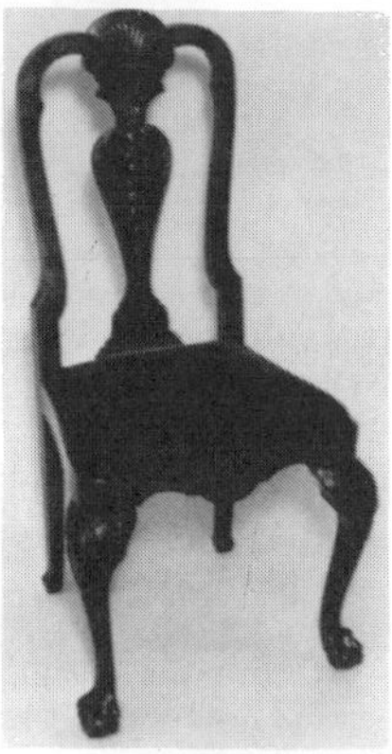

A set of 4 walnut dining chairs.
$800-1,000

Hall Chairs

A Regency carved mahogany hall seat, with reeded ornament, bearing a label 'This forme was purchased at the sale of Admiral Lord Nelson'.
$14,000-16,000

pair of Regency ahogany hall airs, one leg spliced.
,500-2,000

A pair of Regency mahogany hall chairs, with panelled shield backs and shaped seats.
$1,500-2,000

A pair of Regency mahogany hall chairs, with solid concave waisted backs, bowed seats and square tapering legs.
$400-600

Use the Index!
Because certain items might fit easily into any of a number of categories, the quickest and surest method of locating any entry is by reference to the index at the back of the book.
This has fully been cross-referenced for absolute simplicity

Side Chairs

A set of 4 William and Mary black painted bannister back side chairs, New England, some with pieced feet, c1735.
$3,000-4,000

A Queen Anne maple side chair, restoration to 2 returns, and splat shoe, Massachusetts, c1740.
$3,000-4,000

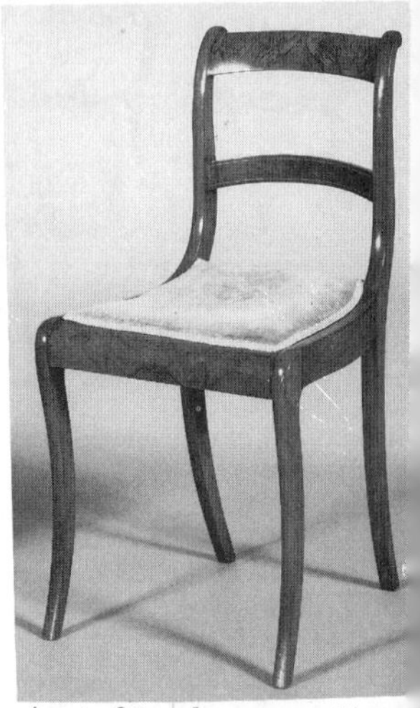

A set of 6 mahogany and bur walnut veneered side chairs, American, c1825.
$1,800-2,500

A set of 4 Federal cherrywood side chairs, various old repairs, Hartfor area, Connecticut, c1800.
$8,000-12,000

A Federal carved mahogany side chair, Massachusetts, c1800.
$10,000-12,000

A Queen Anne carved walnut side chair, one knee return restored and centre stretcher possibly restored, Newport, Rhode Island, c1765.
$22,000-26,000

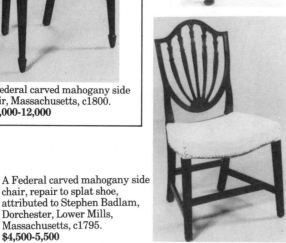

A Federal carved mahogany side chair, repair to splat shoe, attributed to Stephen Badlam, Dorchester, Lower Mills, Massachusetts, c1795.
$4,500-5,500

A Queen Anne walnut slipper cha Boston or Salem, Massachusetts, c1770.
$5,000-8,000

Queen Anne walnut side chair, ınnsylvania, c1740.
,000-7,000

A pair of late Federal carved mahogany side chairs, Baltimore, Maryland, c1815.
$4,000-5,000

A set of 6 fancy painted side chairs, some peeling, Baltimore, Maryland, c1830.
$3,500-4,500

A Chippendale carved walnut side chair, Philadelphia, c1775.
$5,000-7,000

Queen Anne walnut side chair, assachusetts, c1750.
10,000-12,000

A pair of Federal inlaid mahogany side chairs, various old breaks, Baltimore, c1800.
$7,000-8,000

. Federal carved mahogany side nair, probably New York, c1800.
1,000-1,500

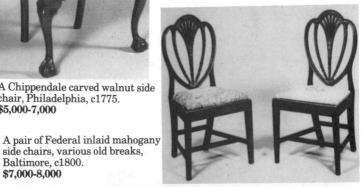

A set of 6 Classical carved and figured maple side chairs, New York State, c1820.
$8,500-10,000

A pair of Federal carved mahogany side chairs, feet on one chair pieced, New York, c1800.
$5,000-6,000

A set of 4 Regency style ebonised and parcel gilt side chairs, the seats variously painted, all stamped GR flanking a crown and variously numbered, late 19thC.
$3,000-4,000

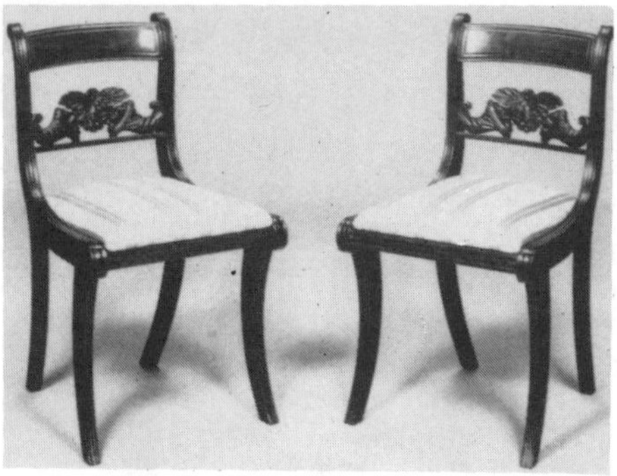

A pair of late Federal carved mahogany side chairs, New York, c1815.
$2,000-3,000

A set of 6 Victorian walnut side chairs, with acanthus carved top rails, bowed seats, on reeded turne[d] front supports.
$2,000-3,000

A Dutch mahogany and marquetry chair, inlaid with foliage and cornucopia.
$600-700

A pair of Dutch painted and gilded side chairs, the shield shaped backs applied with masks and paterae in beaded and bellflower borders, with a central pierced foliate and C-scrolling carved splat, with a central leafy roundel above upholstered seats, late 18thC.
$2,500-3,000

A pair of Chippendale mahogany ribbon back side chairs, damaged, Pennsylvania, c1770.
$2,500-3,500

A Louis XV beechwood chair, with cartouche shaped padded back and serpentine seat, formerly caned.
$700-800

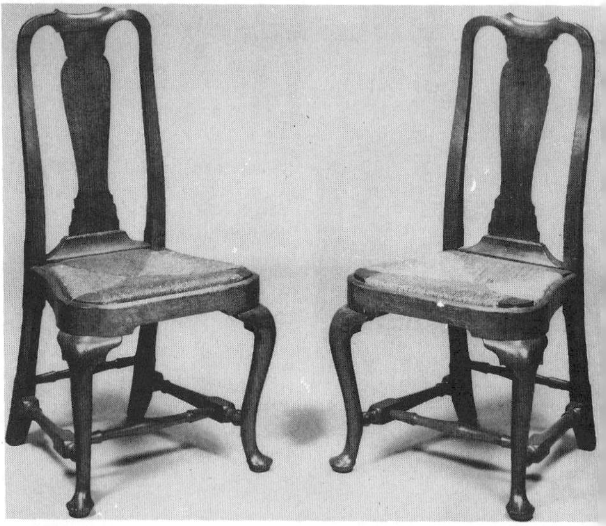

A pair of Queen Anne walnut side chairs, slip-in seat altered for rush Massachusetts, c1750.
$35,000-40,000

hests

Chippendale maple blanket chest, th thumb moulded edge and aped cleats lifting above a maple l, probably Rhode Island, c1775, ½in (120cm).
,000-2,500

A Chippendale walnut chest, fitted with a till, over 3 thumb moulded short drawers, on straight bracket feet, minor crack to top, Pennsylvania, c1770, 49½in (125cm).
$5,000-6,000

Chippendale painted blanket est, with lifting lid, inscribed and ted 1794, Pennsylvania, 49in 24.5cm).
5,000-20,000

A Chippendale figured walnut tall chest of drawers, on shaped bracket feet with a double line inlaid edge, Pennsylvania, c1770, 41in (104cm).
$6,000-8,000

An orange sponge painted blanket chest, the top opening to reveal a compartment with a till, mid-Atlantic States, mid-19thC, 49½in (125cm).
$4,000-5,000

late Federal painted chest with awers, the surface finger painted green, the drawers and ouldings in red, Pennsylvania, 820, 49½in (125cm).
,000-3,000

A Chippendale maple tall chest of drawers, on bracket feet, New England, c1770, 36in (91.5cm).
$4,000-5,000

A Chippendale maple chest of drawers, on straight bracket feet, probably Rhode Island, c1770, 41in (104cm).
$4,000-5,000

A black painted child's blanket chest, with single drawer, some wear, losses and repair to one foot, New England, early 19thC, 24½in (62cm).
$2,500-3,000

A Federal cherrywood chest of drawers, on modified French feet, old repairs to feet, Connecticut, c1810, 42in (106.5cm).
$2,000-2,500

A Federal inlaid mahogany bowfront chest of drawers, small patch to top, North Eastern Massachusetts, c1800, 42in (107cm).
$3,000-4,000

A Federal figured birch and mahogany chest of drawers, New England, c1810, 43in (109cm).
$2,500-3,500

A Federal cherrywood chest of drawers, with 4 cockbeaded and graduated long drawers, over scalloped apron, graphite inscription on backboards Triphem Gorham 1800, Connecticut, 44in (112cm).
$2,500-3,500

A Federal inlaid mahogany chest of drawers, the top with line inlaid edge, with crossbanded satinwood reserve between 2 small drawers, over 3 graduated drawers, on flared French feet, mid-Atlantic States, c1800, 44in (112cm).
$4,000-5,000

A Federal mahogany concave front chest of drawers, with 4 cockbeaded drawers, Coastal New England, c1800, 40in (102cm).
$6,000-7,000

A Federal inlaid mahogany bowfront chest of drawers, with 4 cockbead moulded and graduated drawers, on modified French feet, Massachusetts, c1800, 41½in (104.5cm).
$3,000-4,000

A Federal inlaid mahogany bowfront chest of drawers, the top with inlaid edge, above 4 cockbeaded long drawers, New England, c1800, 39in (99cm).
$3,500-4,500

A Federal inlaid walnut chest of drawers, with 4 line inlaid and cockbead moulded graduated drawers, flanked by line inlaid chamfered corners over a banded apron, Pennsylvania, c1810, 40½i (102cm).
$4,000-6,000

A Federal carved mahogany bowfront chest of drawers, the bowfront with outset rounded corners and applied ring turned moulding, with 4 graduated long drawers flanked by reeded column with fluted waterleaf and star punched capitals, attributed to William Hook, Salem, Massachusetts, c1800, 44in (112cm
$4,000-6,000

A Federal mahogany bowfront chest of drawers, the top with banded edge, 4 graduated long drawers over a shaped apron, Massachusetts, c1800, 43in (109cm).
$3,000-4,000

A Chippendale carved mahogany chest of drawers, minor patches, Philadelphia, c1770, 38in (96.5cm).
$6,000-9,000

A Chippendale walnut chest of drawers, the top with moulded edge above a conforming case, with 4 graduated long drawers, each thumb moulded, on ogee bracket feet, Pennsylvania, c1770, 39½in (100cm).
$10,000-12,000

A Chippendale birch reverse serpentine chest of drawers, 1 rear foot facing replaced, patch to 1 foot, North Eastern, Massachusetts, c1770, 40in (101cm).
$10,000-15,000

\ Chippendale mahogany chest of rawers, on scrolled bracket feet, Jorth Shore, Massachusetts, c1780, 1in (104cm).
5,000-7,000

A Chippendale figured maple tall chest of drawers, several patches to drawers, New England, c1775, 40in (101.5cm).
$5,000-6,000

A Federal inlaid mahogany and bird's-eye maple bowfront chest of drawers, the D-shaped top with banded edge, the 5 graduated drawers with inlaid panels, on French feet, North Shore, Massachusetts, c1800, 41in (104cm).
$7,000-9,000

Federal mahogany bowfront chest drawers, the top with moulded ge, Massachusetts, c1800, 43in 09cm).
,000-5,000

A Federal inlaid mahogany concave front chest of drawers, edged with lightwood banding and with line inlaid drawers, on modified French feet, probably Maryland, c1800, 41in (104cm).
$6,500-7,500

Federal mahogany chest of awers, New England, c1800, 42in 06.5cm).
,000-4,000

A Federal cherrywood tall chest of drawers, the coved cornice above 3 short and 5 long drawers, flanked by chamfered corners, Pennsylvania, c1800, 46in (116cm).
$4,500-5,500

A Federal inlaid mahogany bowfront chest of drawers, the D-shaped top with line inlaid edge, the 4 graduated long drawers with line inlaid panels, minor veneer patches, North Carolina or Virginia, c1800, 40in (101.5cm).
$4,000-5,000

A Queen Anne faded walnut chest, with quarter veneered and broadly crossbanded top, the drawers inlaid with convex herringbone bandings, 37in (94cm).
$3,000-4,000

A laburnum and oyster veneered chest, inlaid with geometric boxwood lines, with 4 long drawers and an undulating apron, on turned bun feet, adapted, late 17thC, 37in (94cm).
$4,000-5,000

A Federal carved mahogany chest of drawers, the graduated long drawers with panelled fronts flanked by fluted pilasters, on turned feet with casters, Philadelphia, c1810, 44in (112cm).
$4,000-5,000

A figured walnut and banded chest, with quarter veneered top, part early 18thC, 42½in (107cm).
$3,000-4,000

A walnut chest, with inlaid and crossbanded quarter veneered top, on turned onion bun feet, parts 18thC, 36in (91.5cm).
$5,000-6,000

A mahogany chest of drawers, early 18thC.
$6,000-8,000

A Dutch marquetry chest of drawers, with decorated brass escutcheons, mid-18thC, 34in (86cm).
$5,000-7,000

A Federal cherrywood and mahogany bowfront chest c drawers, on inverted and ri turned feet with casters, Massachusetts, c1810, 43in (106.5cm).
$4,500-5,500

A laburnum veneered chest, w oak lined featherbanded drawe 18thC, 31in (78.5cm).
$4,000-6,000

A Queen Anne figured walnut chest, inlaid with chevron ban the top crossbanded, on later bracket feet, 39in (99cm).
$6,000-8,000

A walnut chest of drawers, ea 18thC, 33in (84cm).
$14,000-16,000

mahogany dwarf chest, with rushing slide and 4 graduated rawers, parts 18thC, 28in (71cm).
4,000-5,000

n early George II walnut chest, the uarter veneered and crossbanded p above 2 short and 3 long awers, inlaid with ebony and oxwood stringing, 31in (79cm).
4,000-4,500

n early George III mahogany rpentine chest, with moulded lge, 4 long drawers, on ogee racket feet, 38in (96.5cm).
12,000-14,000

Georgian mahogany chest, with rushing slide, over 4 long raduated drawers with brass plate andles, on bracket feet.
4,000-5,000

A late George II mahogany chest, the crossbanded top above a brushing slide and 4 graduated long drawers, on ogee bracket feet, 32½in (82cm).
$5,000-6,000

A George II mahogany chest, fitted with a slide, containing 4 long drawers, on bracket feet, 30in (77cm).
$5,000-6,000

A Georgian mahogany chest of drawers, with green baize lined brushing slide, 2 short and 3 long graduated drawers with brass handles and escutcheons, 33½in (85cm).
$4,000-5,000

A George III mahogany inlaid and laburnum crossbanded chest, the top with geometric stringing, fitted with a slide and 4 long drawers.
$3,000-4,000

An early Georgian walnut chest, the crossbanded top above a slide and 4 graduated drawers, each with the back drawer lining replaced, on later bracket feet, possibly reduced in depth, 29½in (75cm).
$6,000-8,000

An early Georgian walnut chest with crossbanded top, inlaid with chevron lines, on partially replaced bracket feet, 36in (91.5cm).
$4,000-5,000

An early George III mahogany chest, with later moulded top, adapted from the top of a tallboy, 42in (106.5cm).
$1,300-1,500

A George III mahogany chest, with moulded top above a slide and 4 graduated drawers, on bracket feet, 36in (91.5cm).
$4,000-5,000

arlequin set of 6 oak
kshire chairs, 17thC.
00-7,000

An English oak and walnut coffer, with secret compartment, mid-17thC.
$6,000-8,000

A Charles II oak bureau, some alterations, 45in (114cm).
$10,000-12,000

A Charles II oak carved panelled box settle, North Yorkshire, c1680.
$8,000-10,000

Elizabethan oak, walnut and painted
er bedstead, restored, 66in (167cm).
,000-70,000

A harlequin set of 6 Windsor ash and elm chairs, c1830.
$3,500-5,000

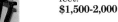

A Jacobean oak chest of drawers, with geometric moulded front, on stile feet.
$1,500-2,000

Villiam and Mary oak
eau, with fitted
erior, on later turned
, 30in (76cm).
,000-25,000

A set of 8 English yew-wood Gothic back chairs, c1820.
$6,000-8,000

A South Wales coffer, 18thC.
$2,000-3,000

An oak bureau with swan neck handles, c1780, 36in (91cm).
$2,000-3,000

A joined oak chest, probably Guilford, Connecticut, 1650-80, 50in (126cm).
$12,000-14,000

A Spanish chestnut coffer, 16th/17thC restorations, 59in (150cm). **$8,000-10,000**

An English carved oak panelled coffer, 17thC.
$2,000-3,000

An English joined pre[s]
cupboard, inlaid with
oak and holly, c1690.
$10,000-14,000

A George III oak cupboard dresser and rack with spice drawers.
$15,000-18,000

A Charles II carved oak coffer with drawer, West Country.
$3,000-5,000

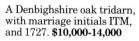

A George I oak writing box on baluster turned stand.
$2,000-3,000

A Denbighshire oak tridarn, with marriage initials ITM, and 1727. **$10,000-14,000**

An English oak dresser wi[th]
rack and cupboards, c1750.
$6,000-10,000

A George III oak low dresser, crossbanded with mahogany, drawers divided by stylised flowerheads, back legs replaced, 74in (188cm). **$10,000-14,000**

A George II oak dresser base, original brasses, good patination.
$10,000-14,000

An oak refectory table, with fluted frieze and baluster legs, initialled HF, part 17thC, 108in (274cm). **$8,000-12,000**

An oak refectory table, with planked top, trestle ends, 18thC, 101in (257cm). **$12,000-15,000**

A Georgian yew-wood tripod table with burr top.
$4,000-6,000

An oak gateleg table, with oval top, 17thC, 64in (164cm). **$13,000-15,000**

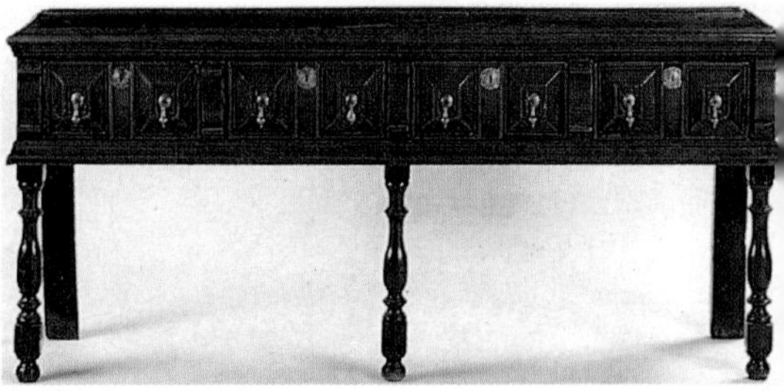

A Charles II oak dresser base, with moulded top and 4 frieze drawers, on baluster front legs, restorations, 70in (177cm). **$20,000-25,000**

A George III oak hanging corner cupboard, with Gothic glazing bars.
$1,200-1,500

An early George II oak gateleg dining table, with oval twin flap top, shaped apron and 6 hipped moulded legs with pad feet, 66in (168cm) wide, extended.
$15,000-18,000

Regency mahogany breakfront bookcase,
:h moulded cornice above 4 ogee arched
ızed doors, 136in (345cm).
5,000-30,000

A George III mahogany and painted bed, 72in (183cm).
$24,000-28,000

A Regency mahogany bookcase, 92in (234cm). **$15,000-18,000**

Regency rosewood bed,
n (181cm).
)0,000-120,000

An oak hanging corner cupboard, with 6 fielded panels, c1750, 27in (68cm) high.
$700-800

An early George III mahogany tester bed. **$12,000-15,000**

mahogany breakfront bookcase,
ise fitted with 3 brushing
ides, 2 cupboards and 8
awers, 96in (244cm).
2,000-15,000

A Transitional bois satiné and parquetry bonheur du jour by Simon Oeben, stamped, 37½in (94cm).
$90,000-100,000

A George III mahogany bookcase, the central secrétaire drawer flanked by 2 other drawers, above 4 panelled doors, 100in (254cm). **$6,000-9,000**

George III mahogany breakfront
ɔokcase, with moulded cornice above
Gothic-glazed doors, the base with
doors enclosing shelves, 100in (254cm).
35,000-40,000

A late George III mahogany breakfront bookcase, secrétaire drawer in the base, 96in (224cm). **$20,000-25,000**

A George III mahogany bookcase, 91in (231cm).
$12,000-15,000

A Regency pollard oak and parcel gilt bookcase, in the manner of Marsh & Tatham, with blue marble tops and gadrooned edges, 53in (134cm).
$28,000-32,000

A Regency rosewood and brass strung open bookcase, the graduated shelves above 2 short brass strung drawers, 37½in (95cm).
$14,000-18,000

A George III bureau bookcase, the hinged leat lined slope enclosing fitte interior, 42in (107cm).
$12,000-15,000

A pair of Regency mahogany open bookcases, filled with various sized leather bound books, adapted, 42in (107cm).
$12,000-15,000

A George III mahogany bureau bookcase, the sloping flap enclosing a fitted interior, above 3 short and 3 long drawers, 48in (122cm).
$8,000-12,000

A George I walnut bure bookcase, the doors enclosing 7 drawers abc sloping flap with well a secret drawers, 40½in (103cm). **$18,000-20,00**

A pair of Regency rosewood and parcel gilt bookcases, with simulated rosewood ends, tops possibly associated, 34in (86cm).
$20,000-25,000

An ormolu mounted and Boulle bookcase, with marquetry inlay, basically mid-18thC, 60in (152cm). **$15,000-20,000**

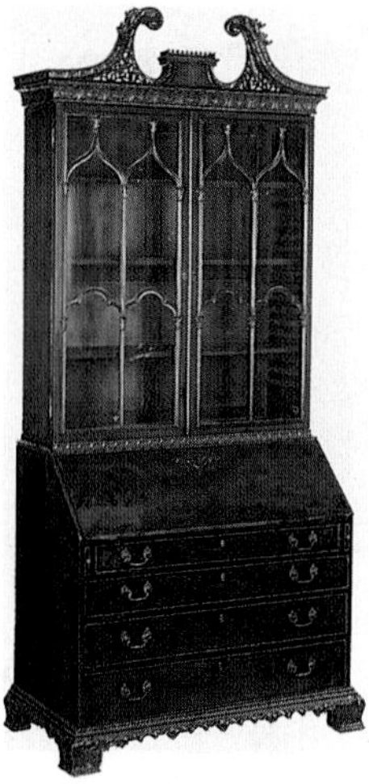

A mahogany bureau bookcase, the hinged slope with fitted interior, 46in (116cm).
$20,000-25,000

A pair of rosewood dwarf bookcases, t friezes applied with giltmetal berried foliage and flowerheads, basically early 19thC, 36in (92cm).
$4,000-6,000

George III satinwood,
ıhogany, marquetry and
ınted secrétaire cabinet,
ıssbanded overall with
ɜewood, restoration, 29in
ɩcm). **$25,000-30,000**

German ormolu mounted
ahogany cylinder bureau, the
caded panelled fall flap
closing 7 drawers, c1800,
'in (119cm).
ɩ0,000-60,000

German stained birch bureau
ıbinet, with shaped arched
ıoulded cornice above panelled
ɔor and 11 drawers, bureau
ith hinged slope above 9
rawers, mid-18thC,
4in (112cm).
15,000-20,000

A George II scarlet and gold lacquer
bureau cabinet, possibly supplied by
Giles Grendey, 40in (101cm). **$500,000+**

l. A George II mahogany bureau
cabinet, sloping front enclosing Gothic
arched pigeonholes and drawers,
46in (115cm). **$12,000-15,000**
r. A George III mahogany
secrétaire bookcase, 31in (77cm).
$15,000-20,000

A George III mahogany cylinder bureau,
the tambour shutter enclosing a
fitted interior with slide and
leather lined panel, later angle
brackets, 39½in (100cm).
$8,000-10,000

A George I figured walnut
bureau cabinet, the mirror
glazed doors enclosing
shelves and pigeonholes,
43in (108cm). **$18,000-20,000**

A Queen Anne burr
walnut bureau
cabinet, later
glazed doors and
later candle slides,
41in (101cm).
$20,000-25,000

A George II figured walnut
bureau cabinet, inlaid with
chequered lines, upper part
and bureau with adjustable
shelves, pigeonholes and
drawers, 44in (112cm).
$45,000-50,000

An Empire ormolu-mounted mahogany secrétaire à abattant, stamped Jacob.D Rue Meslee. **$15,000-18,000**

A Charles X ormolu-mounted mahogany secrétaire à abattant, stamped Durand, 39in (99cm). **$8,000-12,000**

A Scandinavian burr walnut, kingwood a[nd] marquetry bureau, enclosing mahogany fitted interior, late 18thC, 32in (80cm). **$12,000-15,000**

A George I walnut bureau, the sloping flap enclosing fitted interior, 38in (97cm). **$6,000-10,000**

A George I yew wood bureau, with walnut crossbanding, 32in (80cm). **$18,000-20,000**

A George II figured waln[ut] bureau, the sloping flap inlaid with boxwood and ebonised lines, fitted interior repaired, 34in (86cm). **$10,000-15,000**

A George III mahogany secrétaire cabinet, inlaid with shells and chevron banding, 49in (125cm). **$10,000-15,000**

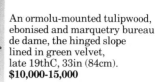

An ormolu-mounted tulipwood, ebonised and marquetry bureau de dame, the hinged slope lined in green velvet, late 19thC, 33in (84cm). **$10,000-15,000**

A walnut bureau, the sloping flap enclosing a fitted interior, the 4 graduated drawers divided by a slide, 26in (66cm). **$8,000-10,000**

A George III mahogany bureau, the gree[n] baize lined slope enclosing a fitted interior, 47½in (120cm). **$8,000-10,000**

George III mahogany sideboard, with
rpentine fronted top, adapted,
4in (110cm). **$6,000-8,000**

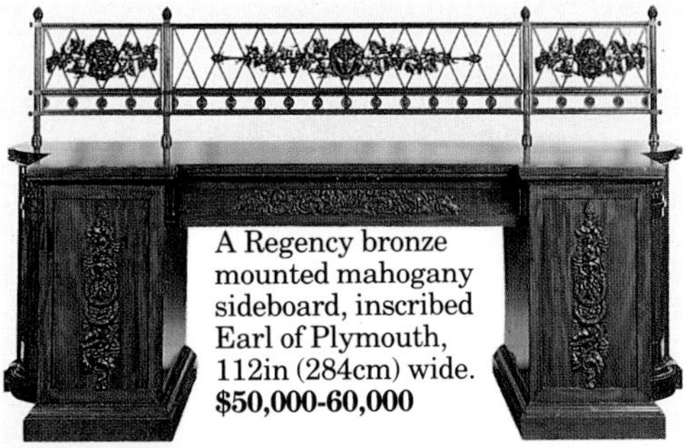

A Regency bronze mounted mahogany sideboard, inscribed Earl of Plymouth, 112in (284cm) wide. **$50,000-60,000**

A Continental neo-classical ormolu-mounted ebonised mahogany bureau à cylindre, stamped Roos, possibly Low Countries, c1840, 62in (155cm). **$8,000-10,000**

late George III mahogany sideboard,
ith crossbanded D-shaped top, 66in
68cm). **$8,000-12,000**

A William IV ormolu-mounted mahogany side cabinet, 66in (168cm). **$35,000-40,000**

Regency mahogany sideboard, inlaid with boxwood lines,
sewood crossbanding, 123in (313cm). **$35,000-40,000**

A Regency mahogany sideboard, 84in (213cm). **$15,000-20,000**

A Louis XIV purpleheart and pewter Boulle bureau Mazarin, inlaid in contre partie with Berainesque strapwork and foliage, the leather lined top with fitted interior, 42½in (107cm). **$12,000-15,000**

A Regency rosewood chiffonier, inlaid with brass lines, 46in (116cm). **$6,000-8,000**

A George III mahogany, tulipwood crossbanded and inlaid sideboard, 60in (152cm). **$6,000-8,000**

A Regency ormolu-mounted rosewood chiffonier, 31in (77cm). **$20,000-25,000**

A Dutch satinwood and marquetry Teestof, late 18thC, 47in (118cm).
$8,000-10,000

A Dutch walnut, ebony and marquetry cabinet on chest, 50in (125cm). **$12,000-16,000**

A pair of ormolu mounted kingwood, mahogany semainier 19in (49cm). **$25,000-30,000**

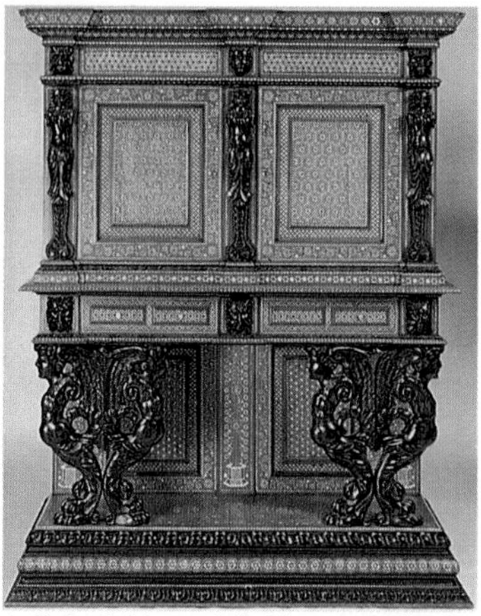

A Colonial ivory inlaid rosewood cabinet on stand, moulded base carved with foliage, 65in (165cm). **$18,000-20,000**

A Queen Anne lacquered cabinet, with gilt chinoiserie scenes, 46in (116cm). **$55,000-60,000**

A Louis Phillipe kingwood, mahogany cabinet, 31in (77cm).
$6,000-8,000

A George I walnut cabinet in 2 parts, the upper part with 2 drawers and 2 false drawers, partly reconstructed in 19thC, 34in (86cm). **$16,000-20,000**

A William and Mary walnut and oyste veneered cabinet, on later feet, 46in (117cm). **$10,000-15,000**

A black and gold lacquer cabinet on stand, 18thC, 45in(114cm).
$16,000-20,000

A French ormolu-mounted, ebonised and red tortoiseshell Boulle meuble d'appui, late 19thC, 60in (154cm).
$8,000-10,000

An ormolu-mounted brass inlaid ebony meuble d'appui, in Boulle style, 73in (186cm).
$16,000-20,000

A Chinese black and gold lacquer cabinet, 17thC, 25in (64cm). **$10,000-15,000**

A Normandy fruitwood armoire, late 18thC, 71in (180cm). **$8,000-10,000**

A Dutch walnut floral marquetry armoire, the panelled doors enclosing shelves and drawers, 78in (198cm). **$35,000-40,000**

A Flemish walnut and marquetry armoire, extensively carved with scrolling foliage, 90in (229cm). **$10,000-15,000**

An Empire mahogany cabinet, mirror-backed hinged top with fitted interior, 21in (53cm). **$16,000-20,000**

A Goanese ivory, ebony and hardwood cabinet on stand, 40in (101cm). **$50,000-60,000**

A Chinese black and gold lacquer coffer, late 17thC, 62in (158cm). **$16,000-20,000**

A Queen Anne lacquer corner cabinet, with enclosed shelves, restored, 42in (107cm). **$6,000-9,000**

A Charles II japanned Vernis Martin cabinet, silvered stand, 64in. **$90,000-100,000**

A Flemish ebony and painted cabinet, enclosing 9 drawers around a cupboard door, restored, late 17thC, 28in (70cm). **$4,000-6,000**

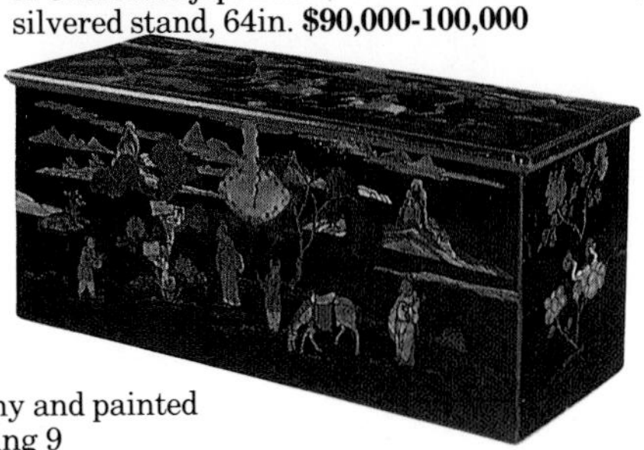

A coromandel lacquer chest, 18thC, 51in (129cm). **$10,000-15,000**

A Louis XV beechwood chair, upholstered seat, formerly caned.
$1,600-2,000

A Regency mahogany desk chair, with deep U-shaped top rail, repaired.
$9,000-11,000

A matched pair of early Louis XV armchairs, upholstered in floral petit point, restored.
$6,000-9,000

A set of 5 Louis XV beechwoo armchairs, extensive repairs and restorations.
$18,000-20,000

A pair of Louis XVI walnut bergères, stamped I. Cheneaux.
$16,000-20,000

A set of 4 Louis XV painted armchairs.
$80,000-90,000

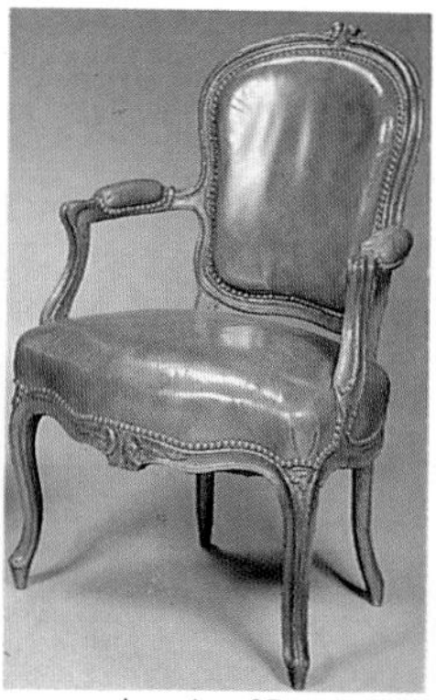

A pair of Louis XV walnut armchairs, stamped Nogaret à Lyon.
$10,000-12,000

A giltwood chais with cartouche shaped back and drop-in seat in floral damask.
$16,000-20,000

A pair of George I armchairs, with arched padded back and shepherds' crook arms, restored. **$70,000-80,000**

A pair of Louis XV gilded walnut armchairs, gilding later. **$55,000-60,000**

An Empire mahogany armchair, the padded seat upholstered in green leather, stamped NI.
$10,000-12,000

A Louis XV beechwood armchair, the moulded frame with rocaille cresting.
$6,000-8,000

A pair of early Louis XV beechwood armchairs.
$6,000-8,000

A walnut open armchair, with floral upholstery, late 17thC. **$6,000-8,000**

‌ueen Anne burr walnut open
ıchair, with gros point
ɔdlework. **$16,000-18,000**

A George I figured walnut
armchair, restored, damaged
foot. **$30,000-35,000**

A William and Mary walnut armchair,
restorations. **$18,000-20,000**

ɟeorge I walnut armchair,
h upholstered drop-in seat,
ɒaired. **$20,000-25,000**

A South German oak and walnut
throne chair, mid-19thC, 59in
(150cm). **$6,000-8,000**

A George II faded mahogany
armchair, upholstered in
silk. **$24,000-30,000**

A set of 8 Directoire mahogany armchairs,
attributed to Georges Jacob. **$140,000-160,000**

ɟeorge I walnut armchair,
ıolstered in petit point
ɔdlework, with shepherds'
ɔk arms and cabriole
s. **$55,000-60,000**

Two Régence
beechwood armchairs,
the frame carved
with shells, scrolls
and foliage.
$7,000-9,000

A pair of Régence
walnut armchairs,
carved with scrolls
and shells.
$16,000-20,000

A pair of Directoire
painted and gilded
armchairs, redecorated.
$14,000-18,000

A George III walnut library armchair, the padded back upholstered in petit point needlework, rear legs stamped WF. **$50,000-70,000**

A set of 10 George III mahogany dining chairs, restorations. **$30,000-35,000**

A pair of George III satinwood armchairs, later blocks. **$35,000-40,000**

A pair of George III armchairs, repaired. **$16,000-18,000**

A pair of George II black and gold armchairs by William and John Linnell, the uprights decorated in gilt with buildings, landscape vignettes. **$200,000-250,000**

A pair of Regency ebonised and gilded armchairs. **$8,000-10,000**

A harlequin set of 8 George III mahogany cockpen armchai some restoration and repairs. **$80,000-90,000**

r. A pair of George III painted armchairs. **$20,000-25,000**

l. A pair of George III mahogany armchairs, restored. **$60,000-70,000**

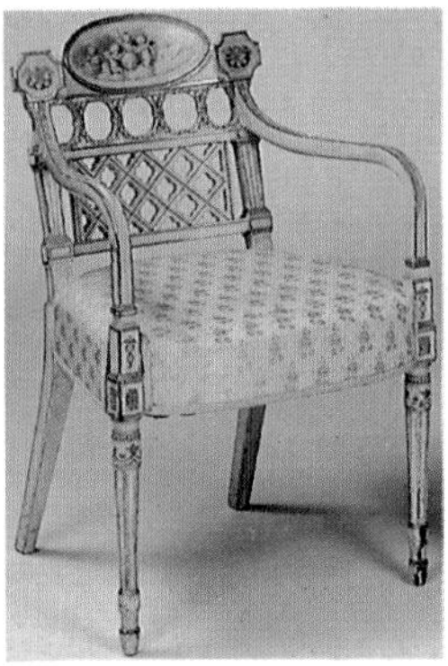

r. Pair of George III mahogany chairs. **$10,000-14,000**

l. A late George III suite of seat furniture. **$250,000-300,000**

A Regency mahogany metamorphic library chair. **$25,000-30,000**

A Regency mahogany tub bergère, the arms carved with ram's head terminals. **$4,000-6,000**

A Regency mahogany armcha
with rosewood crossbanding.
$12,000-15,000

A set of 6 Regency ebonised and parcel gilt armchairs. **$25,000-30,000**

l. A set of 12 Federal mahogany dining chairs, New York, c1800. **$50,000-60,000**

r. A mid-Georgian library armchair, the arms carved with acanthus leaves. **$18,000-20,000**

A pair of George III mahogany armchairs. **$14,000-16,000**

A pair of Regency simulated bronze chairs. **$25,000-30,000**

A pair of Geor
III mahogany
armchairs.
$80,000-90,00

A George III mahogany open armchair. **$6,000-8,000**

r. A pair of George III mahogany armchairs, the vase shaped splats headed by wheat ears. **$8,000-10,000**

l. A set of 4 George IV mahogany armchairs. **$16,000-20,000**

r. A George III mahogany library armchair, restored. **$14,000-16,000**

A pair of William and Mary walnut side chairs, with ornate scrolling frame.
$8,000-10,000

A pair of Anglo-Dutch Queen Anne walnut and marquetry dining chairs.
$6,000-8,000

A pair of Queen Anne burr walnut side chairs, upholstered in gros point needlework.
$18,000-20,000

A set of 6 Queen Anne gilt gesso dining chairs.
$24,000-30,000

A harlequin set of 7 ebony chairs, repaired, c1700, East Indian.
$14,000-16,000

A Maltese rosewood and olive wood armchair, the frame edged with chequered lines.
$10,000-14,000

A Regency mahogany bergère, in the manner of Thomas Hope, re-supported rails.
$10,000-14,000

l. A Mendlesham cherrywood chair with boxwood inlay, c1820.
$8,000-10,000

A set of 4 William IV mahogany tub chairs. **$15,000-18,000**

A pair of mahogany armchairs, the top rails carved with wheat ears. **$15,000-20,000**

A pair of Russian Alexander I armchairs, the top rails carved with scrolling flowerheads.
$6,000-8,000

l. A set of 6 Charles II walnut dining chairs, the frame extensively carved, restorations.
$12,000-14,000

l. A pair of Queen Anne walnut side chairs, brackets replaced. **$10,000-14,000**

A George I walnut side chair, the padded back and seat upholstered in crewelwork. **$10,000-14,000**

A Chippendale carved mahogany armchair, Philadelphia, c1770. **$32,000-40,000**

A set of 3 George I waln chairs. **$50,000-60,000**

r. A set of 14 George II style walnut dining chairs. **$36,000-40,000**

A pair of George I scarlet japanned chairs. **$40,000-50,000**

A set of 3 George I walnut side chairs, gros and petit needlework, restorations. **$8,000-10,000**

l. A pair of Queen Anne walnu side chairs, the splats inlaid with marquetry. **$20,000-25,000**

l. A George II walnut side chair, with cabriole legs and splayed pad feet, partially re-railed. **$4,000-6,000**

A set of 6 George II mahogany and parcel gilt side chairs, in the manner of Robert Mainwaring, extensively carved with acanthus and crested by a pagoda, 24in (61cm). **$350,000-400,000**

A Federal carved mahogar side chair, attributed to Samuel McIntire, Salem, Massachusetts, c1800. **$12,000-16,000**

l. A pair of Queen Anne burr walnut side chairs, upholstered in petit point needlework. **$90,000-100,000**

assembled set of 6 Queen Anne walnut side chairs, :h moulded yoke crest rails, vase shaped splats and loon shaped slip in seats, small repairs, Philadelphia.
)0,000-140,000

A pair of carved mahogany side chairs, signed Brower, New York, c1810, repaired.
$8,000-12,000

pair of George III mahogany ribbon-back ːe chairs, after a design by Thomas ıippendale, the carved pierced backs th scrolling foliage and interlaced bons, the seat rails carved with :kwork, on cabriole legs.
),000-100,000

A harlequin set of 6 George III mahogany dining chairs, some with later blocks.
$10,000-12,000

A matched set of 12 George III mahogany dining chairs, including one armchair, on cabriole legs headed by acanthus on ball and claw feet.
$55,000-60,000

l. A set of 12 George III mahogany dining chairs, with gros and petit point upholstery, seat rails replaced, later front feet.
$50,000-60,000

A set of 6 George III cream painted chairs, some replacements. **$10,000-12,000**

set of 8 mahogany dining chairs, the erced interlaced splats carved with liage, minor variations.
:5,000-30,000

l. A set of 8 early George III mahogany dining chairs, splats carved with foliage.
$8,000-12,000

A set of 6 George III mahogany dining chairs, legs repaired.
$10,000-14,000

l. A set of 4 George III mahogany dining chairs, with carved crest rail.
$6,000-8,000

r. A set of 4 carved walnut frame dining chairs, on cabriole legs, 19thC.
$1,600-1,800

A set of 8 Regency white painted, parcel gilt and lacquer dining chairs.
$20,000-25,000

A set of 8 Regency carved rosewood and brass marquetry dining chairs, on sabre legs.
$14,000-16,000

A George III mahogany side chair, covered in close-nailed buttoned repp.
$2,000-3,000

A set of 6 Victorian painted satinwood side chairs, with bowed padded seats.
$6,000-8,000

A set of 6 George III mahogany dining chair moulded top rail with beaded scrolling ears.
$28,000-32,000

A set of 8 George III mahogany dining chairs.
$18,000-22,000

A set of 8 mahogany dining chairs, the shaped top rail carved with flowerheads and acanthus leaves, later blocks.
$25,000-30,000

A set of 6 George III carv mahogany and fruitwood dining chairs, in the Chippendale taste, one back leg replaced.
$6,000-10,000

l. A set of 12 early Victorian oak dining chairs, the moulded top rails carved with quatrefoils.
$12,000-16,000

l. A pair of George III mahogany dining chairs, the scrolling top rails and ears above pierced carved splats.
$8,000-10,000

Jeorge II mahogany sofa, the padded
ck, arms and seat upholstered in gros
nt needlework, 74in (189cm).
4,000-30,000

Regency and ebonised parcel gilt
adruple chair-back sofa, the top rail
h lion masks and chinoiserie
oration, 66in. **$5,000-7,000**

Regency Gothic giltwood sofa, the
olled arms carved with foliage,
n (185cm). **$25,000-30,000**

eorge III mahogany cockpen settee,
e replacement rails, 42in (107cm).
)00-10,000**

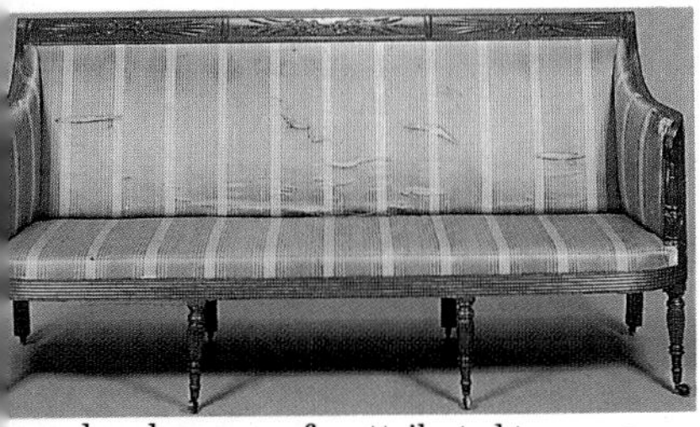

arved mahogany sofa, attributed to
ncan Phyfe, New York, c1810, 77in
5cm). **$50,000-60,000**

A pair of George I walnut settees, covered in stamped and embossed leather decorated in gilt with large flowers and foliage on a blue ground, the cabriole legs with pointed feet, 79in (201cm). **$70,000-90,000**

r. A Queen Anne walnut framed settee, upholstered in gros point floral needlework, the eared cabriole legs with pad feet, 55½in (141cm). **$14,000-18,000**

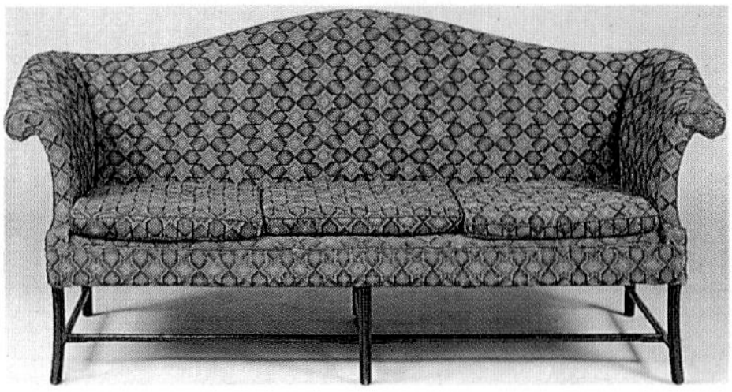

A George III mahogany sofa, the padded back, outscrolled arms and cushions covered in red and green geometric needlework, 87in (220cm). **$25,000-30,000**

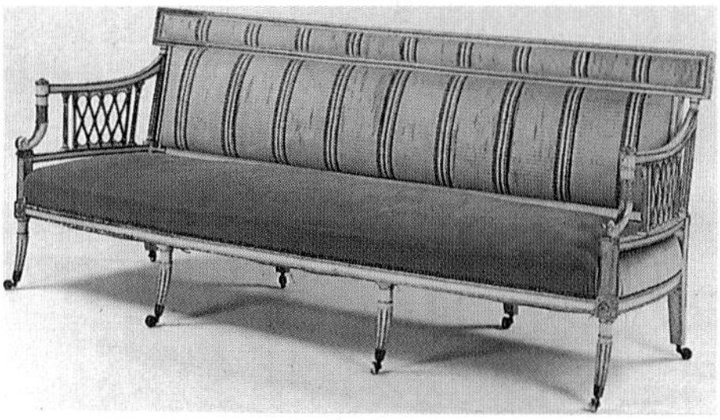

A George III white painted and parcel gilt sofa, covered in yellow, red, green and blue striped silk, some replacements. **$6,000-8,000**

r. An Italian painted and gilded chair, covered in buttoned and braided silk, the scrolled frame painted with flowers, with trade label G.S. Tedeschi, Firenze, mid-19thC, 22in (56cm). **$14,000-16,000**

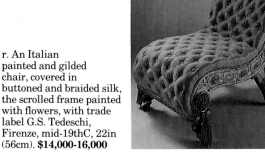

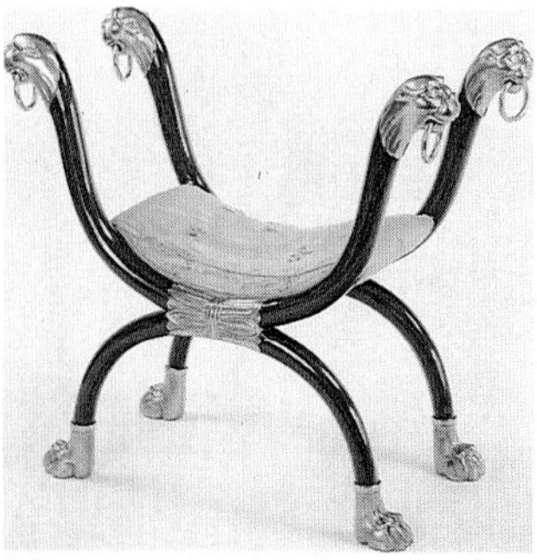

A Regency simulated rosewood and parcel gilt stool, after a design by Thomas Hope, 34in (86cm). **$30,000-35,000**

A mahogany stool with solid panelled seat, 23in (58cm). **$25,000-28,000**

A George IV giltwood stool in Georg style, seat upholstered in green plus and floral needlework, 38in (97cm). **$12,000-15,000**

A Regency ormolu-mounted rosewood stool, supplied by George Bullock for Napoleon's use at New Longwood, 14in (35cm). **$25,000-30,000**

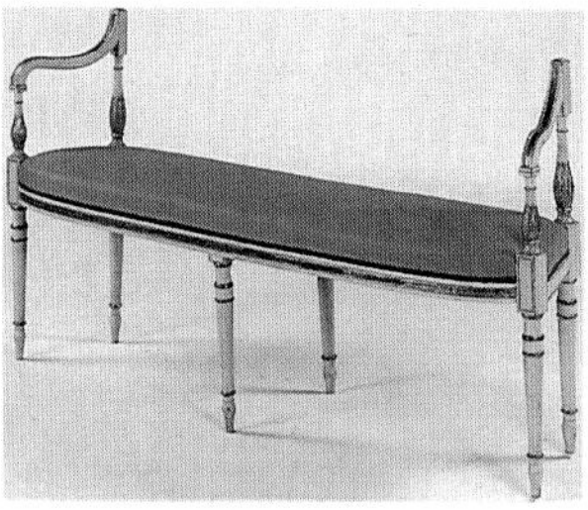

A pair of George III white painted and parcel gilt window seats, 55in (140cm). **$8,000-10,000**

A giltwood banquette of Louis XV st the padded seat covered in red toile de Jouy, the pierced rails carved wit flowerheads, rockwork and scrolling foliage, 44in (111cm). **$6,000-8,000**

A neo-classical white painted and parcel gilt stool, c1825, 28in (70cm). **$7,000-9,000**

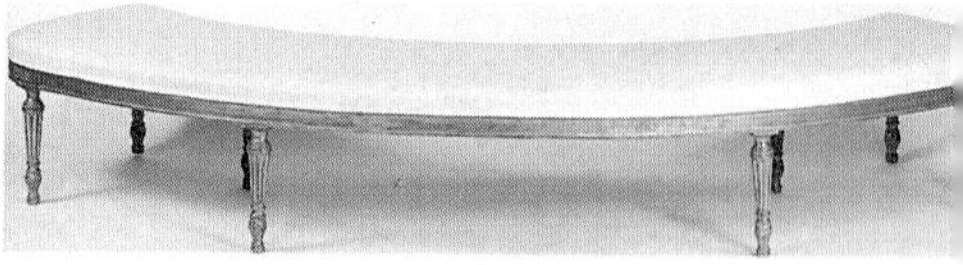

A pair of George III giltwood stools b Thomas Chippendale, on tapering fl legs headed by paterae and baluster feet carved with long leaves, some restoration, 86in (218cm). **$60,000-70,000**

A mahogany X-frame stool, the front with ram mask terminals, 19thC, 29in (72cm). **$6,000-8,000**

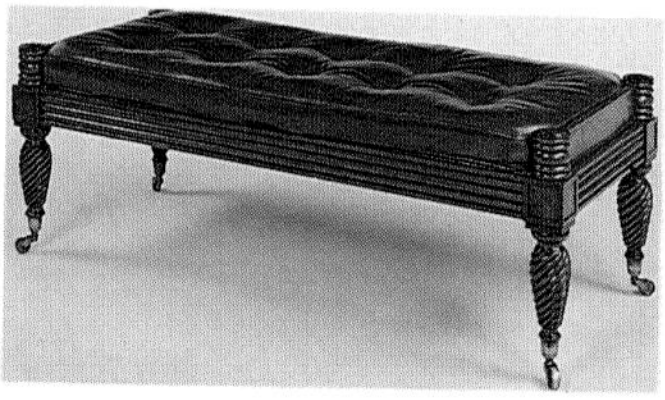

A pair of Regency mahogany stools, on spirally reeded baluster legs, 52in (132cm). **$60,000-70,000**

A Regency mahogany and pa gilt stool, the padded seat covered in striped material, flanked by 4 leopard masks, 32in (81cm). **$25,000-30,000**

A George III mahogany window seat, later blocks, 42in (106cm). **$40,000-50,000**

A George I walnut stool, the seat covered in floral needlework, on cabriole legs and pad feet, 22in (56cm). **$50,000-60,000**

A George I walnut st the seat rails reduced 19½in (49cm). **$10,000-12,000**

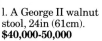

l. A George II walnut stool, 24in (61cm). **$40,000-50,000**

A George III mahogany serpentine chest, inlaid with boxwood and ebony lines, on splayed bracket feet, 48in (122cm). **$6,000-10,000**

A George III mahogany serpentine chest, fitted with a brushing slide, 42in (106cm). **$14,000-16,000**

burr walnut bachelor's
est, with quarter veneered
ding top, 26in (65cm).
2,000-14,000

George III satinwood and
ahogany chest, 38in (97cm).
4,000-16,000

A George III satinwood chest of drawers, crossbanded with kingwood, restored, 37in (94cm). **$8,000-10,000**

A George III mahogany chest, with restorations, 38in (96cm). **$14,000-18,000**

George III mahogany chest,
in (101cm).
20,000-25,000

A William and Mary oyster veneered olivewood chest, boxwood stringing, 38in (97cm). **$15,000-18,000**

A burr walnut secrétaire chest, later moulded crossbanded top, the secrétaire drawer with adapted interior, 34in (86cm). **$8,000-10,000**

l. A Queen Anne figured walnut chest on stand, inlaid with chevron bands, later bun feet, reduced, 42in (107cm). **$8,000-12,000**

r. A George II walnut chest, with quartered chamfered top and 4 graduated drawers, 32in (82cm). **$8,000-10,000**

A Queen Anne walnut chest on stand, Pennsylvania, c1750, 39in (99cm). **$12,000-16,000**

A George III satinwood and inlaid mahogany commode, John Linnell style, 51in (128cm). **$20,000-25,000**

A Louis XV style black and gold japan commode, the drawers decorated with Chinese figures and pavilions, 44in (110cm). **$6,000-10,000**

A George III mahogany serpentine commode, 47in (118cm). **$14,000-16,000**

A mid-Georgian walnut bachelor's chest, with folding top, 30in (76cm). **$28,000-30,000**

A George III harewood and satinwood banded commode, with mahogany lined drawe 38in (95cm). **$15,000-18,000**

A George III mahogany tallboy with brushing slide in the base, 44in (112cm). **$12,000-16,000**

An ormolu-mounted kingwood and marquetry commode, after a model by Riesener, c1900, 80in (202cm). **$20,000-25,000**

A George III mahogany tallboy, the brok scroll pediment flanking a painted coat-of-arms, above a blind fret carved frieze, 47in (118cm). **$14,000-16,000**

A George I burr walnut tallboy, restorations, 49in (123cm). **$25,000-30,000**

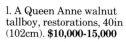

l. A Queen Anne walnut tallboy, restorations, 40in (102cm). **$10,000-15,000**

A George II mahogany commode, the waved moulded top with carved border, 38in (97cm). **$55,000-60,000**

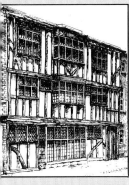

A Régence rosewood palisander and ormolu-mounted commode, 38in (96cm). **$8,000-10,000**

An Italian neo-classical olivewood and marquetry commode, c1775, 49½in (124cm). **$18,000-20,000**

A George III mahogany commode, w rosewood crossbanding, 44in (112cm **$45,000-50,000**

l. A pair of George III satinwood commodes, mahogany crossbanding, inlaid with burr walnut, the angles with bellflowers, 47in (120cm). **$100,000-120,000**

An ormolu-mounted kingwood and marquet commode, the moulded serpentine marble to above 2 drawers 'sans traverse', stamped I.Dubois, 58in (147cm). **$100,000-110,000**

A South German walnut and parquetry commode, mid-18thC, 49½in (124cm). **$20,000-25,000**

r. A Louis XV ormolu-mounted tulipwood commode, with marbled top, stamped 5 times I.B TUART, 50in (126cm). **$15,000-20,000**

A Louis XV kingwood commode, Languedoc marble top, 39in (99cm). **$15,000-18,000**

l. A matched pair of mid-Victorian ormolu and porcelain mounted satinwood and kingwood breakfront commodes, bot with marble tops, 71½in (181cm). **$25,000-30,000**

l. An Italian fruitwood and olivewood commode, with later moulded grey marble top, 18thC, 50in (127cm). **$6,000-8,000**

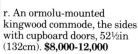

r. An ormolu-mounted kingwood commode, the sides with cupboard doors, 52½in (132cm). **$8,000-12,000**

. Regency mahogany pedestal
esk, 43in (109cm).
8,000-12,000

A George III mahogany partners' desk, the leather lined top with ratchetted reading slope, 60in (152cm).
$14,000-18,000

A George II mahogany kneehole desk, 39in (99cm).
$15,000-20,000

mahogany partners' desk, with 6 frieze
rawers and 2 false end drawers, 60in
152cm). **$10,000-15,000**

An Empire mahogany desk, with leather lined top, 3 frieze drawers each side, 67in (170cm). **$90,000-100,000**

r. A mahogany partners' pedestal desk, late 19thC, 80in (203cm).
$200,000+

l. A black lacquer partners' desk, decorated with chinoiserie scenes, 72in (183cm).
$8,000-10,000

A mahogany partners' desk, 19thC, 54in (137cm). **$6,000-8,000**

A Louis XV brass mounted mahogany cylinder bureau, by Jean-François Dubut, the red leather lined interior with pigeonholes, stamped I.F. Dubut once and JME twice, 58½in (147cm).
$35,000-40,000

\n early Georgian
valnut kneehole
lesk, crossbanded
n yew, 32in (80cm).
;15,000-18,000

l. A Queen Anne carved cherrywood desk, the sloping front with fitted interior, Woodbury, Connecticut, c1750, 44in (110cm). **$20,000-25,000**

r. A George I burr walnut desk, crossbanded and inlaid with feather banding, 31in (78cm). **$50,000-60,000**

mahogany Carlton House desk,
vith 3 frieze drawers, 54½in
138cm). **$15,000-20,000**

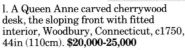

r. A Louis XVI brass mounted mahogany cylinder bureau, the sides with leather lined slides, 64in (162cm). **$12,000-16,000**

A Queen Anne gilt gesso pier glass.
$14,000-16,000

A pair of Régence giltwood mirrors, 44½in (112cm) wide.
$35,000-40,000

A George III giltwood mirror, with scrolling foliate frame with mirrored slips, 64½ by 35in (164 by 89cm).
$60,000-70,000

A giltwood pier glass, possibly Piedmontese, glass largely replaced, c1750, 67in (170cm). **$15,000-20,000**

An Italian carved and gilded tabernacle frame, 17thC.
$6,000-8,000

A Regency giltwood and ebonised girandole, 62 by 49in (157 by 124cm).
$26,000-30,000

A Florentine carved, ebonised and gilded frame, with cherub faces amid foliage, 18thC, 37in (94cm). **$8,000-12,000**

A Georgian carved, white painted and parcel gilt frame, corners with rosettes, 49in (123cm). **$8,000-10,000**

r. A pair of George III giltwood mirrors, with carved frames of entwined rushes, 27in (68cm).
$35,000-40,000

A Dutch double cushion tortoiseshell frame, with ripple moulding, 17thC, 13in (32cm) wide.
$3,000-5,000

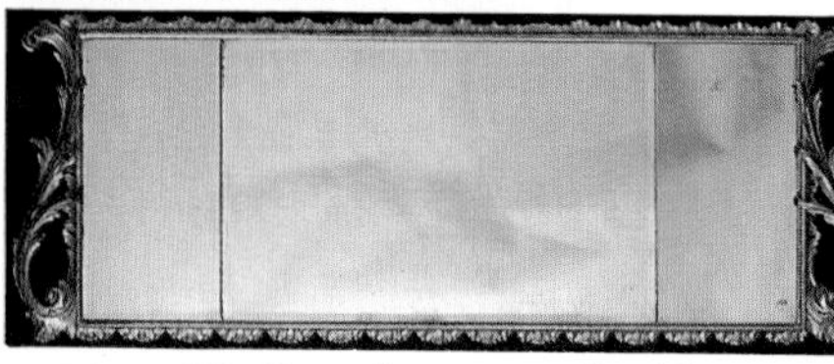

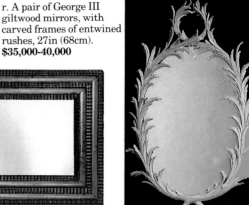

A George III giltwood overmantel, with later bevelled triple plate, 26 by 70in (66 by 178cm). **$14,000-16,000**

r. A George III giltwood mirror, the scrolling foliate cresting surmounted by 'ho-ho' birds on a rockwork base, 43in (109cm).
$20,000-25,000

Spanish steel and gold
yal Presentation mirror,
ted 1782. **$18,000-25,000**

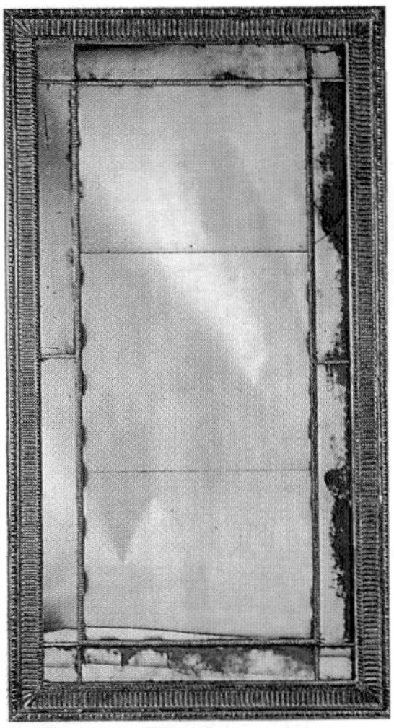

A George III giltwood pier glass, 92 by 51in (234 by 130cm). **$18,000-20,000**

A pair of Roman giltwood mirrors, the frames carved with foliage and scrolls, 84in (213cm). **$10,000-15,000**

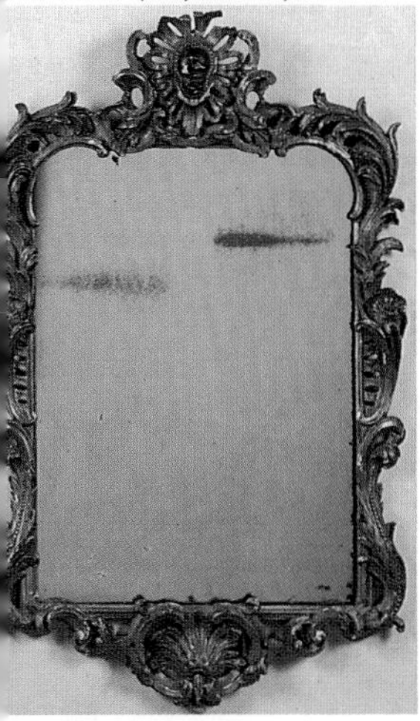

mid-Georgian giltwood
rror, later plate, 29in
3cm). **$10,000-14,000**

A George III giltwood mirror, J. and F. Booker style, 48in (122cm). **$18,000-20,000**

A George III giltwood mirror, with later trellis border, 37in (94cm). **$18,000-20,000**

pair of George III giltwood mirrors,
½in (46cm). **$12,000-16,000**

A George III giltwood mirror, the frame with rockwork, scrolls and foliage, re-gilded, 41in (104cm). **$18,000-25,000**

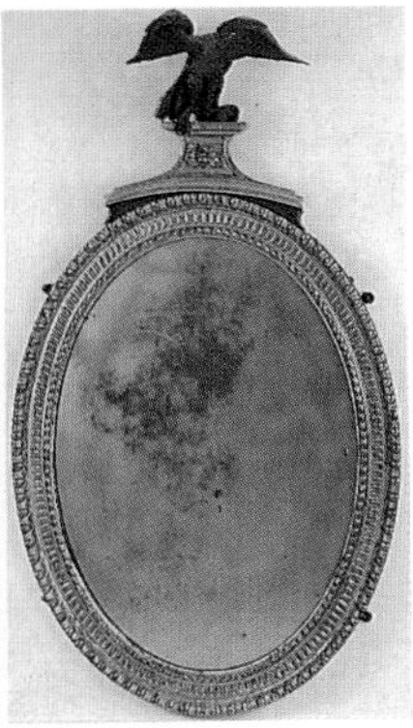

A George III carved giltwood mirror, 33in (83cm). **$6,000-8,000**

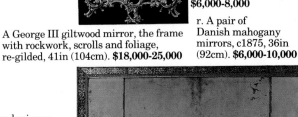

r. A pair of Danish mahogany mirrors, c1875, 36in (92cm). **$6,000-10,000**

r. A gilt-gesso overmantel mirror, 56in (140cm). **$10,000-15,000**

A George III mahogany breakfast table, with satin birch crossbanding, 52in (130cm) diam. **$10,000-15,000**

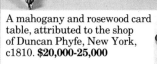

A mahogany and rosewood card table, attributed to the shop of Duncan Phyfe, New York, c1810. **$20,000-25,000**

A Victorian giltmetal and porcelain mounted oak architect's table, 32in (80c
$8,000-10,000

A Regency rosewood card table with ebony and brass inlay, 36in (92cm). **$8,000-12,000**

A Regency rosewood and bra
inlaid breakfast table, 47in (118cm). **$10,000-12,000**

A Regency breakfast table, plinth with gilt brass lotus leaves, 48in (122cm) diam. **$10,000-15,000**

A satinwood card table, folding top crossbanded with kingwood, 38in (97cm). **$15,000-18,000**

r. A Regency rosewood centre table, the top framed with brass lines, 30in (75cm). **$70,000-80,000**

r. A Regency mahogany breakfast table, 47in (119cm). **$10,000-15,000**

r. A Regency rosewood centre table, brass lines, 53in (133cm). **$18,000-20,000**

l. A pair of satinwood and marquetry card tables, 37in (94cm). **$25,000-30,000**

r. A George III mahogany breakfast table, 55in (140cm). **$8,000-12,000**

ı Anglo-Indian ebony and
ɛcimen wood table, 19thC,
ın diam. **$8,000-10,000**

A Victorian black limestone centre table, 31in (77cm).
$8,000-10,000

A Regency brass inlaid rosewood centre table, the inlaid panelled frieze with a drawer flanked by Boulle plaques, 56½in (144cm). **$8,000-12,000**

George III ormolu mounted
ahogany and burr elm centre
ɔle, 42in (105cm).
2,000-16,000

A Sicilian thuya, maple and marquetry centre table, the top centre with a painted panel signed A. Garguilo Sorento, c1880, 40in (101cm).
$18,000-20,000

A Regency rosewood centre table with crossbanded top, inlaid with ebony and brass, 33in (82cm). **$20,000-25,000**

George IV mahogany table
spreading triangular shaft,
ın (119cm). **$8,000-10,000**

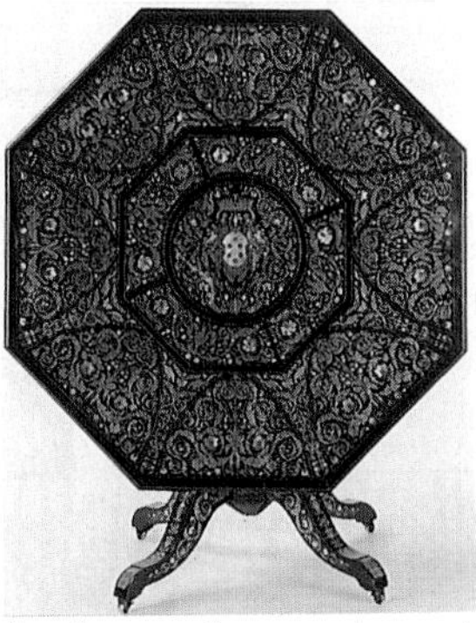

An ebony and marquetry centre table, the top profusely inlaid with mother-of-pearl, c1875, 49½in (126cm).
$18,000-20,000

An Empire ormolu-mounted mahogany centre table, with white marble top and frieze drawer each side, 44in (111cm).
$70,000-80,000

Regency rosewood centre table, the
arble top inlaid with a roundel of
pis lazuli on a pink Breccia marble
ound, 42in (107cm). **$20,000-25,000**

A Victorian papier mâché table, the tip-up top painted with a lakeside scene, 48in (122cm) diam. **$10,000-14,000**

l. An ormolu-mounted table, stamped Wright and Mansfield, and 3561, 36in (92cm).
$12,000-14,000

A pair of Louis XVI giltwood console tables, with mottled grey marble tops, 17in (43cm). **$24,000-30,000**

A Regency simulated rosewood and gilt decorated console table, the top with specimen marbles, 25½in (64cm). **$3,000-4,000**

A pair of George III style mahogany and malachite composition inlaid tables, 42in (106cm). **$10,000-12,0**

A Regency brass inlaid and parcel gilt rosewood table, c1825, 58in. **$18,000-20,000**

A pair of Louis XVI ormolu-mounted ebony and Boulle marquetry console tables, 27in (68cm). **$40,000-50,000**

A George II walnut drop leaf dining table on cabriole legs carved with shells, scrolls and foliage, gateleg repaired, 58in (147cm). **$10,000-14,000**

l. A George III twin pedestal mahogany dining table, top reduced, 87in (221cm) including extra leaves. **$10,000-12,000**

A pair of William IV giltwo console tables, 40in (101cm) **$16,000-18,000**

A George III twin pedestal dining table in mahogany, with a later leaf, 84in (213cm). **$8,000-12,000**

A Regency three pedestal mahogany dining table, tl D-ended top on ring turned shafts and downswept legs, top reduced, 141in (358cm). **$16,000-18,000**

A Georgian solid yew gateleg dining table, with 2 end drawers, 70in (177cm). **$24,000-30,000**

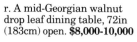

r. A mid-Georgian walnut drop leaf dining table, 72in (183cm) open. **$8,000-10,000**

. George IV satinwood and parcel gilt
ressing table, attributed to Morel and
eddon, 42in (107cm). **$35,000-40,000**

A Regency mahogany three-pedestal dining table, 147½in (374cm) including 2 extra leaves. **$120,000-150,000**

A Regency twin pedestal dining table, the edge banded with mahogany, each quadripartite splayed base banded with ebony and mounted with giltmetal foliate plaques, restorations, 118½in (301cm). **$80,000-90,000**

. Regency mahogany dressing table, with fitted interior
nd easel mirror, 6 false drawers, 38in. **$6,000-8000**

Above. A Regency mahogany dining table, 91in (231cm). **$12,000-16,000**

l. A Regency mahogany dining table, feet replaced, 250in. **$20,000-25,000**

l. A Regency mahogany drum table, the frieze fitted with 4 drawers, 45in (114cm) diam. **$10,000-14,000**

r. A Louis XV kingwood and parquetry dressing table, 35in (88cm). **$10,000-12,000**

l. A mahogany 3-pillar dining table, with brass caps and casters, 175in (444cm). **$24,000-30,000**

r. A Louis XV/XVI kingwood and tulipwood marquetry dressing table, stamped N.Petit JME, late 18thC, 32in (80cm). **$12,000-14,000**

A Regency penwork games table, the ebonised baluster shaft with ivory collars, on ribbed bun feet. **$6,000-10,000**

A Chinese export padoukwood games table, with candle recesses and counter wells, a drawer at each end, 32½in (82cm). **$14,000-16,000**

A Charles X mahogany trictrac table by A. Maigret, the leather lined reversible top inlaid with ebony and ivory squares stamped Maigret, 48in. **$8,000-10,000**

An Anglo-Indian Regency padoukwood games table, inlaid with ebony and bon 51in (130cm). **$25,000-30,000**

A Regency mahogany library table, attributed to Gillows, 2 drawers each side, 60in (152cm). **$24,000-30,000**

A Regency rosewood and brass inlaid table, with crossbanded baize-lined hinged top, above a shaped frieze inlaid with brass lines, 35in (88cm). **$3,000-4,000**

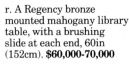

A Charles II walnut gateleg table, on spirally turned supports and scrolled stretchers, 35in (90cm). **$18,000-20,000**

A mid-Georgian walnut triple flap games table, crossbanded top revealing a tea table, a baize-lined playing surface with candl slides and counter wells, 36in (91cm). **$16,000-20,000**

r. A Regency bronze mounted mahogany library table, with a brushing slide at each end, 60in (152cm). **$60,000-70,000**

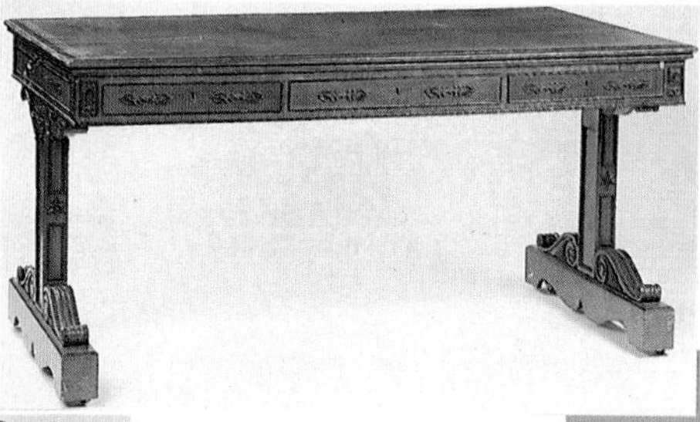

l. A South German walnut and marquetry games table, with enclosed backgammon board, early 18thC, 42½in (106cm). **$10,000-12,000**

r. A George III style satinwood dressing table, cut glass bottles with silver tops, hallmarked London 1912, 35in (89cm). **$35,000-40,000**

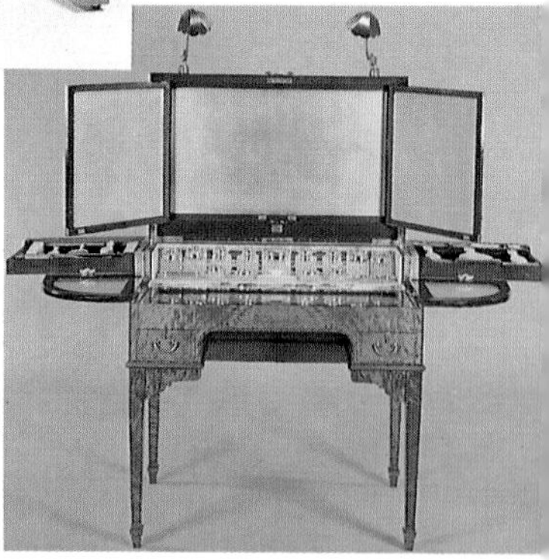

ι George IV mahogany library table,
he top inset with brown leather,
he panelled frieze fitted with 2 double-
nded drawers, 62in (155cm).
20,000-25,000

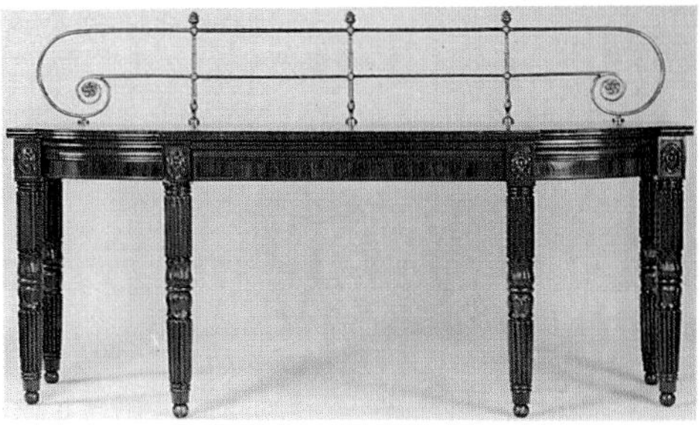

A Regency mahogany and green painted serving table, the scroll ended brass rail with acanthus chased finials, above a breakfront top, 96½in (245cm).
$20,000-25,000

A mid-Georgian mahogany
eading table, with hinged
op and easel support, 28in
72cm). **$8,000-10,000**

A George III mahogany reading table, crossbanded in kingwood, with baize lined brushing slide to the front, 24in (61cm). **$8,000-10,000**

A George III satinwood Pembroke table, crossbanded with rosewood, fitted with a frieze drawer, restorations, 38in (97cm). **$10,000-12,000**

A pair of George III giltwood pier
ables, with bowed Breccia marble tops,
n spirally turned fluted legs carved
vith foliage, 42in (107cm).
$50,000-60,000

A set of 4 Regency rosewood and parquetry tables, brass, pewter and copper inlay, 24in largest. **$8,000-10,000**

A Regency brass-mounted rosewood library table, in the manner of Gillows, 33in (83cm).
$25,000-30,000

A George III mahogany Pembroke table, with crossbanded serpentine top, on moulded cabriole legs, 36in (91cm). **$14,000-16,000**

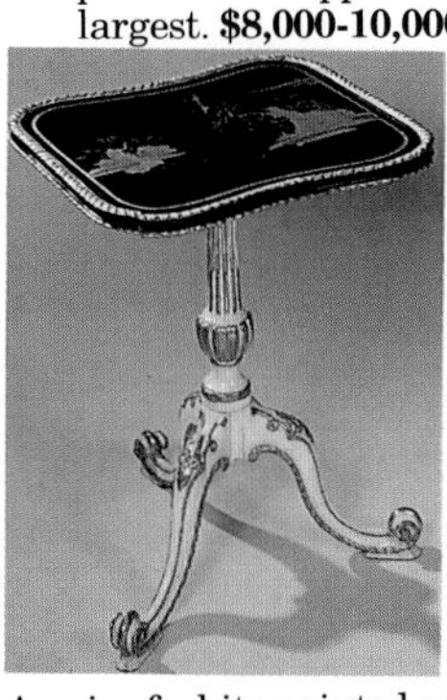

A pair of white painted and gilded occasional tables, tops from Regency polescreens, 18in (46cm). **$6,000-8,000**

r. A George III mahogany reading table, with crossbanded easel top and one frieze drawer, adjustable brass candle sconce, legs repaired, 25in (63cm).
$6,000-8,000

A giltwood side table of George II style, marble top above Vitruvian scrolls, 97in (246cm). **$10,000-14,000**

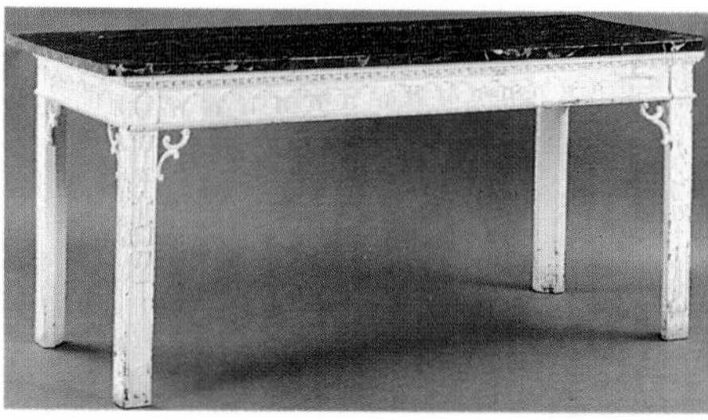

A George III white painted mahogany side table, the mahogany top painted to simulate marble, 75in (190cm **$18,000-25,000**

A George IV mahogany serving table, carved with acanthus and anthemion, 94in (238cm). **$15,000-20,000**

A Regency mahogany and ebonised serving table and matching pedestals, in the manner of George Smith, table 53in (135cm pedestals 21in (53cm). **$25,000-30,000**

A pair of George II side tables, with mottled purple and yellow marble tops, 70in (178cm). **$400,000+**

A George II burr elm side table, 34in (86cm). **$12,000-14,000**

A Georgian yew side table, 31in (78cm). **$10,000-12,000**

A George I burr walnut side table, with crossbanded top, 30in (76cm). **$10,000-14,000**

A George I gilt-gesso side table, with later yellow and black marble top, re-gilt, 37in (93cm). **$12,000-16,000**

A George III satinwood side table, in the manner of Hargraves of Hull, inlaid with satinwood and edged with rosewood, 49in (125cm). **$18,000-20,000**

r. A George II giltwood side table the frieze with Vitruvian scrolls, 51in (128cm). **$35,000-40,000**

ieorge III mahogany side table, with
de antico marble top above fluted
ze, 49in (123cm).
,000-20,000

ieorge III mahogany side table,
cluster column legs and stepped
ıth feet, 72in (183cm).
,000-20,000

ieorge III mahogany side table, with
ulded marble top, 50in (127cm).
,000-50,000

pair of Anglo-Indian ebony side tables,
th later marble top, c1850, 50½in
'6cm). **$12,000-14,000**

George III mahogany side
ɪle, with Portor marble top,
in (144cm). **$55,000-60,000**

A William IV mahogany side table, with Breccia marble top, the frieze carved with key pattern, restorations, 30in (75cm).
$8,000-12,000

A George IV ebonised and parcel gilt side table, the top inset with Italian mosaic panels, 20in (51cm).
$6,000-10,000

A pair of George III mahogany and marquetry tables, 48in. **$40,000-50,000**

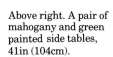

A George III mahogany side table, 39½in (100cm).
$6,000-10,000

Above right. A pair of mahogany and green painted side tables, 41in (104cm).
$14,000-16,000

Below right. A Regency ebony, pollard-oak sofa table, 60in (153cm).
$8,000-12,000

A pair of George III white painted and parcel gilt side tables, with moulded black marble tops, re-gilt, 50in (127cm).
$30,000-35,000

A giltwood side table, with black and grey marble top, 72in (184cm). **$18,000-20,000**

A George IV mahogany side table, the frieze drawer with lozenge fretwork and roundels, 42in (105cm). **$10,000-14,000**

A Regency rosewood sofa table, the top edged with light lines ending in fleur-de-lys in the corners, 58in (146cm). **$12,000-14,000**

A Regency mahogany sofa table, the twin-flap top ebony and brass star pattern band, above 2 panelle frieze drawers, 65in (165cm) open. **$90,000-100,000**

A Regency mahogany sofa table, the panelled frieze fitted with 2 drawers, 63in (160cm) open. **$6,000-8,000**

A Regency rosewood sofa table, the top with crossbanding and edged with boxwood lines, 59in (149cm). **$15,000-20,000**

A Regency rosewood sofa table, crossbanded with satinwood, the frieze with a drawer on each side, with ivory handles, 64½in (164cm) open. **$30,000-35,000**

A Regency rosewood sofa table, crossbanded in calamander, the frieze fitted with 2 drawers, on turned shaft carved with lotus leaves, 57in (144cm). **$10,000-12,000**

A Regency rosewood and parcel gilt sofa table, the top crossbanded with amboyna, restorations, 63in (160cm). **$8,000-12,000**

A Regency rosewood sofa table, the to crossbanded in satinwood, 58in (146c **$4,000-6,000**

A Regency mahogany sofa table, with 2 frieze drawers, 62in (156cm) open. **$10,000-14,000**

A Regency rosewood sofa table, inlaid with boxwood lines, 65in (165cm). **$15,000-20,000**

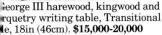

An ormolu-mounted kingwood bureau plat, the undulating frieze fitted with 3 drawers, all legs spliced, mid-18thC, 51in (127cm). **$25,000-30,000**

A Louis Philippe ormolu-mounted mahogany and marquetry bureau plat, stamped G. Durand, 45½in (116cm). **$10,000-14,000**

ꞁeorge III harewood, kingwood and rquetry writing table, Transitional le, 18in (46cm). **$15,000-20,000**

ormolu and porcelain mounted kingwood ·eau plat, the undulating frieze with ·res pattern porcelain plaques, c1850, n (103cm). **$20,000-25,000**

A Federal carved mahogany sewing table, attributed to Samuel McIntyre, Salem, Mass, c1800, 23½in (59cm). **$30,000-40,000**

A flame birch veneer sewing table, attributed to John and Thomas Seymour, Mass., c1800, 21in (52cm). **$25,000-30,000**

ɜeorge III mahogany writing table, th 2 frieze drawers either side, in (150cm). **$15,000-20,000**

A pair of rosewood lamp tables of Regency style, with specimen marble tops, 21½in (54cm). **$6,000-8,000**

A pair of Regency ormolu mounted brass inlaid rosewood lamp tables, George Bullock style, 30in. **$80,000-90,000**

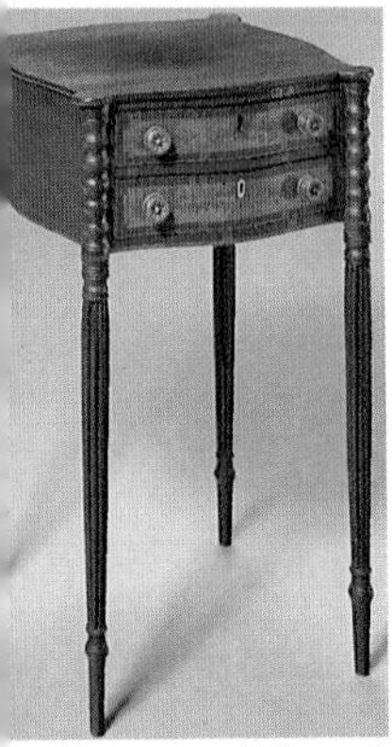

mahogany and flame birch ving table, Mass., c1800, in (45cm). **$30,000-40,000**

A Regency rosewood veneered work/games table, with fitted interior, brass inlaid friezes, 19in (48cm). **$6,000-8,000**

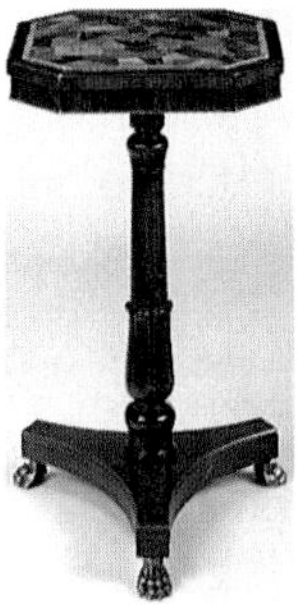

A pair of brass mounted rosewood lamp tables, of Regency style, 20in (50cm). **$8,000-10,000**

A Victorian rosewood artists work table, with needlework drawer, 30in. **$6,000-8,000**

A George II mahogany tripod table, the tip-up top edged with flowerhead border, 31in (78cm). **$40,000-50,000**

A Regency satinwood tripod table, with crossbanded tip-up top, 24in (61cm). **$8,000-10,000**

A pair of Regency rosewood tea tabl inlaid with boxwood lines, 36in (91c **$20,000-30,000**

A George III mahogany tea table, in the manner of Thomas Chippendale, 36in (91cm). **$15,000-18,000**

A George III mahogany tripod table, 28in (70cm). **$8,000-10,000**

A Directoire rosewood tripod table, inlaid with brass lines, stamped B.Molitor, 31in (78cm **$6,000-8,000**

A George III mahogany tea table, 21in (53cm). **$30,000-40,000**

A George III mahogany tripod table, with brass inlaid gallery, restorations, 29½in (74cm) diam. **$45,000-50,000**

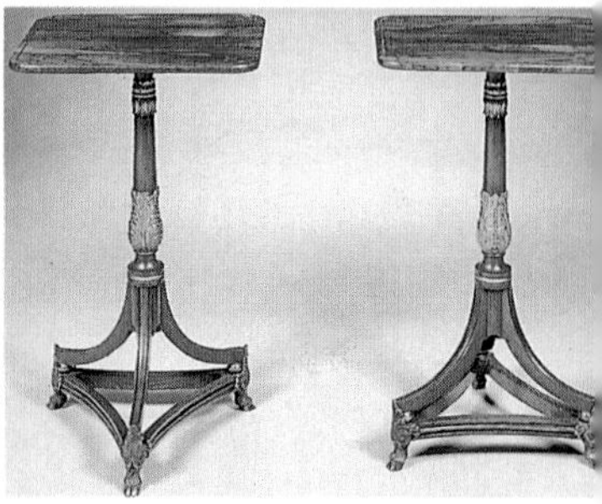

A pair of Regency rosewo and parcel gilt tripod tables, adapted, 17in (43cm). **$15,000-20,000**

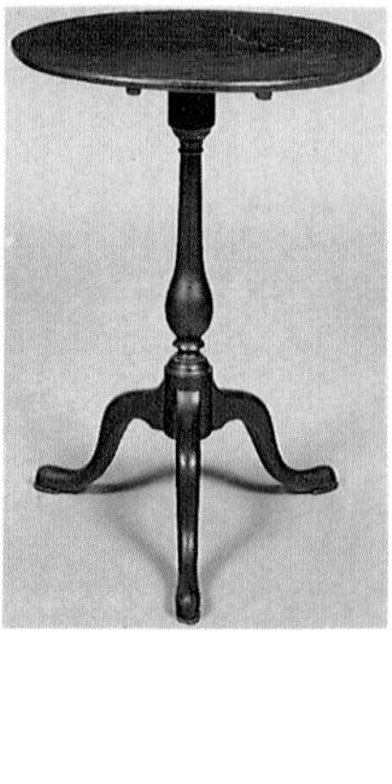

r. A Queen Anne mahogany tilt-top candlestand, by Thomas Burling, New York, c1780, 22in. **$12,000-15,000**

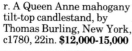

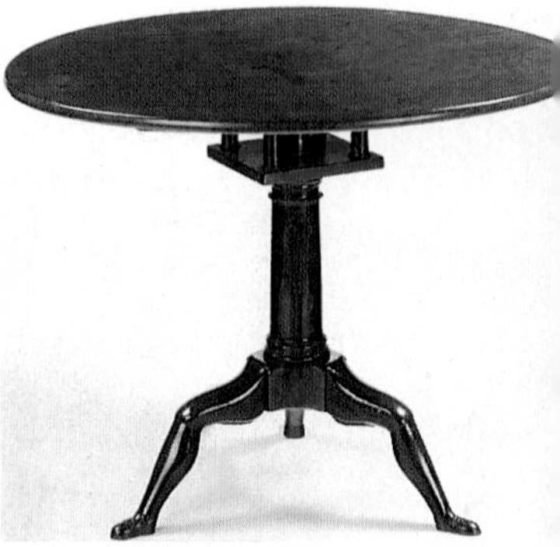

A mid-Georgian mahogan tripod table, with birdcage action on ring turned shaf carved Manx base, 38in (97cm). **$8,000-10,000**

l. A matched pair of Regency calamander, rosewood and satinwood lamp tables, 22 and 22½in (55 and 56cm) diam. **$70,000-80,000**

ʀegency mahogany writing table, in the manner of orge Smith, with leather lined top above a plain ze with 3 drawers on each side, distressed, 65½in 6cm). **$70,000-80,000**

A Regency mahogany writing table, with 2 drawers to each side, 45in (114cm). **$16,000-20,000**

A Regency brass inlaid mahogany writing table, with leather lined top, fitted with 2 frieze drawers, 42½in (107cm). **$30,000-40,000**

A late George III mahogany writing table, crossbanded in tulipwood, fitted with 3 drawers to each side, 56in (142cm). **$50,000-55,000**

A Regency pollard elm writing table, with central leather lined panel, 50in (127cm). **$20,000-24,000**

r. A Regency mahogany writing table, with hinged central compartment, 38in (96.5cm). **$20,000-24,000**

ate George III mahogany iting table, with leather ed top, 42in (107cm). **4,000-18,000**

A late George III mahogany writing table, inlaid with boxwood lines, 25in (63cm). **$3,000-4,000**

A Regency brass inlaid writing table, the top inlaid with fleur- de-lys, 30in (76cm). **$16,000-20,000**

A Regency mahogany writing table, 60in (152cm). **$20,000-24,000**

A Regency mahogany inlaid writing table, 35in (89cm). **$16,000-20,000**

An ormolu mounted mahogany bureau plat, partially remounted, 76in (193cm).
$80,000-90,000

A Regency mahogany writing table, w 2 drawers and a slide to the side, one leg spliced, 36in (91.5cm).
$12,000-14,000

A Louis XV tulipwood writing table, by J. Schmitz, 18in (46cm). **$100,000+**

An ormolu mounted kingwood and mahogany writing table.
$6,000-10,000

A Regency ormolu mounted mahoga writing table, inlaid with ebonised lines. **$22,000-25,000**

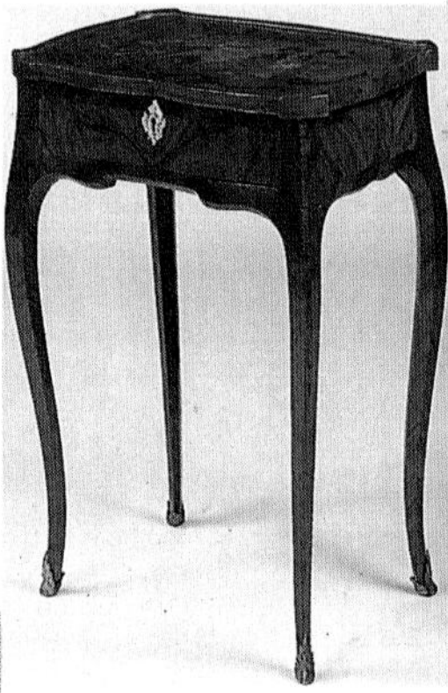

A Louis XV kingwood, walnut, and tulipwood writing table, 19in (48cm).
$20,000-24,000

A French veneered writing table, mid-19thC, 39in (99cm).
$4,000-5,000

A Regency mahogany double-sided writi table, restored, 41in (104cm).
$8,000-10,000

A Charles X mahogany writing table, adapted. **$2,000-3,000**

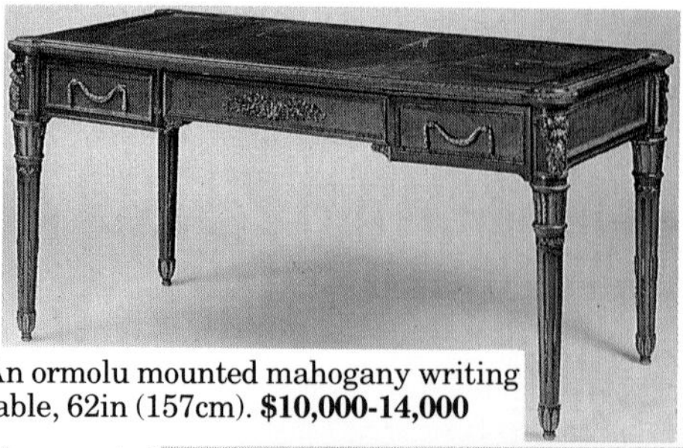

An ormolu mounted mahogany writing table, 62in (157cm). **$10,000-14,000**

A mid-Victorian ormolu mounted ebony, burr walnut and marquetry bureau plat, stamped Gillow. **$18,000-20,000**

An ormolu mounted mahogany bureau plat, with leather lined top and moulded brass border, 57½in (145cm).
$8,000-10,000

ussian neo-classic ormolu and birch
ting table, with later moulded
ichable top, 19thC, 46in (116.5cm).
,000-12,000

A Louis XVI style ormolu mounted mahogany bureau plat. **$12,000-14,000**

An ormolu mounted marquetry and amaranth writing table, late 19thC, 21½in (54cm). **$8,000-10,000**

A Louis XVI mahogany bureau plat, the leather lined top with eagle centre and ebony banding, 53in (134cm). **$35,000-40,000**

ouis XVI ebony and amaranth bureau
t, stamped M. Carlin, 48in (122cm).
0,000-140,000

An ormolu mounted tulipwood and marquetry guéridon, in the style of Topino, 21in (53cm). **$6,000-8,000**

A Chinese black and gold lacquer coffer, 18thC, on later stand with cabriole legs and ball-and-claw feet, 41½in (105cm). **$10,000-12,000**

ouis Philippe ormolu
unted kingwood and
rquetry bureau plat.
000-10,000

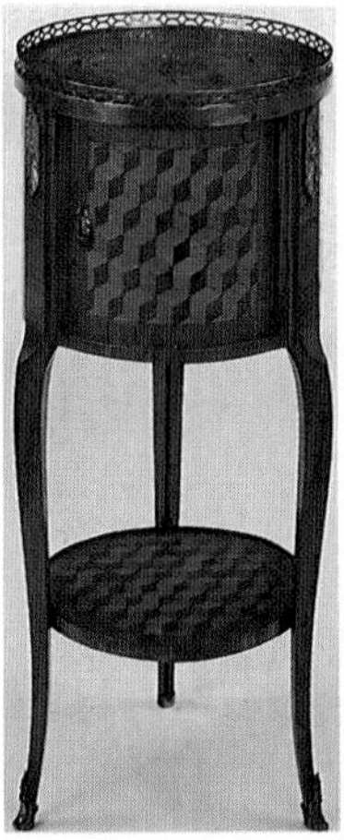

A Regency mahogany wine cooler, the lid inlaid with rosewood, lead lined interior, 27in (68cm). **$3,000-4,000**

Empire ormolu and bronze
éridon, with inset verde
tico marble top, 28in
cm) diam.
0,000-50,000

A Transitional ormolu mounted tulipwood and kingwood guéridon, 14in (35.5cm) diam. **$40,000-50,000**

A Transitional tulipwood and parquetry guéridon, stamped P. Dupre Jme, 13in (33cm). **$18,000-20,000**

An Empire ormolu mounted mahogany and patinated bronze étagère, with verde antico marble top, early 19thC, 24½in (62cm). **$50,000-60,000**

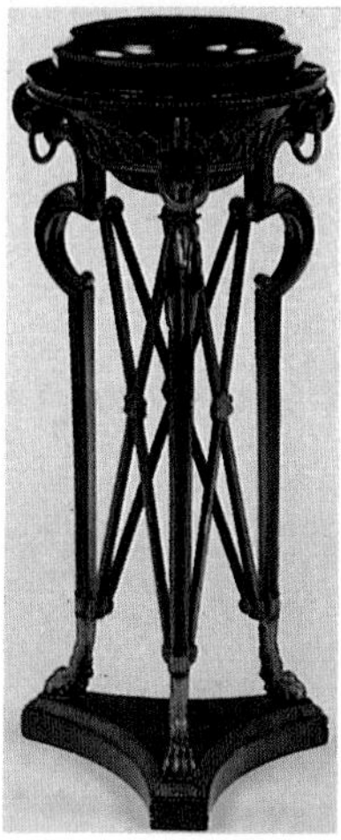

A Regency style ebonised and gilded torchère, the top with milled rim and ozierwork bowl, on scrolled monopodia supports, joined by X-pattern stretchers, 34½in (87cm) high. **$8,000-10,000**

A pair of mahogany wi coolers, the brass boun bodies with zinc lined interiors, one c1800, th other later, 20in (76cm **$7,000-9,000**

A George III mahogany cellaret, with lead lined interior, the brass bound body with carrying handles, 18½in (47cm). **$6,000-8,000**

A George III maple and rosewood tea caddy, the crossbanded twin flap top enclosing a fitted interior, lacking mixing bowl, 12in (30.5cm). **$12,000-14,000**

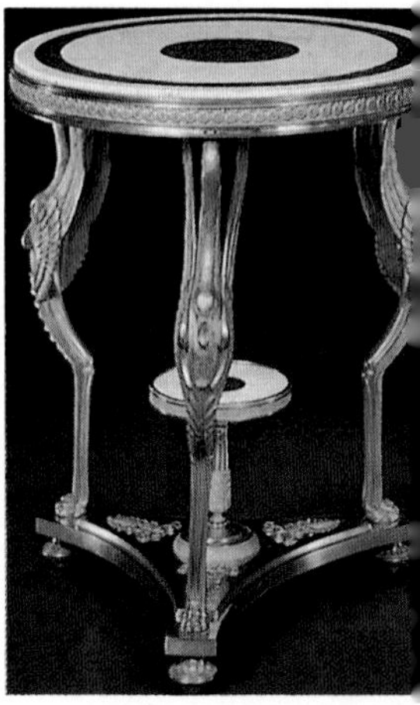

A pair of Empire ormol guéridons, with porphyr verde antico marble top 24in (61cm) diam. **$50,000-60,000**

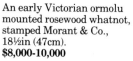

A Louis XVI style ormolu and black marble guéridon, 29in (74cm) diam. **$12,000-14,000**

An early Victorian ormolu mounted rosewood whatnot, stamped Morant & Co., 18½in (47cm). **$8,000-10,000**

A George III mahogany cellaret, the brass bound body with lion mask handles, 25in (63.5cm). **$8,000-10,000**

A pair of Regency rosewood and parcel gilt étagères. **$35,000-40,000**

l. A pair of mahogany veneered pedestals, c1790, 59in (149.5cm). **$20,000-24,000**

A pair or ormolu mounted rhodonite cassolettes, possibly Russian, 9½in (24cm) high. **$8,000-10,000**

A Regency mahogany, ebonised and parcel gilt torchère, with marble top, 14in (35.5cm) diam. **$16,000-20,000**

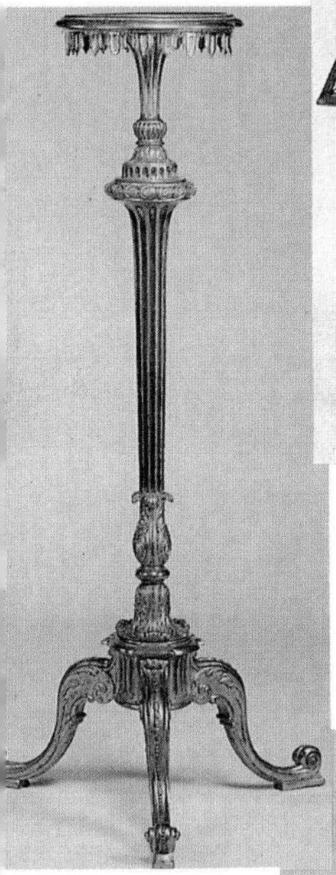

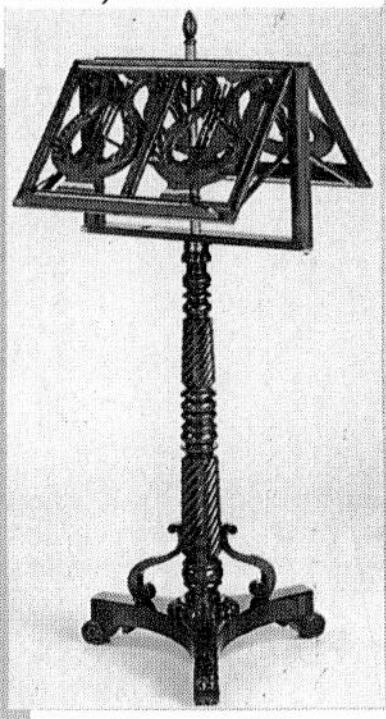

A George IV mahogany duet stand. **$6,000-8,000**

l. A pair of George III giltwood torchères, 52in. **$50,000-60,000**

A Regency mahogany bookstand, 32½in (82cm) diam. **$50,000-60,000**

An Empire ormolu guéridon, with verde antico marble top, 32in (81cm) diam. **$32,000-35,000**

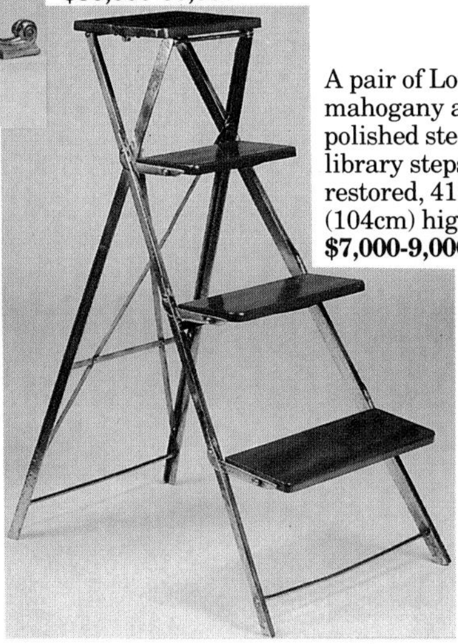

A pair of Louis XVI mahogany and polished steel library steps, restored, 41in (104cm) high. **$7,000-9,000**

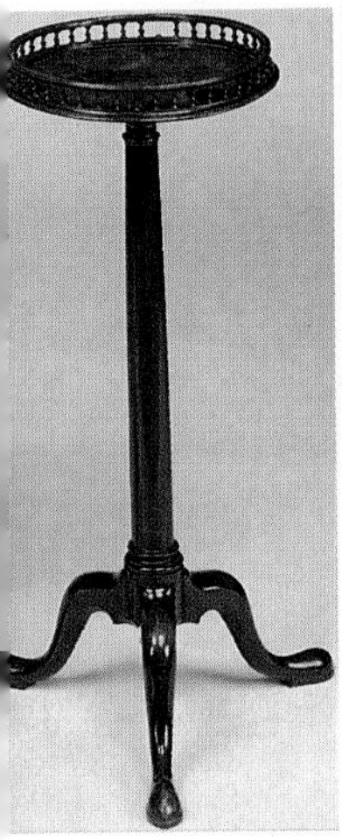

A pair of George II mahogany torchères, restored, 13in (33cm) diam. **$35,000-40,000**

A pair of Regency carved giltwood torchères. **$12,000-16,000**

A pair of giltwood torchères, with octagonal tops, 10in (25.5cm) wide. **$9,000-11,000**

A pine wardrobe, c1850, 70in (177cm).
$1,000-1,200

A pine dressing table, c1870, 39in (99cm) wide.
$500-600

An ash and elm slat back rocking chair, c1860.
$500-600

A pine cupboard c1860, 42in (107 wide.
$1,700-2,000

A pine dresser base, c1870, with reproduction plate rack, 54in (137cm) wide.
$1,500-1,800

A pine and elm tilt-top pedestal table, c1820, 36in (91.5cm) wide.
$500-600

An Irish pine cupboard base, c1870, with reproduction plate rack, 36in (91.5cm).
$1,500-2,000

A Yorkshire pine dresser, c1880, 54in (137cm) wide.
$1,600-2,000

A pine glazed wall corner cupboard, c1870, 30in (76cm)
$600-800

A pine bed, c1820.
$800-1,000

A pine mule che c1860, 39in (99c wide.
$400-500

A pine chest of drawers, c1810, 36in (91.5cm).
$500-600

A satinwood dressing chest, with matching marble topped washstand/chest, c1890. **$1,700-2,000**

A George II pine chimneypiece, with later overmantel, restored, 85in (216cm) wide. **$14,000-16,000**

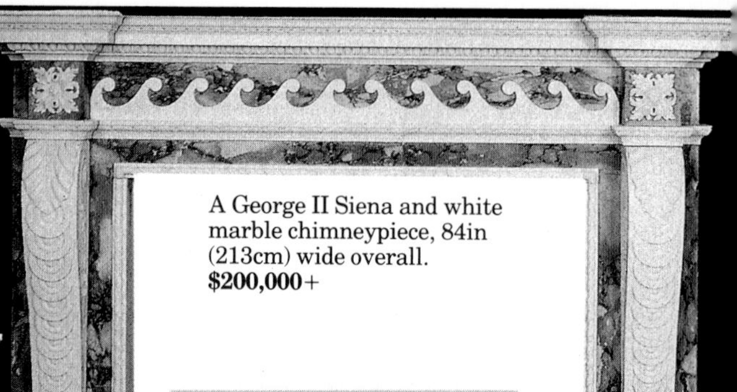

A George II Siena and white marble chimneypiece, 84in (213cm) wide overall. **$200,000+**

An early Victorian mahogany folio sta
labelled J. Kendell & Co., No. 88004, 3
(91.5cm) wide. **$12,000-14,000**

A George II Carrara marble fireplace, 64½in (163cm) wide. **$30,000-40,000**

A Louis XVI grey painted and parcel gilt four-lea
screen with Beauvais tapestry panels, 57in (145c
high. **$6,000-8,000**

A William IV mahogany three-leaf screen, each leaf 55½ by 30½in (141 by 77cm). **$32,000-35,000**

A Regency bronze mounte
mahogany cheval firescree
one foot later, 34in (86cm) wide. **$6,000-8,000**

A George III giltwood wall bracket, with pierced zoomorphic mask, 15½in (39cm) high. **$18,000-20,000**

BRITISH ANTIQUE EXPORTERS LTD

WHOLESALERS, EXPORTERS PACKERS SHIPPERS

HEAD OFFICE: QUEEN ELIZABETH AVENUE, BURGESS HILL, WEST SUSSEX, RH15 9RX ENGLAND

TELEPHONE BURGESS HILL (04 44) 245577 FAX (04 44) 232014

To: Auctioneers, Wholesalers and Retailers of Antique Furniture, Porcelain and Decorative Items.

Dear Sirs

We offer the most comprehensive service available in the UK.

As wholesalers we sell 20 ft and 40 ft container loads of antique furniture, porcelain and decorative items of the Georgian, Victorian, Edwardian and 1930's periods. Our buyers are strategically placed throughout the UK in order to take full advantage of regional pricing.

You can purchase a container from us for as little as £7,500. This would be filled with mostly 1880's to 1930's furniture. You could expect to pay approximately £10,000 to £15,000 for a shipment of Victorian and Edwardian furniture and porcelain. £15,000 to £35,000 would buy a Georgian, Queen Anne and Chippendale style container.

Containers can be tailored to your exact requirements - for example, you may deal only in office furniture and therefore only buy desks, file cabinets and related office items.

Our terms are £1,500 depost, the balance at time of arrival of the container. If the merchandise should not be to your liking for any reason whatsoever, we offer you your money back in full, less one-way freight.

We also have several showrooms where you can purchase individual items.

If you wish to visit the UK yourself and purchase individually from your own sources, we will collect, pack and ship your merchandise with speed and efficiency. Our rates are competitive and our packing is the finest available anywhere in the UK. Our courier-finder service is second to none and we have experienced couriers who are equipped with a car and the knowledge of where to find the best buys.

If your business is buying English Antiques, we are your contact. We assure you of our best attention at all times.

Yours faithfully
BRITISH ANTIQUE EXPORTERS LTD

Norman Lefton
Chairman & Managing Director

DIRECTORS N. LEFTON. (Chairman & Managing). P. V. LEFTON. THE RT. HON. THE VISCOUNT EXMOUTH. A. FIELD. MSC FBOA DCLP FSMC FAAO

REGISTERED OFFICE: 97, CHURCH STREET, BRIGHTON BN1 1UJ REGISTERED No 893406 ENGLAND

BANKERS: NATIONAL WESTMINSTER BANK PLC., 155 NORTH STREET, BRIGHTON BN1 1GN THE CHASE MANHATTAN BANK N.A. 30 ROCKEFELLER PLAZA NEW YORK

ALLIED IRISH BANKS PLC., 20 MARLBOROUGH PLACE, BRIGHTON BN1 1UB

THERE ARE MANY ANTIQUE

... few, if any, who are as quality conscious as Norman Lefton, Chairman and Managing Director of British Antique Exporters Ltd. of Burgess Hill, Nr. Brighton, Sussex.

Nearly thirty years' experience of shipping goods to all parts of the globe have confirmed his original belief that the way to build clients' confidence in his services is to supply them only with goods which are in first class saleable condition. To this end, he employs a cottage industry staff of over 50, from highly skilled antique restorers, polishers and packers to representative buyers and executives.

Through their knowledgeable hands passes each piece of furniture before it leaves the B.A.E. warehouses, ensuring that the overseas buyer will only receive the best and most saleable merchandise for their particular market. This attention to detail is obvious on a visit to the Burgess Hill showrooms where potential customers can view what must be the most varied assortment of Georgian, Victorian, Edwardian and 1930s furniture in the UK. One cannot fail to be impressed by, not only the varied range of merchandise, but also the fact that each piece is in showroom condition awaiting shipment.

As one would expect, packing is considered somewhat of an art at B.A.E. and the manager in charge of the works ensures that each piece will reach its final destination in the condition a customer would wish. B.A.E. set a very high standard and, as a further means of improving each container load, their customer/container liaison dept, invites each customer to return detailed information on the

BRITISH ANTIQUE EXPORTERS LTD,

SCHOOL CLOSE, QUEEN ELIZABETH AVENUE,
BURGESS HILL, WEST SUSSEX RH15 9RX, ENGLAND.

Telephone BURGESS HILL (04 44) 245577.

Fax (04 44) 232014.

Members of L.A.P.A.D.A. and Guild of Master Craftsmen

SHIPPERS IN BRITAIN BUT...

saleability of each piece in the container, thereby ensuring successful future shipments.

This feedback of information is the all important factor which guarantees the profitability of future containers. "By this method" Mr. Lefton explains, "we have established that an average £10,000 container will immediately it is unpacked at its final destination realise in the region of £15,000 to £20,000 for our clients selling the goods on a quick wholesale turnover basis."

When visiting the warehouses various container loads can be seen in the course of completion. The intending buyer can then judge for himself which type of container load would be best suited to his market. In an average 20-foot container B.A.E. put approximately 75 to 100 pieces carefully selected to suit the particular destination. There are always at least 10 outstanding or unusual items in each shipment, but every piece included looks as though it has something special about it.

B.A.E. have opened several new showrooms based at its 15,000 square feet headquarters in Burgess Hill which is 15 minutes away from Gatwick Airport, 7 miles from Brighton and 39 miles from London on a direct rail link, (only 40 minutes journey), the Company is ideally situated to ship containers to all parts of the world. The showrooms, restoration and packing departments are open to overseas buyers and no visit to purchase antiques for re-sale in other countries is complete without a visit to their Burgess Hill premises where a welcome is always found.

BRITISH ANTIQUE EXPORTERS LTD,

SCHOOL CLOSE, QUEEN ELIZABETH AVENUE,
BURGESS HILL, WEST SUSSEX RH15 9RX, ENGLAND.

Telephone BURGESS HILL (04 44) 245577.

Fax (04 44) 232014.

Members of L.A.P.A.D.A. and Guild of Master Craftsmen

A George III mahogany chest, with moulded top above 2 short and 3 long graduated drawers, on bracket feet, 46in (116cm).
$1,600-2,000

A George III mahogany chest, fitted with 4 long graduated drawers with later knob handles, on bracket feet, 35½in (90cm).
$1,600-2,000

A George III mahogany chest, fitted with 2 short and 3 long graduated drawers, on bracket feet, adapted, 37in (94cm).
$1,400-1,800

A George III mahogany serpentine dressing chest, the frieze drawer with a baize lined sliding adjustable ratcheted top concealing fitted compartments, 37in (93cm).
$8,000-10,000

A George III mahogany chest, with a brushing slide and 4 long graduated drawers, on bracket feet, 33in (84cm).
$3,000-4,000

A George III mahogany and ebony strung military secretaire chest, with deep drawer enclosing fitted interior, above 3 long drawers, with carrying handles to the sides.
$4,000-5,000

A George III mahogany chest, fitted with 3 long graduated drawers below a brushing slide, splayed bracket feet, renovated, 33½in (87cm).
$1,600-2,000

A George III mahogany and inlaid serpentine front chest, with decorated gilt brass drop handles, 40in (101.5cm).
$6,000-8,000

A George III mahogany chest, wi brushing slide and 4 long gradua drawers with brass swan neck handles, on bracket feet, 30in (76cm).
$4,000-6,000

A George III black lacquer ches decorated in gilt and red, the to with a moulded edge, bracket fe 45½in (115cm).
$4,000-6,000

A George III mahogany bowfront chest, fitted with 2 short and 2 long drawers, above a serpentine apron, on splayed bracket feet, 36in (91cm).
$800-1,000

A Georgian mahogany chest of drawers.
$8,000-10,000

Regency mahogany bowfront
est, with ebony line inlay to the
ossbanded top, boxwood stringing
the frieze, brass plate swing
ndles, shaped apron and splay
acket feet, 41in (104cm).
,400-1,800

A Regency mahogany bowfront chest, the crossbanded top above 2 short and 3 long drawers, inlaid with boxwood lines, gilt metal handles, and splayed bracket feet, 41in (104cm).
$1,800-2,500

A Regency mahogany bowfront chest, in the manner of Gillows, with moulded eared top and baize lined slide, 42in (106.5cm).
$4,000-6,000

n Anglo-Indian padouk and brass
ound secretaire chest, the hinged
p enclosing a fitted interior, above
long recessed drawers, applied
ith brass studs and pierced brass
lates, with carrying handles to the
des, mid-19thC, 37in (94cm).
4,000-5,000

An inlaid mahogany secretaire chest, fitted with pigeonholes and small drawers with satinwood lined fronts, early 19thC, 47in (119cm).
$2,500-3,000

A two-part brass bound military chest, 19thC, 39in (99cm).
$2,000-3,000

A burr elm bachelor's chest, with hinged top above 4 graduated drawers, 30in (76cm).
$9,000-10,000

A Victorian satinwood chest, the bevelled top above 2 short and 3 long graduated and panelled drawers, on a plinth base with saucer feet, 44in (112cm).
$800-1,200

A Victorian mahogany bachelor's style chest, the fold-over top above 4 graduated drawers, with brass carrying handles, 33in (84cm).
$3,000-4,000

. Scottish apprentice's mahogany
iniature chest, 19thC.
500-800

An oysterwood veneered dwarf chest, inlaid with boxwood lines, on bracket feet, 33in (84cm).
$3,000-4,000

A walnut chest, with quarter veneered top, above 2 short and 3 long drawers, on bracket feet, 33in (84cm).
$2,000-3,000

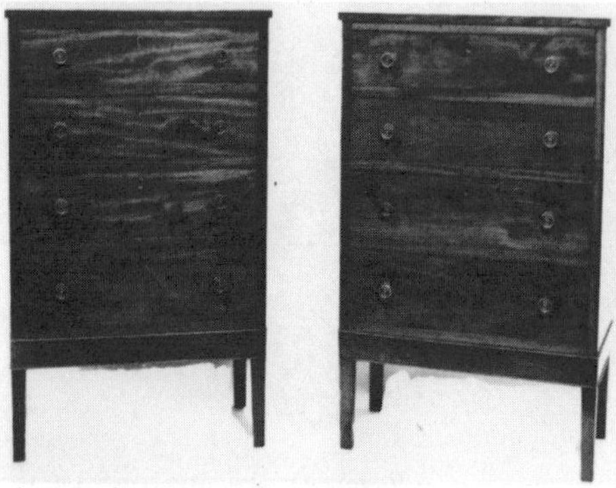

A pair of mahogany dwarf chests, with brass knob handles, on square tapering supports, 20in (51cm).
$1,400-1,800

A chest of drawers, with plate glass top, 28in (71cm).
$400-500

A mahogany chest, with crossbanded serpentine top, a sli and 4 graduated drawers, on bracket feet, 39in (99cm).
$5,000-6,000

A burr walnut chest, with moulded top, above a brushing slide and 4 graduated drawers, 28in (71cm).
$5,000-6,000

A walnut and marquetry chest, with panels of scrolling foliage inlaid on an ebony ground, with moulded top, 2 short and 3 long drawers, on turned feet, 37in (94cm).
$8,000-10,000

An Edwardian mahogany bachelor's chest of drawers, wit boxwood string inlay, oval swin mirror and three-quarter galler 30in (76cm).
$1,400-1,800

Chests-on-Chests

A Queen Anne walnut and herringbone crossbanded tallboy, with replacement brass drop handles and escutcheons and replacement bracket feet, 42½in (107cm).
$12,000-16,000

A George I walnut tallboy, original brass handles and escutcheons, 44in (112cm).
$14,000-18,000

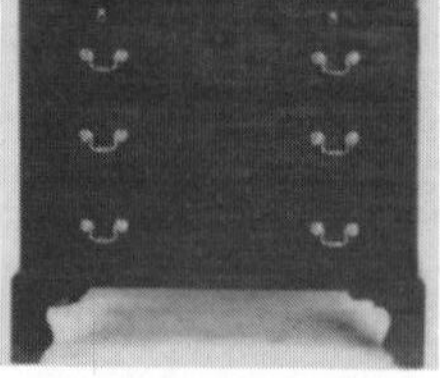

A George II mahogany tallboy, the dentilled moulded cornice above 2 short and 6 long graduated drawers, adapted, 44in (112cm).
$3,000-4,000

An early Georgian mahogany provincial tallboy, with 4 short an 4 long drawers, 40in (102cm).
$4,000-6,000

A George III mahogany tallboy, the upper section with dentil cornice above a blind fret frieze and 2 short and 3 long drawers flanked by fluted canted corners, the lower section with a brushing slide above 3 further drawers, 43½in (111cm).
$3,000-4,000

A George III mahogany tallboy, the bolection moulded cornice and blind fret banded frieze above 2 short and 7 long graduated drawers, on bracket feet, 44in (112cm).
$3,000-4,000

ieorge III figured mahogany lboy, the upper section with a eek key cornice above 2 short and ng drawers, the lower section h a brushing slide above 3 long wers, 44in (112cm).
000-4,000

A George III mahogany tallboy, with dentilled moulded cornice, 43in (109cm).
$6,000-8,000

A late Georgian mahogany tallboy, with 2 small and 5 long graduated drawers.
$2,000-3,000

early George III mahogany lboy, the upper section with ken architectural pediment ve a dentil cornice and blind fret ze, the lower section originally ed with a secretaire drawer, '60, 48in (122cm).
000-8,000

A mid-Georgian mahogany secretaire tallboy, with fitted bottom drawer to the top section, on ogee bracket feet, 44½in (112cm).
$10,000-12,000

A George III mahogany tallboy.
$8,000-10,000

ieorge III fruitwood chest-on-st, with Greek key cornice and ıd fretwork frieze, 2 short and ng graduated drawers, the upper tion with fluted quarter column ners, 46in (116.5cm).
000-7,000

A Victorian camphor wood secretaire chest in 2 sections, incorporating a fully fitted secretaire drawer with fall front, and 2 short and 2 long drawers below, with recessed brassed handles and ebony inlay, on turned supports, 42in (106.5cm).
$5,000-6,000

A black lacquered tallboy, decorated with gilt chinoiserie in white relief, the top section with a moulded cornice, on bracket feet, 48½in (123cm).
$3,000-4,000

A mahogany chest-on-chest, with dentil cornice, reeded canted corners, on bracket feet.
$2,000-3,000

A walnut secretaire tallboy, the t section with a moulded cornice above 3 short and 3 long drawers between fluted angles, the base wi 3 long drawers and inlaid with a concave sunburst, on bracket feet 39½in (100cm).
$8,000-10,000

Chests-on-Stands

A William and Mary walnut and seaweed marquetry miniature chest-on-stand, the top and sides inlaid with geometric sprays, fitted with 2 short and 3 long graduated drawers, the later stand with spirally turned stretchers and bun feet, 19in (48cm).
$9,000-10,000

A William and Mary figured walnut chest-on-stand, with moulded cornice and convex frieze drawer, above a pair of panelled doors with chevron banding, enclosing 11 drawers, the stand fitted with 2 frieze drawers, on spirally turned legs joined by waved stretchers, later bun feet, 43½in (110cm).
$4,000-6,000

A William and Mary walnut chest-on-stand, 43in (109cm).
$3,000-4,000

A figured walnut foliate marquet and penwork chest-on-stand, decorated with flower-swag panel on turned legs joined by a waved stretcher, on bun feet, basically la 17thC, 40in (101.5cm).
$5,000-6,000

A Queen Anne figured walnut chest-on-stand, the bevelled top inlaid with concentric bandings, above 2 short and 3 long lozenge banded drawers, the base with one long drawer and shaped apron, on later bun feet, 39½in (100cm).
$3,000-4,000

A Queen Anne walnut featherbanded chest-on-stand, on later cabriole legs with pointed pad feet, 43in (109cm).
$6,000-8,000

A Queen Anne walnut and burr el chest-on-stand, on later cabriole legs, the back partly replaced, 40i (101.5cm).
$2,500-3,000

;ommodes

. Victorian walnut French style
ımmode, with 3 drawers, marble
ıp, on cabriole legs with carved
ecoration.
,000-1,200

A George III mahogany gentleman's toilet commode, with box top, enclosed fitted interior, various drawers with ebony blind cockbeading and turned knobs, brass carrying handles, 28in (70cm).
$3,000-4,000

A George III mahogany tray top bedside commode, the simulated tambour door above a commode drawer, on square supports, 30in (76.5cm).
$1,200-1,600

A George III mahogany commode,
n the French taste, the serpentine
op above a brushing slide, the
ombé front drawers with cast
endant husk chain brass handles,
2in (106.5cm).
6,000-8,000

A George III mahogany serpentine commode, with 2 short and 3 graduated long drawers, on ogee bracket feet, 51in (130cm).
$6,000-8,000

A bombé commode with 2 drawers, on cabriole legs with gilt metal mounts.
$3,000-4,000

A Continental mahogany fluted cylindrical commode, with interior lid and liner, 19thC, 16in (40cm) diam.
$400-500

A Régence kingwood and fruitwood commode, with moulded distressed bowed 'brèche violette' marble slab above 2 short and 2 long drawers, the sides inlaid, restored, 51in (129cm).
$12,000-14,000

A gilt metal mounted tulipwood petite commode of Transitional style, with canted green marble top, and 2 geometrically inlaid drawers, on cabriole legs, 25in (63cm).
$6,000-8,000

A mahogany serpentine fronted commode, with 2 short and 2 graduated long drawers, the stand carved with foliage and with shell carved cabriole legs and scroll toes, 49in (124.5cm).
$14,000-16,000

A commode converted to 4 graduated drawers, with drop handles, shaped apron and bracket feet, damaged.
$700-800

A black lacquer and gilt chinoiserie decorated bombé commode, in Louis XV taste, with galleried top, the splayed legs with pierced trailing ornament terminating in paw sabots, 19thC, 37in (93cm).
$4,000-6,000

A Louis XV provincial fruitwood commode, with moulded top and 3 drawers, shaped apron and cabriole legs, 51in (130cm).
$10,000-12,000

A Louis XV style rosewood, tulipwood and marquetry bombé commode, applied with ormolu mounts with 'rouge royale' top, above 2 drawers 'sans traverse', on clasp headed cabriole supports and sabots, 48in (122cm).
$3,000-4,000

A Louis XV style kingwood commode, inlaid with marquetry and rosewood bands in boxwood line borders, applied with gilt metal mounts, marble top, 42in (106cm).
$3,000-4,000

A Louis XV style kingwood commode, with bowed moulded mottled ox blood marble top, above 4 graduated long drawers with fluted rounded angles, on moulded feet with pierced ormolu sabots, late 19thC, 32in (81cm).
$5,000-6,000

A Louis XV style rosewood, mahogany and ormolu mounted commode, with 'rouge royale' slab top, with foliate clasp headed angles, on slightly splayed legs with sabots, 31in (78cm).
$1,400-1,600

An Empire mahogany and brass mounted commode, with pierced brass galleried white marble top, 44in (111cm).
$10,000-12,000

An Empire mahogany and brass mounted commode, with contemporary moulded grey marble top, on turned tapering feet with sabots, 35in (89cm).
$6,000-8,000

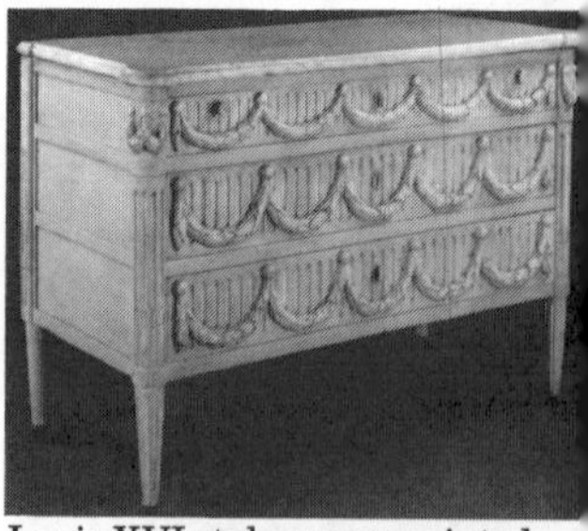

A Louis XVI style cream painted commode, with eared top, 3 long drawers carved with berried foliage swags, on fluted tapering legs, 50in (127cm).
$6,000-8,000

A Louis XVI style brass mounted mahogany commode, with quartered moulded top, above 3 panelled long drawers with stop fluted angles, panelled sides and square tapering legs with spade feet, 47in (119cm).
$5,000-6,000

A Louis XVI brass mounted mahogany commode, with grey marble top, 52½in (133cm).
$7,000-9,000

A Louis XV ormolu mounted tulipwood petite commode, with a grey veined marble top, 25in (63cm).
$8,000-10,000

French bombé kingwood and ory parquetry inlaid toilet mmode, with ormolu mounted coration with double serpentine l, the underside fitted with a irror, the interior with detachable ay, inscribed 'Grade R. de la Paix ', 19thC, 23in (58cm).
,000-4,000

French walnut commode, the short and 2 long drawers with caille cast handles and cutcheons, 44in (111.5cm).
,500-3,000

Dutch ormolu mounted walnut mbé commode, with moulded rpentine grey and white marble p, the 3 drawers with neo-classical m's mask handles and lockplates, te 18thC, 48½in (123cm).
,000-6,000

A French mahogany commode, early 19thC, 16in (40.5cm).
$700-800

A Dutch colonial palisander commode, with grey and white marble top, c1800, 52½in (133cm).
$3,600-5,000

Make the most of Miller's

Miller's is completely different each year. Each edition contains completely NEW photographs. This is not an updated publication. We never repeat the same photograph

A Dutch walnut and marquetry bombé commode, with serpentine top, above 3 drawers with all-over floral and scroll inlays, 47½in (120cm).
$7,000-9,000

A Dutch colonial rosewood commode, with serpentine panelled top, above 3 drawers, on short scroll feet, possibly Cape, mid-19thC, 47in (119cm).
$7,000-9,000

A Dutch walnut bombé commode, with 4 graduated drawers, on bracket feet, 18thC, 38in (96.5cm).
$3,000-4,000

A Dutch mahogany, amaranth and tulipwood banded demi-lune commode, the front with a door containing a lacquer panel depicting a prowling lion beneath a flowering tree, between plum lacquered upright panels, stamped Edwards & Roberts, retailers, late 18thC, 33in (84cm).
$10,000-12,000

A Dutch marquetry bombé commode, the serpentine top inlaid with a basket of flowers, the front inlaid with ribbon tied flowers and birds, 18in (46cm).
$8,000-9,000

A Dutch marquetry bombé commode, the serpentine top inlaid with a basket of flowers, the front inlaid with ribbon tied flowers and birds, 18in (46cm).
$8,000-9,000

A North Italian fruitwood commode, crossbanded with mahogany and inlaid with harewood lines, the mottled inset marble top with foliate carved edge, late 18thC, 51½in (130cm).
$7,000-9,000

A Dutch mahogany and floral marquetry bombé commode, 37in (94cm).
$8,000-10,000

A Danish parcel gilt and stained elm miniature commode, with moulded waved top and 3 drawers, with carved apron and scrolling feet, the sides with carrying handles, 14in (35.5cm).
$5,000-6,000

A Dutch inlaid burr walnut bombé commode, with brass handles and escutcheons, 33in (84cm).
$7,000-8,000

A Swedish ormolu mounted kingwood, walnut and parquetry bombé commode, the drawers crossbanded with tulipwood, the cabriole angles and splayed feet with pierced clasps and sabots, the underside inscribed in pencil K.L. Borgs mahelaffen Nykoping, mid-18thC, 34½in (87cm).
$12,000-16,000

A South German walnut parquetry commode, 18thC, 48in (122cm).
$25,000-30,000

Cupboards – Armoires

A French provincial walnut armoire with arched moulded cornice, the frieze carved with a basket of flowers, 61in (155cm).
$7,000-8,000

An Anglo-Indian padouk cupboard, the 2 panelled doors carved with spandrels and centred by oval paterae, 19thC, 61½in (156cm).
$1,500-2,000

A French provincial chestnut armoire, carved with vines, flowers and acanthus scrolls, early 19thC, 65in (165cm).
$3,000-4,000

A Dutch mahogany armoire, with beaded and foliate carved outlines early 19thC, 69in (175cm).
$8,000-9,000

miniature Dutch gilt metal ›unted mahogany armoire, the ›anelled doors enclosing a fitted :erior, late 18thC, 18½in (47cm).
,000-8,000

A Dutch figured walnut armoire, the canted corners with flat pilasters surmounted by carved capitals, one long drawer with heavy brass handles, early 19thC, 79in (200cm).
$8,000-10,000

A Flemish ebonised armoire, the panelled doors painted with flowers on gilt ground, divided by ripple mouldings with cherubs' heads and carved fruit, basically 17thC, 82in (298cm).
$15,000-18,000

A Louis Philippe ormolu mounted kingwood armoire, the panelled doors filled with brocade within foliate borders, 58in (147cm).
$6,000-7,000

upboards – Bedside

George III mahogany bedside pboard, with tray top above haped panelled doors and a fitted nmode drawer, with handwritten oel: Restored by M.C. Hopwood, Queen Street, Scarborough 1884, ½in (62cm).
,000-4,000

A Sheraton mahogany cupboard, with tambour, false drawer and door below, with side drawer, 18½in (47cm).
$8,000-10,000

A pair of mahogany night tables, the three-quarter galleried tops above a cupboard door, on turned tapered legs, mid-19thC, 18½in (47cm).
$1,200-1,500

A pair of Regency mahogany bedside cupboards, on turned legs, 15½in (40cm).
$4,000-5,000

George III mahogany bowfront dside cabinet, with kingwood and tinwood banding outlined with :inging, 21in (53cm).
,000-2,500

A George III mahogany bedside cupboard, with pierced three-quarter gallery and fall flap, restored, 20in (51cm).
$4,000-5,000

A pair of German mahogany and brass night tables, the square Carrara marble insets above shallow drawers and cupboards, all with brass beading, 16in (40cm).
$2,500-3,000

A Genoese blue and cream painted bombé cupboard, the serpentine top with three-quarter gallery, the sides pierced for handles, decorated overall with blue scrolling foliage, re-decorated, 18in (46cm).
$3,000-4,000

A pair of mahogany bedside cabinets, with three-quarter galleries, different handles, 15½in (40cm).
$5,000-6,000

A pair of satinwood bedside cabinets, outlined with rosewood crossbanding and boxwood and ebonised stringing, the concave doors veneered, 17in (43cm).
$5,000-6,000

Cupboards – Corner

A George III mahogany corner cupboard, the moulded cornice above a Greek key inlaid frieze a a pair of arched fielded panel doo c1800 with later back, 35½in (90c
$1,500-1,800

An early Georgian walnut hangin corner cabinet, with later mirror glazed door, framed by scrolls between canted angles, 24in (61cm
$2,500-3,000

A George III mahogany corner cabinet, with broken scroll pediment, 42in (107cm).
$3,000-4,000

A George III mahogany corner cabinet, with a swan neck pediment carved with foliage and fruit, the panelled doors veneered with ovals, roundels and octagons, with stringing outline, on later ball feet, 44½in (113cm).
$8,000-9,000

A George III mahogany and boxwood strung hanging corner cupboard, the geometrically glazed door enclosing shelves, 30in (76cm).
$1,200-1,500

Georgian inlaid mahogany
ınging corner cupboard, with
:ted shelves, 24in (61cm).
300-1,000

A walnut hanging corner cabinet, with moulded cornice and glazed door, inset with a panel of floral silk on a blue ground, 23in (59cm).
$3,000-4,000

A Dutch marquetry and rosewood corner cabinet, the panel door with lozenge marquetry of flowers, foliate scrolls and butterflies, on bracket feet, early 19thC, 33in (84cm).
$2,000-3,000

Georgian mahogany bowfront
rner cupboard, with 2 banded
ors.
00-1,000

A late Victorian rosewood and marquetry corner cupboard, with pierced gilt metal gallery above bone and marquetry inlaid frieze, 23in (58cm).
$3,000-4,000

A green-painted bowfront corner cupboard, the door painted with an oval medallion of a flower-girl, lover and a spaniel, surrounded by flowers, 28in (71cm).
$2,500-3,000

A mahogany corner cupboard, the doors enclosing fitted internal shelves, 19thC, 51in (130cm).
$1,500-2,000

:upboards – Linen 'resses

An early Georgian dwarf linen press, 46½in (118cm).
$4,000-5,000

Regency mahogany clothes press,
e top section with a cavetto
oulded cornice, the ebonised
aded oval panel doors above
long base drawers, 50in (127cm).
,000-3,000

A Regency mahogany clothes press, inlaid with ebonised lines, 50in (127cm).
$2,500-3,000

A Regency mahogany linen press inlaid with ebony stringing, the panelled cupboard doors above 2 short and 2 long drawers, 55½in (141cm).
$7,000-8,000

A George III mahogany clothes press, the panelled doors inlaid with chequered lines, enclosing a slide, 53in (135cm).
$16,000-18,000

An early Victorian mahogany lin press, by T. Willson, 68 Great Queen Street, London, the 2 crossbanded doors applied with reeded mouldings enclosing slidin trays, 51in (131cm).
$3,500-4,000

A Victorian burr walnut clothes press, with featherbanded lined borders, the top section with a bolection moulded cornice, 54in (137cm).
$2,000-3,000

A mahogany linen press, the dentil cornice above a blind fretwork frieze and a pair of figured cupboard doors, restorations, 50in (127cm).
$800-1,200

A walnut crossbanded and featherstrung linen press, the upper part with a moulded cornice enclosed by a pair of ogee arched moulded panel doors, the lower part with 2 short and 2 long drawers, early 18thC, 66in (167cm).
$3,500-4,000

Cupboards – Wardrobes

An Anglo-Indian rosewood breakfront wardrobe, 19thC, 102in (260cm).
$6,000-8,000

A Regency mahogany breakfron wardrobe, with Gothic arched cornice, crossbanded all over, the central panel doors enclosing 4 sliding trays, 98in (250cm).
$6,000-8,000

A George III mahogany wardrobe, the arched cornice with later turned finials, 95in (242cm).
$4,000-5,000

A Victorian mahogany breakfront wardrobe, the bolection moulded cornice above 4 fielded panel doors, on plinth base, adaptations, 85in (216cm).
$2,000-2,500

Miller's is a price Guide not a price List

The price ranges given reflect the average price a purchaser should pay for similar items. Condition, rarity of design or pattern, size, colour, pedigree, restoration and many other factors must be taken into account when assessing values

Professor James Buckingham

COLLECTION OF ENGLISH PERIOD COPIES

TWIN PEDESTAL DESKS
4′ x 2″ Mahogany £276 Yew £313
5′ x 3″ Mahogany £409 Yew £453
Also available, L-shape Computer Desks with side returns.

SET OF 6 CHAIRS
(4 Single & 2 Carvers)
Mahogany £352
Yew £388

FILING CABINET
2 drawer mahogany £217
2 drawer yew £237
3 drawer mahogany £275
3 drawer yew £310

LOWBOY
Mahogany £244
Yew £262
Walnut £262

7′ DINING TABLE & CENTRE LEAF
Mahogany £210
Yew £280
8′ 8″ Mahogany £295
Yew £357

REVOLVING BOOKCASE
Mahogany £133
Yew £155
Walnut £155

BREAKFAST TABLE
in Mahogany & Yew.
Several sizes from £130

NEST OF 4 TABLES
Mahogany £260
Yew £290

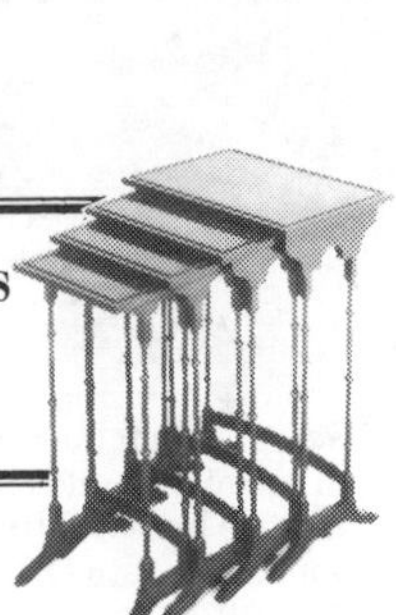

Prices are correct at time of going to publication but may be subject to change.

WHOLESALERS RETAILERS EXPORTERS

Professor James Buckingham

Tel: (04 44) 245577
School Close, Queen Elizabeth Avenue
Burgess Hill, West Sussex (Nr. Brighton) RH15 9RX
Fax (04 44) 232014
ENGLAND

Desks

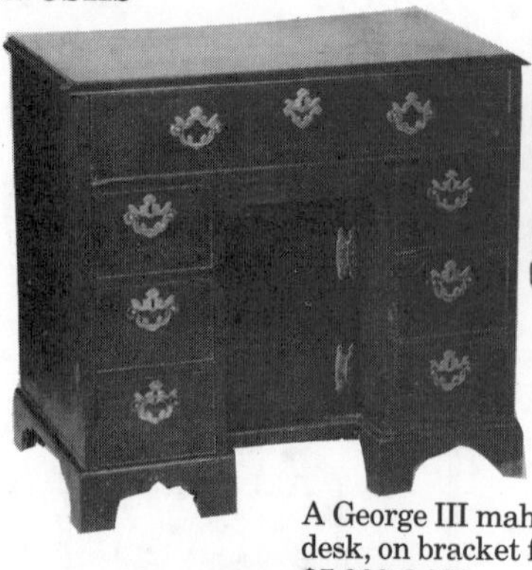

A George III mahogany desk of Carlton House design, the superstructure fitted with a centr enclosed cupboard flanked by 6 drawers and cupboards, the leather-lined top with adjustable ratchet, above 9 graduated drawe 61½in (157cm).
$16,000-20,000

A George III mahogany kneehole desk, on bracket feet, 33in (83cm).
$5,000-6,000

A George III style mahogany partners' kneehole pedestal desk, the inset leather lined top above 9 drawers, the same to the reverse, on bracket feet, 56in (143cm).
$2,500-3,000

A walnut and marquetry kneehole desk, the moulded top centred by an oval floral marquetry panel of a bird, the fall front writing drawer centred by a coat-of-arms flanked by marquetry panels, enclosing fitted interior, marquetry late 17thC, desk reconstructed in mid-19thC, 47in (120cm).
$3,000-4,000

A mahogany pedestal writing desk, with 4 drawers either side, the fall writing slope enclosing pigeonholes, cupboards and drawers, 19thC, 60in (152cm).
$4,000-5,000

A mahogany pedestal desk, in the Georgian style, the top crossbande and inset with frieze drawers, the lower part with 6 drawers and cupboards to either side, 19thC, 68in (173cm).
$14,000-19,000

A George III mahogany desk, inlaid with satinwood and chequered geometric boxwood lines, adaptations, 40in (102cm).
$1,500-2,500

A George III style mahogany pedestal desk, boxwood strung and kingwood crossbanded, the tooled red leather inset top with reeded edge, stamped Maple & Co, 54in (137cm).
$4,000-5,000

A Regency mahogany kneehole desk, inlaid with ebonised lines, adapted, 49in (125cm).
$2,500-3,000

A mahogany pedestal desk, in the Georgian style, the top crossbande and inset with frieze drawers, the lower part with 6 drawers and cupboards to either side, 19thC, 68in (173cm).
$14,000-16,000

mahogany bowfront writing desk
ith inlay, c1890, 47in (120cm).
2,000-2,500

A Victorian pedestal partners' desk, with panelled sides, later crossbanded inlay, c1900, 54in (138cm).
$6,000-7,000

A Victorian mahogany pedestal desk, with graduated drawers, 54in (137cm).
$4,500-5,000

. Victorian mahogany double sided
esk, with drawers and cupboards to
he reverse, 75in (191cm).
8,000-9,000

A Victorian walnut and satinwood crossbanded and line inlaid kneehole desk, with open bookshelf to reverse, damaged, 55in (140cm).
$28,000-32,000

Victorian burr walnut partners'
neehole pedestal desk, with tooled
eather lined top above 9 drawers,
ne reverse with panelled cupboard
oors, 54in (137cm).
10,000-12,000

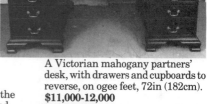

A Victorian walnut desk with 2 drawers, on barley twist supports.
$1,000-1,200

A late Victorian oak partners' desk, the moulded top lined in brown leather, the egg and dart moulded frieze fitted with 6 drawers, 60in (152cm).
$1,800-2,500

A Victorian burr walnut pedestal
lesk, the gallery with spindle back
nd 6 drawers, the fall front with
itted interior, central dummy
rawer and 8 short drawers,
Edwards & Roberts, Wardour
Street, London, 49in (125cm).
3,500-4,000

A Victorian mahogany partners' desk, with drawers and cupboards to reverse, on ogee feet, 72in (182cm).
$11,000-12,000

A Victorian mahogany desk, the moulded top lined in gilt tooled brown leather, above 3 frieze drawers and 8 short drawers, 57in (145cm).
$4,000-5,000

A walnut pedestal partners' desk with drawers, cupboards to reverse, leather top, c1900, 72in (182cm).
$7,000-8,000

A Chippendale carved mahogany secretaire, in 3 parts, the cornice with carved dentilling over a shaped moulding, the middle section with 2 doors opening to reveal a fitted interior, the lower section with 5 drawers, the upper drawer fitted with a writing slide, pen holders and compartments, Southern States, c1770, 41in (104cm).
$18,000-20,000

A Federal inlaid mahogany partners' desk, on square tapering legs with stringing, on brass cuffs with casters, feet reduced, mid-Atlantic States, c1800, 50in (127cm).
$10,500-12,000

A Chippendale walnut and maple desk, the sloping front enclosing a fitted interior, restoration to feet and rear bracket, Massachusetts, c1770, 36in (91.5cm).
$7,000-9,000

A Federal inlaid mahogany tambour desk, the top with moulded edge above a frieze with stringing centering a star above a small door opening revealing a fitted interior, the lower section with hinged writing surface over 3 drawers, on flared French feet, feet pieced, Massachusetts, c1800, 37in (94cm).
$4,000-6,000

A walnut desk with sloping fall front, enclosing fitted interior, above 2 drawers and a shaped frieze, on square tapered legs, 34in (86cm).
$1,200-1,500

An ormolu mounted kingwood and parquetry kneehole desk, with painted leather lined top and channelled border, the kneehole flanked by drawers with ram's mas[k] clasps, 48in (122cm).
$10,000-12,000

Dumb Waiters

A George III mahogany dumb waiter, on a turned spreading shaft and tripod base, with cabriole legs and pad feet, 32in (81cm) high.
$6,000-7,000

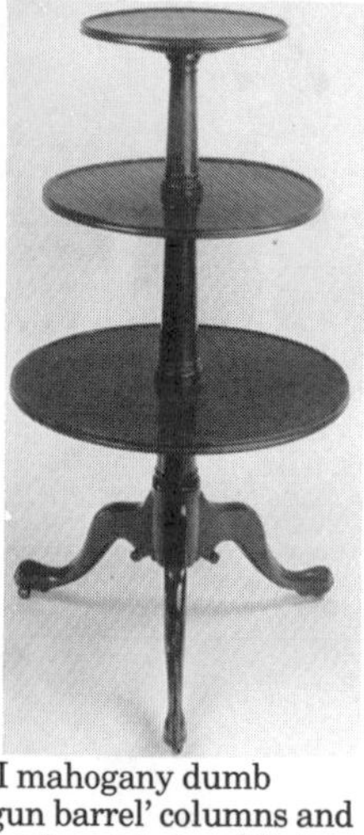

A George III mahogany dumb waiter, on 'gun barrel' columns and tripod base with pointed pad feet, 42in (106cm) high.
$3,500-4,000

A George III mahogany dumb waiter, with 3 stepped tiers on baluster turned stem and cabriol[e] tripod, 46in (116.5cm) high.
$3,000-4,000

A George III style mahogany dumb waiter, on baluster turned columns and cabriole tripod support, 23½in (60cm).
$1,000-1,200

late Regency mahogany dumb
iter, the 2 tiers each with a
rced brass gallery, on solid end
ndards, 46in (116.5cm).
,000-10,000

owboys

Queen Anne walnut
therbanded lowboy, with
ulded and crossbanded top, on
er waved stretcher, 29½in (75cm).
,000-9,000

George I walnut lowboy, fitted
th 3 drawers, on cabriole legs
th pointed pad feet, 32in (81cm).
,000-5,000

George II walnut lowboy, 36in
.5cm).
2,000-14,000

A two-tier mahogany dumb waiter, with brass capped feet and casters, 19thC.
$1,400-1,600

A Queen Anne walnut and featherbanded lowboy, on cabriole legs with fret scroll knee spandrels and ending in pad feet.
$5,000-6,000

A George I style burr walnut lowboy, with featherbanded inlay, on cabriole legs with pad feet, 31in (79cm).
$1,200-1,500

A mahogany lowboy, the frieze fitted with one long and 3 short drawers, on cabriole legs and ball-and-claw feet, basically 18thC, 32in (81cm).
$3,500-4,000

A mahogany three-tier dumb waiter, on ring turned spiral twist carved supports, on a foliate carved tripod with ball-and-claw feet, 25½in (64.5cm).
$1,200-1,600

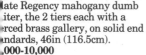

A George I walnut veneered lowboy, 32in (81cm).
$7,000-8,000

A solid burr elm lowboy, the top patched, early 18thC, 27in (68.5cm).
$4,000-5,000

A Georgian mahogany lowboy, c1740.
$5,000-6,000

A mid-Georgian maple lowboy, on scroll headed cabriole legs with shaped pad feet, possibly Irish or American, 36in (91.5cm).
$3,000-4,000

A mid-Georgian walnut lowboy, the top with moulded edge, above a frieze drawer with shaped apron, fitted with 3 other drawers, on cabriole legs with pointed pad feet, 32in (81cm).
$14,000-16,000

A walnut lowboy, with quarter veneered crossbanded top, above frieze drawer and shaped apron, square section cabriole legs, 30in (76cm).
$5,000-6,000

A Dutch walnut lowboy, inlaid with marquetry arabesques, on cabriole legs with shell and bellflower carved headings, basically 19thC, 33in (84cm).
$1,400-2,000

A Dutch mahogany lowboy, 18thC.
$6,000-7,000

Mirrors & Frames

A walnut and marquetry mirror, the frame inlaid with foliage and flowerheads, basically late 17thC with later plate, 20 by 19in (51 b 48cm).
$1,500-1,600

An English carved and gilded frame, with glass, 19 by 15in (48 by 38cm).
$800-1,000

A William and Mary oyster veneered walnut cushion frame mirror, with bevelled plate, 21 b 19in (53 by 50cm).
$2,500-3,500

A cushion frame mirror decorated with marquetry on an ebonised ground, late 17thC with later bevelled plate, 41 by 33½in (104 by 84cm).
$11,000-12,000

A 17thC style ebony veneered and ivory table mirror, set with simulated malachite plaques, 19½in by 14in (50 by 36cm).
$1,000-1,200

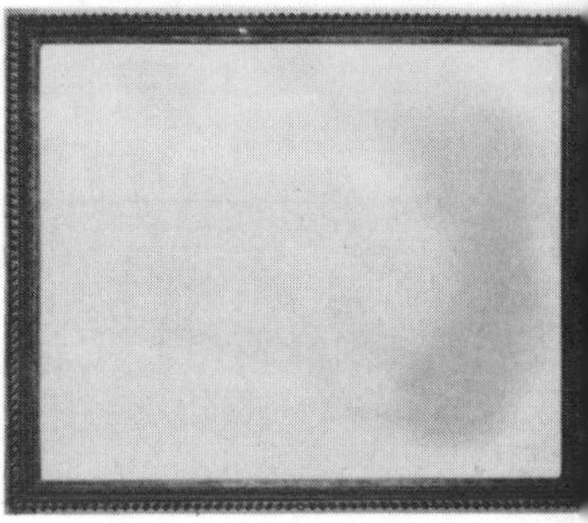

An English carved and gilded frame, 18thC, 61 by 49in (155 by 125cm).
$5,000-6,000

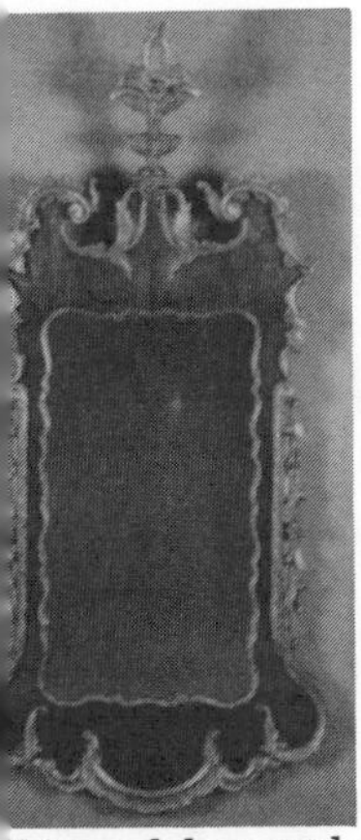

A Classical giltwood pier mirror, the double plate mirror divided by a moulding, American, c1830, 40in (101.5cm).
$1,000-1,200

Chippendale carved giltwood and hogany mirror, late 18thC, ½in (140cm) high.
500-6,500

A pair of carved giltwood looking glasses, one labelled P. Grinnell & Son, Providence R.I., early 19thC, 46in (116.5cm) high.
$20,000-25,000

A plated parcel gilt mirror, the pediment with a seated putto flanked by applied gilt roses and leaves, by Meriden Britannia Company, marked, late 19thC, 22in (56cm) high.
$4,000-5,000

Queen Anne walnut mirror, with rolled pediment and bird carved rs, the plate surrounded by a twood beaded inner frame and oulded outer frame, Baltic States, e 18thC, 30in (76cm).
,500-2,000

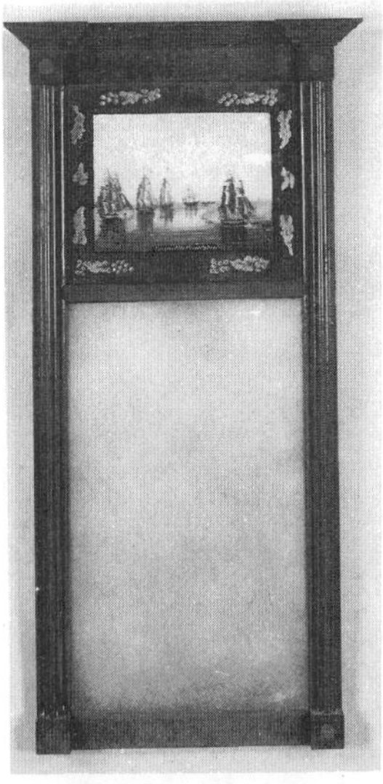

A Federal églomisé mirror, depicting the 'Escape of the Constitution' over the plate flanked by reeded pilasters, now lacking applied rosettes, some repainting to églomisé panel, 34½in (86.5cm) high.
$900-1,200

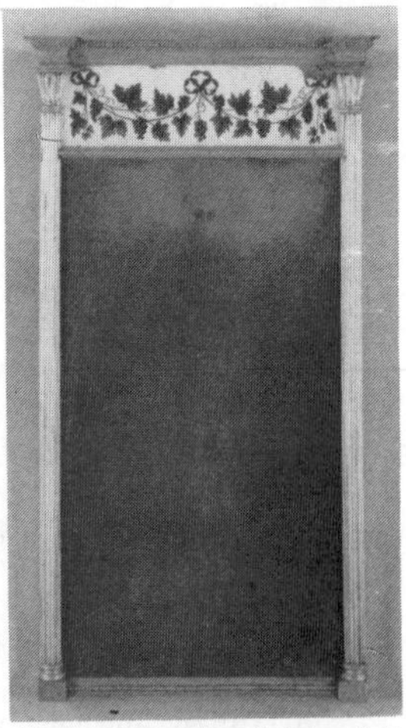

A Federal giltwood and églomisé mirror, Massachusetts, c1820, 30in (76cm).
$1,000-2,000

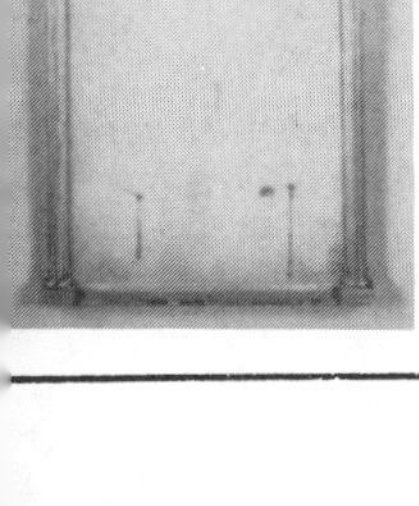

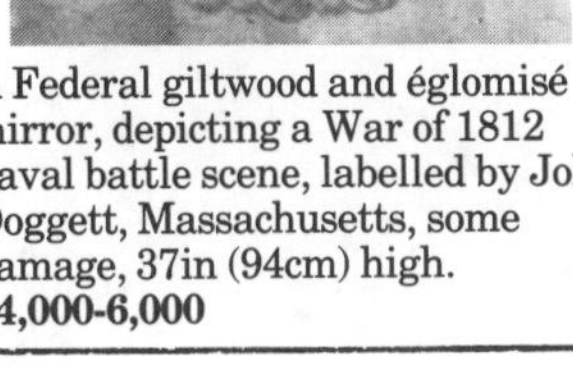

A Federal giltwood and églomisé mirror, depicting a War of 1812 naval battle scene, labelled by John Doggett, Massachusetts, some damage, 37in (94cm) high.
$4,000-6,000

A Georgian style giltwood wall mirror, with carved pierced foliate scroll frame, 52 by 33in (132 by 84cm).
$700-800

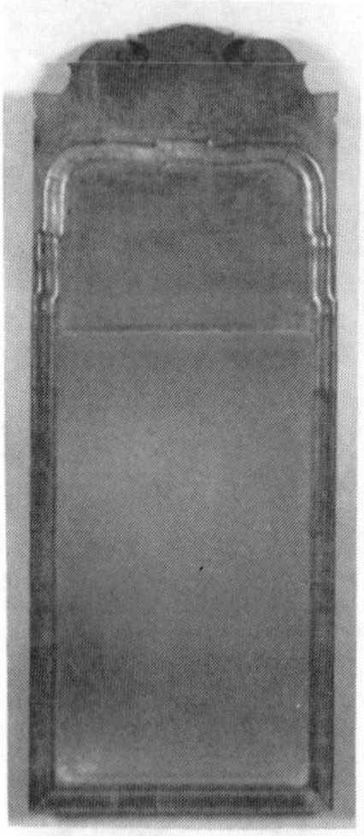

A George II mahogany and giltwood overmantel mirror, the moulded frame edged with gilt carving, minor veneer repair and losses, mid-18thC, 18in (45.5cm) high.
$9,000-11,000

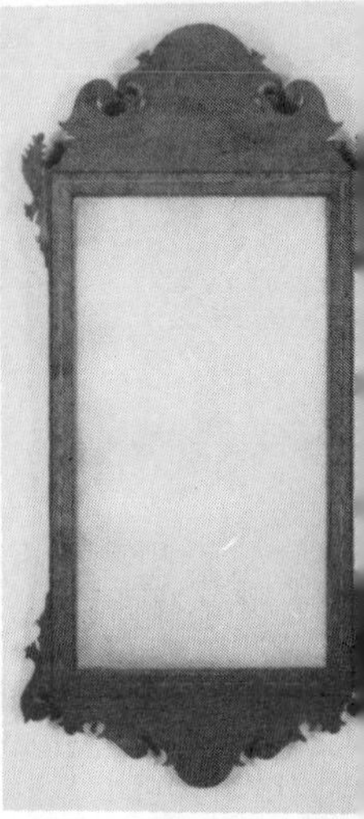

A Queen Anne walnut veneer looking glass, with scalloped crest above a two-part mirror plate within a segmented shaped moulded frame, some loss to crest, English or American, c1740, 43½in (110cm) high.
$5,500-6,500

A Chippendale mahogany mirro the reverse with label for retaile John Elliott & Sons, Philadelphi glass not original, c1805, 48in (122cm) high.
$2,000-3,000

A Chippendale carved mahogany mirror, the frame with applied carved outer moulding enclosing the glass plate, English, c1770.
$6,000-7,000

A Federal giltwood and églomisé panel mirror, probably Boston, Massachusetts, c1810, 35½in (90cm) high.
$1,200-1,500

A pair of late Classical giltwood pier mirrors, labelled by Augustus F. Cammeyer, New York, c1840, 68in (172.5cm) high.
$2,000-3,000

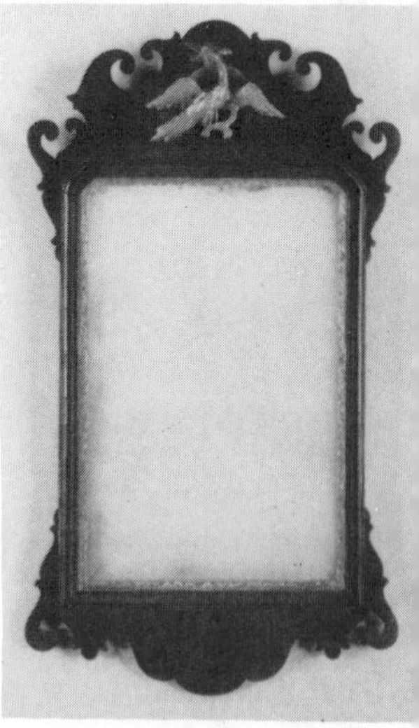

A Chippendale mahogany mirror with scrolled and shaped crest centering a gilt phoenix, the mirr plate within a gilt moulding, glas replaced, American or English, c1770, 30in (76cm) high.
$3,000-4,000

A Federal carved giltwood and églomisé mirror, Massachusetts, c1820, 32in (81cm) high.
$2,500-3,500

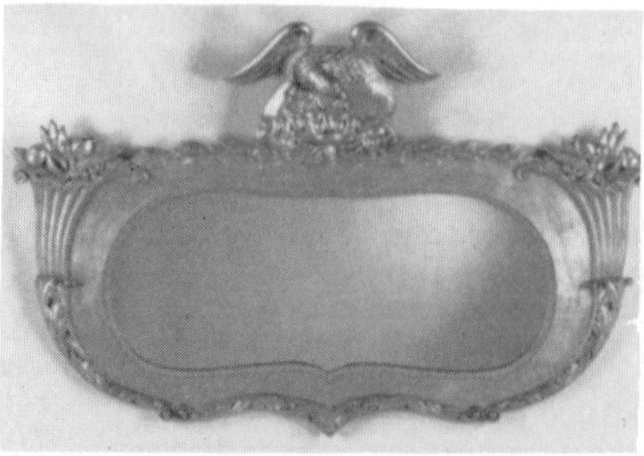

A Classical giltwood overmante mirror, with carved spreadwing eagle above a shaped oval fram enclosing a glass plate, Americ c1850, 33in (84cm) high.
$7,000-8,000

. Queen Anne walnut mirror, in a ıoulded frame with shaped 'esting and apron, applied with S-scroll gilt metal candle :anches, 42 by 18½in (106.5 by 7cm).
',000-8,000

A Queen Anne walnut mirror, in a moulded frame with shaped cresting, the back with wax seal, 37 by 17in (94 by 43cm).
$3,500-4,000

A George I style gilt mirror, 32½ by 18in (82 by 45.5cm).
$5,000-6,000

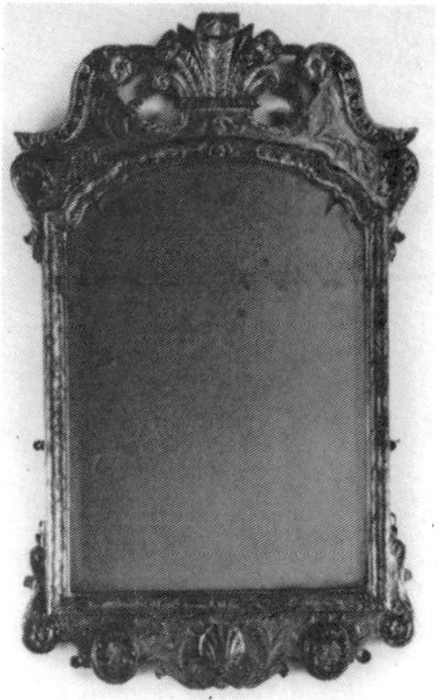

A George I giltwood mirror, with scrolling broken pediment cresting centred by the Prince of Wales' feathers, the waved base with a scallop shell flanked by plated applied clasps, re-gilded, 42½ by 26in (106.5 by 66cm).
$5,000-6,000

. Georgian carved giltwood and esso wall mirror in the :hippendale style, with a pierced resting of a vase of flowers, the urround with C-scrolls and floral ɔliate stems, 56 by 31in (142 by 9cm).
2,500-3,000

A Queen Anne giltwood mirror, the frame with scrolling and foliate rockwork cresting centred by a vase of flowers, re-gilded, 45 by 23in (114 by 58cm).
$1,800-2,500

A walnut and parcel gilt mirror, surmounted by a broken scroll pediment, basically early 18thC with later gilding and cresting, 51 by 25in (130 by 63cm).
$3,000-4,000

A George I giltwood mirror, moulded foliate frame and bevelled plate, the sides with later pierced scrolls, 45 by 24in (114 by 61cm).
$9,000-10,000

Miller's is a price GUIDE not a price LIST

A pair of pier glass, with divided bevelled shaped plates and glazed borders, now with simulated tiles, the plates early 18thC, 85 by 35in (216 by 89cm).
$3,000-3,500

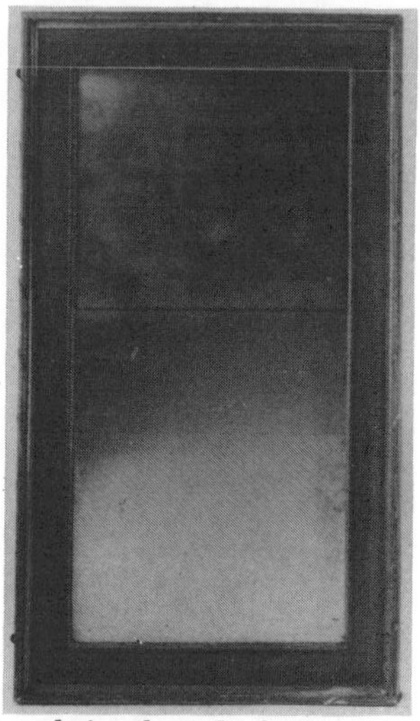

A giltwood pier glass, the frame with ribbon twist reeded edge, the back inscribed in pencil rehung Nov 13, 1931, the plate 18thC, 68½in by 40in (173 by 102cm).
$1,500-1,600

A walnut and parcel gilt mirror, basically mid-18thC, 33 by 17in (8 by 43cm).
$4,000-5,000

A walnut and parcel gilt mirror, in a bolection moulded frame, below a fret carved and 'ho-ho' bird cresting, 18thC, 38½ by 19½in (98 by 49cm).
$1,600-1,800

A George II walnut fret frame looking glass, 38 by 20in (96.5 by 51cm).
$1,600-1,800

A George III style mirror, the sides hung with ribbon tied flowers and fruit, the cresting with a leafy canopy surmounted by C-scrolls, 19thC, 56 by 31½in (142 by 79cm).
$3,500-4,000

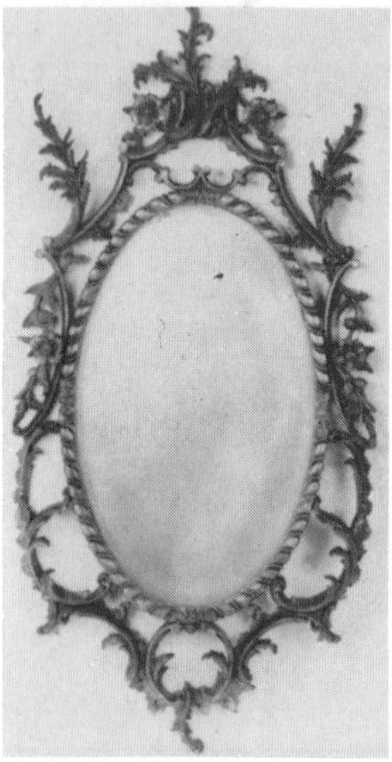

A George III style mirror, the bevelled plate in a gadrooned frame, the surround carved with flowerheads, rocaille, foliage and C-scrolls, 19thC, 53 by 28in (134.5 by 71cm).
$1,800-2,500

A George III giltwood mirror, the plate divided by a moulded slip and foliate joints in a cavetto frame with beading, re-gilded, 67 by 43in (170 by 109cm).
$8,000-9,000

A George III style giltwood mirror with shaped plate, the moulded pierced frame heavily carved, 59 b 37in (150 by 94cm).
$3,000-4,000

Regency carved giltwood convex
rror, surmounted by an
spread eagle on rocky base, 41 by
n (104 by 76cm).
,800-2,500

A Regency mahogany cheval glass, with hinged adjustable plate, on square posts with urn finials and arched downcurved legs, 26in (66cm).
$4,000-5,000

An early Victorian figured mahogany toilet mirror, the serpentine boxed base with a hinged lid and bun feet, the hinges stamped Cope & Austin patent, the bottom rail of the mirror frame inscribed in pencil £3.10.0, 29½in (75cm).
$1,200-1,400

Regency mahogany cheval
rror, the spandrels carved with
iage, 68 by 35½in (172.5 by 90cm).
,000-4,000

A Regency mahogany toilet mirror, the bow shaped frieze inlaid with brass, with 2 frieze drawers and ring turned tapering feet, 22in (56cm).
$550-600

A George III mahogany toilet mirror, the bowed frieze with 3 drawers, 19in (48cm).
$1,800-2,000

Victorian mahogany
eval mirror, on porcelain
sters, 65in (165cm) high.
,200-1,400

Make the most of Miller's

Miller's is completely different each year. Each edition contains completely NEW photographs. This is not an updated publication. We never repeat the same photograph

A Regency giltwood convex mirror, in an ebonised slip and cavetto frame encrusted with balls with associated seahorse cresting, later twisted candle branches with brass nozzles, re-gilded, 32½ by 27in (82 by 68.5cm).
$2,000-3,000

A Victorian bevelled mirror, the pierced brass frame with 3 candle sconces.
$150-200

A giltwood mirror, the frame carved with flowerheads and scrolling foliage, 40 by 31½in (101.5 by 80cm).
$3,000-4,000

A Victorian giltwood and composition overmantel mirror, by 72in (213 by 182.5cm).
$2,000-2,500

A Victorian mahogany cheval mirror, the base fitted with a lidded compartment, on moulded plinth, 74 by 45in (188 by 114cm).
$1,200-1,500

A late Victorian/Edwardian looking glass, the satinwood frame painted with ribbon tied sprays of roses, 31 by 49in (79 by 124.5cm).
$1,200-1,500

A Victorian giltwood overmante mirror in early George III style, by 77in (157 by 195.5cm).
$10,000-12,000

A giltwood mirror, with pierced frame carved with flowerheads, rocaille and foliate scrolls, 53 by 33in (134.5 by 84cm).
$3,000-4,000

A giltwood and composition mirror the pierced frame decorated with lilies, the rockwork cresting centre by a head, the apron with 3 scrollin branches, 57½ by 40in (144.5 by 101.5cm).
$1,400-2,000

A gilt pier mirror, the narrow arched plate with swan neck crest, 56½in (142cm) high.
$800-1,000

Dutch mahogany and marquetry
let mirror, the serpentine base
ed with 2 long drawers, the
ole inlaid with urns of flowers,
350, 27in (69cm).
200-1,400

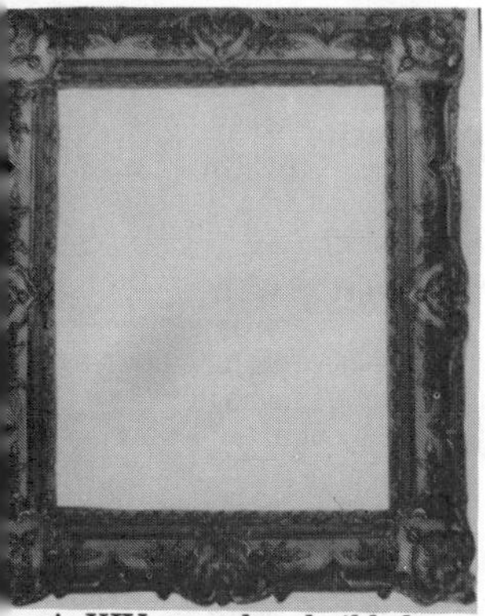

Louis XIV carved and gilded
me, 18 by 21in (45 by 53cm).
000-6,000

Louis XV carved and gilded
me, with scrolling acanthus leaf
sign, 11½in (29cm) wide.
00-700

A Louis XIV carved and gilded frame, 10 by 17in (25 by 43cm).
$3,500-4,000

A Louis XIV carved and gilded laurel leaf corner frame, 28½ by 22in (71 by 55cm).
$4,000-5,000

Did you know
MILLER'S Antiques Price Guide builds up year by year to form the most comprehensive photo-reference system available.

A pair of French carved giltwood pier mirrors and tables, the console tables with Carrara marble tops, mid-19thC, 20in (51cm).
$4,000-5,000

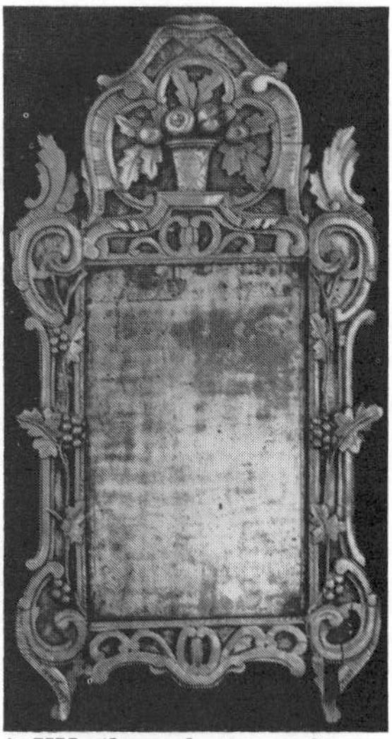

A Louis XV giltwood mirror, the glazed pierced frame carved with C-scrolls and foliage with grapes and vine leaves, border damaged, 41 by 22½in (104 by 56cm).
$2,000-3,000

A Louis XIV carved and gilded frame, the corners with fleur-dy-lys, the sides carved with strapwork, foliage and flowers, 14½ by 18in (36 by 45cm).
$3,000-4,000

An Italian carved and gilded tabernacle frame, with painted scrolling foliate frieze, on a pair of Corinthian columns and similar base, 16thC.
$1,300-1,600

A Florentine carved and gilded frame, with pierced C-scroll borders, late 17thC, 45½ by 33in (115 by 83cm).
$2,500-3,000

A Venetian giltwood and gesso framed mirror, the border inlaid with daisies and foliage raised on a blue ground, within applied barley twist glass mouldings, with later bevelled plate, basically 18thC, 24½in (61cm) high.
$1,200-1,500

An Italian carved and gilded frame, with leaf and flower motifs and strapwork, 17thC, 23½ by 32in (59 by 80cm).
$3,000-4,000

An Italian carved, gilded and painted corner frame, 17thC, 34½ by 26in (86 by 65cm).
$3,000-4,000

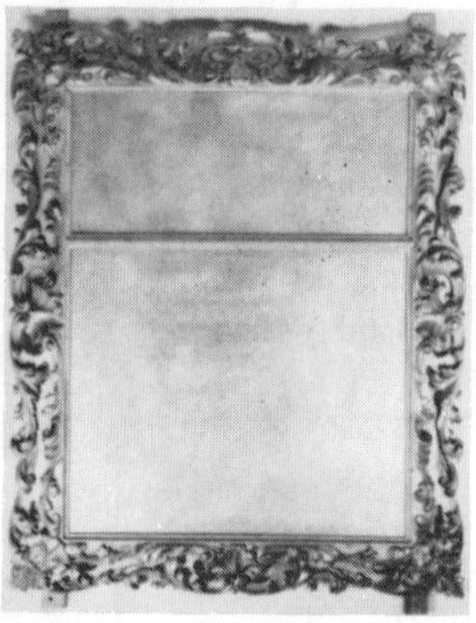

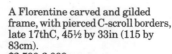

An Italian carved and gilded fram with glass, 17thC, 16 by 12½in (4 by 32cm).
$3,000-4,000

An Italian giltwood mirror, with twin rectangular plates in a frame pierced and carved with scrolling acanthus with grotesque masks to the angles, 19thC, 59 by 50in (150 by 127cm).
$3,000-4,000

A pair of Regency gilt and composition adjustable tripod polescreens, 56in (142cm) high.
$3,500-4,000

A Louis XVI giltwood mirror, the pierced urn cresting with foliate swags and ribbon-tied drapery apron, 34 by 16½in (85 by 41cm).
$1,500-2,500

Screens

A pair of George III mahogany polescreens, each with a glazed panel embroidered in silk with ribbon-tied flowers, both labelled Burlington Fine Arts Club Dec-March 1922-23, and inscribed in red paint 220, the framed panels later, 57in (145cm) high.
$1,000-1,500

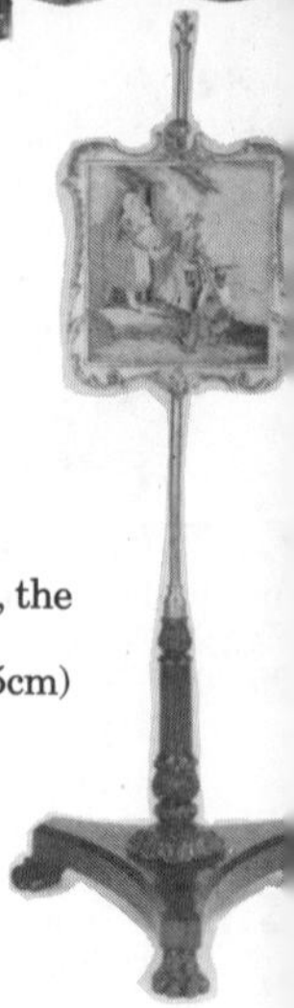

A pair of George IV rosewood polescreens with brass finials, the later giltwood panels with needlework screens, 61in (155cm) high.
$2,500-3,000

A pair of George III mahogany polescreens, with adjustable needlework screens on later poles, with tripod bases, 51in (130cm) high.
$1,400-1,600

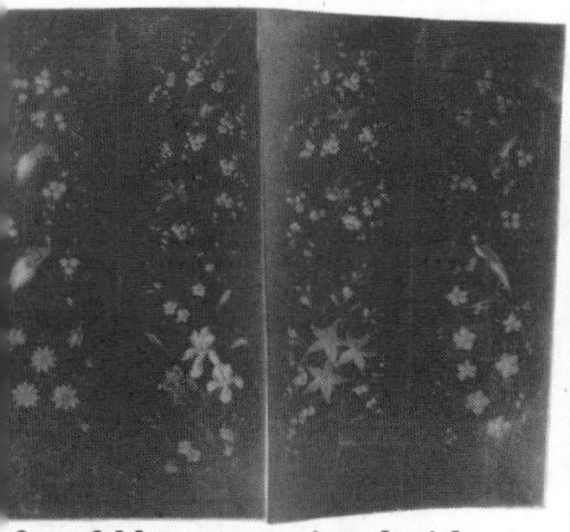

four-fold screen, painted with
otic birds in flowering prunus
anches, 19thC.
00-800

A painted leather four-leaf screen, each leaf painted with urns of flowers and fruit, bold foliate scrolls and trophies framed by drapes, 83in (211cm) high.
$8,000-10,000

An early Victorian mahogany polescreen, 47in (120cm) high.
$200-300

'our-panel red walnut screen,
:h oil on canvas nature studies,
)00, 64in (163cm) high.
,200-1,500

A French giltwood framed three-fold screen, mid-19thC, 76in (193cm) high.
$1,400-1,600

A Regence style walnut firescreen, with gros-point needlework panel, the reverse with a panel of silver thread embroidered silk, in a moulded frame, carved with scrolls and foliage, on scroll feet.
$2,500-3,000

grey-painted screen, with glazed
ints of various houses, above
nulated marble panels, one pane
glass missing, 68in (173cm) high.
,000-5,000

A pair of William IV rosewood polescreens, the panels filled with floral needlework, 55in (140cm) high.
$1,400-1,600

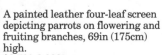

An early Victorian carved rosewood polescreen, with leaf and scroll decorated frame, beadwork flower panel, gilt metal pole and tripod support, 60½in (154cm).
$800-1,000

mahogany polescreen, with
tit-point floral panel on a dark
own ground, 23in (58cm) wide.
00-1,000

A painted leather four-leaf screen depicting parrots on flowering and fruiting branches, 69in (175cm) high.
$2,500-3,000

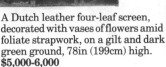

A Dutch leather four-leaf screen, decorated with vases of flowers amid foliate strapwork, on a gilt and dark green ground, 78in (199cm) high.
$5,000-6,000

Settees

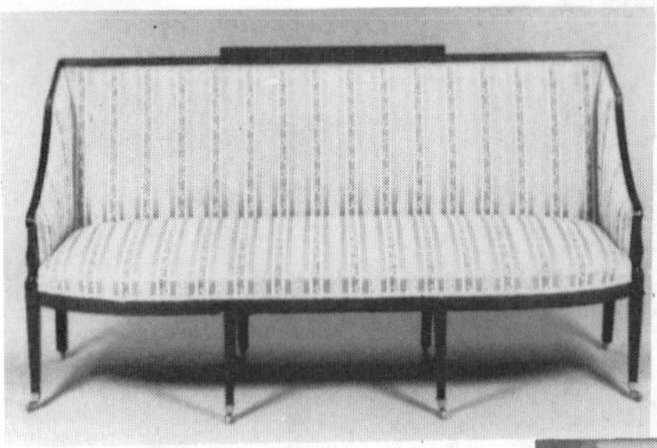

A Federal carved mahogany sofa, with bowed seat, old minor repairs, New York, c1800, 78in (198cm).
$5,000-7,000

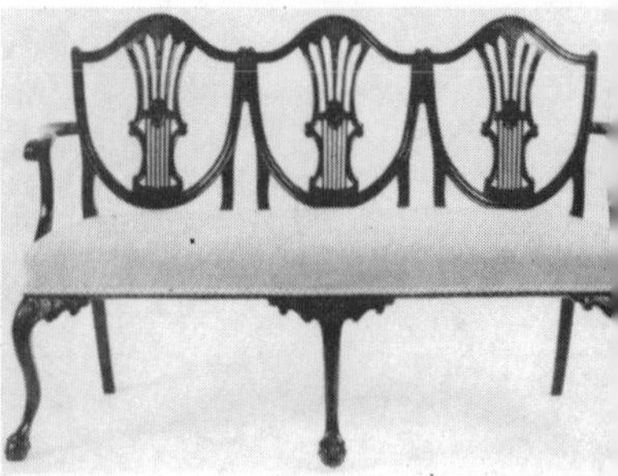

A George III style stained wood triple shield back settee, on acanthus and cabochon headed cabriole legs and ball and claw feet, 63in (160cm).
$1,800-2,500

A Federal carved mahogany sofa, restoration to legs, Massachusetts, c1800, 76in (193cm).
$7,500-8,500

A Regency mahogany scroll end sofa, damaged.
$1,800-2,500

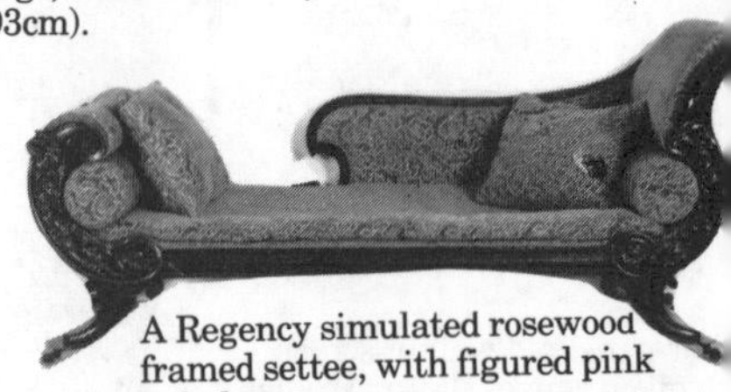

A Regency simulated rosewood framed settee, with figured pink upholstery.
$4,000-5,000

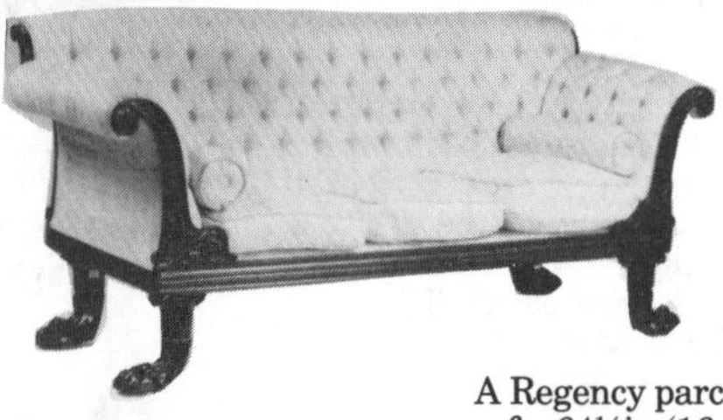

A William IV rosewood sofa, the buttoned back, seat and scrolling side panels upholstered in printed silk repp, on sabre legs with carved paw feet, 86in (219cm).
$6,000-7,000

A Regency parcel gilt and ebonised sofa, 64½in (164cm).
$3,000-4,000

A George III style mahogany triple chairback settee, the shield shaped backs with pierced waisted splats, restored.
$2,000-3,000

Use the Index!

Because certain items might fit easily into any of a number of categories, the quickest and surest method of locating any entry is by reference to the index at the back of the book.
This has been fully cross-referenced for absolute simplicity

A George III beechwood sofa of Louis XV style, with later blocks, formerly painted, 81in (206cm).
$8,000-9,000

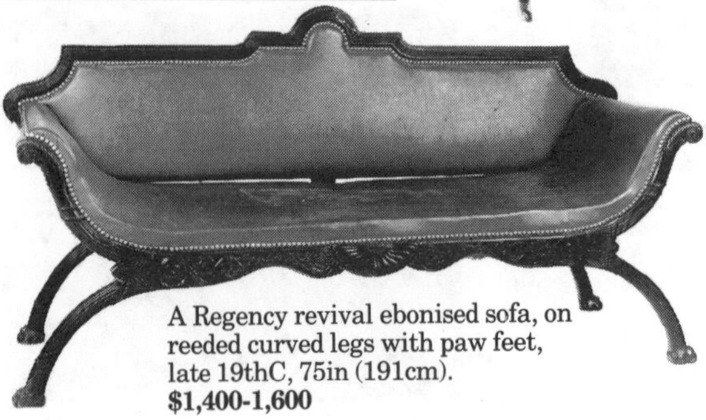

A Regency revival ebonised sofa, on reeded curved legs with paw feet, late 19thC, 75in (191cm).
$1,400-1,600

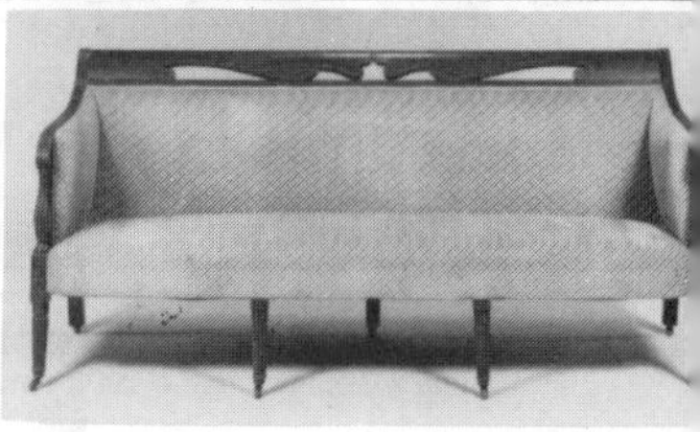

A late Federal mahogany sofa, Massachusetts, c1820, 75½in (192cm).
$4,000-5,000

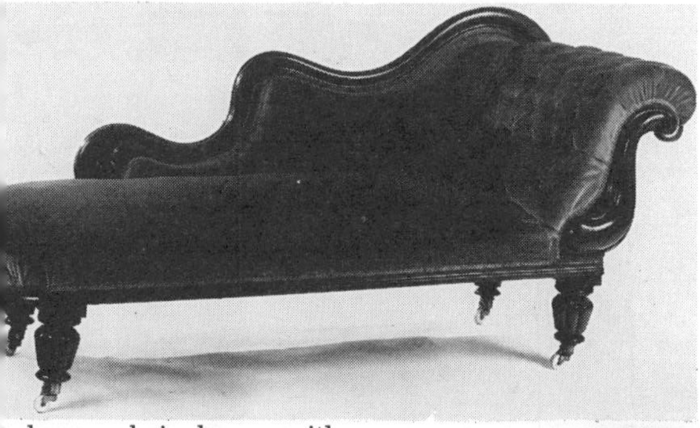

ıahogany chaise longue, with a
ilar lady's and gentleman's
ıchair with arched, bowed backs
l serpentine seats, c1850.
ɒ00-3,000

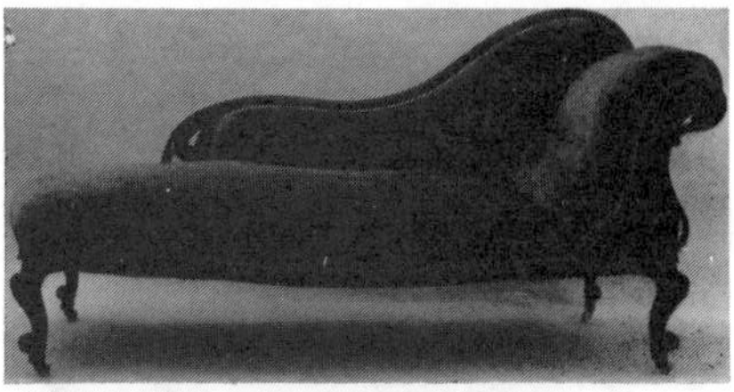

A Victorian walnut framed chaise longue.
$1,400-1,600

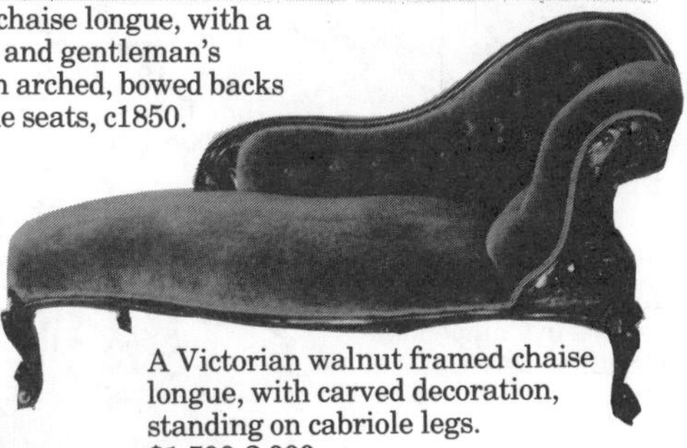

A Victorian walnut framed chaise longue, with carved decoration, standing on cabriole legs.
$1,500-2,000

A Victorian walnut couch, with rose pink upholstery, on French cabriole front supports.
$2,500-3,000

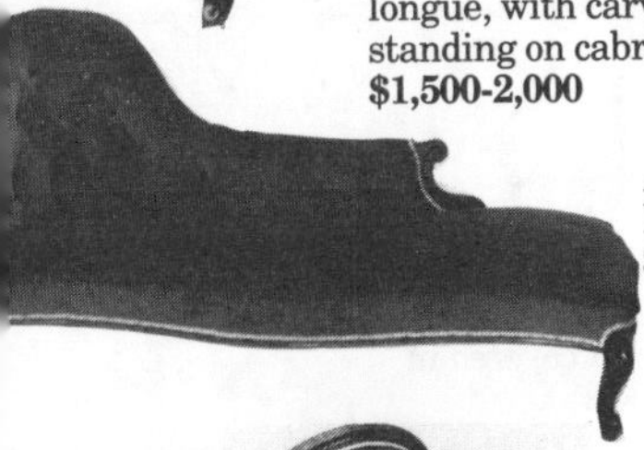

A Victorian rosewood framed chaise longue, 72in (183cm).
$1,400-1,800

A Victorian walnut sofa, upholstered in printed linen, on turned tapering legs, stamped Howard & Sons Ltd, Berners Street and numbered 13106, 77½in (197cm).
$3,000-4,000

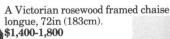

A Victorian walnut chaise longue, with moulded frame, upholstered in blue, carved with foliage, on scrolling cabriole legs, 62in (157cm).
$3,500-4,000

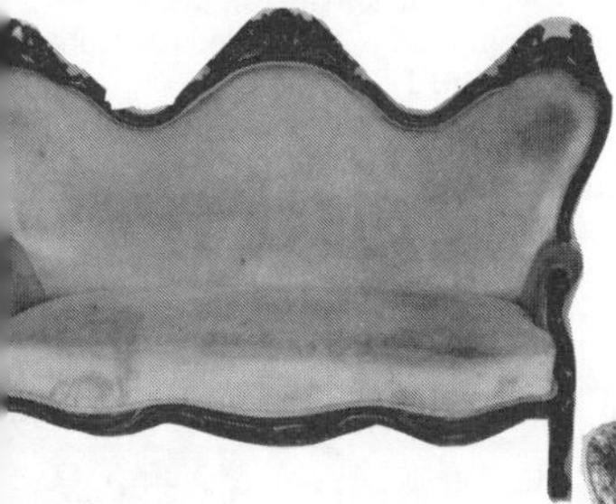

Victorian walnut framed settee,
ı back with floral scrolls and urn
ɔoration, with cabriole legs.
,000-3,000

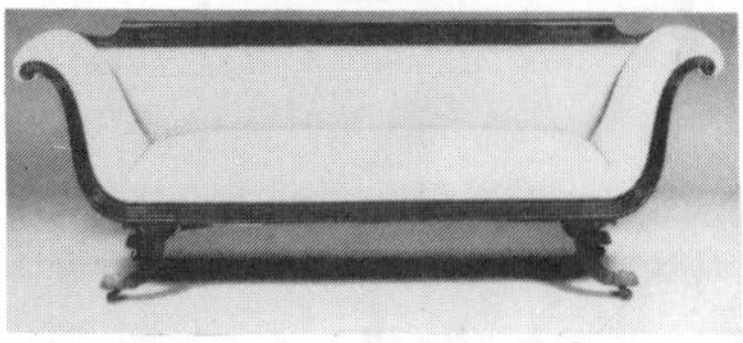

A mahogany sofa, with rolled crest rail above a reeded frieze, Baltimore, c1820, 98in (249cm).
$9,000-12,000

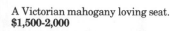

A Victorian mahogany loving seat.
$1,500-2,000

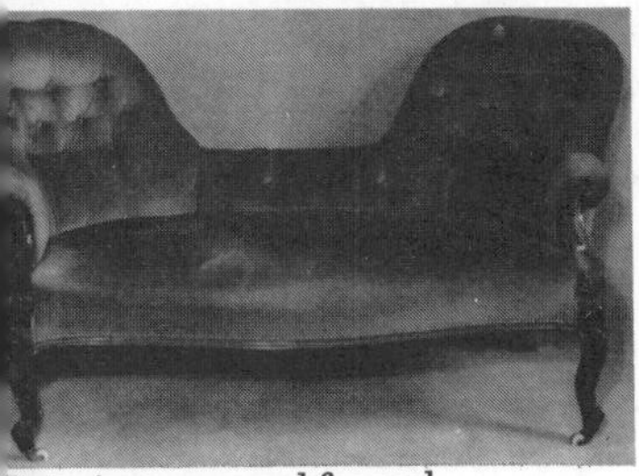

Victorian rosewood framed
ton back settee.
ɜ00-2,000

A Victorian deep buttoned chesterfield, on turned legs.
$2,000-3,000

A Victorian walnut framed conversation sofa, with buttoned backs above carved and pierced foliate scroll splats, on short cabriole legs, upholstery distressed.
$3,500-4,000

A Victorian rosewood framed sett
76in (193cm).
$2,000-3,000

A Victorian walnut framed op
arm settee, decorated with sc
and flowers.
$1,000-1,400

A mahogany framed double chairback settee in Chippendale Gothic style, 42in (107cm).
$1,200-1,400

A beechwood triple chairback settee, the padded seat covered in yellow silk, 65in (165cm).
$3,000-4,000

A late Victorian walnut framed sofa, on square section cabriole legs, 51in (130cm).
$700-900

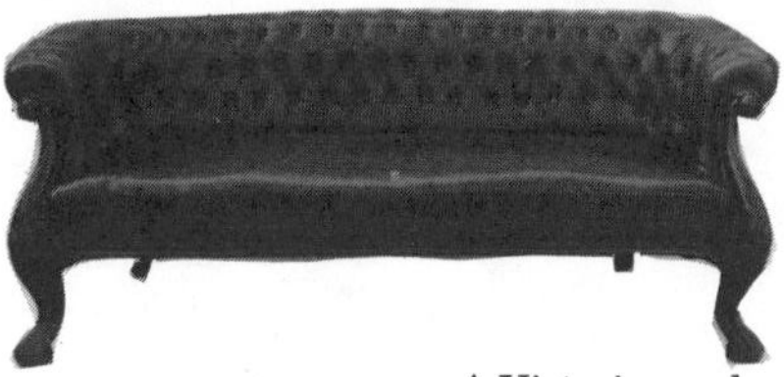

A Victorian walnut framed sette
with leather button back
upholstery, on carved cabriole le
$1,400-1,800

A walnut sofa, upholstered in floral needlework in a moulded frame, on tapering legs, 61in (155cm).
$1,500-2,000

A Chippendale style mahogany open arm settee, profusely carved, above a tapestry upholstered seat and undulating apron, 46in (117cm)
$3,000-4,000

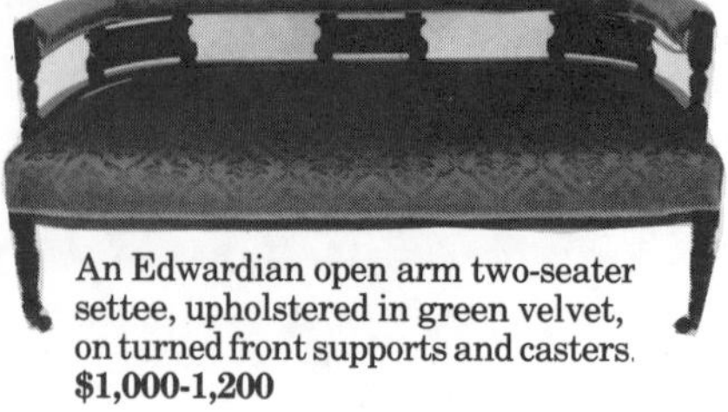

An Edwardian open arm two-seater settee, upholstered in green velvet, on turned front supports and casters.
$1,000-1,200

A walnut framed settee.
$4,000-5,000

Make the Most of Miller's

We do not repeat photographs in Miller's. However, the same item may appear in a subsequent year's edition if our consultants feel it is of interest to collectors and dealers

A Louis XVI style carved giltwood canapé, upholstered in an Aubusson design tapestry, late 19thC, 52in (132cm).
$1,000-1,400

A Louis XVI style gilt suite, upholstered in floral Aubusson tapestry, comprising a canapé and 4 fauteuils, 53in (135cm).
$4,000-5,000

'rench walnut duchesse brisée, acanthus carved legs, mid-19thC.
200-1,600

Shelves

A rosewood shelf with Gothic arched brass gallery and end supports, c1830, 21in (53cm).
$3,000-4,000

A William IV mahogany bookshelf, on baluster supports and a plinth base, 47in (120cm).
$3,500-4,000

pair of mahogany bookshelves, th three-quarter gallery above stepped shelves and a drawer laid with ebony lines, on plinth ise, 27in (68cm).
,000-10,000

A set of mahogany hanging shelves, with 4 graduated tiers and pierced fret sides, with 3 drawers below, 34in (86cm).
$1,000-1,200

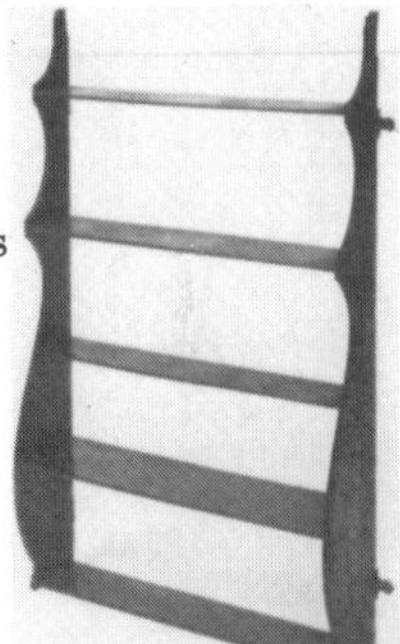

A late Regency mahogany hanging shelf fitment, on reeded graduating supports carved with foliage, 28in (70cm).
$800-1,000

A three-tier display shelf, with shaped upper frieze, early 18thC, 36in (91.5cm).
$800-1,000

Sideboards

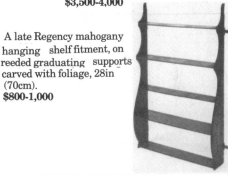

A George III mahogany bowfront sideboard, with 3 frieze drawers, 72in (183cm).
$4,000-5,000

A Georgian mahogany serpentine fronted sideboard, 62in (157cm).
$6,000-8,000

A Federal inlaid mahogany sideboard, with serpentine top, one leg broken, various veneer chips, New York, c1800, 72in (182.5cm).
$5,000-7,000

A Federal inlaid mahogany sideboard, with shaped front, on square tapering legs, 66in (167.5cm).
$8,000-9,000

A Federal inlaid cherrywood sideboard, damage and repairs, probably Connecticut, c1800, 77in (195.5cm).
$8,500-9,500

A Federal mahogany sideboard, the bowed centre with 2 fitted and cockbeaded drawers, flanked by 4 short drawers over central serpentine front, veneer chips, New York, c1810, 74in (188cm).
$2,000-3,000

A Federal inlaid mahogany sideboard, the concave front with 2 short line inlaid drawers above double cupboard doors, flanked by convex line inlaid cupboard doors, feet pieced, Philadelphia, c1800, 77in (195.5cm).
$5,000-7,000

A Federal mahogany sideboard, attributed to Ephraim Haines, Philadelphia, c1810, 65in (165cm).
$11,000-13,000

A late Federal mahogany sideboar with veneered and crossbanded stepped splashboard flanked by brass galleries, old repairs to feet New York, c1810, 73in (185cm).
$14,000-16,000

An Empire carved mahogany and maple sideboard, some veneer loss, top pieced at back, probably New York State, c1820, 64in (162.5cm).
$2,000-4,000

A mahogany bowfront sideboar inlaid with satinwood and foliat spandrels, with crossbanded top 54in (137cm).
$5,000-6,000

A George III mahogany bowfront sideboard with satinwood crossbanded top, with later central shelf, 60in (152cm).
$4,000-6,000

A mahogany sideboard with plain top, on bracket feet, 19thC, 53in (135cm).
$1,500-1,700

Regency mahogany breakfront ideboard, with a deep cellaret rawer simulated as 2 drawers, 6in (193cm).
4,000-6,000

A mahogany sideboard with a divided frieze drawer, flanked on either side by a door edged with boxwood lines, 59½in (151cm).
$3,000-4,000

A Regency mahogany bowfront sideboard with crossbanded top, 54in (137cm).
$12,000-14,000

Regency mahogany sideboard, vith crossbanded breakfront top, 0½in (154cm).
5,000-6,000

A George III mahogany bowfront sideboard, the crossbanded top above a napery drawer, a cellaret and 2 shallow drawers, 72½in (184cm).
$10,000-12,000

A George III mahogany sideboard, inlaid with boxwood lines and crossbanded with rosewood, the semi-elliptical top with later low ledge, 71in (180cm).
$14,000-16,000

A Regency mahogany bowfront sideboard, the crossbanded top with breakfront centre, one back leg spliced, 84in (214cm).
$5,000-6,000

A George III mahogany veneered and inlaid bowfront sideboard, fitted with central drawer flanked by cupboard and cellaret, 50in (127cm).
$3,500-4,000

George III mahogany bowfront deboard, banded in satinwood, the prights inlaid with ovals, on quare tapering legs and spade feet, 2in (183cm).
10,000-12,000

A late Georgian mahogany and boxwood strung serpentine sideboard, inlaid with foliate marquetry ovals, with finialled brass gallery and candle branches, 85in (216cm).
$8,000-9,000

A Regency mahogany sideboard with bowed top, 37½in (96cm).
$10,000-12,000

George IV mahogany breakfront edestal sideboard, outlined with oxwood stringing, 40in (102cm).
2,500-3,000

A George III mahogany serpentine sideboard, outlined with boxwood stringing, 72in (183cm).
$12,000-13,000

Stands

An ormolu-mounted mahogany gueridon, with 'verde antico' marble top, the square undertier centred by a rosette and edged with stiff leaves, basically early 19thC, 20in (51cm).
$3,000-4,000

A mahogany fretwork urn table of George III style, with galleried top, the pierced frieze fitted with a candle slide, on spreading legs headed by scroll brackets and joined by pierced stretchers, 28in (71cm).
$2,500-3,000

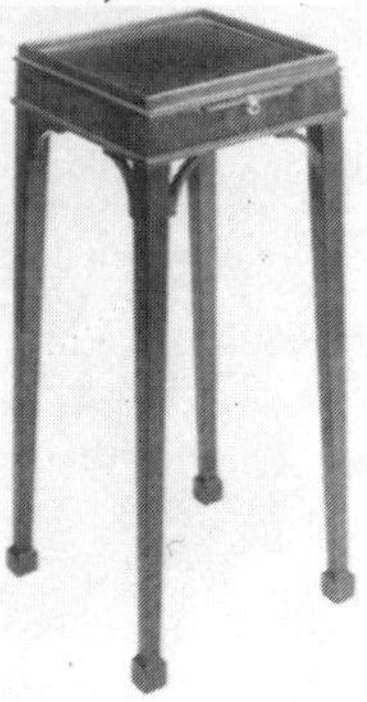

A George III mahogany urn stand with a galleried top, fitted with a candle slide, 12in (30cm).
$2,500-3,000

A walnut umbrella stand, turned and bobbin frame, l 19thC.
$250-300

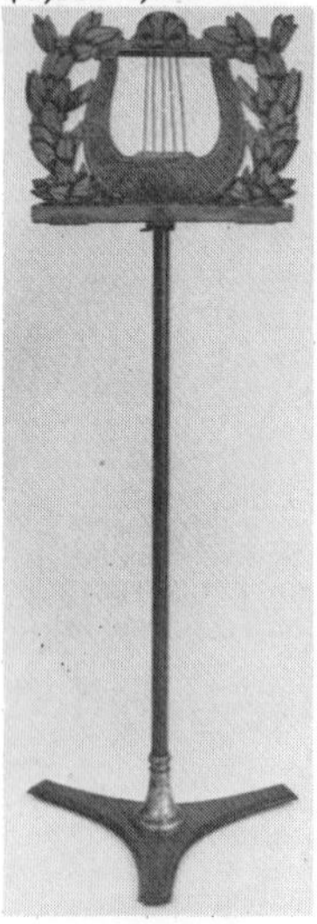

A Regency parcel gilt, maple and brass music stand, the turned shaft with painted iron concave tripod base, 15½in (40cm).
$4,000-5,000

A George IV rosewood duet stand, with lyre filled adjustable top, concave sided base and bun feet, lacking candle sconces, 17½in (45cm).
$3,500-4,000

A Regency mahogany plate and cutlery stand, the top with metal liners and central carrying handle, on turned tapering legs and casters 24½in (62cm).
$5,000-6,000

A Victorian mahogany music sta with turned and part reeded pedestal with decorative scrolled supports.
$1,200-1,500

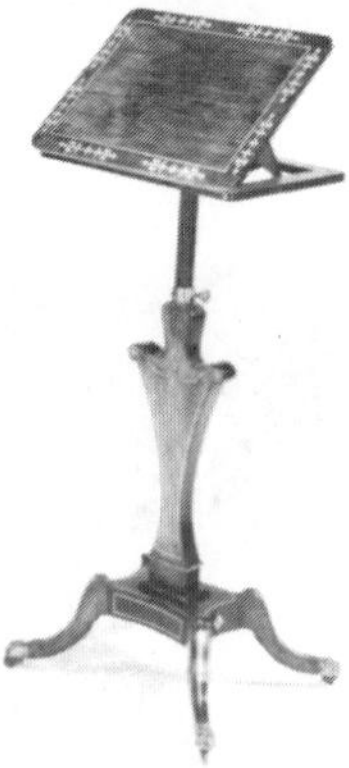

A Regency brass inlaid rosewood reading stand, 18in (46cm).
$1,200-2,000

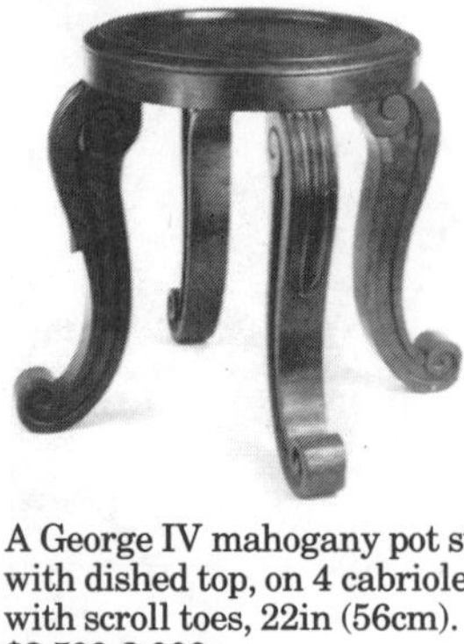

A George IV mahogany pot stand with dished top, on 4 cabriole legs with scroll toes, 22in (56cm).
$2,500-3,000

A pair of rosewood pedestal stands, with inset glazed tops with tapestry panels, basically early 19thC, 15in (38cm).
$1,200-1,600

An early Victorian mahogany f stand, the slatted folding sides baluster X-shaped supports, 31i (79cm).
$4,500-5,000

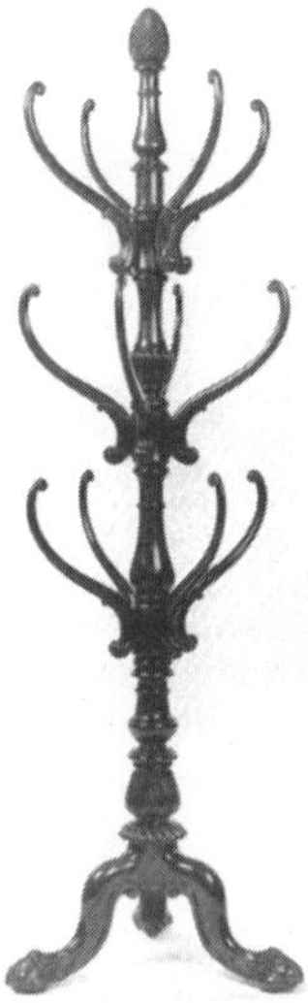

A William IV mahogany hat sta stamped Gillows of Lancaster, 7 (193cm).
$4,000-5,000

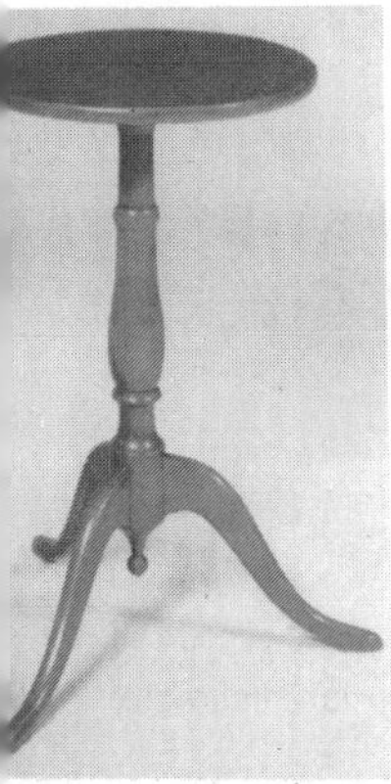

Queen Anne cherrywood
dlestand, Connecticut, c1750,
n (40.5cm) diam.
500-2,500

A Chippendale mahogany stand, Newport, Rhode Island, c1770, 26in (66cm) diam.
$3,500-4,500

A Chippendale mahogany dish-top stand, damaged, Philadelphia, c1780, 21in (53cm) diam.
$4,500-5,500

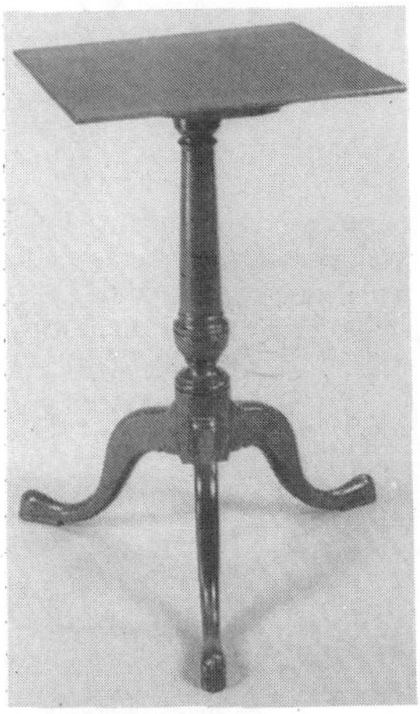

A Federal mahogany tilt-top stand, Massachusetts, c1805, 27½in (70cm) high.
$2,500-3,500

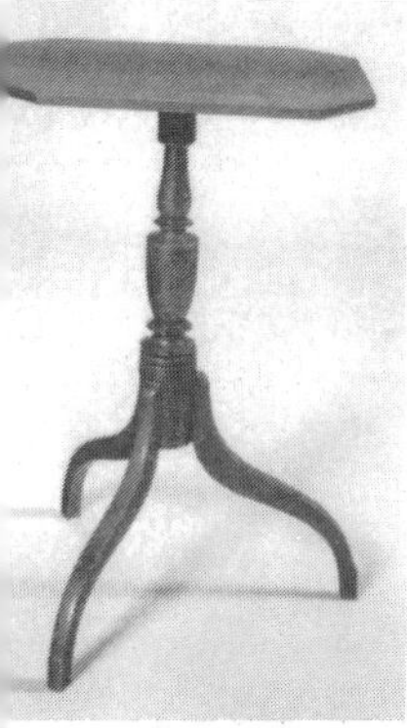

'ederal cherrywood
-top candlestand,
me loss to height,
nnecticut, c1800,
in (71cm) high.
,500-2,000

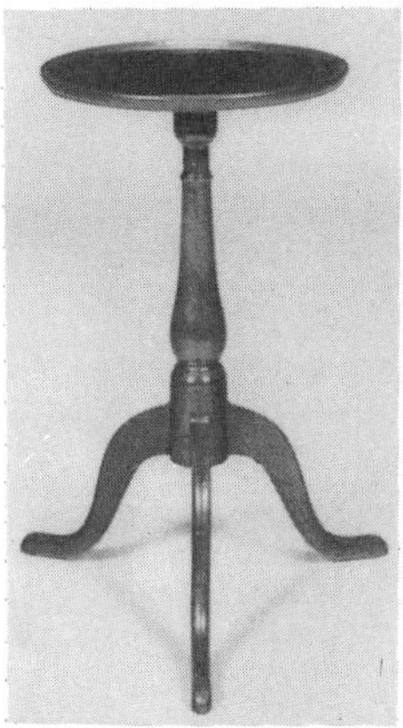

A Chippendale mahogany dish-top stand, probably Rhode Island, c1780, 17in (43cm) diam.
$1,800-2,400

A red painted adjustable candlestand, New England, 19thC, 40in (101cm) high.
$1,500-2,000

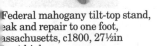

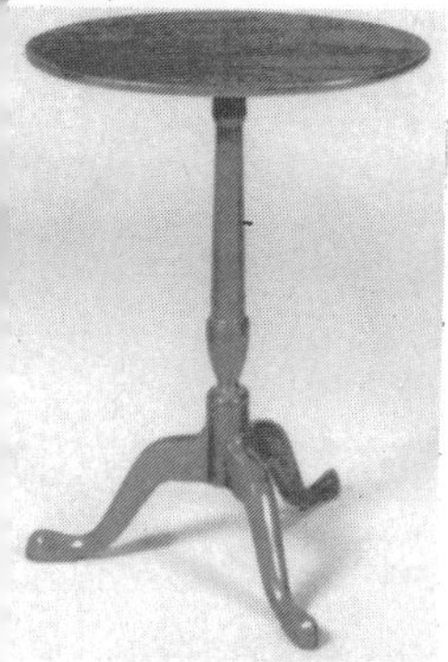

Federal mahogany tilt-top stand,
eak and repair to one foot,
assachusetts, c1800, 27½in
)cm) high.
00-1,200

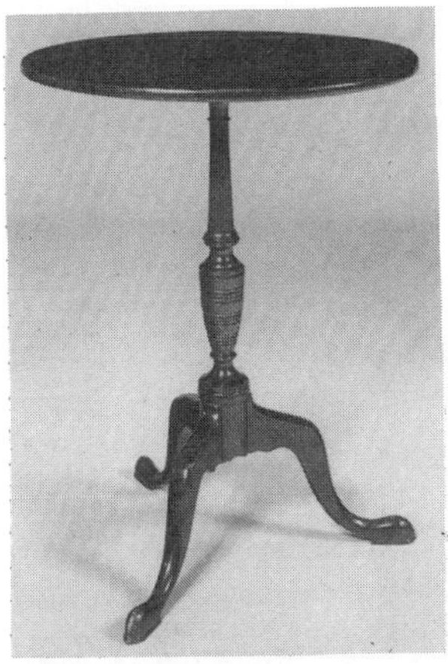

A Federal mahogany candlestand, Massachusetts, c1800, 28½in (73cm) high.
$3,500-4,500

A Federal carved mahogany candlestand, one foot pieced, Massachusetts, c1805, 28in (71cm) high.
$2,500-3,000

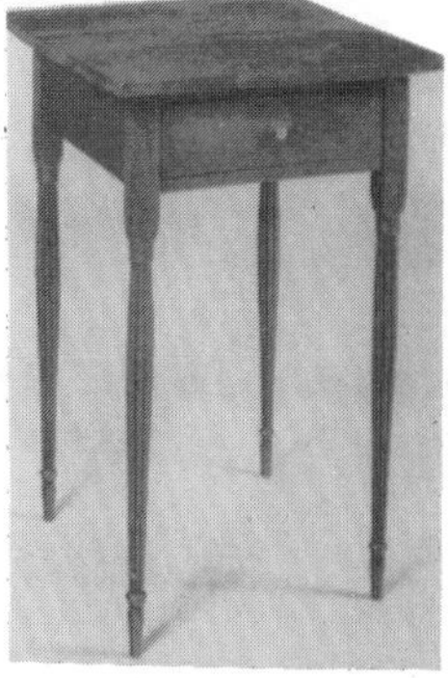

A Federal mahogany stand, Massachusetts, c1800, 28in (71cm) high.
$4,000-5,000

A Federal mahogany stand, top rotated, repairs to feet, probably Massachusetts, c1800, 26½in (68cm) high.
$600-900

Steps

A set of late George III satinwood bedsteps, banded in rosewood, the top 2 treads hinged, with a drawer below, on square tapering legs, 21in (54cm).
$6,000-8,000

A set of late Regency mahogany library commode steps, with 2 hinged treads, on turned tapered legs, 20in (50cm).
$4,000-5,000

A set of Victorian mahogany bedsteps, the carpet lined triple treads with a hinged box top, on turned tapering legs, 22½in (56cm
$1,600-2,000

A late Victorian oak library steps easel, in the neo-classical manner with shell cresting, stamped Hamptons Patent No. 4889, 75in (190cm) high.
$2,500-3,000

Stools

A Queen Anne walnut stool, covered in original needlework, 17½in (44cm) high.
$10,000-12,000

A George III mahogany stool, with padded seat above an undulating frieze, on square chamfered channelled legs, 18in (46cm).
$4,000-5,000

A Regency cane seat black wood and gilt stool, on crossed legs.
$300-400

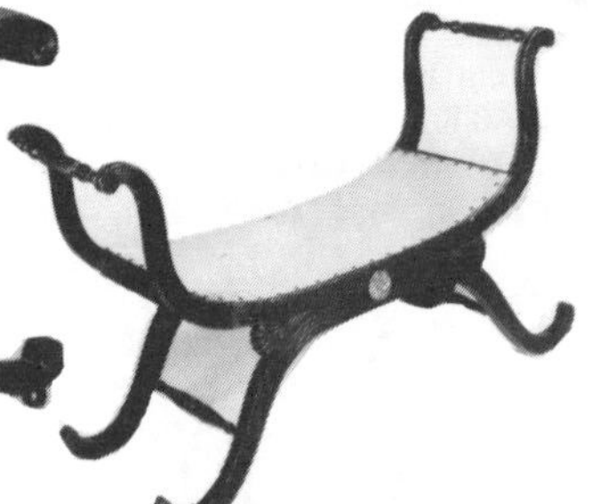

A Regency ebonised window seat, with padded seat in yellow velvet restorations, 45in (115cm).
$4,500-5,000

A Regency rosewood X-frame stool, the padded seat upholstered in striped silk, 24in (61cm).
$4,500-5,000

A Regency simulated rosewood and parcel gilt stool, the dished seat upholstered in silk, one seat rail renewed, 27in (68cm).
$3,500-4,000

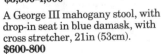

A George III mahogany stool, with drop-in seat in blue damask, with cross stretcher, 21in (53cm).
$600-800

A George III mahogany stool, wit later drop-in seat covered in Hungarian stitch needlework, 19½in (50cm).
$1,400-1,600

A walnut stool, the padded seat upholstered with fragments of verdure tapestry, the seat rails replaced, 20in (51cm).
$1,400-1,600

A William IV mahogany stool, with padded drop-in seat covered in red brocade, on scrolling legs joined by a baluster stretcher, 32½in (83cm).
$2,500-3,000

Regency mahogany piano stool, th seat upholstered in red leather ged in brass, on turned legs joined a stretcher, 13in (33cm) diam.
,000-2,500

A Regency style ebonised stool, on plain supports and turned feet, based on a design by Thomas Hope, 29in (74cm).
$1,000-1,500

A rosewood piano stool, 19thC, 13½in (34cm).
$200-250

A Victorian inlaid rosewood upholstered stool, on stretcher frame.
$350-400

A pair of Dutch walnut and marquetry stools, with turned stretchers, inlaid with flowers and foliage, the seats in later green upholstery, 19thC.
$3,000-4,000

A mahogany window seat of Louis XV style, with scrolling ends and bowed seat, the frame carved with flowerheads, on cabriole legs, 53in (135cm).
$2,500-3,000

A Regency mahogany stool attributed to Gillows, the caned seat with scrolled ends, the moulded scrolling frame with a turned stretcher and ball feet, 20½in (52cm).
$7,000-8,000

A padded stool of Second Empire style, upholstered in blue and white repp, with silk covered cushion and bracket feet, 20in (51cm).
$1,500-1,800

A mahogany stool, with gros and petit point needlework drop-in seat, on cabriole legs and paw feet, 19in (48cm).
$1,200-1,500

Tables – Architects

A mahogany architect's table, with gilt brass candlestick stands to each side, the frieze drawer with divided compartments and a writing slide, brass bail handle, lacking one pillar to rear, 18thC, 36in (91.5cm).
$3,500-4,000

A George III mahogany drawing table, 28in (71cm).
$2,000-3,000

An early Victorian mahogany architect's table, on turned taper legs with brass caps and casters, 32in (81cm).
$4,000-5,000

Tables – Breakfast

A George III mahogany breakfast table, on ring turned tapering legs, with 2 later detachable end leaves, 52½in (133cm) extended.
$700-1,000

A carved rosewood and parcel gilt breakfast table, the snap top with a gadrooned edge and a moulded frieze, on a reeded and foliate knopped column trefoil platform base and reeded acanthus leaf scroll supports and terminating in paw feet, 19thC, 72in (182.5cm) diam.
$8,000-10,000

A Regency style breakfast table with inset leather top, the frieze decorated with porcelain panels, t tripod feet with brass casters, 38i (96.5cm) diam.
$5,000-6,000

A Regency carved mahogany breakfast table, crossbanded in rosewood, with a beaded edge, on ring turned column and reeded splayed legs, with roundel headings terminating in brass cappings and casters, 55in (139cm).
$5,000-6,000

A George III mahogany breakfast table, with snap-top, on baluster column, 48in (122cm).
$1,200-1,400

An Empire carved mahogany breakfast table, with drop leaves and single drawer, on an acanthus carved central pedestal with waterleaf carved sabre legs and carved paw feet, on casters, probably New England, c1830, 36i (91.5cm) long.
$1,500-2,000

A Regency mahogany breakfast table, 49in (124.5cm).
$1,700-2,000

A Regency rosewood breakfast table, with crossbanded and brass inlaid border, on a stepped square section column with brass paw feet, c1815, 48in (122cm) diam.
$6,000-8,000

A Regency mahogany breakfast table, with brass inlay to the edge
$1,700-2,000

:egency mahogany breakfast
le, with tip-up top with reeded
e, turned column and reeded
ıyed quadruple support, with
ss feet and casters, 51in (130cm).
00-4,000

A Regency rosewood breakfast table, 47½in (121cm).
$10,000-12,000

A Regency style rosewood tilt-top breakfast table with brass star and stringing on quatrefoil base with splay feet, brass acanthus leaf mounted, brass toe caps and casters, c1860, 40in (102cm).
$8,000-9,000

William IV rosewood breakfast
ole, 55in (140cm).
500-5,000

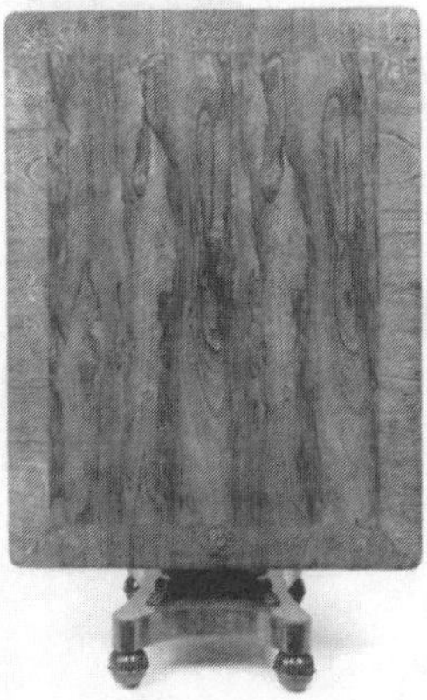

A William IV carved rosewood breakfast table, the crossbanded top with inlaid border on a chamfered column with scroll brackets, quatrefoil base and bun feet, 48in (122cm).
$5,000-6,000

A William IV walnut breakfast table.
$12,000-14,000

Victorian rosewood breakfast
ble.
,000-4,000

Victorian burr walnut breakfast
able, the tip-up top on carved
edestal base and triple supports,
8in (122cm).
3,000-4,000

A Victorian walnut breakfast table, the quarter veneered top of waved outline, on 4 C-scroll supports and flower carved cabriole legs, 56in (143cm).
$3,000-4,000

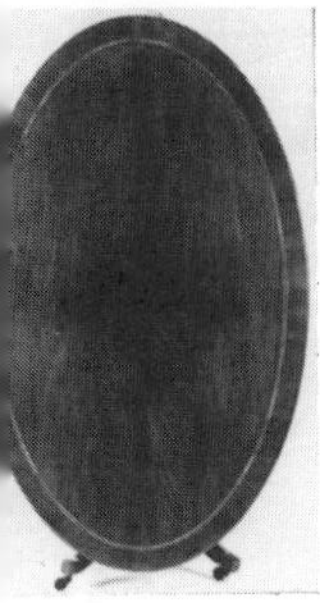

A mahogany breakfast table, with fruitwood crossbanded top, on a gun barrel column and outswept legs, adapted, 60in (152cm).
$1,000-1,200

A Victorian burr walnut table, the top inlaid with boxwood foliate scrolls, on ring turned supports and outswept feet, 53in (135cm).
$1,500-2,000

Tables – Card

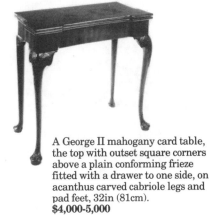

A George II mahogany card table, the top with outset square corners above a plain conforming frieze fitted with a drawer to one side, on acanthus carved cabriole legs and pad feet, 32in (81cm).
$4,000-5,000

A George II mahogany card table, the baize lined top with counter wells, one secret drawer, acanthus carved cabriole legs and ball and claw feet, 32in (81cm).
$4,000-5,000

A George III mahogany card table, with satinwood crossbanded and inlaid fold-over top, inlaid frieze and square tapered legs, 39in (99cm).
$3,500-4,000

A George III card table with crossbanded top, on tapered moulded legs headed by carved rosettes, 42in (107cm).
$1,400-1,800

A late Federal carved mahogany card table, the hinged flap with serpentine front, outset rounded corners and moulded edge above a conforming apron, signed John Dunlap, Antrim, New Hampshire, dated 1817, small moulding repairs, 36in (91.5cm).
$9,000-12,000

A George III style inlaid mahogany card table, 36in (92cm).
$1,500-1,800

A George III satinwood card table, the top inlaid with a shell lunette and crossbanded in rosewood, the legs re-supported, 36in (92cm).
$4,000-5,000

An early George III serpentine card table, the baize lined hinged top with concertina action, raised on hipped tapered legs terminating in pad feet, 36in (92cm).
$3,500-4,000

A Regency rosewood and brass strung card table, with a crossbanded baize lined top, 35in (90cm).
$3,000-4,000

A George III mahogany card table, the serpentine fronted fold-over top crossbanded in satinwood and lined in red baize, 36in (92cm).
$7,000-8,000

A George III mahogany serpentine front card table, with veneers to the front.
$4,000-5,000

A Regency mahogany veneered car[d] table, the D-shaped flap top inlaid with brass stringing, the turned tapering legs with later casters, 36in (92cm).
$2,000-3,000

A Regency walnut and brass inlaid card table.
$10,000-12,000

A late Regency rosewood tilt-top card table, on lion paw feet, 36in (92cm).
$1,000-1,200

A Victorian rosewood card table, with serpentine top above shaped and carved apron, 37in (94cm).
$2,500-3,000

A pair of Sheraton mahogany card tables with crossbanded tops and friezes, 36in (92cm).
$10,000-12,000

A walnut and fruitwood envelope card table, the crossbanded top with an inlaid sunburst opening to reveal a similarly inlaid interior and leaves, probably North Italian, early 19thC, 26in (65cm).
$5,000-6,000

A Dutch marquetry and mahogany card table, on turned pedestal and quatrefoil base, 19thC, 32in (80cm).
$3,000-4,000

Chippendale carved mahogany rd table, with baize lined hinged , on chamfered legs with Gothic t ornament, 37in (94cm).
,000-5,000

A William IV rosewood folding card table, with inlaid baize panel, 36in (92cm).
$1,600-1,800

A Classical mahogany and satinwood card table, the folding top with canted corners swivelling above a conforming skirt with satinwood veneer, the moulded legs with ebonised stringing, on carved lion's paw feet with traces of black paint, patch to one foot, 38in (96.5cm).
$11,000-13,000

A Regency mahogany card table with brass inlay.
$5,000-6,000

A Dutch walnut and marquetry breakfront card table, with fitted drawer, on square tapering line inlaid legs and spade feet, early 19thC, 30in (76cm).
$3,000-4,000

A mid-Victorian inlaid walnut travelling card table, damaged.
$1,500-2,000

A French card table in the manner of Andre Charles Boulle, 19thC.
$1,400-1,600

A Chippendale mahogany card table, with hinged top, New England, c1780, 36in (91.5cm).
$2,000-3,000

A Federal inlaid mahogany card table, with bowed front and serpentine sides, the edge with crossbanding and stringing, probably Newburyport, Massachusetts, c1800, 36in (91.5cm).
$7,500-9,000

A Federal mahogany card table, with brass line inlay, Philadelphia, c1810, 36in (91.5cm).
$5,000-6,000

A Classical figured mahogany card table, Philadelphia, c1810, 36in (91.5cm).
$2,500-3,500

A Federal inlaid mahogany card table, the hinged top edged with stringing, on square tapering line-inlaid legs with husk inlay, New York, c1800, 34in (86cm), open.
$7,000-8,000

A Federal inlaid mahogany and flame birch card table, North Shore, Massachusetts, c1800, 36in (91.5cm), open.
$6,000-7,000

A Federal inlaid mahogany card table, the top with line inlaid edge, 36in (91.5cm).
$3,000-4,000

A late Federal mahogany card table, with conforming flame veneered skirt over a foliate carved lyre base, on carved legs with brass paw feet, Philadelphia, c1820, 36in (91.5cm).
$2,500-3,500

A Federal inlaid mahogany and cherrywood card table, with serpentine hinged top with doub line inlaid edge, Massachusetts, c1800, 36in (91.5cm).
$4,500-6,500

A Federal inlaid mahogany car table, with banded and line inla edge, Massachusetts, c1800, 36i (91.5cm).
$6,000-7,000

A Classical carved mahogany ca table, old damage and one leg pieced, 36in (91.5cm).
$3,500-4,000

A carved mahogany card table, th sabre legs with carved knees and carved paw feet with casters, Boston, Massachusetts, c1820, 36 (91.5cm).
$1,200-1,600

Victorian burr walnut veneered ding card table.
,000-3,000

A Directoire brass mounted mahogany card table, with baize lined top enclosing a compartment with panelled frieze and turned fluted tapering legs, 33in (84cm).
$3,000-4,000

A Louis XV style ebonised and Boulle card table, inlaid throughout in red tortoiseshell and cut brass, with gilt brass mouldings, 34in (86cm).
$3,000-4,000

ouis XV style kingwood and al marquetry flap top card table, green baize lined interior with rquetry crossbanding, 32½in m).
00-4,000

A North Italian walnut and marquetry card table, the folding top with a red velvet interior, inlaid overall with birds and flowers, and crossbanded in fruitwood, 18thC, 35in (88cm).
$12,000-14,000

ables – Centre

late George III mahogany centre ole, the top inset with green baize, e frieze fitted with 2 drawers and ed with 4 false drawers, top and se associated, 44in (110cm).
,000-8,000

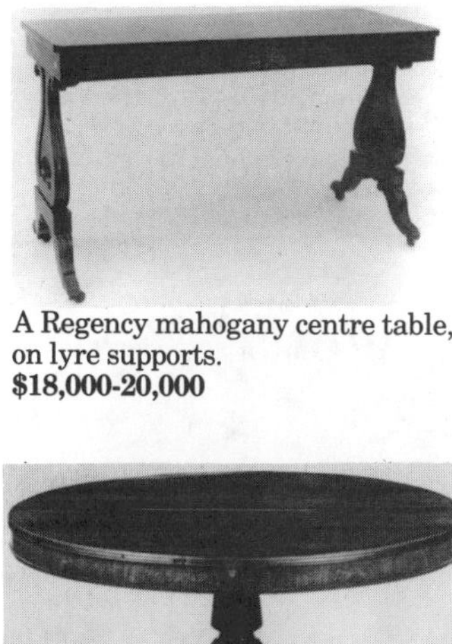

A Regency mahogany centre table, on lyre supports.
$18,000-20,000

A late Regency bird's-eye maple centre table.
$5,000-6,000

A Regency rosewood centre table, the tilt top with channelled brass edge and plain frieze, on turned partially ebonised shaft and quadripartite base edged with beading, on brass paw feet, 49in (125cm).
$12,000-14,000

Regency brass inlaid rosewood ntre table, the top on simulated ewood baluster shaft, 44½in 3cm).
000-8,000

A Regency rosewood centre table, with tip-up top and plain frieze, restorations, 52in (132cm).
$2,500-3,000

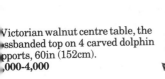

Victorian walnut centre table, the ssbanded top on 4 carved dolphin pports, 60in (152cm).
,000-4,000

A Regency rosewood centre table, the top inlaid with a specimen marble chessboard, the top restored, 27½in (70cm).
$5,000-6,000

An early Victorian gilt and composition centre table, with specimen marble top and flowerhead moulded border.
$4,000-5,000

A pair of Empire tilt-top centre tables, New York, c1835, 27in (69cm) high.
$4,500-5,500

A late Victorian mahogany centre table, with ribbed frieze, 36in (92cm).
$2,000-3,000

An ormolu mounted red tortoiseshell and Boulle centre table, the top inlaid with foliate strapwork, the frieze fitted with a drawer, on cabriole legs with scroll sabots, mid-19thC, 62in (158cm).
$3,000-4,000

A Classical mahogany and gilt marble top centre table, with white marble top, apron inlaid with a border of mother-of-pearl and brass banding, above 3 white marble and gilt column supports, probably New York, c1830, 31in (79cm) high.
$9,000-12,000

A walnut and marquetry centre table, the top inlaid and highlighted in ivory and mother-of-pearl, the border similarly inlaid above a frieze drawer, on Flemish barley twist legs, 41in (104cm).
$4,000-5,000

An Empire mahogany centre table with moulded black fossil marble top on turned spreading supports and concave sided platform base, 32½in (83cm).
$6,000-7,000

A Georgian Irish carved mahogany centre table, on acanthus and female mask headed cabriole supports, reconstructed from a larger table, 34in (86cm).
$4,000-5,000

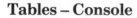

A Scandinavian mahogany centre table, with inlaid top edged with brass, on 3 square tapering legs, mid-19thC, 36in (92cm).
$3,000-4,000

Tables – Console

A Regency parcel gilt and blue painted console table, with mottled salmon pink and ochre marble top, 48in (122cm).
$7,000-8,000

A George IV Irish rosewood conso table, the top inset with green figured marble, the frieze with a bead and reel edge, labelled indistinctly.
$8,000-10,000

pair of Regency rosewood and
nulated rosewood console tables,
. gadrooned legs with square
ntres, later mirror backs and
inth bases, adapted, 37in (94cm).
,000-8,000

A Charles X mahogany console table, with marble top and moulded frieze, 30in (76cm).
$3,500-4,000

A William IV carved rosewood console table, with inset white marble top, the frieze applied with paterae, on acanthus scroll supports and plinth base, 57in (145cm).
$1,500-2,500

pair of giltwood console tables of
uis XV style, with mottled brown
arble slabs, the pierced friezes
rved with C-scrolls and
werheads on scrolling legs edged
th rockwork and pierced foliage,
½in (67cm).
,000-6,000

A Louis XVI carved giltwood console table, with mottled grey marble top, on a scrolling leg carved with acanthus and entrelacs, re-gilded, 24in (62cm).
$1,800-2,500

A pair of early Victorian rosewood console tables, the grey marble slab and egg-and-dart moulded edge above a shallow frieze, on barley twist supports, the mirrored back flanked by foliate pierced sides, on a plinth base, 44½in (113cm).
$5,000-6,000

Louis XV style giltwood console
ole, the eared later marble top
ove a profusely carved frieze, on
briole supports joined with flower
toons and rushes, early 19thC,
in (83cm).
,000-5,000

A cream painted console table, on scrolling foliate legs, 72in (183cm).
$2,000-3,000

A German carved walnut console table, the top with bevelled edge above a leaf carved frieze centred by a relief carved pheasant, on 4 scroll carved supports, late 19thC, 75in (191cm).
$2,500-3,000

ı Italian painted console table, the
aped pietre dura marble top inlaid
various stones, with a red and
llow marble frieze on a scrolling
pport, mid-19thC, 25in (64cm).
,000-6,000

A bleached walnut console table, in the Adam style, the green marble slab above a fluted frieze, 19thC, 72in (183cm).
$3,000-4,000

Tables – Dining

A George II mahogany drop-leaf dining table, with twin flap top above an end drawer, 55in (140cm).
$7,000-8,000

A Federal inlaid mahogany three-part dining table, 103in (261cm) long.
$15,000-20,000

A Regency mahogany dining table, on ring turned columns and hipped outswept legs, 60in (153cm).
$8,000-10,000

A mahogany twin pedestal dining table, basically early 19thC but minor adaptations, 75½in (192cm) including an extra leaf.
$5,000-6,000

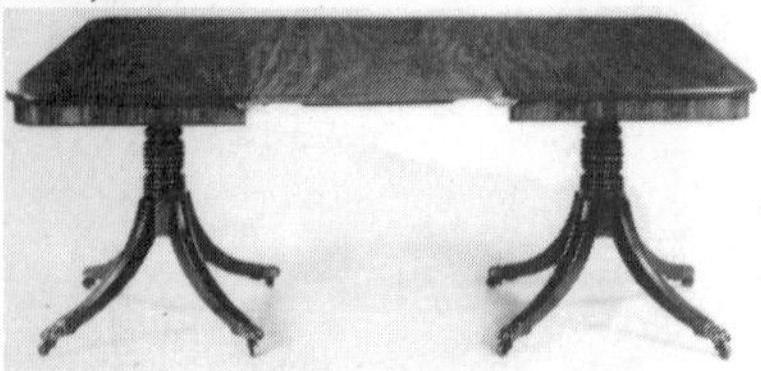

A Regency mahogany dining table, 72in (183cm) including a leaf.
$12,000-15,000

A George III mahogany and inlaid dining table with reeded edged top, 120in (305cm) extended.
$5,000-6,000

A Regency mahogany dining table, the pedestals with turned shaft and reeded quadripartite base, 92in (234cm) including 2 leaves, one later.
$15,000-20,000

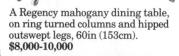

A Georgian triple section mahogany dining table, the centre section with 2 drop leaves, 115in (292cm).
$10,000-12,000

A George III mahogany dining table, on twin reeded splay supports with brass terminals and casters, 104in (264cm) extended.
$20,000-25,000

A George III mahogany D-end dining table, with drop-leaf centre, 110in (280cm) extended.
$7,000-8,000

A George III mahogany dining table, with double gates supporting a detachable drop leaf, the square supports on brass feet and casters, 45in (114cm) diam.
$2,000-2,500

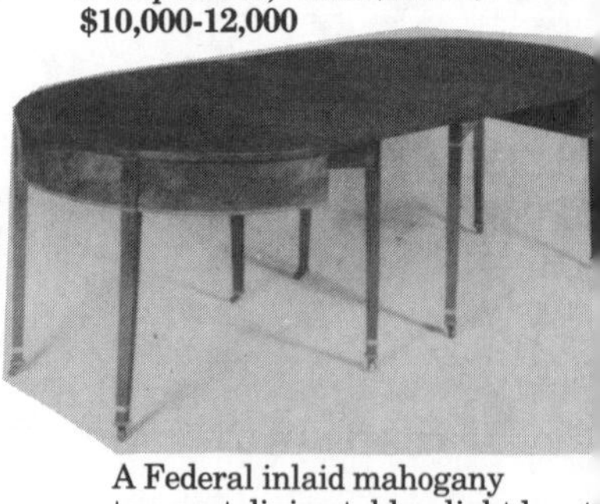

A Federal inlaid mahogany two-part dining table, slight loss t height of legs, Mid-Atlantic State c1800, 89in (226cm) long.
$5,000-7,000

A mahogany twin pedestal dining table of George III style, the rounded rectangular top on turned shafts and splayed legs with brass paw feet and casters, one pedestal early 19thC, 95½in (242cm).
$10,000-12,000

A George III mahogany three-part dining table, on square tapered legs and spade feet, with alterations, c1800, 104in (264cm) extended.
$3,000-4,000

A Regency mahogany dining table, on a ring turned baluster shaft and quadripartite base, with brass caps and casters, 60in (153cm).
$12,000-15,000

'ables – Dressing

George III mahogany kneehole
'essing table, crossbanded with
ahogany and inlaid with boxwood
nes, 39½in (100cm).
12,000-14,000

A Chippendale carved cherrywood dressing table, top reset, drawer sides restored, Connecticut, c1770, 32½in (82.5cm) wide.
$18,000-20,000

A late Victorian figured walnut bedroom suite of 4 pieces, a wardrobe, 61in (155cm) wide, a dressing chest, a washstand and a bedside cabinet.
$1,800-2,000

n Empire mahogany dressing
ıble, with rising swing mirror, gilt
rass mounts, a marble top and
ieze drawers, 28½in (72cm).
5,000-6,000

A South German walnut kneehole dressing table, with a swing mirror in a scroll and flowerhead chased ormolu frame, the superstructure 19thC, the base 18thC and adapted 43in (109cm).
$1,400-2,000

A George III mahogany dressing table, the top crossbanded in satinwood, enclosing an easel-mirror, flanked by lidded compartments, the frieze with a brushing slide, 27in (68cm).
$8,000-10,000

Chippendale cherrywood dressing
ble, fan carved drawer restored,
onnecticut River Valley, c1770,
½in (88cm) wide.
20,000-25,000

A Victorian mahogany dressing table.
$1,400-1,600

A late Federal mahogany dressing table, Salem, Massachusetts, c1820, 39½in (100cm) wide.
$6,000-8,000

Tables – Dropleaf

A Queen Anne mahogany drop leaf table, Massachusetts, c1740, 43½in (11cm) wide.
$3,500-4,500

A Queen Anne mahogany drop leaf table, probably Newport, Rhode Island, c1750, 27½in (70cm) high.
$5,000-7,000

A Queen Anne maple drop leaf table, Massachusetts, c1760, 54in (138cm) wide.
$6,000-7,000

Tables – Drum

A mahogany drum table, with leather lined top and 3 frieze drawers, basically early 19thC, 23½in (60cm).
$6,000-8,000

A George III mahogany drum table, with leather lined top and 2 frieze drawers, flanked by 4 false drawers, on later column, re-supported, 32in (81cm) diam.
£3,500-4,000 *C*

A George III style mahogany drum table, the inset leather lined revolving top with a simulated frieze fitted with 4 drawers, the down curved legs with brass block terminals, 48½in (123cm).
$1,000-1,400

A George IV pollard oak drum table, with brass paw feet and casters, 42in (106.5cm) diam.
$3,000-4,000

Tables – Games

A Regency mahogany games table, with lined fold-over swivel top, on shaped legs terminating with brass toes and casters, 36in (91.5cm).
$1,200-1,400

A mid-18thC mahogany games table, on turned tapered legs with pointed pad feet, joined by a concave platform stretcher, 39in (99cm) closed.
$1,600-2,000

An early Victorian rosewood games table with sliding reversible chess board, backgammon interior, 30in (76cm).
$4,000-5,000

A Victorian burr walnut combined work and games table, with boxwood stringing and marquetry inlay, the interior with corner gaming wells and inlaid markers, 30in (76cm).
$3,000-4,000

. William IV rosewood games and ork table, the folding top opening) reveal a chess board interior, a rawer in the frieze and sliding asket below, applied overall with eading, basket missing, 20in 51cm).
1,200-1,600

A Victorian walnut work/games table, with boxwood and ebony string inlay, the hinged top with chessboard inlay, the fitted interior with central well.
$900-1,000

A Victorian walnut veneered folding games/work table, with inlaid interior, work basket and cabriole legs.
$2,500-3,000

Georgian Irish mahogany games ble, with first fold for cards with a aize lined top, candle and vereign slots, the next for equers and backgammon, nclosing a well for games pieces, 6½in (92cm).
20,000-24,000

A Victorian mahogany bagatelle table, with baize lined playing surface on an adjustable stand, 96in (244cm) extended, including cues and balls, stamped Thurston, 14 Catherine Street, London.
$1,200-1,400

A Victorian figured and inlaid walnut games/work table, with folding top with inlaid chessboard, baize lined interior with 4 wells and Victorian registration mark, 28in (71cm).
$3,000-4,000

Victorian Louis XV style burr lnut and kingwood banded mes table, with ormolu handle d mounts, with cabriole legs, 30in cm).
,500-3,000

Tables – Gateleg

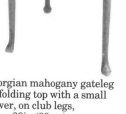

A George III mahogany spider gateleg table, with twin flap top on ring turned legs with conforming stretchers and shaped feet, 30in (76cm) wide, open.
$4,000-5,000

A mid-Georgian mahogany gateleg table, the folding top with a small frieze drawer, on club legs, adaptations, 39in (99cm).
$1,500-2,000

A walnut gateleg table with segmented veneered top, on turned supports joined by a flat stretcher, the top re-supported, 34in (87cm).
$1,400-1,600

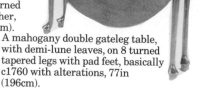

A mahogany double gateleg table, with demi-lune leaves, on 8 turned tapered legs with pad feet, basically c1760 with alterations, 77in (196cm).
$6,000-8,000

Tables – Library

A mahogany library table, the leather lined top with later moulded border, adaptations, 49½in (126cm).
$7,000-8,000

A late Federal mahogany library table, New York, c1820, 57½in (147cm) wide.
$5,000-7,000

A mahogany breakfront library table in 4 parts, 60 by 86in (152 by 219cm).
$10,000-12,000

A Regency rosewood library table fitted with 2 dummy and 2 real drawers, on brass casters, 54in (137cm).
$5,000-6,000

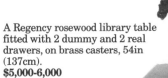

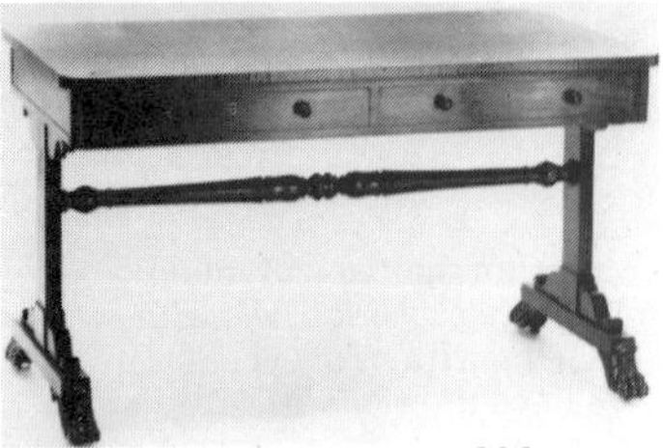

An early Victorian rosewood library table, with 2 frieze drawers each side, 52in (132cm).
$2,000-2,500

A rosewood library table, on twin turned columns and stretcher, with pad feet, 19thC, 47in (120cm).
$1,800-2,000

Tables – Loo

A Victorian burr walnut veneered loo table, with ebonised pattern and boxwood string inlays, on turned reeded supports.
$2,500-3,000

A Victorian rosewood loo table, on cradle shaped base, 60in (152cm).
$3,500-4,000

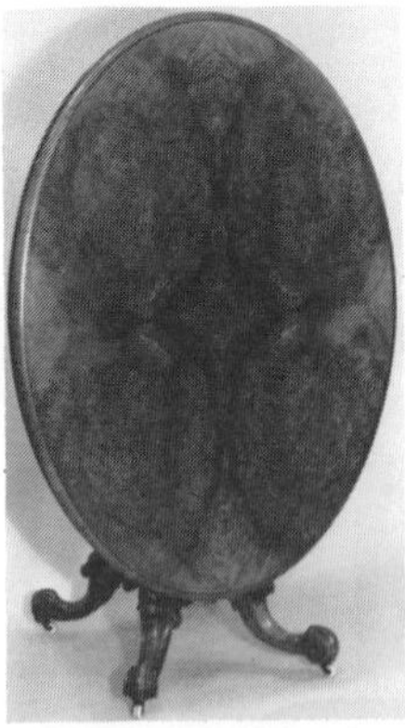

A Victorian burr walnut loo table, on carved scroll legs.
$2,500-3,000

A Victorian figured walnut tip-up top loo table, supported on carved central pillar, with shaped carved legs and original porcelain casters, 54in (137cm).
$2,000-2,500

A rosewood loo table, the top with double thumb moulded edge, on turned column and shaped tripod base, 19thC, 50in (127cm).
$800-1,000

Nests of Tables

A nest of 4 rosewood and satinwood tables, each with a banded and rimmed top, on ring turned column supports and downswept feet joined by a curved stretcher, 18½in (47cm) largest.
$4,000-6,000

Tables – Occasional

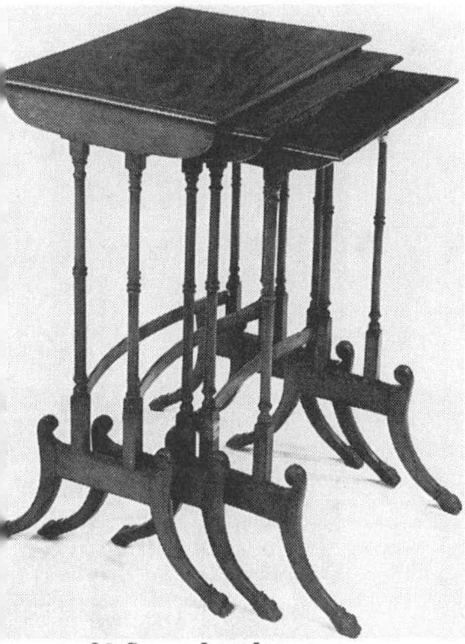

nest of 3 figured mahogany
ccasional tables, 22in (56cm)
rgest.
1,200-1,400

A carved mahogany snap top occasional table, on pillar and tripod base, 19thC.
$1,200-1,400

A Victorian inlaid mahogany occasional table, with inlaid chessboard and floral top, supported on shaped pierced side panels, central turned stretcher and shaped feet, 36in (91.5cm).
$500-600

An Edwardian rosewood occasional table, with marquetry and boxwood string inlay, on scroll supports.
$400-500

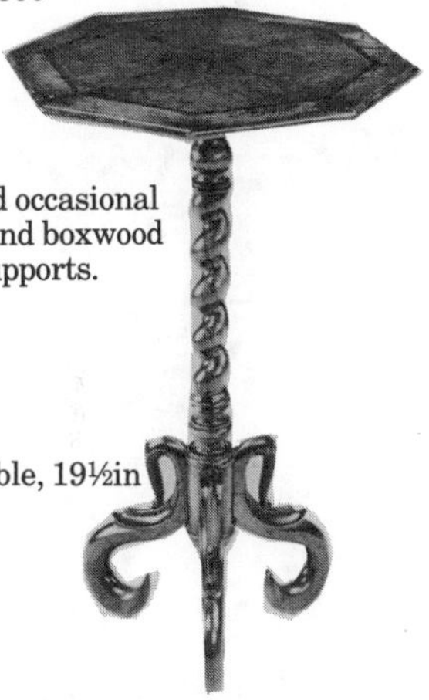

A walnut occasional table, 19½in (49cm).
$10,000-12,000

A Victorian walnut occasional
able, on a baluster turned column
ivided by a galleried tier, with
ircular plinth base, 15½in (39cm)
iam.
$500-600

l. An inlaid kingwood jardinière, mid-19thC.
$1,700-1,900

r. A Louis XVI style marble top mahogany occasional table.
$1,600-2,000

Tables – Pedestal

A William IV quarter veneered walnut pedestal table, on quatrefoil base, 27in (68cm).
$1,600-1,800

Tables – Pembroke

A Georgian inlaid mahogany serpentine Pembroke table, 29in (74cm).
$1,500-1,800

A George III carved mahogany Pembroke table, the hinged top with a moulded edge, with frieze drawer, 40in (101.5cm) extended.
$4,000-6,000

Tables – Pembroke

A George III mahogany Pembroke table, with twin flap top and one frieze drawer, on square tapering legs, 37½in (95cm).
$4,000-5,000

A George III mahogany Pembroke table, on fluted square tapered legs headed by inlaid lozenges, 28in (71cm).
$6,000-7,000

A George III mahogany Pembrok table, inlaid with ebony and boxwood lines, 39in (99cm) open.
$2,500-3,000

A Regency mahogany Pembroke work table, the top inlaid with ebony stringing, 22in (56cm).
$1,200-1,400

A George III mahogany Pembroke table, the frieze drawer with cockbeaded border, 36in (91.5cm) extended.
$600-800

A George III mahogany Pembrok table, with shaped parquetry inla top, banded in rosewood above a frieze drawer, restored, 41in (104cm) open.
$10,000-12,000

A satinwood, tulipwood crossbanded and decorated Pembroke table, early 19thC, 30in (76cm).
$4,000-5,000

A Sheraton period mahogany Pembroke table, with a well figured top, fitted drawer, on square tapering legs with spade feet, 29½in (75cm).
$3,000-4,000

A George III mahogany and ebony strung Pembroke table.
$1,200-1,400

A Regency mahogany Pembroke work table, the top with reeded edge, above 2 drawers, with ring turned tapered legs, 22in (56cm).
$1,300-1,500

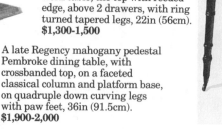

A late Regency mahogany pedestal Pembroke dining table, with crossbanded top, on a faceted classical column and platform base, on quadruple down curving legs with paw feet, 36in (91.5cm).
$1,900-2,000

A Chippendale mahogany Pembroke table, Philadelphia, c1780, 40in (101cm) wide.
$3,500-5,000

A Federal inlaid mahogany Pembroke table, Pennsylvania, c1800, 43in (110cm) wide.
$3,000-4,000

A Chippendale mahogany Pembroke table, Philadelphia, c1780, 37in (95cm) wide.
$2,000-3,000

A Federal inlaid cherrywood Pembroke table, Connecticut, c1800, 39½in (101cm) wide.
$7,500-8,500

A Chippendale applewood Pembroke table, Connecticut, c1790, 36in (92cm) wide.
$1,500-2,000

A Federal mahogany Pembroke table, Massachusetts, c1800, 35in (88cm) wide, open.
$1,000-1,500

A late Federal mahogany Pembroke table, Pennsylvania, c1820, 50in (125cm) wide, open.
$1,000-1,500

A late Federal carved mahogany Pembroke table, Massachusetts, c1820, 44in (112cm) wide, open.
$1,500-2,500

A Regency mahogany Pembroke table, with twin flap top and curved frieze drawer, on a threaded adjustable shaft and downswept tripod base, 36½in (92cm) open.
$3,500-5,000

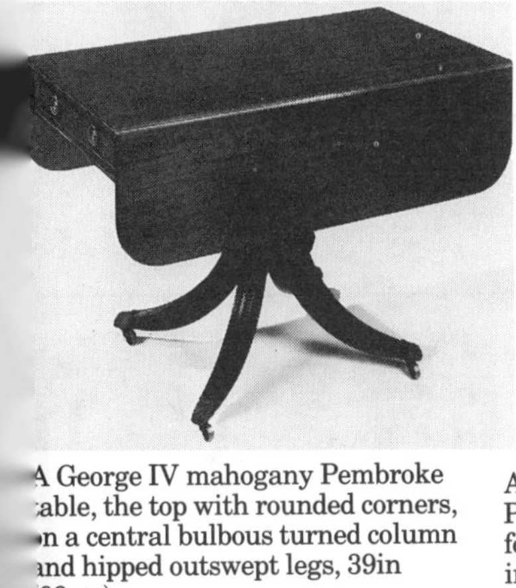

A George IV mahogany Pembroke table, the top with rounded corners, on a central bulbous turned column and hipped outswept legs, 39in (99cm).
$1,000-1,400

A Dutch mahogany and marquetry Pembroke table, the top inlaid with foliage, late 18thC with 19thC inlay, 56in (142cm) open.
$3,500-4,000

A Sheraton mahogany Pembroke table, with a marquetry and satinwood crossbanding, 36in (91.5cm) open.
$7,000-8,000

Tables – Pier

A Classical mahogany pier table, New York, c1820, 39½in (100cm) wide.
$4,000-4,500

A George III mahogany pier table, with boxwood strung and crossbanded top, 32in (81cm).
$1,200-1,300

A Classical mahogany pier table, glass plate broken, New York, c1820, 42in (111cm) wide.
$4,000-4,500

A Classical mahogany and gilt marble top pier table, New York, c1830, 43½in (110cm) wide.
$6,500-7,500

A Regency rosewood and parcel gilt pier table, with mirror backed superstructure, on winged lion monopodia and solid back, damaged, 56in (142cm).
$3,500-4,000

Tables – Reading

A George III satinwood reading table, crossbanded with fiddleback mahogany and rosewood, the easel support top above a cedar lined frieze drawer, previously fitted with a well, 22½in (57cm).
$6,000-7,000

A Victorian mahogany reading table, with adjustable octagonal column and quatrefoil base, 36in (91.5cm).
$800-1,000

A Regency mahogany adjustable reading and writing table, with moulded rim and detachable bookrest, the frieze with a fitted drawer on reeded column and downswept tripod with brass caps and casters, 24in (61cm).
$4,500-5,000

Tables – Serving

A George III mahogany serving table, crossbanded with boxwood stringing, 57½in (145cm).
$5,000-6,000

A George III carved mahogany serpentine serving table, the long frieze drawer with fluting and ribbon tied bellflower and berry garland in relief, 66in (167.5cm).
$11,000-12,000

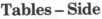

Regency mahogany serving table, the manner of Gillows, the pentine top with 3 frieze wers, 48in (122cm).
000-7,000

A George III mahogany serving table, inlaid with boxwood lines, with 3 frieze drawers flanked by later inlaid ovals, on square tapering legs, 68in (172cm).
$8,000-10,000

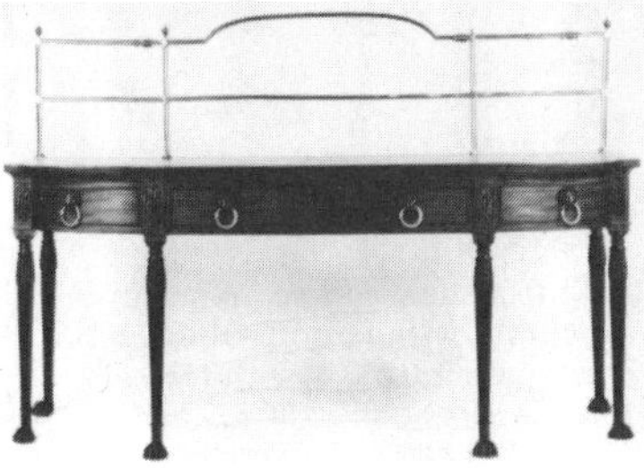

A Regency mahogany breakfront serving table, in the style of George Smith, with brass railed back, bearing a label inscribed 'This sideboard came from the .... at Glastonbury, Somerset', 95in (241cm).
$5,000-6,000

Regency mahogany serving table Gillows of Lancaster, with rieze drawers, 42in (106.5cm).
,000-6,000

Tables – Side

A George II mahogany side table, with moulded top, above 3 frieze drawers, on club legs with pad feet, 30in (76cm).
$4,000-5,000

A George II mahogany side table, with shaped and pierced frieze, the cabriole legs with scroll ears and ball-and-claw feet, later top, 34½in (87cm) open.
$2,000-2,500

George II walnut side table, with ter top, 52½in (133cm).
7,000-20,000

A George III mahogany and satinwood side table, the crossbanded top later painted, 44in (111.5cm).
$8,000-9,000

A George II walnut side table, with later mahogany top, the moulded frieze adapted to 2 later drawers, on acanthus carved cabriole legs and pad feet, 53in (134.5cm).
$4,000-5,000

early Georgian mahogany side ble, on square fret carved legs, ½in (183cm).
,000-9,000

A George III mahogany side table, the frieze fitted with an end drawer, on square tapering legs, 27½in (70cm).
$1,600-2,500

George III mahogany side table, e frieze banded in harewood, with ter green veined serpentine aped marble top, 48½in (123cm).
,000-6,000

A George III mahogany side table, with hinged top enclosing a fitted interior, 37in (94cm).
$3,000-4,000

A Chippendale carved mahogany side table, with later marble top, on ogee chamfered legs with pierced fret spandrels, 34in (86cm).
$7,000-9,000

A Regency mahogany side table, 22in (56cm).
$900-1,200

An Adam period mahogany side table, with a cream figured marble top, 43in (109cm).
$22,000-25,000

A Dutch satinwood and marquetry side table, with mahogany banded top, the deep frieze with a pair of tambour doors, each inlaid with an urn suspended from a ribbon tie flanked by drapery swags, the feet possibly later, 36in (91.5cm).
$3,500-4,000

A pair of mahogany side tables, wit crossbanded top, on square taperin legs headed by inlaid paterae, 35½in (91cm).
$4,000-5,000

A pair of green decorated and carved giltwood side tables, in neo-classical style, with simulated verdé marble tops, 54in (138cm).
$6,000-7,000

An Irish mahogany side table with leaf moulded border, the frieze carved with foliate swags, fitted with 2 drawers, 78in (198cm).
$4,000-5,000

A side table, in the manner of Joseph Chapuis, with mahogar top, 19thC.
$5,000-6,000

A Dutch bois satiné and marquetry side table, in Louis XV style, with inlaid serpentine top, with slender cabriole legs, c1770, 29in (74cm).
$4,000-5,000

A William IV rosewood side table, with bobbin moulded edge, on baluster legs with lappeted foliage, joined by a concave fronted undertier, with gadrooned feet, the back previously panelled, 50½in (128cm).
$4,000-5,000

Empire ormolu mounted
hogany side table, with grey
rble top, the marble distressed,
tored and the stretchers replaced,
½in (97cm).
,000-3,000

A French carved gilt marble top table, 19thC, 24in (61cm).
$1,600-2,000

An Empire brass mounted side table, 22in (56cm).
$2,000-3,000

ables – Sofa

George III mahogany sofa table,
e twin flap top crossbanded with
tinwood, the frieze fitted with
drawers, on solid end standards,
½in (143cm) wide, open.
,000-10,000

A George III mahogany sofa table, with rounded twin flap top, the frieze with a drawer and a false drawer each side, on ribbed panelled trestle supports and ribbed splayed legs, 59½in (151cm) wide, open.
$5,000-6,000

A late George III mahogany sofa table crossbanded with rosewood, the 2 frieze drawers inlaid with boxwood lines, on solid trestle ends and downswept legs, joined by a later stretcher, 55in (140cm).
$8,000-10,000

George III style satinwood sofa
le, inlaid with rosewood bands
d boxwood lines, the down-
rving legs with brass block
minals joined with a tablet cross
etcher, 61in (155cm) extended.
,800-2,000

A late Regency mahogany drop flap table, with ebony line inlay and reeded borders, the 4 sabre supports with brass caps and casters.
$1,800-2,000

A Regency mahogany sofa table inlaid with ebonised lines, the reeded arched splayed legs with foliate caps and casters, restorations, 54in (138cm) wide, open.
$4,000-5,000

Regency mahogany sofa table,
th drop leaf top, reeded lyre
aped supports, wrythen turned
etcher, splayed legs carved with
lised leaves and brass castered
t, 54in (137cm).
,000-10,000

Regency mahogany sofa table
th crossbanded canted top, the
eze with 2 drawers, 66in (168cm).
,000-6,000

A Regency mahogany sofa table, with ebonised stringing, the 2 drawers and 2 dummy drawers with brass knobs, 60in (152cm).
$9,500-10,000

A George IV mahogany sofa table, damaged, 59in (150cm).
$2,500-3,000

A mahogany sofa table, 56in (142cm) wide, open.
$2,000-3,000

A George III mahogany tea table, the top with carved border and one frieze drawer opening to the side, the chamfered square legs headed by pierced scrolling angles, 35½in (90cm).
$3,000-4,000

A Georgian mahogany folding tea table, on tapering legs with pad feet, 36in (92cm).
$5,000-6,000

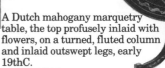

A mahogany sofa table, crossbanded in kingwood, with 2 shallow drawers, centre stretcher and ebony inlaid pillar ends, early 19thC, 56in (142cm).
$4,000-5,000

Tables – Tea

A Chippendale mahogany birdcage tea table, Pennsylvania, c1770, 21½in (54cm) diam.
$3,500-4,500

A William IV rosewood sofa table fitted with 2 short frieze drawers and 2 dummy drawers, on scrolled supports, 60in (152cm).
$3,000-4,000

Tables – Tavern

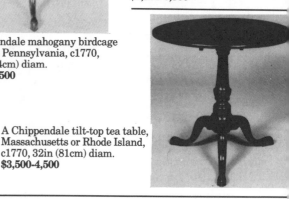

A Queen Anne walnut tavern tabl Philadelphia, c1745, 30½in (77.5cm) wide.
$6,500-7,500

A Chippendale tilt-top tea table, Massachusetts or Rhode Island, c1770, 32in (81cm) diam.
$3,500-4,500

Tables – Tip-top

A walnut and kingwood crossbanded tip-up top table, the top with marquetry inlay, on turned column and triple supports, with scroll and flower carved feet and brass casters, 19thC, 29in (73cm).
$2,500-3,000

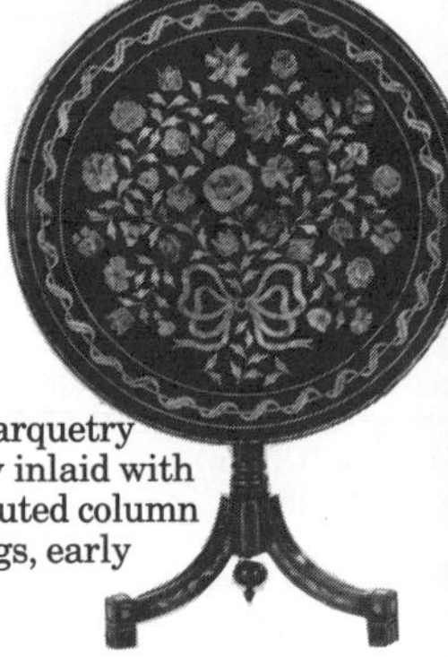

A Dutch mahogany marquetry table, the top profusely inlaid with flowers, on a turned, fluted column and inlaid outswept legs, early 19thC.
$1,800-2,000

A Regency rosewood and brass strung table, 48in (122cm).
$3,500-4,000

ables – Tray

George III mahogany butler's
y, with later stand, 32in (80cm).
,500-3,000

A Regency bamboo tray table, with black lacquered and gilt floral decoration, on later bamboo six-legged folding stand.
$800-1,000

Tables – Tripod

A mahogany dish top tripod table, 18thC, 31½in (79cm).
$2,500-3,000

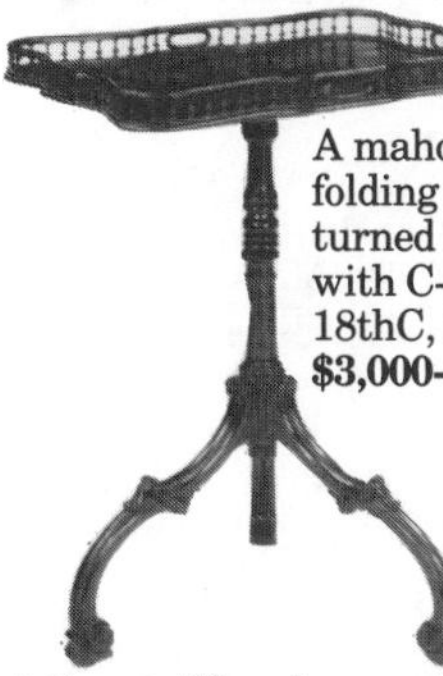

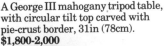

A mahogany tripod table, the folding tray top with a gallery, on a turned shaft, the tripod base carved with C-scrolls and acanthus, part 18thC, 24in (61cm).
$3,000-4,000

eorge II mahogany tripod table,
top with central dished circle
rounded by 9 circles, on a
l-cage support and turned shaft
h cabriole legs and pad feet
ved with foliage, the top
carved and re-shaped, 28½in
cm).
000-3,000

A George III mahogany tripod table, with circular tilt top carved with pie-crust border, 31in (78cm).
$1,800-2,000

A carved mahogany table with specimen marble top, 19thC, 30in (76cm).
$5,000-6,000

A mid-Georgian yew wood tripod table, on cabriole legs with pad feet, 24in (61cm) diam.
$2,000-3,000

A mid-Georgian mahogany table, the tilt top on a baluster shaft and arched down-swept legs, with pointed pad feet, 26in (66cm).
$2,500-3,000

yew wood table, early 19thC,
½in (56cm).
,200-1,400

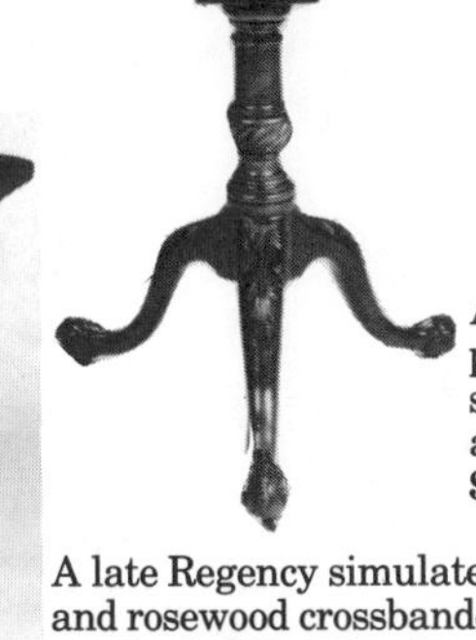

A mahogany tripod table, the pie-crust tilt-top on a bird-cage support and baluster shaft, with ball and claw feet, 29in (74cm).
$3,500-4,000

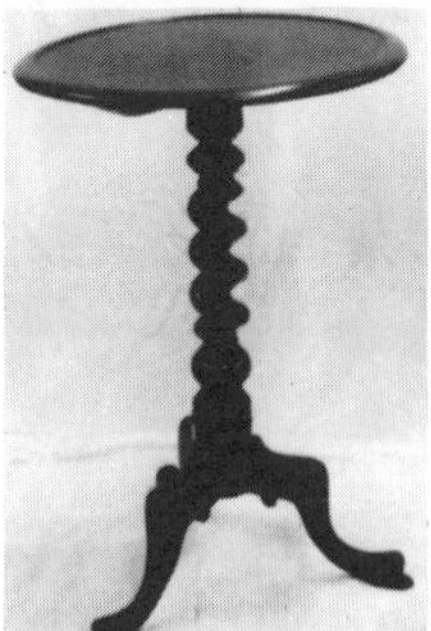

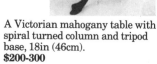

A late Regency simulated rosewood and rosewood crossbanded table, repaired, 24in (60cm).
$800-1,000

A Victorian mahogany table with spiral turned column and tripod base, 18in (46cm).
$200-300

Work/Sewing Tables

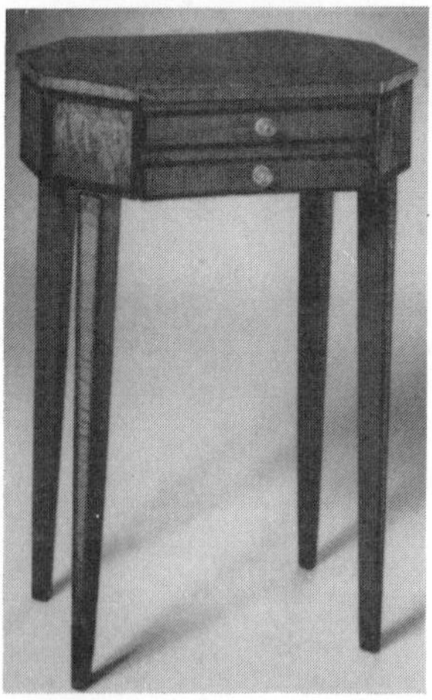

A Federal satinwood veneer sewing table, some restorations, Boston, c1800, 19in (49cm) wide.
$5,000-7,000

A Federal carved mahogany work table, North Shore, Massachusetts, c1800, 19in (49cm) wide.
$9,000-11,000

A Federal mahogany work tabl Mid-Atlantic States, c1800, 25i (64cm) wide.
$3,000-4,000

A Federal inlaid mahogany tambour sewing table, some damage to veneer, New York, c1800, 28½in (72cm) wide.
$3,000-5,000

A late Federal mahogany work table, New York, early 19thC, 24½in (62cm) wide.
$3,000-4,000

A Classical mahogany and burled maple veneer sewing table, Boston, c1810, 24in (61cm) wide.
$8,000-12,000

A late Federal mahogany work table, Baltimore, c1820, 27in (69cm wide, open.
$2,500-3,500

A late Federal mahogany sewing table, Boston, c1825, 29½in (75cm) high.
$2,000-2,500

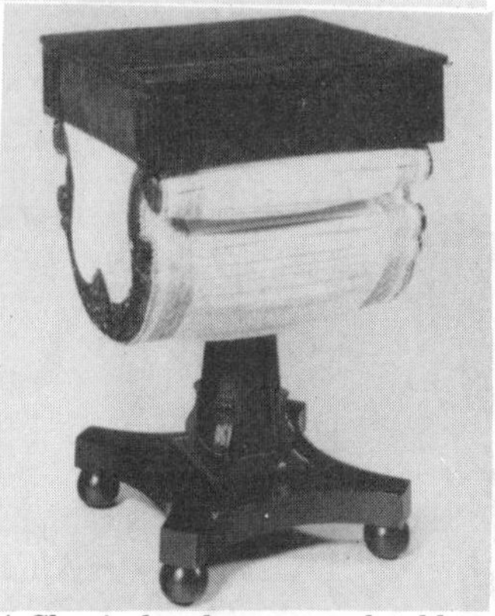

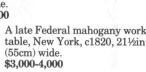

A Classical mahogany work table, Boston, Massachusetts, c1820, 20in (51cm) wide.
$1,800-2,400

A late Federal mahogany work table, New York, c1820, 21½in (55cm) wide.
$3,000-4,000

A Régence boulle bracket clock, signed Boucheret a Paris, restoration, 35in (89cm). **$4,000-5,000**

A Charles II ebony striking bracket clock, signed Joseph Knibb, London, restoration, 12in (32cm). **$70,000-80,000**

Charles II ebony striking bracket clock, ckplate signed J. Knibb, London, Fecit, n (29cm) high. **$40,000-50,000**

nahogany chiming bracket ck, with 8-day 3-train ee movement, 22½in (57cm) gh. **$4,000-5,000**

A Continental stained horn and ormolu mounted grande sonnerie bracket clock, probably Swiss, mid-18thC, 37½in. **$6,000-7,000**

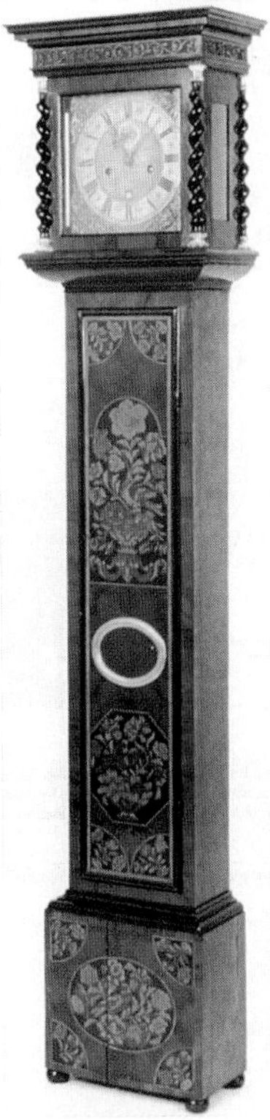

An ormolu musical automaton bracket clock, for the Chinese market, 'nonsense' signature, 22in (57cm) high. **$70,000-80,000**

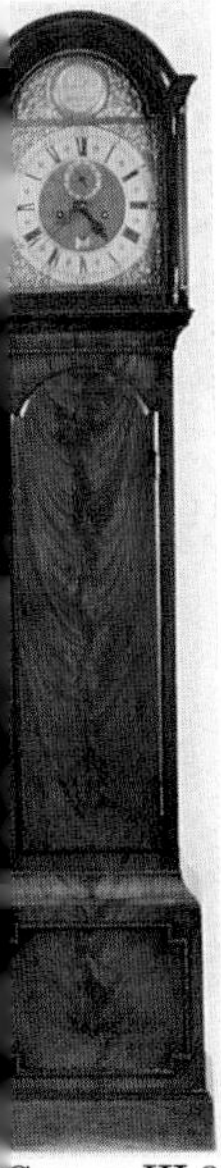

George III 8-day mahogany gcase clock, signed James nd, London, 79in (200cm). **0,000-12,000**

A green and gilt lacquer longcase clock, with 12in brass dial, signed Willm Pridham /London, inscribed 'The Royal/George', the 4-pillar movement with anchor escapement, 86in (219cm) high. **$6,000-7,000**

A walnut and marquetry longcase clock, with 10in brass dial, signed Joseph Windmills, the 8-day 6-pillar movement with anchor escapement, 75in. **$36,000-40,000**

A mahogany longcase clock, the silvered dial signed Robert Fairey, London, 108in (274cm) high. **$35,000-40,000**

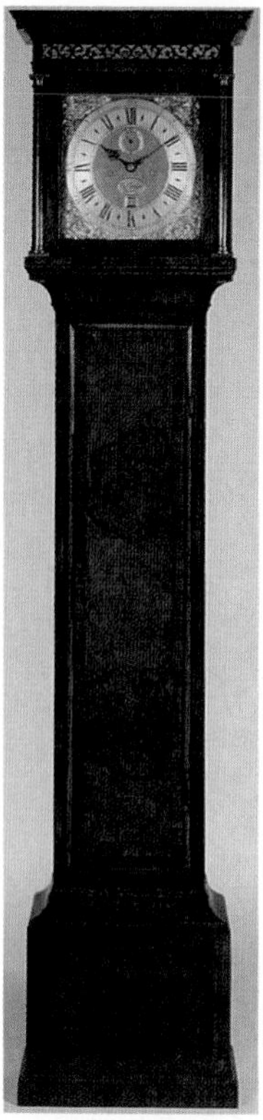

A Queen Anne burr walnut longcase clock, by Tho. Tompion, 80in (203cm).
$90,000-100,000

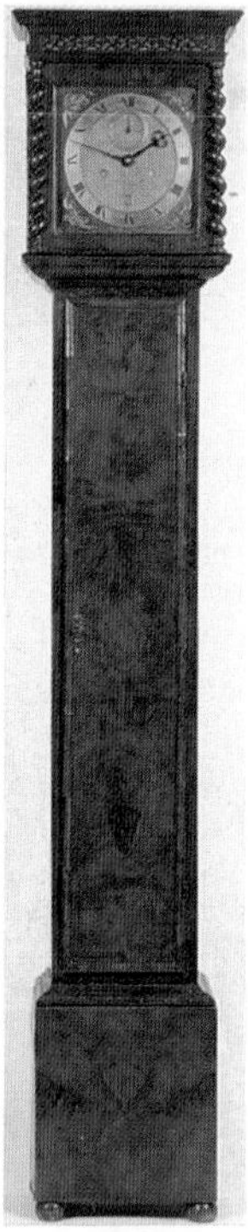

A Charles II walnut longcase clock, the brass dial signed Charles Gretton, Fleet Streete, Londini, restored, c1680, 75in (190cm).
$40,000-50,000

A Queen Anne long-case clock, with 20in dial, signed Edward Cockey, Warminster, 122in.
$140,000-160,000

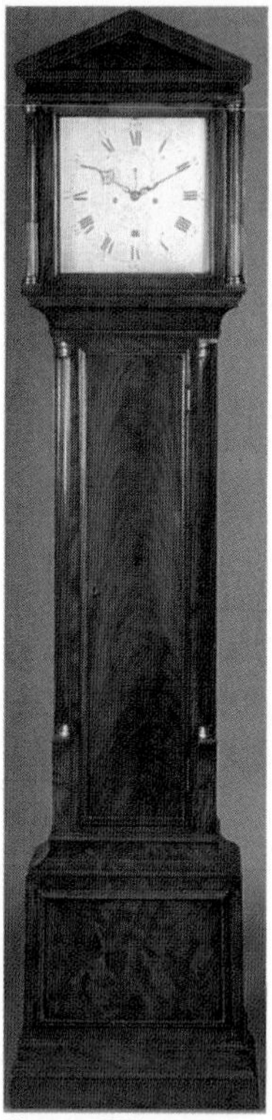

A George III mahogany longcase clock, by Vulliamy, London 525, 85in (216cm).
$60,000-80,000

A Charles II burr walnut month-goi longcase clock, by Joseph Knibb, London, restored, c1675, 80in (203cr
$120,000-140,000

A Charles II burr walnut and marquetry month-going longcase clock, signed John Ebsworth, Londini fecit, restored, 78in (198cm) high.
$32,000-40,000

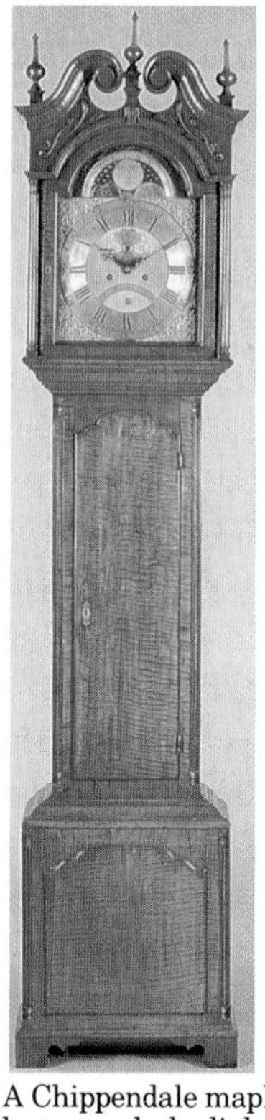

A Chippendale maple longcase clock, dial signed Thomas Wagstaffe, London, case Philadelphia c1780, replacements, 94in (238cm).
$20,000-24,000

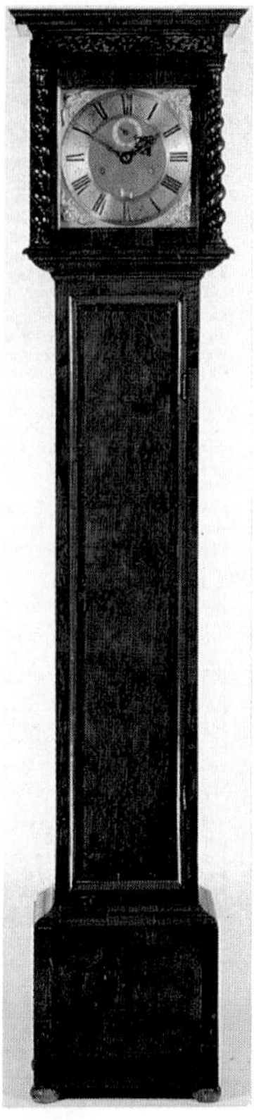

A Charles II walnut longcase clock, the silvered chapter ring signed Cha. Gretton, London, case restored, 75½in (191cm) high.
$24,000-30,000

A walnut marquetry longcase clock, the 11in brass dial signed Wm. Tomlinsc London, late 17thC, 82½in (209cm) high.
$26,000-30,000

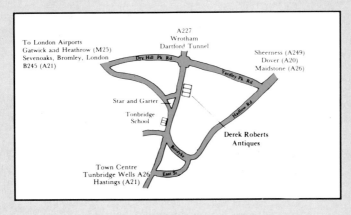

A George III ormolu, Derby biscuit porcelain and white marble mantel clock, the movement by Vulliamy, London, with later enamelled dial, the porcelain damaged and restored, 31½in (80cm) wide.
$70,000-80,000

A George III bronze and ormolu Titus clo
by Matthew Boulton, with later glazed enamel dial, the later movement signed Arnold & Dent, London, 15in (38cm) hig
$50,000-60,000

An ormolu mounted brass inlaid ebony mantel clock, the glazed brass dial signed I. Thuret a Paris, 22½in (57cm). **$20,000-24,000**

A Directoire bronze and ormolu mantel clock, the dial signed a Paris, 17in (43cm) high.
$40,000-50,000

A Louis XVI ormolu urn clock, in the manner of Lepaute, 19in (48cm) high.
$16,000-20,000

A Louis XIV ebon
and boulle mantel
clock, the moveme
signed Thuret a
Paris, 29in (74cm)
high.
$26,000-30,000

A Louis XVI ormolu mantel clock, with glazed enamel dial and striking movement, 20in (51cm).
$16,000-20,000

A Federal mahogany longcase clock, by Reuben Tower, Hingham, c1816.
$100,000-120,000

An Empire ormolu and patinated bronze mantel clock, the dial signed Ledure, Bronzier, a Paris, damaged, early 19thC, 29½in (75cm). **$8,000-10,000**

A George III ormolu and white marble vase clock, by Matthew Boulton. **$4,000-5,000**
A German ormolu mantel clock, 18thC, 11½in (29cm). **$2,000-3,000**

A Louis Philippe ormolu and silver plate garniture, clock 20in (51cm) high.
$6,000-7,000

A Regency bronze, ormolu a marble mantel clock, signe Vulliamy, London, No. 389, 10in (25.5cm) high.
$9,000-10,000

An ormolu mantel clock, signed Bausse Rue de Richilieu, No. 47, 20½in (52cm). **$4,000-6,000**

A Louis XVI ormolu and patinated bronze lyre clock, 27½in (70cm).
$30,000-32,000

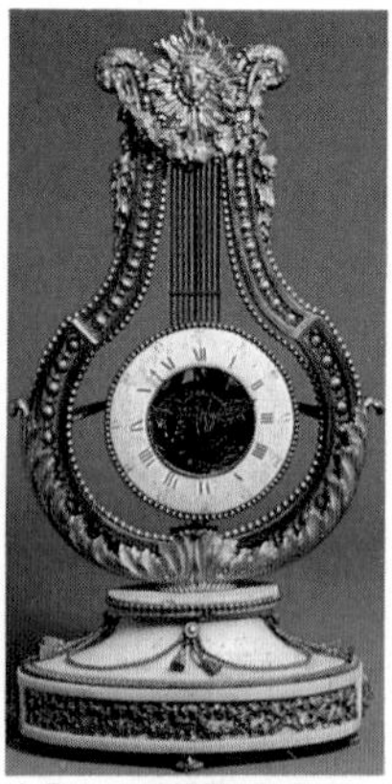

A Louis XVI style ormolu mounted and marble lyre clock, the enamel dial signed Breant a Paris, 21½in (54cm) high.
$12,000-14,000

A grande sonnerie carriage clock, 7in (18cm) high.
$10,000-12,000

A Directoire ormolu mounted biscuit porcelain mantel clock, signed Gavelle L'ainé à Paris, 15½in (39cm) high.
$2,500-3,000

A Louis XVI ormolu clock, the dial signed Furet, H'Ger du Roy, later parts, 12in (30.5cm).
$7,000-9,000

Above. A Viennese silver gilt mounted enamel and wood clock and jewel casket, c1870. **$12,000-14,000**

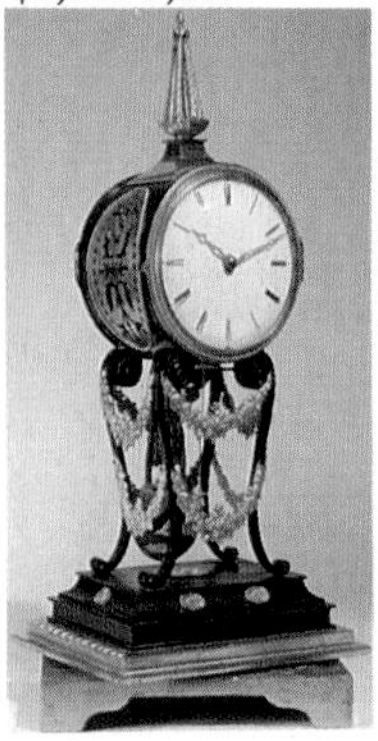

l. A Regency bronzed and giltmetal musical automaton clock, by J. H. Borrell, London, restored, 25in (63cm). **$6,000-8,000**

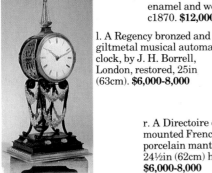

r. A Directoire ormolu mounted French biscuit porcelain mantel clock, 24½in (62cm) high.
$6,000-8,000

An Empire ormolu and bron mantel clock, signed Coeur Pere a Paris, lacking pendulum, 14in (35.5cm).
$10,000-12,000

A Charles X scarlet and parcel gilt tôle peinte clock, 19in (48cm). **$5,000-6,000**

A gold hunter cased grande sonnerie clockwatch, with split second chronograph and perpetual calendar, Swis retailed by Sir John Bennett Ltd., London, No. 2038, 6cm diam. **$70,000-80,000**

An 18ct gold Cartier tank wristwatch, the movement inscribed Bueche-Girod, No. 70. **$2,000-3,000**

l. A gold wristwatch by Patek Philippe, Geneve, the gilt dial with subsidiary seconds, 3.5cm diam. **$4,000-5,000**
r. A gold/steel and diamond set Omega Constellation Chronometer. **$1,400-1,600**

A gold skeletonised cylinder watch, signed, the case marked Paris, 1769, punche JAA, 5cm diam. **$7,000-8,000**

An enamelled gold Austro-Hungarian Imperial presentation watch, signed Patek Philippe, 5cm diam. **$20,000-24,000**

A minute repeating free-sprung lever watch, with perpetual calendar, signed Joseph Player & Son, Coventry, No. 30808, London 1898. **$18,000-20,000**

A gold hunter cased carillon grande sonnerie clockwatch, signed by Louis Elisee Piguet **$36,000-40,000**

An 18ct gold Rolex Cosmograph, No. 1580 727, crystal cracked, 3.7cm diam. **$8,000-10,000**

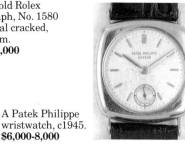

A Patek Philippe wristwatch, c1945. **$6,000-8,000**

An 18ct white gold wristwatch, signed Patek Philipp Geneve, c1987. **$3,500-4,000**

rench lacquered brass
odolite, signed Lenoir à
is, in original fruitwood
rying case, 17½in (44cm)
e, 19thC.
,000-24,000

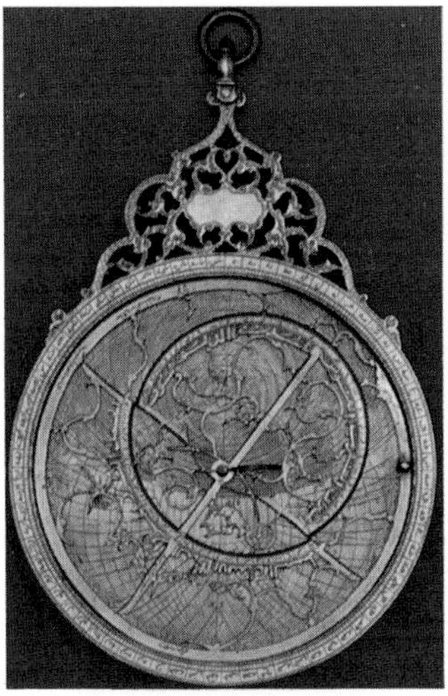

A brass Indo-Persian astrolabe, signed, part missing and replacements, 17thC.
$20,000-30,000

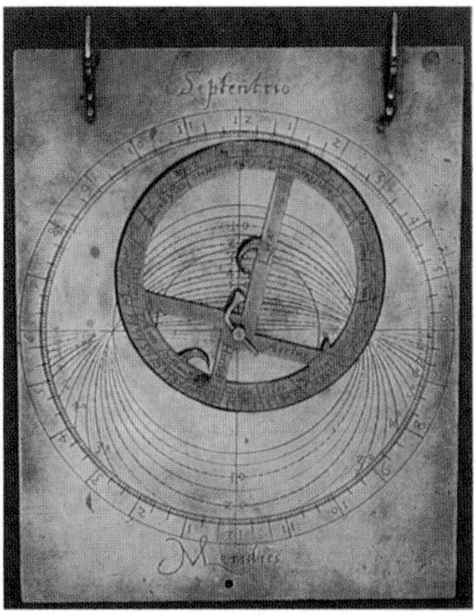

A cast brass simple astrolabe and sundial, unsigned and undated, of the Regiomontanus type.
$36,000-40,000

oxwood nocturnal,
ned Gamaliell Meggison,
ed 1679, crack to one
e, 5in (12.5cm) diam.
000-8,000

A parcel gilt and silvered brass diptych dial, signed Christoph Trechfler Senior Mechanico Anno 1623, 3½in (9cm) long.
$18,000-20,000

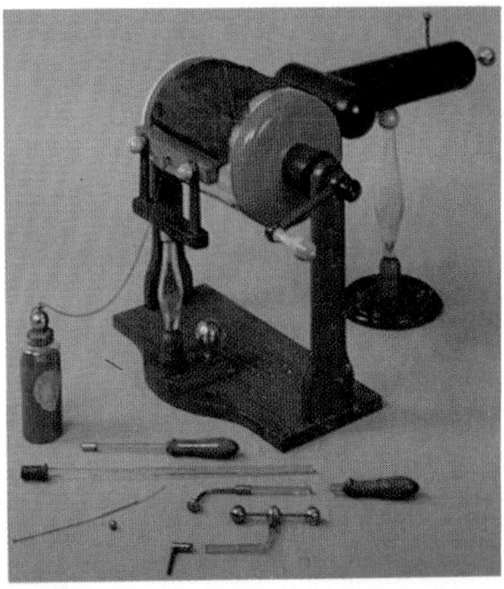

A barrel electrostatic friction generator, supported on twin shaped uprights from the mahogany base, with various collectors and glass rods, in original pine case, early 19thC, 26½in (67cm).
$2,000-3,000

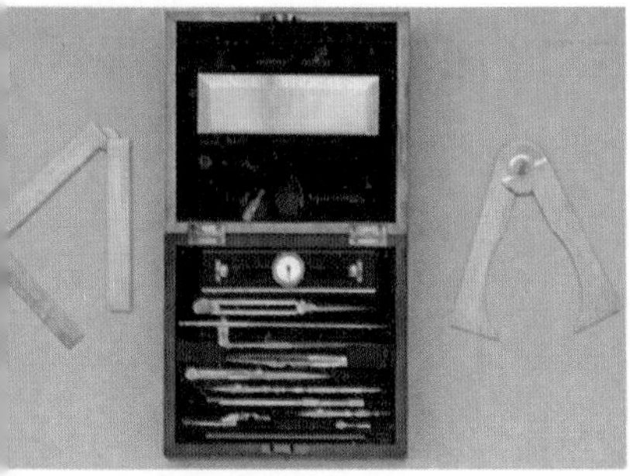

rawing set, with brass
l steel instruments, the
iders, scale and gunners
iper signed G. Adams,
ndon, the micrometer dial
mped Dollond, London,
. 2096, in boxwood strung
gwood crossbanded
hogany case, early 19thC,
(23cm) wide.
,000-6,000

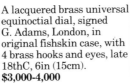

A lacquered brass simple orrery, unsigned, with ivory planets and moon, in mahogany case, 19thC, 8in (20cm).
$3,500-4,000

A lacquered brass universal equinoctial dial, signed G. Adams, London, in original fishskin case, with 4 brass hooks and eyes, late 18thC, 6in (15cm).
$3,000-4,000

A German silver and gilt perpetual calendar, unsigned, possibly 17thC, 2½in (6cm) diam.
$6,000-7,000

A Régence style ormolu and tortoiseshell barometer, stamped F. Lesage.
$7,000-9,000

A pair of early Victorian mahogany glob by Malby & Son, London, c1850, 13½in (34cm) high.
$14,000-16,000

A pair of 3in pocket globes, by Newton, early 19thC, 7in (18cm) high.
$20,000-24,000

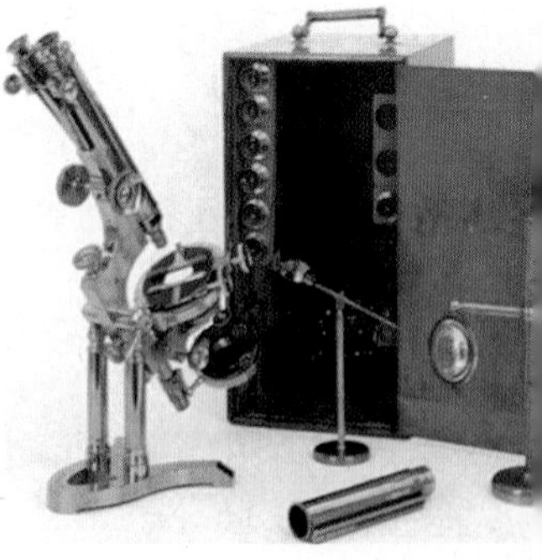

A lacquered brass compoun binocular microscope, signe with accessories in fitted mahogany case, 19thC, 18½ (47cm). **$5,000-6,000**

A lacquered brass compound binocular microscope, signed Powell & Lealand, 170 Euston Rd., London, dated 1872.
$9,000-10,000

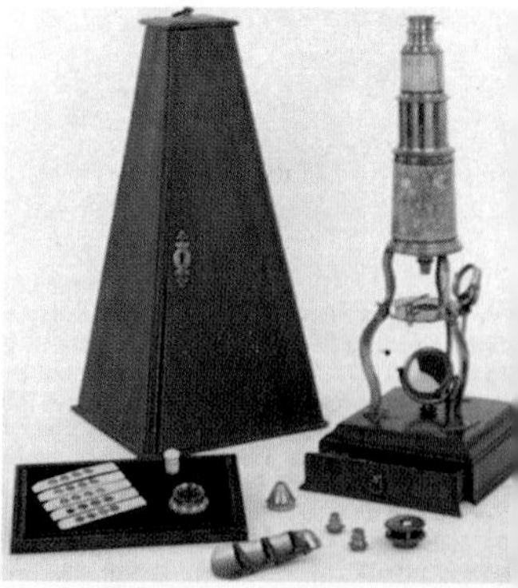

A brass Culpeper-type microscope, unsigned, in mahogany pyramid shaped case, mid-18thC, 16½in (42cm) high.
$6,000-8,000

A Lord Kelvin's pattern reflecting galvanometer, by Elliott Brothers, 100 & 102 St. Martin's Lane, London, late 19thC, 12½in (31cm).
$1,000-1,200

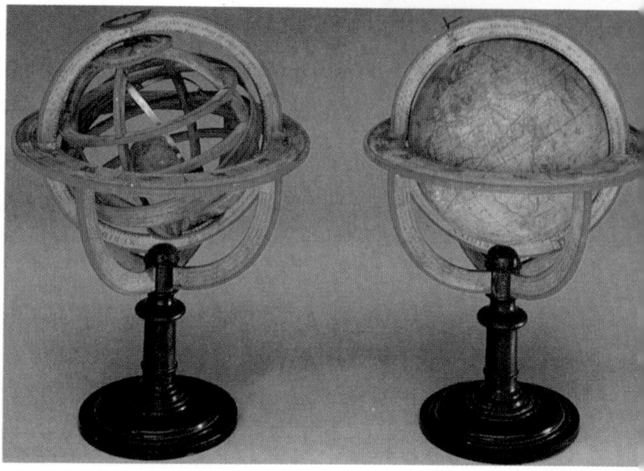

A French Ptolemaic armillary sphere, in the manner of Delamarche, early 19thC, 15in (38cm) high, with paired terrestrial globe. **$7,000-9,000**

ırtle back tile leaded
ss and bronze table lamp,
mped Tiffany, 22in (56cm).
,000-20,000

A laburnum leaded glass and bronze table lamp, stamped Tiffany Studios, New York, 397, 27in (68.5cm) high.
$80,000-90,000

A daffodil leaded glass and bronze table lamp, stamped Tiffany Studios, 22in (56cm).
$24,000-28,000

'avrile glass and bronze
ıle lamp, small repair,
mped Tiffany Studios D856,
n (63.5cm) high.
,000-20,000

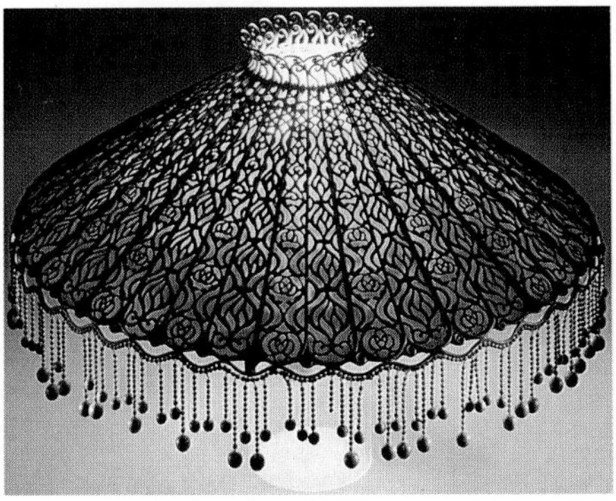

A leaded glass and filigree bronze lamp shade, by Tiffany Studios, 19in (48cm) diam. **$4,000-5,000**

A Tiffany lily Favrile glass and bronze table lamp, 19½in (49cm) high.
$18,000-20,000

visteria leaded glass and
ınze table lamp, stamped
fany Studios, New York,
)6, 27½in (70cm).
0,000-200,000

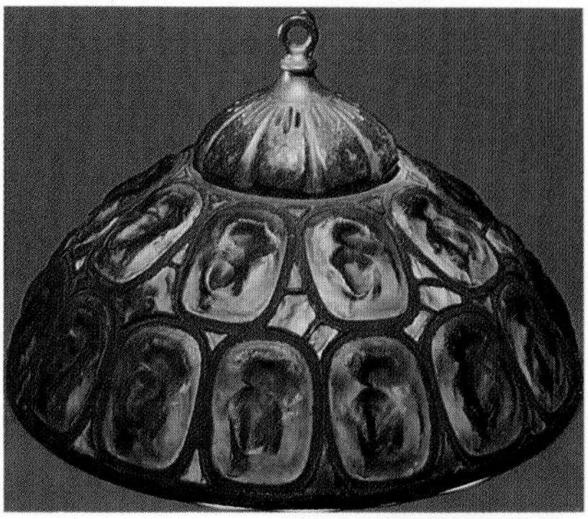

r. A Tiffany turtle back tile and bronze chandelier, 27in (68.5cm) diam.
$20,000-24,000

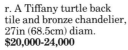

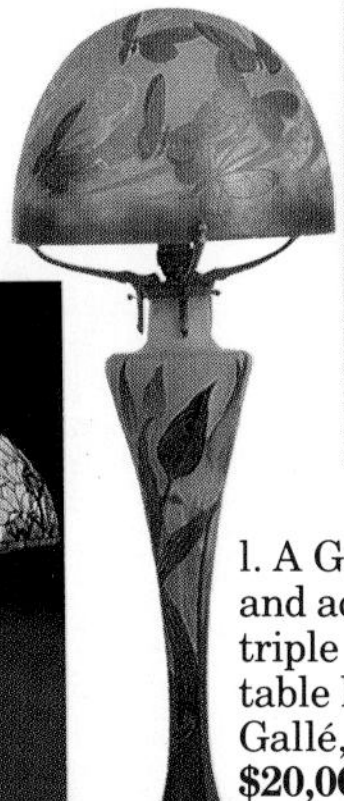

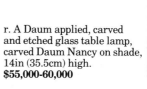

l. A Gallé carved and acid-etched triple overlay table lamp, engraved Gallé, 23½in (60cm).
$20,000-30,000

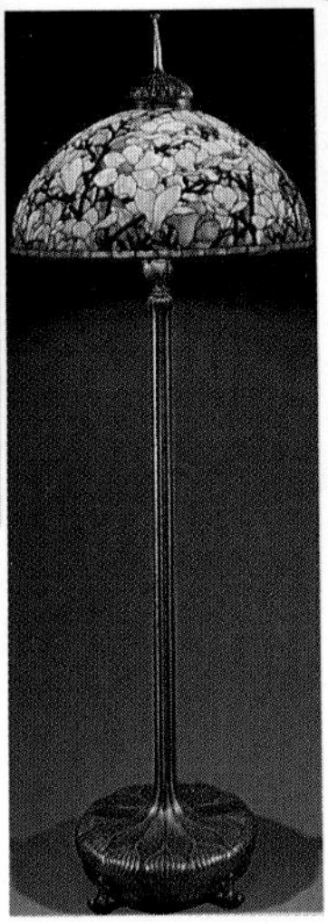

A magnolia leaded glass and bronze floor lamp, stamped Tiffany Studios, 77½in (196cm). **$200,000+**

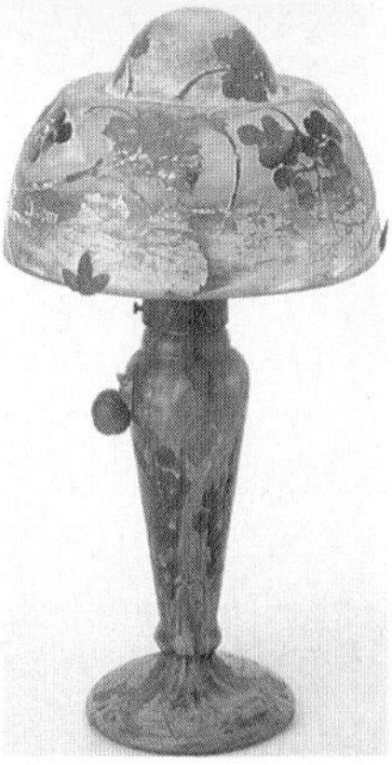

r. A Daum applied, carved and etched glass table lamp, carved Daum Nancy on shade, 14in (35.5cm) high.
$55,000-60,000

A Pilkington Royal Lancastrian lustre vase, decorated by Wm. S. Mycock, potted by E. T. Radford, marked, 1929, 15½in (40cm).
$1,500-2,500

A leaded glass and bronze table lamp, by Duffner & Kimberly, unmarked, 29in (74cm) high.
$8,000-10,000

A majolica simulated bask jardinière, by Holdcroft, on shaped stand, late 19th 11in (28cm) high.
$280-320

A Royal Doulton vase, with presentation inscription 'Presented to Mr. A. Baldwin by his colleagues at Royal Doulton Potteries on the occasion of his marriage, 2nd Sept, 1925', signed by his colleagues. **$360-400**

A Martin Bros. stoneware bird, signed and dated 9-1898, 14½in (36cm).
$10,000-12,000

A daffodil leaded glass and bronze table lamp, impress Tiffany Studios, New York 25882, 22in (56cm) high.
$12,000-14,000

'Paddy', a Royal Doulton character j with musical box playing Irish jig.
$800-900

A Daum Art Deco glass table lamp, acid etched with geometric panels, signed Daum Nancy France on base and shade.
$12,000-14,000

A Martin Bros. stoneware Toby jug, signed Martin Bros, London & Southall, dated 11-1903, 10in (25.5cm).
$6,000-8,000

'Europa and the Bull', a Royal Doulton figure, impressed H. Tittensor, Noke, and 203, 10½in (26cm).
$4,000-6,000

A 15-piece ceramic coffee set, painted mark by Clarice Cliff, Wilkinson Ltd., England, coffee pot 6½in (17cm).
$5,000-6,000

A Carlton tea-for-two service, Anemone patter
$500-600

A selection of Clarice Cliff.
From **$1,000-10,000 each**

A Clarice Cliff Lynton tea-for-two service, c193
$400-500

A Clarice Cliff Bizarre charger, factory marks, 16½in (42cm).
$3,000-4,000

A Clarice Cliff Fantasque Farmhouse vase, c1930, printed F,B, F.S, and N.P. marks, 16½in (42cm).
$8,000-9,000

A Clarice Cliff Applique tea servic one piece cracked.
$11,000-13,000

A Clarice Cliff Bizarre jardinière, painted in the Applique pattern, printed Newport Pottery, Bizarre and Applique marks, 7½in (19cm). **$8,000-9,000**

l. A Carter Stabler Adams vase, 14in (35cm) high.
$500-600
Above. A Susie Cooper sugar bowl, A. E. Gray & Co. Ltd., marked. **$200-250**

A Carter Stabler Adams vase, painted with stylised flowers, crack and repair, impressed mark, painted monogram HY, 16½in (42cm).
$6,000-7,000

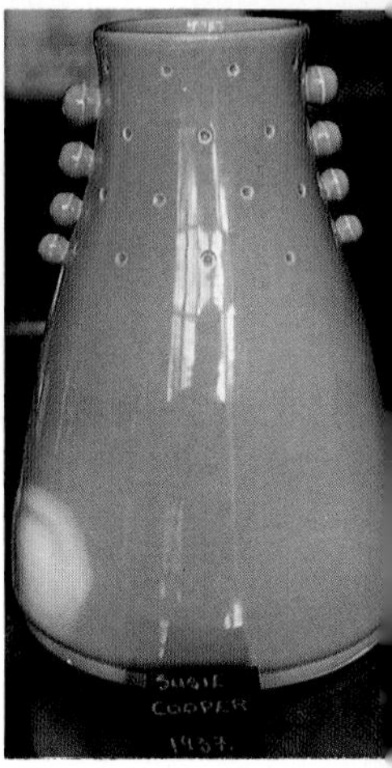

A Susie Cooper studio po incised signature, No. 47 c1937, 9½in (24cm).
$500-600

Two Daum cameo glass vases, cameo mark Daum Nancy, 16½ and 21½in (42 and 54cm).
Left. **$3,500-4,000**
Right. **$6,000-7,000**

A frosted glass vase, 'Lutteurs', relief moulded R. Lalique, engraved France, 5in (12.5cm) high.
$3,000-4,000

A cire perdue glass vase, wheel cut R. Lalique France c1924, 9in (23cm) high.
$80,000-90,000

A black enamelled glass vase, 'Baies', the relief moulding heightened in enamel, intaglio moulded R. Lalique, 10½in (26cm).
$14,000-16,000

A Daum etched and enamelled coupe, signed Daum Nancy, 9in (23cm).
$3,500-4,000

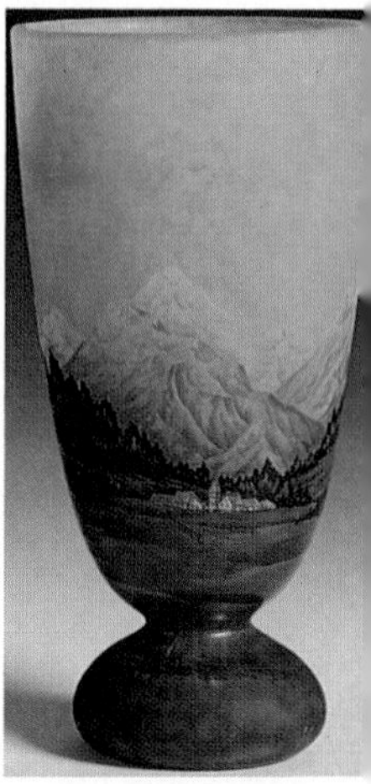

A Daum vase, with overlaid enamel painted alpine scene, enamelled signature Daum Nancy with the cross of Lorraine, 11½in (29cm) high.
$7,000-8,000

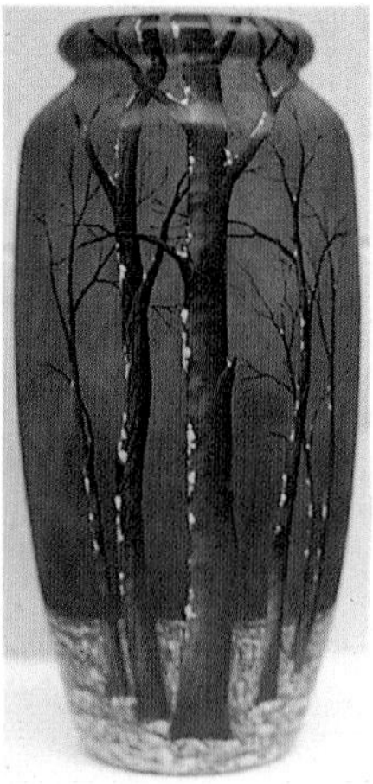

A Daum etched and enamelled vase, signed Daum Nancy, 10½in (26.5cm) high.
$4,000-5,000

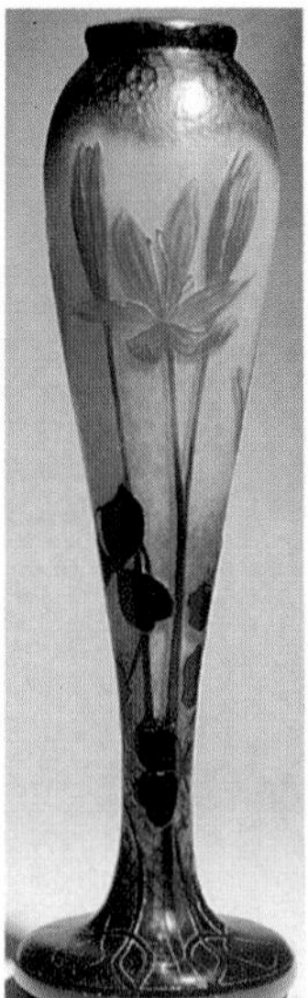

A Daum double overlay and wheel carved martelé vase, engraved signature Daum Nancy with the Cross of Lorraine, 15½in (40cm) high.
$10,000-12,000

An enamelled glass vase, 'Tourbillons', wheel cut R. Lalique, France, engraved No. 973, 8in (20.5cm) high.
$40,000-45,000

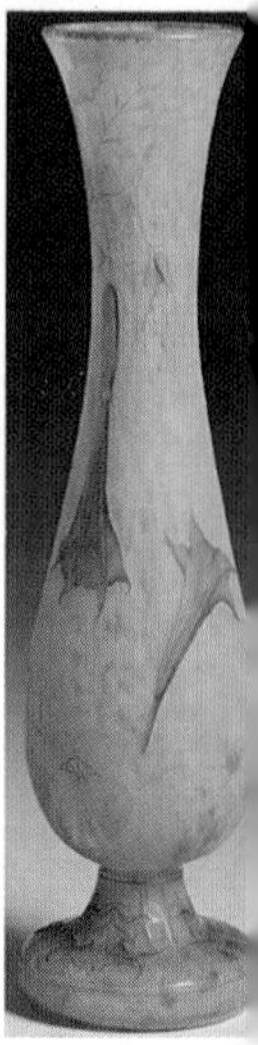

A Daum vase, the frosted ground overlaid with clear glass, gilt signature Daum Nancy with the Cross of Lorraine, 23½in (60cm) high.
$5,000-6,000

A Gallé dragonfly scent bottle, decorated in enamels in the Japanese style, 6in (15cm).
$2,500-3,000

A Daum landscape bowl, amethyst overlaid on yellow/white ground, signed Daum, Nancy, 10in (25.5cm).
$4,000-5,000

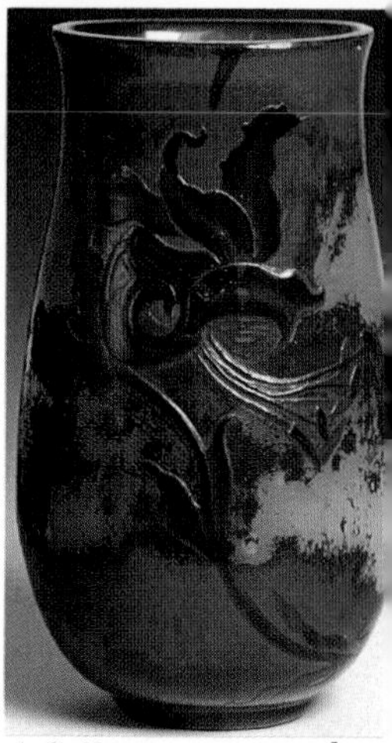

A Gallé vase, engraved Cristallerie de Gallé, 8½in (22cm) high.
$10,000-12,000

A Gallé floral vase, blue and brown overlaid on amber, signed Gallé, 7in (18cm) high. **$5,000-6,000**

A Gallé anemone vase, red overlaid on a frosted clear ground, signed Gallé, 7in (18cm). **$3,000-4,000**

A Daum etched and enamelled jardinièr signed Daum Nancy, 10in (25cm).
$6,000-7,000

A Gallé overlaid vase, signed Gallé, 9in (23cm) high.
$5,000-6,000

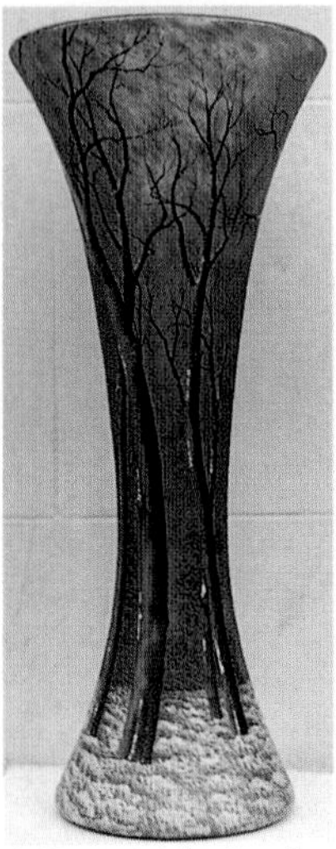

A Daum etched and enamelled landscape vase, signed Daum Nancy, 20in (51cm).
$6,000-7,000

A Gallé clematis overlaid vase, sign Gallé, 9½in (24cm) diam.
$5,000-6,000

A Gallé overlaid fuchsia vase, signed Gallé, 8in (21cm) high.
$6,000-7,000

A Gallé overlaid and acid etched vase, cameo signatur 7½in (19cm) high.
$8,000-9,000

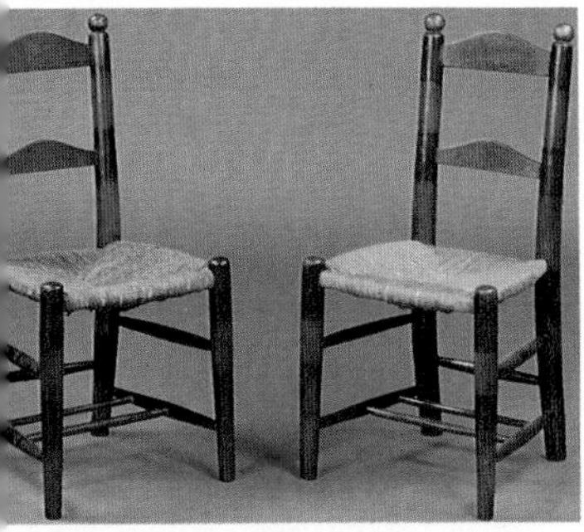

set of 6 J. Walden painted oak side
ıairs, the design attributed to Wm.
urgess.
1,600-2,000

A cast iron, bronze and enamelled table clock, by Albin Müller, 21½in (55cm).
$12,000-14,000

An Austrian Secessionist lacquer and pewter cabinet, inlaid with mother-of-pearl, 64in (161cm) wide.
$10,000-12,000

. laminated birchwood sideboard, designed
y Gerald Summers, 54in (137cm) wide.
6,000-8,000

A Carlo Bugatti rosewood and tooled vellum side chair, decorated with copper and pewter. **$3,000-4,000**

An oak lath armchair, design by Marcel Breuer, for the Bauhaus, Weimar, original fabric replaced, 1924.
$60,000-75,000

Morris & Co., oak bookstand, the rest
ırmounted with carved and turned ball
nd foliate finials, 73in (185cm).
9,000-11,000

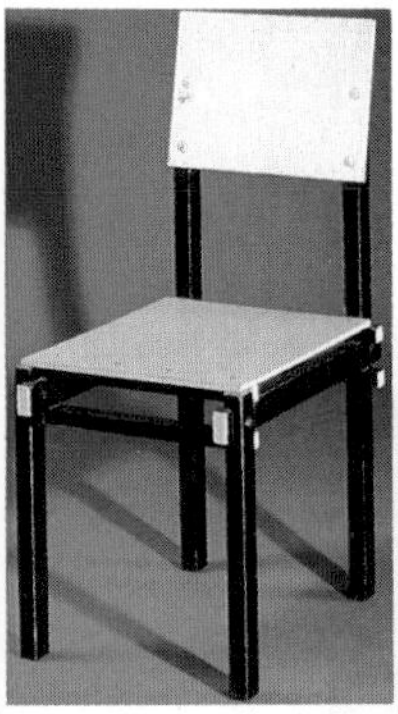

A military chair by Gerrit Rietveld.
$22,000-24,000

A set of 6 Art Deco Macassar ebony arm chairs, attributed to Paul Kiss, the backs formed as 3 upholstered panels with hammered brass top rail.
$12,000-14,000

n oak buffet, designed by M. H. Baillie-Scott, c1898,
28in (327cm).
5,000-10,000

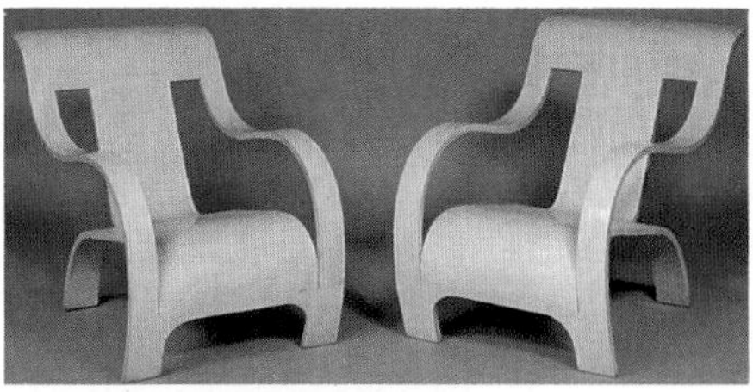

A pair of laminated birchwood open arm chairs, designed by Gerald Summers.
$28,000-30,000

An Aesthetic Movement ebony and lacquer cabinet, signed and stamped Gregory & Co., 62in (158cm).
$4,000-6,000

A Carlo Bugatti ebonised, rosewood an vellum covered games table, the top wi 4 covered wells and inlaid with pewter chessboard, inlaid Bugatti signature, 31½in (79cm). **$24,000-30,000**

An American Arts and Crafts clock, with brass face, c1910.
$1,600-1,800

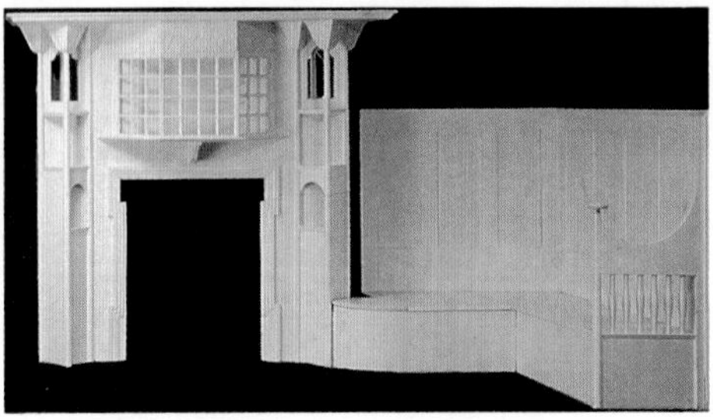

A white painted fire surround and inglenook, designed by M. H. Baillie-Scott, c1898, 83in (211cm) high.
$8,000-12,000

An English walnut dining suite, with yew crossbanding, with labels for Russell & Sons, Broadway, Worcs, c1920, table 66in (167cm) long. **$24,000-30,000**

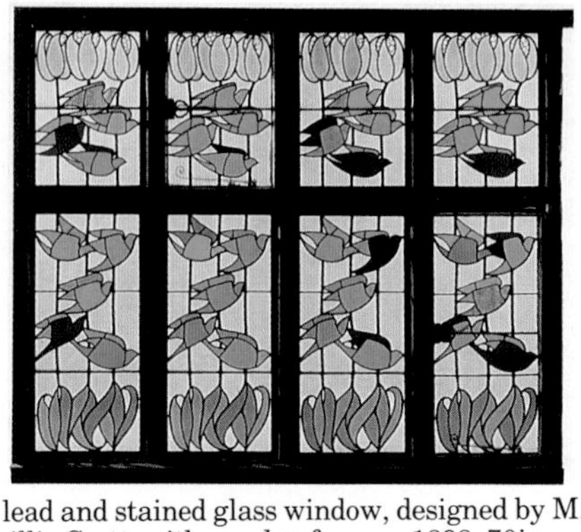

A lead and stained glass window, designed by M. H. Baillie-Scott, with wooden frame, c1898, 70in (177.5cm) high. **$28,000-30,000**

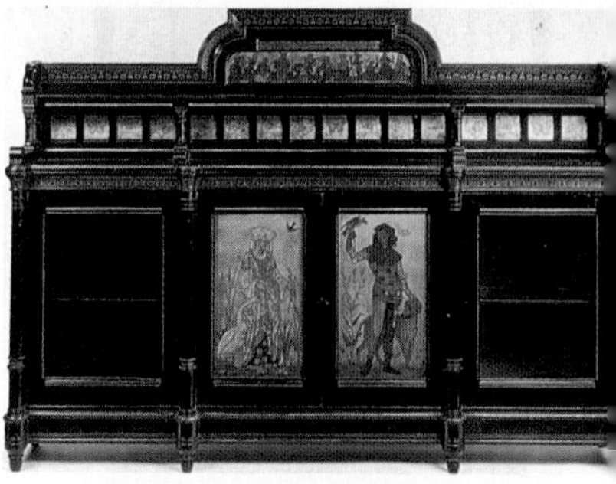

An ebonised and painted sideboard, the painting attributed to Henry Stacy Marks, 78in (198cm) wide.
$6,000-8,000

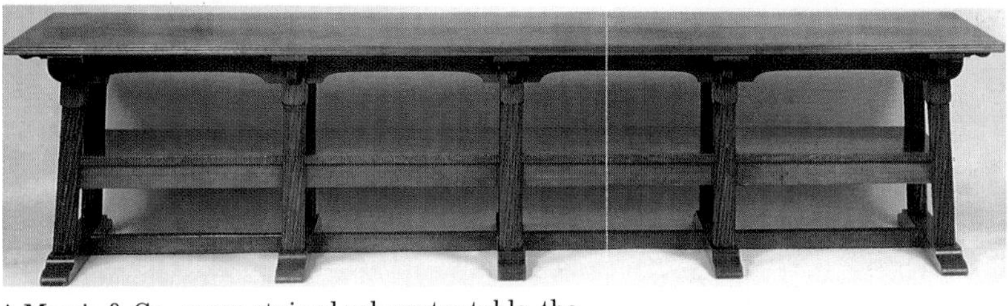

A Morris & Co., green stained oak centre table, the designed attributed to Philip Webb with George Jack, 125in (320cm).
$32,000-36,000

vo chairs by Grand Rapids Bookcase &
ıair Co., under the label 'Lifetime',
912. **$5,000-6,000**

A teak garden suite, comprising a table and 4 chairs, from a design by Ambrose Heal. **$2,000-2,500**

ı extending oak dining table, American
ts & Crafts Movement.
,000-6,000

An oak dining table, probably Liberty & Co., with Pugin influence, c1885. **$2,500-3,500**

l. An oak display cabinet, American Arts & Crafts Movement, c1905.
$2,000-2,500
r. A telephone table and window seat, American Arts & Crafts Movement, c1900.
$500-700 each

A Stickley Bros chair, Grand Rapids, c1910.
$600-700

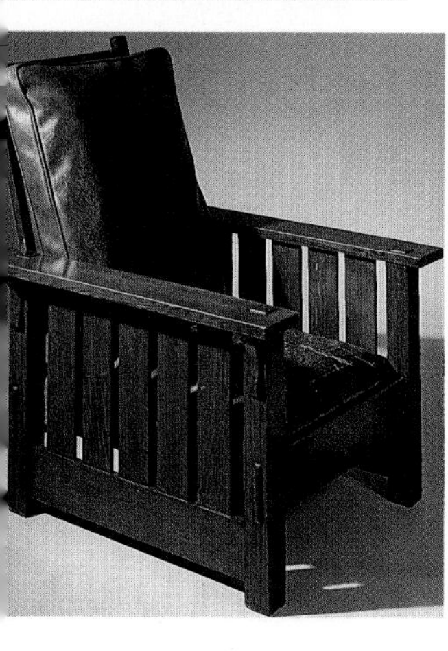

l. An oak Morris Chair, with adjustable back, American Arts & Crafts Movement, c1905. **$2,000-3,000**

Two oak stands and a foot-stool, American, c1905.
$300-600 each

A bronze and ivory figure, 'The Archer', on green onyx base, signed F. Preiss, 8½in (22cm) high.
$10,000-12,000

A bronze and ivory figure, 'Autumn Dancer', signed with F. Preiss monogram, 14½in (37.5cm) high.
$40,000-50,000

Two silver patinated bronze figures, 'Ball Player' and 'Stella', by M. Guira Rivière and Etling, Paris, 22 and 25½ (57 and 63cm) high.
$5,000-6,000 each

A bronze and ivory figure, 'Starlight', on marble base, signed D. H. Chiparus, 23½in (58.5cm). **$24,000-30,000**

A bronze and ivory figure, 'Charm of the Orient', on marble base, signed A. Godard, 19½in (49cm) high.
$18,000-24,000

A bronze and ivory group, 'High Priestes on a white marble plinth, signed on the base A. Bouraine, 24½in (62cm) high.
$36,000-40,000

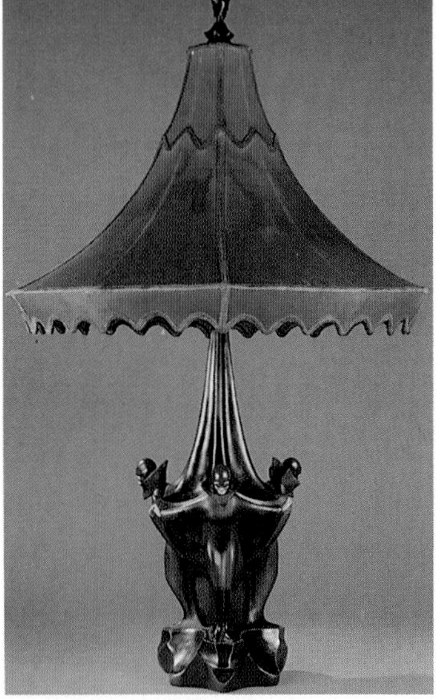

A bronze and ivory table lamp, 'Batwoman', with waxed cotton shade, signed in the bronze Roland Paris, 37in (94cm).
$20,000-30,000

A gilt bronze and silver patinated figure, the bronze base signed E. Barrias, 17in (43cm) high.
$14,000-18,000

A gold patinated bronze and ivory figure, 'Exotic Dancer', on onyx base, signed in the bronze Gerdago, 12in (30.5cm
$30,000-36,000

An English bronze statuette of the Spirit of Ecstasy, by Charles Sykes, 23½in (60cm) high. **$12,000-15,000**

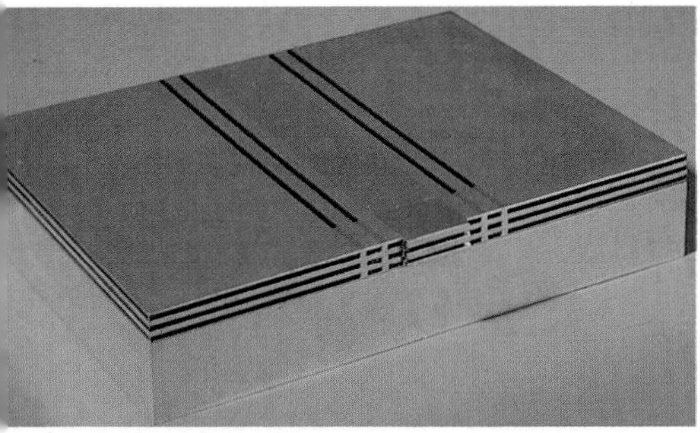

'Asprey silver and gold cigarette box, inlaid with
ck lacquer, stamped, London hallmarks for 1935,
(23cm) wide. **$5,000-6,000**

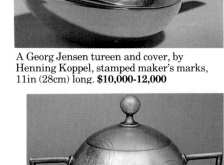

A Georg Jensen tureen and cover, by Henning Koppel, stamped maker's marks, 11in (28cm) long. **$10,000-12,000**

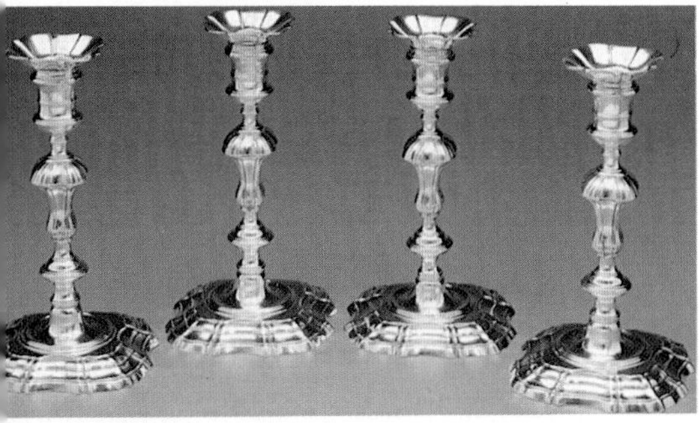

set of 4 George II candlesticks, by William Gould,
ırked on bases and sockets, London 1743, 8in (20.5cm),
oz. **$20,000-24,000**

A Hukin & Heath electroplated bowl and hinged cover, designed by Dr. C. Dresser, c1879, 7½in (19cm). **$20,000-25,000**

set of 4 George I candlesticks, by
Turnbull, 1714. **$24,000-30,000**

A George III pierced cake basket, by Wakelin & Garrard, London 1794, 15in (38cm) wide, 39½oz. **$6,000-8,000**

A pair of George III tea caddies and sugar casket, by Emick Romer, London 1768, 26½oz, in shagreen case by James Wiburd.
$14,000-16,000

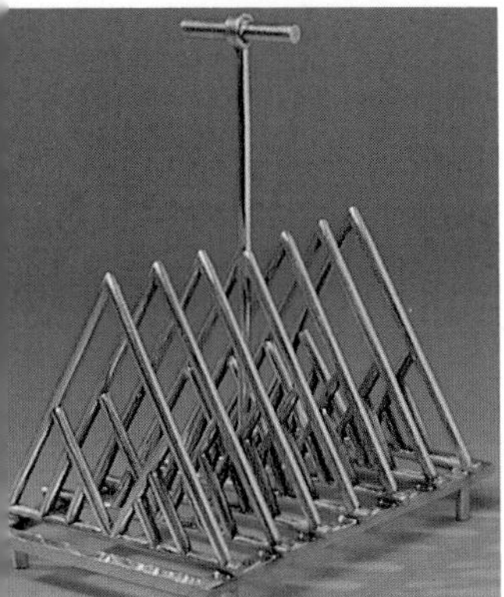

James Dixon & Sons electro-
ıted toastrack, by Chr.
esser. **$30,000-36,000**

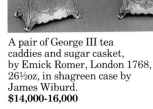

A Hukin & Heath silver sugar basin, designed by Chr. Dresser, marked, c1879, 4½in (12.5cm) diam. **$8,000-10,000**

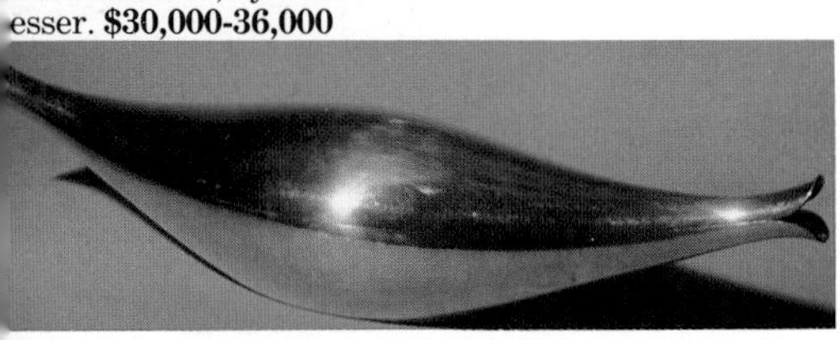

Georg Jensen tureen, designed by Henning Koppel,
ımped, Denmark 1054. **$40,000-50,000**

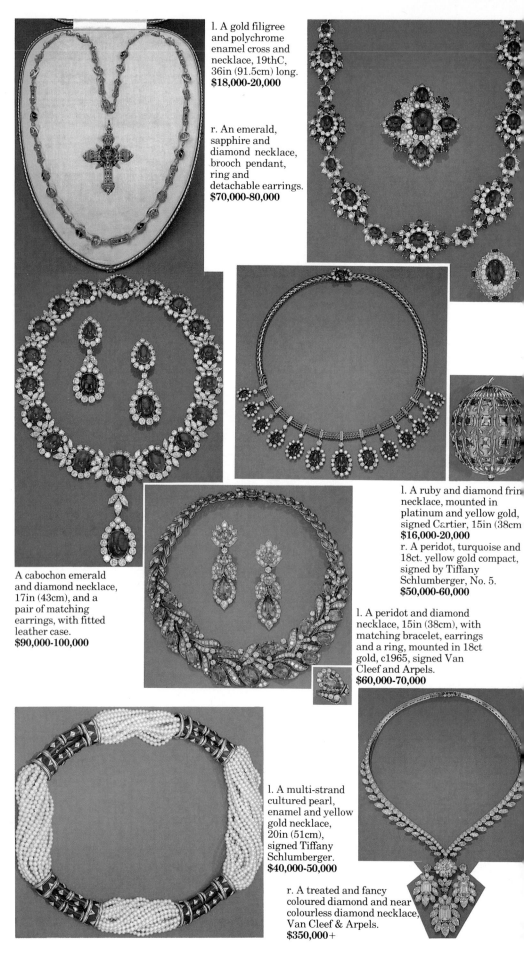

l. A gold filigree and polychrome enamel cross and necklace, 19thC, 36in (91.5cm) long.
$18,000-20,000

r. An emerald, sapphire and diamond necklace, brooch pendant, ring and detachable earrings.
$70,000-80,000

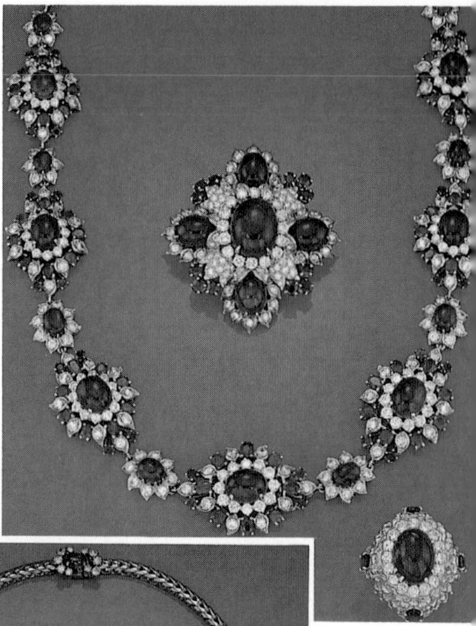

A cabochon emerald and diamond necklace, 17in (43cm), and a pair of matching earrings, with fitted leather case.
$90,000-100,000

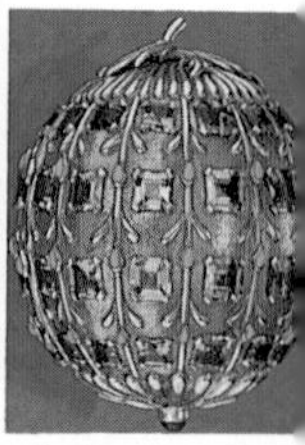

l. A ruby and diamond frin necklace, mounted in platinum and yellow gold, signed Cartier, 15in (38cm
$16,000-20,000

r. A peridot, turquoise and 18ct. yellow gold compact, signed by Tiffany Schlumberger, No. 5.
$50,000-60,000

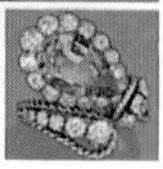

l. A peridot and diamond necklace, 15in (38cm), with matching bracelet, earrings and a ring, mounted in 18ct gold, c1965, signed Van Cleef and Arpels.
$60,000-70,000

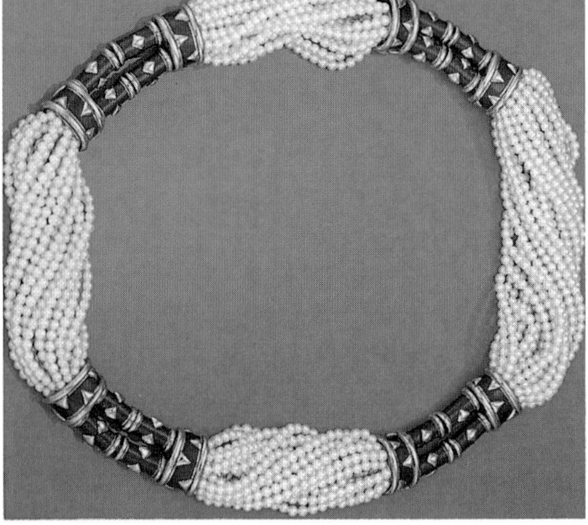

l. A multi-strand cultured pearl, enamel and yellow gold necklace, 20in (51cm), signed Tiffany Schlumberger.
$40,000-50,000

r. A treated and fancy coloured diamond and near colourless diamond necklace, Van Cleef & Arpels.
$350,000+

eorge III satinwood and inlaid
k table, containing a frieze
wer and slide, on squared
ered legs terminating in brass
pings and casters, united by
etchers, 21in (52cm).
000-8,000

A George III mahogany work table, inlaid with boxwood and ebonised lines, the twin flap top above 2 drawers, one fitted, previously with an upholstered well, 38in (95cm) wide, open.
$2,500-3,000

A Regency mahogany work table with a moulded edge, containing a fitted frieze drawer and a sliding well below, on reeded splayed legs united by stretcher.
$3,000-4,000

A Regency pollard elm work/games table, with twin flap top with a reversible centre, inlaid with a chequer board and enclosing a backgammon board, the legs applied with ebonised roundels, 31in (80cm).
$4,000-5,000

Regency rosewood amboyna and
lmwood work table, with banded
above a frieze drawer, on trestle
pports with scroll brackets and
eded bun feet, 23in (59cm).
,000-4,000

A figured mahogany work table, with 2 drop flaps and 2 shallow frieze drawers, the scrolled sabre supports ending in brass caps and casters, 19thC, 16in (40cm).
$1,800-2,000

rench rosewood work table, with
rquetry inlay, on slender
riole supports with gilt metal
unts, 19thC, 18in (46cm).
0-1,000

A rosewood combined work/games table, with folding swivelling baize lined top, backgammon drawer, fitted drawer and pouch, on standard end supports, early 19thC, 20in (51cm).
$1,500-2,000

A William IV rosewood drop-leaf work table, with sliding work compartment, on a U-shaped support with 4 splayed legs, lotus carved toes and casters, 28in (70cm).
$2,000-2,500

A Victorian walnut and marquetry sewing table, the top with chessboard inlay, on tapering column and carved tripod base, 18½in (46cm).
$1,400-1,600

Tables – Writing

A Victorian walnut writing table, with inset leather lined top, above a banded panelled frieze, on reeded turned tapering legs, labelled G. Vaughan & Co., 26 Great Eastern Street, London, 72in (182.5cm) diam.
$3,500-4,000

A Victorian burr walnut writing/card table, the swivel and flap top with serpentine outline and green baize inset, 31in (78cm).
$1,200-1,600

A Victorian walnut writing tabl 49in (125cm).
$5,000-6,000

A late Biedermeier mahogany and parcel ebonised writing table, the angles applied with Egyptian busts on incurved legs and paw feet joined by an X-stretcher supporting a stepped platform, 35in (89cm).
$6,000-8,000

A North Italian rosewood and parquetry writing table, the top inlaid with key pattern border, the frieze slide with gilt tooled leather writing panel, 18thC, 39in (99cm).
$10,000-12,000

A French Empire style mahogany bureau plat.
$7,000-8,000

An Empire style mahogany and brass writing desk, with leather lined top, central frieze drawer, 2 short drawers and a deep drawe on turned tapered fluted legs, 51i (129.5cm).
$4,000-5,000

A kingwood and tulipwood writing table, with leather lined top, the sides inlaid with musical trophies and the back with false drawers, possibly Swedish, 47in (119cm).
$7,000-8,000

Teapoys

A William IV rosewood teapoy, with 4 lidded caddies and 2 mixing bowls, 19in (48cm).
$4,000-5,000

A Regency mahogany and ebony teapoy, the hinged top enclosing 4 lidded compartments, 15in (38cm).
$800-1,200

A William IV Colonial carved rosewood teapoy, on square foliat column, quatrefoil platform and scroll feet, 18½in (48cm).
$1,000-1,200

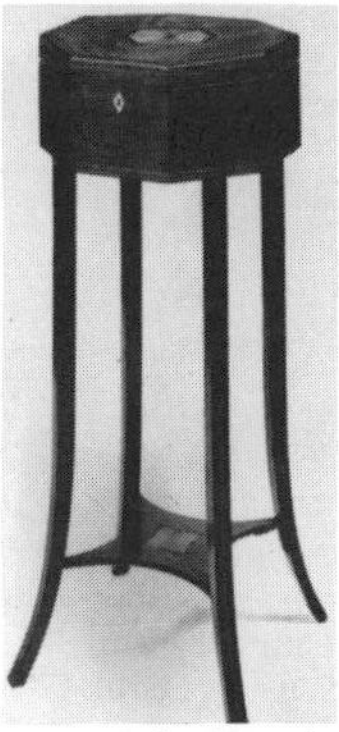

A Regency mahogany teapoy, rossbanded in rosewood and with bony and boxwood stringing, with itted interior, 32in (81cm) high.
$2,000-2,500

Washstands

A mahogany washstand, early 19thC, 30in (76cm).
$1,600-2,000

A Federal inlaid mahogany corner basin stand, North Shore, Massachusetts, branded on back N Pierce, c1800, 22½in (57cm) wide.
$3,500-4,500

A washstand, with lifting top to eveal rising mirror, inlaid panel loors and drawers below, 19thC.
1,200-1,400

A Georgian inlaid corner washstand, with 4-piece blue and white toilet set.
$800-900

A Federal inlaid mahogany corner washstand, restoration to legs, New York, c1800, 24in (61cm) wide.
$10,000-12,000

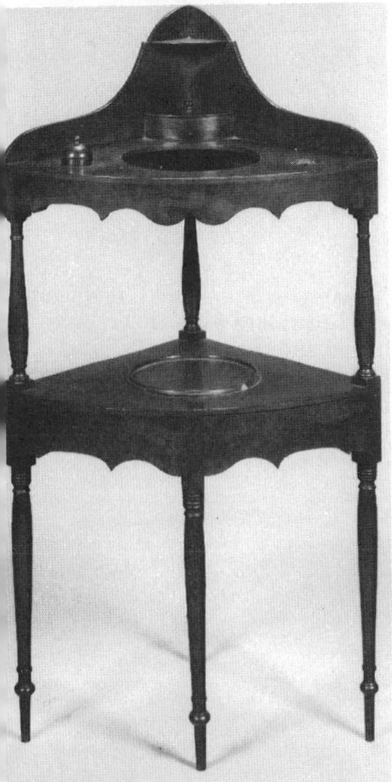

late Federal mahogany corner ashstand, repairs, New York, 820, 23½in (60cm) wide.
,500-2,000

Whatnots

A Regency mahogany two-tier whatnot, with lattice sides, on turned supports and turned tapering legs with brass caps and casters, 18in (46cm).
$5,000-6,000

A Victorian walnut whatnot, with adjustable writing slope.
$3,500-4,000

A Victorian whatnot, with barley twist side supports, shaped shelves with inlaid decorative panels.
$1,000-1,200

Wine Coolers

A George II mahogany wine cooler with metal liner, brass carrying handles, and a small drawer, 18½in (46cm) high.
$4,000-5,000

A George III mahogany and brass bound wine cooler, with lion mask ring handles, separate stand, on turned legs and casters, 25in (63cm).
$3,000-4,000

A George III mahogany and brass bound octagonal wine cooler, 18in (46cm).
$4,000-5,000

A George III mahogany and brass bound wine cooler, 18in (46cm).
$6,000-7,000

A George III brass bound mahogany wine cooler of hexagonal form, 17in (43cm).
$6,000-7,000

A Georgian crossbanded mahogany and line inlaid wine cooler, brass bound and with brass carrying handles, lined interior and tap to base, on a stand with chased brass ball and claw feet, 18in (46cm).
$3,500-4,000

A Regency fiddleback mahogany wine cooler of sarcophagus form, the panelled sides outlined with red mouldings, 30in (76cm).
$1,500-1,800

A Regency lift top cellaret, with reeded corner panels, 23in (58cm).
$1,500-1,800

A Regency mahogany sarcophagus shaped cellaret, with Egyptian style corners, 29in (73cm).
$4,500-5,000

A Regency mahogany cellaret, wit rising lid and zinc lined fitted interior, with lion mask ring drop handles, on paw feet.
$3,000-4,000

iscellaneous

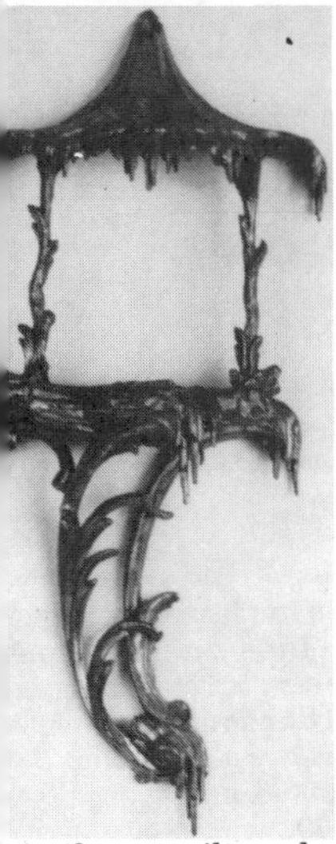

air of rococo giltwood wall ckets in the Chippendale taste, h pagoda canopies hung with les, on twin branch uprights, the cy bases with foliate scrolls ow, 23½in (59cm).
500-4,000

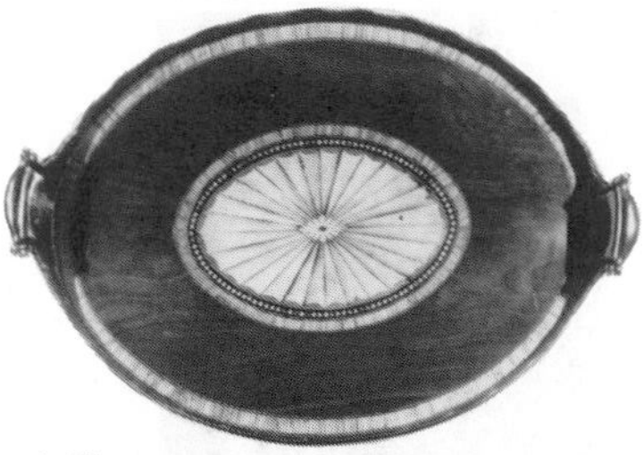

A Sheraton period mahogany tray, with wavy edged sides, satinwood crossbanding and satinwood and harewood inlay, 32in (80cm).
$4,000-5,000

A Georgian mahogany waste paper basket, with a brass swivel handle and blind fretwork decoration against a green linen backing, 13in (32cm) high.
$1,500-2,000

A Charles X burr ash bidet, the hinged top rail enclosing compartments, the interior lacking bowl, with deep frieze, on square straight legs, 31½in (79cm) high.
$2,000-3,000

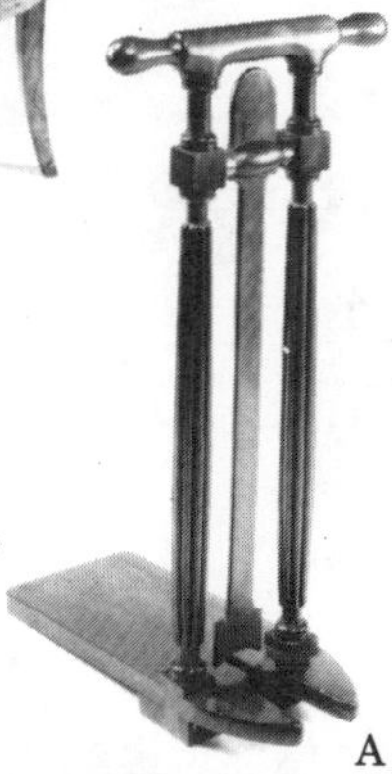

A Victorian mahogany boot-jack, turned hand rail, on ribbed supports, 31½in (79cm) high.
$2,800-3,200

A Dutch fruitwood and parquetry jardinière, of serpentine bombé shape with detachable tin liner and cabriole legs, 20in (51cm) high.
$2,000-3,000

ir of mahogany paper baskets, ret-pierced sides with Gothic es, on bracket feet, 17in (43cm).
00-7,000

A giltmetal mounted kingwood and tulipwood jardinière, with detachable tin liner with inlaid panels, 49in (125cm).
$7,000-8,000

Regency style ebony and ulated rosewood jardinière, with achable tin liner, 29in (73cm).
000-4,000

Biedermeier tapestry frame, with ustable open top on trestle ends ed by a moulded stretcher, fitted h 3 small drawers, on splayed t, 41in (104cm).
000-4,000

Miller's is a price Guide not a price List

The price ranges given reflect the average price a purchaser should pay for similar items. Condition, rarity of design or pattern, size, colour, provenance, restoration and many other factors must be taken into account when assessing values. When buying or selling, it must always be remembered that prices can be greatly affected by the condition of any piece. Unless otherwise stated, all goods shown in Miller's are of good merchantable quality, and the valuations given reflect this fact. Pieces offered for sale in exceptionally fine condition or in poor condition may reasonably be expected to be priced considerably higher or lower respectively than the estimates given herein

ARCHITECTURAL ANTIQUES

Fireplaces

A Victorian fireplace, 37in (94cm).
$600-1,000

An Art Nouveau fireplace with tiles, 37in (94cm).
$700-900

A Victorian iron and brass firegr of bowed outline, the railed front flanked by scrolled standards, wi lions' head finials on paw feet, th domed canopy with acanthus scrolls, 26in (66cm).
$2,000-3,000

A Regency blackened iron fire surround and grate, 43in (109cm).
$6,000-7,000

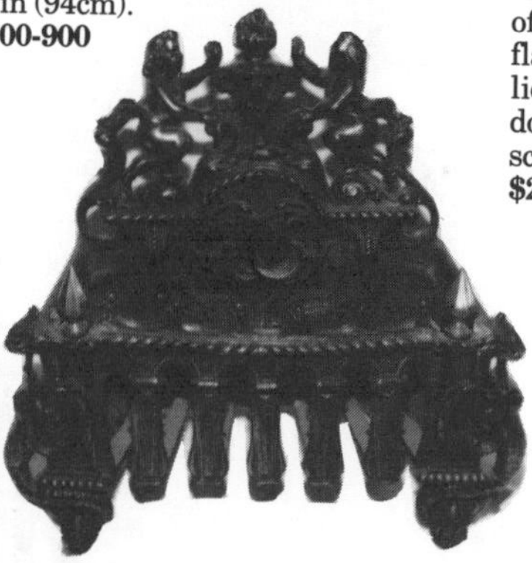

A small fire basket, 14in (35cm).
$500-700

A brass and steel firegrate wi serpentine basket, on square supports, the back plate broke 27½in (69cm).
$3,000-4,000

A tin plated miniature fire surround and grate, with moulded uprights and lintel, 12in (31cm).
$500-700

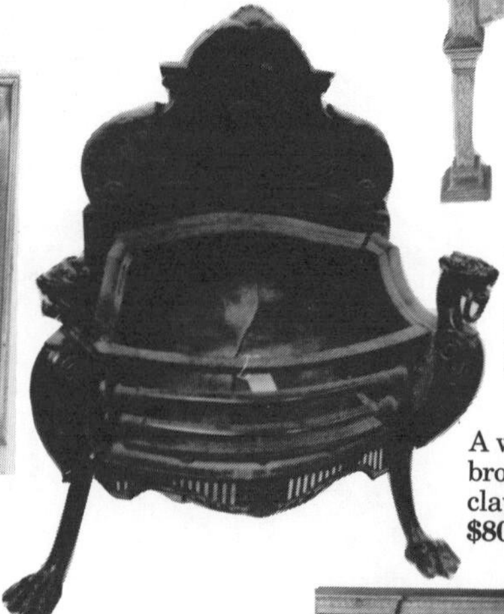

A wrought iron back firegrate, w bronze lion's head decoration, on claw feet, 26in (64cm).
$800-1,000

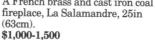

A French brass and cast iron coal fireplace, La Salamandre, 25in (63cm).
$1,000-1,500

A George III style fireplace, with moulded foliate cornice, the panelled sides with flowerheads ar foliage, 75½in (192cm).
$10,000-12,000

ieorge III style cast iron and
ss firegrate, late 19thC, 36in
cm).
000-4,000

A steel fireplace, centred with the cypher of George III, flanked by the royal arms, with swags above and fleur-de-lys below, 32½in (81cm).
$1,800-2,500

An Adam style brass and steel serpentine fronted firegrate, 19thC, 32in (80cm).
$3,000-4,000

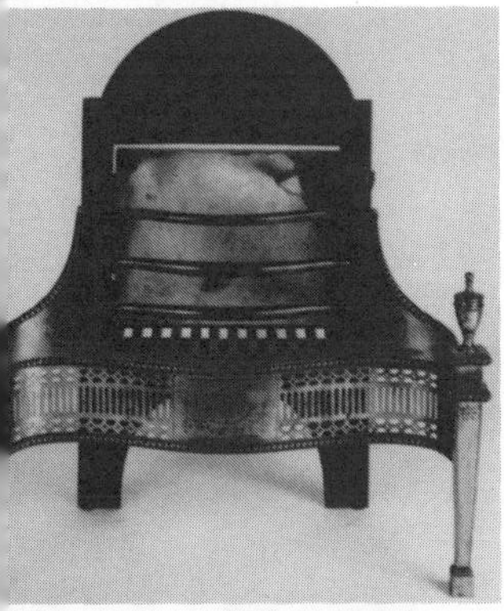

Adam style steel firegrate, the
ed front above a pierced
entine frieze, flanked by
ering uprights, with urn shaped
als, the arched backplate centred
vinged figures at a sacrificial
r, 27in (68cm).
000-4,000

A brass and cast iron serpentine grate, the supports formed as griffin caryatids, on ball and claw feet, 19thC, 33in (83cm).
$3,000-4,000

An Adam style polished steel and cast iron firegrate, with raised backplate of architectural design, 33in (83cm).
$1,500-2,500

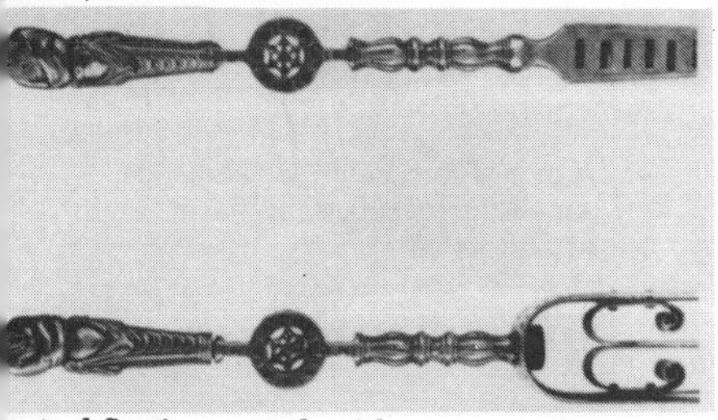

) steel fire irons, each with a
ss grip, 18thC.
0-800

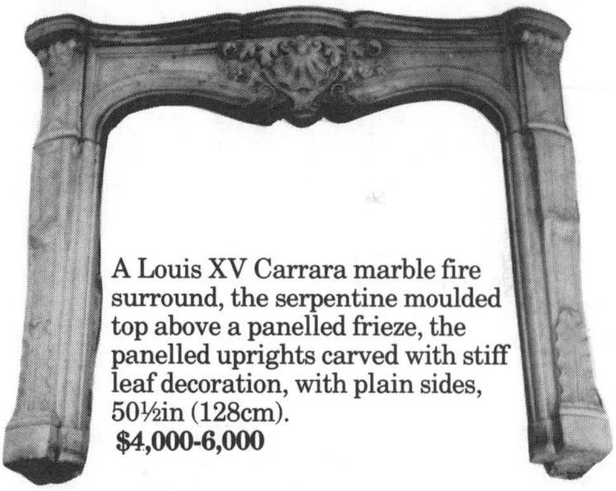

A Louis XV Carrara marble fire surround, the serpentine moulded top above a panelled frieze, the panelled uprights carved with stiff leaf decoration, with plain sides, 50½in (128cm).
$4,000-6,000

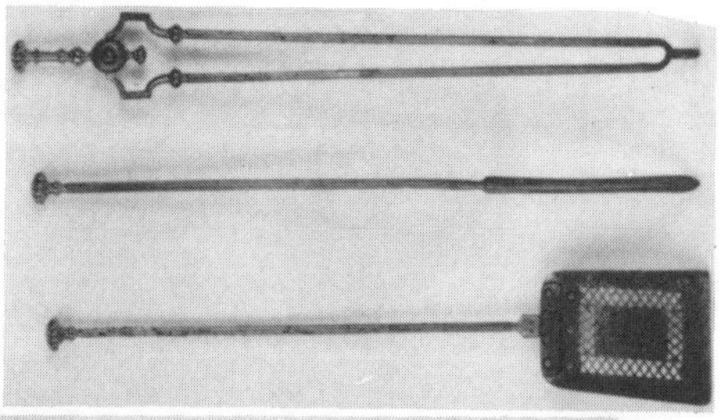

A set of 3 Georgian steel fire irons, the reeded shafts with lobed grips.
$1,000-1,200

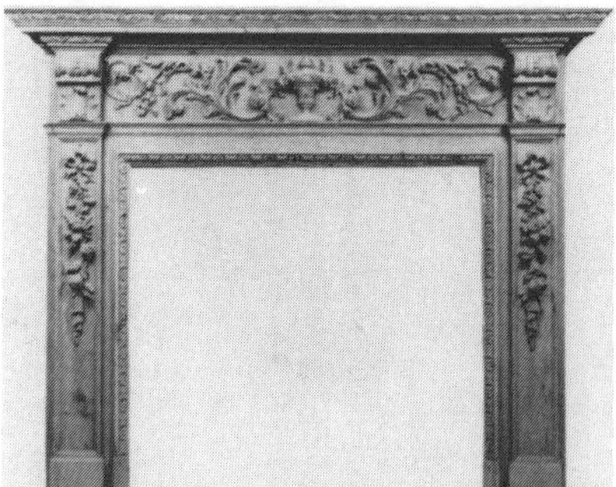

A pine chimneypiece, with frieze centred by an urn with scrolling foliage, the jambs carved with flowers and fruit, mid-19thC, 78½in (200cm).
$5,000-6,000

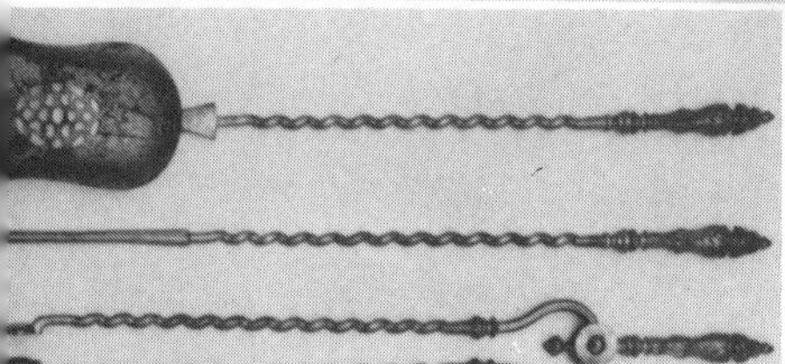

et of steel fire irons, the spirally
ned shafts applied with acanthus
chased ormolu grips.
0-600

A pair of Federal brass andirons, probably New York, c1800, 27½in (70cm) high.
$1,300-1,500

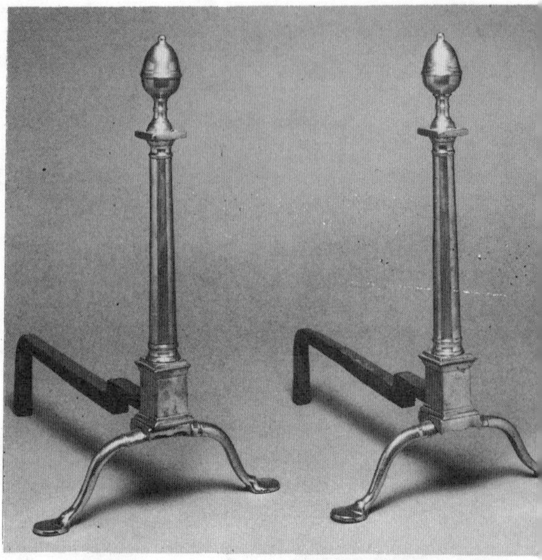

A pair of Federal brass andirons, American, c1810, 19in (48cm) hig
$1,200-1,500

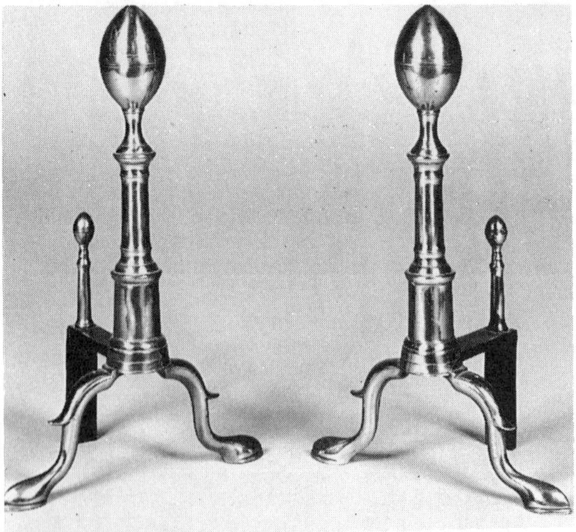

A pair of bell metal andirons, billet bars shortened, American, late 18thC, 17in (43cm) high.
$1,000-1,500

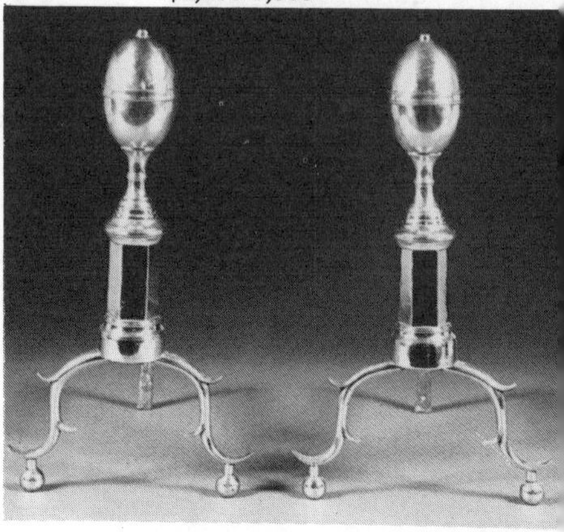

A pair of Federal brass andirons, American, c1800, 21in (54cm) high.
$1,500-2,000

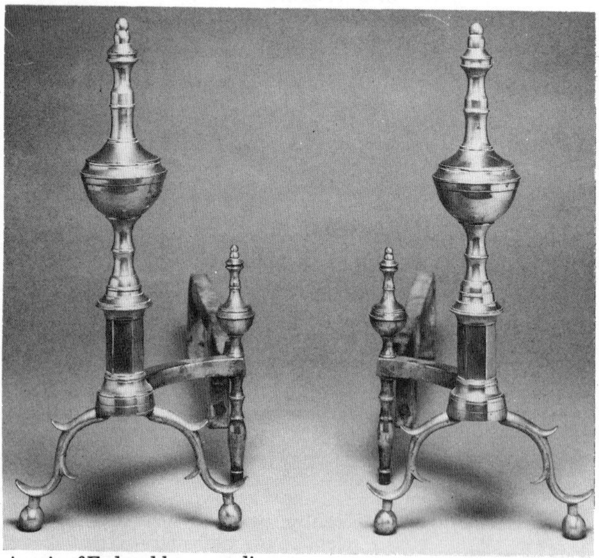

A pair of Federal brass andirons, New York, c1800, 21in (54cm) high.
$2,000-2,500

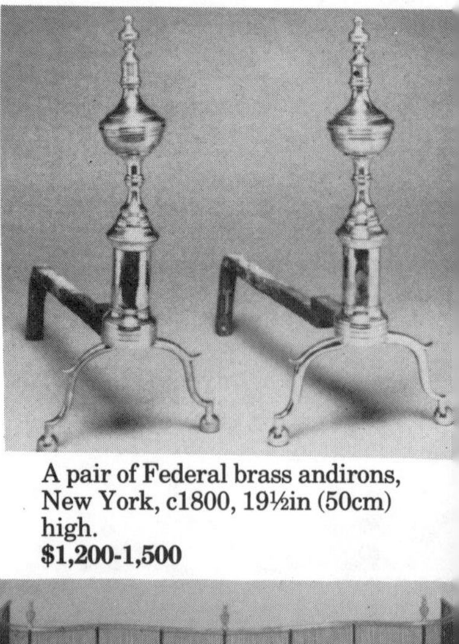

A pair of Federal brass andirons, New York, c1800, 19½in (50cm) high.
$1,200-1,500

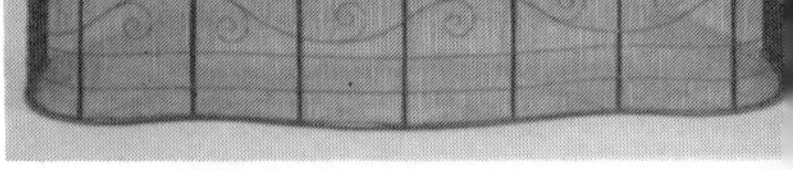

A Federal brass and wire fire fende American, early 19thC, 55in (140cm) wide.
$3,000-4,000

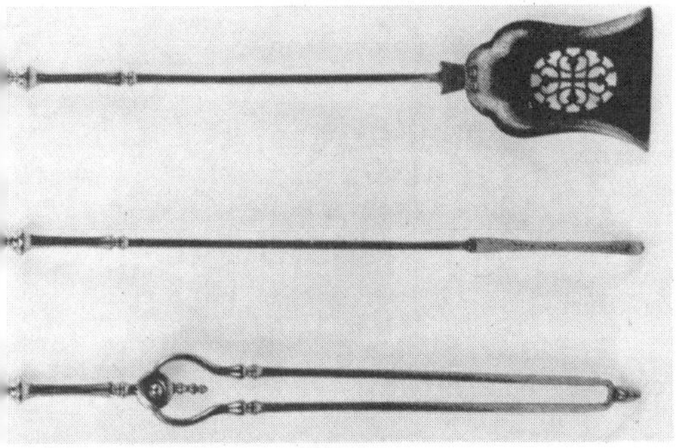

;et of 3 George III polished steel
; irons, with a faceted handle and
ned shaft, 29in (73cm) long.
)0-1,000

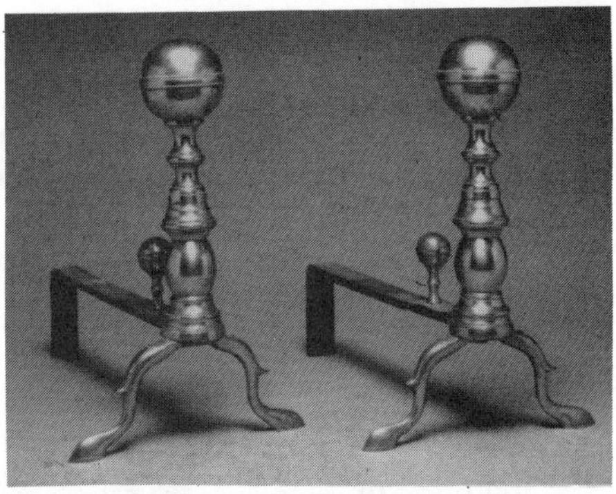

A pair of Federal brass andirons, probably Boston, c1820.
$700-1,000

A pair of beech bellows, boldly carved with a group of Hercules and the Hydra of Lerna, the bronze spout with a chased dragon's head, 40in (101.5cm).
$1,000-1,200

pair of French bronze and ormolu
enets, the bases with foliate
rced bowed frieze panels flanked
fitted uprights, early 19thC, 13in
3cm) high.
,000-4,000

A pair of brass and cast iron andirons, with fluted urn surmounts, on hoof feet, 19thC, 18in (45.5cm) high.
$1,000-1,200

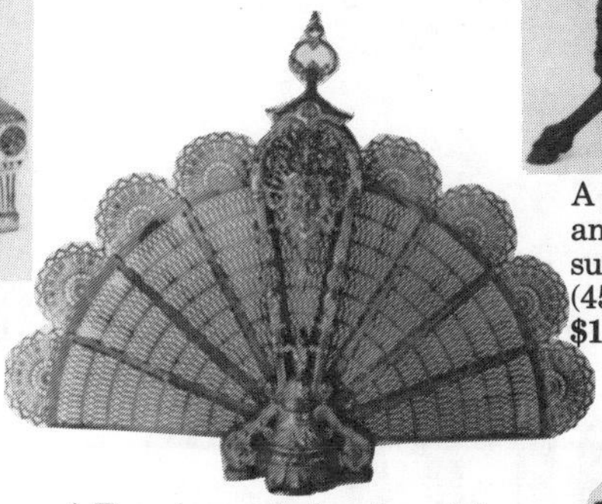

A French ormolu fan shaped fire screen, the frame with a chased satyr mask and entwined dolphin carrying handle, on scroll feet, 19thC, 34in (86cm) high.
$1,000-1,200

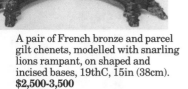

A pair of French bronze and parcel gilt chenets, modelled with snarling lions rampant, on shaped and incised bases, 19thC, 15in (38cm).
$2,500-3,500

A pair of Louis XVI design ormolu and white marble chenets, on fluted D-end bases, with foliate frieze panels, 19thC, 12in (30.5cm).
$700-1,000

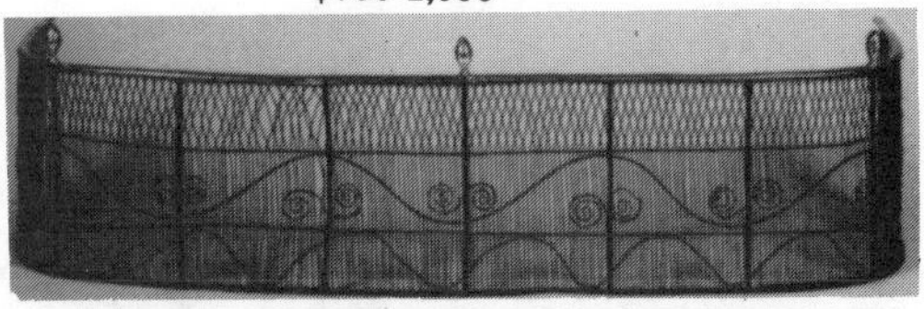

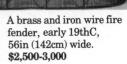

A brass and iron wire fire fender, early 19thC, 56in (142cm) wide.
$2,500-3,000

pair of cast iron figural andirons,
nerican, 19thC, 20in (51cm) high.
,000-6,000

A pair of Federal brass andirons with matching firestools, Boston, c1820, 19in (48cm) high.
$2,500-3,500

Miscellaneous

A brass lion door knocker, 8in (20cm).
$150-200

A brass door lock, 8in (20.5cm).
$200-300

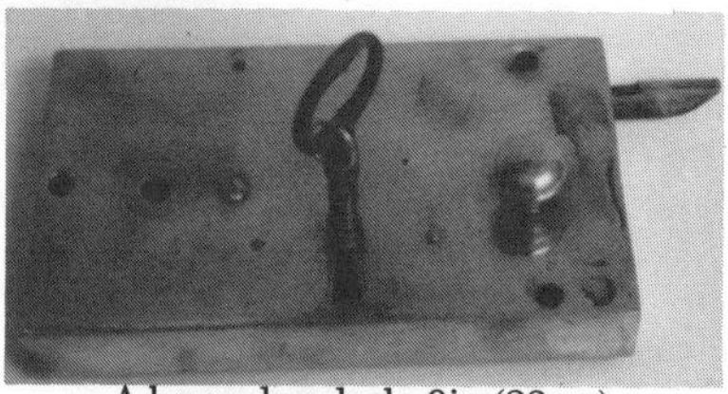

A brass door lock, 9in (23cm).
$200-300

A brass and marble bell pull, 9i (23cm) high.
$150-250

A French door lock, 6in (15cm).
$250-300

A pair of brass all-in-one finger plates, escutcheons and handles, 16in (40.5cm).
$100-200

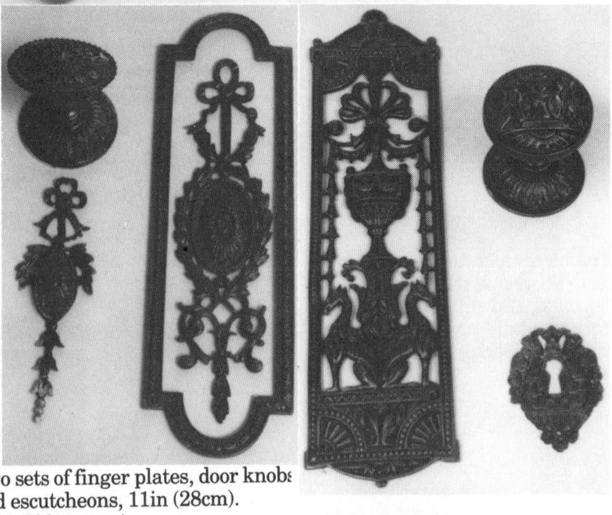

Two sets of finger plates, door knobs and escutcheons, 11in (28cm).
$200-300 per set

A pair of brass locks, 10½in (26.5cm).
$250-300

An Oriental brass door handle, 5in (12.5cm).
$200-300

A green painted tôle fountain, with arcaded gallery and glazed panels, the water spout formed as a gilt flowerhead, 19thC, 39in (99cm).
$3,500-4,000

A Victorian pitc pine pulpit.
$200-400

Miller's is a price GUIDE not a price LIST

noulded copper weathervane, odelled in the form of a running rse, American, 19thC, 31in cm) long.
500-2,000

A moulded copper weathervane, modelled in the form of a rooster on an arrow, traces of gilding, tail cut down, American, 19thC, 25in (63.5cm).
$1,200-1,500

A weathered white marble figure of a young scholar, with raised pince nez, attributes of the arts and science at his feet, 34in (86cm) high.
$3,000-4,000

noulded copper weathervane, odelled in the form of a leaping g, with traces of gilt, L.W. shing & Sons, Waltham, assachusetts, late 19thC, 20in cm) long.
0,000-12,000.

A moulded copper weathervane, in the form of a horse, with traces of yellow paint, American, late 19thC, 34in (86cm) long.
$5,000-7000

A set of 4 lead figures of putti, depicting the Seasons, 19thC, 20in (51cm) high.
$3,000-4,000

A moulded copper weathervane, modelled in the form of a fish, American, early 20thC, now mounted on a barrel base, 18in (46cm).
$1,000-1,500

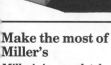

A pair of stone lions, 19thC.
$2,000-2,500

Make the most of Miller's

Miller's is completely different each year. Each edition contains completely NEW photographs. This is not an updated publication. We never repeat the same photograph

A Federal carved and painted pine exterior doorway, disassembled and in need of repair, Trenton, New Jersey, c1800, 120in (330cm) high.
$2,000-3000

A medieval oak door frame.
$1,400-1,600

A stained glass window, coloured in black, yellow and blue, with inscription, 33½in (85cm) wide.
$1,000-1,200

A pair of stone garden urns, 24½in (62cm) high.
$1,200-1,400

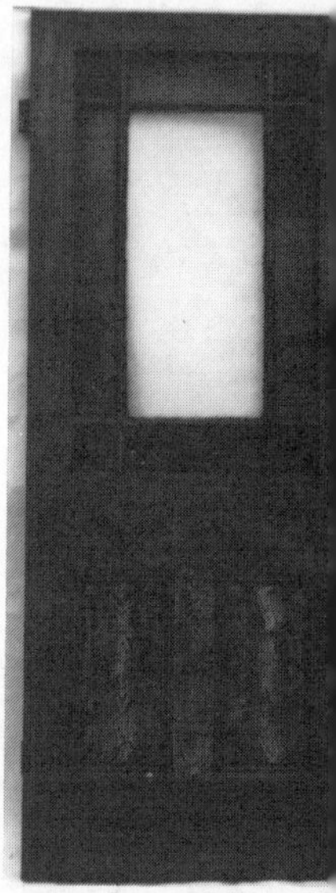

A Victorian pine door, with comb grain design, and blue and red gla 80 by 32in (203 by 81cm).
$130-170

A pair of white painted cast iron garden urns, 31in (79cm).
$1,700-2,000

A Japanese style stone garden lantern, the acorn top above a cylindrical shaft and domed base, 56½in (143cm) high.
$650-800

A pair of lead urns of Adam design, with fluted ovoid bodies and covers with urn finials, 25in (63.5cm) high
$1,600-1,800

A pair of black painted cast iron urns, in the manner of Claude Ballin, 2 horns lacking, 19thC, 31½in (80cm) high.
$6,000-10,000

These urns were taken from designs by Louis XIV's goldsmith, Claude Ballin, the originals remain to this day in the Palace of Versailles.

A Japanese style stone garden lantern with ball finial, circular domed top above an octagonal bo on arcaded base, 36in (91.5cm) hi
$600-800

A pair of marble urns, damaged, 31in (78cm) high.
$1,500-2,500

A ship's lantern, 22in (30.5cm).
$200-300

An Edwardian stained glass lantern, 12in (30.5cm).
$150-250

A pair of sandstone urns, 21in (53cm) high.
$1,600-1,800

A pair of white painted cast iron chairs, with pierced and cast spoon backs, on cabriole legs.
$700-800

A white painted wrought and cast iron bench, with scrolled ends, on X-shaped supports with cross stretcher and octagonal pad feet, 72in (182cm).
$1,000-1,200

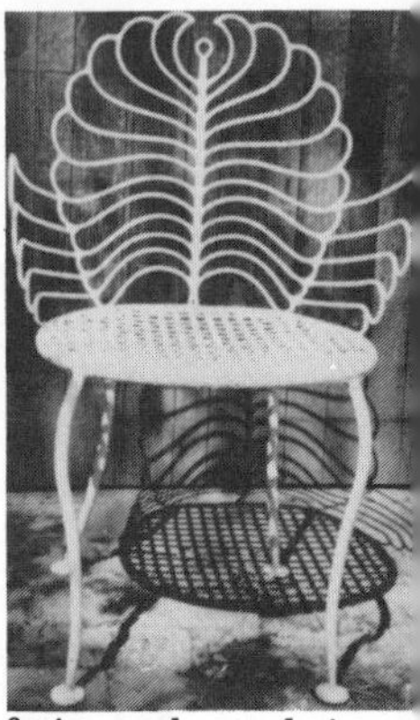

A pair of wire-work armchairs, w winged arm rests.
$500-800

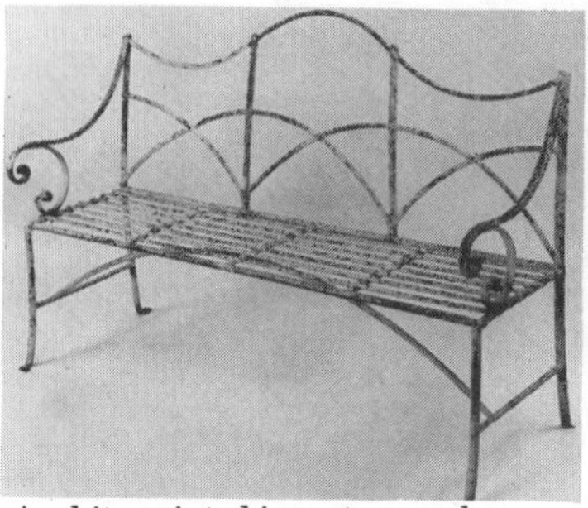

A white painted iron strapwork garden bench, early 19thC, 67in (169cm).
$4,000-5,000

A blue painted wrought iron lyre-shaped seat, with arched feet and scroll frieze, 52½in (133cm).
$1,800-2,500

A wrought iron armchair, with spoon back and spiral spring back and seat, with down curved scroll arm rests.
$200-300

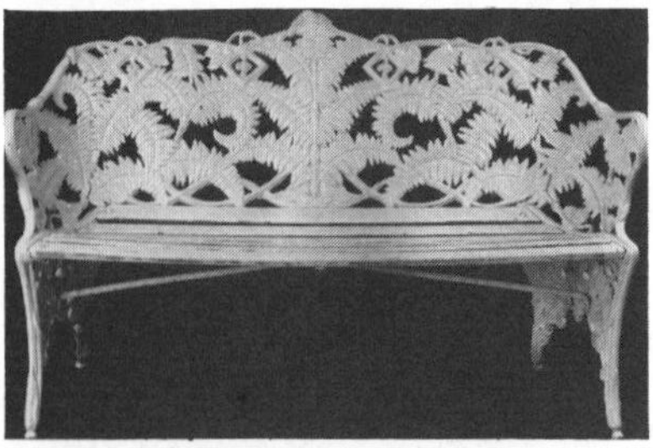

A Victorian Coalbrookdale cast iron garden bench, with fern leaf design, wooden slatted seat, manufacturer's mark on the back, 57in (146cm).
$1,400-1,800

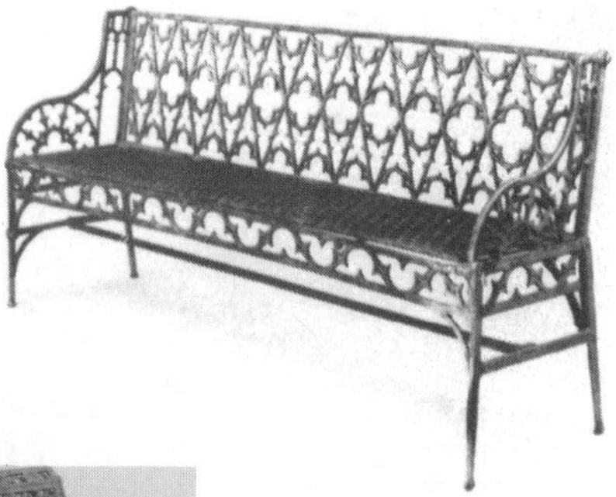

A cast iron and trellis work garden bench, early 19thC.
$2,500-3,000

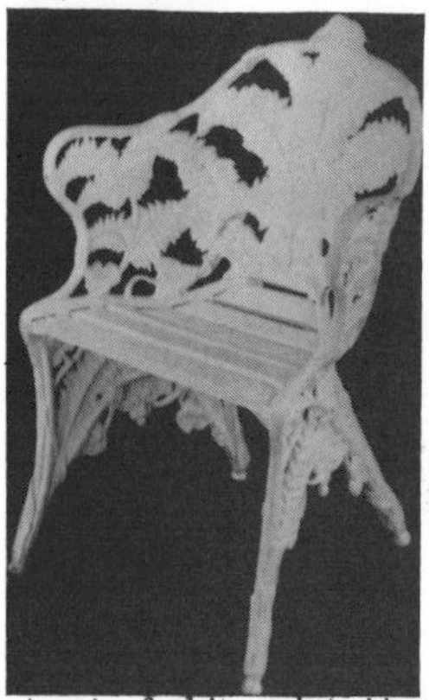

A pair of white painted bronze fern leaf pattern armchairs, with down curved arm rests and wood slatted seats.
$3,000-4,000

A cast iron nasturtium pattern garden bench, the back and ends pierced and cast with foliage, damaged back, 19thC.
$1,000-1,400

A cast iron bench, with pierced back of Indian influence, down curved arms, wooden seat and pierced apron, 19thC, 46½in (117cm).
$2,000-3,000

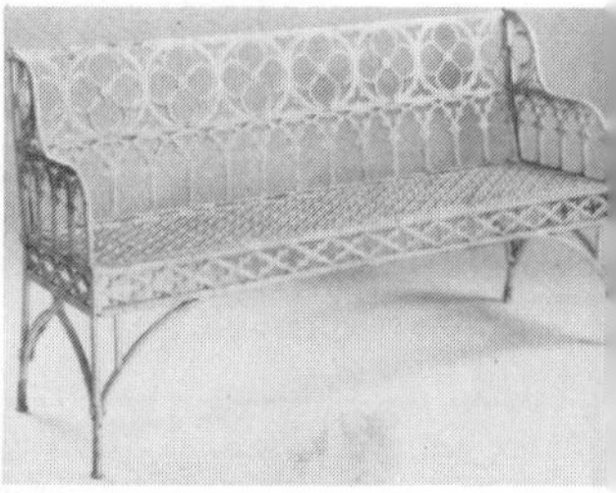

A Regency white painted cast iron garden bench, the seat rail with cusped trellis work, on legs joined by arched stretchers, 61in (155cm).
$3,000-4,000

Two Staffordshire blue terracotta finials, tallest 18in (46cm) high.
$40-60 each

A pair of finial roof tiles.
$300-500

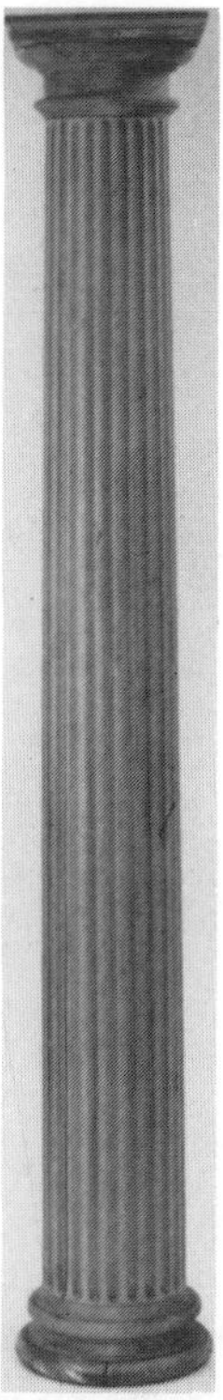

A pair of stripped pine columns, 77in (196cm) high.
$2,000-2,500

. sandstone church stoup, 35in
9cm) wide.
2,000-3,000

A pair of Victorian terracotta gate cappings.
$700-900

A barn cooling vent, 30in (76cm) high.
$160-250

An oak tread staircase, with 18 reads, barley sugar twist uprights around a central turned oak olumn, 139in (354cm).
$3,000-4,000

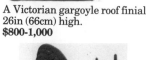

A Victorian gargoyle roof finial, 26in (66cm) high.
$800-1,000

A pair of Georgian porch columns, with traces of gold leaf decoration.
$1,200-1,500

Make the most of Miller's

When a large specialist well-publicised collection comes on the market, it tends to increase prices. Immediately after this, prices can fall slightly due to the main buyers having large stocks and the market being 'flooded'. This is usually temporary and does not affect very high quality items

Mrs. Pankhurst chained to the railings, 68in (172.5cm) high.
$100-200

A brass bell pull, 4in (10cm).
$200-250

Two timber framed dog kennels, 60in (152cm) high.
$200-250

A timber framed gazebo/summer house, with 2 leaded light stained glass windows, single door with matching window, fitted internally with slatted seats, 120in (304cm) high.
$2,000-2,500

A white metal aviary, with tin pagoda top and spike finial, 19thC, 106in (269cm).
$2,000-2,500

A wicker dog kennel with canvas cover, 28in (71cm) high.
$150-250

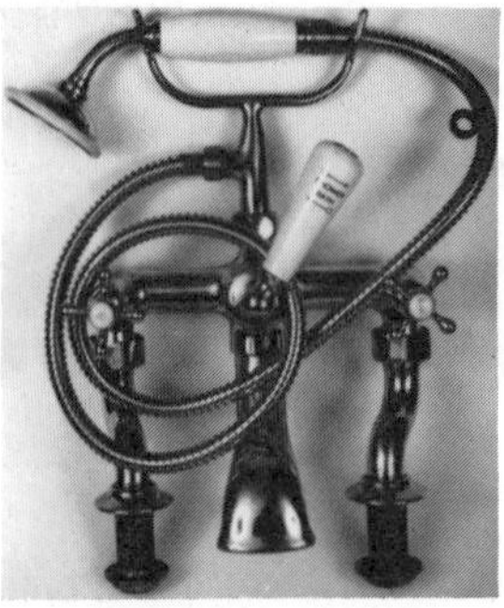

Brass taps and shower unit, c1925.
$180-250

A Victorian W.C. with pump action flush, 17in (43cm) high.
$500-700

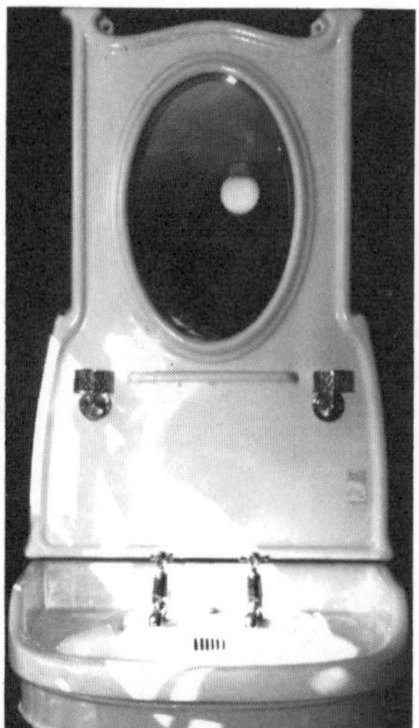

A ceramic sink with mirror, 27in (68cm) wide.
$700-900

A Victorian painted W.C., 'The Puritas Washdown Closet', 16in (41cm).
$1,300-1,500

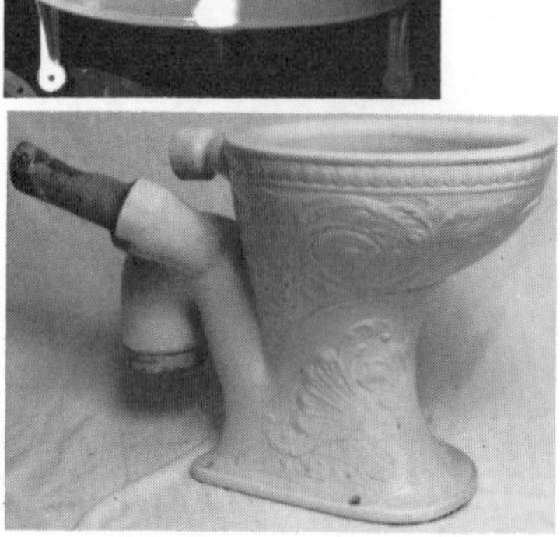

A Victorian Doulton & Co Ltd., W.C., 'the Simplicitas', 17in (43cm)
$1,000-1,200

Make the Most of Miller's

CONDITION is absolutely vital when assessing the value of an antique. Damaged pieces on the whole appreciate much less than perfect examples. However a rare, desirable piece may command a high price even when damaged

LOCKS

,ongcase :locks

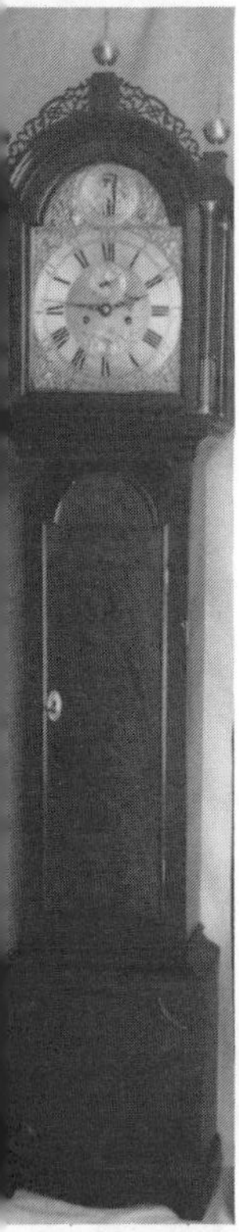

mahogany 8-day ngcase clock, the pillar movement ith a raised apter ring, the conds ring with engraved centre low 12 O'clock, gned by Henry ker of Mallin low West alling), 88in 23.5cm).
0,000-12,000

enry Baker orked from 1768-

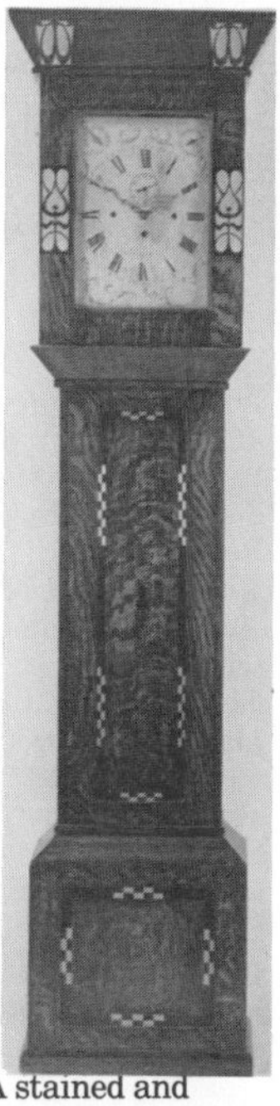

A stained and inlaid oak longcase clock, inlaid with ebonised and pewter scrolling motifs, the panelled front inset with ebonised and mother-of-pearl stringing, the door with central ebonised mouse motif, with multiple chiming movement, the face with black enamelled Roman chapters, 91in (230cm).
$3,000-4,000

A walnut veneered longcase clock, with inlaid decoration, 8-day movement, and brass arch dial, London, 18thC.
$7,000-9,000

A carved oak longcase clock, with arched brass dial, 8-day chiming movement and second hand, maker James B. Banks.
$6,000-7,000

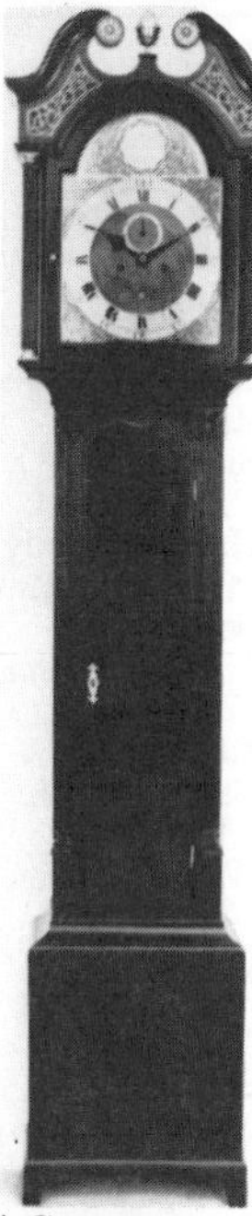

A Georgian mahogany longcase clock, with Edinburgh type case, with 8-day movement, c1780, 86in (219cm).
$11,000-13,000

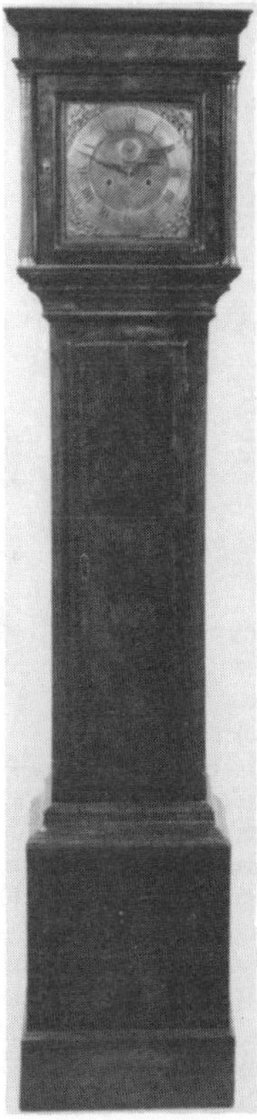

. walnut longcase ock, the trunk oor with erringbone inlay nd crossbanding, e dial with raised apter ring, graved John arnett, Tavistock, e 8-day ovement striking a bell, with endulum and brass cased eights, mid-8thC, 82in 08cm).
,000-5,000

A carved oak longcase clock, with arched brass dial, 8-day chiming movement and second hand, maker James B. Banks.
$5,000-6,000

A mahogany 8-day longcase clock, the trunk inlaid with rosewood, tulipwood and satinwood, the 5-pillar movement with breakarch dial and strike/silent, raised chapter ring and recessed seconds dial and date aperture, the dial signed Nichs. Blondel a Guernsey, 81in (207cm).
$9,000-11,000

A Georgian mahogany longcase clock, by John Ellicot, London, 8-day movement with deadbeat escapement, c1760, 96in (244cm).
$14,000-16,000

HINTS TO DATING LONGCASE CLOCKS

Dials

8in square	to c1669	Carolean
10in square	from c1665-1800	
11in square	from 1690-1800	
12in square	from c1700	from Queen Anne
14in square	from c1740	from early Georgian
Broken-arch dial	from c1715	from early Georgian
Round dial	from c1760	from early Georgian
Silvered dial	from c1760	from early Georgian
Painted dial	from c1770	from early Georgian
Hour hand only	to c1680	
Minute hand introduced	c1663	
Second hand	from 1675	post-Restoration
Matching hands	from c1775	George III or later

Case finish

Ebony veneer	up to c1725	Carolean to early Georgian
Walnut veneer	from c1670 to c1770	Carolean to mid-Georgian
Lacquer	from c1700 to c1790	Queen Anne to mid-Georgian
Mahogany	from 1730	from early Georgian
Softwood	from 1690	from mid-Georgian
Mahogany inlay	from c1750	from mid-Georgian
Marquetry	from c1680 to c1760	from Carolean to mid-Georgian
Oak	always	

A George III mahogany longcase clock, the dial signed John Berry, London, with 5-pillar rack striking movement with anchor escapement and alarm pulley to one side, with securing bracket to the backboard, case restored, 95in (242cm).
$12,000-14,000

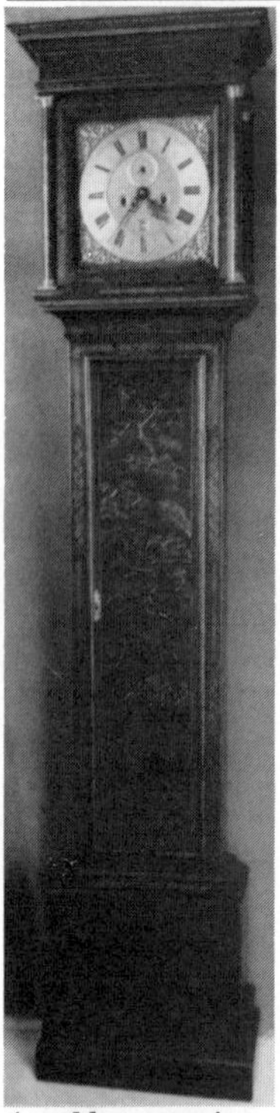

A red lacquer pine longcase clock, with 5-pillar rack striking movement and brass dial, by J. Barron of Hermitage, London, c1720, 85in (216cm).
$11,000-12,000

A mahogany and rosewood crossbanded longcase clock, the painted dial with rolling moon in arch, seconds ring and date aperture, the spandrels depicting the 4 continents, signed Benj. Bell, Uttoxeter, the 8-day movement striking on a bell, with pendulum and 2 weights, 90in (229cm).
$1,800-2,400

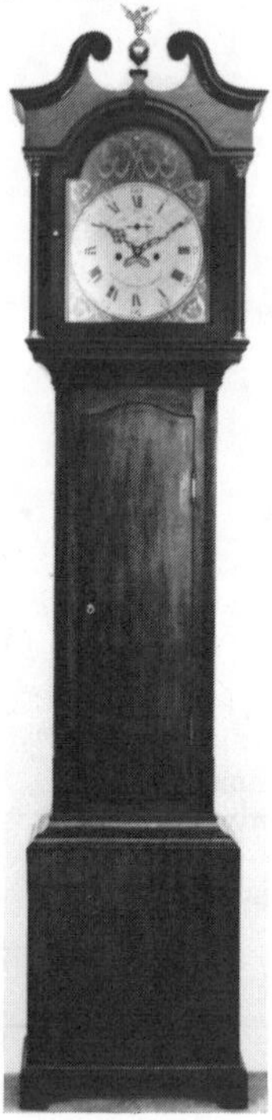

A Georgian mahogany longcase clock, with 8-day movement and painted dial, by Alexander Crawford, Scarborough, c1790, 90in (229cm).
$6,000-7,000

An 8-day chiming clock, with arched brass dial, silvered chapter ring, signed Thos. Bartholomew, London, matt centre with seconds dial, strike/silent and Westminster chimes/chime on 10 bells/chime on 8 bells dials, 110in (279cm).
$5,000-7,000

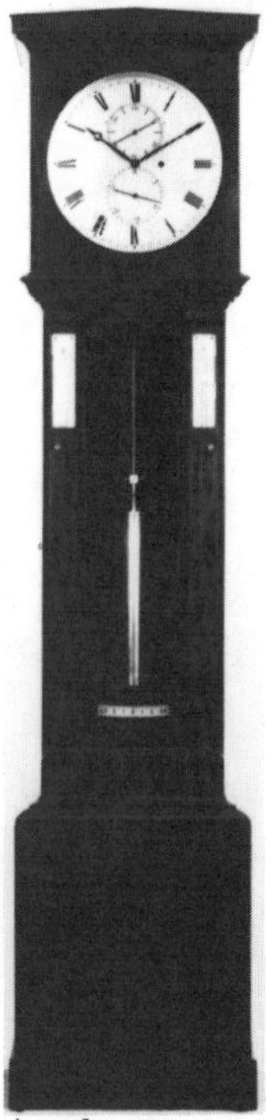

A mahogany longcase clock with barometer, the 8-day movement with deadbeat escapement and maintaining power, by Brysons, Edinburgh, c1860, 85in (216cm).
$12,000-14,000

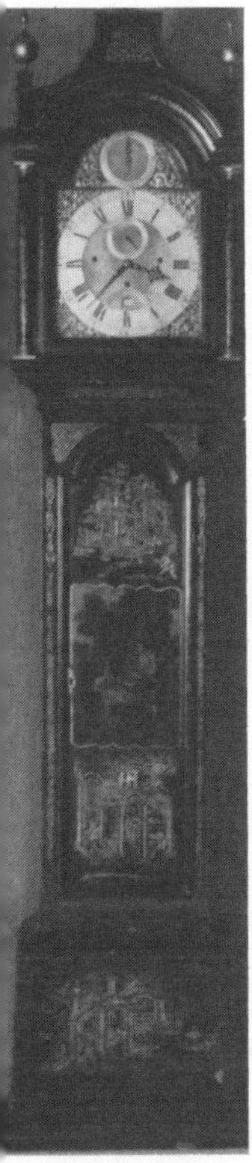

A green lacquer musical longcase clock, the 3-train movement chimes the quarters on 6 bells and plays either a Polonaise or a Minuet on 8 bells and 16 hammers at the hour, the brass dial with tune selection in the arch, seconds ring, date aperture and strike/silent lever, signed Charles Coulon of London, 90in (229cm).
$22,000-26,000

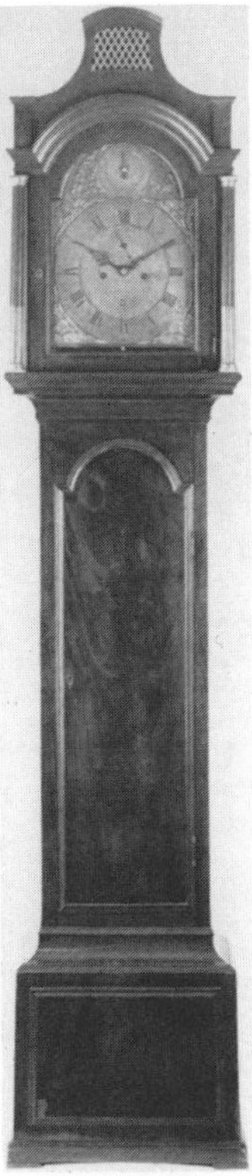

A George III mahogany longcase clock, the arched brass dial with brass chapter ring, signed Ellicott, London, with recessed subsidiary seconds and date aperture and strike/silent, the 5-pillar movement with anchor escapement, 90in (229cm).
$7,000-9,000

A mahogany longcase clock, by Henry Fish, Royal Exchange, London, late 18thC, 94in (238cm).
$10,000-12,000

A walnut longcase clock, the 8-day striking movement with anchor escapement, the brass dial with subsidiary dial and date aperture, silvered chapter ring and chased spandrels, inscribed Dan. Delander, London, early 18thC, 90in (228cm).
$13,000-15,000

Daniel Delander worked in Devereux Court and Fleet Street. He was apprenticed in 1692, free of the Clockmaker's Company 1699 and died in 1733.

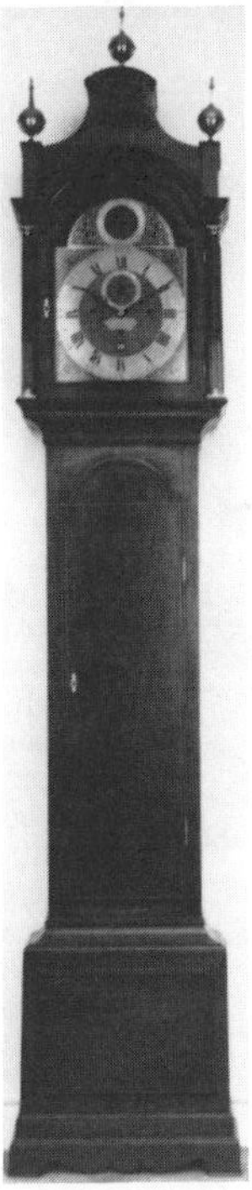

A Georgian mahogany longcase clock, with 3-train movement, quarter striking on 8 bells, by Henry Fish, Royal Exchange, London, c1760, 101in (255.5cm).
$20,000-24,000

A mahogany and chequered strung longcase clock, with arched dial, seconds ring and date aperture, signed R. Fox, Pontypool, the 8-day movement striking on a bell with weights and pendulum, mid-19thC, 86½in (219cm).
$3,000-4,000

A walnut and marquetry longcase clock, the hood with later parcel gilt angle columns, the dial with silvered chapter ring with inscription Chas. Gretton, Londini Fecit, the 5-ringed pillar rack striking movement with anchor escapement, associated and adapted, 82in (208cm).
$5,000-9,000

Price

Prices vary from auction to auction – from dealer to dealer. The price paid in a dealer's shop will depend on:
1) what he paid for the item
2) what he thinks he can get for it
3) the extent of his knowledge
4) awareness of market trends
It is a mistake to think that you will automatically pay more in a specialist dealer's shop. He is more likely to know the 'right' price for a piece. A general dealer may undercharge but he could also overcharge.

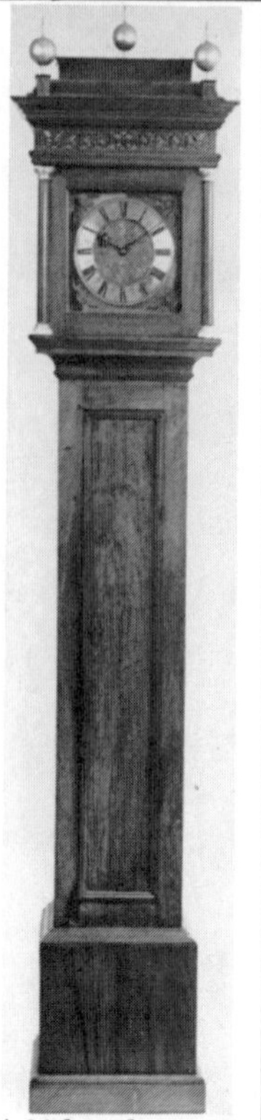

A 30-hour longcase clock, the brass dial signed Thomas Tompion, Londini, with silvered chapter ring, the movement of lantern form, originally designed for verge escapement, now with anchor and long pendulum, the later walnut case with restored hood, 92in (234cm).
$16,000-20,000

A mahogany 8-day longcase clock, the brass dial with raised chapter ring and spandrels and recessed seconds ring, by James Smythe, Woodbridge, 77in (196cm).
$6,000-8,000

An 8-day marquetry longcase clock, by John Wise, London, with square brass dial, anchor escapement and outside locking plate, striking the hours on a bell, 87in (221cm).
$5,000-7,000

A George III mahogany longcase clock, inscribed by John Wyke of Liverpool, with brass dial plate, moonphase aperture, subsidiary dials for seconds and date, the 8-day movement striking on a bell, 95in (241cm).
$7,000-8,000

A George III mahogany longcase clock, the case in the style of Gillows, the dial signed W. Wilson Kendal, the 4-pillar rack striking movement with anchor escapement, 95in (241cm).
$6,000-8,000

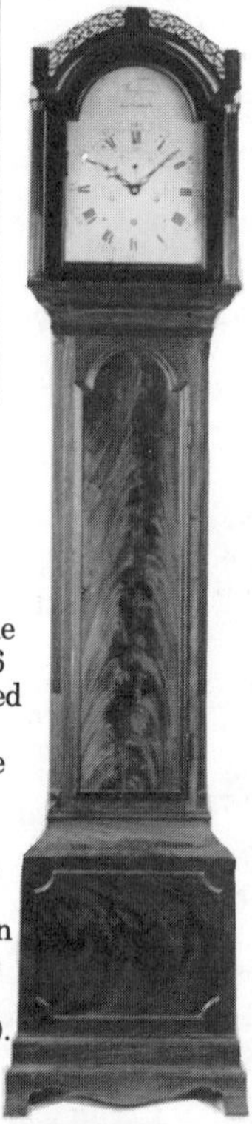

A mahogany month-going longcase clock, the plates united by 6 latched ring turned pillars, outside countwheel strike and anchor escapement, numbered 338 on the backplate, inscribed Tompion London, with late 18thC silvered dial, 86in (218cm).
$20,000-24,000

A mahogany and marquetry longcase clock, with brass dial, raised silvered chapter ring, signed Brounker Watts, London, the 4-ringed pillar movement with inside countwheel striking on a bell, with pendulum and 2 weights, 83in (210cm).
$4,000-6,000

A George III Lancashire mahogany longcase clock, the painted dial signed William Wilson Kendal, the 4-pillar rack striking movement with anchor escapement, 96in (243cm).
$6,000-8,000

Longcase/Tallcase Clocks

In the United States longcase clocks are commonly referred to as "tallcase". Both terms are equally correct and are becoming interchangeable

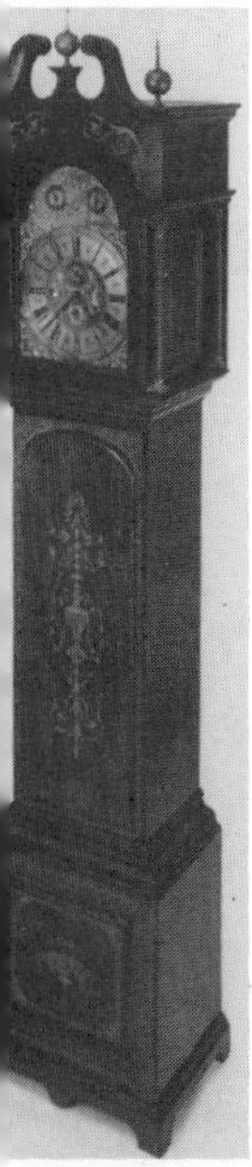

ı 8-day
ıhogany and
.aid longcase
·ck, with silvered
apter ring,
conds dial,
ime/silent and
hittington
ime/
estminster
ime dials in the
ch, the 4-pillar
ovement with
ing, striking and
iming trains,
iming and
iking on 8 bells
d 5 gongs, and
th anchor
capement, in
ahogany case,
ossbanded in
tinwood, 101in
56cm).
,000-8,000

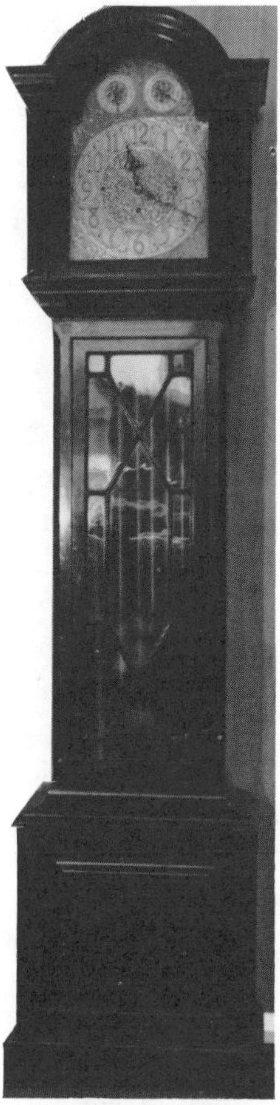

An Edwardian chiming longcase clock on 9 tubular bells, with brass fretwork dial and Arabic numerals.
$6,000-7,000

A mahogany longcase clock, the arched dial with convex centre, signed, with subsidiary seconds and date crescent, rolling moon in the arch, 8-day 4-pillar rack striking movement with anchor escapement, c1800, 93in (236cm).
$4,000-5,000

A lacquered longcase clock, with stylised pagoda top surmounted by a gilt cockerel finial, the dial with raised chapter ring, inner quarter hour ring, the 30-hour posted frame movement with countwheel strike on a bell, 85in (216cm).
$2,500-3,200

A Georgian mahogany longcase clock, with divided dentil moulded pediment and fret carved frieze, stamped Webbs, Gorey.
$3,000-4,000

A George III oak longcase clock, the brass and silvered dial with subsidiary dial and date aperture, and 8-day striking movement, 87in (221cm).
$2,000-3,000

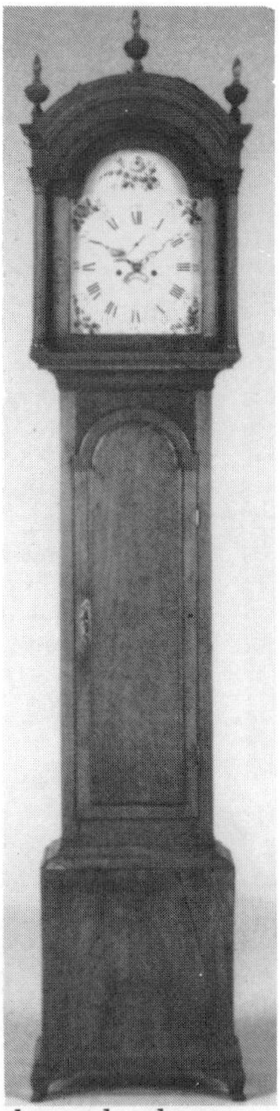

A Federal carved mahogany longcase clock, with white painted dial with Arabic and Roman chapter rings enclosing sweep seconds and calendar day rings, with painted spandrels, 96in (243cm) high.
$13,000-15,000

A walnut and marquetry longcase clock, by F. G. Lubert of Amsterdam, 18thC, 94in (238cm).
$8,000-10,000

An Edwardian mahogany inlaid longcase clock, with brass arch dial, the 3-train chiming movement on 4 gongs.
$5,000-6,000

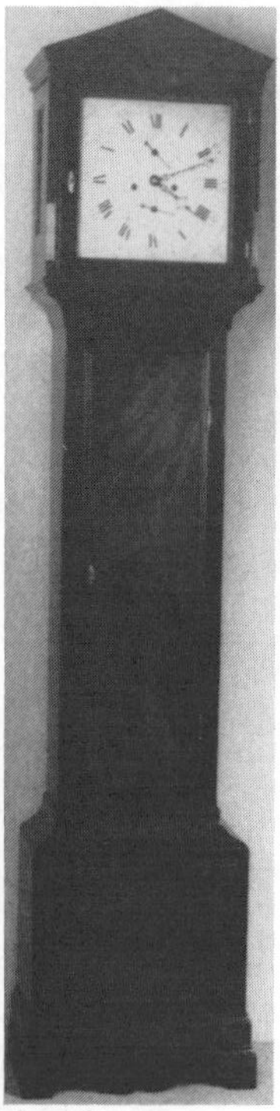

A mahogany longcase clock, the 5-pillar movement with rack strike on a bell, the silvered brass dial with subsidiary dials for seconds and date, London, 83in (210cm).
$10,000-12,000

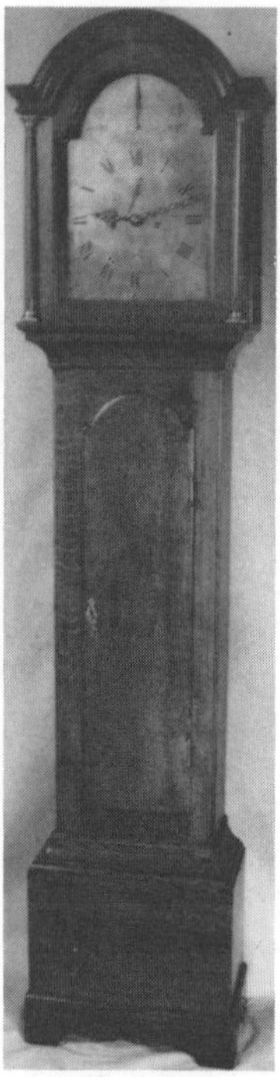

An oak 8-day longcase clock, the 5-pillar movement with engraved flat brass dial with strike/silent regulation, seconds ring and date aperture, 80in (203cm).
$4,000-6,000

Regulators

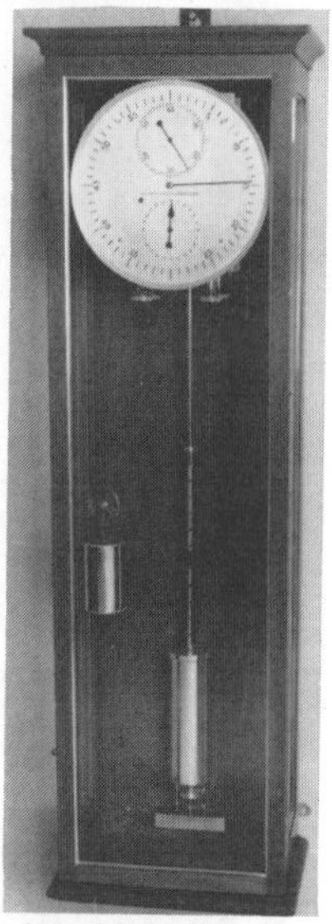

A teak cased wall regulator, by T. Cooke & Sons of London and York, the silvered brass dial with 24-hour ring, the pendulum of Buckneys form of zinc/steel compensation with concentric tubes of zinc and steel pierced out to provide rapid transference of heat and cold, 54in (137cm).
$12,000-14,000

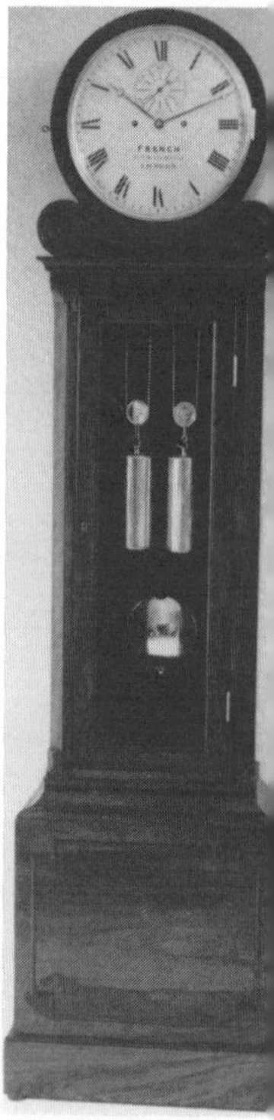

A rosewood striking longcase regulator, the 5-pillar movement with Graham deadbeat escapement, Harrisons maintaining power, the engraved, silvered brass dial signed French, Royal Exchange, London, 75in (190cm).
$10,000-12,000

Santiago James Moore French worked at the Royal Exchange in Sweetings Alley and was a member of the Clockmaker's Company from 1810-40.

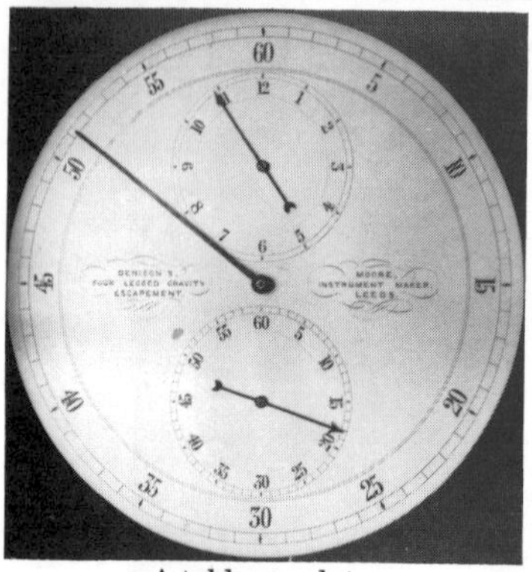

A longcase regulator by Moore of Leeds, the 4-legged gravity escapement mounted externally to the backplate, with 5-spoke wheelwork and side winding, the dial signed, in an oak case with removable hood.
$10,000-12,000

A table regulator with strike on a gong, the case veneered in zebra wood, the movement with lost beat detented escapement mounted externally to the backplate, with silvered brass dial, signed Geo. McLean, Glasgow, mid-19thC, 18½in (47cm).
$10,000-12,000

A George III astronomical longcase regulator, by Richard Roe of Midhurst, with silvered brass breakarch dial with aperture showing annual and zodiaccal calendars, the 2 minute hands showing mean and solar time.
$14,000-16,000

ɪracket Clocks

ı early Regency bracket clock, by
ːdward & Collier, with 2-train
ɔvement, c1815, 16in (40.5cm).
ɪ,000-5,000

late Victorian walnut case
ıiming bracket clock, with silvered
ıapter ring and ormolu dial
amped Goldsmiths Co., Regent
:., London, 35in (89cm), including
:racket.
;,000-6,000

\ George III ebonised striking
ɪracket clock, the dial with white
ːnamel chapter disc and blued steel
ıands, signed Haley & Son, London,
he 5-pillar twin fusee movement
ıow wire lines, with anchor
ːscapement, adapted and
ıssociated, 13½in (34cm).
;4,000-5,000

A George III mahogany verge bracket clock, the twin fusee movement striking and repeating on a bell, signed by William Gatford of Uxbridge, c1770, 17in (43cm).
$24,000-28,000

A mahogany and brass inlaid bracket clock, with painted dial, twin fusee movement with anchor escapement, signed Thos. Glase, Bridgnorth, 19thC, 19in (48cm), with wall bracket.
$1,800-2,500

A mahogany bracket clock, by Gravell & Tolkien, London, numbered 3694, with a 2-train movement striking and repeating on a bell, anchor escapement, the engraved and silvered brass dial with strike/silent regulation, with carrying handles, early 19thC, 25½in (64cm).
$10,000-12,000

An ebony cased bracket clock, with 7in (18cm) brass dial, the 5-pillar 8-day movement with anchor escapement and chain fusee going and striking the hours on a bell, inscribed Robert Halsted, London, restored and altered, early 18thC, 13½in (33cm).
$3,000-4,000

A George III mahogany bracket clock, with strike/silent dial and subsidiary seconds, 2-train movement striking the hours on a bell, inscribed George Jamison, Charing Cross, London, 20½in (52cm).
$6,000-8,000

HINTS TO DATING BRACKET CLOCKS

Dials

Square dial	to c1770	pre-George III
Broken arch dial	from c1720	George I or later
Round/painted/silvered	from c1760	George III or later

Case finish

Ebony veneer	from c1660 to c1850	Carolean to mid-Victorian
Walnut	from c1670 to c1870	Carolean to Victorian
Marquetry	from c1680 to c1740	Carolean to early Georgian
Rosewood	from c1790	from mid-Georgian
Lacquered	from c1700 to c1760	Queen Anne to early Georgian
Mahogany	from c1730	from early Georgian

A George III red japanned striking bracket clock, restored, possibly associated, 18½in (47cm).
$6,000-10,000

A Regency Gothic mahogany bracket clock, the case with brass and ebony line inlay, the repainted dial signed Bentley & Beck, Royal Exchange, London, with strike/silent, the movement by Handley & Moore, 4167, chiming on 8 bells and hour strike on further bell, anchor escapement with micrometer regulated pendulum, adapted, 23in (58cm).
$2,500-3,000

An ebonised bracket clock, by John Berry, London, with pull quarter repeat, verge escapement and calendar to the arch, c1720.
$9,000-11,000

A Georgian mahogany bracket clock, the painted dial signed D. Evans, London, with subsidiaries for date and strike/silent, the twin fusee movement now converted to anchor escapement, 20½in (52cm).
$3,000-4,000

A Victorian 8-day bracket clock with strike and chiming double fusee movement, chiming on 8 bells, the oak case enriched with gilded metal lion mask and foliate mouldings, the silvered dial engraved John Durden, London, 30in (76cm).
$3,000-4,000

A Regency rosewood bracket clock, with 2-train movement striking and repeating on a bell, signed Earnshaw, London, 119 High Holborn.
$2,800-3,500

A Georgian fruitwood striking bracket clock, the dial inscribed John Ellicott, London, the twin fusee movement now wire lines, with pull quarter repeat on 6 bells, now converted to anchor escapement, 15½in (39cm).
$7,000-9,000

A Regency ebonised breakarch brass inlaid bracket clock, the 2-train movement striking and repeating on a bell, with strike/silent regulation, the painted dial signed H. Knight, and numbered 2243, 17in (43cm).
$3,000-4,000

An English bracket clock, by Moginie of Pimlico, with painted dial, raised brass decoration to the front, brass carrying handles and surmounted by a brass ball finial, with 2-train movement, striking and repeating on a bell, 20½in (52cm).
$3,600-5,000

A bracket clock, by Thomas Page, London, with painted dial, 8-day twin wire fusee movement striking on a bell, in mahogany case with brass mounts, early 19thC.
$2,500-3,000

A George III mahogany striking bracket clock, the engraved brass dial plate set with enamelled chapter disc, signed Isaac Rogers, London, 15½in (38cm).
$4,000-5,000

An ebony veneered striking bracket clock, with silvered chapter ring, signed Jno. Le Roux, London, the 5-pillar movement now converted to anchor escapement, 16½in (42cm).
$2,000-3,000

A late George III mahogany miniature bracket timepiece alarm, the engraved silvered dial signed Perigal, Coventry Street, London with central alarm disc, chain fusee movement with verge escapement, pull wind alarm on bell, plain backplate, restored, 9½in (24cm).
$7,000-9,000

An ebonised verge bracket clock, by Wasborn, London, the 2-train movement striking and repeating on a bell and also fitted with an alarm, the dial with mask spandrels, date aperture and mock bob and Dutch style chapter ring, 15in (38cm).
$13,000-15,000

A Regency bracket clock, with brass inlaid rosewood case, the white dial signed Purvis, North Audley Street, Grosvenor Square, with 8-day fusee movement, c1830, 13in (33cm).
$8,000-9,000

An early Victorian papier mâché bracket clock, with glazed enamel dial, the case painted with flowers and highlighted with mother-of-pearl, 30in (76cm).
$1,200-1,500

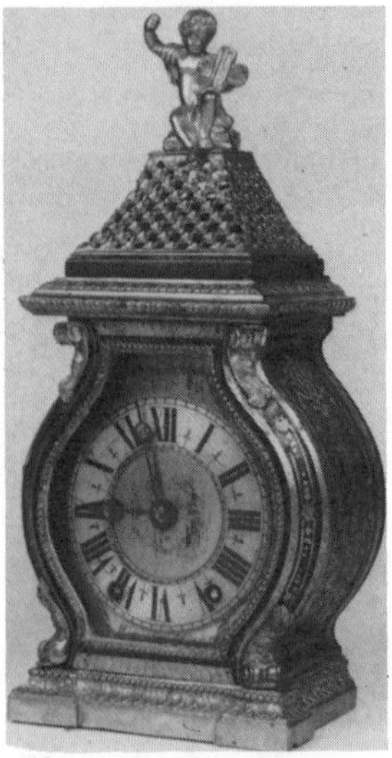

A late Louis XIV scarlet boulle miniature bracket clock, the sides with Bérainesque panels inlaid with pewter and brass, the silvered chapter ring signed Margotin a Paris, the movement with shaped plates, twin going barrels, lantern pinions, rack strike and now converted to anchor escapement, later canopy and finial figure, 14½in (37cm).
$2,000-3,000

Carriage Clocks

An engraved carriage clock, striking and repeating on a gong, signed Aubert & Co., 2 Regent Street, London and numbered 3428, with enamelled dial, c1845, 6in (15cm).
$5,000-6,000

A gilt brass striking carriage clock, with uncut bimetallic balance to lever platform, strike/repeat and alarm on gong, white enamel dial, blued spade hands, subsidiary alarm ring, 6in (15cm).
$1,000-1,200

An 8-day miniature carriage timepiece, in brass case, with white enamel dial, and lever platform escapement, dial cracked, 3in (7.5cm).
$400-500

A carriage timepiece, with white enamel dial, the 8-day movement with platform lever escapement, dial cracked, 4½in (11cm).
$200-300

A silver cased minute repeating carriage clock, the white enamel dial inscribed E. White, 32 Haymarket, London, 3½in (9cm), with travelling case and original key.
$7,000-9,000

A repeating carriage clock, with white enamel dial, the 8-day movement with silvered lever platform escapement striking on a gong, 5½in (14cm).
$800-900

A gilt metal bamboo striking carriage clock, with strike/repeat and alarm on gong, cloisonné enamel dial with birds and bees amidst flowers on a blue ground, 7in (18cm).
$3,000-4,000

A gilt brass month-going carriage timepiece, the ivorine dial with subsidiary seconds at XII, bevelled surround, Corinthian case, composite, 5in (12.5cm).
$1,000-1,200

A brass miniature carriage timepiece, with white enamel dial oval case with scroll handle, 3in (7.5cm).
$1,300-1,500

A repeating alarm carriage clock, in engraved case for the Chinese market, with silvered lever platform escapement and striking on a bell, with the alarm bell in the base, 5½in (14cm).
$2,500-3,000

A silver plated carriage timepiece, with underslung lever platform, single train movement with silvered dial and repoussé panel beneath, in a case with husk chased columns and bands of fluting, the handle with lion masks, c1860, 6in (15cm).
$900-1,200

A miniature silver and enamel arriage timepiece, lever scapement backplate stamped TC, the case decorated with lilac namel over a machined ground, with white borders, 2in (5cm).
1,400-1,600

A French brass carriage clock, with 8-day striking movement and repeat, 7in (18cm), in case.
$800-900

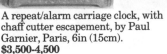

A repeat/alarm carriage clock, with chaff cutter escapement, by Paul Garnier, Paris, 6in (15cm).
$3,500-4,500

A gilt metal quarter striking carriage clock, signed No. 3995, Le Roy & Fils Hgers du Roi Paris, with plain gilt balance to gilt lever platform, quarter strike/repeat on 2 bells, signed enamel dial, c1850, 6in (15cm).
$2,500-3,000

A Drocourt grande sonnerie calendar and alarm carriage clock, with white enamel dial, the 8-day movement with silvered platform lever escapement striking on 2 bells with a change lever in the base, 5½in (14cm), with leather carrying case.
$4,000-5,000

A Continental silver miniature carriage timepiece, with enamel dial, the case decorated with repoussé flowers, marked London 1895, 4in (10cm).
$900-1,200

A French brass grande sonnerie carriage clock, the lever movement chiming on 2 gongs, with push repeat and numbered 24861, with enamel dial, 7in (18cm).
$3,000-4,000

striking carriage clock, with hite enamel dial, 8-day movement ith lever platform escapement triking on a gong, the backplate earing the trademark LF, Paris, in (15cm).
500-700

An 8-day alarm repeating clock, the lever movement striking on a gong, the backplate numbered 10360, and inscribed Leroy & Fils, 13 & 15 Palais Royal, the white enamel dial with subsidiary alarm pointer, 19thC, 6in (12cm).
$2,000-3,000

A gilded French carriage clock, signed L. Leroy et Cie à Paris, numbered 23063, the movement striking and repeating on a gong, 9in (23cm), with leather travelling case.
$6,000-8,000

A gilt brass and engraved grande sonnerie carriage clock, the silvered lever platform stamped No. 308 JS, movement with strike/repeat on 2 gongs, alarm on bell, white enamel dial, the platform by Soldano, 6½in (17cm), with case.
$5,000-7,000

A French gilt brass grande sonnerie carriage clock, chiming on 2 gongs, with alarm and push repeat, numbered 166, with enamel dial, 19thC, 7in (18cm).
$3,000-4,000

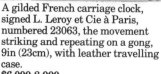

An 8-day repeating carriage clock, the movement striking on a gong with replacement platform, the gilt dial with fretwork and an enamel chapter ring, with gilt brass case, late 19thC, 6½in (16.5cm).
$1,000-1,200

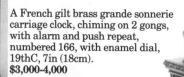

A French carriage clock, with white enamel dial, 8-day movement with lever escapement and bi-metallic compensated balance wheel, striking and repeating on a bell, 6in (15cm), with travelling case.
$2,000-3,000

A French gilt brass carriage clock, the movement with replaced lever platform, striking on a gong, with alarm and push repeat, numbered 3532, the enamel dials with an engraved gilt mask, 19thC, 7½in (19cm), with leather travelling case.
$1,200-1,400

A brass cased carriage clock, with polychrome champlevé enamel panels, with French 8-day striking movement, numbered 2441, 19thC, 7in (18cm).
$1,200-1,400

A gilt brass and porcelain striking carriage clock, 4in (10cm).
$2,500-3,000

A French carriage clock, with alarm, hour and half-hour repeating movement, the white dial with subsidiary alarm dial, late 19thC, 6in (15cm), with travelling case.
$1,200-1,400

A French brass carriage clock, with 8-day movement, 7in (18cm).
$1,200-1,400

lantel Clocks

French brass and silvered mantel ock, the porcelain dial, inscribed attaneo & Co., Paris, with floral orcelain panel below, the 8-day ovement striking on a gong, 15in 8cm).
;00-900

A Louis XV ormolu mounted kingwood mantel clock, the enamel dial signed Baret a Brevanne, later movement, reveneered, 17½in (44cm).
$1,200-1,400

A French mantel clock, veneered with rosewood and decorated with floral inlay and boxwood stringing, the 2-train movement with silk suspension and countwheel strike on a bell, signed Dupont of Paris, and numbered 600, mid-19thC, 9½in (24cm).
$1,800-2,500

A South German mahogany cuckoo mantel clock, with cuckoo in arch, white painted dial, the twin going barrel movement striking on a gong, stamped S. Kansrer, Furtwangen, 19in (46cm).
$1,200-1,400

A Regency mahogany and brass inlaid mantel timepiece, the white enamel dial signed Saddleton, Lynn, 11in (28cm).
$1,300-1,400

A French striking electric mantel clock, inscribed A.T.O. J. Bouyssou Cahors, the movement with curved soft iron core pendulum oscillating between 2 coils, the electro-magnetic striking system mounted on the backplate striking on a bell, 13½in (34cm).
$1,200-1,500

A Victorian mahogany mantel clock, the white painted dial inscribed Yonge & Son, Strand, London, the twin fusee movement with shaped plates and engraved border, striking on a bell, some damage and repairs, 18½in (47cm).
$2,500-3,500

A Louis XV style mantel clock, the gilt dial signed Gorohé Paris, the 8-day movement numbered 541 with outside countwheel striking the hours and half-hours on a bell, the back plate also signed, the case veneered in tortoiseshell inlaid with cut brass and with gilt metal mounts, early 19thC, 22½in (56cm).
$1,800-2,000

Federal mahogany pillar and :roll mantel clock, labelled Eli erry & Sons, Plymouth, onnecticut, c1820, 31in (79cm) igh.
2,000-2,500

A French mantel clock, with porcelain panels, the 2-train movement striking on a bell, stamped Japy Freres Medaille d'honneur, initialled F & PF and numbered 111, 12in (30.5cm).
$4,000-5,000

A French mantel clock, by M. Roy, Paris, with 8-day striking movement, the ormolu case mounted with 13 Sèvres porcelain panels, mid-19thC, 20in (51cm), on giltwood plinth.
$4,000-5,000

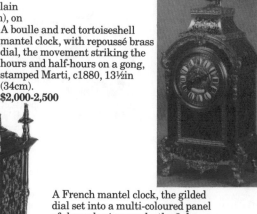

A boulle and red tortoiseshell mantel clock, with repoussé brass dial, the movement striking the hours and half-hours on a gong, stamped Marti, c1880, 13½in (34cm).
$2,000-2,500

A French mantel clock, the gilded dial set into a multi-coloured panel of champlevé enamels, the 8-day movement striking the hours and half-hours on a bell and signed R & C London & Paris, No. 569, late 19thC, 9½in (24cm).
$2,000-3,000

A French ormolu and Sèvres style porcelain mantel clock, the 8-day striking movement stamped Rollin a Paris, No. 436, 19thC, 15in (38cm), on an ebonised base, under a glass dome.
$2,000-3,000

A Federal mahogany mantel clock, with white painted dial and gilt spandrels above an églomisé panel, restoration to églomisé, repair to crest, labelled Seth Thomas, Plymouth, Connecticut, early 19thC, 29in (74cm) high.
$1,500-2,000

A French ormolu mantel clock, by Stainville & Robin, Paris, c1850, 19in (48cm).
$700-800

A French mantel clock, the movement with countwheel strike on a bell, stamped Vincenti et Cie on the backplate and signed in full Thomas a Paris, c1840, 8½in (21cm).
$1,500-1,700

A French white marble and ormolu mounted mantel clock, on marble plinth with cupids drinking from a fountain, 19thC, 15in (38cm).
$1,800-2,500

A French ormolu and white marble mantel clock, the enamel dial with pierced gilt hands, 19thC, 27½in (70cm).
$2,500-3,000

An Empire style ormolu and bronze mantel clock, the frieze with Apollo in his chariot, the movement signed 8829 3 9 and dated 1889, 15in (38cm).
$600-800

A Louis XV style white marble and ormolu mounted lyre-shaped clock, with white enamel and swagged dot dial and swinging paste-set bezel, the 8-day movement striking on a bell, 16½in (42cm).
$3,000-4,000

Charles X mahogany and ormolu ounted mantel clock, the silvered apter ring with gilt foliate cast ezel and centre, pierced grille low, the 8-day movement striking a bell, 16in (41cm).
1,000-1,400

A French red tortoiseshell and boulle mantel clock, with gilt cast ormolu mounts, with gilt cast dial, the 8-day movement striking on a bell, 18in (45.5cm).
$1,200-1,400

A French gilt mantel clock, with white enamel dial, with blue numerals and blued steel moon hands, the 8-day movement with countwheel strike on bell, bell and pendulum lacking, 18in (46cm).
$600-800

A French ormolu mantel clock, with enamel dial, 19thC, 21½in (54cm).
$1,600-2,000

A French mantel clock, with silvered brass dial, signed Examd by Barraud and Lunds, 44 Cornhill, London, No. 4274, in a walnut case, 10½in (27cm).
$2,000-3,000

French Third Empire bronze antel clock, the 8-day movement riking on a bell, inscribed J.B. elettrez, 62 Rue Charlot, Paris, ith a white enamel dial, the case ith a Roman Emperor standing by plinth, above a classical frieze, 9thC, 21in (53cm).
400-600

A French ormolu and porcelain mantel clock, on giltwood base, 19thC, 14in (35.5cm), with an oval ebonised base under a glass dome.
$1,800-2,000

A French ormolu and enamel mantel clock, the enamel dial with pierced gilt mask, the case with bowed front flanked by turned and decorated Corinthian columns, 19thC, 12in (30.5cm).
$2,000-2,500

Lantern Clocks

A brass wall lantern clock, inscribed Robt. Higgs London, the 30-hour weight driven movement with verge escapement and alarm, 8in (20cm).
$2,000-2,500

A 2-train full size spring-driven lantern clock, with ting tang quarter strike on 2 bells, with engraved dial and raised chapter ring, late 19thC, 15½in (38cm).
$2,000-3,000

An English lantern clock by Barnard Dammant of Colchester, the engraved dial with raised chapter ring, now fitted with 2-trai chain fusee movement, early 18th 15in (38cm).
$2,000-3,000

Skeleton Clocks

A brass cathedral skeleton clock, on white marble base with bun feet, the silvered chapter ring with Roman numerals, the 6 spoke movement with chain fusee and passing strike on a bell, 19thC, 21in (53cm), with glass dome.
$1,600-1,800

A brass skeleton timepiece,with silvered chapter ring, the fusee movement with 6 spoked wheels and anchor escapement, on 4 turned supports under a glass shade, on later ebonised base, 19thC, 15in (38cm).
$1,200-1,500

An English twin fusee scroll frame skeleton clock, striking on a bell mounted above the movement, with engraved and silvered brass chapter ring, with glass dome and brass inlaid rosewood base, 19thC, 17in (43cm).
$5,000-6,000

A chain fusee skeleton timepiece with 7 turned frame pillars with dished brass collets, 6 spoke wheel work and passing strike on a bell, with engraved and silvered chapter ring, on a rosewood base, 18½in (46cm).
$2,500-3,000

A skeleton clock, with plain engraved and silvered brass chapter ring, on a rosewood base, 14in (35cm).
$2,500-4,000

A brass skeleton clock, inscribed 'George Orpwood, 1838, Improved Lever', with single train fusee movemer and lever escapements, 19thC, 9½in (24cm).
$1,500-2,000

An unsigned skeleton clock, possibly Strutt & Wigstons, 13in (33cm), on burr elm base.
$9,000-10,000

Wall Clocks

An English fusee wall clock with heavy moulded cast brass bezel and mahogany surround, 12in (31cm) painted dial, original ground signed by Cohen of Hastings, c1830, 14½in (36cm).
$1,400-1,800

An English fusee wall clock, with painted dial and original ground signed Brown, 104 Praed St, Paddington, (London), 14½in (37cm).
$1,500-1,800

HINTS TO DATING WALL CLOCKS

Dials

Square	to c1755	George II or later
Broken arch	from c1720 to c1805	early to late Georgian
Painted/round	from c1740	George II or later
Silvered	from c1760	George III or later

Case finish

Ebony veneer	from c1690	to William and Mary
Marquetry	from c1680 to c1695	from Carolean to William and Mary
Mahogany	from c1740	from early Georgian
Oak	always	

wall clock with alarm, 9½in (cm) engraved and silvered brass l with centre sweep minute hand, ur and alarm hands, signed De La lle & Christie, Cannon St, ndon, in rosewood drum case, ½in (33cm) diam.
,000-5,000

mes and Thomas De La Salle corded as working in Cannon reet 1816-40 and William Christie London 1825-40.

An inlaid mahogany wall clock with rosewood crossbanding and double brass stringing, the silvered brass dial signed George Muston, Small Street, Bristol, c1840, 25½in (65cm).
$3,000-4,000

A striking Act of Parliament clock, with black lacquered trunk, signed Ino.Wilson, Peterborough, the door decorated with gilt chinoiserie, the 8-day movement striking on a bell with anchor escapement, 18thC, 56½in (142cm).
$3,000-4,000

An Act of Parliament clock by John Watts of Guernsey, 1777, the five-pillar movement with anti-clock wind, 4 wheel train, and counterbalance for the hands, with oval brass cased weight, 48in (122cm).
$14,000-16,000

A Regency single fusee drop trunk wall clock, with brass stringing and brass inlay, the movement with shaped plates and convex painted dial with Roman numerals on the original ground, with convex brass bezel, 25in (64cm).
$2,000-3,000

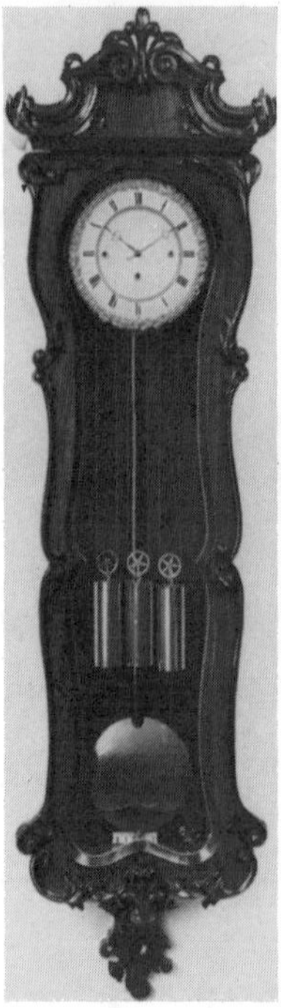

A grande sonnerie Vienna wall clock, the rosewood and ebonised case decorated with carved scrolls, with enamel dial, pierced steel hands, triple weight movement with deadbeat escapement, 19thC, 49in (123cm).
$7,000-8,000

A Vienna wall clock by Gustav Becker, with 2-part dial, striking movement in elaborate carved walnut case, 58in (145cm).
$1,000-1,200

A Dutch inlaid staartklock, with 11in (28cm) embossed dial, anchor escapement, countwheel striking and alarum work, the oak case inlaid with birds and flowers, the break arch hood flanked by pilasters with Corinthian capitals, 49½in (124cm).
$3,500-4,500

A French clock garniture, 8-day movement with out countwheel striking on a b stamped Villamesens, Pa 19thC, the clock 20in (51
$2,000-3,000

Garnitures

A Charles X Sienna marble and bronze mounted composite clock garniture, surmounted by a bronze group depicting The Oath of Horatio, the gilt dial with engine turned centre, moon hands, the 8-day movement with outside countwheel strike on a bell and silk suspension, the clock 19in (48cm).
$4,000-5,000

A French ormolu cloc garniture, with white enamelled dial, countwheel striking hours and half-hours a bell, flanked by a pair of 2-light candela 19thC, the clock 11in (28cm).
$1,500-1,800

A Victorian g spelter clock garniture, wi printed Limo panels, with French 8-day 2-train movement, c1870, clock 16½in (42cm)
$1,000-1,200

A French white marble and gilt metal mounted composite clock garniture, the 8-day movement with outside countwheel strike on a gong, the clock 16in (40.5cm).
$900-1,000

A French clock garniture, with 8-day striking movement, white enamel dial and heavily decorated ormolu case with Sèvres porcelain flowered panels, 19thC, the clock 17½in (43cm), with matching candelabra.
$5,000-6,000

Louis XVI style white marble
lock garniture, with gilt bronze
ounts and French drum
ovement, late 19thC, the clock
4in (35.5cm).
1,600-2,000

A French four-hour régulateur de table, the twin going barrel movement striking on bell with 3-rod grid iron pendulum, the enamel dial signed Leroy et fils Pals, Royal Grie, Montpensier 13-15 Paris, 211 Regent Street London, 22in (56cm).
$6,000-7,000

A Japanese double-foliot weight-driven table clock, in brass case, the bronzed chapter ring with Japanese numerals, the twin verge movement with countwheel strike on bell, one heavy brass-cased weight, 26in (66cm).
$5,000-6,000

able Clocks

Japanese table clock in glazed
itan wood case, the gilt dial with
gle steel hand, adjustable
apter ring and 2 date apertures,
verge movement surmounted by
lance wheel and bell, with chain
see going and spring barrel
iking train with outside
untwheel, 19thC, 7½in (19cm), in
ed of restoration.
,000-8,000

A South German rococo table clock, with rocaille carved giltwood frame, the dial with pewter chapter ring, front swinging pendulum to verge escapement, above twin going barrel movement, with twin countwheel quarter strike on 2 vertically planted bells, 21in (53cm).
$3,500-4,500

iscellaneous

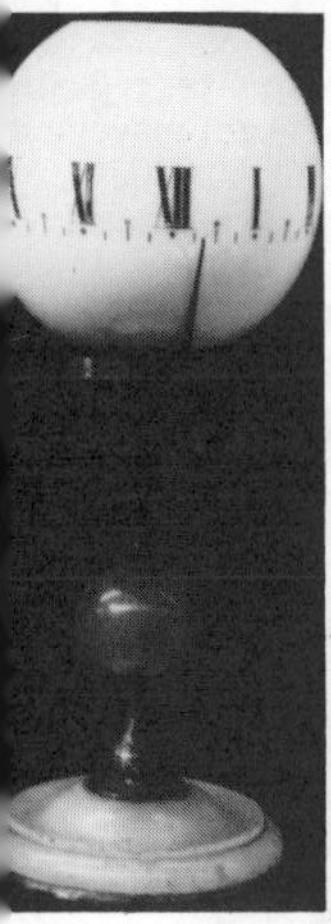

A Victorian nightlight clock, with glass shade on alabaster and brass pillar, 9½in (24cm).
$450-550

An American wagon spring clock of 8-day duration, the movement powered by a laminated spring, by Birge & Fuller, Bristol, Connecticut, U.S.A. signed on the movement, 26in (66cm).
$5,000-6,000

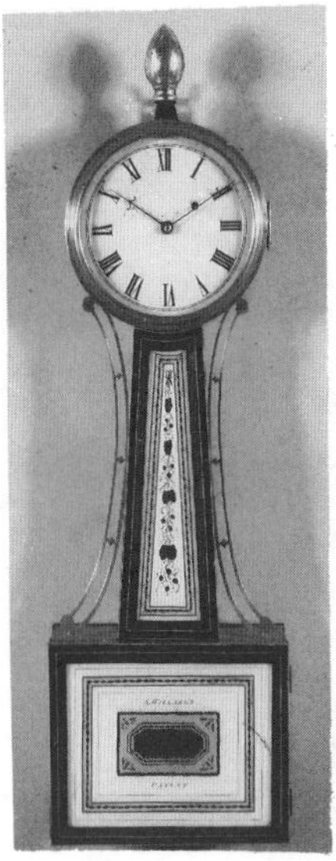

A Federal inlaid mahogany églomisé banjo clock, with gilt acorn finial, the églomisé panel inscribed S. Willard's patent, bottom base board replaced, Massachusetts, early 19thC, 33in (84cm) high.
$4,500-5,500

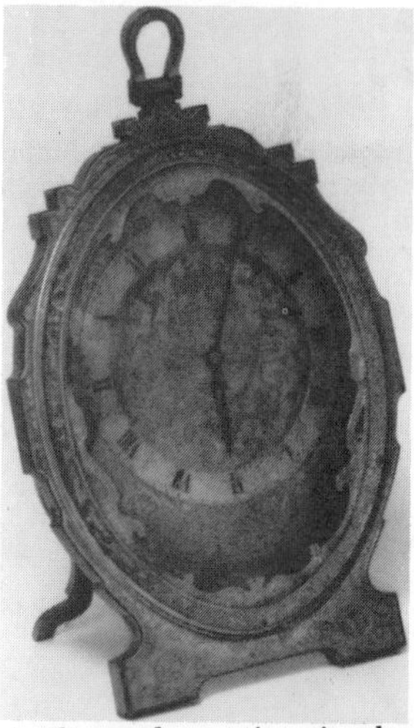

A gilt metal strut timepiece by Thomas Cole, with silvered dial engraved with fruit and scrolls, retailer's Tessier & Son, the case engraved and numbered 971, 19thC, 6in (15cm).
$1,500-1,600

A French exhibition piece, with steel frame, hour striking train with 24 hour countwheel on the right, in a glazed brass framed case, mid-19thC, 54in (136cm).
$18,000-20,000

A gilt timepiece and barometer desk set, with engraved gilt dial plate, the enamelled dial with Roman and Arabic numerals, with timepiece movement and platform lever escapement, the barometer flanked by 2 thermometers with Fahrenheit and Centigrade scales, 7in (17cm).
$800-1,000

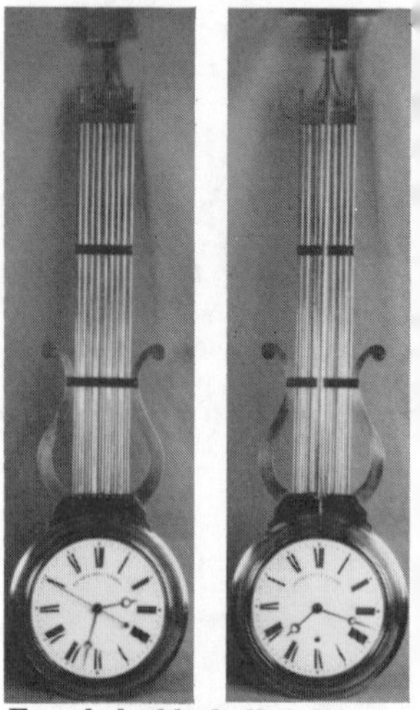

A French double dialled shop window clock, signed C.H. Chaumont a Paris, the 2 enamelled 10in (25cm) dials surrounded by a heavy brass beze 51in (128cm).
$13,000-14,000

A steam hammer clock in gilt brass and bronzed case, the silvered dial with raised Arabic numerals, the two-train movement striking on a bell, movement defective, 19thC, 18in (46cm).
$3,000-4,000

A French automaton clock in the form of a stern of a ship, the two-train movement striking on a gong which bears the stamp of S. Marti et Cie, and Medaille d'Or G.L.T. Brt. S.G.D.G. Paris, c1880, 11½in (29cm).
$5,000-7,000

Watches

A gold pair cased quarter repeatir cylinder watch, the gilt movemen signed Allam London 2620, diamond endstone to engraved masked cock, steel cylinder, brass 'scape wheel, repeating via 2 hammers on bell, gilt dust cover white enamel dial, gold arrow hands, inner case stamped TH, London 1808, 5.2cm.
$1,400-1,800

A lever watch, signed Robert Cocker, Preston, No. 303, in plain silver open face case, hallmarked Chester 1867, 6.8cm.
$1,400-1,500

A gold pair cased ruby cylinder watch, signed Alexr. Cumming, London 834, both cases plain, London 1771, casemaker IR, 5.4cm.
$4,000-5,000

A gold commemorative coin watcl inscribed on reverse, the milled ed with pushpiece to reveal the watc movement, with brushed gilt dial signed Garrard, 1980, 3.4cm, wit fitted box.
$2,000-3,000

gold fusee lever watch, with gilt
-plate movement, signed W. Davis
Sons, No. 12580, 84 King William
:reet, City, London, in plain case
ith milled band, London 1860,
1cm.
,000-1,200

A gold duplex watch, the gilt movement signed Desbois & Wheeler, London No. 2968, blued steel spring with bimetallic wishbone compensation curb, gilt dust cap, white enamel dial, open faced consular case, London 1818, casemaker DW, 5.6cm.
$1,200-1,400

An 18ct gold lever pocket watch, in engine turned hunter case, the white enamel dial signed Charles Frodsham, numbered 03384ADFMSZ, 5.5cm.
$1,500-1,600

An 18ct. gold lever pocket watch with stop mechanism, in plain consular case, with gold hands, signed Frères Sinderby, London, with rack lever escapement and jewelled pallets, some damage, late 18thC, 5.3cm.
$1,400-1,600

silver pair case verge pocket
atch in repoussé outer case with
lded cast decoration, the cracked
hite enamel dial with letters
rming the name Robert Carns, the
lge of the backplate signed Richd.
vingham, London, the inner case
allmarked London 1777, 5cm.
,000-1,200

A gold verge watch, signed Thomas Revis, Bedford, hallmarked London 1814, 4.8cm.
$1,200-1,400

A sector watch, in white metal keyless case, with gold hands with jump-back action, the frosted gilt movement inscribed Record Watch Company Tramelan, 5.9 by 7cm.
$2,500-3,000

. lever deck watch, with plain
ickel case, signed H. Williamson
.td., London 54444F, c1885, 5.8cm.
500-600

A dress pocket watch, by Gounouilhou & Francois, Geneve, with engine turned silver dial, in floral and foliate engraved and enamelled gold case with black background, 4cm.
$900-1,000

A Swiss 18ct gold and enamel cylinder watch, with engraved gold dial, the back decorated with dark blue enamel, set with rose diamond flowers, 3.5cm, with gold and enamel fob.
$900-1,200

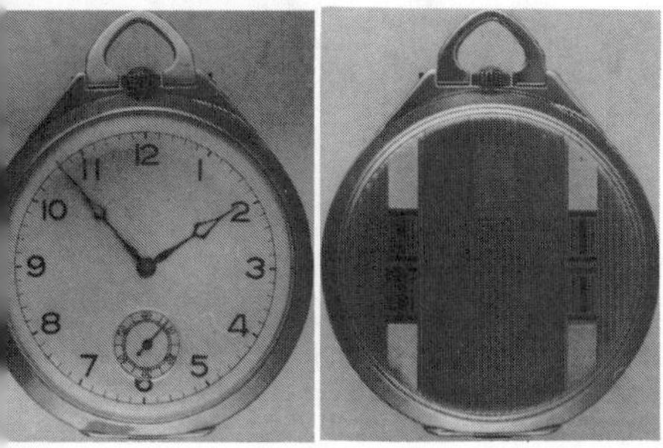

A Swiss lever dress watch, by Paul Ditisheim, in a gold and enamel open face case, c1930, 4.6cm.
$900-1,000

An American gold keyless pocket watch, the white enamel dial signed A.W. Co., Waltham, the movement inscribed Appleton, Tracy & Co., 5.2cm.
$1,100-1,200

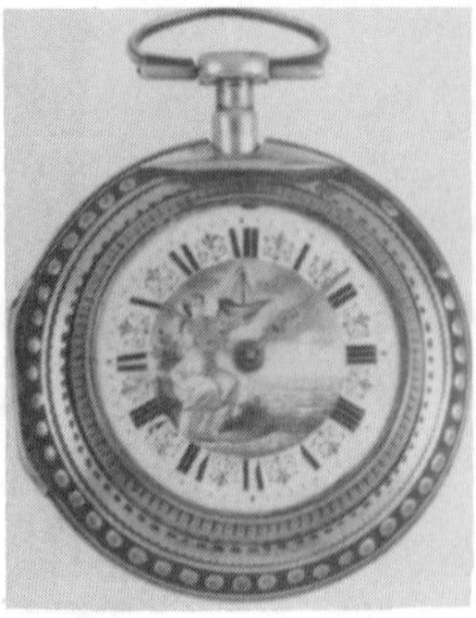

A South German horn and silver pair case verge pocket watch, signed Michael Ehrnstofer Timelham, No. 312 on backplate, some damage, 18thC, 6.2cm.
$1,400-1,500

A French open face silver verge watch for the Turkish market, decorated with translucent green enamel and signed Jn. LeRoy a Paris, and numbered 3459, 18thC.
$1,000-1,200

Wristwatches

An Ebel gold, diamond and tiger's-eye set wristwatch, with snakeskin strap, 3cm square.
$3,000-4,000

A stainless steel Breitling chronograph wristwatch, with black dial, numbered 765, 4cm.
$800-1,000

A World War II Italian Navy wristwatch, by Rolex, inscribed Radiomir Panerai, the case numbered 1010014 3645, with wi leather strap and steel buckle, 4.6cm.
$3,000-3,500

A Swiss lady's platinum and diamond wristwatch, on moire ribbon strap.
$400-600

An 18ct gold chronograph wristwatch, signed Eberhard and Co., La Chaux de Fonds, the case numbered 1012990, 3.9cm.
$3,000-4,000

An 18ct gold wristwatch, with cabochon winder, the brushed dial signed Baume and Mercier, Geneve 3.3cm.
$1,600-1,800

A gold perpetual calendar and moonphase wristwatch, by Patek Philippe, Geneve, c1948, 3.4cm.
$65,000-70,000

An 18ct gold gentleman's wristwatch, signed Piaget, with integral 18ct gold Piaget strap and clasp, 3.1cm, with presentation case.
$3,000-4,000

AROMETERS
tick

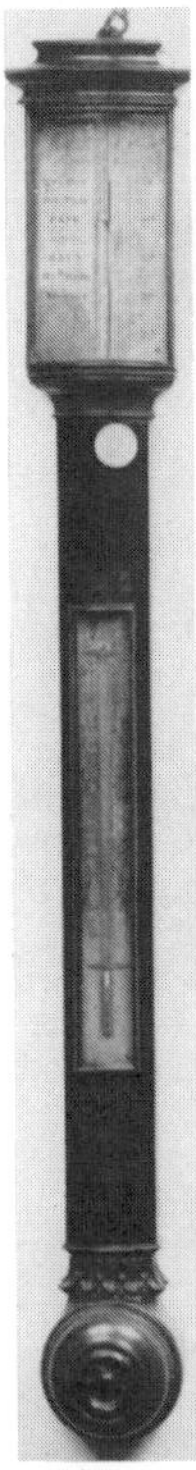

A Georgian mahogany bowfront mercury barometer, the silvered dial with vernier inscribed J. Pastorelli, Gable St, Liverpool, boxed thermometer with silvered scale, 37½in (94cm).
$4,500-5,000

A mahogany stick barometer by Ronchetti, Manchester, with ivory register in round arch top case, lacking mercury, 36in (90cm).
$900-1,000

An Admiral Fitzroy's barometer, in a carved oak case.
$900-1,000

> **Price**
> ***Prices vary from auction to auction – from dealer to dealer. The price paid in a dealer's shop will depend on:***
> ***1) what he paid for the item***
> ***2) what he thinks he can get for it***
> ***3) the extent of his knowledge***
> ***4) awareness of market trends***
> ***It is a mistake to think that you will automatically pay more in a specialist dealer's shop. He is more likely to know the 'right' price for a piece. A general dealer may undercharge but he could also overcharge***

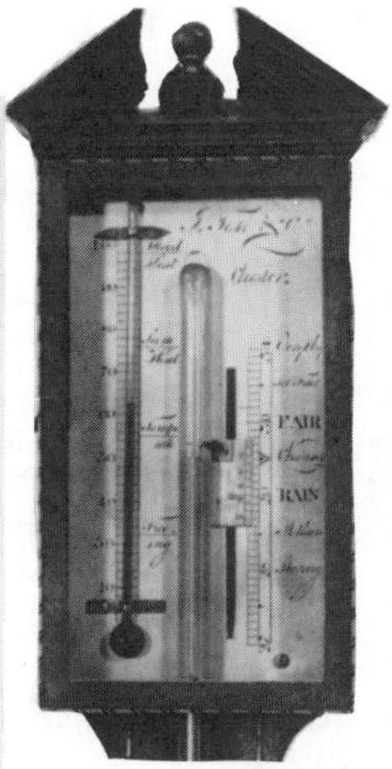

A mahogany stick barometer with herringbone veneer and rope inlay, silvered scale with adjustable pointer, J. Testi & Co, Chester, early 19thC.
$1,500-2,000

mahogany stick barometer by . Bolongaro, Manchester, c1800, 7½in (94cm).
,500-1,800

'heel

A Victorian mahogany wheel barometer, with boxwood stringing and floral and shell inlays, the boxed thermometer with silvered scale in Fahrenheit, the 8in (20cm) dial inscribed A. Corti, Fecit, 38in (97cm).
$900-1,000

A Regency rosewood banjo barometer and thermometer, decorated with simulated brass inlay, by Bellairs, Spalding, 41in (103cm).
$400-500

Victorian rosewood wheel arometer with white enamel dial, mperature gauge, Adshead & Son, udley, 39in (99cm).
300-400

> **Make the most of Miller's**
> ***Miller's is completely different each year. Each edition contains completely NEW photographs. This is not an updated publication. We never repeat the same photograph***

A heavily carved oak wheel barometer, with temperature gauge, Cremonini, Wolverhampton, 19thC, 45in (113cm).
$500-600

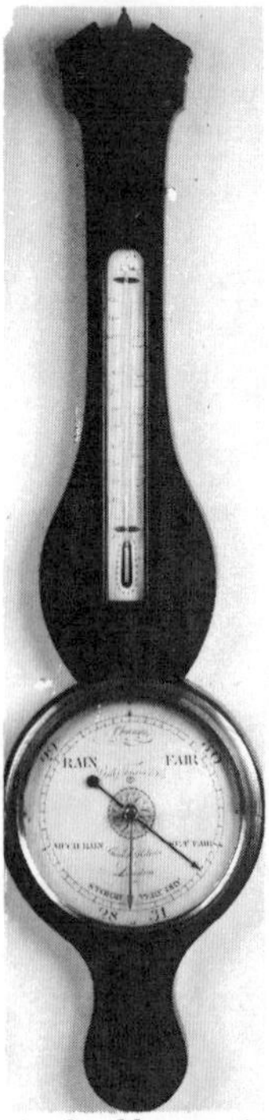

A Victorian rosewood inlaid with mother-of-pearl wheel barometer, with temperature gauge, Laffrancho, Ludlow, 39in (99cm).
$400-500

A French Empire barometer with painted dial inscribed Barometre/ Thermometre Selon Reaumur, blu steel pointer and mercury thermometer, in ebonised gilt woo frame, the crest carved with an eagle displayed within a garland o laurel, 34½in (86cm).
$2,500-3,000

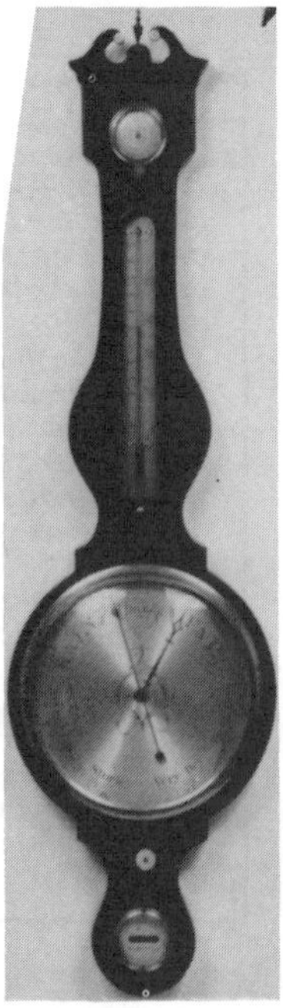

A mahogany wheel barometer with boxwood and ebony inlay, hygrometer, boxed thermometer with silvered Fahrenheit scale, the 10in (25cm) dial with spirit level inscribed Rowe, Cambridge, 42in (106cm).
$1,000-1,500

A wheel barometer with edgeline stringing and a thermometer with engraved and silvered scale, signed Gally Tarone & Co, Grevil St, Holborn, London, early 19thC, 39in (99cm).
$1,500-2,000

Chronometers

A Continental chronometer in gold open faced case, with polished steel regulator, gold train and escape wheels, white enamel dial with subsidiary seconds, blue steel hands, hallmarked London 1861, 5cm.
$2,000-3,000

A 2-day chronometer by Arnold and Dent, the engraved dial with blued steel hands, c1835, 6in (15cm) square.
$7,000-8,000

A rare 2-day marine chronometer by Barwise, in 2 tier mahogany b the silvered dial with 3 rings for hours, minutes and seconds, signe Barwise, London, number 65, ear 19thC, 9cm.
$10,000-12,000

A 2-day marine chronometer, inscribed Charles Shepherd, maker to the Admiralty, 588, 19thC, in a rosewood case.
$3,500-4,000

Make the Most of Miller's

In Miller's we do NOT just reprint saleroom estimates. We work from realised prices either from an auction room or a dealer. Our consultants then work out a realistic price range for a similar piece. This is to try to avoid repeating freak results – either low or high

Iiscellaneous

An aneroid barometer by J. H. Steward, 46 Strand, London, the ebonised and brass mounted case enclosing the mechanism, with silvered dial, each day with individual recording stylus, the underside stamped 138, late 19thC, 9in (24cm).
$600-800

A lacquered brass and burnished steel barograph, by J. Brown, 76 St. Vincent St, Glasgow, with thermometer and carved drawer in glazed mahogany case, 19½in (50cm) wide.
$1,300-1,500

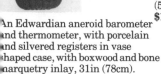

An Edwardian aneroid barometer nd thermometer, with porcelain nd silvered registers in vase haped case, with boxwood and bone narquetry inlay, 31in (78cm).
1,200-1,500

SCIENTIFIC INSTRUMENTS

Dials

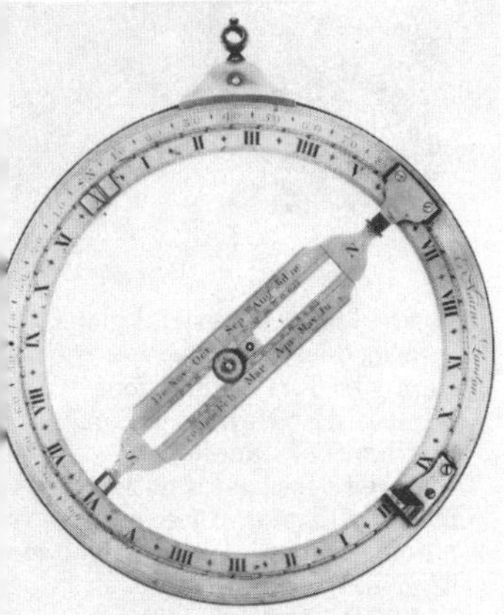

A universal equinoctial ring dial, signed E. Nairne, London, on the meridian ring with sliding ring suspension and calibrated with twin N and S quadrant scales, the pivoted equinoctial ring with twice XII hours, 18thC, 10in (24.5cm) diam.
$3,500-4,000

A plated brass reproduction Butterfield-type dial, with inscription J.L. Jonker Nederhorst den Berg, with folding bird gnomon and compass, 9in (23cm).
$300-400

A brass universal equinoctial ring dial, signed on the meridian ring Edm. Culpeper Fecit, 18thC.
$3,000-4,000

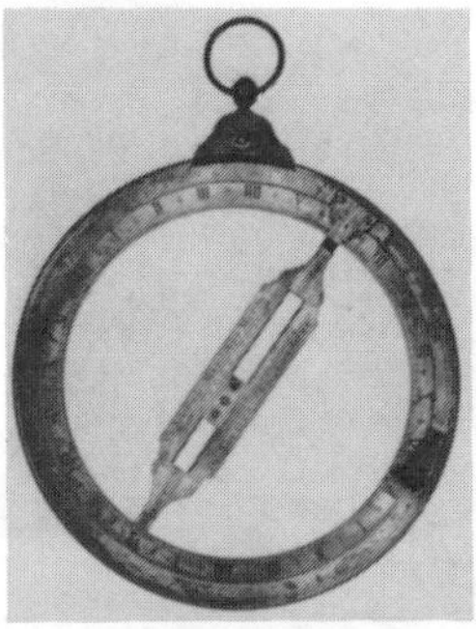

A brass equinoctial ring dial, signed Dollond, London, on the meridian ring and further engraved Standish Grady, Esq., 1807, with 0°-90° scales, the silvered equinoctial ring engraved on the face and inner edge with a 24-hour scale, early 19thC, 9in (23cm) diam.
$3,000-4,000

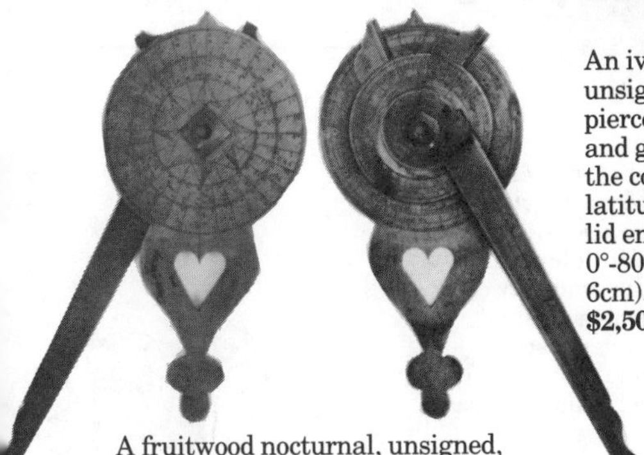

A fruitwood nocturnal, unsigned, 17thC, main plate 4in (10.5cm) diam.
$5,000-6,000

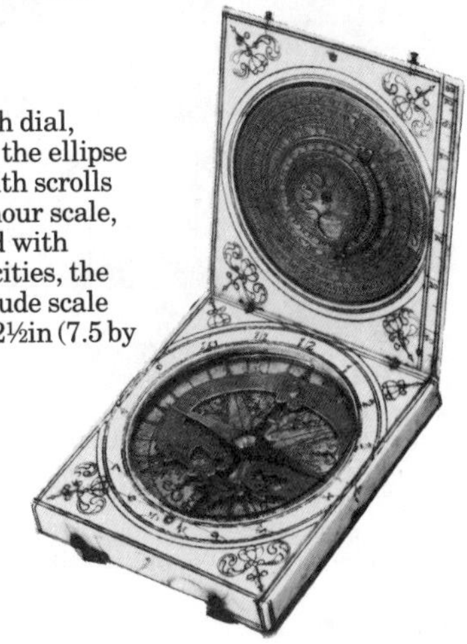

An ivory azimuth diptych dial, unsigned, of Bloud-type, the ellipse pierced and decorated with scrolls and graduated with an hour scale, the compass card printed with latitudes of continental cities, the lid engraved with a latitude scale 0°-80°, 17th/18thC, 3 by 2½in (7.5 by 6cm).
$2,500-3,500

A brass bearing dial, by C. Weilbach & Co., Copenhagen, with 2 folding sights, gimbal mounted with wall bracket, 11in (28cm) high.
$80-100

Globes

A 2¾in (7cm) terrestrial globe, with label inscribed 'A Terrestrial Globe, G. Adams, No.60 Fleet Street, London', with coloured paper gores showing ocean currents and Anson's track, New Holland ill defined and New Zealand as only part, in fishskin case, the interior with celestial chart, late 18thC.
$4,000-5,000

A 15in (38cm) celestial globe, by J & W Cary, 181 Strand, Londo dated 1818, with forward information to 1820, 39in (99cm high.
$6,000-7,000

A 13in (33cm) terrestrial globe, the maker's label inscribed C. Adami's Erdglobus neu bearbeitet und gezeichnet von H. Kiepert, marked with ocean currents, steamship routes and trans-ocean cables, needle lacking, 19thC, 26½in (67cm) high.
$2,500-3,000

A Malby's terrestrial globe, on 3 turned legs, late 19thC.
$200-250

A 3in (7.5cm) terrestrial globe, inscribed Newton's New & Improved Terrestrial Globe, published by Newton & Son, 66 Chancery Lane, London, the coloured paper gores with ocean tracks of Captain Briscoe and others, restored, 19thC, 4in (10cm high, in treen case.
$1,800-2,500

A 3in (7.5cm) pocket celestial globe, by Newton, with replacement brass meridian circle, hour ring and in a fishskin covered case, the interior o the lid with sky diagram, on mahogany stand, 19thC.
$3,500-4,500

A 4in (10cm) terrestrial globe, inscribed, with brass meridian circle signed Jernig Fecit, on oak table stand, the underside of the cruciform stretchers bearing an inscription dated 1896, 6in (15cm) high.
$6,000-7,000

Surveying

A lacquered brass theodolite, signed on the horizontal plate Crichton, London, the telescope with rack and pinion focusing, with level and dust cap located on the limb between twin clamps, with vertical half-circle, the silvered scale graduated 90°-0°/0°-60° with vernier read out, in fitted mahogany case, 19thC, 11in (28cm) wide.
$1,800-2,500

The case bears a presentation inscription to Archd. Reid, 1842.

\An oxidised, lacquered brass and ilvered miniature theodolite, igned on the compass rose, Casella, Maker to the Admiralty ınd Ordnance, London, No. 4675, he compass box with silvered dial, dge bar needle on jewelled pivot ınd graduated bubble level, with ccessories in fitted mahogany case, ate 19thC, 7in (17.5cm) wide.
$1,000-1,200

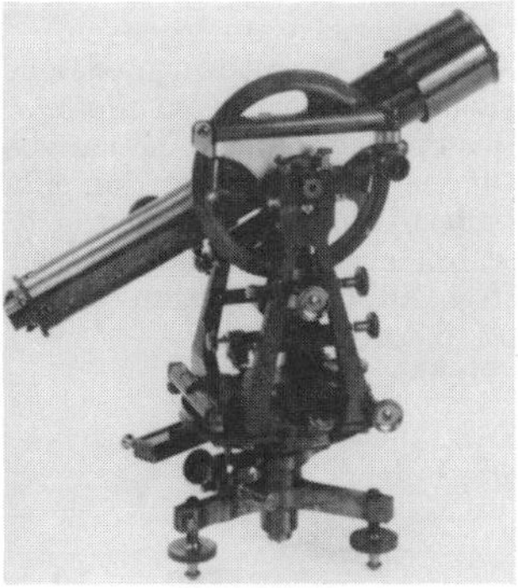

An oxidised brass transit theodolite, by Troughton & Simms, located with the 5in (12.5cm) vertical circle on axis with level and twin verniers on A-frames over the horizontal circle with silvered scale, twin verniers, magnifiers and bubble level signed, with trough compass, tripod attachment with 3 levelling screws and other accessories in fitted mahogany case, 23in (59cm) high, with leather outer case.
$1,400-1,600

A Swiss brass theodolite, signed on the silvered compass dial Bmy Gourdon a Geneve, the primary telescope with axis located on twin supports, with vertical arc engraved 45°-0°/0°-45° with vernier scale, in original case, 19thC, 13in (33cm) high.
$3,500-4,000

An Italian black enamelled and lacquered and oxidised brass surveying level, signed Guiseppe Spano & Figlio, Napoli, 1840, the telescope with rack and pinion focusing mounted on twin adjustable supports with sights, 19thC, 18in (46cm) wide, with accessories and maker's trade label in fitted case.
$1,200-1,400

black enamelled brass transit ıeodolite, signed on the silvered ompass dial R.W. Street, Commerl. d, Lambeth, London, the telescope vith rack and pinion focusing and raduated level, 19thC, 12½in 32cm) wide, with fitted mahogany ase, with associated mahogany and rass tripod.
1,000-1,200

A Swiss oxidised brass plane table alidade theodolite, signed Kern & Cie AARU Suisse, with some accessories including a ray shade, trough compass and plane table level, in fitted pine case, late 19thC, 22½in (57cm).
$3,000-4,000

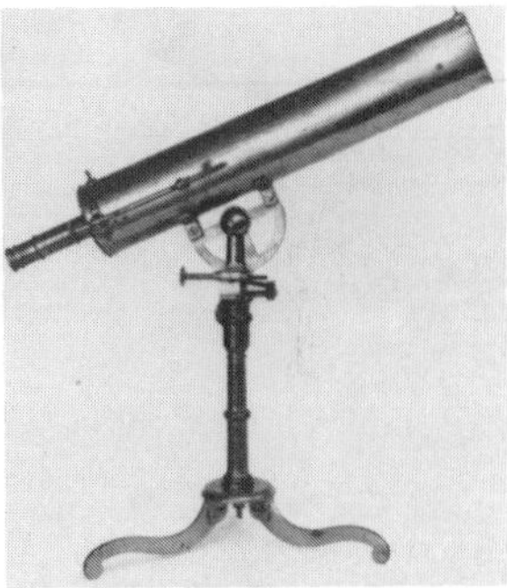

A lacquered brass 2¾in (7cm) reflecting telescope, signed on the eyepiece backplate J. Bird, London, contained in original mahogany case, 18thC, 23in (58cm).
$1,800-2,500

'elescopes

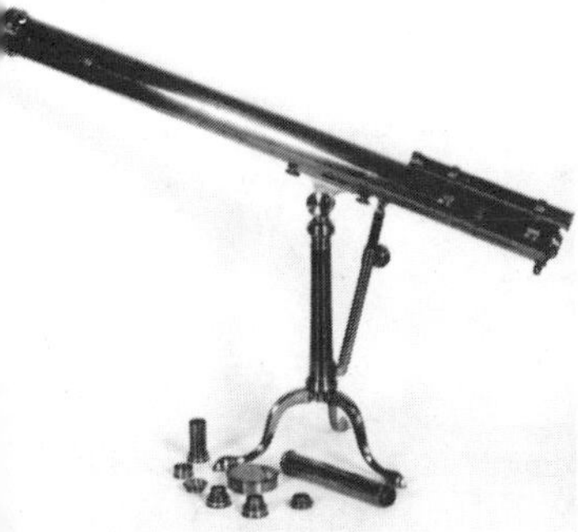

A 3in (7.5cm) Cary brass refracting telescope on stand, stamped on the tube Cary, 181 Strand, London, focusing by rack and pinion, supported by a bracket above tapering column with supporting strut above folding tripod base, tube 43½in (109.5cm) long, in mahogany case with 6 oculars.
$3,500-4,500

A brass telescope, with 2 tripod stands and one table stand, by P. H. Dallmeyer, London.
$8,000-9,000

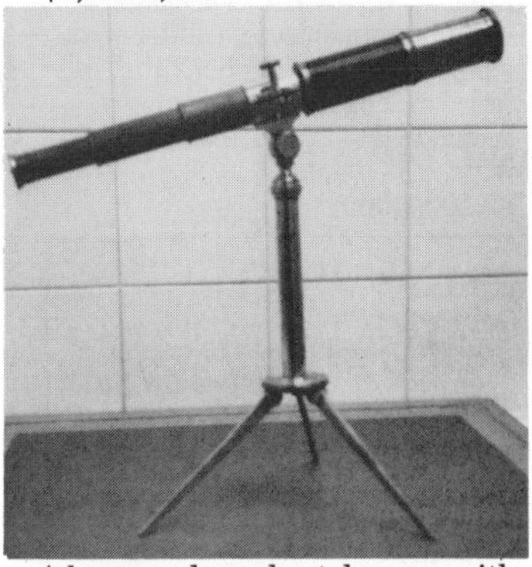

A brass and wooden telescope, with brass stand, c1860, 21in (53cm) extended.
$300-400

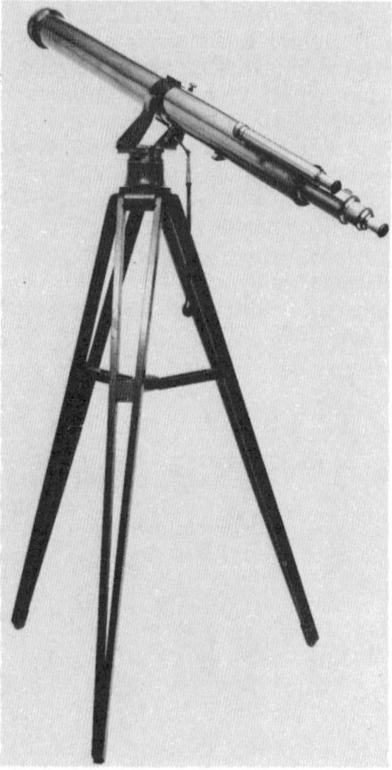

A lacquered brass 5in (12.5cm) refracting telescope, by T. Cooke & Sons York, with star finder telescope, lens hood, dust cap and extensive range of eyepieces and sun shades and other accessories, with associated mahogany and brass tripod, in 2 pine cases, 19thC, 75½in (192cm) long.
$3,000-4,000

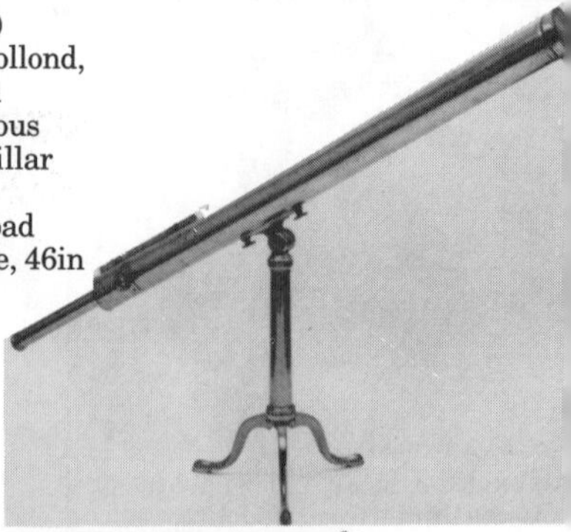

A lacquered brass 2⅝in (7cm) refracting telescope, signed Dollond, London, with rack and pinion focusing, star finder and various lenses, raised on a tapering pillar support and tripod stand, the cabriole legs terminating in pad feet, 19thC, in mahogany case, 46in (116.5cm) long.
$1,400-1,600

A brass 3in (7.5cm) refracting telescope, by S &B Solomons, London, with rack and pinion focusing, on an equatorial mount with engraved circles, verniers and scales, late 19thC, the body tube 41in (104cm) long.
$2,500-3,000

Microscopes

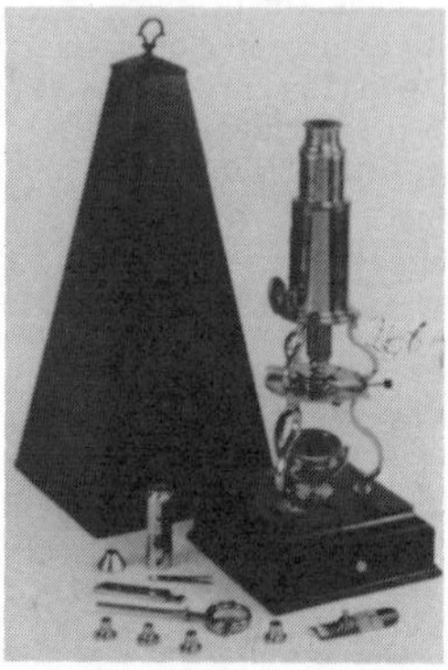

A brass Cuff-type compound monocular microscope, the cruciform stage signed G. Adams, Inst Maker to His Majesty, with eyepiece, dust slide, amber tinted field lens, mounted on a mahogany plinth base with drawer containing 5 objectives, slides and other items in a pyramid shaped mahogany case, 18thC, 18½in (47cm) high.
$3,000-4,000

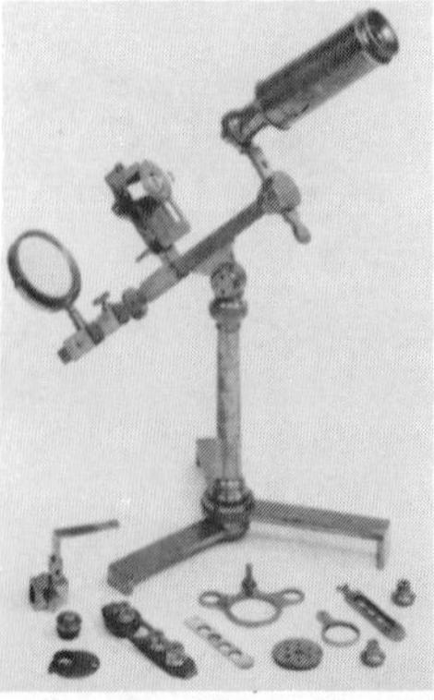

A lacquered brass Jones' Most Improved compound monocular microscope, signed on the folding stand W & S Jones, 30 Holborn, London, with various accessories including an objective slider with 4 objectives and 2 lieberkuhn, in fitted mahogany case, some damage, late 18thC, 12½in (32cm) wide.
$2,500-3,000

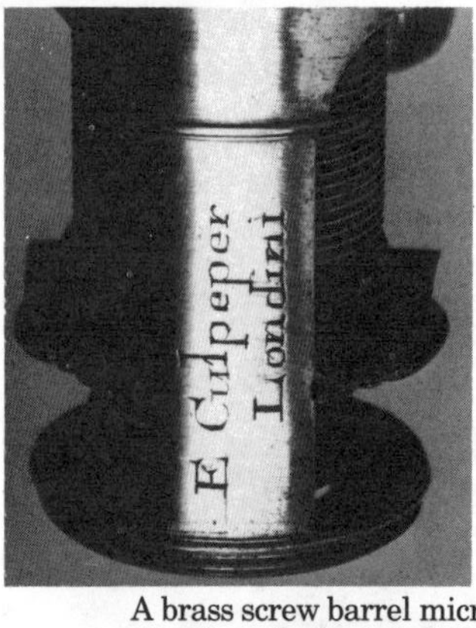

A brass screw barrel microscope, signed on the body tube E Culpeper Londini, the pillar stand with adjustable articulated arm with concave mirror, raised on a part-engraved Y-shaped folding stand, defective, early 19thC.
$12,000-13,000

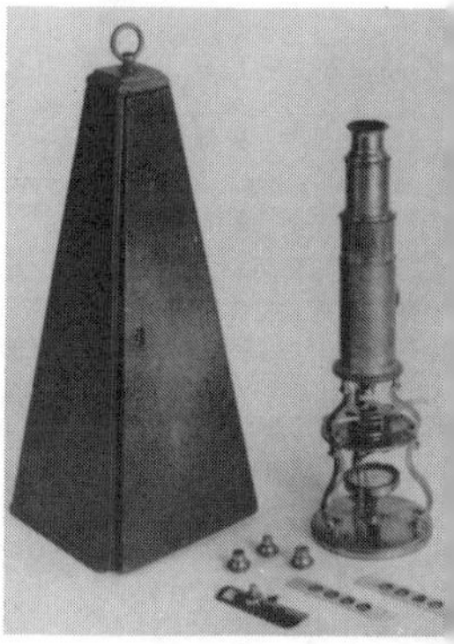

A lacquered brass Culpeper-type microscope, the stage signed Silberrad, Aldgate, London, with 4 objectives, ivory sliders, fish plate, sprung stage forceps and other items, in pyramid shaped mahogany case, 19thC, 13in (33cm).
$1,200-1,400

Use the Index!

Because certain items might fit easily into any of a number of categories, the quickest and surest method of locating any entry is by reference to the index at the back of the book.
This has been fully cross-referenced for absolute simplicity.

brass travelling micrometer
eading microscope, by Troughton
: Simms Ltd., the stage with
ngraved scale operated by spring
ension, the frame united by
pillars, in mahogany case, 19thC,
in (20cm) wide.
200-300

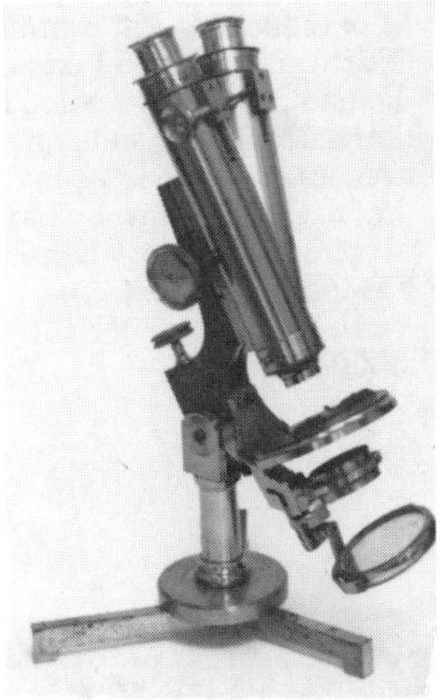

A brass binocular microscope, by Watson & Sons, with Ross Zentmayer stage and tripod base, engraved No. 1518, 313 High Holborn, London, in mahogany fitted case with 8 lenses, 19thC, 14in (35.5cm).
$900-1,200

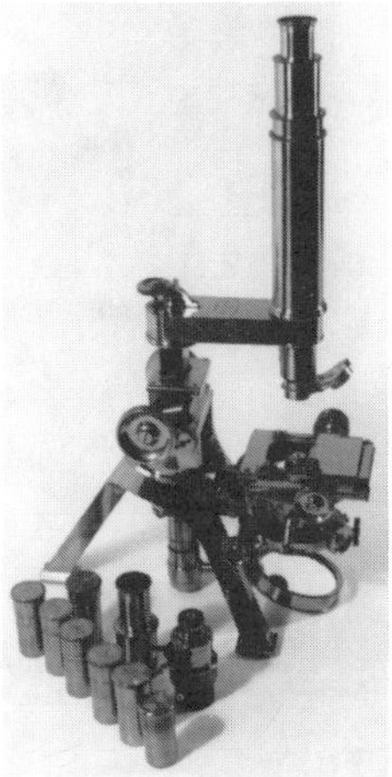

A brass microscope, by Powell & Lealand, cased with accessories.
$4,000-5,000

)ental nstruments

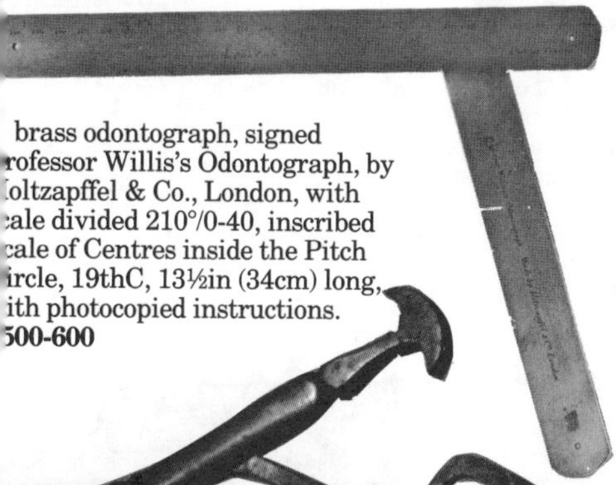

brass odontograph, signed
rofessor Willis's Odontograph, by
oltzapffel & Co., London, with
cale divided 210°/0-40, inscribed
cale of Centres inside the Pitch
ircle, 19thC, 13½in (34cm) long,
ith photocopied instructions.
500-600

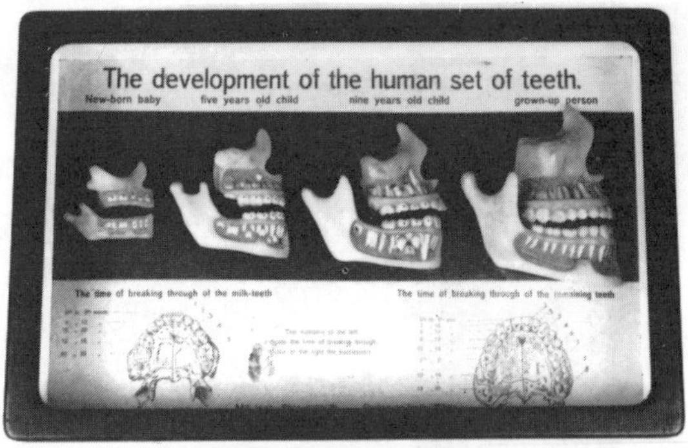

A German wax model showing the development of human teeth, c1910.
$400-500

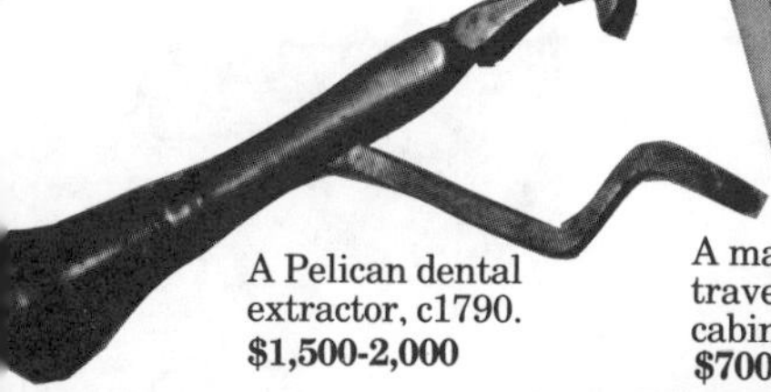

A Pelican dental extractor, c1790.
$1,500-2,000

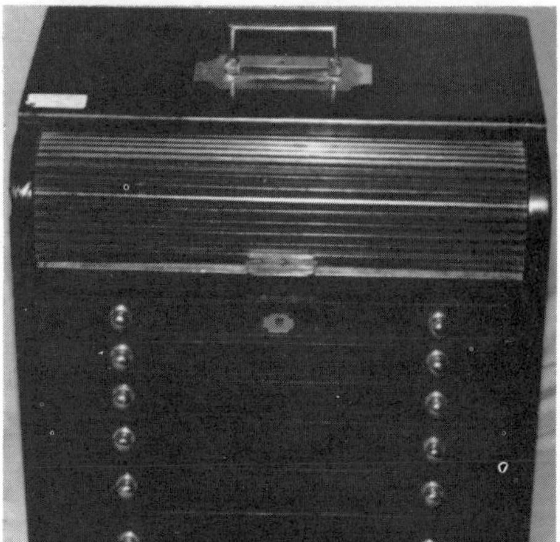

A mahogany roll-top travelling dental cabinet, c1890.
$700-800

ledical nstruments

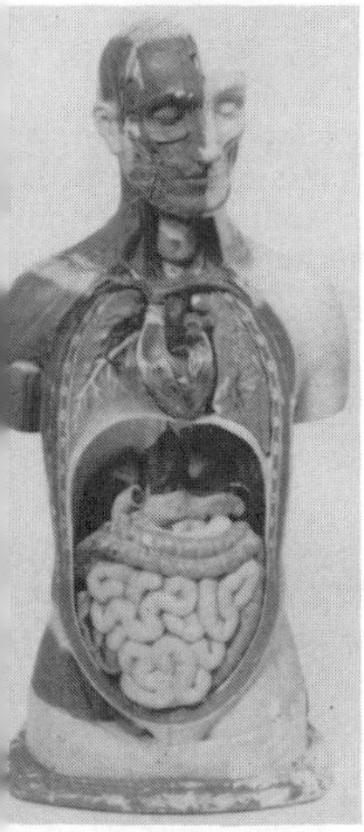

painted plaster of Paris male
iedical torso, the insides
etachable, late 19thC, 30in (76cm)
igh.
200-250

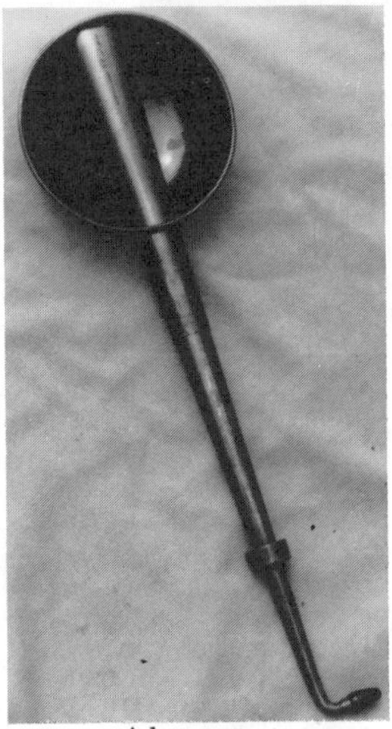

A brass ear trumpet, c1910.
$140-160

A pair of tortoiseshell framed spectacles, c1890.
$150-200

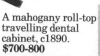

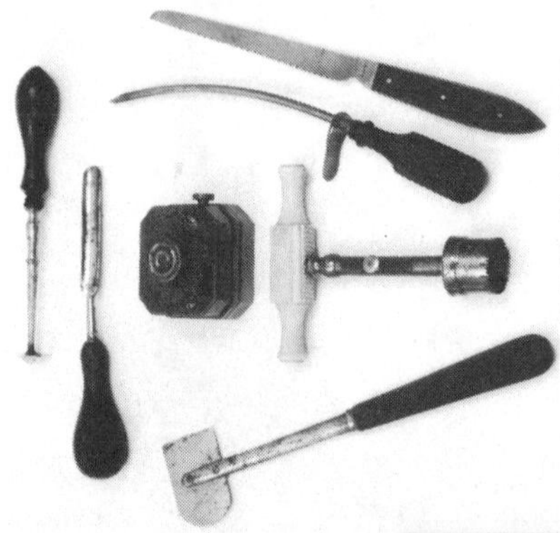

A part surgical kit, containing a scarificator, signed Ferris & Co., Ponstol, 2 ebony handled Listan knives by Weiss, London, various trocars and probes, ebony handled knives, a Heys saw by Savigny, a trephine with ivory handle, a finger saw and other items, in a mahogany case, 19thC.
$600-800

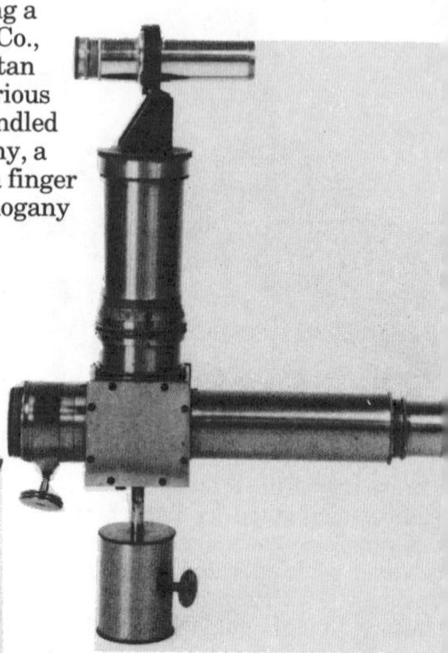

A lacquered brass solar eyepiece, of Steinheil of Munich pattern, and signed on the miniature eyepiece, with prism, micrometer scale, balance weight and draw tubes, in original pine carrying case, 13in (33cm) long.
$2,000-2,500

A set of steel and ebony handled trepanning instruments, signed Chappell & MacLeod, comprising a brush with ivory handle signed Durroch, London, and other items, in fitted mahogany case, late 18thC, 9½in (24cm) wide.
$1,300-1,500

Viewers

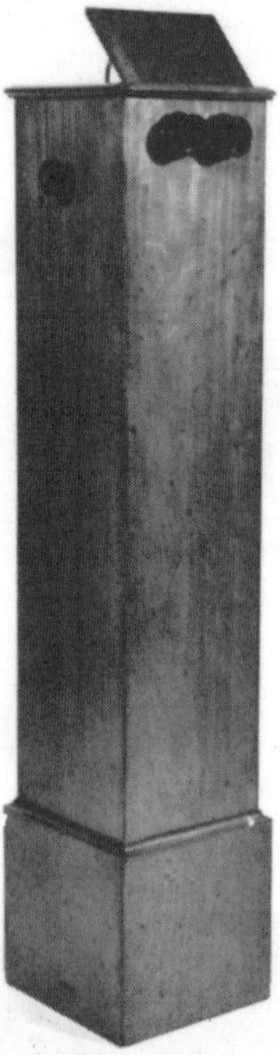

A Victorian walnut and ebonised stereoscopic viewer in pedestal cabinet, twin hinged flaps to the top, skirting plinth support, 48in (122cm) high, and a quantity of glass stereoscopic slides.
$700-800

A wood polyscope peepview, with multifacet viewing lens and single slide in holder, box 9½in (24cm) long.
$100-120

A mahogany viewer, by Kinora, London, with inlaid gilt decoration turned wood handle and internal clockwork mechanism, mounted on an ornate metal stand with a mahogany base, and 2 Kinora reel 14in (36cm) high.
$2,500-3,000

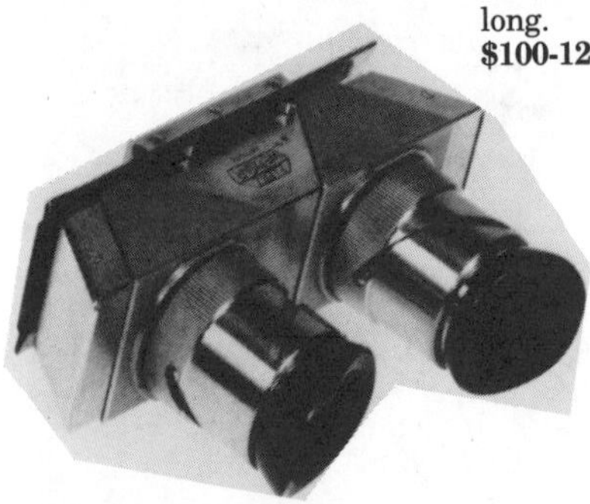

A Votra stereo transparency viewer, by E. Leitz, Wetzlar, in maker's fitted plush lined box.
$1,300-1,500

A 4-person Viewmaster stereoviewer demonstration unit, by Sawyers Europe, Belgium, built into a globe with the legend 'The world at your fingertip' on a base giving details of each viewer 'Adventure', 'Science', 'Cartoon', 'Travel', the globe on rotating stand with internal electric illuminant.
$700-900

Iiscellaneous

steel balance with brass pans and collection of weights, and a trade abel for James Rubridge, in nahogany box, late 18thC, 7in 18cm) wide.
150-200

A brass kaleidoscope, signed on the body tube Spurin, 37 New Bond Strt, with one object plate, mirrors possibly replaced, early 19thC.
$800-1,200

A steel balance, with glass pans and brass weights, with trade label for Young & Son, in oak case, early 19thC, 8in (20.5cm).
$100-150

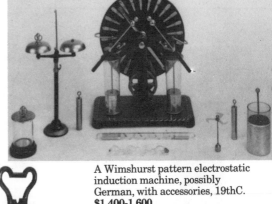

A Wimshurst pattern electrostatic induction machine, possibly German, with accessories, 19thC.
$1,400-1,600

A brass and iron spectrometer, the tubes with rack and pinion focusing, adjustable slit, 3 prisms on rotating centre table, the base with 2 engraved circles and adjustable feet, late 19thC, 16½in (42cm) diam.
$700-900

A George III mahogany waywiser, by William Watkins, St. James's Street, London, with 7in (18cm) silvered dial, wheel 32in (81cm) diam.
$4,000-5,000

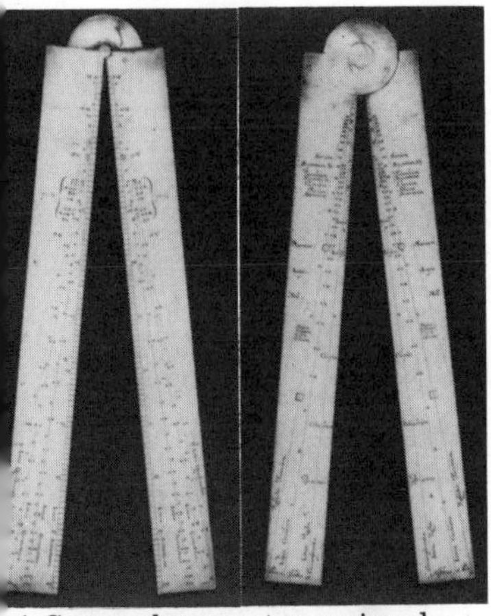

A German brass sector, unsigned, engraved with maker's monogram, constructed of riveted sheet with various ratio scales, symbols, with locking and brass hinge pins, early 17thC, 22½in (57cm).
$5,000-6,000

Miller's is a price Guide not a price List

The price ranges given reflect the average price a purchaser should pay for similar items. Condition, rarity of design or pattern, size, colour, pedigree, restoration and many other factors must be taken into account when assessing values.

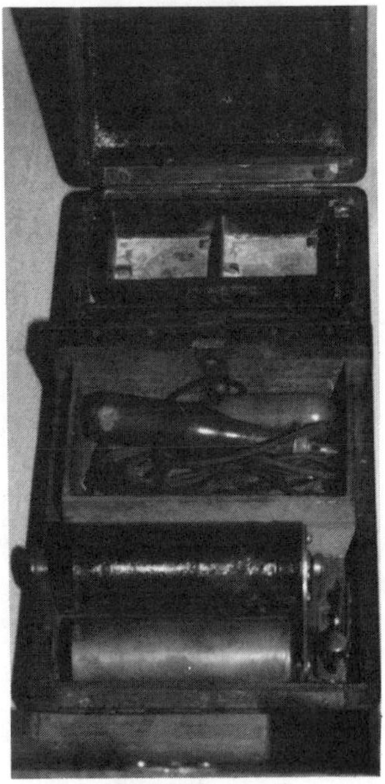

An electric shock machine, c1850.
$100-200

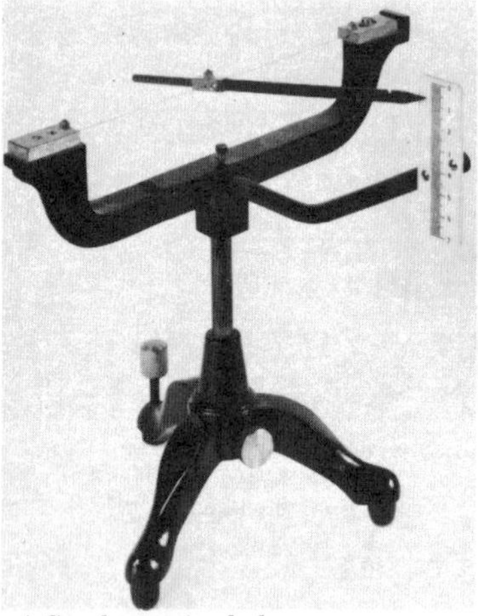

A Searles torsion balance apparatus, by W. G. Pye & Co. Ltd., on black enamelled stand and accessories, 11in (28cm) wide.
$400-500

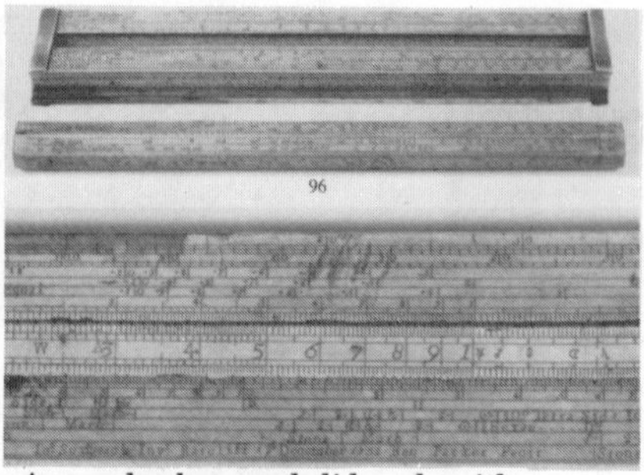

A complex boxwood slide rule with stamped signature, Ios. Suxfpeach Invr. Ratcliff 1st December 1752, Ben Parker fecit, the main body of the rule stamped with a calendar scale, scales for spirits and wine, mathematical symbols, 2 sliders missing, 18thC, 12in (30.5cm) long.
$1,000-1,200

Cameras

A brass bound camera obscura prism head by R. & J. Beck Ltd London, with internal prism and mounting flange.
$1,800-2,000

A mahogany studio portrait camera on stand, by Billelif, Manchester, with 12¾in (32cm) plate, 19thC.
$1,200-1,500

A Ticka camera with viewfinder, by Houghtons Ltd., London.
$300-400

A Brins patent detective camera, Pat No. 17143/517, circa 1891, damaged, in fitted case.
$4,000-5,000

An 8½ by 6½in (22 by 17cm) mahogany folding plate camera, with integral changing box with light tight sleeves and internal folding light tight flap, opening flap in camera base and a brass bound lens, camera with plaque inscribed Walter Lawley, 78 Farringdon St., London EC.
$1,000-1,200

A roll film Baby Sibyl camera No. B303, by Newman and Guardia, London, with a Carl Zeiss Tessar f4.5 75mm lens No. 182632, in maker's leather case.
$800-1,000

A complete Solomon and Grant Patent Magnesium lamp with double magnesium reels, clockwork draw-fan mechanism, metal reflector, all mounted on metal legs, with wooden handle, lamp with inscribed metal plaque, Magnesium Lamp, J Solomon, Brevete SGDC, 22 Red Lion Square, London, No. 4754.
$1,500-1,800

Patented October 31, 1864, No. 2690.

A cream enamelled Polyfoto camera, type P.F.O. MKII No. 527, by Williamson Manufacturing Co. Ltd., London, with maker's plaque.
$200-300

A 1in (2.5cm) diam. Telephot Button Camera No. 2230, by The British Ferrotype Co., England, with lens developing section and buttons.
$700-1,000

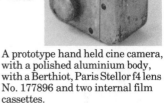

A quarter plate 'Vesca' camera No. 11692, The Stereoscope Co., London, with green leather bellows and a C P Goerz Celor f4.8 90mm lens No. 292572 and roll-film back, in a fitted leather case.
$400-500

A prototype hand held cine camera, with a polished aluminium body, with a Berthiot, Paris Stellor f4 lens No. 177896 and two internal film cassettes.
$500-600

Kodak No. 4 folding roll-film mera, No. 7778, pat. date May 5th 385, 5 by 4in (13 by 10cm) film, ausch & Lamb compur shutter and aroon bellows, contained in black ather covered mahogany case ith brass fittings.
00-600

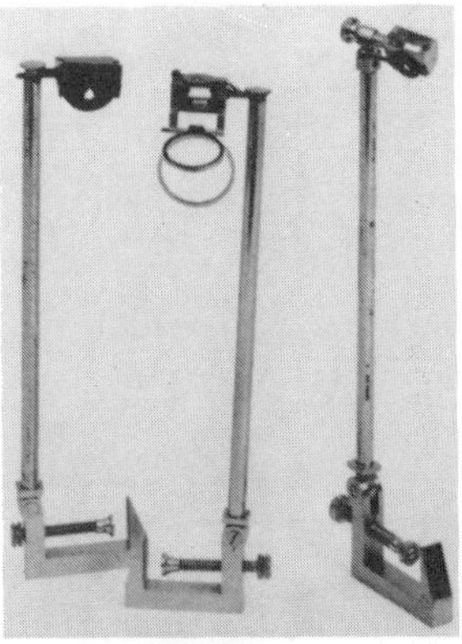

Three camera lucidas, 2 in fitted cases.
$400-500

A 35mm Canon X-ray camera, by Seiki-Kogaku, Japan, No. 3087 with sliding metal plate shutter, pull-chain wind-on mechanism and a Seiki-Kogaku R-Serenar f1.5 5cm lens No. 3447, camera body and back also stamped, camera body lacks leather covering.
$1,200-1,500

3 by 4cm. roll film Piccolo camera o. 188 with simple lens, wheel ops and guillotine time and stantaneous shutter, by hoto-Opera, Paris.
00-800

he camera made use of newly troduced Kodak roll film for the lding Pocket Kodak. It is similar to e cone Kodak camera in shape and nish.

A 35mm Luftwaffen Robot camera No. F59961-5, by O. Berning and Co., Germany, with a Robot-Schneider Tele-Xenar f3.8 7.5cm lens No. 1813722, and extended winding knob, with backplate engraved Luftwaffen-Eigentum.
$500-600

A Hasselblad 500 C/M crystal glass replica camera by Victor Hasselblad A.B., Gothenburg, Sweden.
$400-600

This crystal glass replica Hasselblad camera was awarded to Mr. George Alt of Lake Forest, Illinois, U.S.A. as the winner of a Hasselblad competition. Alt, as owner of Hasselblad 1000F camera serial number CS10604 held the lowest serial numbered working camera in the United States within that category.

A grey Rolleiflex T camera No. T2132008, by Franke and Heidecke, Braunschweig, with a Heidosmat f2.8 75mm viewing lens No. 3006165 and a Zeiss Tessar f3.5 75mm taking lens No. 2706178 set into a Synchro-Compur shutter, in a leather e.r.c.
$500-600

A plastic model of a studio camera by Asanuma & Co., Japan, with inset Copal clock, in the style of a Japanese made wooden studio camera.
$150-200

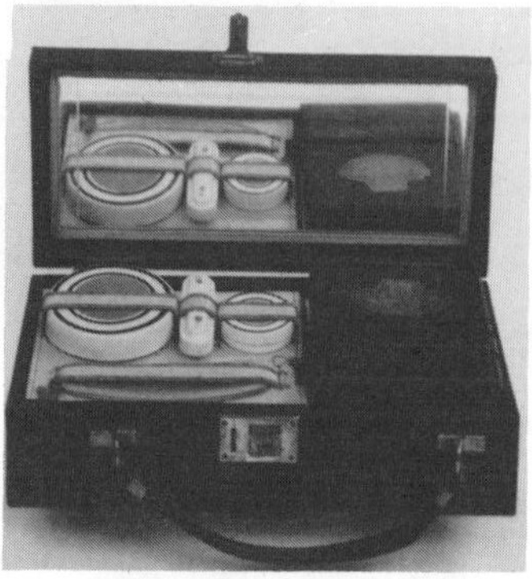

A Photo-Vanity outfit comprising a make-up set and box camera, by Agfa-Ansco, U.S.A., all built-in to a black leather vanity case, with waist level finder on one edge of the case and lens on one other side of the case.
$5,000-6,000

The vanity case contains a lipstick, powder, rouge and comb and mirror set into the case lid. The Vanity case was apparently made by Q.L.G.Co., and fitted with an Ansco camera.

A 16mm Teleca combined camera and binocular, by Tokiwa Seiko Co., Japan, with a Telesigmar f4.5 3.5in (9cm) taking lens and side mounted binocular viewing lenses mounted on a tripod.
$2,500-3,000

A16mm Micro 16 disguised camera, by Wm. R. Whittaker Co. Ltd., Los Angeles, U.S.A., No. 17772, contained within a cigarette packet.
$150-200

A 126 cartridge Mick-A-Matic Deluxe novelty camera, by Child Guidance Products Inc., NY, U.S.A. in maker's original box, c1971.
$120-140

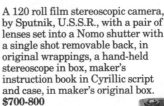

A 2¼ by 3¼in (6 by 8cm) Riley technical duorail camera, by Riley Research Co., Santa Monica, U.S.A., model B No. 781 with a polished aluminium body with a Wollensak Velostigmatic 101mm f4.5 lens No. 501683 set into a Rapax shutter.
$700-800

A 120 roll film stereoscopic camera, by Sputnik, U.S.S.R., with a pair of lenses set into a Nomo shutter with a single shot removable back, in original wrappings, a hand-held stereoscope in box, maker's instruction book in Cyrillic script and case, in maker's original box.
$700-800

RT NOUVEAU

eramics

lish with a lady, by Ernst
iallis, Vienna, c1900, 8½in
cm) high.
,000-1,400

A William de Morgan tile, painted in brown and yellow with a sailing boat, impressed Sand's End mark, mounted as a teapot stand, 7in (18cm) square.
$800-1,000

A William de Morgan tile, painted in black with a stylised Dodo, impressed Sand's End pottery mark, mounted as a teapot stand, 7in (18cm) square.
$600-700

jardinière.
,600-2,000

Two French bisque plaques, 5 by 4in (12.5 by 10cm).
$40-60 each

A William de Morgan tile, painted in red lustre with stylised carnations, with painted signature W de Morgan & Co, Fulham, London, 8in (20.5cm) square.
$350-400

A Watcombe pottery vase, in green and red, c1950, 8in (20.5cm).
$100-160

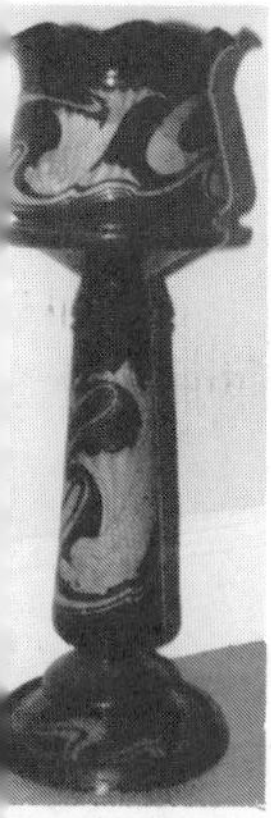

Bretby jardinière,
corated with fish.
00-1,000

A Dutch jardinière and stand, decorated in batik-style with flowers, foliage and trellis panels, supported on a broad cylindrical stand, signed Corona Holland, 39in (99cm).
$1,200-1,400

A pair of Bretby ware vases, with grey metal finish, c1900, 8½in (22cm).
$80-100

An Eltonware jar and cover, with floral design in shades of blue and green, c1890, 6½in (16.5cm).
$400-600

An Eltonware jug, with central gold lustre decoration of a fish and wings, base with monogram for George Masters, 7in (18cm) high.
$1,400-1,600

A Linthorpe pottery ewer, designed by Christopher Dresser, the reddish body glazed on the shoulders with streaked milky-green and brown, marked Linthorpe 'HT' and facsimile signature, 9½in (24cm) high.
$400-600

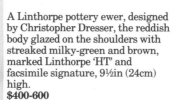

A Wade vase, with colourful floral decoration, c1930, 9in (23cm).
$40-80

An Eltonware jardinière, with triple loop handles, signed Elton, 10in (25.5cm) high.
$1,500-2,000

An Eltonware jug, with fruit design in shades of green and red, c1890, 6½in (16cm).
$400-600

Elton, Sir Edmund Harry (1846-1920). English art potter who in 1883 succeeded to a baronetcy and inherited Clevedon Court in Somerset where, with the aid of an assistant potter, **G. Masters,** he made earthenware vessels decorated with flower patterns in coloured slips (blue, red or green). His products, known as 'Elton ware', were shown at the Arts and Crafts Exhibition Society of which he was a member

An Eltonware pre-Columbian shaped jug, with floral decoration and butterflies in shades of green, c1885, 8½in (22cm) high.
$450-600

An Eltonware vase in gold 'crackle' with black slip underneath, c1910, 5½in (14cm).
$700-900

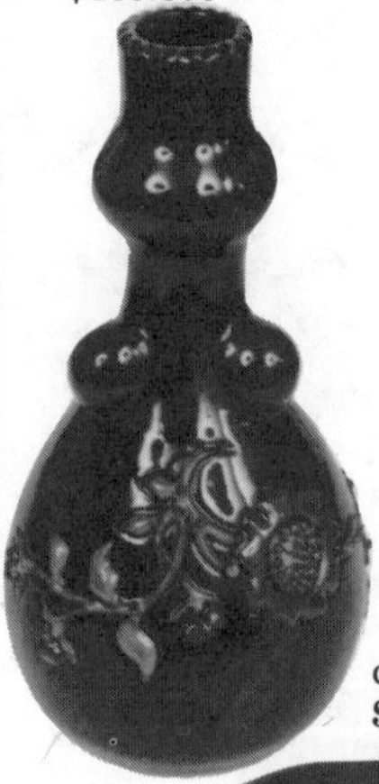

An Eltonware vase, with sunflowers in shades of blue, c1900, 8in (20cm).
$450-600

An Eltonware vas with daffodil desig in shades of blue, green and brown, c1890, 7in (18cm
$200-350

An Eltonware trefoil shaped jug, in shades of purple and red, c1900, 6in (15cm).
$700-800

An Eltonware jug, in green slip with gold crackle, c1910, 6½in (16cm).
$450-600

An Eltonware gourd shaped vase, with insects design in shades of purple and red, c1885, 9½in (24cm).
$450-600

An Eltonware vase, wit bird and leaf design in shades of green, blue and yellow, c1900, 10in (25.5cm).
$600-900

An Eltonware 'crackle' jug, c1921, 7in (18cm).
$600-900

This jug was made after Elton died by his son, and is signed Elton with a cross.

Did you know

MILLER'S Antiques Price Guide builds up year by year to form the most comprehensive photo-reference system available.

An Eltonware three-handled vase, with floral decoration in shades of blue and brown, c1900, 7½in (19cm).
$400-600

An Eltonware vase, with red rose design, signed, 12in (30.5cm).
$1,200-1,400

An Eltonware long necked vase with rare flower design in shades of blue and green, 19½in (50cm).
$1,400-1,800

Elton used rare flowers which grew in the grounds of Clevedon Court, with a profusion of Sunflowers – hence the so called Sunflower Pottery.

An Eltonware serpent vase, with applied sunflower decoration, marked, 10½in (27cm).
$400-500

\n Eltonware vase, ith sunflower lesign in shades of lue and green, :1890, 12in (30.5cm).
$1,200-1,400

An Eltonware vase with kingfisher design, signed, c1885, 18in (46cm).
$1,400-1,800

The original price label of 25/– is still intact.

An Eltonware biscuit glazed plaque, signed.
$600-700

'locks

Liberty & Co., 'Tudric' pewter nepiece, showing the influences of F. A. Voysey, impressed Tudric .01, 13½in (34cm).
,000-6,000

A Foley Intarsio ceramic clock, the case painted in blue, turquoise, green, brown and yellow enamels, with maidens representing day and night, printed maker's mark, 11½in (29cm).
$1,800-2,000

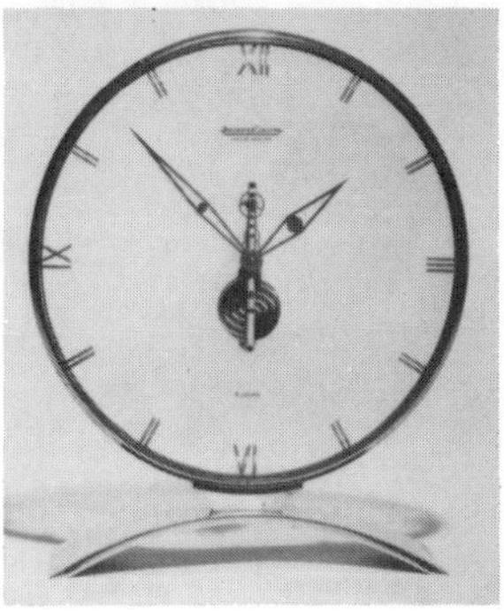

A Jaeger-Le Coultre 8-day mantel clock, with Roman chapters, the transparent glass discus-shaped body with chrome rim and foot, printed Jaeger-Le Coultre Fabriqué en Suisse, 8 Jours, 9in (23cm).
$1,200-1,400

A Lalique clock, the satin finished glass moulded with love birds in blossoming branches, with brown stained decoration, the dial with glass face, monogrammed ATO and black enamelled chapters, slightly chipped corner, with moulded signature R. Lalique, 8½in (21.5cm) wide.
$2,000-3,000

A Liberty & Co., hammered pewter clock, decorated with stylised tree and foliate panels, the copper clock face with black enamel Roman chapters and turquoise enamel centre, stamped 01154 English Pewter, 7in (18cm) high.
$1,400-2,000

A Liberty & Co., Tudric pewter clock, with enamelled copper dial and black enamel Roman numerals, flanked by shaped columns, stamped marks Tudric English Pewter, Liberty & Co., 0761, 8½in (21cm) high.
$2,000-3,000

An Arts and Crafts clock, retailed b Liberty & Co., with Hamburg American Clock Co., movement, 14in (35.5cm).
$1,000-1,200

Figures

A Goldscheider figure of a boy, Petri, Austrian, c1920, 10in (25.5cm) high.
$500-600

A pair of Edwardian bisque novelties, c1900, 5in (12.5cm) high.
$300-400

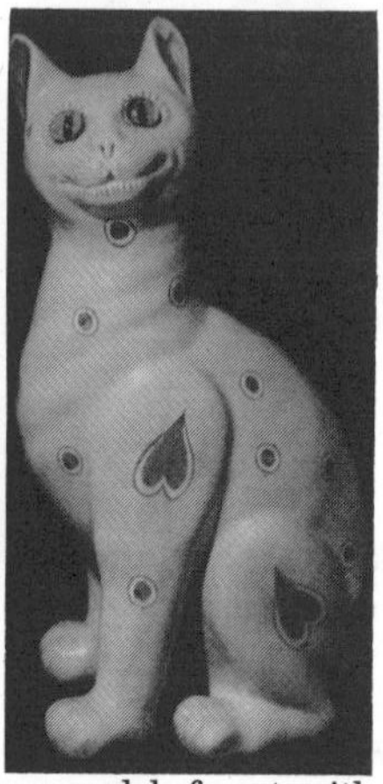

A Gallé faience model of a cat, with green glass eyes, painted with blue and white motifs reserved against a yellow ground, partial signature, 13in (33cm).
$800-1,000

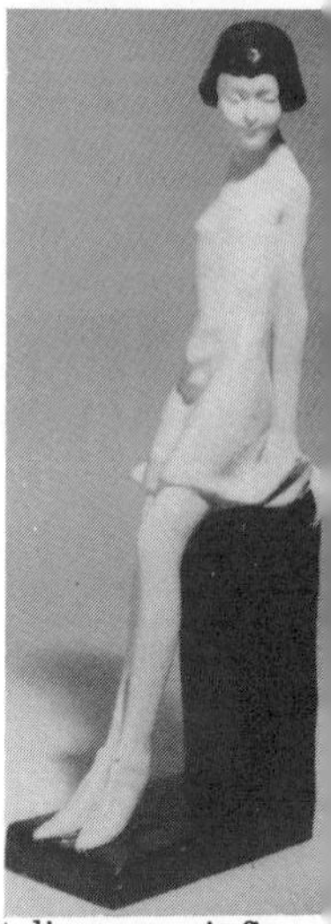

An Italian ceramic figur her hair, the post and th base enamelled black, signed E. Mazzolani, the base enamelled with E.I monogram and Milano, 1929, with paper labels, one of which typed L'Edizionie di Sole 5 Copie, 18in (45.5cm).
$2,000-3,000

A pair of gilt bronze figures of peasant girls with broken urns, incised signature Germain, 17½in (43cm) high, on later bases.
$2,500-3,000

HOW TO USE MILLER'S

Unless otherwise stated, any description which refers to 'a set' or 'a pair' includes a valuation for the entire set or the pair, even though the illustration may show only a single item.

Furniture

An Arts and Crafts armchair, retailed by Liberty & Co., with rush seat, c1895.
$600-800

A mahogany chair, c190
$1,800-2,000

An Arts and Crafts desk, by Shapland & Petter of Barnstaple, c1905.
$1,500-2,000

A Gallé walnut and marquetry side table, the top inlaid in various fruitwoods, with inlaid signature Gallé, 21in (53cm) long.
$1,200-1,400

Heal's limed oak dining room
ite, comprising dining table,
leboard, 6 chairs, including one
mchair, and a serving trolley,
ith inset manufacturer's label,
935.
,000-5,000

An Arts & Crafts armchair, c1900.
$1,600-1,800

An American Arts and Crafts mahogany occasional table, c1910.
$600-800

Victorian Aesthetic Movement
onised chair, similar to a Fred
addox design for Floris & Co.
00-1,000

An Arts and Crafts oak chair, Glasgow School, c1900.
$1,400-1,600

An oak revolving bookcase, the design attributed to Richard Norman Shaw, the top carved with the inscription 'The Tabard Inn, the true university of these days is a collection of books', 73in (186cm) high.
$2,500-3,500

A George Walton oak armchair, the tapering back splat with heart-shaped piercing, the out curving arms and rush seat on square section legs joined by plain stretchers.
$3,000-3,500

A pair of Liberty & Co., oak side chairs, designed by Archibald Knox, with engraved plaques Liberty & Co., Ltd., London W.
$900-1,000

air of limed oak chairs, by Heals,
908.
00-1,000

l. An oak tabouret, by the Grand Rapids Bookcase and Chair Co., c1910.
$400-600

r. An oak tabouret, by Stickley Brothers, Grand Rapids, c1905.
$600-800

An oak tea table, inlaid with ebony, with 4 fold down shelves.
$800-1,000

A Gustav Stickley oak armchair, c1903.
$1,200-1,400

A Gustav Stickley oak settee, c1903.
$4,500-5,000

A stained beech table with pegged construction, Liberty's, c1905.
$550-650

An Arts and Crafts mahogany armchair, c1900.
$800-1,000

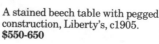

A set of 5 Gordon Russell oak dining chairs and an armchair, with drop-in seats, on tapering square section legs joined by plain stretchers.
$3,500-4,000

An American Arts and Crafts oak magazine/book rack, by the Lake Craft Shops, Sheboygan, Wisconsi c1905.
$1,600-2,000

An oak occasional table, by Heals. **$500-600**

An oak sofa/table, the table top swivels down to reveal settee, c1910.
$1,800-2,000

An inlaid mahogany writing desk, the single frieze drawer with brass drop handles, leather top, 33in (84cm).
$1,000-1,200

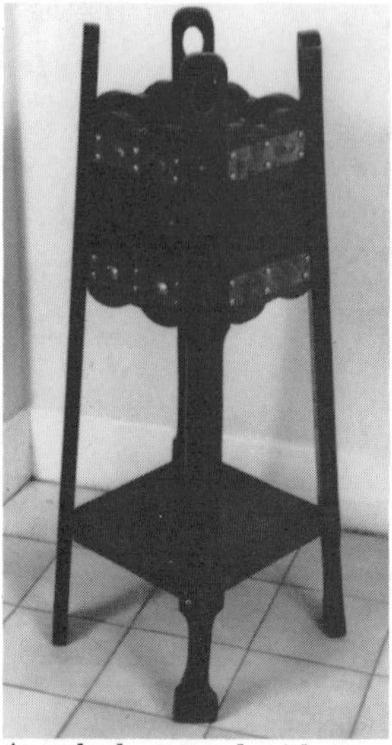

An oak plant stand, with copper banding, c1900, 36in (91.5cm) higl
$400-600

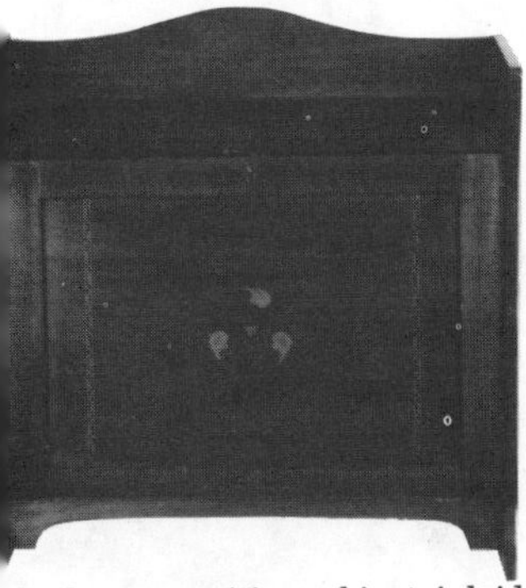

 mahogany writing cabinet, inlaid ith stained woods and stringing, 1905, 19in (48cm).
500-600

A mahogany display cabinet, inlaid in coloured woods with stylised roses, on tapering supports, 42in (106cm).
$1,600-1,800

A Victorian Aesthetic Movement ash wardrobe, the fielded panel doors inset with Minton Hollins pottery tiles painted with birds, butterflies and floral sprays, 57½in (145cm) wide.
$2,500-3,000

n English oak wall cabinet, with uitwood marquetry panel of a aiden above stylised foliage, anked by shaped shelves with racket supports, 15½in (40cm).
900-1,000

An Edwardian mahogany marquetry inlaid display cabinet, 59in (150cm).
$2,500-3,000

A smoking cabinet, by Shapland and Petter, c1905, 18in (46cm).
$600-800

An Arts and Crafts jewellery box, c1905.
$500-600

A walnut umbrella stand, with hammered copper panel, probably by Shapland and Petter of Barnstaple, c1905, 21in (53cm).
$900-1,000

A Gordon Russell table, with moulded Y-shaped brackets and arched block feet, joined by elaborately moulded stretcher, with manufacturer's label, inscribed Cabinet Maker J. Driessche, April 23rd, 1929, 53in (135cm) long.
$5,000-6,000

An American Arts and Crafts prairie school desk, c1905.
$1,600-2,500

In the Furniture section if there is only one measurement it usually refers to the width of the piece

Glass

A Gallé two-handled bowl, the green tinted glass with polychrome enamelled floral spray, dragonfly and water lily decoration, with gilt and enamel borders, signed E. Gallé Nancy déposé, 9½in (24cm) high.
$2,500-3,000

A pair of Loetz glass vases, 4½in (11cm).
$600-800

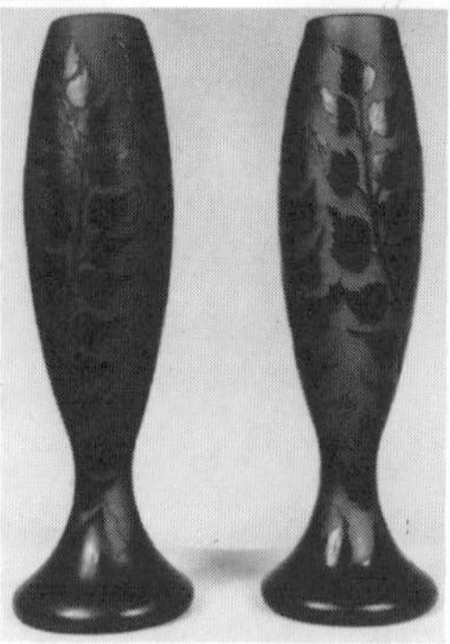

A pair of Gallé cameo glass vases, with brown foliage on an amber ground, signed, 20½in (52cm).
$3,500-4,000

A Gallé cameo glass vase, of tinted amber and overlaid with blue and amethyst glass acid etched with fir trees and mountains, signed Gallé in cameo, 5½in (14cm).
$1,800-2,000

A Gallé carved, acid etched and enamelled cameo vase, the pale amber glass with polychrome striations, overlaid with dark amber vines, with green enamel decoration, carved signature Gallé, 9in (24cm).
$3,000-3,500

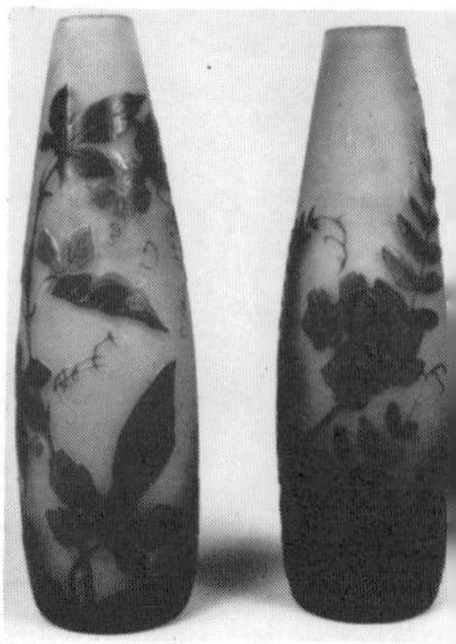

l. A Gallé cameo glass vase, overlaid with amber columbine on a yellow ground, signed, 7in (18cm).
$1,100-1,200

r. A Gallé cameo vase, overlaid in red on a yellow ground, signed, 7in (18cm).
$1,300-1,400

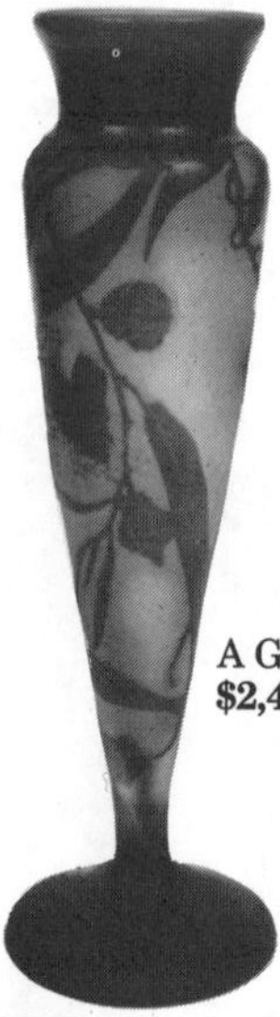

A Gallé cameo vase, 12in (30.5cm).
$2,400-3,000

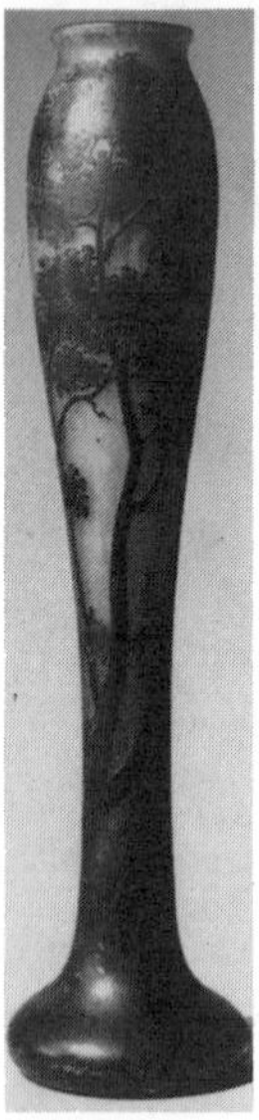

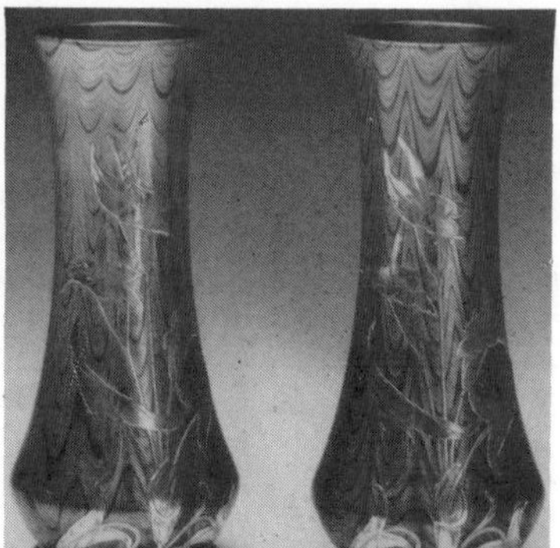

A pair of Loetz iridescent glass vases, decorated overall with blue and purple swags, overlaid in silver with lily-like flowers, inscribed Loetz, Austria, 7in (18cm).
$4,000-5,000

A Daum carved and acid etched double overlay vase, the amber mottled glass overlaid with red and dark amethyst trees in a lake landscape, carved signature Daum Nancy with the Cross of Lorraine, 28½in (72cm).
$4,000-5,000

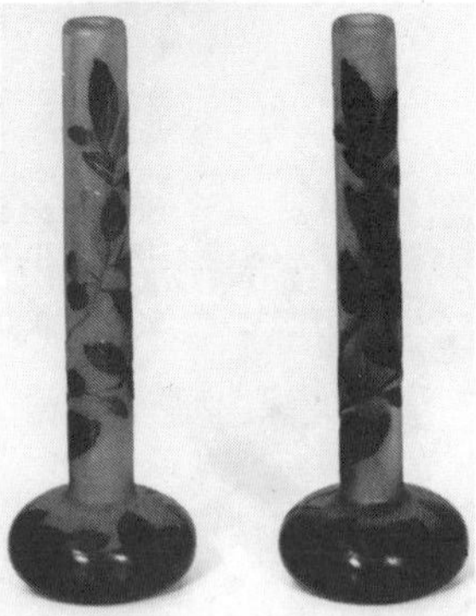

Two Gallé cameo glass vases, with signatures, 7in (23cm).
$1,600-1,700

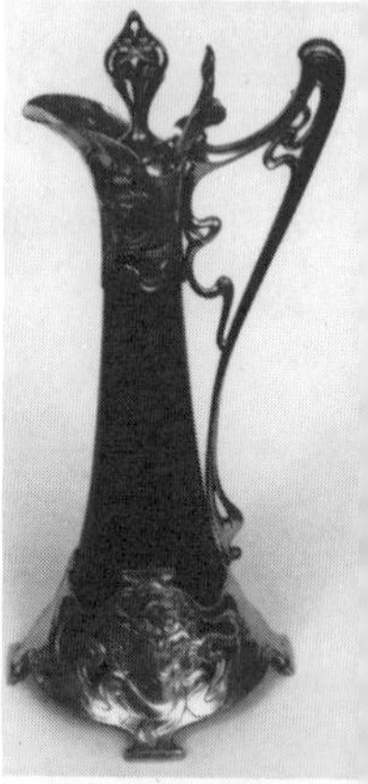

A green glass and silver plate claret jug, marked W.M.F. AS 1/10 EP, 16½in (42cm).
$1,200-1,500

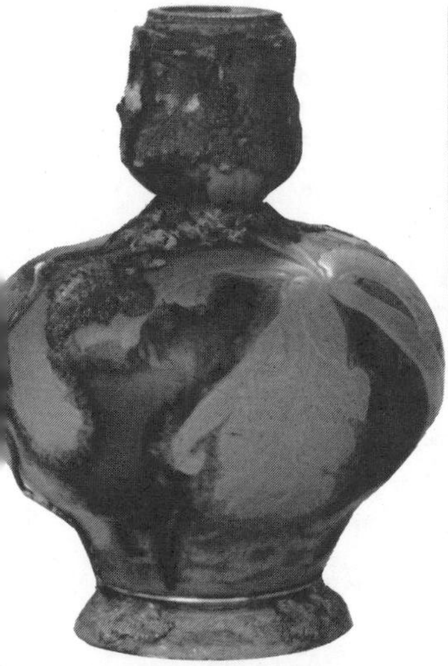

Daum four-overlay bulbous aped cameo vase, in opal over blue er ruby over citrine, carved with nvulvulous floral decoration, with plied metalwork vine neck, foot d trailwork to the body, repair to ck, signed to base Daum Nancy th Cross of Lorraine, c1900, 11in 3cm).
,000-5,000

An American vase, in green glass with silver overlay, decorated with orchids and arabesques, the mounts marked 999/1000, 14in (35.5cm). **$1,000-1,200**

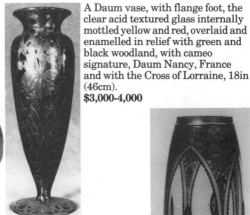

A Daum vase, with flange foot, the clear acid textured glass internally mottled yellow and red, overlaid and enamelled in relief with green and black woodland, with cameo signature, Daum Nancy, France and with the Cross of Lorraine, 18in (46cm).
$3,000-4,000

A pair of enamelled glass vases, by Faschulle Haida, 13in (33cm).
$600-800

ewellery

a silver and enamel pendant, c1900.
100-200

An Arts and Crafts pendant, in the Medieval style, with rubies, sapphires, emeralds and pearls and picked out in coloured enamels, 6in (15cm) overall length.
$800-900

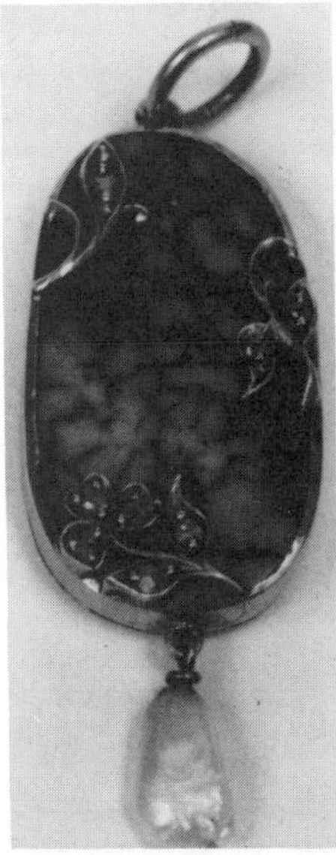

A silver and turquoise pendant, with baroque pearl drops and diamonds.
$400-600

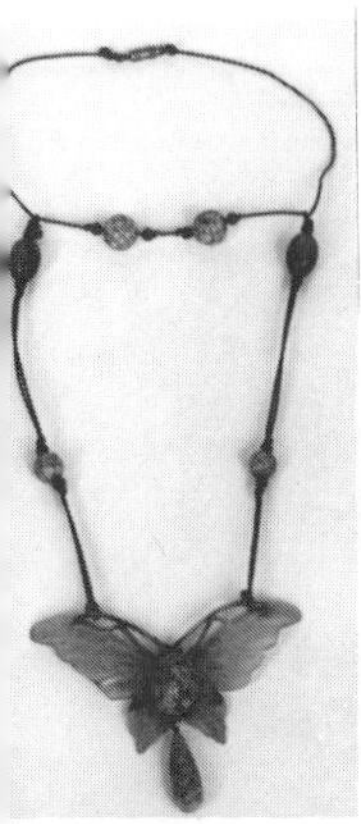

a horn and turquoise necklace, igned Bonté.
600-800

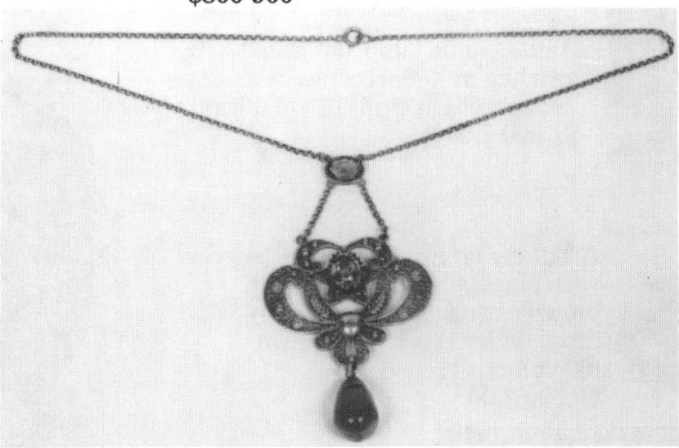

A pendant with amethysts.
$160-300

Lamps

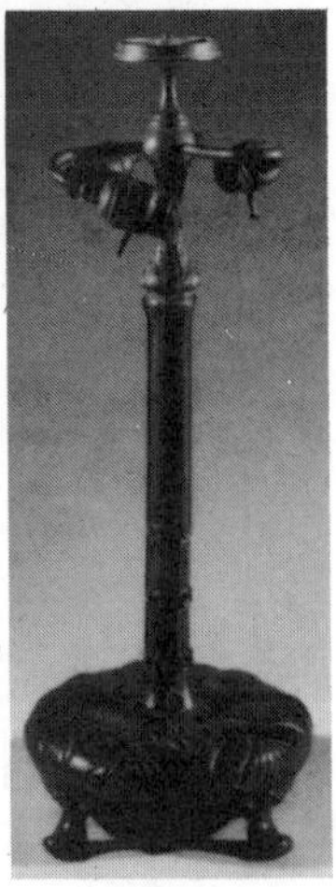

A Tiffany bronze library table lamp base, with brown patina, on 4 raised feet and stylised decoration of petals and vines, stamped Tiffany Studios New York 357, 22½in (57cm).
$6,000-7,000

An Almeric Walter pâte-de-verre panel, mounted as a table lamp, the pale amber glass tinged with amethyst, with moulded decoration of a fish amongst seaweed, fitted for electricity, moulded signature A. Walter Nancy, 8½in (21.5cm).
$2,000-3,000

A Daum etched glass and wrought iron table lamp, with mottled orange glass shade, the shade etched Daum Nancy, France, base stamped Katona, 12in (30.5cm) high.
$7,000-8,000

A Lallemant vase mounted as a table lamp, with polychrome painted decoration, illustrating a nursery rhyme, with painted signature T. R. Lallemant, France, 9½in (24cm).
$700-800

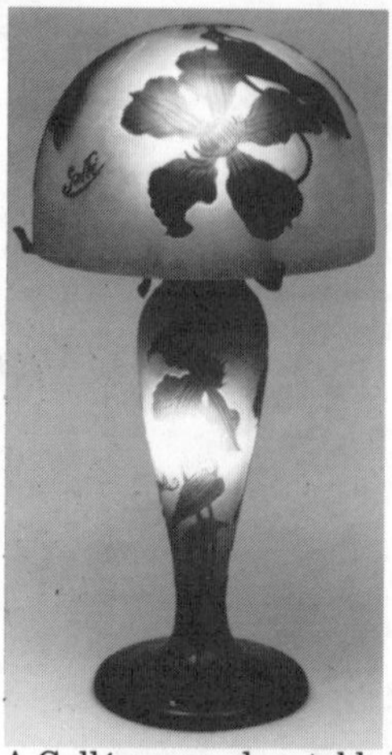

A Gallé cameo glass table lamp and shade, in purple glass on a yellow stained and frosted ground, each piece signed Gallé, 13in (33cm).
$13,000-14,000

A Guerbe Le Verrier green patinated, bronzed metal figural lamp, on veined marble base, inscribed Guerbe stamped Le Verrier Paris, shade etched Daum Nancy, France, 15in (38cm).
$1,500-1,600

A Gallé carved and acid etched double overlay hanging light, overlaid with green and dark amber pendant clematis, the metal suspension rod with decorated foliage, with carved signature Gallé, 14in (35cm).
$16,000-18,000

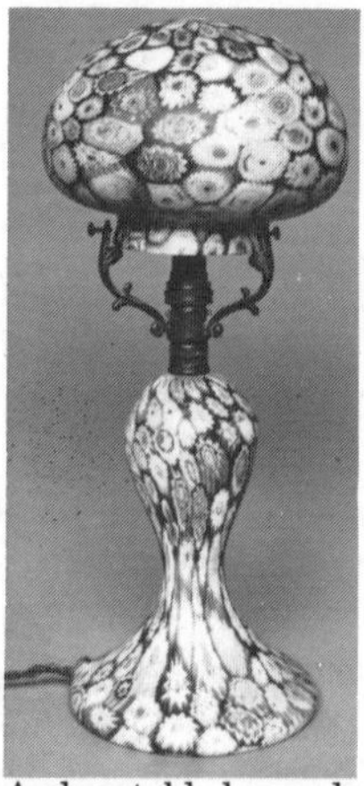

A glass table lamp, decorated with swirling millefiori canes, with brass fittings, slight chip, 13½in (34cm).
$1,000-1,600

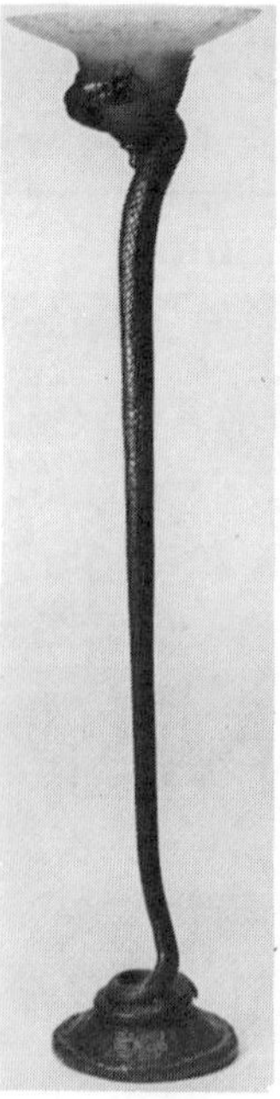

A Tiffany bronze table lamp base, with pineapple decoration with brown patina, stamped Tiffany Studios New York 366, 23½in (60cm).
$6,000-7,000

A glass and bronze floor lamp, in the manner of Edgar Brandt and Daum, cast as a cobra rising from a basketwork base, its neck coiled around a mottled, frosted orange glass shade with wide everted rim, 64in (162cm).
$4,000-5,000

An American Arts and Crafts prairie school wall lantern, c1900
$700-800

letal

W.M.F. pewter matchbox cover.
0-80

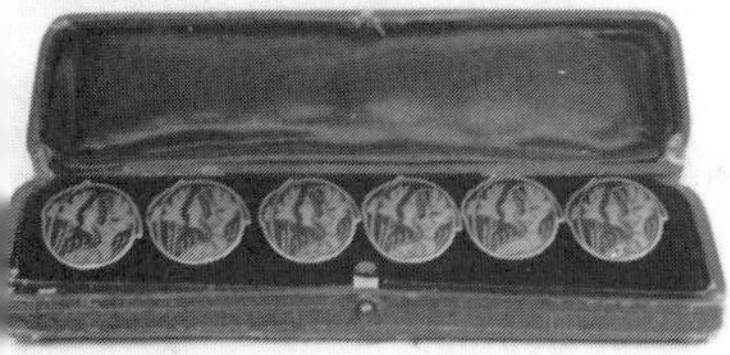

set of silver buttons.
50-250

wrought iron and copper
ndlestick, c1910, 13½in (34cm).
250-350

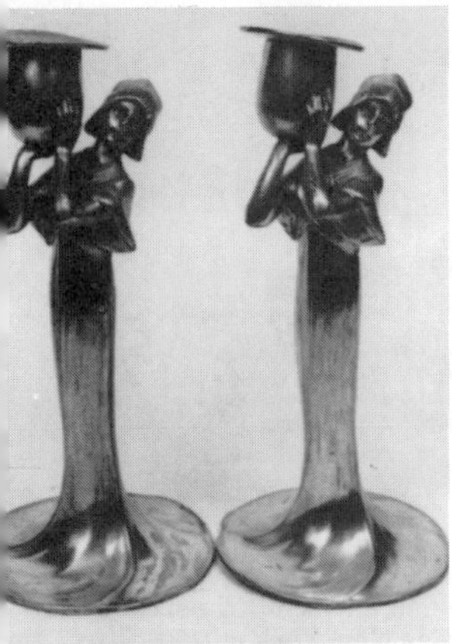

pair of W.M.F. pewter
ndlesticks, 8½in (22cm).
300-1,200

An Arts and Crafts copper candlestick, with 3 garnets inset on the stem.
$150-250

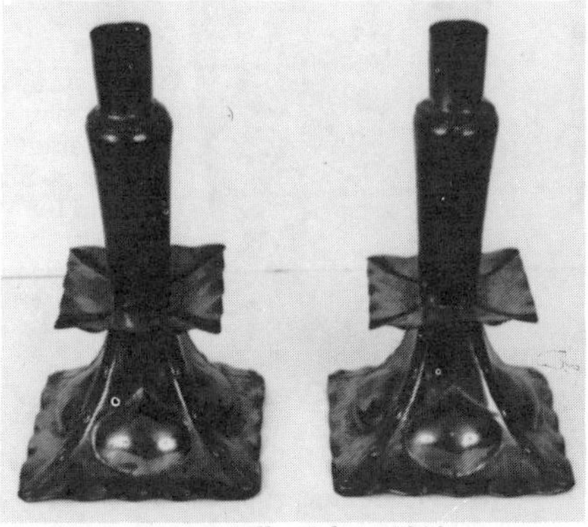

A pair of copper candlesticks, c1910.
$200-250

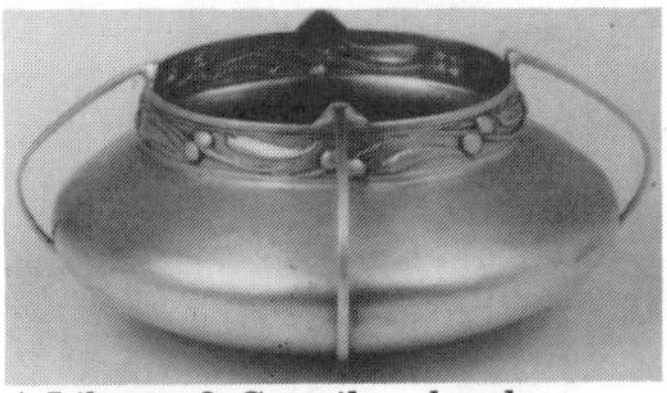

A Liberty & Co., silver bowl, stamped L & Co., and London, hallmarks for 1898, 2½in (6.5cm) high, 247 grammes.
$1,200-1,300

A copper bowl, by Keswick School of Industrial Arts, 16in (40.5cm) wide.
$500-600

A pair of Edwardian Arts and Crafts candlesticks, by James Dixon, Sheffield 1907, 8½in (22cm).
$1,400-1,500

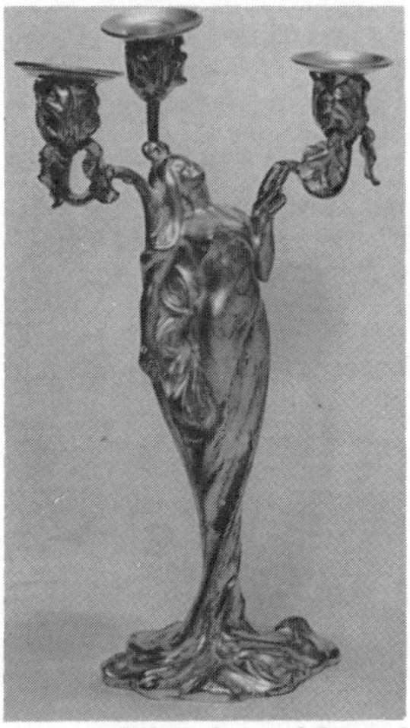

A pair of plated metal figural candlesticks, stamped marks on base 'B.G' and crown and Imperial 4572, signed on base C. Bonneford.
$3,000-4,000

An Arts and Crafts copper bowl, possibly by the Birmingham Guild of Handicraft, 7½in (19cm) high.
$600-700

A German pewter fruit comport, with glass liner, marked, 12½in (32cm) wide.
$600-800

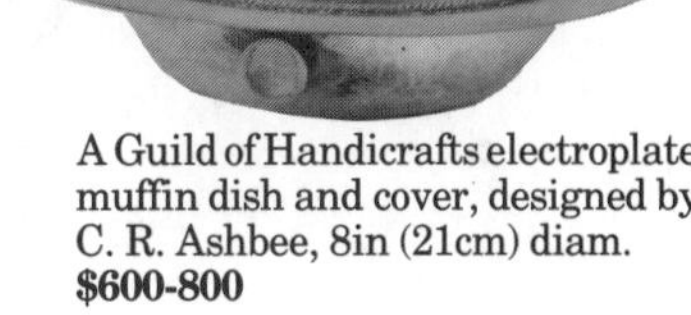

A Guild of Handicrafts electroplated muffin dish and cover, designed by C. R. Ashbee, 8in (21cm) diam.
$600-800

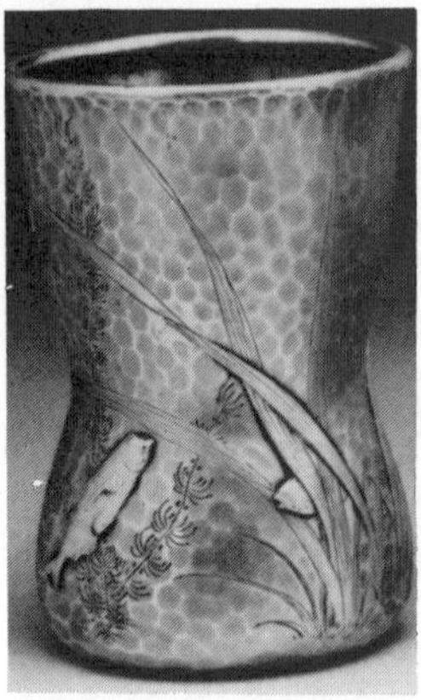

A pair of beakers, with an applied mid-rib and applied initials WWM, by Lebolt, Chicago, c1920, 3½in (9cm) high, 9oz.
$500-600

A beaker with hammer-faceted surface, applied with fish against an engraved and chased seagrass, bruised, Tiffany & Company, New York, c1880, 4in (10cm) high, 5.5oz.
$1,200-1,600

A sugar bowl in the Japanese taste, the hammer-faceted surface applied with 2 copper crabs and one silver clam shell, against chased seagrass, by Tiffany & Company, New York, c1880, 2in (5cm) high, 4.5oz.
$1,000-1,200

A pair of beakers, the hammer-faceted surface applied with a stylised monogram within a circle, with later engraved initials WWM, by Chicago Silver Co., c1930, 4½in (11cm), 11oz.
$500-600

A pair of salt and pepper casters in the Persian taste, by Tiffany & Company, New York, c1870, 4in (10cm) high, 4oz.
$1,500-2,000

A pair of salt and pepper casters, decorated in the Japanese taste, by Tiffany & Company, New York, c1875, 5in (12.5cm) high, 7.5oz.
$9,000-11,000

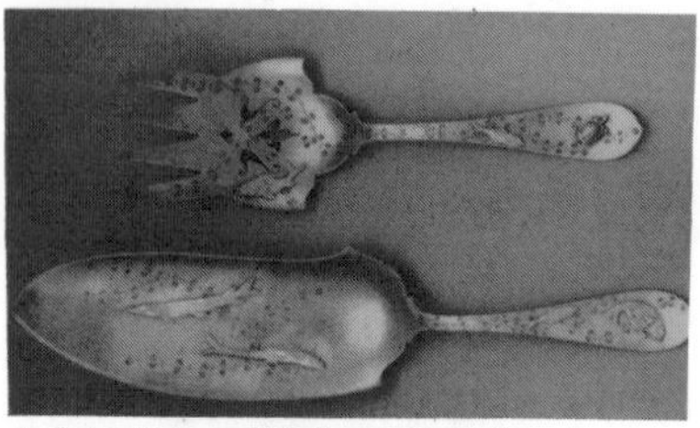

A fish slice and fork, engraved and chased with seaweed and applied with cast fish and a turtle, by Tiffany & Co., New York, c1878, slice 11½in (29cm) long, 8oz.
$3,000-4,000

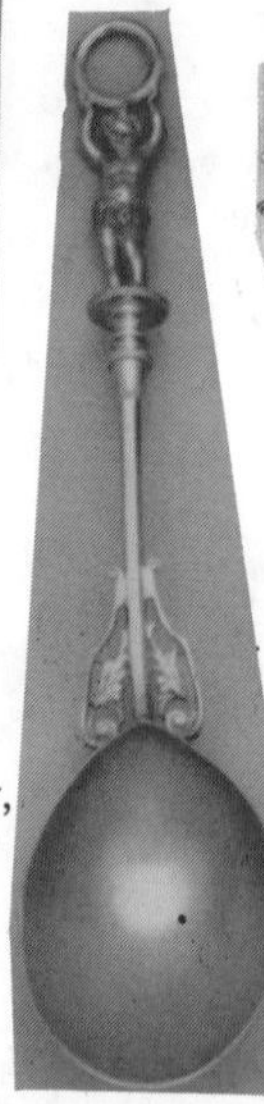

Five American servers, 2 by Gorham, the others by Tiffany, Wood & Hughes, c1860, 9in to 15½in (23 to 39cm) long, 22oz.
$1,200-1,500

A set of 4 compotes, with applied shell and scroll rims, by Tiffany & Co., New York, c 1880, 7in (18cm) diam, 38oz.
$2,000-3,000

A three-piece tea service, by Tiffany & Co., New York, c1895, teapot handle loose, teapot 4½in (11cm) high, 20.5oz gross.
$2,000-3,000

Chrysanthemum pattern
.tware service, comprising 102
eces, monograms removed, by
ffany & Co., New York, c1885,
4oz. weighable silver.
1,000-13,000

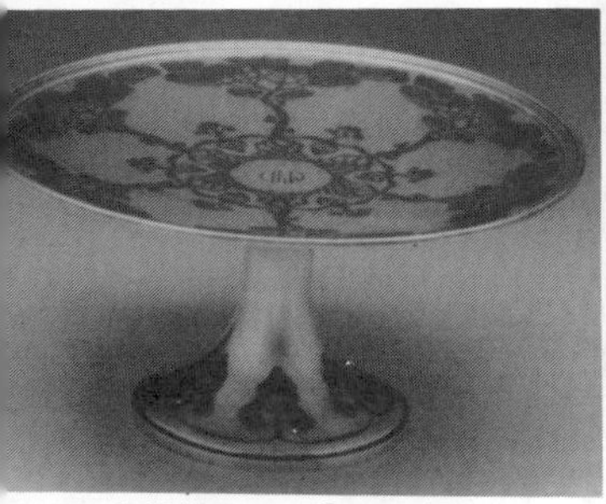

copper inlaid tazza, the centre
ith small monogram, by Tiffany &
)., New York, c1910, 8½in (21cm)
am, 16.5oz gross.
,500-3,000

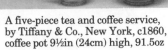

repoussé water jug, the base
graved with a monogram, by
ffany & Co., New York, 1886, 8in
0.5cm) high, 26oz.
,000-8,000

waiter, by Tiffany & Co., New
ork, c1885, 9in (23cm) wide,
.5oz.
0,000-12,000

A compote, by Tiffany & Co., New York, c1858, with later engraved monogram, 10in (25.5cm) diam, 31.5oz.
$4,000-5,000

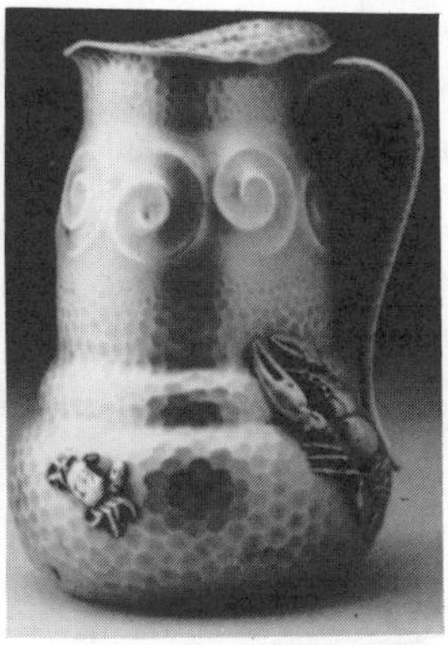

A repoussé jug, by Tiffany & Co., New York, c1880, 6in (15cm) high, 11.5oz.
$5,500-6,500

A five-piece tea and coffee service, by Tiffany & Co., New York, c1860, coffee pot 9½in (24cm) high, 91.5oz gross.
$5,000-6,000

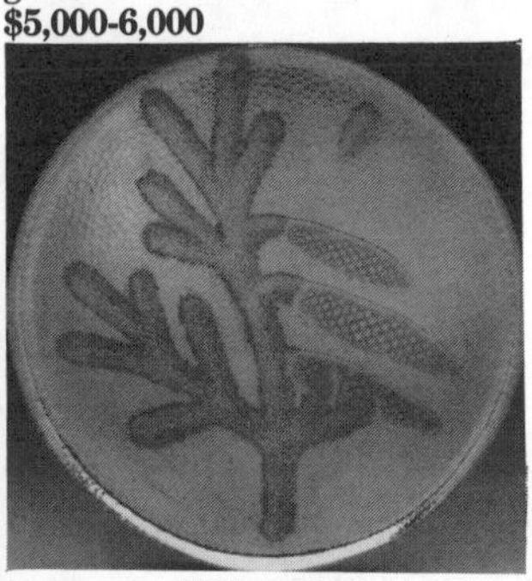

A tray, by Tiffany & Co., New York, c1885, 16in (40.5cm) diam, 64oz.
$10,000-12,000

A tea tray, by Tiffany & Co., New York, c1855, 28in (71cm) long, 108oz.
$5,000-7,000

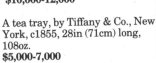

A repoussé compote, by Tiffany & Company, New York, c1890, 9in (23cm) diam, 33.5oz.
$6,000-7,000

A repoussé water jug, the base with later engraved script monogram, by Tiffany & Co., New York, c1880, 8in (2.5cm) high, 29oz.
$4,500-5,500

A wine cooler, by Tiffany & Company, New York, c1875, 13in (33cm) high, 88oz.
$11,000-13,000

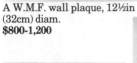

A pair of silver picture frames, Chester hallmarked, 12in (30.5cm) high.
$1,400-2,000

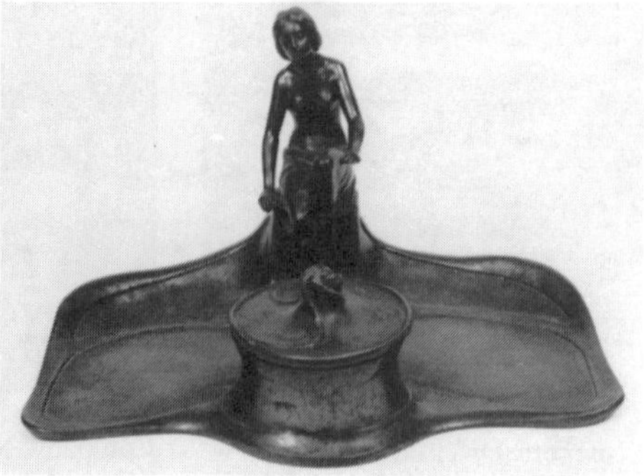

A bronze inkwell, 8½in (22cm).
$600-800

An Arts and Crafts tobacco jar, c1900.
$400-500

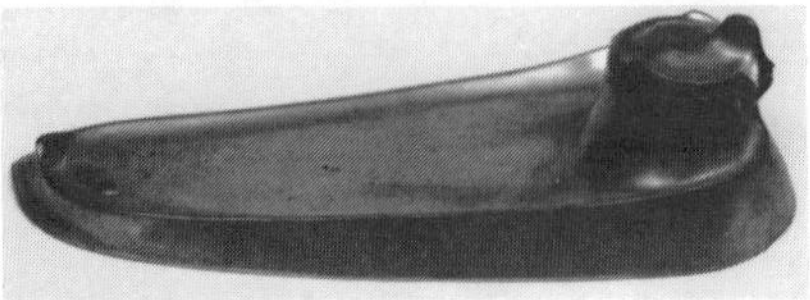

A German pewter inkstand and well, 11in (28cm).
$80-150

A pewter wall plaque, 5in (12.5cm) diam.
$60-100

A spelter figure on a tray, 6½in (16.5cm).
$100-150

A W.M.F. jug with lid, 13½in (34cm).
$400-800

A W.M.F. wall plaque, 12½in (32cm) diam.
$800-1,200

A Newlyn School copper plat stamped Newlyn, c1900, 10i (25.5cm) dian
$300-60

A pewter wall plaque, 5in (12.5cm). diam.
$60-100

A W.M.F. tray with figure in relie 15½in (39cm).
$600-900

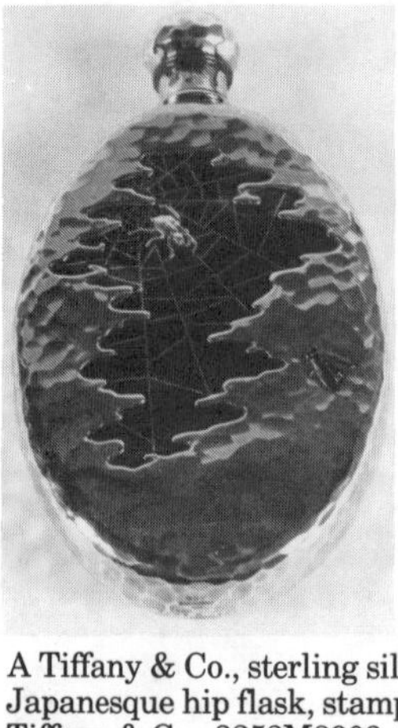

A Tiffany & Co., sterling silver Japanesque hip flask, stamped Tiffany & Co., 3252M8903, Sterling silver and other metals, 5½in (14cm).
$3,000-4,000

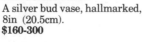

A silver bud vase, hallmarked, 8in (20.5cm).
$160-300

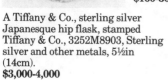

A Scottish pewter teapot stand, 7in (18cm) square.
$40-80

Austro-Hungarian silver sideboard dish, early
hC, 32in (81cm), 156oz.
,000-50,000

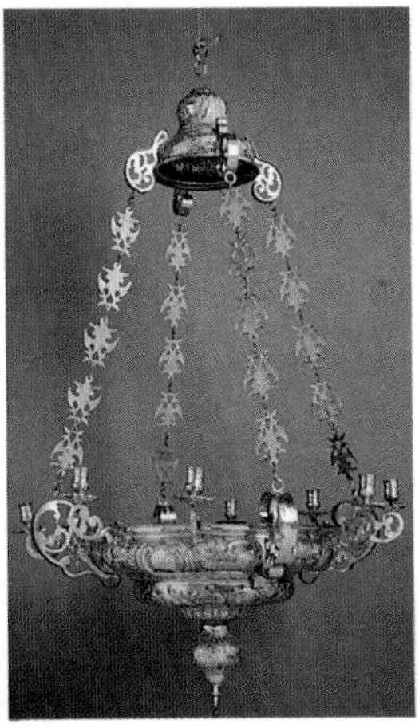

A Spanish chandelier, by Vincent Gargallo, marked, late 18thC, chain links and candle branches possibly later, 20½in (52cm) diam, 242oz gross.
$8,000-10,000

A George IV epergne, by Matthew Boulton, fully marked, Birmingham 1820, 15½in (39cm) high, 122oz.
$14,000-16,000

Continental silver gilt sideboard dish,
border late 17thC, altered c1830,
marked, 34oz. **$4,000-6,000**

A set of 5 George III meat dishes, by Benjamin Smith & Digby Scott, London c1805, largest 22in (56cm), 387oz.
$26,000-30,000

A pair of Victorian presentation candelabra, by C. F. Hancock, London 1866, 40in (102cm) high, 873oz.
$130,000-150,000

George IV tray, by Paul Storr,
ndon 1820, 28in (71cm) long,
oz. **$18,000-24,000**

A German silver gilt rose-water dish, maker's mark, c1640, 24in (61cm), 88.5oz.
$36,000-40,000

Spanish footed dish, apparently
lladolid, maker's mark, dated 1655,
in (24cm), 15.5oz. **$22,000-26,000**

r. A pair of Victorian silver gilt flasks, by James Garrard, fully marked, London 1890, 25½in (65cm) high, 315oz.
$80,000-100,000

The Large-Mifflin family tea and coffee service, by J. Richardson Jr, Philadelphia, 1799, 106oz 10dwt. **$90,000-100,000**

A sugar bowl and cream jug, by Tiffany & Co., New York, c1876, jug 4in (11cm) high, 11oz 10dwt. **$10,000-15,000**

A Victorian tea and coffee service, by Edward Cornelius Farrell, London 1845, 227oz gross. **$14,000-18,000**

A George IV inkstand, by Edward Bart London 1825, marked, 13in (33cm) wid 78oz. **$12,000-16,000**

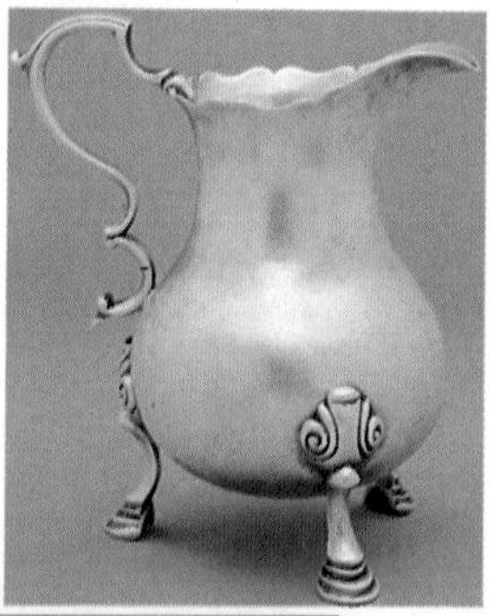

r. A cream jug, by Myer Myers, New York, 1745-76, marked, 4in (10cm) high, 4oz. **$14,000-16,000**

A George III soup tureen and cover, by Robert Makepeace & Richard Carter, London 1777, 13in (33cm) long, 98oz. **$10,000-12,000**

A Victorian tea and coffee service, by George Angell, London, c1866, marked, 114oz gross. **$8,000-10,000**

l. A George III soup tureen and cover, by Andrew Fogelberg, London 1774, marked, 14in (36cm) wide, 103oz 10dwt. **$18,000-20,000**

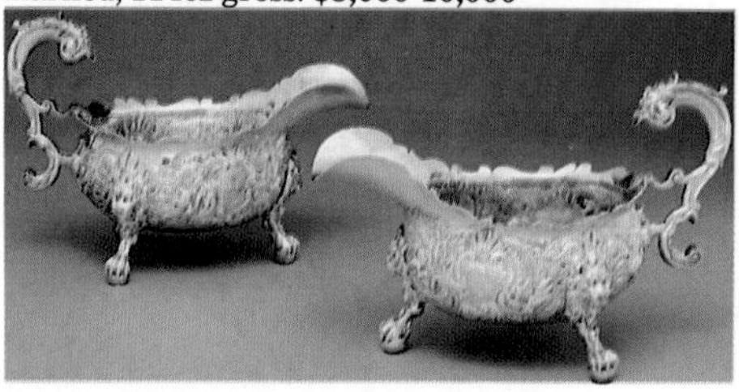

A pair of George II sauceboats, by John Payne, London 1752, 9½in (24cm) long, 47oz. **$12,000-16,000**

r. A pair of George III soup tureens and covers, by George Methuen, London 1760, 16in (41cm) long, 186oz. **$30,000-40,000**

A selection of pewter items.
From **$50-300 each**

A silver plated teapot, with bird's head spout, 19thC.
$200-300

An early Victorian Sheffield plate chamberstick, 7in (18cm).
$200-300

A porringer, by Paul Revere, mark struck on inside of bowl, Boston c1770, 5½in (14cm) diam, 8.5oz.
$18,000-20,000

A Victorian racing trophy, The Royal Hunt Cup 1845, by John S. Hunt of Hunt & Roskell, London 1844, on wood plinth, 24in (61cm).
$36,000-40,000

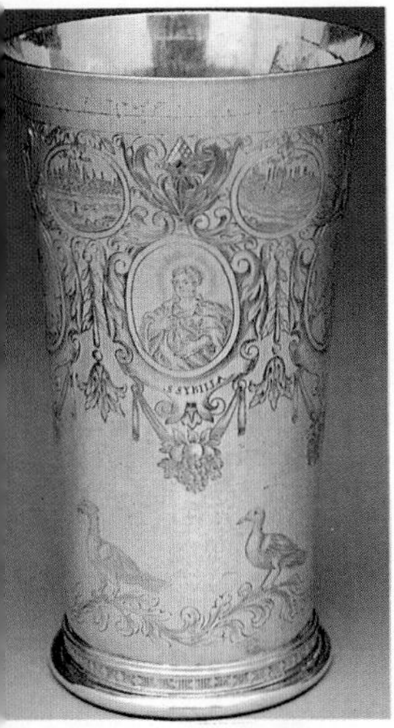

l. A German silver gilt beaker, by Joannes Jacobus Hultz, Cologne, dated 1717, 8½in (21.5cm) high, with domed cover, by Sebastian Crespel, London 1843.
$40,000-50,000

r. A set of 5 pewter plates, with bull's head crests, by James King, c1718, and 2 pewter bowls by Robert Nicholson, c1690, 9½in (23cm) diam.
$800-1,200

r. An enamelled Exposition vase, by Tiffany & Co, 1893.
$35,000-40,000

l. Two George II Irish cups and covers. **$22,000-26,000**

A George IV soup tureen and cover, with George III stand, 174oz. **$12,000-14,000**

A French bronze group of a stag attacked by a panther, cast from a model by A. L. Barye, signed on base, 19thC, 14in (36cm) high. **$5,000-6,000**

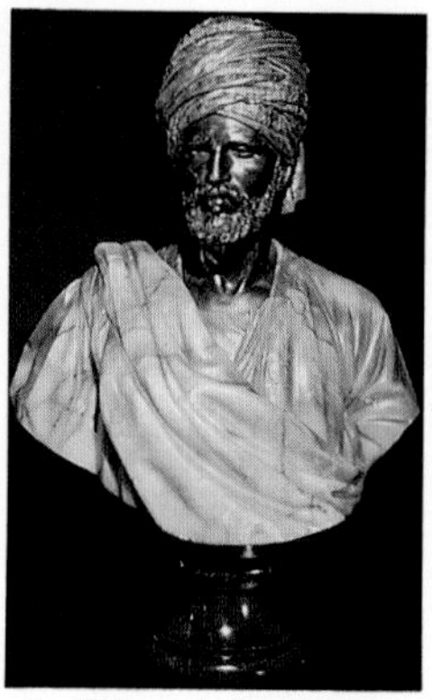

A pair of French bronze parcel gilt and enamelled busts, signed Cordier, on red marble socles, 19thC, 34in (86cm). **$400,000+**

An Empire ormolu and bronz chenet, attributed to Thomire plinth dated 1803, 16in (41cm **$10,000-12,000**

A French bronze group showing Fame, with coats-of-arms, attributed to Charles Gabriel Lemire, 18thC, 17in (43cm) high. **$50,000-60,000**

A Venetian gilt bronze statue of Neptune, in the style of Girolamo Campagna, 16thC, 17in (42cm). **$13,000-17,500**

An Anglo-Florentine bronze model of a horse by Francesco Fanelli, on marble base, 17th 6in (15cm). **$60,000-70,000**

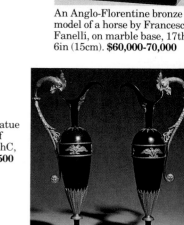

A pair of Empire ormolu and bronz ewers, with mottled green marble bases, 18in (45cm) high. **$8,000-10,000**

A French bronze group of Nessus and Deianeira, early 18thC, 16½in (41cm) high. **$40,000-50,000**

An English New Sculpture bronze statue of Perseus, from a model of F. W. Pomeroy, signed, late 19thC, 20½in (51cm) high. **$28,000-32,000**

r. An Irish bronze statue of Mr. Gladstone, cast from a model by Albert Bruce-Joy, 19thC, 38in (97cm) high. **$7,000-9,000**

›air of Empire ormolu stands, by P. P.
›mire, previously with glass bowls,
›cribed, 14½in (37cm) high.
›000-10,000

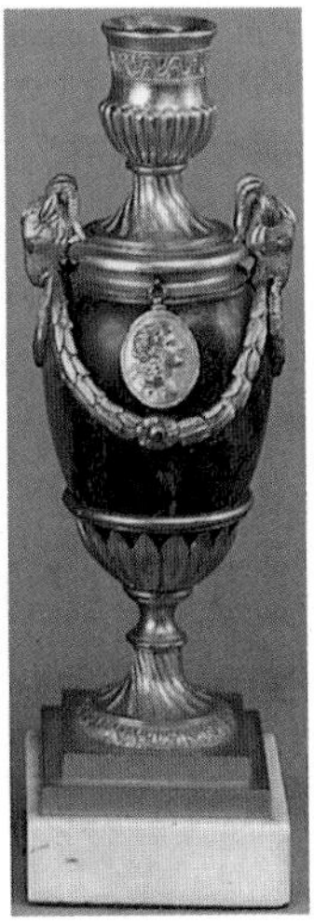

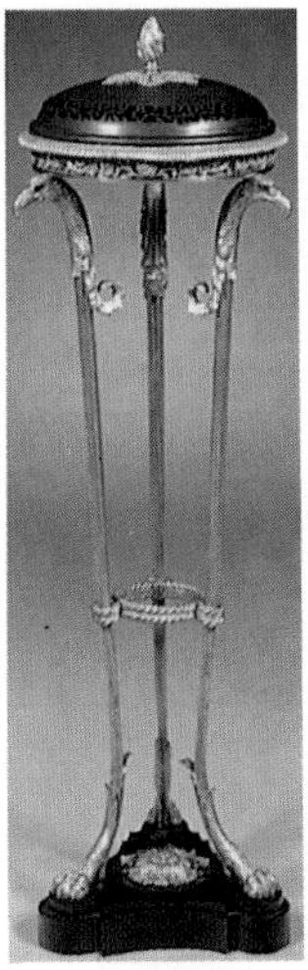

Above. A pair of George III ormolu mounted blue john cassolettes. **$16,000-20,000**
Right. A late Louis XVI ormolu and bronze brûle parfum, 35in. **$16,000-20,000**

A pair of Directoire bronze and ormolu brûle parfums, 16½in (42cm). **$28,000-32,000**

›pair of ormolu mounted
›vres porcelain vases,
› porcelain late 19thC,
› (23cm) high.
›8,000-20,000

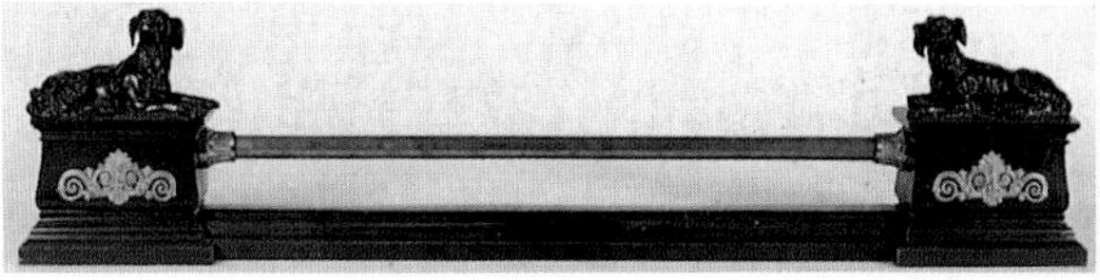

An Empire adjustable ormolu and bronze fender, with a pair of recumbent spaniels, 51in (130cm) wide.
$5,000-6,000

A pair of Louis XVI ormolu and bronze chenets, with later finials, 21in (53cm) wide.
$10,000-12,000

A pair of George III ormolu mounted blue john cassolettes, 10in (25.5cm) high.
$16,000-20,000

›pair of early
›uis XVI bronze
›d ormolu candle-
›cks, 12in
›.5cm) high.
›4,000-40,000

Above. A pair of Continental neo-classic urns, early 19thC, fitted for electricity, 17in (43cm) high.
$10,000-12,000
Right. A pair of Régence of ormolu mounted rock crystal obelisks, the ormolu early 18thC, 23½in (60cm) high.
$36,000-40,000

Above. A French ormolu male figure, 52in (132cm) high. **$80,000-90,000**
Right. A pair of ormolu chenets, 18thC, 10in (25.5cm) high.
$8,000-12,000

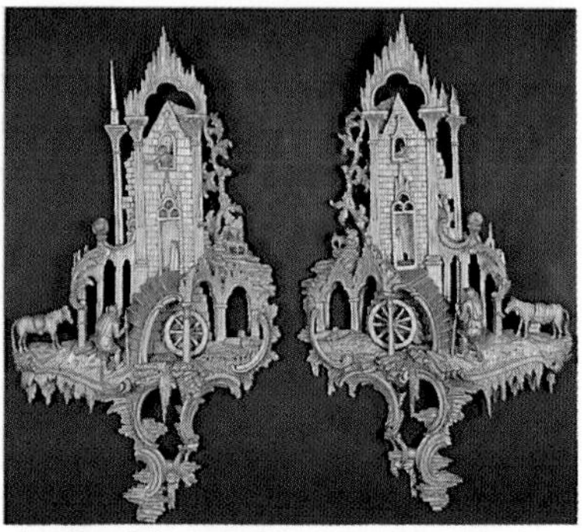

A pair of George III giltwood appliques, after a design by Thomas Johnson, 38 by 22in (97 by 55cm). **$20,000-25,000**

A French terracotta bust of Marguerite Bellanger, signed A. Carrier-Belleuse, 19thC, 28in (69cm). **$18,000-20,000**

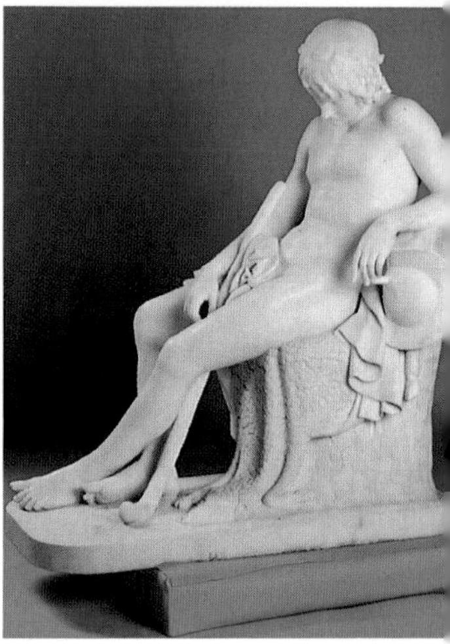

A British marble statue of a shepherd boy, by J. Gibson, repairs, 19thC, 45in (114cm). **$100,000-110,000**

A pair of Continental ormolu mounted marble ewers, c1775, 12in (30cm). **$8,000-10,000**

A polychrome and giltwood figure of Archangel Gabriel, 18thC, 31in. **$10,000-12,000**

r. A Regency painted plaster model of George III, by L. Gahagan, 11in (28cm) high. **$6,000-8,000**

A pair of Venetian painted and gilded blackamoor stands, supporting a moulded round platform, 31in (78cm). **$25,000-30,000**

A Louis XVI ormolu-mounted ornam with a bust of embracing lovers, 14in (35cm). **$14,000-16,000**

A marble bust of the First Earl of Stradbroke, c1811, 27½in. **$32,000-36,000**

A Regency ormolu and slate tazza, with 3 dolphin supports, 16in (41cm) wide. **$20,000-25,000**

l. A George III marble urn, by Matthew Boulton, 16in (41cm). **$40,000-50,000**

A pair of ormolu-mour white marble ewers, 1 (33cm). **$14,000-16,00**

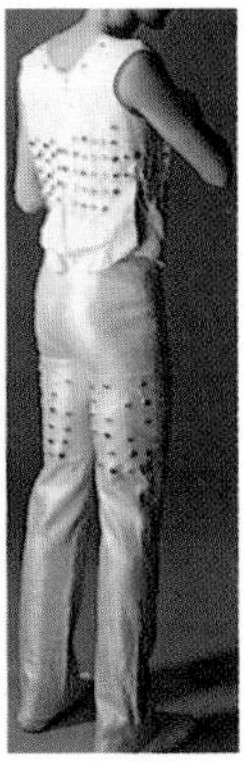

Two pairs of Michael Jackson's shoes, signed. **$4,000-8,000 each**

Michael Jackson's silver lamé stage suit, with iridescent glass decoration and matching bolero top. **$6,000-8,000**

vis Presley's suit, with mé cape, accompanied by letter of authenticity. **28,000-30,000**

A 5in gauge model of the D.R. 4–4–0 tank locomotive, by D. G. Sutcliffe, 34½in (87cm) long. **$8,000-10,000**

10¼in gauge model of the G.N.R. Ivatt 4–2 Atlantic locomotive and tender o. 251, old damage, 116in (294cm) long. **3,000-10,000**

A Tri-ang M.G. Magic Midget racer, with clockwork motor, 1934, 15½in **$2,500-3,000**

A Carette hand painted open tourer, with clockwork mechanism, 1907, 8½in (22cm). **$18,000-20,000**

bisque headed bébé, by mile Jumeau, the head npressed D8, the body with èbè du Bon Marché sticker, 1875. **$4,000-6,000**

A Gunthermann trio of musical clowns, c1890, 12in (30.5cm). **$8,000-10,000**

A bisque headed doll, by Schoenau & Hoffmeister, with composition jointed body, c1910. **$150-200**

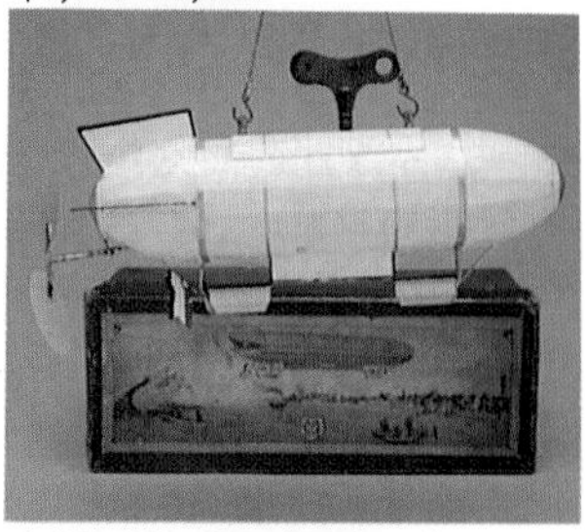

A Marklin hand painted airship, with clockwork motor, 1909, 10in (26.5cm). **$10,000-12,000**

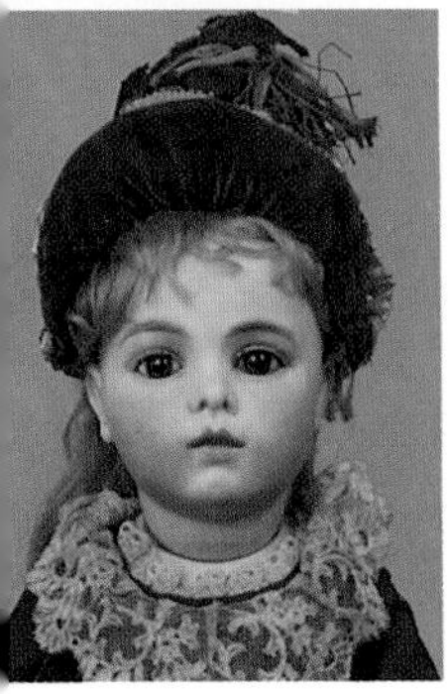

Left. A bisque headed bébé, damaged, marked BRU Jne 6, 18½in (47cm) high. **$20,000-24,000**

l. A Gunthermann racing car, c1904, 12in (30cm). **$50,000-60,000**

A Marklin water tanker, ma in 1919, 22in (55cm) long. **$32,000-40,000**

A Macdonald's Cut Golden Bar tobacco tin, c1900. **$60-80**

A French clockwork tramcar, by C. Rossignol, c1905. **$9,000-10,000**

A German horseless carriage, by Bing, c1899, 9in (23cm). **$35,000-40,000**

A miniature cocoa bean, c1890. **$120-150**

r. A 'caravan' biscuit tin, Jacob & Co, c1937. **$360-440**

A Sharp's 7lb toffee tin, with Mr. Kreemy Nut. **$100-150**

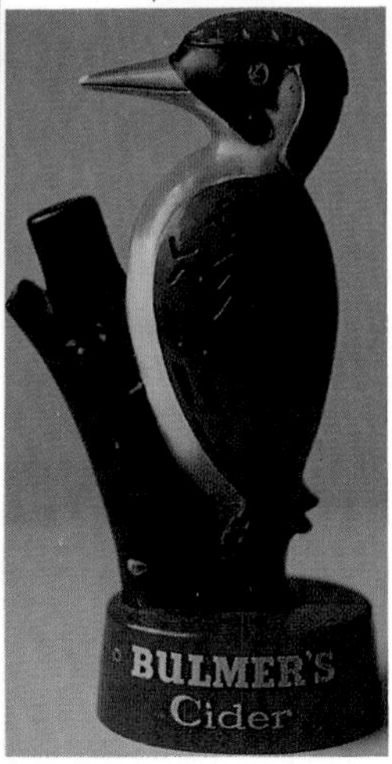

A Bulmer's Cider advertising figure. **$80-100**

An Edwardian enamelled sign. **$180-220**

l. A Pimm's advertising figure. **$100-120**

A Shieldhall, Heath Brown Flake tobacco tin, early 20thC. **$40-60**

L. S. W. R.
LEHMANN
U.S. MAIL
HEINZ
57 VARIETIES
PEARS SOAP
OXO
UNITED MOTOR BUS COMPANY LTD.
DINKY TOYS
260
CARTER PATERSON
EXPRESS PARCELS TRAFFIC
LNER

A 1955 Mercedes-Benz 300L lightweight Gullwing coupé, Registration No. XYN 215, Chassis No. 1980405500840, Engine No. 5500800, left hand drive.
$600,000+

A 1930 Lagonda 3-litre low chassis tourer, Registration No. WB 3582, Chassis No. Z3SB.SS Z9632, Engine No. Z1376. **$100,000-120,000**

A 1964 Jaguar E-Type 3.8 litre roadster, Registration No. ENP 359B, Chassis No. 850780, Engine No. RA 4249-9.
$50,000-60,000

A c1925 Hispano-Suiza H6B four-seater tourer, with replica coachwork c1970, Registration No. 506 JLB, Engine No. 300929. **$100,000-160,000**

A 1923 Hispano-Suiza H6B two-door sports saloon, coachwork by Vanden Plas c1930, Registration No. XN 9813.
$80,000-100,000

A 1915 Morgan eight-seater station wagon, coachwork by Martin & Parry, Detroit, Chassis No. P6910848, Engine No. 1904.
$16,000-20,000

A 1936 Lagonda LG 45 Le Mans replica, Registration No. DFP 244, Chassis No. 12166/G10, Engine No. LG45/295/83.
$140,000-160,000

A 1951 Allard J2 competition roadster, Chassis No. J.1852.
$180,000-200,000

A 1949 Healey Silverstone two-seater roadster, Registration No. MZ 8306, Engine No. B2887.
$80,000-100,000

A 1913 Sunbeam 12/16 three-door sports phaeton, Chassis No. 6224, Engine No. 6750.
$80,000-100,000

French gilt paper workbox, the interior ith scissors, silver etui and scent ottle, the silver French, late 19thC arks, 16½in (42cm) wide. **$3,000-4,000**

A Victorian oak decanter box, signed Harry Payne, 1888, decanters and glasses missing, 22in (55cm). **$6,000-7,000**

An Empire brass mounted mahogany 'necessaire de voyage', c1800, 14in (35cm) wide. **$18,000-20,000**

stoneware pot, inscribed Alison Britton '88, 11in (28cm) high. **12,000-2,400**

A spherical porcellaneous form by Gabriele Koch, signed, 16in (41cm). **$700-800**

A stoneware form, by Ewen Henderson, 20½in (51.5cm) high. **$4,000-5,000**

An Anglo-Indian ivory veneered game box, he interior with backgammon board and 3 oxes containing chess set and draughts, arly 19thC, 18in (45cm). **$3,000-4,000**

A Raku handbuilt figure, Cat Column, inscribed J. Crowley, 12½in (31.5cm). **$600-700**

An enamelled gold singing bird box, with fusee and chain movement, Geneva, c1825, 4in. **$40,000-50,000**

A stoneware bottle, by Hans Coper, impressed HC seal, c1971, 5½in (14.5cm) high. **$18,000-20,000**

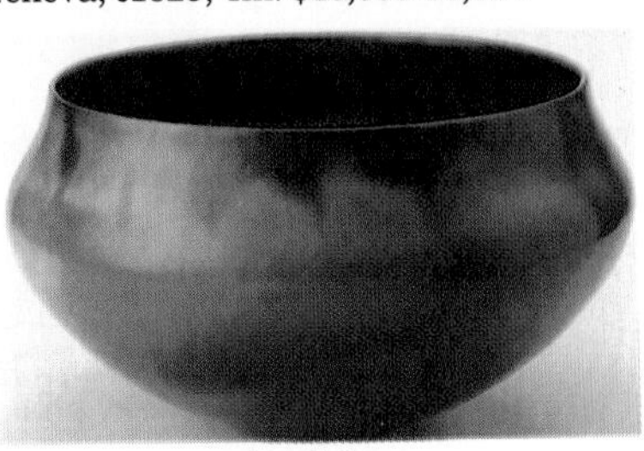

A porcellaneous bowl, by Gabriele Koch, signed, 16in (41cm) diam. **$1,600-1,800**

A porcelain bowl by Lucie Rie, c1978, 9in (22cm) diam. **$7,000-8,000**

A bronze statue of Cautopates, 1stC A.D., 2½in (6cm) high. **$8,000-12,000**

A Gandhara grey Schist head of a Bodhisattva, slight damage, 2nd/3rd Century, 20½in (52cm) high. **$25,000-30,000**

A polished black basalt foundation tablet of Ur-Nammu, c2100 B.C., 2½in (6cm) wide. **$60,000-70,000**

A Roman marble bust of Socrates, 1st-2nd Century AD, 18in (45cm). **$18,000-20,000**

A Romano-Egyptian painted plaster head of a female, 1st-2nd Century A.D., 8in (20cm) high. **$7,000-9,000**

An administrative tablet, with 10 cases of text, 2in (5cm) wide. **$35,000-40,000**

An Etruscan bronze bust of a winged siren, wing restored, early 4th Century B.C., 4in (10cm) high. **$8,000-12,000**

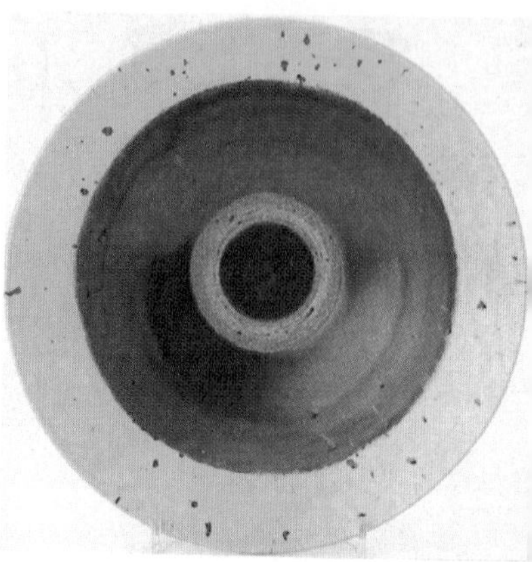

A stoneware bowl by Lucie Rie, slightly pitted, impressed LR seal, c1955, 10in (25cm) wide. **$5,000-6,000**

An earthenware bowl form, by Martin Smith, 1987. **$1,200-1,600**

l. An administrative tablet, with 17 cases of text in all, 2½in (6cm) wide. **$60,000-70,000**

ı Attic black amphora, .ded red and white for tail, c530 B.C., 15in (37cm) gh. **$35,000-40,000**

A marble group of a satyr and Dionysos, damaged, early 3rd Century A.D., 26½in (67cm) high. **$40,000-80,000**

An Attic black figure amphora, chipped and repainted, c510 B.C., 16½in (42cm) high. **$18,000-24,000**

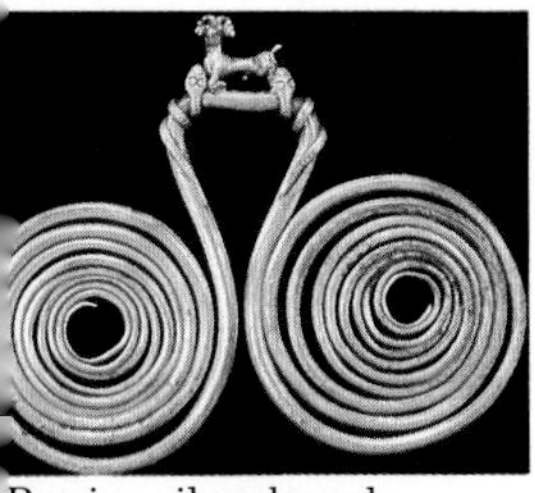

Persian silver brooch, nprising 2 coiled rpents, c1200 B.C., 5in 3cm) wide. **2,000-24,000**

An Attic red figure kylix, by the H.P. painter, minor restoration, c500 B.C., 4½in (11.5cm) high. **$140,000-160,000**

An Etruscan 'impasto' ware stand, repaired, late 7th Century B.C., 14½in (36cm) high. **$10,000-12,000**

l. A gesso-painted wood sarcophagus, framed, Ramesside, Dynasty XIX-XX, 63in (159cm) high. **$60,000-70,000**

ı Attic black figure ıochoe, minor repairs, rly 5th Century B.C., ı (23cm). **$260,000-300,000**

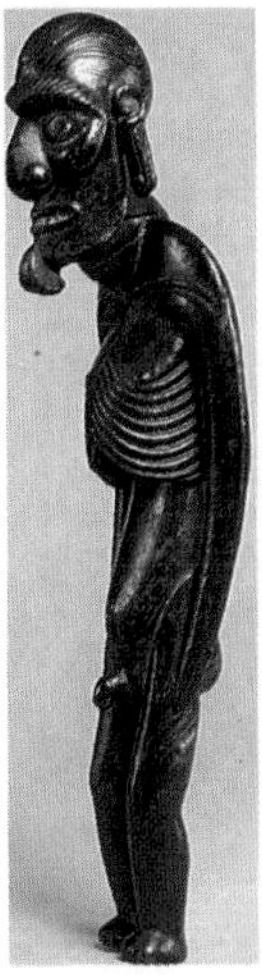

An Easter Island figure, neck repaired, 17½in (44cm) high. **$90,000-100,000**

An inscribed bronze vessel, reign of Utuhegal, King of Uruk, c2123-2113 B.C., 6in (15cm) high. **$200,000+**

ı Attic black figure cup, nor restoration, c550 B.C., ı high. **$80,000-90,000**

l. An American Indian spoon, the handle carved as an otter, the tail forming the bowl, 13in (33cm) long. **$4,000-5,000**

A lacquer Christian portable shrine, old damage and restored, Momoyama period. **$110,000-120,000**

A gold lacquer Kodansu, unsigned, 19thC, 4½in (11cm) high, with fitted hinoki box. **$10,000-12,000**

A lacquer Christian portable shrine, old wear and damage, Momoyama period, 8½in (21cm) high. **$90,000-100,000**

A lacquer Kodansu, the hinged door opening to reveal 3 drawers, slight old wear, 19thC, 4½in (11cm) high. **$6,000-8,000**

A lacquer robe chest, old wear and restored, c1700, 25½in (64cm) wide, on later stand. **$20,000-24,000**

A lacquer tray, with silver mounts, signed Somei (Muneaki), late 19thC, 12in (30.5cm) wide. **$8,000-10,000**

A pair of six-panel screens, Tosa School, Scenes fr
the tale of Genji, early 17thC, 142in (362cm) wide.
$70,000-80,000

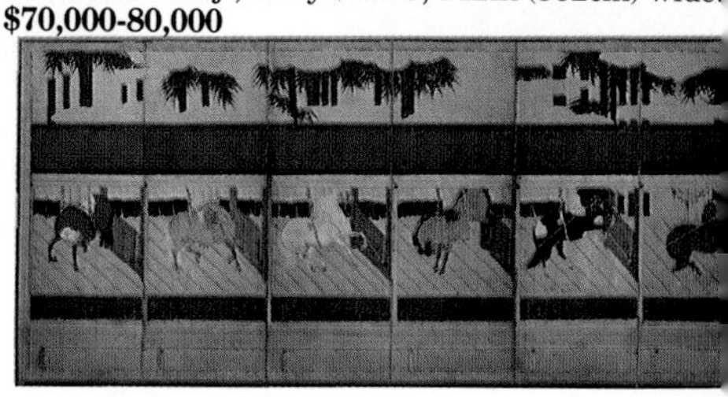

A six-leaf screen in Kano style in Sumi, old dama
retouched, unsigned, 17thC, 23½in (59.5cm) high
$90,000-100,000

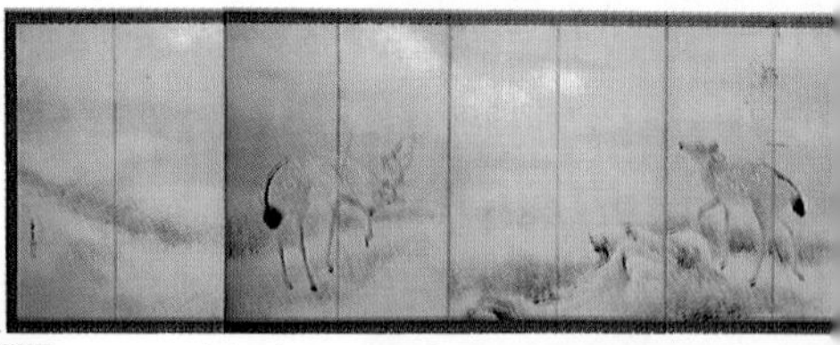

An eight-panel screen, attributed to Yo
Buson, 1716-83, signed Shunsei, 176in
(449cm) long. **$120,000-140,000**

A pair of six-panel screens, Tosa Scho
late 17thC, 104in (264cm) long.
$36,000-40,000

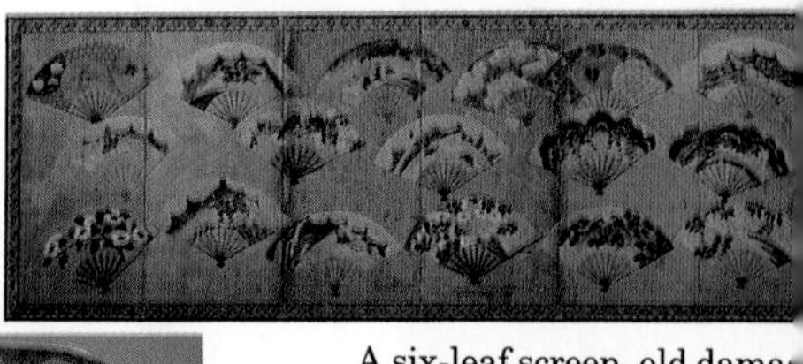

A six-leaf screen, old dama
and repairs, unsigned, c170
41in. **$16,000-20,000**

An export lacquer writing cabinet, o
wear and damage, late 16thC, 34in
(86.5cm) wide, with fitted wood stan
$280,000+

gold and silver inlaid
ronze animal form support,
'arring States, 5in (12.5cm)
igh. **$100,000-120,000**

An archaic bronze beaker, Shang Dynasty, 11in (27cm) high, fitted box.
$16,000-20,000

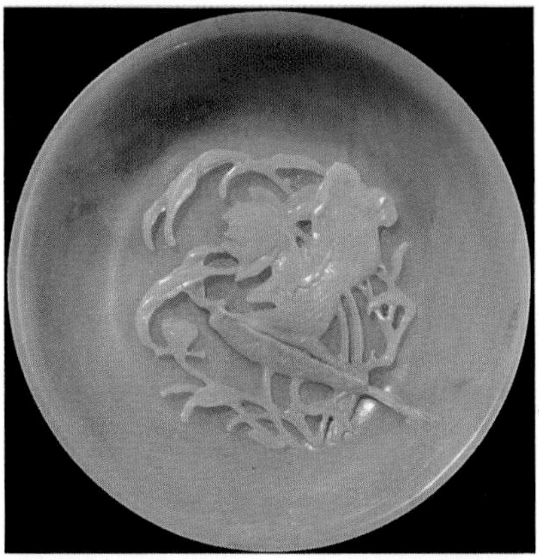

A celadon jade bowl, 18thC, 6½in (16cm) diam. **$10,000-12,000**

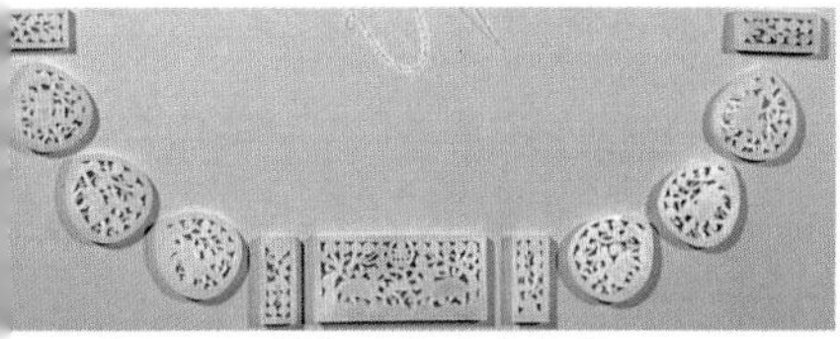

complete set of 20 white jade belt
aques, in various shapes and sizes,
e broken, Ming Dynasty, fitted box.
8,000-20,000

A Mughal white jade bowl, carved in shallow relief, 18th/19thC, 6½in (16.5cm) diam.
$12,000-14,000

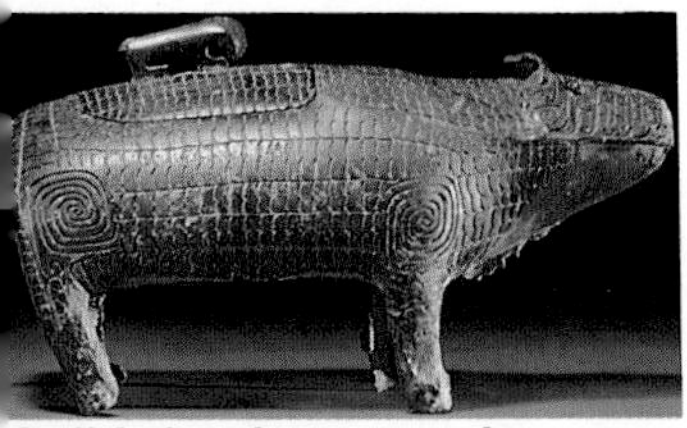

buffalo form bronze vessel
nd cover, damage, Shang
ynasty, probably pre-Anyang,
2½in (31.5cm) long.
3,000,000+

A Kashmir double metal figure of Samvara, damaged, 9th Century 7in (18cm). **$12,000-14,000**

An ivory and lacquer figure, replacements, signed Komin, late 19thC, 6in (15.5cm).
$10,000-12,000

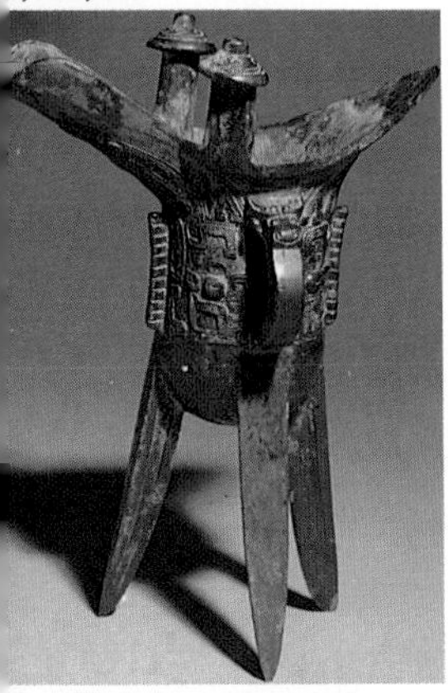

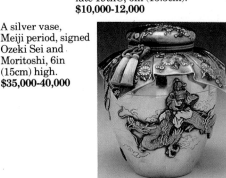

n archaic bronze tripod
bation vessel, some
alachite encrustation and a
ictogram behind the handle,
hang Dynasty, 8in (20.5cm)
igh. **$12,000-14,000**

A South Indian bronze figure of Krishna Nagaraja, corrosion and damage, 26½in (67cm) high.
$14,000-16,000

A silver vase, Meiji period, signed Ozeki Sei and Moritoshi, 6in (15cm) high.
$35,000-40,000

A pale celadon jade bowl, natural flaw, 18thC, 6in (15cm), wood stand.
$28,000-32,000

A pale celadon jade bowl, carved in the interior with a bat, on ruyi bracket feet, 7½in (19cm) wide across handles, wood stand. **$25,000-30,000**

A pair of ruby overlay white Beijing glass jars and covers, 19thC, 7in (17cm) high. **$7,000-9,000**

A gilt bronze censer formed as a qilin, repaired, Qianlong, 9in (23cm) high. **$25,000-30,000**

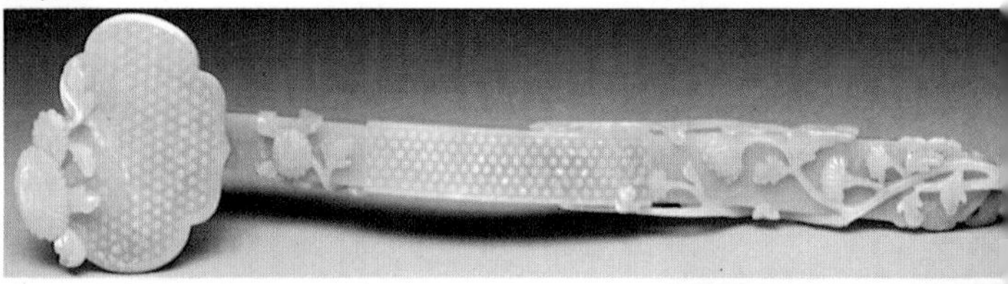

A mottled greyish green jade ruyi sceptre, repaired, 18thC, 17in (42cm) long. **$8,000-10,000**

A pale celadon jade plaqu both sides deeply carved, 18thC, 15in (37.5cm) high **$10,000-13,000**

A Tibetan bronze figure of Samvara, 16thC, 3in (8cm). **$3,000-4,000**

r. A gold and silver cylinder, Warring States, 5½in (13.5cm). **$40,000-50,000**

An agate bowl and cover, 6in (15cm) across the handles. **$1,800-2,000**

A pale celadon jade figure of a bea Han Dynasty, 2in (5cm) long. **$70,000-80,000**

A gold and silver inlaid bronze tiger form weight, Han Dynasty, 2in (5cm) wide. **$20,000-30,000**

A gilt bronze Taotie mask and ring handle, Warring States, 6in (15cm). **$26,000-30,000**

l. A pair of jade bowls, 19thC, 7in (17cm) diam, with box. **$5,000-7,000**

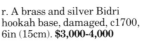

r. A brass and silver Bidri hookah base, damaged, c1700, 6in (15cm). **$3,000-4,000**

ɔale celadon jade censer, some natural
ws, 17th/18thC, 5in (12cm) square,
od stand. **$2,000-2,500**

A vase and cover, Mid Qing Dynasty, 9½in (24cm) high. **$14,000-18,000**

A celadon jade double cylinder vase and cover, 18thC, 8in (20cm). **$50,000-60,000**

white jade tripod censer and cover,
tural flaw, Qianlong, 7½in (19.5cm)
de. **$20,000-24,000**

A pale celadon vase and cover, Qianlong, 14in (35cm). **$30,000-40,000**

A jadeite ding and cover, incised Qianlong four-character mark, 10½in (27cm) high. **$50,000-60,000**

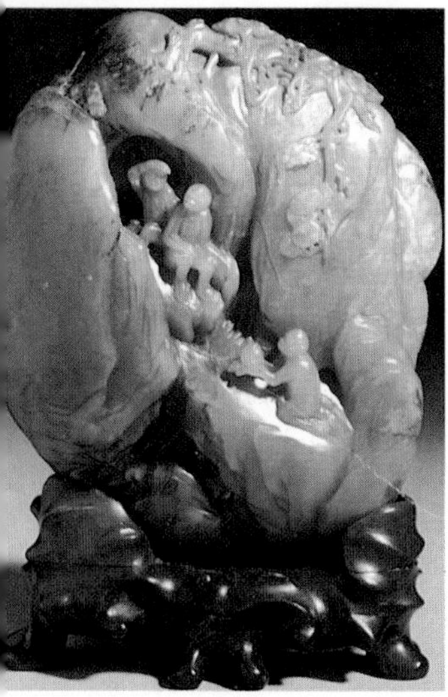

celadon and jade boulder
ountain, 17thC, 6in (15cm)
gh, wood stand and box.
4,000-16,000

A celadon jade phoenix and magnolia vase, Qing Dynasty, 8in (21cm). **$6,000-8,000**

A pair of jade vases and covers, 9in (23cm) high. **$20,000-24,000**

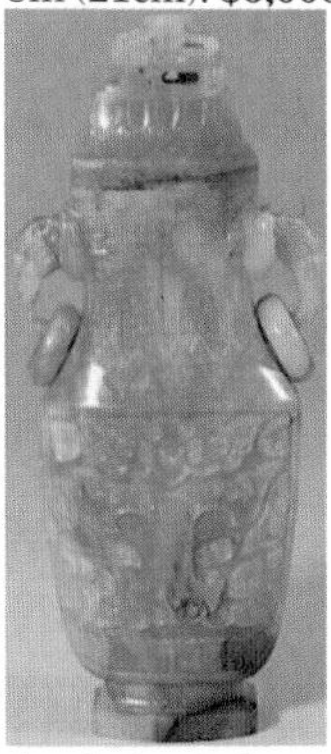

A celadon jade vase and cover, 10½in (26.5cm) high. **$4,000-6,000**

ı Imperial jade box and
ver, Qianlong, signed
roll dated AD 1821.
0,000-60,000

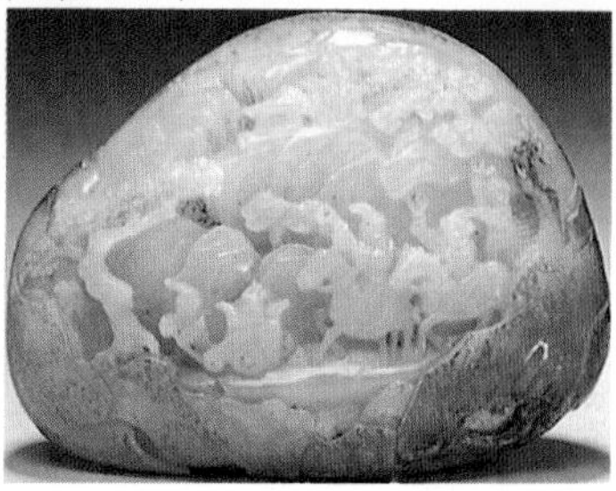

r. A jade pebble form mountain, 5in (12.5cm) long. **$8,000-10,000**

A pair of ormolu and Meissen porcelain twin light candelabra, the naturalistic branches with soft paste porcelain flowers and parrots, the porcelain 18thC, 10in (25cm) high. **$6,000-8,000**

A silk Kesi robe, fastened with 4 loop and metal ball toggles, yellow silk lining, 19thC, 55in (140cm). **$5,000-7,0**

An ormolu and biscuit porcelain clock garniture, clock movement signed F. Marti Paris 1900, candelabra 18in (45cm) high. **$8,000-10,000**

r. A giltmetal and cut glass eight-light chandelier, early 19thC, 48in (120cm) high. **$4,000-5,000**

A Festival doll of a samurai in armour, with attendant, 19thC figures, 18thC brocade, 37 and 21in. **$16,000-18,000**

A pair of William IV bronze colza oil lamps, Bright & Co, (Late) Argand & Co, 10½in (26cm). **$20,000-25,000**

A pair of George III giltwo wall lights, Thomas Johns style, 32in (81cm) high. **$14,000-18,000**

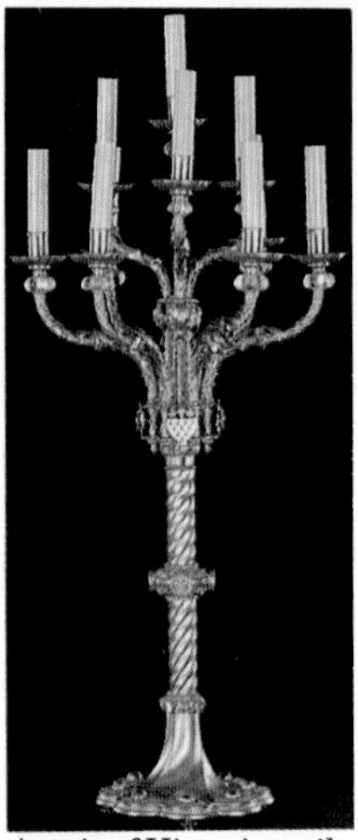

A pair of Victorian giltmetal candelabra, by John Hardman, Birmingham, with pedestals, 74in. **$35,000-40,000**

A pair of painted, parcel gilt 9-light candelabra, 82in (208cm) high. **$3,500-4,000**

A pair of Venetian parcel gilt lanterns, 19thC, 36in (91cm) high. **$5,000-7,000**

r. A cloisonné vase and cover, signed Kyoto Namikawa, Meiji period, 3in (7.5cm), with stand. **$8,000-10,000**

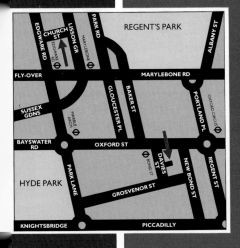

A pair of Louis XVI ormolu and marble candelabra, 27in (68.5cm) high.
$12,000-14,000

A pair of Empire bronze and ormolu candelabra, stamped Rabiat, 49½in (125cm) high.
$50,000-60,000

A pair of ormolu and silvered metal candlesticks, stamped, late 19thC, 7in (18cm) high. **$12,000-14,000**

A pair of early George III ormolu urn candelabra, 16in (40.5cm) high.
$35,000-40,000

A pair of early Louis XV bronze and ormolu candelabra, 19in (48cm) hig
$60,000-80,000

r. A pair of Louis XVI bronze and ormolu candelabra, 17½in (44cm) high.
$14,000-16,000

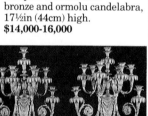

A pair of Louis XVI style ormolu and marble candelabra, 19thC, 39in (99cm). **$16,000-20,000**

A pair of George III ormolu and marble vase candelabra, 21in. **$140,000-160,000**

A pair of Louis XV ormolu and Chinese porcelain candlesticks, the porcelain possibly 18thC, 9in (23cm) high, including plinths.
$20,000-24,000

A pair of Louis XVI style ormolu and marble candelabra, mid-19thC, 34in. **$4,000-5,500**

A pair of Regency bronze and ormolu candlesticks.
$100,000-120,000

A Regency giltwood chandelier, 54in (137cm) diam.
$18,000-20,000

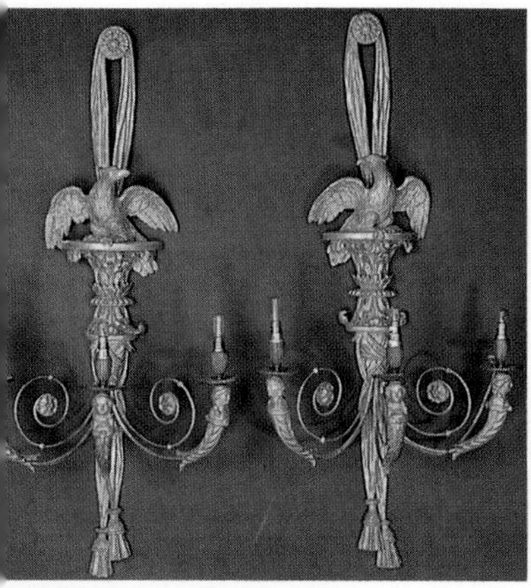

pair of George III giltwood and
nposition wall lights, fitted for
ctricity, 37in (95cm) high.
3,000-20,000

l. A George III ormolu mounted glass hanging lantern, 11½in (29cm) wide.
$7,000-9,000

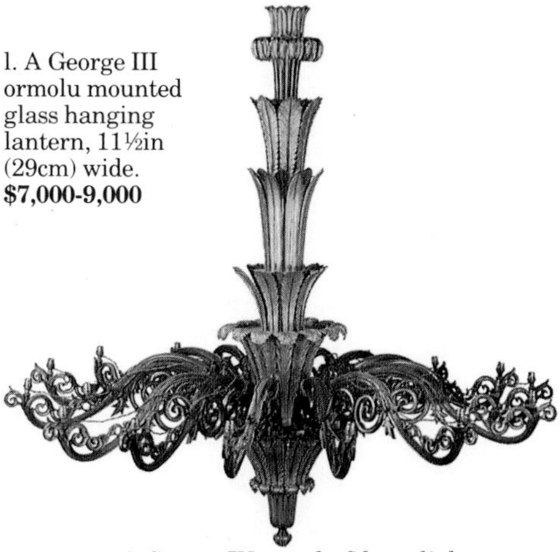

A George IV ormolu fifteen-light chandelier, fitted for electricity, 78in (198cm) high.
$45,000-50,000

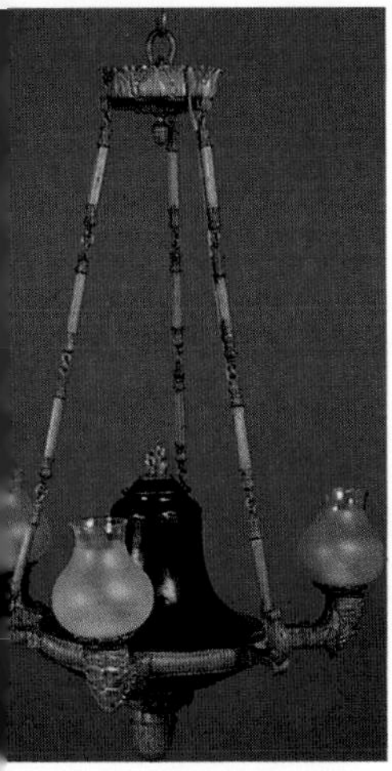

Regency ormolu and bronze
za oil chandelier, with
sted glass shades, 37in
cm) high. **$12,000-14,000**

A Regency ormolu and cut glass eight-light chandelier, 36in (91.5cm) high.
$13,000-15,000

A pair of Regency ormolu, cut glass and Wedgwood porcelain candlesticks and candelabra. l. & r. **$1,600-1,800**
c. **$6,000-8,000**

A pair of Charles X ormolu and patinated bronze lamps, c1825, 27in (68cm) high.
$16,000-18,000

A pair of Empire style ormolu-mounted rock crystal lamps, 20in (51cm) high.
$25,000-30,000

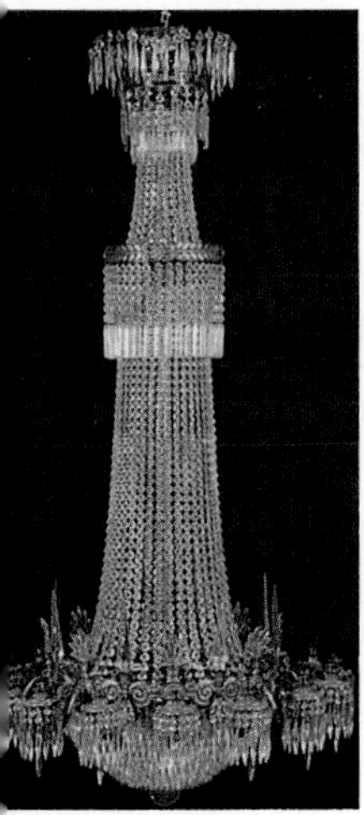

Regency ormolu
d cut glass 16-
ht chandelier,
in (234cm) high.
5,000-70,000

A Louis XV ormolu, cut glass and rock crystal nine-light chandelier, mid-18thC, 44in (110cm). **$25,000-30,000**

r. A pair of Continental ormolu, cut glass and rock crystal girandoles, 27½in (68cm). **$14,000-18,000**

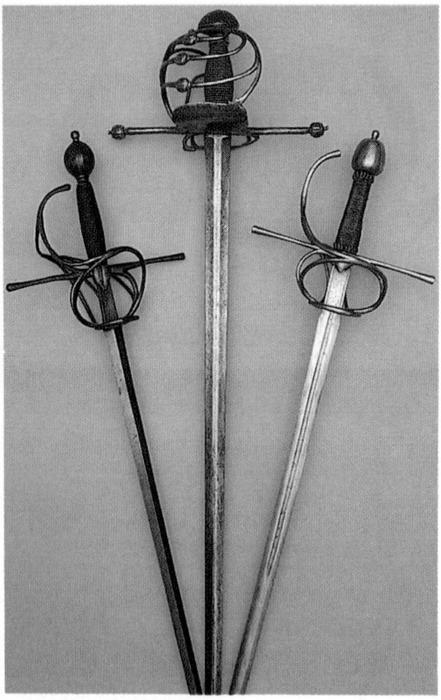

Two Continental rapiers and a broadsword, mid-17thC.
$2,000-2,500 each

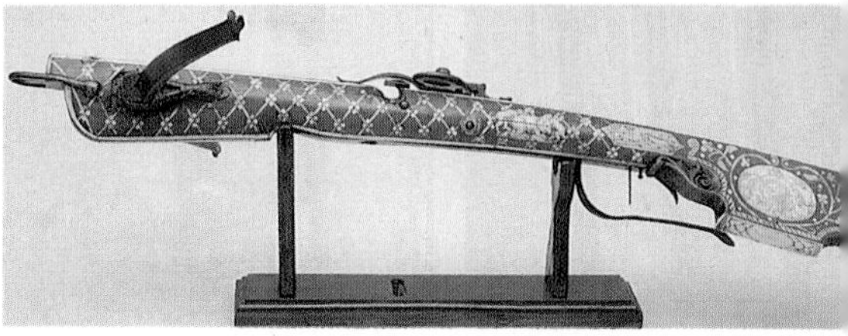

A German crossbow, some inlay restored, 17thC, 25in (63.5cm) long.
$4,500-5,000

A Lowland-Scots dagger, 17thC. **$11,000-13,000**

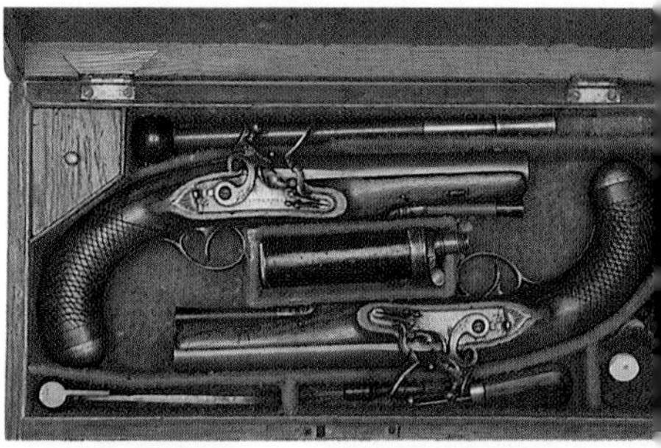

A pair of 16-bore flintlock pistols, b Tatham & Egg. **$4,000-5,000**

The Victoria Cross group to Lieutenant, later Capta William Leefe Robinson, Royal Flying Corps, late Worcester Regiment and memorabilia. **$200,000+**

An officer's shako, of the 10th Light Dragoons, c1855.
$3,500-4,000

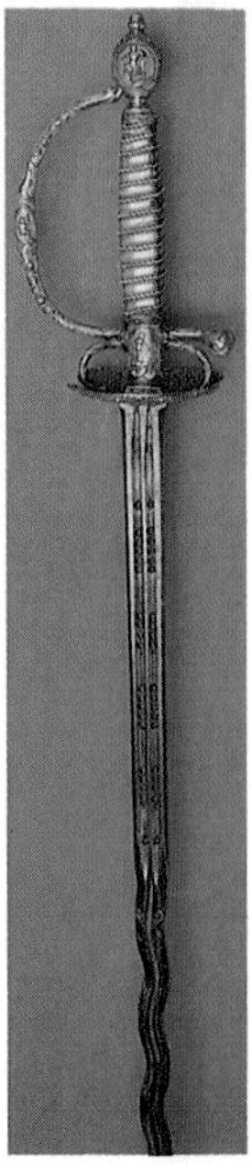

A French small sword, with associated blade, engraved 'Vivat", c1770, 39in (99cm) long.
$11,000-12,000

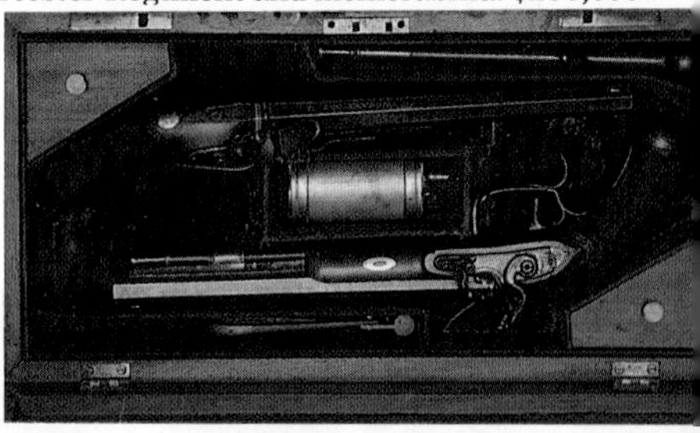

A pair of 34-bore flintlock duelling pistols, by D. Egg, c1795, 14½in (37cm) long. **$6,000-8,000**

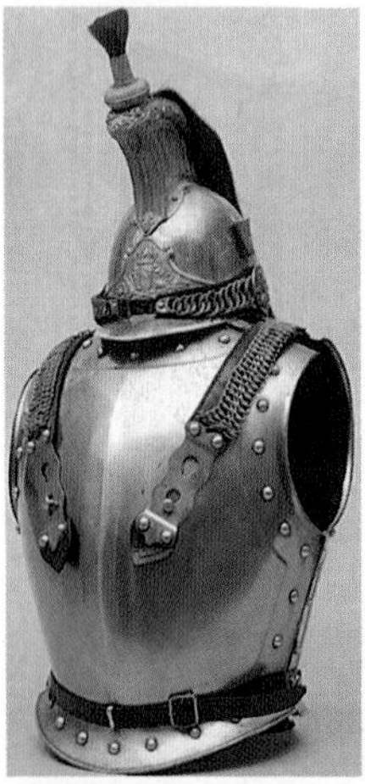

l. A French Guard Cuirassier officer's helmet, breast and back-plate, c1870.
$5,000-6,000

An Imperial German Garde du Corps parade helmet, and undress gilt fluted spike and mount.
$12,000-14,000

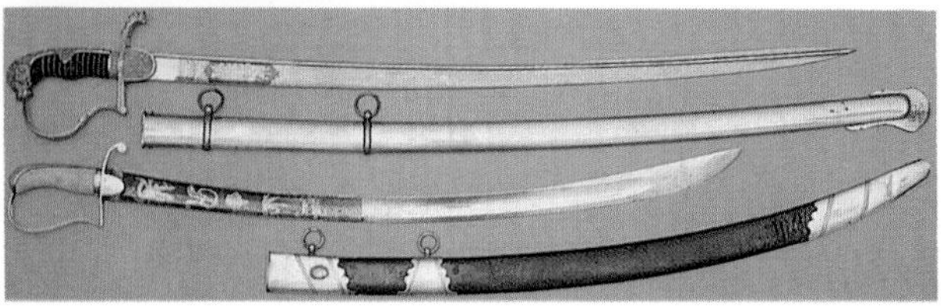

An Imperial German Cavalry officer's sword and a British Cavalry officer's sword.
$1,600-1,800 each

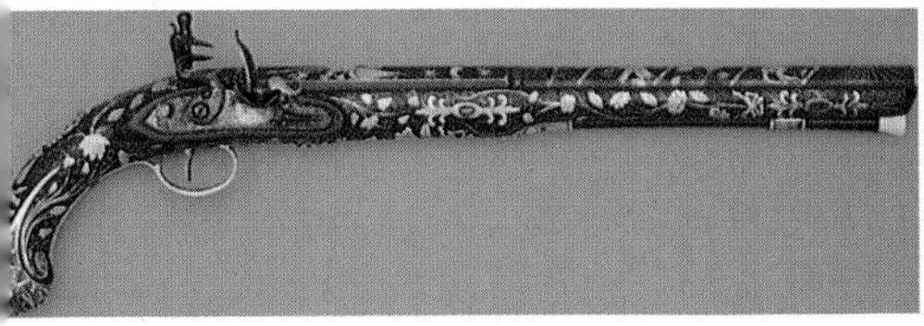

silver mounted flintlock presentation
stol, with two-stage sighted barrel,
laid with engraved silver trophies of
ms and foliage, by Rundell, Bridge &
ndell, London, London silver hallmarks
· 1802, maker's mark of Moses Brent,
½in (55cm).
,000-10,000

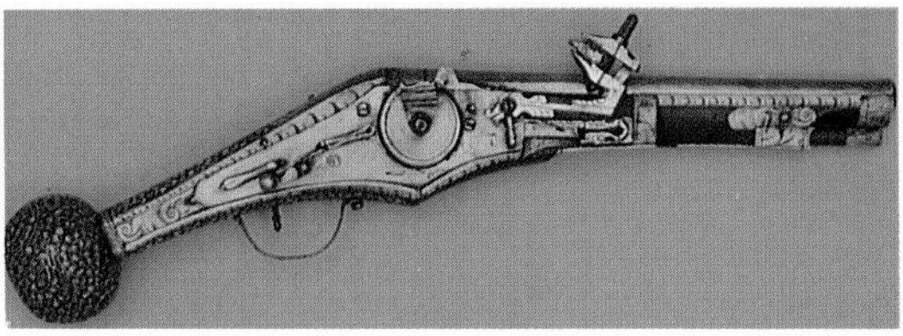

A German wheel-lock pistol, struck with maker's mark and initials 'INS', probably Thuringian, dated 1577, and later horn tipped wooden ramrod, 21in (54cm).
$14,000-16,000

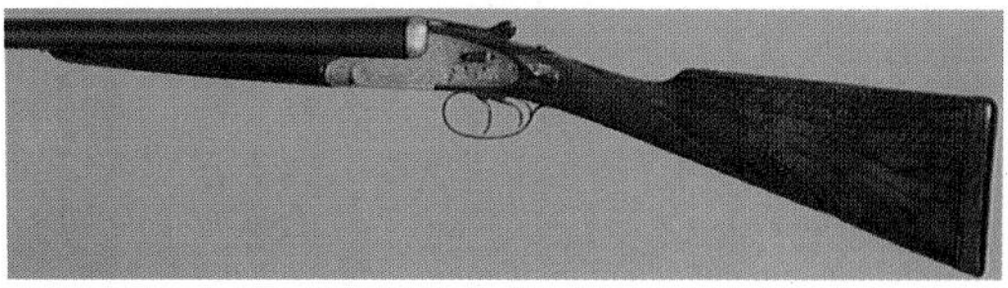

A pair of 12-bore Royal Brevis self-opening sidelock ejector guns by Holland & Holland, No. 33017/8, 1935, 28in (71cm) barrels, with oak and leather case.
$45,000-50,000

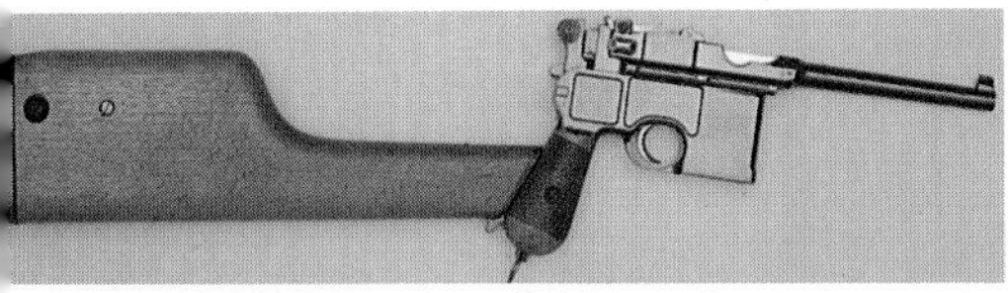

7.63mm civilian Mauser model 96 semi-
tomatic pistol, No. 2103, 5½in (12.5cm)
rrel. **$2,000-3,000**

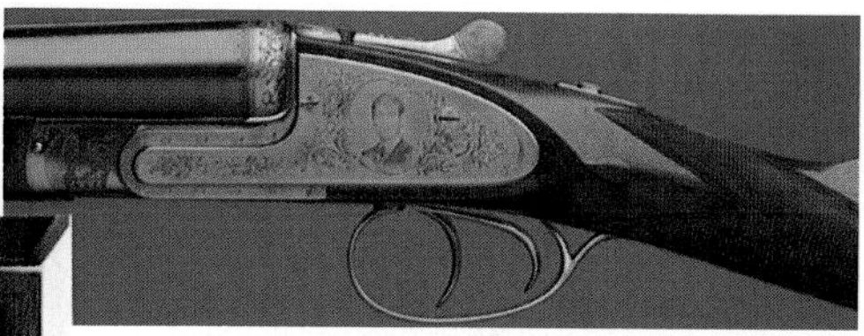

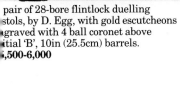

A 12-gauge D.B. hammerless sidelock ejector gun, by Westley Richards, No. 19704, built to commemorate the marriage of HRH Prince Andrew to Sarah Ferguson, 23rd July, 1986.
$20,000-24,000

pair of 28-bore flintlock duelling
stols, by D. Egg, with gold escutcheons
graved with 4 ball coronet above
itial 'B', 10in (25.5cm) barrels.
,500-6,000

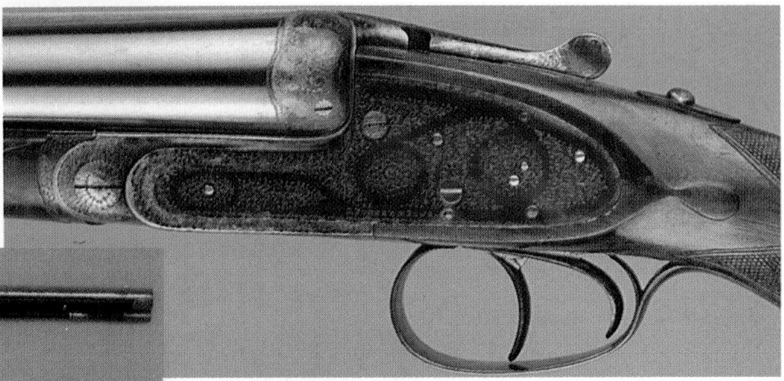

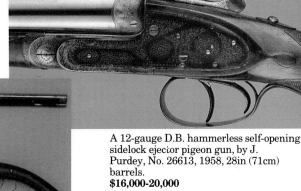

A 12-gauge D.B. hammerless self-opening sidelock ejector pigeon gun, by J. Purdey, No. 26613, 1958, 28in (71cm) barrels.
$16,000-20,000

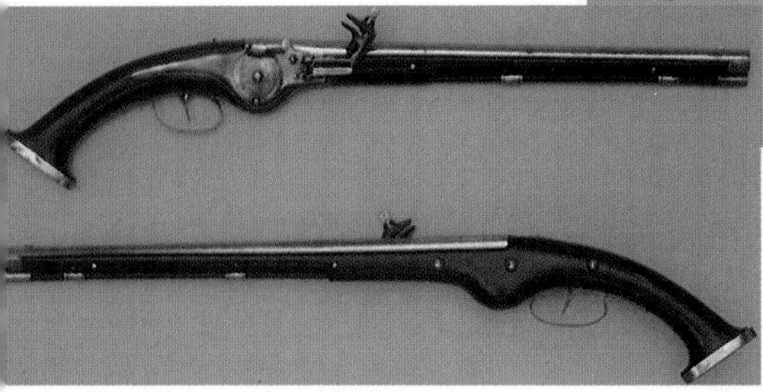

pair of Dutch long wheel-lock holster
stols, maker's mark and initials 'TK',
pairs, c1640, 42in (107cm).
2,000-14,000

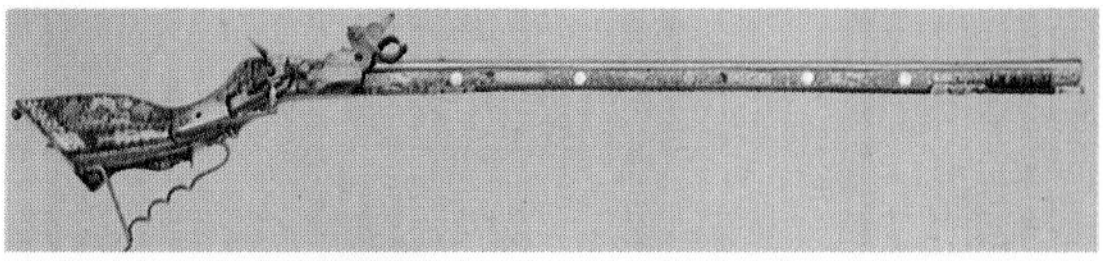

A .32in East German wheel-lock birding rifle Tschink, c1650, 43in (109cm).
$9,000-10,000

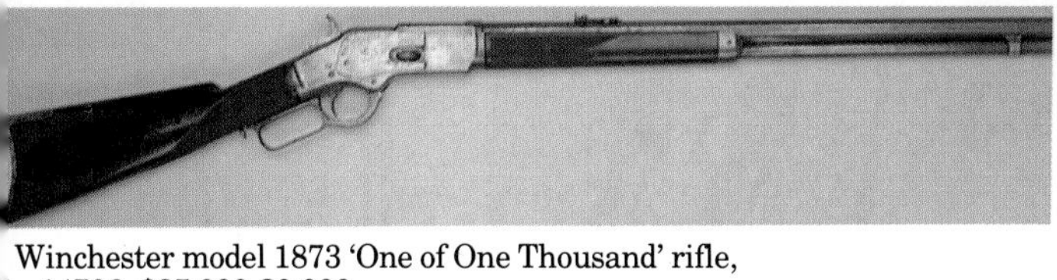

Winchester model 1873 'One of One Thousand' rifle,
o. 14706. **$25,000-30,000**

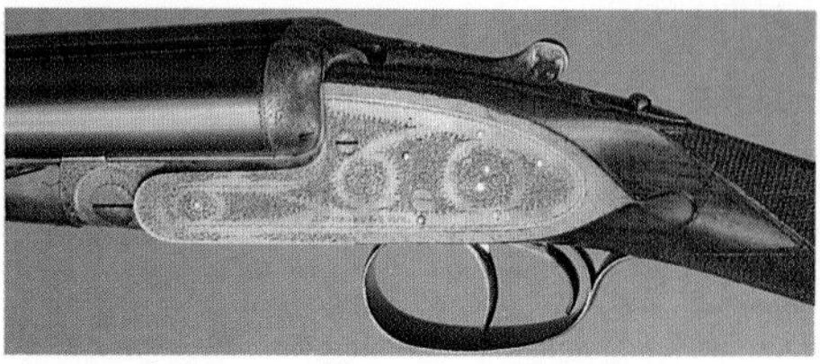

A pair of 12-bore self-opening sidelock ejector guns, by J. Purdey, No. 25679/80, 1939, 30in (76cm) barrels. **$60,000-70,000**

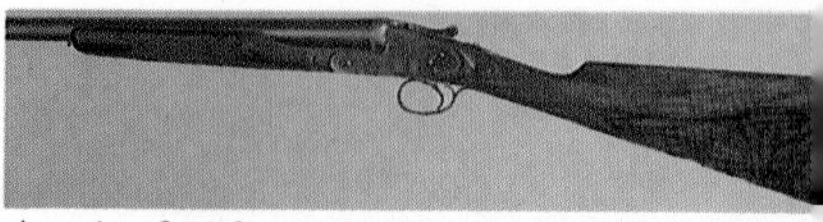

A pair of 12-bore single trigger self-opening sidelock ejector guns, by J. Purdey, No. 28171/2, 1977, 26in (66cm) barrels. **$70,000-80,000**

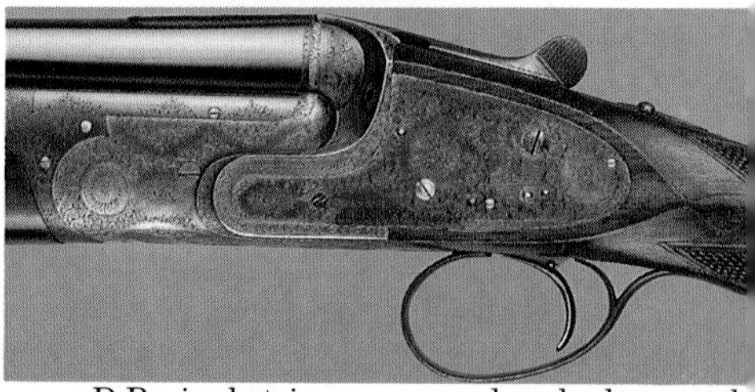

A 12-gauge D.B. single trigger over-and-under hammerl sidelock ejector gun, by Boss, No. 8338, 1935, 28in (71cm) barrels. **$35,000-40,000**

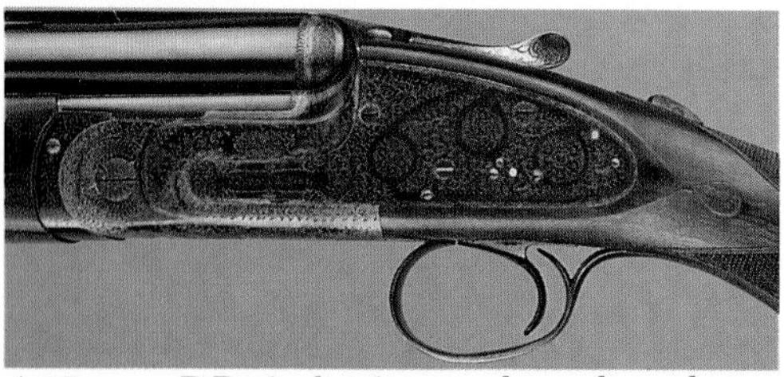

A 12-gauge D.B. single trigger under-and-over hammerless sidelock ejector gun, by J. Purdey, No. 27879, 1976, 28in (71cm) barrels. **$32,000-40,000**

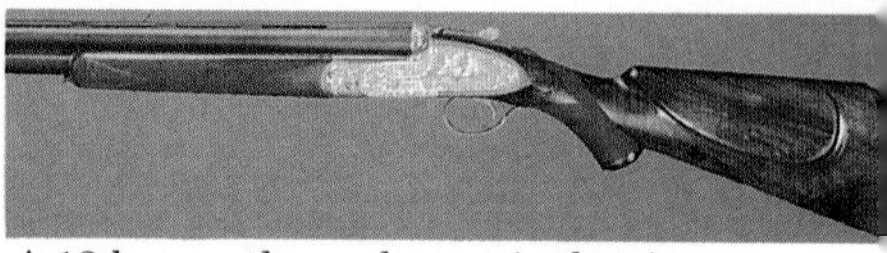

A 12-bore under-and-over single trigger sidelock ejector pigeon gun, by J. Purdey, No. 26735, engraved by K. C. Hunt, 1959 and later. **$60,000-70,000**

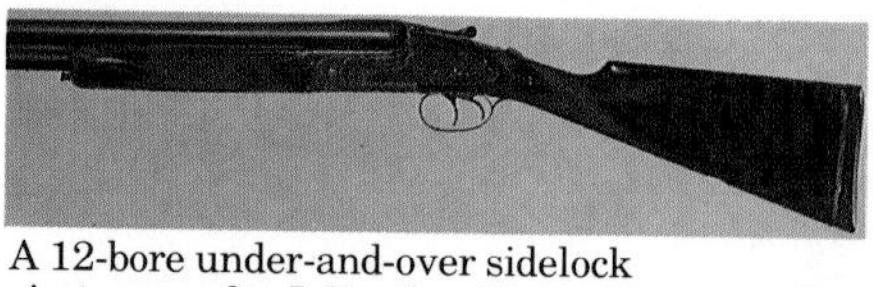

A 12-bore under-and-over sidelock ejector gun, by J. Purdey, No. 28089, 1975. **$40,000-50,000**

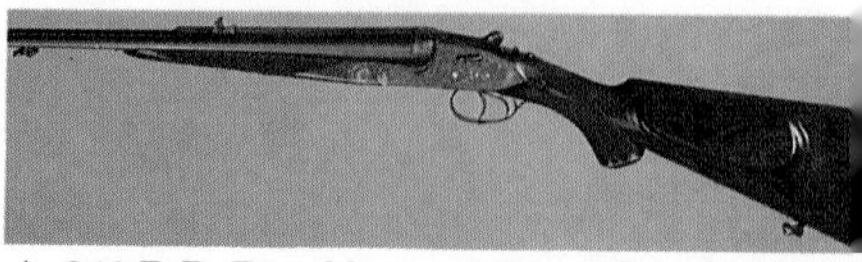

A .240 D.B. Royal hammerless sidelock ejector rifle, by Holland & Holland, No. 31036, 25in (63.5cm) barrels. **$22,000-30,000**

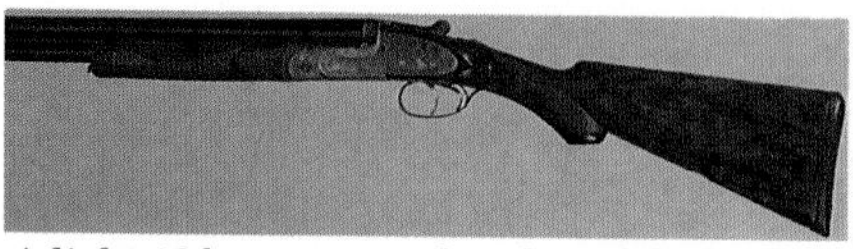

A light 16-bore over-and-under sidelock ejector gun, by J. Woodward, No. 6803, 1927. **$30,000-35,000**

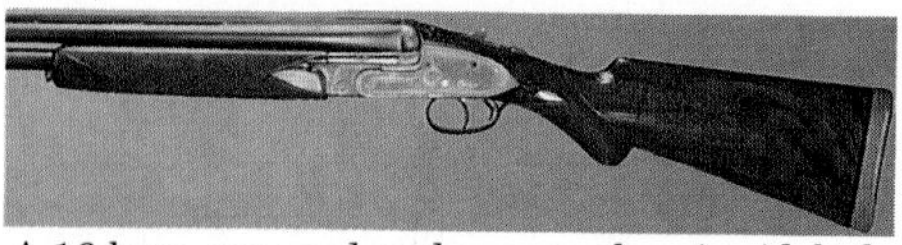

A 16-bore over-and-under sextuple grip sidelock ejector pigeon gun, by J. Purdey, No. 23055, inscribed in gold 'Dr. E.C. Moore, Los Angeles, California', 1926, 30in (76cm) barrels. **$20,000-24,000**

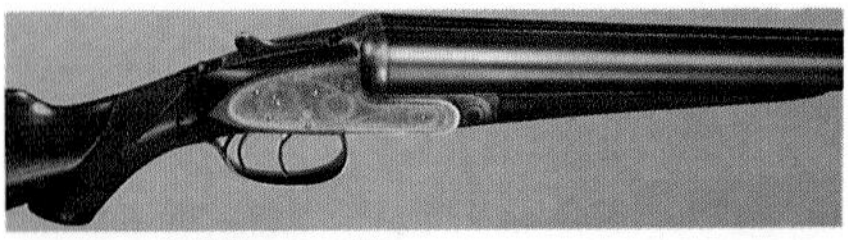

A pair of 12-bore self-opening sidelock ejector guns, by J. Purdey, No. 22865/6, 30in (76cm) barrels. **$40,000-50,000**

A 12-gauge D.B. hammerless self-opening sidelock ejector gun, by J. Purdey, No. 22566, 1924, 30in (76cm) barrels. **$12,000-16,000**

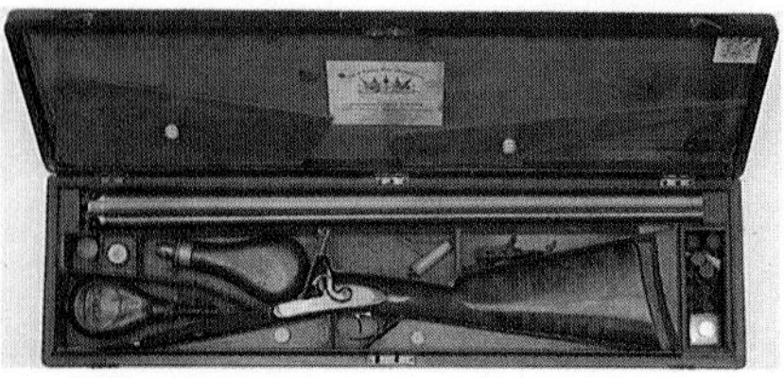

A 12-bore double barrelled percussion sporting gun, by George & John Deane, No. 30 King William St, London Bridge, cased. **$2,500-3,000**

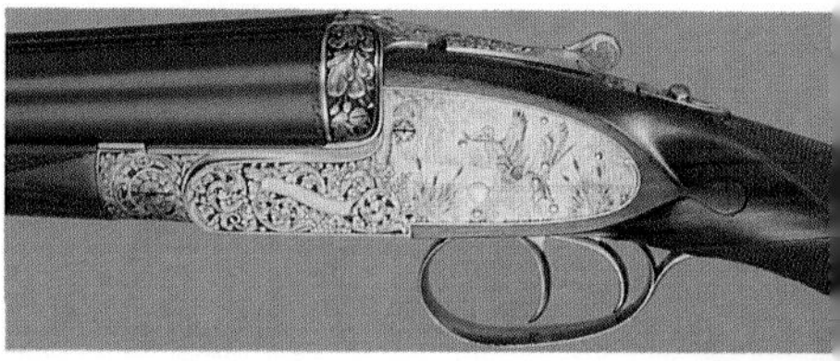

A 12-bore self-opening sidelock ejector gun of Purde type, by Peter Chapman, No. 6446, 1986, 28in (71cr barrels. **$28,000-32,000**

:hree-piece demi-tasse service on
ray, by Tiffany & Co., New York,
)04, coffee pot 11in (28cm) high,
oz.
,000-6,000

A pair of bread trays, by Tiffany & Co., New York, c1895, 16in (40.5cm) wide, 81oz.
$5,000-6,000

A covered butter dish, the base with engraved inscription dated 1879, by Tiffany & Co., New York, 5in (12.5cm) high, 16oz.
$2,000-3,000

)anish silver dish-on-stand,
ırked, 5½in (14cm).
)0-400

A water jug, by Tiffany & Co., New York, c1880, 8in (20.5cm) high, 30oz.
$3,000-3,500

A Liberty 'Tudric' loving cup.
$400-500

A pewter photograph frame, 8in (20.5cm) high.
$160-250

A German pewter mirror, 18in (45.5cm) high.
$800-1,200

A four-piece tea and coffee service, by Tiffany & Co., New York, c1870, coffee pot 9in (23cm) high, 79oz gross.
$5,000-6,000

A Georg Jensen silver tazza, 7½in (19cm) high.
$1,600-2,500

A W.M.F. silver plated petrol cigarette lighter.
$150-200

A pewter tea service, designed by Archibald Knox for Liberty's, with cane handles, 1903.
$2,500-3,000

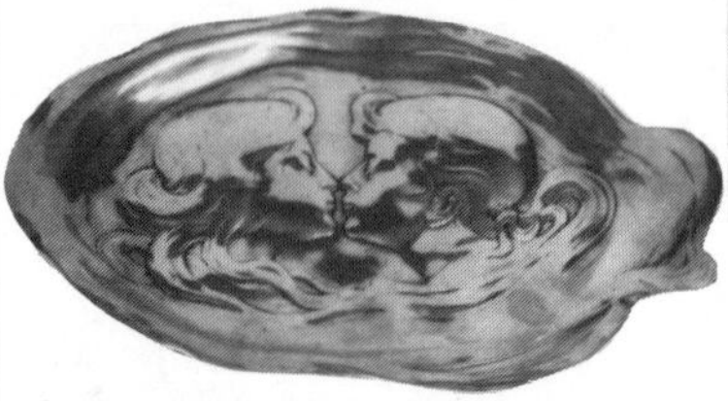

A pewter tray, 11in (28cm).
$160-300

A German pewter inkwell, 11in (28cm) wide.
$75-150

A W.M.F. electroplated pewter teaset, W.M.F. marks, hot water jug 7in (17.5cm).
$600-1,000

Moorcroft

Two Moorcroft figures, one in maroon and blue, the other in green, pink and yellow, printed Moorcroft, Made in England, 10½in (26.5cm) high.
$400-600

These figures were made from Churchill moulds and fired in Moorcroft colours at the Moorcroft factory in 1985.

A Moorcroft pottery Coronation mug, 1937.
$250-300

A Moorcroft two-handled pottery comport, decorated in the Pansies pattern with pink and blue flowers and green foliage on a dark blue ground, impressed marks, signed i green, 6in (15cm) high.
$800-1,000

A Moorcroft clock, Eventide pattern, c1925, 5in (12.5cm) high.
$3,000-4,000

A Moorcroft jug, produced to commemorate the Coronation of King George VI and Queen Elizabeth, May 12, 1937, impressed mark with initials, 7in (17.5cm).
$800-1,000

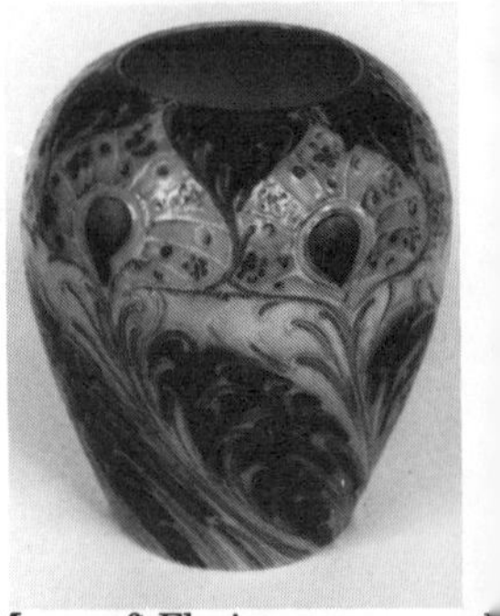

A Moorcroft Florianware peacoc vase, in blue, yellow and green, Florianware stamp, signed, c190 5½in (14cm).
$2,000-2,500

Moorcroft floral jardinière, 5½in
4cm) high.
.20-160

. Moorcroft Florianware jug, in
nades of blue with silver plated lid
lorianware stamp, signed, c1898,
in (20.5cm).
300-1,000

Moorcroft plate, part of the Royal
acht service, impressed and
gned, 6in (15cm).
60-100

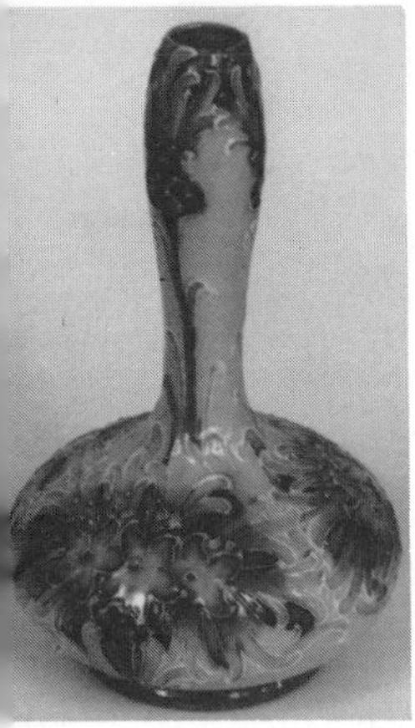

A Moorcroft vase, with cornflowers in shades of blue, Florianware stamp, signed, c1900, 5in (12.5cm).
$400-600

A Moorcroft platter, decorated in white and blue on a flambé ground, incised signature, 12in (30.5cm) diam.
$500-600

A Moorcroft Claremont vase, in green and red, made for Liberty, signed W. Moorcroft, c1903, 6in (15cm).
$1,600-2,000

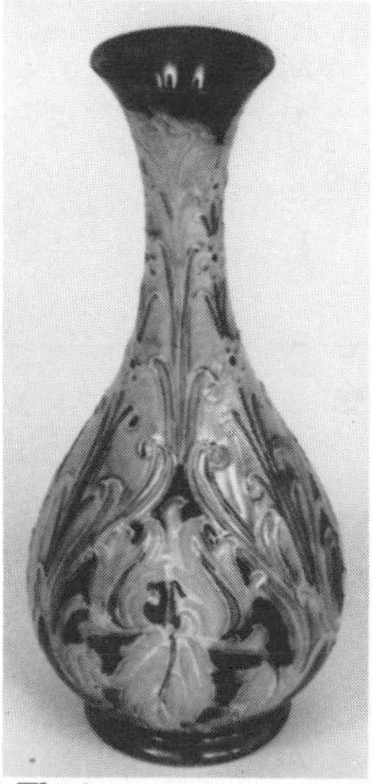

A Moorcroft Florianware vase, with iris and forget-me-nots, Florianware stamp, signed, c1900, 6in (15cm).
$900-1,000

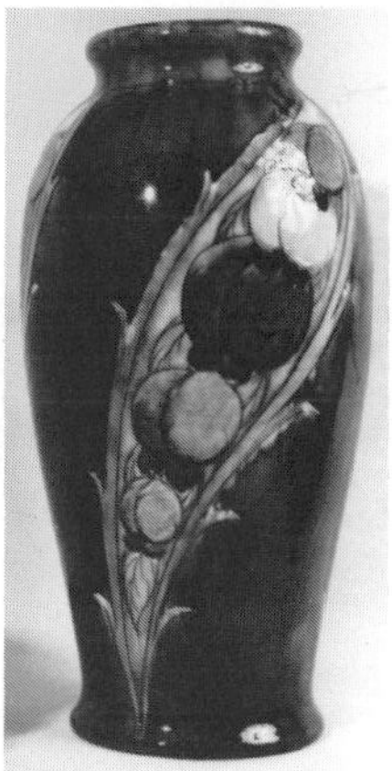

A Moorcroft vase, signed and dated 1929, 22in (56cm).
$2,500-3,000

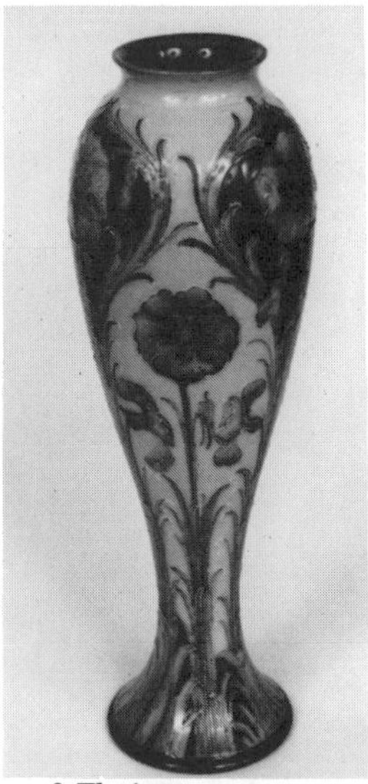

A Moorcroft Florianware poppy vase, in shades of blue, Florian stamp, signed W. Moorcroft, c1898, 11½in (29cm).
$1,000-1,400

A Moorcroft pottery vase, painted with red, beige and purple cornflowers and green foliage, on blue/green ground, green signature on base, 12in (30cm).
$1,500-1,700

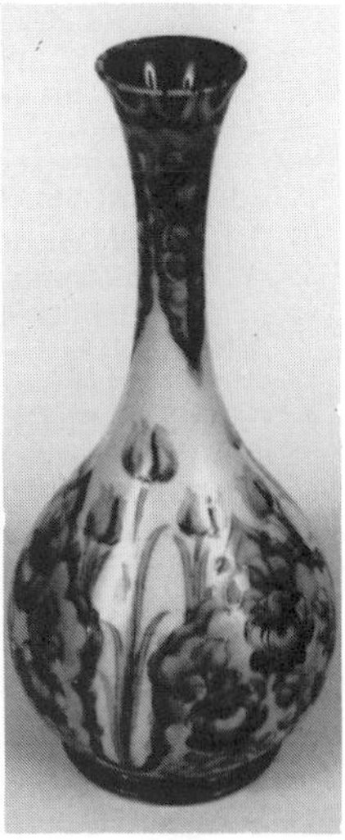

A Moorcroft Florianware Macintyre vase, 10in (25.5cm).
$1,500-2,000

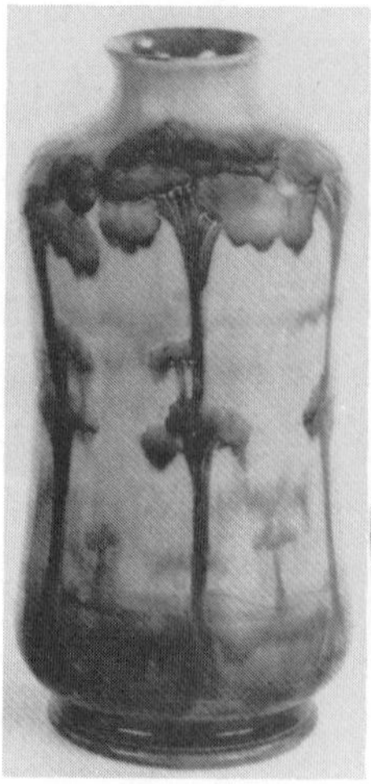

A pair of Moorcroft pottery vases, decorated in the Hazeldene pattern with tall blue and green trees and hilly landscape, on a yellow/green ground, cracks to body of one vase, printed marks for Liberty & Co., signed in green W. Moorcroft des, 9½in (24cm).
$1,300-2,000

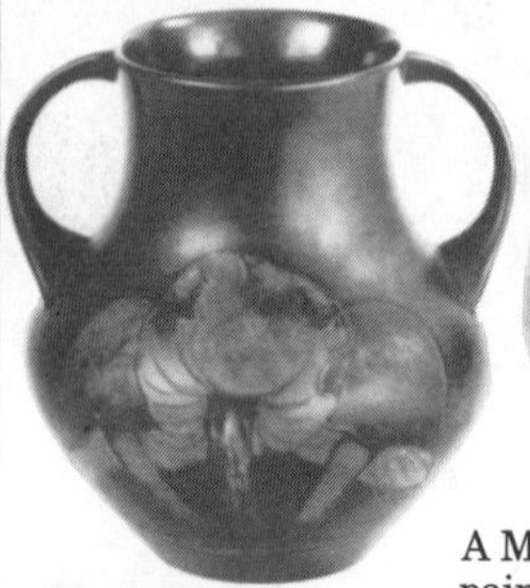

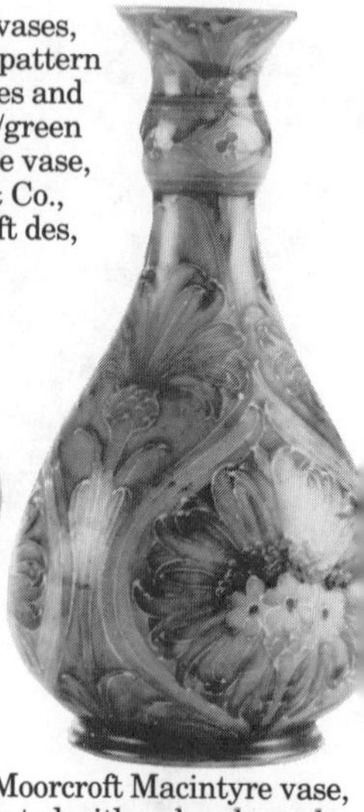

A Moorcroft vase, painted in shades of red, green, yellow, white and blue on a dark blue ground, impressed marks, 17in (43cm).
$1,500-1,700

A Moorcroft two-handled pottery vase, decorated in the Claremont pattern, with toadstools under a deep flambé glaze, impressed marks, signed in green, 7in (18cm).
$2,000-3,000

A Moorcroft Macintyre vase, painted with red and purple cornflowers with green foliag Macintyre trade mark on bas and green signatures, 10in (25cm).
$1,400-1,600

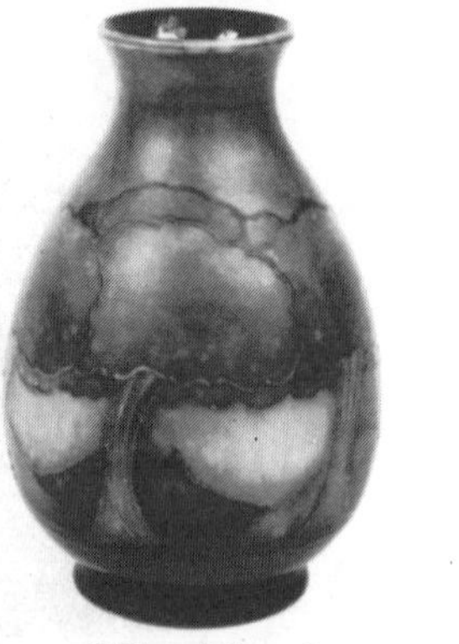

A Moorcroft Eventide pottery vase, decorated with green and brown trees and green hills, against a flame coloured sky, stamped marks, signed in blue, 10in (25cm).
$1,000-1,400

A pair of Moorcroft Tudric vases, decorated with trees against a dark blue ground, with flared pewter bases, No. 01310, 9in (23cm).
$2,000-3,000

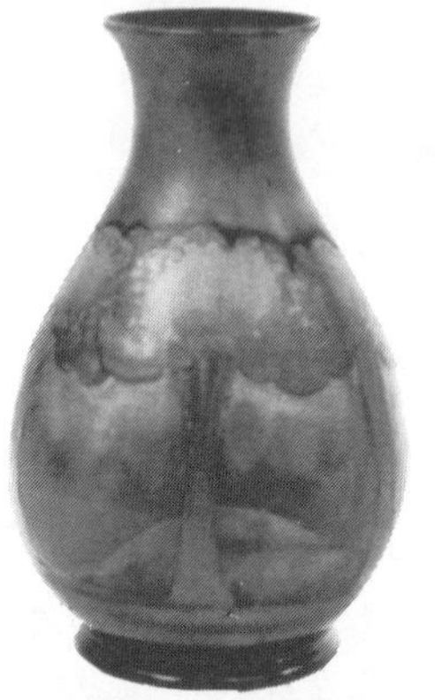

A Moorcroft Eventide pottery vase, decorated with green and brown trees and green hills against a flam coloured sky, impressed marks, signed in blue, 9½in (24cm).
$1,400-1,800

MACINTYRE/ MOORCROFT

- ★ first Art Pottery produced in 1897. Early wares marked Macintyre and/or W Moorcroft des
- ★ William Moorcroft established his own works in 1913
- ★ 1913-21 wares impressed MOORCROFT BURSLEM with painted W.Moorcroft signature
- ★ after 1916 impressed ENGLAND
- ★ 1921-1930 impressed MADE IN ENGLAND
- ★ 1930-1949 paper label, BY APPOINTMENT, POTTER TO H.M. THE QUEEN used
- ★ 1949-1973 label states BY APPOINTMENT TO THE LATE QUEEN MARY
- ★ rivals copied patterns and colours

Posters

'Coffee Bean', a pair of costume designs by Erté, painted in yellow, orange, black and shades of brown on buff paper, signed in ink, one with pencil notes and slight rubbing, mounted and framed, 13 by 9½in (34 by 24cm).
$3,000-4,000

'Evening Gown', by Erté, a serigraph printed in colours, heightened with silver gilt, signed in pencil Erté and numbered 167/30 framed, 17½in by 13in (45.5 by 33.5cm).
$1,300-2,000

cent Bottles

cameo glass perfume bottle, gned, 6½in (17cm).
00-600

A Gallé enamelled clear glass scent bottle and stopper, decorated in the Islamic style with beaded roundels and scrolled crosses in blue, white and red enamel with gilding, small chips to stopper, signed in gilt Gallé a Nancy, 4in (10cm), and a Gallé clear glass scent bottle and stopper, enamelled and gilded with flowers in white and blue, the stopper enamelled with a dragonfly in blue and white, some deterioration to enamel, and chip to base, signed in gilt Cristallerie Emile Gallé, Nancy, 5in (12cm).
$1,400-1,500

Iiscellaneous

n Austrian brass inlaid rosewood riting folder, with watered silk iterior, 11 by 9in (28 by 23cm).
400-500

An Arts and Crafts mahogany three-leaf screen, each panel inset with embossed leather panels, painted in green and heightened with gilt, each panel above reeded panels, 78in (196cm) high.
$3,500-4,000

An Arts and Crafts silver mounted oak pepper mill, the silver bands attached by brass screws, with Peugeot Freres Brevets steel grinding mechanism, stamped maker's marks GHW and Sheffield hallmarks for 1898, 4in (10cm) high.
$250-300

Brunelleschi, 5 cards, all from series 31.
$250-300

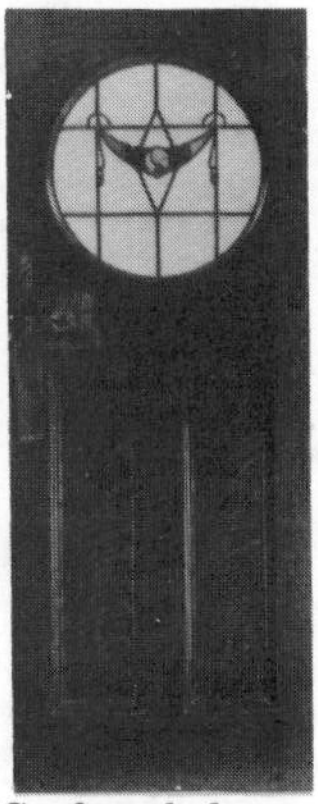

A pair of Arts and Crafts oak doors, each inset with leaded glass panels, with pewter lock plates, 78in (196cm) high.
$900-1,200

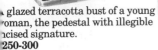

Miller's is a price Guide not a price List

The price ranges given reflect the average price a purchaser should pay for similar items. Condition, rarity of design or pattern, size, colour, pedigree, restoration and many other factors must be taken into account when assessing values

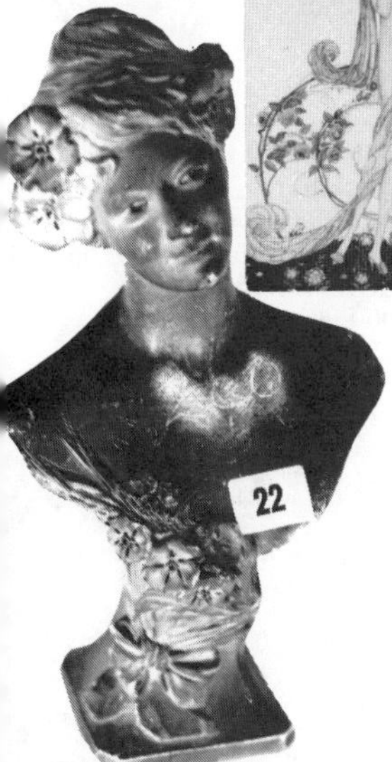

glazed terracotta bust of a young oman, the pedestal with illegible ncised signature.
250-300

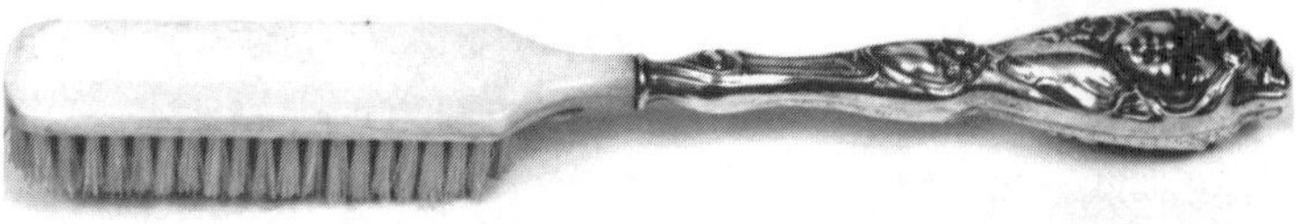

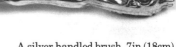

A silver handled brush, 7in (18cm).
$100-200

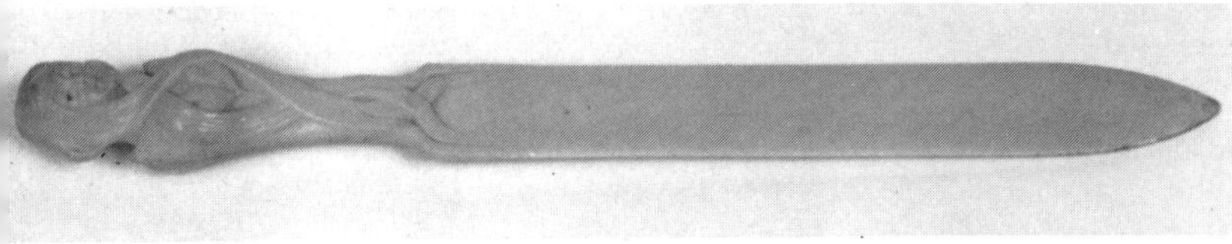

An ivory paper knife, 10in (25.5cm).
$160-250

Alphonse Mucha, 2 cards from Seasons of the Year series, with 3 others.
$250-300

A marquetry panel, attributed to Charles Spindler, in various natural and stained woods, image area 10 by 27in (25 by 69.5cm), framed.
$1,000-1,400

A German white metal centrepiece, with glass trough, stamped 14515, 800 WTB, 10½in (26.5cm) long, 250 grammes without liner.
$600-1,000

A French plated centrepiece, formed by two maidens standing back-to-back, holding outwards the hems of their skirts, poised above a flower form base, inscribed Carlier, 11½in (29.5cm) high
$500-600

A fawn painted on marble, initialled DJH, 10 by 7½in (25.5 by 19cm).
$80-140

Doulton

A Doulton Lambeth stoneware ewer, by Hannah Barlow, impresse mark and initialled HBB 56 LR18 9½in (24cm) high.
$600-800

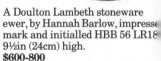

A Doulton Lambeth three-handled loving cup, attributed to Hannah Barlow, heightened in blue against a buff ground, restored, impressed marks, 7½in (19cm).
$350-400

A Doulton teapot, decorated with cats, rats and mice, by Hannah Barlow, in blue, green, brown and buff, c1880, 6in (15cm).
$1,100-1,200

A Doulton Lambeth stoneware jug and 2 matching beakers, by Emily E. Stormer, incised and decorated with beadwork, glazed in shades of brown, green, blue and white, each with silver rim, impressed and incised marks, 10in (25cm).
$600-800

A Doulton Lambeth mug, 1876, 6in (15cm).
$250-300

A pair of Doulton Lambeth vases, b Hannah Barlow, incised with a frieze of horses and donkeys between borders of stylised light and dark green leaves on a brown ground, some chips, incised and impressed marks HBB and assistants, 14½in (37cm).
$1,400-1,500

Doulton Lambeth stoneware jug, George Tinworth, the buff ound with incised blue, green olling foliage and applied werheads, mounted with silver n and lid, hallmarks for Sheffield 73, impressed marks and incised monogram to base, 11½in cm).
00-800

A Doulton Lambeth baluster jug, by Hannah Barlow, in shades of brown, green and cream, mounted with a silver rim and lid, hallmarks for London 1894, restored incised and impressed marks HBB, 7½in (19cm).
$400-600

A Doulton Lambeth stoneware jug, by George Tinworth, glazed in green, blue, brown and white, mounted with a silver rim and hinged cover with Hukin and Heath Birmingham hall marks for 1877, impressed and incised marks, 10in (25.5cm).
$1,600-1,800

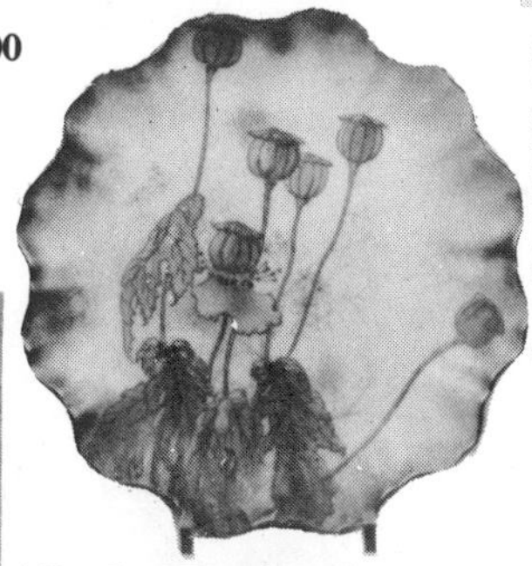

A Doulton Burslem dessert service, comprising 5 cake stands and 12 dessert plates, painted in pink, purple, light green, blue and gilt, damaged, printed and painted marks, plates 8½in (22cm) diam.
$3,000-4,000

Doulton Lambeth stoneware ver rimmed lemonade set, mprising a jug and a pair of akers, all moulded in relief, jug in (24cm).
00-900

A Doulton Lambeth stoneware jug and 2 beakers, by George Tinworth, glazed in green, blue and brown, each with white metal mount to rim, G.T. monogram to body, impressed date 1882, and incised marks to base, 9½in (24cm).
$700-800

A Doulton Lambeth faience wall plaque, 'First Come First Served', painted by Esther Lewis in naturalistic colours, impressed and painted marks, numbers 242, 17in (43cm) diam.
$800-900

Doulton Lambeth stoneware jug, Hannah Barlow, incised with ats above a band of blue and green ylised leaves, Doulton Lambeth ark dated 1878, incised HBB and sistants, 8in (21cm).
00-1,000

A Doulton faience jardinière and stand, moulded in high relief with foliate rococo designs, the baluster stand with fluted waist, painted in muted enamel colours, slight restoration to bowl, late 19thC, 18in (45cm) high.
$1,000-1,200

A Doulton Lambeth stoneware vase, by Edith D. Lupton, with incised stylised flowers and beadwork, glazed in shades of brown, yellow and blue, impressed and incised marks, 13in (33cm).
$900-1,000

A pair of Doulton Lambeth stoneware vases, by Hannah Barlow, in shades of blue and green, slight chips to rims, incised and impressed marks HBB and assistants, 8in (20cm).
$500-600

A Doulton Lambeth stoneware vase, by Mark V. Marshall, glazed in shades of blue, brown, green and white surrounded by green and brown foliage, bead and flowerhead decoration, restored, incised and impressed marks, 11½in (29cm).
$250-300

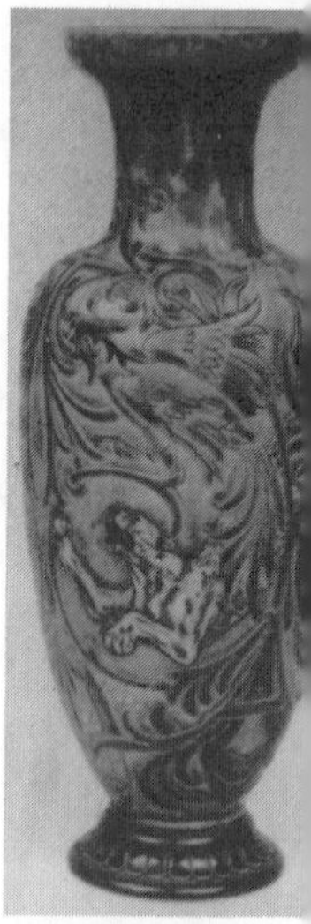

A Doulton Lambet vase by Florence Barlow, incised wi lions heightened i white glaze, in sha of green and brow all on a mottled green ground, impressed and incised marks, 18i (45.5cm).
$1,400-1,600

A pair of Doulton stoneware vases, decorated by Elizabeth A. Sayers, dated 1878, impressed and inscribed marks, 9½in (24.5cm).
$400-600

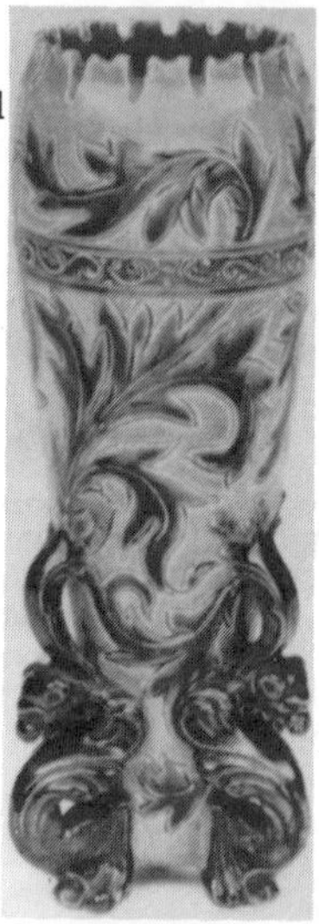

A Doulton stoneware vase, by Mark V. Marshall, incised with green glazed foliage on a light blue ground, the base supported by 3 dark brown grotesque beasts in full relief, incised marks, 8in (21cm).
$1,000-1,200

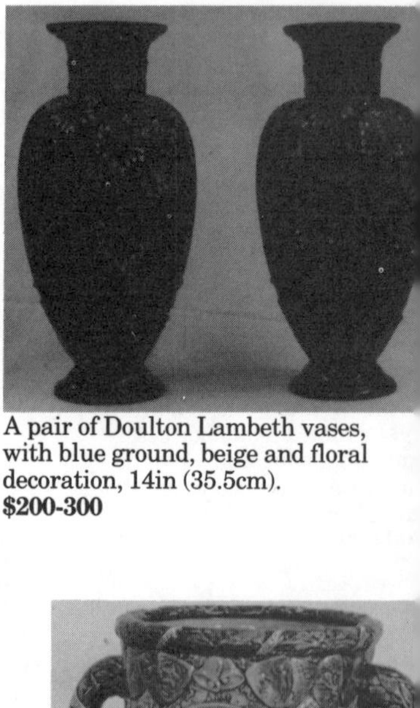

A pair of Doulton Lambeth vases, with blue ground, beige and floral decoration, 14in (35.5cm).
$200-300

Royal Doulton

A Whieldon ware Nightwatchman's series jug, hair crack, D1460, c1903.
$100-120

Fortune Teller, a character jug, designed by G. Sharpe, D6523, printed marks, 2½in (6cm) high.
$300-400

A commemorative jug, c1905, 8in (20.5cm).
$450-500

A two-handled loving cup, King George V and Queen Mary, 1935, limited edition 450/1000, with certificate.
$700-800

ed-haired Clown, a character jug
esigned by H. Fenton, D5610,
rinted marks, 6in (15cm) high.
2,000-2,500

ony Weller, a musical character
g, designed by L. Harradine and
. Fenton, D5888, printed marks,
in (15cm) high.
600-800

ondolier, a character jug, designed
y D. Biggs, D6595, printed marks,
½in (6cm) high.
300-400

gly Duchess, a character jug,
esigned by M. Henk, D6603,
rinted marks, 4in (10cm) high.
350-400

Paddy, a musical character jug, designed by H. Fenton, D5887, printed marks, 6in (15cm) high.
$500-600

Granny — toothless, a character jug, designed by H. Fenton and M. Henk, D5521, printed marks, 7in (19cm) high.
$200-400

Pearly boy, a small character jug, designed by H. Fenton, printed and painted marks, 3in (8cm) high.
$3,000-4,000

Courtier, a porcelain figure designed by L. Harradine, HN1338, with original lamp base, cracks and chips, printed and painted marks, 4½in (11cm).
$1,600-1,800

Sunshine Girl, a porcelain figure designed by L. Harradine, HN1344, printed and painted marks, 5in (12.5cm).
$1,800-2,000

Contentment, a figure designed by L. Harradine, HN572, slight chip, printed and painted marks, 7in (18cm).
$1,000-1,200

Dulcinea, designed by Leslie Harradine, HN1419, introduced 1930, withdrawn 1938, 5½in (14cm).
$1,500-1,600

The Goose Girl, designed by L. Harradine, HN559, introduced 1923, withdrawn 1938, 8in (20.5cm).
$1,500-1,600

Ibraham, a figure, HN2095, withdrawn 1955.
$500-600

Farmer Bunnykins, a porcelain figure, D6003, printed and painted marks, 7in (18cm).
$1,500-1,600

Carpet Seller, a figure, HN1464, withdrawn 1969
$300-500

Angela, a porcelain figure designed by L. Harradine, HN1204, printed and painted marks, 7in (18cm).
$1,200-1,300

Clarissa, a porcelain figure designed by L. Harradine, HN1525, printed and painted marks, original paper label, 10in (25cm).
$500-600

King Charles, a porcelain figure designed by C. J. Noke and H. Tittensor, HN404, cane missing, printed marks, 17in (43cm).
$500-800

Abdullah, a figure, HN2104, withdrawn 1962.
$400-500

Teenage, a figure designed by M. Davies, HN2203, printed and painted marks, 7in (18cm).
$200-300

A Moorish Minstrel, designed by C. J. Noke, HN364, introduced 1920, withdrawn 1938, firing crack to base, 14in (35.5cm).
$2,500-3,000

Three porcelain figures of dachshunds, HN1128, HN1141 and HN1970, and 3 other figures by various makers, chips.
$400-600

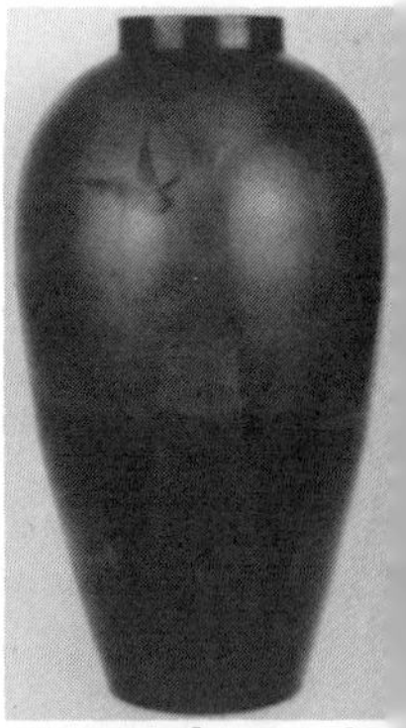

A flambé baluster vase, decorated i black against a rich flambé ground printed and impressed marks, 20in (51cm) high.
$500-600

Grandma, a figure, introduced 1950, withdrawn 1959, 7in (18cm).
$350-400

hepherd, a porcelain figure, IN751, restored, printed and ainted marks, 7½in (19cm).
500-700

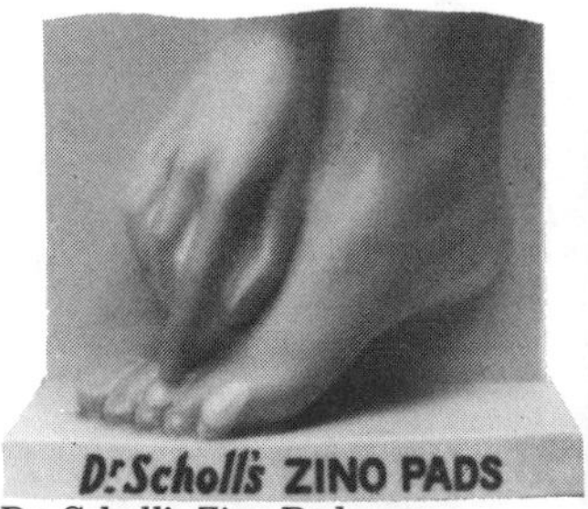

Dr. Scholl's Zino Pads, an advertising counter display model, slight chip, printed marks, 8in (20.5cm).
$300-400

Jack Point (a variation), a white glazed figure, hairline cracks, R.D. printed mark to base, incised 269, impressed No. 269, 16½in (42cm).
$1,700-1,900

A golfing vase, decorated in yellow on a red ground, 8in (20.5cm).
$250-300

George Robey, a jug modelled as the music hall artist, hat missing and damage to head, printed Royal Doulton mark, painted monogram to base, 10in (25cm).
$1,400-1,600

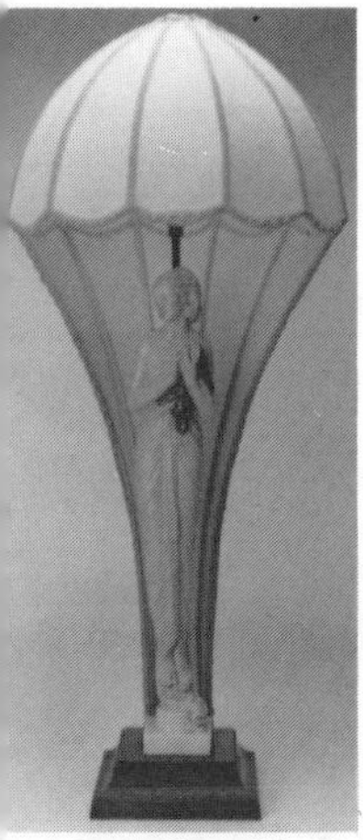

pring, designed by Richard Garbe, IN1827 second version, introduced 937, withdrawn 1949, converted to table lamp with silk shade, 18in 45.5cm).
5,000-6,000

A boxed set of napkin rings, comprising the Dickens figures: Mr. Pickwick, Mr. Micawber, Fat Boy, Tony Weller, Sam Weller and Sairey Gamp, crack to Tony Weller, printed marks.
$2,000-3,000

A Royal Doulton stoneware teapot and cover, by George Tinworth, the finial modelled as a seated frog, glazed in shades of green and brown, restored, impressed and incised marks, 5in (12.5cm).
$600-800

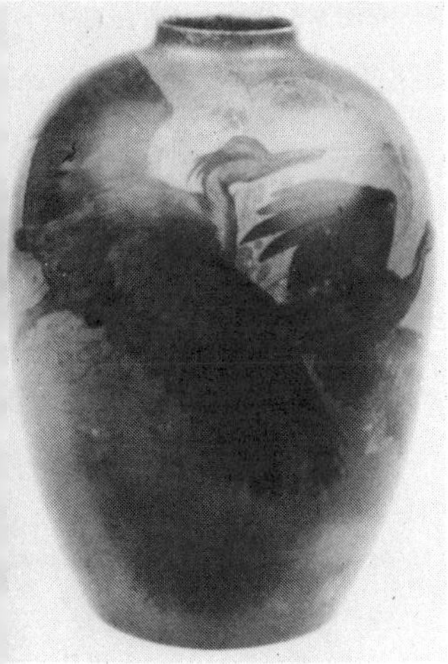

A 'Sung' vase, painted with crested erons in flight, with purple and ink plumage against a speckled ed and amber sky above a urquoise base, cracked, printed Royal Doulton Flambé, painted Noke Sung, 12½in (32cm).
900-1,000

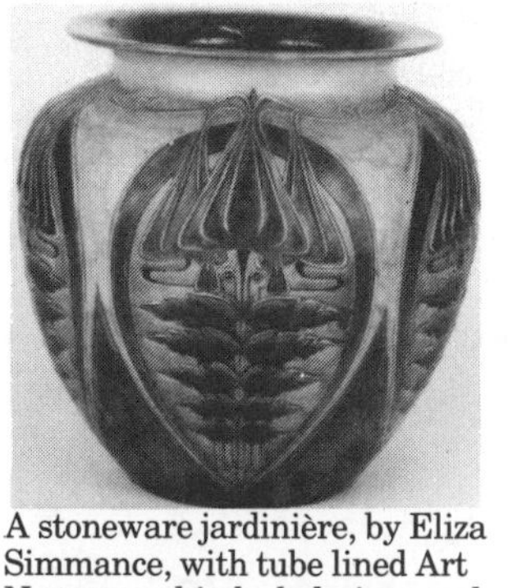

A stoneware jardinière, by Eliza Simmance, with tube lined Art Nouveau whip-lash designs and leaves, glazed in shades of blue, green, brown and yellow, impressed and incised marks, 12½in (31cm).
$1,000-1,200

A model of a seated rabbit, his ear cocked, glazed in white and grey with black and yellow detailing, 4in (10cm).
$700-800

A Kingsware Dewars Whisky flask, decorated in colours against brown, with Charles Edward Stuart in Highland dress, holding a glass, 'Bonnie Prince Charlie' inscribed on the front, with metal and cork stopper, printed marks, 7in (18cm).
$180-250

A vase, painted by J. H. Plant, with gilt rim, named on base Hilchurn Castle, green printed marks, 6in (15cm).
$600-800

A Lalique stained opalescent table clock, 'Inseparables', moulded signature, 4in (11cm).
$1,800-2,400

An amethyst tinted frosted and polished car mascot, 'Grand Libellule', damaged, repaired, etched R. Lalique, France, 8½in (21cm).
$3,000-4,000

ART DECO

Lalique Glass

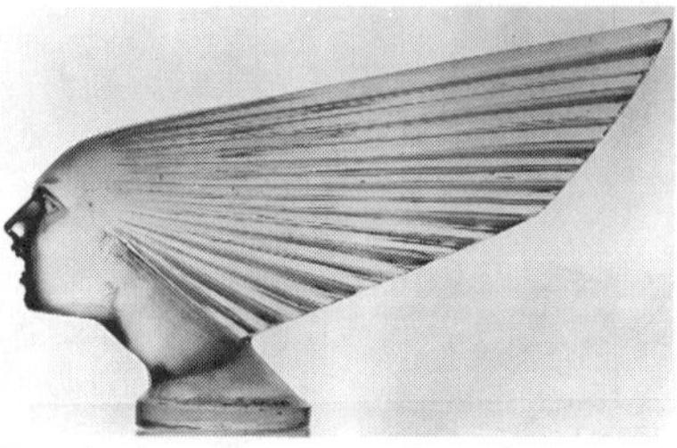

A satin glass car mascot of amethyst tint, 'Victoire', on Brèves Gallery chromium plated base, damaged, moulded R. Lalique, France, 10in (26cm).
$12,000-13,000

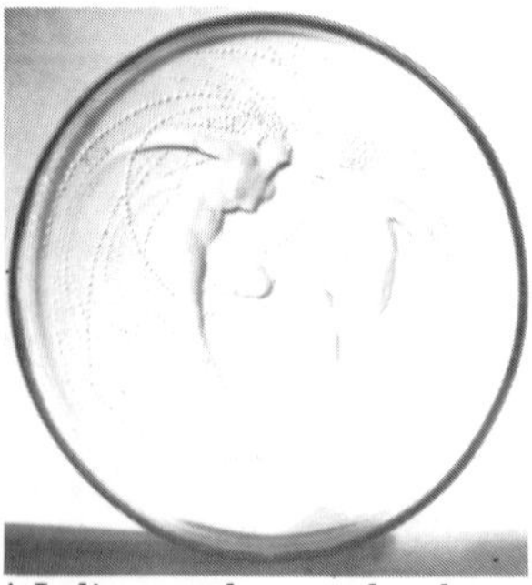

A Lalique opalescent glass box and cover, 'Deux Sirènes', moulded R. Lalique, engraved France No. 43, 10in (26cm) diam.
$4,000-6,000

An opalescent clear and blue-stained bowl, 'Perruches', stencilled R. Lalique, France, 9in (23.5cm) diam.
$4,000-6,000

A frosted and opalescent bowl, signed on base R. Lalique, France, c1930, 3½in (9cm).
$800-1,000

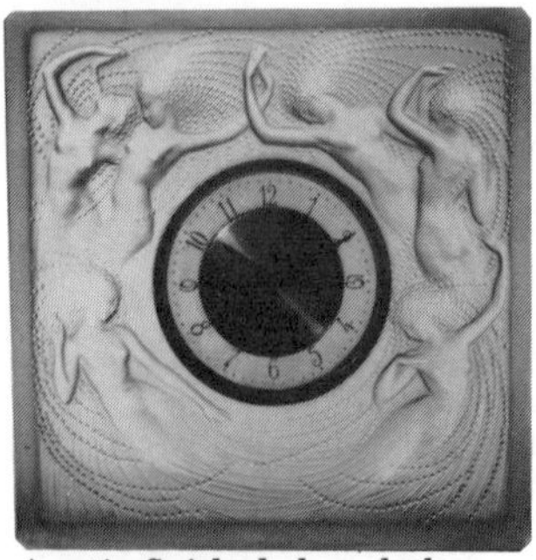

A satin-finished glass clock, 'Sirènes', with acid stamped signature R. Lalique, France, 11in (28cm).
$6,000-8,000

A clear glass box and cover, 'Coquilles', heightened with grey staining, moulded Lalique, 3in (7cm) diam.
$1,800-2,000

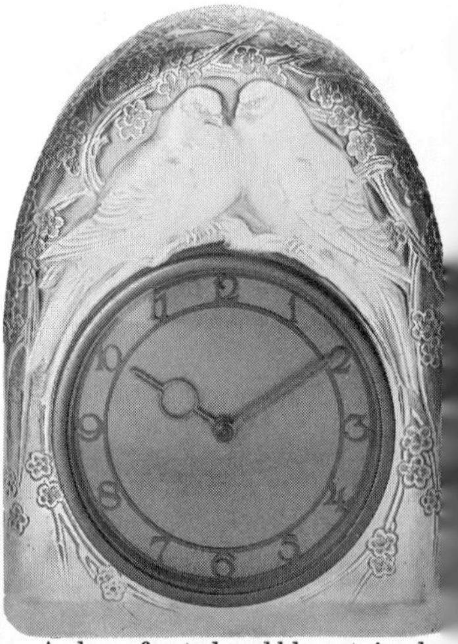

A clear, frosted and blue-stained clock, 'Deux Colombes', moulded R. Lalique, etched France, 8½in (22.2cm) high.
$3,500-4,000

. blue stained opalescent bowl, 'erruches', acid-stamped signature . Lalique, France, 9in (23.5cm) iam.
4,000-5,000

A car mascot, 'Perche', moulded signature R. Lalique, 6in (16cm) long.
$1,200-1,600

A clear and satin polished mascot, 'Longchamps', damaged, moulded R. Lalique, France, 5in (12.5cm).
$12,000-13,000

. clear and frosted table clock, Pierrots', stencilled R. Lalique, 'rance, 5in (12.5cm).
1,800-2,000

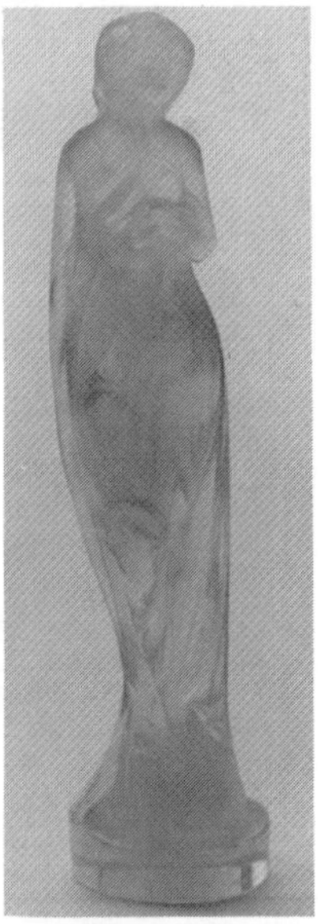

A Lalique opalescent statuette, 'Moyenne Voilée', engraved R. Lalique, France, 5½in (14cm).
$4,000-6,000

A Lalique cockerel mascot, signed, 8in (20cm) high.
$2,500-3,000

.n amethyst tinted polished car nascot, 'Têtes d'Éperviers', with hromium plated base, damaged, noulded Lalique, France, 2½in 6.5cm).
$1,400-1,600

A clear frosted and sienna-stained chalice, damaged, engraved Lalique, 7in (18cm) high.
$3,000-4,000

A set of 8 wine glasses, stem moulded with bunches of grapes, with engraved signatures R. Lalique, France, 5in (13cm).
$1,700-1,800

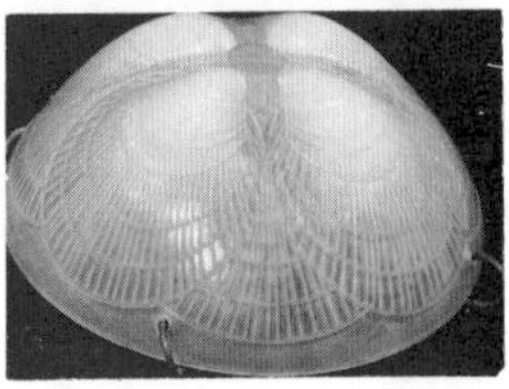

An opalescent and frosted glass hanging shade with gilt metal suspension cords, wheel-cut R. Lalique, France, and engraved No. 385 in script, 12in (30cm) diam.
$900-1,000

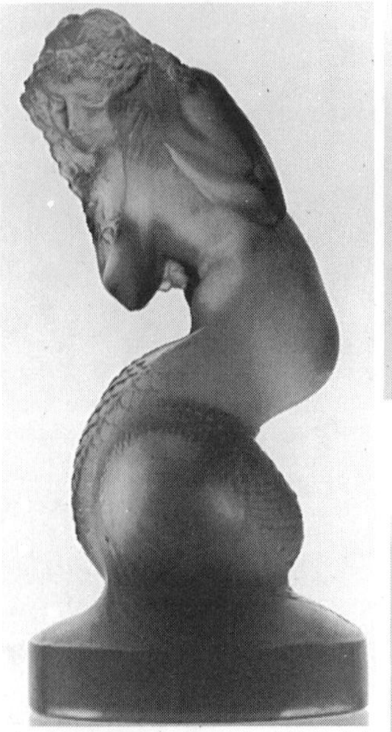

An opalescent statuette, 'Naiade', moulded R. Lalique, 5in (13cm) high.
$7,500-8,500

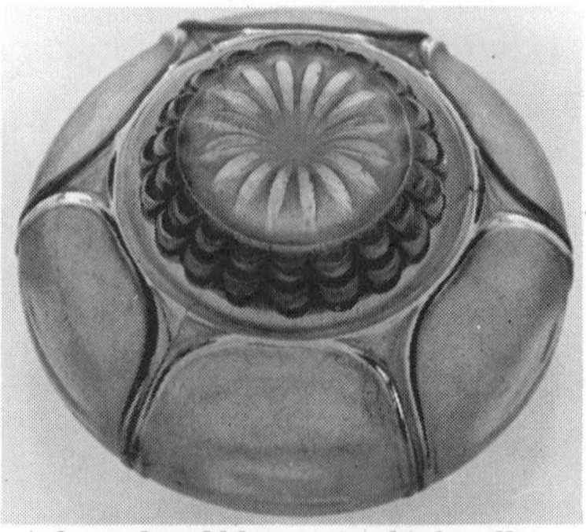

A frosted and blue-stained inkwell, 'Nénuphar', etched script mark R. Lalique, 2½in (7cm) diam.
$1,000-1,200

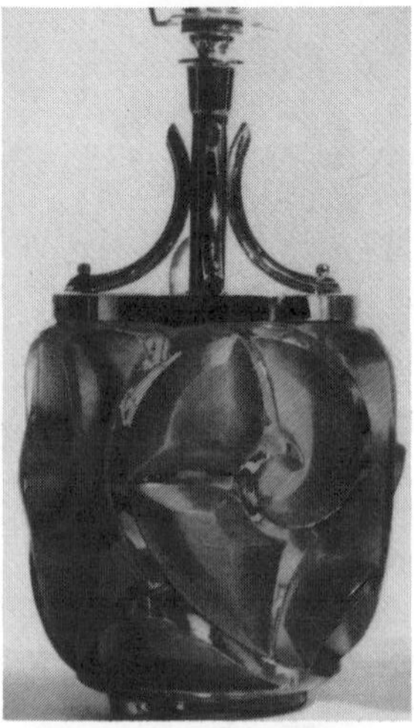

An amber glass lampbase, moulde in deep relief with stylised branches engraved signature R. Lalique, France, 8in (20cm) high.
$5,000-6,000

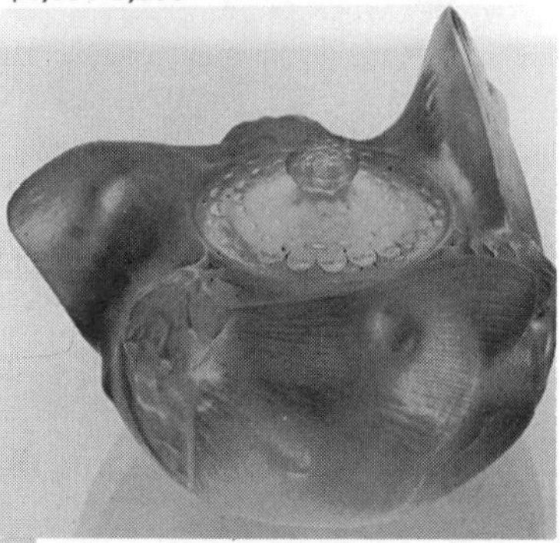

A frosted inkwell and cover, 'Trois Papillons', moulded R. Lalique, 3½in (9.5cm) wide.
$1,200-1,400

A drinking set, 'Hespérides', with electroplated carrying basket, the glass with acid-stamped signatures R. Lalique, jug 8½in (22cm) high.
$2,000-2,500

A set of 6 clear glass footed beakers, moulded with bands of leaping fish stained in blue, stencilled R. Lalique, 3½in (9cm).
$600-800

A clear and sepia-stained claret jug and stopper, the handle moulded as a satyr mask with horns, etched script mark R. Lalique pour Cusenier, 9½in (24cm) high.
$1,800-2,400

Did you know
MILLER'S Antiques Price Guide builds up year by year to form the most comprehensive photo-reference system available.

A 17-piece drinking set, with moulded motif incorporating 2 male nudes, with acid-stamped and engraved signatures R. Lalique, France, No. 5084.
$4,000-5,000

A plafonnier with gilt-metal mounts and suspension chains, damaged, moulded signature R. Lalique, 20½in (52cm) diam.
$4,000-6,000

A lampbase, 'Marisa', the milky-white glass moulded with fish, engraved signature R. Lalique, France, 9in (23cm) high.
$3,000-4,000

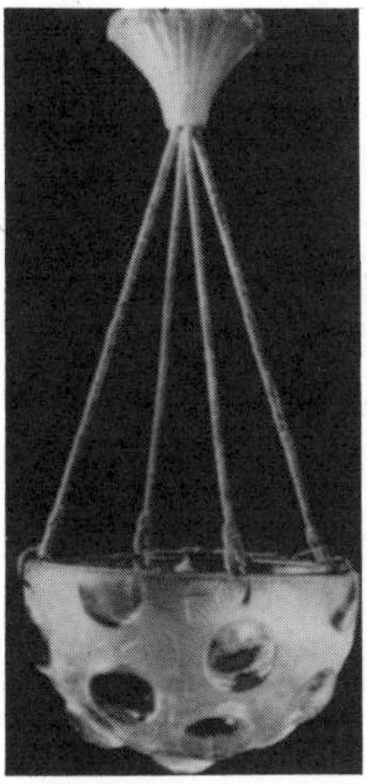

A plafonnier, moulded and engraved signatures R. Lalique, 12½in (32cm) diam.
$2,000-2,400

An amber pendant, with the head of a young woman, etched Lalique, 1½in (4cm) high.
$800-1,000

An opalescent pendant, moulded with a spray of lily of the valley, moulded Lalique, 1½in (4.5cm) long.
$900-1,000

A glass pendant, moulded with a woman and a dove, engraved signature R. Lalique, France.
$600-700

A frosted glass hanging shade, 'Acanthus', inscribed R. Lalique, France, 18in (45cm) diam.
$1,800-2,400

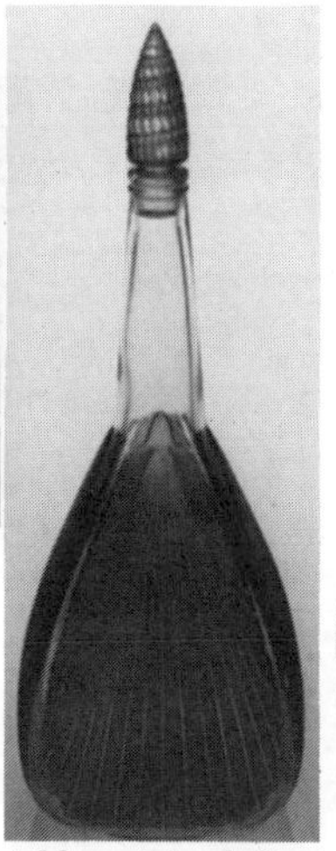

A blue-stained, frosted and clear decanter, 'Carafe Coquilles', engraved R. Lalique, France, with applied retailer's label, 13½in (34cm) high.
$2,500-3,000

A clear and frosted scent bottle, 'Tulipes', with traces of sienna staining, moulded R. Lalique, France, 3in (7.5cm) high.
$600-700

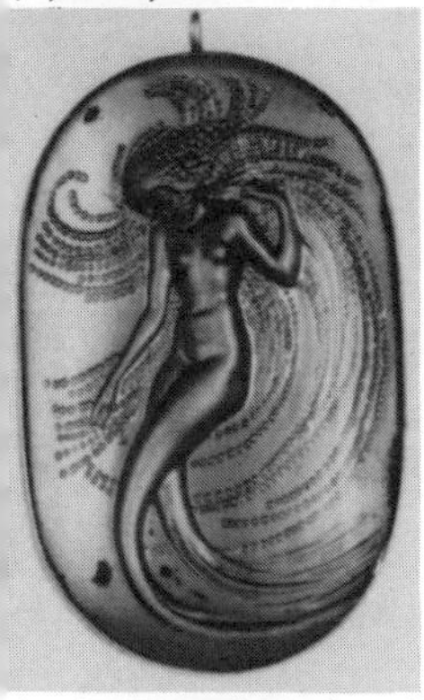

A mirror-pendant, the white metal mounted glass with a sea-sprite, the reverse with bevelled edged mirror, the frame stamped Lalique, 3½in (9cm) long.
$1,000-1,200

A frosted pendant, in the form of a perfume amphora, the 2 handles pierced for suspension, with floral stopper, engraved R. Lalique, 1½in (4cm) high.
$3,500-4,000

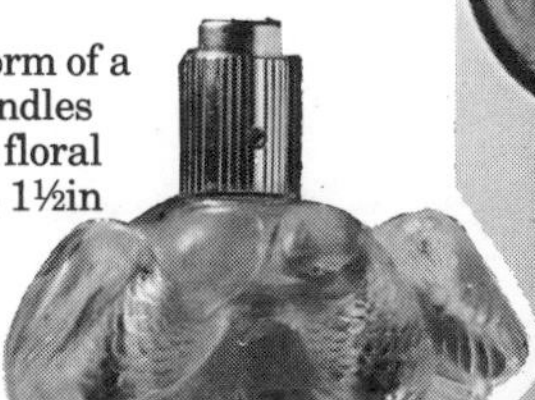

A frosted glass atomiser with gilt metal collar and plunger, marked Lalique, France, in block capitals, 3½in (9.5cm) wide.
$1,000-1,200

An amber glass pendant, engraved R. Lalique, 2½in (6cm).
$1,000-1,300

An amber-stained scent-bottle and stopper, 'Pan', with moulded signature R. Lalique and inscribed Lalique, 5in (13cm) high.
$1,800-2,400

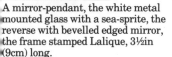

A frosted glass atomiser, enamelled in orange, moulded R. Lalique, France, mounts stamped Le Parisien, 5½in (13.5cm) high.
$400-500

A black glass scent bottle and stopper, moulded at each corner with a woman in long dress, moulded mark Lalique, Ambrl D'Orsay, 5in (13cm) high, original box.
$3,000-4,000

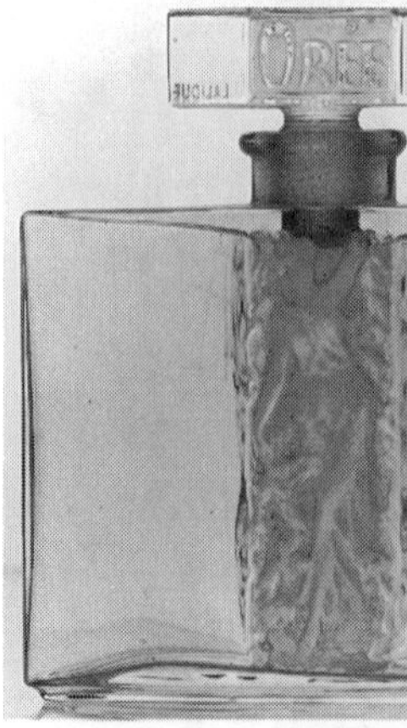

A clear and frosted bottle, 'Oree', the stopper moulded with the words Oree, Claire Paris, engraved Lalique on stopper, 3in (8cm) high.
$3,000-4,000

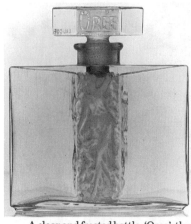

A black glass bottle, 'NN' (Nuit Noir), the bottle with central panel moulded with the words Le Parfum NN Forvil, moulded R. Lalique, 3½in (9cm) high.
$9,000-10,000

A clear and frosted glass scent bottle and stopper, 'Amphyrite', traces of brown staining, moulded marks Lalique, 4in (10cm) high.
$2,000-2,500

A clear and russet-stained bottle, 'La Belle Saison', for Houbigant, moulded R. Lalique, 5½in (14.5cm) high.
$3,000-4,000

A clear glass scent bottle for Molinard, 'Le Baiser du Faune', outer ring for scent, intaglio moulded R. Lalique, 6in (15cm) high.
$7,000-9,000

A clear glass scent bottle, with tiara stopper, for Roger et Gallet, stopper moulded Lalique, 3in (8cm) high.
$13,000-14,000

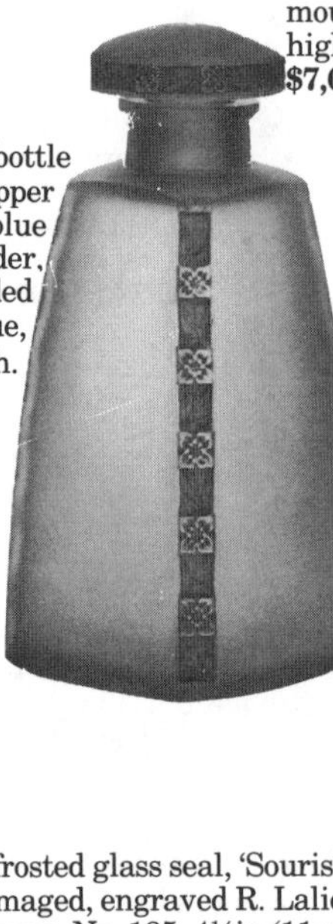

A cologne bottle 'Fleurettes', the stopper decorated with blue stained flower border, damaged, moulded signature Lalique, 8in (20cm) high.
$700-800

A glass perfume bottle, the stopper moulded as the full-figure of a maiden, moulded Lalique, with extended L, 4in (10cm) high.
$2,500-3,000

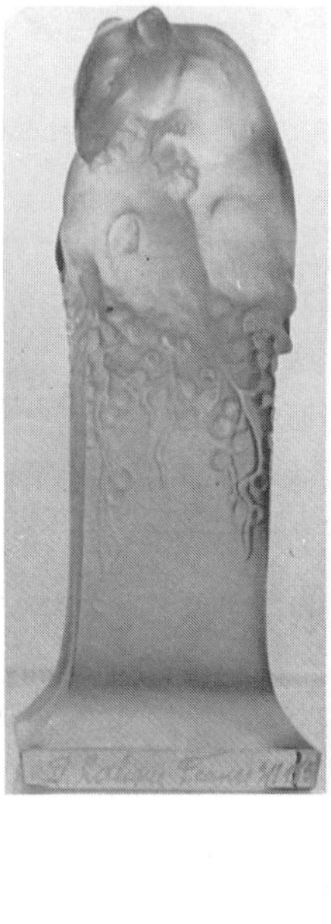

A frosted glass seal, 'Souris', damaged, engraved R. Lalique, France, No. 185, 4½in (11cm).
$3,000-4,000

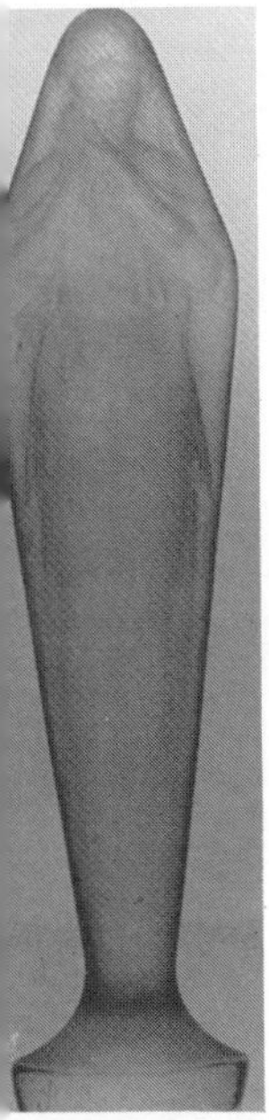

A clear glass scent bottle, for Worth, 'Requête', the stopper moulded with W, moulded Lalique, France, 3½in (9cm) high.
$1,300-1,500

A glass vase, 'Pierrefonds', engraved signature R. Lalique, France No. 990, 6in (15.5cm) high.
$3,000-4,000

frosted seal, 'Figurine Mains ointes', moulded as a female figure, tched R. Lalique, 3½in (9.5cm) igh.
700-800

A pair of brass table mirrors, in the manner of R. Lalique, 20in (50cm) high.
$2,500-3,000

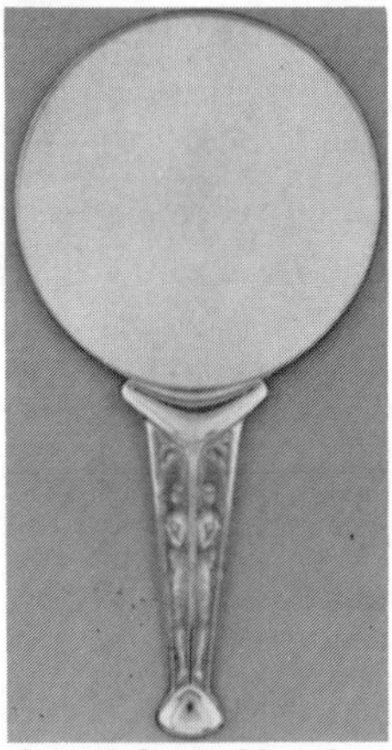

A glass and metal hand mirror, stamped on metal Lalique, 12in (30cm) long, in original case.
$6,000-7,000

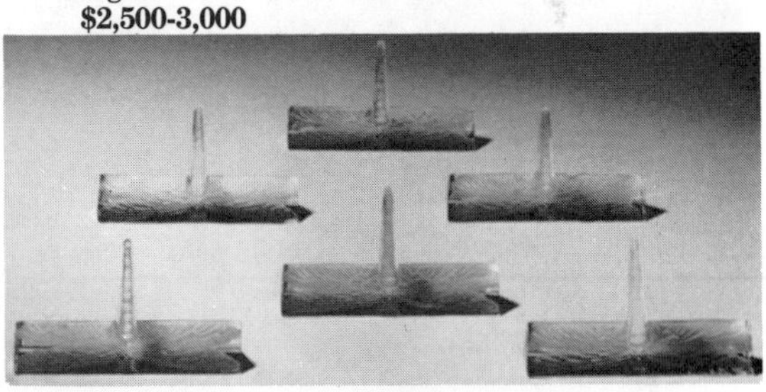

A set of 6 knife rests, each with a satin-finished dragon-fly, damaged, engraved signature R. Lalique, 4in (10cm) long.
$3,200-4,000

black polished glass seal, 'Tête 'Aigle', engraved R. Lalique, 'rance No.175, 3in (8cm) high.
1,600-1,800

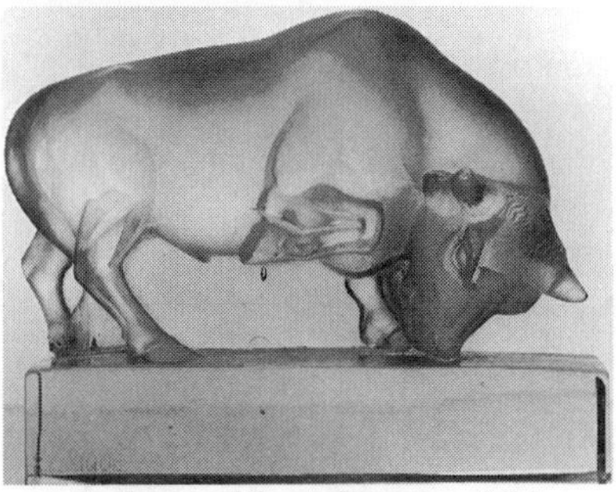

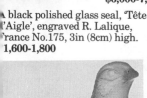

A clear and frosted paperweight, 'Taureau', stencilled R. Lalique, France, 3½in (8.5cm) high.
$900-1,100

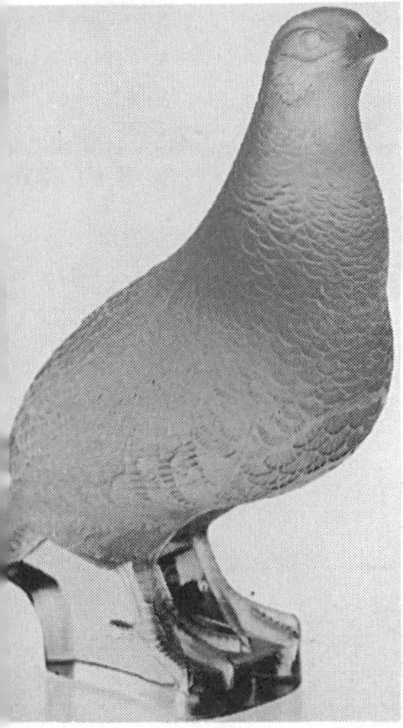

A frosted table decoration, 'Perdrix', moulded as a French partridge, stencilled R. Lalique, France, 7in (17.5cm) high.
$700-800

A clear and frosted vase, 'Faune', the stem moulded as the head of Bacchus, 2 exaggerated horns forming curved handles, stencilled R. Lalique, France, 12½in (32cm) high.
$3,500-4,000

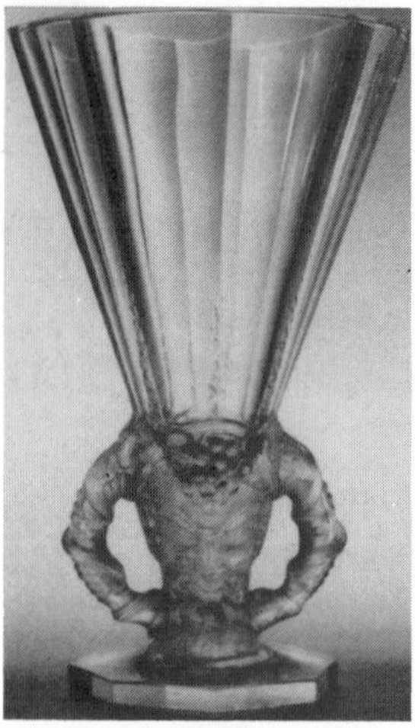

A two-handled vase, 'Faune', acid-stamped signature R. Lalique, France, 12in (30cm) high.
$4,500-5,200

A two-colour stained vase, 'Martins Pêcheurs', green stained Kingfishers perched in grey stained flowering branches, engraved and moulded signature R. Lalique, 9½in (24.5cm) high.
$6,000-7,000

A vase, 'Marisa' with graduated bands of fish, damaged, engraved signature R. Lalique, France No. 1002, 9in (23cm) high.
$6,000-7,000

A pair of Lalique candlestick damaged, 9in (23cm) high.
$2,000-3,000

A frosted and polished glass vase, 'Martins Pêcheurs', with green and grey staining, damage, moulded R. Lalique, 9½in (24.5cm) high.
$3,000-4,000

An opalescent blue-stained vase, 'Oléron', etched script mark R. Lalique, France No. 1008, 3½in (9.5cm) high.
$1,000-1,200

A brown stained vase, 'Milan', engraved signature R. Lalique, France No. 1025, 11in (28cm) high.
$3,000-4,000

An opalescent blue-stained vase, 'Tournesol', etched script R. Lalique, France, 4½in (11.5cm) high.
$1,200-1,300

Ceramics

A Czechoslovakian fac mask,c1930, 8½in (21c
$300-400

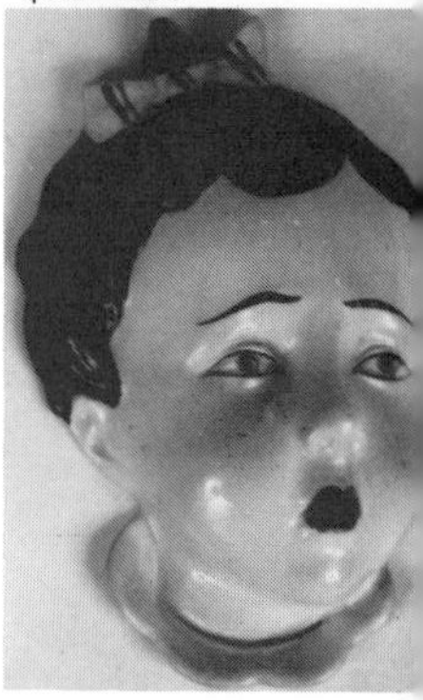

A Royal Dux face mask, c1930, 7½in (19cm).
$200-300

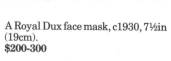

C. Copes & Co. face mask, 1930, 7in (17.5cm).
100-200

An Austrian face mask, 8in (20cm).
$200-350

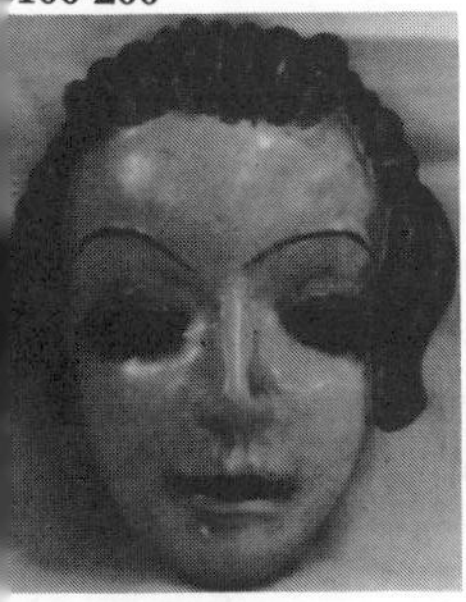

Goldscheider face mask, ½in (16cm).
250-300

A Japanese flask, entitled Just a Little Nip, c1900.
$80-120

Ladies used to keep them in their handbags or muffs.

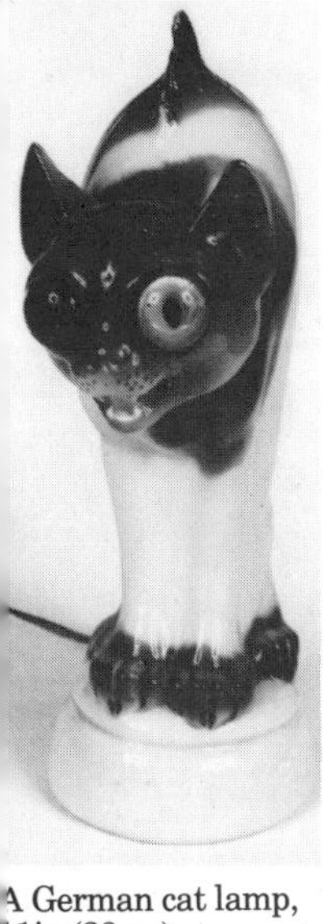

German cat lamp, 1in (28cm).
$300-500

A Susie Cooper coffee pot, 5in (13cm).
$60-70

Milk jug, 2½in (6.5cm).
$15-20

A Grays pottery jug, A.923, 7½in (19cm).
$60-100

A Barker Bros. hand-painted jug, 6in (15cm).
$90-100

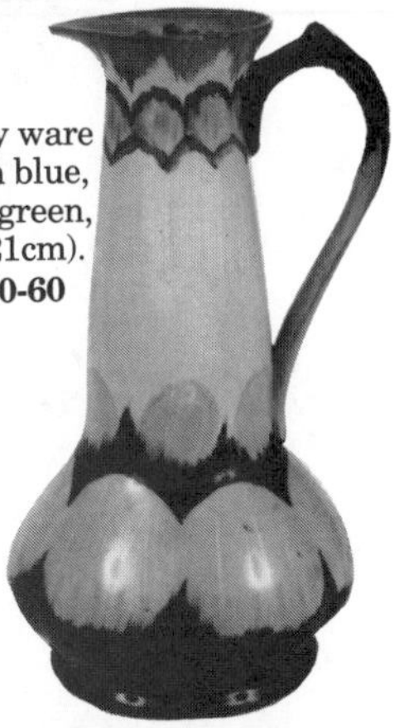

A Hancock's ivory ware jug, decorated in blue, yellow and green, 8½in (21cm).
$50-60

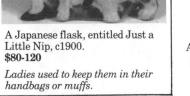

A Susie Cooper tea cup and coffee cup.
$20-30 each

A Susie Cooper coffee set, pot 8in (20cm) high.
$150-200

A Shelley 22-piece tea service, with yellow phlox pattern.
$900-1,000

A Torquay pottery jug, 5in (13cm).
$60-70

A green teapot in the form of a car, c1930.
$150-160

A Grays pottery dish, 14in (35cm) wide.
$150-200

A Lingardware teapot in yellow, 7½in (19cm).
$100-130

A cube teapot by G. Clews Ltd. in orange, c1930, 4in (10cm).
$40-50

A Simple Simon teapot.
$130-150

A Carltonware grey teapot, c1950, 9½in (24cm) wide.
$60-70

A Burleigh ware biscuit barrel with the Susie Cooper pattern, with plated lid and handle, 7½in (19cm).
$120-200

A Myott biscuit barrel, 7½in (19cm).
$80-120

A Shelley tea cup, saucer and plate.
$250-300

A Burleigh ware plaque in the form of a galleon, in matt green glaze, 13in (33cm).
$60-120

A Grays pottery jam pot, with Pharaoh's mark, 4½in (12cm).
$40-50

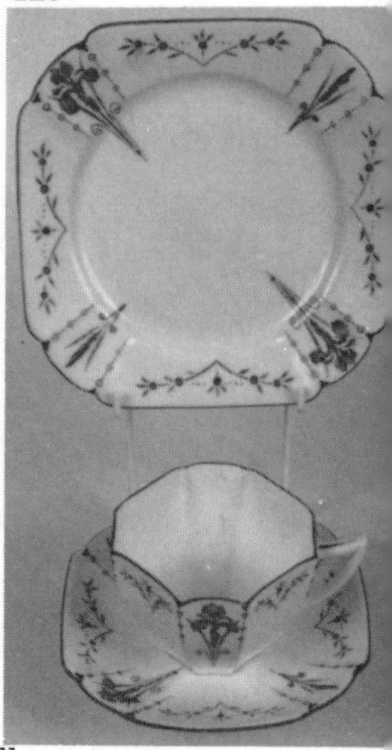

A Shelley tea cup, saucer and plate with the Blue Iris design.
$100-120

A Grays flower trough, 9in (24cm).
$120-200

ɅAn Arthur Wood vase in orange, nauve, yellow and green, c1930, 9in 24cm).
60-120

A Keith Murray vase in green, 1933.
700-800

This vase in either blue, white or traw coloured would be $1,000-,300

Clarice Cliff

A Bizarre table decoration, 'Age of Jazz', hairline crack, rubber stamp mark, 8in (20cm) high.
$7,000-8,000

A Crown Derby vase in dark red, 9½in (24cm) wide.
$50-60

A Crown Devon lotus type jug, c1930, 13in (33cm).
$400-450

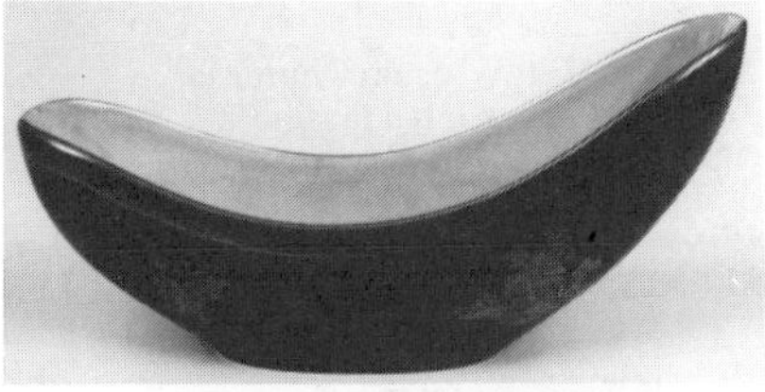

A Crown Derby dark red vase with gilt trim, 9in (23cm) wide.
$60-70

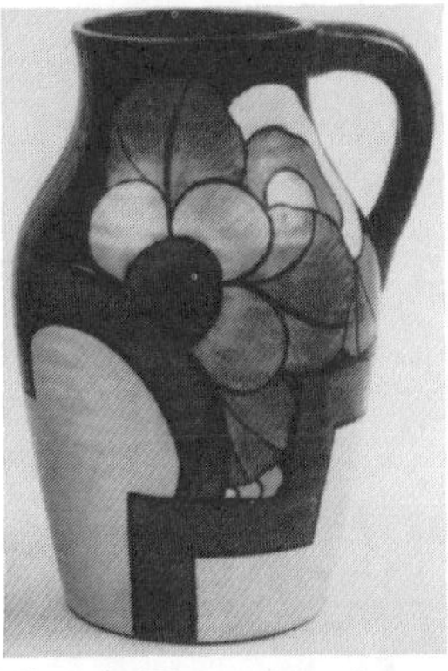

A Latona Bizarre lotus jug decorated in the Dahlia pattern, painted in black, green, pink, blue and yellow on a matt ground, rubber stamp mark, painted Latona, 12in (30cm).
$4,000-5,000

A Crown Devon glazed turquoise vase with gilt trim, 5½in (14cm).
$60-70

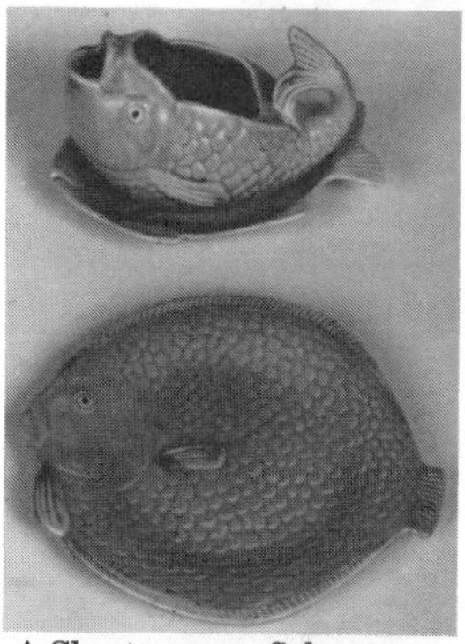

A Shorter ware fish set comprising 6 plates, a dish and a sauce boat, plates 9in (24cm) wide.
$150-200

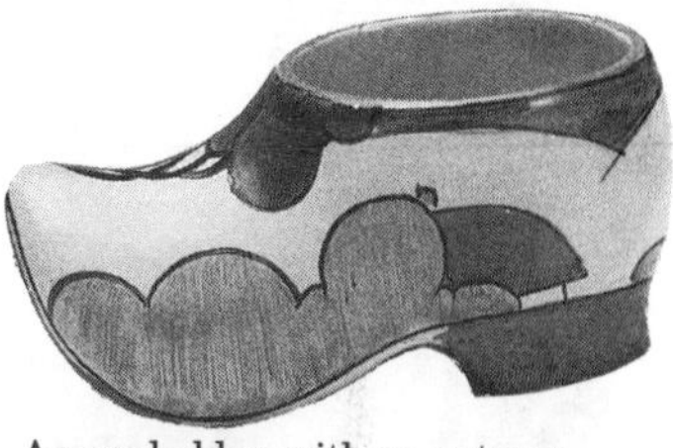

A posy holder, with an autumn design of trees and a house, 5½in (13cm) long.
$500-700

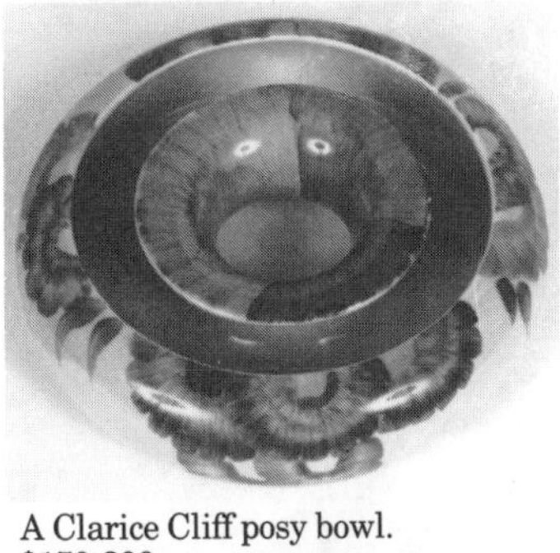

A Clarice Cliff posy bowl.
$150-200

A Clarice Cliff vase with My Garden pattern, 5in (14cm).
$500-700

A Clarice Cliff jam pot with pine trees.
$200-300

A Clarice Cliff Bizarre vase, with hand-painted design in colours, Wilkinson's shape No. 370, 6in (15cm).
$900-1,000

A Clarice Cliff globular vase, painted with the Summerhouse design, 6in (15cm).
$3,000-4,000

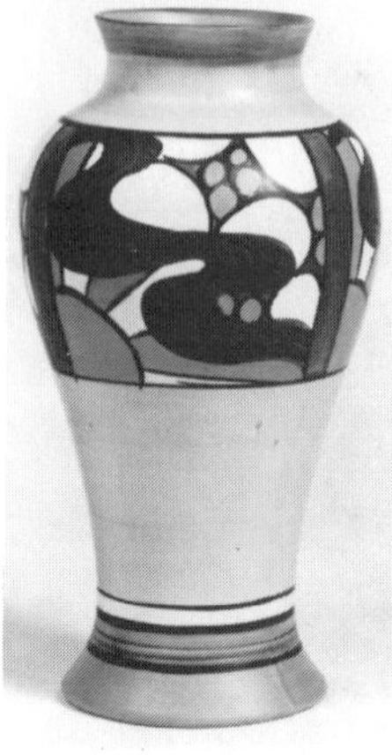

A Fantasque vase, painted in colours, with the Sunrise pattern, printed F, F.S, W.L. marks and gilt Lawleys, Regent Street stamp, c1929, 9in (23cm).
$1,400-1,600

A Clarice Cliff Winston Churchill Toby jug, with printed facsimile signature mark and Royal Staffordshire, Wilkinson, No. 47, 12in (30cm).
$1,500-1,600

A vase inscribed on base 'Cafe a Lait', hand-painted, Bizarre by Clarice Cliff, Newport Pottery, England, 9in (21cm).
$1,000-1,200

A Clarice Cliff cruet, 3in (7.5cm).
$40-60

A Clarice Cliff vase, painted in colours with a central frieze of stylised leaves, printed factory marks and facsimile signature, 10in (25cm).
$1,400-1,600

Ceramic Figures

A Goldscheider figure of a lady dancing, 16in (40cm).
$600-800

A Goldscheider figure, by Dakon, 13in (33cm).
$2,000-3,000

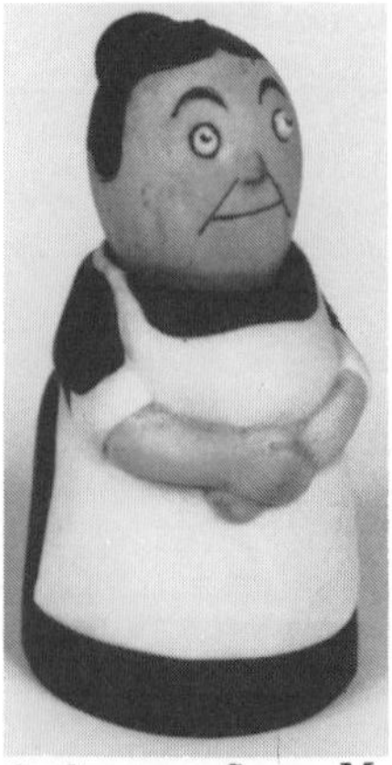

A Carltonware figure, Mrs. Bun, designed by John Hassall.
$400-500

ronze & Ivory igures

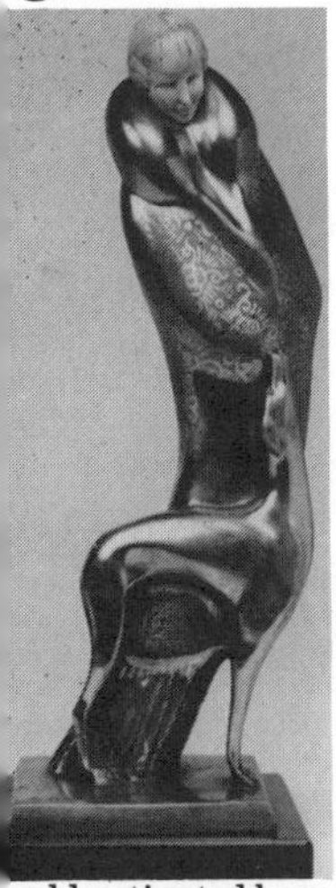

gold patinated bronze and ivory oup, 'Elegant', cast and carved om a model by S. Bertrand, on onze plinth and black marble ise, slightly chipped, signed Bertrand, 12in (31cm).
,000-6,000

A pair of bronze figures by P. Laurel, 11½in (29cm) high.
$3,000-4,400

A marble and bronze figure by Lothar, signed.
$4,000-5,000

A bronze figure, 'Speedskater', cast from a model by Carl Fagerberg, signed on the bronze plinth Carl Fagerberg, Stockholm and dated April 1932, 20½in (51cm).
$5,000-7,000

This piece was commissioned for a competition and exhibition commemorating the 1932 Los Angeles Olympic Games and bears its original exhibition label on the underside of the base.

A bronze and ivory figure of the poet Dante, cast and carved from a model by D. H. Chiparus, signed in the bronze D. H. Chiparus, 28in (70cm).
$6,000-10,000

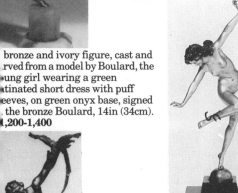

A bronze and ivory figure, cast and carved from a model by Lorenzl, on green onyx base, stamped Lorenzl, Made in Austria, 13½in (35cm) high.
$3,000-4,000

bronze and ivory figure, cast and rved from a model by Boulard, the ung girl wearing a green tinated short dress with puff eeves, on green onyx base, signed the bronze Boulard, 14in (34cm).
,200-1,400

A bronze and ivory figure by Lorenzl, 12½in (32cm) high.
$1,600-2,400

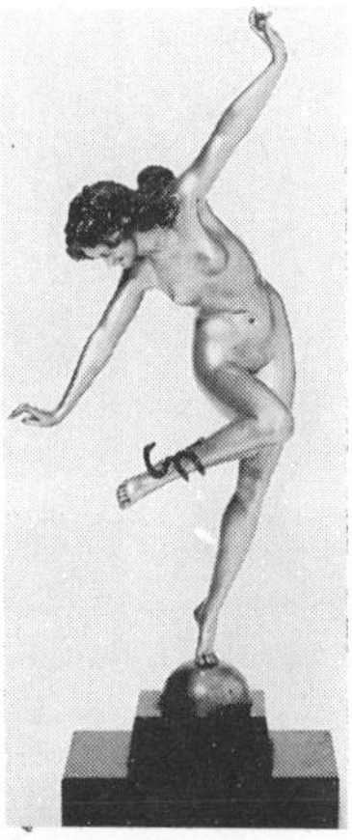

A cold painted bronze figure, unmarked but attributed as a model by Colinet, the girl poised on one leg with a green serpent entwined round her ankle, 20in (50cm).
$3,000-4,000

A cold painted bronze and ivory figure, cast and carved from a model by Lorenzl, on a geometric green and black onyx base, signed Lorenzl, 10in (25.5cm) high.
$2,000-3,000

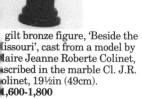

gilt bronze figure, 'Beside the issouri', cast from a model by laire Jeanne Roberte Colinet, iscribed in the marble Cl. J.R. olinet, 19½in (49cm).
,600-1,800

A bronze figure, 'Cleopatra', cast from a model by D. H. Chiparus, signed in the bronze Chiparus, 19in (48cm) wide.
$8,000-12,000

A green-patinated bronze and ivory figure, 'Juggler', cast and carved from a model by Jaeger, signed in the bronze Jaeger and stamped Vrai Bronze Deposé, 36½in (93cm) high.
$4,000-8,000

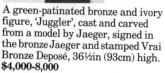

An ivory figure, carved in the style of Ferdinand Preiss, 2½in (6.5cm).
$900-1,000

A bronze figure, by Philippe, signe 8½in (22cm) high.
$1,200-2,000

A bronze and ivory figure, 'Page Boy', cast and carved from a mode by Prof. Otto Poertzel, cold painte green cape, bronze foot and striat marble base, signed in the bronze Prof. O. Poertzel, 11½in (29cm).
$3,000-4,000

A bronze and ivory figure, by Tereszczuk.
$1,200-1,800

A bronze and ivory figure, signed Philippe, 16in (41cm) high.
$8,000-12,000

A bronze figure, 'Radha', by Philippe, 22in (56cm) high.
$6,000-8,000

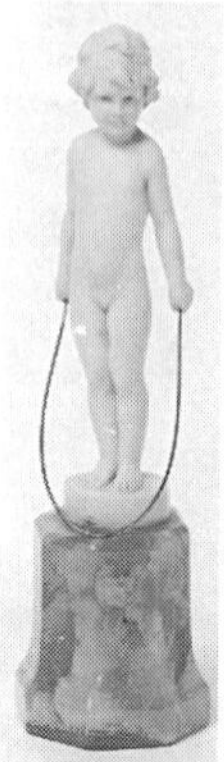

An ivory figure, 'Girl with Skipping Rope', carved from a model by Ferdinand Preiss, signed F. Preiss, 6in (15cm).
$900-1,200

A bronze figure of a nude girl, cast from a model by Lorenzl, veined marble base, with overall muted silver-coloured patination, signed Lorenzl, 25in (64cm) high.
$4,000-5,000

A bronze figure, by Philippe, 9in (23cm) high.
$600-1,000

An ivory figure, carved from a model by P. Philippe, on a brown onyx striated pedestal base, the base inscribed P. Philippe, 9in (23cm) high.
$5,000-6,000

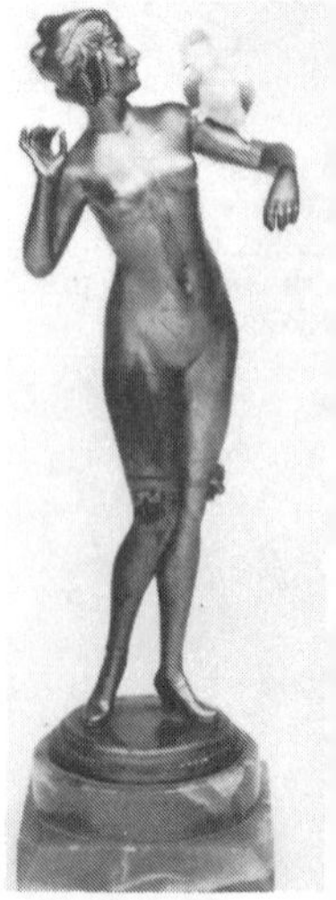

A gilt bronze and ivory figure, cas and carved from a model by H. Keck, on an onyx base, signed in the bronze H. Keck, with foundary mark, 12in (30.5cm) high.
$1,300-1,600

Furniture

A drinks cabinet, veneered in burr walnut, with 4 cupboards and a slide, 42in (106cm).
$1,400-1,600

An oak cabinet designed by Ambrose Heal, inset with circular manufacturer's label Heal & Son Makers, London W., 44in (113cm).
$5,000-6,000

A stained black and limed oak Ashanti-style stool, 20½in (52cm) high.
$500-600

An English walnut centre table, 31in (78.5cm).
$1,400-1,600

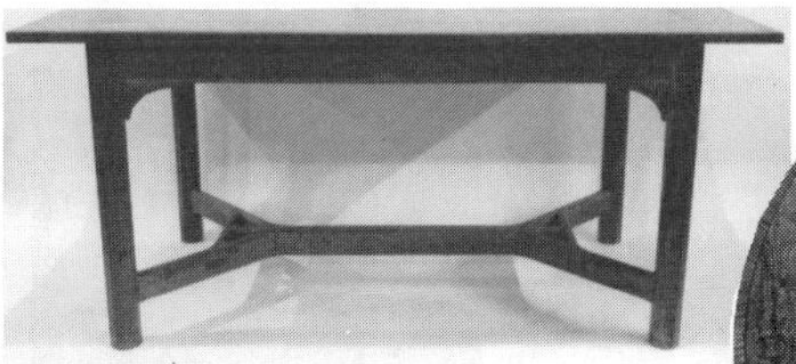

A quartered oak dining table, designed by Gordon Russell, made by G. Cooke, with label to underside, c1923, 66 by 33in (167 by 84cm).
$5,000-6,000

A small gilt and upholstered salon chair attributed to Jules Leleu, upholstered in beige fabric.
$3,400-4,000

A walnut dining table, with walnut veneer, 71in (179cm) long.
$1,400-1,800

An oak and chestnut sideboard by Gordon Russell, fitted with 2 drawers, cabinet maker P. J. Wade, c1927, 52½in (136cm).
$4,000-5,000

An English Egyptian-style bed, the headboard with beaten copper panel, 42in (108cm).
$1,200-1,400

A walnut veneered circular display cabinet, 45in (114cm).
$700-900

An Austrian Secessionist painted writing table and chair, 23in (58cm).
$5,000-6,000

A maple veneered side table, 40in (100cm) long.
$1,200-1,400

A set of 4 'Brno' chairs, designed by Mies van der Rohe.
$2,000-2,400

Glass

An Austrian overlaid and carved glass drinking set, comprising 12 small beakers and a decanter, the amethyst tinted glass overlaid in pink with carved geometric patterns, decanter 13in (33cm).
$1,200-1,600

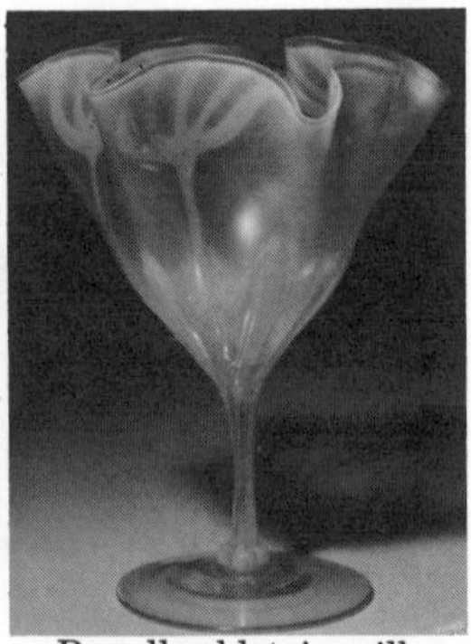

A James Powell goblet, in milky vaseline glass, the stem flaring into a flower-form bowl with wavy rim, decorated with milky striations, 8in (20cm).
$1,000-1,200

A liqueur set in green glass, 10in (25.5cm).
$100-200

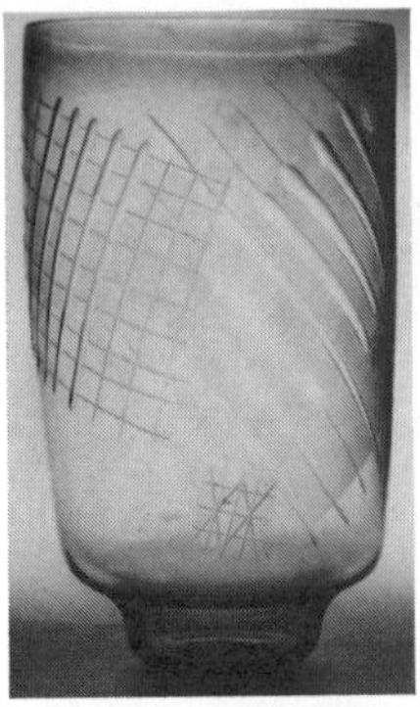

A Christopher Williams 'cut dust' vase, in green tinted clear glass, wheel engraved acid-etched and polished with linear geometric panels, engraved Christopher Williams, 923, Glasshouse 1986, 14½in (36cm).
$800-1,000

A pair of plafonniers, the clear and satin finished glass with striated acid-etched decoration, with 3 gilt metal suspension cords, signed Daum Nancy France, with the Cross of Lorraine, 14½in (6.5cm) diam.
$3,000-4,000

A green glass and chromium plated cake stand, 8in (20cm) high.
$30-40

A James Powell carafe, the clear glass cone shaped body with cup rim, applied notched band, 7½in (19cm) high.
$160-250

A vase, decorated with a man and 5 maidens, enamelled in red, blue, yellow and green on a carved ground, with enamel signature K. Poner, 40, 15½in (40cm) high.
$3,000-4,000

A rose coloured dessert servi
$50-60

Jewellery

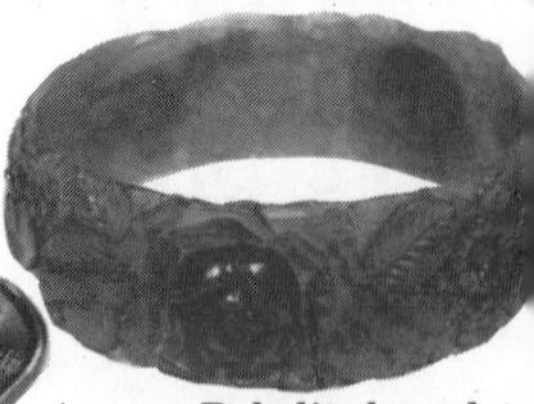

A green Bakelite bracelet.
$10-20

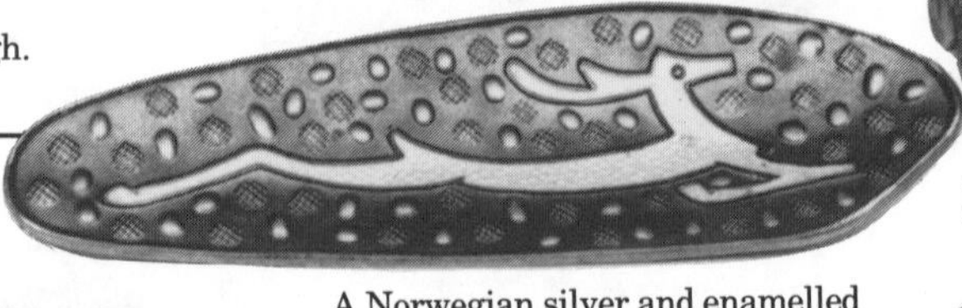

A Norwegian silver and enamelled brooch, 3in (8cm).
$60-100

A gold ring set with rubies, c1930.
$400-600

A set of three Bakelite brooches.
$10-20 each

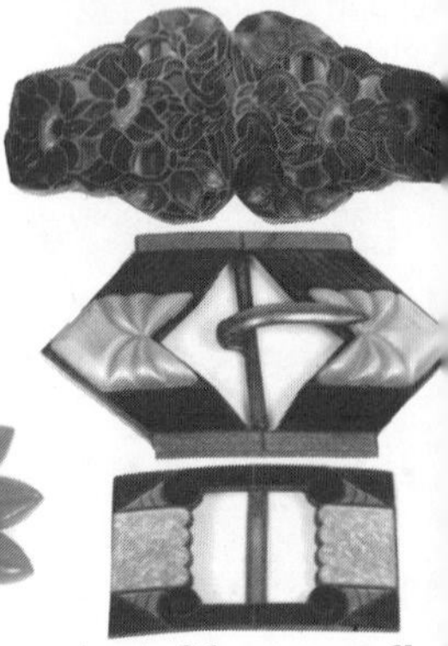

A set of three enamelle buckles.
$40-100 each

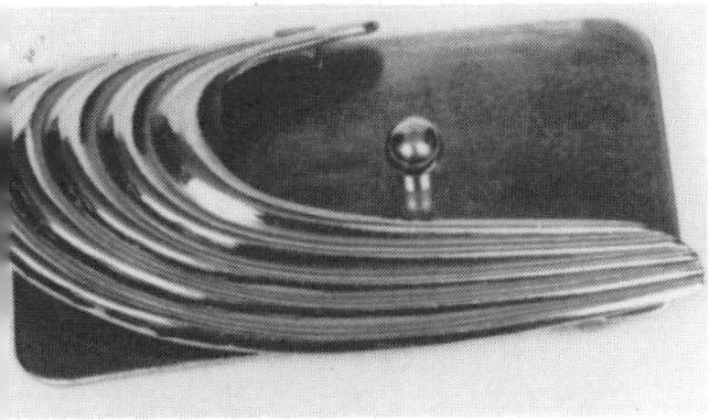

silver buckle.
5-30

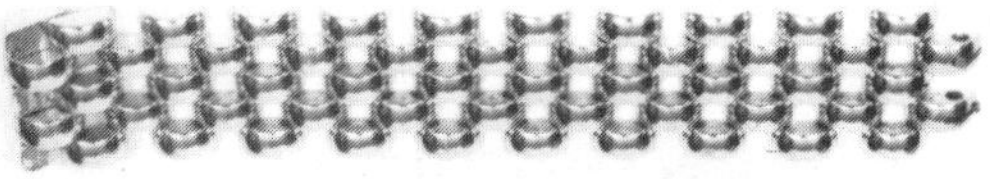

A silver coloured linked bracelet.
$100-200

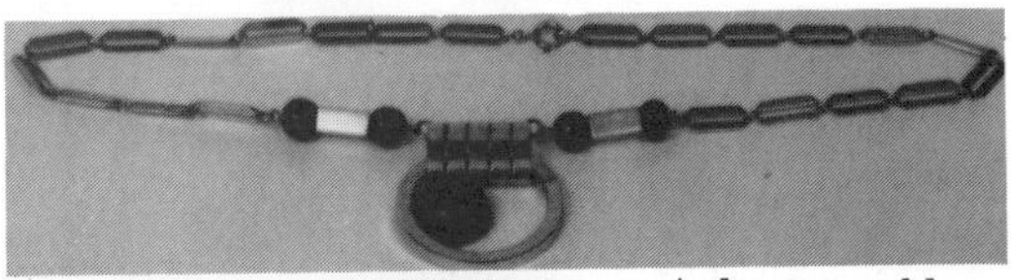

A chrome necklace, with red beads.
$80-160

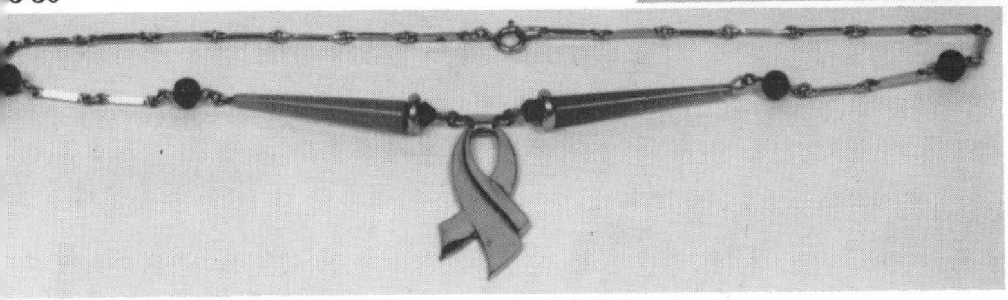

A silver necklace set with green stones.
$80-100

A chrome necklace, with green beads.
$80-160

A chrome and red beaded necklace.
$80-160

letal

A chrome jam and marmalade set, c1930.
$30-40

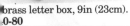

brass letter box, 9in (23cm).
.0-80

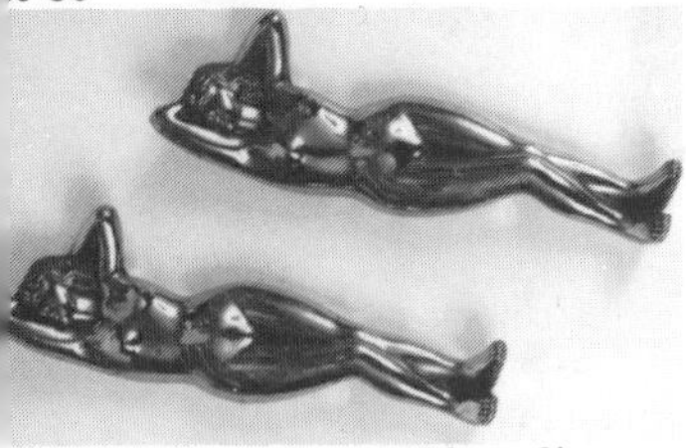

pair of chrome posy holders, 6in 5cm) long.
10-60

A chrome cruet set, 8in (20cm) wide.
$60-80

A chrome cake basket with etched glass, 11½in (29cm) wide.
$80-120

A silver and enamel rouge pot, c1930.
$60-100

A tortoiseshell and silver compact, 2in (5cm) diam.
$140-180

A four-piece chrome tea service.
$90-100

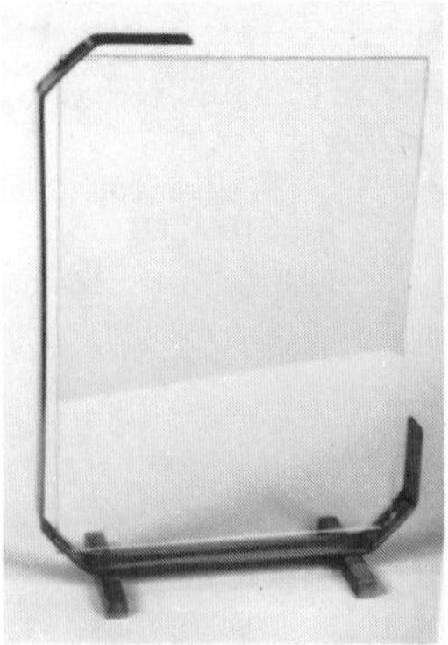

A chrome picture frame, 10½ by 7½in (27 by 19cm).
$80-120

A chromium plated cruet, 2½i (6cm) high.
$20-30

A chromium plated cake stand, 8in (20cm) high.
$30-40

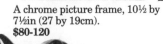

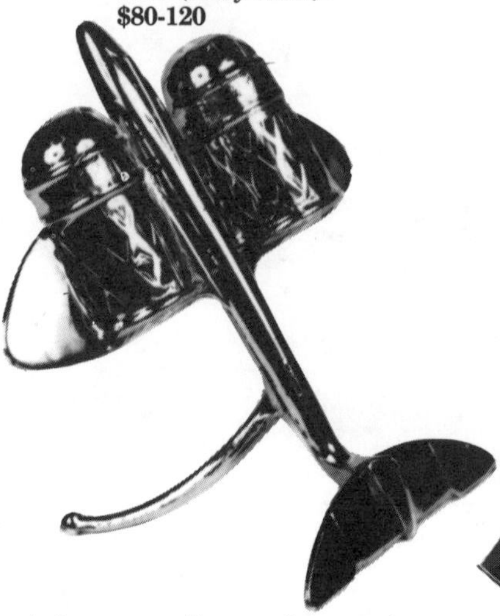

A chrome novelty aeroplane cruet, c1950, 4½in (11cm) high.
$60-100

A Dunhill shagreen cigare lighter, c1930, 2in (5cm).
$40-80

A pair of chrome candlesticks, trimmed with green Bakelite, 5in (13cm).
$80-120

A clock garniture.
$400-500

A chrome desk lamp, 18in (46cm
$180-240

Miscellaneous

A simulated tortoiseshell cigarette case, with watch inset, 4 by 3in (10 by 8cm).
$60-100

A clock garniture.
$300-400

A clock garniture.
$400-500

An alarm clock, by Phinney-Walker, 5½in (14cm) high.
$60-100

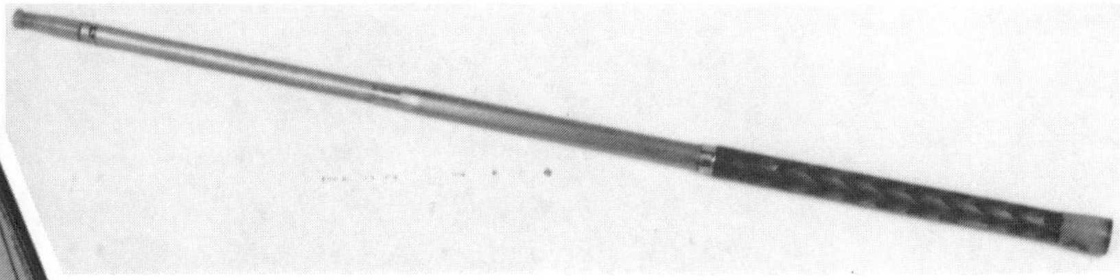

An extending cigarette holder, enamel and amber, c1930, 13½in (34cm).
$60-100

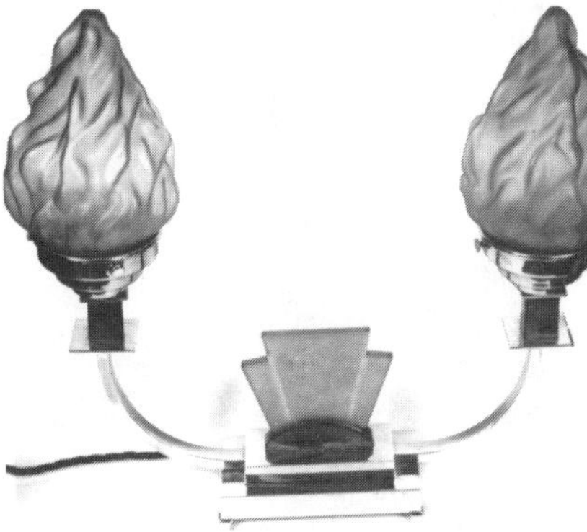

A chrome double lamp, with pink torch shades, 17in (43cm) high.
$150-200

A spelter figure lamp, with golden crackle glass, 21in (53cm).
$500-600

A clock garniture.
$400-500

A chrome electric clock, 10in (26cm) wide.
$120-160

chrome table lamp, with peach
ade, 17in (43cm).
50-200

A French lamp on onyx base with brass birds, 8½in (22cm) wide.
$200-240

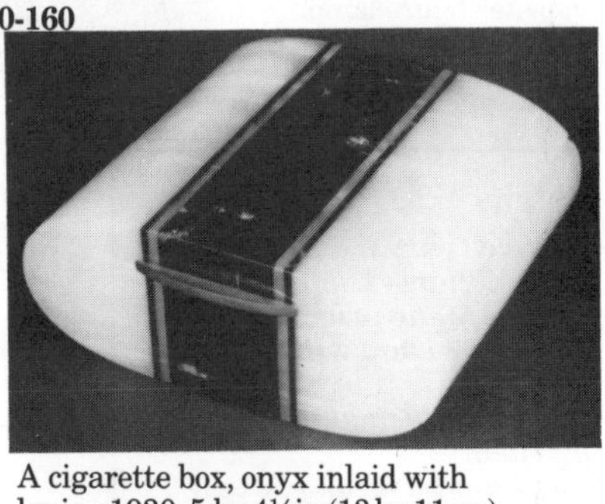

A cigarette box, onyx inlaid with lapis, c1930, 5 by 4½in (13 by 11cm).
$200-400

clock, 13in (33cm) wide.
300-500

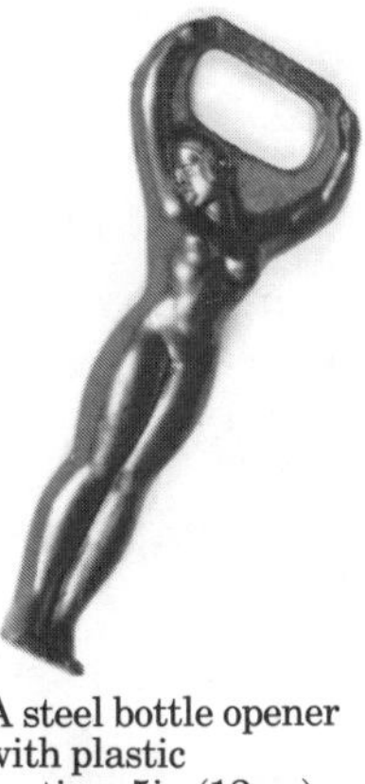

A steel bottle opener with plastic coating, 5in (12cm).
$60-80

A clock garniture.
$500-600

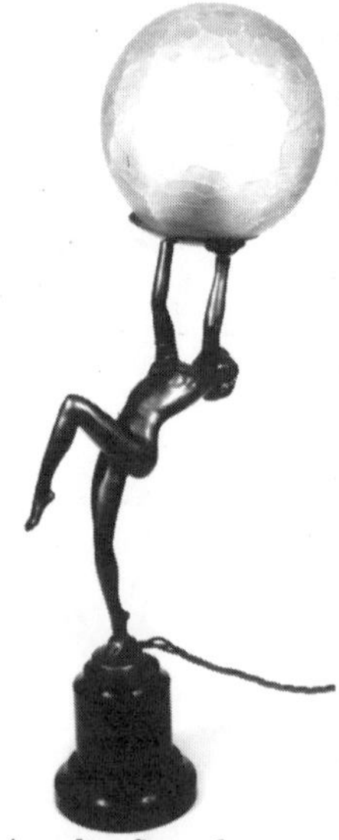

A spelter figure lamp, 22½in (57cm).
$700-800

A spelter figure lamp, with pink globe, 25in (64cm) high.
$600-800

A clock garniture.
$450-500

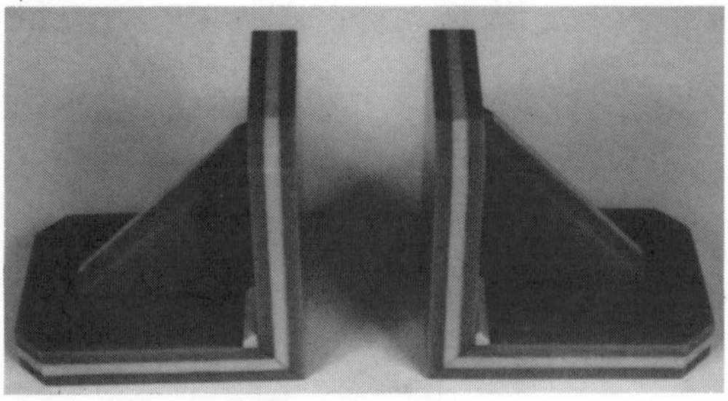

A pair of blue and cream Bakelite bookends, c1930.
$200-300

A clock garniture.
$500-600

An electric clock, chrome with green glass, 4½in (12cm) high.
$120-160

A Bakelite biscuit barrel and
$35-50

A perspex yacht, 5½in (14cm) high.
$60-100

A chrome brush and crumb tray, 8in (20cm) high.
$100-140

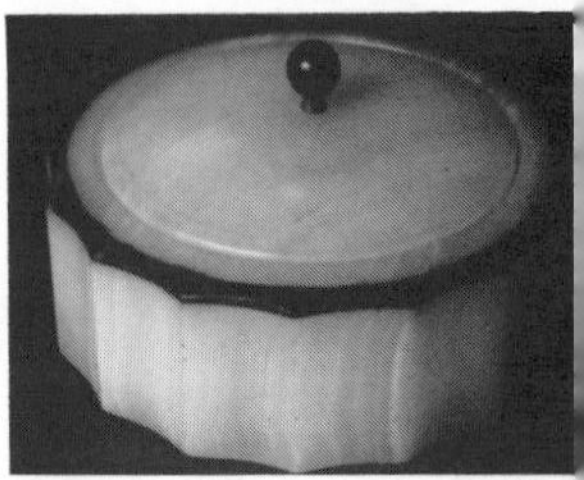

An onyx powder bowl, trimmed wi malachite, c1930, 4in (10cm) dian
$250-300

A perspex clock, with orange base and peach face, 8½in (22cm) high.
$60-100

Price

Prices vary from auction to auction – from dealer to dealer. The price paid in a dealer's shop will depend on:
1) what he paid for the item
2) what he thinks he can get for it
3) the extent of his knowledge
4) awareness of market trends
It is a mistake to think that you will automatically pay more in a specialist dealer's shop. He is more likely to know the 'right' price for a piece. A general dealer may undercharge but he could also overcharge.

ILVER
askets

George III swing handled sugar
ısket, by Andrew Fogelberg,
ıgraved with a paterae band and
itials, the oval stem to a shaped
blong foot, London 1794, 5oz.
,000-1,300

A George III bread basket, engraved with a crest, by Henry Green and Charles Aldridge, 1765, 14½in (36.5cm) long, 43oz.
$8,000-10,000

A George III bread basket, on moulded foot, engraved with a monogram, by John Vere and William Lutwyche, 1766, 14in (35.5cm), 32oz.
$6,000-8,000

A George III bread basket, engraved with a coat-of-arms, by John Vere and William Lutwyche, 1765, 13½in (34cm), 29oz.
$4,000-5,000

An American cake basket, marked sterling, c1900, 15in (38cm) high, 52oz.
$3,000-4,000

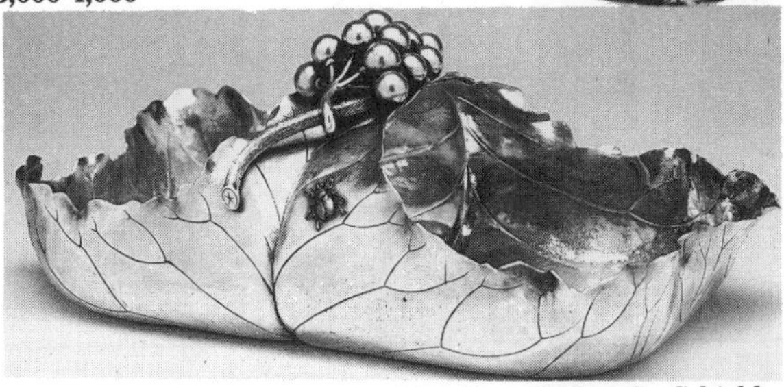

A leaf form basket, by Schiebler, New York, the matt finished interior with traces of gilding, c1885, 10½in (26cm) wide, 17.5oz.
$6,000-7,000

A cake basket, by Marquand and Company, New York, repairs to rim and handle, c1835, 11½in (29cm) diam, 39.5oz.
$5,000-6,000

pair of fan shaped sweetmeat
ıskets, Birmingham 1911, 5in
2.5cm) high.
100-500

Beakers

A pair of beakers, by William Gale & Son, New York, engraved with script initials 'HHV', each marked, 1865, 3½in (9cm) high, 10.5oz.
$1,000-1,200

A set of 3 beakers, by Alfred and George Welles, Boston, each engraved on the front with Script 'W', each marked, c1810, 3½in (9cm) high, 11.5oz.
$1,000-1,200

A pair of beakers, by Eli C. Garner, Lexington, Kentucky, engraved with script initials 'JMH', each marked, after 1838, 3½in (9cm) high, 8.5oz.
$1,500-2,000

Bowls

A porringer, by Adrian Bancker, New York, the front later engraved with a crest over initials, the base engraved 'CBD', some repair, marked on base, c1750, 7½in (19cm) long, 8.5oz.
$1,700-2,000

A porringer, by Jonathan Otis, Newport, the pierced handle engraved 'S. Coggeshall', repair to handle join, marked in centre of bowl and back of handle, c1760, 8in (20.5cm) long, 8.5oz.
$3,000-3,500

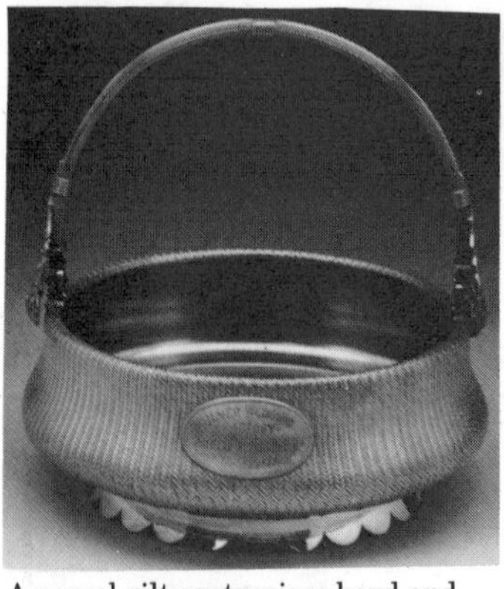

A parcel gilt centrepiece bowl and cream jug, by Wood & Hughes, New York, with presentation inscription, c1880, the bowl 9in (23cm) diam.
$900-1,200

A porringer, by William Simpkins, Boston, the handle engraved with the initials 'THP', repair to handle join, marked W. Simpkins, c1750, 8in (20.5cm) long, 7.5oz.
$2,000-2,500

A footed bowl, by John and/or Joel Sayre, New York, one side with a bright cut and roulette work oval cartouche enclosing script initials 'JPM', marked twice on base, c1810, 6½in (17cm) diam, 12oz.
$1,500-2,000

A Martelé bowl, by Gorham Manufacturing Company, Providence, signed W. C. Codham, marked, c1902, 11in (28cm) diam, 28oz.
$5,000-6,000

A footed fruit bowl, by Whiting Manufacturing Company, North Attleboro or Newark, marked, c1885, 8½in (22cm) diam, 21.5oz.
$7,500-8,000

A porringer, by Samuel Tingley, New York, one side with early scrip monogram 'FLM', initial touch struck on either side of handle join c1765, 8in (20cm) long, 9.5oz.
$7,000-8,000

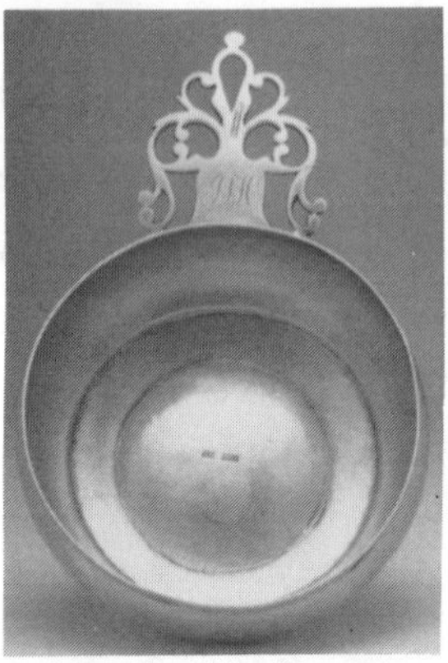

A porringer, by John Hancock, Boston, the pierced handle engrav in script 'JSH', damage to handle join, marked on handle and inside bowl, c1760, 8in (20.5cm) long, 8o
$2,500-3,000

A mixed metal centrepiece bowl an serving spoon, by Whiting Manufacturing Company, North Attleboro or Newark, both marked c1880, the bowl 8in (20.5cm) diam, 26oz.
$8,000-10,000

entrepiece bowl, by Samuel Kirk
on, Baltimore, one side with
er monogram, original removed,
rked, c1880, 11in (28cm) high,
5oz.
000-4,000

A William III bleeding bowl, the handle engraved with a cypher, by Robert Timbrell, 1701, 7½in (19cm), 6oz.
$3,000-4,000

A seafood bowl, attributed to Ball, Black & Co., New York, the bowl interior gilt, marked 'English Sterling', c1865, 13in (33cm) long, 19.5oz.
$1,500-2,000

An Edwardian porringer in the 18thC taste, fitted with a glass liner, D. & J. Welby, London 1903, 6½in (16cm), 8.25oz free.
$300-400

A bowl, by Herman W. Glendenning for Stone Associates, Gardner, Massachusetts, c1930, 10½in (27cm) diam, 29oz.
$3,000-4,000

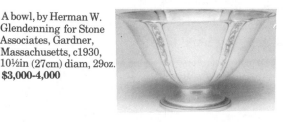

A centrepiece bowl, by Milton A. Fuller, Inc., New York/Palm Beach, marked, c1900, 14in (35.5cm) diam, 68oz.
$4,500-5,000

oxes

o small silver boxes, each with
achable cover, with enamelled
nted plaque, the bodies
mingham, the plaques South
ffordshire, damaged, c1780, 2in
m) wide.
200-1,500

A George III silver gilt shell shaped vinaigrette, Matthew Linwood, Birmingham 1806.
$300-400

A William IV silver-gilt gilt-lined vinaigrette, Nathaniel Mills, Birmingham 1837, 1½in (4cm).
$900-1,000

George IV gilt-lined snuff box, the
se and sides engine-turned, I.J.
ndon 1828, 3½in (9cm).
,800-2,000

A Victorian silver-gilt vinaigrette, by Nathaniel Mills, Birmingham 1836, 2in (5cm).
$500-600

Candelabra

A candelabrum in the neo-classical taste, Sheffield 1896, 21in (53.5cm), 55oz of weighable silver.
$4,000-5,000

A pair of Corinthian column five-light candelabra, by The Goldsmiths and Silversmiths Co. Ltd., 1939, 18½in (47cm), weight of branches 100oz.
$9,000-10,000

A pair of three-branch candelabra, Spink and Son, London 1960, 16½i (42cm), 96oz.
$3,500-4,000

Candlesticks

Four George III candlesticks, by Jonathan Alleine, 1773 and 1774, 9½in (25cm), 71oz.
$10,000-12,000

A George III gadrooned chamber candlestick, by Jonathan Alleine, London 1772, 7in (18cm), 12.25oz.
$1,500-1,700

Four George III Corinthian colu candlesticks, by Ebenezer Coker 1761 and 1762, 12in (30.5cm).
$12,000-14,000

A pair of George II candlesticks, by John Cafe, 1753, the nozzles unmarked, 9½in (24cm), 42oz.
$4,000-5,000

Four George III candlesticks, 2 by William Cafe, 1762, and 2 by Ebenezer Coker, 1765 and 1766, 11in (28cm), 101oz.
$6,000-8,000

A pair of George III candlesticks, by Matthew Boulton, Birmingham 1809, engraved with scratch weights 15:10 and 15:7, 12in (30.5cm).
$3,000-4,000

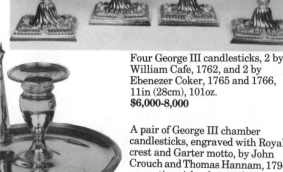

A pair of George III chamber candlesticks, engraved with Royal crest and Garter motto, by John Crouch and Thomas Hannam, 1794, one extinguisher by another, maker's mark indistinct, 5½in (14cm) diam, 19oz. 9dwt.
$3,000-4,000

ur Victorian candlesticks,
aker's mark JW and EH, Sheffield
45, 10½in (27cm).
,000-7,000

A pair of Victorian plain candlesticks in the Charles II taste, engraved with initials, by George Fox, 1867, Britannia Standard, 10½in (27cm), 40oz.
$3,000-4,000

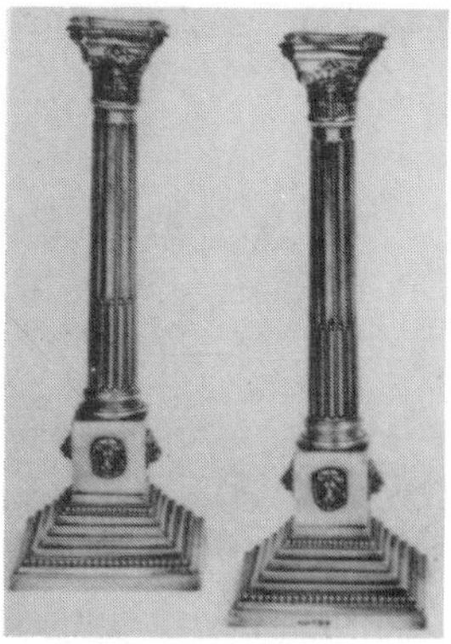

A pair of Corinthian capital candlesticks, with beaded stepped square bases decorated with lions' masks, 14in (35.5cm), 33oz.
$1,300-1,400

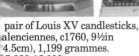

A pair of Maltese candlesticks, by Lebrun, c1790, 8½in (21.5cm), 725 grammes.
$4,000-5,000

pair of Louis XV candlesticks,
alenciennes, c1760, 9½in
4.5cm), 1,199 grammes.
15,000-16,000

A pair of German table candlesticks, c1760, 7in (18cm), 20oz.
$5,000-6,000

asters

set of 3 George I casters, maker's
ark S.W. for Samuel Welder or
arling Wilford, 1724, largest 7in
8cm), 19oz.
,000-7,000

A William IV sugar caster, by Paul Storr, London 1832, 6½in (17cm), 6.25oz.
$2,400-3,200

An Edwardian sugar caster, H.B., London 1906, 8½in (21cm), 10oz.
$500-600

A late Victorian sugar caster, Charles Stuart Harris, London 1889, Britannia Standard, 8in (20cm), 11.75oz.
$700-800

A late Victorian sugar caster, by William Hutton & Sons Ltd., London 1897, 8½in (22.5cm), 13.25oz.
$700-800

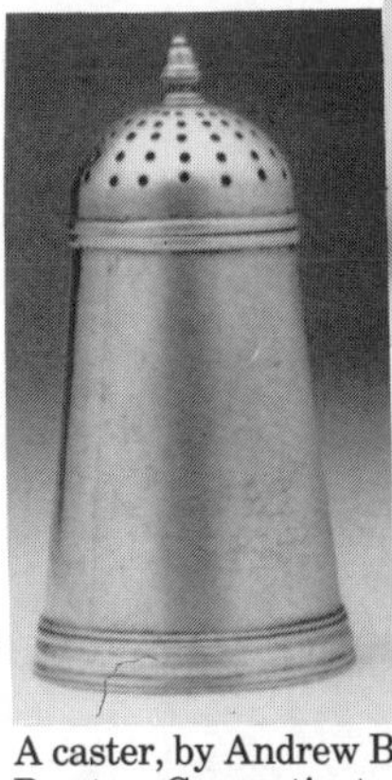

A caster, by Andrew Billings, Preston, Connecticut or Fishkill or Poughkeepsie, New York, the base engraved 'JWR', marked on base A Billings with pseudo hallmarks, c1790, 4in (10cm) high, 3.5oz.
$8,000-10,000

Centrepieces

A table centrepiece, London 1911, 6½in (17cm) high, 50.5oz.
$1,800-2,400

A George III eight-branch openwork epergne, by Thomas Pitts, 1780, 12¼in (31cm), 70oz.
$16,000-18,000

A William IV vine centrepiece, by John Tapley, 1836, 17½in (44.5cm), 106oz.
$8,000-10,000

Coffee & Chocolate Pots

A George II coffee pot, by Ayme Videau, 1741, 8½in (22cm), 26oz gross.
$8,000-10,000

A George II coffee pot, engraved with a coat-of-arms and crest, by John Swift, 1759, 11¼in (28.5cm), 33oz gross.
$4,500-5,000

The arms are those of Chichester, for Arthur, 1st Marquess of Donegal, 1739-99.

A George III coffee pot, by Orlando Jackson, 1771, 13½in (34.5cm), 34oz gross.
$6,000-8,000

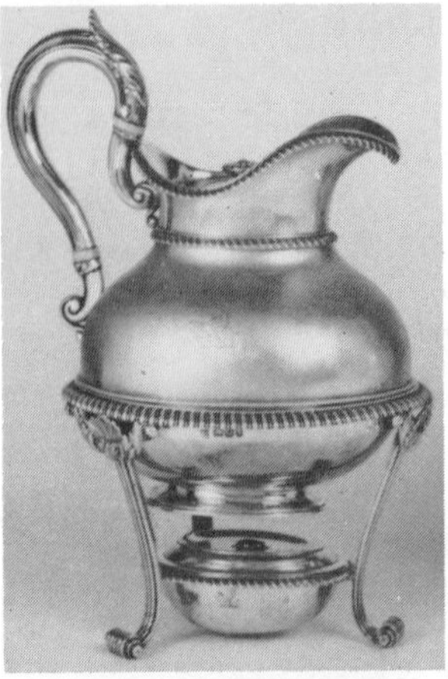

A George III coffee pot, stand and lamp, the coffee pot and lamp engraved with a crest, by Benjamin and James Smith, 1811, 10in (26cm), 37oz gross.
$2,000-3,000

A George II coffee pot, engraved with a coat-of-arms, within a rococo cartouche, Dublin, c1740, 9in (23cm), 31oz gross.
$5,000-7,000

The arms are those of Johnson, Ireland.

A George III chocolate pot, by Frances Stamp, 1780, 12in (30.5cm), 31oz gross.
$5,000-7,000

SILVER

Some dates of importance in study of silver:–

- ★ 1660 restoration of Charles II – beginning of great era of domestic English silver
- ★ c1670 influence of acanthus leafage and fluted baroque
- ★ 1685 The Revocation of the Edict of Nantes – brought Huguenot silversmiths to England
- ★ 1697 introduction of Britannia standard. Lasted until 1702
- ★ 1740s early signs of rococo
- ★ 1750s revival of chinoiserie
- ★ 1760s influence of neo-classicism
- ★ 1800-20 tendency to add decoration to plainer style
- ★ 1820s revival of rococo style
- ★ by 1830s machines much in use
- ★ 1880s Arts and Crafts movement – influence of Art Nouveau

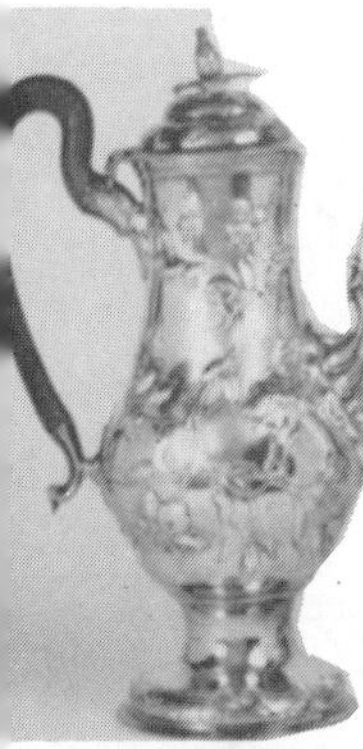

A George III coffee pot, engraved with a monogram, by William Reynolds, Cork, c1770, 12in (30.5cm), 35oz gross.
$6,000-8,000

A George IV coffee pot, by George Hunter II, London 1827, 8½in (21.5cm), 22oz gross.
$1,400-1,600

A Danish coffee pot, with presentation inscription dated 1855, 8½in (22cm), 35.25oz.
$500-700

ı early Victorian coffee pot, by essrs. Barnard, London 1838, ½in (27cm), 29oz.
,300-1,500

Did you know
MILLER'S Antiques Price Guide builds up year by year to form the most comprehensive photo-reference system available.

A Victorian pedestal coffee pot, by Messrs. Barnard, London 1882, 9½in (25cm), 18.5oz gross.
$1,000-1,200

French coffee pot, c1840, 6½in 7cm).
00-1,200

A Queen Anne coffee pot, engraved with a coat-of-arms within a drapery cartouche, by Richard Bayley, 1711, 10in (25cm), 28oz gross.
$8,000-10,000

The arms are those of Warham, Osmington, Co. Dorset.

ups

pair of George III tumbler cups, aker's mark of Hester Bateman ver-striking another, 1787, 2in cm), 5oz.
,000-6,000

A George I two-handled cup and cover, engraved with a coat-of-arms within a foliate scroll cartouche, by Bowles Nash, 1721, Britannia Standard, 10in (26cm), 49oz.
$5,000-7,000

The arms are those of Lippingcott and Wyberry, Co. Devon.

A George II two-handled baluster cup and cover, engraved with a coat-of-arms within a rococo cartouche, by Edward Wakelin, 1752, the cover unmarked, the foot stamped, Lambert Coventry St. London, 12½in (31.5cm), 85oz.
$12,000-14,000

The arms are those of Bagge, presumably for Thomas Bagge, a client of Parker and Wakelin.

Cutlery

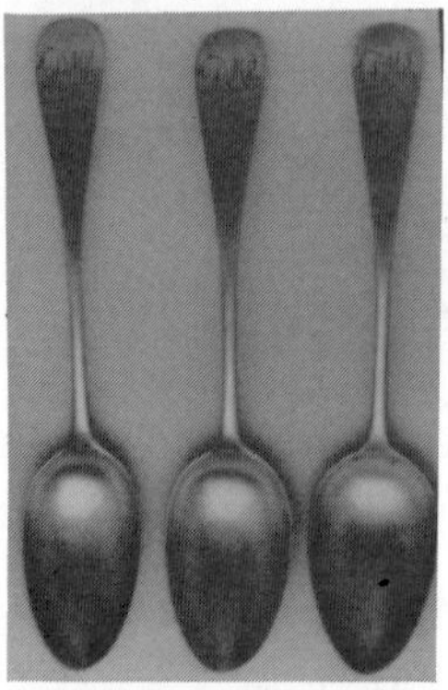

A set of tablespoons, by Paul Revere II, Boston, engraved with initials 'DMS' in foliate script, each marked 'Revere', c1790, 9in (23cm) long, 11oz.
$15,000-20,000

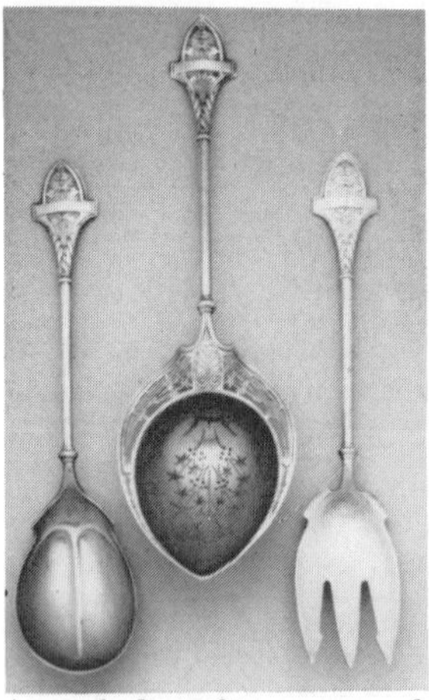

A matched set of 14 servers and a set of 6 dessert spoons, by Gorham Manufacturing, Providence, each marked, c1868, ladle 11½in (29cm) long, 32oz.
$2,000-3,000

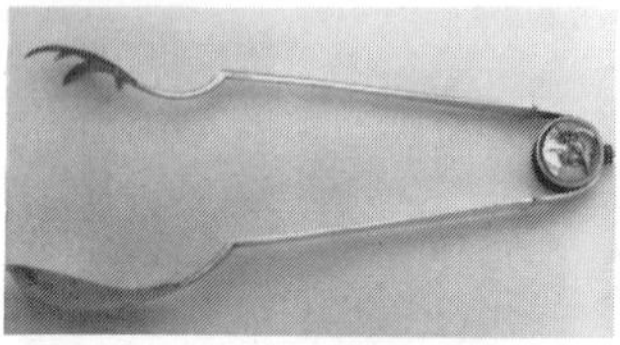

A pair of medallion ice tongs, by Gorham, Providence, marked, c1865, 11½in (29cm) long, 6oz.
$2,500-3,000

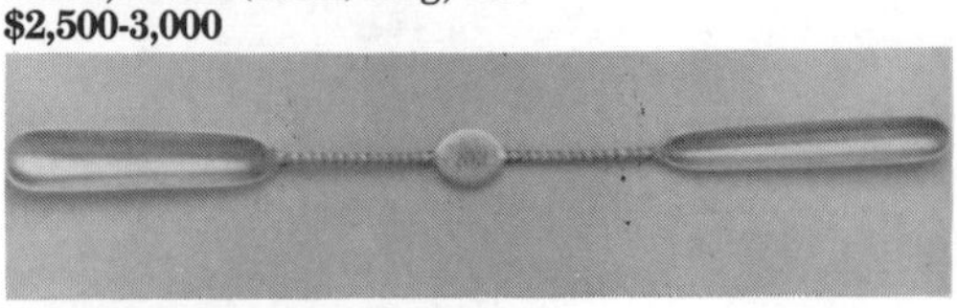

A rare marrow scoop, by Gale & Willis, New York, engraved 'RRS' in fine script, marked with maker's name and 'Sterling', c1840, 11in (28cm) long, 1oz.
$1,500-2,000

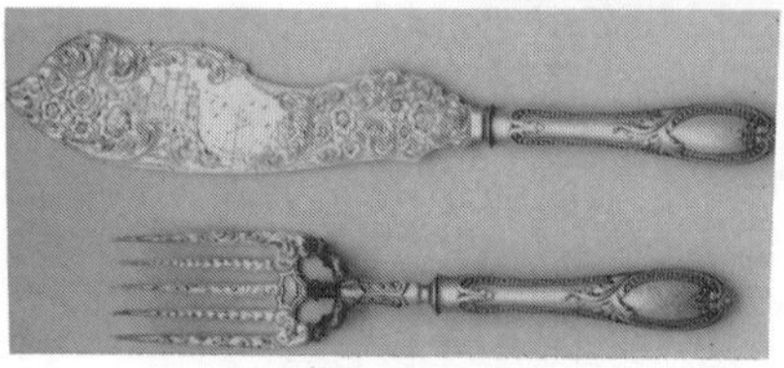

A pair of engraved fish servers, by Albert Coles, New York, slice marked, c1850, slice 12in (30.5cm) long, 8oz gross.
$550-750

A group of medallion servers and flatware, various makers, comprising: 2 soup ladles, an ice cream server and 6 matching spoons, 2 flat servers, a basting spoon, a serving fork, a small pierced ladle, a cheese knife, a fluted serving spoon, 2 tablespoons, 11 nut picks, a pastry fork and a salt spoon, c1865, 51oz.
$4,500-5,000

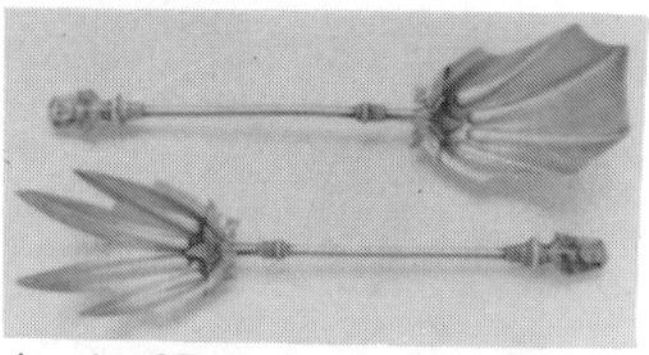

A pair of Egyptian style servers, by Gorham Manufacturing Company, Providence, each marked, c1865, 10in (25.5cm) long, 5oz.
$2,500-3,000

Three American servers, by Whiting Manufacturing Co., Albert Coles and George Sharp, each marked, late 19thC, 9 to 11in (23 to 28cm) long, 11oz.
$2,000-3,000

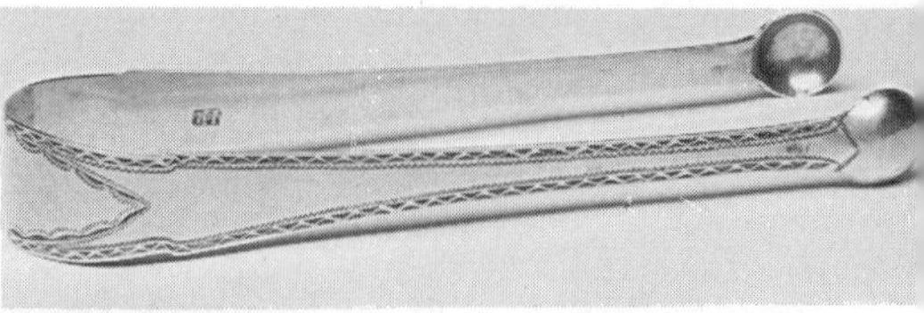

A pair of sugar tongs, by Joseph Richardson, Philadelphia, mark struck twice inside arms, c1784, 6i (15cm) long, 1oz.
$500-600

A set of 3 Egyptian Revival serve by Gorham, Providence, each marked, c1865, slice 12½in (31cm long, 9.5oz.
$1,500-2,500

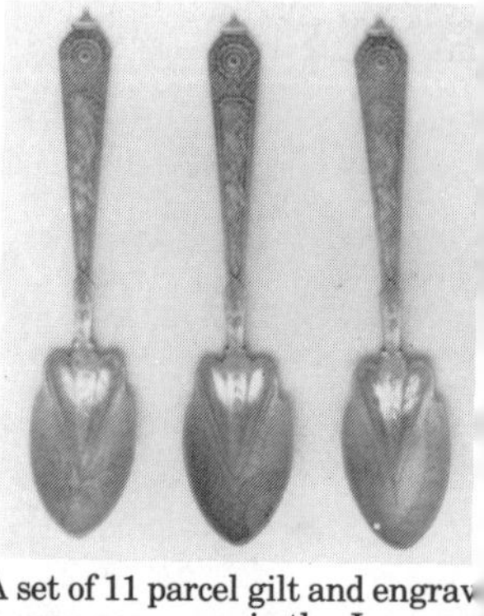

A set of 11 parcel gilt and engrav ice cream spoons, in the Japanese taste, by Gorham, Providence, ea marked, c1875, 6in (15cm) long, 9.5oz.
$3,000-4,000

A pair of American salad servers, unmarked, c1865, 11in (28cm) long 7.5oz.
$2,000-2,500

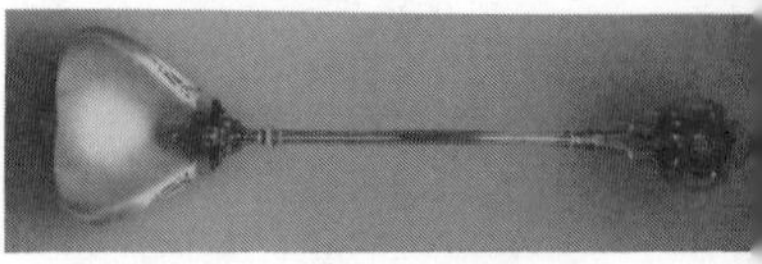

A soup ladle, by George Sharp or Joseph Bailey, Philadelphia, marked, c1850, 14½in (36cm) long, 9.5oz.
$2,500-3,000

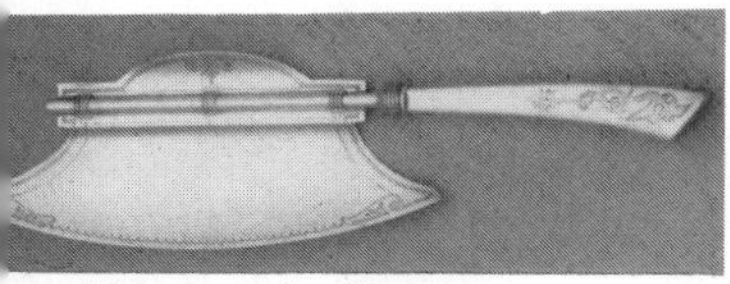

.et of 7 servers, by Gorham
.nufacturing, Providence,
.rked, c1865, slice 11in (28cm)
g, 21.5oz.
000-3,000

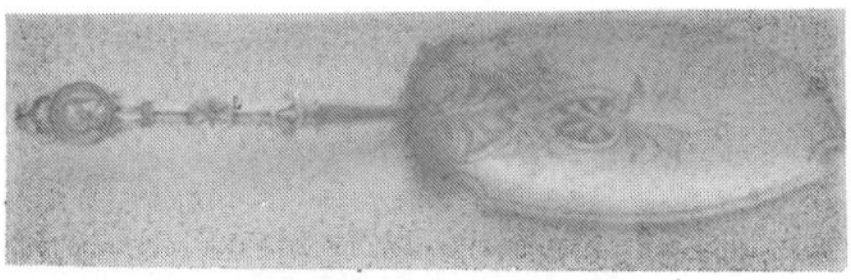

A fish slice, probably by Schulz & Fischer, retailed by Anderson and Randolph, San Francisco, c1868, marked by retailer, 12½in (32cm) long, 4oz.
$500-600

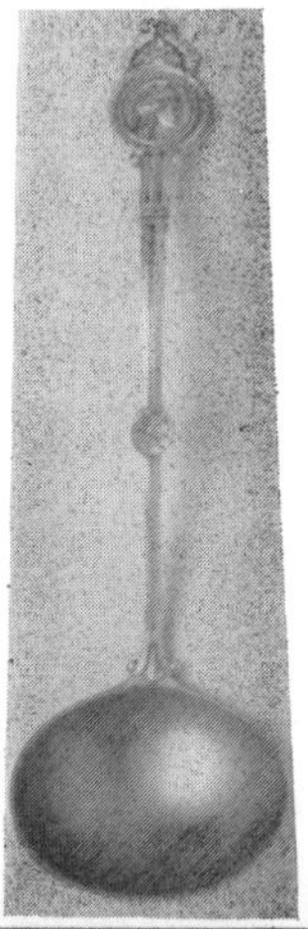

A soup ladle, probably by Schulz and Fischer, San Francisco, marked 'Coin', c1868, 13in (33cm) long, 6.25oz.
$500-600

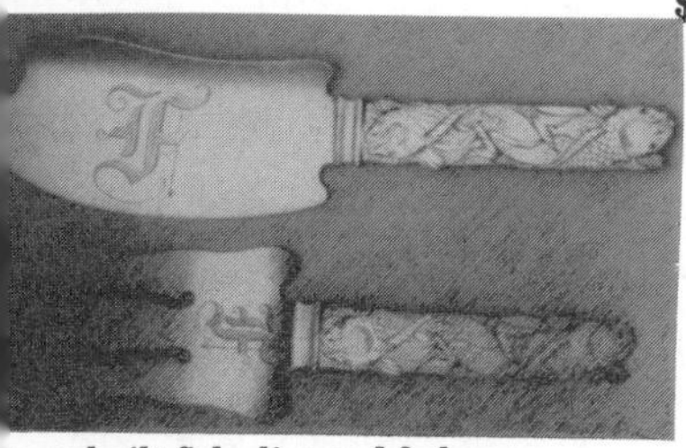

.parcel gilt fish slice and fork,
.nerican, engraved with the initial
. marked Sterling Pat. Etching,
.885, slice 11½in (29cm) long, 8oz.
.000-2,000

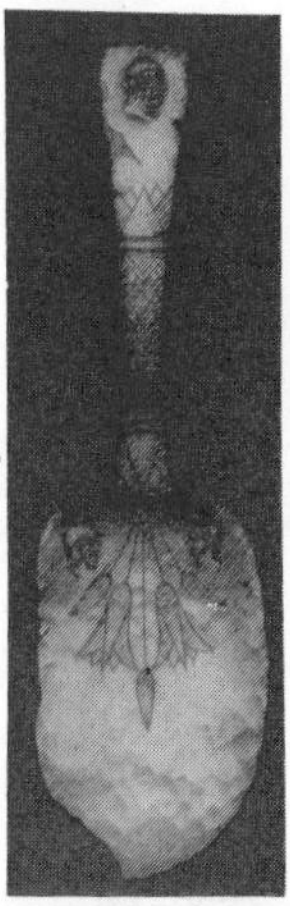

An Egyptian style slice, by Shiebler, New York, marked, c1885, 11in (28cm) long, 7oz.
$3,000-4,000

A set of 5 serving pieces and a set of 14 seafood forks and a similar fork, in the Japanese taste, by Gorham, Providence, each marked, c1880, slice 9in. (23cm) long, 25.5oz.
$2,500-3,000

.pair of leaf shaped servers, a leaf
.aped ice cream slice and a set of 9
.atching spoons, the servers by
.dlich, the dessert pieces by
.iebler, each marked. c1885, the
.rvers 9in (23cm) long 14.5oz.
.500-4,000

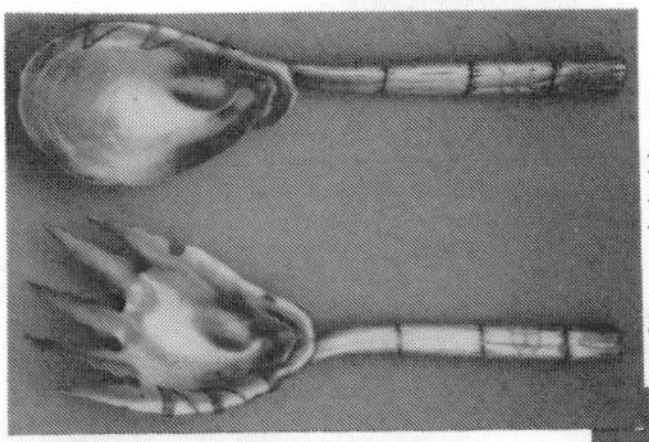

A pair of salad servers, by Gorham, Providence, handles later engraved with initials, each marked, c1880, 10in (25cm) long, 7oz.
$6,500-7,000

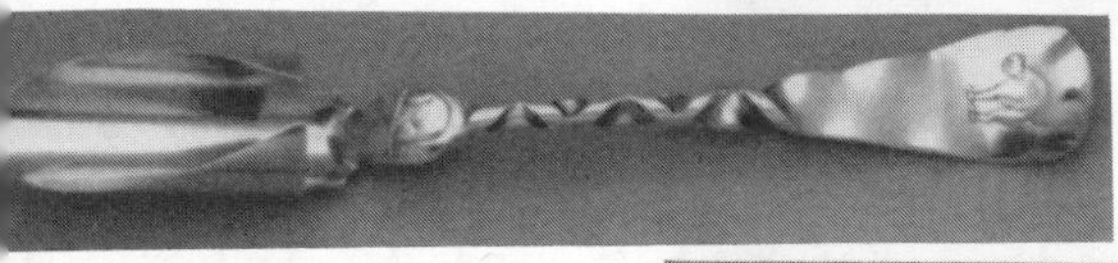

.cheese scoop and a set of 4 servers,
. Whiting Manufacturing Co.,
.orth Attleboro or Newark,
.riously monogrammed, worn
.arks, c1885, 7 to 10½in (18 to
..5cm) long, 16.5oz.
.000-1,500

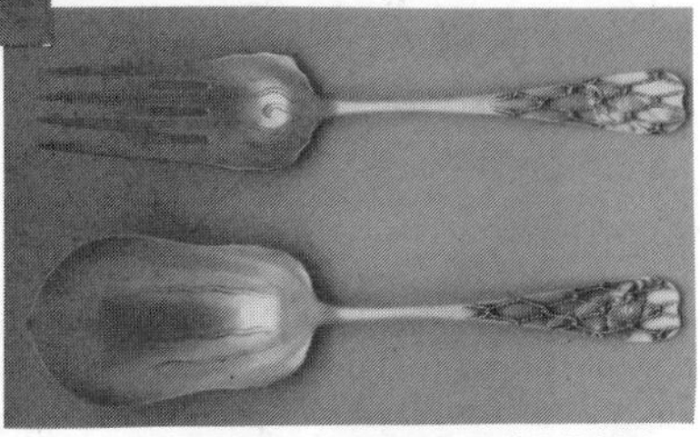

A pair of salad servers, by Whiting Manufacturing Co., North Attleboro or Newark, marked, c1885, 9in (23cm) long, 5.5oz.
$2,500-3,000

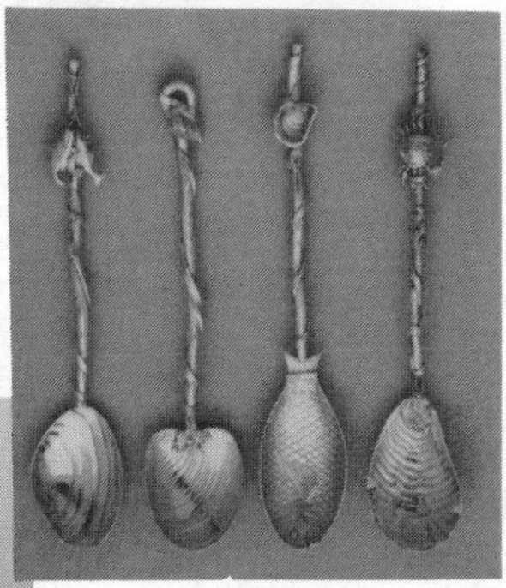

A pair of condiment servers and a set of 4 condiment spoons, by Gorham, Providence, each marked, c1885, 5½in (14cm) long, 3.5oz.
$1,500-2,000

A Victorian pierced vine pattern dessert service, comprising: 18 spoons, 18 forks, 18 knives, 18 ice-cream spoons, 18 coffee spoons, a serving spoon, by Robert Roskell, Allan Roskell and John Hunt, 1882 and 1883, weight without knives 115oz.
$10,000-12,000

Did you know
MILLER'S Antiques Price Guide builds up year by year to form the most comprehensive photo-reference system available

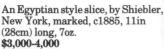

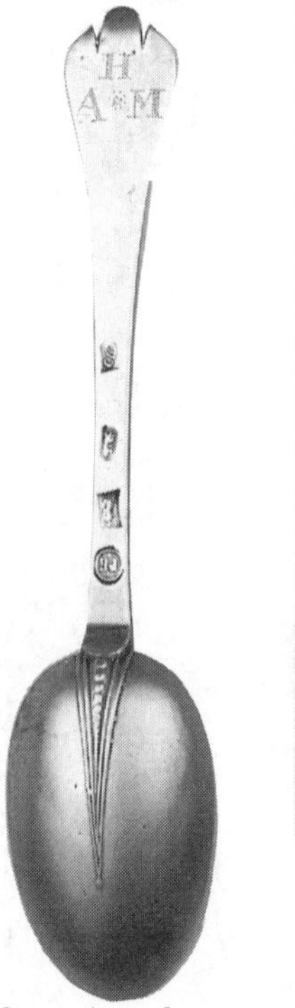

A Queen Anne dog nose spoon, John Sutton, London 1711.
$240-360

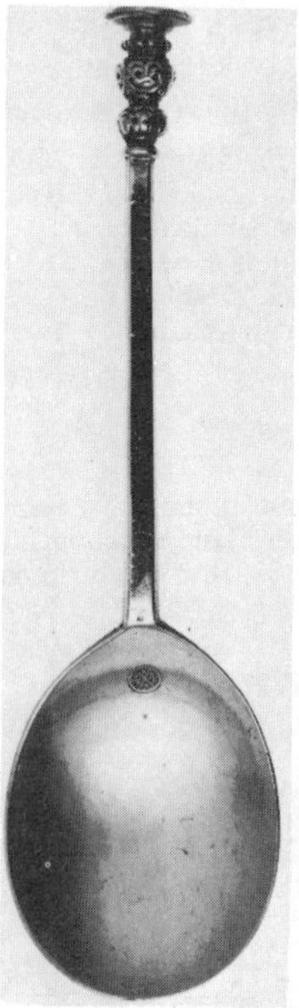

A seal-top spoon, the seal pricked with initials I.S., the back of the bowl with date and initials 1651 A.T., probably Provincial, marked only in the bowl with a wheel enclosing 6 pellets, c1650.
$1,200-1,400

A pair of Victorian silver-gilt grape scissors, by John and Henry Lias, London 1845, with a fitted case.
$1,000-1,200

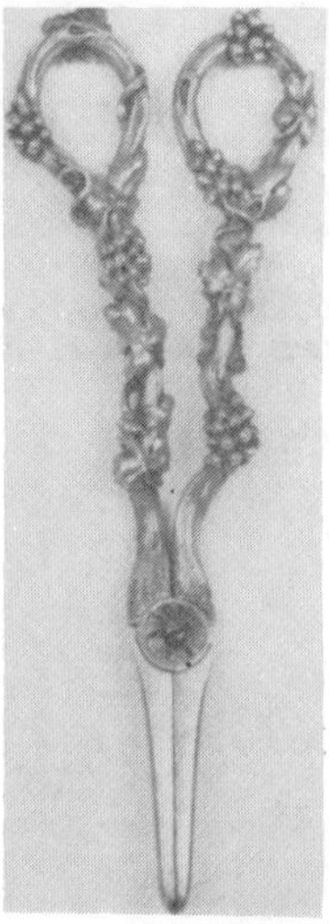

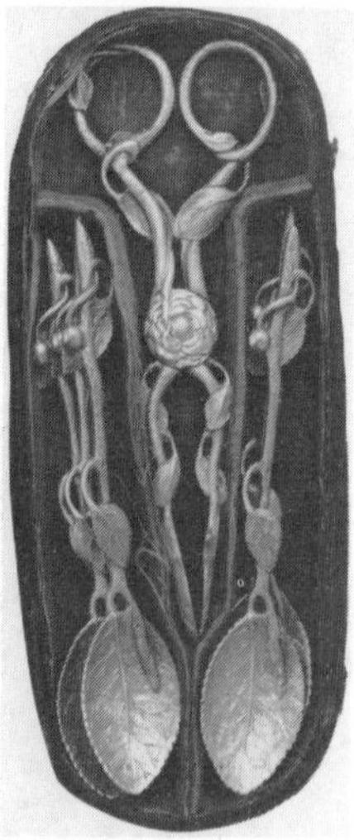

A set of 6 naturalistic teaspoons and a pair of matching sugar scissors, apparently unmarked, c1750, original case.
$700-800

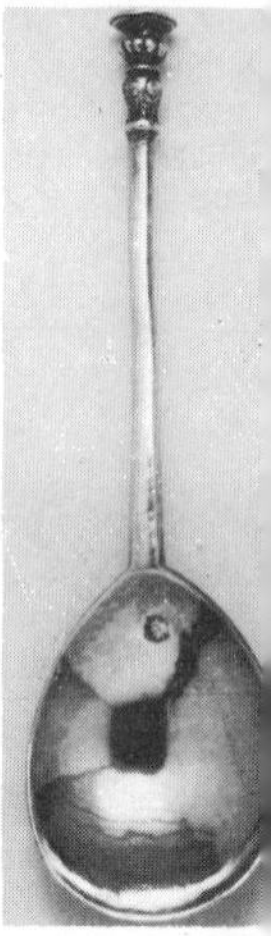

A James I seal-top spoon, maker's mark indistinct, 1607.
$1,000-1,200

A George II lemon strainer, unmarked, c1740, 10½in (26.5cm) long, 4oz 12dwt.
$600-800

A George III lemon strainer, Michael Fowler, Dublin, c175 9½in (24.5cm), 3oz 18dwt.
$1,000-1,200

A silver-gilt Coburg pattern dessert service, comprising 38 pieces, the knives and forks by Paul Storr, 1815, 1816 and 1817, the spoons by John Aldwinckle and Thomas Slater, 1890, the serving spoons with erased maker's mark, in fitted wood case, 66oz.
$8,000-10,000

A composite fiddle, thread and shell pattern table service, some engraved with a crest, 1817, 1841, 1845, comprising: 38 spoons, 40 forks, 18 teaspoons, one single struck, a butter knife, 4 salt spoons, single struck, 12 table knives with stainless steel blades, 12 modern dessert knives, 215oz.
$12,000-14,000

A George III old English pattern table service, comprising 60 piec by Eley and Fearn, 1804, the tab forks 1805, 78oz.
$8,000-10,000

poons – Caddy

William IV Kings pattern caddy oon, maker JW, Birmingham 31, 3in (7.5cm).
00-150

A George III caddy spoon, by William Bateman, London 1817, 3in (7.5cm).
$100-120

A George III caddy spoon, London 1816, 3in (7.5cm).
$160-200

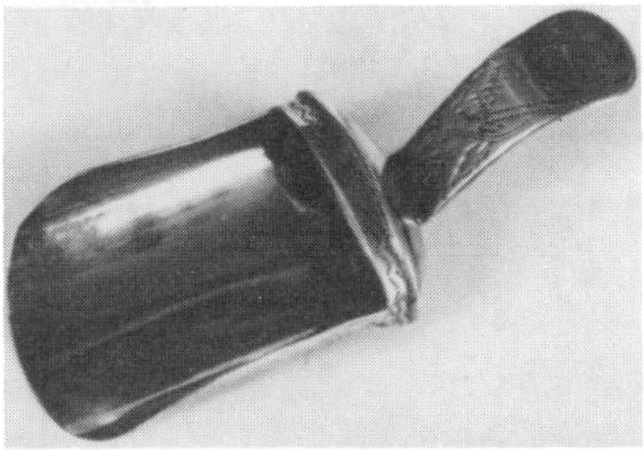

A George III caddy spoon, with gilt bowl and engraved handle, by Cocks & Bettridge, Birmingham 1805, 2½in (6cm).
$400-500

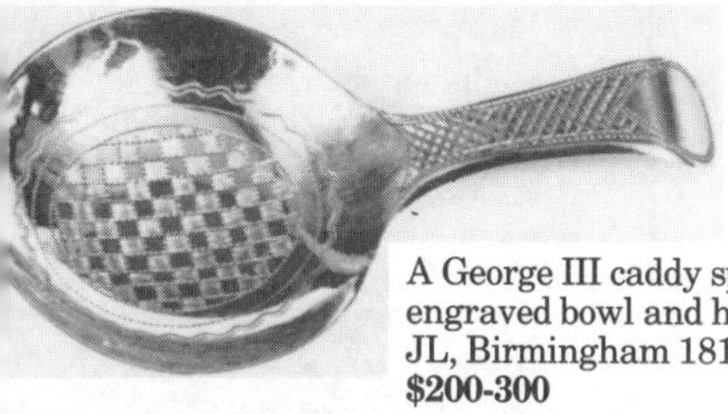

A George III caddy spoon, with engraved bowl and handle, maker JL, Birmingham 1810.
$200-300

A George IV caddy spoon, by John, Henry and Charles Lias, London 1828.
$250-300

ishes

silver gilt covered dish, by Samuel irk & Son, Baltimore, with graved monogram, marked, obably c1850, 6in (15cm) diam, oz.
,000-1,500

A Charles II sweetmeat dish, engraved with a crest, maker's mark E.T., with a mullet below, 1660, 9in (23cm) wide, 4oz.
$2,500-3,500

A set of 12 George II plates, engraved with the contemporary arms and motto of the Earls of Sackville, by Jonathan le Sage, London 1750, 9½in (24cm), 207oz.
$20,000-24,000

George III meat dish, engraved ith a coat-of-arms within the rder of the Bath motto, 2 coronets d a crest, the reverse later graved with the initials of King eorge V, by Benjamin and James mith, 1811, 20in (51cm) wide, 96oz.
,000-6,000

A George III meat dish, maker's initials H S (or S H), 19½in (49.5cm), 82oz.
$2,500-3,000

A George III entrée dish, cover and detachable handle, by Philip Rundell, 1819, 10in (25.5cm).
$2,000-3,000

A compote, by Gorham, Providence, one side engraved 'EGS', marked, c1860, 13½in (34cm) wide, 33oz.
$2,000-3,000

A medallion compote, by Gorham, Providence, engraved with a script inscription 'EOB from CAB', marked, c1865, 9in (23cm) diam, 22oz.
$700-1,000

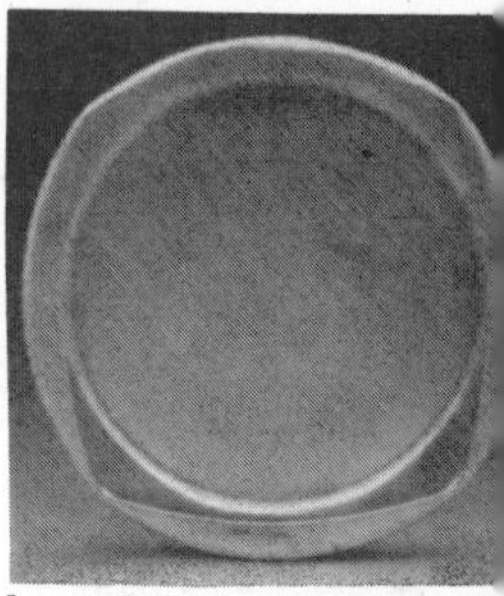

A large dish, by The Kalo Sh Chicago, marked, c1915, 13½ (34cm) diam, 31.5oz.
$4,000-5,000

A pair of entrée dishes, by Porter Blanchard, Calabasas, California, each marked, 20thC, 10in (25.5cm) long, 37.5oz.
$1,500-2,000

A condiment dish, by Wood & Hughes, New York, the handle engraved with initial 'M' and dates '1861-1886', the interior gilt, marked, 6½in (16cm) long, 3oz.
$500-800

A medallion butter dish, by Gorham, Providence, the domed cover with a finial, with decorative silver liner, marked, c1865, 6in (15cm) diam, 16oz.
$1,000-1,500

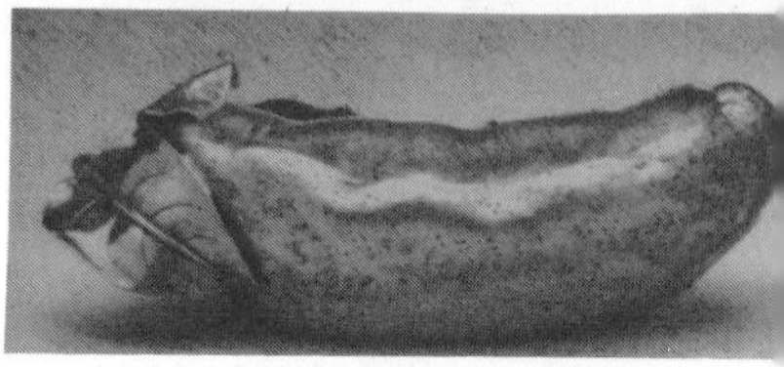

An olive dish, by Gorham, Providence, in the form of a curve olive on a stem with 3 leaves forming a handle, the interior gilt the exterior decorated with punchwork, with small script monogram, marked, 1884, 4.5oz.
$1,500-2,000

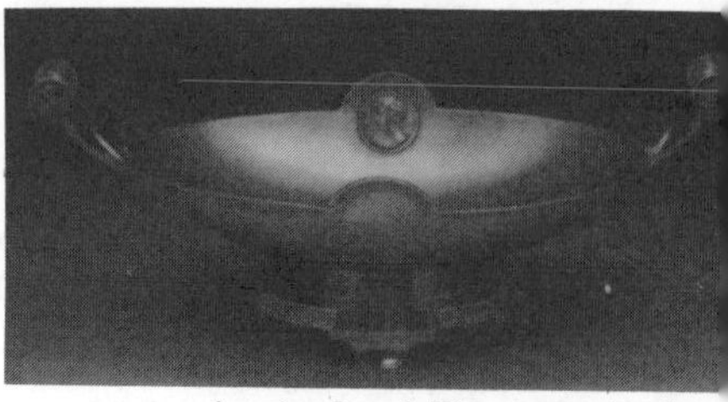

A pair of medallion compotes, by Gorham, Providence, marked, c1865, 14in (35.5cm) wide, 51.5oz.
$3,000-5,000

A shell form dish, by Ball, Black & Co., New York, with hinged cover, break to one foot, marked, c1860, 2in (5cm) high, 4oz.
$900-1,200

Miller's is a price Guide not a price List

The price ranges given reflect the average price a purchaser should pay for similar items. Condition, rarity of design or pattern, size, colour, pedigree, restoration and many other factors must be taken into account when assessing values

ıkstands

early Victorian inkstand, on ell and scroll feet, fitted with a ver mounted rib cut glass inkwell, atching bottle and central wafer , with contemporary esentation inscription, Robinson, kins and Aston, Birmingham 45, 13in (33cm), 30oz.
500-1,700

A William IV inkstand, with 2 silver mounted glass wells and a central wafer box with detachable taperstick and conical extinguisher, engraved with a crest, by Matthew Boulton and Plate Co., Birmingham 1831, the extinguisher by Robinson, Edkins and Aston, date letter indistinct, 9in (23cm) wide, 21oz.
$3,000-4,000

A George III inkstand, on lion's paw feet, fitted with silver mounted glass wells and central taperstick, engraved with a crest, by John and Thomas Settle, Sheffield 1817, 10½in (27cm) wide, 25oz.
$4,000-5,000

Victorian inkstand, stamped with ews of Windsor Castle, fitted with entral taperstick, blue glass kwell and matching pounce pot, th detachable covers, the kstand with contemporary esentation inscription, J.T., rmingham 1842, 6in (15cm).
,800-2,500

A Mexican inkstand, with 4 vases and covers and a bell, engraved with trailing vines, scrolls and masks, Mexico c1770, with the assay master's mark of Jose Antonio Lince y Gonzalez, 12in (30cm), 1,437 grammes.
$8,000-10,000

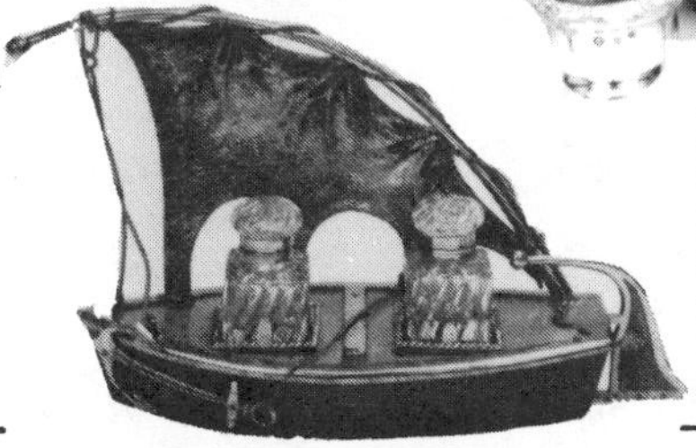

A novelty double inkstand, modelled as a yacht with polished wood hull and gilt rigging, 12in (30.5cm).
$800-900

ugs

George III hot water jug, later ased with rococo flowers and rolling foliage, Charles Wright, ondon 1774, 12in (30.5cm), 7.75oz. **$1,400-1,500**

A Georgian cream jug, London 1809, 4½in (11cm) high.
$400-500

A George III hot water jug, with wicker covered scroll handle and domed hinged cover with vase shaped finial, later chased, John Denziloe, London 1781, 12in (30.5cm), 25oz gross.
$1,400-1,500

A late Victorian cow cream jug with plain hinged cover, London 1897, 6in (15cm), 6.5oz.
$900-1,000

A George III cream jug, with reeded border and angled handle, by Urquart and Hart, London 1801, 4in (10cm) high, 4oz.
$400-500

A jug by Robert Evans, Boston, the base engraved 'In Remembrance of the Family Estate in Federal Street', marked, c1800, 7½in (19cm) high, 17.5oz.
$5,500-6,000

A water jug, by Fletcher & Gardiner, Philadelphia, the side engraved with foliate script initials 'DSC', bruised, marked, c1820, 11in (28cm) high, 39oz.
$3,000-4,000

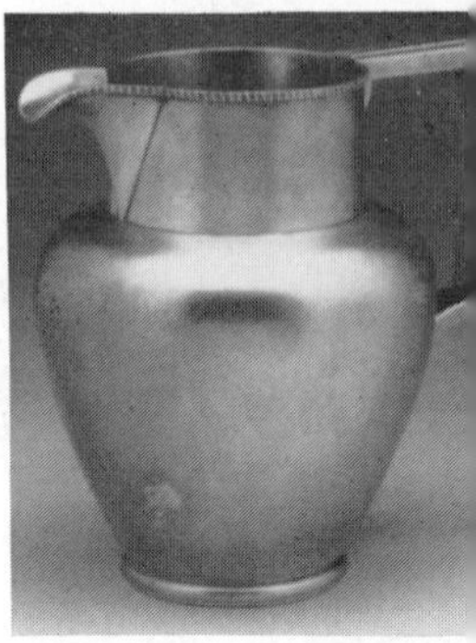

A jug by William Seal, Philadelph marked, c1810, 8in (20.5cm) high 35oz.
$3,500-4,000

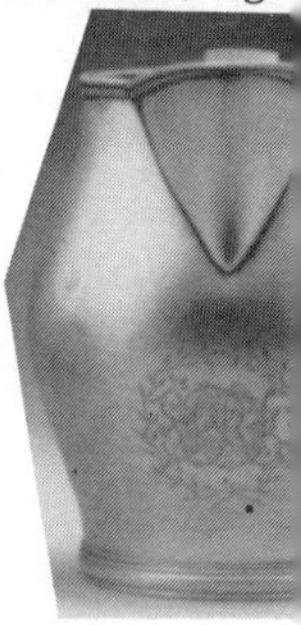

A pair of American jugs, the fro engraved with a wreath enclosir initials 'SRF', bruised, unmarke c1815, 6½in (16cm) high, 35oz.
$3,500-4,000

A pair of ewers, by Frederick Marquand, New York, with wreath of roses centering the initials 'EMK', each marked, c1835, 14½in (37cm) high, 78.5oz.
$7,000-8,000

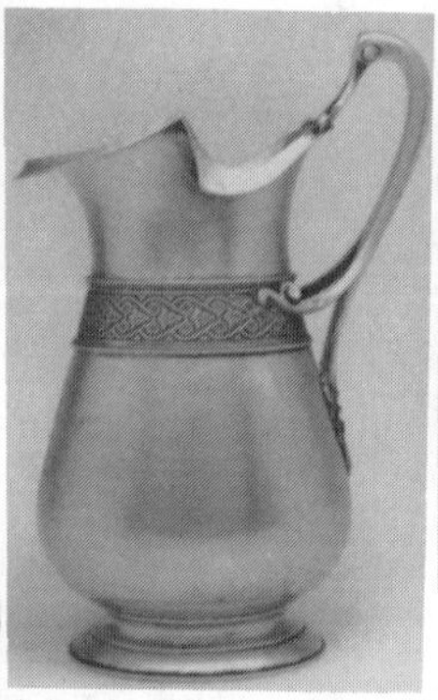

A jug by Whiting Manufacturing Co., North Attleboro or Newark, the front with an inscription dated 1870, marked, 12in (30.5cm) high, 34oz.
$1,500-2,000

A jug by Gorham, Providence, c1865, with later inscription dated 1879, marked, 9½in (23cm) high, 14.5oz.
$900-1,000

A trophy ewer, by Whiting Manufacturing Company, North Attleboro or Newark, with etched inscription 'Seawanhaka Corinthian Yacht Club, Third Class Sloops and Cutters, Cutter Clara, June 19th 1886, New York Bay', marked, 10½in (26cm) high, 30oz.
$3,000-4,000

A jug by Dominick & Haff, New York or Newark, marked, 1879, 8in (20cm) high, 31oz.
$9,000-10,000

A water jug, attributed to Whiting Manufacturing Company, North Attleboro or Newark, damage to rim, marked with retailer's mark Wm. Wilson & Son, c1880, 7in (18cm) high, 26.5oz.
$4,000-5,000

A jug by Lebkuecher & Co., Newark, engraved with inscriptio marked, c1901, 10in (25.5cm) high 32.5oz.
$4,000-5,000

:ontinental novelty cream jug, delled as a bust of Napoleon, his forming the 2 spouts, import rks for London 1899, 4in (10cm), .
0-800

A George IV cream jug, engraved with a crest, by Paul Storr, 1821, 5in (12.5cm) high, 9oz.
$3,000-4,000

A Victorian jug, chased in high relief, the hinged domed cover with detachable mare and foal finial, the short spout cast and chased with a dog's head and foliage, engraved with presentation inscription dated 1872, by Robert Hennell, 1863, 16in (40.5cm), 104oz.
$6,000-8,000

n American pitcher, with applied roll rim and leaf capped scroll andle, Black Starr & Frost, New ork, c1890, 9in (23cm), 28oz.
700-900

A Victorian beaded and spiral fluted hot water jug, with a foliate decorated spout, polished wood handle and domed hinged cover with sprial twist finial, George Lambert, London 1880, 11in (29cm), 21oz gross.
$900-1,000

A water jug, by the Randahl Shop, Chicago, c1915, with script monogram 'MHL', marked, 8½in (21.5cm) high, 25.5oz.
$1,200-1,500

A George III oil and vinegar stand, the bottle holders pierced with slats and applied with rosettes, drapery swags and beaded borders, fitted with silver mounted glass bottles, each with leaf capped scroll handle, hinged cover and shell thumbpiece, by Robert Hennell, 1775, the bottle mounts unmarked, 9in (23cm) high, 15oz.
$3,000-4,000

A jug by Peter L. Krider, Philadelphia, c1870, with mark of Clark & Biddle, 11in (28cm) high, 40oz.
$3,000-4,000

A Martelé jug, by Gorham Manufacturing Company, Providence, marked, 1908, 9in (23cm) high, 43oz.
$10,000-12,000

A Continental cream jug, modelled as a bellowing bull, the hinged cover chased with a bee, import marks, 5in (12.5cm), 5.5oz.
$700-800

Models

Two Victorian figures of Mr. Punch, each holding an ivory baton, one with hinged hat, the other with detachable hat, by Charles and George Fox, 1844 and 1845, both with registration mark, one stamped Thomas's Bond Street, each on shaped wood stand, 8in (20.5cm) high overall, 19oz gross.
$4,000-5,000

A pair of Continental model figur based on those in the Hofkirche, Innsbruck, on foliate pierced base and with ivory faces, import mark 1926, 8in (21cm), 28oz gross.
$4,000-5,000

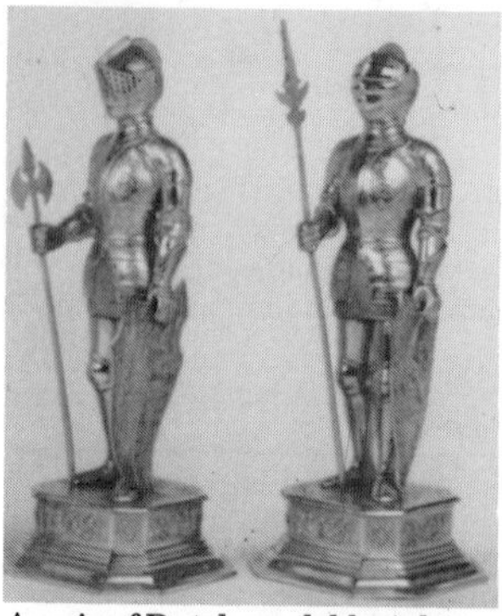

A pair of Dutch model knights, representing England and Holland, each holding a shield-of-arms, import marks, 1929, 9in (23cm) high, 26oz.
$3,500-4,000

A pair of Continental silver gilt models of a knight and his lady, with ivory faces, import marks for 1924, 19in (45cm) high, 180oz gross.
$14,000-16,000

An Eastern articulated fish, with hinged head and engraved scales and fins, 11in (28cm).
$700-800

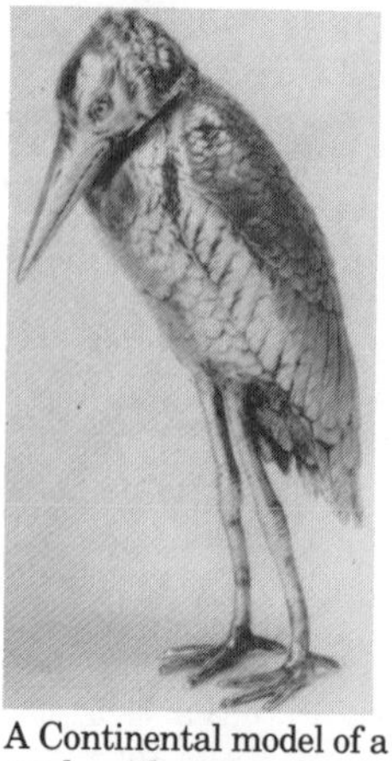

A Continental model of a Maribou stork, with stamped and chased plumage and detachable head, bearing import marks for London 1906, 11in (28cm), 18oz.
$900-1,000

A pair of cast and chased model grouse, 7in (18cm), 40.25oz.
$2,000-3,000

A pair of Continental models of a cock and a hen pheasant, each wi realistically chased plumage and hinged wings, late 19thC, 14 and 18in (35.5 and 45.5cm) long, 1,419 grammes.
$8,000-10,000

Mugs & Tankards

A cann by John Burt, Boston, engraved with contemporary owner's initials 'MW', body engraved with inscription 'Polley Wallingford's', repair to foot, marked, c1740, 5in (13cm) high, 10oz.
$1,500-2,000

A medallion mug, by Gorham, Providence, c1865, with inscription and later inscription, marked, 3in (7.5cm) high, 4oz.
$500-800

Queen Anne tankard and cover, th scroll handle and stepped med cover with plume umbpiece, engraved with a later est, by Adam Billon, Cork, c1710, in (19cm) high, 21oz.
,000-9,000

e crest is that of Newenham of olmore, Co. Cork. John ewenham was Lord Mayor of Cork 1671.

George II mug, engraved with a est, by Richard Zouch, London 737, 13oz.
,400-1,600

Use the Index!

Because certain items might fit easily into any of a number of categories, the quickest and surest method of locating any entry is by reference to the index at the back of the book.
This has been fully cross-referenced for absolute simplicity

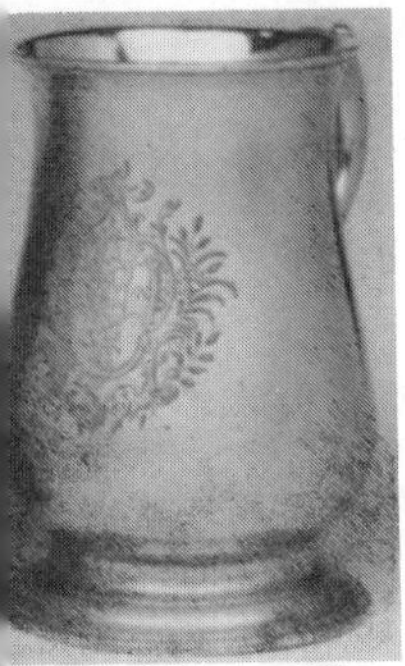

pair of George III mugs, engraved ith a coat-of-arms within a foliate croll cartouche, by Francis Crump, 763, 4½in (11cm) high, 15oz.
4,000-5,000

A cann by Jacob Hurd, Boston, marked Hurd near handle join, c1745, 5in (12.5cm) high, 11oz.
$3,500-4,000

A mug by Gorham, Providence, marked, 1881, 4in (10cm) high, 8oz.
$2,000-2,500

A George III baluster tankard, with hinged domed cover and openwork scroll thumbpiece, by Thomas Whipham and Charles Wright, 1768, 8in (20.5cm) high, 31oz.
$4,000-5,000

A cann, probably New York, engraved with contemporary owner's initials 'EAC', unmarked, mid-18thC, 3½in (9cm) high, 7.5oz.
$900-1,200

A George III tankard and cover, the domed cover with openwork scroll thumbpiece, engraved later with initials, maker's mark B.M. 8in (20.5cm) high, 24oz.
$3,500-4,000

A George III tankard, with engraved armorial to front and double scroll handle, the hinged cover with open shaped thumbpiece, by John Kentember, London 1767, 26oz.
$3,500-4,000

A William IV tankard, with foliate scroll handle terminating in a greyhound's mask, Barnard Bros, 1835, 9in (23cm) high, 39oz.
$2,000-3,000

A Victorian gilt lined pint tankard, E & E Barnard, London 1866, 5½in (14cm), 12oz.
$900-1,000

Salts

A George I pepper pot, the pierced cover with bayonet fittings, probably London 1720, Britannia Standard, 4in (10cm).
$300-400

A pair of George II salt cellars, each engraved with crest and Baron's coronet, by George Wickes, 1745, 23.5oz.
$9,000-10,000

Four George II salt cellars, engraved with a crest, by James Morrison, 1759, with 4 salt spoons with shell bowls and foliate stems, unmarked, c1760, 34oz.
$9,000-10,000

A George III mustard pot, with shaped bracket handle, blue glas liner and domed hinged cover, engraved with a monogram and coronet, John Gould, London 180 4in (10cm).
$400-500

A set of 4 George III parcel gilt sa cellars, engraved with a crest, by Rebecca Emes and Edward Barnard, 1808, 4in (10cm) long, 14oz 18dwt.
$3,000-4,000

A pair of Victorian novelty pepperettes, one formed as a Harlequin the other as a court jester, one with pierced detachable head, the other with detachable hat, by James Barclay Hennell, 1877, the jester's hat by Robert Hennell, 1867, 5in (12.5cm) high, 11oz.
$1,800-2,000

A pair of George III Scottish mustards, engraved with the Gr crest, with blue glass liners, by W & P Cunningham, c1810, 9oz.
$1,000-1,200

A pair of Victorian novelty pepperettes, formed as Mr & Mrs Punch, by John Round and Son Ltd., Sheffield 1896, and another as Mr. Punch's dog, Toby, by Charles Stuart Harris, 1869, stamped with registration mark, 4in (10cm), 6oz.
$1,800-2,000

Make the most of Miller's

Unless otherwise stated, any description which refers to 'a set' or 'a pair' includes a valuation for the entire set or the pair, even though the illustration may show only a single item.

. set of 4 George III parcel gilt salt ellars, each engraved with a crest nd initial, by William Fountain, 808, 4in (10cm) long, 12oz 12dwt.
6,000-7,000

A pair of George IV salts with gilt linings, London 1823, 11oz 8dwt.
$700-800

Salvers

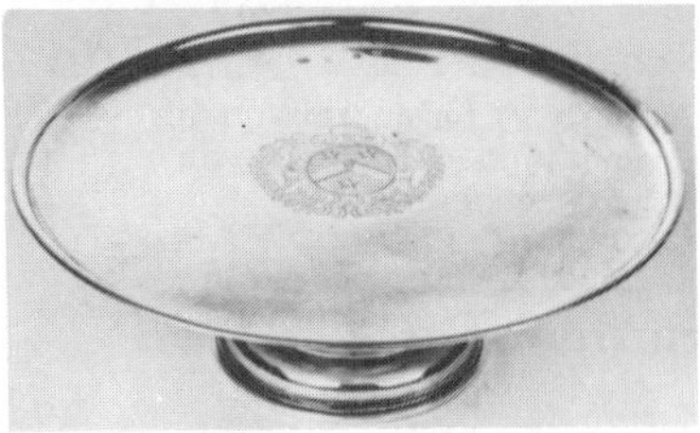

A Queen Anne salver, engraved with a coat-of-arms within a cartouche, by Anthony Nelme, 1703, 10½in (27cm), 26oz 3dwt.
$4,000-6,000

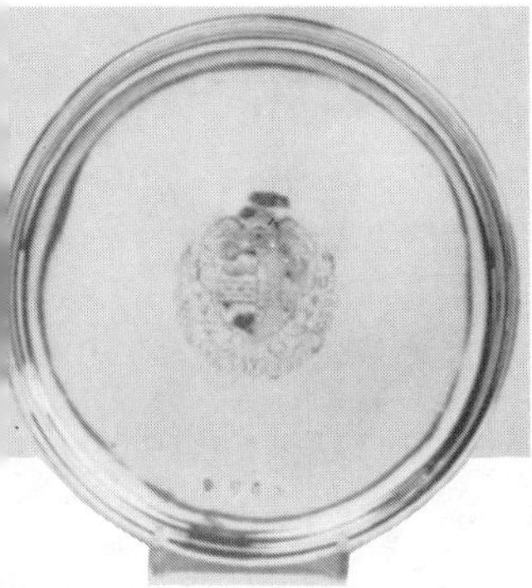

A George I salver, on central preading foot, engraved with a oat-of-arms in a baroque cartouche, y Thomas Folkingham, 1717, 9in 23cm), 16oz.
4,000-6,000

The arms are those of Cooke mpaling another.

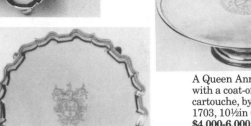

A George II salver, with moulded border, later engraved with coat-of-arms, by Simon Pantin, 1730, 11in (28cm), 27oz.
$6,000-7,000

The arms are those of Theed, incorrectly blazoned.

A George I salver, on 4 curved bracket feet, engraved with a coat-of-arms within a baroque cartouche, by Peter Archambo, 1723, Britannia Standard, 12in (30.5cm), 36oz.
$22,000-25,000

The arms are those of Sealy impaling Samson, Nottingham.

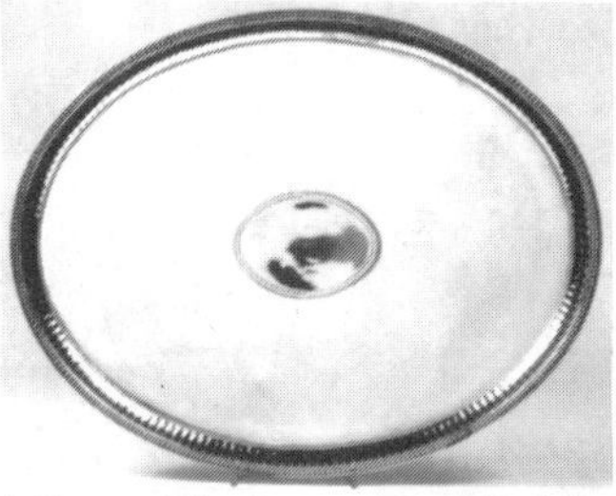

A George III salver, engraved with a vacant cartouche, by John Scofield, 1781, 18in (45.5cm) wide, 62oz.
$5,000-6,000

A George III salver, on ball-and-claw eet, engraved with a coat-of-arms n a rococo cartouche, by John Carter, 1775, 14in (35.5cm), 45oz.
3,000-4,000

The arms are those of Marsh mpaling Bennett.

A William IV salver, on 4 acanthus foliage and scroll feet, the border cast with masks, shells and foliage, maker's mark T.W., c1831, 22½in (57cm) diam, 166oz.
$8,000-9,000

. George III salver and matching vaiter, engraved with contemporary ouble armorials, on ball-and-claw eet, by Ebenezer Coker, London 772, 26oz.
4,000-5,000

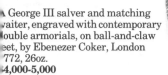

An early Victorian waiter, with presentation inscription, 9½in (24cm), London 1859.
$500-600

A Victorian salver, with applied rococo shell and scroll border, the ground engine-turned and engraved with strapwork, a crest and a motto, Charles Boyton, London 1866, 12in (30.5cm), 29oz.
$700-800

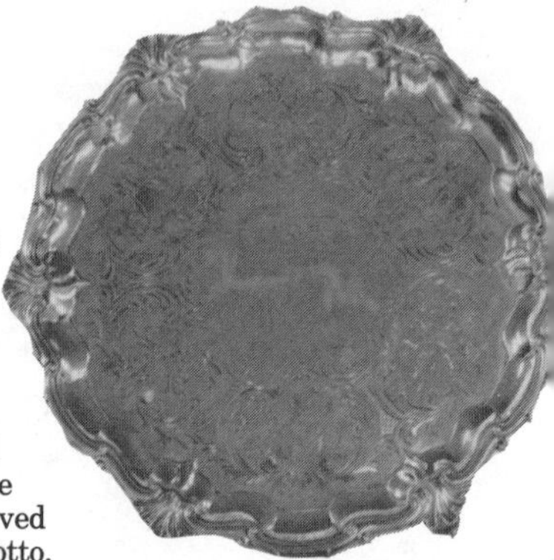

A Victorian salver, with embossed scroll and shell border, on foliate and scroll tab feet, London 1850, 12½in (32cm), 25oz.
$1,000-1,200

Sauceboats

A pair of double lipped sauceboats, each on spreading foot and with beaded borders, by Henry Chawner, 1786, 8½in (22cm) wide, 18oz.
$3,000-4,000

A George II sauceboat, with shaped rim and leaf capped double scroll handle, the body later chased with rococo scrolling foliage and engraved with a monogram, London 1736, 6½in (16cm), 8.75oz.
$500-600

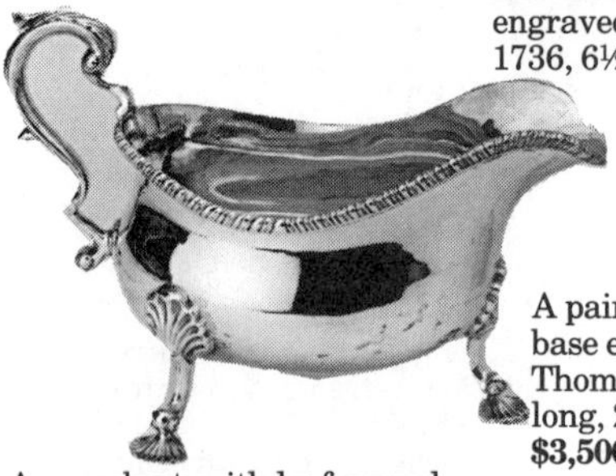

A sauceboat, with leaf capped double scroll handle and 3 fluted scroll and shell legs, Barnards, London 1901, 8½in (22cm), 15oz.
$500-600

A pair of George II sauceboats, the base engraved with initials, by Thomas Jeanes, 1749, 8in (20.5cm) long, 22oz.
$3,500-4,000

A pair of George II sauceboats, engraved with a crest, maker's mark W.R., 1759.
$8,000-10,000

A George III argyle, engraved with a crest and ducal coronet, by Henry Greenway, 1795, 6in (15cm), 24oz.
$10,000-12,000

Services

A George III three-piece composite moulded tea service, the teapot by Thomas Paine Dexter, London 1806, the milk jug and sugar basin possibly by a maker with initials G.H., London 1812, teapot 7in (18cm), 29.25oz gross.
$1,200-1,300

A three-piece composite Scottish Regency and George IV tea service the gilt-lined milk jug and sugar basin by Robert Gray & Son, Edinburgh 1815, the teapot, Edinburgh 1820, 6in (16cm) high, 55oz.
$3,000-4,000

ı William IV three-piece tea ervice, the milk jug and sugar asin gilt-lined, by James Vaterhouse, Sheffield 1832, teapot in (18cm) high, 48.75oz.
2,000-2,500

A five-piece tea and coffee service, by Samuel Kirk & Son, Baltimore, each marked except cream jug and sugar bowl, c1885, coffee pot 17in (43cm) high, 140oz gross.
$6,000-7,000

A late Victorian three-piece tea service, by J.S., Dublin 1900 and 1901, teapot 5½in (14cm) high, 39.75oz.
$800-1,000

ı late Victorian four-piece tea and offee service, by Gibson and angman, London 1895, coffee pot ½in (24cm) high, 60oz gross.
3,000-4,000

ı three-piece tea service, Sheffield 1904, 37oz.
700-800

A Victorian tea and coffee service in the 18thC taste, coffee biggin with ivory scroll handle on a stand with burner, the teapot on a stand, by Frederick Brasted, London 1876, coffee biggin 11in (28cm) high overall, and a pair of George II fiddle pattern sugar tongs, engraved with a monogram, London 1822, 66.75oz gross.
$3,000-4,000

A composite William IV and early Victorian four-piece tea and coffee ervice, London 1835 and 1839, ,230 grammes gross.
3,000-4,000

A Victorian tea and coffee service, by Robert Garrard, 1858, with a salver on three scroll feet, engraved with a presentation inscription, by Ebenezer Coker, 1757, in fitted wood case, 11½in (29cm) diam, 95oz gross.
$6,000-7,000

The inscription records the presentation of the salver with the tea and coffee service to Revd. Arthur George Warner, 1873.

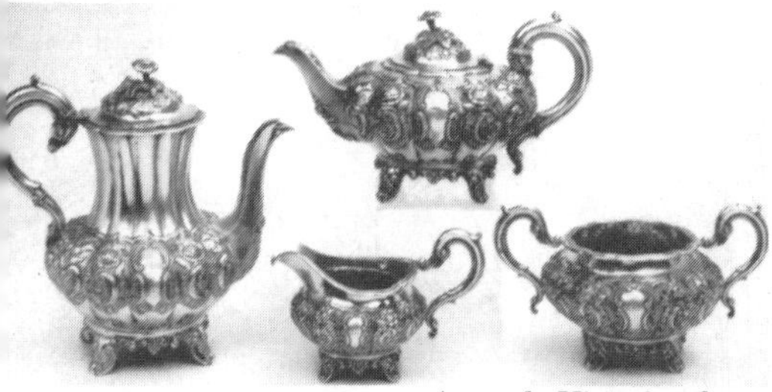

An early Victorian four-piece tea service, engraved with a crest and monogram, by William Hunter, London 1838, coffee pot 9½in (25cm) high, 73.75oz gross.
$4,000-5,000

A three-piece tea service and a coffee pot, by Joel and John Sayre, probably New York City, the tea service engraved in script 'MP', the coffee pot engraved 'TED', each marked, c1810, the teapot 7in (18cm) high, 78.5oz gross.
$4,000-5,000

A five-piece tea and coffee service by Simon Chaudron, Philadelphia, each engraved with a coat-of-arms, crest and motto 'SPES Pennsylvania', teapot and sugar bowl marked, c1810, coffee pot 8in (20cm) high, 118.5oz gross.
$6,000-9,000

A seven-piece tea and coffee service with tray, by William B. Durgin Company, Concord, New Hampshire, each engraved with a script monogram, each marked, c1900, tray 31in (79cm) wide, 393.5oz gross.
$9,000-10,000

A three-piece tea service, by Arthur L. Hartwell for Stone Associates, Gardner, Massachusetts, marked, c1920, teapot 6in (15cm) high, 26.5oz.
$5,000-6,000

A five-piece tea and coffee service, by Gorham, Providence, the waste bowl engraved on one side 'Harriet S. Richards from her Father', one finial detached, each marked, c1850, 116.6oz.
$3,500-4,000

A composite three-piece teaset, by Richard Sawyer, teapot Dublin 1844, sugar bowl and cream jug, Dublin 1839, 63oz.
$1,500-2,500

A three-piece tea service, by H. Haddock, Boston, later engraved 'Fanny Mackie 1851' and 'Carolyn B Mackie', each marked, teapot 7in (18cm) high, 67oz gross.
$2,500-3,000

A four-piece tea and coffee service, by Samuel Kirk, Baltimore, each engraved with script initial 'D', each marked with name touch and Baltimore assay marks, c1825, coffee pot 13in (33cm) high, 177oz gross.
$5,000-6,000

A five-piece tea and coffee service, by Wood & Hughes, New York, the cream jug and waste bowl with gilt interiors, cream jug engraved 'Willets', 4 monograms lightly erased, each marked, c1870, 8½in (22cm) high, 80oz gross.
$3,000-4,000

A five-piece tea and coffee service, by Wood & Hughes, New York, in the Aesthetic taste, each marked, c1875, coffee pot 6in (15cm) high, 84.5oz gross.
$6,000-7,000

A three-piece tea service with gadroon border, Sheffield 1929, 44oz gross. **$700-800**

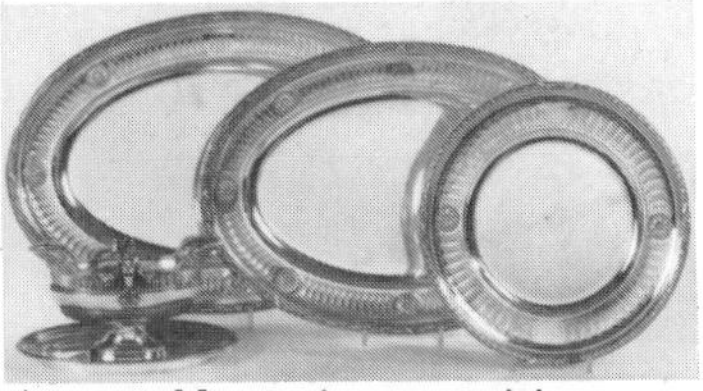

A part table service, comprising: 2 meat dishes, sauce boat and stand, by Odiot, a dish, by George Keller, Paris, c1880, 11in (28cm) diam, 4,878 grammes.
$8,000-10,000

A part dinner service, comprising: sauce boat and stand, a dessert stand and 5 dishes, Paris, c1880, 7,283 grammes.
$7,000-9,000

A four-piece tea and coffee set, Sheffield 1968, 88oz.
$1,500-2,000

French seven-piece tea and offee-service, late 19thC, tea-urn, 5½in (65cm) high, 7,812 grammes.
15,000-20,000

A three-piece tea service, Birmingham 1936, 25½oz.
$700-1,000

A five-piece tea and coffee service in he early 18thC taste, each ngraved with a monogram, the tea ervice by Charles Stuart Harris nd Sons, London 1933, the coffee ot and hot milk jug by a different naker, London 1931, coffee pot 8in 20cm) high, and a pair of sugar ongs engraved with a monogram, 1.25oz.
1,500-1,600

A four-piece tea service, Sheffield 1933, hot water jug 7½in (19cm) high, 57oz gross.
$3,000-4,000

Tea Caddies

A George III tea caddy, by Robert Hennell, 1782, 4½in (12cm) high, 13oz.
$4,000-5,000

An oval tea caddy, by Hester Bateman, London 1784, 5in (12cm), 10.5oz.
$1,500-1,600

pair of early ictorian tea caddies nd covers, by Charles ox, London 1838, ½in (14.5cm), 39 grammes.
4,000-5,000

Miller's is a price Guide not a price List

The price ranges given reflect the average price a purchaser should pay for similar items. Condition, rarity of design or pattern, size, colour, provenance, restoration and many other factors must be taken into account when assessing values. When buying or selling, it must always be remembered that prices can be greatly affected by the condition of any piece. Unless otherwise stated, all goods shown in Miller's are of good merchantable quality, and the valuations given reflect this fact. Pieces offered for sale in exceptionally fine condition or in poor condition may reasonably be expected to be priced considerably higher or lower respectively than the estimates given herein

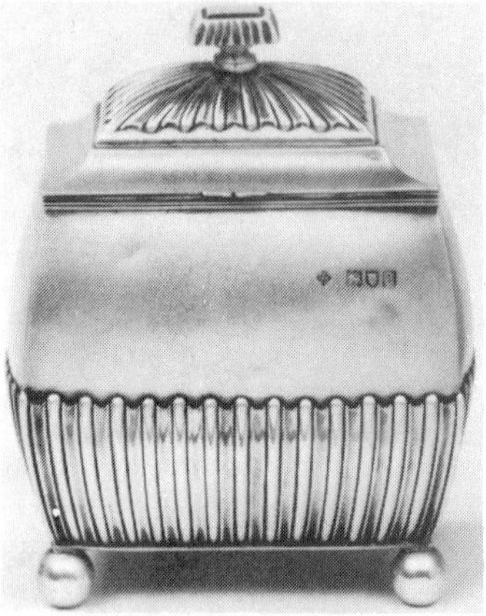

A late Victorian gilt-lined tea caddy, engraved with a diamond registration mark, by Henry Wilkinson & Co. Ltd., London 1896, 4in (11cm), 8.5oz gross.
$700-800

A Victorian tea caddy and cover, by F.A.P., London 1896, 3½in (9cm) high.
$400-500

An Edwardian tea caddy, by H.M., Birmingham 1910, 3in (8cm).
$300-400

A George III tea urn, engraved with a coat-of-arms and crest, by Francis Butty and Nicholas Dumee, 1769, 21in (54cm), 93oz.
$6,000-8,000

The arms are those of Hare, Co. Norfolk, impaling another.

Tea Kettles

A George II kettle, stand and lamp on triangular stand, the kettle, spirit-stand and lamp by George Wickes, 1738, the spirit-stand with maker's mark only struck 4 times, the triangular stand by Robert Abercrombie, 1738, 90oz gross.
$13,000-15,000

A George II windshield for a kettle-stand, engraved with a coat-of-arms, crest and motto, maker's mark probably IR overstruck with that of Thomas Hemming, 1764, 5in (12.5cm) high, 21oz.
$1,800-2,000

The arms are those of Vane impaling another.

Teapots

A George III teapot, by Benjamin Smith, Snr., 1807, 40oz gross.
$6,000-8,000

A George III teapot and stand, engraved with a monogram, by Peter and Ann Bateman, 1791, 26oz gross.
$4,000-5,000

A Regency teapot, by Samu
Hennell, London 1815.
$900-1,000

A George II bullet-shaped teapot, engraved with a crest and initials WFS, by William Aytoun, Edinburgh 1743, assay master, Edward Lothian, 20oz gross.
$3,000-4,000

A George III teapot, the undersic engraved 'This teapot belonged t Margaret, Lady Fairfax', by Johr Emes, London 1800, 6½in (17cm 17oz gross.
$1,000-1,500

Trays

A small tray, by Whiting Manufacturing Company, Newark, the centre engraved with a seascape with Japanese fishermen in a boat, marked, c1880, 5in (12.5cm) long, oz gross.
1,000-2,000

A salver, by Dominick & Haff, New York, square with rounded corners, marked, 1882, 10in (25.5cm) square, 21oz.
$2,500-3,000

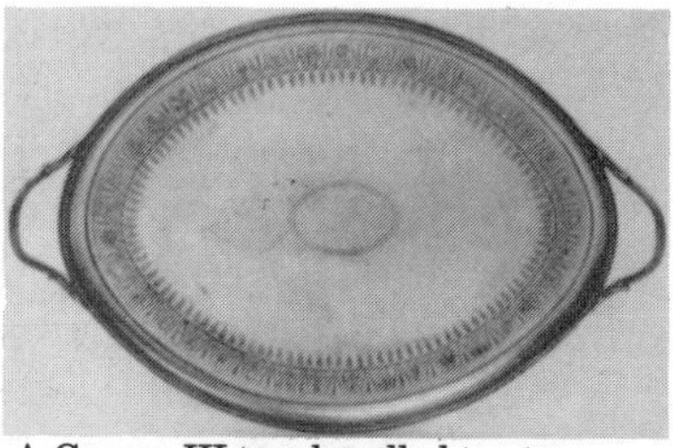

A George III two-handled tea tray, bright cut with a frieze of acorns, fruit, flowers and foliage, John Hutson, London 1795, 20½in (52cm), 48.75oz.
$400-600

A tray, by Porter Blanchard, Calabasas, California, marked on reverse, 20thC, 20in (51cm) long, 69.5oz.
$4,000-5,000

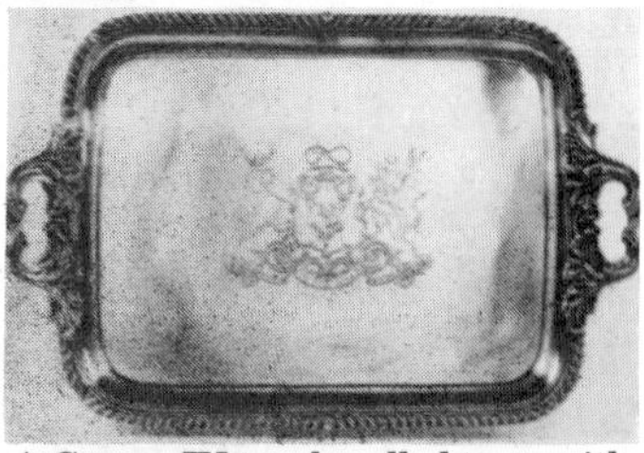

A George IV two-handled tray, with gadrooned moulded border, engraved with a coat-of-arms, by Robert Garrard, c1828, 24in (61cm) wide, 118oz.
$8,000-10,000

The arms are those of Cavendish with Compton in pretence.

A tea tray, by L. C. Shellabarger, marked, 1933, 30in (76cm) long, 180.5oz.
$6,000-7,000

Tureens

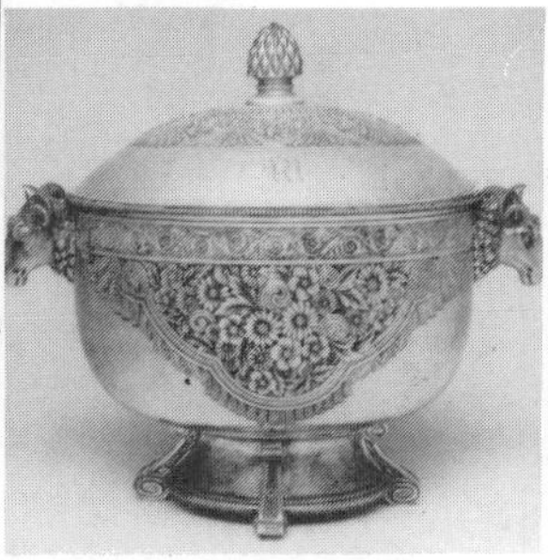

A soup tureen, by Gorham Manufacturing Company, Providence, in the Aesthetic taste, marked, 1875, 15in (38cm) wide, 94.25oz.
$14,000-15,000

A sauce tureen, by W. K. Vanderslice & Company, San Francisco, California, marked, c1865, 7in (18cm) high, 20oz.
$2,500-3,000

A George III soup tureen and cover, the domed cover with ostrich and chapeau crest finial, engraved with a coat-of-arms, crests and an inscription, by Peter, Ann and William Bateman, 1802, 14½in (37cm), 89oz.
12,000-14,000

A covered tureen, by Whiting Manufacturing Co., North Attleboro or Newark, c1878, 8in (20.5cm) high, 51.5oz.
$4,000-5,000

A George III soup tureen and cover, with detachable snake finial, later chased overall and engraved with a coat-of-arms, the cover engraved twice with a crest, by Paul Storr, 1807, 11½in (29cm) high, 144oz.
$20,000-22,000

A George IV soup tureen and cover, engraved with a coat-of-arms, by R. Emes and E. Barnard, 1827, 11in (28cm) diam, 88oz.
$6,000-8,000

A William IV soup tureen and cover, on foliage and scroll feet, with shell border, scroll handles and fluted domed cover with foliage finial, engraved with a crest, by J. C. Edington, 1835, 11in (28cm) diam, 126oz.
$10,000-12,000

Toys & Miniature Pieces

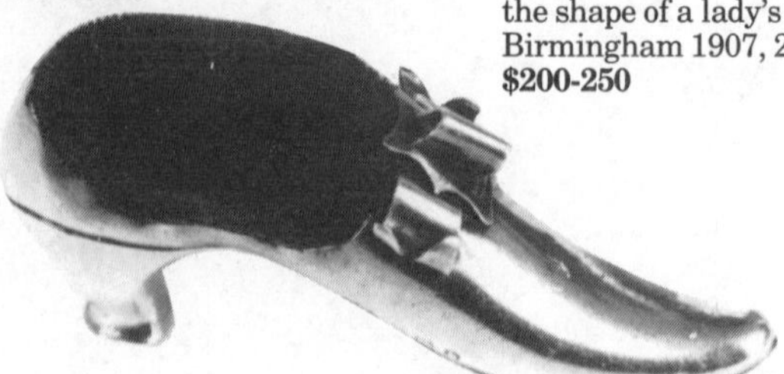

An Edwardian silver pincushion, in the shape of a lady's shoe, Birmingham 1907, 2in (5cm) long.
$200-250

A set of 4 novelty smoker's companions, formed as Mr. Punch, by Walter and John Barnard, 1896, 5½in (14cm) high, 30oz.
$8,000-10,000

Miscellaneous

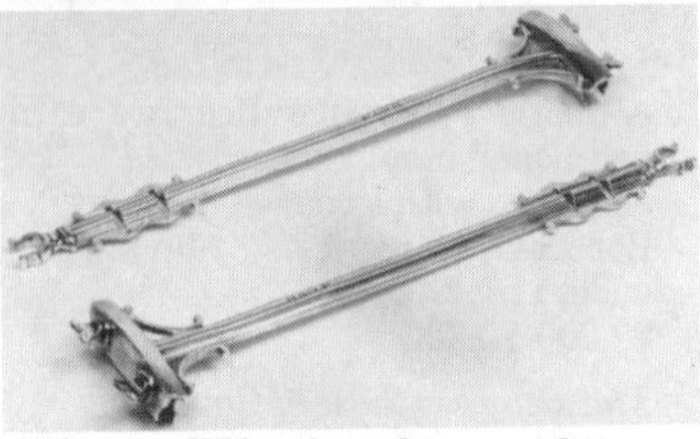

A George III beef machine, with scroll brackets to the curved dish clamps, with moulded stems and pierced and scroll tops surmounted by U-shaped spit rests, by Thomas Hemming, 1773, 12in (30.5cm) long, 14oz 16dwt.
$3,000-4,000

A Victorian cast and chased novelty pepperette, modelled as a kitten with a gilt bow around its neck, engraved with a diamond registration mark, Robert Hennell, London 1875, 3in (7.5cm), 3.75oz.
$1,200-1,400

A George III silver gilt fireman's arm badge, chased in the centre with a royal crown above clasped hands and 'No.4' below, the border engraved 'Hand in Hand Fire Office Instituted 1696', by Hester Bateman, 1776, 6in (15cm) high, 5oz 8dwt.
$9,000-10,000

A George IV table bell, by Thomas Robinson, 1821, 4in (10cm) high, 6oz.
$3,000-4,000

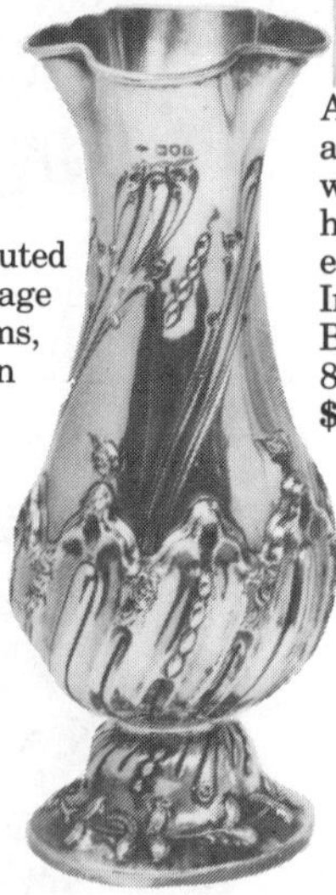

A pair of late Victorian spiral fluted vases, chased with scrolling foliage and with moulded quatrefoil rims, C. C. Pilling, London 1901, 9½in (24cm), 23oz.
$1,300-1,500

A pair of George III snuffers, with honeysuckle cast handle and wrigglework border decoration, Birmingham 1776.
$700-800

A model of a stag, with removable head, London import mark for 1910, 10½in (26cm) high, 20oz.
$1,600-1,800

An Edward VII officer's silver mounted pouch, Birmingham 1903.
$400-500

bud vase, by Gorham, Providence, ngraved with stylised monogram, ıarked, 1869, 7in (17cm) high, 7oz.
500-800

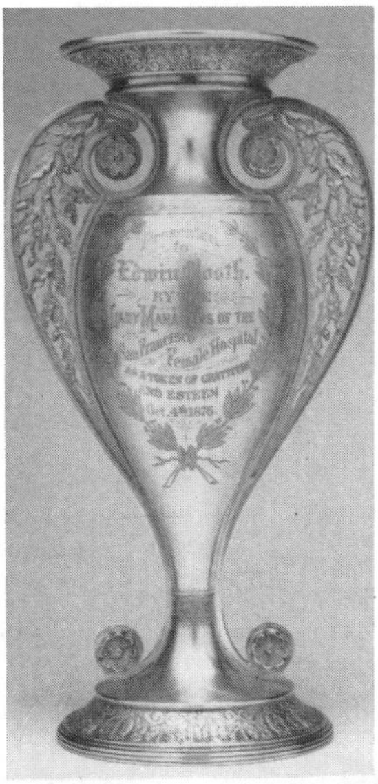

A presentation vase, by W. K. Vanderslice, San Francisco, the interior of the neck gilt, marked, c1876, 12in (30cm) high, 31.5oz.
$3,500-4,000

A medallion silver and gold belt buckle, by Shiebler, New York, c1885, 1.5oz.
$1,600-2,000

A silver gilt belt buckle, by Shiebler, :1880, 2 watch fobs and a brooch, ›uckle 2½in (6cm) long, 2oz gross.
$1,000-1,200

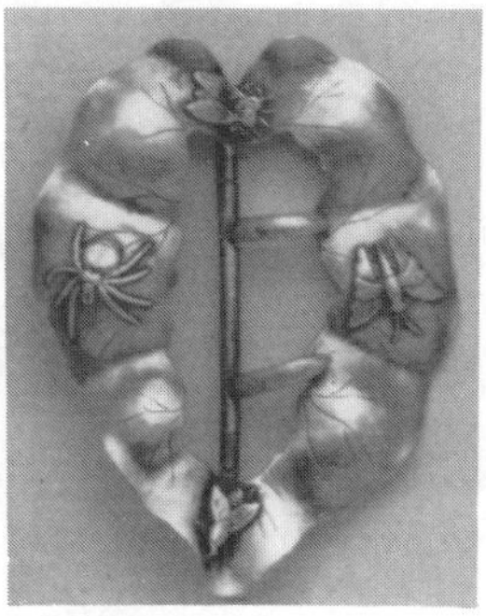

A leaf form belt buckle, by Frank M. Whiting, North Attleboro, c1885, 3in (8cm) long, 1oz.
$500-600

A belt buckle and a garter buckle, by Shiebler, New York, c1885, 1.5oz gross.
$180-200

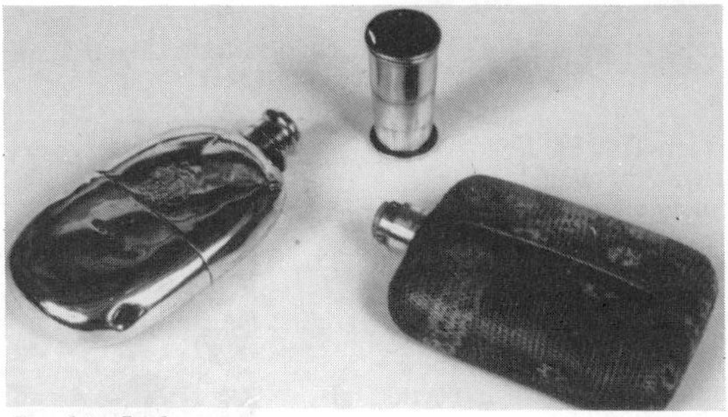

Two hip flasks:
l. Birmingham assay 1884, 5in (12.5cm) long.
r. By Sampson Mordan, c1890.
$500-600 each

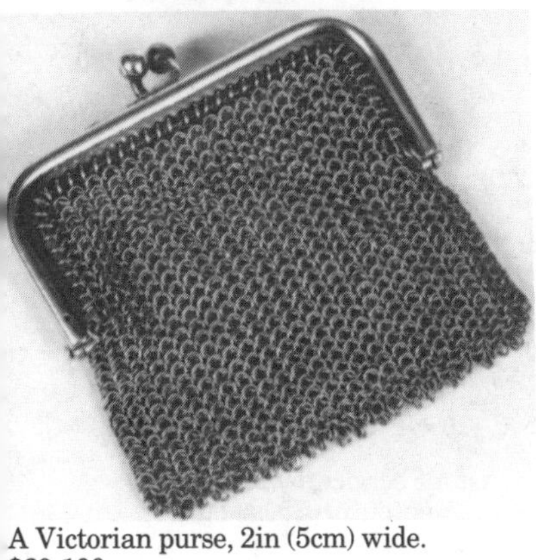

A Victorian purse, 2in (5cm) wide.
$60-100

A Victorian purse, 4½in (11cm) wide.
$150-200

Miller's is a price Guide not a price List

The price ranges given reflect the average price a purchaser should pay for similar items. Condition, rarity of design or pattern, size, colour, provenance, restoration and many other factors must be taken into account when assessing values. When buying or selling, it must always be remembered that prices can be greatly affected by the condition of any piece. Unless otherwise stated, all goods shown in Miller's are of good merchantable quality, and the valuations given reflect this fact. Pieces offered for sale in exceptionally fine condition or in poor condition may reasonably be expected to be priced considerably higher or lower respectively than the estimates given herein

SILVER PLATE

Candlesticks

A set of 6 Victorian candlesticks, by Thomas Bradbury, London 1897, 1898, the candelabra 16in (41cm) high.
$7,000-9,000

A Victorian Sheffield plate four-light candelabrum, 28in (71cm).
$800-1,000

A pair of George IV candlesticks, by John and Thomas Settle, Sheffield 1822, 6½in (16.5cm).
$1,000-1,200

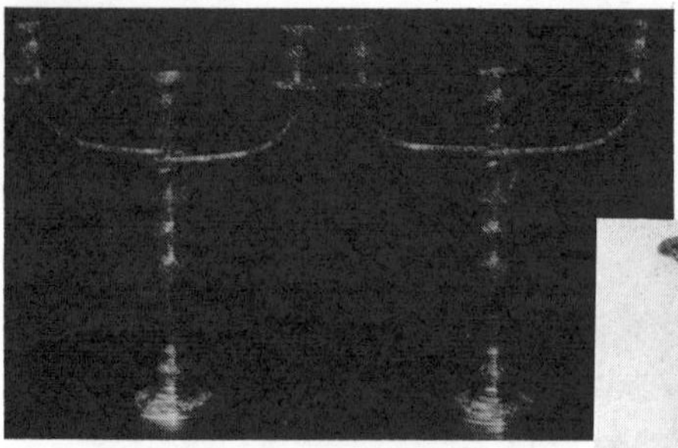

A pair of Victorian electroplated candelabrum, repaired, 23½in (72cm).
$600-800

A pair of three-light plated candelabra of Corinthian column form, with beaded and stepped square bases, the swirling branches supporting Corinthian capitals, the centre capital with a torch cover, 23in (58cm).
$1,200-1,500

A pair of George III Sheffield plate candlesticks, 12½in (32cm).
$800-1,000

A pair of old Sheffield plate three-light candelabra, the removable candle branches formed of a central column with flambeau snuffer and two S-scroll branches, one pair of branches socketed to form one five-light candelabrum, double sun marks, Matthew Boulton & Co., 23½in (60cm) high.
$1,000-1,200

A plated centrepiece compote, by Gorham, Providence, c1867, repaired, 13in (32cm) high.
$450-600

Services

A plated seven-piece tea and coffee service, by Rogers, Smith & Co, New Haven, c1875, coffee pot 11in (27cm) high.
$600-700

A plated part tea service, by Reed and Barton, Taunton, c1875, sugar bowl 8in (20cm) high.
$400-500

Victorian four-piece tea service, heffield, c1893.
1,400-1,600

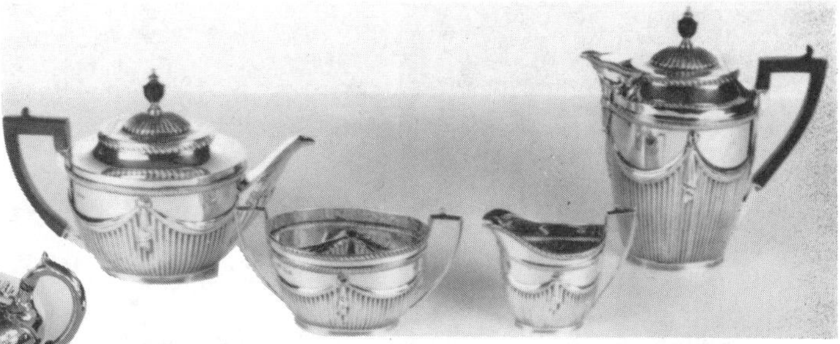

Victorian four-piece coffee ervice, Elkington & Co.
300-400

set of 4 old Sheffield plate entrée ishes, covers and handles, each ith two-handled hot water stand nd cover, with detachable foliage andles, each engraved with a oat-of-arms, by Waterhouse & Co., 1835, 15in (38cm) wide.
9,000-10,000

he arms are those of McGeough ond, of Drumsill, N. Ireland.

Tureens

A pair of early Victorian Sheffield plate crested entrée dishes.
$400-600

A set of 4 old Sheffield plate sauce tureens and covers, the domed covers with detachable handles, engraved twice with a crest, by T. and J. Creswick, c1820, 9in (23cm) wide.
$6,000-8,000

A pair of old Sheffield plate venison dishes, each on lion's paw and foliage feet and with shell, foliage and gadrooned borders, each engraved with 2 crests, by Waterhouse & Co., c1835, 22 and 23in (56 and 58.5cm) wide.
$3,000-4,000

Iiscellaneous

n old Sheffield plate cup and cover, ngraved with a coat-of-arms, with eaded knop finial and fluted order, presentation engraving to e side 'For the Best Two Acres of abbages, Kiplin, 1770', 13in 3cm) high.
900-1,200

A late Victorian Armada pattern ewer, with presentation inscription, by Elkington & Co., c1899, 18in (46cm) high.
$4,000-6,000

An old Sheffield plate coffee biggin, with everted foliate border and foliate finial to domed panelled cover, foliate scroll handle, on pierced foliate bracket feet, c1830.
$200-400

A plated tea tray in the Japanese taste, by Pairpoint, New Bedford, c1875, 21in (52.5cm) wide.
$900-1,000

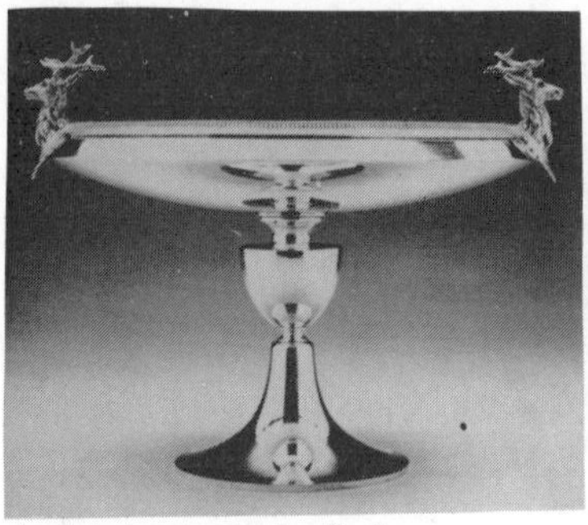

A plated compote, by Gorham, Providence, c1870, 11½in (29cm) diam.
$1,200-1,500

A plated basket, by Simpson, Hall & Miller, Wallingford, Connecticut, c1885, 8in (20cm) wide.
$600-900

A plated water jug on a stand, with pair of goblets, by Meriden Britannia Co, c1875, 20½in (51cm high.
$2,800-3,000

A parcel gilt plated cake basket, by Pairpoint, New Bedford, c1875, 10in (26cm) long.
$400-500

A plated compote, by Meriden Silver Plate Co., c1875, 10in (26cm) diam.
$500-600

A plated jewel box with pin cushic by Reed and Barton, Taunton, c1875, 11in (27cm) high.
$400-500

A plated water jug and goblet on stand, by Reed and Barrow, Taunton, c1875, repaired, jug 16½in (41.5cm) high.
$1,000-1,200

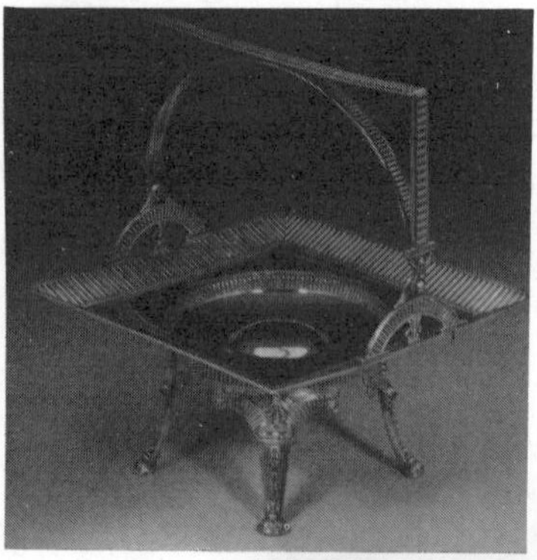

A plated cake basket, unmarked, c1875, 10in (25cm) square.
$600-700

A plated smoking stand, by Pairpoint, New Bedford, c1875, 9in (23cm) wide.
$200-250

A plated cake basket, unmarked, c1875, 11in (27cm) wide.
$400-500

plated dog's head inkwell, by
eriden Britannia Co, c1875, 7in
3cm) high.
,800-2,000

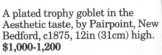

A plated parcel gilt compote, by Simpson, Hall, Miller & Co, Wallingford, c1875, 10in (25cm) diam.
$550-650

A plated trophy goblet in the Aesthetic taste, by Pairpoint, New Bedford, c1875, 12in (31cm) high.
$1,000-1,200

A plated centrepiece bowl, by Reed and Barton, Taunton, late 19thC, 15in (38cm) wide.
$700-900

plated basket, by Simpson, Hall,
iller & Co, Wallingford, c1875,
½in (16cm) wide.
00-900

A plated dish, by James W. Tufts, Boston, c1875, 11½in (28cm) diam.
$300-400

A plated compote, by Reed and Barton, Taunton, c1875, 14½in (36.5cm) high.
$450-550

plated covered punch bowl on a
and, with 12 goblets, by Reed and
arton, Taunton, c1875, the bowl
in (40cm) high.
,800-2,000

A plated elephant's head inkwell, by Meriden Britannia Company, late 19thC, 6½in (16cm) long.
$600-700

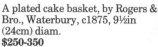

A plated cake basket, by Rogers & Bro., Waterbury, c1875, 9½in (24cm) diam.
$250-350

A parcel gilt plated dish, by Middleton Plate Co, c1875, 9½in (24cm) long.
$450-550

A plated cat's head inkwell, by Meriden Silver Plate Co, c1875, 8½in (21cm) long.
$2,500-3,000

A pair of silver plated coaching lamps, with simulated flame finials over bulbous embossed and pierced domes, the bodies with engraved glass panels, complete with plated brackets, fitted for electricity, 19thC, 30in (76cm) high.
$40,000-50,000

A plated nut bowl, by Meriden Britannia Company, c1875, 11in (27cm) high.
$2,000-2,500

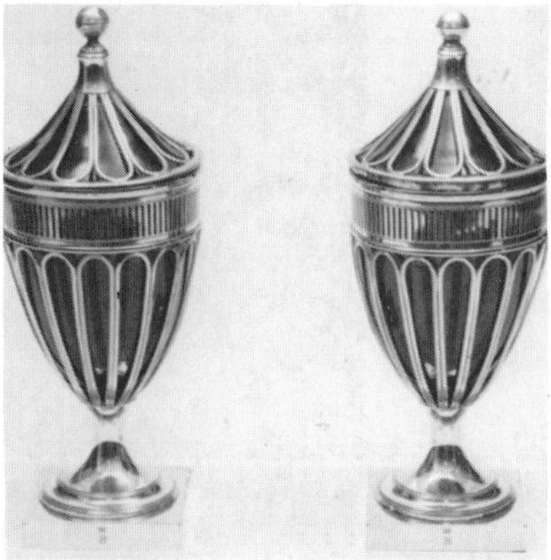

A pair of Adam design Sheffield urns, with blue glass liners, lined domed detachable covers with ball finials, one liner damaged, early 19thC.
$3,000-4,000

JUDAICA

A silver Ethrog box, with applied plaques, depicting the Migdal David, the Akedat Yitschak, and the Western Wall, the cover inscribed in Hebrew, with cast handle, stamped Bezalel Jerusalem, 5in (13cm), 479 grammes.
$2,500-3,000

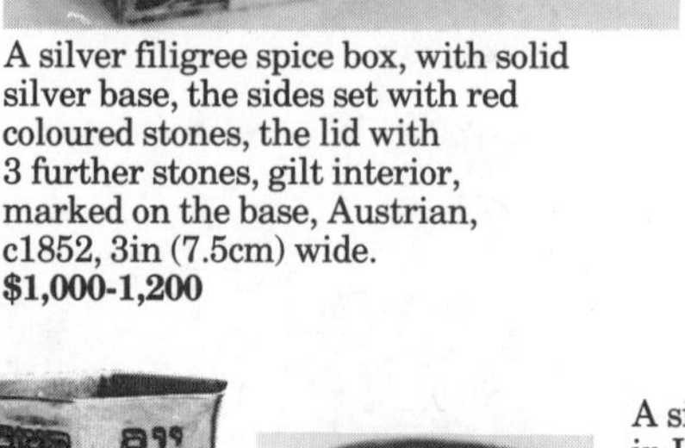

A silver filigree spice box, with solid silver base, the sides set with red coloured stones, the lid with 3 further stones, gilt interior, marked on the base, Austrian, c1852, 3in (7.5cm) wide.
$1,000-1,200

A silver Kiddush beaker, inscribe in Hebrew, maker's mark AA Moscow, 1894, 5in (13cm) high, 140 grammes.
$600-1,000

A silver Kiddush beaker, engraved with Holy Land vignettes, the base stamped with quality mark 12, probably Polish, 19thC, 3½in (9cm) high, 159 grammes.
$2,500-3,000

A silver Kiddush cup, the rim with Hebrew inscription, German, standard mark 800 on base, probably late 19thC, 5in (13cm) high, 128 grammes.
$1,000-1,200

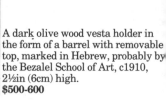

A dark olive wood vesta holder in the form of a barrel with removable top, marked in Hebrew, probably by the Bezalel School of Art, c1910, 2½in (6cm) high.
$500-600

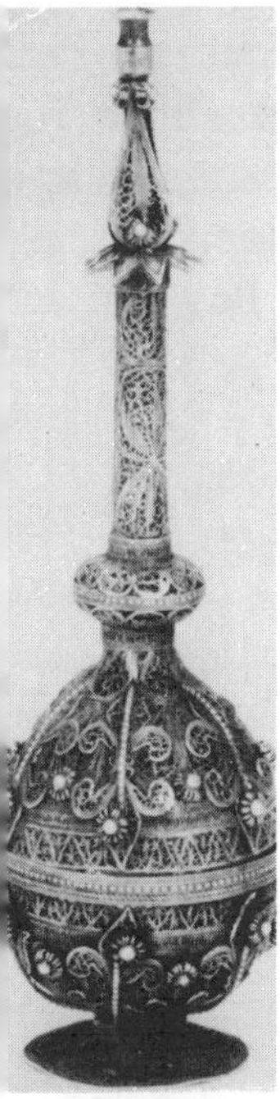

A Middle Eastern filigree spice container, the filigree body overlaid with a floral decoration and small silver beads, slight damage, c1860, 8in (20.5cm).
$1,400-1,500

A Dutch pewter wedding plate, on 4 supports, the centre engraved and with Hebrew inscription, dated in Hebrew 1822, the reverse stamped with a touchmark of Daniel ten Winkel, The Hague, The Netherlands, 8in (20.5cm) wide.
$700-800

A Bezalel silver Megillat Esther case, decorated with scenes from the Purim story and with quotations from the scroll of Esther, the body and thumpiece inscribed in Hebrew, 17½in (44cm) long.
$2,000-2,500

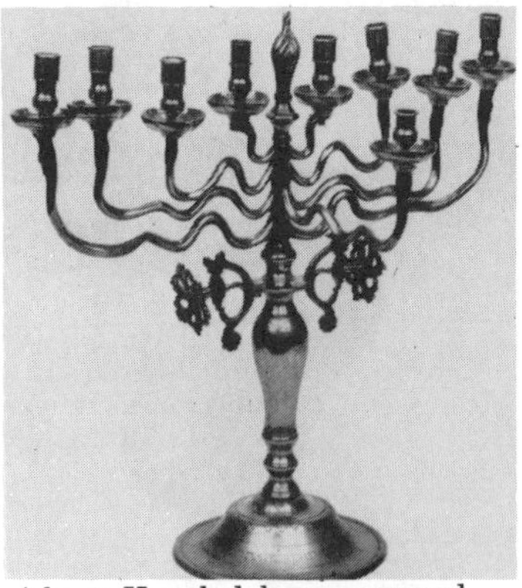

A brass Hanukah lamp, engraved with Hebrew inscription, dated 1836, probably German, 21½in (55cm) high.
$6,000-8,000

German Sabbath lamp, uspended from an ornate cast hook nd cast chain, the oil tray with spouts joined to the drip tray, 1820, 6in (15cm) high.
500-600

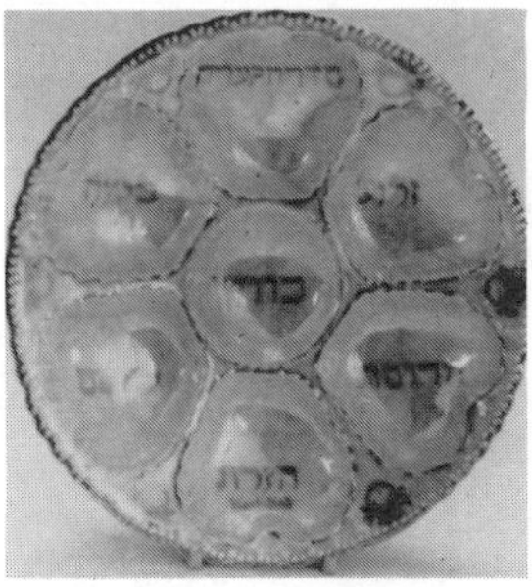

An Austrian porcelain Seder dish, with 7 wells marked in gilt with the foods of the Passover, and with the added inscription 'Karlsbad', decorated in gilt, c1890, 8½in (22cm).
$1,200-1,400

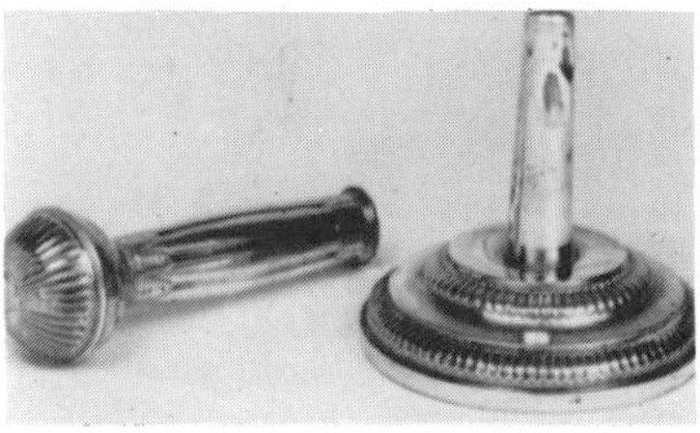

A Queen Anne Torah mount, by John Ruslen, 1708, and a silver handle with fluted stem and partly fluted finial, leopard's head erased, c1710, the stand 5in (12.5cm) high.
$6,000-8,000

A silver mounted wood, bone and mother-of-pearl Torah pointer, with silver hand and engraved mounts with swirling silver inscribed mount with the name of the owner in Hebrew, unmarked, Polish, 19thC, 15in (38cm).
$600-700

late Victorian silver plated and ilt Torah breast plate, set with oloured glass stones, inscribed Presented by Simon & Darren haw', suspended from a chain, ome damage, c1880, 7in (18cm) igh.
500-600

A pair of German parcel gilt silver Rimmonim, with pierced decoration and a lion rampant finial, maker's mark probably ING, Nuremberg, c1766, 15in (38cm) high, 1,185 grammes.
$20,000-24,000

A silver spice tower, with a hinged door, surmounted by a spire with wirework columns, hung with a bell, Russian marks, 19thC, 12½in (31cm) high, 177 grammes.
$300-400

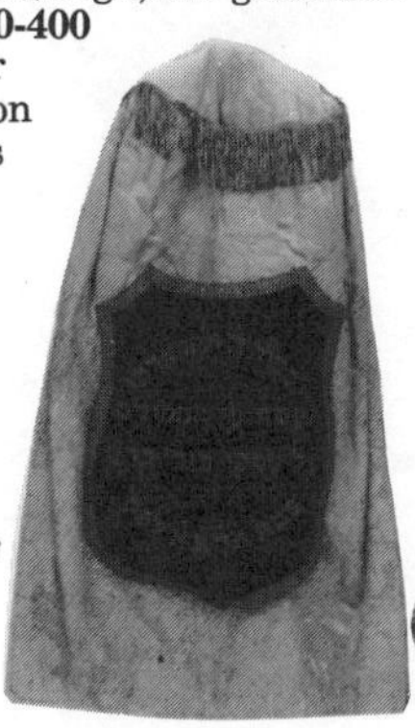

A gold coloured silk damask Torah mantle, with brown silk velvet applique, with Hebrew text in silver thead, dated Pesach 1931, 34in (87cm).
$400-500

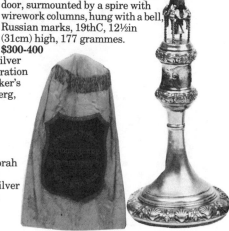

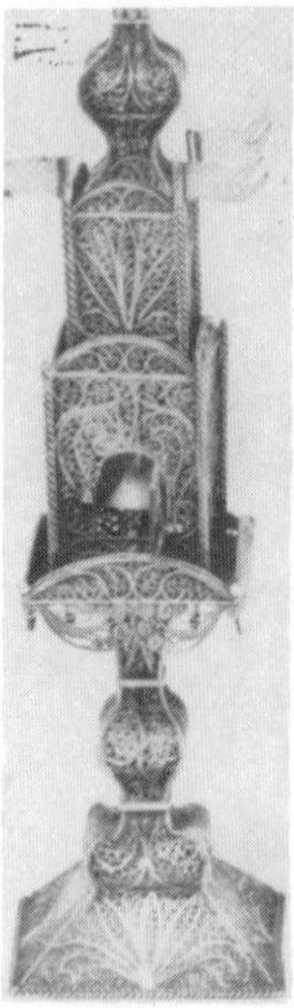

An Austro-Hungarian spice tower, the interior fitted with a bell, 1819, 10in (25.5cm).
$600-700

A silver Torah double crown, decorated with foliate ornaments, the finial shaped as a spread eagle, possibly Polish, unmarked, 18th/19thC, 10½in (26cm) diam, 1,280 grammes.
$2,000-2,500

A silver Esther scroll holder and scroll, the fine filigree sleeve set with coloured stones, the handwritten scroll of Esther in black ink on 5 sewn parchment sheets in 22 columns, probably Italian, c1840, 8½in (22cm) long.
$4,000-5,000

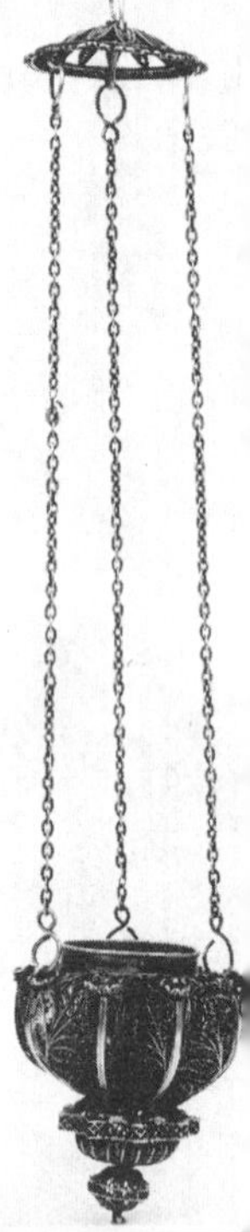

A silver filigree eternal light, decorated with foliate ornaments on 3 chains, possibly Russian, c1869, 3in (8cm) diam, 174 grammes.
$1,500-1,600

A silver plated Polish Hanukah lamp, with detachable shamush and oil jug, late 19thC, 10½in (26cm) wide.
$300-400

Wine Antiques

A set of 4 old Sheffield plate beaded, pierced and bright cut wine coasters, each engraved with a crest, 5½in (14cm).
$1,800-2,500

A set of 4 George III wine coasters, on turned wood bases, engraved with a crest, by Richard Morton & Co., Sheffield, 1778.
$7,000-9,000

A set of 3 stoneware barrels, moulded with Royal Arms, Prince of Wales feathers, fruiting vines and cold painted in red, green, black and gilt, 13in (33cm) high.
$800-900

A wine cooler, by Gorham, Providence, dated 1867, 11in (27cm) high, 80.5oz.
$7,000-8,000

Four George IV wine coasters, each engraved with 2 crests, 2 by Rebecca Emes and Edward Barnard, 1820 and 1826.
$9,000-10,000

A pair of early Victorian Sheffield plate decanter stands, with turned wood bases an baize lined central bosses.
$700-800

\ Flemish verdure hunting
apestry, woven in silks and
vools, cut and shut, early
.7thC, 108 by 80in (274 by
03cm). **$16,000-18,000**

A pair of Aubusson entre
fenêtres, repaired, 157 by
100in (398 by 252cm).
$12,000-14,000

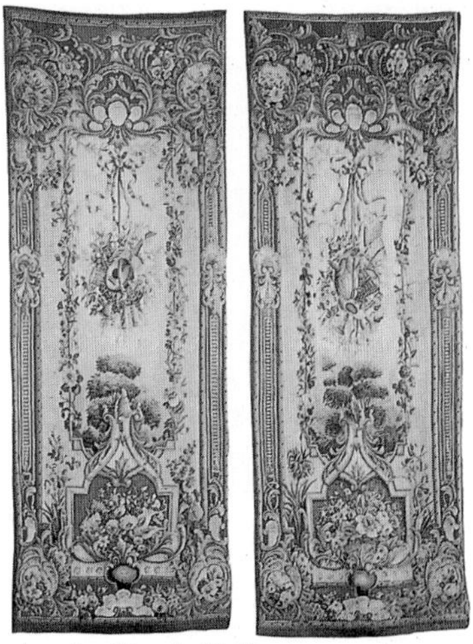

A pair of Louis Philippe
Aubusson portières, 133½ by
50in (338 by 127cm).
$10,000-12,000

A verdure tapestry fragment, 16thC,
12½ by 59½in (108 by 151cm),
n later parcel gilt, gesso and
grained frame. **$8,000-10,000**

l. A Flemish tapestry woven in silks
and wools, 18thC, 122in (310cm) long.
$18,000-20,000
r. A pair of tapestry panels, 84in
(213cm) long. **$60,000-70,000**

A Beauvais tapestry woven in
silks and wools, 18thC, 85 by
56in (216 by 142cm).
$6,000-8,000

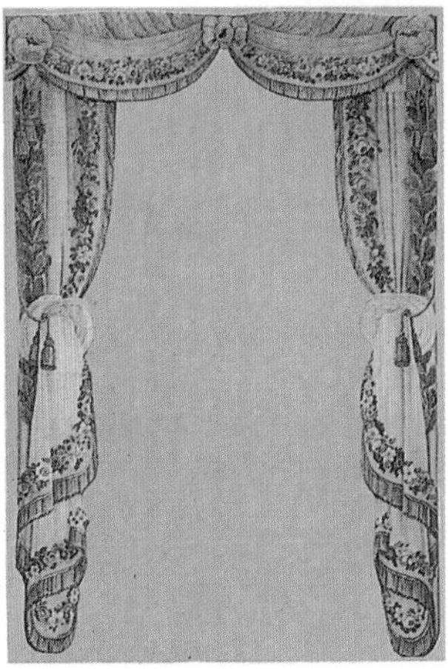

A set of 4 Louis Philippe
Aubusson portières, 133in
(337cm). **$12,000-14,000**

A pair of Louis Philippe Aubusson
portières, c1875, 129 by 49½in (327 by
126cm). **$10,000-12,000**

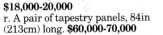

A Brussels tapestry, woven in
wools and silks, 17thC, 274in
(696cm) long.
$30,000-35,000

A Vienna Du Paquier beaker, painted with Imperial Russian arms, the interior gilt, c1755, 3in (7.5cm) high. **$10,000-12,000**

Six dinner plates and four serving dishes from The Kremlin Service, commissioned by Tsar Nicholas I, from the Imperial Porcelain Factory, gilding and paint worn, 1836. **$26,000-30,000**

Two soup plates, painted and gilded, by the Imperial Porcelain Factory, Paul I period, 9½in (24cm) diam. **$2,000-3,000**

Two dinner plates, from the service of the Order of St. Alexander Nevsky, by the Imperial Porcelain Factory, Alexander II period, 9½in (24cm) diam. **$5,000-7,000**

A Soviet porcelain cup and saucer, painted with stylised flowers, leaves and a butterfly, marks of Imperial Porcelain Factory, and later State Porcelain Factory, dated 1921, saucer 6½in (16cm). **$5,000-7,000**

A Soviet propaganda porcelain plate, marks of Imperial Porcelain Factory, Alexander II period, and State Porcelain Factory, 1919, No. 281, 10in (25.5cm). **$6,000-8,000**

A Suprematist cup and saucer, by the Dulevo Porcelain Factory, export mark, c1925, saucer 4½in (11cm) diam. **$8,000-10,000**

An export armorial plate, from the service of Empress Catherine The Gre of Russia, gilding rubbed and chipped, c1740, 9in (23cm) diam. **$12,000-15,000**

A porcelain plate, painted with a rose, gilding worn, marked overglaze Archangelski, 1827, 9in (23cm) diam. **$10,000-12,000**

A Soviet propaganda porcelain plate, minor restoration, Imperial Porcelain Factory and State Porcelain Factory marks, 1922. **$4,000-6,000**

A porcelain plate, painte with roses, marked overglaze Archangelski, 9in (23cm) diam. **$9,000-12,000**

Soviet propaganda
ɔrcelain plate, dated
919, 9½in (24cm).
3,000-10,000

c. A porcelain plate from the Yacht service, Paul I period, 9½in (24cm). **$1,500-2,000**
l. & r. Two porcelain plates from the Arabesques Service, Catherine II period. **$16,000-18,000**

. Soviet propaganda porcelain
late, by Imperial Porcelain
'actory, dated 1921, 10in
25cm). **$12,000-14,000**

A Soviet propaganda porcelain plate, inscribed 'He who does not work does not eat', dated 1922, 9½in. **$14,000-16,000**

A Soviet propaganda porcelain plate, by Adamovich, dated 1921, 9½in (24cm).
$10,000-12,000

ı Soviet propaganda porcelain
late, by Imperial Porcelain
'actory, dated 1921, 10in
25cm). **$10,000-12,000**

A Soviet propaganda porcelain plate, Imperial Porcelain Factory, 1921. **$14,000-16,000**

Two Wurtemburg Service porcelain plates. **$3,000-4,000**

ı Soviet propaganda porcelain
mperial and State Porcelain
'actory marks, dated 1921,
½in (24cm). **$8,000-10,000**

A porcelain plate, gilding restored, marked Archangelski 1827, 9in (23.5cm).
$6,000-8,000

A Soviet propaganda porcelain plate, The Red Star, by M. Adamovich, State Porcelain Factory. **$25,000-30,000**

A Soviet propaganda porcelain plate, by Lomonosov Porcelain Factory, marked, 10in (25cm). **$18,000-20,000**

A Suprematist plate, by the Lomonosov Factory, marked Made in Russia, inscribed July 29, N. Suetin, 7in (18cm). **$8,000-10,000**

A Soviet porcelain dish, blue overglaze interlaced initials, c1928, 12½in (32cm). **$8,000-10,000**

A porcelain tea set, painted with the coat-of-arms of Count Panzini of Mantua, by the Imperial Porcelain Factory, Catherine the Great period, c1780, teapot 4in (10cm) high. **$14,000-16,000**

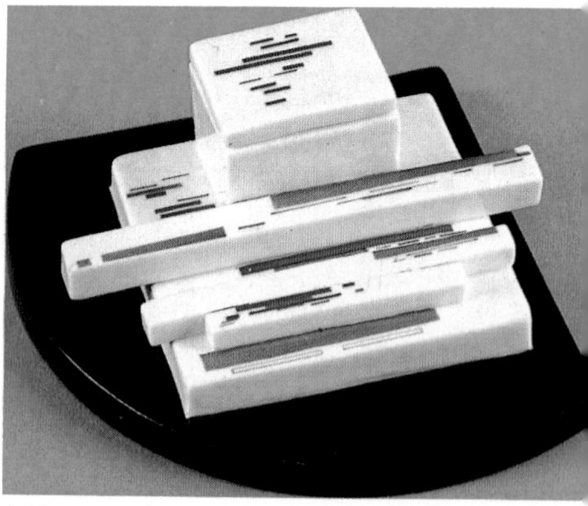

A Suprematist porcelain inkwell, by the Lomonoso Porcelain Factory, green underglaze mark, and re overglaze mark, c1926, 5½in (14cm). **$20,000-24,000**

Twelve cups and saucers and a two-handled bowl, by the Imperial Porcelain Factory, Alexander II period. **$25,000-30,000**

Part of the Orlov porcelain toilette service, with gold monogram, by the Imperial Porcelain Factory, impressed and incised marks, pots 3in (7.5cm) high. **$18,000-24,000**

A pair of Russian Imperial porcelain vases, 1801-55, 27in. **$40,000-50,000**

A Suprematist dish, marks of Imperial and State Porcelain Factories, c1926, 11in (28cm). **$24,000-30,00**

A tazza from the service of Grand Duke Konstantin Nikolaevich, by the Imperial Porcelain Factory, Nicholas I period. **$6,000-8,000**

A Soviet propaganda plate, marks of Imperial and State Porcelain Factories, 1921, 9in (23cm). **$6,000-8,000**

ilver mounted Favrile
lescent glass vase,
bergé and Tiffany Studios,
. **$60,000-70,000**

A silver mounted presentation vase, the porcelain by the Imperial Porcelain Factory, the mounts Fabergé, c1915, 19in (49cm).
$60,000-70,000

A Russian Empire malachite and ormolu centre table, c1840, 35in (89cm) diam.
$45,000-50,000

enamel and silver
sk folio, by
chinnikov, Moscow
93, 16in (40.5cm)
gh.
,000-7,000

A silver mounted mahogany tea table, Fabergé mounts, c1900. **$90,000-100,000**

Twelve Meissen porcelain-handled knives, forks and spoons, some cracked, c1750, in embossed fitted leather cases.
$50,000-60,000

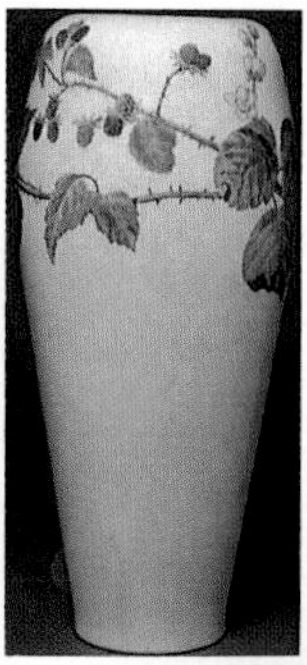

A vase by the Imperial Porcelain Factory, dated 1904, 18½in (47cm) high.
$5,000-6,000

A brass mounted mahogany commode, stamped on back, c1870, 32½in (82cm).
$30,000-40,000

Russian Karelian birch
binet, early 19thC,
in (117cm) wide.
,000-8,000

An ormolu mounted malachite table, late 19thC, 27in (68.5cm) diam.
$22,000-24,000

r. An ormolu mantel clock, signed Paul Buhré, St. Petersbourg, mid-19thC, 29in (74cm) high.
$5,000-6,000

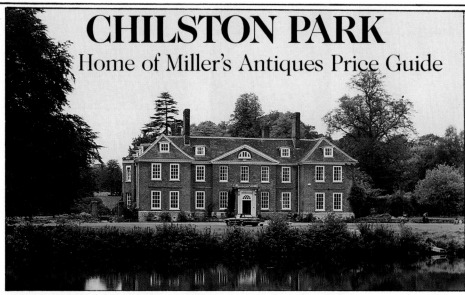

The Private Dining Room...
English cooking and fresh food are the main principles of Chilston's excellent Dining Room. Breakfast, for instance, might include porridge, kidneys, bacon, scrambled and coddled eggs, kippers, kedgeree and muffins. A baron of beef, roast saddle of lamb, game, hams...and a variety of proper puddings feature on the menu.

The Reception Hall...
Atmosphere, warmth and light flickering from chandeliers welcome you to Chilston. Gleaming wood, bright with the patina of age, sets off a gathering of family portraits...dogs doze in front of a blazing log fire...and your hosts wait to receive you.

The Drawing Room...
With an emphasis placed upon comfort, the Drawing Room provides a quiet retreat. Somewhere to rest after a journey or a day's entertainment...to take tea in the afternoon or foregather with friends for a drink before dinner...and to relax completely at the end of the day.

The Bedrooms...
There are 25 bedrooms at Chilston, all of which have private bathrooms en suite. All are luxuriously appointed and delightfully furnished and guests are quite likely to find themselves in a four-poster bed. A special degree of personal comfort is provided by traditional hot-water bottles, complete with hand-knitted woollen covers.

An enamel silver gilt kovsh, marked Fedor Rückert, Moscow, 1899-1908, retailed by Ovchinnikov, 13½in (34cm) long. **$28,000-32,000**

A pair of plique-à-jour enamel kvoshi, marked Ivan Khlebnikov, Moscow, c1900, 7in (18cm). **$10,000-12,000**

A guilloche enamel gold and silver mounted table clock, marked Fabergé, St. Petersburg, c1890, 7in. **$24,000-30,000**

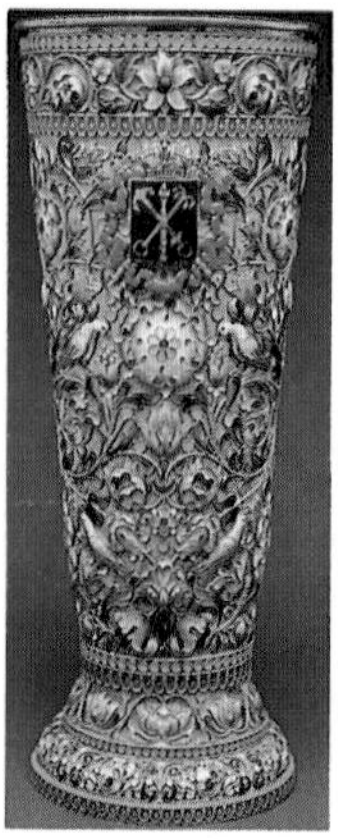

An enamel silver gilt beaker with St. Petersburg coat-of-arms, Ovchinnikov warrant, c1890, 11in (29cm). **$28,000-32,000**

A pair of plique-à-jour gilt and enamelled beakers, by P. Ovchinnikov, Imperial warrant, Moscow, 1899-1908, 4in (9.5cm) high. **$10,000-12,000**

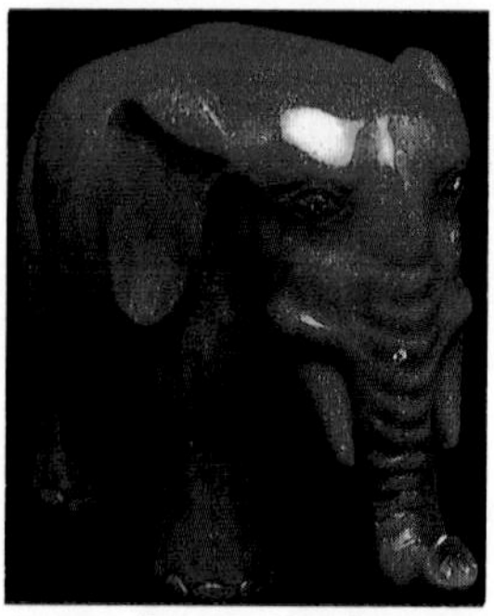

A carved purpurine figure of an elephant, Indian variety, curled trunk inset with a single diamond, by Fabergé, c1900, 4in (10cm) high. **$110,000-120,000**

A silver and enamel Imperial presentation portfolio, marked with the Imperial Warrant of Ovchinnikov, Moscow, 1894, 12in (30cm) wide. **$14,000-16,000**

A guilloche enamel silver gilt table clock, marked Fabergé, St. Petersburg, c1880, 4½in (11.5cm) wide. **$35,000-40,000**

A guilloche enamel desk clock, seed pearl bexel enclosing dial, marked Fabergé, St. Petersburg, c1900, 5in. **$28,000-30,000**

A plique-à-jour enamel and silver table lamp, marked Grachev, St. Petersburg, c1890, 20in (53cm). **$25,000-30,000**

A gold and guilloche enamel picture frame, marked Fabergé, St. Petersburg, c1890, 4in (10cm) high. **$46,000-50,000**

\ six-piece enamel and silver gilt tea ınd coffee service, marked Antip Kuzmichev, 'loscow, 1899-1908. **$18,000-20,000**

Two Elizabeth Petrovna gilt presentation kovshi;
l. Unmarked, c1750, 10in (25cm), 445gr. **$16,000-18,000**
r. D. Mochalkin, Moscow, 1758, 631gr. **$18,000-20,000**

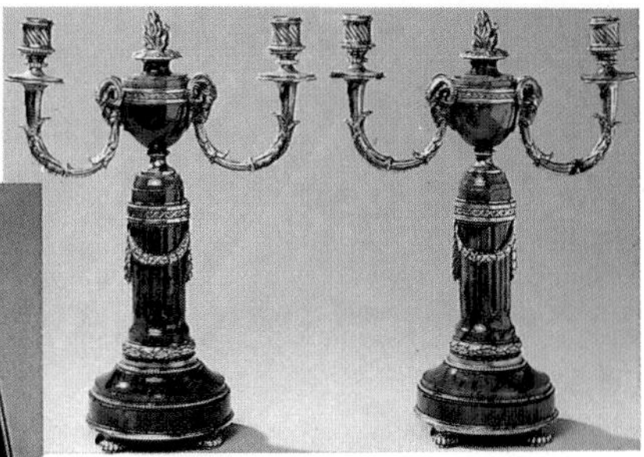

A pair of silver mounted nephrite candelabra, by Fabergé, c1890, 13in (33cm). **$70,000-80,000**

\ matching enamel silver gilt ıugar box and tea caddy, c1900. **$5,000-7,000**

A gold mounted guilloche enamel frame, St. Petersburg, c1890, 6in (15cm) high. **$35,000-40,000**

\n enamel and silver gilt icon)f the Virgin Kazanskaya, Moscow ı900. **$5,000-7,000**

An Elizabeth Petrovna parcel gilt Imperial kovsh, initialled G.I. Moscow 1751, 12½in (32cm) long, 646gr. **$25,000-30,000**

A niello silver gilt box, Popov factory, c1770, 4in (10cm) long, 272.5 grammes. **$14,000-16,000**

An enamel silver gilt tea service, marked Semenova, Moscow, c1910. **$8,000-10,000**

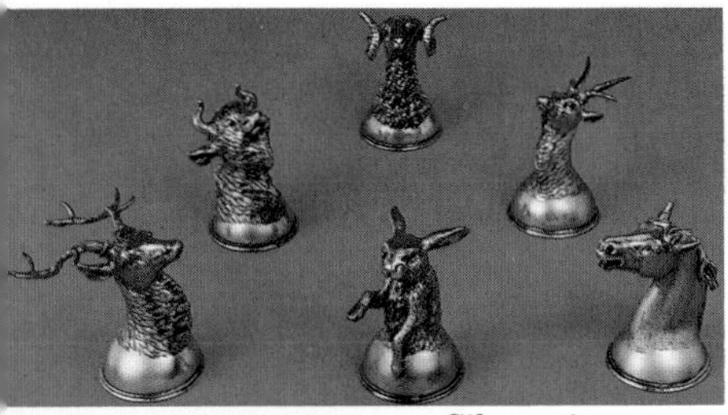

Silver stirrup cups in animal form, Samuel Arnd, St. Petersburg, 1863, 3in (8cm) high. **$4,000-5,000 each**

r. A silver 15-piece liquor service, St. Petersburg, 1880, gross weight 111oz. **$8,000-10,000**

A cloisonné enamel and silver gilt cruet, by Khlebnikov, Imperial Warrant Moscow, c1880, 12in (30cm). **$12,000-14,000**

A triptych painted in 17thC style, with semi-precious stones and mother-of-pearl, 18thC, 20in (50cm) high. **$25,000-30,000**

A portrait miniature of Alexander II, Czar of Russia, by Gustav Rockstuhl, signed and dated 1860, 5in (13cm). **$3,000-4,000**

A bound copy of Alex II Coronation ritual, 1856. **$15,000-20,000**

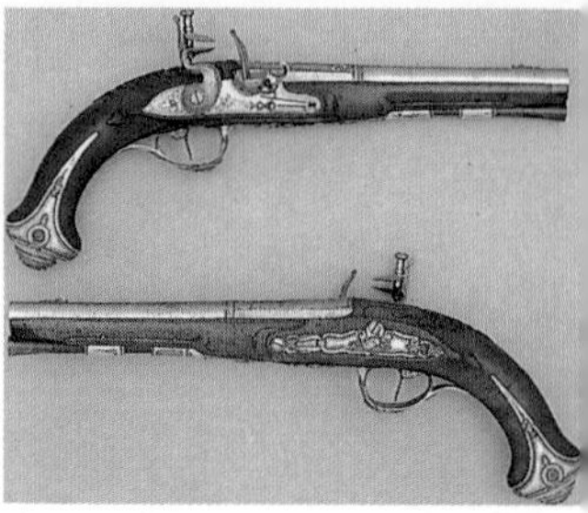

A pair of Russian flintlock holster pistols, unsigned, repaired, c1770, 15½in (39cm). **$25,000-30,000**

Seven portrait miniatures of the children of Czar Alexander II, on gold mounts, marked St. Petersburg, 1858, 6in (15cm) high. **$30,000-35,000**

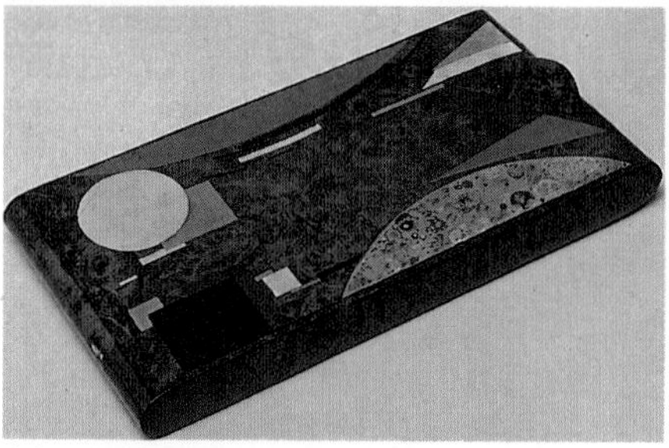

A birchwood cigarette case, decorated by Sergei Chekhonin, 6½ by 3½in (16.5 by 9cm). **$12,000-14,000**

An enamel parcel gilt icon of St. Basil the Great and St. Anisia, Moscow 1908-17, 12in (31cm) high. **$6,000-8,000**

A Fabergé peridot and diamond necklace, bracelet and ear-rings, pendant missing, St. Petersburg, 1899-1903, necklace 15in (38cm) long. **$45,000-50,000**

An icon, Tikhvin, Mother of God, painted in the classical style of the Moscow School, c1500, 39 by 30½in (98 by 77cm). **$15,000-20,000**

Two papier mâché lacquer Easter eggs, painted with the Resurrection, some wear, 19thC, 6in (16cm) high.
l. **$5,000-7,000**
r. **$7,000-9,000**

A white marble bust of Prince Alexander Borisovich Kurakin, possibly by F. I. Chubin, 29in (74cm) high. **$15,000-20,000**

A neo-classical design Axminster carpet, c1800, 379in (962cm) long. **$300,000+**

An Afshar rug, 77in (195cm) long. **$14,000-18,000**

An Aubusson carpet, repaired, mid-19thC. **$28,000-32,000**

r. An Afshar rug, worn and colour run, c1920, 68 by 50in (172 by 127cm). **$4,000-6,000**

A Louis Philippe Aubusson carpet, 191in (485cm) long. **$14,000-18,000**

An Afshar rug, 64 by 44in (163 by 111cm). **$16,000-20,000**

A Napoleon III Aubusson carpet, 239in (607cm) long. **$40,000-44,000**

r. An Agra carpet, 137in (347cm) long. **$14,000-18,000**

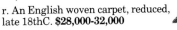

An Aubusson tapestry carpet, 248in (630cm). **$8,000-10,000**

r. An English woven carpet, reduced, late 18thC. **$28,000-32,000**

A Napoleon III Aubusson woven carpet, 161in (408cm) long.
$14,000-16,000

A Napoleon III Aubusson carpet, 324 by 222in (822 by 563cm).
$9,000-11,000

A Bakhtiari carpet, reduced in width, slight corrosion, 210 by 148in (787 by 376cm). **$18,000-20,000**

A Bakhtiari carpet of Qashqai design, with inscription cartouche at one end dated AH 1331 (AD1913), 275 by 151in (698 by 383cm). **$20,000-24,000**

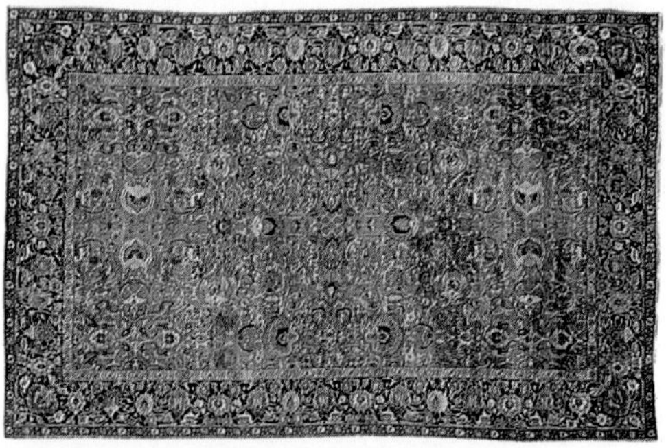

An Agra carpet, slight wear, 199 by 127in (505 by 322cm). **$10,000-12,000**

An Aubusson carpet, 141 by 97in (358 by 245cm). **$28,000-32,000**

l. A Bakhtiari carpet, minor repairs, 220 by 145in (558 by 368cm).
$16,000-20,000

Bidjar carpet, with allover Herati
ttern, worn, c1880, 217 by 139in
51 by 353cm).
4,000-28,000

A Bergama rug, worn, repaired and mounted, early 18thC, 59in (150cm) long.
$10,000-12,000

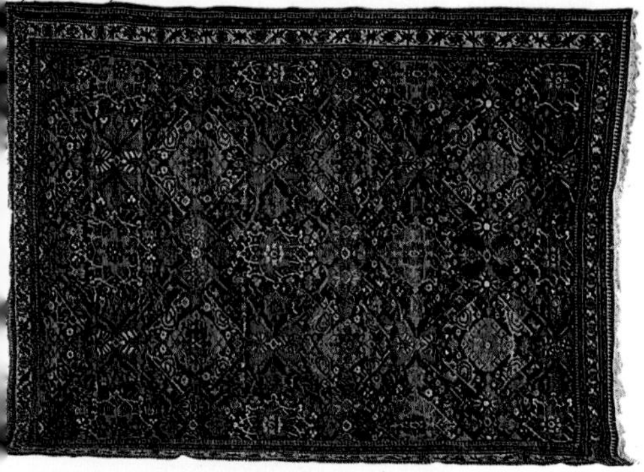

Bakhtiari carpet, 186 by 146in (472
y 370cm). **$12,000-16,000**

A Bidjar carpet, 264 by 133in (670 by 337cm). **$20,000-24,000**

r. A Chadjli rug, 119 by 44in (302 by 111cm).
$6,000-8,000

. Bergama rug, worn, replaced kilim at
ne end, repaired and mounted, early 18thC,
4in (163cm) long.
32,000-35,000

A Bakshaish carpet, reduced end guard borders, worn selvedges, late 19thC, 159 by 136in (403 by 345cm).
$16,000-20,000

A Daghestan rug, the ivory ground with stylised flowers, some wear, c1875, 52 by 42in (132 by 107cm).
$5,000-7,000

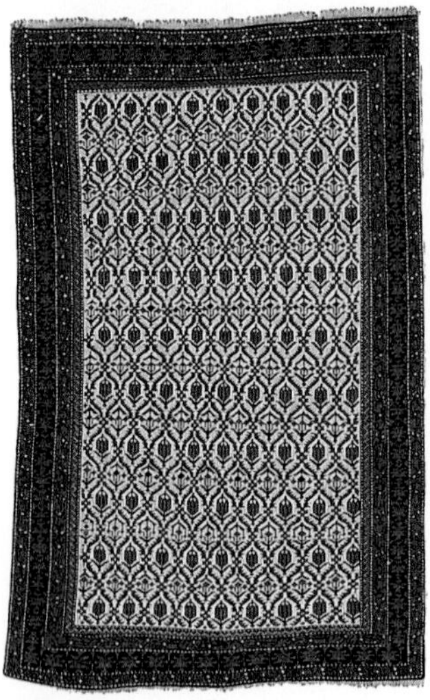

A Daghestan rug, some wear, c1875, 71 by 47in (180 by 120cm). **$3,500-4,000**

A Daghestan rug, the navy blue ground with allover pattern of latchhook devices, some wear, repairs, c1875, 58 by 44in (147 by 112cm). **$3,500-4,000**

A Bidjar carpet, the indigo field with cypress trees and flowering plants, in a brick red floral spray border, 141 by 78in (358 by 198cm).
$12,000-16,000

A Fereghan Sarouk rug, the red ground with allover Herati pattern, surrounded by blue primary border of palmettes, c1920, 79 by 52in (201 by 132cm).
$6,000-8,000

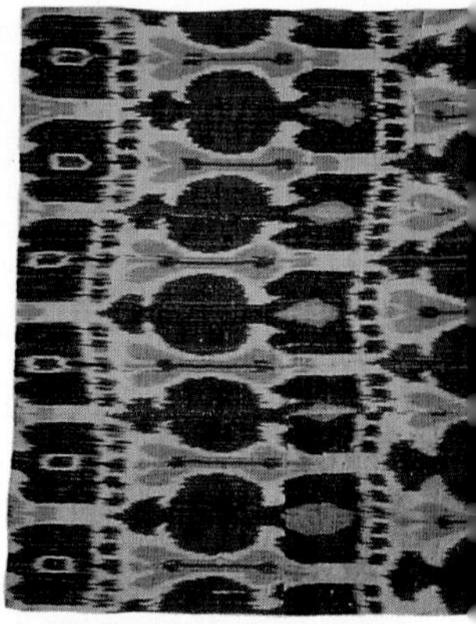

A silk Ikat technique wall hanging, Emirate of Bokhara, c1930, 48 by 71in (120 by 180cm). **$400-600**

A Fereghan carpet, the navy blue ground with allover Herati pattern, some wear, repaired, c1900, 149 by 107in (379 by 272cm).
$8,000-10,000

A Bidjar carpet, the camelhair ground covered by a navy blue pendant stepped centre medallion, c1900, 146 by 104in (370 by 264cm). **$12,000-15,000**

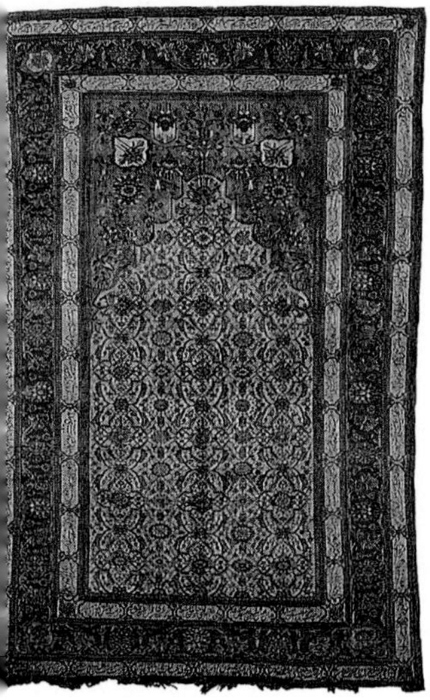

silk Fereghan prayer carpet,
paired and crease wear,
0 by 79in (304 by 200cm).
0,000-70,000

A Fereghan rug, slight damage to one side, 116 by 72in (294 by 182cm).
$5,000-7,000

A Gabbeh rug, c1920, 74 by 43in (188 by 109cm).
$2,000-2,500

Bidjar carpet, repaired,
5 by 138in (622 by 350cm).
5,000-40,000

A silk Hereke carpet, slight wear, c1920, 192 by 132in (487 by 355cm).
$24,000-30,000

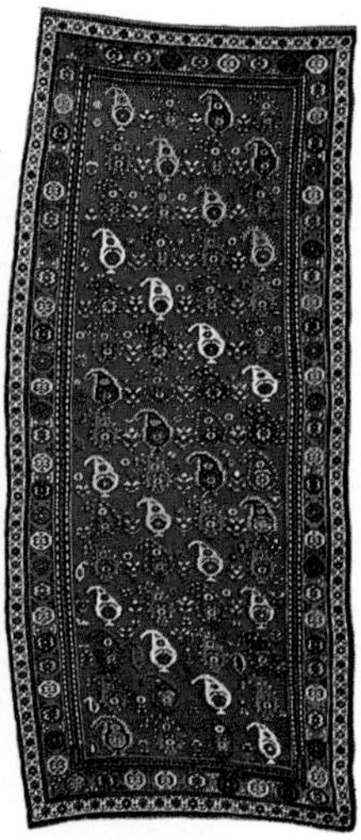

A Gendje rug, slight wear, late 19thC,
5in (190cm) long. **$8,000-10,000**
A Gendje rug, 124in (314cm).
4,000-6,000

l. A Fereghan Sarouk carpet, slight wear and stains, late 19thC, 160in (406cm) long. **$8,000-10,000**
r. A Gendje rug, old repairs, late 19thC, 92in (233cm).
$8,000-10,000

A South Caucasian prayer rug, even wear and repairs, c1840, 53 by 33in (135 by 83cm). **$5,000-6,000**

A Herat rug, the claret ground with an allover Shah Abbas design, surrounded by a navy blue primary border of palmettes, repaired, c1600, 83 by 55in (211 by 140cm). **$90,000-100,000**

A silk Herez rug, the rust ground with the Tree of Life and various animals, slight wear, outer border missing, c1875, 54in (137cm) wide. **$18,000-20,000**

A Herez carpet, the black field with palmettes and flowerheads, some wear and damage, 288 by 156in (580 by 399cm). **$10,000-12,000**

A Herez carpet, the stepped rust field with palmettes and angular foliate stems, within ivory and terracotta spandrels, 159 by 91in (404 by 231cm). **$7,000-9,000**

A Herez carpet, the rust ground with gold central medallion, some wear, loss to end borders, c1920, 125 by 96in (318 by 244cm). **$7,000-9,000**

A Herez carpet, the rust ground covered with a pattern of vines, palmettes and rosettes, surrounded by a navy blue border of rosettes, even wear, slight loss to end guard borders, c1900, 141 by 108in (358 by 274cm). **$10,000-12,000**

Herez rug, some wear, in (188cm) long. **,000-10,000**

A Kazak rug, small repair, damaged ends, 1886, 94in (238cm). **$9,000-11,000**

A silk and metal thread Istanbul rug, 77in (196cm) long. **$30,000-40,000**

Kazak rug, ends damaged d repaired, 79in (200cm). **4,000-16,000**

A Karabagh rug, some wear and re-piling, c1875, 93in (236cm) long. **$3,000-4,000**

A Herez carpet, areas of wear and repair, 131in (332cm) long. **$11,000-13,000**

Manchester Kashan prayer g, with a Tree of Life, ight wear, c1920, 79in 00cm) long. **1,000-13,000**

A silk warp Isfahan carpet, c1945, 140in (355cm) long. **$25,000-30,000**

Approx 1,000 knots per sq. in.

A Chelaberd Karabagh rug, breaks to selvedge and loss to kilim, c1900, 91in (231cm). **$12,000-16,000**

A Kazak rug, the tomato red field with green and blue medallions, 100 by 65in (254 by 165cm). **$20,000-25,000**

A Bessarabian kilim, the ivory field with floral sprays in a black flowering vine border, 93 by 68in (236 by 173cm). **$7,000-9,000**

A Kazak rug, with allover stars and trelliswork pattern, c1880, 76 by 52in (193 by 132cm). **$8,000-10,000**

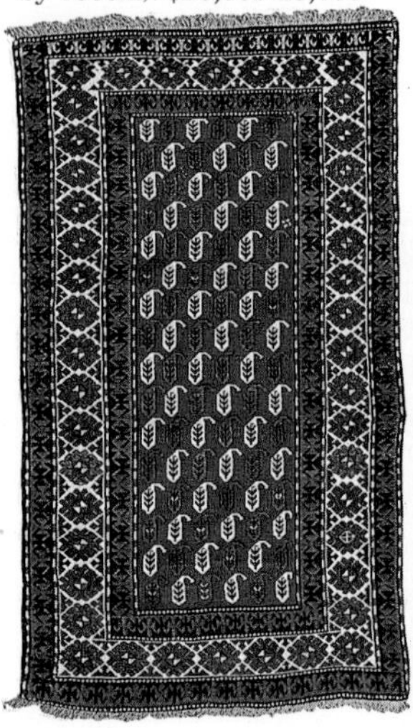

A Kazak rug, the red field with blue and ivory floral boteh, one corner repaired, 92 by 52in (234 by 132cm). **$4,000-6,000**

A Khamseh Confederacy rug, with allover pattern of birds and flowers, even wear, c1875, 73 by 52in (185 by 132cm). **$3,000-4,000**

A Konya long rug, with central five-part ivory outlined medallion, slight wear, c1900, 143 by 50in (365 by 127cm). **$4,000-6,000**

A Persian wool rug, Malagan, Hamadan district, c1920, 75 by 37in (190 by 95cm). **$1,200-1,500**

A Kazak runner, the navy blue ground covered with a Shah Abbas pattern, slight wear, c1880, 152 by 42in (386 by 107cm). **$10,000-12,000**

A Khotan silk rug, the indigo field with golden yellow sprays, embroidered fringes, 98 by 63in (249 by 160cm). **$8,000-10,000**

Qashqai rug, 83 by 60in
10 by 152cm).
,000-10,000

A Mogham rug, slight wear, late 19thC, 77 by 63in (195 by 160cm).
$6,000-8,000

A Zejwa Kuba rug, c1900, 96 by 55in (244 by 140cm).
$6,000-7,000

Savonnerie style pile carpet, woven in various colours,
:e 18thC, 165 by 157in (419 by 398cm).
0,000-45,000

A Zejwa Kuba rug, slight wear and repairs, late 19thC, 70in (177cm) long.
$8,000-10,000

Qashqai mille fleurs
ayer rug, with kilim strip
one end, 84in (213cm)
ng. **$50,000-60,000**

A Lenkoran rug, 127 by 43in (322 by 109cm).
$7,000-8,000

A Nain carpet, with ivory silk highlights, contemporary, 150in (381cm) long. **$10,000-12,000**

A Shirvan prayer rug, wear and repairs, c1860, 60 by 47in (152 by 119cm).
$8,000-10,000

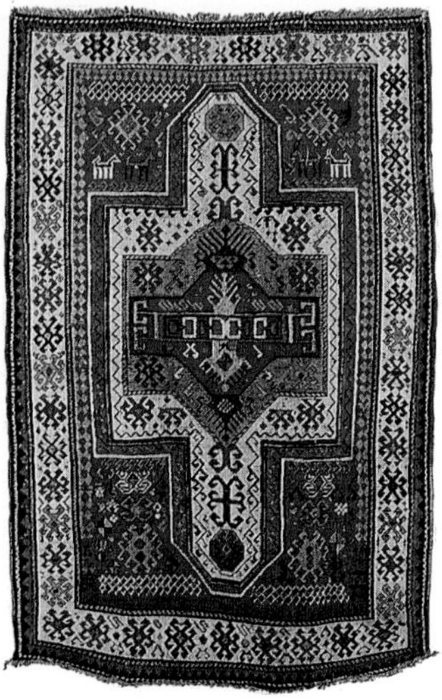

A Sewan Kazak rug, worn, late 19thC, 85 by 56in (216 by 142cm).
$5,000-6,000

A Shakhrizyabz Suzani silk embroidery, small breaks, 94in (238cm).
$11,000-13,000

A Senneh rug, with a kilim strip at each end, 58in (147cm) long.
$4,000-6,000

A Shirvan rug, slight damage to ends, 135in (342cm) long. **$12,000-16,000**

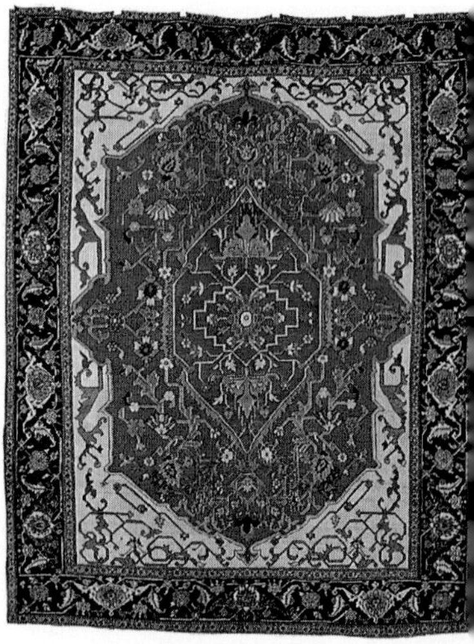

A Serapi carpet, some wear, c1875, 141 by 113in (358 by 287cm). **$20,000-25,000**

A Serapi carpet, with 5 narrow decorative guard borders, slight wear, c1875, 168in (426cm) long. **$20,000-24,000**

A Serapi carpet, slight wear, c1880, 155in (393cm).
$18,000-20,000

Susani with central octagonal floral
edallion with radiating floral sprays,
e broad border with flowering plants,
ght staining, 88 by 80in (224 by
4cm). **$8,000-10,000**

A Shirvan Kelleh, the ivory border with hooked vine, dated AH 1333/AD 1914, 134 by 69in (340 by 175cm). **$7,000-9,000**

A silk Tabriz prayer rug, the ivory field with various figures, the 2 blue floral columns supporting a burgundy mihrab, slight wear, 72 by 53in (183 by 135cm). **$12,000-14,000**

Soumak carpet, the red ground with
arge navy blue medallions, slight
ar, c1875, 100 by 88in (254 by
4cm). **$10,000-12,000**

A Turkish prayer rug, Bergama, some repairs, c1830, 65 by 49in (165 by 125cm). **$6,000-8,000**

A Lesghi Shirvan rug, the red ground with 2 rows of Lesghi stars, surrounded by a narrow floral border, slight wear, c1875, 73 by 41in (186 by 104cm). **$5,000-7,000**

A Sileh carpet, with stylised ivory and
navy dragon, slight damage and repairs,
c1875, 76in (193cm) wide. **$10,000-12,000**

A Marasali Shirvan rug, the blue ground with various figures and animals, flanked by stylised snakes, small repairs, c1875, 54 by 44in (137 by 112cm). **$5,000-7,000**

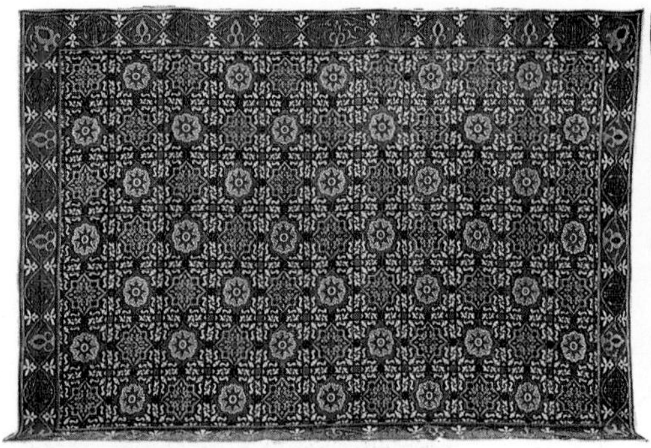

A Turkish carpet, the medium brown field with allover design of palmette octagons and stars, 192 by 140in (488 by 354cm).
$12,000-16,000

l. A Spanish carpet, slight staining, inscribed RFT and MD 1969, 201in (510cm) long. **$10,000-12,000**
r. A Yarkand carpet, 155in (393cm) long.
$14,000-16,000

A Chinese dragon carpet, the blue ground with a pair of dragons at each end and a circular one in the centre, slight wear and mothing, early 20thC, 122in (309cm) long. **$20,000-24,000**

A Chinese pillar rug, with a pair of five-claw dragons, some wear, c1875, 96in (243cm). **$6,000-8,000**

A Tabriz carpet, c1920, 162in (411cm) long.
$8,000-10,000

A Chinese carpet, with the 8 horses of Mu Wang surrounded by key fret border, 106in (269cm) long.
$11,000-13,000

A Chinese wool rug, Baotou district, c1920, 43in (110cm) long.
$700-900

A Tekke Turkoman carpet, worn, 108in (274cm) long.
$6,000-8,000

Flemish verdure tapestry,
›ven in silks and wools,
›rly 17thC, 125in (318cm)
ıg. **$15,000-21,000**

A needlework picture or cushion, worked in silk in tent stitch with the Life of Abraham signed 1634, E.P., 22in (56cm) high, in glazed tortoiseshell frame.
$16,000-18,000

A Brussels tapestry, cut and shut, later slip, restorations, 17thC, 115in (292cm) high. **$14,000-16,000**

Brussels tapestry,
oven in silks and
ools, cut and shut,
te 16thC, 139in
53cm) high.
,000-10,000

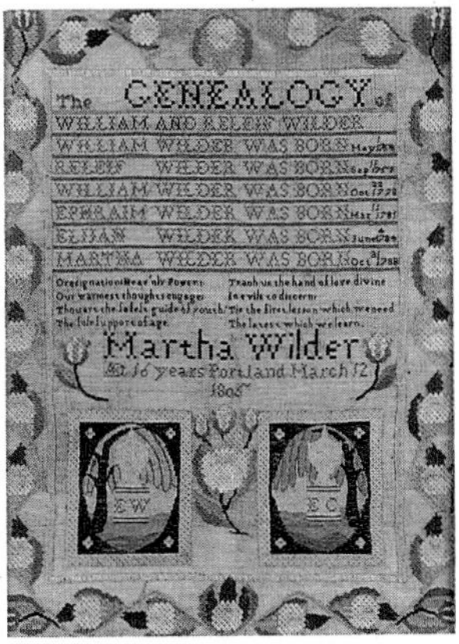

A needlework sampler, signed 'Martha Wilder', Portland, Maine, 1805, 24in (61cm) high. **$10,000-12,000**

An embroidered wool coverlet, restored, c1825, 99in (241cm) high. **$12,000-14,000**

r. A silk-on-silk embroidered coat-of-arms, by Elizabeth Flower, Philadelphia, c1765, 12in (30.5cm) high.
$32,000-40,000

An American appliqued cotton quilted coverlet, some browning, c1820, 98in (249cm).
$4,000-5,000

l. A four-colour wool and cotton jacquard coverlet, Daniel Snyder, Hanover Township, Pennsylvania, 1839, 92in (233cm) long.
$2,500-3,000

r. An American appliqued cotton quilted coverlet, some foxing, c1825, 92in (233cm).
$6,000-7,000

An American Mennonite pieced cotton quilted coverlet, c1890, 75 by 80in (190 by 203cm).
$6,000-8,000

A Chinese saddle cover, early 20thC, 53in (134.5cm) long.
$500-600

An American appliqued and stuffed album quilt, 1850.
$140,000-160,000

An American appliqued and embroidered cotton pictorial quilted coverlet, 1932, 84in (213cm). **$50,000-60,000**

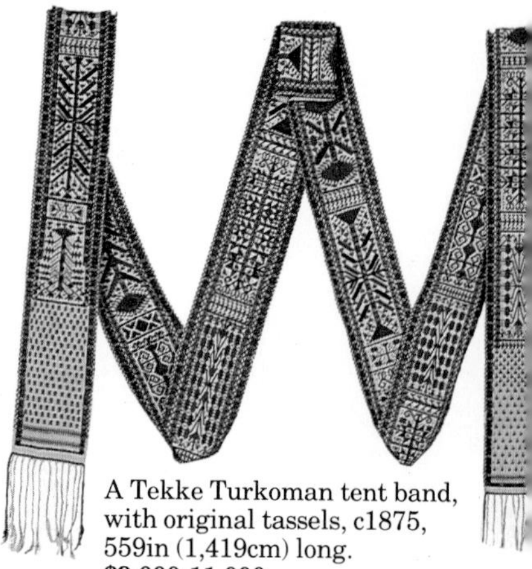

A Tekke Turkoman tent band, with original tassels, c1875, 559in (1,419cm) long.
$9,000-11,000

Ladies silk Ikat technique dresses, Emirate of Bokhara, Uzbekistan, c1900, l. **$600-700**
r. **$900-1,000**

An American pieced cotton quilted coverlet, worn, c1830, 120in (304cm).
$6,000-7,000

An American pieced and embroidered silk and velvet coverlet, c1880, 89in (226cm).
$10,000-12,000

A pair of Yomud Turkoman asmalyks, worn and stained, late 19thC, 48in (122cm) wide.
$8,000-10,000

A set of 4 George IV wine coasters, the sides chased with trailing vines and with shell and scroll everted rims, with turned wood bases, by S. C. Younge & Co., Sheffield, 1827.
$4,000-5,000

A set of 6 George IV Scottish wine coasters, on turned wood bases, the sides cast and chased with trailing vines and with fluted borders, the print engraved with a crest and motto, by Robert Gray & Son, Glasgow, 1820.
$16,000-18,000

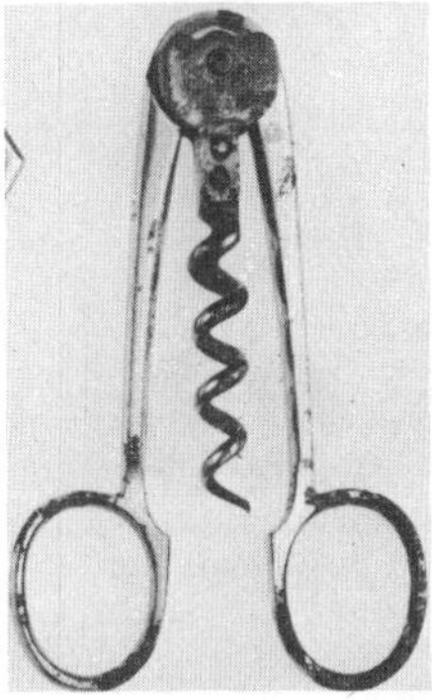

A pair of scissor-type champagne wire nippers and corkscrew combination.
$160-200

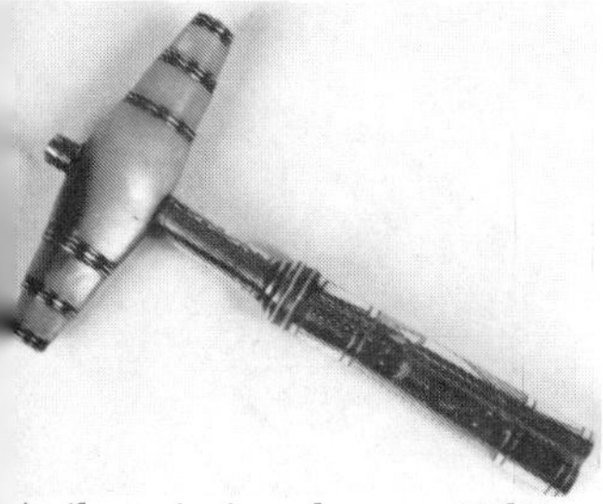

A silver picnic corkscrew, 18thC.
$500-600

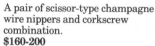

A corkscrew with finger ring, c1880, 6in (15cm).
$30-50

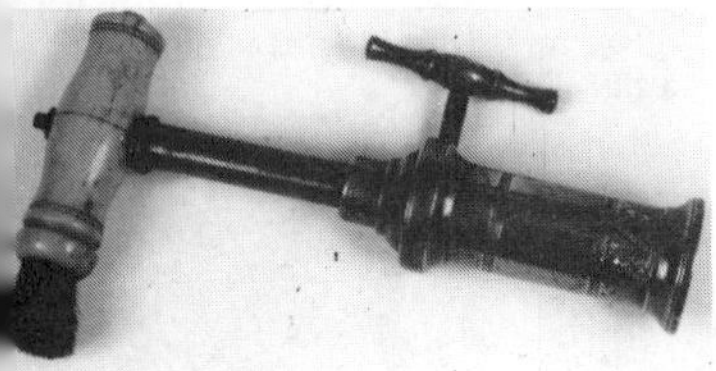

A king screw with arms, marked 'Dowler', c1840.
$500-700

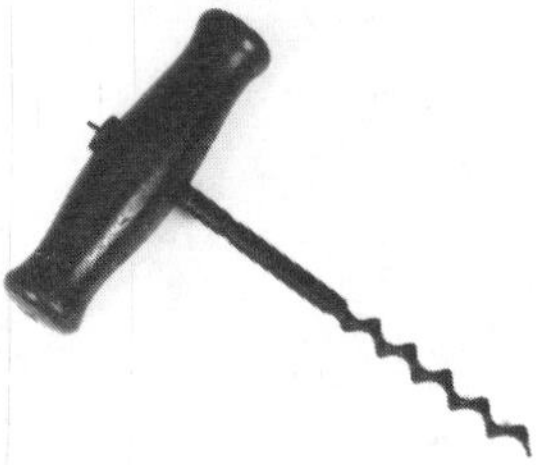

A wooden handled corkscrew, 19thC, 5½in (14cm).
$20-40

A Thomason corkscrew, with coat-of-arms, 19thC.
$300-400

A Weirs Patent multi-lever corkscrew.
$120-160

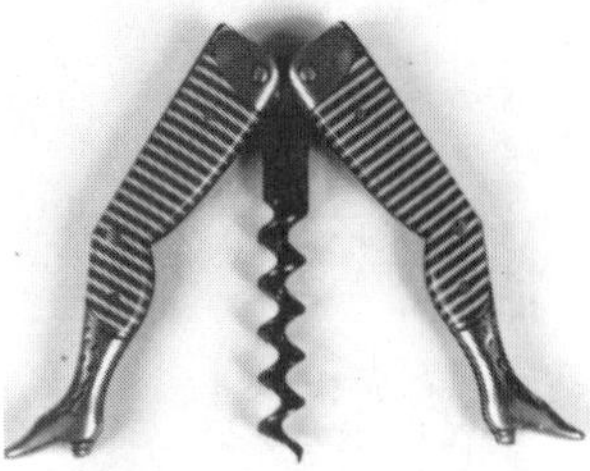

A German enamelled corkscrew, c1900.
$300-400

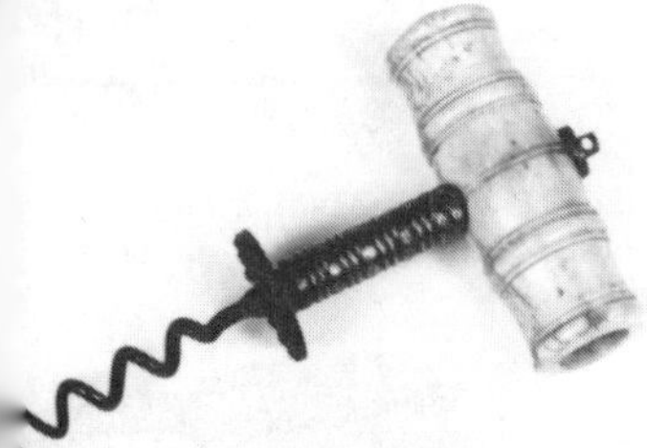

A baluster stemmed corkscrew, with turned bone handle, 5½in (14cm).
$80-120

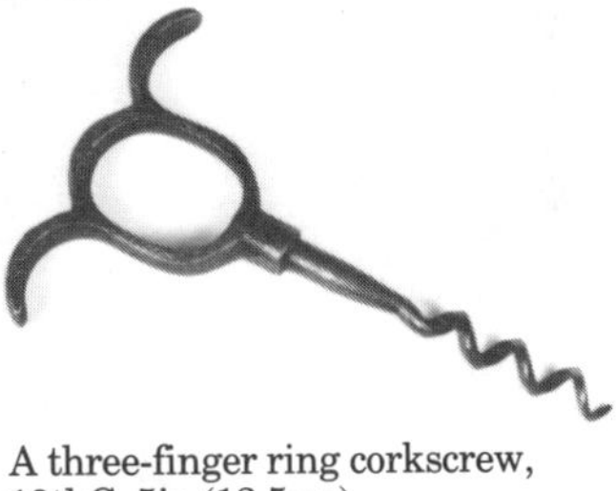

A three-finger ring corkscrew, 19thC, 5in (12.5cm).
$20-30

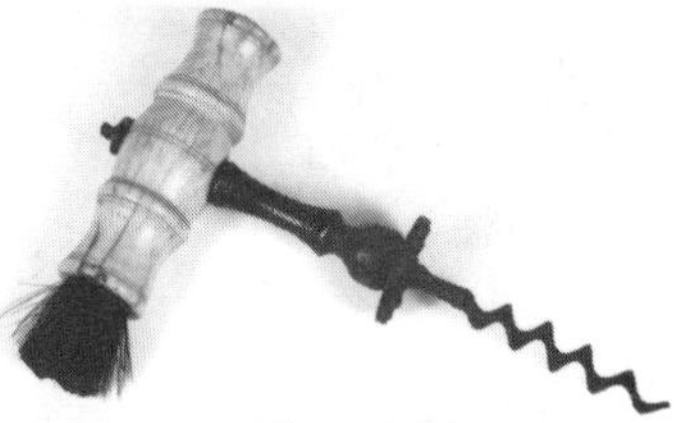

A corkscrew with turned bone handle, 6in (15cm).
$100-140

A Universal 4-finger corkscrew, 1870, 5in (12.5cm).
$80-140

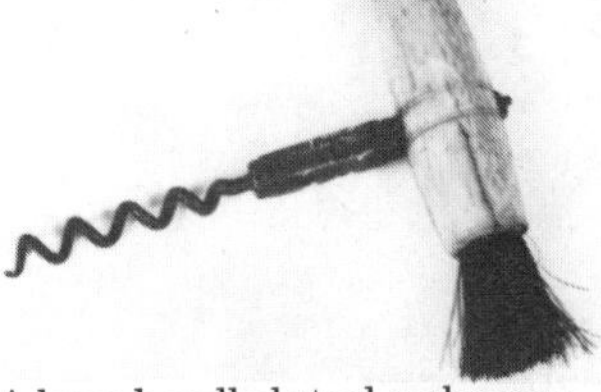

A bone handled steel corkscrew, with brush, 5½in (14cm).
$60-100

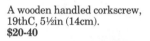

An English champagne tap, 7in (18cm).
$100-140

METAL
Pewter

A pewter measure, 2½in (6cm) high.
$45-70

A pewter box, 3in (7.5cm) diam.
$20-40

A pewter tazza, 8in (20.5cm) diam.
$60-100

A German flagon with lid, c1800 9in (23cm) high.
$350-400

A pair of Regency pewter candlesticks, c1810, 9in (23cm) high.
$500-600

A pewter warming dish, with blue and white liner, 11in (28cm) diam.
$80-120

A pewter serving dish, with 2 pairs of servers, 19in (48cm) wide.
$450-500

An English pewter charger, with all-over hammered decoration, c1700, 18in (46cm) diam.
$400-500

An English pewter charger, c1690, 18in (46cm) diam.
$400-500

A Scottish flagon, c1780, 10in (25.5cm) high.
$450-550

A pewter measur 2in (6cm) high.
$14-20

A French flagon with lid, 18thC, 9½in (24cm) high.
$400-500

A Scottish pewter charger, c1800, 15in (38cm).
$300-400

A set of 3 pewter measures, quart, pint and ½ pint, 19thC.
$250-300

A pair of English pewter quart jugs, c1840, 6½in (16.5cm) high.
$300-400

A pewter tankard.
$150-200

A pewter measure, 19thC, 3in (7.5cm).
$40-100

n English pewter tankard, c1920,
n (12.5cm).
50-200

A set of 6 pewter half pint tankards, c1840, 4in (10cm).
$400-450

A collapsible pewter drinking vessel, 3in (7.5cm) high.
$20-30

pewter measure, 19thC, 4in
0cm).
'0-90

Brass

A pair of French brass candlesticks, 18thC, 9½in (24cm).
$1,400-1,500

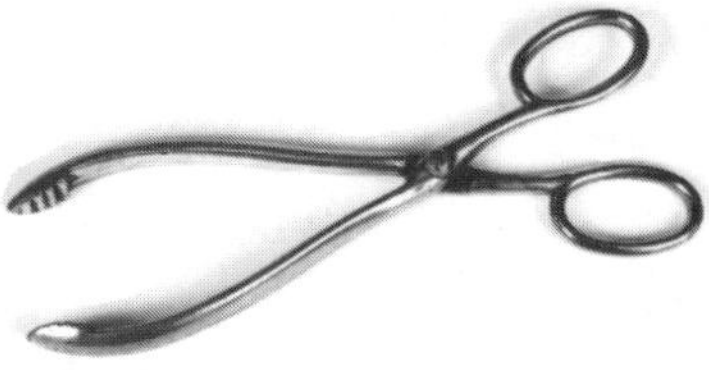

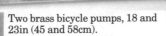

A pair of brass tongs.
$20-30

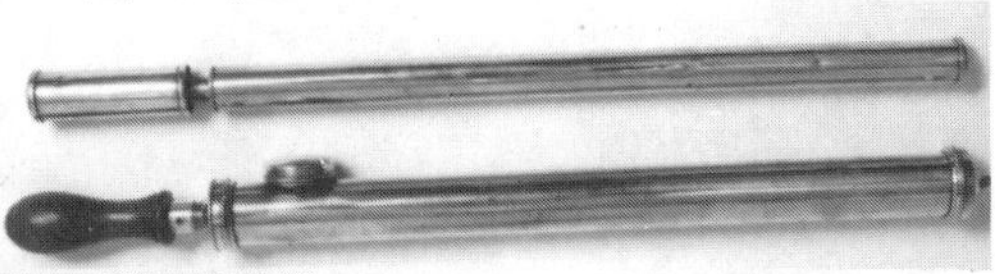

Two brass bicycle pumps, 18 and 23in (45 and 58cm).
$60-80 each

A brass parrot cage, early 19thC, 42in (106.5cm).
$1,000-1,200

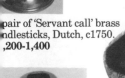

pair of 'Servant call' brass
ndlesticks, Dutch, c1750.
,200-1,400

A selection of 19thC horse brasses.
$20-50 each

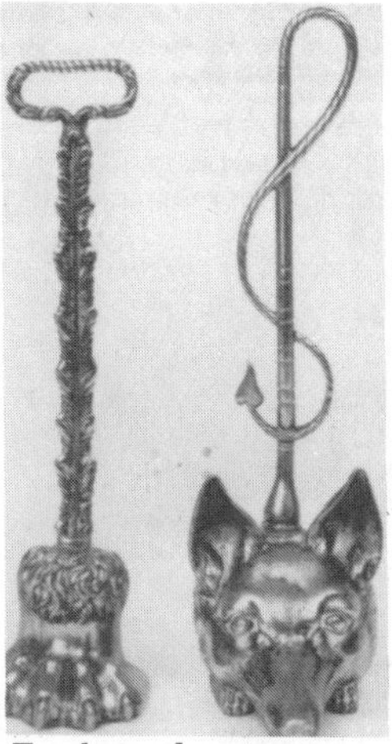

Two brass doorstops, 17in (43cm) high.
$200-300 each

A pair of Victorian lacquered brass banker's beam balance scales, by W & T Avery Ltd., on mahogany base with drawer, 35in (89cm) high.
$500-600

An Oriental brass vase.
$40-80

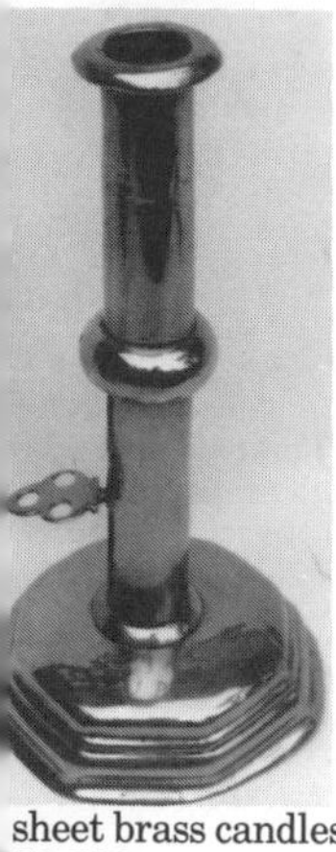

sheet brass candlestick, c1700.
:50-300

A brass bowl with coloured stones, 19thC, 8in (20cm) diam.
$60-100

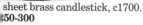

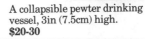

A Victorian brass trivet, 9in (23cm).
$40-80

Bronze

A Roman bronze head of a Flavian lady, 17th/18thC, 14½in (37cm) high.
$16,000-20,000

A French bronze bust of Napoleon, attributed to Noel Ruffier, signed Noel R, on turned marble and ormolu socle, 4in (10cm) high.
$600-1,000

A French bronze figure of Psyche, patina worn, base signed Math. Moreau, late 19thC, 26½in (67cm) high.
$3,500-4,000

A pair of bronze figures of dancers, 12in (30.5cm) high.
$1,300-1,500

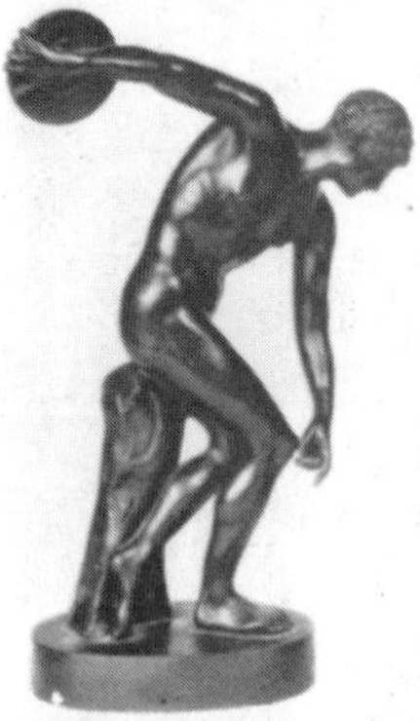

A bronze figure, early 19thC, 9½in (24cm) high.
$600-700

A French bronze bust of a young child, signed Jul(es) Lagae, 19thC, 11in (28cm) high, on rouge marble stand.
$800-900

A pair of Equestrian hunting groups of Francois I of France and his Queen, on veined marble bases, 19thC, 16in (40.5cm) high.
$4,000-5,000

A Roman bronze statuette of the infant Mercury, from the workshop of Francesco Righetti, the infant god with wings in his hair and a purse in his hand, late 18thC, 9in (23cm) high.
$3,000-4,000

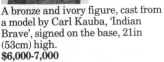

A bronze and ivory figure, cast from a model by Carl Kauba, 'Indian Brave', signed on the base, 21in (53cm) high.
$6,000-7,000

A bronze model of an eagle with a crane caught in its talons, unsigned, late 19thC, 34½in (88cm) wide.
$1,800-2,500

An Anglo-Florentine bronze of Africa, attributed to Francesco Fanelli, the continent depicted as a negress, with an elephant mask, 17thC, 5in (13cm) high.
$5,000-6,000

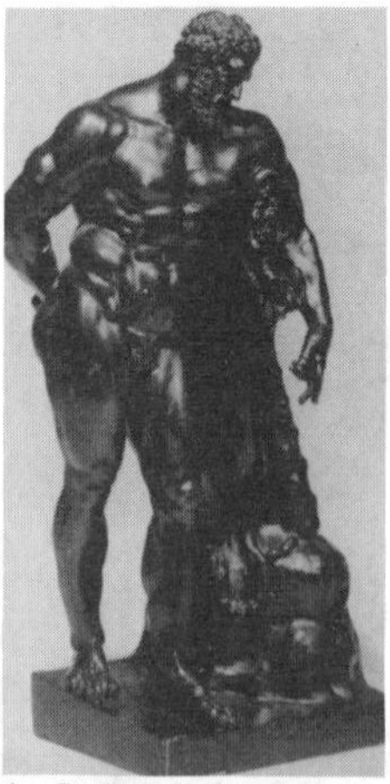

An Italian bronze group of the Farnese Hercules, fig leaf damaged, late 18thC, 13½in (34cm) high.
$7,000-8,000

A pair of bronze vase oil lamps, with twin scroll handles and applied with goat maskheads, acanthus and neo-classical ornament, c1840.
$1,400-2,000

n Italian or French gilt bronze
gure of a wild boar, on red marble
ase, 19thC, 4½in (12cm) high.
2,500-3,000

A Roman bronze model of Christ and Saint Paul, hole for suspension, late 15thC, 3½in (8cm) diam.
$2,000-2,500

A French or Italian bronze profile of The Virgin, inscribed within the beaded border, traces of gilt and pierced for suspension, 17thC, 8in (20cm) high.
$500-800

A Roman bronze figure of Bacchus, standing by a tree stump with a panther, repaired, 18thC, 14in (36cm) high.
$4,000-6,000

Regency bronze Argand table
amp, 12½in (31cm) wide.
800-1,000

An Italian bronze model of a panther, tail missing, 16thC, on wooden plinth, 8½in (21cm) high.
$8,000-9,000

A bronze model of an elephant with ivory tusks, tusks reglued, signed Toho, late 19thC, 18in (46cm) long.
$1,800-2,500

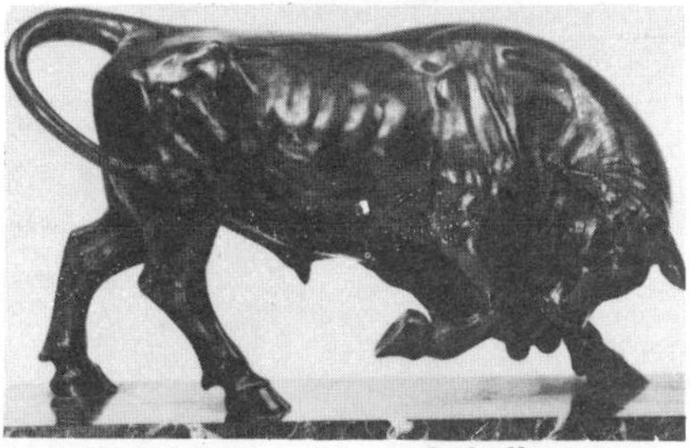

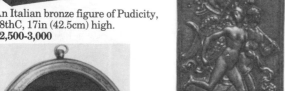

A French bronze figure of a bull, 16in (40.5cm) long.
$700-800

n Italian bronze figure of Pudicity,
8thC, 17in (42.5cm) high.
2,500-3,000

A bronze figure of a young discus thrower, early 19thC, 7½in (19cm) high.
$500-600

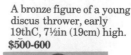

A North Italian bronze satyr's head door knob, late 16th/early 17thC, 6½in (16.5cm).
$3,000-4,000

A Paduan bronze plaque of Mars and Victory, by Moderno, hole for suspension, surface slightly worn, early 16thC, 2½in (7cm) high.
$5,000-6,000

pair of French bronze medallions
Baccantes, signed Clodion, in
molu frames with loops for
spension, early 19thC, 8in (20cm).
,000-6,000

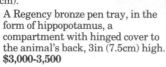

A Regency bronze pen tray, in the form of hippopotamus, a compartment with hinged cover to the animal's back, 3in (7.5cm) high.
$3,000-3,500

Copper

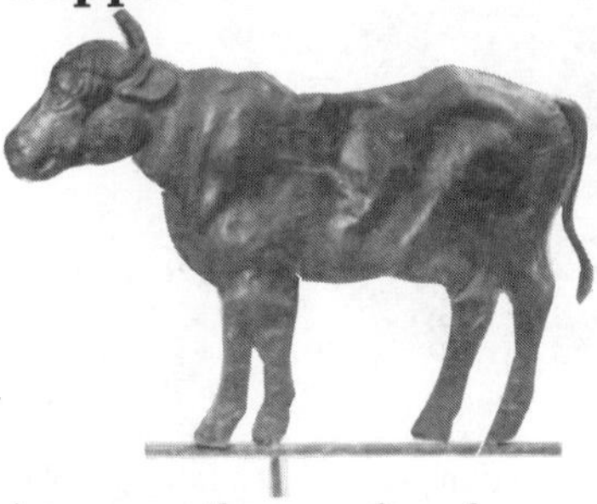

A copper weather vane, formed as a figure of a cow, 31in (79cm) wide.
$400-600

A George III copper and brass tea kettle, with twin ebonised handles.
$400-500

A copper plant holder, 6½in (17cm) high.
$50-60

A copper kettle.
$60-100

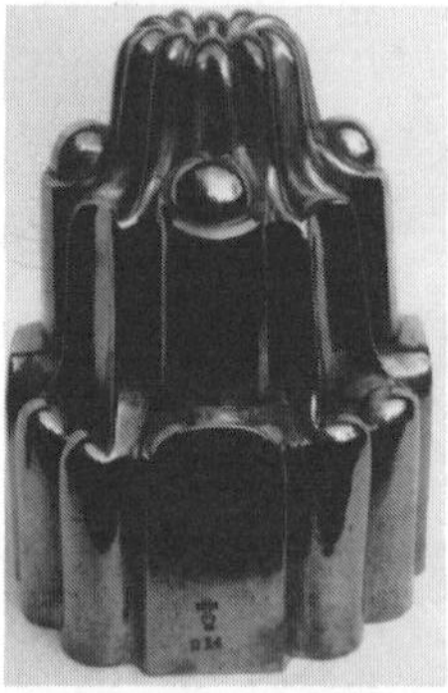

A Victorian copper jelly mould.
$160-200

Iron

A Regency iron and brass door knocker, c1830.
$120-150

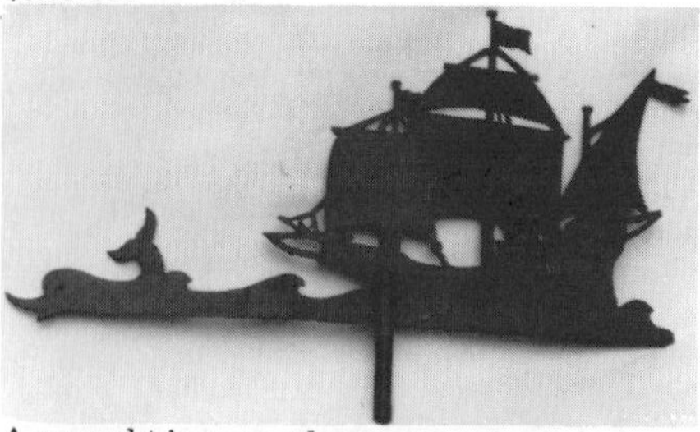

A wrought iron weather vane.
$200-250

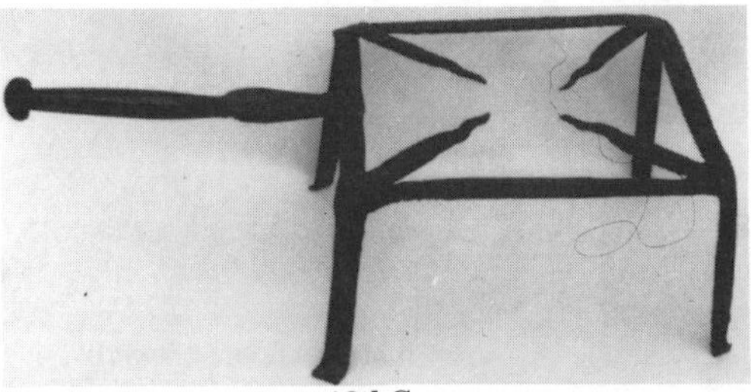

A wrought iron trivet, 18thC.
$150-200

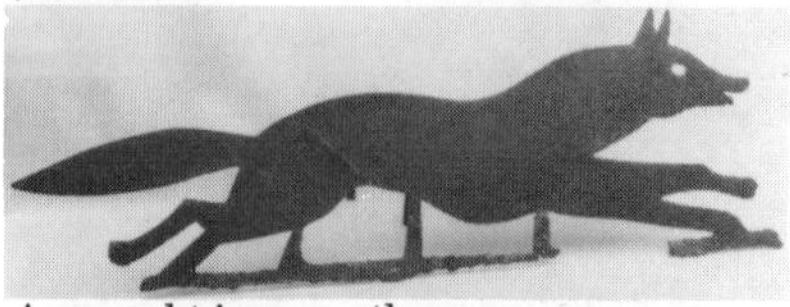

A wrought iron weather vane, 18thC.
$300-350

Two wrought iron firebacks:
l Tudor coat-of-arms, c1600.
r. James I, dated 1619.
$600-1,000 each

A wrought iron adjustable pot hook, c1760.
$60-80

An iron and brass door knocker, c1800.
$100-120

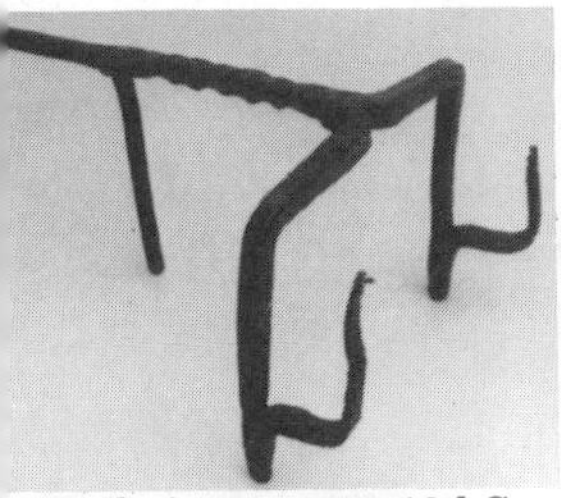

wrought iron toaster, 18thC.
50-200

An English wrought iron trivet, c1800.
$100-120

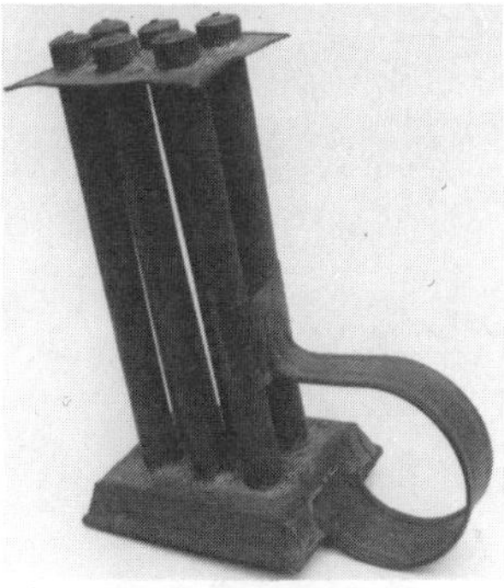

A tin candle mould, c1830.
$140-160

set of late Regency cast iron elves, with lyre-shaped supports d leaf cast finials, 34½in (85cm) de.
,000-5,000

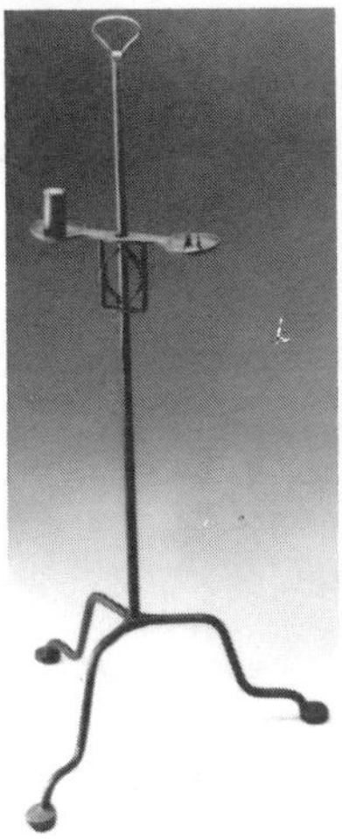

Irish iron candlestand, c1760.
000-1,200

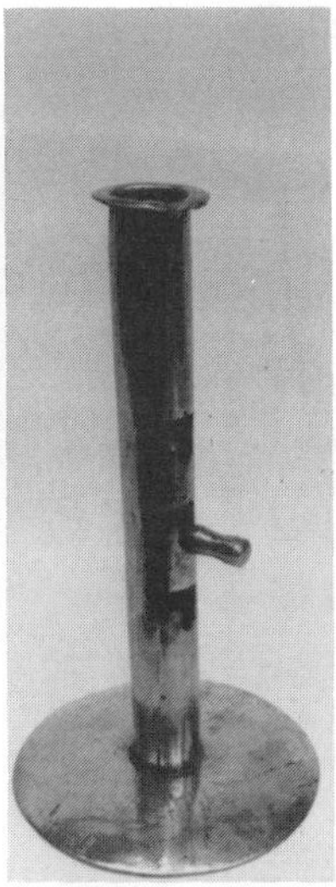

A sheet iron candle-holder, c1800, 9in (23cm) high.
$160-180

An ormolu triptych folding photograph frame, to take 15 miniatures, 19thC, 11in (29cm) high.
$400-500

rmolu

French ormolu plaque applied th sunburst surmount, with pework and scroll border, 19thC, in (63cm) high.
00-1,000

An Empire ormolu wall bracket, formerly part of a chandelier, 6½in (16cm) wide.
$800-900

A Regency ormolu cylindrical cover, the domed top with pineapple finial, 7½in (19cm) high.
$2,000-3,000

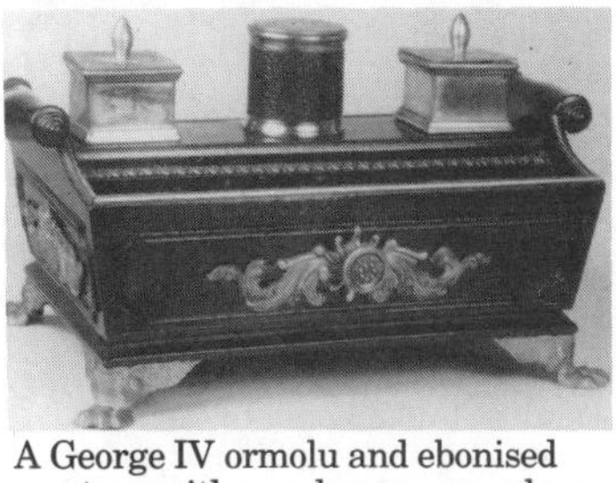

A George IV ormolu and ebonised pen tray with one drawer, one glass liner missing, 13½in (34cm) wide.
$2,000-3,000

A pair of French gilt ormolu candelabra, 19thC.
$1,000-1,200

A pair of ormolu chenets of Louis XVI style, with flaming urn finials and bow-and-arrow trophies, on faceted tapering legs and foliate feet, 12in (31cm) high.
$1,500-2,000

Miscellaneous

A pair of tôle peinte chestnut urns, early 19thC, 10in (26cm) high.
$6,000-8,000

A brass and tôleware twin light desk lamp, 25in (64cm) high.
$500-700

A German statuette of a huntsman, influenced by Simon Troger, on wood stand, c1800, 7½in (19cm).
$3,000-4,000

IVORY

Ivory & Shell

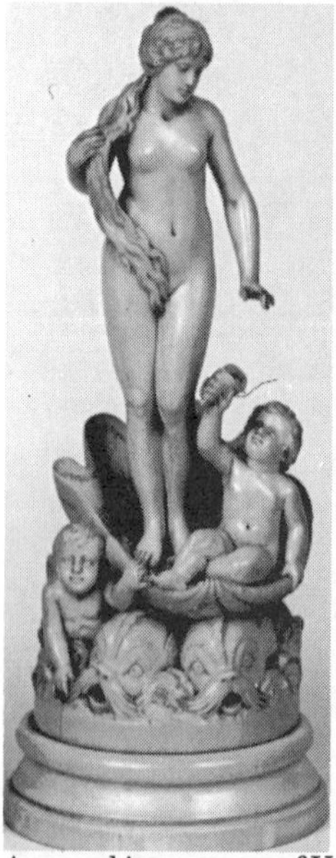

A carved ivory group of Venus, mid-19thC, 10in (26cm) high.
$4,000-6,000

A carved ivory figure of the Virgin and Child, in the French Gothic style, 19thC, 19in (49cm).
$6,000-8,000

A set of 4 carved ivory figures, emblematic of the Four Senses, Sight, Touch, Taste and Hearing, 11½in (29cm). **$8,000-10,000**

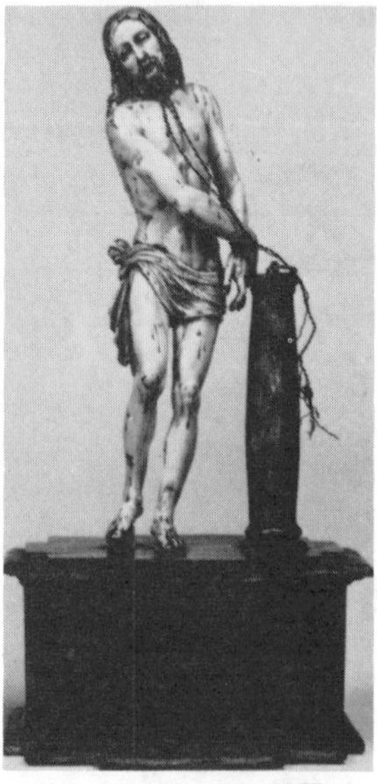

A Spanish statuette of Christ as man of sorrows at the column, 17thC, 14in (35cm) high.
$3,000-4,000

A pair of Italian Comedy figures, on wood socles, 5½in (14cm).
$1,500-2,000

A German tankard shaft with cavorting putti, attributed to the workshop of J. J. Betzoldt, late 17thC, 5in (13cm) high.
$4,000-5,000

A Colonial group of the Virgin, Christ Child and St. John the Baptist, 18thC, 9½in (25cm) wide.
$4,000-6,000

An English bust of Mrs. Emmeline Pankhurst, by A. G. Walker, signed on the back, early 20thC, 6½in (16.5cm).
$6,000-8,000

Arthur George Walker (1861-1939), R.A., exhibited at the Royal Academy from 1884 onwards. He made a monumental bronze figure of Mrs. Pankhurst, which was erected in 1930, in Victoria Gardens. Mrs. Emmeline Pankhurst (1858-1928) founded the Women's Social and Political Union in 1903, and was a celebrated suffragette.

MARBLE

An English marble bust of Lady Antonina Le Despenser, by John Bacon, inscribed Antonina, the only daughter of Francis, Baron Le Despenser, also Philopatria and signed behind the right shoulder J. Bacon, early 19thC, 28in (71cm).
$30,000-35,000

A pair of Indian vases on stands, each in 3 sections, 19thC, 32in (82cm) high.
$1,000-1,500

A weathered white marble figure of Aphrodite, 18th/19thC, 36in (92cm).
$1,000-1,500

A French marble group of cupids, after an 18thC original, 19thC, 25in (64cm).
$3,500-4,500

An Italian figure of Venus, 19thC, 47in (121cm) high.
$3,000-4,000

A Flemish relief of the Mater Dolorosa, by Laurent Delvaux, damaged, 18thC, 13 by 9in (33.5 by 23.5cm).
$1,000-1,500

A figure of a recumbent infant, incised A. Bertuzzi Roma, 1877, 19thC, 20in (51cm).
$3,000-4,000

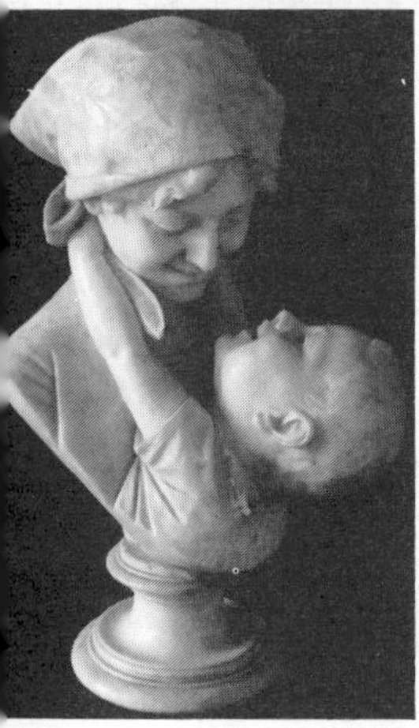

An Italian bust of a mother and her child, signed, E. Fiaschi, socle repaired, 19thC, 22½in (57cm).
$1,400-1,600

An Austrian group of a dancing bacchante with a faun, by Theodor Friedl, damaged, late 19thC, 53in (136cm) high.
$30,000-40,000

Terracotta/Stone

A pair of terracotta herms, 19thC, 58in (148cm).
$1,500-2,000

A French group, incised Clesinger, early 19thC, 25½in (65cm).
$3,000-4,000

A carved stone standing figure of the Virgin and Child, 59½in (151cm).
$30,000-40,000

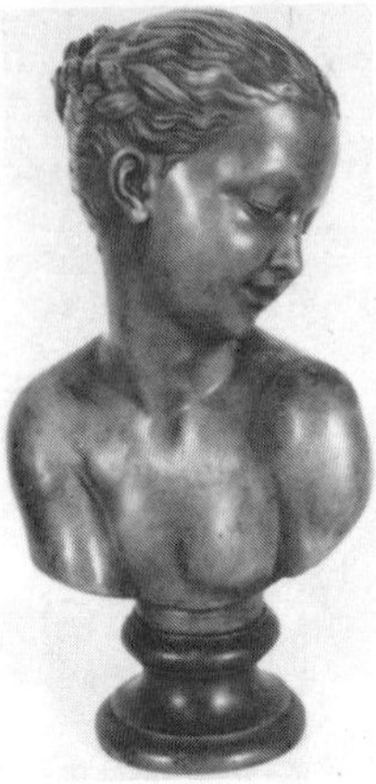

A bust of a young woman, incised La Ronte, impressed 222 mark, 18in (46cm).
$500-600

An English terracotta statue of the Art of Painting, damaged, signed, A. Drury 1886, 15½in (39.5cm).
$1,000-1,500

A French relief of the See-saw, aft Clodion, 19thC, 12 by 12½in (30 b 32cm).
$1,000-1,200

A French group, in the manner of Clodion, damaged, 19thC, 12½in (32cm).
$5,000-6,000

A Davenport two-handled jardinière, 10in (24cm).
$1,500-2,000

A Greek figure of a seated youth, c3rd Century BC, 6in (14.5cm).
$2,000-2,500

A French buff plaque of a satyress with 2 babies, in the style of Marin c1800, 5 by 6in (13 by 16cm).
$800-1,000

A pair of brown glazed stoneware figures, stamped Earnley Irons, Leeds, 40in (101cm) long.
$2,500-3,000

A French maquette for a monumental group of 3 classical females, mid-19thC, 8in (21cm).
$1,500-2,000

A Louis XVI Frenc maquette for a funeral monument 18thC, 7in (18.5cm).
$2,000-3,000

A French group of a young maiden, damaged, by Clodion, late 18thC, 15½in (40cm).
$15,000-20,000

A French bust of a little boy, signed on shoulder, A. Pajou, c1800, 17in (43cm).
$10,000-12,000

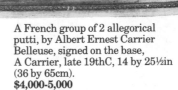

A French group of 2 allegorical putti, by Albert Ernest Carrier Belleuse, signed on the base, A Carrier, late 19thC, 14 by 25½in (36 by 65cm).
$4,000-5,000

A French bust of a Prince in armour, signed Chinard, 19thC, 26in (66cm).
$5,000-6,000

/oodcarvings

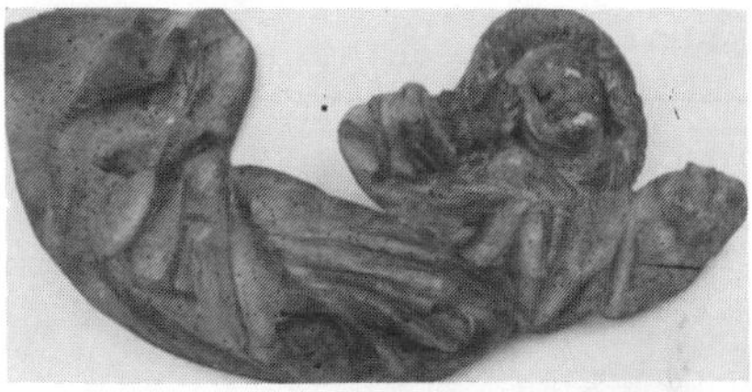

A South German carved limewood angel awakening from sleep, with incised hair, c1500, 17½in (44cm) wide.
$3,000-4,000

A pair of Flemish oak carved caryatids, 17thC, 18in (46cm) high.
$600-800

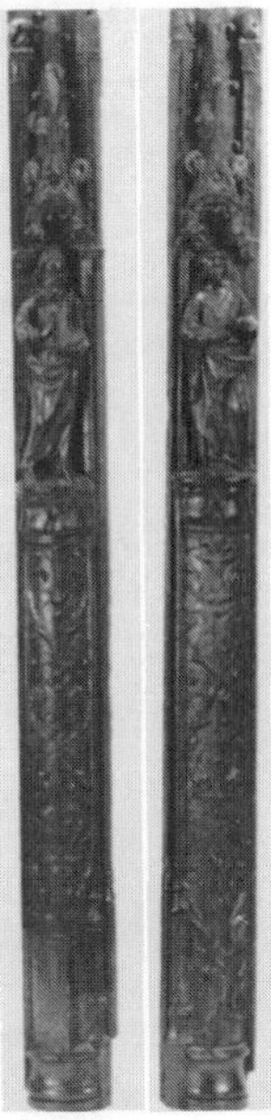

A pair of Franco-Flemish Gothic oak pilasters, depicting St. John the Baptist and another saint, damaged and restored, early 16thC, 59in (147cm) high.
$1,800-2,500

German boxwood statue of the ırnese Hercules, left toes missing, 'thC, 13½in (34cm) high.
,000-4,000

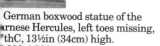

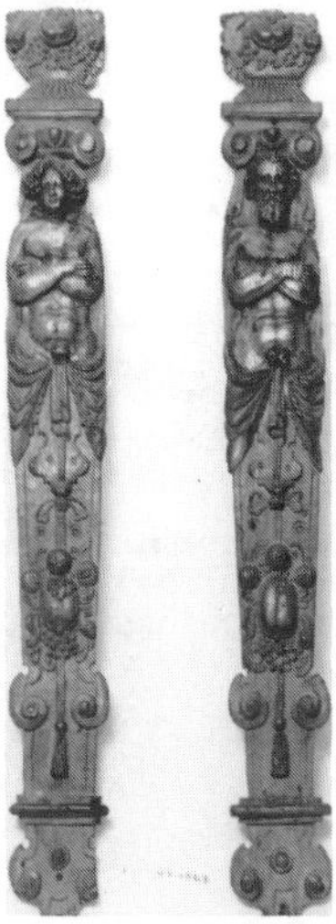

A pair of Flemish oak carvings, 17thC, 42in (105cm) high.
$1,500-2,000

A carved walnut figure of a heraldic lion, with traces of original gilding and polychrome, 16thC, 23½in (59cm) high.
$4,000-5,000

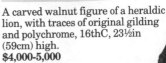

:arved giltwood and polychromed gle perched on a rock, on concave twood base, 18thC, 37in (93cm) de.
,000-1,500

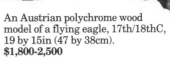

An Austrian polychrome wood model of a flying eagle, 17th/18thC, 19 by 15in (47 by 38cm).
$1,800-2,500

ANTIQUITIES

Metalware

An East Persian copper inlaid bronze bucket, the exterior engraved and inlaid, one dent, slight damage, 12thC, 6½in (16cm) high.
$6,000-8,000

An Ummayad bronze polycandelon, with associated attachment chains, Spain, c10thC, 8½in (21cm) diam.
$3,000-4,000

A copper inlaid bronze pumice holder in the form of a lion, restoration, 12thC, 6in (16cm) long.
$4,000-6,000

Pottery

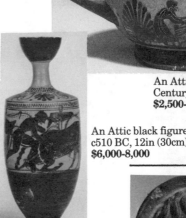

An Attic black figure cup, 5th Century BC, 8in (21cm) wide.
$2,500-3,000

A Nishapur bowl, the white interior with stylised inscription, repaired, 10thC, 10in (26cm) diam.
$3,000-4,000

An Attic black figure Lekythos, c510 BC, 12in (30cm) high.
$6,000-8,000

An Etruscan hollow terracotta head of a youth, 3rd-2nd Century BC, 9in (23cm).
$1,500-2,000

Miscellaneous

A clear glass bottle, wheel cut with 3 rows of circles, extensive polychrome iridescence, mouth repaired, Nishapur, 10thC, 5½in (14cm) high.
$7,000-8,000

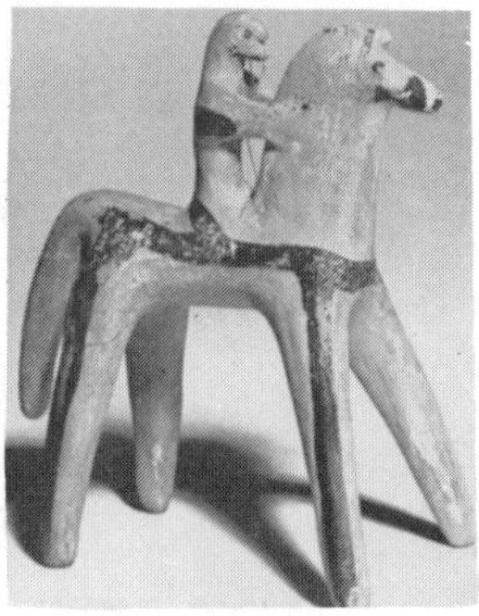

An archaic Greek terracotta horse and rider, decorated in black, 6th Century BC, 4in (10cm) high.
$2,500-3,000

A Mamluk enamelled clear glass beaker, with a gold band of enamelled figures, restored, late 13thC, 7in (18cm) high.
$4,000-6,000

A Cypriot painted terracotta figur of a horse and rider, some repair a restoration, 8th-7th Century BC, 9½in (24cm) high.
$2,000-3,000

DOLLS

Dolls – Wooden

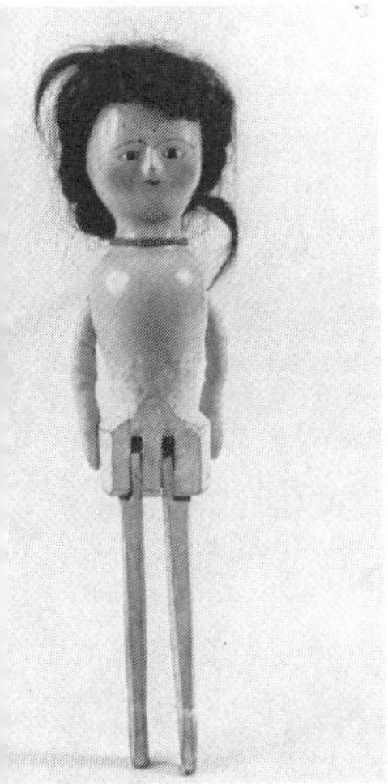

A wooden doll, with natural brown plaited wig, held with a nail, the turned body with cloth arms tapering into squared hips and the straight legs peg jointed at the hip, redressed, late 18thC, 12in (30.5cm).
$1,000-1,200

A painted wooden Grödenthal doll, with yellow comb, green painted shoes and wearing contemporary striped dress edged with green braid, c1837, 10in (25.5cm).
$600-800

A Charles II wooden doll, with bright pink rouged cheeks, brown eyes, vertical upper lashes and a single brush stroke for each eyebrow, blonde horsehair wig, the cream painted body jointed at the hips and knees, with neck join, rust marks and hole at rear of torso, probably the remains of the wire for turning the head, the painted wooden arms sewn to short upper arm sections, dressed in contemporary green patterned silk bodice with silver gilt braid decoration, laced up the back, the overskirt of warp patterned striped cream and deep pink silk, the petticoat of plain yellow silk taffeta, lined with paper and decorated with silver gilt braid and a pink and white silk braid to match the skirt, her undergarments consisting of a plain linen shift, a later madder printed linen shift early 18thC, and yellow silk stockings to match her petticoat, with the same silver gilt braid around her ankles, remains of original cap in green, pink and yellow silk with linen lace edging, feet missing, clothes dusty and some wear, c1680, 13in (33cm), and a glazed mahogany case with pagoda shaped top, 27in (69cm) high.
$160,000+

This doll appears to be the earliest known example of the work of the maker of 'Lord and Lady Clapham'.

Wax

A poured wax headed figure of a man, with inset hair, eyelashes, eyebrows and moustache, the composition body with wax hands, dressed in workman's blue boiler suit, with manufacturer's label, on a wooden plinth, c1910, 22in (56cm).
$400-800

A Victorian wax doll, with fair hair, fixed blue eyes, composition body, wearing pink dress trimmed with broderie anglaise, 29in (74cm) high, in glazed display case.
$600-800

CHARACTER DOLLS

- ★ in 1909 Kammer & Reinhardt introduced a large number of character dolls
- ★ these were modelled from life, showing all the nuances of childish temperament
- ★ a model was made and then a mould taken, which was used about fifty times
- ★ Simon and Halbig cast and painted the heads for many other manufacturers, including Kammer & Reinhardt, such heads are marked K & R, Simon & Halbig, or K & R, S & H and the model number
- ★ early K & R character dolls are of exceptional quality
- ★ the French had remained supreme in the manufacture of dolls, in the 19thC, with Jumeau one of the main exponents
- ★ however, from the 1890s the Germans had perfected equal skills
- ★ after K & R introduced their characters many other makers followed: Heubach, Armand Marseille, Bruno Schmidt, Kestner, and S.F.B.J. (the Societe Francaise de Fabrication de Bebes et Jouets)
- ★ obviously these dolls were expensive and so they were hardly produced in large quantities
- ★ K & R Model 117 is usually considered to be one of the most desirable; in fact any 'pouty' doll is highly collectable
- ★ the most common is model 126
- ★ there are more Heubach characters than any other
- ★ as one gets nearer to the First World War quality tends to decrease and character dolls produced after the war are in many cases, poor quality

Bisque

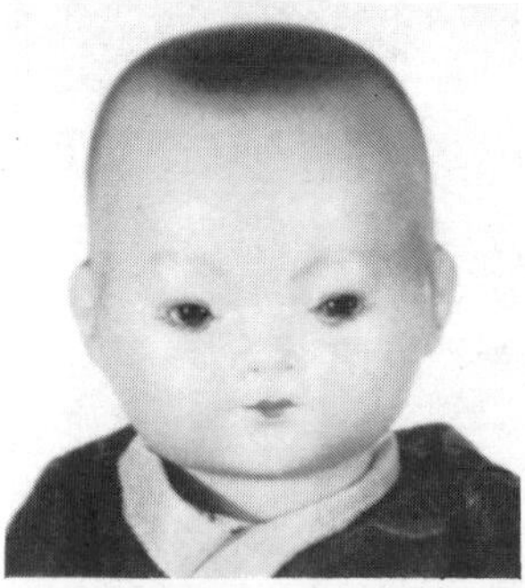

A bisque headed baby doll, modelled as an Oriental, with brown sleeping eyes, the bent limbed composition body dressed in original kimono, marked A Ellar M 10 K, the head 3in (7.5cm) high, in original box.
$1,200-1,400

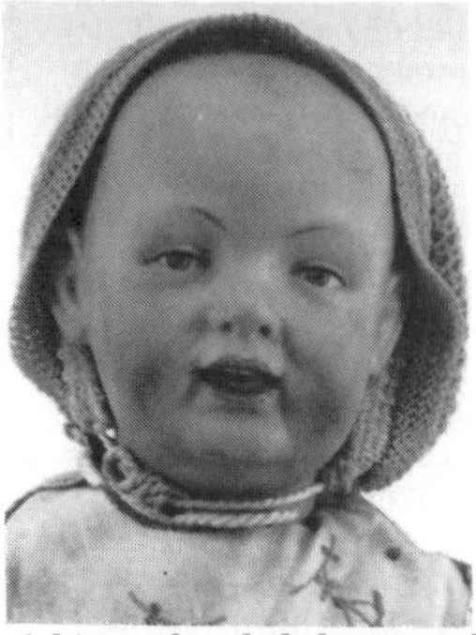

A bisque headed character baby doll, with painted grey eyes, moulded brush stroked hair and bent limbed composition body with painted toes, marked F.S. and Co., 1267/40, 16in (40.5cm) high.
$800-1,000

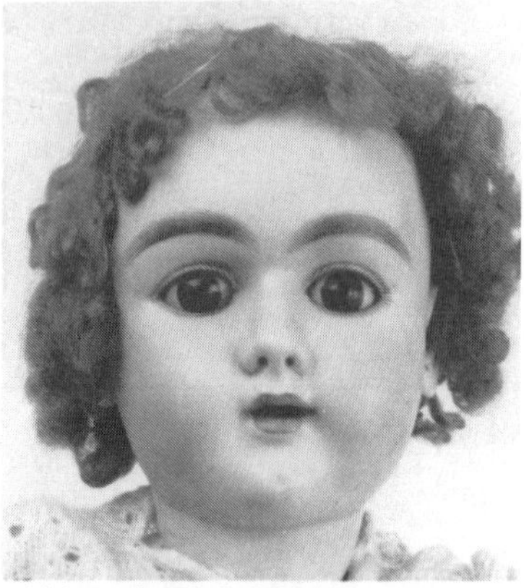

A bisque headed child doll, with brown sleeping eyes, pierced ears and blonde wig, the jointed wood and composition body in knitted outfit, marked 109 15 DEP, the body stamped Handwerck, 28in (71cm).
$800-1,000

An all bisque character doll, with moulded short blonde hair, side glancing googlie eyes, jointed at shoulder and hip, wearing pink edged tunic and trousers, moulded blue socks and brown shoes, marked 147 12½, by Hertel Schwab & Co., 5in (12.5cm).
$500-600

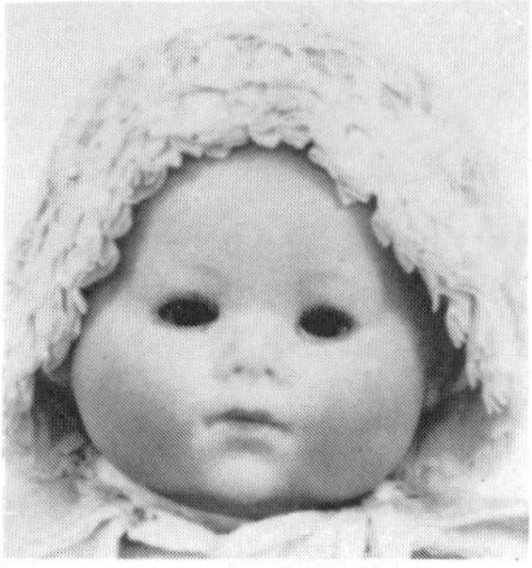

A bisque headed character baby doll, with blue sleeping eyes and stuffed body, marked 3 H S, 16in (40.5cm).
$500-700

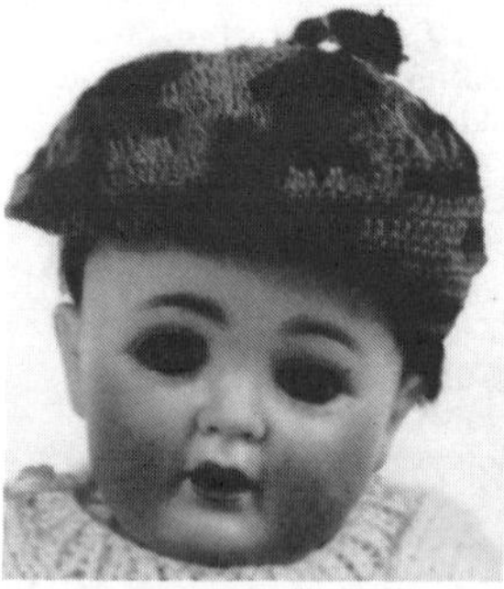

A bisque headed character doll, with brown sleeping eyes, brown mohair wig, the bent limbed composition body dressed as a boy, marked K & Co 262, 14in (35.5cm).
$800-1,000

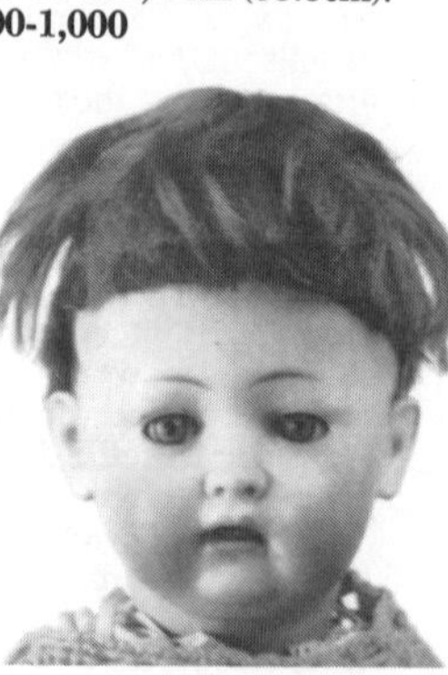

A bisque headed character baby doll, with blue lashed sleeping eyes, brown mohair wig, the bent limbed composition body in blue knitted dress and white underwear, marked K & W 1010 IV 6 by König & Wernicke, 14½in (37cm).
$700-800

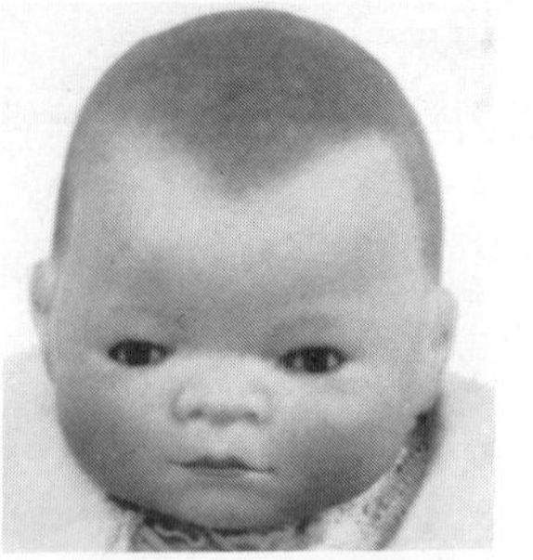

A bisque headed baby doll, with blue sleeping eyes, the cloth body with celluloid hands, in a cream sil and lace baby gown and carrying cape, marked Copr. by Grace S. Putnam, 12in (30.5cm).
$900-1,200

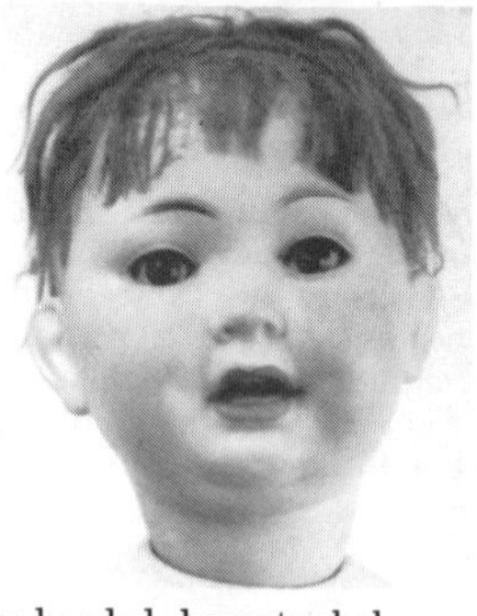

A bisque headed character baby doll, with brown lashed sleeping eyes and composition baby's body with voice box, marked 914 12 by Otto Reinicke, 22in (56cm).
$700-800

A Victorian bisque headed bab doll, 5in (12.5cm).
$100-150

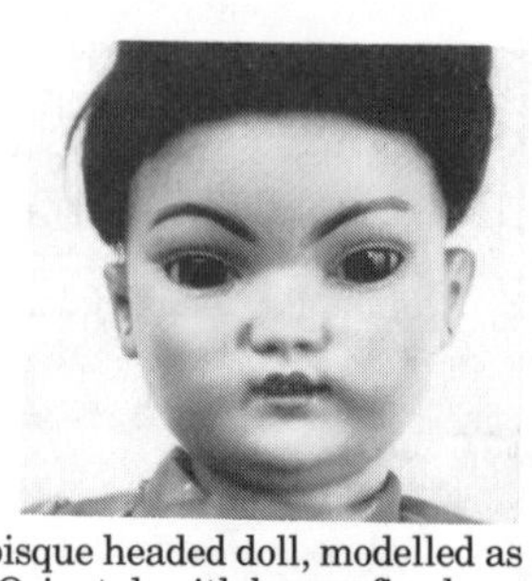

A bisque headed doll, modelled as an Oriental, with brown fixed eyes, pierced ears and brown mohair wig, the jointed wood and composition body dressed in gold and green silk jacket and skirt, damage, marked SH 1199 Dep 6, head 4in (10cm) high.
$1,000-1,200

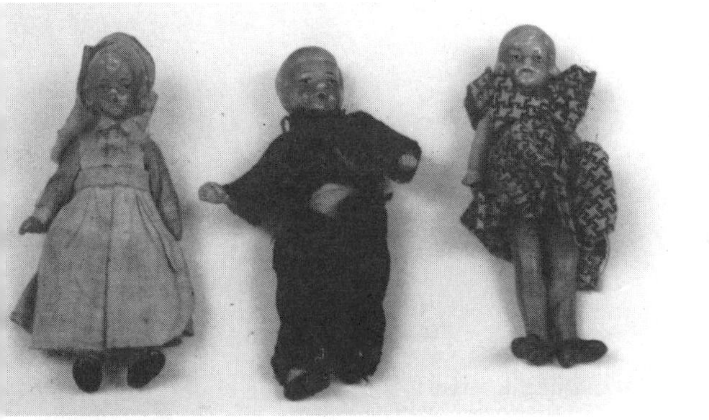

Three German bisque dolls.
$80-100 each

A bisque shoulder head with fixed blue eyes, with blonde curls, the shoulder plate pierced 4 times, marked 60, 8in (20.5cm) high.
$700-900

A bisque headed character doll, with blue lashed sleeping eyes, blonde mohair wig, the composition toddler body in frilled dress and velvet cape, marked Porzellan Fabrik Burggrub Princes Elizabeth 3½, 16½in (42cm).
$1,800-2,400

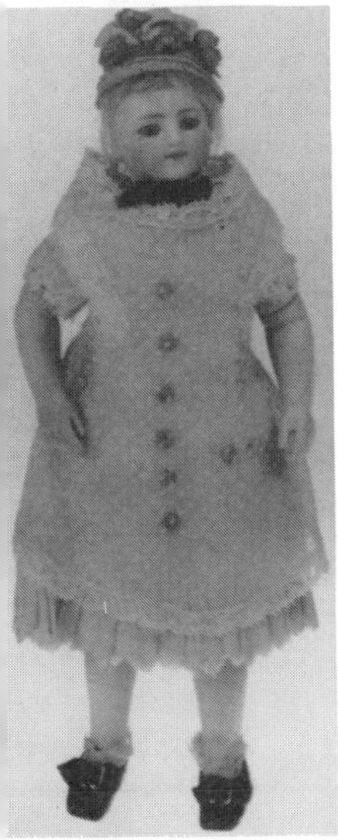

A bisque swivel headed Parisienne, modelled as a child, with blue eyes, pierced ears and blonde mohair wig, the stuffed body with bisque limbs, in original white dress trimmed with silk buttons and pleated frill, spotted muslin apron, straw hat and bronze shoes, 9½in (24cm) high.
$2,500-3,500

A bisque shoulder headed doll, with fixed blue eyes and brown mohair wig, the stuffed body with composition limbs, dressed in tartan woollen dress and white underwear, 17½in (44cm) high.
$900-1,200

A bisque headed doll, with brown sleeping eyes, the composition body in original pink satin dress and white felt hat, 6in (15cm).
$500-600

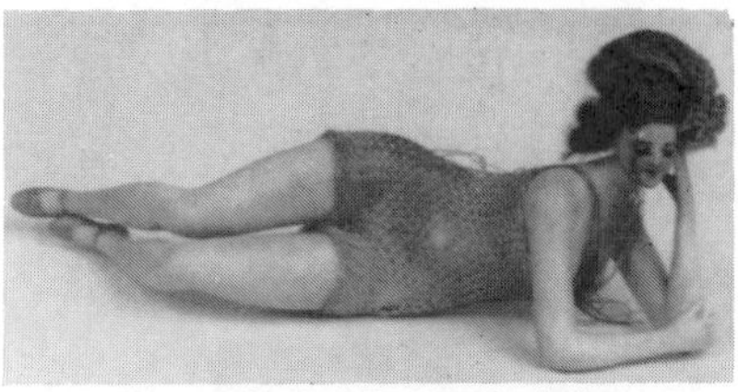

A bisque reclining figure of a lady, in a bathing suit, marked 4072, 4½in (11cm) long.
$500-700

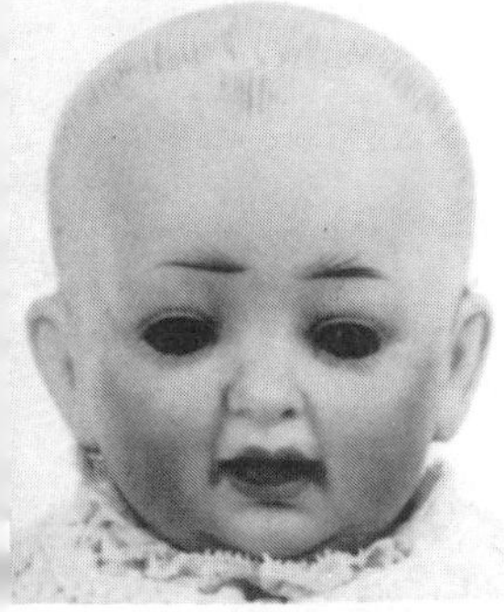

A bisque headed character baby doll, with blue sleeping eyes, moulded hair, wearing a nightgown, marked 2 142, 12in (30.5cm).
$500-700

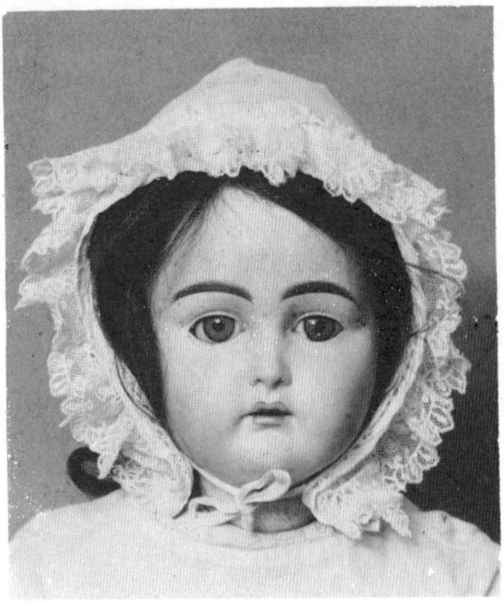

A bisque headed child doll, with blue sleeping eyes and brown wig, the jointed wood and composition body in whitework dress, white bonnet and underwear, marked 191 17, 31in (79cm) high.
$1,200-1,400

A pair of bisque dolls house dolls, with inset brown eyes, jointed at neck, shoulder and hip, with moulded blue socks and brown and black shoes, with chip at neck, 3½in (9cm) high.
$1,000-1,200

A pair of bisque bonnet headed dolls, with moulded pink turbans, the bodies in contemporary white net angel costumes, decorated with tinsel and gold paper flowers and leaves, 11in (28cm).
$600-800

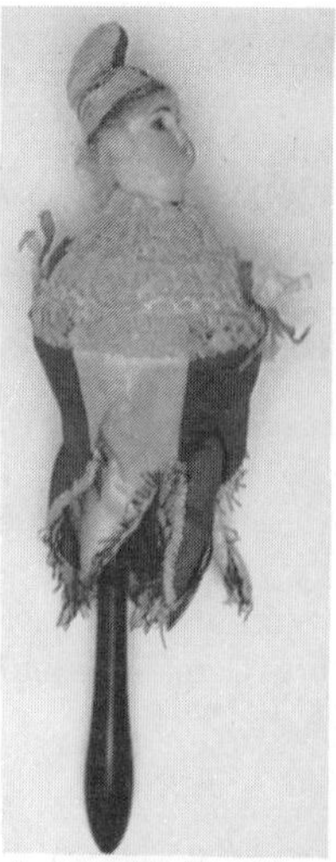

A bisque headed puppet doll, with closed mouth, fixed blue eyes and feathered brows, dressed in original red and white silk outfit, with musical movement, 13in (33cm) high.
$800-1,000

Make the Most of Miller's

Every care has been taken to ensure the accuracy of descriptions and estimated valuations. Price ranges in this book reflect what one should expect to pay for a similar example. When selling one can obviously expect a figure below. This will fluctuate according to a dealer's stock, saleability at a particular time, etc. It is always advisable to approach a reputable specialist dealer or an auction house which has specialist sales

An all bisque baby doll, with painted blue eyes, blonde mohair wig, jointed at shoulder and hips, dressed in regional Greek costume, marked 3, 7½in (19cm) high.
$400-500

A pair of bisque dolls, with movable arms, 4in (10cm) high.
$10-20

A pair of bisque headed dolls house dolls, one with brown head and sleeping eyes, the composition body with moulded pink shoes and white socks, in original red and white dress, the pink headed doll with moulded yellow shoes and black socks, in original white petticoat, 5in (12.5cm).
$700-900

Bru

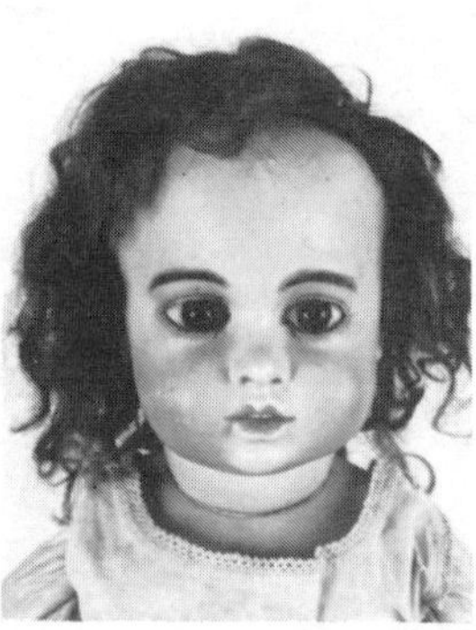

A bisque headed bébé, with fixed brown eyes and mohair wig, on modern gusseted kid body with bisque shoulder plate and hands, dressed in underwear, head damaged, circle dot mark of Bru, 20in (51cm).
$1,000-1,200

A Bru Jeune bisque headed doll, with original sheepskin wig over cork pate, blue paperweight eyes, pierced ears, open/closed mouth with painted upper teeth and kid leather body gusseted at the hip and knee, with bisque forearms, some damage to hip joints, impressed on neck and shoulder BRU JNE 6, 19in (48cm).
$35,000-40,000

Gebruder Heubach

A bisque figure of a seated boy, wearing a bathing cap and trunks, impressed with Gebruder Heubach sunburst and 4859, 11½in (29cm).
$1,400-1,600

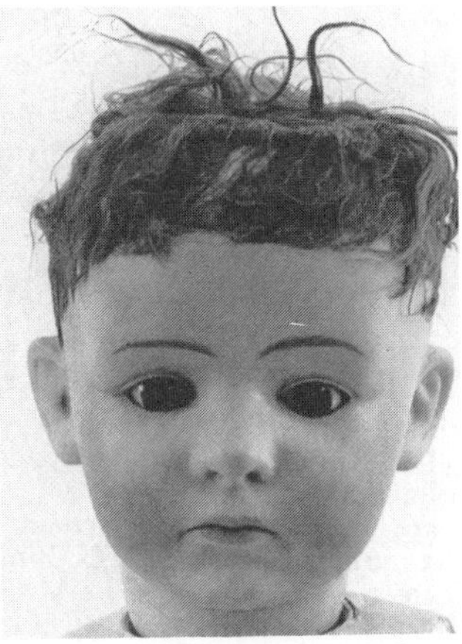

A bisque headed character baby doll, with brown sleeping eyes and baby's body, neck damaged, marked 7246, Gebruder Heubach sunburst and 12, 23in (58cm).
$4,000-5,000

A bisque figure of a baby in a shoe, damaged, marked with Gebruder Heubach sunburst DEP 37, 12in (30.5cm) high.
$1,600-1,800

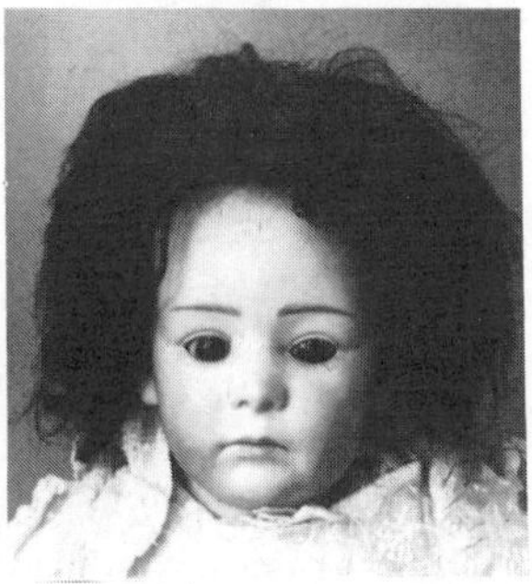

A bisque headed character doll, with brown sleeping eyes and brown mohair wig, the bent limbed composition body dressed in white embroidered organza, marked 7246, 11 Gebruder Heubach sunburst, 21½in (55cm).
$3,500-4,000

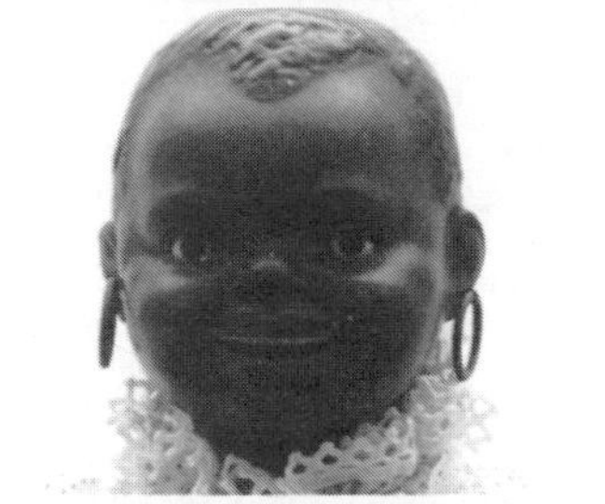

A black sprayed bisque headed doll, with brown sleeping eyes, moulded brows, pierced ears and moulded curly hair, the composition toddler body dressed in red and white, some overpainting, marked Heubach Koppelsdorf 418.3/0, 14in (35.5cm).
$800-1,000

A bisque headed character boy doll, with moulded blonde curls, blue intaglio eyes, the jointed body wearing shorts, knitted socks, a jersey, floppy hat and leather belt and harness, with Gebruder Heubach sunburst, and 7622, 12½in (32cm).
$1,200-1,600

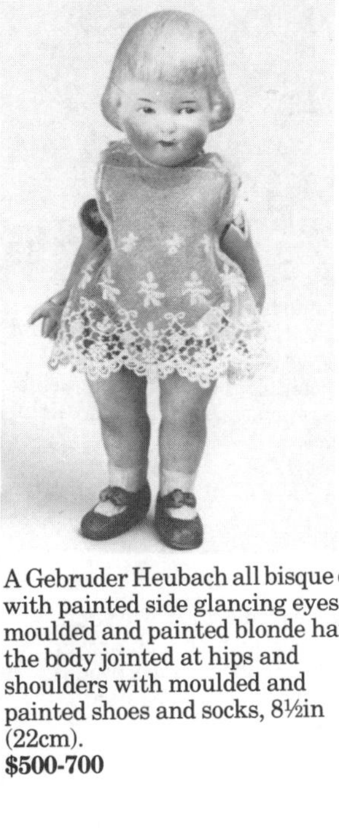

A Gebruder Heubach all bisque doll, with painted side glancing eyes, moulded and painted blonde hair, the body jointed at hips and shoulders with moulded and painted shoes and socks, 8½in (22cm).
$500-700

Jumeau

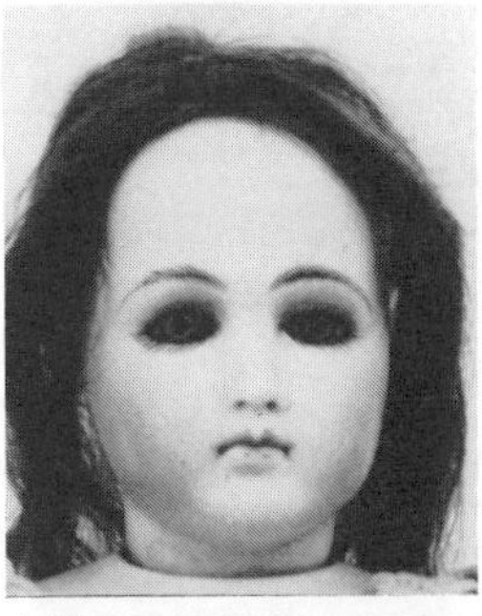

A bisque swivel-headed Parisienne, with blue eyes, feathered brows and brown mohair wig, stuffed body with white bisque arms, dressed in underwear, woollen suit and hat, chip to shoulder plate, possibly Jumeau, 6½in (42cm).
$900-1,200

A bisque headed bébé, with heavy feathered brows, blue paperweight eyes, fair wig, the jointed wood and composition body in red silk sailor dress, hat and shoes, slight damage, marked 7, stamped in red Depose Tête Jumeau body marked with Bébé Jumeau Diplome d'Honneur sticker, 19in (48cm).
$2,000-4,000

J. D. Kestner

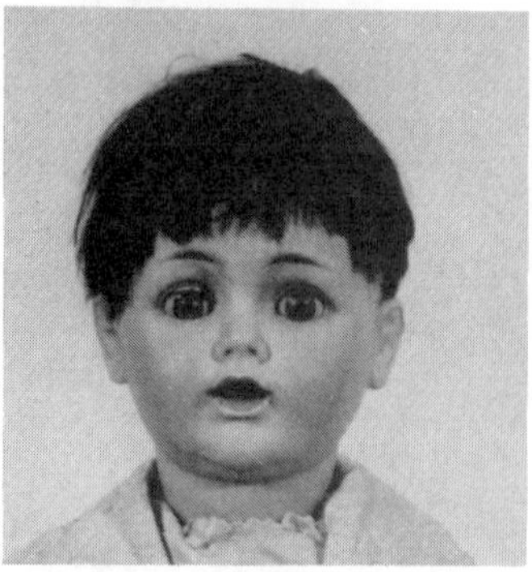

A bisque headed character baby doll, with blue sleeping eyes, brown short wig, on a larger jointed composition body, dressed in blue and cream, marked 25764, by J.D. Kestner, 36in (91.5cm).
$900-1,000

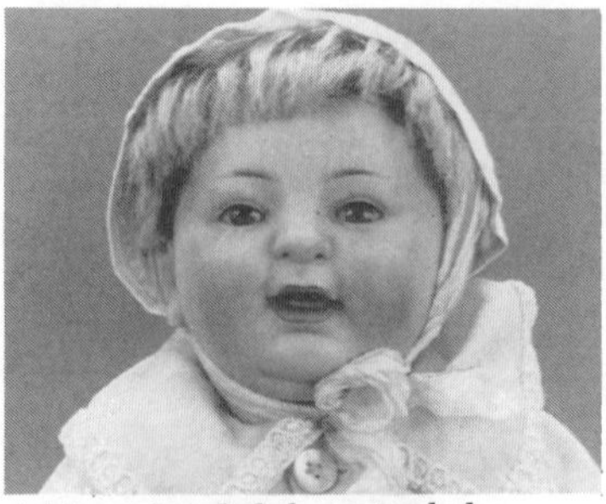

A bisque headed character baby doll, with blue sleeping eyes, blonde mohair wig and bent limbed composition body dressed in cream coat and hat, marked 211 JDK, 15in (38cm).
$900-1,000

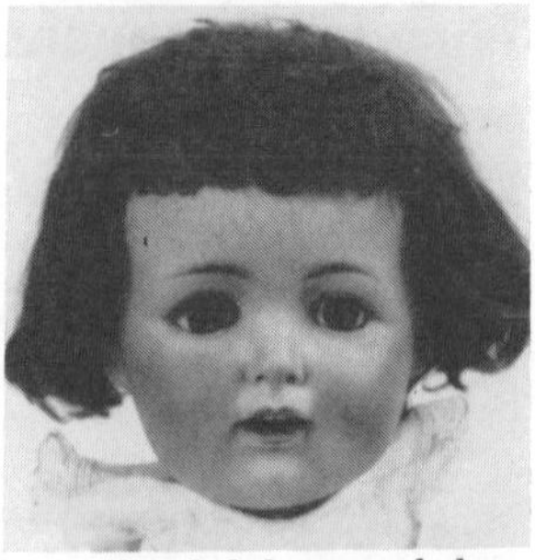

A bisque headed character baby doll, with blue lashed sleeping eyes, golden brown mohair wig, the bent limbed composition body in whitework dress, cape and bib, eye flake, marked JDK, 27in (69cm).
$1,400-1,600

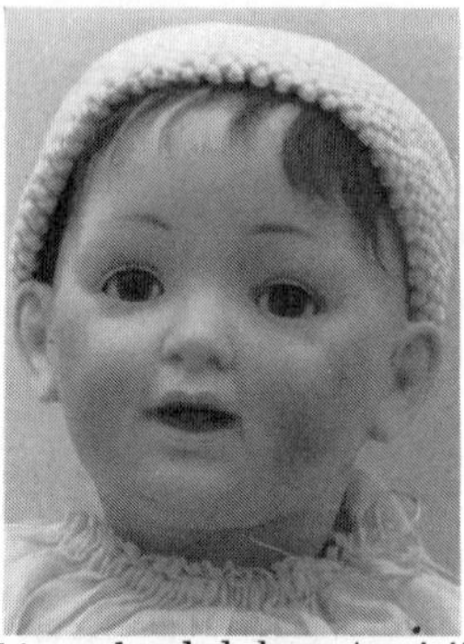

A bisque headed character doll 'Laurence', with brown sleeping eyes, brown mohair wig and bent limbed composition body, dressed in white, arms repainted, marked JDK 211, 19in (48cm).
$1,200-1,400

A bisque headed character doll, 'Pitman', with googlie eyes, blonde mohair wig and jointed composition toddler body, dressed in knitted suit and leather shoes, marked C.7. JDK, 221 Gesgesch, 11½in (29cm).
$6,000-7,000

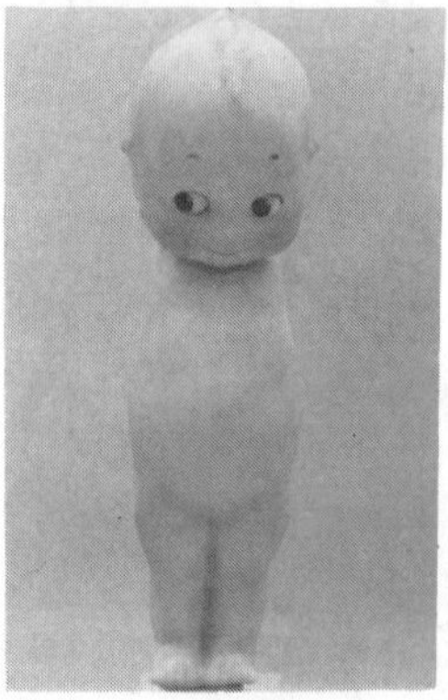

An all bisque doll, jointed at the shoulders, with painted eyes, blue painted wig, chip to shoulder, arms detached, marked 2 on arms, by Kestner, 8in (20.5cm).
$500-700

An all bisque googlie eyed doll, with painted blue eyes and blonde mohair wig, the body jointed at shoulders and hips, dressed in contemporary cotton print dress and straw hat, legs marked 179 3/0, by Kestner, 6in (15cm).
$1,200-1,400

Armand Marseille

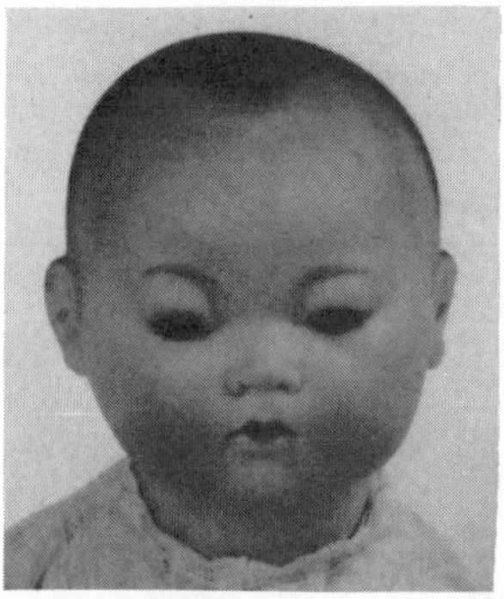

A bisque headed Oriental baby doll, with brown sleeping eyes, the bent limbed composition body in white organdie dress, marked AM 353/ 41E, 17in (43cm).
$1,600-1,800

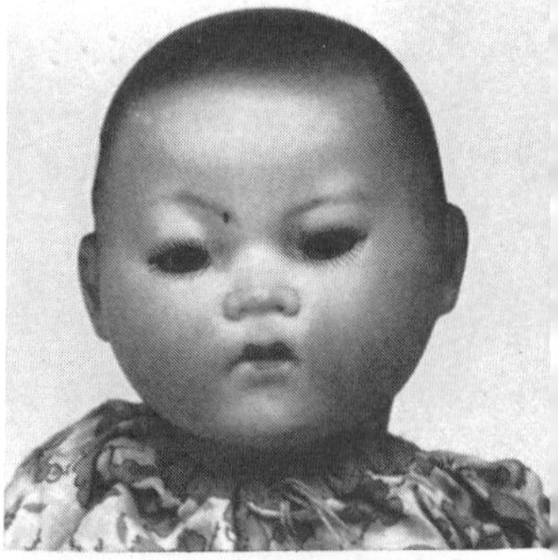

A bisque headed character baby doll, with brown sleeping eyes and black sprayed hair, the yellow composition body dressed in print dress, marked AM 353/2K, 10½in (27cm).
$1,000-1,200

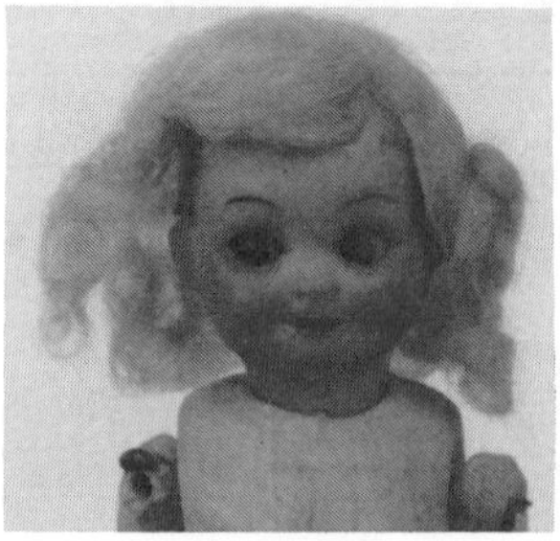

A bisque headed googlie eyed doll, with blue eyes, blonde mohair wig and straight limbed composition body with moulded and painted shoes and socks, marked AM 253 11/0, 7in (18cm).
$800-1,000

S.F.B.J.

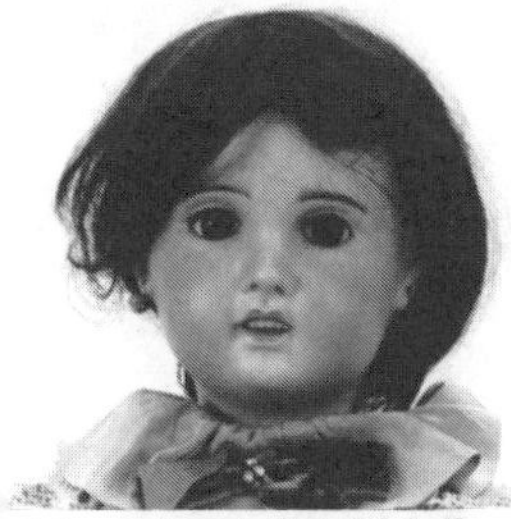

A bisque headed child doll, with brown lashed sleeping eyes, pierced ears and brown wig, the jointed wood and composition body dressed in blue, marked SFBJ Paris II, 26in (66cm).
$1,000-1,200

A composition doll, in original costume, by S.F.B.J., c1930, 10in (25.5cm).
$100-120

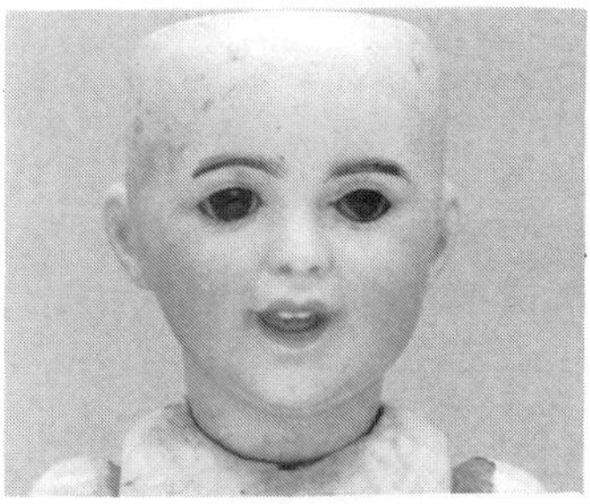

A bisque headed character baby doll, with sleeping dark eyes, marked SFBJ 236 Paris 4, 12½in (32cm).
$400-600

Simon & Halbig/ Kammer & Reinhardt

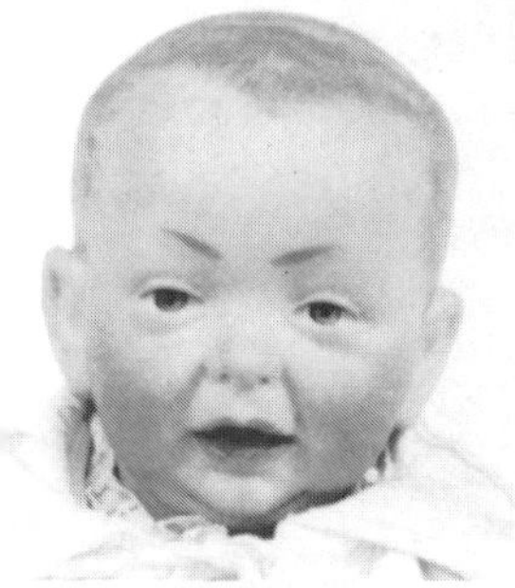

A bisque headed character baby doll, with painted hair and features, dressed in white, marked 36 K*R 100, 15in (38cm).
$900-1,200

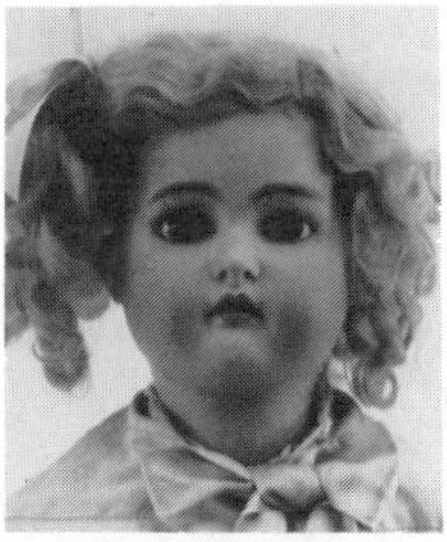

A bisque headed child doll, with blue lashed sleeping eyes and blonde mohair wig, the jointed wood and composition body in whitework dress, blue lace trimmed cape and underwear, marked K*R Simon & Halbig 80, 31in (79cm).
$1,800-2,000

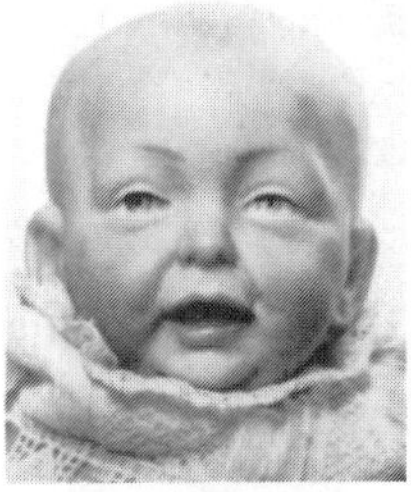

A bisque headed character baby doll, with blue painted eyes, wearing robes, marked 28 K*R 100, 10½in (27cm), with spare clothes.
$800-1,000

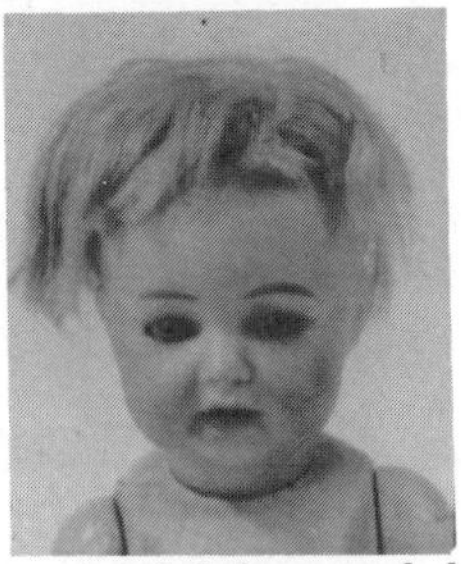

A bisque headed character baby doll, with blue sleeping eyes, blonde mohair wig and bent limbed composition body, slight flaw on forehead, marked K*R 122 26, 10in (25.5cm).
$600-800

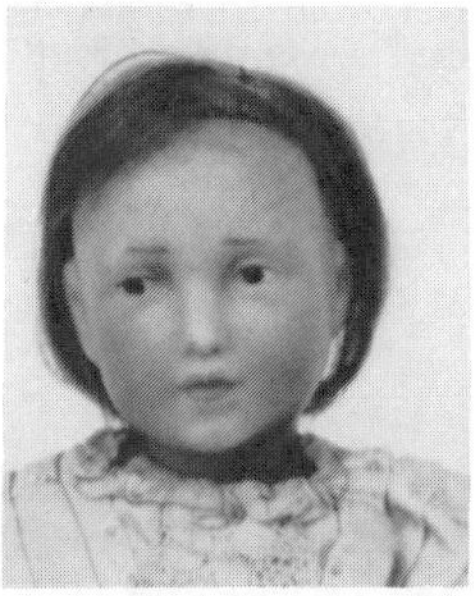

A bisque headed character doll, with painted eyes and fair mohair wig, the jointed composition toddler body dressed in cream silk and lace, marked K*R 109, 10in (25.5cm).
$2,500-4,000

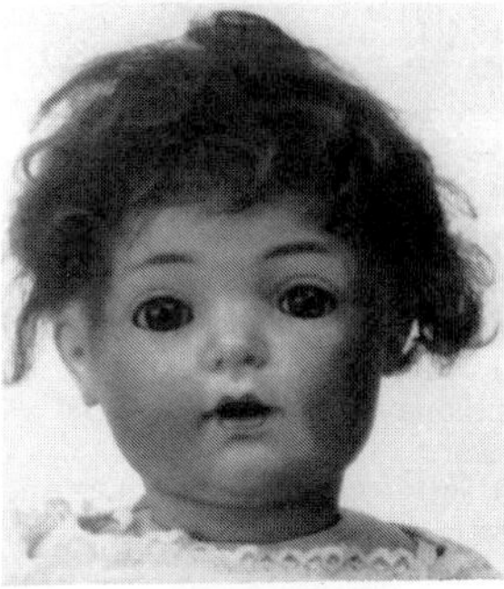

A bisque headed character baby doll, with sleeping blue eyes, brown mohair wig and bent limbed composition body dressed in white, slight wig pulls, marked K*R Simon & Halbig 121 50, 19in (48cm).
$1,200-1,500

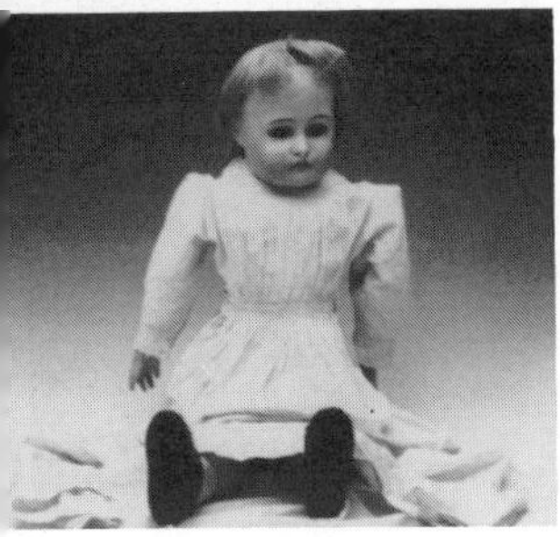

A bisque headed doll, with sleeping brown eyes, fair hair, on composition body with ball jointed articulated limbs, impressed K&R, 28in (71cm).
$800-1,000

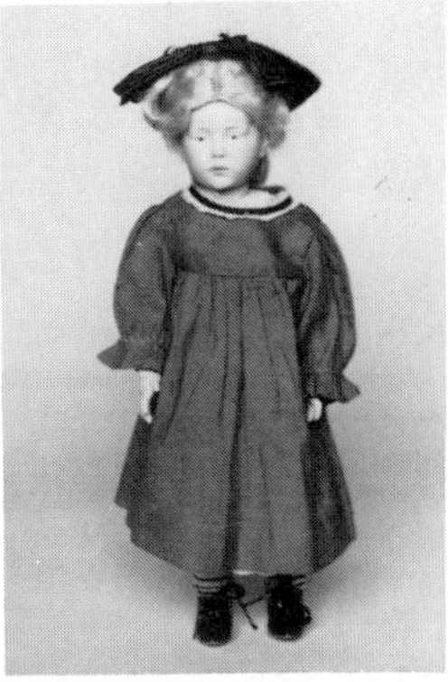

A Kammer & Reinhardt character doll, with blonde mohair wig, hands restored, c1910, 12in (30.5cm).
$4,000-5,000

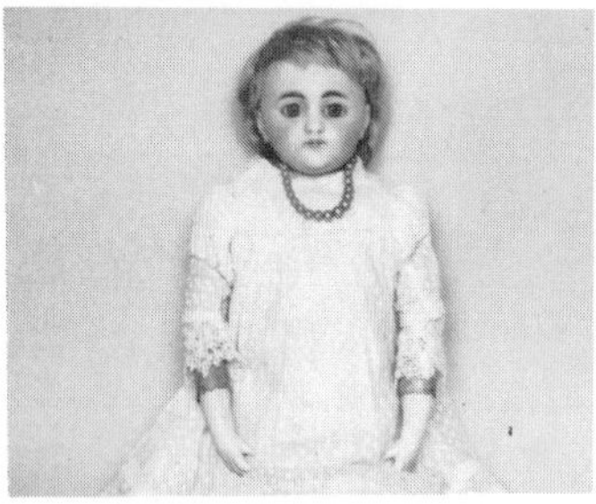

A Simon & Halbig doll, marked S & H 905, 18in (46cm).
$3,000-4,000

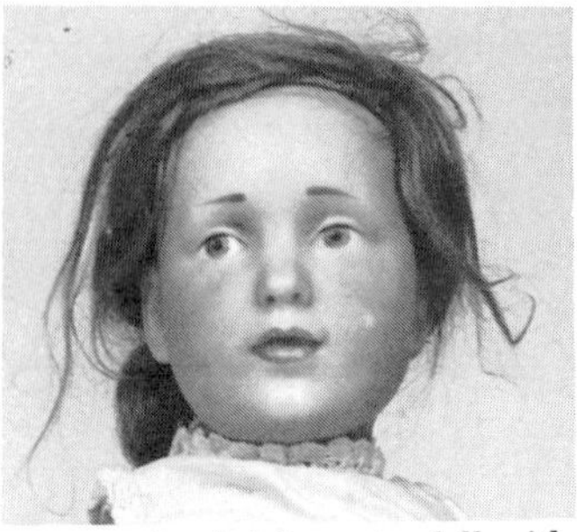

A bisque headed character doll, with blue painted eyes and blonde mohair wig, the jointed composition body dressed in white, rub on cheek and wig pulls, marked K*R 109, 16in (40.5cm).
$8,000-12,000

Jules Steiner

A bisque headed bébé, with blue sleeping eyes operated by a lever, long blonde wig, the fixed wrist wood and composition body with inoperative voice box, damage and firing crack, impressed SIE C1 and stamped in red J. Steiner BSGDGJ, J. Bourgoin Succ, 16in (40.5cm).
$1,500-1,800

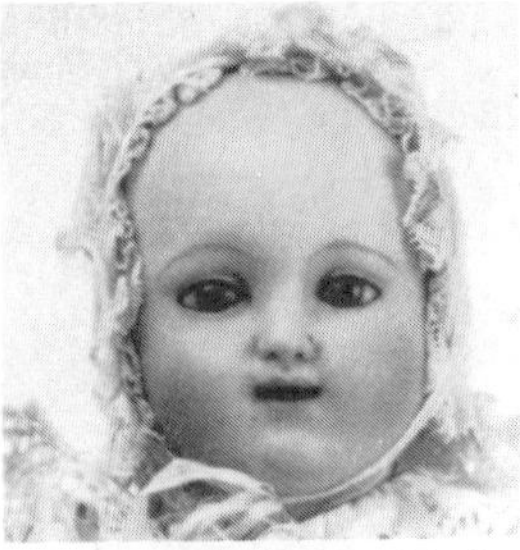

A bisque headed bébé, with fixed blue eyes, feathered brows and domed head, the kid covered body with walking mechanism, composition arms and legs, dressed in baby gown, cape and bonnet, by Jules Nicholas Steiner, c1890, 16in (40.5cm).
$1,200-1,600

Dolls Houses

A wooden dolls house, the façade printed to simulate yellow brickwork and stone, opening to reveal 4 rooms with fireplaces, by Silber and Fleming, 29in (74cm) high.
$600-800

A mahogany dolls house, opening to reveal 4 rooms, late 19thC, 47in (119cm) high.
$3,000-4,000

A model of a Georgian house, the casement windows revealing a fully fitted interior of 14 rooms, mounted on a velvet covered base and in a glass case, the case 19in (48cm) wide.
$1,200-1,500

A printed paper on wood dolls house, opening at the sides to reveal 4 rooms, lacks base, repainted woodwork, marked 3592, 28in (71cm) wide.
$400-600

A painted wooden dolls house, the brickwork overpainted, opening to reveal 6 rooms, mid-19thC, 60in (152cm) high.
$5,000-6,000

A Victorian dolls house, 16in (40.5cm) wide.
$400-500

TOYS

Automata

A bisque headed hand-operated automaton, ringing handbells, dressed in original red velvet outfit, trimmed with gold braid, with musical movement, hairline to head, one bell missing, head marked 12/0, 15in (38cm).
$1,000-1,200

A German printed and painted mechanical clown, with clockwork mechanism, slightly worn, c1925, 5in (12.5cm) long.
$500-600

A bisque headed automaton doll, seated playing a piano, with composition body, the doll impressed SFBJ 60 Paris 8/0, 13½in (34cm) wide.
$900-1,100

An animated action machine, 'The Band', by the Chicago Coin Machine Co., in need of restoration, 28in (71cm) high.
$900-1,000

Cinderella and Prince Charming dancing automaton, c1945, 5in (12.5cm).
$50-60

A musical automaton doll, in the form of a magician, with crimson box base enclosing the movement, requires restoration, 15in (38cm) high.
$2,000-2,500

A bisque headed musical automaton, as the music plays she raises the lid of the basket to show another doll turning from side-to-side in a basket of flowers, by Lambert, re-dressed, arms replaced, the head stamped Tête Jumeau, 19in (48cm) high.
$6,000-8,000

Teddy Bears

A cinnamon plush covered bear, with black boot button eyes, hump and elongated limbs with growler, Steiff button in ear, c1904, 29in (74cm).
$4,000-6,000

A Steiff brown plush covered teddy bear, with boot button eyes, hump and elongated limbs, slight wear, growler inoperative, 21in (53cm).
$700-900

A honey plush covered teddy bear, with boot button eyes, hump and elongated limbs, growler inoperative, replaced paw pads, Steiff button in ear, c1903, 14in (35.5cm).
$1,800-2,500

A red plush teddy bear, with button eyes and felt pads, dressed as a Russian, voice box inoperative, front paws recovered in chamois leather, Steiff button, c1910, 13in (33cm).
$30,000+

The Steiff factory at Giengen have no records of making a line of red bears and suggest that it was a special order made in very limited quantities.

A dark gold plush covered teddy bear, with brown glass eyes, brown felt pads and hump, Steiff button, c1920, 19½in (50cm).
$800-1,200

A golden plush covered teddy bear with hump, elongated limbs and growl, Steiff button in ear, 16in (40.5cm).
$700-1,000

A blonde plush covered teddy bear, with boot button eyes, hump and elongated limbs, with Gebruder Bing button on side, Nuremberg, c1910, 11½in (29cm).
$1,000-1,200

A musical teddy bear, 15in (38cm).
$800-1,000

A golden plush covered teddy bear, with boot button eyes, cut muzzle, hump and elongated limbs, Steiff button in ear, 16in (40.5cm).
$3,000-4,000

A blonde plush covered teddy bear, with boot button eyes, long arms and felt pads, c1910, 10½in (26cm).
$700-900

A teddy bear, 14in (35.5cm).
$60-80

A teddy bear, c1930, 21in (53cm).
$120-160

A golden plush covered teddy bear, with hump and elongated limbs, Steiff button in ear, 14in (35.5cm).
$800-1,000

.ead Soldiers

:lastolin, 70mm scale, General
'ield Marshal Goring in Luftwaffe
ıniform, together with other
fficers, some fatigue.
;500-700

Tinplate

An American tinplate toy, by
Unique Art Manufacturing Co.
Ltd., 8½in (22cm) high.
$400-500

\ printed and painted tinplate
imousine, 'Ebomotor', with
lockwork mechanism, by Eberl,
1909, rear doors broken, 11in
28cm), in original box, lid torn.
;3,000-4,000

A lithographed and painted saloon
car, with clockwork mechanism, in
original box, damaged, by Burnett,
No. BL5892, c1912, 7½in (19cm).
$300-500

A clockwork painted tinplate
battleship, 'Cruiser' No. 640/65,
with clockwork mechanism, by
Fleischmann, main details missing,
worn, c1936, 25½in (64cm) long.
$4,000-5,000

Kadi' EPL no.723, with flywheel
nechanism, in original paintwork,
y Lehmann, c1910, 7in (18cm).
$1,000-1,200

A Triang Minic clockwork mother
and pram, in original box, c1950.
$160-200

A painted tinplate negro, carrying
bunches of bananas, with concealed
clockwork mechanism, on metal
wheels, original paintwork worn,
probably by Distler, c1930.
$400-600

\ lithographed tinplate motorbike
vith Indian Chief rider,
No. 3158/3, by Wells, clockwork
nechanism, in original paintwork,
original box, c1930.
$1,000-1,200

A lithographed tinplate racing
motorbike and rider, The Ace Rider,
by Wells, with clockwork
mechanism, in original box, c1948,
7in (18cm).
$500-600

A Lehmann wind-up tinplate toy,
'Baulky Mule'.
$250-300

A painted tinplate Colonial soldier, with clockwork mechanism, original paintwork, probably by F. Martin, helmet chipped, clothing frayed, c1900.
$1,300-1,500

A printed and painted gardener with wheelbarrow, 'Tap Tap', EPL No. 560, with clockwork mechanism, by Lehmann, c1920, 6in (15cm) long.
$600-800

A lithographed and painted pedal car, EPL No. 684, with clockwork mechanism, in original paintwork, by Lehmann, c1920.
$400-600

A printed and painted tinplate 'Autobus', EPL No. 590, open Berlin type double-deck omnibus, with clockwork mechanism, in original paintwork, lacks driver, by Lehmann, c1912, 8in (20.5cm) long.
$1,500-2,000

A Tipp Limousine, lithographed and painted, with clockwork mechanism, damaged, c1928, 7in (17cm) long.
$200-300

A printed and painted saloon car, with clockwork mechanism, in original box, by Chad Valley, c1930, 9½in (23.5cm).
$500-700

A painted tinplate roadster, 5 HP Citroën, with clockwork mechanism, damaged, French, c1932.
$1,000-1,500

A printed and painted tinplate land speed record car, 'Sunbeam Silver Bullet', with clockwork mechanism, in original paintwork, by Gunthermann, c1931, 22in (56cm).
$800-1,000

A Gunthermann printed and painted tourer, with clockwork mechanism, c1928.
$2,000-2,500

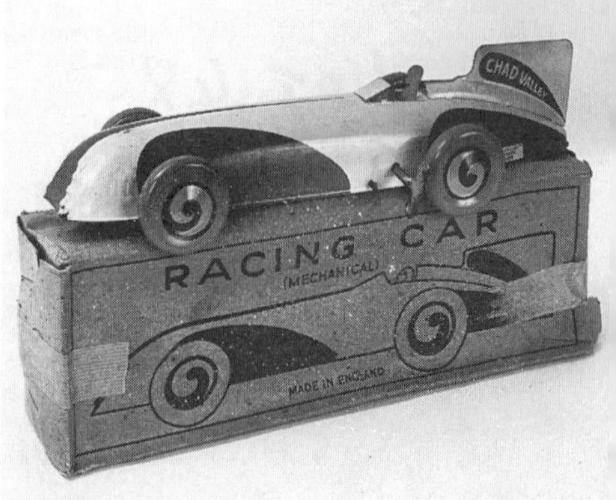

A painted Grand Prix racing car, with clockwork mechanism, in original box, by Chad Valley, 1930s, 11½in (29.5cm).
$400-500

A clockwork wheeled toy, with composition head, as he moves along he raises his rifle and fires, A. Theroude plate on the mechanism, distressed, 8½in (22cm) high.
$800-1,000

A clockwork tinplate Popeye, probably German, poor condition, c1930.
$200-300

A bisque headed clockwork clown, damaged and mechanism inoperative, head marked 3, 16in (40.5cm) high.
$800-1,000

A Chad Valley No. 46 'All Winners' Gift Set, in original box.
$200-300

A Dinky No. 439 Ford D. 800 snow plough and tipper truck, in original box.
$100-200

Dinky Supertoys, comprising No. 501 Foden diesel 8-wheel wagon, No. 502 Foden flat truck, No. 503 Foden flat truck with tailboard, No. 504 Foden 14-ton tanker and No. 505 Foden flat truck with chains.
$700-1,000

A Dinky No. 513 Guy flat truck with tailboard, c1950.
$200-400

Two Dinky Supertoys, damaged.
$900-1,000

Four French Dinky toy lorries, in original boxes, c1960.
$700-800

A Dinky No. 22b Sports Coupé, c1933.
$600-700

Three Dinky Supertoys No. 948 Tractor-Trailer McLeans, all in original boxes.
$1,000-1,200

A Dinky No. 514 Guy Van, chipped, in original box.
$1,000-1,500

A Dinky No. 918 Guy Van, transfer damaged, in original box.
$200-500

A Dinky pre-war 28 series, No. 28m Wakefields Oil van, 1st type, restored.
$200-500

A Dinky commercial vehicle, boxed, c1960.
$200-300

A Dinky No. 514 Guy Van, chipped, boxed, c1950.
$500-700

A Dinky 28 series, No. 28n Meccano van, 1st type, damaged, c1935.
$900-1,000

Minic pre-war commercial vehicles, comprising No. 22M Carter Paterson van, No. 10M delivery lorry, in original paintwork and boxes.
$400-500

A repainted Dinky 28 series, 28g Kodak van, 1st type, c1936.
$300-500

A Minic No. 56ME Rolls Royce sedan, electric, boxed, c1938.
$1,500-2,000

A Distler Electro Matic 7500 car, boxed, c1955.
$1,000-1,200

A Dinky 28 series, No. 28k Marsh and Baxters van, 1st type, slight damage, c1935.
$1,000-1,500

A Dinky set of 6 No. 27 tramcars, boxed, c1935.
$600-1,000

A Meccano motorcar constructor outfit No. 2, with clockwork mechanism, damaged, c1937.
$800-1,000

Four lithographed tinplate motorbikes, all in original paintwork, c1946.
$800-1,000

A Minic, No. 52M single deck bus, original paintwork and box, c1935.
$300-400

A tinplate toy stage coach, 26in (66cm) long.
$500-700

A felt doll modelled as a gnome, with yes/no mechanism, by Schuco, 7in (18cm) high.
$400-500

Miscellaneous

A short plush covered carton nodding Boston terrier, with pull growl and lower jaw movement, on wheels, French, c1910, 22in (56cm) long.
$700-1,000

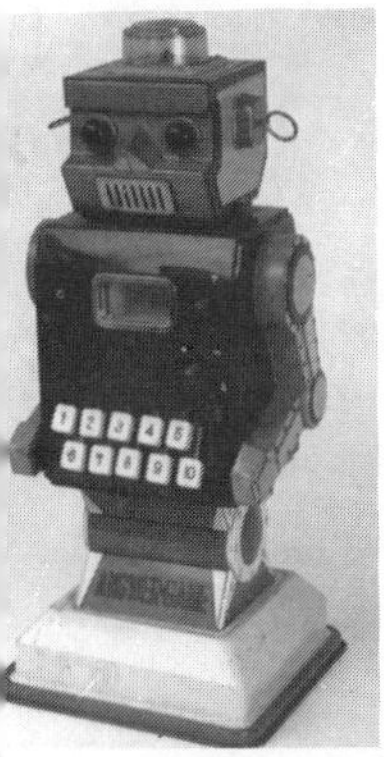

An Answer-Game lithographed and painted tinplate robot, in original paintwork, by Ichida, Japan, 1960s, 14½in (36.5cm).
$700-1,000

A Steiff lion on wheels, c1913, 13in (33cm).
$500-700

A painted felt headed pull-along toy, with squeaker and body movement, by Steiff, 8in (20cm) long.
$700-800

A German humorous composition toy, mid-19thC, 6½in (16cm) long.
$1,500-2,000

Two Steiff bulldogs, largest 9½in (25cm) high.
$500-600

A nodding bulldog, French, c1910, 18½in (47cm) long.
$1,000-1,200

A plush covered donkey on wheels, with blank Steiff button in ear, c1904, 22in (56cm) high.
$800-1,000

A clown, damaged, 1950s, 9in (23cm) high.
$100-150

A skin covered horse on wheels, c1890, 16in (47cm) high.
$700-1,000

A marotte with 3 dancing children, with bisque heads and wooden bodies, in original clothing, music needs attention, 11in (28cm) high.
$900-1,000

A Britains Mammoth Circus, set No. 1444, with special display box, c1935.
$1,000-1,500

A painted wood Noah's Ark, damaged, by Erzegebirge, Germany, c1890, 18in (46cm) long.
$800-1,000

A papier mâché and wood tumbling toy, German, mid-19thC, the box 4½in (11cm) high.
$500-800

A Britains hunting series, set No. 234, in original box, some pieces replaced, c1938.
$500-700

A group of chromolithographic paper on wood skittles, 2 missing, 10½in (27cm) high.
$200-300

A painted wood toy post chaise, Continental, possibly Dutch or French, from 1750, 16in (41cm) high.
$2,000-3,000

A Merit Dan Dare Rocket Gun set in original box, c1950.
$150-200

A coloured lithograph on cardboard toy shadow theatre, German, late 19thC, 18½in (47cm) wide.
$700-800

A Dan Dare radio station, in original box.
$150-200

Elastolin zoo animals, approx. 35 pieces, some damaged.
$1,300-1,500

A Lines Bros. pedal car, with wooden body and chassis, No. LB 2376, 1930s, 47in (119cm) long.
$1,500-2,000

A painted wood Noah's Ark, damaged, by Erzegebirge, Germany, c1870, 14½in (37.5cm) long.
$800-1,000

A Schoenhut Humpty Dumpty circus, in original paintwork, slight damage, c1903.
$500-1,000

MODELS

Air

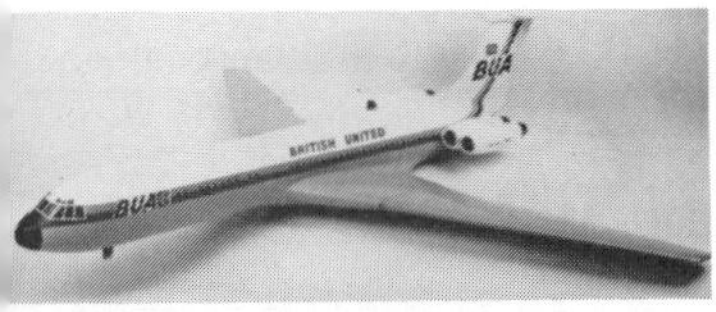

A scale model of a British United VC10, made for display purposes, 1960.
$200-300

A 1:16 scale matchstick model of the Supermarine Spitfire Mark II, Serial No. P8088 NKK, by D A Edgar, 22in (56cm) long.
$500-700

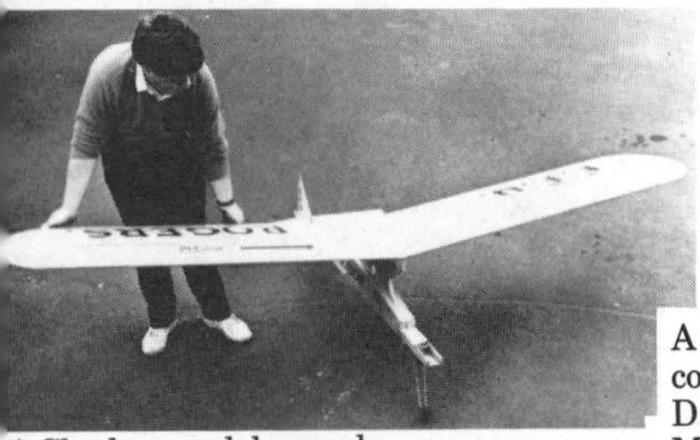

A Shadow model aeroplane, 2 channel aircraft, c1945, wingspan 120in (304cm). **$200-300**

Sea

A model of HMS Victory made from matchsticks, 84in (213cm) long.
$1,200-1,500

An early Marklin station, Harrogate, c1902, 40in (101cm).
$3,500-4,500

A rake of 4 twin bogie corridor coaches and baggage car forming D.R. Rheingold Express, by J & M Models, Sturminster Newton, some spares, original boxes.
$4,000-5,500

Land

An early Carette 3-rail electric twin tram car unit, original paintwork, damged, c1904.
$3,000-4,000

A Marklin central railway station, Central-Bahnhof, original paintwork, c1901.
$6,000-7,000

A Hornby 3½in (9cm) gauge live steam spirit fired model of George Stephenson's Rocket locomotive and tender, in original box.
$700-1,000

A Marklin M.R. 1st class bogie coach, some damage, c1904.
$1,300-1,500

An electric scale model of a De Dion Bouton tourer, by W Hatswell, Southend, c1900, 13 by 23in (33 by 58cm).
$1,500-1,600

A Marklin 3-rail electric model of the G.W.R. 4–6–2 Pacific locomotive and bogie tender No. 111, 'The Great Bear', with a circle of track and power unit, damaged, c1909.
$8,000-10,000

A gauge 1 3-rail electric model of the L.M.S. 0–4–0 standard tank locomotive No. 112, c1920.
$500-600

A Bing for Bassett-Lowke clockwork model of the L.&N.W.R. 4–4–2, Precursor tank locomotive, c1912.
$1,000-1,500

A spirit fired steam engine, by Doll et Cie, in need of restoration, c1920, 12in (30.5cm).
$200-300

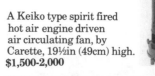

A Marklin 3-rail electric model of the Paris-Orleans Railway E.1. electric locomotive, lacks pantograph, c1919.
$1,500-2,500

A Hornby 3-rail electric model of the L.M.S. 4–4–0 No. E220 locomotive and tender No. 1185, in original box, c1936.
$1,500-1,700

A Keiko type spirit fired hot air engine driven air circulating fan, by Carette, 19½in (49cm) high.
$1,500-2,000

A Bing clockwork model of the L.S.W.R. 0–4–4 M7 tank locomotive No. 109, damaged, c1909.
$2,000-3,000

A Marklin 3-rail electric model of the 2 car diesel unit Hamburg Flyer, Ref. No. T.W. 12970, c1937.
$1,300-1,500

Bing for Bassett-Lowke gauge 1 -rail electric model of the G.C.R. -6–0 locomotive and tender No. 423, Sir Sam Fay, slight hipping, c1914.
3,000-4,000

A Bing for Bassett-Lowke live steam spirit fired model of the G.N.R. 4–4–2, Atlantic locomotive and tender No. 1442, boiler scorched, c1912.
$2,500-3,000

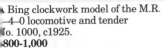

A Bing for Bassett-Lowke 3-rail electric model of the L.&N.W.R. 4–4–0 locomotive and tender, c1905.
$1,700-2,500

Bing clockwork model of the M.R. –4–0 locomotive and tender No. 1000, c1925.
800-1,000

An unpainted mainly nickel silver model of an L.N.E.R. Class A8 4–6–2 side tank locomotive, fitted Bond's motor, 3½ by 11½in (9.5 by 30cm).
$400-500

A Leeds Model Company clockwork model of the S.R. 0–6–0 goods locomotive and tender No. B350, finished in S.R. black livery, in original box, c1933.
$800-1,000

A Bassett-Lowke gauge 0 3-rail electric model of the B.R. Class 7P 4–6–2 locomotive and tender No. 70004, William Shakespeare, 3½ by 19½in (9.5 by 49.5cm).
$5,000-6,000

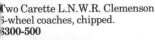

Two Carette L.N.W.R. Clemenson -wheel coaches, chipped.
$300-500

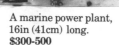

A marine power plant, 16in (41cm) long.
$300-500

A Bing for Bassett-Lowke gauge 2 clockwork model of the G.W.R. 4–4–0 locomotive and tender No. 3410, Sydney, damaged, c1905.
$2,000-2,500

A Hornby gauge 0 Carr's biscuit van, in original paintwork, damaged, c1927.
$300-400

A Marklin D.R. baggage van No. 18081, c1938.
$300-500

GAMES

Chess Sets

A Staunton carved ivory chess set, with a crimson morocco halma board, each king inscribed Jacques, London, 3½in (9cm) high.
$2,000-3,000

A Chinese export lacquer games cabinet containing chess and backgammon, damaged, Canton, 19thC, 18in (46cm) wide.
$3,500-4,000

A middle Eastern folding games table, top damaged, 33½in (85cm wide.
$1,000-1,500

Musical Instruments

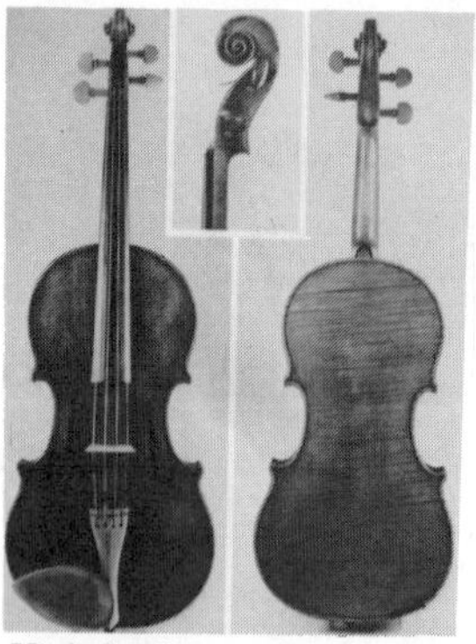

A Viola by George Craske, bearing the label Made by George Craske, and sold by William E Hill & Sons, London, c1860, length of back 15½in (39.5cm), in shaped case.
$5,000-7,000

A violin by François Pique, labelled Pique rue de Grenelle d'honoré, au coin de celle des deux écus, No. 35 à Paris 1815, length of back 14in (35.8cm).
$30,000-35,000

An English Viola, by Joseph Panormo, unlabelled, length of bac 15½in (38.5cm).
$20,000-30,000

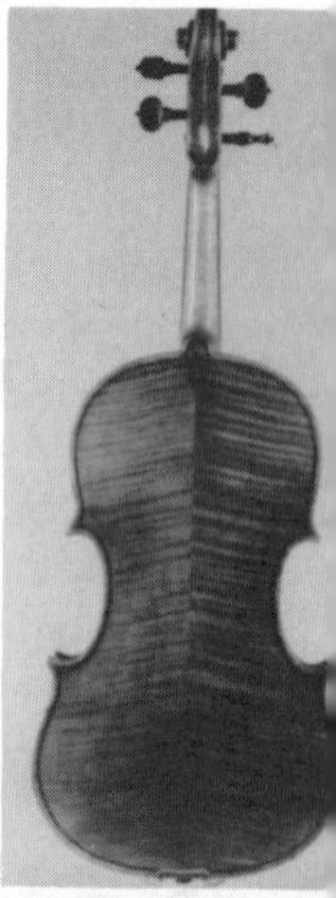

An Italian Viola by Romeo Antoniazzi, labelled Antoniazzi Romeo Cremonese / fece a Cremona l'anno 1918 and branded AR below the back button, length of back, 16½in (42cm), in case.
$12,000-14,000

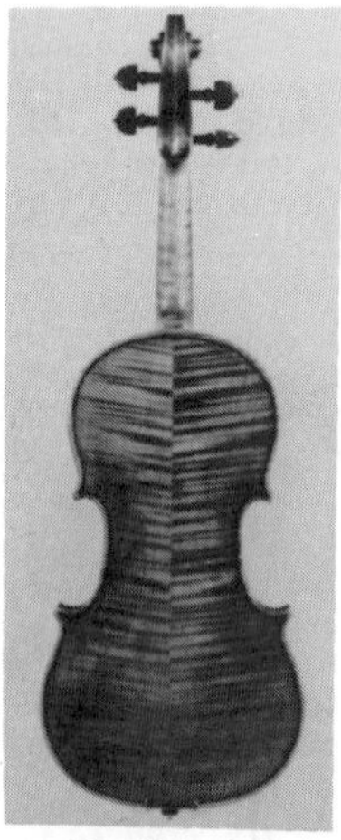

An English violin by William Luff, labelled William H Luff, Maker, London 1978, length of back 14in (35.5cm), in case.
$9,000-10,000

A violin by William H Luff, London, dated 1983, length of back 14in (35.5cm), in case.
$8,000-10,000

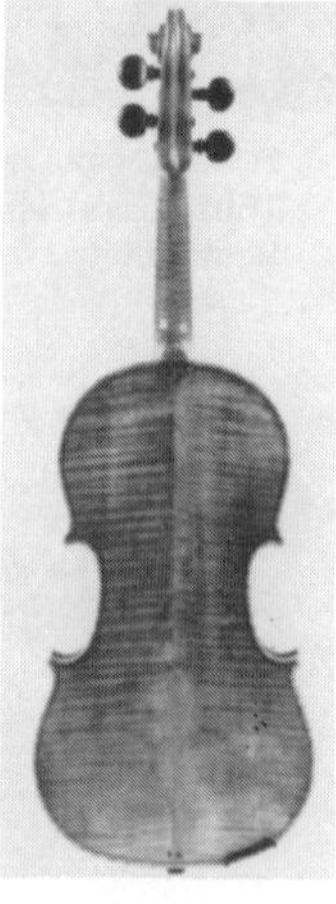

A violin, labelled Rocca, c1850, length of back 14in (35.5cm), in case.
$6,000-8,000

MAKE THE MOST OF MILLER'S

Miller's is completely different each year. Each edition contains completely NEW photographs. This is not an updated publication. We never repeat the same photograph.

violoncello signed Made by John Wm.
wen, Leeds Oct, 1904, No. 15 cello,
ngth of back 30in (76.4cm), in bag
ith bow.
.0,000-12,000

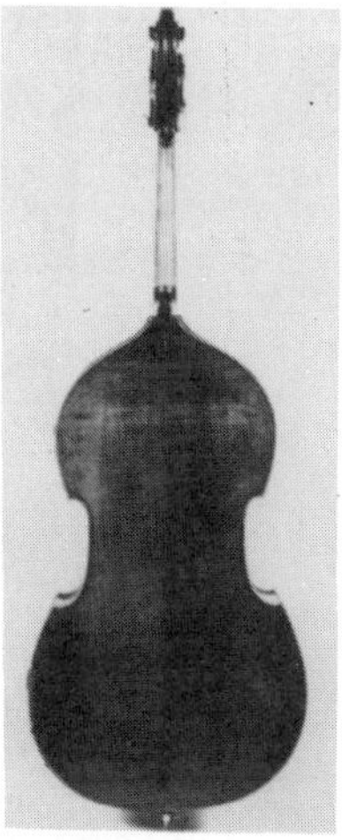

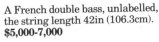

A French double bass, unlabelled, the string length 42in (106.3cm).
$5,000-7,000

A French child's violoncello, unlabelled, c1880, length of back 19½in (49.6cm), in fitted case.
$4,000-5,000

An Italian violoncello attributed to Giuseppe Marconcini, labelled Giuseppe Marconcini, fecit Ferrara anno 1812, length of back 29½in (75.5cm).
$40,000-60,000

Gors & Kallman baby grand
iano, No. 55519, 60in (152.5cm).
3,000-4,000

A Ritzmar mahogany baby grand piano, No. 1801.
$2,500-4,000
A mahogany stool, 19thC, 42in (106.5cm) long.
$1,000-1,500

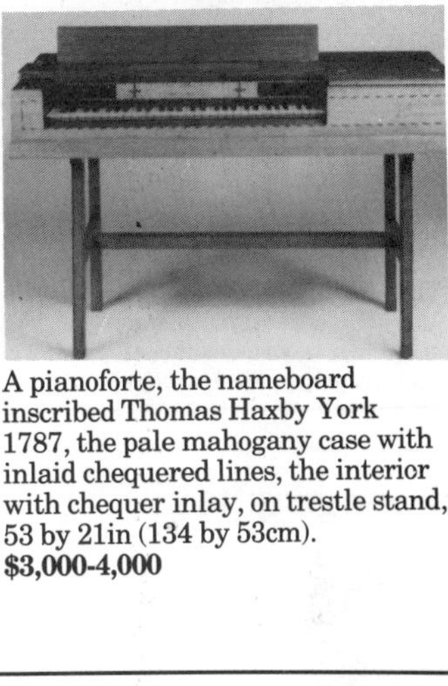

A pianoforte, the nameboard inscribed Thomas Haxby York 1787, the pale mahogany case with inlaid chequered lines, the interior with chequer inlay, on trestle stand, 53 by 21in (134 by 53cm).
$3,000-4,000

Iusical Boxes

simulated rosewood musical box,
tunes, some damage.
400-600

. cylinder musical box, with 15 note
rgan playing 8 airs, c1870.
4,000-5,000

A hidden drum and bell cylinder musical box, playing on 6 bells, c1860.
$3,000-4,000

A Symphonion disc musical box, in walnut case, with 12 discs, c1885, 9½in (24cm).
$2,000-3,000

A Polyphon 11in (28cm) musical box, with 9 discs, c1875, 8in (20.5cm) high.
$2,400-3,000

A 15¾in (40cm) Olympia table disc musical box, with comb movement, in mahogany case with colour print in lid and 30 discs.
$9,000-10,000

A 15½in (39cm) German polyphon disc musical box, with 40 discs, c1900, 21½in (54cm) wide.
$3,000-4,000

A Swiss bells-in-sight cylinder musical box in rosewood case, late 19thC, 16 by 9in (40 by 23cm).
$900-1,000

A Swiss giltmetal singing bird box, with key, slight damage to enamelling, 19thC, 4in (10cm) wide, cased.
$6,000-8,000

A Swiss giltmetal singing bird box with key, slight damage to enamelling, 19thC, 4in (10cm) wid cased.
$6,000-7,000

Phonographs

An Edison Gem phonograph, with horn and 12 cylinders.
$500-700

Gramophones

A Gramophone Company Junior Monarch gramophone, with morning glory horn, slight damage.
$1,200-1,400

A Deccalion gramophone in mahogany case, on Chippendale design stand, with Salon soundbo c1923, 34in (85cm) high.
$1,000-1,200

An HMV double spring Monarch gramophone, 1911 model, with fluted oak horn, damage, repairs.
$2,000-3,000

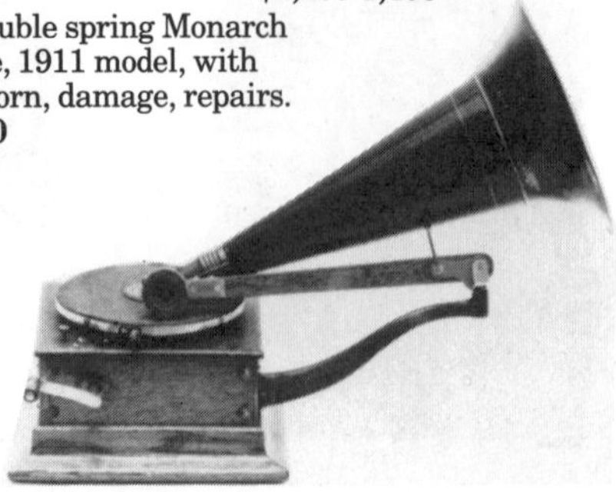

A Victor Type R talking machine, No. 805, with Victor Concert soundbox, restorations.
$1,000-1,200

Miscellaneous

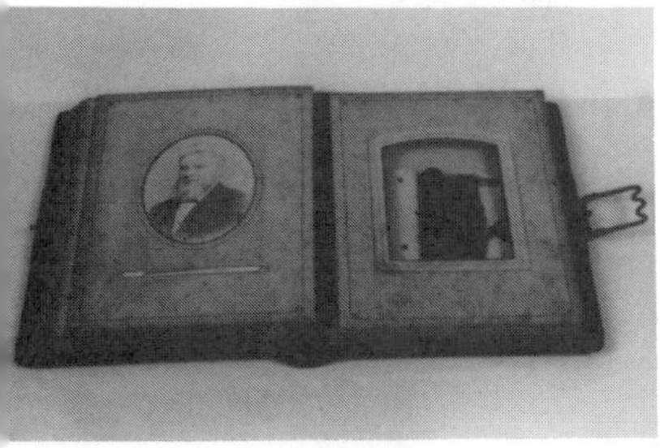

musical photograph album with
wo-air movement, c1885.
500-700

A papier mâché snuff box, signed
Samuel Raven, 18thC.
$700-900

A Georgian inlaid
mahogany candle
box.
$900-1,000

oxes

Russian cigar box, with troika
ene, c1860, 4in (11cm) square.
00-600

A Scottish Mauchline snuff box,
with hunting dog scene.
$150-200

A George III mahogany and chequer
strung knife box, fitted with an
18thC 48-piece cutlery set, box
14½in (37cm) high.
$4,000-5,000

painted snuff box, signed by
tobwasser, 18thC.
1,000-1,500

A Georgian snuff box.
$300-400

A shoe snuff box.
$400-600

snuff box in the form of a horse's
ead, with ivory teeth, 18thC, 3½in
cm) long.
600-1,400

A mastiff tobacco box.
$1,000-2,000

Miller's is a price Guide not a price List

The price ranges given reflect the average price a purchaser should pay for similar items. Condition, rarity of design or pattern, size, colour, pedigree, restoration and many other factors must be taken into account when assessing values.

A mahogany hanging candle box, with fretwork pediment, mid-19thC, 21in (53cm) high.
$200-300

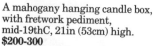

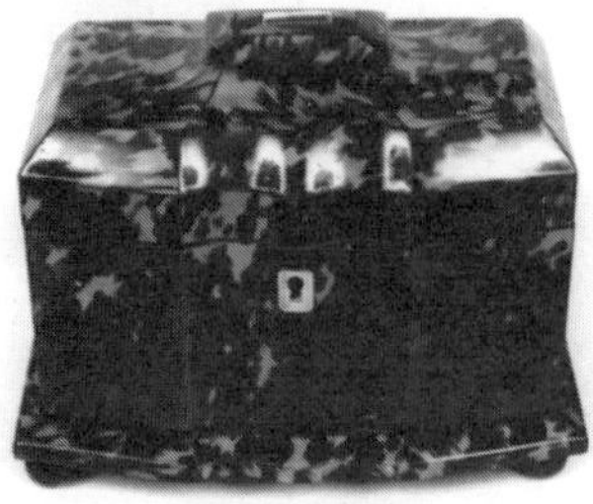

A Regency tortoiseshell tea caddy.
$800-1,200

A curled paper tea caddy, 18thC.
$1,500-1,600

A fruitwood tea caddy, with metal lock and hinge, partly stained red, 18thC, 4½in (11cm) high.
$4,000-5,000

A Sheraton tea caddy, painted with foliate swags, 5in (14cm).
$800-900

A powder box, the lid inset with a painting on ivory, early 20thC.
$700-800

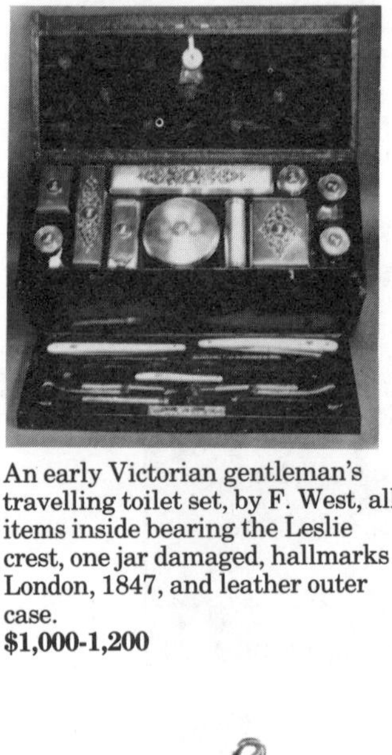

An early Victorian gentleman's travelling toilet set, by F. West, all items inside bearing the Leslie crest, one jar damaged, hallmarks London, 1847, and leather outer case.
$1,000-1,200

A Victorian biscuit box, with swan finial, on 4 paw feet.
$250-350

A Victorian zebra wood toilet box, by Charles Henry, Manchester, with jewel drawer below the fitted interior, London hallmarks, 1866.
$900-1,000

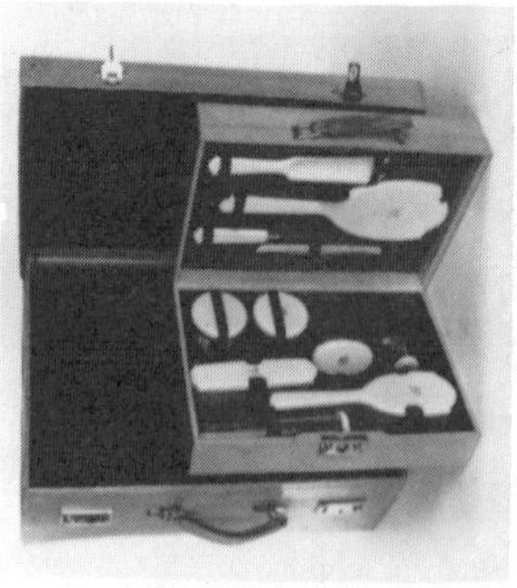

A hide dressing case, with silver and ivory bottles and fittings, in separate case.
$900-1,000

A Victorian cut glass and plated biscuit box, on bun feet.
$150-200

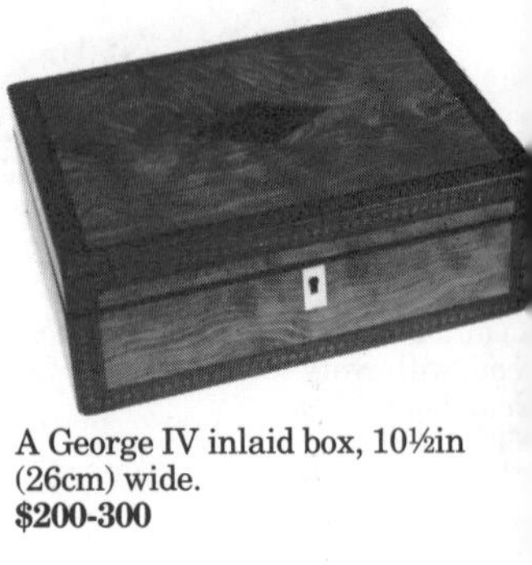

A George IV inlaid box, 10½in (26cm) wide.
$200-300

walnut box, inlaid with shell and
ıother-of-pearl, 14in (36cm) wide.
150-200

A Regency penwork casket, decorated with flowerheads and leaves, with giltmetal drop ring handles and ball feet, 11½in (29cm).
$1,300-1,500

An owl box, 3in (7.5cm) high.
$80-140

. George III mahogany brass bound
ıilitary box, with ebony inlay,
7½in (44cm) wide.
350-450

A rosewood workbox, with fitted interior, 19thC, 12½in (32cm) wide.
$250-350

mahogany writing slope with
ıcret drawer, 19thC, 20in (50cm)
ide.
500-700

A satinwood inlaid jewellery box, 9in (23.5cm) wide.
$250-350

A Victorian rosewood box inlaid with pewter and mother-of-pearl, 11½in (29cm).
$150-200

A Victorian burr walnut and brass box, 8½in (21cm) wide.
$250-350

Regency tea caddy, c1820,
200-250

A walnut brass bound table writing slope, with fitted interior.
$400-500

A walnut box, 11in (28cm).
$150-200

A Newlyn copper box, 3in (7.5cm) diam.
$150-250

A Russian box, restored, c1860.
$300-400

A gold coloured metal patch box, se with diamonds and sapphires, Tiffany & Co.
$1,400-1,500

A William IV rosewood writing slope, inlaid with mother-of-pearl, with secret drawers.
$500-600

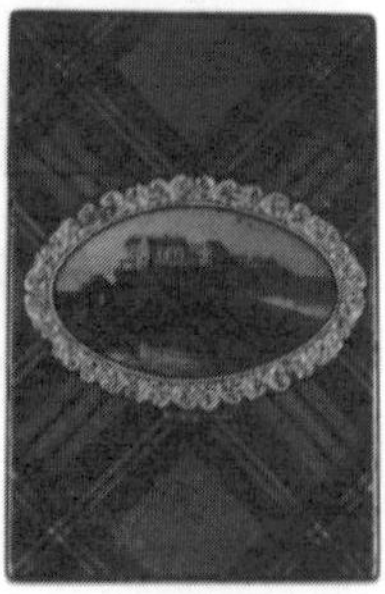

A hand painted Mauchline card case, depicting Stirling Castle in the cartouche.
$300-400

A George III ivory box strung with ebony, 8in (20cm) wide.
$400-600

l. A Victorian mahogany domestic medicine box, with 10 bottles and fitted drawer.
$600-700

r. A mahogany travelling medicine box, fitted with bottles, 19thC.
$500-700

TRANSPORT

Vehicles

A 1925/26 Matchless R-Model 250cc solo motorcycle, engine No. 1026.
$6,000-8,000

A 1919 Chevrolet 490 four-seater tourer, chassis No. 294541.
$10,000-12,000

A 1940 Buick series 40 two-door coupe, coachwork by Fisher, engine No. 4 3871836.
$25,000-30,000

Make the most of Miller's

Price ranges in this book reflect what one should expect to pay for a similar example. When selling one can obviously expect a figure below. This will fluctuate according to a dealer's stock, saleability at a particular time, etc. It is always advisable to approach a reputable specialist dealer or an auction house which has specialist sales.

\ 1959 Jaguar XK150S roadster,
ngine No. VS 1255/9.
80,000-100,000

A Victorian pram.
$250-350

1934 Austin Seven saloon,
gistration No. AMG 347, restored.
,000-7,000

A late Victorian iron tricycle, 82in (208cm) long.
$800-1,000

\ Penny Farthing bicycle, the front
vheel with 'Solar' sponge tyre, the
ron backbone with mounting step,
eather saddle and 'T' handle bars,
ront wheel 53in (136cm) diam.
3,500-4,000

'ar Mascots

glass nymph, Vitesse, on winged
luminated base and wood stand,
½in (29cm) high.
,000-6,000

Miscellaneous

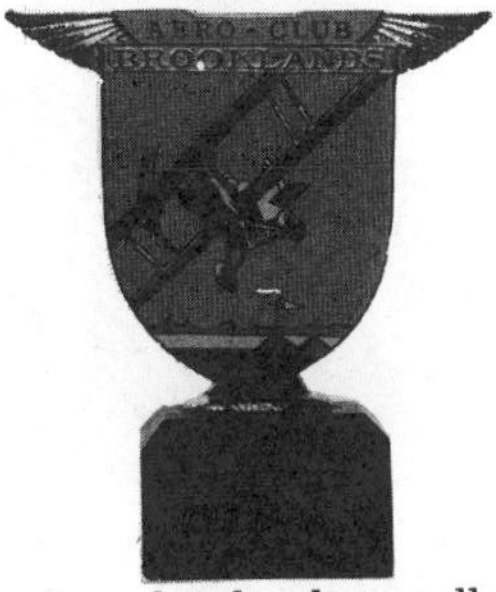

A chromium plated and enamelled Aero-Club Brooklands badge, stamped 164, 3½in (9.5cm) high.
$1,800-2,000

A chromium plated and enamelled Brooklands Automobile Racing Club badge, stamped 894, 3½in (9.5cm) high.
$1,200-1,600

Caledonian Railway, second device, on blue panel, 20in (51cm).
$200-500

M.R. final device, 20in (51cm).
$100-150

Cambrian Railways, Prince of Wales plumes, 15 by 16in (38 by 41cm).
$200-300

LEATHER & LUGGAG

A nickel plated Michelin tyre pressure gauge, contained in original printed tinplate box depicting Bibendum and an early motorist, original instructions.
$300-400

An early brass Austin winged steering wheel on radiator cap, indistinct mark, 4in (10cm) high.
$1,200-1,800

Leather & Luggage

A crocodile skin suitcase, 24in (61cm) long.
$500-600

A Louis Vuitton wardrobe tru labelled, No. 782259, 44in (111.5cm) long.
$3,500-4,000

A Louis Vuitton wardrobe trunk, covered with LV material, labelled, 40in (102cm) long.
$4,000-5,000

SPORT

Fishing

An Eaton and Deller brass reel, engraved with owner's initials, c1850, 2½in (6cm).
$100-200

A brass reel, fitted with a reversible brass handle, c1860, 5in (12.5cm).
$100-150

A Paton of Perth rosewood and bra trolling reel, with half-circle brass brake fitting into an extended rim the drum, c1890, 5in (13cm).
$150-200

A Carter of London Jardine brass and ebonite reel, with nickel silver rims, c1890, 4in (10cm).
$80-120

A Malloch Sun and Planet brass reel, with ebonite back plate and nickel silver rims, c1890, 4in (10cm).
$120-160

A Hardy Field aluminium alloy reel, with ivorine handle, c1900, 2½in (7cm).
$200-300

A Hardy Perfect reel, duplicated Mk. II, c1930, 3in (7cm).
$120-160

A Hardy Uniqua wide drum salmon fly reel, with horseshoe latch, c1930, 3½in (9cm).
$80-100

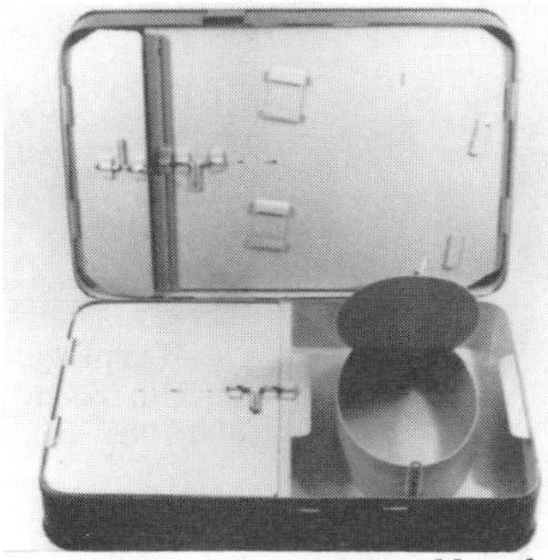

A Hardy black japanned lure box, restored, c1930, 7in (18cm).
$40-60

A J. W. Young Gildex multiplying bait casting reel, with level wind control and patented hinged alloy foot, c1960.
$30-40

An Illingworth No. threadline casting reel, fitted with line, in plush lined case.
$700-800

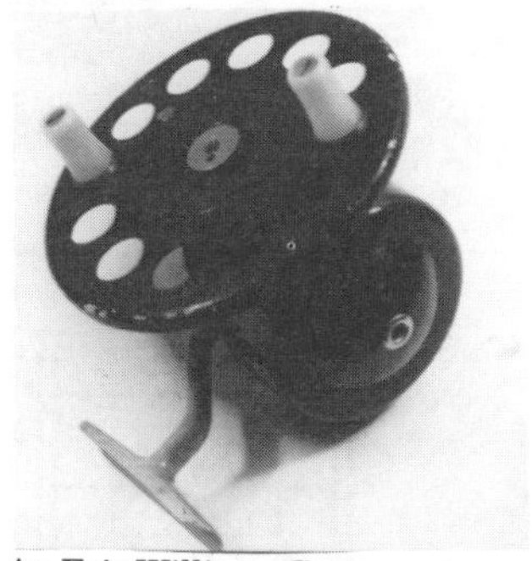

An Eric Williams Centrecaster, patent number 1018130, post-war, 4in (11cm).
$30-40

An unnamed salmon fly reel in nickel silver, with a pair of folding brass handle knobs, c1915, 4in (10cm).
$60-100

A Palace Superb casting reel, late 1940s.
$40-60

A Hardy St. George reel, 3-screw drum latch, agate line-guard, c1930s, 3in (7.5cm).
$120-160

A French fixed spool reel, The Willmouth, late 1940s.
$20-30

A Hardy Neroda fly box, with fitted interior, c1950.
$40-60

A Hardy Perfect fly reel, wartime model, 4in (10cm).
$120-160

A Hardy Perfect all brass fly reel, with brass ball-bearings, in original condition with hand trade mark, 2½in (6cm).
$400-600

An Allcock Bell big game sea reel, in dark and pitted condition, c1930, 6in (15cm).
$40-60

A stuffed and mounted pike, in natural reeded river setting in glazed display case, 42in (105cm) wide.
$700-900

l. An unnamed drum fly reel, with central drag control and ivorine handle, c1930, 3in (8cm).
$30-40

r. An Ogden Smith Exchequer fly reel, with double reverse tapered composition handle, red agate lineguard, restored, c1940, 3in (8cm).
$50-70

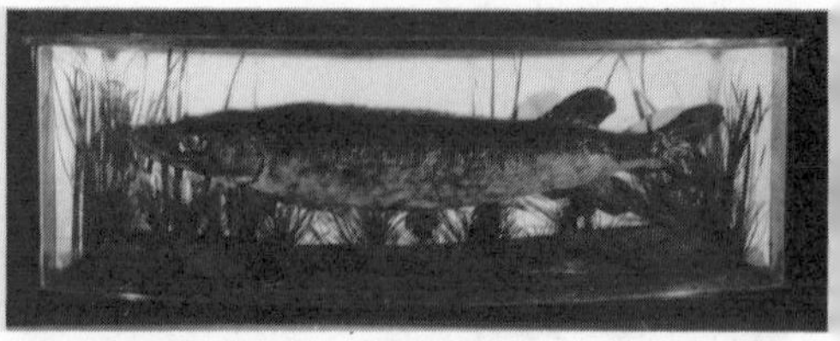

A stuffed pike in a bowfronted case, fish 33in (83cm) long.
$600-700

A Hardy Bouglé trout fly reel, with ivorine handle, 1906 check, 3in (8cm).
$600-800

Golfing

A pair of American tinplate 'Jocko the Golfer', clockwork toys, 6½in (16.5cm) long.
$600-800

A tinted glass panel, the centre section painted with a golfing scene, c1900, 38in (96.5cm) high.
$5,000-6,000

A 9ct. L.U.G.C. replica golf championship cup, London hallmark 1910, 6in (15cm) high, 8½oz, on ebony plinth with presentation plaque.
$2,000-3,000

Miscellaneous

A commemorative cotton handkerchief, printed with 2 football teams, c1890, 26 by 28in (66 by 71cm).
$800-1,000

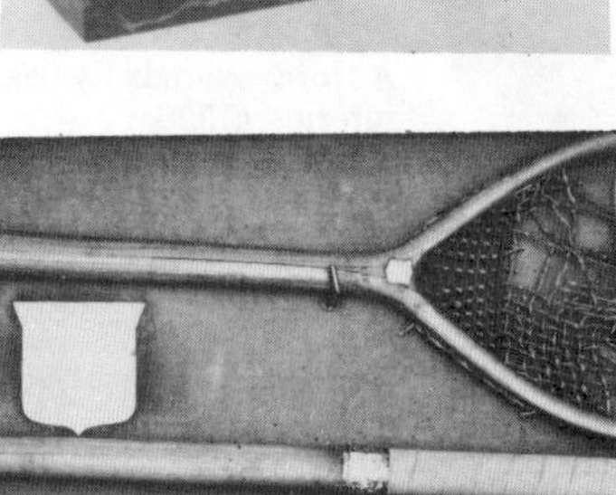

A bronze figure of a skier, on marble plinth, 12½in (32cm) long.
$1,000-1,200

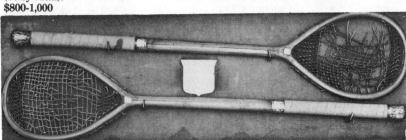

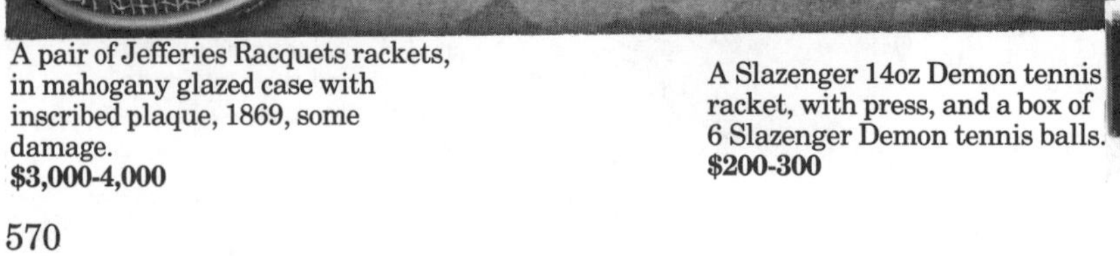

A pair of Jefferies Racquets rackets, in mahogany glazed case with inscribed plaque, 1869, some damage.
$3,000-4,000

A Slazenger 14oz Demon tennis racket, with press, and a box of 6 Slazenger Demon tennis balls.
$200-300

Crafts

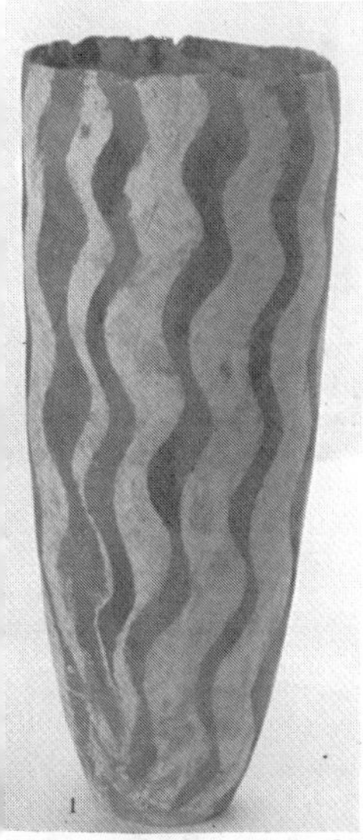

A blue and white striped vase, by Nancy Angus, painted NA signature, 13in (33cm) high.
$200-300

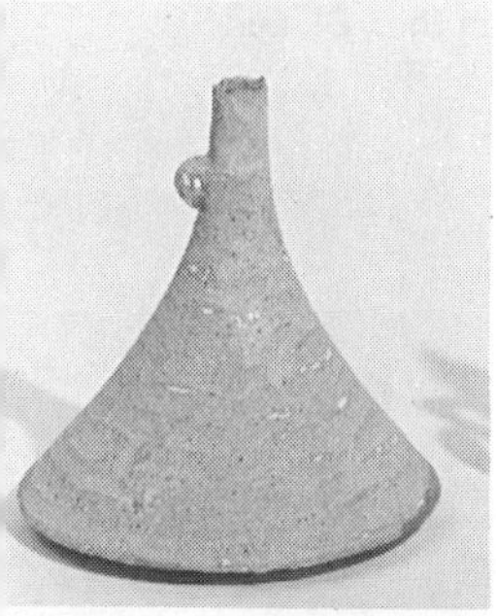

A blue vase by Peter Beard, impressed PFB seal, 5½in (14.5cm).
$60-140

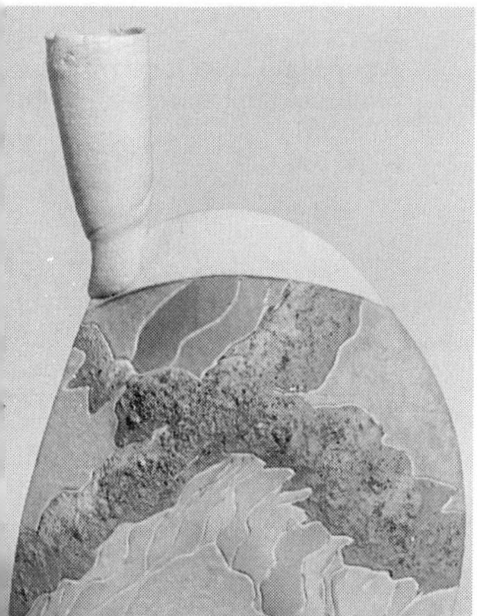

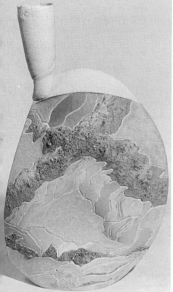

A porcelain assymetrical form, in white with blue, pink and green incised decoration, painted J. Bevan signature, 15in (38cm) high.
$100-200

A porcelain plant holder, with blue and green floral and foliate decoration, by Brigitte Appelby, 7in (18cm) high.
$100-200

An olive green stoneware teapot by Terry Bell-Hughes, potter's impressed seal, 7½in (18.5cm).
$100-140

A teapot by Tony Bennett, with green frog-like impression on one side and Tony Bennett seal on the other, 9in (23cm).
$120-180

A stoneware bowl by Michael Cardew, the interior with combed decoration, impressed MC and Wenford Bridge seals, 11in (27.5cm) diam.
$1,200-1,400

A stoneware bowl by Michael Cardew, with mushroom coloured glaze, impressed MC and Wenford Bridge seal, 10½in (26.5cm).
$1,200-1,400

A stoneware teapot by Michael Cardew, impressed MC and Wenford Bridge seal, 9½in (24cm) high.
$1,200-1,400

A stoneware dish by Michael Cardew, the interior with olive green, brown and lustrous iron glazes, exterior unglazed, firing cracks, impressed MC and Wenford Bridge seals, 14½in (36.5cm).
$200-300

A press moulded vessel, The Princess and the Dragon, by Stephen Dixon, 13in (33cm) diam.
$240-320

A winged bird vase by Neil Ions, painted signature, 7in (18cm).
$80-120

A teapot by Wally Keeler, embossed seal, 9in (23cm).
$300-400

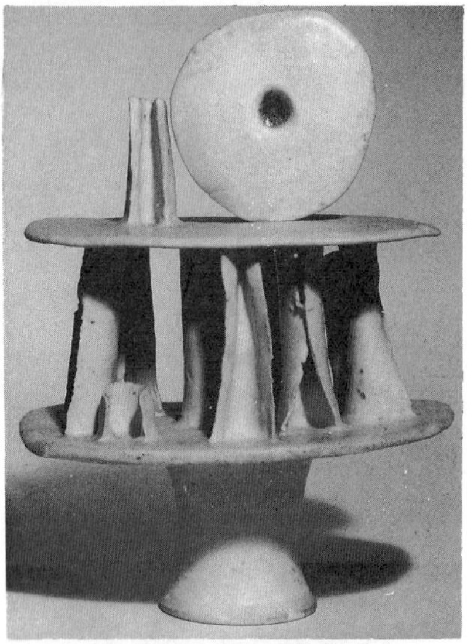

A porcelain hand built form by Ruth Duckworth, painted R monogram, 11in (28cm).
$1,600-1,800

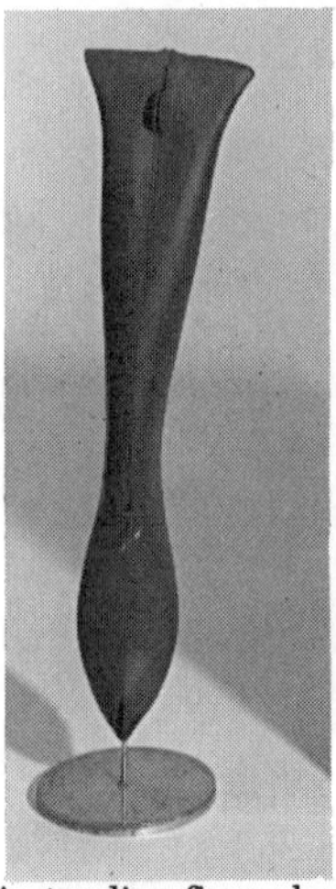

A standing figure by Mo Jupp, 9in (22cm).
$140-200

A stoneware bowl by Bernard Leach, small rim chip, BL and St. Ives seals, 6in (15cm).
$2,500-3,000

A porcelain bowl form by Peter Simpson, impressed seal, 5½in (13.5cm).
$600-700

A stoneware bottle vase by Bernard Leach, impressed BL and St. Ives seals, 9in (22.5cm).
$5,000-6,000

A stoneware bottle by Andrew Marshall, impressed M seal, 9½in (24cm).
$80-140

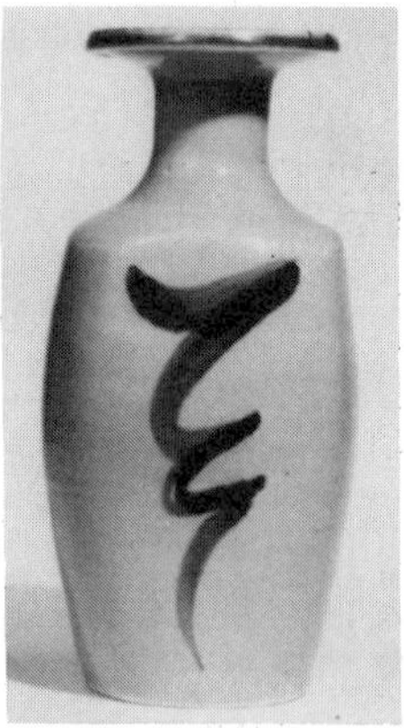

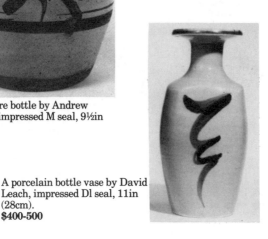

A porcelain bottle vase by David Leach, impressed Dl seal, 11in (28cm).
$400-500

A vase by John Maltby, painted signature, 9½in (24cm).
$150-200

A black, red and green bowl by Janice Tchalenki, 10in (25cm) diam.
$200-300

A Louis Wain porcelain vase, painted with green, terracotta and black, moulded marks Louis Wain, printed Made in England, Rd. No. 638315, 3½in (9cm) high.
$600-800

A Louis Wain porcelain vase, in the shape of a stylised cat, painted Louis Wain, made in England, 5½in (14.5cm).
$800-1,000

A Louis Wain porcelain pig vase, painted marks Louis Wain, Rd. No. 638320, 5in (12cm).
$600-1,000

Tribal Art

A Fiji lenticular Kava bowl, dark glossy patina, 21in (52cm).
$700-900

A Samoan Kava bowl, with inscription, dark glossy patina, repaired, 19in (47cm) diam.
$600-800

A boat group by Thomas Ona, 12in (30cm).
$1,500-1,800

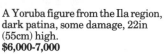

A Maori feather box, 15½in (39cm).
$2,000-3,000

A Yoruba figure from the Ila region, dark patina, some damage, 22in (55cm) high.
$6,000-7,000

Three Yoruba figures, by Thomas Ona Odulate of Ijebu Ode, 10in (25cm).
$1,200-1,600

TRIBAL ART

A Yoruba Epa helmet mask, the elaborate coiffure painted in blue, from Oshogbo, 39in (98cm) high.
$3,000-4,000

A New Ireland Malagan figure, Totok, painted with red, black and white, damaged, 31½in (79cm) high.
$7,000-8,000

A Dogon female figure, damaged, 15in (38cm).
$12,000-13,000

A Benin bronze belt mask, loop below for attachment, loop above missing, c1800, 6in (16cm).
$3,000-4,000

A Chokwe female figure, with incised scarification, hatched Lunda coiffure, dark patina, 11½in (29cm).
$700-800

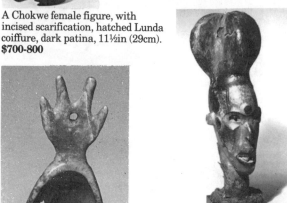

A Yoruba head-dress for Egungun, from the Adugbuloge carving house, Abeokuta, 10in (26cm) high.
$700-900

An Ogoni mask, with articulated lower jaw, black patina, repaired, 10in (26cm).
$240-300

A Luba Shankadi stool, dark glossy patina, c1900, 15in (38cm).
$5,000-7,000

An Ekoi skin-covered mask head-dress, the open mouth with filed teeth, minor damage, 17in (42cm) high.
$2,000-2,500

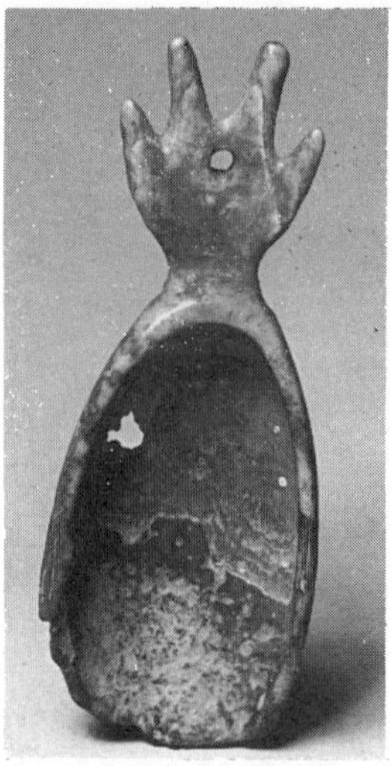

An Archaic Eskimo spoon, Old Bering Sea Culture.
$300-400

A Chokwe stool, the legs engraved with basketweave design, with hide seat, 18in (45cm) wide.
$2,000-3,000

TEXTILES

Costume

A dress of fawn ribbed silk, trimmed with grey silk binding and bows, with a petticoat similarly trimmed and gathered to form a high bustle, c1870.
$400-500

A shallow crowned wide-brimmed hat of woven straw, covered in ivory silk, slight wear, mid-18thC.
$4,000-5,000

An ivory silk Christening robe, 3 cotton baby robes, 3 ivory flannel baby's petticoats and a collection of linen.
$200-250

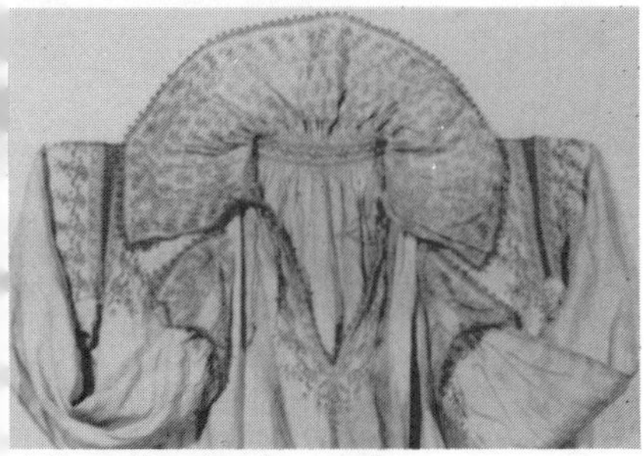

A linen chemise, damaged, 17th/18thC, Portuguese.
$400-500

A green silk damask open robe and petticoat, c1775.
$6,000-10,000

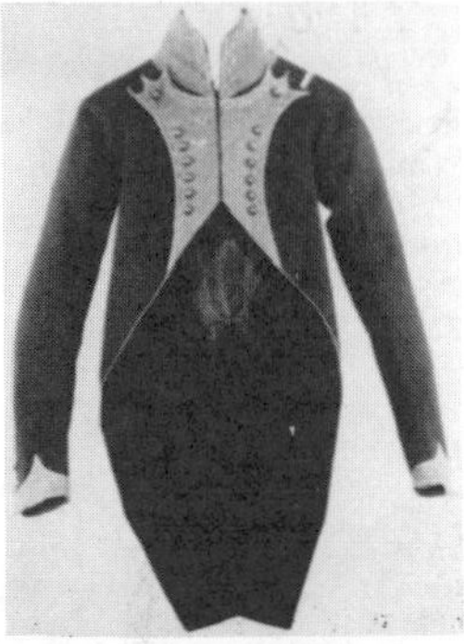

An officer's dress of dark blue facecloth with crimson facings, and silver leaf embroidery, with a pair of crimson breeches, moth damage, 1 button missing, c1805.
$5,000-6,000

Worn by a Guard of Honour at Liège to receive Napoleon.

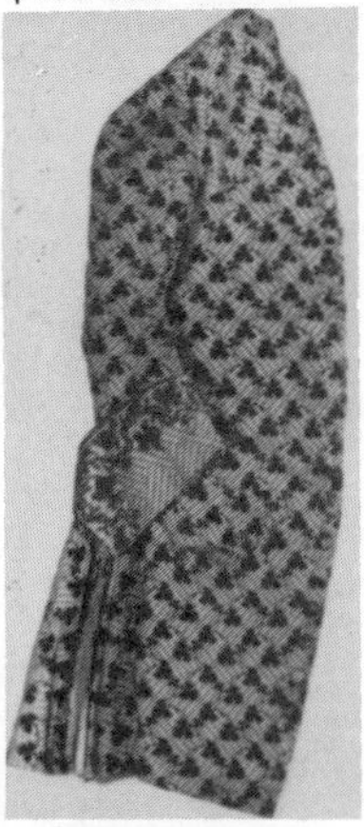

A ciselé velvet coat, alterations, c1740.
$2,000-3,000

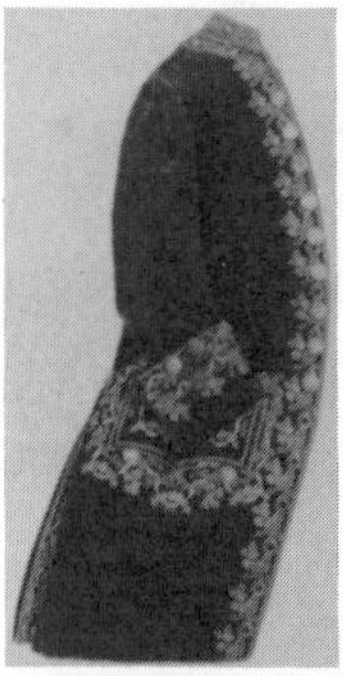

An embroidered brown velvet coat, and breeches, c1770.
$1,200-2,000

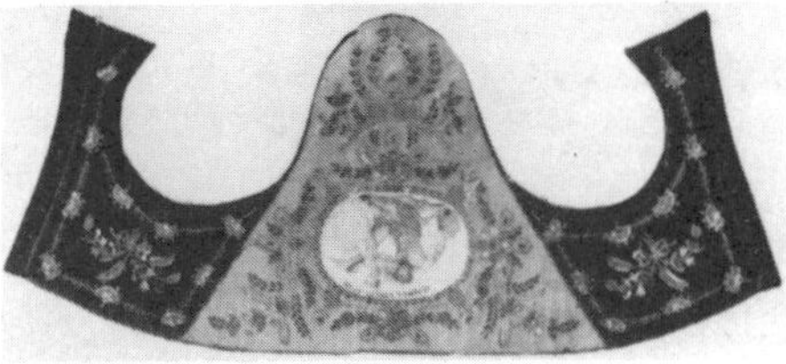

A black and blue silk embroidered wedding belt, motto 'Omnia vincit amor', Swiss or French, c1790.
$200-500

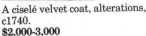

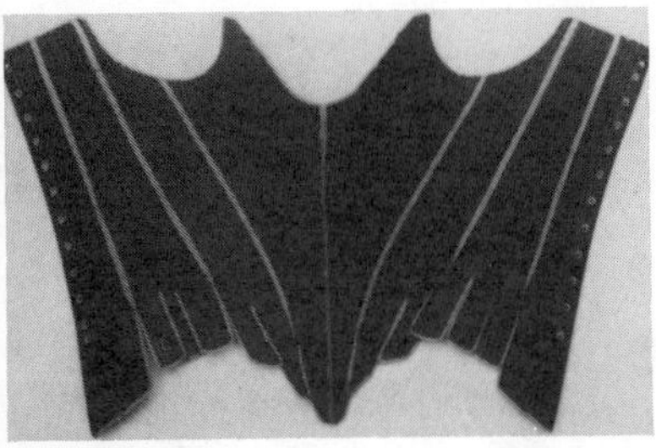

A brown canvas boned corset, c1770.
$6,000-7,000

A yellow cotton banyan, damaged, late 18thC.
$2,000-4,000

A waistcoat of black satin, lined with white glazed cotton, c1840.
$400-500

A girl's dress of white muslin, 1840s.
$400-500

A pair of black velvet shoes, c1790.
$400-800

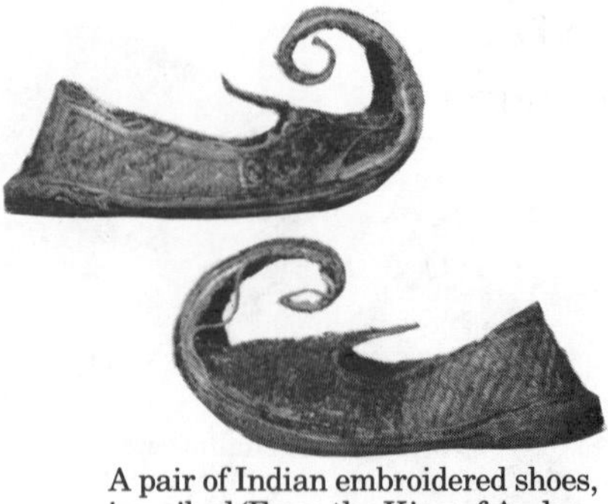

A pair of Indian embroidered shoes, inscribed 'From the King of Andes Palace at Lucknow, 1857', worn.
$400-500

A pair of shoes, embroidered with green and pink cottons with a check design, c1720.
$7,000-8,000

A pair of gentleman's slippers with a square domed toe, worn and faded, one inscribed inside 'George II's slippers', c1720.
$2,500-3,000

These are believed to have belonged to HM King George II.

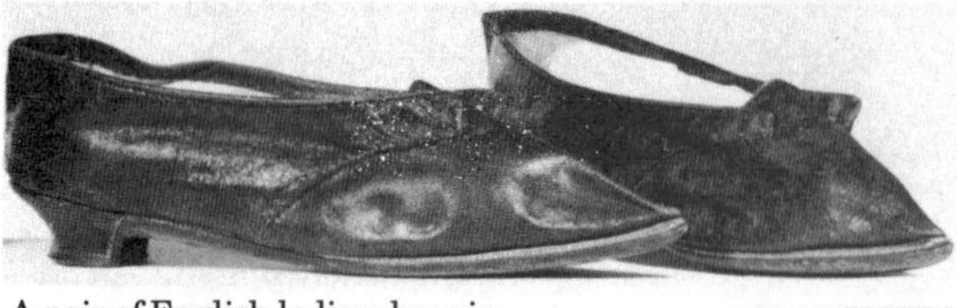

A pair of English ladies shoes in grape coloured leather, c1790.
$2,500-3,000

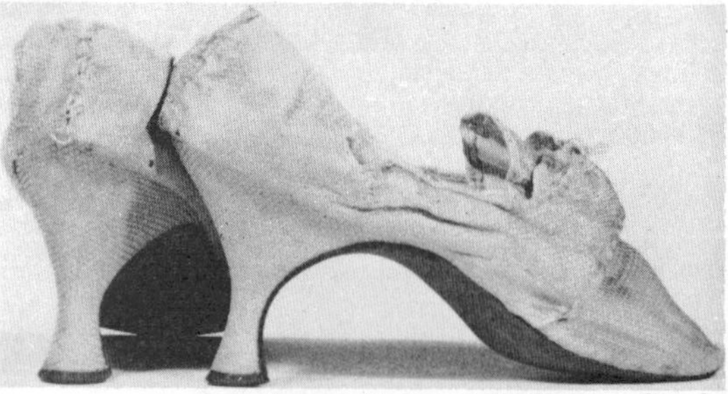

A pair of ladies pink silk shoes, lined with ivory kid, worn, c1770.
$2,500-3,000

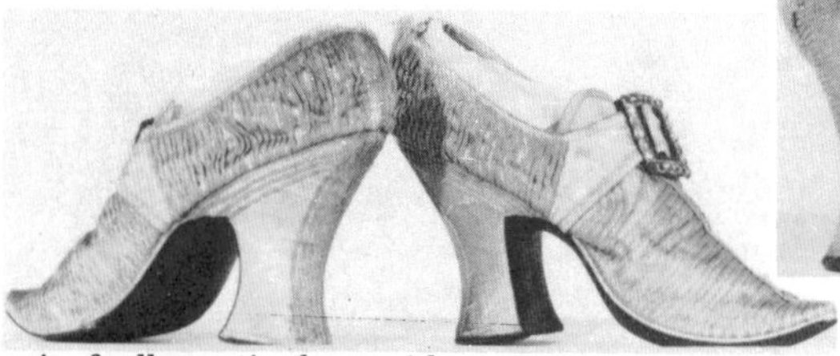

A pair of yellow satin shoes, with a blue and white paste buckle, a few stones missing, c1730.
$10,000-12,000

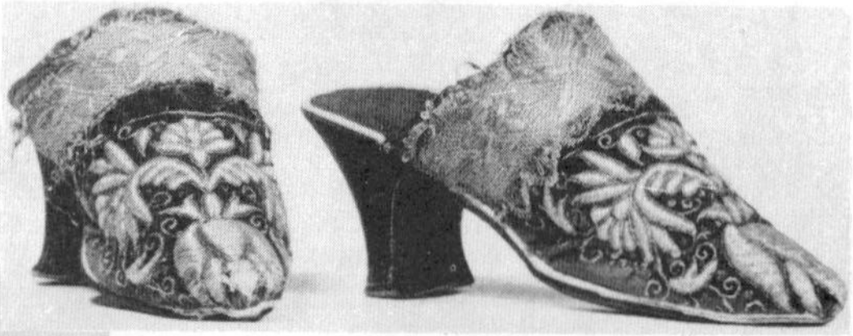

A pair of mule slippers of embroidered maroon velvet, c1700.
$25,000-30,000

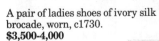

A pair of ladies shoes of ivory silk brocade, worn, c1730.
$3,500-4,000

Three pairs of gaiters, repairs, c1800.
$600-700

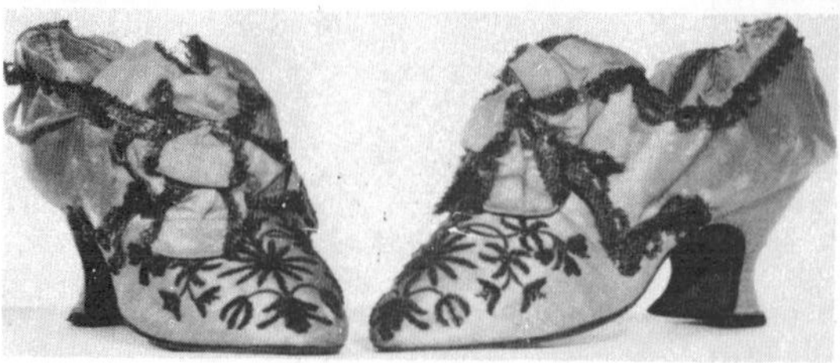

A pair of pink silk shoes, the toes embroidered with sequins and metal braid, faded, slight wear, c1760.
$8,000-10,000

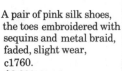

A Chinese court vest in midnight blue silk, embroidered in coloured silks and gilt thread.
$800-1,000

A Chinese lady's informal jacket of red silk, lined in pale blue silk.
$1,400-1,600

A Chinese dragon robe of blue kossu silk, 18thC.
$3,500-4,000

Embroidery

A Charles II trumpet banner of crimson damask, applied with the Royal Arms in blue and crimson satin, c1660, 20 by 23in (50 by 58cm), framed and glazed.
$8,000-12,000

A mirror-frame embroidery, worked in brightly coloured silks, c1660, 18 by 23in (46 by 57cm), on a canvas ground.
$6,000-8,000

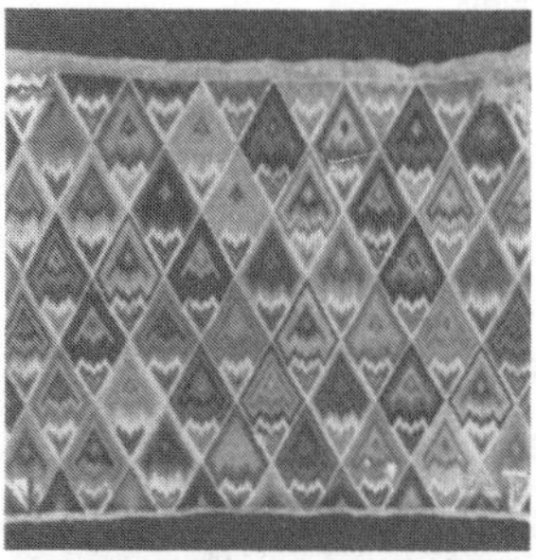

A set of 3 embroidered chair covers worked in coloured wools, mainly pink, with the inscription Sarah Woods, 1781, 14 by 19in (35 by 48cm).
$600-800

Lace

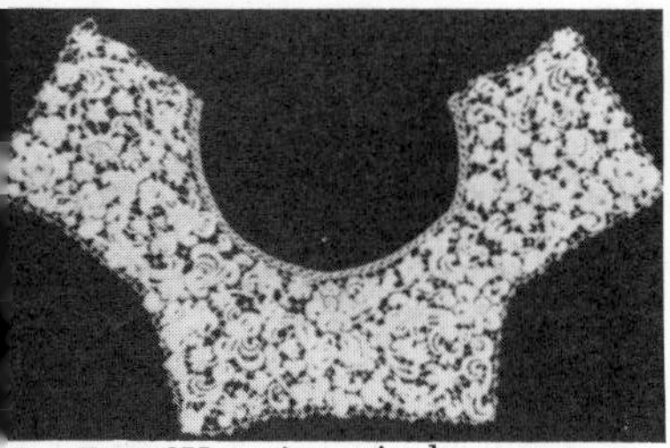

A collar of Venetian raised needlelace, 17thC with 19thC alterations.
$800-1,000

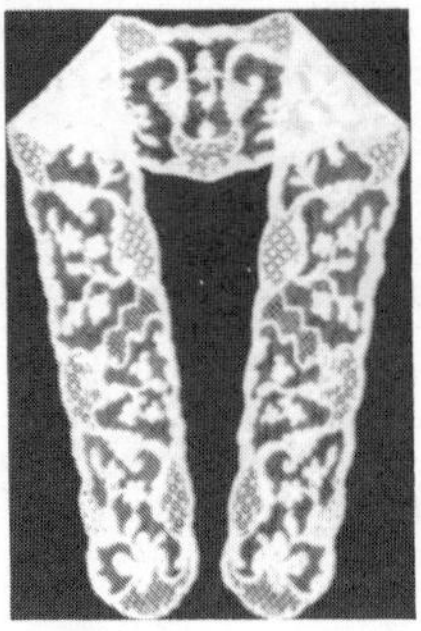

A lappet of Valenciennes bobbin lace, 18thC.
$400-600

A collection of lace including a single point de gaze lappet, 18thC.
$250-300

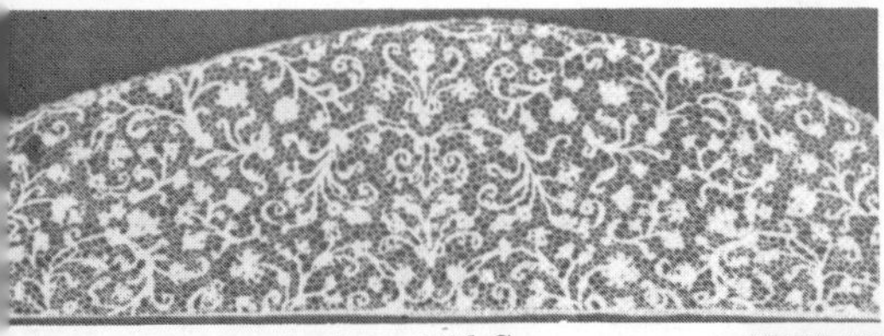

A collar of point plat lace, 17thC, with 19thC alterations.
$300-400

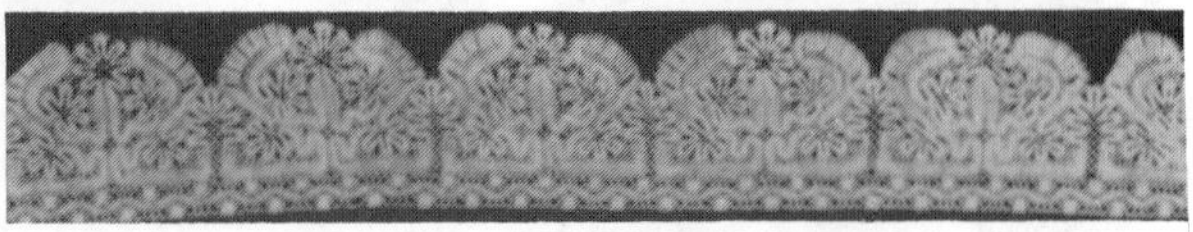

A collection of lace including a border of bobbin lace, possibly 18thC.
$500-600

A collection of lace including a Limerick veil and a fragment of 18thC Valenciennes edging.
$300-400

Covers

An appliqued cotton quilted coverlet, worked in Rose of Sharon pattern, probably Pennsylvania, mid-19thC, 82 by 80in (205 by 200cm).
$900-1,000

A wool and cotton overshot double woven Jacquard coverlet, the border inscribed 'Memorial Hall, Centennial', c1876, 78in (198cm) square.
$400-600

A pieced wool quilted coverlet, worked in the Diamond in the Square pattern, Lancaster County, Pennsylvania, c1910, 75in (191cm) square.
$1,000-1,500

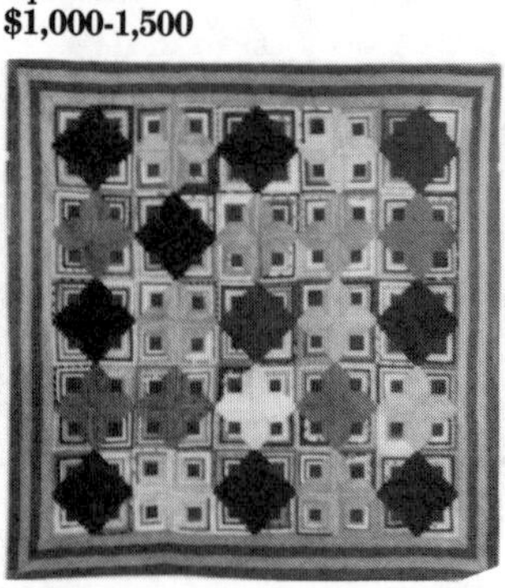

A Mennonite pieced wool quilted coverlet, Lancaster County, Pennsylvania, c1910, 96in (244cm) square.
$2,500-3,500

A pieced wool coverlet, possibly Mennonite, Pennsylvania, early 20thC, 68 by 86in (173 by 219cm).
$2,000-3,000

A wool and cotton double woven coverlet, American, c1830, 80½ by 83in (204 by 211cm).
$600-800

A pieced and appliqued cotton quilted coverlet, with central crest of the Hawaiian monarchy and inscription, some wear, c1870, 81½in (207cm) square.
$8,000-10,000

The translation of the inscription, 'The life of the land is preserved in the righteous', is the motto of Hawaii.

An appliqued cotton album quilt top, Maryland, c1850, 85½ by 84in (218 by 216cm).
$5,000-7,000

An appliqued cotton quilted coverlet, Kentucky, c1850, 85 b 109in (216 by 277cm).
$1,000-1,200

A pair of pieced and appliqued quilted cotton coverlets, American, c1930, 78 by 88in (198 by 224cm).
$2,000-3,000

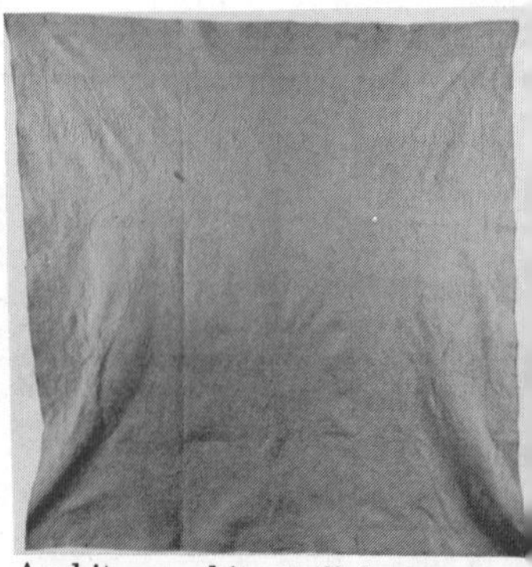

A white-on-white stuffed cotton quilt, with a pattern of meandering vines, floral blossoms and corner pineapples, signed 'Mary Young, August 23, 1821', 100in (254cm) square.
$12,000-15,000

A Mennonite pieced wool quilted coverlet, Cumberland County, Pennsylvania, c1900, 90in (229cm) square.
$3,000-5,000

An Amish pieced cotton quilted coverlet, Mid-Western, c1910, 76 by 89in (193 by 226cm).
$2,500-3,500

An Amish pieced cotton quilted coverlet, with the Broken Star pattern, probably Indiana, c1930, 86in (219cm) square.
$3,000-4,000

An Amish pieced cotton quilted coverlet, with Star patterns, in slate blue, maize and black, some staining, Kalona, Iowa, 1921, 74 by 80in (188 by 203cm).
$5,000-6,000

An Amish pieced cotton quilted coverlet, worked in Sunshine and Shadow pattern, Lancaster County, Pennsylvania, c1930, 84 by 88in (213 by 224cm).
$4,000-5,000

An Amish pieced wool quilted coverlet, slight wear, Lancaster County, Pennsylvania, c1920, 72 by 80in (183 by 203cm).
$5,000-6,000

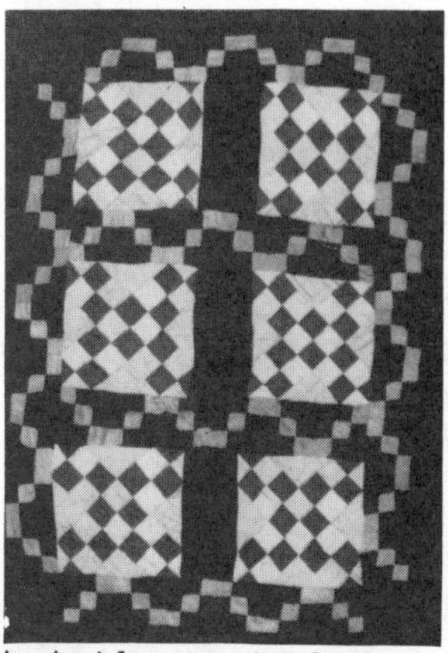

An Amish cotton pieced crib coverlet, probably Ohio, early 20thC, 53 by 40in (133 by 100cm).
$1,100-1,300

An applied cotton coverlet top, Pennsylvania, mid-19thC, 86in (219cm) square.
$500-700

A wool and cotton Jacquard coverlet, attributed to Jefferson Co, NY, with 'Patience Mendell 1837' bottom right hand corner, damaged, 92½ by 78in (235 by 198cm).
$1,200-1,500

A wool and cotton Jacquard coverlet, Emanuel Meily, Lebanon, Pennsylvania, 1848, 88 by 94in (224 by 238cm).
$1,200-1,500

A pieced cotton quilted coverlet, early 19thC, 106 by 90in (270 by 229cm).
$2,000-2,500

A wool and cotton double woven Jacquard coverlet, worn and fraying, mid-19thC, 65 by 67in (165 by 170cm).
$400-500

Use the Index!

Because certain items might fit easily into any of a number of categories, the quickest and surest method of locating any entry is by reference to the index at the back of the book.
This has been fully cross-referenced for absolute simplicity

Samplers

A needlework sampler, with the inscription 'Elizabeth Bennett Aged 11 years', with 'S. Betts, Instructress' lower right, mid-19thC, 17 by 16in (43 by 40cm).
$700-900

A needlework sampler, with verse and inscription 'Polly Biship Born December 6th 1800, Cumberland County, August 29th, 1813', 16½ by 11½in (41 by 29cm).
$800-1,000

A needlework picture, with religious verse and inscription 'Martha James's work finish'd in the year 1762', some damage, 17 by 12in (43 by 31cm).
$1,000-1,200

A needlework picture, attributed to Miss Patten's School, Hartford, Connecticut, c1800, 17 by 21in (43 by 53cm).
$1,200-1,500

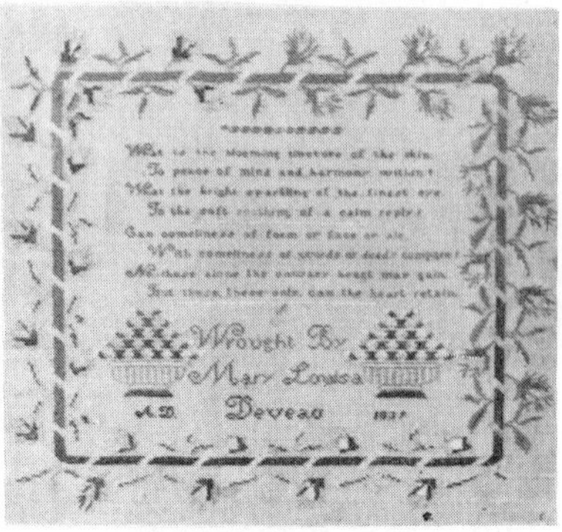

A needlework picture, with verse and inscription 'Wrought by Mary Louisa Deveau, 1839', the whole surrounded by a floral and trailing vine border, 16½ by 18½in (41.5 by 46cm).
$700-900

A needlework picture, with poem and inscription 'Sarah Bane's work wrought AD 1830 in the ninth year of her age', probably Chester County, Pennsylvania, 25½ by 23½in (64 by 58cm).
$6,000-7,000

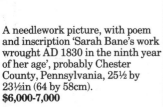

A silk-on-silk needlework picture, c1800, 10 by 14in (25 by 35cm).
$1,800-2,000

A sampler by Eliza Andrews, worked in coloured silks, early 19thC, 17 by 13in (43 by 33cm), framed and glazed.
$600-800

A needlework sampler by Mary Ann Burgess, aged 9 years, 1829, 17½ by 18in (43 by 45cm), framed and glazed.
$700-800

Victorian sampler by Mary 'arris, aged 9 years, 1845, with an questrian figure of the Duke of Brunswick, 13 by 10in (33 by 5.5cm).
2,500-3,000

A sampler by Martha Mabe, 1837, worked in coloured silks with the caption 'Milton Lodge, the seat of Sir J Asterley Bart Norfolk', 18 by 13in (46 by 33cm), framed and glazed.
$4,000-5,000

A sampler worked in coloured silks, inscribed Emily White, aged 11, 1825, 14 by 12in (35 by 31cm), framed and glazed.
$1,800-2,000

A sampler by Mary Bateman, 1739, worked in coloured silks, 9 by 10in (23 by 25cm), framed and glazed, re-applied.
$12,000-14,000

A pair of map samplers, by Sarah Fitkin, 1794, embroidered in coloured silks, 21 by 17in (53 by 43cm), framed and glazed.
$1,200-1,400

A sampler inscribed Miss Frances Cullen, aged 8 years, 1832, worked in coloured silks, 13 by 12in (33 by 31cm), framed and glazed.
$900-1,000

A darning sampler by Maria Jesup, 1799, the linen ground embroidered in red, green and ochre silks, 18 by 17in (45 by 42cm), framed and glazed.
$1,800-2,000

A silk needlework sampler by Mary Noble, aged 13 years, 1830, in original painted frame.
$2,000-2,500

A stumpwork picture, the central needlepoint panel depicting Elijah being fed by ravens, 17thC, 11½ by 15½in (29 by 39cm), framed and glazed.
$4,000-5,000

Tapestries

A Flemish tapestry, top border missing, 17thC, 129 by 94in (329 by 240cm).
$2,500-3,000

A Victorian woolwork tapestry, 44 by 37½in (110 by 96cm).
$900-1,000

A fragment of Flemish tapestry, adapted, 80 by 68in (205 by 173cm).
$8,000-10,000

Two Gobelins tapestry borders, woven in shades of brown and yellow, 17thC, 141 by 10in (358 by 25cm).
$1,200-1,600

A tapestry sofa cover, woven in bright colours, French, 18thC, 30 by 75in (75 by 191cm).
$5,500-6,000

A Flemish tapestry depicting a king and attendants, possibly Arras, bottom border slightly reduced, 17thC, 200 by 94in (507 by 238cm).
$18,000-20,000

A pair of Brussels tapestry borders, woven in colours against a brown ground, mid-19thC, 18 by 72in (45 by 183cm).
$2,500-3,000

Miscellaneous

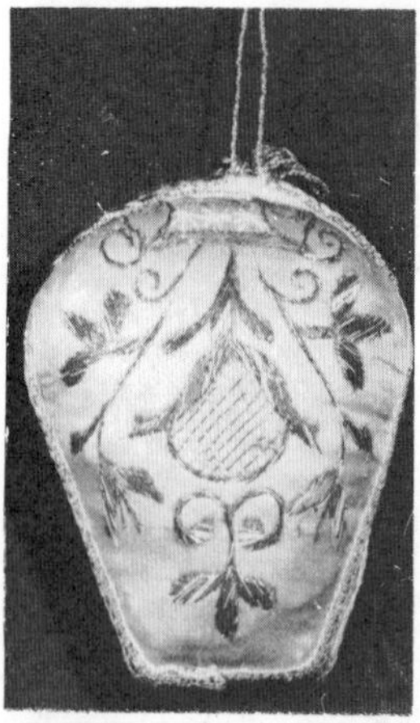

A needlecase of salmon pink silk, embroidered with silver thread, early 18thC.
$80-120

A purse of ivory coloured silk, c1830, 7 by 5in (18 by 13cm).
$800-1,000

A shield-shaped purse of ivory coloured silk, embroidered in gilt thread, trimmed with gold braid, 18thC.
$500-600

A Chinese ivory silk cover, embroidered in coloured silks, early 19thC, 100in (254cm) square.
$800-1,000

A pictorial hooked rug, American, dated 1898, 35 by 56in (90 by 142cm).
$2,000-2,500

Price

Prices vary from auction to auction – from dealer to dealer. The price paid in a dealer's shop will depend on:
1) what he paid for the item
2) what he thinks he can get for it
3) the extent of his knowledge
4) awareness of market trends
It is a mistake to think that you will automatically pay more in a specialist dealer's shop. He is more likely to know the 'right' price for a piece. A general dealer may undercharge but he could also overcharge

'ans

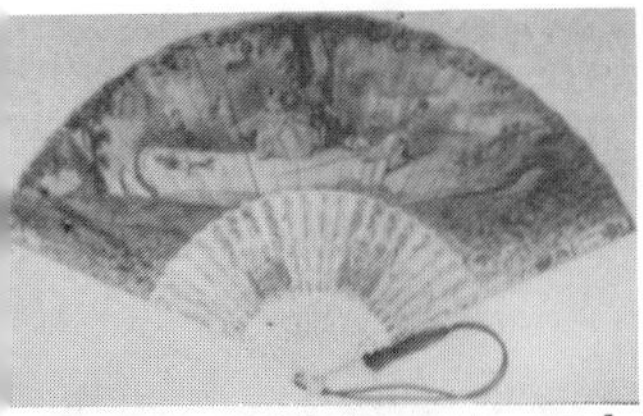

A fan painted with figures in a park, .he ivory sticks carved, pierced and ›ainted, worn, c1760, 10½in (26cm).
$1,000-1,500

A Canton fan, the leaf painted with a Chinese port, the ivory sticks carved and pierced with figures, damaged and repaired, c1850, 11in (28cm), in fitted lacquer box labelled Ayun.
$2,000-2,500

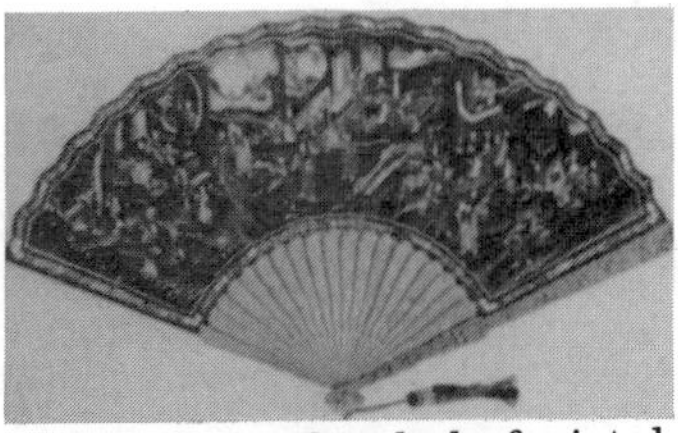

A large Canton fan, the leaf painted with figures, the sandalwood sticks carved and pierced, damaged, c1860, 18in (45.5cm), with contemporary box and glazed fan case.
$1,000-1,200

A fan with carved and painted ivory sticks, European, worn and repaired, c1740, 11in (29cm).
$900-1,000

A chicken skin fan, painted with a view of the Pantheon, Rome, repaired, c1780, 10in (25cm).
$2,500-3,000

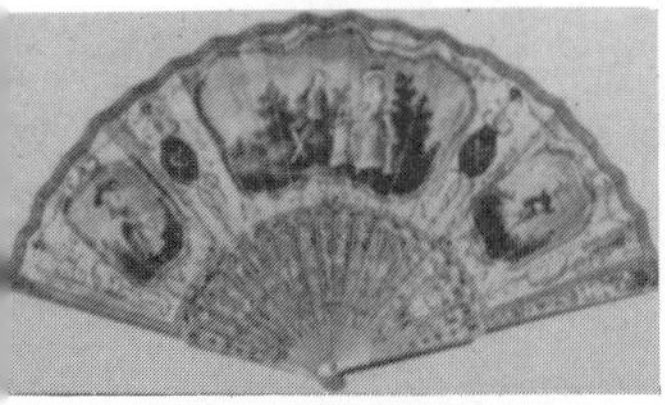

A fan, the satin leaf painted with 3 vignettes of figures, edged with sequins, c1780, 11in (29cm).
$600-800

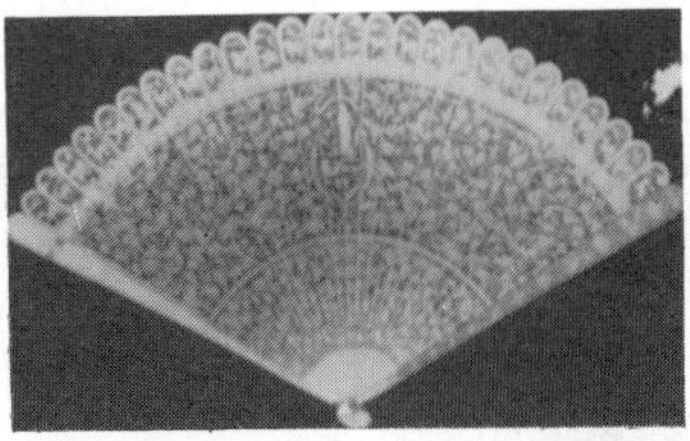

A Canton ivory brisé fan, carved and pierced, the border with a frieze of birds and beasts, the guard sticks with flowers, c1790, 10in (25.5cm).
$4,000-5,000

A fan painted with figures, the ivory sticks carved, pierced and backed with red foil, damaged, c1740, 12in (30cm).
$1,000-1,500

A fan with ivory sticks, the guard sticks carved with dolphins and eagles, Italian, c1740, 11in (29cm) in later box.
$1,300-1,500

A fan painted with a classical scene, the ivory sticks carved, pierced and painted with shells, fruit and insects, c1740, 10in (25cm).
$1,800-2,000

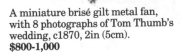

A chicken skin leaf fan, with ivory sticks clouté with mother-of-pearl and piqué with silver, damaged, c1720, 11in (29cm).
$1,500-2,500

A miniature brisé gilt metal fan, with 8 photographs of Tom Thumb's wedding, c1870, 2in (5cm).
$800-1,000

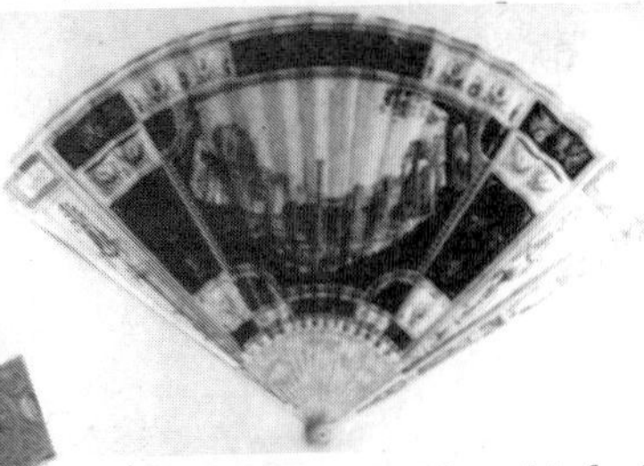

An Italian fan, the chicken skin leaf painted, the ivory sticks carved with figures and pierced, c1805, 8½in (22cm).
$1,600-1,800

A Canton brisé fan, painted with figures, rubbed, c1820, 8in (20cm).
$1,000-1,400

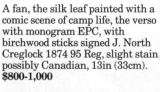

A fan, the silk leaf painted with a comic scene of camp life, the verso with monogram EPC, with birchwood sticks signed J. North Creglock 1874 95 Reg, slight stain possibly Canadian, 13in (33cm).
$800-1,000

A black lace fan of Chantilly type lace, with horn sticks, one guard stick set with the gilt metal inscription 'Janie', c1890, 13½in (34cm).
$900-1,000

A Canton carved and pierced ivory brisé fan, the filigree guard sticks enamelled in blue and green, one guard stick broken, c1800, 10in (25.5cm), in an embroidered fan case, with box.
$1,000-1,400

A Canton ivory brisé fan, carved and pierced with pagodas, flowers, fruit and figure c1820, 7½in (19cm).
$1,000-1,200

A dagger fan, the double cockade leaf enclosed in a leather sheath, with leather handle, rubbed, c1874, 10½in (26.5cm).
$160-250

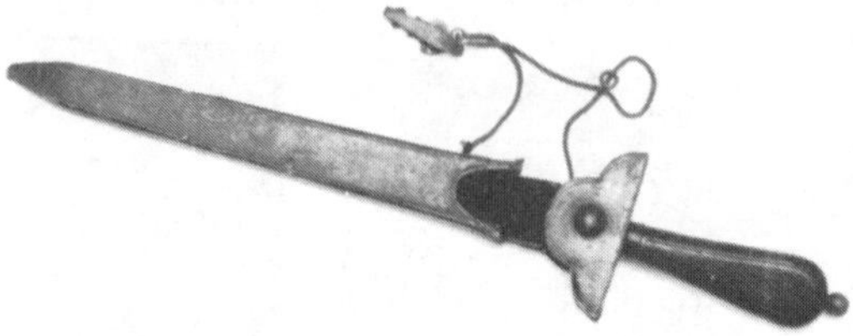

A Cantonese fan, painted with figures with ivory faces, with carved and pierced sandalwood sticks, white feather trimmed, 19thC, in a black and gilt lacquered case.
$600-800

A pair of pen-work face screens, decorated in the chinoiserie taste, applied with ring turned ivory handles, 9in (23cm) wide.
$600-800

A fan, the leaf lithographed with racing scenes, with wooden sticks, 1873, 11in (28cm).
$3,000-4,000

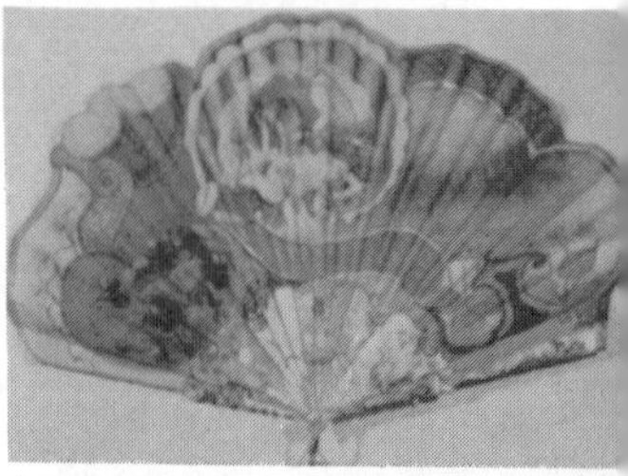

A fan, the shaped leaf painted with a woman wearing a violet trimmed bonnet and with gauze insertions, painted with violets and embroidered with sequins, the mother-of-pearl sticks carved and painted with violets, signed Jebagnes, c1905, 9½in (24cm).
$4,000-5,000

A fan painted with 18thC scenes, the mother-of-pearl sticks painted with vignettes of country scenes, c1890, 11in (28cm), in fitted Duvelleroy box.
$1,200-1,500

Pine Furniture

Beds

A child's cot, c1880, 56in (141cm) wide.
$450-550

Bookcases

A pine bookcase, 83in (211cm) wide.
$2,500-3,000

Chairs

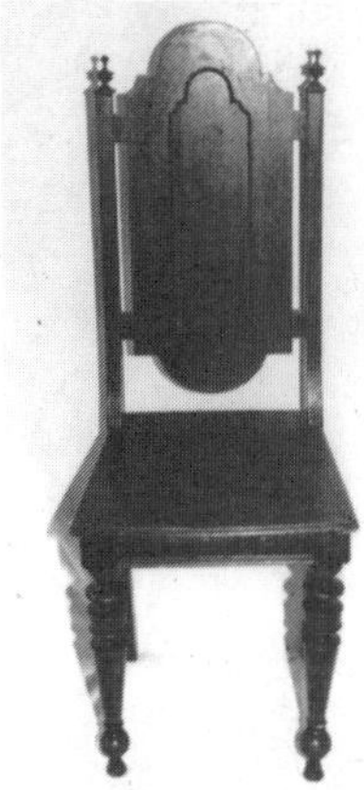

A pair of painted chairs, 17in (43cm) wide.
$1,000-1,200

An Irish fools chair, 19in (48cm) wide.
$200-300

A child's chair, 18in (46cm) wide.
$300-400

A child's high chair, 33in (84cm) high.
$800-1,000

An Irish famine chair, c1840.
$500-600

A panel back settle, c1790, 76in (193cm) wide.
$650-850

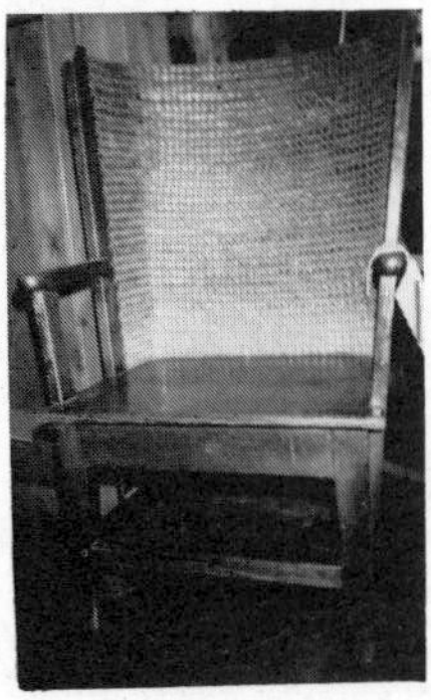

A pine and wicker Orkney chair, 19thC.
$350-400

Chests

A pine 3 height chest, c1820, 39in (99cm) wide.
$450-500

A pine 4 height chest, c1860, 45in (111cm) wide.
$600-700

A pine chest of drawers with simulated bamboo decoration, 40in (101cm) wide.
$1,200-1,500

A pine 4 drawer chest, c1890, 39in (99cm) wide.
$500-600

A pine chest of drawers, 42in (104cm).
$800-1,000

A nest of drawers, 18in (46cm).
$500-600

A collectors cabinet, 29in (74cm).
$1,000-1,200

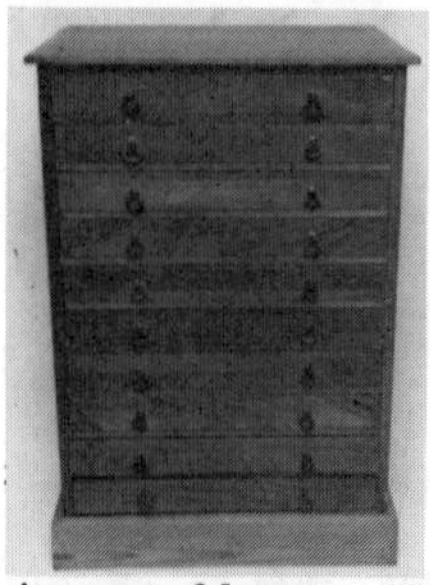
A pine nest of drawers, 19½in (50cm).
$500-600

A pine flight of 29 hand dovetailed drawers, English, c1870.
$700-800

A shop counter, c1880, 109in (277cm).
$1,500-1,700

Cupboards

A pine 2 door corner cupboard, English, c1800, 36in (91.5cm).
$3,000-4,000

A pine corner cupboard, c1800, 42in (104cm).
$1,200-1,500

A pine barrel back and front 4 door corner cupboard with slide at waist, Lincolnshire, c1820, 38in (96.5cm).
$3,000-4,000

A small cupboard with glass do
26in (66cm).
$400-500

An astragal glazed corner cupboard, c1800, 39in (99cm).
$700-800

A pine cupboard with astragal glazed door, 32in (89cm).
$1,100-1,500

A bow front corner cupboard, c1780
34in (86cm).
$1,200-1,500

An astragal glazed pine corner cupboard, 39in (99cm).
$2,000-3,000

A pine corner cupboard, 18thC. (86.5cm).
$1,000-1,200

A small pine chiffonier, 33½in (85cm).
$600-1,000

A pine 2 door food cupboard, Burgundy, c1840, 34in
$1,300-1,500

A linen press, c1840, 49in (124cm).
$1,000-1,200

A Danish caddy top cupboard, c1870, 31in (79cm).
$600-700

A hanging corner cupboard, c1790, 37in (94cm).
$600-800

An Austrian painted pine cupboard, 55in (140cm).
$3,500-4,000

An architectural cupboard, c1780, 50in (127cm).
$1,500-2,000

A Danish secretaire, c1880, 38in (96.5cm).
$1,500-1,700

A pine livery cupboard, 19thC.
$1,300-1,500

An Irish pine food cupboard, 49in (124cm).
$2,000-3,000

An Irish panelled food cupboard, c1790, 53in (135cm).
$3,500-5,000

Desks

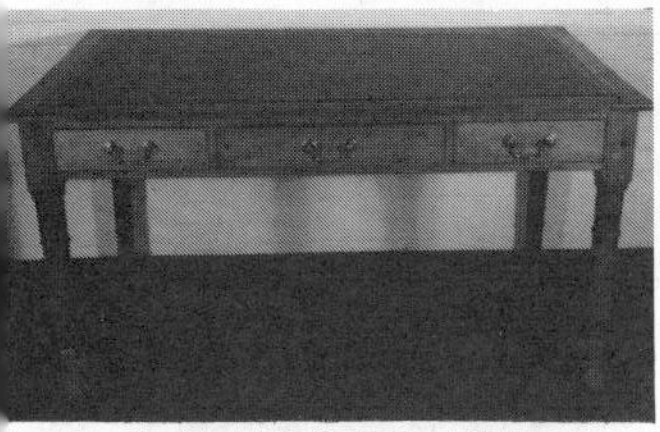

A pine desk, c1870, 59in (150cm).
$300-500

A small pine desk, 26in (66cm).
$1,000-1,300

A bureau, c1840, 43in (135cm).
$2,000-2,300

A pine knee-hole desk with gallery back and original pot knobs, c1880, 50in (127cm).
$1,000-1,300

A pine and faux bamboo (beechwood turned to look like bamboo) escritoire, French, 39in (99cm).
$700-1,000

A Victorian pedestal partners desk, c1880, 60in (152cm).
$4,000-5,000

Dressers

A French Buffet, c1820, 66in (167cm).
$800-1,000

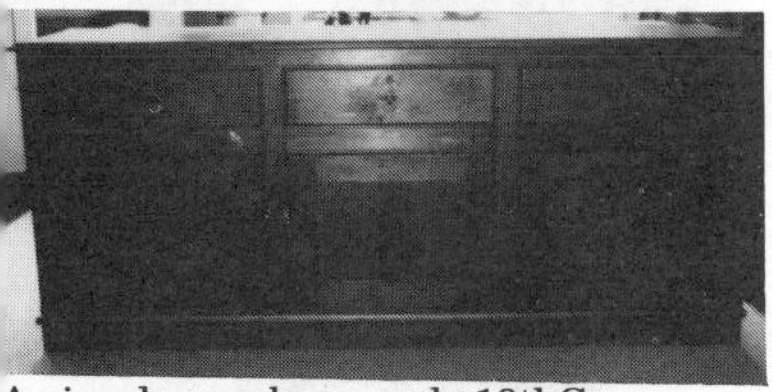

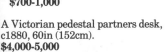

A pine dresser base, early 19thC, 83in. (211cm).
$1,200-1,300

An Irish fiddle front dresser, c1840, 57in (145cm).
$1,300-1,500

A small Irish dresser, c1880, 37in (94cm).
$1,000-1,200

A French buffet, c1860, 54in (138cm).
$1,000-1,200

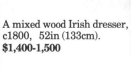

A mixed wood Irish dresser, c1800, 52in (133cm).
$1,400-1,500

An Irish pine 1 piece dresser original feet and cornice, c1840.
$1,400-1,600

An Irish pine dresser, c1850.
$2,000-2,500

A Victorian pine dolls dresser, French, 19½in (50cm) high.
$80-100

A carved pine Buffet a Deux Corps, from Normandy, 52in (133cm).
$5,500-6,500

A pine dresser with glazed rack, 61in (154.5cm).
$1,600-2,000

A large pine potboard dresser, c1860, 122½in (311cm).
$3,000-4,000

Dressing Tables

A pine dressing-chest with matching marble top and tiled back wash-stand, c1870, both 36in (91.5cm).
$1,700-2,000

A pine dressing table and wash-stand, c1880.
$1,300-1,500

A pine satin-wood dressing-chest, c1895, 45in (111cm).
$700-1,000

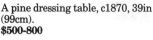

A pine dressing table, c1870, 39in (99cm).
$500-800

Mirrors

A carved pine mirror holder, 3 sections, 47in (116cm).
$800-1,000

A carved pine mirror, 34in (86.5cm) high.
$2,000-2,500

Settles

A pine settle, 18thC, 46in (114cm).
$1,500-1,700

An Irish pine high back settle, c1870, 72in (183cm).
$1,000-1,200

A high back pine settle, 45in (111cm).
$1,200-1,500

Sideboards

A pine break-front sideboard, c1890, 66in (167cm).
$1,200-1,500

A pine sideboard, 73in (185cm).
$1,200-1,500

Stools

An elm kitchen stool, c1860, 18in (46cm) high.
$50-100

Tables

A low pine coffee table, 47in (116cm) long.
$500-700

A pine console table, 58in (147.5cm).
$1,200-1,500

An Irish table, c1860, 31in (79cm).
$200-300

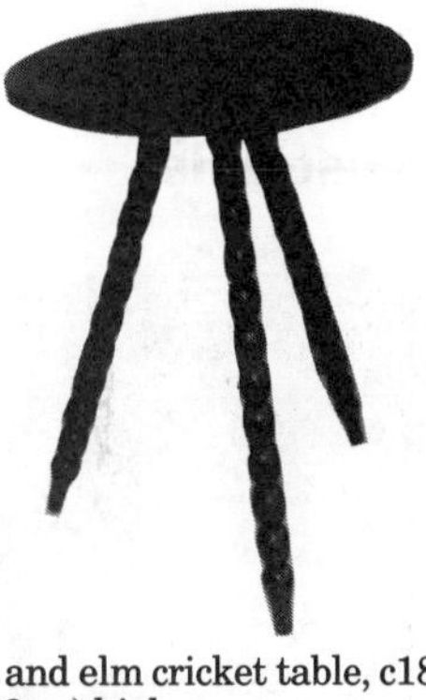

A pine and elm cricket table, c1840, 26in (66cm) high.
$150-200

A carved pine and limewood console table, 47in (116cm).
$2,000-3,000

A pine and elm tilt-top pedestal table, c1840, 36in (91cm).
$500-600

A pine hunt table, American , used for cutting up game after hunting, 74in (187cm).
$400-500

Wardrobes

A large pine wardrobe, 67in (170cm).
$1,200-1,500

A pine wardrobe with 2 drawers under, c1880, 48in (147cm).
$800-1,000

A pine marriage armoire from Normandy, 62in (157cm).
$5,000-6,000

A pitch-pine and pine wardrobe, c1880, 46in (142cm).
$800-1,000

A Danish armoire, c1880, 44in (137cm).
$700-800

A pine wardrobe, 44in (137cm).
$600-800

A French panelled armoire, c1840, 60in (152cm).
$1,000-1,200

A pine wardrobe, 41½in (108cm).
$800-1,000

Washstands

A pine tiled-back washstand, c1870, 36in (91.5cm).
$500-600

A pine washstand, c1830, 31in (79cm).
$400-600

Miscellaneous

A carved bear with flower holder, 22in (56cm) high.
$600-700

A child's trolley, late 17thC, 20in (51cm).
$1,200-1,500

Eleven carved pine fairground gallopers, German, 19thC, 2 sizes, smallest 36in (91.5cm).
$10,500-14,000

A carved doorway, 59in (150cm).
$5,500-6,500

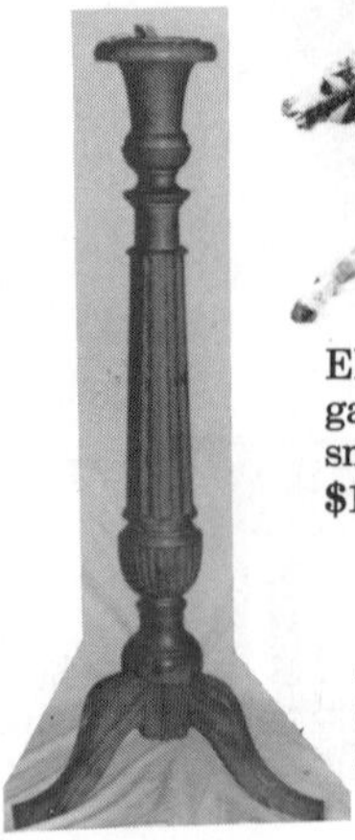

A pine torchère, 60in (152cm).
$300-500

Kitchenalia

A brass bushell measure, with channelled sides and 2 baluster carrying handles, inscribed Potter, Poultry, London 19thC, 25in (63.5cm) wide.
$4,000-5,000

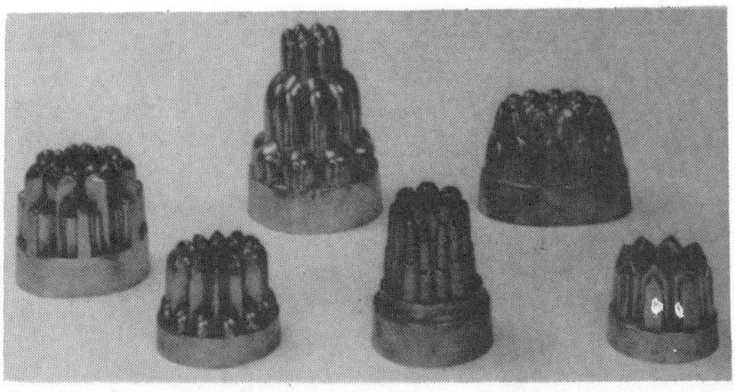

Six various copper jelly moulds.
$400-500

A Georgian style mahogany combined spoon rack and box, the base banded in brass, 21in (53.5cm) high.
$400-500

A Scandinavian butter dish, the lid pegged between volute uprights, the body with extensive foliate carving, on spayed supports, incised MKF and dated 1798, 8½in (22cm) diam.
$1,200-1,400

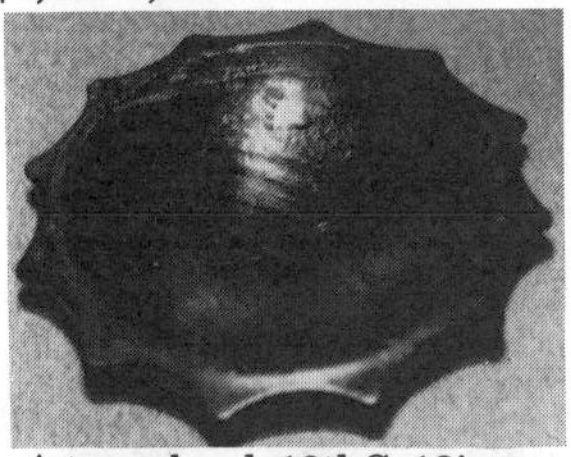

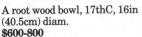

A treen bowl, 19thC, 12in (30.5cm). **$140-200**

A root wood bowl, 17thC, 16in (40.5cm) diam.
$600-800

The Dining Room

A treen bowl, 19thC, 26in (66cm).
$140-200

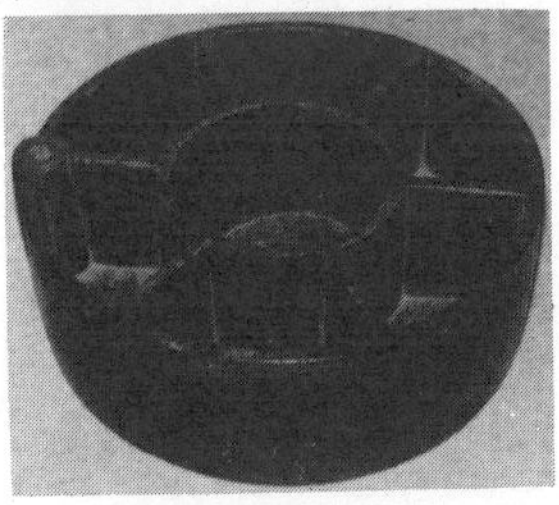

A treen spice bowl, lid missing, 19thC, 23in (58cm).
$160-200

Sundry Trades

A Norris A50 annealed iron smoother with gunmetal lever and twin thread Patent adjustment.
$300-400

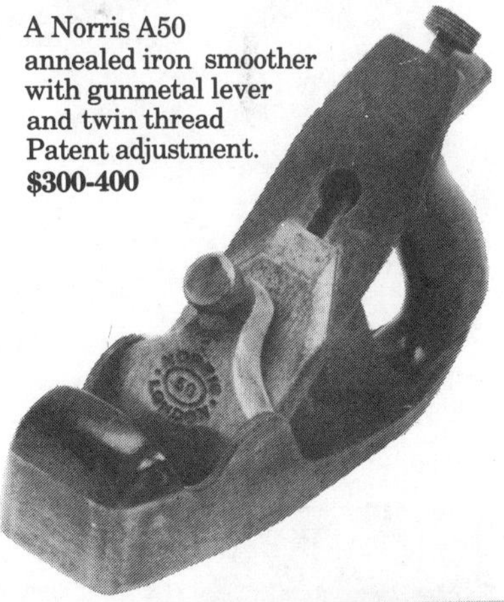

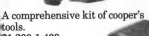

A comprehensive kit of cooper's tools.
$1,200-1,400

A dovetail iron mitre plane, by Moon, with rosewood infill, unsnecked James Cam cutter and replacement wedge, 10in (25.5cm) long.
$400-500

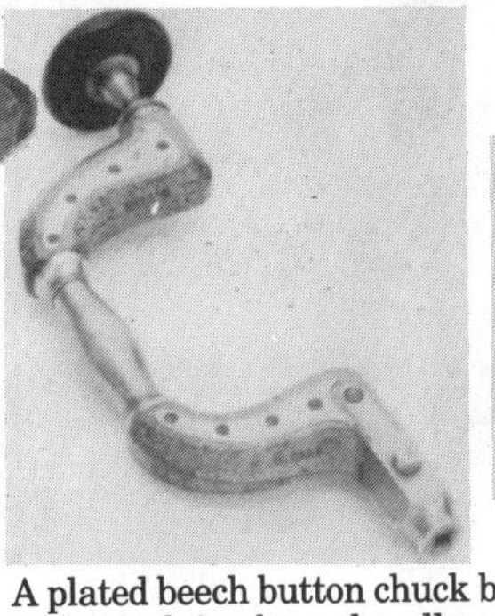

A plated beech button chuck brace, with revolving brass handle and ebony head on brass baluster.
$700-800

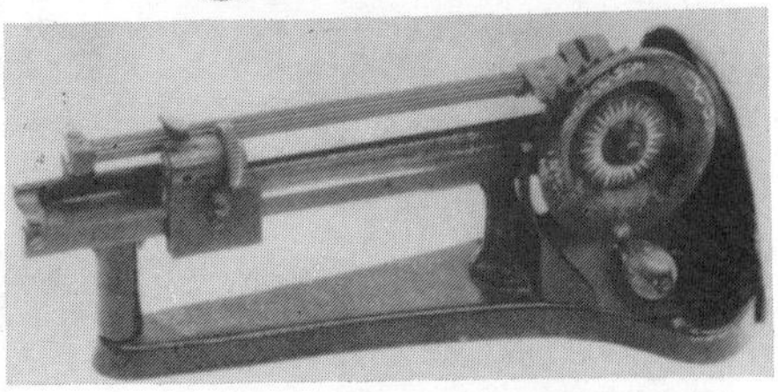

A Guhl's Patent 'Jupiter' rotary pencil sharpener, with gilt on black finish, 13in (33cm) long.
$400-500

EPHEMERA

Pop Ephemera

A signed page from the premier programme for the film 'Help!', signed by the 4 Beatles and other personalities, mounted, framed and glazed, 14 by 11in (36 by 29cm).
$5,000-6,000

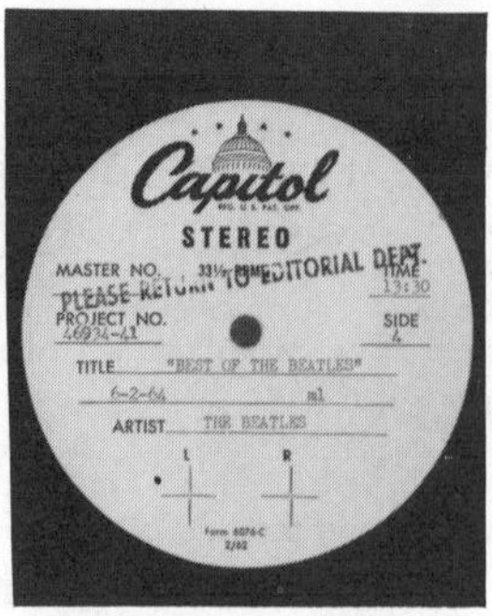

A set of 2 double-sided acetates, 'Best of the Beatles', Capitol Records, 6.2.64.
$5,000-6,000

Four lifesize figures of The Beatles as they appeared in the film 'Yellow Submarine', 81in (203cm) high.
$2,500-3,000

A bronze bust of John Lennon by John Somerville, limited edition 30/50, on wooden base, c1985, sculpture 19½in (49cm) high.
$1,400-1,600

Beatles wallpaper, 1963, 96in (244cm) long.
$80-100

An Art Deco enamel and chrome clock belonging to John Lennon and Yoko Ono, 9½ by 8½in (24 by 21cm).
$2,000-2,500

The Beatles album cover, 'Let It Be', signed by the Beatles, together with presentation gold record, mounted, framed and glazed, 18½ by 29½in (46 by 74cm).
$3,000-4,000

A pair of Beatles sneakers, manufactured by Wing Dings, USA, unused.
$250-300

A Chuck Berry presentation silver disc, for the Golden Decade Vol. 1, c1975.
$300-500

Elvis Presley's Christmas Album on the USA RCA label, c1957.
$200-400

An R.I.A.A. multi-platinum Sales Award presentation record and tape for The Jacksons 'We are the World' LP, presented to Tito Jackson.
$3,000-4,000

A matador style suit worn by Tom Jones at Caesar's Palace, Las Vegas, c1970.
$1,400-1,600

An original press kit for a Sex Pistols LP.
$300-500

multi-coloured blue print shirt
orn by Elvis Presley in the late
960s.
900-1,200

An Eastern style green and gold robe, belonging to Elvis Presley.
$3,000-4,000

Paul Cook of the Sex Pistols black Gretsch drum kit, two signed drumsticks.
$6,000-10,000

A presentation gold disc for the Ferry Aid single 'Let It Be', presented to Boy George, c1987.
$1,400-1,500

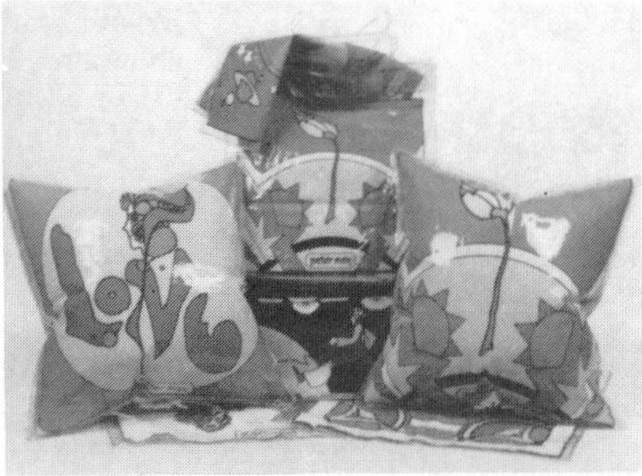

A collection of 6 Peter Max psychedelic inflatable plastic cushions and holdall.
$200-300

osters

EPPING FOREST
Cheap return tickets are issued from London and many G.E. section Suburban Stations to
BEAUTY SPOTS IN ESSEX

pping Forest.
200-300

L.B.S.C.R. Excursion from London, on linen, June 1901.
$1,000-1,200

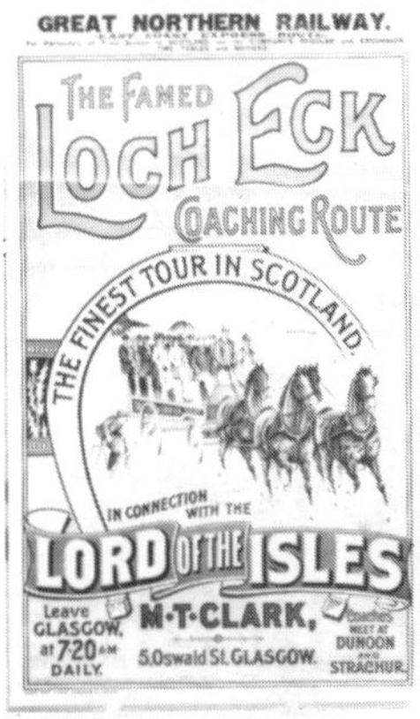

G.N.R., The Famed Loch Eck.
$1,000-1,200

C.W.S. Crumpsall, A Lucky Dip, Crumpsall Cream Crackers, 24 by 18in (61 by 46cm).
$1,800-2,500

G.N.R. original poster design, Skegness, signed, published 1911, 28 by 20in (78 by 51cm).
$5,000-6,000

B.R. Clear Road Ahead, Monmouth Castle.
$400-500

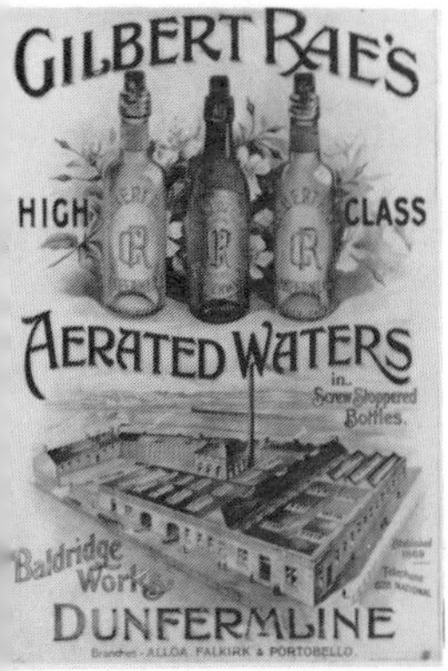

ilbert Rae's High Class Aerated
Vaters printed sign, embossed, 28
y 20in (71 by 51cm).
900-1,100

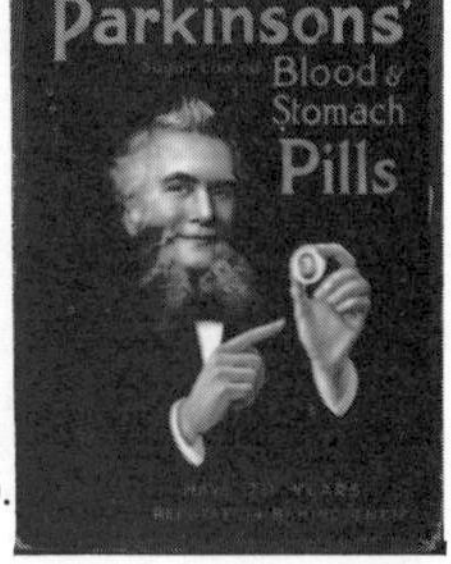

Parkinsons' Sugar Coated Pills showcard, 19 by 15in (48 by 38cm).
$200-300

Macfarlane Lang's Biscuits showcard, 31in (79cm) high, framed.
$400-500

Brass Metal Polish showcard, 20 by 13in (51 by 33cm).
$400-500

Lazenby's Specialities showcard, 29 by 36½in (74 by 92cm), in original frame.
$1,000-1,200

A German identification poster, 1941, 60 by 34in (152 by 86cm).
$50-60

Robin Starch showcard, 15 by 10½in (38 by 26cm).
$700-900

Olympic Ale showcard, published Brussels 1937, 18 by 12½in (46 by 31cm).
$60-80

Four illustrated circus advertising bills, c1820, each mounted on card.
$900-1,200

An illustrated circus advertising bill, c1809, mounted on card.
$400-500

Bluebell Metal Polish showcard, 15 by 21in (38 by 53cm).
$60-80

R. Fry & Co's Table Waters, 20 by 15in (51 by 38cm).
$900-1,200

L.M.S. Central Wales, Best Way Series No. 28.
$1,000-1,200

Jones Sewing machines enamel sign, 32 by 34½in (81 by 87cm).
$500-600

L.M.S. Southend-on-Sea, Series No. 24. **$1,000-1,200**

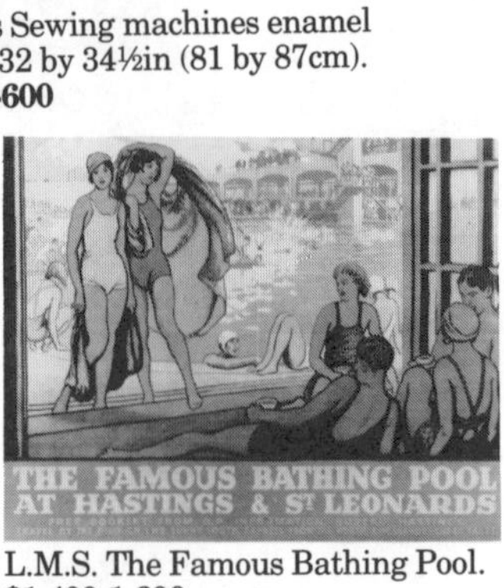

L.M.S. The Famous Bathing Pool.
$1,400-1,600

L.M.S. Great Yarmouth and Gorleston-on-Sea, Best Way Series No. 35.
$1,200-1,400

Miscellaneous

Old design coke cans, c1960/70.
$20-50

A Coca Cola bamboo and glass tray, c1930s.
$100-150

A Coca Cola tray, c1970.
$20-50

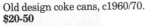

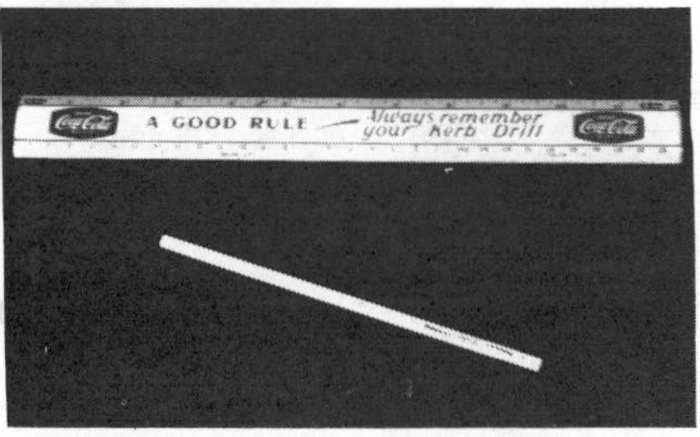

A Coca Cola ruler and pencil, ruler, c1950.
$30-50

A frothy coke bottle, c1970.
$5-10

A Coca Cola embroidered patch.
$20-30

ORIENTAL

Bamboo

A Chinese bamboo carving of a lady, smaller figure at her side, 17th/18thC, 14in (36cm) high.
$500-700

Cloisonné & Enamel

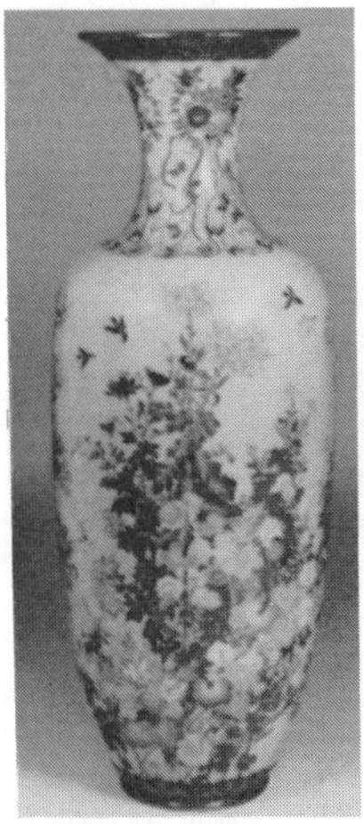

A cloisonné vase, damaged, late 19thC, 53in (136cm) high.
$5,000-10,000

A Kinozan vase, painted Kin-ko-zan sei, Meiji period, 6½in (17cm).
$2,000-3,000

A Japanese cloisonné teapot and cover, 5½in (14cm) long.
$500-700

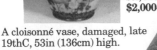

An enamel Yixing bottle with a sunken biscuit panel with a gilt inscription, covered with a cobalt-blue glaze, late Qing Dynasty. **$1,200-1,500**

A cloisonné box and cover, Meiji period, 3½in (9.3cm) wide.
$3,000-5,000

Furniture

A Thai gilt decorated ebonised hardwood cabinet.
$1,500-2,000

A small iron cabinet, inlaid Dai Nippom Kisto Jiu Komai Seisu, Meiji period, 3½in (8.5cm).
$3,000-5,000

A black lacquer cabinet decorated in hiramakie and inlaid mother-of-pearl, damaged, late 17thC.
$4,000-5,000

An oriental carved hardwood and shibayama cheval grate screen, 28in (71cm) wide.
$300-500

An oriental hardwood display cabinet.
$3,000-5,000

A pair of Chinese red lacquered cabinets, 27½in (70cm) wide.
$2,000-3,000

A Chinese red lacquered cabinet.
$3,000-4,000

A cabinet on a stand, decorated in hiramakie, okibirame and aogai, late 17thC, the stand late 18thC, both damaged.
$15,000-20,000

A jade screen, Qing Dynasty, wood frame and stand, 11 by 9in (27.5 by 23cm).
$1,000-1,500

A lacquer robe-chest, damaged, late 18thC, 25 by 17 by 15in (63 by 42 by 38cm).
$4,000-5,000

A pair of Chinese lacquered lanterns on stands, 89in (222cm).
$1,500-2,000

A Chinese black and gold lacquer 4 leaf screen, early 19thC, 75½ by 17½ (191 by 45).
$5,000-6,000

A Chinese hardwood centre table with inset rouge marble top and undertier, 19th C, 24in (61cm).
$1,500-2,000

A mother-of-pearl inlaid screen, mid-Qing Dynasty, some restoration, 36 by 40in (92 by 102cm).
$2,000-3,000

. black lacquer cabinet and stand, amaged, late 19thC, 28 by 18½ by 3in (72 by 47 by 33cm).
12,000-15,000

\ nest of 3 tables in damascus work.
1,000-1,500

Glass

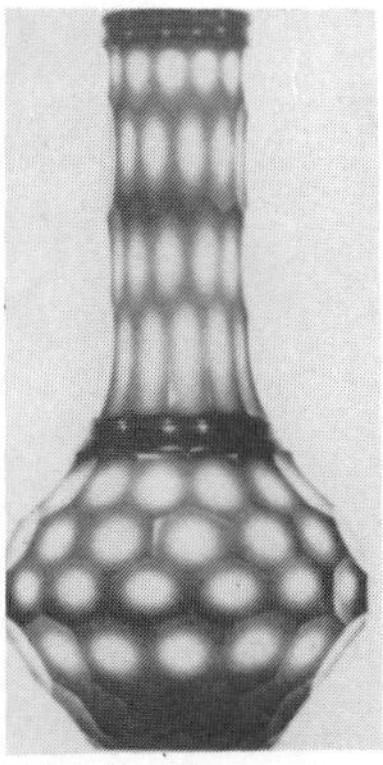

A Beijing turquoise and white vase, 9½in (25cm) high.
$3,000-4,000

A glass bottle with stopper, c1850.
$500-1,000

Inros

A natural wood 3 case inro, damaged, unsigned, 19thC, 3in (7.5cm) diam.
$5,000-7,000

A single-case inro, damaged, 19thC, 3in (7.5cm) wide.
$2,500-3,000

A four-case inro, damaged, signed Gyokkosai, 19thC, 3½in (8.5cm).
$2,000-2,500

A Japanese inro, signed Komin, 19thC, 3½in (9cm).
$3,500-5,000

A two-case brown lacquer inro, damaged, 19thC, 3in (8cm).
$2,000-2,500

.vory

n ivory carving f a fisherman and oy, Meiji period, ½in (22cm).
4,000-5,000

A Shibayama style ivory carving of a caparisoned elephant, Meiji period, 6in (16cm) long.
$6,000-8,000

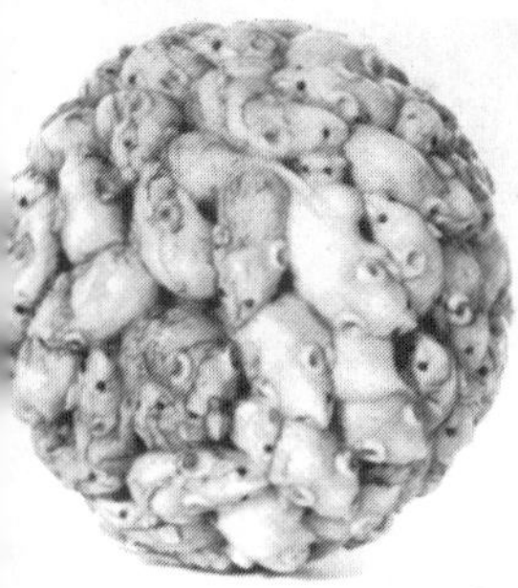

. Japanese ivory ball, signed leiyu, 2½in (7cm) wide.
1,000-1,500

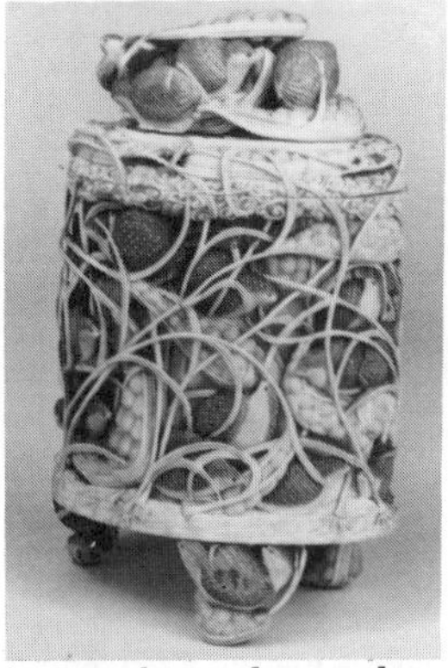

An ivory box and cover, damaged, late 19thC, 8in (20cm).
$5,000-5,500

An ivory group of the shichifukujin, and 3 attendants, signed Jogyoku, late 19thC, 8½in (21.5cm) long.
$3,500-5,000

An Okimono of a lady carrying a boy, damage, signed Tomochika and kakihan, late 19thC, 7in (17.5cm).
$1,000-1,500

A carving of a tradesman, minor damage, signed Toshimitsu, Meiji period, 7in (18cm) high.
$2,000-2,500

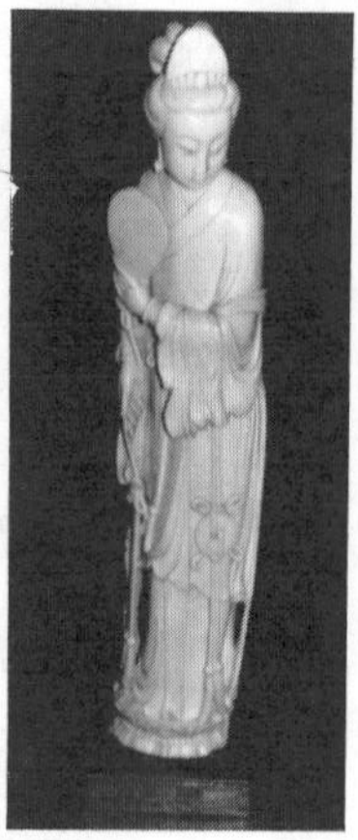

A Chinese carving of Kuan Yin, 19th and 20thC, 8½in (21.5cm).
$1,300-1,500

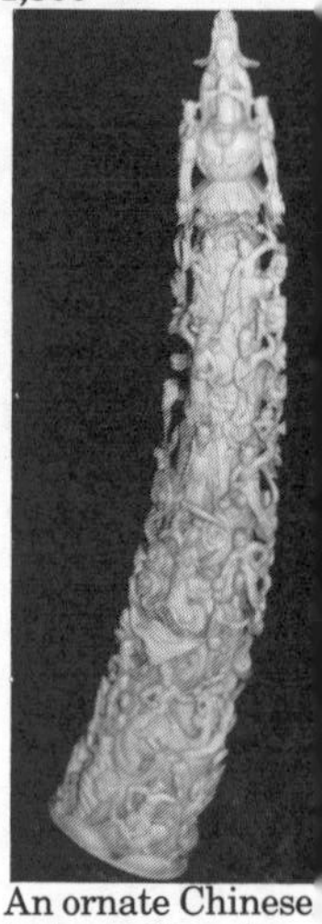

An ornate Chinese tusk carving of figures in relief, 17½in (44cm) high.
$300-500

A Tanto and attached kozuka mounted in ivory, signed Shungyoku, late 19thC, 19in (48cm).
$3,000-4,000

Jade

A white jade bottle, late 18th/early 19thC.
$800-1,000

A celadon jade figure of Buddha, 19thC, 6in (16cm).
$1,000-1,500

A Chinese carved green jade figure 7in (18cm) high.
$500-600

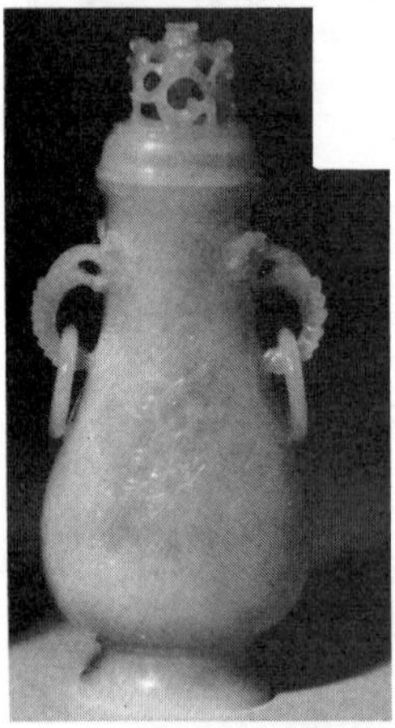

A pale celadon jade vase and cover, 19thC, 6in (16cm).
$2,500-3,500

An emerald green and lavender-flecked white jade figure, 10in (25.5cm).
$4,500-5,500

A carved jade brush holder, 19thC, 3½in (9cm).
$800-1,000

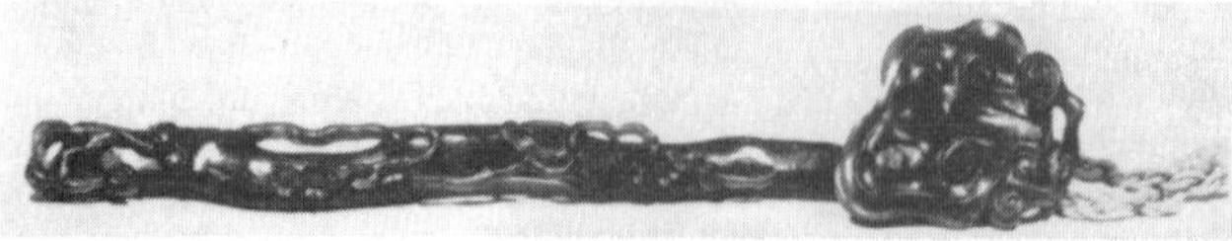

A Chinese green jade ruyi sceptre, 15in (38cm) long.
$1,000-1,200

Lacquer

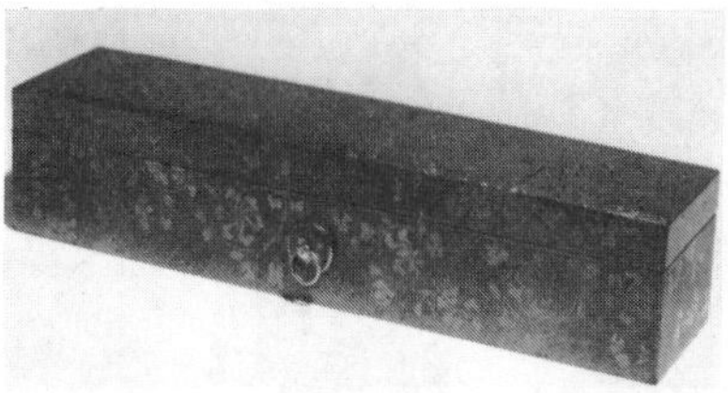

A lacquer naga-fubako, damaged, late 18th/early 19thC.
$800-1,000

A red lacquered and chinoiserie mirror, 37½ by 17in (95 by 43cm).
$2,500-3,000

A lacquer bundai, minor scratches, 19thC, 9in (24cm).
$3,500-4,500

A pair of Japanese bronze toads, late 19thC, 2½in (7cm).
$700-800

Metal

A bronze figure of a warrior, and another of a hunter, damaged, both signed Yoshimitsu, Meiji period.
$2,500-3,000

A Japanese bronze model of a tiger, signed, 19in (48cm) long.
$1,000-1,200

A bronze jardinière, minor damage, signed Dai Nihon Genryusai Seiya zo, Meiji period, 19½in (50cm) diam.
$9,000-10,000

A pair of bronze koro modelled as quail, detachable covers, signed Hozan, 5½in (14cm).
$500-1,000

A Japanese bronze model of a crayfish, late 19thC, 17in (43cm).
$1,500-2,000

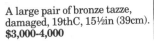

A large pair of bronze tazze, damaged, 19thC, 15½in (39cm).
$3,000-4,000

A Chinese bronze gu beaker vase, 17thC, 10in (25cm).
$400-500

A silver vase and domed cover, base missing, 19thC, 12½in (31.5cm).
$6,000-7,000

A pair of inlaid bronze vases, Meiji period, 13½in (34.5cm).
$3,000-4,000

Netsuke

An ivory netsuke of a recumbent karashishi, 19thC, 2in (5cm) long.
$300-500

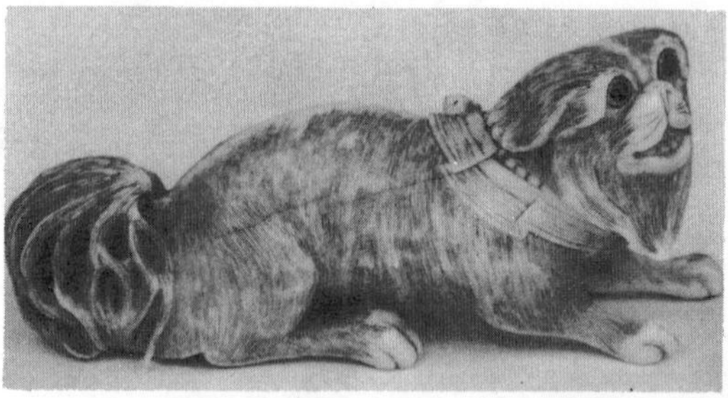

An ivory netsuke of a Pekinese, 19thC, 3½in (9cm) long.
$1,500-2,000

An ivory netsuke of 3 figures, signed Tomochika, 19thC, 2in (5cm).
$1,500-2,000

A wood netsuke, signed Masaraku (Shoraku), 19thC, 1½in (4cm).
$1,500-2,000

An ivory netsuke of Momotaro, signed Mitsuyuki, 19thC, 2in (5cm).
$1,000-1,500

Wood

A wood and Shibayama style caparisoned elephant, Meiji period, 8in (21cm) long.
$2,500-3,500

A Japanese wooden figure, 14in (36cm).
$400-500

A boxwood carving of an eagle attacking a monkey, damaged, signed Jisen, late 19thC, 6½in (16.5cm).
$2,500-3,500

Miscellaneous

A Chinese album of 11 rice paper paintings, 19thC.
$4,000-6,000

A Ming stone head of the Goddess Guanyin, 16thC, 10in (26cm) high.
$700-1,000

An early Victorian papier mâché tray, 32in (81cm) long.
$800-1,000

An early Victorian black lacquered work table, 31in (79cm) high.
$1,000-1,500

A Victorian papier mâché tray, 29in (74cm) wide.
$2,000-2,500

An early Victorian black and gilt papier mâché oval tray, 24½in (62cm) wide.
$1,200-1,500

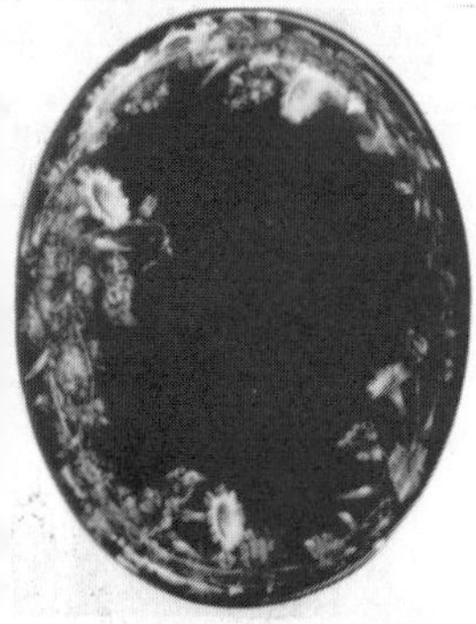

A Victorian papier mâché tray, 31in (79cm) wide.
$1,000-1,300

A papier mâché table, 16in (40.5cm) wide.
$600-800

Papier Mâché

A Victorian papier mâché workbox, 14in (35.5cm) high.
$1,000-1,500

A George IV papier mâché tray, stamped on the reverse, by Jennens and Bettridge, 30½in (78cm) wide.
$800-1,000

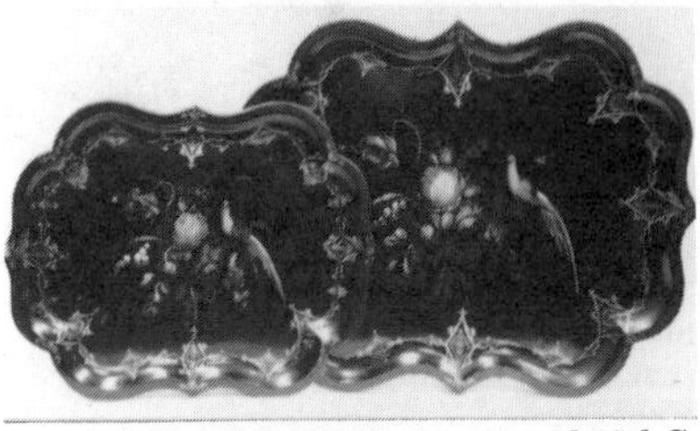

Two papier mâché trays, mid 19thC, largest, 32½in (83cm).
$1,200-1,500

An early Victorian papier mâché table, 28in (71cm) wide.
$800-1,000

A graduated set of 3 early Victorian papier mâché trays, stamped B Walton & Co. warranted, largest, 32in (81cm).
$7,000-8,000

A black lacquered papier mâché tray, by Jennens & Bettridge, 19thC, 25 by 19½in (63.5cm by 50cm).
$1,300-1,500

Sewing

A Bradbury's Wellington hand machine.
$350-500

A Princess of Wales lockstitch machine, by Newton Wilson.
$6,000-7,000

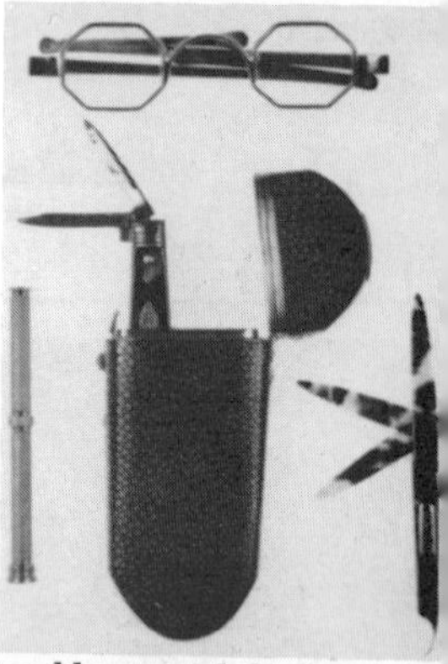

A gold mounted shagreen etui by J Butler & Co., London, a tortoiseshell pen-knife by Robinson, 19thC, 5in (12cm) long.
$3,000-4,000

A Monarch lockstitch sewing machine by Smith & Co., Soho, London.
$300-500

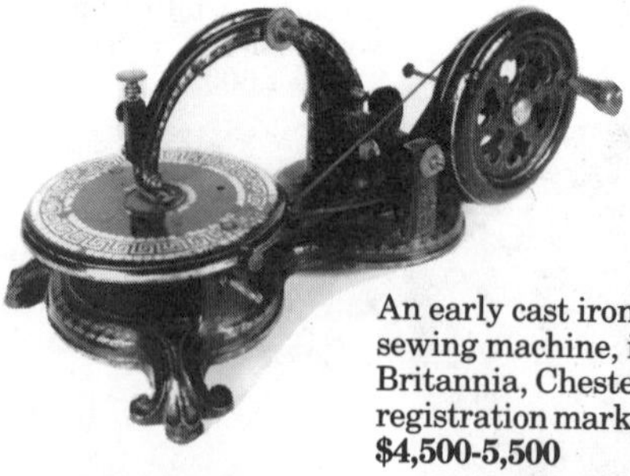

An early cast iron hand operated sewing machine, inscribed Britannia, Chester, with Victorian registration mark, 18in (46cm) long.
$4,500-5,500

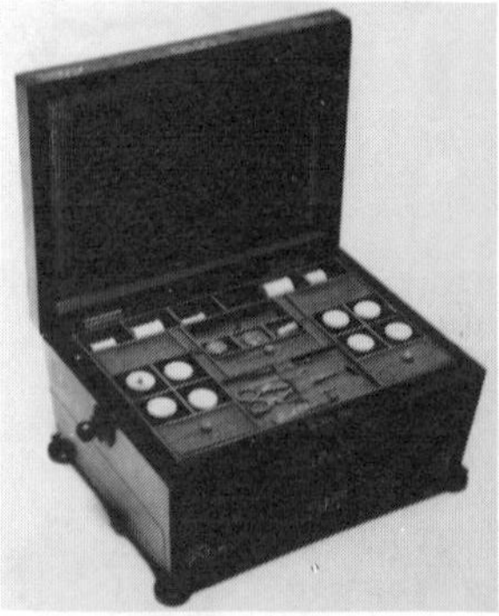

A late Regency rosewood musical sewing box, 15in (38cm) wide.
$2,000-2,500

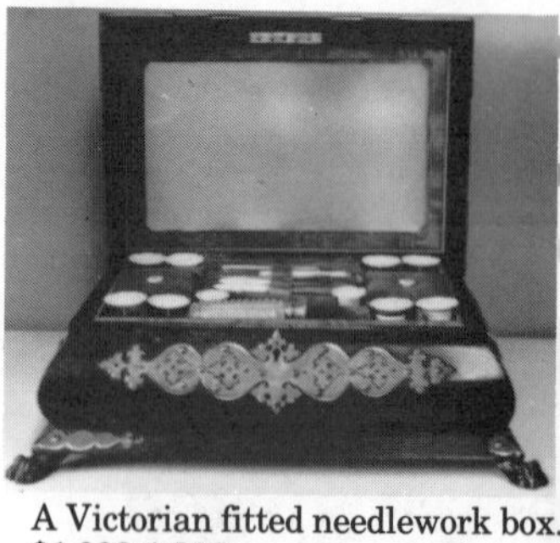

A Victorian fitted needlework box.
$1,000-1,300

A Victorian sewing box of exotic timbers, fitted interior missing, c1860, 13½in (34cm) wide.
$400-600

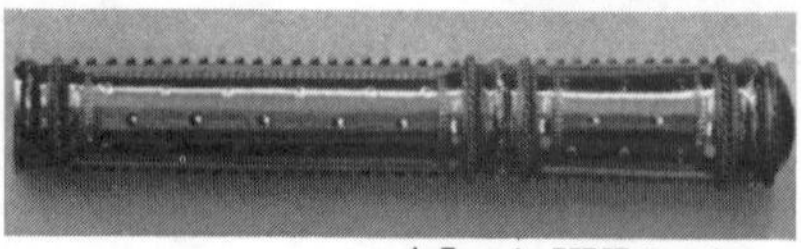

A Louis XVI 2-colour gold bodkin case.
$1,000-1,500

A Louis XVI gold and blue enamel bodkin case.
$2,000-2,500

RMS & ARMOUR

rmour

Cromwellian pikeman's armour, mprising pot with two-piece skull, reastplate and backplate.
1,000-1,600

A suit of Japanese black lacquered metal armour, c1620, contained in a lacquered paper and wood armour box, with iron loop handles, clasp and lock, the sides gilded, 15in (38cm) wide.
$14,000-20,000

A composite Cuirassier's armour, mainly 17thC and Victorian with later elements.
$4,000-5,000

A Japanese suit of composite armour, some defects overall.
$1,200-1,800

annon

Polish bronze cannon barrel, ecorated with the arms of Poland nd Lithuania and with the date 547, on later brass mounted ooden carriage of 16thC type with pen trail, 18in (45.5cm) barrel.
10,000-12,000

cast iron cannon, c1850, 38in 96.5cm) barrel.
600-700

pair of signal cannon, three-stage on barrels with flared muzzles, unded cascubels, mounted on eir iron mounted four-wheeled epped carriages, 27½in (70cm) arrels.
2,000-3,000

Crossbows

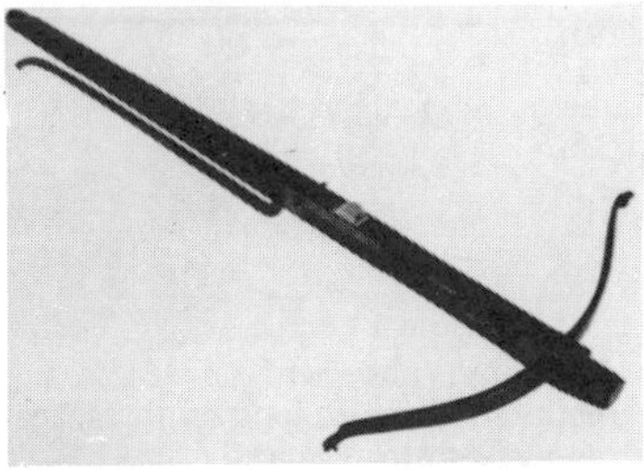

A Spanish crossbow, with light steel bow struck with mark, 16thC, 33in (84cm).
$2,500-3,000

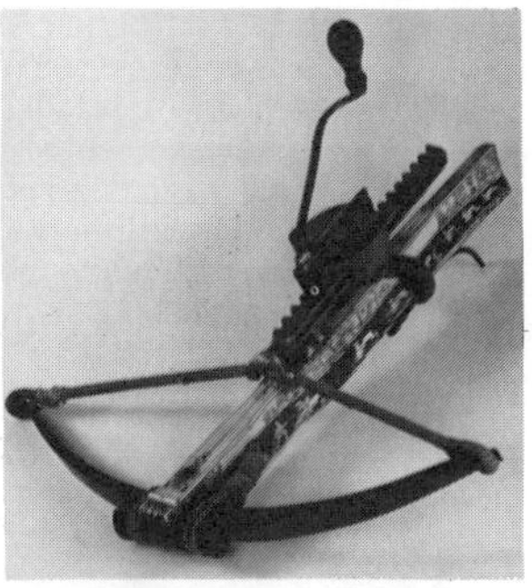

A German sporting crossbow, mid-17thC, with short robust steel bow, perhaps later, and a cranequin, mid-16thC.
$10,000-12,000

Edged Weapons – Knives

A hunting knife, with nickel silver hilt, marked Joseph Rodgers & Sons, Cutlers to Their Majesties, No. 6 Norfolk Street, Sheffield, in leather scabbard with nickel silver mounts, the chape and belt loop missing, some pitting, 19thC, 12½in (31.5cm) blade.
$600-700

Swords

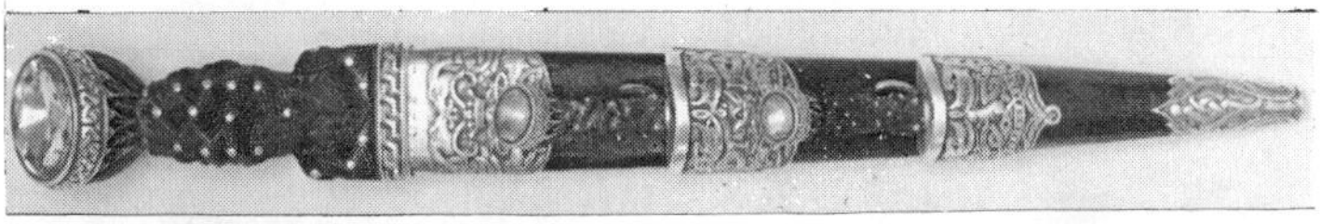

A Scottish silver mounted Regimental dirk, the blade by Brook & Son, George Street, Edinburgh, embossed with regimental badges, 12in (30.5cm) blade, complete with a companion knife and fork, hallmarked Edinburgh 1900.
$2,000-2,500

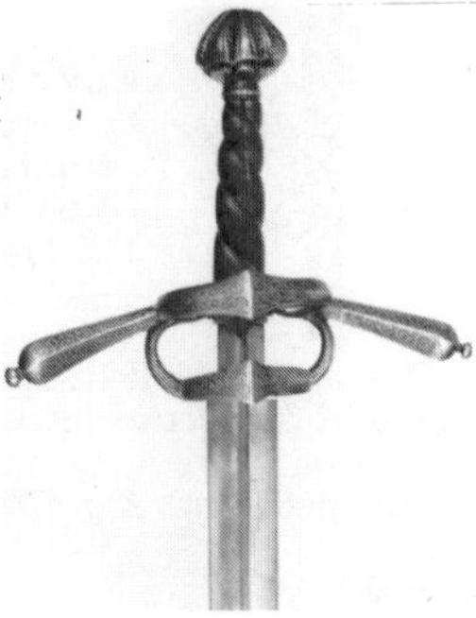

A Victorian broadsword, in mid-16thC Saxon style, the hilt etched overall with scrolling foliage, 42½in (107cm) blade.
$300-500

An American Confederate Naval officer's sword, by Firmin & Sons, 153 Strand and 13 Conduit Street, London, with brass hilt, the inside of the guard engraved R. H. Pearson, with wire bound fishskin grip, 30in (76.5cm) blade, in brass mounted leather scabbard, damaged.
$9,000-10,000

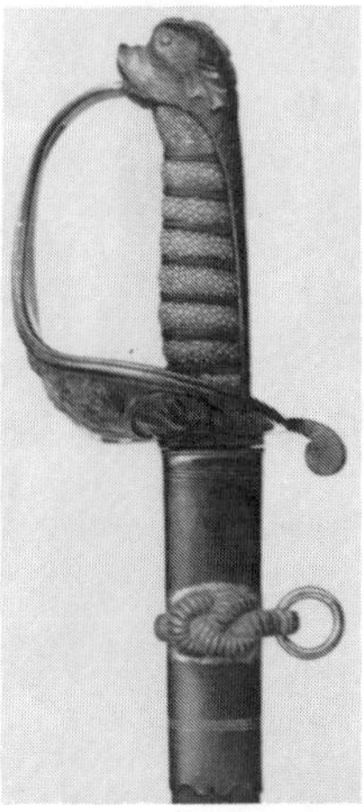

A silver mounted romantic sword, with diamond section blade, silver hilt in the form of St. George slaying the dragon, 24½in (61.5cm) blade, in cloth covered scabbard with silver mounts embossed with scrolling foliage, the locket with belt hook.
$2,000-3,000

An Italian 'crab's claw' broadsword, early 17thC, 33½in (85.5cm) blade.
$1,200-1,400

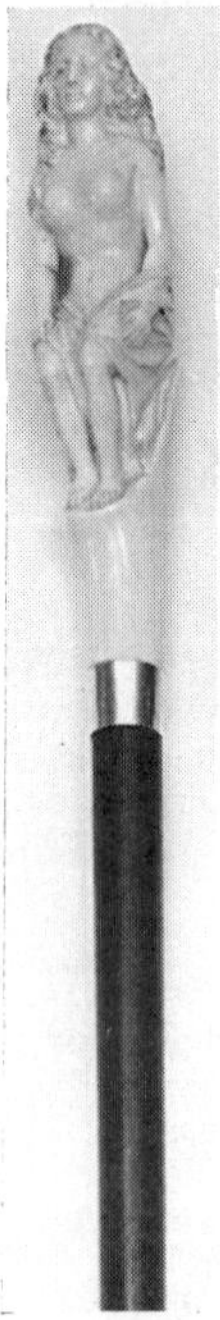

A swordstick, the triangular section etched with scrolls, the ivory hilt carved as a seated semi-clad maiden, gold ferrule bearing Russian hallmarks, the malacca cane with white metal tip, 16in (40.5cm).
$1,200-1,400

A Hungarian hunting sword, wit ivory grip bound with roped silve wire, and decorated silver guard, engraved with the motto 'Vivat Pandvr' and 2 verses in German, some damage, c1750, 21in (53cm blade.
$500-600

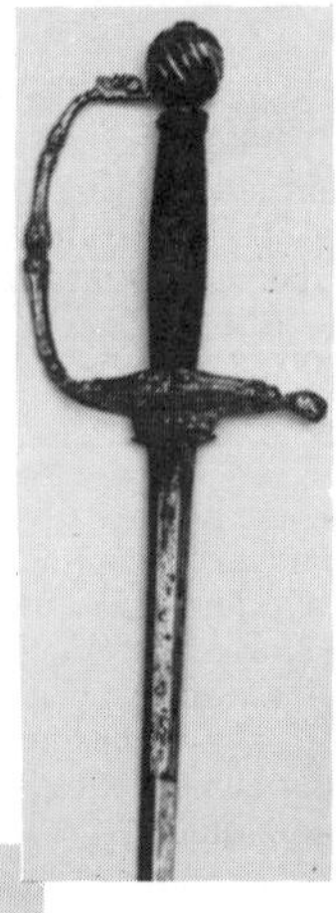

An Indian sabre, with silver mounted hilt with long quillons, the heavy ivory grip carved as 2 crouching demons, 32in (81cm) blade, contained in its cloth covered scabbard with silver mounts embossed and pierced with birds amidst foliage, scabbard damaged.
$700-800

A steel hilted smallsword, inlaid with silvered brass scrollwork, with wooden grip bound with twisted iron wire, silver rubbed, probably Dutch, late 17thC, 30in (76cm) blade.
$1,200-1,400

Swords – Eastern

▶ A Khanjar, with double fullered blade, and carved jade hilt, in leather scabbard with gilt mounts embossed with scrolls and foliage, 13in (33cm) blade.
$1,200-1,400

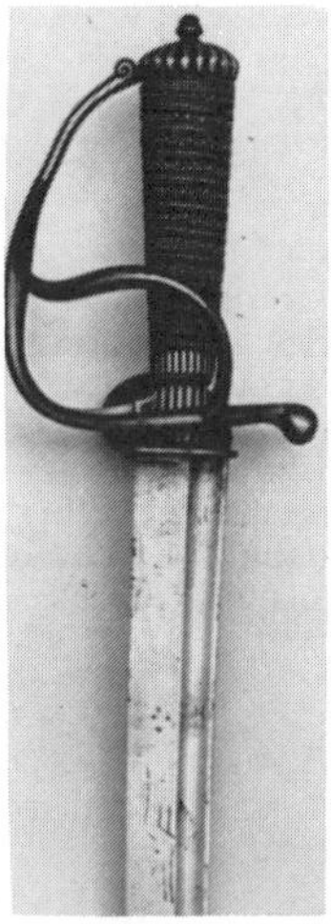

A silver hilted hanger, with curved single edged blade, double edged towards the point, with shagreen covered wooden grip bound with twisted silver wire, in original leather covered wooden scabbard, with silver chape and locket, engraved with maker's name in full, by Stephens, Temple Gate, London, silver hallmarks for 1745, 27½in (70cm) blade.
$1,200-1,500

An Italian silver hilted smallsword, engraved 'Gio Pietro Clavbera', and 'Di Solinga Me Fecit', Roman silver marks, mid-18thC, 30in (76cm) blade.
$1,000-1,200

An Indo-Persian Khanjar, with hilt carved from 2 pieces of opaque white nephrite, the blade with pierced ricasso reinforcing plate, median rib and thickened point for chain mail piercing, in velvet covered sheath, damaged, 10in (25.5cm) blade.
$1,800-2,500

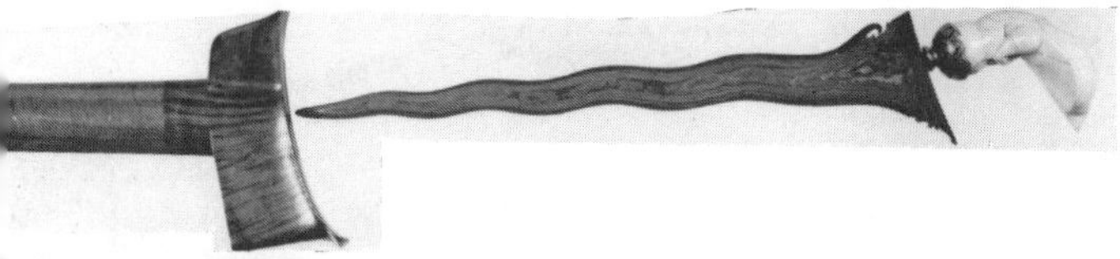

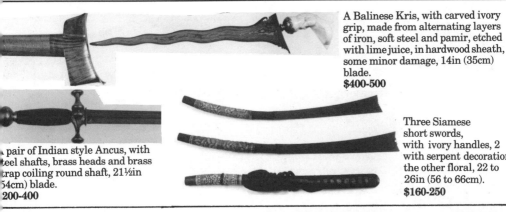

A Balinese Kris, with carved ivory grip, made from alternating layers of iron, soft steel and pamir, etched with lime juice, in hardwood sheath, some minor damage, 14in (35cm) blade.
$400-500

pair of Indian style Ancus, with teel shafts, brass heads and brass trap coiling round shaft, 21½in 54cm) blade.
200-400

Three Siamese short swords, with ivory handles, 2 with serpent decoration, the other floral, 22 to 26in (56 to 66cm).
$160-250

Rifles

A lightweight 12-bore assisted opening sidelock ejector gun, by S. Grant, No. 17095, 1932, 28in (71cm) barrel.
$10,000-12,000

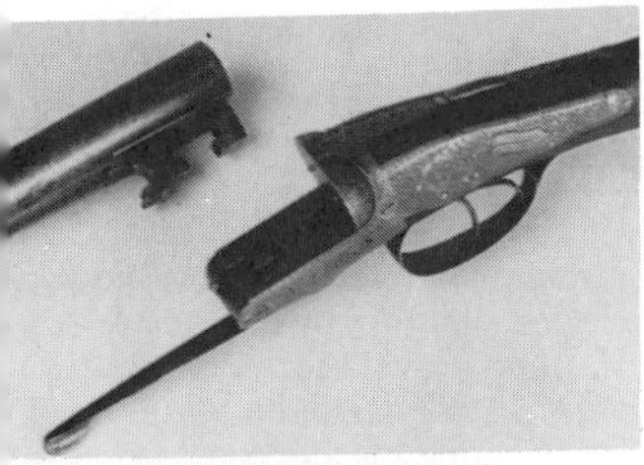

n alternate cocking helical nainspring hammerless 12-bore un, No. 6169, the backlocks signed F Beesley/From Purdey's', London roof marks, proof exemption, hortened barrels 23½in (60cm).
2,000-3,000

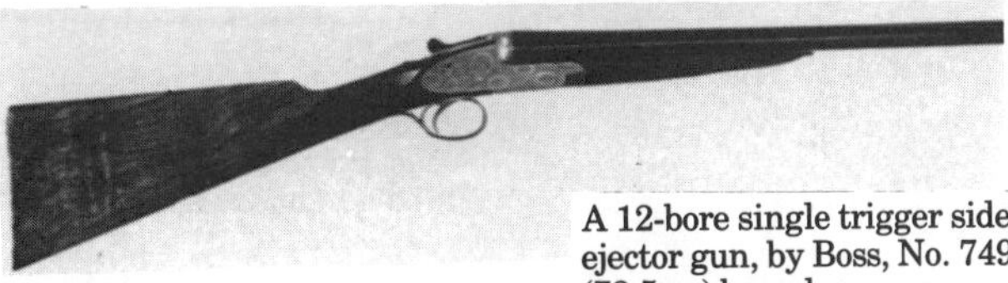

A 12-bore single trigger sidelock ejector gun, by Boss, No. 7490, 29in (73.5cm) barrel.
$14,000-16,000

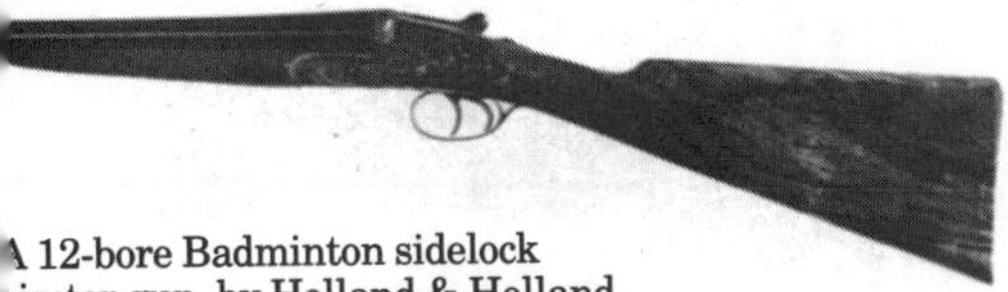

A 12-bore Badminton sidelock ejector gun, by Holland & Holland, No. 34826, rolled edge triggerguard, full engraving of bold foliate scrollwork with ribbons and flowers, full hardening colour and blueing, well-figured stock, 1983, 28in (71cm) barrel.
$16,000-20,000

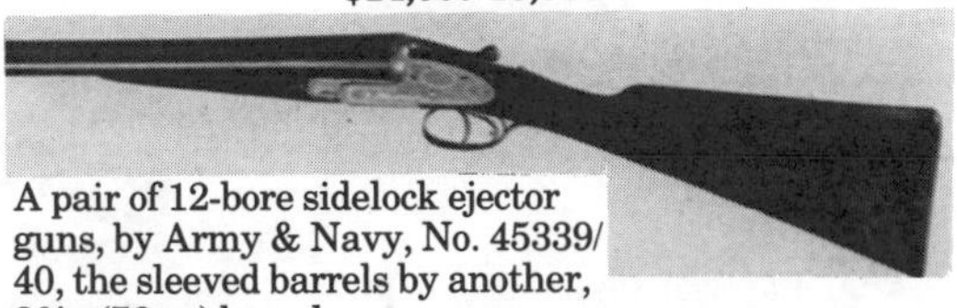

A pair of 12-bore sidelock ejector guns, by Army & Navy, No. 45339/40, the sleeved barrels by another, 30in (76cm) barrel.
$7,000-9,000

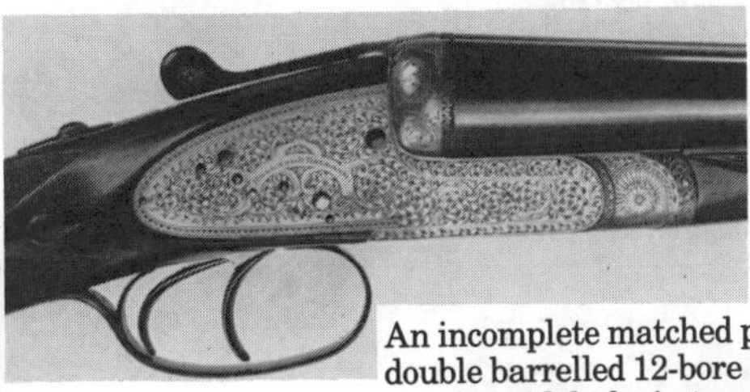

An incomplete matched pair of double barrelled 12-bore assisted opening sidelock ejector shotguns, by Boss & Co., Nos. 4916 and 5509, contained in baize lined brass bound oak and leather case.
$16,000-20,000

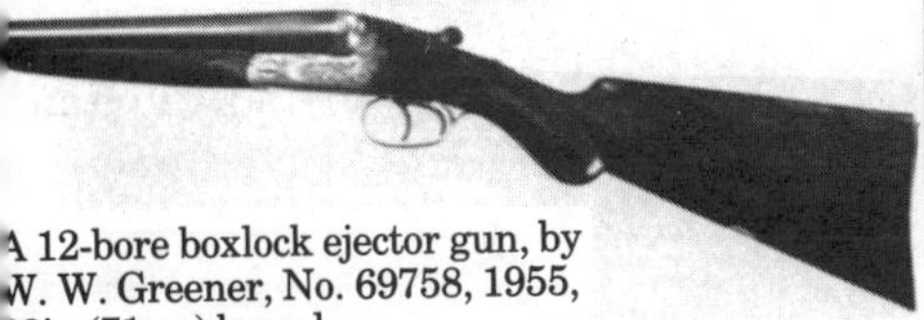

A 12-bore boxlock ejector gun, by W. W. Greener, No. 69758, 1955, 28in (71cm) barrel.
$4,000-5,000

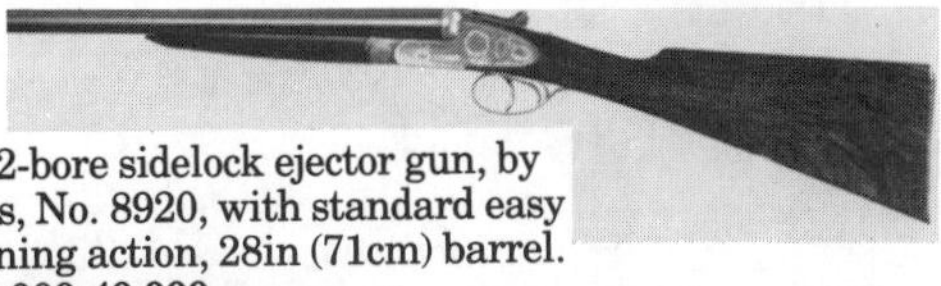

A 12-bore sidelock ejector gun, by Boss, No. 8920, with standard easy opening action, 28in (71cm) barrel.
$30,000-40,000

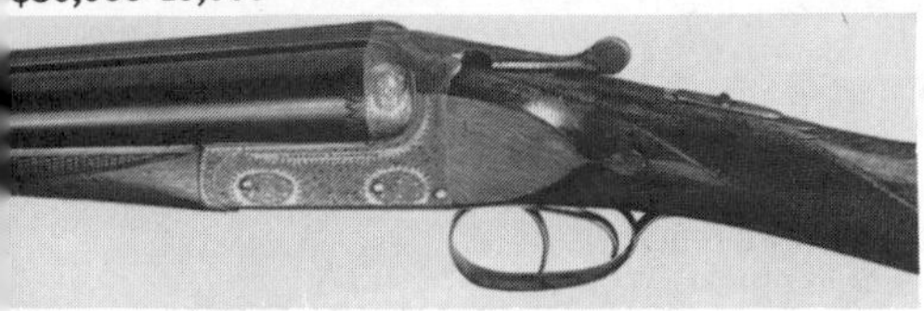

A 16-bore boxlock ejector gun, by Clabrough & Johnstone, No. 12983, 28in (71cm) barrel.
$3,000-4,000

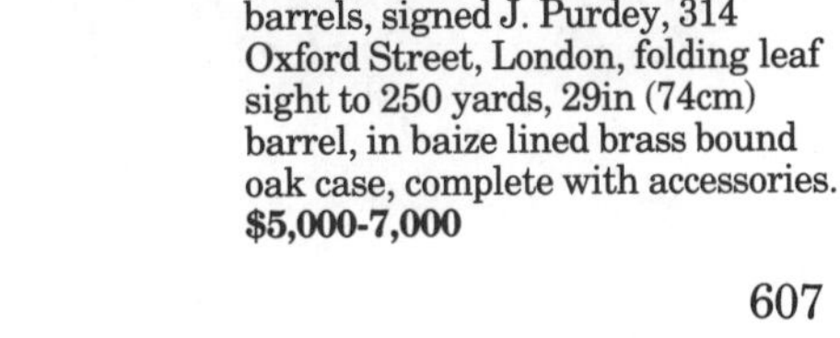

A double barrelled 40-bore percussion rifle, sighted damascus barrels, signed J. Purdey, 314 Oxford Street, London, folding leaf sight to 250 yards, 29in (74cm) barrel, in baize lined brass bound oak case, complete with accessories.
$5,000-7,000

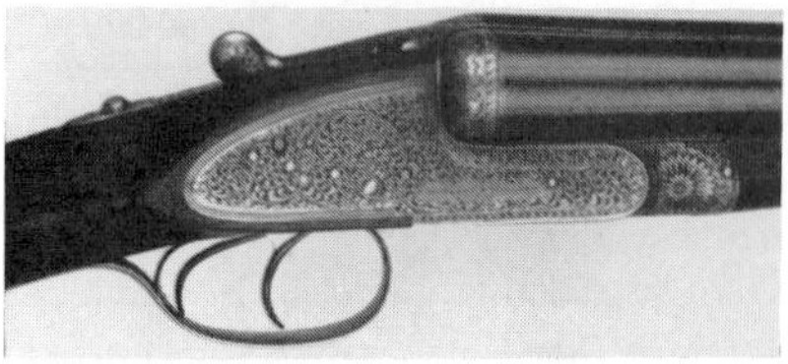

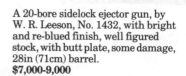

A 12-bore Royal sidelock ejector gun, by Holland & Holland, No. 27246, with hand detachable locks, 30in (76cm) barrel.
$15,000-17,000

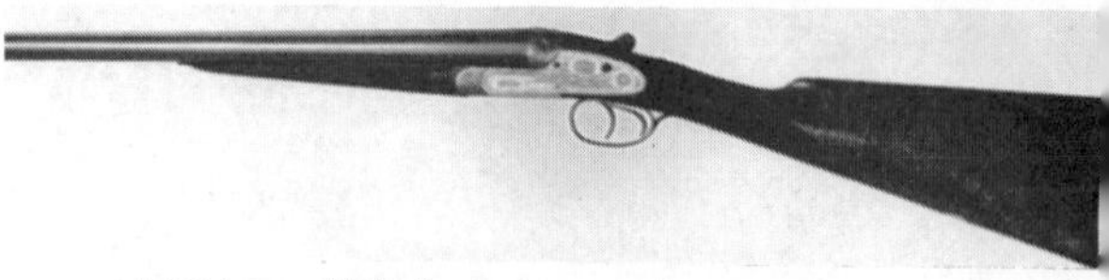

A 20-bore sidelock ejector gun, by W. R. Leeson, No. 1432, with bright and re-blued finish, well figured stock, with butt plate, some damage, 28in (71cm) barrel.
$7,000-9,000

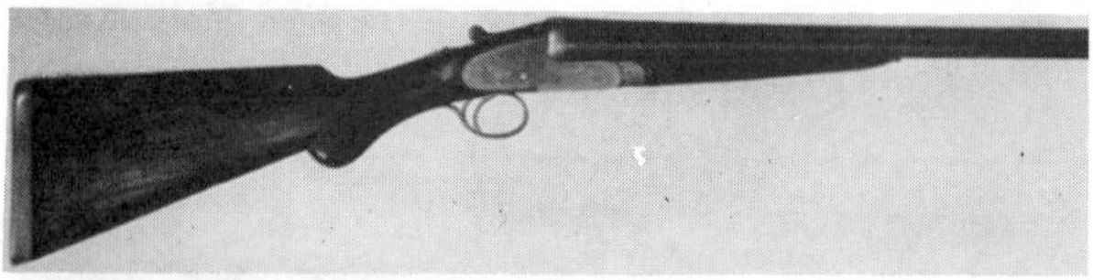

A 12-bore single trigger sidelock ejector gun, by Boss, No. 6904, 29in (73.5cm) barrel.
$20,000-24,000

The engraving is most probably the work of Jack Sumner.

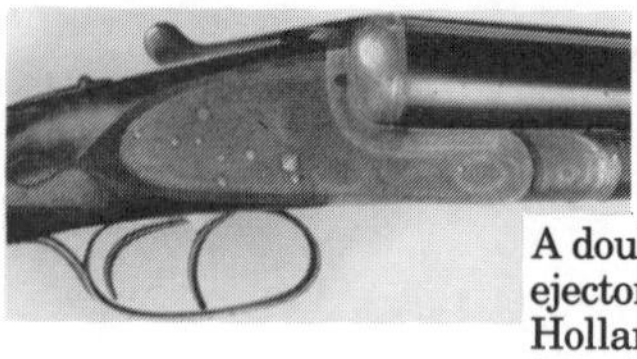

A double barrelled 12-bore sidelock ejector shotgun, by Holland & Holland, Royal model, No. 22019, 28in (71cm) barrel, in baize lined brass bound leather case.
$11,000-13,000

A 12-bore double barrel boxlock shot gun, non-ejector, with walnut stock and leather case, by Frederick Williams, London and Birmingham.
$600-800

Pistols

An Imperial Russian .70cal flintlock holster pistol, made at the Tula Arsenal and dated 1833, the escutcheon bearing the Royal Cipher of Czar Nicholas I, 9½in (24cm) barrel.
$600-800

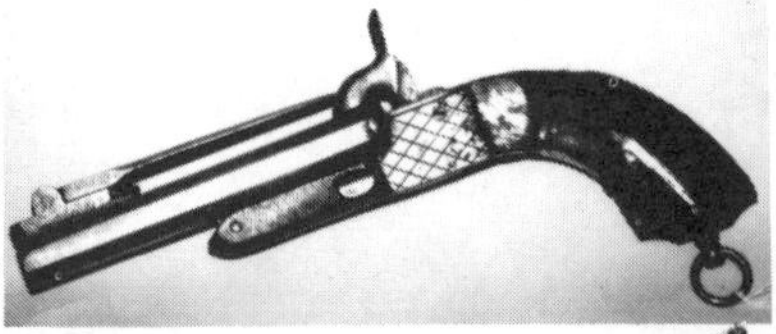

A large calibre flintlock pistol.
$250-350

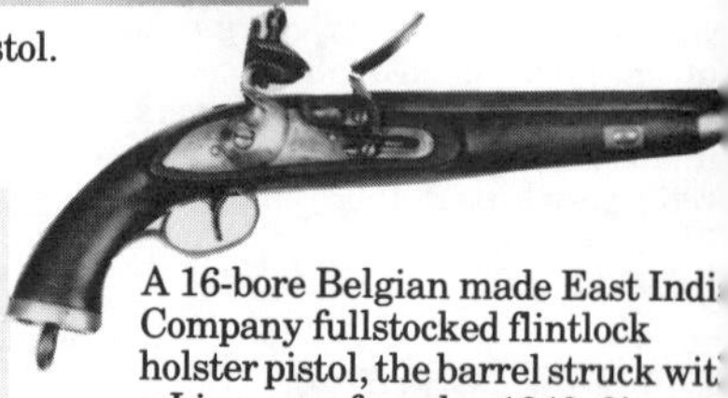

A 16-bore Belgian made East India Company fullstocked flintlock holster pistol, the barrel struck with a Liege proof mark, c1840, 9in (23cm) barrel.
$500-600

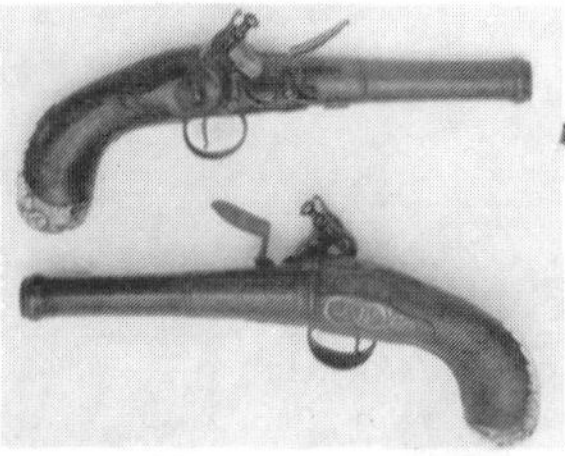

A pair of Queen Anne cannon barrelled flintlock pistols, with scrolling silver wire inlay, silver butt caps in the form of leopards heads, 4½in (11cm) barrel.
$6,000-8,000

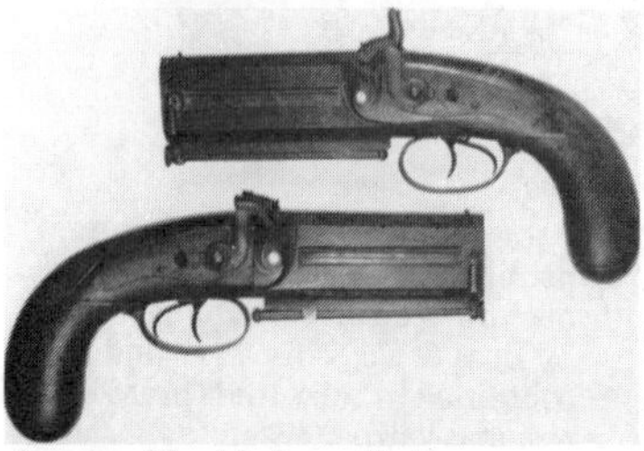

A pair of double barrelled percussion over-and-under pistols, with octagonal barrels and engraved muzzles, engraved London, bottled scroll engraved back action locks, signed Smith, hammer spurs lacking from one pistol, 4½in (11cm) barrel.
$1,600-1,800

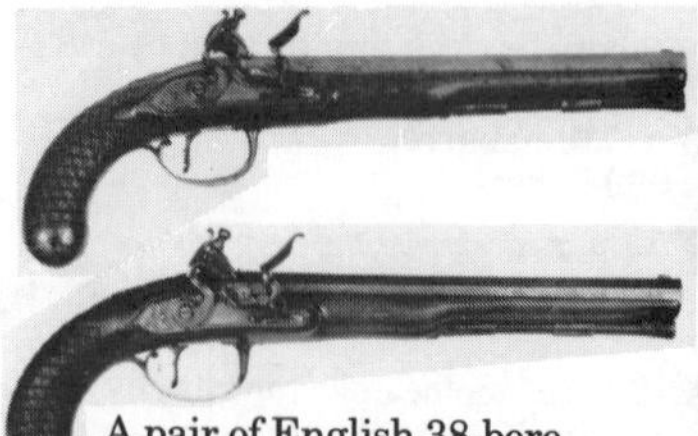

A pair of English 38-bore fullstocked flintlock duelling pistols, by Durs Egg, Royal Gunmaker, London, the breeches with gold vents, single gold bands and gold poincons with a crown, c1810, 10in (25.5cm) barrel.
$8,000-10,000

A three-barrel revolving percussion pistol, with iron nipples, covers, hammer, trigger and guard, signed Nakajima Nagaharu saku, 19thC, 11in (28cm).
$9,000-11,000

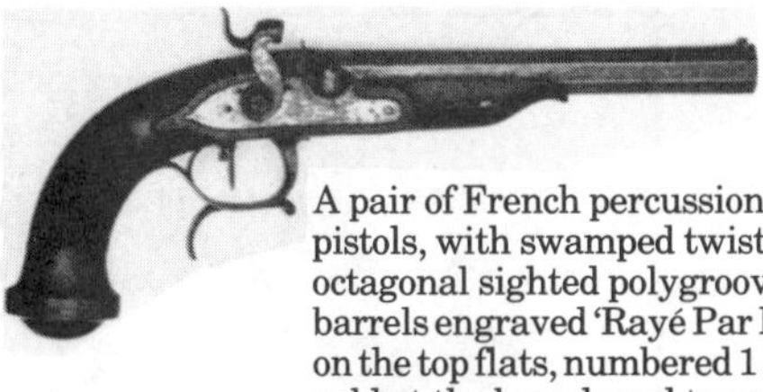

A pair of French percussion target pistols, with swamped twist octagonal sighted polygroove rifled barrels engraved 'Rayé Par Le Page' on the top flats, numbered 1 and 2 in gold at the breech and tangs, gold lines, engraved flat locks, St. Etienne proof marks, early 19thC, 15in (38cm).
$3,500-4,000

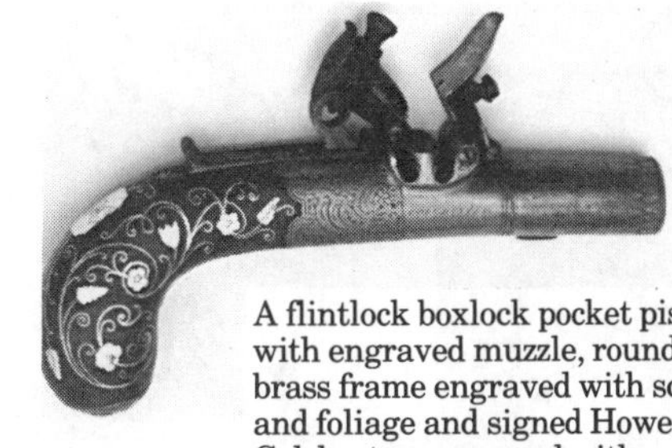

A flintlock boxlock pocket pistol, with engraved muzzle, rounded brass frame engraved with scrolls and foliage and signed Howe, Colchester, engraved with owner's initials, silver butt cap embossed with scrolls, 1½in (4cm) barrel.
$800-1,000

A flintlock boxlock cannon barrelled pistol, three-stage turn off barrel with ringed muzzle, scroll engraved frame signed Barbar, London, sliding trigger guard safety, slab sided wood butt inlaid with scrolling silver wire, 2in (5.5cm) barrel.
$600-700

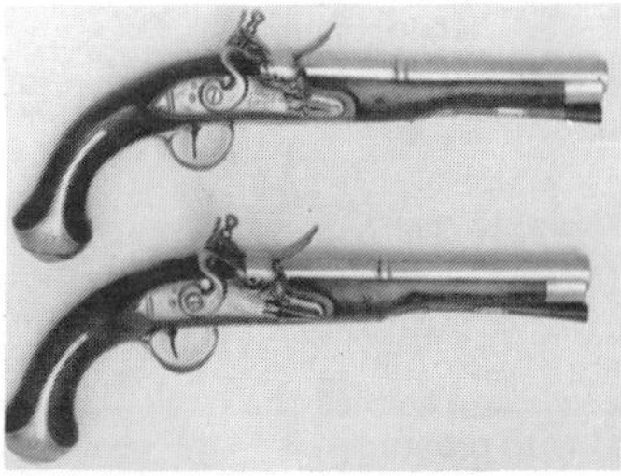

A pair of brass barrelled flintlock holster pistols, two-stage barrels, border engraved stepped locks, signed Richards, 8½in (22cm).
$1,600-2,000

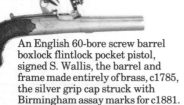

An English 60-bore screw barrel boxlock flintlock pocket pistol, signed S. Wallis, the barrel and frame made entirely of brass, c1785, the silver grip cap struck with Birmingham assay marks for c1881.
$700-900

Revolvers

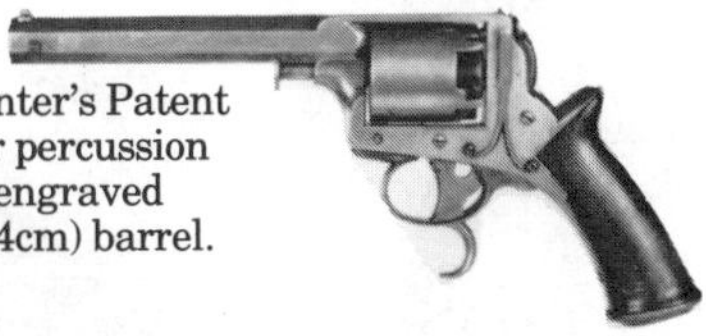

A 54-bore William Tranter's Patent five-shot double trigger percussion revolver, the top strap engraved 'Pattern 1856', 5½in (14cm) barrel.
$2,000-2,500

A .380CF William Tranter's Patent solid frame five-shot double action pocket revolver, serial No. 53773, retailed by Kerr & Co., King William St, London, 3in (7.5cm) barrel.
$400-500

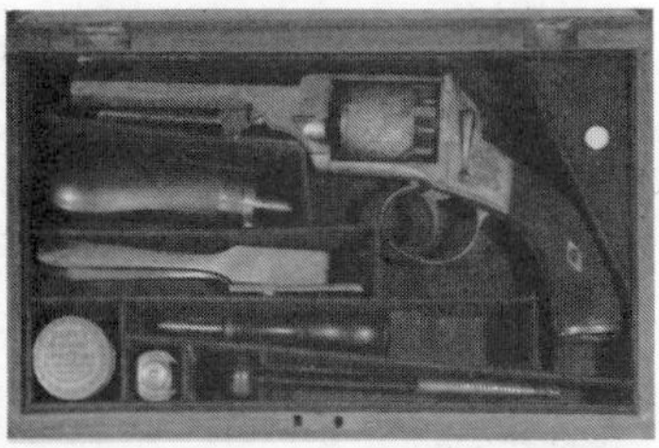

A six-shot 80 bore percussion revolver, sighted octagonal barrel engraved with scrolls and signed Frederick J. Smith & Co., London, 5in (13cm) barrel, in lined mahogany case complete with accessories.
$1,000-1,200

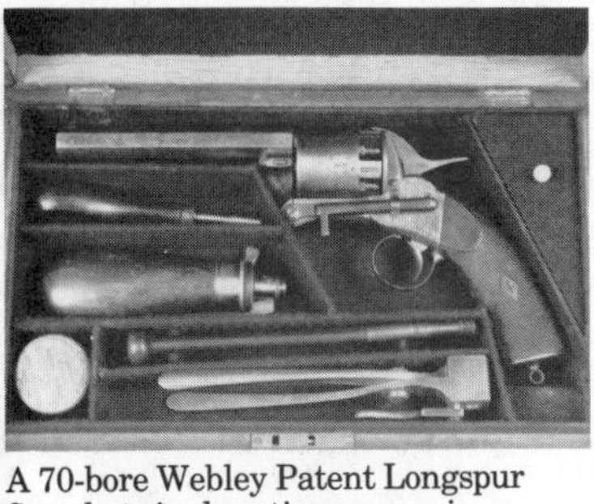

A 70-bore Webley Patent Longspur five-shot single action percussion revolver, serial No. 951, retailed by Pritchett, 86 St. James St. London, Hawksley patent top revolver flask with graduated charger, William Davis single cavity brass bullet mould, Eley cap tin and rosewood handled nipple wrench, some damage, 5in (12.5cm) barrel.
$1,000-1,200

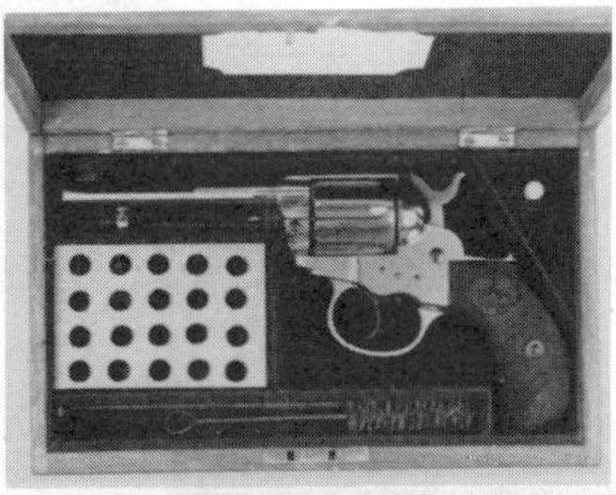

A .38 five-shot Colt Lightning revolver, No. 6951, London address on barrel, steel parts plated overall, chequered grips with Colt medallion, London Black Powder Proof, contained in lined case.
$4,000-6,000

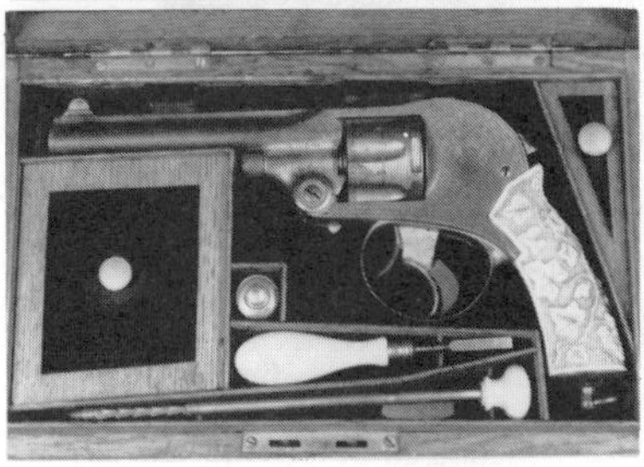

A .476cal Kynoch Gun Factory six-shot hammerless double trigger army revolver, serial No. 143, marked, 6in (15cm) barrel.
$4,000-6,000

Helmets

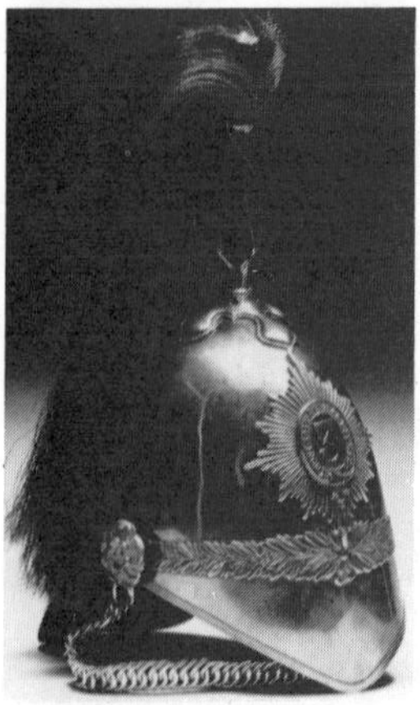

A Third Dragoons brass helmet, with plume and chin strap, 13½in (34cm) high.
$1,000-1,400

An English Civil War steel lobster tail helmet, with adjustable nose guard and pointed peak and 2 ear flaps, 17thC.
$900-1,000

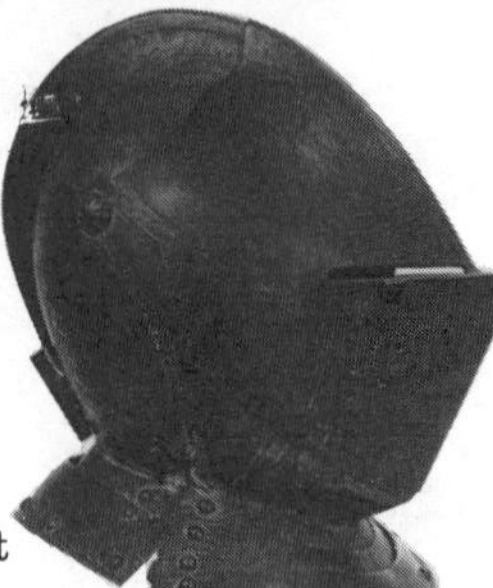

An Italian etched close helmet, the one piece skull with prominent roped comb and brass plume pipe at base, worn and pitted throughout, late 16thC, 12in (30.5cm) high.
$12,000-14,000

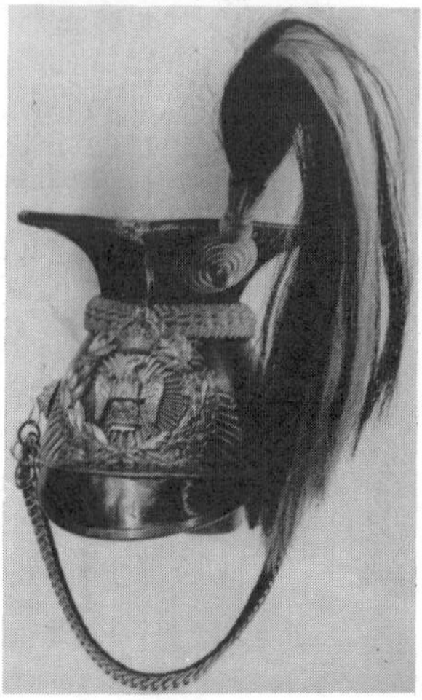

An officer's lane cap of the Bedfordshire Yeomanry, the internal leather headband marked SBR 056, upper lining missing, with a gilt burnished chin chain and a black and white hair plume with matt gilt socket.
$7,000-9,000

An officer's Victorian gilt helmet of the 7th (The Princess Royal's) Dragoon Guards, with black and white hair plume, enamel and small tag missing from plate and lining from chin chain, with stand.
$1,500-2,000

A British Infantry officer's blue cloth full dress spiked helmet of The Middlesex Regiment (1st Volunteer Battalion), c1890.
$1,000-1,200

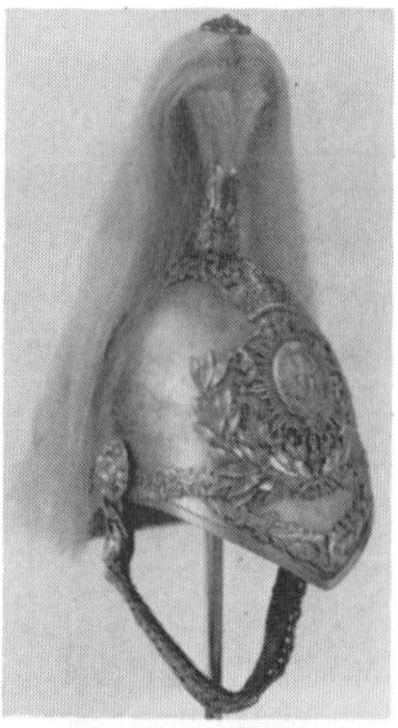

A Victorian officer's helmet of the North Somerset Yeomanry, silver plated skull with gilt fittings and white horsehair plume, complete with its tin named Captain Astley.
$1,600-2,000

An Imperial German/Bavarian staff officer's Pickelhaube, polished leather with gilt brass mounts with Bavarian coat-of-arms, c1890.
$2,000-3,000

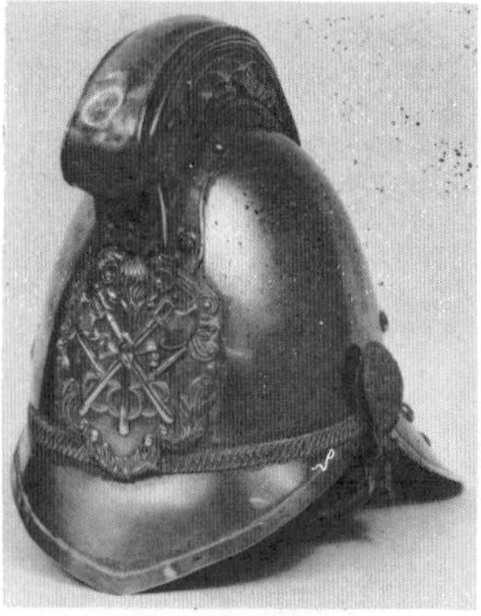

A brass Fire Brigade helmet of Merryweather pattern, with brass chin scales and general pattern plate.
$500-600

A French brass fireman's helmet, c1880.
$400-500

Powder Flasks

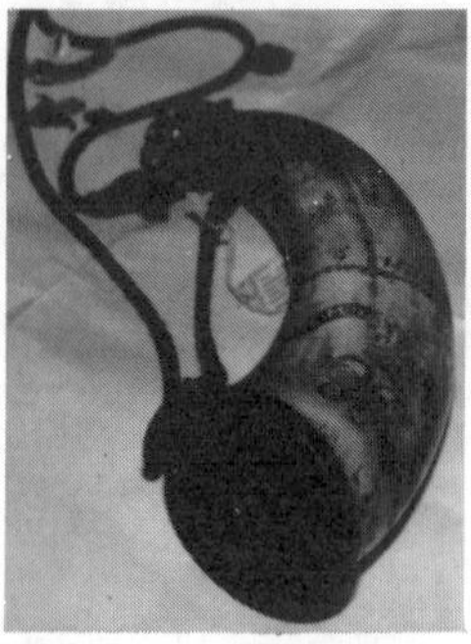

A British George III engraved powder horn, used in the American War of Independence, engraved with battle scenes.
$800-900

Miscellaneous

A Georgian officer's campaign basin, the brass bound mahogany case with hinged lid and silver plated liner, the escutcheons with lifting handle engraved M. General Pack, the base with 4 screw holes for attachment of legs.
$1,600-1,800

An Eley & Kynoch ammunition board, with metallic and paper dummy cartridges and components, mounted on grey card around a Nobel disc, framed and glazed, 30in (76cm) high.
$3,000-4,000

An Eley Sporting and Military cartridge board, with metallic and paper dummy cartridges and components, on grey card with Eley roundel, oak framed and glazed, 31½in (80cm) high.
$4,000-6,000

Jewellery

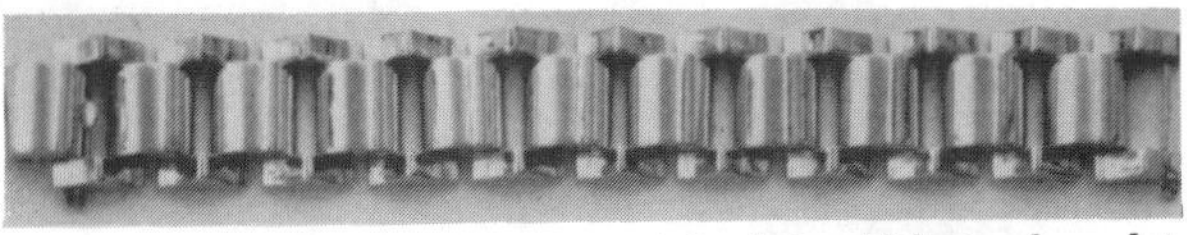

A 'tank track' design bracelet.
$1,200-1,400

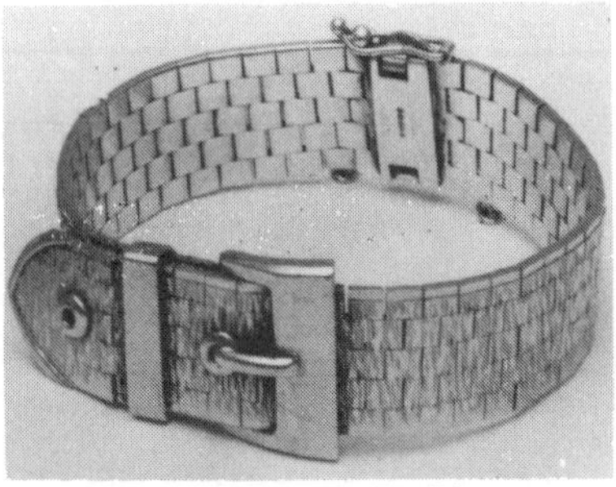

A 9ct gold buckle design flexible textured bracelet.
$500-600

Scottish agate bracelets.
$400-900 each

An 18ct gold textured woven link flexible bracelet.
$1,200-1,400

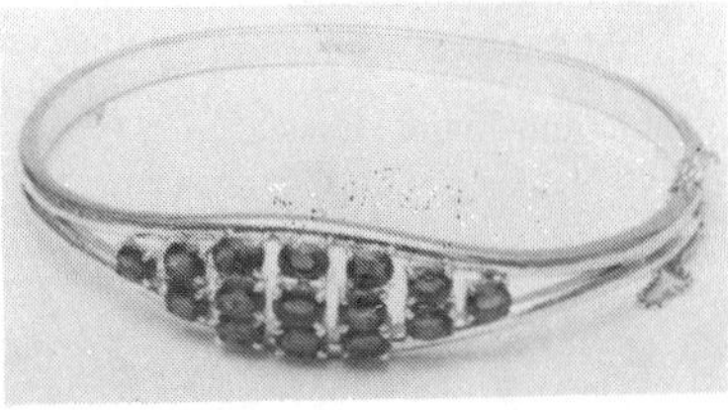

An oval ruby cluster half-loop hinged bangle.
$1,000-1,200

Two silver and green enamel bracelets.
$300-400 each

A panel bracelet with applied pierced decoration depicting figures in various occupations.
$900-1,200

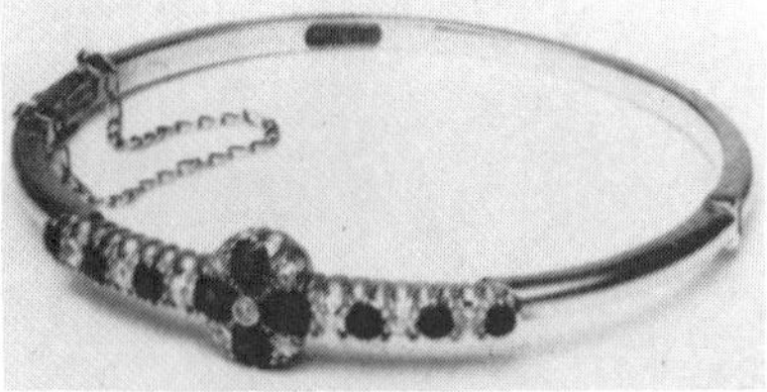

A diamond and sapphire cluster and line hinged bangle.
$1,800-2,000

PRICE

Prices in jewellery can vary enormously

1. According to age and condition
2. The basic materials from which it is made
3. Whether it is hand made or mass produced
4. The quality of the stones set in the items
5. Whether the item is at present fashionable

The last consideration could be the most important of all, because, although fashions go in cycles, it may be many years before an unfashionable item becomes marketable once again. The only value often in these instances is that of the basic materials from which the item is made, i.e. Scrap Value

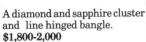

A rose diamond and pearl flowerspray brooch.
$800-900

A silver and agate crested brooch.
$700-800

A step cut peridot solitaire brooch with diamond six-stone shoulders.
$1,200-1,400

Three Scottish agate and silver brooches.
$300-700 each

An agate and gold brooch.
$800-900

An agate and silver star brooch.
$350-400

A diamond double line brooch with 2 applied opal, rose diamond and black enamel star motifs.
$1,200-1,400

An agate and silver brooch.
$600-700

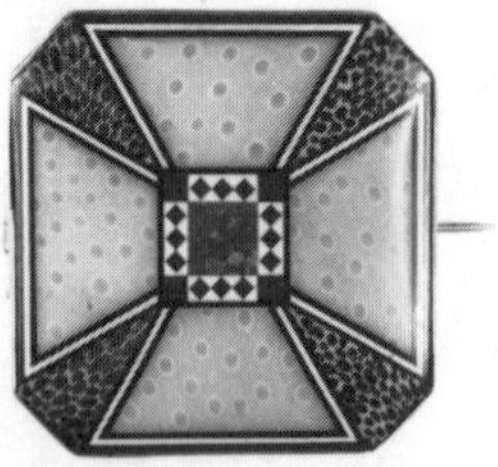

A silver and enamel brooch.
$500-600

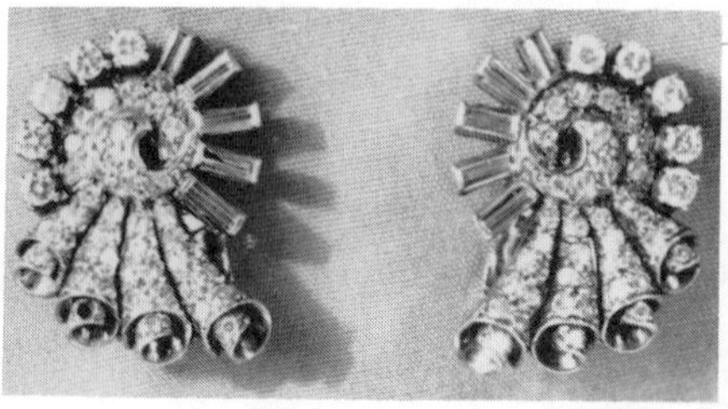

A pair of white gold diamond dress clips, with 5 baguettes and 5 brilliant cut diamonds around a pavé set spiral and scrolls.
$3,000-4,000

A Victorian 15ct gold diamond set filigree bar brooch and matching earrings.
$800-900

A diamond and ruby cluster horseshoe spray brooch.
$800-1,000

A diamond, calibre diamond, rose diamond, half pearl, sapphire and triangular sapphire double clip brooch, one stone deficient.
$2,500-3,000

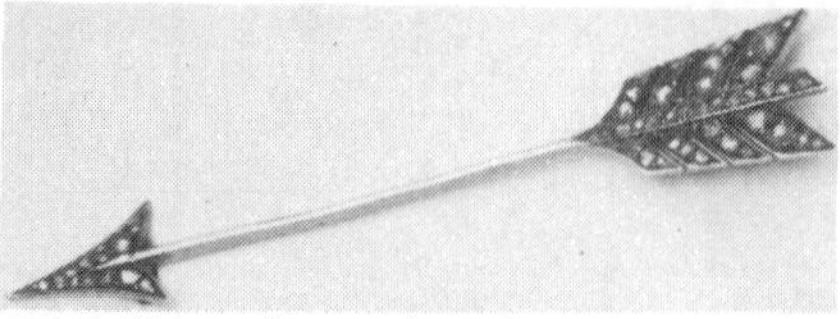

A rose diamond arrow brooch.
$400-600

A rose diamond, floral spray brooch.
$600-800

A diamond and rose cluster star brooch.
$900-1,000

An oval shell cameo brooch depicting flora, the ground with engraved decoration, in a fitted case.
$1,500-1,800

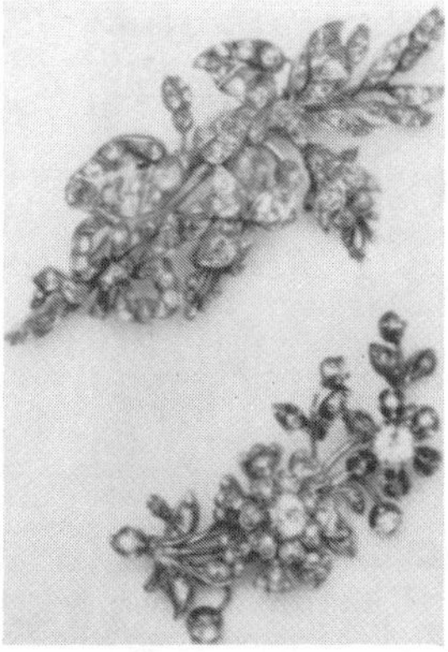

A diamond and rose diamond ribbon and flowerspray brooch.
$1,800-2,500

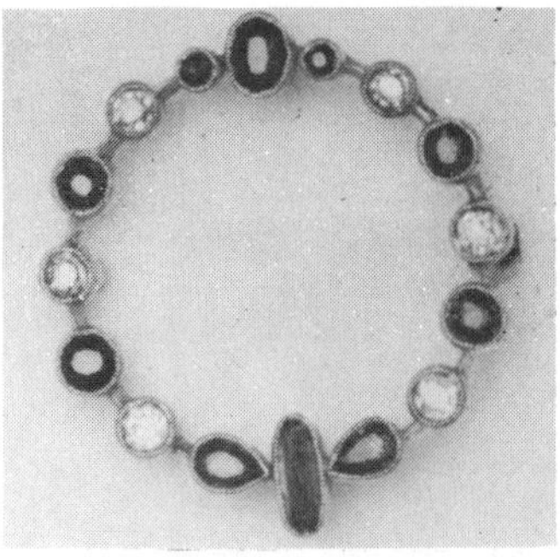

A diamond, ruby and sapphire open circle brooch.
$900-1,000

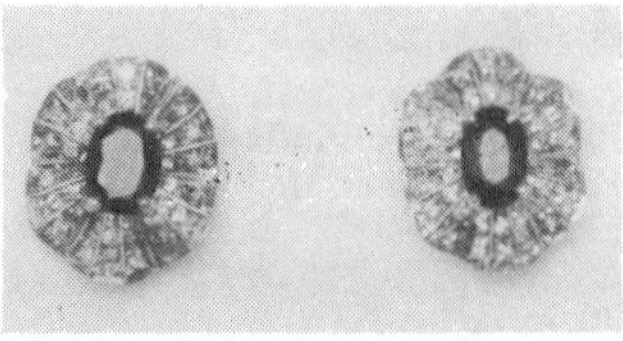

A pair of sapphire solitaire earrings with diamond wave borders.
$600-800

A pair of Art Deco diamond earrings.
$1,800-2,500

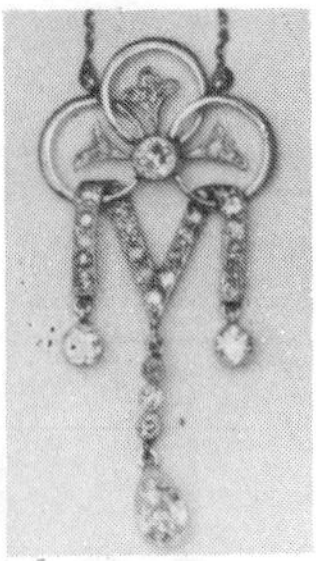

A diamond pendant, on platinum chain, in a case.
$3,000-4,000

An Edwardian gold and diamond pendant, set with 2 hoops of pavé set stones, 4 pear shaped collet set diamonds to the centre and bow above, with chain.
$5,000-6,000

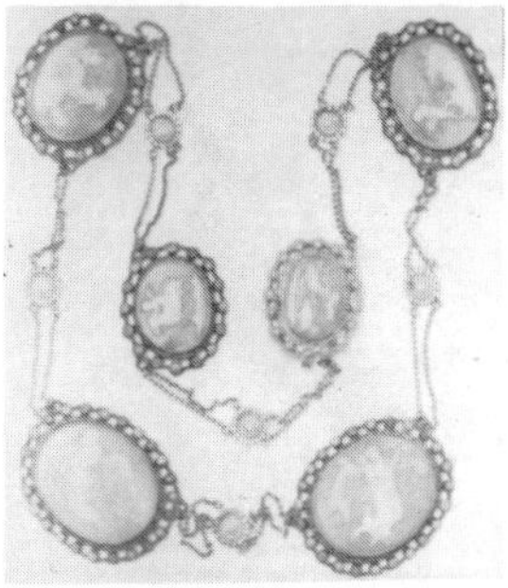

A two colour mounted shell cameo six panel necklace, with foliate chain link dividers, each panel depicting a classical scene.
$1,400-1,600

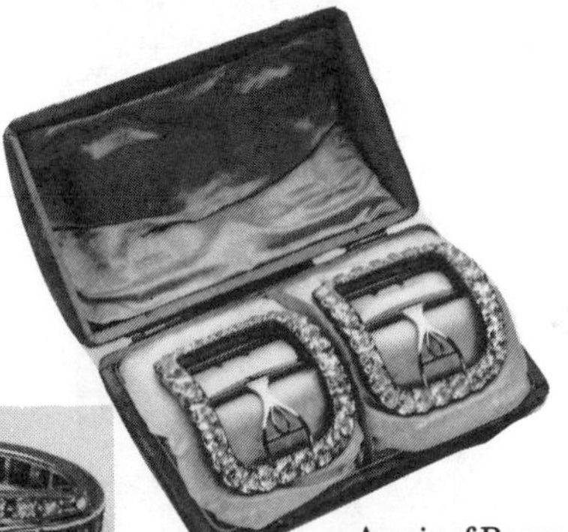

A pair of Regency paste buckles, in original fishskin case.
$800-900

A diamond, calibre sapphire and calibre ruby triple eternity ring, size N, stones deficient.
$800-1,000

A shaped locket pendant with applied diamond star and diamond set ground.
$900-1,000

A diamond three stone ring.
$1,400-1,600

A diamond solitaire ring, with diamond three stone shoulders.
$3,000-3,500

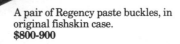

A diamond 3 stone gipsy ring.
$1,600-1,800

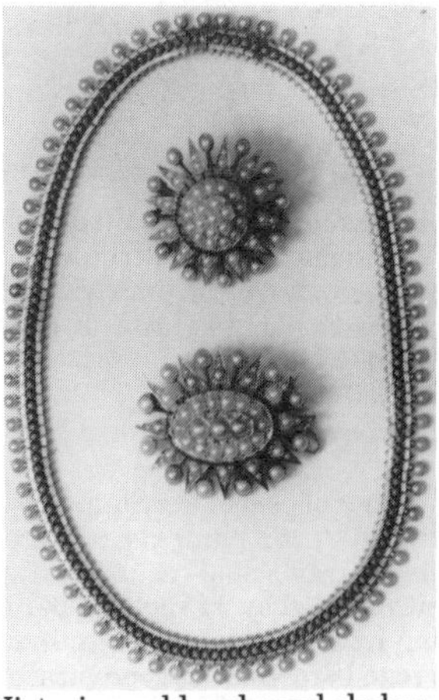

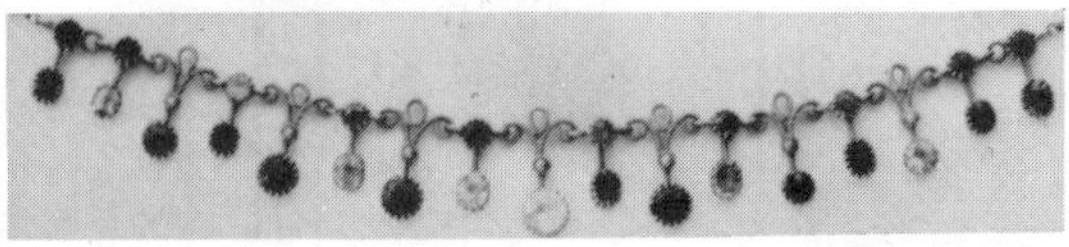

A sapphire, demantoid, garnet, amethyst and multi-gem fringe necklace.
$1,400-1,600

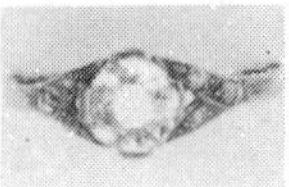

A diamond solitaire ring, with rose diamond three stone shoulders.
$900-1,000

A Victorian gold and pearl choker, and 2 brooches with rose cut diamond and pearl centres, c1870.
$4,000-5,000

RUSSIAN

Icons and Works of Art

A Greek icon of Saint Nicholas, flanked by diminutive figures of the Saviour and the Mother of God, painted in pale colours on gold ground, 17thC, 15 by 12in (38 by 30.5cm).
$11,000-13,000

A Greek icon of Saints Mercurius Tifon and Matrona, Balkan School, 11 by 8½in (28 by 21cm).
$3,000-4,000

A Russian icon of the Vladimir Virgin and Child, with crowned halo, covered by an unmarked silver riza with hanging tsata, 10½ by 8½in (27 by 22cm).
$1,600-2,500

A Greek icon of St. Catherine, inscribed and dated, late 17thC, 19½ by 15½in (50 by 40cm).
$1,600-2,000

A Greek icon, depicting 5 Prophets, with a multitude of Saints in rows behind, bearing an inscription and dated 1664.
$1,600-1,800

A Russian icon of the Virgin 'banish my sorrows', prayers reproduced in full below, 18thC, 13 by 10½in (33 by 26cm).
$400-500

Mother of God of the Sign, centred by the Virgin painted realistically in the traditional manner, surrounded by 9 Prophets, painted in vivid colours on gold ground with green borders with appropriate inscriptions of the names of the prophets, late 18thC, 16½ by 13½ (42 by 34cm).
$1,800-2,000

A set of 3 small icons of Saint Nicholas of Mojaisk, Saint Catherine and Saint Alexis the man of God, each carved from walrus tusk in the traditional manner, each mounted on wooden panel with suspension rim, Archangel, c1700, 6 by 4in (15 by 10cm).
$4,000-5,000

A Russian icon of the Vladimir Mother of God, early 18thC, 12½ by 10½in (31.5 by 26cm).
$1,200-1,400

A Greek icon of Saint Harlampios, holding a book of gospels, 18thC, 9½ by 7in (24 by 18cm).
$800-1,000

A painted Russian icon of Virgin of Joy, 18thC, 12½ by 11in (31.5 by 28cm).
$900-1,200

A Greek icon of the Dormition, in the traditional manner and painted in bright colours on gold ground, 18thC, 11 by 8in (28 by 20.5cm).
$1,800-2,500

Saint Paraskeva, wearing a crown of martyrdom held by 2 angels, on a silver background, red borders, Provincial, c1800, 15 by 12½in (38 by 31.5cm).
$800-1,000

Mother of God Joy to Those Who Grieve, flanked by angels, the sick, naked and infirm, with Christ Pantocrator above, silver background, early 119thC, 17 by 14in (43 by 35.5cm).
$900-1,000

A Greek icon of the 3 doctor Saints, Kosmos, Damian and Panteleimion, painted in bright colours on gold ground, c1800, 13 by 8½in (33 by 21.5cm).
$2,500-3,000

An icon of Mother of God of the Three Joys, centred by Saint Joseph, with Saint Elisabeth on his right holding the infant John the Forerunner, on his left Mother of God holding the infant Christ, early 19thC, 12 by 11in (30.5 by 28cm).
$1,000-1,200

Weep Not Mother of Mine, The Saviour and Mother of God, painted in Palekh manner on gold ground, some paint loss, c1800, 14 by 12in (35.5 by 30.5cm).
$900-1,200

Mother of God Smolenskaya, traditionally painted in vivid colours in 16thC style, gold background, some paint loss, 19thC,
13 by 11in (33 by 28cm).
$1,200-1,400

Resurrection of 12 Cardinal Feasts, painted in traditional manner, in vivid colours on gold ground, early 19thC, 21 by 18in (53 by 46cm).
$4,000-6,000

A Greek icon of the Decollation of Saint John the Baptist, the Saint depicted bending over a tray held by Salome, painted in bright colours on gold ground, restoration, c1800, 12 by 9½in (30.5 by 24cm).
$3,000-4,000

A Russian icon of the Resurrection, surrounded by festival scenes, the Trinity above the Evangelists in the corners, Palekh School, some damage, early 19thC, 21½ by 17½in (54 by 44cm).
$3,000-4,000

A Russian icon of St. Nicholas, surrounded by miniatures of scenes from his life, early 19thC, 12½ by 10½in (31 by 26.5cm).
$1,400-1,600

A Russian icon of Christ Pantocrator, overlaid with a silver gilt riza, 19thC, 10½ by 8in (27 by 21cm).
$1,200-1,400

A Russian icon of Christ Pantocrator, covered by an engine turned silver riza with enamel corner plaques, 19thC, 10½ by 8½in (26.5 by 22cm).
$900-1,100

A Russian icon of the Vernicle, covered by a silver and enamel riza, by Ovchinnokov, dated 1878, 5½ by 4½in (14 by 11cm).
$1,300-1,500

A Russian icon showing the Virgin of the Sign, early 19thC, 21 by 18in (53 by 46cm).
$2,500-3,000

A Russian icon, depicting the entry into Jerusalem, Palekh School, c1820, 10½ by 9in (27 by 23cm).
$2,000-2,500

Saint Nicholas, painted holding an open Book of Gospels, flanked by Jesus Christ and Mother of God, with a finely chased and engraved oklad embellished with champlevé enamel cornerpieces and inscription plaque, the halo applied with repoussé mitre engraved with the Deisis, by Khlebnikov, Moscow, 1880, 17½ by 14½in (44 by 37cm).
$4,000-5,000

A Russian icon of the Kasanskaya Mother of God, overlaid with a silver gilt riza, 19thC, 10½ by 9in (27 by 23cm).
$1,000-1,200

Mother of God of Kazan, painted on gold ground with simulated floral borders, 19thC, 16½ by 13½in (42 by 34cm).
$2,000-2,500

Mother of God of Vladimir, painted on brown ground, in the Palekh manner, with silver oklad, dated Moscow 1892, maker's mark Cyrillic B.A.C, 12 by 10½in (30.5 by 27cm).
$3,000-4,000

A Russian icon of the Smolenskaya Mother of God, overlaid with a silver gilt riza, 19thC, 9 by 7in (23 by 18cm).
$800-900

A silver mounted carved topaz icon of Christ the Saviour, inscribed in Russian 29 April 1870, 3½in (9cm) high.
$800-1,000

Saint Mary Magdalene, wearing a red Maphorion and a green chiton, on green background with brown borders, the icon forms part of a Church Iconastas, 19thC, 24½ by 10in (62 by 26cm).
$1,600-2,000

Mother of God of the Sign, painted in the traditional manner of the Palekh School, in vivid colours on gold ground, a cherubim and seraphim in the upper corners, 19thC, 14 by 11½in (35.5 by 29cm).
$1,400-1,600

An icon centred by cast bronze crucifix let into the panel, flanked by painted representations of the Mother of God and Saint Nicholas, the 2 Marys and Saint John and Saint Longinus, the Guardian Angel and 3 further Saints on the borders, 19thC, 21 by 17in (53 by 43cm).
$1,800-2,500

Mother of God of Vladimir, painted in shades of brown in 16thC style, with gilt metal repoussé and engraved oklad, haloes embellished with paste, 3 white enamel inscription plaques, 19thC, 14 by 12in (35.5 by 30.5cm).
$1,800-2,500

A Russian icon of the Virgin of Kazan, covered by a baroque silver gilt riza, dated 1853, 9 by 7in (23 by 18cm).
$700-800

A Greek icon of the Descent of the Holy Ghost (Pentecost), painted in bright colours against architectural background, the Holy Ghost above, on gold ground, 19thC, 20 by 15in (51 by 38cm).
$4,000-5,000

Mother of God of the Sign, traditionally painted on silver ground with red borders, Provincial, 19thC, 14½ by 12in (37 by 30.5cm).
$1,100-1,400

The resurrection, depicted in the centre by 12 scenes of the Passion, the whole painted in miniature in the Palekh manner, the borders with inscriptions of the festivals and floral design, vivid colours on gold ground, 19thC, 12 by 10in (30.5 by 25cm).
$3,200-4,000

A Russian icon of the Mother of God Troyeruchica, 8 by 6in (20.5 by 15cm).
$400-500

Miscellaneous

A porcelain biscuit bust of the Count Vladimir Borisovich Freedericks, by the Imperial Porcelain Factory, 1906, 14in (35.5cm) high.
$6,000-7,000

A Russian porcelain figure of a peasant sowing grain, wearing an iron red jerkin, striped breeches and shoes tied with laces, incised script on base, 20thC, 7in (18cm) high.
$1,000-1,200

A pair of porcelain figures, wearing traditional costume and dancing on a naturalistic ground, by the Kornilow Factory, 1843-60, 8in (20cm).
$2,000-3,000

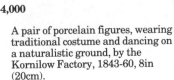

A Russian Nicholas I mahogany centre table, on shaped legs and claw feet, 56in (142cm) wide.
$3,000-4,000

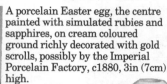

A porcelain Easter egg, the centre painted with simulated rubies and sapphires, on cream coloured ground richly decorated with gold scrolls, possibly by the Imperial Porcelain Factory, c1880, 3in (7cm) high.
$1,200-1,400

A porcelain Easter egg, one side painted with pink cyclamen on a white ground, 19thC, 4in (10cm).
$1,000-1,200

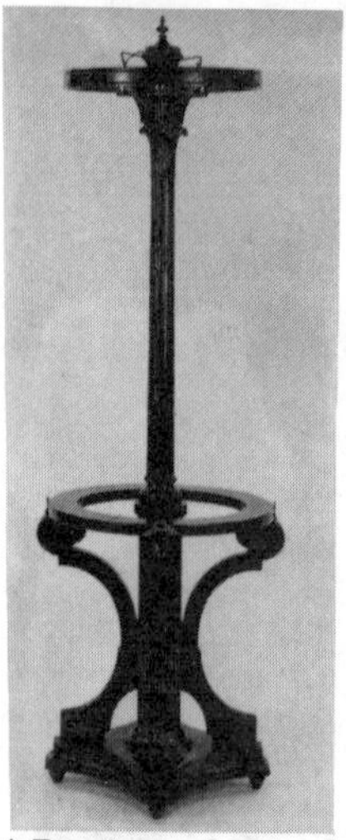

A Russian mahogany hat stand, the base with later glass shelves and scrolling supports on bun feet, fitted for electricity, lacking coat hooks, 75in (190cm) high.
$400-600

A Russian ivory sewing box, the inner panel applied with a later needlework panel, enclosing a lidded compartment, the frieze drawer below, extensively fitted with needleworking accessories, late 18thC, 10½in (26cm) wide.
$2,000-2,500

A porcelain Easter egg, painted within a gold rim, amidst purple ground with gold stylised flowers, gold slightly rubbed, 3in (7.5cm) high.
$3,500-4,000

An ivory plaque of Nicholas I, signed in Cyrillic and dated, 4in (10cm) high.
$2,500-3,000

An ormolu mounted malachite mantel clock and urn, inset with a clock, enriched with fluted and foliate neck, handles and base, 19thC, 19in (48cm).
$5,000-6,000

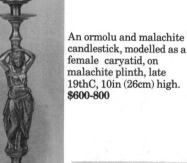

An ormolu and malachite candlestick, modelled as a female caryatid, on malachite plinth, late 19thC, 10in (26cm) high.
$600-800

A brass ashtray, the centre with Imperial Eagle and Russian inscription 'War 1914' and signature K. Fabergé, 4in (10cm) diam.
$1,600-1,800

A bronze equestrian group of a troika sled bearing 3 moujiks, after E. Lanceray, 12in (30.5cm).
$2,000-3,000

A bronze candlestick in the form of a lantern lighter, stamped in Cyrillic, 19thC, 10in (25cm) high.
$900-1,000

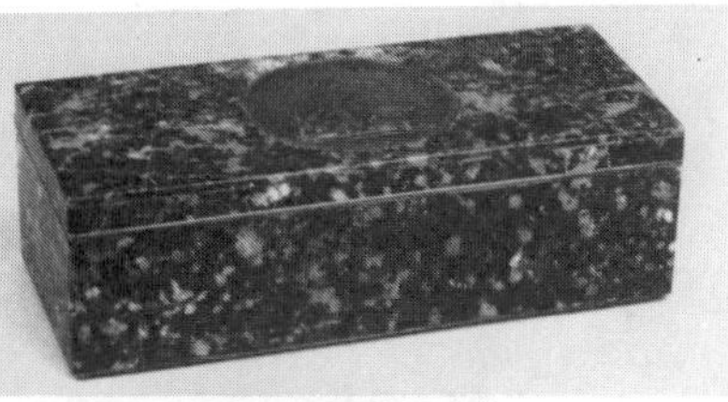

A lapis lazuli box, the hinged cover set with a bronze medal commemorating the Battle near Elizabeth's Field, after the design of Count Fedor Tolstoī, early 19thC, 7½in (19cm) long.
$2,000-3,000

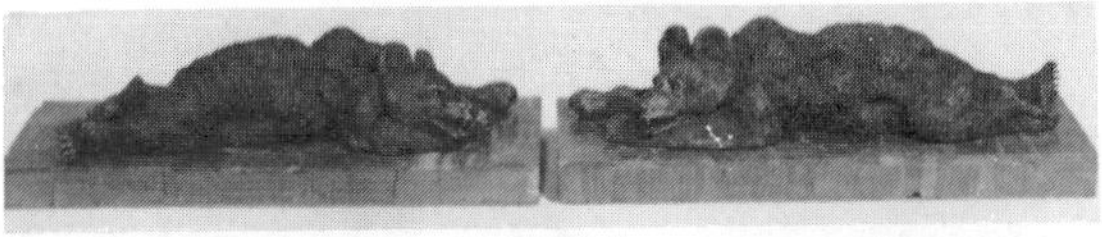

A pair of bronze bears on malachite bases, stamped in Cyrillic Grizar, 8in (20.5cm) wide.
$4,000-5,000

A malachite box, with metal hinge, 19thC, 2½in (6.5cm) wide.
$300-400

A bronze equestrian group of a cossack and his love, seated on a horse, after E. Lanceray, with F. Chopin foundry mark, 14½in (36.5cm) high.
$4,000-5,000

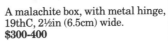

A bronze equestrian figure of the cossack's farewell, after E. Lanceray, with F. Chopin foundry marks, 15½in (39cm) high.
$3,500-4,000

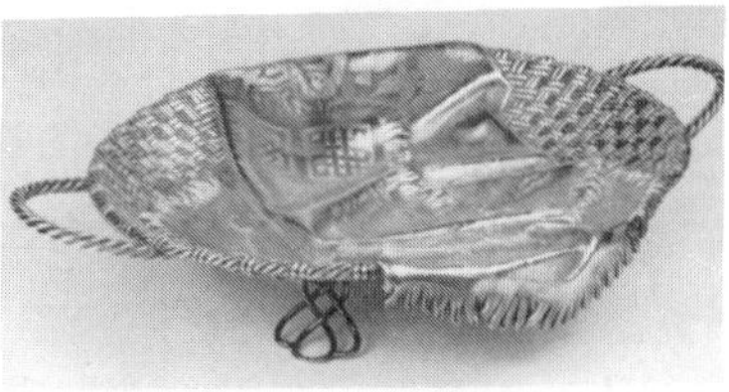

A silver trompe l'oeil basket, with twisted ropework handles and 4 pierced feet, minor damage, possibly Piotr Loskutov, Moscow, 1882, 16in (40.5cm) long, 723 grammes.
$3,000-4,000

A silver beaker, repoussé and chased with 2 eagles above swags and garlands, by Andrei Dementiev and unrecorded maker's Cyrillic initials, Moscow, 1795, 3in (7.5cm) high, 75 grammes.
$700-900

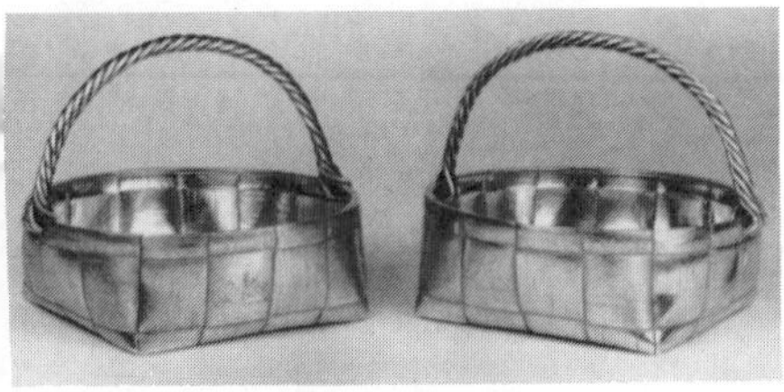

A pair of silver trompe l'oeil baskets, with twisted ropework handle and gilt interior, engraved with 2 crests, by N. Ianichkin, St. Petersburg, 1886, 6in (15cm) diam, 657 grammes.
$9,000-10,000

A silver beaker, repoussé and chased with 3 eagles amidst scrolls, with gilt interior, Moscow, unrecorded maker's initials EK and B.A., 1769, 2½in (6cm) high, 42 grammes.
$1,200-1,400

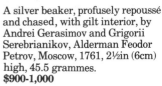

A pair of silver candlesticks, Minsk, 1873, 15in (38cm) high, 1,354 grammes.
$4,000-5,000

A silver beaker, repoussé and chased with scrolls on partly matted ground, Moscow, unrecorded maker's initials B.A., c1790, 2in (5cm) high, 47 grammes.
$1,200-1,400

A silver beaker, profusely repoussé and chased, with gilt interior, by Andrei Gerasimov and Grigorii Serebrianikov, Alderman Feodor Petrov, Moscow, 1761, 2½in (6cm) high, 45.5 grammes.
$900-1,000

A Lukutin lacquered dish, painted with a scene of a troika, 8in (20cm) wide.
$800-1,000

A Russian silver tea caddy, 4in (10cm) high.
$800-1,000

A composite silver tea service, by Aleksei Kvasnikov, Savary, and unrecorded maker's initials IRS, St. Petersburg, 1834 and 1839, the teapot 5½in (14cm) high, 1,877 grammes gross.
$2,500-3,000

A silver coffee service, comprising a coffee pot with ivory finial, a two-handled covered sugar bowl and a milk jug, by Gratchev Brothers, with the Imperial warrant, St. Petersburg, 1887, coffee pot 7in (18cm) high, 1,210 grammes gross.
$3,500-4,000

A three-piece silver tea service, with gilt interiors, by V. Morozov, with Imperial warrant, St. Petersburg, 1893, the teapot 6in (15cm) high, 1,014 grammes gross.
$1,500-2,000

A silver samovar on stand, engraved with the coat-of-arms of the family of the Princess Meshcherskii, some damage, by Gubkin, Moscow c1845 and Carl Magnus Stähle, St. Petersburg 1841, the samovar 18in (45.5cm) high, 5,604 grammes.
$30,000-40,000

Two papier mâché lacquer napkin rings, one with a view of the Kremlin from the banks of the Neva, the other of a peasant woman and her horse, by the Lukutin Factory, late 19thC.
$800-900

A seven-piece niello tea service, most of the pieces nielloed with views of the Kremlin Cathedrals, by Vasilii Semenov, Moscow 1887, the teapot 5½in (14cm) high, 1,042 grammes, in original fitted wood case applied with silver plaque engraved AR 1888.
$6,000-8,000

A pair of silver and champlevé enamel lemon tea spoons, late 19thC.
$800-900

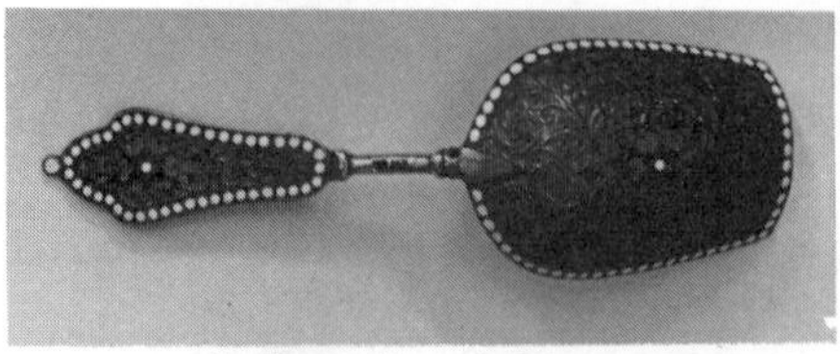

A silver gilt and cloisonné enamel spoon.
$500-600

l. A papier mâché lacquer snuff box, the cover the painted portrait bust of Peter the Great, the interior with a tin lining, some damage, 19thC, 4in (10cm) long.
$1,000-1,200

r. A papier mâché match-case holder, painted with a peasant woman, by the Lukutin Factory, 19thC.
$600-800

DIRECTORY OF INTERNATIONAL AUCTIONEERS

This directory is by no means complete. Any auctioneer who holds frequent sales should contact us for inclusion in the 1991 Edition. Entries must be received by April 1990. There is, of course, no charge for this listing. Entries will be repeated in subsequent editions unless we are requested otherwise.

America

Acorn Farm Antiques,
15466 Oak Road, Carmel,
IN 46032
Tel: (317) 846-2383

ALA Moanastampt Cain (David H Martin),
1236 Ala Moana Boulevard,
Honolulu, HI 96814

Alabama Auction Room Inc,
2112 Fifth Avenue North,
Birmingham, AL 35203
Tel: (205) 252-4073

B Altman & Co,
34th & Fifth Avenue, New York,
NY 10016
Tel: (212) OR 9 7800 ext 550 & 322

Ames Art Galleries,
8729 Wilshire Boulevard, Beverly Hills, CA 9021
Tel: (213) 655-5611/652-3820

Arnette's Auction Galleries Inc,
310 West Castle Street,
Murfreesboro, TN 37130
Tel: (615) 893-3725

Associated Appraisers Inc,
915 Industrial Bank Building,
Providence, RI 02906
Tel: (401) 331-9391

Atlanta's ABCD Auction Gallery (Clark, Bate and Depew),
1 North Clarendon Avenue,
Antioch, IL 30002
Tel: (312) 294-8264

Bakers Auction,
14100 Paramount Boulevard,
Paramount, CA 90723
Tel: (213) 531-1524

Barridoff Galleries,
242 Middle Street, Portland,
ME 04 101
Tel: (207) 772-5011

C T Bevensee Auction Service,
PO Box 492, Botsford, CT 06404
Tel: (203) 426-6698

Frank H. Boos Gallery, Inc.,
420 Enterprise Ct., Bloomfield Hills, MI 48013

Richard A Bourne Co Inc,
Corporation Street, PO Box 141/A,
Hyannis Port, MA 02647
Tel: (617) 775-0797

Bridges Antiques and Auctions,
Highway 46, PO Box 52A,
Sanford, FL 32771
Tel: (305) 323-2801/322-0095

George C Brilant & Co,
191 King Street, Charleston,
SC 29401

R W Bronstein Corp,
3666 Main Street, Buffalo,
NY 14226
Tel: (716) 835-7666/7408

Brookline Auction Gallery,
Proctor Hill Road, Route 130,
Brookline, NH 03033
Tel: (603) 673-4474/4153

Brzostek's Auction Service,
2052 Lamson Road, Phoenix,
NY 13135
Tel: (315) 678-2542

Buckingham Galleries Ltd,
4350 Dawson Street, San Diego,
CA 92115
Tel: (714) 283-7286

Bushell's Auction,
2006 2nd Avenue, Seattle,
WA 98121
Tel: (206) 622-5833

L Butterfield,
605 W Midland, Bay City,
MI 48706
Tel: (517) 684-3229

Butterfield,
808 N La, Cienega Boulevard, Los Angeles, CA 90069

Butterfield & Butterfield,
1244 Sutter Street, San Francisco,
CA 94109
Tel: (415) 673-1362

California Book Auction Galleries,
358 Golden Gate Avenue, San Francisco, CA 94102
Tel: (415) 775-0424

C B Charles Galleries Inc,
825 Woodward Avenue, Pontiac,
MI 48053
Tel: (313) 338-9023

Chatsworth Auction Rooms,
151 Mamaroneck Avenue,
Mamaroneck, NY 10543

Christie, Manson & Wood International Inc,
502 Park Avenue, New York
Tel: (212) 826-2388 Telex: 620721

Christie's East,
219 East 67th Street, New York,
NY 10021
Tel: (212) 570-4141

Representative Offices:
California:
9350 Wilshire Boulevard, Beverly Hills, CA 902 12
Tel: (213) 275-5534

Florida:
225 Fern Street, West Palm Beach,
FL 33401
Tel: (305) 833-6592

Mid-Atlantic:
638 Morris Avenue, Bryn Mawr,
PA 19010
Tel: (215) 525-5493

Washington:
1422 27th Street NW, Washington,
DC 20007
Tel: (202) 965-2066

Midwest:
46 East Elm Street, Chicago,
IL 60611
Tel: (312) 787-2765

Fred Clark Auctioneer Inc,
PO Box 124, Route 14, Scotland,
CT 06264
Tel: (203) 423-3939/0594

Cockrum Auctions,
2701 North Highway 94,
St Charles, MO 63301
Tel: (314) 723-9511

George Cole, Auctioneers and Appraisers,
14 Green Street, Kingston,
NY 12401
Tel: (914) 338-2367

Coleman Auction Galleries,
525 East 72nd Street, New York,
NY 10021
Tel: (212) 879-1415

Conestoga Auction Company Inc,
PO Box 1, Manheim, PA 17545
Tel: (717) 898-7284

Cook's Auction Gallery,
Route 58, Halifax, MA 02338
Tel: (617) 293-3445/866-3243

Coquina Auction Barn
40 S Atlantic Avenue, Ormond Beach, FL 32074

Danny's Antique Auction Service (Pat Lusardi),
Route 46, Belvidere, NH 07823
Tel: (201) 757-7278

Douglas Galleries,
Route 5, South Deerfield,
MA 01373
Tel: (413) 665-2877

William Doyle,
175 East 87th Street, New York,
NY 10128
Tel: (212) 427-2730

DuMochelle Art Galleries,
409 East Jefferson, Detroit,
MI 48226
Tel: (313) 963-6255

John C Edelmann Galleries Inc,
123 East 77th Street, New York,
NY 10021
Tel: (212) 628-1700/1735

Robert C Eldred Co Inc,
Box 796, East Dennis, MA 02641
Tel: (617) 385-3116/3377

The Fine Arts Company of Philadelphia Inc,
2317 Chestnut Street,
Philadelphia, PA 19103
Tel: (215) 564-3644

Fordem Galleries Inc,
3829 Lorain Avenue, Cleveland,
OH 44113
Tel: (216) 281-3563

George S Foster III,
Route 28, Epsom, NH 03234
Tel: (603) 736-9240

Jack Francis Auctions,
200 Market Street, Suite 107,
Lowell, MA 01852
Tel: (508) 441-9708

S T Freeman & Co,
1808 Chestnut Street,
Philadelphia, PA 19103
Tel: (215) 563-9275

Col K R French and Co Inc,
166 Bedford Road, Armonk,
NY 10504
Tel: (914) 273-3674

Garth's Auctions Inc,
2690 Stratford Road, Delaware,
OH 43015
Tel: (614) 362-4771/369-5085

Gilbert Auctions,
River Road, Garrison, NY 10524
Tel: (914) 424-3657

Morten M Goldberg,
215 N Rampart Street, New Orleans, LA 70112
Tel: (504) 522-8364

Gramercy Auction Galleries,
52 East 13th Street, New York,
NY 10003
Tel: (212) 477-5656

Grandma's House,
4712 Dudley, Wheatridge,
CO 80033
Tel: (303) 423-3640/534-2847

The William Haber Art Collection Inc,
139-11 Queens Boulevard,
Jamaica, NY 11435
Tel: (212) 739-1000

Charlton Hall Galleries Inc,
930 Gervais Street, Columbia,
SC 29201
Tel: (803) 252-7927/779-5678

Hampton Auction Gallery,
201 Harwick Street, Belvidere,
NH 07823
Tel: (201) 475-2928

Hanzel,
1120 S Michigan Avenue, Chicago,
IL 60605
Tel: (312) 922-6234

Harbor Auction Gallery,
238 Bank Street, New London,
CT 06355
Tel: (203) 443-0868

Harmer's of San Francisco Inc,
49 Geary Street, San Francisco,
CA 94102
Tel: (415) 391-8244

Harris Auction Galleries,
873-875 North Howard Street,
Baltimore, MD 21201
Tel: (301) 728-7040

Hart,
2311 Westheimer, Houston,
TX 77098
Tel: (713) 524-2979/523-7389

Hauswedeil & Nolte,
225 West Central Park, New York,
NY 10024
Tel: (212) 787-7245

G Ray Hawkins,
7224 Melrose Avenue, Los Angeles, CA 90046
Tel: (213) 550-1504

Elwood Heller & Son Auctioneer,
151 Main Street, Lebanon,
NJ 08833
Tel: (201) 23 62 195

William F Hill Auction Sales,
Route 16, East Hardwick,
VT 05834
Tel: (802) 472-6308

Leslie Hindman,
215 West Ohio Street, Chicago,
IL 60610
Tel: (312) 670-0010

The House Clinic,
PO Box 13013A, Orlando, Fl 32859
Tel: (305) 859-1770/851-2979

Co Raymond W Huber,
211 North Monroe, Montpelier,
OH 43543

F B Hubley Et Co,
364 Broadway, Cambridge,
MA 02100
Tel: (617) 876-2030

Iroquois Auctions,
Box 66, Broad Street, Port Henry,
NY 12974
Tel: (518) 942-3355

It's About Time,
375 Park Avenue, Glencoe,
IL 60022
Tel: (312) 835-2012

Louis Joseph Auction Gallery (Richard L Ryan),
575 Washington Street, Brookline,
MA 02146
Tel: (617) 277-0740

Julia's Auction Service,
Route 201, Skowhegan Road,
Fairfield, ME 04937
Tel: (207) 453-9725

Sibylle Kaldewey,
225 West Central Park, New York,
NY 10024
Tel: (212) 787-7245

Kelley's Auction Service,
PO Box 125, Woburn, MA 01801
Tel: (617) 272-9167

Kennedy Antique Auction Galleries Inc,
1088 Huff Road, Atlanta,
GA 30318
Tel: (404) 351-4464

DIRECTORY

Kinzie Galleries Auction Service,
1002 3rd Avenue, Duncansville,
PA 16835
Tel: (814) 695-3479

La Salle,
2083 Union Street, San Francisco,
CA 94123
Tel: (415) 931-9200

L A Landry (Robert Landry),
94 Main Street, Essex, MA 01929
Tel: (603) 744-5811

Jo Anna Larson,
POB 0, Antioch, IL 60002
Tel: (312) 395-0963

Levins Auction Exchange,
414 Camp Street, New Orleans,
LA 70130

Lipton,
1108 Fort Street, Honolulu,
HI 96813
Tel: (808) 533-4320

F S Long & Sons,
3126 East 3rd Street, Dayton,
OH 45403

R L Loveless Associates Inc,
4223 Clover Street, Honeoye Falls,
NY 14472
Tel: (716) 624-1648/1556

Lubin Galleries,
30 West 26th Street, New York,
NY 10010
Tel: (212) 924-3777

Main Auction Galleries,
137 West 4th Street, Cincinnati,
OH 45202
Tel: (513) 621-1280

Maison Auction Co Inc,
128 East Street, Wallingford,
CT 06492
Tel: (203) 269-8007

Joel L Malter & Co Inc,
Suite 518, 16661 Ventura
Boulevard, Encino, CA 91316
Tel: (213) 784-7772/2181

Manhattan Galleries,
1415 Third Avenue, New York,
NY 10028
Tel: (212) 744-2844

Mapes,
1600 West Vestal Parkway,
Vestal, NY 13850
Tel: (607) 754-9193

David W Mapes Inc,
82 Front Street, Binghamton,
NY 13905
Tel: (607) 724-6741/862-9365

Marvin H Newman,
426 South Robertson Boulevard,
Los Angeles, CA 90048
Tel: (213) 273-4840/378-2095

Mechanical Music Center Inc,
25 Kings Highway North, Darien,
CT 06820
Tel: (203) 655-9510

Milwaukee Auction Galleries,
4747 West Bradley Road,
Milwaukee, Wl 53223
Tel: (414) 355-5054

Wayne Mock Inc,
Box 37, Tamworth, NH 03886
Tel: (603) 323-8057

William F Moon & Co,
12 Lewis Road, RFD 1, North
Attleboro, MA 02760
Tel: (617) 761-8003

New England Rare Coin Auctions,
89 Devonshire Street, Boston,
MA 02109
Tel: (617) 227-8800

Kurt Niven,
1444 Oak Lawn, Suite 525, Dallas,
TX 75207
Tel: (214) 741-4252

Northgate Gallery,
5520 Highway 153, Chattanooga,
TN 37443
Tel: (615) 842-4177

O'Gallerie Inc,
537 SE Ash Street, Portland,
OR 97214
Tel: (503) 238-0202

Th J Owen & Sons,
1111 East Street NW, Washington,
DC 20004

Palmer Auction Service,
Lucas, KS 67648

Park City Auction Service,
925 Wood Street, Bridgeport,
CT 06604
Tel: (203) 333-5251

Pennypacker Auction Centre,
1540 New Holland Road,
Kenhorst, Reading, PA 19607
Tel: (215) 777-5890/6121

Peyton Place Antiques,
819 Lovett Boulevard, Houston,
TX 77006
Tel: (713) 523-4841

Phillips,
867 Madison Avenue, New York,
NY 10021
Tel: (212) 570-4830

525 East 72nd Street, New York,
NY10021
Tel: (212) 570-4852

Representative Office:
6 Faneuil Hall, Marketplace,
Boston, MA 02109
Tel: (617) 227-6145

Pollack,
2780 NE 183 Street, Miami,
FL 33160
Tel: (305) 931-4476

Quickie Auction House,
Route 3, Osseo, MN 55369
Tel: (612) 428-4378

R & S Estate Liquidations,
Box 205, Newton Center,
MA 02159
Tel: (617) 244-6616

C Gilbert Richards,
Garrison, NY 10524
Tel: (914) 424-3657

Bill Rinaldi Auctions,
Bedell Road, Poughkeepsie,
NY 12601
Tel: (914) 454-9613

Roan Inc,
Box 118, RD 3, Logan Station,
PA 17728
Tel: (717) 494-0170

Rockland Auction Services Inc,
72 Pomona Road, Suffern,
NY 10901
Tel: (914) 354-3914/2723

Rome Auction Gallery (Sandra A
Louis Caropreso),
Route 2, Highway 53, Rome,
GA 30161

Rose Galleries Inc,
1123 West County Road B,
Roseville, MN 55113
Tel: (612) 484-1415

Rosvall Auction Company,
1238 & 1248 South Broadway,
Denver, CO 80210
Tel: (303) 777-2032/722-4028

Sigmund Rothschild,
27 West 67th Street, New York,
NY 10023
Tel: (212) 873-5522

Vince Runowich Auctions,
2312 4th Street North, St
Petersburg, FL 33704
Tel: (813) 895-3548

Safran's Antique Galleries Ltd,
930 Gervais Street, Columbia,
SC 29201
Tel: (803) 252-7927

Sage Auction Gallery,
Route 9A, Chester, CT 06412
Tel: (203) 526-3036

San Antonio Auction Gallery,
5096 Bianco, San Antonio,
TX 78216
Tel: (512) 342-3800

Emory Sanders,
New London, NH 03257
Tel: (603) 526-6326

Sandwich Auction House,
15 Tupper Road, Sandwich,
MA 02563
Tel: (617) 888-1926/5675

San Francisco Auction Gallery,
1217 Sutter Street, San Francisco,
CA 94109
Tel: (415) 441-3800

Schafer Auction Gallery,
82 Bradley Road, Madison,
CT 06443
Tel: (203) 245-4173

Schmidt's Antiques,
5138 West Michigan Avenue,
Ypsilanti, MI 48 197
Tel: (313) 434-2660

K C Self,
53 Victory Lane, Los Angeles,
CA 95030
Tel: (213) 354-4238

B J Selkirk & Sons,
4166 Olive Street, St Louis,
MO 63108
Tel: (314) 533-1700

Shore Galleries Inc,
3318 West Devon, Lincolnwood,
IL 60659
Tel: (312) 676-2900

Shute's Auction Gallery,
70 Accord Park Drive, Norwell,
MA 02061
Tel: (617) 871-3414/238-0586

Ronald Siefert,
RFD, Buskirk, NY 12028
Tel: (518) 686-9375

Robert A Siegel Auction Galleries
Inc,
120 East 56th Street, New York,
NY 10022
Tel: (212) 753-6421/2/3

Robert W Skinner Inc,
Main Street, Bolton, MA 01740
Tel: (617) 779-5528

585 Boylston Street,
Boston, MA 02116
Tel: (617) 236-1700

C G Sloan & Co,
715 13th Street NW, Washington,
DC 20005
Tel: (202) 628-1468

Branch Office:
403 North Charles Street,
Baltimore, MD 21201
Tel: (301) 547-1177

Sotheby,
101 Newbury Street, Boston,
MA 02116
Tel: (617) 247-2851

Sotheby Park Bernet Inc,
980 Madison Avenue, New York,
NY 10021
Tel: (212) 472-3400

1334 York Avenue, New York,
NY 10021

171 East 84th Street, New York,
NY 10028

Mid-Atlantic:
1630 Locust Street, Philadelphia,
PA 19103
Tel: (215) 735-7886

Washington:
2903 M Street NW, Washington,
DC 20007
Tel: (202) 298-8400

Southeast:
155 Worth Avenue, Palm Beach,
FL 33480
Tel: (305) 658-3555

Midwest:
700 North Michigan Avenue,
Chicago, IL 60611
Tel: (312) 280-0185

Southwest:
Galleria Post Oak,
5015 Westheimer Road, Houston,
TX 77056
Tel: (713) 623-0010

Northwest:
210 Post Street, San Francisco,
CA 94108
Tel: (415) 986-4982

Pacific Area:
Suite 117, 850 West Hind Drive,
Honolulu, Hawaii 96821
Tel: (808) 373-9166

Stack's Rare Coin Auctions,
123 West 57th Street, New York,
NY 10019
Tel: (212) 583-2580

Classic Auction Gallery
(formerly Sterling Auctions),
62 No. 2nd Avenue, Raritan,
NJ 08869
Tel: (201) 526-6024

Stremmel Auctions Inc,
2152 Prater Way, Sparks,
NV 89431
Tel: (702) 331-1035

Summit Auction Rooms,
47-49 Summit Avenue, Summit,
NJ 07901

Superior Stamp & Coin Co Inc,
9301 Wiltshire Boulevard,
Beverly Hills, CA 90210
Tel: (213) 272-0851/278-9740

Swann Galleries Inc,
104 East 26th Street, New York,
NY 10021
Tel: (212) 254-4710

Philip Swedler & Son,
850 Grand Avenue, New Haven,
CT 06511
Tel: (203) 624-2202/562-5065

Tait Auction Studio,
1209 Howard Avenue,
Burlingame, CA 94010
Tel: (415) 343-4793

Tepper Galleries,
110 East 25th Street, New York,
NY 10010
Tel: (212) 677-5300/1/2

Louis Trailman Auction Co,
1519 Spruce Street, Philadelphia,
PA 19102
Tel: (215) K1 5 4500

Trend Galleries Inc,
2784 Merrick Road, Bellmore,
NY 11710
Tel: (516) 221-5588

Trosby Auction Galleries,
81 Peachtree Park Drive, Atlanta,
GA 30326
Tel: (404) 351-4400

Valle-McLeod Gallery,
3303 Kirby Drive, Houston,
TX 77098
Tel: (713) 523-8309/8310

The Watnot Auction,
Box 78, Mellenville, NY 12544
Tel: (518) 672-7576

Adam A Wechsler & Son,
905-9 East Street NW,
Washington, DC 20004
Tel: (202) 628-1281

White Plains Auction Rooms,
572 North Broadway, White
Plains, NY 10603
Tel: (914) 428-2255

Henry Willis,
22 Main Street, Marshfield,
MA 02050
Tel: (617) 834 7774

The Wilson Galleries,
PO Box 102, Ford Defiance,
VA 24437
Tel: (703) 885-4292

Helen Winter Associates,
355 Farmington Avenue,
Plainville, CT 06062
Tel: (203) 747-0714/677-0848

Richard Withington Inc,
Hillsboro, NH 03244
Tel: (603) 464-3232

Wolf,
13015 Larchmere Boulevard,
Shaker Heights, OH 44120
Tel: (216) 231-3888

Richard Wolffers Inc,
127 Kearney Street, San
Francisco, CA 94 108
Tel: (415) 781-5127

Young,
56 Market Street, Portsmouth,
NH 03801
Tel: (603) 436-8773

Samuel Yudkin & Associates,
1125 King Street, Alexandria,
VA 22314
Tel: (703) 549-9330

Australia

ASA Stamps Co Pty Ltd,
138-140 Rundle Mall, National
Bank Building, Adelaide, South
Australia 5001
Tel: 223-2951

Associated Auctioneers Pty Ltd,
800-810 Parramatta Road,
Lewisham, New South Wales 2049
Tel: 560-5899

G J Brain Auctioneers Pty Ltd,
122 Harrington Street, Sydney,
New South Wales 2000
Tel: 271701

Bright Slater Pty Ltd,
Box 205 GPO, Lower Ground
Floor, Brisbane Club Building,
Isles Lane, Brisbane, Queensland
4000
Tel: 312415

Christie, Manson & Woods
(Australia) Ltd,
298 New South Head Road, Double
Bay, Sydney, New South Wales
2028
Tel: 326-1422

William S Ellenden Pty Ltd,
67-73 Wentworth Avenue,
Sydney, New South Wales 2000
Tel: 211-4035/211-4477

Bruce Granger Auctions,
10 Hopetoun Street, Huristone
Park, New South Wales 2193
Tel: 559-4767

Johnson Bros Auctioneers & Real
Estate Agents,
328 Main Road, Glenorchy,
Tasmania 7011
Tel: 725166 492909

James A Johnson & Co,
92 Boronia Road, Vermont,
Victoria 3133
Tel: 877-2754/874-3632

Jolly Barry Pty Ltd,
212 Glenmore Road, Paddington,
New South Wales 2021
Tel: 357-4494

James R Lawson Pty Ltd,
236 Castlereagh Street, Sydney,
New South Wales
Tel: 266408

Mason Greene & Associates,
91-101 Leveson Street, North
Melbourne, Victoria 3051
Tel: 329-9911

Mercantile Art Auctions,
317 Pacific Highway, North Sydey,
New South Wales 2060
Tel: 922-3610/922-3608

James R Newall Auctions Pty Ltd,
164 Military Road, Neutral Bay,
New South Wales 2089
Tel: 903023/902587 (Sydney ex)

P L Pickles & Co Pty Ltd
655 Pacific Highway, Killara, New
South Wales 2071
Tel: 498-8069/498-2775

Sotheby Parke Bernet Group Ltd,
115 Collins Street, Melbourne,
Victoria 3000
Tel: (03) 63 39 00

H E Wells & Sons,
326 Rokeby Road, Subiaco, West
Australia
Tel: 3819448/3819040

Young Family Estates Pty Ltd,
229 Camberwell Road, East
Hawthorn, Melbourne 2123
Tel: 821433

New Zealand

Devereaux & Culley Ltd,
200 Dominion Road, Mt Eden,
Auckland
Tel: 687429/687112

Alex Harris Ltd,
PO Box 510, 377 Princes Street,
Dunedin
Tel: 773955/740703

Roger Moat Ltd,
College Hill and Beaumont Street,
Auckland
Tel: 37 1588/37 1686/37 1595

New Zealand Stamp Auctions,
PO Box 3496, Queen and
Wyndham Streets, Auckland
Tel: 375490/375498

Alistair Robb Coin Auctions,
La Aitken Street, Box 3705,
Wellington
Tel: 727-141

Dunbar Sloane Ltd,
32 Waring Taylor Street,
Wellington
Tel: 721-367

Thornton Auctions Ltd,
89 Albert Street, Auckland 1
Tel: 30888 (3 lines)

Daniel J Visser,
109 and 90 Worchester Street,
Christchurch
Tel: 68853/67297

Austria

Christie's,
Ziehrerplatz 4/22, A-1030 Vienna
Tel: (0222) 73 26 44

Belgium

Christie, Manson & Woods
(Belgium) Ltd,
33 Boulevard de Waterloo, B-1000
Brussels
Tel: (02) 512-8765/512-8830

Sotheby Parke Bernet Belgium,
Rue de l'Abbaye 32, 1050 Brussels
Tel: 343 50 07

Canada

A-1 Auctioneer Evaluation
Services Ltd,
PO Box 926, Saint John,
NB E2L 4C3
Tel: (508) 762-0559

Appleton Auctioneers Ltd,
1238 Seymour Street, Vancouver,
BC V6B 3N9
Tel: (604) 685-1715

Ashton Auction Service,
PO Box 500, Ashton, Ontario,
KOA 180
Tel: (613) 257-1575

Canada Book Auctions,
35 Front Street East, Toronto,
Ontario M5E 1B3
Tel: (416) 368-4326

Christie's International Ltd,
Suite 2002, 1055 West Georgia
Street, Vancouver, BC V6E 3P3
Tel: (604) 685-2126

Miller & Johnson Auctioneers Ltd,
2882 Gottingen Street, Halifax,
Nova Scotia B3K 3E2
Tel: (902) 425-3366/425-3606

Phillips Ward-Price Ltd,
76 Davenport Road, Toronto,
Ontario M5R 1H3
Tel: (416) 923-9876

Sotheby Parke Bernet (Canada)
Inc,
156 Front Street, Toronto, Ontario
M5J 2L6
Tel: (416) 596-0300
Representative:
David Brown,
2321 Granville Street, Vancouver,
BC V6H 3G4
Tel: (604) 736-6363

Denmark

Kunsthallens,
Kunstauktioner A/S,
Købmagergade 11 DK 1150
Copenhagen
Tel: (01) 13 85 69

Nellemann & Thomsen,
Neilgade 45, DK-8000 Aarhus
Tel: (06) 12 06 66/12 00 02

France

Ader, Picard, Tajan,
12 rue Favart, 75002 Paris
Tel: 261.80.07

Artus,
15 rue de la Grange-Batelière,
75009 Paris
Tel: 523.12.03

Audap,
32 rue Drouot, 75009 Paris
Tel: 742.78.01

Bondu,
17 rue Drouot, 75009 Paris
Tel: 770.36.16

Boscher, Gossart,
3 rue d'Amboise, 75009 Paris
Tel: 260.87.87

Briest,
15 rue Drouot, 75009 Paris
Tel: 770.66.29

de Cagny,
4 rue Drouot, 75009 Paris
Tel: 246.00.07

Charbonneaux,
134 rue du Faubourg Saint-
Honoré, 75008 Paris
Tel: 359.66.57

Chayette,
10 rue Rossini, 75009 Paris
Tel: 770.38.89

Delaporte, Rieunier,
159 rue Montmartre, 75002 Paris
Tel: 508.41.83

Delorme,
3 rue Penthièvre, 75008 Paris
Tel: 265.57.63

Godeau,
32 rue Drouot, 75009 Paris
Tel: 770.67.68

Gros,
22 rue Drouot, 75009 Paris
Tel: 770.83.04

Langlade,
12 rue Descombes, 75017 Paris
Tel: 227.00.91

Loudmer, Poulain,
73 rue de Faubourg Saint-Honoré,
75008 Paris
Tel: 266.90.01

Maignan,
6 rue de la Michodière, 75002 Paris
Tel: 742.71.52

Maringe,
16 rue de Provence, 75009 Paris
Tel: 770.61.15

Marlio,
7 rue Ernest-Renan, 75015 Paris
Tel: 734.81.13

Paul Martin & Jacques Martin,
3 impasse des Chevau-Legers,
78000 Versailles
Tel: 950.58.08

Bonhams, Baron Foran,
Duc de Saint-Bar, 2 rue Bellanger,
92200 Neuilly sur Seine
Tel: (1) 637-1329

Christie's, Princess Jeanne-Marie
de Broglie,
17 rue de Lille, 75007 Paris
Tel: (331) 261-1247

Sotheby's, Rear Admiral J A
Templeton-Cotill, CB,
3 rue de Miromesnil, 75008 Paris
Tel: (1) 266-4060

Monaco

Sotheby Parke Bernet Group,
PO Box 45, Sporting d'Hiver, Place
du Casino, Monte Carlo
Tel: (93) 30 88 80

Hong Kong

Sotheby Parke Bernet (Hong
Kong) Ltd,
PO Box 83, 705 Lane Crawford
House, 64-70 Queen's Road
Central, Hong Kong
Tel: 22-5454

Italy

Christie's (International) SA,
Palazzo Massimo Lancellotti,
Piazza Navona 114, 00186 Rome
Tel: 6541217

Christie's (Italy) SR1,
9 Via Borgogna, 20144 Milan
Tel: 794712

Finarte SPA,
Piazzetta Bossi 4, 20121 Milan
Tel: 877041

Finarte SPA,
Via delle Quattro, Fontane 20,
Rome
Tel: 463564

Palazzo International delle Aste ed
Esposizioni SPA,
Palazzo Corsini, Il Prato 56,
Florence
Tel: 293000

Sotheby Parke Bernet Italia,
26 Via Gino Capponi, 50121
Florence
Tel: 571410

Sotheby Parke Bernet Italia,
Via Montenapoleone 3, 20121
Milan
Tel: 783907

Sotheby Parke Bernet Italia,
Palazzo Taverna, Via di Monte
Giordano 36, 00186 Rome
Tel: 656 1670/6547400

The Netherlands

Christie, Manson & Woods Ltd,
Rokin 91, 1012 KL Amsterdam
Tel: (020) 23 15 05

Sotheby Mak Van Waay BV,
102 Rokin 1012, KZ Amsterdam
Tel: 24 62 15

Van Dieten Stamp Auctions BV,
2 Tournooiveld, 2511 CX The
Hague
Tel: 70-464312/70-648658

DIRECTORY

Singapore & Malaysia

Victor & Morris Pte Ltd,
39 Talok Ayer Street, Republic of Singapore
Tel: 94844

South Africa

Ashbey's Galleries,
43-47 Church Street, Cape Town 8001
Tel: 22-7527

Claremart Auction Centre,
47 Main Road, Claremont, Cape Town 7700
Tel: 66-8826/66-8804

Ford & Van Niekerk Pty Ltd
156 Main Road, PO Box 8, Plumstead, Cape Town
Tel: 71-3384

Sotheby Parke Bernet South Africa Pty Ltd,
Total House, Smit and Rissik Streets, PO Box 310010, Braamfontein 2017
Tel: 39-3726

Spain

Juan R Cayon,
41 Fuencarral, Madrid 14
Tel: 221 08 32/221 43 72/222 95 98

Christie's International Ltd,
Casado del Alisal 5, Madrid
Tel: (01) 228-9300

Sotheby Parke Bernet & Co,
Scursal de Espana, Calle del Prado 18, Madrid 14
Tel: 232-6488/232-6572

Switzerland

Daniel Beney,
Avenue des Mousquines 2, CH-1005 Lausanne
Tel: (021) 22 28 64

Blanc,
Arcade Hotel Beau-Rivage, Box 84, CH-1001 Lausanne
Tel: (021) 27 32 55/26 86 20

Christie's (International) SA,
8 Place de la Taconnerie, CH-1204 Geneva
Tel: (022) 28 25 44

Steinwiesplatz,
CH-8032 Zurich
Tel: (01) 69 05 05

Auktionshaus Doblaschofsky AG,
Monbijoustrasse 28/30, CH-3001 Berne
Tel: (031) 25 23 72/73/74

Galerie Fischer,
Haldenstrasse 19, CH-6006 Lucerne
Tel: (041) 22 57 72/73

Germann Auktionshaus,
Zeitweg 67, CH-8032 Zurich
Tel: (01) 32 83 58/32 01 12

Haus der Bücher AG,
Baumleingasse 18, CH-4051 Basel
Tel: (061) 23 30 88

Adolph Hess AG,
Haldenstrasse 5, CH-6006 Lucerne
Tel: (041) 22 43 92/22 45 35

Auktionshaus Peter Ineichen,
CF Meyerstrasse 14, CH-8002 Zurich
Tel: (01) 201-3017

Galerie Koller AG,
Ramistrasse 8, CH-8001 Zurich
Tel: (01) 47 50 40

Koller St Gallen,
St Gallen
Tel: (071) 23 42 40

Kornfeld & Co,
Laupenstrasse 49, CH-3008 Berne
Tel: (031) 25 46 73

Phillips Son & Neale SA,
6 Rue de la Cité, CH-1204 Geneva
Tel: (022) 28 68 28

Christian Rosset,
Salle des Ventes, 29 Rue du Rhone, CH-1204 Geneva
Tel: (022) 28 96 33/34

Schweizerische Gesellschaft der Freunde von Kunstauktionen,
11 Werdmühlestrasse, CH-8001 Zurich
Tel: (01) 211-4789

Sotheby Parke Bernet AG,
20 Bleicherweg, CH-8022 Zurich
Tel: (01) 202-0011

24 Rue de la Cité, CH-1024 Geneva
Tel: (022) 21 33 77

Dr Erich Steinfels, Auktionen,
Rämistrasse 6, CH-8001 Zurich
Tel: (01) 252-1233 (wine) & (01) 34 1233 (fine art)

Frank Sternberg,
Bahnhofstrasse 84, CH-8001 Zurich
Tel: (01) 211-7980

Jürg Stucker Gallery Ltd,
Alter Aargauerstalden 30, CH-3006 Berne
Tel: (031) 44 00 44

Uto Auktions AG,
Lavaterstrasse 11, CH-8027 Zurich
Tel: (01) 202-9444

West Germany

Galerie Gerda Bassenge,
Erdener Strasses 5a, D-1000 West Berlin 33
Tel: (030) 892 19 32/891 29 09

Kunstauktionen Waltraud Boltz,
Bahnhof Strasse 25-27, D-8580 Bayreuth
Tel: (0921) 206 16

Brandes,
Wolfenbütteler Strasse 12, D-3300 Braunschweig 1
Tel: (0531) 737 32

Gernot Dorau,
Johann-Georg Strasse 2, D-1000 Berlin 31
Tel: (030) 892 61 98

F Dörling,
Neuer Wall 40-41, D-2000 Hamburg 36
Tel: (040) 36 46 70/36 52 82

Roland A Exner,
Kunsthandel-Auktionen,
Am Ihmeufer, D-3000 Hannover 91
Tel: (0511) 44 44 84

Hartung & Karl,
Karolinenplatz 5a, D-8000 Munich 2
Tel: (089) 28 40 34

Hauswedell & Nolte,
Pöseldorfer Weg 1, D-2000 Hamburg 13
Tel: (040) 44 83 66

Karl & Faber,
Amiraplatz 3 (Luitpoldblock), D-8000 Munich 2
Tel: (089) 22 18 65/66

Graf Klenau Ohg Nachf,
Maximilian Strasse 32, D-8000 Munich 1
Tel: (089) 22 22 81/82

Numismatik Lanz München,
Promenadeplatz 9, D-8000 Munich 2
Tel: (089) 29 90 70

Kunsthaus Lempertz,
Neumarkt 3, D-5000 Cologne 1
Tel: (0221) 21 02 51/52

Stuttgarter Kunstauktionshaus,
Dr Fritz Nagel,
Mörikestrasse 17-19, D-7000 Stuttgart 1
Tel: (0711) 61 33 87/77

Neumeister Münchener Kunstauktionshaus KG,
Barer Strasse 37, D-8000 Munich 40
Tel: (089) 28 30 11

Petzold KG- Photographica,
Maximilian Strasse 36, D-8900 Augsburg 11
Tel: (0821) 3 37 25

Reiss & Auvermann,
Zum Talblick 2, D-6246 Glashütten im Taunus 1
Tel: (06174) 69 47/48

Gus Schiele Auktions-Galerie,
Ottostrasse 7 (Neuer Kunstblock), D-8000 Munich 2
Tel: (089) 59 41 92

Galerie,
Paulinen Strasse 47, D-7000 Stuttgart 1
Tel: (0711) 61 63 77

J A Stargardt,
Universitäts Strasse 27, D-3550 Marburg
Tel: (06421) 234 52

Auktionshaus Tietjen & Co,
Spitaler Strasse 30, D-2000 Hamburg 1
Tel: (040) 33 03 68/69

Aachener Auktionshaus, Crott & Schmelzer,
Pont Strasse 21, Aachen
Tel: (0241) 369 00

Kunstauktionen Rainer Baumann,
Obere Woerthstrasse 7-11, Nuremburg
Tel: (0911) 20 48 47

August Bödiger oHG,
Oxford Strasse 4, Bonn
Tel: (0228) 63 69 40

Bolland & Marotz,
Feldören 19, Bremen
Tel: (0421) 32 18 11

Bongartz Gelgen Auktionen,
Münsterplatz 27, Aachen
Tel: (0241) 206 19

Christie's International Ltd,
Düsseldorf:
Alt Pempelfort 11a, D-4000 Düsseldorf
Tel: (0211) 35 05 77

Hamburg:
Wenzelstrasse 21, D-2000 Hamburg 60
Tel: (4940) 279-0866

Munich:
Maximilianstrasse 20, D-8000 Munich 22
Tel: (089) 22 95 39

Württenberg:
Schloss Langenburg, D-7183 Langenburg

Sotheby Parke Bernet GmbH,
Munich:
Odeonsplatz 16, D-8000 Munich 22
Tel: (089) 22 23 75/6

Kunstauktion Jürgen Fischer,
Alexander Strasse 11, Heilbronn
Tel: (07 131) 785 23

Galerie Göbig,
Ritterhaus Strasse 5 (am Thermalbad ad Nauheim)
Tel: (Frankfurt) (611) 77 40 80

Knut Günther,
Auf der Kömerwiese 19-21, Frankfurt
Tel: (611) 55 32 92/55 70 22

Antiquitaeten Lothar Heubel,
Odenthaler Strasse 371, Cologne
Tel: (0221) 60 18 25

Hildener Auktionshaus und Kunstgalerie,
Klusenhof 12, Hilden
Tel: (02103) 602 00

INDEX